D1060858

UNIVERSITY CASEBOOK SERIES®

SCIENTIFIC EVIDENCE IN CIVIL AND CRIMINAL CASES

SEVENTH EDITION

ANDRE A. MOENSSENS, J.D., LL.M.
Douglas Stripp Professor of Law Emeritus
University of Missouri at Kansas City
Professor of Law Emeritus, University of Richmond
Forensic Consultant

BETTY LAYNE DESPORTES, J.D., M.S.
Benjamin & DesPortes, P.C.
Richmond, Virginia

STEVEN D. BENJAMIN, J.D.
Benjamin & DesPortes, P.C.
Richmond, Virginia

FOUNDATION
PRESS

© 1973, 1978, 1986, 1995, 2007 FOUNDATION PRESS
© 2013 by THOMSON REUTERS/FOUNDATION PRESS
© 2017 LEG, Inc. d/b/a West Academic
    444 Cedar Street, Suite 700
    St. Paul, MN 55101
    1-877-888-1330

Printed in the United States of America

ISBN: 978-1-63460-714-8

The authors dedicate the 7th edition of this book to:

To my children, Monique, Jacqueline, Michele, Suzanne and Mark, and to my most patient, caring, and loving spouse Ann
Andre A. Moenssens

To scientists and their endless quest for knowledge
Betty Layne DesPortes

To public defenders for their tireless fight to ensure justice
Steven D. Benjamin

PREFACE TO THE SEVENTH EDITION

The term scientific evidence covers a range of opinion testimony varying widely in probative value, weight, and persuasiveness. Some disciplines allow the formulation of an opinion with near mathematical precision; others are less certain and are intermixed with examiner subjectivity. The various techniques and methodologies, however, share a common mode of introduction in civil and criminal cases: the expert witness. Data generated in laboratories or other facilities have no real meaning in the law until given voice by the expert witness. The effectiveness of the presentation of that scientific evidence is limited by a factor independent of the scientific strength of the testimony: the ability of counsel to present the scientific evidence consistent with the comprehension level of the trier of fact. The presentation of the expert testimony must be appropriate to the trier of fact's ability to understand the testimony and to apply the testimony to the issues in the case. To ensure the most effective presentation of the evidence, lawyers must first understand it. That is the purpose of this book: to assist legal scholars and practitioners in obtaining a concise understanding of the most commonly encountered types of expert testimony and the potential legal issues that might arise in the presentation of such testimony.

The first edition of *Scientific Evidence in Civil and Criminal Cases* was published in 1973. The six prior editions were issued during the four decades in which the legal field comfortably embraced scientific evidence and then began to grapple with questions of reliability of the "scientific" evidence being offered at trial. After the *Daubert* trilogy of cases in the mid-1990s provided the admissibility standards to be enforced through the trial court's gatekeeping function, additional scrutiny was focused on the scientific evidence offered in civil trials, but the criminal justice system remained relatively unaffected by the decisions. Scientific evidence continued to be readily admitted and largely unchallenged in criminal trials, particularly in the traditional forensic science pattern comparison fields that relied on subjective assessments by experts mostly retained by the prosecution.

The legal acceptance of scientific evidence was also reflected in the "main-streaming" of science, especially forensic science involving crime scene reconstruction or analysis, through television shows and movies. Forensic scientists, both fictitious and real, starred in television shows as omniscient crime-fighters. Since the mid-1990s, the hundreds of wrongful convictions exposed by DNA evidence and the media coverage of these innocent individuals being released from decades of incarceration added to the aura of scientific evidence as the final, unassailable arbiter of justice. With the popularization of forensic science and its emergence in the cultural lexicon, jurors and attorneys came to expect scientific evidence to be presented in cases even though few understood the actual capabilities and limitations of the scientific techniques used.

This seventh edition follows the publication of the 2016 President's Council of Advisors on Science and Technology (PCAST) report, *Forensic Science in Criminal Courts: Ensuring Scientific Validity of Feature-Comparison Methods.* Consistent with the 2009 National Academy of Sciences Report on the state of forensic science in the United States, *Strengthening Forensic Science in the United States: A Path Forward,* the PCAST report was highly critical of the lack of validation in several pattern comparison disciplines. While federal agencies, particularly the National Institute of Standards and Technology and the National Commission on Forensic Science, have funded and promoted research and standard development efforts, the forensic science community remains largely self-regulated. It remains the obligation of attorneys and the courts to ensure that the scientific evidence presented is based on properly applied and validated methodologies. The capabilities and limitations of forensic science techniques are discussed extensively in this edition to assist legal practitioners in assessing scientific evidence in the most commonly encountered forensic science disciplines. To improve the focus of the book on current techniques and methods, the book has been restructured. Less frequently encountered disciplines and the extensive historical and philosophical discussion of behavioral evidence have been removed. Chapters on other disciplines, such as Digital Forensics and Forensic Psychiatry and Psychology, have been completely rewritten. Although the book covers a wide breadth of forensic science disciplines, the field of forensic science covers a vast array of disciplines and techniques, far too many to be encompassed in one book. The approach to the assessment of the reliability and validity of the forensic science methods in this book, however, can be applied to any method or technique used in other forensic science disciplines.

Consistent with the evolution of the use of scientific evidence in civil and criminal cases, the line-up of co-authors of this book has changed over four decades. Professor Fred E. Inbau, who was the inspiration for the first edition, regrettably passed away in 1998. His lifelong commitment to scientific evidence is memorialized in the continued publication of this book. Professors James E. Starrs, Carol E. Henderson, and Carl E. Edwards, who have contributed so much to the forensic science community and the legal profession, left to focus on independent publishing ventures and on guiding the next generation of leaders in forensic science and the law. Sharon G. Portwood, who contributed to the behavioral sciences chapters of the fifth edition, has also continued teaching and contributing to publishing in the field. This seventh edition adds another practicing attorney as editor and resumes the practice of involving subject matter experts in the review and update of the specific discipline chapters.

With the addition of these contributors, Fred Inbau's inspiration of a book to integrate science and the law in a practical and accessible format for legal scholars and professionals shall continue.

ANDRE A. MOENSSENS
BETTY LAYNE DESPORTES
STEVEN D. BENJAMIN

January 2017

SUMMARY OF CONTENTS

TABLE OF CONTENTS

TABLE OF CASES

UNIVERSITY CASEBOOK SERIES®

SCIENTIFIC EVIDENCE IN CIVIL AND CRIMINAL CASES

SEVENTH EDITION

CHAPTER 1

SCIENTIFIC EVIDENCE AND EXPERT TESTIMONY[1]

I. INTRODUCTION

§1.01 SCOPE OF THE CHAPTER

Scientific evidence is an important component of both civil and criminal litigation, providing the trier of fact with information necessary to resolve issues in the case. The significance of primary evidence in the case is not always apparent, and may require clarification and explanation to make it fit in a party's presentation to a trier of fact. In other words, sometimes the significance of evidence is often far removed from common experience and understanding.

---

[1] The Authors thank Judge Roderick Kennedy, former Chief Judge of the New Mexico Court of Appeals (ret.), for his help in updating this chapter. Judge Kennedy has taught forensic evidence as an adjunct at the University of New Mexico School of Law, and is a Fellow of the American Academy of Forensic Sciences. He is a Professional Member of the Chartered Forensic Science Society (UK), and the 2003 recipient of its JB Firth Memorial Medal and Lecture. His CLE series on skeptically evaluating scientific evidence received the New Mexico Bar's "Peak Award of Excellence" in 2011.

1

Accordingly, attorneys must present the evidence in ways that make relevant concepts accessible to both the judge and the jury. To this end, attorneys use expert witnesses to conceptualize and explain the connnections between various facts and evidence for the jury. The roles of educator, reporter, and interpreter of scientific evidence are regularly assigned to expert witnesses.[2] The interaction between the law and scientific or other expertise is not always without controversy and both scientists and legal professionals express frustration over the conflicts in terminology, methodology, and attitudes.[3]

As a general rule of evidence, a witness may testify only to facts personally observed or known by that witness.[4] Witnesses are generally prohibited from providing opinion testimony, although exceptions are made for opinion testimony based on common observation such as distances and speed.[5] Over time, issues arose in litigation that required analysis and explanation of facts in cases by persons having specialized knowledge or experience: an expert witness. An expert at common law was a witness who, by virtue of their knowledge and skill could give their opinion without having firsthand knowledge of the facts of the case,[6] where the opinion was relevant, and sufficiently reliable to promote a safe result for the proceeding.[7] An expert may also educate the fact finder in relevant principles of science or other specialties that the fact finder may itself apply to the case.[8] Thus, an expert may testify not only as to personal observation, but also as to opinions and

---

[2] *See* Ronald L. Carlson et al., *Evidence: Teaching Materials For An Age of Science and Statutes*, 6th ed., LexisNexis, 2007 at p. 291.

[3] On the differences between law and science generally, *see* Noreen L. Channels, SOCIAL SCIENCE METHODS IN THE LEGAL PROCESS (1985); Lee Loevinger, "Science, Technology, and Law in Modern Society," 26 JURIMETRICS 1 (1985); Steven Goldberg, "The Reluctant Embrace: Law and Science in America," 75 Geo. L. J. 1341 (1987); Mark R. Patterson, "Conflicts of Interest in Scientific Expert Testimony," 40 Wm. & Mary L. Rev. 1313 (1999).

[4] F.R.E. Rule 602 (2011)("A witness may testify to a matter only if evidence is introduced sufficient to support a finding that the witness has personal knowledge of the matter. Evidence to prove personal knowledge may consist of the witness's own testimony."). Excluded from the application of this rule are the bases of opinions given by experts.

[5] *See* F.R.E. Rule 701 (2011), limiting testimony by a non expert in the form of an opinion to one based on the witness's perception, and not based on any type of knowledge within the scope of Rule 702.

The issue of lay witnesses providing opinion evidence has become controversial as prosecutors have used the testimony of law enforcement agents as to the meaning of "drug jargon" such as "key" (for kilogram) and "snow" (for cocaine) as lay witness opinion. *See* United States v. Johnson, 617 F.3d 286 (4th Cir. 2010)(excluding such testimony); United States v. Cruz, 363 F.3d 187, 197 (2d Cir. 2004)(admitting some drug jargon interpretation testimony but excluding general interpretation testimony of witness statements). For an excellent discussion of problems with expert testimony in drug jargon cases, *see* United States v. Mejia, 545 F.3d 179 (2d Cir. 2008).

[6] Tal Golan, *Laws of Men and Laws of Nature*, Harvard University Press, 2004 at p. 42 (*quoting* John Henry Wigmore, *A Treatise on the Anglo-American System of Evidence*, 2d ed., 1923, at Vol. 4, p. 105). Wigmore articulated a common-law standard dating to the 18th century, with particular reference to the case of *Folkes v. Chadd* (1782), as discussed on Golan, id., Chap. 1, *passim*.

[7] Learned Hand, "Historical and Practical Considerations Regarding Expert Testimony," 15 Harv. L. Rev. 40, 46 (1901)

[8] F.R.E. Rule 702 (2011), Advisory notes.

conclusions based on facts received from sources other than personal perceptions, and based on knowledge exceeding that of "the average juror."[9]

From the Fourth century B.C.E. where medical experts testified in Athens,[10] through the middle ages where courts employed juries of expert tradesmen to apply their expertise to cases within their specialized knowledge, experts have given courts the benefit of their training and experience.[11] The earliest reported use of expert testimony in this country occurred when a certain Dr. Brown, testifying at a heresy trial, ventured the "scientific" opinion that the victims had been bewitched by the defendant.[12] From that questionable American beginning, the scope of expert opinion testimony offered in civil and criminal trials has exploded to include any subject remotely relevant to triable issues, as has the ubiquity with which experts are called to the stand.

Being mindful that experts are valuable precisely because of their specialized knowledge that is beyond that possessed by the fact finder, it was inevitable that mischief would result. The problem, as noted in an editorial *Nature* published in 1885, was not that an expert would utter untruths, but "that by the emphasis by which he laid on certain statements, and by what has been defined as a highly cultivated faculty of evasion, the effect was actually worse than if he had."[13] Because of the great power experts wield by virtue of their knowledge and expertise, the need to exercise judicial control over the admission of expert testimony became an issue.[14] As more scientific and technical evidence was offered, the chances of it being based on erroneous foundations and put to erroneous use, increased as well. Standards for admissibility evolved in the common law; general acceptance of a

---

[9] *See, e.g.,* Town of Rochester v. Town of Chester, 3 N.H. 349, 358 (1826) ("On questions of science, or trade, or others of the same kind. . .persons of skill may speak not only to facts, but are allowed also to give their opinions in evidence."); F.R.E. rule 702, Advisory Committee Notes ("There is no more certain test for determining when experts may be used than the common sense inquiry whether the untrained layman would be qualified to determine intelligently and to the best possible degree the particular issue without enlightenment from those having a specialized understanding of the subject involved in the dispute.")(*citing* Mason Ladd, "Expert Testimony," 5 Vand. L. Rev. 414, 418 (1952).

[10] John Pearn, "Hammurabi's Code: A primary datum in the conjoined professions of medicine and law," 84(3) Medico-Legal Journal 125–131 (2016) at p. 129.

[11] Tal Golan, *Laws of Men and Laws of Nature*, Harvard University Press, 2004 at p. 19. "If matters arise in our law which concern other sciences or faculties, we commonly apply for the aid of that science or faculty, which it concerns. Which is an honorable and commendable thing in our law. For thereby it appears that we don't despose all other sciences but our own, but we approve of them and encourage them, as things worthy of commendation." Id. at p. 18 (*citing* Buckley v. Thomas (1554)).

[12] Learned Hand, "Historical and Practical Considerations Regarding Expert Testimony," 15 Harv. L. Rev. 40, 46 (1901).

[13] "The Whole Duty of a Chemist" 33 (839) Nature 74 (1885).

[14] Bert Black, "A Unified Theory of Scientific Evidence," 56 Fordham L. Rev. 592 (1988).

scientific method or theory by a relevant community,[15] with variations, was broadly used.

In 1975, Congress adopted the Federal Rules of Evidence,[16] both codifying and supplementing the common law of evidence, drawing new attention to the admissibility of expert testimony in the Federal courts. By the 1990's, books such as *Galileo's Revenge* by Peter Huber[17] had associated the ubiquity of expert witnesses in civil litigation with the rise of a newly-coined phenomenon of "junk science," drawing intense scrutiny to both the quality of experts and the testimony they provided in court. In 1993, in *Daubert v. Merrell Dow Pharmaceuticals,*[18] the United States Supreme Court reevaluated the evidentiary standards for expert testimony.

This chapter will discuss the nature and admissibility of scientific evidence and expert testimony broadly without limitation to any particular discipline or specialty. The most widely-used admissibility standards[19] will be discussed in the chronological order in which the courts took cognizance of them, including what has been called "the *Daubert* revolution," establishing the primacy of the rules of evidence in the admission of expert testimony and scientific evidence. The 2009 National Academy of Sciences (NAS) Report,[20] and the 2016 President's Council of Advisors on Science and Technology (PCAST) Report,[21] detailing issues with the validity and reliability of several forensic science disciplines used in criminal cases, and suggesting the adoption of common standards for their employment will be discussed. These reports demonstrate both the limitations of forensic science evidence and the frequent inability of its consumers, the legal community, to deal with its responsible use in the service of justice. The reports also generally serve as models for inquiries into the reliability of scientific evidence and the opinions of expert witnesses necessary for admissibility determinations.

---

[15] *See, e.g.,* Frye v. United States, 293 F. 1013, 1014 (D.C. Cir. 1923).

[16] Pub. L. 93–595, § 1, Jan. 2, 1975, 88 Stat. 1926.

[17] Peter Huber, Galileo's Revenge: Junk Science in the Courtroom, New York: Basic Books, 1991.

[18] 509 U.S. 579 (1993).

[19] *See generally* Mark McCormick, "Scientific Evidence: Defining a New Approach to Admissibility," 67 Iowa L.Rev. 879 (1982); Andre A. Moenssens, "Admissibility of Scientific Evidence-An Alternative to the Frye Rule," 25 Wm. & Mary L. Rev. 545 (1984); Carlton Bailey, "The Admissibility of 'Novel Scientific Evidence' in Arkansas: Does Frye Matter?," 52 Ark. L. Rev. 671 (1999); National Conference of Lawyers and Scientists, Symposium on Science and the Rules of Evidence, 99 F.R.D. 187 (William A. Thomas, ed. 1983); National Conference of Lawyers and Scientists, Symposium on Science and the Rules of Legal Procedure, 101 F.R.D. 599 (William A. Thomas, ed. 1983); David L. Faigman, et. al., *Modern Scientific Evidence: The Law and Science of Expert Testimony,* Vols. 1–5, Eagan, MN: West (2011).

[20] Committee on Identifying the Needs of the Forensic Science Community, National Research Council of the National Academies, *Strengthening Forensic Science in the United States: A Path Forward,* The National Academies Press: Washington D.C., 2009.

[21] Executive Office of the President, President's Council of Advisors on Science and Technology, "Forensic Science in Criminal Courts: Ensuring Scientific Validity of Feature-Comparison Methods," September 2016.

The chapter will also address practical considerations in determining when an expert witness will be helpful to a case; how to find and retain an expert; and the role of expert testimony, and the obligations of the attorney with respect to it, in the context of both pretrial and trial phases of litigation of civil and criminal cases. In terms of trial procedures, the chapter will discuss the impact of Supreme Court decisions concerning a criminal defendant's right to confront forensic science experts, as well as the general direct and cross-examination issues with respect to expert testimony.

II. ADMISSIBILITY STANDARDS[22]

While courts have admitted the opinions of experts as evidence for several centuries, the theoretical basis in the law for doing so developed much later. At first, a variety of admissibility standards seemed to exist, and it is perhaps not wrong to ascribe the courts' attitudes toward expert testimony of a fairly novel nature as applying a "market place" criterion: if a person was skilled enough in a profession or trade to be able to make a living, then the individual would be considered an expert and their testimony would be admissible.[23] However, by the late 1800s, patterns of evaluating expert evidence began to emerge that are recognizable today, including the rule requiring expert opinions to be founded upon evidence that the witness possessed superior "experience, skill or science," and the idea that unfounded expert qualifications or opinion were not worthy of credence.[24] In the event that more than one expert testified, and the opinions were conflicting, it was (and still is) within the power of the jury to give any opinion such weight the jury believed was merited.[25] As courts afforded the power to the jury to weigh expert opinions, the courts recognized that standards were needed to judge the quality of an expert's opinion, and ultimately, the admissibility of the expert testimony.

---

[22] The admissibility standards discussed herein are specific to expert testimony. Additional admissibility hurdles that apply to all evidence, such as the restrictions in Federal Rule of Evidence 403 and similar rules, will not be discussed. *See* FRE Rule 403 ("Although relevant, evidence may be excluded if its probative value is substantially outweighed by the danger of unfair prejudice, confusion of the issues, or misleading the jury, or considerations of undue delay, waste of time, or needless presentation of cumulative evidence.").

[23] In Marcy v. Barnes, 82 Mass. 161 (1860), the court stated that a photographer who examined handwritings in connection with his business, with an intent to detect forgeries, was qualified to give an opinion about the genuineness of a disputed signature.

[24] "Much of the testimony relied on consists of the mere opinion of witnesses who are evidently unlearned in the scientific principles of which they speak; who can have no pretensions to be experts; and whose opinions, therefore, are in some instances plainly unfounded, and in all instances unworthy of credit, because we have no evidence that they had any such experience or education as would entitle us to rely on them." Carr v. Town of Northern Liberties, 35 Pa. 324, 327 (1860).

[25] *See, e.g.,* Getchell v. Lindley, 24 Minn. 265, 266 (1877).

§1.02   THE *FRYE* TEST

1.   GENERAL APPLICATION

In 1923, the federal circuit court in the District of Columbia evaluated the admissibility of evidence of results from a "deception test" offered by the defendant in a murder case. An expert witness offered testimony that blood pressure involuntarily changes when a person attempts to deceive, and that by measuring blood pressure during questioning the expert could determine whether the person was providing deceptive answers. At the time of trial, this theory and method was a novel kind of expertise.[26] The circuit court affirmed the trial court's exclusion of the expert's testimony, using a criterion that is now known as the "*Frye* test" or the "general acceptance test."[27] This test represents an articulation of the general requirements of common law for the admission of expert testimony by measuring the quality of the underlying theory and method behind the expert's opinion against community standards.

> Just when a scientific principle or discovery crosses the line between the experimental and demonstrable stages is difficult to define. Somewhere in this twilight zone the evidential force of the principle must be recognized, and while courts will go a long way in admitting expert testimony deduced from a well-recognized scientific principle or discovery, the thing from which the deduction is made must be sufficiently established to have gained general acceptance in the particular field in which it belongs.[28]

The principle enunciated in *Frye* initially was given scant attention by other courts, partly because of its limitation to screening novel scientific techniques. For several decades it was known only for its holding that lie detector testimony is inadmissible.[29] The premise that the expert testimony was required to spring from an "well-recognized" scientific principle that was "sufficiently established to have gained general acceptance" acquired no immediate cachet. There was no mention of *Frye* in the legislative history for the 1975 Federal Rules of Evidence.[30] In civil cases, *Frye* would not be cited as a guiding principle

---

[26] *See generally* Andre Moenssens, "Frye v. United States" in WILEY ENCYCLOPEDIA OF FORENSIC SCIENCE, (Jamieson A. & Moenssens A.A., eds) 2009 & online updates.

[27] For a concise history of the background and conduct of the Frye case, see Tal Golan, *Laws of Men and Laws of Nature*, Harvard University Press, 2004 at pp. 242–253.

[28] Frye v. United States, 293 F. 1013, 1014 (D.C. Cir. 1923).

[29] "Courts cited *Frye* only five times in published opinions before World War II, mostly in polygraph cases. After World War II, *Frye* was cited six times before 1950, twenty times during the 1950s, and twenty-two times in the 1960s." Paul C. Giannelli, "Forensic Science: Why No Research?" 38 FORDHAM URBAN L. J. 503–518, 511 n. 50 (2010) (citations omitted).

[30] Paul C. Giannelli, Daubert: Interpreting the Federal Rules of Evidence, 15 Cardozo L. Rev. 1999, 2000–2001 (1994).

until 1984, and was mentioned in less than half a dozen civil cases.[31] In criminal cases, by contrast, *Frye* became the polestar to guide the admission of test results from dozens of widely varied techniques that poured out of the growing number of crime laboratories starting in the 1970s. Ultimately, *Frye* became "the dominant standard for determining the admissibility of novel scientific evidence at trial."[32]

The *Frye* test was intended to represent a conservative approach to admitting evidence based on newly-developed scientific theories.[33] This approach was considered desirable under the view that jurors are easily awed by conclusions voiced by experts with impressive credentials. A 1926 survey of members of the American Psychological Association concerning the detection of deception seemed to demonstrate that the "relevant community" was less troubled by the reliability of the deception test than of a credulous juror being "bewitched by charlatans."[34]

In practice, the standard of "general acceptance in the particular field" under *Frye* proved difficult to define and inadequate in guaranteeing the reliability of the scientific evidence. Attorneys and courts grappled with what constituted the relevant "field" of expertise[35] and there was disagreement about whether "general acceptance" was intended to address the methodology or the expert's conclusions.[36] The D.C. Circuit Court later noted that under *Frye*, "the prime focus is on counting scientists' votes, rather than on verifying the soundness of a scientific conclusion."[37] The emphasis on "vote counting" can be counterproductive in assessing the validity and reliability of a scientific methodology. New developments made by imaginative workers in a field may be considered radical by their more conservative colleagues, who reject the new developments regardless of their worth. On the other hand, workers in a novel area sharing a common goal may develop a technique and they may subsequently advocate its reliability to further their professional goals.[38] These points have been central to criticisms of the courts' handling of some pattern comparison techniques in criminal cases.

---

[31] For a detailed discussion of the application of *Frye* in civil and criminal cases between 1923 and 1993, *see* Kenneth Chesebro, "Galileo's Retort: Peter Huber's Junk Scholarship," 42 Am. U. L. Rev. 1637, 1693–1696 (1993).

[32] Daubert v. Merrill Dow Pharmaceuticals, 509 U.S. 579, 585 (1993).

[33] People v. Kelly, 17 Cal.3d 24, 130 Cal.Rptr. 144, 549 P.2d 1240 (1976).

[34] Tal Golan, *Laws of Men and Laws of Nature*, Harvard University Press, 2004 at p. 252.

[35] The court in *Frye* decided that the polygraph belonged in the fields of physiology and psychology, though neither field has claimed the technique.

[36] David E. Bernstein, "Frye, Frye, Again: The Past, Present, and Future of the General Acceptance Test," 41 Jurimetrics J. 385–407 (2001).

[37] Jones v. United States, 548 A. 2d. 35, 42 (D.C. 1988).

[38] Andre A. Moenssens, "Requiem for the 'General Acceptance' Standard in Forensic Science—Some Whimsical Thoughts on the Battle of *Frye* vs. The Federal Rules of Evidence," in Cyril H. Wecht, ed. *Legal Medicine Annual*, W.B. Saunders Co., 1982 at pp. 275, 279–280.

The now-discredited forensic disciplines of voice recognition, bullet lead analysis, and microscopic hair comparison, and the heavily criticized practice of bitemark comparisons, were accepted by the practitioners who used the techniques. Advocates whose adversarial positions in criminal cases (generally the prosecution) depended on the practitioners to establish that the techniques were generally accepted in their field to admit the "scientific" evidence. For years, courts accepted the evidence generated by these techniques under *Frye*.[39] Upon the application of more objective scrutiny by the broader scientific community to the theories and practices involved in these disciplines, a lack of robust validation for these practices was demonstrated.

As the laboratory-proven science of DNA comparison became a standard by which the quality of validation and reliability of "scientific" methods and techniques were judged, assumptions about the "scientific" underpinnings of forensic disciplines faltered. As DNA analysis contributed to proving the existence of wrongful convictions in cases that had employed forensic "science" to associate the defendant with evidence in the case, it also cast doubt on the evidence derived from these practices. Many of these practices were based in experiential expertise and subjective analysis; some (except for bitemark comparisons) are now almost entirely abandoned, despite having "general acceptance" among the practitioners in those narrow disciplines, and years of acceptance by courts.

2.   MODIFICATIONS

Some state courts rejected a strict adherence to the *Frye* decision.[40] Other courts, while nominally bound by *Frye,* ignored its dictates when they felt that the general acceptance test would produce an inappropriate result. For example, in *People v. Williams*,[41] the court held that when a test was unknown in the medical profession generally, but accepted by a narrow specialty within medicine, its results would be admissible.[42] The court recognized that medical specialization made it impossible for some tests to become widely known and accepted in the

---

[39] *See, e.g.,* U.S. v. Wright, 37 C.M.R. 447 (1967)(voice identification); Section 4.08(1) discussing bullet lead analysis in Chapter 4 "Firearm and Toolmark Evidence," *infra*; Section 7.11 discussing hair analysis in Chapter 7 "Trace Evidence: Materials," *infra*; and Section 11.09 discussing bitemark comparisons in Chapter 11 "Forensic Odontology," *infra*.

[40] *See, e.g.,* People v. Hampton, 746 P.2d 947 (Colo. 1987)(*Frye* is to be used only for polygraph evidence and not for behavioral science evidence—here rape trauma syndrome evidence, which was held admissible); State v. Hall, 297 N.W.2d 80 (Iowa 1980)(*Frye* rejected, mandating showing of reliability of the evidence on an *ad hoc* basis and admitting blood splatter analysis evidence); State v. Klindt, 389 N.W.2d 670 (Iowa 1986)(*Frye* again rejected when dealing with serologist, anthropologist, and statistician evidence).

[41] 331 P.2d 251 (Cal.1958).

[42] The case involved the development, by a physician, of the Nalorphine (Nalline) pupil test to determine narcotic addiction. *See* Stanley E. Grupp, "The Nalline Test I:Development and Implementation," 61 J. CRIM. L., CRIMINOLOGY & POLICE SCI. 296 (1970); "The Nalline Test II: Rationale," 61 J. CRIM. L., CRIMINOLOGY & POLICE SCI. 463 (1970); "The Nalline Test III: Objections, Limitations and Assessment," 62 J. CRIM. L., CRIMINOLOGY & POLICE SCI. 288 (1971).

general field of medicine, but gave no guidance on factors to be considered when dealing with experimental testing tailored to the requirements of a specific investigative problem. In 1968, a Florida appellate court provided that guidance. *Coppolino v. State*[43] was replete with scientific evidence for both the defense and the prosecution, including scientific tests which had been specifically devised by a pathologist to reveal the presence of a certain chemical in body tissue. The test was previously unknown among pathologists, and expert witnesses for the opposing side testified to its lack of proven reliability. The court nevertheless upheld the admissibility of the test results. The court concluded that novel test results, specifically devised to explore a given problem, are not necessarily inadmissible simply because the profession at large is not yet familiar with them. Admission of the novel test results was based on the expert's explanation of the already-accepted principles underlying the analysis and a description of the technique that would permit reproduction of the results by other researchers. In this way, *Frye* jurisprudence also came to include the concepts of validation of techniques according to objective scientific criteria and an assessment of a technique's reliability in practice.

With the passage in 1975 of the Federal Rules of Evidence, questions continued about whether the *Frye* concept of "general acceptance" within a relevant community remained a viable one. Legal commentators also criticized the increasingly apparent failure of courts to reliably assess whether "good science" was being presented at trial.[44] A good example of the courts' movement away from the limited scope of *Frye* to focus on reliability of the theory and method underlying the expert's testimony appears in *United States v. Downing*.[45] In *Downing*, the Third Circuit Court of Appeals reversed the trial court's exclusion of testimony concerning the reliability of eyewitness identifications. In analysis foreshadowing practice that developed a decade later, the court conditioned admission of the evidence on preliminary scrutiny of the reliability of the scientific principles on which the testimony rested.[46] The court pointed out that *Frye* was sufficiently vague to permit manipulating the "relevant scientific community" to obtain the level of

---

[43] 223 So.2d 68 (Fla. App. 1968), *appeal dismissed* 234 So.2d 120 (Fla.1969), *cert. denied*, 399 U.S. 927 (1970).

[44] *See, e.g.*, Giannelli, "The Admissibility of Novel Scientific Evidence: Frye v. United States, A Half Century Later, 80 Colum. L. Rev. 1197 (1980); Bert Black, "A Unified Theory of Scientific Evidence," 56 Fordham L. Rev. 592 (1988).

Some commentators complained that "junk science" was flooding the courtrooms. *See* Peter Huber, "Junk Science in the Courtroom," FORBES, Jul. 8, 1991 at 68 ("with the backing of 'expert' testimony from a doctor and police department officials, a soothsayer who decided she had lost her psychic powers following a CAT scan persuaded a Philadelphia jury to award her $1 million."). However, Huber's work was itself strongly criticized. One author referred to Huber's methodology in outlining the problem of "junk science" in the courtroom as "little better than that of the charlatans he criticizes." Jeff Lewin, "Calabresi's Retort: Peter Huber's Junk Scholarship," 21 Hofstra L. Rev. 183 (1992).

[45] 753 F. 2d 1224 (3d Cir. 1985).

[46] 753 F.2d at 1226.

agreement needed.[47] Instead, the court recognized the "more flexible approach" to admissibility afforded by Federal Rule of Evidence 702, and suggested an inquiry focusing on:

> (1) the soundness and reliability of the process or technique used in generating the evidence, (2) the possibility that admitting the evidence would overwhelm, confuse, or mislead the jury, and (3) the proffered connection between the scientific research or test result to be presented, and particular disputed factual issues in the case.[48]

Turning the analysis from the vague standards of internal reference in a relevant scientific community to a more broad and objective assessment of reliability and helpfulness represented a significant shift of focus.[49]

§1.03 THE *DAUBERT* STANDARD

As courts were debating the viability of *Frye* following the enactment of the Federal Rules of Evidence, a tort case was working its way through the federal courts in California. It involved two infant plaintiffs, their mother, and the father of one of the children, whose last name was Daubert. They had sued the manufacturer of the drug Bendectin, prescribed to alleviate the discomfort of morning sickness, alleging that the drug caused limb reduction birth defects. The drug company moved for summary judgment based on thirty studies done on Bendectin that had not found a statistically significant relationship between the drug and birth defects. The plaintiffs' experts, based on a reanalysis of the same studies argued they showed a possible link. The Ninth Circuit Court of Appeals, in affirming the district courts' exclusion of the plaintiffs' expert testimony, held the testimony of the plaintiffs' experts did not satisfy the *Frye* "general acceptance" test as measured in the relevant scientific community of epidemiologists.[50] The case was appealed to the United States Supreme Court and multiple amici briefs were filed: fourteen supporting the defendant, six in support of the plaintiffs, and two supporting neither party.

With a plethora of legal and policy arguments before it, the Supreme Court ignored most of them in reaching its holding in *Daubert v. Merrell Dow Pharmaceuticals*,[51] simply referred to hereafter as

---

[47] 753 F.2d at 1236.

[48] 753 F.2d at 1237.

[49] During this period of time, the Carnegie Commission on Science, Technology and Government noted a dearth of interdisciplinary input to judicial decisionmaking on the use of scientific evidence in the courts and called for reform. *Science and Technology in Judicial Decision Making: Creating Opportunities and Meeting Challenges,* Carnegie Corporation of New York, March 1993 (available at: https://www.carnegie.org/publications/science-and-technology-in-judicial-decision-making-creating-opportunities-and-meeting-challenges/)(last accessed January 3, 2017).

[50] Daubert v. Merrell Dow Pharm., 727 F.Supp. 570 (S.D.Cal.1989), 951 F.2d 1128 (9th Cir.1991).

[51] 509 U.S. 579 (1993).

Daubert. The Court focused solely on whether the *Frye* rule survived the enactment of the Federal Rules of Evidence.[52] Holding unanimously that it did not, the Court concluded that expert testimony is no longer inadmissible merely because it has not gained general acceptance in the scientific field in which it belongs. In *Daubert*, the Supreme Court squarely relegated *Frye* to history as far as federal trials were concerned, stating that "a rigid 'general acceptance' requirement would be at odds with the 'liberal thrust' of the Federal Rules and their general approach to relaxing the traditional barriers to opinion testimony."[53] In its decision, the Supreme Court mandated that instead of "general acceptance," the court must determine the "scientific reliability" of expert opinion evidence using the following mechanism:

> Faced with a proffer of expert scientific testimony, then, the trial judge must determine . . . whether the expert is proposing to testify to (1) scientific knowledge that (2) will assist the trier of fact to understand or determine a fact in issue. This entails a preliminary assessment of whether the reasoning or methodology underlying the testimony is scientifically valid and of whether that reasoning or methodology properly can be applied to the facts in issue.[54]

To assist the trial court in making the legal decision on admissibility of proffered expert opinion testimony, the trial judge should examine the following factors: (1) whether the type of evidence can be and has been tested by a scientific methodology;[55] (2) whether the underlying theory or technique has been subjected to peer review and has been published in the professional literature;[56] (3) how reliable

---

[52] The rule at issue in the case was Federal Rule of Evidence 702. The rule has been amended several times since *Daubert*, most recently in 2011. The rule currently provides:

Rule 702. Testimony by Expert Witnesses

A witness who is qualified as an expert by knowledge, skill, experience, training, or education may testify in the form of an opinion or otherwise if:

    (a) the expert's scientific, technical, or other specialized knowledge will help the trier of fact to understand the evidence or to determine a fact in issue;

    (b) the testimony is based on sufficient facts or data;

    (c) the testimony is the product of reliable principles and methods; and

    (d) the expert has reliably applied the principles and methods to the facts of the case.

[53] 509 U.S. at 588–589 (internal quotations omitted).

[54] 509 U.S. at 592–593 (internal citations omitted).

[55] This has been interpreted to mean that the theory on which the testimony relied has been empirically tested. The Court cited Karl Popper's criterion for the scientific status of a theory or methodology to be its falsifiability. *See* Karl R. Popper, *Conjectures and Refutations: The Growth of Scientific Knowledge*, New York, NY: Routledge (1963).

See Ann C. Smith, "Daubert v. Merrell Dow Pharmaceuticals," in WILEY ENCYCLOPEDIA OF FORENSIC SCIENCE, (Jamieson A. & Moenssens A.A., eds) 2009 & online updates.

[56] "The term peer review literature generally refers to professional journals or periodicals, wherein inclusion of an article has preliminarily been screened by other scientists who deem it worthy to be submitted for comment and scrutiny to the relevant scientific community. Published works, which the Court considered to be one aspect of 'peer review,' receive even more analysis and critical comment. . . ." Ann C. Smith, "Daubert v. Merrell Dow

the results are in terms of a potential error rate;[57] (4) the existence and maintenance of standards controlling the technique's operation; and finally (5) a consideration of general acceptance.[58] "A reliability assessment does not require, although it does permit, explicit identification of a relevant scientific community and an express determination of a particular degree of acceptance within that community."[59] The Supreme Court stressed that the new test was a flexible one with no controlling factor and in which other factors could be considered.[60] The "scope of a Daubert hearing [on admissibility] is not limited to an appraisal of an expert's credentials and techniques but also entails an examination of his conclusions to determine whether they flow rationally from the methodology employed. If perscrutation reveals 'that there is simply too great an analytical gap between the data and the opinion proffered,' the expert's testimony should be excluded."[61]

The consideration of additional factors than those specifically voiced in *Daubert* quickly arrived. On remand to the Ninth Circuit, the issue of whether the plaintiffs' expert had performed his statistical calculations mainly for the purpose of litigation was discussed. This "for purposes of litigation" work was contrasted with the work of the defendants' experts whose epidemiological analysis was done in the course "of research they have conducted independent of litigation."[62] While the Ninth Circuit stopped short of holding that "good science" must be done independently of litigation, it said that "preexisting research unrelated to the litigation provides the most persuasive basis for concluding that opinions ... were derived by the scientific method."[63] Thus, a proffer of expert testimony that is not based on

---

Pharmaceuticals," in WILEY ENCYCLOPEDIA OF FORENSIC SCIENCE, (Jamieson A. & Moenssens A.A., eds) 2009 & online updates.

   See also Andre Moenssens, "Peer Review as Affecting Opinion Evidence," in WILEY ENCYCLOPEDIA OF FORENSIC SCIENCE, (Jamieson A. & Moenssens A.A., eds) 2009 & online updates.

   [57] "To what extent the theory or conjecture is likely to be wrong. . . .Error rates, when they exist, are meaningful in that they help confirm the degree of confidence [in] the scientific conclusions. . . ." Ann C. Smith, "Daubert v. Merrell Dow Pharmaceuticals," in WILEY ENCYCLOPEDIA OF FORENSIC SCIENCE, (Jamieson A. & Moenssens A.A., eds) 2009 & online updates.

   [58] 509 U.S. at 592–594.

   [59] 509 U.S. at 594 (quoting United States v. Downing, 753 F.2d 1224, 1238 (3d Cir.1985)).

   [60] On remand, Judge Alex Kozinski, who wrote the first and subsequent *Daubert* opinions in the Ninth Circuit, found that the proffered expert evidence did not meet the *Daubert* factors either. Calling the post-*Daubert* era a "Brave New World" and his role in imposing upon judges a "far more complex and daunting task" than under *Frye*, Judge Kozinski again affirmed the earlier decision to grant summary judgment. *See* Daubert v. Merrell Dow Pharm., 43 F.3d 1311 (9th Cir.1995)(on remand).

   [61] Samaan v. St. Joseph Hospital, 670 F.3d 21, 32 (1st Cir. 2012)(internal citations omitted).

   [62] Daubert v. Merrell Dow Pharmaceuticals, Inc., 43 F. 3d 1311, 1317 (9th Cir.1995).

   [63] Id.

independent research "must come forward with other objective, verifiable evidence that the testimony is based on 'scientifically valid principles,'" that the court took to mean scrutiny through peer review and publication in a reputable journal.[64]

1. NON-SCIENTIFIC EXPERT TESTIMONY

While *Daubert* decided the admissibility standard for civil and criminal cases in federal courts only, the ruling also had a great impact in states with evidence codes based upon the Federal Rules of Evidence and even in states that had previously followed the general acceptance rule of *Frye*. However, questions remained whether the new standard also governed the admissibility of expert testimony not clearly grounded in science. One court observed:

> The distinction between scientific and non-scientific expert testimony is a critical one. By way of illustration, if one wanted to explain to a jury how a bumblebee is able to fly, an aeronautical engineer might be a helpful witness. Since flight principles have some universality, the expert could apply general principles to the case of the bumblebee. Conceivably, even if he had never seen a bumblebee, he would still be qualified to testify, as long as he was familiar with its component parts.
>
> On the other hand, if one wanted to prove that bumblebees always take off into the wind, a beekeeper with no scientific training at all would be an acceptable expert witness provided a proper foundation were laid for his conclusions. The foundation would not relate to formal training, but to his firsthand observations. In other words, the beekeeper does not know any more about flight characteristics than the juror, but he has seen a lot more bumblebees than they have.[65]

The bumblebee analogy may provide some insight into the distinction between scientifically schooled experts and non-scientist expert witnesses, but it is not always helpful. Perhaps it was for that reason that some state courts suggested avoiding the *Daubert* quandary by applying the decision's factors only to "novel scientific evidence." In doing so, courts began to differ in determining whether a given field of expertise was "novel,"[66] or even whether it was "science."[67]

---

[64]   43 F.3d at 1318.

[65]   Berry v. City of Detroit, 25 F.3d 1342, 1349–1350 (6th Cir.1994).

[66]   *Contrast* Meador, 674 So.2d at 834 (HGN is not "novel") *with* People v. Leahy, 8 Cal.4th 587, 34 Cal.Rptr.2d 663, 882 P.2d 321 (1994) (HGN is "novel").

[67]   *See, e.g.,* State v. Meador, 674 So.2d 826 (Fla.App.1996)(holding that the horizontal gaze nystagmus test is "scientific" evidence under the state's *Frye* test, but recognizing that other jurisdictions consider it simply lay observational evidence not based on scientific expertise).

The debate about non-scientific expert testimony was settled decisively in 1999 when the United States Supreme Court handed down its decision in *Kumho Tire Co. v. Carmichael*.[68] The plaintiffs had experienced a tire blowout in their minivan and sought to make their case through the testimony of a tire failure expert that a defect in the tire's design or manufacture caused the blowout. Applying the *Daubert* factors, the trial court excluded the testimony of the mechanical engineer because the expert's methodology in determining tire failure was unreliable and not generally accepted in the relevant community of experts. The Eleventh Circuit reversed the trial court's decision and held that *Daubert* applied only to "scientific" opinions.[69] The Supreme Court unanimously rejected the Eleventh Circuit's reasoning and stated unequivocally that the *Daubert* standard applied to experts whose testimony might be either of a technical nature or based on "other specialized knowledge."[70] The Court reiterated that the *Daubert* factors to determine evidentiary reliability constituted a flexible guideline only and not a definitive checklist.[71] The Court recognized that for some professions there might well be other criteria by which reliability could be examined more appropriately.[72] In addition, the Court made clear that the examination of reliability potentially extended to theories, methods based on those theories, and the conclusions an expert reached.[73]

2. STANDARDS OF REVIEW

Between *Daubert* and *Kumho,* and after some division of opinion in the circuit courts, the issue of the appropriate standard of review for a trial court's Daubert admissibility decision was addressed by the Supreme Court. The lower courts had split on whether the admissibility decision was a question of law to be reviewed de novo on appeal or an exercise of judicial discretion entitled to deference on appeal. In *General Electric v. Joiner,*[74] the second case of the Daubert "trilogy", the US Supreme Court determined that the decision to admit or exclude expert opinion remained solely within the trial court's discretion, and that

---

[68] 526 U.S. 137 (1999); See generally Ann C. Smith "Kumho Tire v. Carmichael," in WILEY ENCYCLOPEDIA OF FORENSIC SCIENCE, (Jamieson A. & Moenssens A.A., eds) 2009 & online updates.

[69] Carmichael v. Samyang Tire, Inc., 131 F.3d 1433, 1435 (11th Cir. 1997).

[70] 526 U.S. at 148.

[71] Id. at 151 (the list of *Daubert* factors "was meant to be helpful, not definitive. . . . Indeed, those factors do not all necessarily apply even in every instance in which the reliability of scientific evidence is challenged.").

[72] For a thorough discussion of the history and application of the *Daubert* trilogy, *see* Margaret A. Berger, "The Admissibility of Expert Testimony," in Federal Judicial Center, *Reference Manual on Scientific Evidence*, 3rd ed., Washington, DC: National Academies Press (2011) at pp. 11–36.

[73] 526 U.S. at 149.

[74] 522 U.S. 136 (1997).

review by an appellate court encompasses both the expert's methodologies and conclusions.[75]

§1.04   JURISDICTIONAL CONSIDERATIONS

The United States Supreme Court opinions discussed in the previous section apply only in federal civil and criminal trials because they interpret the meaning of Federal Rule of Evidence 702. Many of the states which have evidence rules patterned upon Federal Rule 702 have decided to follow *Daubert*.[76] A number of *Frye* jurisdictions, however, have chosen to retain *Frye*,[77] although that number is dropping.[78] Some states adopted a hybrid approach.[79] Even in the states that have not adopted *Daubert*, the decisions of the United States Supreme Court interpreting Rule 702 have had an impact, not always on the decision of admissibility, but certainly as a way of evaluating the probative value of the evidence.[80] Furthermore, even true *Frye* states are reinterpreting the "general acceptance" standard as one that requires perhaps more proof of reliability than merely acceptance by the users of the test.[81]

---

[75] 522 U.S. at 146.

[76] *See, e.g.,* Paul C. Giannelli, *Daubert in the States*, Faculty Publications. Paper 349 (1998) (available at: http://scholarlycommons.law.case.edu/faculty_publications/349)(last accessed November 17, 2016); Lukjan v. Commonwealth, 358 S.W.3d 33 (Ky. App. 2012)(Kentucky Rule of Evidence 702 mirrors the federal counterpart); State v. Coon, 974 P.2d 386, 394 (Alaska 1999)(adopting the *Daubert* standard for admissibility of scientific evidence); State v. Porter, 241 Conn. 57, 698 A.2d 739 (1997), *cert. denied*, 523 U.S. 1058 (1988)(same).

[77] *See, e.g.,* Montgomery Mut. Ins. Co. v. Chesson, 399 Md. 314, 327, 923 A.2d 939, 946 (Ct. App. 2007)("Maryland adheres to the standard set forth in Frye v. United States, 293 F. 1013 (D.C. Cir. 1923), for determining the admissibility of scientific evidence and expert scientific testimony."); People v. David Banks, 2016 IL App (1st) 131009 (Nov. 9, 2016)("In Illinois, the admission of expert testimony is governed by the standards expressed in Frye"); Grady v. Frito-Lay, Inc. 576 Pa. 546, 557, 839 A.2d 1038, 1044 (2003)("the Frye rule will continue to be applied in Pennsylvania")

[78] *See* Motorola Inc. v. Murray, 2016 D.C. App. LEXIS 382 (DC App. 2016)(adopting FRE 702 to replace Frye as the admissibility standard in the District of Columbia).

[79] West Virginia, which has evidence rules patterned upon the Federal Rules, has chosen to follow *Daubert* for "scientific evidence," but rejected *Kumho* for all non-scientific expert opinion evidence. *See* Watson v. Inco Alloys Int'l, Inc., 209 W.Va. 234, 545 S.E.2d 294 (2001). Commenting on the decision, see the article by Chief Justice Robin Jean Davis, "Admitting Expert Testimony in Federal Courts and its Impact on West Virginia Jurisprudence," 104 W.V. L. Rev. 485 (2002).

[80] *See* Turner v. State, 953 N.E.2d 1039, 1050 (Ind. 2011)("We therefore find Daubert helpful, but not controlling, when analyzing testimony. . . . In light of the differences between Indiana Rule 702 and Federal Rule 702, we have previously declined to follow Kumho Tire in applying the Daubert reliability analysis to non-scientific expert testimony.")

[81] In Illinois, which has retained *Frye*, an appellate court used a "*Frye*-plus-reliability" test for the admission of novel scientific evidence. In Harris v. Cropmate Co., 302 Ill.App.3d 364, 375, 706 N.E.2d 55, 64–65 (1999), the court suggested trial judges are required to make a six-inquiry approach, the final point of which sounds remarkably like *Daubert*:

Is the evidence "reliable?" Even when proponents can make a colorable claim that a particular scientific technique or method has been accepted by the appropriate scientific community, trial courts still may not delegate their authority to the scientific community . . . In serving as gatekeepers to keep out scientific evidence that constitutes nothing but 'junk science' or mere speculation, trial courts should constantly be asking, does the proffered witness have sufficient information . . . to render a *reliable* opinion? Courts should remember that they need not—and should

Another jurisdictional consideration is the subject matter requirement in the admission of expert testimony.[82] In most common law jurisdictions, experts are adduced as witnesses to assist the trier of fact (judge or jury) in areas outside their common knowledge.[83] In federal courts, which must follow Federal Rule of Evidence 702, and in state courts that have adopted a similar rule, the codified admissibility standard is a more liberal formulation of the subject matter requirement. FRE 702 does not impose an "outside the common knowledge" requirement; instead, it requires that the expert testimony "assist the trier of fact."[84] Some states impose different standards in civil and criminal cases. For example, in Virginia the rules of evidence provide:

(a)   Use of Expert Testimony.

(i) In a civil proceeding, if scientific, technical, or other specialized knowledge will assist the trier of fact to understand the evidence or to determine a fact in issue, a witness qualified as an expert by knowledge, skill, experience, training, or education may testify thereto in the form of an opinion or otherwise.

(ii) In a criminal proceeding, expert testimony is admissible if the standards set forth in subdivision (a)(i) of this Rule are met and, in addition, the court finds that the subject matter is beyond the knowledge and experience of ordinary persons, such that the jury needs expert opinion in order to comprehend the subject matter, form an intelligent opinion, and draw its conclusions.[85]

---

not—accept an expert's opinion on the basis of *ipse dixit*, i.e. such a thing is so because [the witness says] it is so.

[82] *See* United States v. Needham, 604 F.3d 673, 680 (2d Cir. 2010)("a jury is capable of concluding based on its lay knowledge that cocaine is imported into the United States"); *but see* Rosenfield v. Oceania Cruises, Inc., 654 F.3d 1190 (11th Cir. 2011)(expert testimony erroneously excluded under FRE 702 because "matters of slip resistance and surface friction" are beyond the understanding and experience of the average lay juror).

[83] *See* Bond v. Commonwealth, 226 Va. 534, 311 S.E.2d 769 (1984)(when the evidence, exclusive of expert testimony, is sufficient to enable a jury of laymen to reach an intelligent conclusion, expert testimony is inadmissible).

[84] *See* State v. Chapple, 135 Ariz. 281, 292–293, 600 P.2d 1208, 1219–1220 (1983)(the standard in Rule 702 "is not whether the jury could reach some conclusion in absence of the expert evidence, but whether the jury is qualified without such testimony to determine intelligently and to the best possible degree the particular issue without enlightenment from those having a specialized understanding of the subject.")(internal citations omitted); Hampton v. State, 588 N.E.2d 555, 558 (Ind. App. 1992)("Portions of the [expert testimony] were beyond the common knowledge and experience of the average lay person, but portions of it were also inherently understandable.").

[85] Rules of the Supreme Court of Virginia Rule 2:702.

§1.05   OUT-OF-COURT CHALLENGES

Daubert doubtless had a great impact on civil litigation, where federal judges took their "gatekeeping role" seriously, rigorously evaluating the bases for validating experts' theories, often to the detriment of plaintiffs' experts.[86] The impact in criminal cases was less profound. In the aftermath of *Kumho*,[87] some commentators and courts anticipated a tide of successful *Daubert* challenges in criminal cases based on the lack of rigorous systematic research to validate the basic premises of the underlying techniques of some forensic science disciplines.[88] Judges in criminal cases, however, did not respond with the same vigorous scrutiny of the scientific evidence reliability as was seen in civil cases. One venerable commentator stated that the courts' approach to admissibility questions overemphasized how data was produced to a point that distracted court and counsel from what the scientific evidence might actually prove.[89] Both the tide of challenges and the exclusion of forensic science evidence in criminal cases failed to materialize. Whether due to inadequate scientific training of attorneys, funding limitations,[90] or force of habit, the seismic shift in the admission of such evidence did not materialize following *Daubert* and

---

[86] *See, e.g.,* Margaret A. Berger, "Upsetting the Balance Between Adverse Interests: The Impact of the Supreme Court's Trilogy on Expert Testimony in Toxic Tort Litigation," 64 L. & CONTEMPORARY PROBLEMS 289, 290 (2001)(noting that Federal Judicial Center studies had reported 65% of counsel as stating that judges are less likely to admit expert testimony since *Daubert*).

[87] As is customary whenever a new decision is announced, differing interpretations on its scope were issued. *Compare* David Crump, "The Trouble with Daubert-Kumho: Reconsidering the Supreme Court's Philosophy of Science," 68 Mo. L. Rev. 1 (2003), Edward J. Imwinkelried, " 'Peer Dialogue' The How and What of 'Appropriate Validation' Under Daubert: Reconsidering the Treatment of Einstein and Freud," 68 Mo. L. Rev. 43 (2003), *with* Paul R. Rice, "Peer Dialogue: The Quagmire of Scientific Expert Testimony: Crumping the Supreme Court's Style," 68 Mo. L. Rev. 53 (2003).

[88] *See* Randolph N. Jonakait, "The Meaning of Daubert and What that Means for Forensic Science," 15 Cardozo L. Rev. 2103, 2117 (2004)("[I]f *Daubert* is taken seriously, then much of forensic science is in serious trouble."); Barry C. Scheck, "DNA and Daubert," 15 Cardozo L. Rev. 1959, 1959 (2004)("*Daubert* calls upon courts to undertake a much more sophisticated and informed analysis of scientific evidence than Frye v. United States."); *see also* Margaret A. Berger, "Procedural Paradigms for Applying the Daubert Test," 78 Minn. L. Rev. 1345, 1354 (1994)("Considerable forensic evidence made its way into the courtroom without empirical validation of the underlying theory and/or its particular application. Courts never required some of the most venerable branches of forensic science—such as fingerprinting, ballistics, and handwriting—to demonstrate their ability to make unique identifications.")

See United States v. Hines, 55 F. Supp. 2d 62, 67 (D. Mass. 1999)(*Daubert* and *Kumho* invited "reexamination even of 'generally accepted' venerable, technical fields" such as handwriting comparison); United States v. Hidalgo, 229 F. Supp. 2d 961, 966 (D. Ariz. 2002)("Courts are now confronting challenges to testimony, as here, whose admissibility had long been settled.")

[89] Margaret Berger, "Expert Testimony in Criminal Proceedings: Questions Daubert Does Not Answer", 33 Seton Hall L. Rev. 1125 (2003).

[90] *See* Peter J. Neufeld, "The (Near) Irrelevance of *Daubert* to Criminal Justice: And Some Suggestions for Reform," 95 AM. J. PUB. HEALTH S107 (2005)("Defense lawyers generally fail to build a challenge with appropriate witnesses and new data. Thus, even if inclined to mount a *Daubert* challenge, they lack the requisite knowledge and skills, as well as the funds, to succeed").

Kumho.[91] While the anticipated seismic shift in the admissibility of forensic science evidence in criminal cases languished, challenges to the evidence were being raised in other contexts.

1.   NATIONAL ACADEMY OF SCIENCES

Since the 1990s, exonerations of wrongly convicted innocent persons through use of DNA evidence post-trial revealed a prevalence of faulty forensic analyses and testimony about them. Observers noted that while DNA had been extensively verified through scientific research, other areas of forensic science had not. In 2006, Congress authorized the National Academy of Sciences (NAS) to study the various practices involved in forensic science services in the country. The mandate to study forensic science was broad based, requiring the study to focus on existing resources and needs of the forensic science community, evaluate best practices, and assist in the development in the use of forensic technologies and techniques. A Committee was appointed by NAS in the fall of 2006 to implement the congressional mandate. The Committee was composed of members of academia and the forensic science community, lawyers, judges, and scientists. Its project would have as its main purpose: "Identifying the Needs of the Forensic Science Community." Eight meetings were held throughout 2007 and 2008, at which experts from all sectors of the various evidence examination disciplines were invited to make presentations. The presenters included law enforcement officials, scientists, medical examiners, crime laboratory personnel, defense attorneys, law professors and other academics, private practitioners in forensic science, educators, and representatives of relevant professional organizations.

The Committee's report, (hereinafter "2009 NAS Report") was publicly revealed on February 18, 2009.[92] Its conclusion was dire:

> The bottom line is simple: In a number of forensic disciplines, forensic science professionals have yet to establish either the validity of their approach or the accuracy of their conclusions, and the courts have been utterly ineffective in addressing this problem.[93]

---

[91] *See* Paul C. Giannelli, Edward J. Imwinkelried and Joseph L. Peterson, "Reference Guide on Forensic Identification Expertise," in Federal Judicial Center, *Reference Manual on Scientific Evidence*, 3d ed., Washington, DC: National Academies Press (2011) at pp. 55–127. *See also* D. Michael Risinger, "Navigating Expert Reliability: Are Criminal Standards of Certainty Being Left on the Dock?" 64 ALB. L. REV. 99, 149 (2000); Mark Page, Jane Taylor, and Matt Blenkin, "Forensic Identification Science Evidence Since *Daubert*: Part I—A Quantitative Analysis of the Exclusion of Forensic Science Identification Evidence," 56 J. FORENSIC SCI. 1180–1184 (2011); Mark Page, Jane Taylor, and Matt Blenkin, "Forensic Identification Science Evidence Since *Daubert*: Part II—Judicial Reasoning in Decisions to Exclude Forensic Identification Evidence on Grounds of Reliability," 56 J. FORENSIC SCI. 913–917 (2011).

[92] Committee on Identifying the Needs of the Forensic Science Community, National Research Council of the National Academies, *Strengthening Forensic Science in the United States: A Path Forward*, The National Academies Press: Washington D.C., 2009.

[93] NAS Report at p. 53.

When the report became available, it detailed some of the alarming findings that forensic scientists had anticipated and raised additional ones. The reaction in the forensic science community was generally supportive of the report's recognition that forensic science services are grossly underfunded and that additional research was needed to validate forensic science technique and their applications. Neither of these two points came as any surprise. The report's other findings and recommendations, however, roiled the forensic science and legal communities and resulted in media frenzy over the "serious problems" and the "seriously deficient" forensic science system in the United States.[94]

After reviewing the current state of forensic science services and highlighting some widely publicized false attributions of incriminating evidence,[95] the Committee members concluded that the criminal justice system places an overreliance on expert witness testimony that is not based on scientifically validated methodologies. The Committee further concluded that expert witnesses in at least some of the forensic science disciplines are largely untrained in scientific methods; are susceptible to prosecutorial bias; and lack adequate training, education, and certification. These deficiencies were found more in those disciplines that have long been accepted uncritically by courts wherein its practitioners seek to individualize certain types of evidence as having a "positive" connection to a suspect. These disciplines are sometimes referred to as "comparative evidence" methods. The examiners sometimes justified their conclusions on the basis of some mantra such as "nature never duplicates itself," "no two snowflakes are alike," and "everything in nature is different," whether those proffered justifications could be shown to apply to the specific forms of evidence.

As a result of the findings by the Committee, the report presented thirteen recommendations, of which the most far-reaching and controversial recommendation was the creation of a new and independent federal agency to provide oversight of the forensic science community. The existing voluntary self-regulating oversight provided by professional organizations was found by the Committee to produce too much fragmentation and insufficient leadership to meet the needs of the forensic science community and the criminal justice system. The proposed new federal agency—the National Institute of Forensic Science

---

[94] Nell Greenfield-Boyce, "Report: Forensics Rife with 'Serious Problems'," NPR All Things Considered, February 18, 2009 (available at: http://www.npr.org/templates/story/story.php?storyId=100813367)(last accessed January 3, 2017); Pete Williams, "Crime Labs Are Seriously Deficient, Report Says: National Academy of Science Says Only DNA Evidence is Dependable," NBC News, February 18, 2009 (available at: http://www.nbcnews.com/id/292585 76/ns/us_news-crime_and_courts/t/crime-labs-are-seriously-deficient-report-says/#.WGwSbbG ZNm8)(last accessed January 3, 2017).

[95] Among other examples of the failings in forensic science, the 2009 NAS Report cites the erroneous identification by leading FBI experts of Brandon Mayfield as the person whose latent fingerprint was associated with the Madrid, Spain train bombing, the frauds of the late West Virginia State Police Crime Laboratory examiner Fred Zain in the early 1990s, suspected bite mark cases, and the Houston, Texas laboratory scandal. 2009 NAS Report at pp. 42–48.

(NIFS)—was deemed essential for "a more central, strategic, and integrated approach to forensic science at the national level."[96] The report envisioned NIFS as an independent agency, to be removed from law enforcement control or prosecution affiliation, with specific and wide-ranging purposes designed to standardize and regulate forensic science service.[97]

Concerning the scientific validity of forensic science disciplines, the Committee found little support in science for "individualization" testimony offered in fingerprint, firearm, tool mark, bite mark, and some trace evidence opinions. Several times the Report repeated the finding that "[w]ith the exception of nuclear DNA analysis . . . no forensic method has been rigorously shown to have the capacity to consistently, and with a high degree of certainty, demonstrate a connection between evidence and a specific individual or source."[98] The Report analyzed the strengths and weaknesses of several forensic science disciplines.[99] While recognizing that some of the well-established evidence evaluations of crime laboratories are based on solid scientific principles and are supported by solid bases of theory and research,[100] other techniques:

> have been developed heuristically. That is, they are based on observation, experience, and reasoning without an underlying scientific theory, experiments designed to test the uncertainties and reliability of method, or sufficient data that are collected and analyzed scientifically.[101]

In the courts, the report immediately gained attention through multiple citations in the United States Supreme Court's opinion in *Melendez-Diaz v. Massachusetts*,[102] although the majority decision insisted that it was not relying on "the deficiencies of crime-lab analysts shown by this report to resolve the constitutional question presented in this case."[103] The report continued to be cited in federal and state cases, primarily in support of defense challenges to the admissibility of forensic science evidence, but the majority of courts have denied these challenges or at most limited some of the expert conclusions expressed before

---

[96]   2009 NAS Report at p. 56.

[97]   Id. at pp. 81–82.

[98]   Id. at p. 7.

[99]   The report's observations and conclusions as to specific methods are addressed throughout this book within the discussion of the individual disciplines.

[100]   The report mentions DNA analysis, serology, forensic pathology, toxicology, chemical analysis, and digital and multimedia forensics. 2009 NAS Report at p. 128.

[101]   Id.

[102]   557 U.S. 305, 129 S.Ct. 2527 (2009). The case is discussed in Section 1.13(1) *infra*.

[103]   557 U.S. at 319 n. 6, 129 S.Ct. at 2537 n. 6.

juries.[104] The decisions overwhelmingly consider the "deficiencies of crime-lab analysts" to be the proper subject of cross-examination.[105]

The majority sentiment of commentators and the forensic community at the time the NAS Report was issued seemed to be that while the report provided many beneficial suggestions for improvements in forensic science, the most ambitious recommendations were economically unattainable or doomed by institutional opposition.[106] Although federal legislation was introduced in 2011 and 2012 to further many of the recommendations, including the creation of a federal agency to provide oversight of forensic science, the legislation was not enacted.[107] One area that has received federal support is the development of standards and policies to improve the quality of forensic science services. The National Institute of Standards and Technology (NIST) has created the Organization of Scientific Area Committees (OSAC) to support the development and promulgation of forensic science consensus documentary standards and guidelines, and to ensure that a sufficient scientific basis exists for each discipline.[108] Additionally, Congress authorized and funded the creation of the National Commission on Forensic Science (NCFS)[109] in the Department of Justice, and in partnership with NIST "to promote scientific validity, reduce fragmentation, and improve federal coordination of forensic science."[110] Since its inception, the NCFS has promoted the development of standards of practice in the forensic sciences, as well as addressing issues of training, accreditation of laboratories, case reporting, standardizing terminology, and other subjects of concern to the integrity of using forensic science in criminal cases.[111] As of December 2016, the NCFS has adopted over 35 documents in the areas of accreditation and proficiency testing, interim solutions, scientific

---

[104] *See* United States v. Taylor, 663 F. Supp.2d 1170 (D. N.M. 2009); *but see* State v. Ward, 364 N.C. 133, 694 S.E.2d 738 (2010)(finding the visual inspection of pills was insufficiently reliable method of identification).

[105] *See* United States v. Council, 777 F. Supp.2d 1006, 1012 (ED Va. 2011); United States v. Aman, 748 F. Supp.2d 531 (ED Va. 2010); United States v. Stone, 2012 US Dist. LEXIS 8973 (ED Mich. 2012).

[106] Conference Report, "The Good, the Bad, the Ugly: The NAS Report on Strengthening Forensic Science in America," 50 SCI. & JUST. 8–11 (2010).

[107] In response to the recommendations of the National Academy of Sciences and other calls for reform, Senator Patrick Leahy introduced the Criminal Justice and Forensic Science Reform Act of 2011. Senator Rockefeller introduced the Forensic Science and Standards Act of 2012. Neither bill was enacted.

[108] *See* https://www.nist.gov/topics/forensic-science/organization-scientific-area-committees-osac (last accessed January 3, 2017). The NIST OSAC Subcommittee work is discussed in the specific discipline chapters of this book. The PCAST Report, discussed *infra*, criticized the NIST OSAC effort as suffering from a lack of independent input and oversight, and a dearth of statisticians to assist in validation efforts. PCAST Report, *infra* note 113, at p. 126.

[109] https://www.justice.gov/ncfs (last accessed December 26, 2016).

[110] Id.

[111] *See* https://www.justice.gov/ncfs/work-products.

inquiry and research, mediolegal death investigation, reporting and testimony, human factors, and training on science and law.[112]

2. PRESIDENT'S COUNCIL OF ADVISORS ON SCIENCE AND TECHNOLOGY

Although federal resources have been directed to address the NAS Report recommendations concerning the development of standards and policies for improving the practice of forensic science, the NAS Report's statements on the apparent lack of scientific validity of several disciplines were not immediately addressed in a centralized manner. As of 2015, the question still seemed open as to whether establishing the validity of forensic science methods had been addressed since the 2009 NAS report had suggested that changes be made. In 2015, the President's Council of Advisors on Science and Technology (PCAST) was asked to respond to the following presidential question:

> whether there are additional steps on the scientific side, beyond those already taken by the Administration in the aftermath of the highly critical 2009 National Research Council report on the state of the forensic sciences, that could help ensure the validity of forensic evidence used in the Nation's legal system.[113]

The PCAST Committee assessed the state of forensic science following the NAS Report in 2009 and remarked on studies that had called into serious question the validity of forensic techniques previously regarded as "reliable," including microscopic hair analysis, bullet-lead evidence, fingerprint analysis, and bitemark evidence. The PCAST Report noted that the research showed that experts' reports and testimony frequently overstated the quality of the analysis and the significance of the results obtained.[114] In hair analysis cases, "FBI examiners had provided scientifically invalid testimony in more than 95 percent of cases where

---

[112] Id. One of the more interesting recommendations has been to prohibit the use of the term "reasonable scientific certainty" in expert testimony as unnecessary, idiosyncratic, and confusing to jurors. See NCFS, "Recommendations to the Attorney General Regarding the Use of the Term "Reasonable Scientific Certainty," Approved by the Commission March 22, 2016 (available at: https://www.justice.gov/ncfs/file/839726/download)(last accessed January 3, 2017). On September 6, 2016, the Attorney General announced that "Department forensic laboratories will review their policies and procedures to ensure that forensic examiners are not using the expressions 'reasonable scientific certainty' or 'reasonable [forensic discipline] certainty' in their reports or testimony. Department prosecutors will abstain from use of these expressions when presenting forensic reports or questioning forensic experts in court unless required by a judge or applicable law." Office of the Attorney General, "Memorandum for Heads of Department Components," September 6, 2016 (available at: https://www.justice.gov/opa/file/891366/download)(last accessed January 5, 2017).

[113] Report: "Forensic Science in Criminal Courts: Ensuring Scientific Validity of Feature-Comparison Methods", Executive office of the President, President's Council of Advisors on Science and Technology, 2016, p. 1 (available at https://obamawhitehouse.archives.gov/sites/default/files/microsites/ostp/PCAST/pcast_forensic_science_report_final.pdf)(last accessed March 3, 2017).

[114] Id. at p. 3.

that testimony was used to inculpate a defendant at trial."[115] The report also recognized that based on the FBI review of hair analysis cases, "in March 2016, the Department of Justice announced its intention to expand to additional forensic-science methods its review of forensic testimony by the FBI Laboratory in closed criminal cases."[116]

PCAST examined the "foundational validity"[117] and "validity as applied"[118] of seven forensic disciplines: DNA Analysis of single-source and simple-mixture samples, DNA Analysis of complex-mixture samples, Bitemark Analysis, Latent Fingerprint Analysis, Firearm Analysis, Footwear Analysis, and Hair Analysis. The specific conclusions of the PCAST Report as to each discipline are discussed in later chapters of this book,[119] but for the majority of the disciplines, the report found that both the foundational validity and the validity as applied in case work of these forensic science methods was insufficiently established.[120] The report called for more validation research, except for bitemark analysis, because it "consider[ed] the prospects of developing bitemark analysis into a scientifically valid method to be [so] low" that expending resources was unwarranted.[121]

Importantly for the legal profession, PCAST pointed out that the legal standard for evidentiary reliability of scientific evidence depends directly on "standards of scientific validity."[122] Since FRE 702 requires admissibility decisions to take into account reliable principles and methods and their reliable application to the case at bar, PCAST suggests looking at these concepts through their lens of "foundational validity" and "validity as applied."[123] These considerations would be based on the "appropriate scientific criteria for the scientific discipline to which it belongs."

---

[115] Id.

[116] Id.

[117] "Foundational validity for a forensic-science method requires that it be shown, based on empirical studies, to be repeatable, reproducible, and accurate, at levels that have been measured and are appropriate to the intended application. Foundational validity, then, means that a method can, in principle, be reliable. It is the scientific concept we mean to correspond to the legal requirement in Rule 702(c), of 'reliable principles and methods.' " Id. at pp. 4–5.

[118] "Validity as applied means that the method has been reliably applied in practice. It is the scientific concept we mean to correspond to the legal requirement, in Rule 702(d), that an expert 'has reliably applied the principles and methods to the facts of the case.' " Id. at p. 5.

[119] Footwear comparison analysis is not discussed in this book. PCAST found that "there are no appropriate empirical studies to support the foundational validity of footwear analysis to associate shoeprints with particular shoes based on specific identifying marks (sometimes called "randomly acquired characteristics"). Such conclusions are unsupported by any meaningful evidence or estimates of their accuracy and thus are not scientifically valid." PCAST did not evaluate the foundational validity of class characteristic (shoe size, shoe brand) analysis of footwear. Id. at p. 117.

[120] Id. at 4–5.

[121] Id at 9.

[122] Id., p. 142, quoting Daubert v. Merrill Dow, n. 9 ("in a case involving scientific evidence, *evidentiary reliability* will be based on *scientific validity*." (emphasis in original)

[123] Id.

Scientific validity and reliability require that a method has been subjected to empirical testing, under conditions appropriate to its intended use, that provides valid estimates of how often the method reaches an incorrect conclusion. For subjective feature-comparison methods, appropriately designed black-box studies are required, in which many examiners render decisions about many independent tests (typically, involving "questioned" samples and one or more "known" samples) and the error rates are determined. Without appropriate estimates of accuracy, an examiner's statement that two samples are similar—or even indistinguishable—is scientifically meaningless: it has no probative value, and considerable potential for prejudicial impact. Nothing—not personal experience nor professional practices—can substitute for adequate empirical demonstration of accuracy.[124]

Additionally, PCAST addressed the courts' tendency to treat long-standing forensic science techniques as valid because they have been regarded as such by the courts for long periods of time. It concluded that "[w]hen new facts falsify old assumptions, courts should not be obliged to defer to past precedents: they should look afresh at the scientific issues."[125]

It did not take long for the PCAST report to meet resistance from forensic laboratories and prosecutors. The suggestion that serious efforts at validation were necessary before pattern-matching evidence would be admissible, together with suggestions as to how that validation should be conducted occasioned an explosion of ire from law enforcement. US Attorney General Loretta Lynch quickly expressed her confidence that current forensic practices were based on sound science and legal reasoning, and announced that while the Department of Justice appreciated PCAST's "contribution to the field of scientific inquiry, the department will not be adopting the recommendations related to the admissibility of forensic science evidence."[126] The

---

[124] Id., p. 143.

[125] Id. at p. 144. In criminal cases, it has been common for courts to note that certain forensic techniques are so long standing as to entitle their validity to such deference that the court, rather than requiring the proponent of the evidence to demonstrate its validity, shifts the burden to the opponent to demonstrate its unreliability. See, e.g., State v. Fuentes, 2010-NMCA-027, 147 N.M. 761, 228 P.3d 1181("We are persuaded that, in the present matter, the district court appropriately exercised its discretionary authority in finding that the reliability of the science in question could properly be taken for granted. The science underlying the firearm forensics and tool mark analysis techniques employed in the present matter has long been held reliable in New Mexico. . . However, Defendant failed to persuade us that the district court erred with it assumed the reliability of the science underlying the firearm forensics and tool mark analysis. . .[he] did not set forth any basis for calling into question the reliability of the science underlying these techniques.") In light of the PCAST findings generally, (and specifically with regard to toolmark examination in *Fuentes*) it may be that such a tendency is about to be overtaken by a return to requiring a preliminary showing of reliability by the expert's proponent.

[126] http://www.wsj.com/articles/white-house-advisory-council-releases-report-critical-of-forensics-used-in-criminal-trials-1474394743.

National District Attorneys' Association "slammed" the legitimacy of the report, stating, "PCAST has taken it upon itself to usurp the Constitutional role of the Courts and decades of legal precedent and insert itself as the final arbiter of the reliability and admissibility of the information generated through these forensic science disciplines."[127] Whether the findings, and more importantly the reasoning, of the PCAST report will influence the courts in making admissibility decisions remains to be seen.

III. CONSIDERATIONS IN SELECTING EXPERTS

§1.06   CIVIL CASES

An expert can function in many capacities with respect to scientific evidence: first, as an analyst to examine the physical evidence; second, as a consultant to evaluate the quality of the evidence on the other side or to assist the attorney in constructing the case for trial using expert testimony; third, as a testifying witness who gives an opinion based on the information uncovered through examination. When scientific evidence may be a vital part of a case, the selection of the appropriate expert or experts is critical.[128] The attorney should understand the nature of the expertise that they will need for the case and what sort of expert to retain. Vetting the expert's qualification and reviewing the work is an important responsibility of the attorney.[129] Equally important are the ethical and procedural requirements that govern attorney and expert conduct, including required disclosures in the course of litigation. Jurisdictional rules differ on confidentiality of attorney-expert communications and as to what materials must be disclosed during various stages of the proceedings.

The availability of experts in civil cases, for either the plaintiff or the defense, is so prevalent that the difficulty lies in discerning the most qualified experts. Personal referrals by other lawyers who have dealt with similar issues, or the client's own contacts in industry, often direct a litigator to appropriate and available experts. For those who cannot avail themselves of these sources, there are commercial providers who offer to furnish lists of witnesses in thousands of fields of

---

[127] www.ndaa.org/pdf/NDAA%20Press%20Release%20on%20PCAST%20Report.pdf (last accessed February 26, 2017).

[128] *See generally* Carol Henderson and Kurt W. Lenz, "Expert Witnesses: Selection and Investigation," in WILEY ENCYCLOPEDIA OF FORENSIC SCIENCE, (Jamieson A. & Moenssens A.A., eds) 2009 & online updates.

[129] *See, e.g.,* Drake v. Portuondo, 553 F.3d 230, 232 (2d Cir. 2009)(convictions reversed because testimony of government's witness as to fictional syndrome of sexual dysfunction—picquerism—"which was, medically speaking, nonsense"—also lied about his credentials); People v. Cornille, 95 Ill.2d 497, 448 N.E.2d 857 (1983).

expertise.[130] Universities and colleges have many researchers in wide varieties of specialties. Government regulatory agencies that publish reports, studies, and articles in the area they regulate may direct lawyers to specific subject specialists who are cited in their reports for their authoritative research.

The duty to verify credentials and check claims made in biographical sketches rests squarely on the attorney retaining the expert.[131] There have been many instances where expert witnesses have lied about their credentials, experience, and professional affiliations.[132] Often, these deceptions have come to light only when the expert witness is investigated for other misconduct.

§1.07 CRIMINAL CASES

1. PROSECUTION

Experts working for the prosecution conventionally fulfill one of four purposes in the criminal case: (1) to identify contraband or prohibited items (such as drugs or firearms); (2) to associate, through comparison or analysis, physical evidence to the accused or to the victim (such as fingerprints, DNA, or other trace evidence); (3) to prove mental state by way of psychological or psychiatric evidence, or by toxicological evidence of alcohol or drug influence; or (4) to prove the criminal circumstances of unobserved or suspicious death by means of autopsy examination.

Prosecutors have a considerable advantage based on their access to the resources of local, state, and federal law enforcement and related agencies to obtain, identify, or use the expert assistance needed in cases. Experts are often involved in the investigation stage of the case, working with detectives, suggesting investigative paths, and evaluating the culpability of suspects.[133] This close relationship between law enforcement and forensic scientists has frequently been cited in recent years as a motivational detriment to an expert's independence and objectivity.[134] If the prosecution or law enforcement agency attempts to

---

[130] For example, the Technical Advisory Service for Attorneys (TASA) offers over 10,000 categories of expertise available at www.tasanet.com (last accessed January 4, 2017) and Claims Providers of America publishes The National Directory of Expert Witnesses with an online directory at http://national-experts.com (last accessed January 4, 2017). Other specific professional organizations are cited in the discipline specific chapters of this book.

[131] People v. Cornille, 95 Ill.2d 497, 448 N.E.2d 857 (1983).

[132] For some early writings on that issue, see, James E. Starrs, "Mountebanks Among Forensic Scientists," in *Forensic Science Handbook,* Vol. II (Saferstein, ed., 1988); Andre A. Moenssens, "Novel Scientific Evidence in Criminal Cases: Some Words of Caution," 84 J. CRIM. L. & CRIMINOLOGY, 801 (1993); Kuzma, "Criminal Liability for Misconduct in Scientific Research," 25 U.Mich.J.L.Ref. 357 (1992); James E. Starrs, "The Misbehaving Expert: The Law Turns Turtle," SCI. SLEUTHING REV., Spring 1993, p. 1.

[133] William C. Thompson, "What role should investigative facts play in the evaluation of scientific evidence?" 43 Australian J. For. Sci. (2–3) 123 (2011).

[134] *See* 2009 NAS Report at p. 185; Peter Neufeld, "Have You No Sense of Decency?," 84 J. Crim. L. & Criminology 189 (1993); D. Michael Risinger, et al., "The Daubert/Kumho

influence the expert's investigation or interfere with defense access to the expert, this attempt may provide grounds for the reversal of a conviction on appeal. In *State v. Beecroft*,[135] the Minnesota Supreme Court reversed a murder conviction in "the interests of justice" because state actors (prosecutors and law enforcement officials) interfered with the defendant's ability to consult with and call expert witnesses by suggesting to medical examiners who worked for the state that it would be a "conflict of interest" to assist the defense:

> Our analysis of Beecroft's claims on appeal must be considered in the context of the historic role of coroners and medical examiners and their important function and obligations in our modern criminal justice system. Any such analysis must take into account the independence, autonomy, and neutrality that we expect from medical examiners. This perspective takes on added importance given that the conduct of certain state actors in this case reflects what appears to be a growing point of view within Minnesota's law enforcement and prosecution communities that it is a "conflict of interest" for medical examiners to consult with or testify at the request of criminal defendants. It is not a conflict of interest for a medical examiner to consult with criminal defense attorneys or testify at a criminal defendant's request. Indeed, such activity is authorized and protected by law. *See* U.S. Const. amend. VI (protecting a criminal defendant's right to present witnesses in his defense); U.S. Const. amend. XIV (protecting a person's right to due process).[136]

2. INDIGENT DEFENDANTS

For a non-indigent criminal defendant, the defense has the same access to hire experts as civil parties, though the defense usually does not have the guidance of crime laboratory specialists that is freely available to prosecutors. However, in some jurisdictions, laboratories and medical examiner offices will discuss cases freely with defense counsel. Professional associations of criminal defense attorneys, such as the National Association of Criminal Defense Lawyers (NACDL), also assist attorneys with expert witness referrals through listserves and other resources.[137]

For indigent defendants, the access to experts is more challenging. Within public defender systems, money may be separately allocated for

---

Implications of Observer Effects in Forensic Science: Hidden Problems of Expectation and Suggestion," 90 Cal. L. Rev. 1 (2002); Paul C. Giannelli, "The Abuse of Scientific Evidence in Criminal Cases: The Need for Independent Crime Laboratories", 4 VA. J.Soc. Policy & L. 439, 457–62 (1997).

[135] 813 N.W.2d 814 (Minn. 2012).

[136] Id. at 831.

[137] www.nacdl.org (last accessed January 4, 2017).

expert assistance, but resources for most public defenders are so limited that they must seek funds from the court on a case-by-case basis. Although most courts now recognize a constitutional or statutory right to expert assistance at state expense for indigent defendants,[138] the promise of adequate access to expert witnesses is widely regarded as illusory.[139] The showing required to obtain this funding varies widely among jurisdictions and can be very restrictive. For example, in Virginia the defense must make a sufficient showing that the assistance of the expert is likely to be a "significant factor" in the defense and that the defense will be prejudiced by the denial of assistance.[140] This type of "particularized showing" can be difficult to produce without expert review of the evidence in the context of the case; realistically, an expert is needed to get an expert appointed, a true catch-22 for the indigent criminal defendant.

§1.08   COMPELLING AN EXPERT TO TESTIFY

The majority of states have held that the expert may be subpoenaed to give a professional opinion based upon facts observed and opinions arrived at *prior* to being subpoenaed, even though the witness will not be compensated with an expert witness fee.[141] However, an expert may not ordinarily be required to engage in any additional study or preparation. In instances where special preparation is not required in order to enable the expert to arrive at an opinion, or when the expert has previously formed an opinion based upon facts within his knowledge, the opinion is treated as any other testimonial evidence. Another view allows the expert to refuse to testify except to

---

[138] Although the United States Supreme Court recognized that "[t]here can be no equal justice where the kind of trial a man gets depends on the amount of money he has," Griffin v. Illinois, 351 U.S. 12, 19 (1956), it took decades for the Court to clearly articulate that an indigent defendant may be entitled to the appointment of an expert. *See* Ake v. Oklahoma, 470 U.S. 68 (1985)("Justice cannot be equal where, simply as a result of his poverty, a defendant is denied the opportunity to participate meaningfully in a judicial proceeding in which his liberty is at stake.") (psychiatric expert) It took another decade for some jurisdictions to hold that the indigent defendant may be entitled to the appointment of other forensic experts. *See* Husske v. Commonwealth, 252 Va. 203, 476 S.E.2d 920 (1996)(A state must, upon request, provide indigent defendants with "the basic tools of an adequate defense" and "in certain instances, these basic tools may include the appointment of non-psychiatric experts.")

In states where a constitutional right to expert assistance has not been specifically recognized, there is a generally a statutory right to such assistance. *See* Alaska Stat. Ann. § 18.85.100(a) (2): an indigent defendant is entitled to be provided "with the necessary services and facilities of [appointed] representation, including investigation and other preparation."

Some states have found both a constitutional and statutory duty to provide expert assistance. *See* State v. Cornell, 179 Ariz. 314, 878 P.2d 1352 (1994).

[139] *See, e.g.,* Paul Giannelli, "Ake v. Oklahoma: The Right to Expert Assistance in a Post-Daubert, Post-DNA World,"89 Cornell L. Rev. 1305, 1310–13 (2003–2004).

[140] Husske v. Commonwealth, 252 Va. 203, 476 S.E.2d 920 (1996).

[141] Flinn v. Prairie County, 60 Ark. 204, 29 S.W. 459 (1895); People v. Conte, 17 Cal.App. 771, 122 P. 450 (1912); People v. Speck, 41 Ill.2d 177, 242 N.E.2d 208 (1968); Ramacorti v. Boston Redevelopment Authority, 341 Mass. 377, 170 N.E.2d 323 (1960); In re Hayes, 200 N.C. 133, 156 S.E. 791 (1931); Nielsen v. Brown, 232 Or. 426, 374 P.2d 896 (1962); Summers v. State, 5 Tex.App. 365 (1879); Ealy v. Shetler Ice Cream Co., 108 W.Va. 184, 150 S.E. 539 (1929); Stevens v. Desha County, 1993 WL 44622 (Ark.App.1993).

facts he has personally observed.[142] A third group of cases holds that an expert may be required to testify to facts and opinions in all circumstances even when compensated only as an ordinary witness.[143]

Many of the cases dealing with compelling an expert witness to testify involve civil controversies. For example, in *Gugliano v. Levi*,[144] the defendant's expert who had rendered a report that was favorable to plaintiff's position was then subpoenaed by the plaintiff. In reversing, the court called this an "improper trial tactic" inasmuch as the plaintiff did not lack expert evidence to prove his own case and the opposing expert's testimony was available from other sources. Federal Rule of Civil Procedure 26(b)(4)(D)[145] protects experts, and their opinions, from compelled testimony and discovery save under narrow circumstances:

> (D) Expert Employed Only for Trial Preparation. Ordinarily, a party may not, by interrogatories or deposition, discover facts known or opinions held by an expert who has been retained or specially employed by another party in anticipation of litigation or to prepare for trial and who is not expected to be called as a witness at trial. But a party may do so only:
>
> > (i)   as provided in Rule 35(b); or
> >
> > (ii) on showing exceptional circumstances under which it is impracticable for the party to obtain facts or opinions on the same subject by other means.

The Rule, however, does not protect tangible items, such as photographs, in the possession of the non-testifying expert.[146] The courts have split on whether the identity of a non-testifying expert is protected by this rule.[147]

Different considerations apply when dealing with criminal cases. If, for example, an examiner in a public crime laboratory has made an

---

[142] Agnew v. Parks, 172 Cal.App.2d 756, 343 P.2d 118 (1959); Buchman v. State, 59 Ind. 1 (1877); Hull v. Plume, 131 N.J.L. 511, 37 A.2d 53 (1944); People ex rel. Kraushaar Bros. & Co. v. Thorpe, 296 N.Y. 223, 72 N.E.2d 165 (1947); Pennsylvania Co. for Insurances on Lives & Granting Annuities v. Philadelphia, 262 Pa. 439, 105 A. 630 (1918); Bradley v. Poole, 187 Va. 432, 47 S.E.2d 341 (1948). *But see*, Cooper v. Norfolk Redevelopment and Housing Authority, 197 Va. 653, 90 S.E.2d 788 (1956).

[143] Ex parte Dement, 53 Ala. 389 (1875); Board of Comm'rs of Larimer County v. Lee, 3 Colo.App. 177, 32 P. 841 (1893); Dixon v. State, 12 Ga.App. 17, 76 S.E. 794 (1912); Dixon v. People, 168 Ill. 179, 48 N.E. 108 (1897); Swope v. State, 145 Kan. 928, 67 P.2d 416 (1937); and Barnes v. Boatmen's Nat. Bank, 348 Mo. 1032, 156 S.W.2d 597 (1941); *See also*, 8 Wigmore, *Evidence*, § 2203. (J. McNaughton Rev.1961); 4 Jones, *Evidence*, § 879 (5th ed. 1958).

[144] 24 A.D.2d 591, 262 N.Y.S.2d 372 (1965). The court said: "The practice [of calling an opponent's consulting expert without a showing of difficulty in obtaining other expert testimony] thrusts the expert into the intolerable position of working for both sides, and into violation of his 'ethical obligation not to accept a retainer from the other side." Id. at 374. *See also*, Glenn v. Plante, 269 Wis.2d 575, 676 N.W.2d 413 (2004), reversing where it had not been established preliminarily that the testimony was "uniquely necessary."

[145] Current as of December 2016.

[146] *See, e.g.*, McCusttian v. LG Elecs. U.S.A., Inc. 2016 U.S. Dist. LEXIS 55884 (M.D. Ala. 2016).

[147] *See* In re Welding Fume Prods. Liab. Litig., 534 F. Supp.2d 761, 767–768 (N.D. Ohio 2008) (detailing the split in the circuit courts).

analysis of evidence and furnished a report of its findings to the prosecutor, the defense is entitled to call the prosecution expert as a defense witness. In *Flores v. State*,[148] a crime laboratory director who had performed an examination refused to testify for the defense unless retained as its expert. The Texas Court of Criminal Appeals held that the trial judge erred in refusing to instruct the witness to testify, under penalty of contempt if he refused, as to the examination he had already conducted, citing defendant's Sixth Amendment right to the compulsory process of witnesses.

§1.09   ETHICAL RESPONSIBILITIES

1.   EXPERT

When selecting, preparing, and presenting expert testimony on scientific evidence, an attorney must be aware of the lawyer's own ethical obligations as well as of the ethical constraints on an expert's conduct.[149] Unless the expert's employment mandates a code of conduct, the ethical obligations will derive from the ethics codes of certifying bodies or professional associations.[150] For example, members of the American Academy of Forensic Sciences (AAFS) are prohibited from making material misrepresentations of their education, training, or expertise; or of the data and scientific principles upon which their professional opinions are based.[151] The National Commission on

---

[148] 491 S.W.2d 144 (Tex.Crim.App.1973).

[149] *See generally* Andre Moenssens, "Ethics: Codes of Conduct for Expert Witnesses," in WILEY ENCYCLOPEDIA OF FORENSIC SCIENCE, (Jamieson A. & Moenssens A.A., eds) 2009 & online updates.

[150] *See, e.g.,* National Association of Medical Examiners Bylaws, Article Ten, Code of Ethics and Conduct (2005) (provides that members of NAME shall conform to the published ethics of the American Medical Association); The National Society of Professional Engineers Code of Ethics (2006) (setting forth fundamental canons, rules of practice, and professional obligations); The American Board of Criminalistics Bylaws, Article IV.5.4 (2006) (rules of professional conduct which must be complied with by applicants and diplomates).

[151] AAFS Bylaws, Article II, Section 1 provides:

"As a means to promote the highest quality of professional and personal conduct of its members and affiliates, the following constitutes the Code of Ethics and Conduct which is endorsed by all members and affiliates of the American Academy of Forensic Sciences:

  a.   Every member and affiliate of the Academy shall refrain from exercising professional or personal conduct adverse to the best interests and objectives of the Academy. The objectives stated in the Preamble to these bylaws shall be to promote professionalism, integrity, and competency in the membership's actions and associated activities; to promote education for and research in the forensic sciences; to encourage the study, improve the practice, elevate the standards and advance the cause of the forensic sciences; to promote interdisciplinary communications; and to plan, organize and administer meetings, reports and other projects for the stimulation and advancement of these and related purposes.

    (a)   No member or affiliate of the Academy shall materially misrepresent his or her education, training, experience, area of expertise, or membership status within the Academy.

Forensic Science has recommended a code of professional responsibility for forensic science and forensic medicine service providers,[152] and on September 6, 2016, the Department of Justice adopted a new code of professional responsibility for Department forensic laboratories.[153]

Some courts have sanctioned experts for their unethical behavior. In *Schmidt v. Ford Motor Co.*,[154] the court banned the plaintiff's accident reconstruction expert from testifying in federal court in Colorado because he had conveyed intentionally misleading information in depositions and informal conversations with defense expert. The expert also concealed his knowledge from the defendant that one of the plaintiffs had tampered with the evidence.

Expert witnesses may be held civilly responsible for their negligent professional behavior.[155] Expert witness malpractice causes of action have been allowed in jurisdictions including New Jersey, Texas, California, Missouri, and Louisiana.[156] Some courts have granted immunity to court appointed experts.[157]

2. ATTORNEY

Attorneys' ethical obligations are contained in each state's Rules of Professional Conduct or Code of Professional Responsibility. While no specific rule deals directly with attorneys and expert witnesses, some of the American Bar Association Model Rules of Professional Conduct are applicable. California is the only state that has not adopted rules similar to the format of the ABA Model Rules.[158] Some of the model

---

> (b)   No member or affiliate of the Academy shall materially misrepresent data or scientific principles upon which his or her conclusion or professional opinion is based.
>
> (c)   No member or affiliate of the Academy shall issue public statements that appear to represent the position of the Academy without first obtaining specific authority from the Board of Directors."

The AAFS Bylaws are available at: https://www.aafs.org/wp-content/uploads/Bylaws.pdf (last accessed January 4, 2017).

[152] National Commission on Forensic Science, "Recommendation to the Attorney General National Code of Professional Responsibility for Forensic Science and Forensic Medicine Service Providers, Adopted March 22, 2016 (available at: https://www.justice.gov/ncfs/work-products-adopted-commission) (last accessed January 4, 2017).

[153] The new code is attached to the Office of the Attorney General, "Memorandum for Heads of Department Components," September 6, 2016 (available at: https://www.justice.gov/opa/file/891366/download) (last accessed January 5, 2017).

[154] 112 F.R.D. 216 (D.Colo.1986).

[155] *See generally* Carol Henderson and Kurt W. Lenz, "Malpractice Actions Against Experts, " in WILEY ENCYCLOPEDIA OF FORENSIC SCIENCE, (Jamieson A. & Moenssens A.A., eds) 2009 & online updates.

[156] *See* Ronson v. David S. Talesnick, CPA, 33 F.Supp.2d 347 (D.N.J.1999); James v. Brown, 637 S.W.2d 914 (Tex.1982); Mattco Forge, Inc. v. Arthur Young & Co., 52 Cal.App.4th 820, 60 Cal.Rptr.2d 780 (1997); Murphy v. A.A. Mathews, 841 S.W.2d 671 (Mo.1992); Marrogi v. Howard, 805 So.2d 1118 (La. 2002).

[157] *See* Reimers v. O'Halloran, 678 N.W.2d 549 (ND 2004); Huges v. Long, 242 F.3d 121 (3d Cir. 2001).

[158] The American Bar Association maintains statistics on the adoption of the model rules and links to the Ethics Rules in each state (available at: http://www.americanbar.org/groups/

rules which impact upon an attorney's use of expert witnesses are the following:

Rule 3.3 (Candor toward the Tribunal) requires the attorney to investigate the background of expert witnesses to avoid putting on perjured testimony regarding their credentials.[159]

Rule 3.4 (Fairness to Opposing Party and Counsel) prohibits an attorney from fabricating evidence; assisting a witness to testify falsely; offering an inducement to a witness that is prohibited by law; making frivolous discovery requests; or failing to make a reasonably diligent effort to comply with a legally proper discovery request.

Rule 3.8 (Special Responsibilities of a Prosecutor) specifies that the prosecutor's role as a "minister of justice" requires the making of timely disclosure of evidence or information that will negate evidence of guilt or mitigate guilt. Therefore, if fraud is uncovered relating to the expert's acts or knowledge it must be disclosed.

Rule 4.1 (Truthfulness in Statements to Others) prohibits an attorney from making false statements of material fact or law to a third person, such as an expert witness

Rule 5.3 (Responsibilities Regarding Nonlawyer Assistance) applies to experts as well as paralegals, and extends to situations where the lawyer is in essence ratifying the unethical conduct of the expert.

Rule 8.3 (Reporting Professional Misconduct) requires the attorneys to report unethical conduct of other attorneys. Therefore, if the opposing party's counsel knowingly uses an expert discovered to be a fraud, counsel is obligated to report the other lawyer to the grievance committee.

Rule 8.4(a)–(d) (Misconduct) states that it is professional misconduct to violate or attempt to violate the Model Rules; commit a criminal act that reflects adversely on a lawyer's honesty, trustworthiness, or fitness; engage in conduct involving dishonesty, fraud, deceit, or misrepresentation; or engage in conduct that is prejudicial to the administration of justice.

Model Rules 1.1 (Competence) and 1.3 (Diligence) require an attorney to seek out expert services necessary for a client's representation. In

---

professional_responsibility/publications/model_rules_of_professional_conduct.html)   (last accessed January 4, 2017).

[159] Attorneys must also be careful of a "diploma mill": a credentialing company that has questionable qualification procedures. *See* Mark Hansen, "Expertise to Go," ABA J., Feb. 2000, at 44. *See also*, Barbara A. Lee, "Who Are You? Fraudulent Credentials and Background Checks in Academe," 32 J.C. & U. L. 655 (2006) and Sandra R. Sylvester, "Calling Prosecutors to Arms," 37 Prosecutor 8 (Sept./Oct. 2003).

addition to an ethical violation, the failure of a criminal defense attorney to obtain the services of expert witnesses or to challenge the prosecution's expert testimony may constitute the ineffective assistance of counsel.[160] An attorney is also responsible for the preparation of his or her own witnesses, including expert witnesses.[161]

In 2012, the American Bar Association Litigation Section proposed a resolution adopting guidelines for the retention of expert witnesses in litigation.[162] Although the resolution was not adopted by the ABA, it contains a helpful compendium of suggestions concerning the retention and preparation of expert witnesses for trial. The American Bar Association standards relating to the Administration of Criminal Justice also set forth standards for prosecutors[163] and defense counsel[164] to follow when working with expert witnesses in criminal trials. The standards provide that the attorney should respect the expert's independence, not dictate the formation of the expert's opinion, and that paying excessive or contingent fees is unprofessional conduct. A lawyer may not promise an expert a fee contingent on the outcome of the case, nor may an attorney share fees with an expert.[165] In may also be an ethical violation to fail to pay an expert's fee absent an express disclaimer of responsibility.[166]

Attorneys have been sanctioned for abusing an expert witness on cross-examination. In *Florida Bar v. Schaub*, a prosecutor was suspended from the practice of law for thirty days for improperly eliciting irrelevant testimony from the defense's expert witness, a

---

[160] *See, e.g.,* Commonwealth v. Millien, 474 Mass. 417, 50 N.E.3d 808 (2016) ("where the prosecution's case rested almost entirely on medical expert testimony, the defendant was denied his constitutional right to effective assistance of counsel because, by not providing the jury with the other side of [the debate on shaken baby syndrome], his attorney's poor performance 'likely deprived the defendant of an otherwise available, substantial ground of defense.'"); Commonwealth v. Epps, 474 Mass. 743, 53 N.E.3d 1247 (2016) (same). *See also* United States v. Hebshie, 754 F. Supp. 2d 89 (D. Mass. 2010)(counsel ineffective for failing to challenge the validity or reliability of the arson evidence offered by the state); Wilkins v. State, 146 P.3d 709 (Kan.App.2006)(counsel failed to consult with or hire a forensic expert to counter a forensic anthropologist and forensic dentist hired by the State); Turpin v. Bennett, 272 Ga. 57, 525 S.E.2d 354 (2000)(defense lawyer provided ineffective assistance by failing to move for a continuance when it became obvious that an expert witness whom the lawyer called to present testimony supporting the insanity defense was himself mentally impaired).

See also Harrington v. Richter, 131 S.Ct. 770 (2011) (recognizing that "[c]riminal cases will arise where the only reasonable and available defense strategy requires consultation with experts or introduction of expert evidence, whether pretrial, at trial, or both.").

[161] In re Warmington, 568 N.W.2d 641, 669 (Wis. 1997) (attorney disbarred for, among other things, "failing to supervise the preparation of an expert witness.").

[162] http://www.abajournal.com/files/2012_hod_annual_meeting_101.pdf (last accessed December 22, 2016).

[163] Standard 3–3.3, ABA Standards for Criminal Justice, Third Ed.

[164] Standard 4–4.4, ABA Standards for Criminal Justice, Third Ed.

[165] Dupree v. Malpractice Research, Inc., 179 Mich.App. 254, 445 N.W.2d 498 (1989). See also, First National Bank of Springfield v. Malpractice Research, Inc., 179 Ill.2d 353, 228 Ill.Dec. 202, 688 N.E.2d 1179 (1997); Model Rule 5.4(a).

[166] Copp v. Breskin, 56 Wash.App. 229, 782 P.2d 1104 (1989)(the court cited ABA Model Rules of Professional Conduct 1.8(e) and 4.4 as authority). *Cf.* Boesch v. Marilyn M. Jones & Associates, 712 N.E.2d 1061 (Ind.App.1999).

psychiatrist. The prosecutor insulted the witness, ignored the court's rulings sustaining defense objections, and inserted his personal opinions on psychiatry and the insanity defense into his questioning.[167]

Court rules, such as Rule 11 of the Federal Rules of Civil Procedure, may also provide for sanctions to punish a knowing filing of a false and misleading pleading, or the failure to disclose a contrary expert opinion.[168]

IV. TRIAL AIDS

§1.10   DISCOVERY AND DISCLOSURE IN CIVIL CASES

1.   GENERAL CONSIDERATIONS

As with admissibility standards, jurisdictions vary in their rules of discovery. Rule 26 governs only civil discovery in federal courts and most federal district courts have adopted local rules that impose additional requirements in their individual courts governing the timing of disclosures.[169] Many jurisdictions have patterned their rules after Rule 26, but the interpretation of those rules are governed solely by the

---

[167] 618 So.2d 202 (Fla.1993). In another case, Ross v. Colorado National Bank of Denver, 170 Colo. 436, 463 P.2d 882, 887 (1969), the court stated, "Rigid and searching cross-examination, however, does not license the cross-examiner to reach into the realm of improper hearsay questions which tend to demean an expert witness and his school of training by implications of incompetence and corruption."

[168] Schering Corp. v. Vitarine Pharmaceuticals, Inc., 889 F.2d 490 (3d Cir.1989).

[169] *See, e.g.,* Local Rule 26 for the United States District Court in the Eastern District of Virginia (available at: http://www.vaed.uscourts.gov/localrules/LocalRulesEDVA.pdf) (last accessed January 4, 2017):

(D) Expert Disclosures:

(1) Agreement Upon Disclosure: Counsel are encouraged to agree upon the sequence and timing of the expert disclosures required by Fed. R. Civ. P. 26(a)(2). All such agreements must be in the form of a consent order entered by the Court.

(2) Timing of Mandatory Disclosure: Absent such a consent order or unless ordered otherwise, the disclosures required by Fed. R. Civ. P. 26(a)(2) shall be made first by the plaintiff not later than sixty (60) days before the earlier of the date set for completion of discovery or for the final pretrial conference, if any, then by the defendant thirty (30) days thereafter. Plaintiff shall disclose fifteen (15) days thereafter any evidence that is solely contradictory or rebuttal evidence to the defendant's disclosure.

(3) Completion of Disclosure: Whether accomplished by agreement pursuant to Local Civil Rule 26(D)(1) or pursuant to the schedule set by Local Civil Rule 26(D)(2), all parties shall complete all forms of expert disclosure and discovery not later than thirty (30) days after the date upon which plaintiff is, or would be, required by Fed. R. Civ. P. 26(a)(2)(C) to disclose contradictory or rebuttal evidence.

(4) General Provisions: For purposes of this Local Rule, counter-claim plaintiffs, cross-claimants, and third-party plaintiffs shall be plaintiffs as to all elements of the counterclaim, cross-claim, or third-party claim. Answers to interrogatories directed at clarification of the written reports of expert witnesses disclosed pursuant to Fed. R. Civ. P. 26(a)(2) shall be due fifteen (15) days after service.

case law of that jurisdiction. In any civil matter, the civil procedure rules of the jurisdiction and any cases interpreting those rules must be the primary source of guidance for discovery obligations.

Since the adoption by the Supreme Court of the Federal Rules of Civil Procedure in 1937,[170] and throughout many subsequent amendments, discovery has become an important part of the civil litigation process. It replaced pleadings as the primary means by which parties learned of some factual information and formulated issues in the case. When it comes to discovery of experts, and information held by them, two opposing views have traditionally been advocated. The first view is that which favors liberal discovery, leading to a narrowing of the triable issues prior to trial and the avoidance of surprise. The opposing view regards the retention and consultation of experts by an attorney as part of a professional and competent pretrial preparation that should be kept confidential; to do otherwise would be to reward the incompetent and less resourceful advocate. Adherents of this latter view suggest various rationales for prohibiting discovery of information in the possession of the expert: (1) an expert who is consulted in preparation of trial gains knowledge about the case that should be covered by the attorney-client privilege; (2) even if the expert's knowledge is not within the evidentiary privilege, it should nevertheless come under the "work product" rule; and (3) to permit an opponent to discover information collected at great expense and with considerable resourcefulness is unjust.

The modern view, exemplified by the Federal Rules of Civil Procedure provisions on discovery, have taken a position favoring discovery, and have sought to prevent abuses and exploitation through provisions permitting the courts to issue protective orders and direct the demanding attorneys to make payment of fees and expenses to the party retaining the expert.[171] The Federal Rules do distinguish between experts called as witnesses ("testifying experts") and experts who are not called as witnesses ("consulting experts").

2.   FEDERAL RULE 26

Significant and massive changes in Federal Rule 26 and other Rules of Civil Procedure have occurred over the years, continuing through 2015.[172] To summarize the most important aspect of federal civil discovery, litigants must disclose to their opponent, without being

---

[170] The rules first went into effect in 1938. *See* McLaughlin, "Discovery and Admissibility of Expert Testimony," 63 Notre Dame L. Rev. 760 (1988) (discussing the historical developments leading to the rule affecting experts).

[171] The 2015 amendments to the Rules of Civil Procedure eliminated any reference to discovery of the "subject matter" of the case and defined the scope of discovery as that which is "relevant" to any claim or defense and "proportional to the needs of the case." FRE Rule 26(b) (1).

[172] The Federal Rules of Civil Procedure are available at: http://www.uscourts.gov/sites/default/files/rules-of-civil-procedure.pdf (last accessed January 4, 2017).

asked to do so, a variety of types of essential information about pending litigation. The most significant portions of Rule 26 pertaining to expert witnesses will be discussed.[173]

The initial disclosures in Rule 26(a)(2) are mandatory in all cases and require no court intervention or judicial order. The parties are required to provide the information listed in the rule on a voluntary basis and in a writing that is signed and formally "served." Subdivision (B) of Rule 26(a)(2) sets out in great detail the type of information that must be contained in an expert report or provided in appendices to the report. To comply with the requirements of this subdivision, experts must continually update their curriculum vitae as they author new publications and are retained to testify as expert witnesses in other cases during the specified periods of time—10 years and 4 years, respectively.

Rule 26. Duty to Disclose; General Provisions Governing Discovery

(a) REQUIRED DISCLOSURES.

. . . .

    (2) *Disclosure of Expert Testimony.*

        (A) *In General.* In addition to the disclosures required by Rule 26(a)(1), a party must disclose to the other parties the identity of any witness it may use at trial to present evidence under Federal Rule of Evidence 702, 703, or 705.

        (B) *Witnesses Who Must Provide a Written Report.* Unless otherwise stipulated or ordered by the court, this disclosure must be accompanied by a written report—prepared and signed by the witness—if the witness is one retained or specially employed to provide expert testimony in the case or one whose duties as the party's employee regularly involve giving expert testimony. The report must contain:

            (i) a complete statement of all opinions the witness will express and the basis and reasons for them;

            (ii) the facts or data considered by the witness in forming them;

            (iii) any exhibits that will be used to summarize or support them;

            (iv) the witness's qualifications, including a list of all publications authored in the previous 10 years;

---

[173] *See generally* Andre Moenssens, "Discovery of Expert Findings in the United States: Federal Civil Cases," in WILEY ENCYCLOPEDIA OF FORENSIC SCIENCE, (Jamieson A. & Moenssens A.A., eds) 2009 & online updates.

(v)   a list of all other cases in which, during the previous 4 years, the witness testified as an expert at trial or by deposition; and

(vi) a statement of the compensation to be paid for the study and testimony in the case.

(C) *Witnesses Who Do Not Provide a Written Report.* Unless otherwise stipulated or ordered by the court, if the witness is not required to provide a written report, this disclosure must state:

(i)   the subject matter on which the witness is expected to present evidence under Federal Rule of Evidence702, 703, or 705; and

(ii)   a summary of the facts and opinions to which the witness is expected to testify.

(D) *Time to Disclose Expert Testimony.* A party must make these disclosures at the times and in the sequence that the court orders. Absent a stipulation or a court order, the disclosures must be made:

(i)   at least 90 days before the date set for trial or for the case to be ready for trial; or

(ii) if the evidence is intended solely to contradict or rebut evidence on the same subject matter identified by another party under Rule 26(a)(2)(B) or (C), within 30 days after the other party's disclosure.

(E) *Supplementing the Disclosure.* The parties must supplement these disclosures when required under Rule 26(e).

. . . .

(4)   *Form of Disclosures.* Unless the court orders otherwise, all disclosures under Rule 26(a) must be in writing, signed, and served.

Apart from the preparation of reports, experts who will testify may also have their depositions[174] taken prior to trial. Rule 26(b)(4)—Trial Preparations: Experts provides:

(b)   DISCOVERY SCOPE AND LIMITS.

. . . .

(4)   Trial Preparation: Experts.

(A) Deposition of an Expert Who May Testify. A party may depose any person who has been identified

---

[174] *See generally* Rhonda M. Wheate, "Discovery: Depositions" in WILEY ENCYCLOPEDIA OF FORENSIC SCIENCE, (Jamieson A. & Moenssens A.A., eds) 2009 & online updates.

as an expert whose opinions may be presented at trial. If Rule 26(a)(2)(B) requires a report from the expert, the deposition may be conducted only after the report is provided.

The following provisions were added in December, 2010, to ensure that the expert's opinions and factual bases remain subject to scrutiny, while protecting counsel's mental theories or impressions.

> (B) Trial-Preparation Protection for Draft Reports or Disclosures. Rules 26(b)(3)(A) and (B) protect drafts of any report or disclosure required under Rule 26(a)(2), regardless of the form in which the draft is recorded.

> (C) Trial-Preparation Protection for Communications Between a Party's Attorney and Expert Witnesses. Rules 26(b)(3)(A) and (B) protect communications between the party's attorney and any witness required to provide a report under Rule 26(a)(2)(B), regardless of the form of the communications, except to the extent that the communications:

>> (i) relate to compensation for the expert's study or testimony;

>> (ii) identify facts or data that the party's attorney provided and that the expert considered in forming the opinions to be expressed; or

>> (iii) identify assumptions that the party's attorney provided and that the expert relied on in forming the opinions to be expressed.

Rules 26(b)(4)(B) and (C) provide work product protection for drafts of expert reports and communications between counsel and the expert, subject to the limited exceptions. Discovery into the expert's opinions, including their development, factual foundation, or basis, remains permissible. For example, proper areas of inquiry include, among other things, the expert's testing methods, the expert's communications with individuals other than counsel, and any alternate methods or approaches that the expert elected not to use. Protected materials may still be discovered if "the party has a substantial need for the discovery and cannot obtain the substantial equivalent without undue hardship."

For experts who are consulted by attorneys for trial preparation but who are not expected to testify, the following special provision applies in Rule 26(b)(4):

> (D) Expert Employed Only for Trial Preparation. Ordinarily, a party may not, by interrogatories or deposition, discover facts known or opinions held by an expert who has been retained or specially employed by another party in anticipation of

litigation or to prepare for trial and who is not expected to be called as a witness at trial. But a party may do so only:

(i)   as provided in Rule 35(b); or

(ii)   on showing exceptional circumstances under which it is impracticable for the party to obtain facts or opinions on the same subject by other means.

When a witness has been retained in anticipation of litigation but is not expected to testify as a witness for the retaining party, such as a consulting expert, discovery can be had only upon showing of "exceptional circumstances." An exception is made for Rule 35 physical and mental examinations of persons.[175]

In most cases, experts are entitled to be compensated reasonably for the time they will be required to expend responding to discovery requests. This compensation is to be provided by the litigant seeking the disclosure of information and Rule 26(b)(4) provides:

(E)   Payment. Unless manifest injustice would result, the court must require that the party seeking discovery:

(i)   pay the expert a reasonable fee for time spent in responding to discovery under Rule 26(b)(4)(A) or (D); and

(ii)   for discovery under (D), also pay the other party a fair portion of the fees and expenses it reasonably incurred in obtaining the expert's facts and opinions.

§1.11   DISCOVERY AND DISCLOSURE IN CRIMINAL CASES

1.   GENERAL CONSIDERATIONS

As with civil discovery, jurisdictions are governed by their own individual rules for criminal discovery.[176] Some state discovery rules are patterned after Federal Rule 16[177] (discussed *infra*), others on the American Bar Association Recommended Standards for Criminal Discovery,[178] and some have "open file" discovery. "Open file" discovery

---

[175] Rule 35 provides, in part that the court "where the action is pending may order a party whose mental or physical condition—including blood group—is in controversy to submit to a physical or mental examination by a suitably licensed or certified examiner. The court has the same authority to order a party to produce for examination a person who is in its custody or under its legal control."

[176] *See generally* Andre Moenssens, "Discovery in the United States: Criminal Cases," in WILEY ENCYCLOPEDIA OF FORENSIC SCIENCE, (Jamieson A. & Moenssens A.A., eds) 2009 & online updates.

[177] *See, e.g.,* Ala.R.Crim.P. 16; Del.Sup.Ct.Crim.R. 16; West's Fla.Crim.R.Proc. 3.220; Mass. R. Crim. P. 14, N.J.Crim.Prac.R. 3:13–3; N.C.Gen.Stat. § 15A–903(a) & § 15A–905(b); N.D.R.Crim.P. 16; Ohio Crim.R.Proc. 16; R.I.Sup.Ct.R.Crim.P. 16; S.C.R.Crim.P. 5; S.D.C.L. Ch. 23A-13; Tenn.R.Crim.P. 16.

[178] *See* American Bar Association Standards for Criminal Justice (3d ed. 1992); Alaska R. Crim P.16; Ariz. R.Crim. P. 15.1, 15.2; Colo. R.Crim.P. 16; Me. R.Crim.P. 16; Md. R.Crim. P. 4–263; N.Y.-McKinney's Crim.Proc.L.§§ 240.20 & 240.30; Or. Rev. Stat. 135.815, 135.835; Vt. R.Crim. P. 16. The key difference between the Standards and Federal Rule 16 is the absence in the former of prosecutorial discovery based upon reciprocity. Under the ABA provisions, the

permits the defense access to all of the evidence and information obtained by the prosecution. Additionally, court interpretation can strongly influence what practice is followed under a given rule. For example, in Kentucky, the motion by a defendant for discovery of the prosecution's expert evidence should almost automatically be granted. This follows from *James v. Commonwealth*,[179] where the Supreme Court of Kentucky chastised the prosecution for not releasing the reports of a chemist in a narcotics case. The court stated: "A cat and mouse game whereby the Commonwealth is permitted to withhold important information requested by the accused cannot be countenanced."[180]

Constitutional provisions, particularly the due process guarantees in the Fifth and Fourteenth Amendments, also govern required disclosures by the prosecution. In recent years, there has been a trend toward accepting, in criminal matters, the general purposes of disclosure and discovery in civil actions: preventing surprise at trial; narrowing the issues to be tried; and speeding the administration of justice by encouraging settlement (e.g., plea bargaining) of those cases where both sides know the strength or weakness of the evidence. Pretrial discovery also provides a means whereby defense counsel is able to equalize the imbalance of resources available to the state by gaining access to both the expert's evidence, but also information concerning its generation and underlying data.[181]

Rule 16 of the Federal Rules of Criminal Procedure will be discussed in some detail, since these provisions have been models for many revisions in state criminal discovery rules.[182] When examining the laws of all fifty states, it becomes evident that a majority of states have adopted statutes and court rules that specifically allow some

---

prosecutor's right to obtain discovery is not conditional on the defendant's request. Also, in the Standards only the prosecution need seek a court order to obtain discovery and neither the prosecution nor the defense must show that the other intends to introduce the expert information at trial to discover that material.

[179] 482 S.W.2d 92 (Ky.1972).

[180] Id. at 94. But thereafter, the Kentucky court expressed another view as to the scope of the accused's entitlement in Bussey v. Commonwealth, 697 S.W.2d 139 (Ky.1985) (in prosecution for attempted sodomy of daughter, defendant was not entitled to disclosure of psychiatric files of defendant's son where psychiatrist's testimony was not based on the contents of those files) and Milburn v. Commonwealth, 788 S.W.2d 253 (Ky.1989) (defendant not entitled to advance notice of firearms examiner's testimony as far as its being consistent with certain findings in his report, where the report was made available to the defendant prior to trial, and where the opinion was drawn directly from the findings in the report).

[181] As Justice Benjamin Cardozo stated in People ex rel. Fordham Manor Reformed Church v. Walsh, 244 N.Y. 280, 291, 155 N.E. 575 (1927), "Disclosure is the antidote to partiality and favor."

[182] Not all states have dealt specifically with discovery of scientific information by statute nor does this Chapter detail each jurisdiction's laws and rules separately. It is incumbent upon each lawyer to be familiar with the court rules and procedural statutes and mechanisms adopted within the jurisdiction where the litigation is occurring. When local authority is not mentioned, an extrapolation from the pronouncements regarding general criminal discovery will nevertheless be useful.

pretrial discovery of expert information for both prosecution and defense. Reference to these other sources will be given where helpful. For those states that have not adopted specific rules, case law may provide a guide for an understanding of the state's approach to expert discovery.

2. FEDERAL RULE 16

Pretrial discovery in federal criminal cases is covered by Rule 16 of the Federal Rules of Criminal Procedure. Rule 16 has two separate provisions covering discovery of experts retained by the defendant and those experts retained or employed by the prosecution.[183]

The provision for defendant's discovery of expert information from the prosecution is contained in Rule 16(a)(1)(F) and (G):

(F) Reports of Examinations and Tests. Upon a defendant's request, the government must permit a defendant to inspect and to copy or photograph the results or reports of any physical or mental examination and of any scientific test or experiment if:

(i) the item is within the government's possession, custody, or control;

(ii) the attorney for the government knows—or through due diligence could know—that the item exists; and

(iii) the item is material to preparing the defense or the government intends to use the item in its case-in-chief at trial.

(G) Expert Witnesses. At the defendant's request, the government must give to the defendant a written summary of any testimony that the government intends to use under Rules 702, 703, or 705 of the Federal Rules of Evidence during its case-in-chief at trial. If the government requests discovery under subdivision (b)(1)(C)(ii) and the defendant complies, the government must, at the defendant's request, give to the defendant a written summary of testimony that the government intends to use under Rules 702, 703, or 705 of the Federal Rules of Evidence as evidence at trial on the issue of the defendant's mental condition. The summary provided under this subparagraph must describe the witness's opinions, the bases and reasons for those opinions, and the witness's qualifications.

---

[183] For an interesting aspect of expert categorization, *see* United States v. Bel-Mar Laboratories, Inc., 284 F.Supp. 875 (E.D.N.Y.1968) (for purposes of Rule 16, experts who are government employees and experts who are retained by the government are treated alike).

Under this provision, discovery is activated by the "request" of the defendant.[184] A request is often made and complied with extra-judicially; however, in the case of a dispute over discovery either party may move for an order denying, restricting, or deferring discovery or inspection. Rule 16 grants courts the power to regulate discovery.

Once the defendant makes a request, the rule provides that the government shall permit the defendant to inspect or copy the results of reports of medical or scientific tests.[185] However, for the rule to apply, the expert information must be in the control of the government, the prosecution must know of its existence, and the information requested by the defendant must be material to the preparation of his defense or it must be intended to be introduced at the trial by the prosecution in the case-in-chief.[186] The final restriction is intended to prevent the defendant from conducting a "fishing expedition" through the voluminous reports of the government. It also protects the work efforts of the advisor-expert from disclosure, thus encouraging full case investigations by the prosecution. Of course, the defendant will eventually receive expert information from the prosecution which is material and favorable to the defense under the *Brady* rationale, even if the expert is not expected to testify.[187]

---

[184] Absent a request by the defense, the prosecution has no obligation to disclose this information. *See* United States v. Walker, 657 F.3d 160, 175 n. 12(3d Cir. 2011) (noting that, ironically, the defendant had filed a *pro se* motion to compel discovery, but it had been stricken by the court since he was represented by counsel and counsel made no such request from the prosecution).

[185] *See* United States v. Hearst, 412 F.Supp. 863 (N.D.Cal.1975) (reports of prosecution and defense psychiatrists to be exchanged between the parties).

Despite the broad language of the statute, there are limitations on the scope and content of discoverable material. *See, e.g.*, United States v. Orzechowski, 547 F.2d 978 (7th Cir.1976), cert. denied 431 U.S. 906 (1977) (prosecution not required to produce internal memoranda of Drug Enforcement Administration relating to testing of alleged cocaine products since such reports had not been made in connection with any particular prosecution); United States v. Beaver, 524 F.2d 963 (5th Cir.1975), cert. denied 425 U.S. 905 (1976) (court did not err in permitting fingerprint testimony on the ground that the government, while furnishing defendant with a fingerprint report, failed to provide prior to trial the specific points of identification and the number of matching points).

What constitutes a "report" or "results" may be an issue of dispute. *See, e.g.*, United States v. Dennison, 937 F.2d 559 (10th Cir.1991) (psychiatrist's notes taken during discussion with defendant were not discoverable medical reports or results); United States v. Peters, 937 F.2d 1422 (9th Cir.1991) (examination of Federal Rule 16(b) and Hawaii District Court Rule 345–1(b) where expert made no written findings of his review of photographs and medical records).

[186] In United States v. Lambert, 580 F.2d 740 (5th Cir.1978), certain evidence was held to be outside the scope of the discovery order since it was introduced not as part of the government's case-in-chief, but as impeachment evidence during cross-examination of the defendant.

[187] Brady v. Maryland, 373 U.S. 83 (1963), discussed in Section 1.11(3) *infra*. Courts consistently distinguish between information discoverable under Fed. R.Crim. Proc. 16(a) (1) and that required to be disclosed under the *Brady* doctrine. See generally, Weatherford v. Bursey, 429 U.S. 545 (1977). The distinction between the two rules was articulated in United States v. Kaplan, 554 F.2d 577, 579–80 (3d Cir.1977) ("Where documentary evidence is exculpatory, it may be within both *Brady* and Rule 16, but nonexculpatory records are obtainable in advance of trial only by virtue of Rule 16. It is conceivable that some documents which are not covered by Rule 16, e.g., a Jencks Act statement, may be *Brady* material because of their content.").

The provision for the prosecution's discovery of expert information from the defense is contained in Fed. Rule 16(b)(1)(B) and (C):

(B) Reports of Examinations and Tests. If a defendant requests disclosure under Rule 16(a)(1)(F) and the government complies, the defendant must permit the government, upon request, to inspect and to copy or photograph the results or reports of any physical or mental examination and of any scientific test or experiment if:

(i) the item is within the defendant's possession, custody, or control; and

(ii) the defendant intends to use the item in the defendant's case-in-chief at trial, or intends to call the witness who prepared the report and the report relates to the witness's testimony.

(C) Expert Witnesses. The defendant must, at the government's request, give to the government a written summary of any testimony that the defendant intends to use under Rules 702, 703, or 705 of the Federal Rules of Evidence as evidence at trial, if—

(i) the defendant requests disclosure under subdivision (a)(1)(G) and the government complies; or

(ii) the defendant has given notice under Rule 12.2(b) of an intent to present expert testimony on the defendant's mental condition.

This summary must describe the witness's opinions, the bases and reasons for those opinions, and the witness's qualifications.

The prosecution should possess, and the defense should specifically request all documents resulting from the collection of physical evidence, its transmission to the expert for analysis, standards and procedures used by the expert in its analysis, bench notes concerning the conduct of the analysis, and standards concerning how the data obtained by the analysis is gathered and reported. At least one current commentator has pointed out that giving the ubiquity of scientific evidence used to prove presumptive guilt—DWI alcohol tests, for instance—access to the underlying facts and data for scientific testing is a matter of due process.[188]

These provisions are nearly identical to those for discovery by the defense except that they contain a reciprocity clause. That is, the prosecution can discover the expert information from the defense only if the defendant first requests disclosure of similar information from the

---

[188] Andrea L. Roth, "Machine Testimony" Yale L.J. (forthcoming): UC Berkeley Public Law Research Paper No. 2893755 (January 4, 2017)(available at SSRN: https://ssrn.com/abstract=2893755)(last accessed February 27, 2017).

government and the government has complied with the request. If the defendant has triggered Subdivision (b)(1)(B), the prosecution may request the information it desires. However, the reports or test results which are sought must be within the control of the defense *and* there must be the intention to introduce such evidence at trial. Also, the prosecution may seek only the results or reports of medical or scientific tests that were made in connection with the case.

3.   CONSTITUTIONAL REQUIREMENTS

a.   *Due Process*

Even though there is no direct constitutional requirement for pretrial discovery in criminal cases,[189] a constitutional duty in the area of disclosure was first recognized by the United States Supreme Court in 1935.[190] Although there is no constitutional right to discovery generally, a criminal defendant has due process rights under the Fifth and Fourteenth Amendments which require the prosecutor to disclose certain evidence. In *Brady v. Maryland*, the Supreme Court held that upon defense request the prosecution must disclose evidence favorable to the defendant that is material to guilt or punishment.[191] In *United States v. Bagley*, the Court held that the prosecution's duty to disclose *Brady* material arises regardless of a specific request by the defense.[192] Evidence is exculpatory if it can be used by the defendant for impeachment purposes.[193] The prosecution's duty to disclose exculpatory information includes all information known to the attorney for the state and any agent of the state,[194] if that information is not equally accessible to the defense.[195] "Whether the nondisclosure was a

---

[189] *See* Weatherford v. Bursey, 429 U.S. 545 (1977) (there is no general constitutional right to discovery in a criminal case). *See also*, Wardius v. Oregon, 412 U.S. 470 (1973) ("the Due Process Clause has little to say regarding the amount of discovery which the parties must be afforded."). *Accord* United States v. LaRouche, 896 F.2d 815 (4th Cir.1990), cert. denied 496 U.S. 927 (1990) (criminal defendants do not have a "general" constitutional right to discovery); Strickler v. Commonwealth, 241 Va. 482, 404 S.E.2d 227 (1991) (no constitutional right to discovery even where a capital offense is charged).

[190] Mooney v. Holohan, 294 U.S. 103 (1935) (a criminal conviction procured by state prosecuting authorities solely by the use of perjured testimony knowingly used by them in order to procure the conviction, is without due process of law and in violation of the Fourteenth Amendment).

[191] 373 U.S. 83, 87 (1963).

[192] 473 U.S. 667 (1985); Kyles v. Whitley, 514 U.S. 419, 433 (1995).

[193] Id. at 676; Robinson v. Commonwealth, 231 Va. 142, 150, 341 S.E.2d 159, 164 (1986)

[194] Kyles v. Whitley, 514 U.S. 419, 437 (1995) ("the prosecutor has a duty to learn of any favorable evidence known to the others acting on the government's behalf in the case, including the police.").

[195] Price v. Thurmer, 514 F.3d 729, 731–732 (7th Cir. 2008)(no *Brady* violation when prosecution did not disclose indictment against court-appointed expert psychologist for Medicare fraud because indictment was matter of public record and accessible to defense attorneys).

result of negligence or design, it is the responsibility of the prosecutor" to seek and disclose exculpatory evidence.[196]

The prosecutor's responsibility to fulfill the constitutional obligations of *Brady* means that all information concerning the expert and the expert's analysis that is favorable to the defense must be disclosed. For most experts, the exculpatory nature of scientific findings that do not implicate the defendant is readily recognized as *Brady* material and all experts acting in good faith would expect this information to be provided to the defense. This would include DNA results that do not match the defendant's profile, drug analysis that does not indicate the presence or requisite amount of controlled substances, blood testing that is negative for the presence of alcohol or drugs, and other similar "clear" exculpatory results. However, *Brady* materials also include information that is not so "clear" in that it does not conclusively exonerate the defendant but supports a claim of innocence.[197] *Brady* also requires disclosure of information useful for *impeachment.* Any information that would suggest problems with an analysis, such as the failure to follow protocols[198] or indications of contamination in the results, would also need to be disclosed to the defense. Anything potentially impacting the results of the analysis would need to be disclosed.

The more controversial information covered by *Brady* would be the impeachment information concerning the analyst. The Rules of Evidence are quite broad as to what can be used to impeach a witness.[199] All information relevant to impeachment as to job-performance *and to general credibility* must be disclosed. (*See* Section 1.13(3)(a) *infra*). This disclosure would include negative information on job performance, proficiency test failures, the failure to pass certification tests, criminal convictions, prior inconsistent statements, drug use, alcohol abuse, and any information supporting an inference that the witness's ability to observe or relate details is compromised.

The government also has a limited duty to preserve evidence. In *California v. Trombetta*, the United States Supreme Court held that due process requires the government to preserve evidence "that might

---

[196] Giglio v. United States, 405 U.S. 150, 154 (1972). The Brady obligation extends to information in the possession of the prosecution or its agents. If the expert is not considered a part of the prosecution team, *Brady* does not require information in the possession of the expert to be disclosed. Avila v. Quarterman, 560 F.3d 299, 308–309 (5th Cir. 2009)(no *Brady* violation when government did not disclose opinion of expert witness because expert witness was not considered arm of prosecution).

[197] *See* Gonzales v. McKune, 247 F.3d 1066, 1077 (10th Cir. 2001)(information about lack of sperm in semen sample collected from victim was exculpatory even though it did not conclusively exonerate defendant who did not have low sperm count).

[198] *But see*, United States v. Sanchez-Florez, 533 F.3d 938, 941 (8th Cir. 2008)(evidence that fingerprint lab technician used improper lab procedures not favorable to an accused because defendant's fingerprints were not found even through the use of the improper procedure).

[199] *See, e.g.,* Federal Rules of Evidence, Rules 607–713.

be expected to play a significant role in the suspect's defense."[200] The evidence must (1) "possess an exculpatory value that was apparent before the evidence was destroyed;" and (2) "be of such a nature that the defendant would be unable to obtain comparable evidence by other reasonably available means."[201] If the evidence is merely potentially exculpatory, the defendant must show bad faith in the destruction to establish a denial of due process.[202] The burden to establish the apparent exculpatory value is difficult to establish. The courts have found no due process violation for the destruction of a rape kit two years after the crime because the police had no suspects and the evidence was not exculpatory at that time,[203] or for the destruction of a semen sample when another assailant remained at large so the "negative DNA test" did not fully exculpate the defendant.[204]

Additionally, the due process clause bars discovery by the prosecution unless there is reciprocal discovery for the defense. In *Wardius v. Oregon*,[205] the United States Supreme Court held unconstitutional a state law requiring a defendant to notify the prosecution if he intended to give an alibi defense, and to give the names of any witnesses that would be called to support such a defense, where there was no corresponding duty on the prosecution to give the defense the names of witnesses that would be called by the prosecution to rebut the defendant's alibi. The Court stated that "the Due Process Clause of the Fourteenth Amendment forbids enforcement of alibi rules unless reciprocal discovery rights are given to criminal defendants."[206] In view of *Wardius,* any prosecutorial discovery system, including discovery of scientific information, must also provide for similar discovery rights for the defendant.

The constitutional protection of due process has also been invoked in connection with scientific evidence by criminal defendants seeking relief from convictions based on flawed scientific evidence. In *Albrecht v. Horn*, the Third Circuit Court of Appeals suggested that a petitioner may claim that scientific evidence introduced at trial violated his due process rights upon a showing that the evidence "infect[ed] his entire trial with error of constitutional dimensions."[207] The petition for relief is

---

[200] 467 U.S. 479, 488 (1984).

[201] Id. at 488–489; *see* Yarris v. County of Delaware, 465 F.3d 129, 142–143 (3d Cir. 2006)(due process violation where government left DNA evidence it knew to be exculpatory in a paper bag under a detective's desk, destroying the evidence).

[202] Arizona v. Youngblood, 488 U.S. 51, 58 (1988).

[203] Monzo v. Edwards, 281 F.3d 568, 580 (6th Cir. 2002).

[204] Hubanks v. Frank, 392 F.3d 926, 931 (7th Cir. 2004).

[205] 412 U.S. 470 (1973).

[206] Id. at 472. The court further stated that "discovery must be a two-way street." Id. at 475.

[207] 485 F.3d 103, 124 n. 7 (3d Cir. 2007)(*quoting* Murray v. Carrier, 477 U.S. 478, 494 (1986)).

not a "free-standing innocence claim," but a due process claim.[208] Relying on this rule, the court in *Lee v. Houtzdale* granted habeas relief to a defendant whose conviction rested on flawed arson analysis, which the government conceded had been rendered invalid by subsequent scientific developments.[209] The Ninth Circuit joined the Third Circuit in recognizing that habeas petitioners can allege a due process violation from the introduction of flawed expert testimony at trial in *Gimenez v. Ochoa*, but denied relief to the petitioner in that case finding that "permitting the prosecution's experts to testify based on a triad-only theory of [shaken baby syndrome]" was not so unfair that it violated the constitutional provisions.[210] In 2016, the Washington Court of Appeals vacated a 2003 conviction based on "the medical community's now generally accepted understanding of brain trauma in children directly contradicts the medical theories that were relied upon to convict her."[211]

b. Protection Against Self-Incrimination

It is generally accepted now that rules requiring the defendant to submit to limited pretrial discovery by the prosecution do not, by themselves, violate the Fifth Amendment protection against self-incrimination. However, when Rule 16 of the Federal Rules of Criminal Procedure was amended in 1966 to allow for discovery of defense evidence by the prosecution as a condition to the defendant obtaining disclosure of government evidence, serious Fifth Amendment questions were raised which remain important for more than historical reasons. Justices Black and Douglas dissented from the promulgation of the new discovery rule by the Supreme Court. Their dissents were directed toward the Fifth Amendment aspects of conditioning defense discovery upon reciprocal discovery being allowed the prosecution.[212] However, their arguments are presumably even stronger against nonreciprocal discovery where the prosecution has a right to discover defense evidence independent of a triggering defense request.

For present purposes, it is sufficient to note that limited discovery of defense evidence is constitutional.[213] Nevertheless, the Fifth Amendment right to be free from self-incrimination limits prosecutorial discovery.[214] The controversial issues in criminal cases involve the scope

---

[208] Lee v. Houtzdale SCI, 798 F.3d 159, 162 (3d Cir. 2015)(*interpreting* Lee v. Glunt, 667 F.3d 397, 403 n. 5 (3d Cir. 2012).

[209] 798 F.3d at 167.

[210] 821 F.3d 1136, 1145 (9th Cir. 2016).

[211] In re Pers. Restraint of Fero, 192 Wn. App. 138, 153, 367 P.3d 588, 595 (2016).

[212] *See* United States v. Fratello, 44 F.R.D. 444 (S.D.N.Y.1968); Comment, "Prosecutorial Discovery Under Proposed Rule 16," 85 Harv. L. Rev. 994 (1972). Under the current federal rule, no court involvement is required although a defense request to discover government evidence remains necessary to trigger prosecutorial discovery.

[213] *See* Williams v. Florida, 399 U.S. 78 (1970) (upholding constitutionality of state notice of alibi statute in the face of a Fifth Amendment claim).

[214] *See* United States v. Ryan, 448 F. Supp. 810 (S.D.N.Y.1978), affirmed 594 F.2d 853 (2d Cir.1978), cert. denied 441 U.S. 944 (1979) (if a defendant demands discovery of the government, he waives protection against self-incrimination as far as documents are

of the waiver of Fifth Amendment protections when certain issues are raised by the defense, such as a mental state defense. A criminal defendant who raises mental state as a guilt or penalty phase issue generally waives the Fifth Amendment privilege against self-incrimination "to the extent necessary" to permit a proper examination of that condition.[215] Courts, however, may be asked to decide what limits may properly be placed on prosecutorial access to court-ordered examinations and their results before the defendant actually introduces mental state evidence at trial.[216]

4.   PROCEDURES

As already noted, the federal system and most states have adopted provisions specifically dealing with pretrial discovery of expert information. These rules and statutes contain their own procedures and timelines for obtaining discovery which normally consist of written requests to the other party or motions to the court. Typically, discovery is conducted by motion in criminal cases. The overwhelming majority of modern criminal discovery rules do not allow civil-type depositions of an opponent's expert witness. Rather, specific disclosure of test results and reports is mandated. Florida, Iowa, Indiana, Nebraska, and Missouri[217] allow for discovery depositions of experts in addition to the specific information that must be disclosed under the rules. In this regard, it should be pointed out that Florida and Missouri allow additional oral depositions for *defendants* only, whereas Iowa and Indiana allow depositions by the prosecution conditioned upon reciprocity. Nebraska, however, allows either prosecution or defense to request the court to allow additional discovery by deposition if the pretrial oral examination would assist in the preparation of the case.

If permitted as part of the procedure accompanying the filing of a pretrial discovery motion or request for permission to take the deposition of a witness, counsel may require, by the service of a subpoena duces tecum, that an expert called to testify produce specified books, papers, documents, or other things in the expert's possession. The documents or objects sought by the subpoena duces tecum should be particularly described. Also, a party should be prepared to make a showing of materiality and relevance. These latter requirements may be difficult to fulfill if the subpoenaing party is unaware of the contents of the requested item. In jurisdictions with modern expert discovery provisions, the subpoena duces tecum will be of little use since those

concerned although he is still free to refuse to testify and is entitled to the appropriate standard charge in such regard).

[215] Buchanan v. Kentucky, 483 U.S. 402, 422–423 (1987).

[216] *See* Section 16.12(1) in Chapter 16: Forensic Psychiatry and Psychology discussing the implications of the Fifth Amendment in cases involving mental health evidence.

[217] Fla. R.Crim. P. 3.220(d); Burns' Ind. Code Ann., 35–37–4–3; 56 Iowa Code Ann. § 813.2, Rule 12; Mo. R.Cr. P. 25.12; Neb.Rev.Stat. § 29–1917.

rules specifically state books, papers, reports, and other documents may be otherwise obtained. While there is often a subpoena duces tecum provision in those jurisdictions, such as Rule 17(c) of the Federal Rules of Criminal Procedure, the provision is rarely necessary in light of the specific disclosure scheme established for expert witness materials.

§1.12 PRETRIAL PREPARATION

Prior to conferring with the expert about anticipated testimony, an attorney should obtain a full written report of the expert's findings, and familiarize herself with relevant texts concerning the forensic discipline and techniques used in any analysis that will supply evidence at trial. The widely-held belief that attorneys and judges are ill-prepared to understand or use expert evidence is compounded by the expert's likely unfamiliarity with procedures in court, requiring that attention be paid to educating experts on how to clearly convey dense and technical information to a lay audience without losing important details.[218] Although obtaining a copy of the report may entail further expenditure, it is beneficial in preparation for the pretrial conference and trial. The report may also be instrumental in bringing about a negotiated settlement of the charge.

At some time prior to trial an attorney must schedule a conference with the expert. At the pretrial attorney-expert conference, the attorney can explain to the witness the purposes of the witness' testimony.[219] This serves to focus the scope of the expert's attention to the relevant facts and the evidentiary theory of the case. The conference also gives the attorney an opportunity to ask any questions based upon the expert's previously submitted written report. Documents, photographs, and tangible evidence intended to be introduced should be reviewed to assure that the identification can be proved as a predicate to the introduction of the evidence at trial. Demonstrative exhibits such as models, charts, or diagrams should be examined and discussed. Experts should be prepared to deal with cross-examination questions based upon any books, articles, or treatises expressing views contrary to those expressed by the expert. The expert's own publications should also be reviewed for opinion that suggests a conclusion different from the one the witness has reached in the case. This change in opinion is of little impeachment value and may be used advantageously if the expert can relate facts demonstrating how technological advances led to the formation of the new opinion.

[218] National Institute of Justice, Focus Group on Scientific and Forensic Evidence in the Courtroom, p. 4 (2007)(available at: https://www.ncjrs.gov/pdffiles1/nij/grants/220692.pdf)(last accessed December 27, 2016).

[219] Suggested reading on courtroom expectations and demeanor: Thomas G. Gutheil, *The Psychiatrist as Expert Witness,* 2d ed., American Psychiatric Publishing, 2009; Harold A. Feder and Max M. Houck, *Feder's Succeeding as an Expert Witness,* 4th ed., CRC Prece, 2008; Dan Poynter, *Expert Witness Handbook-Tips and Techniques for the Litigation Consultant,* Revised ed., Para Publishing, 2012; Stanley L. Brodsky, *Testifying in Court: Guidelines and Maxims for the Expert Witness,* American Psychological Association, 1991.

Experts likely do not possess the legal knowledge of court rules and procedures sufficient to write their own examination for an attorney. However, pretrial advice from the expert on the precise wording of the questions asked on direct examination can be of great assistance. The expert may also suggest cross-examination questions for an opposing expert. Complex explanatory terminology can be rephrased and simplified into layman's language for a more understandable presentation to the trier of fact. Above all, the attorney who is familiar with an expert's discipline and the scope of the possibilities in examinations of the type involved in the case will be better prepared for trial.

§1.13   TRIAL TESTIMONY

Any party to a case can call expert witnesses, and the court has the right to call a witness on its own, or at the request of a party.[220] The court also has the right to examine any witness, regardless of who calls the witness.[221] In the event the court uses either of these provisions, objections to the court's examination may be made at the time, or at the next opportunity when the jury is not present.[222]

1.   CONFRONTATION[223]

The Sixth Amendment of the United States Constitution guarantees the accused in criminal prosecutions the right "to be confronted with the witnesses against him." This right is referred to as the right to confrontation and the provision is known as "the Confrontation Clause." In *Melendez-Diaz v. Massachusetts*,[224] the United States Supreme Court continued the reformation of the Confrontation Clause begun four years before in *Crawford v. Washington*.[225] In *Crawford*, the Court had held that the constitutional protections of the Confrontation Clause extended to all "testimonial statements," and that the right to confrontation was not satisfied by any inherent reliability of the statements to be presented. Instead, the right to confrontation required that the reliability of the statements be assessed by the in-court presentation of witness testimony subjected to the rigors of cross-examination.

What constitutes "testimony" or testimonial statements is still hotly contested and beyond the scope of this chapter. In *Melendez-Diaz*, the Court continued to define "testimonial statements," holding that

---

[220] FRE Rule 614(a).

[221] FRE Rule 614(b).

[222] FRE Rule 614(c).

[223] *See generally* Betty Layne DesPortes, "Melendez-Diaz v. Massachusetts—The Admissibility of Laboratory Reports," in WILEY ENCYCLOPEDIA OF FORENSIC SCIENCE, (Jamieson A. & Moenssens A.A., eds) 2009 & online updates.

[224] 557 U.S. 305 (2009).

[225] 541 U.S. 36 (2004).

laboratory reports of forensic analysis fell within the "core class of testimonial statements." Thus, the analysts were "witnesses" for purposes of the Sixth Amendment, entitling the defendant to "be confronted with" them at trial.[226] The admission of the forensic reports over the defendant's objection without the in-court testimony of the analysts violated Melendez-Diaz's Sixth Amendment right to confrontation. The Court's opinion in *Melendez-Diaz* firmly rejected the notion that forensic laboratory analysts, or expert witnesses of any kind, were exempt from the protections of the Confrontation Clause. The Court refuted the classification of forensic analysts as "non-accusatory" witnesses, finding no support for such a distinction in the Sixth Amendment itself or in prior case law.[227] Similarly, the Court noted that the Confrontation Clause does not contain a distinction for "ordinary" or "conventional" witnesses that would exclude expert witnesses from its reach.[228] In commentary that should have surprised no forensic analyst or legal practitioner, the Court emphasized that forensic evidence is not uniquely immune from the influences that affect any witness testimony: bias, dishonesty, mistake, and fraud.[229] Therefore, it could not be immune from the process mandated by the Sixth Amendment to ensure reliability: confrontation.

In June 2011, the United States Supreme Court continued the Confrontation Clause revolution in forensic science evidence. In *Bullcoming v. New Mexico*,[230] a five-justice majority held that the right to confrontation is not satisfied by calling a supervisor or "surrogate" expert to merely read the lab report of another person's analysis.[231] Although the supervisor in *Bullcoming* could speak from personal knowledge about the laboratory's general procedures, he had not participated in or observed the performance of any part of the testing on the blood sample involved in the case.[232] The majority opinion rejected the reasoning of the New Mexico Supreme Court that had concluded the report's author was a "mere scrivener" for the gas chromatograph performing the blood analysis.[233] The Court emphasized that the report did more than merely recite the numbers yielded by the machine; it amounted to a certification of the manner in which the analysis was conducted.[234] Although the supervisor could discuss the machine and laboratory procedures generally, only the individual analyst knew about the specific analysis in the case.[235]

---

[226] 557 U.S. at 311.

[227] 557 U.S. at 313.

[228] 557 U.S. at 315.

[229] 557 U.S. at 318–320.

[230] 564 U.S. 647 (2011).

[231] 564 U.S. at 652.

[232] 564 U.S. at 661–662.

[233] 564 U.S. at 659.

[234] 564 U.S. at 660.

[235] 564 U.S. at 661.

In June 2012, the United States Supreme Court issued another 5–4 decision concerning the application of the Confrontation Clause to forensic science evidence to resolve the question left open in *Bullcoming*: whether the prosecution could introduce the conclusions in one analyst's laboratory report through another expert witness who also performed part of the analysis. *Williams v. Illinois*[236] involved a DNA expert testifying, based in part on an analysis conducted by another person, that the evidentiary DNA profile matched the DNA profile of the defendant. The Illinois Supreme Court held that this arrangement did not violate the confrontation clause because the statements in the report did not need to be admissible (as the bases of the testifying expert's opinion). Although the Court upheld the decision of the Illinois Supreme Court, that court's reasoning was not endorsed. Five justices held that "[t]here is no meaningful distinction between disclosing an out-of-court statement so that a factfinder may evaluate the expert's opinion and disclosing that statement for its truth." Instead, the majority of the court affirmed the conviction based on the conclusion that the original lab report in the case was not testimonial. Reciting many of the arguments of the dissenters in *Melendez-Diaz* and *Bullcoming*, the four-justice plurality reasoned that the original lab report which contained just the unassociated evidentiary DNA profile (from a vaginal swab of an alleged rape victim), did not accuse the defendant of a crime. The testifying expert conducted the "incriminating" analysis that compared the evidentiary DNA profile with the defendant's DNA profile and concluded the two profiles matched. With Justice Thomas's concurrence in which he found the lab report to be insufficiently "formal"[237] or "solemn" because it was not sworn or attested, the majority view of five justices affirmed the conviction.

With the *Williams* addition to complete the *Melendez-Diaz* trilogy on forensic science evidence, the Confrontation Clause continues to prohibit the introduction, over defense objection, of "formal" laboratory reports. Formal laboratory reports are ones which typically involve testing by just one analyst and are incriminating on their face, such as drug, blood alcohol, fingerprints, and some autopsies. However, the results or subsidiary reports used to generate a final incriminating report will probably not be testimonial and can be relied upon by an expert in providing testimony at trial. In a multi-step analytical method, it will probably be sufficient for the prosecution to produce the

---

[236] 132 S.Ct. 2221 (2012).

[237] In a footnote, Justice Thomas makes clear that the "formality" of the report cannot be altered by efforts to "evade the formalized process" by reformatting a report. 132 S.Ct. at 2260 n. 5 (Thomas, J. concurring)(quoting Davis v. Washington, 547 U.S. 813, 838 (2006)).

expert who conducted the final interpretational analysis, who will presumably be the author of the final report.[238]

A developing area of confrontation discussion concerns the admissibility of autopsy reports when the examining pathologist does not appear at trial and the evidence is offered through a surrogate. The question is whether the report constitutes inadmissible testimonial hearsay; a question on which courts are quite divided.[239] A work-around may exist when the testifying pathologist can look at the record of an autopsy, conclude it is sufficient for him or her to review, reach an independent conclusion based on the record presented, and state their opinions as to their findings, including cause and manner of death.

2.   Direct Examination

a.   *Qualification*

An expert witness is permitted to testify not only to facts but also to his opinions and conclusions drawn from the facts. As a predicate to opinion testimony, however, it must be demonstrated by proof that the witness is qualified from observation, study, or actual experience to speak as an expert. Federal Rule of Evidence 702 provides that an expert witness is one qualified "by knowledge, skill, experience, training, or education." Most state evidence provisions contain identical or similar provisions. Qualification establishes no more than the basis of the witness's ability to give an opinion, but does not reflect on the validity or the quality of that opinion,[240] which may be vigorously examined or attacked when rendered from the witness stand.

Before testifying, the expert witness must be found "qualified" by the court to testify as an expert witness through a demonstration by the proponent of the expert's opinion.[241] Qualification is predicated on the witness's testimony deriving from his or her "knowledge, skill, experience, training, or education."[242] In jurisdictions that have adopted

---

[238] *See* Jeffrey Fisher, "The Holdings and Implications of Williams v. Illinois," SCOTUSblog (Jun. 20, 2012, 2:20 PM) (available at: http://www.scotusblog.com/2012/06/the-holdings-and-implications-of-williams-v-illinois)(last accessed July 1, 2012).

[239] *See* People v. Lewis, 806 N.W. 2d 295 (Mich. 2011) (pointing out that there has been no definitive answer to the question of whether autopsy reports are testimonial hearsay, and that the US Supreme Court has previously denied cert. in Craig v. Ohio 549 US 1255 (2007)). *See also* Daniel J. Capra & Joseph Tartakovsky, "Autopsy Reports and the Confrontation Clause: A Presumption of Admissibility," 2 Va. J. Crim. L 62. (2014) (arguing for a presumption of admissibility); Marc D. Ginsburg, "The Confrontation Clause and Forensic Autopsy Reports— A Testimonial," 74 La. L. Rev. 117 (2013–4) (arguing that reports are testimonial and should be excluded).

[240] United States v. Laurienti, 611 F.3d 530, 547(9thCir.2010) (holding that qualification is no imprimatur of quality of testimony, but no more than a reflection that basic compliance with the requirements of Rule 702 have been met).

[241] *See, e.g.,* Fed.R.Evid.104(a) ("In General. The court must decide any preliminary question about whether a witness is qualified, a privilege exists, or evidence is admissible. In so deciding, the court is not bound by evidence rules, except those on privilege.").

[242] *See* FRE Rule 702 (2011) (requiring expert witness to David E. Watson, PC v. United States, 668 F.3d 1008 (8th Cir. 2012)("The government's witness, as a general engineer for the

the 2000 amendments to Rule 702, or adhere to *Daubert* criteria, the proponent of the testimony must also be prepared to demonstrate that the expert's specialized knowledge will be helpful to the trier of fact, based on sufficient facts or data, and the result of validated methodology that has been applied to the case at hand.[243]

The scope of the trial court's discretion in determining whether a witness qualifies as an expert is quite broad. Nevertheless, even after the trial judge rules (or indicates) that the witness is competent to testify as an expert, the trier of fact (jury or judge) determines what weight to assign to the testimony, and expert witnesses are not deemed any more "credible" than lay witnesses under the law. This equality of testimonial value is the source of a current controversy over whether to qualify expert witnesses in the presence of the jury.[244]

Experts' qualifications to testify may be established in a number of ways at trial. A recital of qualifications and a formal tender of the witness as expert in open court in the presence of the jury is commonly requested by the proponent of the testimony. This has the tactical advantage of emphasizing the "expert" status of the witness, potentially giving more weight to their testimony than the law allows. In recent articles, this has begged the question as to whether such a ruling by the judge amounts to improper vouching for the witness. Some courts have abandoned the practice as a result. Pre-trial motions in limine, by which the party proffering the expert pre-qualifies the expert to testify outside the presence of the jury, is another procedural method that seems to be gaining ground in the literature. This procedure has been endorsed by the American Bar Association[245] and the National Commission on Forensic Science.[246] Once qualified, the court may or may not, according to its discretion and relevant law, ever inform the jury that a particular witness is an expert.

In practice, the process of establishing the qualifications of a witness can be very routine. Typically, the attorney will ask questions

---

IRS, spent about 40 percent of his time dealing with compensation issues and had worked on about 20 to 30 reasonable compensation cases; even if the witness's education and training was not specifically tailored to compensation issues, he certainly had demonstrated practical experience qualifying him as *an* expert in the field."); United States v. Haywood, 363 F.3d 200, 210–211 (3d Cir. 2004) (holding that police officer who was a resident of the Virgin Islands had sufficient knowledge to testify that beer sold by bar originated in the mainland United States).

[243] FRE Rule 702 (b-d) (2011).

[244] *See,* e.g., Cynthia Ford, "Tender Is the Night: Should Your Expert Be?" 38 Mont. Law. 21 (2013) (discussing whether formal tender and acceptance by the court unduly emphasizes the witness's special status as against the equal weight given by law to expert testimony).

[245] ABA Civil Trial Practice Standard 14 (2007).

[246] National Commission on Forensic Science, "Views of the Commission on Judicial Vouching," Adopted June 21, 2016 ("The Commission is of the view that it is improper and misleading for a trial judge to declare a witness to be an expert in the presence of the jury.") (available at: https://www.justice.gov/ncfs/work-products-adopted-commission) (last accessed January 4, 2017).

drawn from the expert's resume to elicit the following types of information:

1. employment history and current position;

2. formal education, training, licenses, certifications;

3. continuing education and professional organization membership;

4. leadership positions in the relevant fields;

5. writings, publications, lectures and teaching;

6. experience in the field; and

7. prior qualifications as an expert witness.[247]

If qualification is challenged or if the opposing counsel wishes to demonstrate deficiencies in the expert's credentials, opposing counsel will ask additional questions of the expert.[248] If the witness's qualifications are accepted by the court, direct examination begins in which the expert's data, examinations, and opinions are disclosed. An expert witness will be qualified to provide opinions in a specific field or fields that are relevant to the subject of inquiry in the case, and opposing counsel may object if the expert attempts to provide testimony outside the field(s) of qualification.[249]

b.   Ultimate Issue

As a general rule of common law, an expert who testifies to cause and effect from an analysis of the facts must state the expert's conclusion in the form of an opinion rather than as absolute fact. This rule has been extended by a line of cases establishing the inadmissibility of testimony from an expert witness in the form of an opinion or inference which embraces the ultimate issue or issues to be decided by a jury. The common law "ultimate issue" rule, therefore, prohibits any witness, including an expert, from giving an opinion on the ultimate issue in the case. The rationale underpinning this rule is that a witness should not invade the province of the jury.[250]

The problem regarding the ultimate issue limitation is simply that in complex cases involving issues beyond the comprehension of a lay jury, an expert's opinion on the ultimate issue is needed to assist the

---

[247] Andre Moenssens, "Direct Examination of Experts," in WILEY ENCYCLOPEDIA OF FORENSIC SCIENCE, (Jamieson A. & Moenssens A.A., eds) 2009 & online updates.

[248] State v. Owens, 167 Wash. 283, 9 P.2d 90 (1932); *contra* People v. Sawhill, 299 Ill. 393, 132 N.E. 477 (1921).

[249] United States v. Smallwood, 456 Fed. Appx. 563 (6th Cir. 2012) (although witness had experience in toolmarks generally, she had no specific training or experience with knife marks and the trial court's decision to exclude the expert as unqualified under FRE 702 was upheld). *But see* Rodriguez v. State, 30 A.3d 764, 769 (Del. 2011)(fingerprint expert qualified as an expert in tire tracks and shoe prints because he took an FBI course that also covered those topics, studied a learned treatise on the topics, and "the analytic process is similar").

[250] Shreve v. United States, 103 F.2d 796 (9th Cir.1939), cert. denied 308 U.S. 570 (1939), *but see*, United States v. Johnson, 319 U.S. 503 (1943), rehearing denied 320 U.S. 808 (1943).

jury to reach a verdict. Rule 704 of the Federal Rules of Evidence rejected the ultimate issue doctrine, with the exception of certain mental state opinions in criminal cases.[251]

It must also be noted that not all courts have followed the pattern of rejection of the ultimate issue rule. In *Bond v. Commonwealth*,[252] the Virginia Supreme Court refused to follow the trend and retained the ultimate issue prohibition in criminal cases:

> We are not prepared to reject the ultimate issue prohibition . . . in a criminal case such as this where life or liberty often turns upon inferences raised by circumstantial evidence. The process of resolving conflicting inferences, affected as it is by the credibility of the witnesses who supply such evidence, is the historical function of a jury drawn from a cross-section of the community. We are unwilling to entrust that function to experts in the witness box.[253]

The traditional Virginia view was reinforced in *Llamera v. Commonwealth*[254] where the trial court had permitted a police officer who qualified as an expert in the sale, distribution, marketing, packaging, and effects of narcotics, to testify that in his opinion the cocaine seized from the defendant was packaged in a way that "suggested that the owner of the cocaine was a person who sold cocaine." The Supreme Court rejected the prosecution's view that the expert's use of the word "suggest" was a qualification, not a statement of fact on the ultimate issue: "We consistently have held that the admission of expert testimony upon an ultimate issue of fact is impermissible because it invades the function of the fact finder."[255]

c.   Bases of Opinion

A hearsay question arises when the expert bases an opinion on information given by someone else. Hearsay evidence is defined as testimony or written evidence of an out-of-court statement offered for the truth of the matters asserted therein, and thus relying on the credibility of the out-of-court declarant. As a general principle of law, all hearsay evidence is inadmissible unless the hearsay falls within one of a long list of recognized exceptions to the hearsay rule—exceptions created out of necessity or because the hearsay was uttered under circumstances evidencing some guarantee of trustworthiness. At common law, in criminal cases experts were prohibited from testifying

---

[251] *See* Section 16.11(3) in Chapter 16: Forensic Psychiatry and Psychology for additional discussion of this issue.

[252] 226 Va. 534, 311 S.E.2d 769 (1984).

[253] 226 Va. at 538, 311 S.E.2d at 772.

[254] 243 Va. 262, 414 S.E.2d 597 (1992).

[255] The Virginia Rules of Evidence, adopted in 2012, abolished the ultimate issue prohibition in civil cases, but retained the prohibition in criminal cases. Rules of the Supreme Court of Virginia Rule 2:704.

to an opinion based in whole or in part upon information received from others. But as with the ultimate issue rule, this prohibition has eroded, culminating in a rejection of the prohibition in the Federal Rules of Evidence:

Rule 703. Bases of an Expert's Opinion Testimony

An expert may base an opinion on facts or data in the case that the expert has been made aware of or personally observed. If experts in the particular field would reasonably rely on those kinds of facts or data in forming an opinion on the subject, they need not be admissible for the opinion to be admitted. But if the facts or data would otherwise be inadmissible, the proponent of the opinion may disclose them to the jury only if their probative value in helping the jury evaluate the opinion substantially outweighs their prejudicial effect.

Rule 705. Disclosing the Facts or Data Underlying an Expert's Opinion

Unless the court orders otherwise, an expert may state an opinion—and give the reasons for it—without first testifying to the underlying facts or data. But the expert may be required to disclose those facts or data on cross-examination.

Rule 703 specifically provides that an expert may give opinion testimony based on facts and data, including reports by others, even though this information may be inadmissible, provided "experts in a particular field would reasonably rely on those kinds of facts or data." Opinions based on information received from others not present in court would normally be inadmissible under the rules prohibiting hearsay testimony, but the federal rules of evidence chose to focus not on hearsay prohibitions, but on the reliability of such information as accepted within a professional discipline. Note that Rule 703 prohibits the disclosure of underlying facts without judicial permission if they would otherwise be inadmissible.

It must be recognized that in criminal cases because of the constitutional right of confrontation guaranteed in the Sixth Amendment, evidence that may be admissible under a recognized hearsay exception may still violate the confrontation right. This is the heart of the Supreme Court's decisions in the *Melendez-Diaz* trilogy. The bases of the expert's opinion do not become immune from a confrontation clause challenge just because the evidence forms the bases of the expert's opinion; if the evidence is testimonial and would otherwise violate the Confrontation Clause, the expert's opinion testimony does not provide a loophole for admission.

d.   Chain of Custody

The chain of custody rule provides that the party seeking to introduce into evidence the results of expert analysis has the burden of proving that the specimen or object analyzed was, in fact, derived or taken from the particular person or place alleged. In short, this constitutes a warranty that the object analyzed is from a known source and has not been subject to tampering or manipulation. This proof, which is of particular importance in criminal cases, is customarily adduced by testimony which traces the location and custody of the specimen from the time it was secured by law enforcement officers or agents of the state until it is offered in evidence. The chronicle of custody includes (1) the initial possession of the specimen or object by an officer, (2) the journey to the laboratory, (3) the method of storage at the laboratory prior to analysis and (4) the retention, whenever feasible, of the unused portion of the specimen or the object after analysis and up to the time of trial. It must also be established, as a prerequisite to admissibility of the evidence specimens, that they were in fact the same ones taken from the place or person in question, so that not only unbroken possession, but also the original source, can be established with certainty.[256]

Chain of custody is an essential requirement of proof in any case involving such materials as bullets, cartridge cases and weapons, fingerprints, hair, stained clothing, drugs, and blood specimens. In most cases the chain of custody can be sufficiently proven by the testimony of the investigator who secured the specimen or object and the analyst who examined it. The investigator's testimony establishes that he collected the exhibit, identified and placed it in a sealed container which was also marked for identification, and that the exhibit remained in the witness's custody or control until placed in the mail or in a laboratory receptacle such as a lock box. The expert removes the specimen or object from the mail or laboratory receptacle and analyzes it. Tangible objects which are not consumed in the analysis are marked for identification by the analyst and secured until the time of trial so that they will be admissible in addition to testimony concerning the analysis. For example, in the case of blood specimens from an impaired driving suspect, there must be legal proof that the specimen taken by a physician, nurse, or laboratory technician was the same specimen analyzed by the expert. The defense, of course, must also be prepared to demonstrate a proper chain of custody concerning analytical test specimens which are the subject of a defense expert's testimony.

When a break exists in the chain of custody of a specimen which was linked by scientific analysis to the defendant in an inculpatory fashion, it may be reversible error to admit opinion testimony based

---

[256] For a comprehensive discussion of admissibility attacks on testimony by chain of custody witnesses and weight attacks on the chain of custody, *see,* Imwinkelried, *The Methods of Attacking Scientific Evidence,* 3rd ed. (1997). See generally Andre Moenssens, "Chain of Possession of Tangible Evidence," in WILEY ENCYCLOPEDIA OF FORENSIC SCIENCE, (Jamieson A. & Moenssens A.A., eds) 2009 & online updates.

upon the analysis.[257] It is important to determine in each case whether the break affects the validity of the expert's findings. However, the practicalities of proof may not require a party offering certain evidence to negate the remotest possibility of substitution or alteration; all that need be established is a reasonable certainty that there has been no substitution, alteration, or tampering with the specimen.[258]

3. CROSS EXAMINATION

"[A] primary interest secured by [the Sixth Amendment] is the right of cross-examination."[259] Emphasizing the primacy of that interest, the United States Supreme Court has stated that "[t]he very integrity of the judicial system and public confidence in the system depend upon full disclosure of all of the facts, within the framework of the rules of evidence."[260] Invoking the Constitution of Virginia and statutory law, the Supreme Court of Virginia has also recognized that "[o]ne of the most zealously guarded rights in the administration of justice is that of cross-examining an adversary's witnesses."[261] Anything that might call into question an important aspect of the witness's testimony may be explored on cross-examination:[262] qualifications, ability to observe or recall, bias, prior statements, prior criminal acts, or character for untruthfulness may be explored.[263]

a. Competency and Credibility[264]

It is clear that each side has the right to cross examine the opposition's expert as to qualifications and matters which may impeach the credibility of the expert's opinion. For expert witnesses, counsel

---

[257] In Robinson v. Commonwealth, 212 Va. 136, 183 S.E.2d 179 (1971), panties, a blouse, and some pubic hair specimens were collected from a rape victim by a registered nurse at the hospital. The officers who received the evidence from the nurse and those who analyzed it testified at the trial, but the nurse was not called as a witness. The court held that the chain of custody was fatally defective and the expert testimony should not have been admitted.

[258] Beck v. State, 651 S.W.2d 827 (Tex.App.1983)(when there is no evidence that a technician improperly tested a blood sample in an involuntary manslaughter prosecution, the fact that the doctor testified he could not remember whether he took the blood sample of the defendant or whether it was taken by someone else in his presence does not affect the admissibility of the specimen, but goes only to its weight).

See also, People v. Mascarenas, 666 P.2d 101 (Colo.1983)(taking what has become the generally recognized approach to the necessity for an intact chain of custody).

[259] Douglas v. Alabama, 380 U.S. 415, 418 (1965).

[260] United States v. Nixon, 418 U.S. 683, 709 (1974).

[261] Moore v. Commonwealth, 202 Va. 667, 669, 119 S.E.2d 324, 327 (1961).

[262] A witness can be impeached both on direct and cross-examination by any party, even the party who calls the witness (see FRE Rule 607), but impeachment generally occurs during cross-examination of the opposing party's witness.

[263] See FRE Rules 608–610.

[264] After impeachment on cross-examination, a witness's credibility may be rehabilitated on redirect or through separate witnesses. Prior to cross-examination, however, it is improper to attempt to "bolster" the witness's credibility by offering evidence solely to enhance the witness's credibility. See Andre Moenssens, "Expert Testimony: Limitation on Scope— 'Improper Bolstering' Rule," in WILEY ENCYCLOPEDIA OF FORENSIC SCIENCE, (Jamieson A. & Moenssens A.A., eds) 2009 & online updates.

"may seek to explore potential weaknesses in the expert's qualifications, question the appropriateness and accuracy of the methods of examination used, explore potential insufficiency and inaccuracy of the data obtained, and throw doubt on the credibility of the conclusions."[265] Cross-examination can be an effective way to test the accuracy and relevance of an opinion or assertion based upon an expert's examination of evidence. Its efficacy, however, depends upon the skill and experience of the attorney, and quality of the attorney's preparation. The caliber and preparation of the expert witness will also determine the effectiveness of any impeachment attempts.

Whenever counsel has advance knowledge that a certain expert witness will appear for the other side, an effort should be made to learn as much as possible about the prospective witness.[266] A good source of information is often the expert whom the cross-examiner intends to use in the presentation of her own case. Experts in the same specialty can best appraise the competency and integrity of the expert who will testify. On-line legal databases can now be searched for experts' histories, and searching for case law containing an expert's name is occasionally productive to discover previous testimony. Similarly, experts' online presence by way of social media can also provide much information about their background and work. Since various fields within the forensic sciences are fairly restricted numerically, most experts are familiar with the others who are working in the field, or who have testified for the opposing side. Thus, they become a fertile source of information about others working in the same discipline and can assist the lawyer by providing information about the opposing witnesses. Checking with appropriate scientific associations or organizations may also be productive. By checking with the professional associations, an attorney may discover whether an expert has been sanctioned by the association for ethics violations. Most professional associations have codes of ethics and ethics committees to investigate and sanction instances of unethical professional conduct. An attorney should also consult with certifying bodies in the field. A search should also be made of publications authored by the anticipated expert witness. Whatever a proposed witness for either side has written should be read, especially the material pertaining to the particular subject of his testimony.

The expert may be questioned on other issues relevant to job performance such as results of proficiency testing, job evaluations, and results on certification exams. Also, the expert witness should expect to be cross-examined on non-job performance issues relevant to the

---

[265] Andre Moenssens, "Cross-Examination of Experts," in WILEY ENCYCLOPEDIA OF FORENSIC SCIENCE, (Jamieson A. & Moenssens A.A., eds) 2009 & online updates.

[266] For example, learning about specific prior conduct of the expert in other cases can provide ammunition for attacking credibility. *See* Navarro de Cosme v. Hospital Pavia, 922 F.2d 926 (1st Cir.1991).

credibility of all witnesses: criminal conduct;[267] prior inconsistent statements; and defects in capacity, contradiction, and bias. This seems to be the most difficult aspect of cross-examination for experts to comprehend. Understandably, experts would prefer for the entire focus of the testimony to be the analysis and the conclusions reached, but some experts fail to appreciate that they are witnesses presenting testimony and opinions to the jury. The credibility of a witness is always relevant, whether the witness testifies to known facts or expert opinions. The jury must assess the credibility of the witnesses and they cannot reliably do that if they do not have all information relevant to credibility. Some experts believe their general credibility is irrelevant because "they are testifying about the facts," but all witnesses provide factual testimony and the jury must decide whether they believe a witness's recitation of the "facts." If a witness is addicted to alcohol— which would impact both the ability to observe events and to accurately recall and relate those events—the jury needs to have that information, whether the witness is simply an eyewitness to a crime or an expert witness analyzing physical evidence from the crime. There simply is no difference in a credibility assessment between a witness testifying that a car was blue and a witness testifying that a color test used in drug analysis was blue.

It is important to remember that bias is a permissible area of impeachment for any witness, including expert witnesses. An accused has a right to cross-examine prosecution witnesses to show bias or motivation and that right, when not abused, is absolute."[268] The law concerning cross-examination for bias focuses on the permissible inferences to be drawn from the evidence.[269] There is no requirement that the witness actually receive a benefit for his testimony; likewise, the witness need not even admit that he hopes such a benefit will be forthcoming. What are relevant are any facts from which the trier of fact might infer that the witness hopes his testimony will garner him a benefit. If a witness believes he will benefit from testifying, whether or not the prosecution has actually promised the benefit, he has a bias and a motive to favor the prosecution with his testimony. The defendant is entitled to cross-examine a witness as to circumstances which would permit an *inference* of bias to try to establish that bias. "[T]he partiality

---

[267] *See* United States v. Ignasiak, 667 F.3d 1217, 1237–1238 (11th Cir. 2012)(describing as valuable impeachment evidence against the government's expert witness that he abused his government authority and committed acts which could have been charged as felonies when he used a counterfeit badge and his US Marshal credentials to pose as an on-duty US Marshal to carry firearms on commercial planes).

[268] Brown v. Commonwealth, 246 Va. 460, 463–64, 437 S.E.2d 563, 564–65 (1993)(defendant entitled to cross-examine a witness concerning his expectation of leniency in pending cases to establish bias and motive to testify); *see also* Brandon v. Commonwealth, 22 Va. App. 82, 467 S.E.2d 859 (1996)(disposition of juvenile charges admissible to show bias); Banks v. Commonwealth, 16 Va. App. 959, 434 S.E.2d 681 (1993)(specific acts of misconduct relevant to show bias or a motive to testify).

[269] *See* Davis v. Alaska, 415 U.S. 308, 316 (1974)(explaining the importance of opportunity to expose on cross-examination a bias, prejudice, or ulterior motive of the witness).

of the witness is subject to *exploration* at trial, and is always relevant as discrediting the witness and affecting the weight of his testimony."[270]

b. Treatises

There are two rules concerning the use of books or written authorities on cross-examination to impeach or discredit an expert witness where the authorities are in fact contrary to the witness's testimony. The first rule allows questioning of an expert regarding knowledge of an authoritative statement in a textbook or compilation of relevant data if it can be demonstrated that the witness relied upon the written authority. The more liberal rule—and federal practice—permits cross-examination when the expert admits that the particular book offered is a standard authority. The latter rule[271] allows the expert to be cross-examined and impeached from standard books, pamphlets, and articles in his field even though the expert did not rely on the particular book in reaching his opinion. The predicate for cross-examination from a book requires that the book be authenticated as authoritative. If the expert does not acknowledge the work as authoritative, the attorney may wish to call his own expert to do so.

In some jurisdictions the book itself is not admissible as substantive evidence, and the admissibility of excerpts is limited to impeachment.[272] The data recited is not offered for its truth; hence, it is not deemed hearsay. However, in a number of jurisdictions, particularly those that have adopted the federal rules of evidence,[273] authoritative treatises or professional publications may be used as substantive evidence in direct examination as well as impeaching evidence on cross-examination.[274] The theory of such a rule is that reliable writings, as with reliable oral testimony, should be considered admissible as evidence because the authors have staked their professional reputation

---

[270] Davis, 415 U.S. at 316 (internal quotations and citations omitted) (emphasis added).

[271] *See* Darling v. Charleston Community Memorial Hospital, 50 Ill.App.2d 253, 200 N.E.2d 149 (1964), affirmed 33 Ill.2d 326, 211 N.E.2d 253 (1965).

[272] *See* Rules of the Supreme Court of Virginia Rule 2:706(b), applicable to criminal cases: "Where an expert witness acknowledges on cross-examination that a published work is a standard authority in the field, an opposing party may ask whether the witness agrees or disagrees with statements in the work acknowledged. Such proof shall be received solely for impeachment purposes with respect to the expert's credibility."

[273] Under FRE 803(18), a statement contained in a treatise, periodical, or pamphlet is not excluded by the rule against hearsay if:

1. the statement is called to the attention of an expert witness on cross-examination or relied on by the expert on direct examination; and

2. the publication is established as a reliable authority by the expert's admission, or testimony, by another expert's testimony, or by judicial notice.

Evidentiary rules typically provide, as does FRE 803(18), that while passages from authoritative texts may be admitted substantively by being read in evidence, they may not be received as exhibits.

[274] *See* Lewandowski v. Preferred Risk Mutual Ins. Co., 33 Wis.2d 69, 146 N.W.2d 505 (1966); State v. Nicolosi, 228 La. 65, 81 So.2d 771 (1955); Stoudenmeier v. Williamson, 29 Ala. 558 (1857); Kan.Code of Civil Procedure, § 60:401 (1964); S.C.Code, § 26:142 (1952); and Uniform Rules of Evidence, Rule 63(31).

on the reliability of those statements. The federal rule (FRE 803(18)), which allows substantive evidence of writings that are established as reliable authority by expert testimony or judicial notice, does not require that the expert rely on the text or even recognize it as authoritative. Its rationale is founded on the case of *Reilly v. Pinkus*,[275] where the Supreme Court pointed out that the testing of a witness's professional competence would be incomplete without an opportunity to explore the witness's attitude toward the authoritative or generally accepted textbooks in his field.

When cross-examination from scientific texts is contemplated, the lawyer sponsoring the witness should caution the expert beforehand not to admit the authority of any book with which the witness is not sufficiently familiar to make that judgment. The opposition is thus put to the proof of showing its authenticity in a different manner. Experts should also be advised to ask to examine the book, its date of publication, and edition before conceding it to be authoritative.

§1.14   IMPROVING JURY COMPREHENSION

The effectiveness of expert testimony in jury trials is limited by a factor independent of the strength of the expert's testimony: the jurors' comprehension level. If the presentation of the expert testimony is not appropriate to the jurors' ability to understand the testimony and to apply the testimony to the issues in the case, the expert evidence is, at best, useless. The inability to comprehend the expert testimony may lead the jurors to misapply the expert testimony, thereby negatively affecting the party's position at trial and thwarting the interests of justice. It is the obligation of the attorneys and the court to ensure that the jurors understand the expert testimony and are able to competently use the evidence to reach a proper verdict. The primary means to assist jurors in understanding expert testimony are through jury *voir dire*, presentation of the evidence, and jury instructions.

1.   JURY VOIR DIRE

The purpose of jury *voir dire* is to obtain information relevant to prospective jurors' experiences to impanel a fair and appropriate jury. *Voir dire* seeks to discern a potential juror's bias or inability to judge the evidence and to apply the relevant law. This information can aid counsel in tailoring the presentation of the expert evidence to the jurors' capabilities and limitations, enabling a more effective presentation of the expert testimony involved in the case. "*Voir dire* provides a means of discovering actual or implied bias and a firmer basis upon which the parties may exercise their peremptory challenges intelligently."[276]

---

[275] 338 U.S. 269 (1949).

[276] J.E.B. v. Ala. Ex rel. T.B., 511 U.S. 127, 143–144 (1994). *Voir dire* conducted by attorneys has been shown to be more effective than *voir dire* conducted by judges in uncovering biases that are potentially disqualifying because jurors are more candid in their

Although the relatively low level of scientific and technical literacy in the general population and the legal profession[277] may make underlying reliability concepts (such as validation, uncertainty measurement, and statistical association) somewhat difficult to initially comprehend, the information is necessary for the jurors' proper determinations of the weight to accord the expert testimony, and to avoid misleading the jurors about the significance of the evidence. To decrease possible confusion of the issues, the parties should strive to present expert testimony in terms and using concepts familiar to the jurors. Additional questioning to ascertain jurors' prior experiences with the scientific or technical field will permit more effective presentations of expert evidence, and more informed jury decisions concerning such evidence.[278] The scope and extent of the questioning should always be tailored to the specific issues in controversy in the case.

In cases involving contested expert testimony, *voir dire* should include questions relevant to the nature of the case and the experiences of the jurors. Questions should ascertain the prospective jurors' qualifications with respect to the expert testimony, including the jurors' preconceptions about the scientific or technical field involved, and familiarity with the concepts and factors relevant to determining the probative value of the expert evidence. The following factors should be addressed in *voir dire*:[279]

1. Experiences with general scientific or technical principles, including specialized training or education in science and experience with laboratory practices;

2. Experiences with the specific scientific or technical principles relevant to the specific scientific discipline utilized in the case [chemistry, toxicology, engineering, etc.];

3. Any preconceptions about the subject of the expert testimony;

4. Any bias for or against experts, the scientific or technical field involved, including whether expert testimony will be accepted or rejected without consideration.

---

responses to attorneys. Susan E. Jones, "Judge versus Attorney-Conducted Voir Dire," 11 L. & Human Behav. 131 (1987).

[277] 2009 NAS Report at pp. 234–238.

[278] In some cases, the complexity of the expert evidence or the seriousness of the potential penalties may warrant providing a written questionnaire for prospective jurors. A written questionnaire allows expanded inquiry into these areas and provides enhanced opportunities for jurors to supply detailed responses.

[279] These factors are contained within the American Bar Association House of Delegates Resolution 101D, adopted Midyear Meeting 2012.

2. PRESENTATION OF EVIDENCE

The legal system requires an integrated system of expert evidence and the law. Trial attorneys must approach expert evidence with better education, skill, and knowledge than they have demonstrated in the past. Judges and juries cannot properly assess the weight of the expert testimony if attorneys do not adequately investigate, offer, and present such evidence. In any complex case involving contested scientific or technical issues, or any case where the expert testimony is difficult to comprehend, the parties and the court should be encouraged to find innovative solutions to facilitate jury understanding. Proposed solutions include accommodations in the trial structure to permit expert witnesses from both sides to testify sequentially and permitting jurors to actively participate in questioning the expert witnesses.

Adversarial legal systems rely on lawyers representing the interests of the parties and can lead to two problems with jury comprehension: battles of experts and isolation of the jurors. When the parties present dueling experts, research has shown that the expert evidence may simply be disregarded by jurors, who believe both experts have been discredited.[280] To avoid this nullification of expert testimony, counsel should strive to improve the jurors' understanding of the underlying principles to assist the jurors in resolving the conflicting issues. Ways to improve juror comprehension involve engaging the jurors in the trial through questions, note-taking, and visual presentations.

Steps that can improve jury comprehension of scientific evidence include permitting juror questions, note-taking, and technology assistance. In most jurisdictions within the United States, it is a matter of judicial discretion as to whether jurors may submit questions for the witnesses, and the practice is rarely used.[281] Not only does this reluctance have the potential to hamper a jury's comprehension of expert evidence, it also increases the burden on legal counsel to adequately examine and cross-examine expert witnesses by anticipating what information the jurors will find persuasive and how to make that information accessible to them.[282] Unlike juror questioning, juror note-taking is widely used. Research has shown that note-taking improves

---

[280] *See* Scott E. Sundby, "The Jury as Critic: An Empirical Look at How Capital Juries Perceive Expert and Lay Testimony," 83 Va. L. Rev. 1109 (1997).

[281] Hon. Gregory E. Mize, Paula Hannaford-Agor & Nicole L. Waters, "The State-of-the-States Survey of Jury Improvement Efforts: A Compendium Report," National Center for State Courts (April 2007) (reporting that approximately 11% of federal courts and 15% of state courts permit juror questions during trial) (available at: http://www.ncsc-jurystudies.org/state-of-the-states-survey.aspx) (last accessed January 4, 2017).

[282] It also removes an opportunity for the court and counsel to learn of jury confusion or difficulties with the evidence. *See* Howard Ross Cabot & Christopher S. Coleman, "Arizona Jury Reform: A View from the Trenches," Ariz. J. (July 12, 19991). *See also United States ex rel. DiGiacomo v. Franzen*, 680 F.2d 515, 516 (7th Cir. 1982)(jury submitted the following question to the judge: "Has it been established by sampling of hair specimens that the defendant was positively proven to have been in the automobile?").

comprehension.[283] In all United States jurisdictions, jury note-taking is expressly permitted or allowed by judicial discretion[284] and the majority of jurisdictions regularly allow jurors to take notes.[285] Preliminary instructions may be required to ensure jurors use the notes properly.[286] In addition to juror questions and note-taking, the use of visual presentations of evidence have been shown to improve the presentation of complex evidence.[287]

3. JURY INSTRUCTIONS

The goals of jury instructions are to increase the legal accuracy of verdicts, and thereby avoid reversals, and to improve juror comprehension of presented evidence. The 2009 NAS Report criticizing the subjectivity and lack of scientific validity for some areas of forensic science generated discussion about the appropriateness of limiting instructions for scientific evidence. The majority of courts follow model jury instructions which address expert testimony generally and without distinction between "subjective" and "objective" bases. Some courts have prohibited the use of "scientific" or "science" in referring to opinions in these fields to avoid misleading the jury,[288] or have removed the label "expert" from the instructions.[289] But these evidence-specific restrictions are not commonly used, despite the duty imposed on the trial courts to ensure jurors understand the law they are to apply, the issues they will

---

[283] Larry Heuer & Steven Penrod, "Juror Notetaking & Question Asking During Trials," 18 L. & Human Behav. 121 (1994). *See generally* G. Thomas Munsterman, Paula L. Hannaford-Agor & G. Marc Whitehead, *Jury Trial Innovations* (2d ed. 2006).

Research from mock trials indicates, however, that just permitting note-taking did not improve comprehension, but note-taking in conjunction with other innovations such as question-asking did improve comprehension. B. Michael Dann, Valerie P. Hans & David H. Kaye, "Can Jury Trial Innovations Improve Juror Understanding of DNA Evidence?" 255 NIJ Journal (November 2006) (available at: http://www.nij.gov/journals/255/trial_innovations. html)(last accessed January 4, 2017).

[284] The only jurisdictions which were reported in 2007 to have express prohibitions against jury note-taking were South Carolina and Pennsylvania. *See* Hon. Gregory E. Mize, Paula Hannaford-Agor & Nicole L. Waters, "The State-of-the-States Survey of Jury Improvement Efforts: A Compendium Report," National Center for State Courts p. 32 (April 2007). South Carolina has case law indicating this is actually a matter of judicial discretion, see *State v. Trent*, 234 S.C., 26, 156 S.E.2d 527 (1959), and Pennsylvania court rules were amended in 2008 to permit note-taking. *See* Pa. R. Crim. Proc. Rule 644.

[285] Hon. Gregory E. Mize, Paula Hannaford-Agor & Nicole L. Waters, "The State-of-the-States Survey of Jury Improvement Efforts: A Compendium Report," National Center for State Courts p. 32 (April 2007).

[286] *See* Esaw v. Friedman, 217 Conn. 553 (1991)(trial court has discretion to permit the jurors to take notes, but if it is allowed a precautionary instruction must be given).

[287] Lederer, "Courtroom Technology" 19 Criminal Justice 15, 15–19 (2004); B. Carney and N. Feigenson, "Visual Persuasion in the Michael Skakel Trial: Enhancing Advocacy through Interactive Media Presentations" 19 Criminal Justice 22 (2004).

[288] United States v. Starzecpyzel, 880 F.Supp. 1027, 1038 (S.D.N.Y. 1995).

[289] *See* United States v. Gutierrez-Castro, 805 F. Supp.2d 1218,1234–1235 (D. NM 2011)(fingerprint examiner not qualified as an "expert" before the jury and "expert" reference removed from jury instructions to avoid influencing jury assessment of weight of the evidence).

be asked to determine, and the factors they may properly consider in determining those issues.[290]

When expert witnesses give testimony in jury trials, juries are instructed as to the legal effect of having evidence given by persons who have special skills and knowledge. These "pattern" jury instructions generally tell jurors to weigh expert testimony no more than other witness testimony, accepting all or part of the testimony as they see fit.[291] Pattern jury instructions, while reducing reversals by using language from appellate opinions setting legal standards, do not necessarily track the specific issues of the case and do not improve juror comprehension or help them to properly assess the weight of the evidence. This is particularly true with expert evidence. Few pattern jury instructions address the factors jurors may use in determining the weight of the evidence or guide jurors on the proper use of expert testimony concerning scientific or technical results. Instructions should be provided to jurors that are tailored to the facts of each individual case and where expert evidence is contested, the instructions should reflect the evidence presented and the factors affecting the reliability of that evidence. Preliminary instructions should be used to provide guidance on the contested expert issues to improve juror comprehension.[292]

Jury instructions, to the extent relevant in the particular case, should inform jurors that they may consider the following factors in evaluating the weight to be attributed to the expert testimony:[293]

1. The extent to which the particular analysis used by the examiner is founded on a reliable methodology that has been properly validated;

2. The extent to which the examiner followed the methodology during the analysis;

---

[290] *See also* Taylor v. Commonwealth, 186 Va. 587, 592, 43 S.E.2d 906, 909 (1947)("It is always the duty of the court at the proper time to instruct the jury on all principles of the law applicable to the pleadings and the evidence."); Williams v. Lynchburg Traction and Light Co., 142 Va. 425, 432, 128 S.E.2d 732, 734 (1925)(The trial court's "imperative duty [to properly instruct the jury as to the law] . . . is one which can neither be evaded nor surrendered.").

[291] *See, e.g.,* New Mexico Rules Annotated, Uniform Jury Instruction 13–213 (2005). This instruction has most of the elements common to these instructions:

The Rules of Evidence do not ordinarily permit a witness to testify as to an opinion or conclusion. However, a witness who is qualified as an expert in a subject may be permitted to state an opinion as to that subject. After considering the reasons stated for an opinion, you should give it such weight as it deserves. You may reject an opinion entirely if you conclude that it is unsound.

This rule applies to allow the jury to totally disregard the expert's opinion even if it is uncontradicted. Strickland v. Roosevelt Co. Rural Elec. Co-op, 1982-NMCA-184, 99 N.M. 335, 657 P.2d 1184, cert. denied, 463 U.S. 1209, 103 S. Ct. 3540, 77 L. Ed. 2d 1390 (1983).

[292] *See* Principle 6 C, American Bar Association Principles for Juries and Jury Trials, 2005.

[293] These factors are similar to the factors contained within the ABA Criminal Justice Section Report to the House of Delegates on Proposed Resolution (101C) adopted at the ABA Midyear Meeting, February, 2012, pp. 12–13.

3. The extent to which the particular analysis relies on human interpretation;

4. The extent to which the analysis in this case may have been influenced by the possibility of bias;

5. The extent to which the analysis in this case followed standards established by reputable and knowledgeable organizations;

6. The qualifications of the examiner;

7. Whether the handling and processing of any physical evidence that was used in the analysis was sufficient to protect against contamination or alteration of that evidence;

8. The extent to which the examiner's methodology is generally accepted within the relevant scientific or technical community;

9. The reasons given by the examiner for the opinion;

10. Whether the examiner has been certified in the relevant field by a recognized body that evaluates competency by testing;

11. Whether any facility used by the examiner during the analysis was accredited by a recognized body if accreditation is appropriate for that type of facility;

12. The extent to which the examiner has complied with applicable ethical obligations;

13. Whether the physical observations made by the examiner are observable by others;

14. Other evidence of the accuracy of the examiner's conclusions;

15. The known nature of error associated with the examiner's methodology;

16. The fact that the nature and degree of error associated with the examiner's methodology (why and how often incorrect results are obtained) cannot or has not been determined;

17. The estimation of uncertainty (the range of values encompassing the correct value at a defined confidence interval) associated with the examiner's methodology.

Courts traditionally state their belief that juries follow instructions,[294] so one view is that jury instructions on expert witnesses are important. Research has raised doubt, however, that jury instructions have an

---

[294] *See, e.g.,* Richardson v. Marsh, 481 U.S. 200, 206 (1987) (emphasizing the "invariable assumption of the law that jurors follow their instructions").

impact on verdict decisions.[295] Ignoring the implications of judicial vouching (if an expert is qualified as such by the court in the presence of the jury) versus the common jury instruction for a moment, research suggests that "jurors appear insensitive to variables indicative of the actual validity and accuracy of a forensic technique, including testimony concerning whether a technique has been empirically validated (or not) and whether evidence is offered that the technique is known to make errors (or not)."[296] While it is beyond the scope of this chapter to talk at length about problems of juror cognition or comprehension, clearly attorneys should take steps to make jury instructions as clear and comprehensible as possible to jurors.

V. RESOURCES

§1.15   BIBLIOGRAPHY OF ADDITIONAL RESOURCES

Ronald J. Allen, "Expertise and the Supreme Court: What Is the Problem?," 34 Seton Hall L.Rev. 1 (2003).

Peter D. Barnett, *Ethics in Forensic Science: Professional Standards for the Practice of Criminalistics* (2001).

Jason Borenstein, "Science, Philosophy, and the Courts," 13 St. Thomas L. Rev. 979 (Summer 2001).

Terry Carter, "M.D. with a Mission: a Physician Battles Against Colleagues He Considers Rogue Expert Witnesses," 90 A.B.A. J. 40 (Aug. 2004).

David S. Caudill and Lewis H. LaRue, "A Non-Romantic View of Expert Testimony," 35 Seton Hall L. Rev. 1 (2004).

Mark P. Denbeaux and D. Michael Risinger, "Kumho Tire and Expert Reliability: How the Question You Ask Gives the Answer You Get," 34 Seton Hall L.Rev. 15 (2003).

Federal Judicial Center, National Academy of Sciences, *Reference Manual on Scientific Evidence*, 3d Ed., 2011 (available for download at: http://www.fjc.gov/public/home.nsf/pages/1448)(last accessed December 27, 2016).

Paul C. Giannelli, "Prosecutors, Ethics, and Expert Witnesses," 76 Fordham L.Rev. 1494 (2007).

---

[295] Eastwood, J., Caldwell, J. "Educating Jurors About Forensic Evidence: Using an Expert Witness and Jury Instructions to Mitigate the Impact of Invalid Forensic Science Testimony", 60 J. For. Sci 1523 (2015).

[296] N.J. Schweitzer, "Communicating Forensic Science", NIJ Final Report/Executive Summary for Project 2008-DN-BX-0003, 2016 at p. 11 (available at: https://www.ncjrs.gov/pdf files1/nij/grants/249804.pdf) (last accessed January 4, 2017).

Paul C. Giannelli, "Ake v. Oklahoma: The Right to Expert Assistance in a Post-Daubert, Post-DNA World," 89 Cornell L. Rev. 1305 (Sept. 2004).

Paul C. Giannelli, "Expert Qualifications: Who Are These Guys?" 19 A.B.A. CRIM. JUST. MAG. 70 (Spring 2004).

Paul C. Giannelli, "False Credentials," 16 A.B.A. CRIM. JUST. MAG. 40 (Fall 2001).

Michael H. Graham, "The Expert Witness Predicament: Determining 'Reliable' Under the Gatekeeping Test of Daubert, Kumho, and Proposed Amended Rule 702 of the Federal Rules of Evidence," 54 U. Miami L. Rev. 317 (Jan. 2000).

Laurel J. Harbour, "Increasing Judicial Scrutiny of Expert Testimony in Toxic Tort Cases," 30 Washburn L.J. 428 (1991).

Jeffrey L. Harrison, "Reconceptualizing the Expert Witness: Social Costs, Current Controls and Proposed Responses," 18 Yale J. on Reg. 253 (Summer 2001).

Edward J. Imwinkelried, "The Relativity of Reliability," 34 Seton Hall L.Rev. 269 (2003).

David H. Kaye, David E. Bernstein and Jennifer L. Mnookin, *The New Wigmore: A Treatise on Evidence: Expert Evidence*, 2d ed., Aspen Publishers, 2010.

Taylor C. Mascovitz, "Evidence: Expert Witness Qualification is a Fact and Circumstances Determination," 35 Suffolk U.L. Rev. 705 (Dec. 2001).

Joelle Anne Moreno, "What Happens When Dirty Harry Becomes an (Expert) Witness for the Prosecution?" 79 Tul. L. Rev. 1 (Nov. 2004).

Dale A. Nance, "Reliability and the Admissibility of Experts," 34 Seton Hall L.Rev. 191 (2003).

Myrna S. Raeder, "See no Evil: Wrongful Convictions and the Prosecutorial Ethics of Offering Testimony by Jailhouse Informants and Dishonest Experts," 76 Fordham L. Rev. 1413 (2007).

Andrea L. Roth, "Machine Testimony" (January 4, 2017). Yale Law Journal, Forthcoming; UC Berkeley Public Law Research Paper No. 2893755. Available at SSRN: https://ssrn.com/abstract=2893755 (accessed 2/27/17).

Michael J. Saks, "Scientific Evidence and the Ethical Obligations of Attorneys (Toward More Reliable Jury Verdicts? Law, Technology and Media Developments Since the Trials of Dr. Sam Sheppard)," 49 Clev. St. L. Rev. 421 (Summer 2001).

Michael J. Saks, "The Aftermath of Daubert: An Evolving Jurisprudence of Expert Evidence," 40 Jurimetrics J. 229 (2000).

Bruce D. Sales and Daniel W. Shuman, *Experts in Court: Reconciling Law, Science, and Professional Knowledge* (2005).

Joseph Sanders, "Expert Witness Ethics," 76 Fordham L. Rev. 1539 (2007).

Ryan M. Seidemann, "Closing the Gate on Questionable Expert Witness Testimony: a Proposal to Institute Expert Review Panels," 33 S.U. L. Rev. 29 (Fall 2005).

Dan Simon, *In Doubt: The Psychology of the Criminal Justice Process*, Harvard University Press, 2012.

Christopher Slobogin, "Doubts About Daubert," 57 Wash. & Lee L. Rev. 919 (2000).

Christopher Slobogin, "The Structure of Expertise in Criminal Cases," 34 Seton Hall L. Rev. 105 (Winter 2003).

Jennifer Turner, "Going After the 'Hired Guns': Is Improper Expert Witness Testimony Unprofessional Conduct or the Negligent Practice of Medicine?" 33 Pepp. L. Rev. 275 (Winter 2006).

Laurie Weiss, "Expert Witness Malpractice Actions: Emerging Trend or Aberration?" 15 PRAC. LITIG. 27 (Mar. 2004).

CHAPTER 2

DEMONSTRATIVE EXHIBITS

I. INTRODUCTION

§2.01 SCOPE OF THE CHAPTER

Testimony concerning scientific evidence can be difficult to convey to the trier of fact because of the complexity of the underlying scientific principles and the relative tedium of data presentations. For expert witnesses, using visual aids during testimony to present or explain the scientific results can vastly improve juror comprehension and retention. Studies have shown that visual aids can greatly improve juror recollection of evidence since jurors recall approximately 15% of what they hear and 85% of what they see.[1] These visual aids are a form of demonstrative evidence.

The term "demonstrative evidence" is used frequently, but with misleading or inconsistent results. Common demonstrative aids, such as photographs, charts, models, etc., may or may not be labeled "demonstrative," and may or may not be admitted into the record as evidence. The ambiguity in defining "demonstrative evidence" and the

---

[1] *See* Robert F. Seltzer, "Evidence and Exhibits at Trial," *Practising Law Inst., Preparation & Trial of a Toxic Tort Case* (1990) at p. 373; Robert F. Seltzer, "Effective Communication: Seeing is Believing," *Practising Law Inst., Product Liability of Manufacturers* (1988) at p. 599. *See also* Romano, John F. "The Media Plan for Trial—Selection and Presentation of Dynamic Demonstrative Evidence" 1 Ann.2001 ATLA-CLE 1071 (2001); Jason M. Lynch and Iris Eytan, "The Importance of Visual Presentation at Trial," 60 The Champion 14 (2016) at nn. 1–3 and accompanying text.

impact of that ambiguity on evidence rules and legal precedent will be discussed in subsequent sections, but for purposes of this chapter the term "demonstrative exhibit" will be used to refer to any item or device used to aid the trier of fact in understanding the issues at trial. The word "evidence" has been replaced with "exhibit" to reflect the variety of circumstances in which these items are presented at trial.

Demonstrative exhibits are used to assist the trier of fact to better understand a pertinent aspect of a case. Demonstrative exhibits are distinguished from oral testimony, but may be derived from such testimony. For example, a diagram may be created from an expert witness's description of the sequence of testing. Demonstrative exhibits are also separate from, but may incorporate or be derived from, physical evidence. A handgun used in an alleged crime is physical evidence. A schematic of that weapon presented at trial to help explain how the gun works is a demonstrative exhibit. Similarly, a broken bone is physical evidence; an x-ray showing the broken bone is a demonstrative exhibit. A shoe print in the dirt is physical evidence, but a cast of that mark shown to a jury is a demonstrative exhibit. If that cast is used to create a model of the shoe which is then compared to a shoe worn by an accused, the results of the comparison may the subject of expert testimony. The expert may create photographs during her examination of the model and the recovered shoe to illustrate her opinions concerning similar tread patterns. The cast, the model, and the photographs created during the expert examination are all possible sources of demonstrative exhibits.

The most frequent purpose of the demonstrative exhibit is to augment, illustrate, or otherwise provide a visual aid to the jurors so they can more effectively comprehend the oral testimony. The evidence is the testimony of the witness. The demonstrative exhibit merely helps the jury follow and better understand the words spoken by the witness. Since scientific evidence may involve complicated scientific principles, terminology unfamiliar to non-scientists, or extensive testing results, demonstrative exhibits are frequently used to convey unfamiliar complex material in expert testimony in a simplified visual format. Demonstrative exhibits prepared by an expert witness are "well nigh indispensable to the understanding of a long and complicated set of facts."[2]

Sometimes the demonstrative exhibit provides substantive evidence apart from the oral testimony of a witness. Photographs or other images may be relied upon by the expert witness in reaching her opinion. For example, crime scene photographs or video documenting bloodstains may be analyzed by a bloodstain pattern expert to provide a theory on the sequence of events. The crime scene photographs and video are not just illustrative of the expert's opinion, but supply the factual basis for her conclusions. Computer simulations or re-enactments, such as those used in some accident reconstructions, illustrate an expert's opinion and

---

[2]   Conford v. United States, 336 F.2d 285, 287 (10th Cir. 1964).

supply substantive information about what occurred. In those circumstances, the demonstrative exhibit is substantive evidence and not merely illustrative of other evidence.

This chapter will discuss the relevant legal principles concerning demonstrative exhibits and the specific issues involved with several types of demonstrative exhibits. The discussion will be limited to demonstrative exhibits commonly used or created in connection with scientific expert testimony. Demonstrative exhibits used by lay witnesses or counsel[3] are beyond the scope of this chapter, although many of the legal principles discussed would also apply to such exhibits.

§2.02 "DEMONSTRATIVE EVIDENCE" DEFINITIONS

As the Seventh Circuit Court of Appeals recognized in 2013, "[t]he term 'demonstrative' has been used in different ways that can be confusing and may have contributed to [errors in the trial courts]."[4] Although demonstrative exhibits are used frequently in cases, rules of evidence[5] do not define "demonstrative evidence" and case law has not developed consistent guidance for attorneys and judges concerning demonstratives.[6] Absent consistent guidance and a uniform lexicon for addressing the issue, "trial judges arrived at vastly different conclusions

---

[3] Demonstratives used by lay witnesses and counsel, such as "day-in-the-life" videos in personal injury cases, can be persuasive devices at trial. *See* Grimes v. Employers Mutual Liability Ins. Co., 73 F.R.D. 607, 610 (D. Ala. 1977)("The films illustrate, better than words, the impact the injury has had on the plaintiff's life in terms of pain and suffering and loss of enjoyment of life. While the scenes are unpleasant, so is the plaintiff's injury."); Chilton Davis Varner & James Matheson McGee, "A Thousand Words: The Admissibility of Day-in-the-Life Videos," 35 Tort & Ins. L.J. 175, 175 (Fall 1999)("Motion pictures or videos in personal injury trials have become almost commonplace today"). *See generally* Ryan E. Ferch, "Helping the Jury: An Argument for Sending Summary Demonstrative Evidence into the Jury Room," 1:2 J. of Court Innovation 263 (2008).

[4] Baugh v. Cuprum S.A. De C.V., 730 F.3d 701, 706 (7th Cir. 2013). The court in *Baugh* recognized that the inconsistent definitions had prevented legal scholars from articulating coherent evidentiary standards for demonstrative evidence. Ultimately, the court declined to reconcile past uses of the term and focused on the specific procedural facts of the case, noting that the exhibit had not been admitted into evidence, and therefore, should not have been provided to the jury during deliberations. The court reversed the verdict for the defense and the retrial resulted in a $11million verdict for the plaintiff. Baugh v. Cuprum S.A. De C.V., 2015 U.S. Dist. LEXIS 171282 (N.D. Ill. December 22, 2015).

[5] *See* notes 17–19 *infra* and accompanying text.

[6] Legal scholars have also contributed to the confusion by using inconsistent definitions of demonstrative evidence in commentary. "There are at least three definitions of demonstrative evidence in current use." Christopher B. Mueller and Laird C. Kirkpatrick, Evidence § 9–32, 1142 (5th ed. 2012)(citing Melvin Belli, "Demonstrative Evidence: Seeing is Believing," 16 Trial 70 (1980)). "[T]here is not even a settled definition of the term." Robert D. Brain and Daniel J. Broderick, "The Derivative Relevance of Demonstrative Evidence: Charting Its Proper Evidentiary Status," 25 U.C. David L. Rev. 957, 960 (1992). *See also* Thomas R. Mulroy, Jr. and Ronald J. Rychiak, "Use of Real and Demonstrative Evidence at Trial," 33 Trial Law.'s Guide 550, 555 (1989); 2 Kenneth S. Brown, McCormick on Evidence § 214 (6th ed. 2006)).

about the categorization, admissibility, and use of demonstrative evidence."[7]

Inconsistency in the definitions of demonstrative evidence partially derive from the attempts to categorize evidence. Most commentators use three categories of evidence, but differ on the specific categories. One theory classifies evidence as:

(1) "verbal"—oral testimony at trial;

(2) "real" —objects that played "an actual or direct role in the incident or transaction" giving rise to the cause of action; and,

(3) "demonstrative"—"all nonverbal evidence that is not real evidence."[8]

Other commentators describe evidence as:

(1) testimonial;[9]

(2) documentary; and,

(3) demonstrative, with "demonstrative" defined as evidence "tendered for the purpose of rendering other evidence more comprehensible to the trier of fact"[10] or "used to explain or illustrate testimony (or other evidence) that is already in the record."[11]

A variation of this categorization scheme further distinguishes "demonstrative evidence" (admitted) from "illustrative evidence" (not admitted).[12]

Other commentators used only two categories of evidence, but again differ on the two categories. One theory classifies evidence as:

(1) testimony; or

(2) demonstrative—which includes both real evidence and "exhibits meant to help illustrate the testimony."[13]

---

[7] Maureen A. Howard and Jeffrey C. Barnum, "Bringing Demonstrative Evidence in from the Cold: The Academy's Role in Developing Model Rules," 88 Temple L. Rev. 513–549 (2016).

[8] David S. Santee, "More than Words: Rethinking the Role of Modern Demonstrative Evidence," 52 Santa Clara L. Rev. 105, 110–111 (2012)(citing and quoting McCormick on Evidence §§ 213–214 (Kenneth S. Broun et all. Eds. 6th ed. 2006)).

[9] Some criminal defendants have challenged crime scene and autopsy photographs and videotapes as "testimonial" evidence subject to the Sixth Amendment right to confrontation citing language from the Supreme Court's decision in *Bullcoming*, that "document[s] created solely for an 'evidentiary purpose,' . . . made in aid of a police investigation, ran[k] as testimonial." Bullcoming v. New Mexico, 564 U.S. 647, 664 (2011)(internal quotations and citations omitted). Courts have unanimously rejected this argument. *See* State v. Smith, 367 P.3d 420, 432 (N.M. 2016).

[10] 2 McCormick on Evidence § 212 (5th ed. 1999).

[11] 22 Charles Alan Wright & Kenneth W. Graham, Jr., *Fed. Prac. & Proc.* § 5172 (2d ed. 2012).

[12] *See, e.g.*, Ronald Jay Allen et al., *Evidence: Text, Problems, and Cases* (5th ed. 2011) at p. 192.

Another theory broadly categorizes evidence as:

(1) substantive—which includes both testimony and real evidence that is "adduced for the purpose of proving a fact in issue;" or,

(2) demonstrative—which "carries no independent probative value [and merely] illustrate[s] the testimony of a witness to help jurors under stand difficult factual issues."[14]

Whether evidence is classified in two, three, or four categories, "demonstrative evidence" has either been defined very narrowly or very broadly. At the broadest, demonstrative evidence definitions encompass any physical evidence.[15] At the narrowest, "demonstrative evidence" is an exhibit that is not admitted as evidence, but is merely displayed at trial to help the trier of fact understand the substantive evidence in a case.[16]

Adding to the ambiguity of the definition of demonstrative evidence, or perhaps reflecting it, the Federal Rules of Evidence do not use the term "demonstrative."[17] The term is mentioned in the 1972 advisory committee's notes to Federal Rule of Evidence 611(a): "Item (1) restates in broad terms the power and obligation of the judge as developed under common law principles . . . [and] covers such concerns as . . . the use of demonstrative evidence. . . ."[18] State rules of evidence also do not specifically address demonstrative evidence. One state, Maine, addresses

---

[13] Stephanie Gree, "50 Shades of Prejudicial: Reexamining Demonstrative Evidence through State v. Jones," 45 U. Tol. L. Rev. 319, 325 (2014)(citing Morgan C. Smith, "Litigation Tip: The Best Way to Get Demonstrative Evidence Admitted at Trial," Cogent Legal Blog, January 19, 2012)(available at: http://cogentlegal.com/blog/2012/01/litigation-tip-the-best-way-to-get-demonstrative-evidence-admitted-at-trial/ (last accessed August 15, 2016)).

[14] *See* Steven C. Marks, "The Admissibility and Use of Demonstrative Aids," 32 The Brief 24, 25 (2003)(internal citations omitted). *See also* Jennifer L. Mnookin, "The Image of Truth: Photographic Evidence and the Power of Analogy," 10 Yale J.L. & Human. 1, 67 (1998)(describing the "generally understood" definition of demonstrative evidence as "that evidence addressed directly to the senses without intervention of testimony . . . Such evidence . . . [that] illustrates some verbal testimony and has no probative value in itself.")(citing Black's Law Dictionary 432 (6th ed. 1990)).

[15] *See, e.g.,* Finley v. Marathon Oil Co., 75 F,3d 1225, 1231 (7th Cir. 1996)(using demonstrative evidence" as synonym for physical exhibits).

"Demonstrative evidence" has been used to refer to both illustrative and real evidence in Virginia. *See* Kehinde v. Commonwealth, 1 Va. App. 342, 338 S.E.2d 356 (1986)(doll used as a replica for the child victim described as "demonstrative" evidence); *contrast* Jones v. Commonwealth, 228 Va. 427, 441–442, 323 S.E.2d 554, 561–562 (1984)(bag of jewelry from crime scene described as "demonstrative" evidence).

[16] *See, e.g.,* United States v. Janati, 374 F.3d 263, 273 (4th Cir. 2004)(demonstrative "charts or summaries may include witnesses' conclusions or opinions, or they may reveal inferences drawn in a way that would assist the jury. But . . . in the end they are not admitted as evidence.")(internal citations omitted); United States v. Milkiewicz, 470 F.3d 390, 396–398 (1st Cir. 2006). *See also* Robert D. Brain & Daniel J. Broderick, "The Derivative Relevance of Demonstrative Evidence: Charting Its Proper Evidentiary Status," 25 U.C. Davis L. Rev. 957, 961 (1992)("Demonstrative proof has only a secondary or derivative function at trial: it serves only to explain or clarify other previously introduced, relevant substantive evidence.").

[17] The complete Federal Rules of Evidence can be searched and downloaded at: https://www.rulesofevidence.org (last accessed August 11, 2016).

[18] Rule 611, Advisory Committee Notes, 1972 Proposed Rules, *Federal Criminal Code and Rules*, Thomson Reuters, 2016 Revised Edition at p. 303.

the use of "illustrative aids," defined as objects or depictions that are not admissible as evidence.[19]

As a result of the lack of a uniform definition and applicable evidentiary standards, jurisdictions are inconsistent in their identification and use of demonstrative exhibits. Several fundamental legal principles guide the analysis applied by courts when demonstrative exhibits are presented at trial.

II. LEGAL PRINCIPLES

§2.03   USE V. ADMISSION

In order to apply the proper legal standard applicable to a particular demonstrative exhibit, the first issue to consider is whether the exhibit is being used during a witness's testimony as an illustrative aid or the exhibit is being admitted as substantive evidence.[20] Demonstrative exhibits used as illustrative aids at trial are objects, pictures, models, or other devices intended to clarify or depict aspects of a witness's testimony to the trier of fact. Demonstrative aids that seek to directly establish the truth or falsity of an alleged fact contain substantive evidence.[21]

Identifying the purpose of the exhibit will provide some guidance in determining the applicable legal standards, including foundational requirements and evidence rules.[22] Identifying the purpose of the exhibit, however, is not decisive in determining the applicable legal standards. Ambiguous terminology and individual court practices have contributed to the variances in how demonstrative exhibits are handled

---

[19]   Maine Rules of Evidence 616 provides in part: "(a) Otherwise inadmissible objects or depictions may be used to illustrate witness testimony or counsel's arguments. (b) The court may limit or prohibit the use of illustrative aids as necessary to avoid unfair prejudice, surprise, confusion, or waste of time. (c) Opposing counsel must be given reasonable opportunity to object to the use of any illustrative aid prepared before trial. (d) The jury may use illustrative aids during deliberations only if all parties consent, or if the court so orders after a party has shown good cause." Maine Rules of Evidence (available at: http://www.courts. maine.gov/rules_adminorders/rules/text/mr_evid_plus_2015-9-1.pdf)(last accessed August 12, 2016).

[20]   United States v. Wood, 943 F.2d 1048, 1055 (9th Cir. 1991)("When considering the admissibility of exhibits of this nature, it is critical to distinguish between charts or summaries *as evidence* and charts or summaries *as pedagogical devices.*")(internal citations and quotations omitted).

[21]   Security camera footage is an example of a demonstrative exhibit that may supply substantive evidence. An exhibit which is introduced as substantive evidence without accompanying witness testimony is sometimes described as a "silent witness" to the activity or information depicted. Knapp v. State, 9 N.E.3d 1274, 1282 (Ind. 2014). *See generally* Steven I. Bergel, " 'Silent Witness Theory' Adopted to Admit Photographs Without Percipient Witness Testimony," 19 Suffolk U. L. Rev. 353 (1985); James McNeal, "Silent Witness Evidence in Relation to the Illustrative Evidence Foundation," 37 Okla. L. Rev. 219 (1984).

[22]   Baugh, 730 F.3d at 708 ("The distinction is important in determining whether evidentiary standards apply and whether the item will be available to the jury during deliberations.").

by the courts.[23] Some courts routinely "admit" into evidence illustrative aids that have no substantive evidentiary value, and some appellate cases have discussed the "admission" of purely illustrative aids.[24] The method of handling demonstrative exhibits will vary not only by the purpose of the item (illustrative v. substantive evidence), but also by the particular practice of the individual court.[25] Evidentiary rules vary by jurisdiction and courts have differed on the evidentiary standards to be applied to demonstrative exhibits. The law and practice of the jurisdiction and the individual court should be considered on a case-by-case basis.[26]

§2.04   Use at Trial

Demonstrative evidence, when the term is used in the narrowest sense to denote illustrative aids, is not generally admitted into evidence and the admissibility standards in rules of evidence should not be applicable.[27] In such circumstances, the decision to permit the use of the illustrative aid is committed to the "sound discretion" of the trial judge.[28] The foundational requirements imposed for the use of a

---

[23] Maureen A. Howard and Jeffrey C. Barnum, "Bringing Demonstrative Evidence in from the Cold: The Academy's Role in Developing Model Rules," 88 Temple L. Rev. 513, 521(2016)("Confusion as to nomenclature, characterization, and admissibility adds to the uncertainty as to whether demonstrative evidence is formally admitted into evidence and whether jurors get to review the object in their deliberations.").

[24] *See* United States v. Bray, 139 F.3d 1104, 1111–1112 (6th Cir. 1998)("We note in passing that in appropriate circumstances not only may such pedagogical-device summaries be used as illustrative aids in the presentation of evidence, but they may also be admitted into evidence"); United States v. Towns, 913 F.2d 434, 445–446 (7th Cir. 1990)(upholding admission of ski mask and gun for demonstrative purposes as replicas of the mask and gun reportedly used). *See also* State v. Pangborn, 836 N.W.2d 790, 797 (Neb. 2013)("We historically have discussed the use of demonstrative exhibits in terms of admissibility. . . . But the use of such terminology can be misleading.").

[25] For discussion of the variety of court procedures for handling exhibits during jury deliberations, *see* Ryan E. Ferch, "Helping the Jury: An Argument for Sending Summary Demonstrative Evidence into the Jury Room," 1:2 J. of Court Innovation 263 (2008).

[26] For a discussion of applicable law by jurisdiction, *see* Fred Lane and Scott Lane, *Lane Goldstein Trial Technique, 3rd ed.* §§ 2:75, 11:160 and § 12:29 (updated 2012). *See also* Barbara E. Bergman and Nancy Hollander "Demonstrative Evidence" 3 Wharton's Criminal Evidence § 16:23 (15th ed., updated 2011). Any compilation of jurisdictional law, however, may not reflect the inconsistencies of the underlying appellate case law. "Demonstrative evidence used for illustrative purposes is handled differently from jurisdiction to jurisdiction and sometimes from courtroom to courtroom." Roger Park, David Leonard, Aviva Orenstein and Steven Goldberg, *A Student's Guide to the Law of Evidence as Applied in American Trials*, 3d ed., 2011 at pp. 583–584. "The inconsistency in lexicon and definition leads to further confusion as to admissibility and use because appellate courts' discussion of acceptable discretionary practice rules for one type of evidence labeled demonstrative often conflict with other courts' practice rules." Maureen A. Howard and Jeffrey C. Barnum, "Bringing Demonstrative Evidence in from the Cold: The Academy's Role in Developing Model Rules," 88 Temple L. Rev. 513, 523 (2016).

[27] *See* Baugh, 730 F.3d at 708. *See also* David S. Santee, "More than Words: Rethinking the Role of Modern Demonstrative Evidence," 52 Santa Clara L. Rev. 105, 119–121 (2012).

[28] *See, e.g.,* Commonwealth v. Walter, 406 N.E.2d 1304, 1309 (Mass. App. Ct. 1980); State v. Panghorn, 836 N.W.2d 790, 801 (Neb. 2013); Commonwealth v. Moore, 279 A.2d 179, 184–185 (Pa. 1971). *See also* Peoples v. Commonwealth, 147 Va. 692, 705, 137 S.E. 603, 606–607 (1927)(explaining that the use of "means of illustration, such as exhibiting to the jury models, tools, weapons, implements, etc., is a matter of every day practice. A discretion is

demonstrative exhibit for illustrative purposes are (1) that the exhibit is a "fair and accurate" representation of the evidence it purports to depict; and, (2) that the item will assist the trier of fact.[29]

If the exhibit does not fairly depict the information or is unduly prejudicial, the court will prohibit the use of the demonstrative exhibit. In *Rodd v. Raritan Radiologic Associates*,[30] the New Jersey appellate court reversed a plaintiff's verdict because the trial judge permitted use of super-magnified computer images as exhibits in a case. At issue in the case was whether the defendants were negligent in failing to detect cancerous growths in radiological images. The applicable standard of care required the defendants to review the images at 2.5 power magnification. The exhibits used by the plaintiffs, however, were magnified many times greater than the 2.5 power magnification. The defendant argued that the super-magnified images made the cancerous growths obvious and implied that the defendants failed to act with reasonable care. The court held that the use of the exhibits was "unduly influential, potentially confusing, susceptible of being accepted as substantive evidence, and was clearly capable of producing an unjust result" because the images were magnified greater than the images actually reviewed by the defendants.[31]

§2.05 ADMISSION

If the demonstrative exhibit is not merely used at trial, but admitted into evidence, different foundational requirements may apply. Generally, the admission of evidence requires showings of (1) authenticity, (2) relevance, and (3) reliability.[32] Of the three elements for admissibility of demonstrative exhibits, courts have been relatively consistent in their standards for establishing only one element: authenticity.

---

vested in the trial court to prevent an abuse of the use of such illustrations, and unless there has been such an abuse, [the appellate] court will not interfere.").

[29] Knapp v. State, 9 N.E.3d 1274, 1282 (Ind. 2014); Dunkle v. State, 139 P.3d 228, 247 (Okla. Crim 2006); State v. Farner, 66 S.W.3d 188, 209 (Tenn. 2001); Clark v. Cantrell, 529 S.E.2d 528, 536 (S.C. 2000); Sommervold v. Grevlos, 518 N.W.2d 733, 738 (S.D. 1994); Nachtsheim v. Beech Aircraft, 847 F.2d 1261 (7th Cir. 1988); Smith v. State, 491 N.E.2d 193, 195 (Ind. 1986). *See also* 5 Christopher B. Mueller & Laird C. Kirkpatrick, Federal Evidence § 9:22 (4th ed. 2012).

[30] 860 A.2d 1003 (N.J. Super. Ct. App. Div. 2004).

[31] 860 A.2d at 1011–1012.

[32] Other rules or statutory requirements, such as timely disclosure and notice obligations, may bar admission of evidence that meets these general requirements. *See* Caprio v. Commonwealth, 254 Va. 507, 510, 493 S.E.2d 371, 373–374 (1997)(chart proffered by an expert illustrating the results of DNA tests was improperly admitted where the Commonwealth failed to notify and provide a copy of the chart to opposing counsel at least 21 days before trial as required by Va. Code § 19.2–270.5).

Similarly, admissibility may also be established by statute. *See, e.g.,* D.C. Code § 50–2209.01(b)(2010)("Recorded images taken by an automated traffic enforcement system are prima facie evidence of an infraction and may be submitted without authentication).

1. Authentication

For the first element of admissibility, courts apply Federal Rule of Evidence 901(a) and analogous state evidence rules[33] and case precedents. Federal Rule of Evidence 901 provides that "the proponent must produce evidence sufficient to support a finding that the item is what the proponent claims it is." The authentication element[34] requires proof that the exhibit is a fair and accurate representation of what the exhibit purports to portray[35] or that it was produced through a reliable process.[36] For demonstrative exhibits, this proof is generally accomplished through testimony from a witness with knowledge of what the exhibit represents or how it was produced. For example, a photograph of a scene can be authenticated by someone familiar with the scene or by the photographer.

At least one court has imposed additional requirements to authenticate computer-generated substantive evidence. In *State v. Swinton*,[37] the Connecticut Supreme Court adopted a six-factor test for authentication of computer-generate evidence: "(1) the computer equipment is accepted in the field as standard and competent and was in good working order, (2) qualified computer operators were employed, (3) proper procedures were followed in connection with the input and output of information, (4) a reliable software program was utilized,

---

[33] *See, e.g.,* Commonwealth v. Serge, 586 Pa. 671, 896 A.2d 1170, 1171 (Pa. 2006), cert. denied, 549 U.S. 920 (2006)(discussing PaR.E. 901 (a) and stating that demonstrative evidence may be authenticated by testimony "that a matter is what it is claimed to be").

[34] Some courts apply the authentication requirement of authenticity as part of the admissibility standard without reference to the terms "authenticity" or "authentication." *See, e.g.,* Hetzer-Young v. Elano Corp., 2016 Ohio 3356, 2016 Ohio App. LEXIS 2244 (2016)(holding that video did not meet the admissibility standard because there was no testimony that the video contained a sound "substantially similar to the sound [the eyewitness] heard immediately before [the crash]").

[35] *See* Gosser v. Commonwealth, 31 S.W.3d 897 (Ky. 2000)(authentication of a computer animation that illustrates an eyewitness's statement does not require proof of how the data was gathered and inputted, but does require the witness to testify that the animation is consistent with their recollection).

[36] In the past, some courts imposed an additional foundational step for admission of demonstrative exhibits as substantive evidence where the images depicted were not separately witnessed by an individual, such as surveillance video footage, under the "silent witness" theory. The authentication of such demonstrative exhibits required a showing that the item is substantially unaltered.

"[A]n adequate foundation must show that the original has been preserved without change, addition, or deletion and that, if a copy is introduced into evidence, there must be a cogent explanation of any copying such that the court is satisfied that during the copying process there were no changes, additions, or deletions." People v. Flores, 406 Ill.App.3d 566, 577, 941 N.E.2d 375, 385 (2010).

Subsequent cases abandoned this requirement and clarified that the "silent witness" theory of substantive demonstrative evidence requires that "a witness need not testify to the accuracy of the image depicted in the photographic or videotape evidence if the accuracy of the process that produced the evidence is established with an adequate foundation." People v. Taylor, 956 N.E.2d 431, 438 (2011).

[37] 268 Conn. 781 (2004).

(5) the equipment was programmed and operated correctly, and (6) the exhibit is properly identified as the output in question."[38]

2. RELEVANCE AND RELIABILITY

For the two remaining elements of admissibility, the courts have not been consistent in their application of evidentiary standards establishing the relevance and reliability of demonstrative evidence. The most common evidence rules applied in this context will be discussed below.

a. Federal Rule of Evidence 611(a): Effective for Determining the Truth

Federal courts frequently discuss the admission of demonstrative exhibits by reference to Federal Rule of Evidence 611(a):[39]

> Rule 611.   Mode and Order of Examining Witnesses and Presenting Evidence
>
> (a) Control by the Court; Purposes. The court should exercise reasonable control over the mode and order of examination of witnesses and presenting evidence so as to:
>
> (1)   make those procedures effective for determining the truth;
>
> (2)   avoid wasting time; and
>
> (3)   protect witnesses from harassment or undue embarrassment.

The rule only directs federal courts to exercise reasonable control over the presentation of demonstrative exhibits to ascertain the truth while avoiding needless consumption of time. Some state courts have imposed a similar latitude for trial judges in admitting and controlling the manner of presentation of demonstrative exhibits.[40]

In *Johnson v. United States*,[41] the Fourth Circuit Court of Appeals applied Rule 611(a) to uphold the district court's admission of a summary chart prepared by a detective that concerned the organizational structure of the alleged drug conspiracy. The district court qualified the detective as an expert "with regard to the modes of distribution, packaging, weights, prices, and the use of narcotics"

---

[38]   268 Conn. at 811–812 (internal quotation marks omitted).

[39]   *See* United States v. Salerno, 108 F.3d 730, 744 (7th Cir. 1997)(demonstrative aids are admitted under Rule 611 "to clarify or illustrate testimony"). *See also* United States v. Pinto, 850 F.2d 927, 935 (1988); United States v. Possick, 849 F.2d 332, 339 (8th Cir. 1988); United States v. Gardner, 611 F.2d 770, 776 (9th Cir. 1980); United States v. Scales, 594 F.2d 558, 563–564 (6th Cir. 1979).

Rule 611(a) has also been cited as controlling the use of demonstrative exhibits at trial. *See* Baugh v. Cuprum S.A. De C.V., 730 F.3d 701, 708 (7th Cir. 2013).

[40]   *See* Meurling v. County Trans. Co., 230 F.2d 167, 168 (2d Cir. 1956); State v. Feaster, 716 A.2d 395, 436 (NJ 1998).

[41]   54 F.3d 1150 (4th Cir. 1995).

pursuant to Federal Rules of Evidence 702.[42] After considering Rule 702, the Fourth Circuit determined that the detective based the chart on testimony from other witnesses who described various transactions and did not use any "specialized knowledge" in the preparation of the chart so Rule 702 was inapplicable.[43] The Fourth Circuit held that pursuant to Rule 611(a) the district court was within its discretion in allowing the chart into evidence.[44] In reviewing the district court's decision, the appellate court relied on the following "guiding principles": (1) whether the exhibit "aids the jury in ascertaining the truth," and (2) the possible prejudicial effect of allowing the exhibit into evidence.[45]

Although courts have permitted the "admission" of demonstrative exhibits under Rule 611(a), some courts have also required an instruction on the manner in which the jury may consider the exhibit to ensure that the jury is not relying on the exhibit as substantive evidence, but on the evidence on which the exhibit was based.[46] In these cases, although the exhibits were admitted as evidence at trial, the exhibits were not actually considered part of the evidence. Commentators have noted that federal standard jury instructions in several circuits tell jurors that "illustrative exhibits" are not evidence and have cautioned courts not to refer to "admitting" the exhibits, but to "allowing" the use of exhibits, under Rule 611(a).[47] In *United States v. Janati*, the Fourth Circuit Court of Appeals departed from its earlier language in *Johnson* and noted that "displaying [demonstrative exhibits] is always under the supervision of the district court under Rule 611(a), and in the end they are not admitted as evidence."[48]

b. Federal Rules of Evidence 401, 402, and 403: Relevance and Prejudicial Effect

The Federal Rules of Evidence do not specifically mention demonstrative evidence, but provide for the admission of evidence generally in Rules 401 and 402:

---

[42] 54 F.3d at 1156.

[43] 54 F.3d at 1158.

[44] The appellate court also noted the "lack of cohesion among the federal courts as to the guiding principles involved in reviewing the admissibility of such a summary chart." Id.

[45] 54 F.3d at 1159.

[46] 54 F.3d at 1159–1160 (admission of summary chart not error where court provided instructions to the jury that the jury must weigh the evidence underlying the exhibit).

See also United States v. Casamento, 887 F.2d 1141, 1151 (2d Cir. 1989)(use of demonstrative exhibit allowed "so long as the judge properly instructs the jury that it is not to consider the [exhibits] as evidence."); United States v. Goldberg, 401 F.2d 644, 647–648 (2d Cir. 1968)(admission of charts into evidence not abuse of discretion where court instructed jury that charts were not "independent" evidence, and, instead, were only representations of other admitted evidence).

[47] *See* David S. Santee, "More than Words: Rethinking the Role of Modern Demonstrative Evidence," 52 Santa Clara L. Rev. 105, 121 and n. 90 (2012)(discussing the standard jury instructions used in the 5th, 6th, 7th, and 8th Circuits).

[48] 374 F.3d 263, 273 (4th Cir. 2004).

Rule 401.   Test for Relevant Evidence

Evidence is relevant if:

(a) it has any tendency to make a fact more or less probable than it would be without the evidence; and

(b) the fact is of consequence in determining the action.

Rule 402.   General Admissibility of Relevant Evidence

Relevant evidence is admissible unless any of the following provides otherwise:

- the United States Constitution;
- a federal statute;
- these rules; or
- other rules prescribed by the Supreme Court.

Irrelevant evidence is not admissible.

Additionally, Rule 403 places the following limitation on the admission of evidence:

Rule 403.   Excluding Relevant Evidence for Prejudice, Confusion, Waste of Time or Other Reasons

The court may exclude relevant evidence if its probative value is substantially outweighed by a danger of one or more of the following: unfair prejudice, confusing the issues, misleading the jury, undue delay, wasting time, or needlessly presenting cumulative evidence.

Together, these three rules and analogous state evidence rules provide the standards applied by some courts for establishing the relevance and reliability of demonstrative exhibits.[49] In *Verizon Directories Corp. v. Yellow Book USA, Inc.*, the trial court discussed both the history of demonstrative exhibits and the application of Rule 611(a) by prior courts before holding that a demonstrative exhibit "should generally be admitted as evidence . . . if it satisfies the requisites of Rules 402 and 403 of the Federal Rules of Evidence."[50] The court found that although the claim in the case (misleading advertising) was relatively simple, "[t]he methods of proof . . . involve complicated statistical data and expert testimony" so the demonstrative exhibits were necessary to assist the jury.[51]

In applying Rule 401, 402, and 403, courts have emphasized the importance of the reliability of the demonstrative exhibit to prevent misleading the jury. "The overriding principle in determining if any evidence, including demonstrative, should be admitted involves a

---

[49] *See, e.g.,* Commonwealth v. Hawk, 551 Pa. 71, 709 A.2d 373 (1998)(the trial court must decide first if the evidence is relevant and, if so, whether its probative value outweighs its prejudicial effect)(applying Pennsylvania rule of evidence).

[50] 331 F. Supp.2d 136, 142 (E.D. NY 2004).

[51] 331 F.Supp. 2d at 141.

weighing of the probative value versus the prejudicial effect."[52] In *Harris v. State*, the defense sought to introduce a computer animation reflecting an accident reconstructionist's theory that the defendant had only run over her husband once (supporting an accident defense) as opposed to multiple times (supporting the murder charge).[53] The animation did not use a model or dummy to represent the body and had an "X" to indicate the location of the critical blood stain. Texas Court of Appeals applied state evidence rules analogous to the Federal Rules of Evidence to uphold the trial court's exclusion of a computer animated demonstrative exhibit due to the danger of unfair prejudice outweighing the probative value because of the omission of anything indicating the location of the body.[54]

III. Examples of Demonstrative Exhibits

§2.06   Replicas of Physical Evidence

Although exact definitions vary, "real" evidence is generally understood as physical items that were directly involved in the incident giving rise to the case.[55] The array of real evidence can include everything from microscopic skin cells to a collapsed building. In some cases, bringing the actual item of real evidence to trial is not feasible for logistical or financial reasons and the litigants choose to use replicas of the physical items. In other circumstances, such as when the physical item involved in the incident was not recovered, a replica of the item may be introduced in order to demonstrate a particular feature or as an illustrative aid for the jury.

In *People v. Powell*,[56] witnesses testified that the murderer used a firearm with an unusual shell ejection and collection feature. A firearm consistent with this description was recovered from the defendant but could not be definitively linked to the incident. The state sought to introduce the firearm as a demonstrative exhibit during the testimony of the expert witness who examined the firearm. On appeal, the defendant argued that the firearm was not unique and without evidence specifically linking the firearm to the murder, the introduction of the demonstrative exhibit was more prejudicial than probative. The appellate court concluded that the trial court did not abuse its discretion in admitting the firearm as a demonstrative exhibit "for the sole purpose of demonstrating how its shell catcher operated" and

---

[52]   Commonwealth v. Serge, 586 Pa. 671, 682, 896 A.2d 1170, 1177 (2006).

[53]   152 S.W.3d 786 (Tex. App. 2004).

[54]   152 S.W.3d at 793–794.

[55]   *See* David S. Santee, "More than Words: Rethinking the Role of Modern Demonstrative Evidence," 52 Santa Clara L. Rev. 105, 110–111 (2012).

[56]   2015 IL. App. (5th) 120258-U, 2105 Ill. App. Unpub. LEXIS 2979 (2015).

instructing the jury that the exhibit was used "to better illustrate a particular feature of a weapon allegedly used in this case."[57]

Courts have permitted a plethora of replicas to be used by experts to illustrate their opinions. For example, courts allowed experts to use a styrofoam head to illustrate a bullet's trajectory,[58] a medical examiner to use a bed to demonstrate that the rope was too short for the victim to hang herself,[59] an expert to use a Smith & Wesson nine-millimeter pistol not recovered at the scene to demonstrate how that type of gun ejected shell casings,[60] and a medical examiner to use a golf club similar to one found in the defendant's apartment to show that it could have been the type of weapon used to inflict the injury pattern on the victim.[61]

§2.07 IMAGES AND RECORDINGS

1. CONVENTIONAL

Photography is a potent tool for conveying facts to a jury. The history of forensic photography is the history of the camera itself.[62] By the 1830s, daguerreotypes were being used to provide pictures of arrested persons (mug shots) in Belgium. The use of mug shots to identify individuals has survived to this day. Photographs were also used to record scenes of crimes and accidents, of bodies and wounds, of suspect documents and checks, and of other items of evidence. By 1900, the United States Supreme Court ruled on the admissibility of enlarged photographs. In *United States v. Ortiz*, the Court held that the enlargement was sufficiently authenticated by the photographer's testimony regarding the process, methodology, and equipment used in the enlargement.[63] Shortly thereafter, courts were looking at stereoscopic photographs, photomicrographs, photomacrographs, and x-rays.[64]

As photographic techniques became more sophisticated, still photographs were made through a microscope of hairs, fibers, paint

---

[57] 2015 IL. App. at *P70, 2015 Ill. App. Unpub. LEXIS at **39.

[58] State v. Reid, 164 S.W.3d 286, 344 (Tenn. 2005); Mackall v. Commonwealth, 236 Va. 240, 254, 372 S.E.2d 759, 768 (1988)(medical examiner allowed to use knitting needle in a Styrofoam head to illustrate bullet trajectory since "probably shortened the time needed to describe the bullet's points of entry and exit and its course through the head and made it easier for the jury to understand the medical examiner's description.").

[59] State v. Stanley B. Hill, 2013 Tenn. Crim. App. LEXIS 742, 2013 WL 4715115, at *10–11 (Aug. 30, 2013).

[60] Jones v. Commonwealth, 2007 Va. App. LEXIS 265 (2007).

[61] Lynch v. State, 2007 Tex. App. LEXIS 4107 (Tex. App. Amarillo 2007).

[62] For a brief history of forensic photography, *see* Robert C. Sanders, "History of Forensic Imaging" in Edward M. Robinson (ed.), *Crime Scene Photography,* 2d ed., Academic Press, 2010.

[63] 176 U.S. 422, 430 (1900).

[64] *See* State v. Matheson, 103 N.W.137 (Iowa 1905)(x-ray admissible to demonstrate the location of a bullet lodged near the victim's spine).

chips, tool marks, and other minute items of trace evidence.[65] The advent of color photography, stereophotography, and infrared[66] and ultraviolet picture taking,[67] sometimes in conjunction with the use of a microscope, also permitted the taking of photographs of small details that the human eye could not distinguish.[68]

Although courts historically have not been consistent with their reasoning or the application of evidence rules in allowing the use or admission of photographs at trial,[69] photographs are common exhibits in civil and criminal cases. Originally, photographs were used or admitted under a theory that they illustrated witness testimony, but "[o]ver the course of the twentieth century, an alternative theory for admissibility . . . emerged—a "silent witness" theory that recognize[d] photographs to be substantive evidence."[70] Both theories continue to be

---

[65] The use of filters (physical or electronic) to alter contrast is important to many forensic scientists, including fingerprint and forensic document examiners. The fingerprint examiner may use a filter to photograph a latent fingerprint developed on a multicolored surface, such as a magazine cover. By using a filter of essentially the same color as the background (magazine cover illustration), the examiner can make that background appear to be white or light gray, so that the fingerprint developed with black powder can be studied. The document examiner may use contrast filters to photograph endorsement signatures on cancelled checks to view signatures under bank stamps.

[66] The word "infrared" indicates that type of radiation which adjoins the red rays of the visible spectrum. While infrared radiation cannot be seen by the human eye, responsive photographic emulsions and digital sensors can detect infrared waves making infrared radiation particularly useful to forensic scientists to photograph evidence. Infrared photography can distinguish among inks and reveal blood stains and powder burns on clothing or under paint. See Andrew Farra, Glenn Porter and Adrian Renshaw, "Detection of Latent Bloodstains Beneath Painted Surfaces Using Reflected Infrared Photography," 57(5) J. FORENSIC SCI. 1190–1198 (2012).

[67] Using fluorescent powder on multicolored surfaces that are dusted for fingerprints may render them visible under ultraviolet light without distracting backgrounds. Bodily secretions such as urine, semen, perspiration, and pus often glow when illuminated with ultraviolet rays, thus permitting the detection of otherwise invisible traces on clothing. In the forensic document examination field, obliterated writings can often be rendered visible by exposure to ultraviolet rays.

[68] Microscopic vision differs from photographic enlargement in a number of ways. A microscope enlarges a very small portion of a larger whole. The greater the microscope's power of magnification, the smaller the portion of an object being enlarged. A similar result can be obtained with a photographic enlargement, but the enlarged detail is unlikely to have the desired resolution. When a camera is fitted to a microscope and an object is photographed, the result is called a photo*micro*graph. Photomicrographs are used in firearm comparison analysis, trace evidence examination, and other fields which use comparative microscopy and microanalysis.

[69] At a minimum, courts have used five characterizations for photographs: "real evidence, tantamount to real evidence, substantive evidence, representative evidence, and demonstrative evidence." Maureen A. Howard and Jeffrey C. Barnum, "Bringing Demonstrative Evidence in from the Cold: The Academy's Role in Developing Model Rules," 88 Temple L. Rev. 513 (2016) at p. 531–532 (internal citations omitted).

For a detailed discussion of the history of photographic evidence and its handling by the courts, see Jennifer L. Mnookin, "The Image of Truth: Photographic Evidence and the Power of Analogy," 10 Yale J.L. & Human. 1 (1998). The following legal treatises also catalogue the evidentiary status and characterizations of photographs offered into evidence: Christopher B. Mueller and Laird C. Kirkpatrick, *Evidence Under the Rules: Texts, Cases, and Problems* (8th ed. 2014); Jack B. Weinstein, John H. Mansfield, Norman Abrams and Margaret A. Berger, *Evidence: Cases and Materials* 157–160 (9th ed. 1997).

[70] Jennifer L. Mnookin, "The Image of Truth: Photographic Evidence and the Power of Analogy," 10 Yale J.L. & Human. 1, 73 (1998). For cases discussing the "silent witness" theory of admissibility, see Knapp v. State, 9 N.E.3d 1274, 1282 (Ind. 2014); Brooks v.

used by the courts and the prevalence of photographs in criminal and
civil cases has been estimated at approximately half of all cases in the
United States.[71] The admission of other images, such as more
sophisticated medical imaging,[72] and recordings, such as
audio/videotapes,[73] followed and currently use the same evidentiary
theories.[74]

2. DIGITAL

Conventional photography uses mechanical shutters focusing light
onto a piece of film to create a negative; the negative is then developed
into a print through a chemical process.[75] Digital cameras focus light into
a semiconductor device to record information in binary code that develops
into pixels forming an image through interpretation by a computer.[76]
Once in the digital format of binary code, the information "can be stored,
accessed, retrieved, manipulated, organized, and [transmitted]"[77] with
relative ease, causing concerns about reliability in the legal community.[78]
Alteration of digital images generally does not require advanced training
or equipment, making digital images much "easier to modify, particularly
in terms of time and skill, than [conventional] images."[79]

In 1997, the International Association for Identification (IAI), a
professional organization that certifies forensic photographers and crime
scene photographers, adopted Resolution 97–9, declaring that

Commonwealth, 15 Va. App. 407, 410, 424 S.E.2d 566, 569 (1992); Midland Steel Prods. v.
International Union, 573 N.E.2d 98 (Ohio 1991); Ferguson v. Commonwealth, 212 Va. 745,
746, 187 S.E.2d 190, *cert. denied*, 409 U.S. 861 (1972).

[71] Ronald Carlson, Edward Imwinkelried, Julie Seaman and Erica Beecher-Monas,
Evidence: Teaching Materials for an Age of Science and Statutes, 7th ed., LexisNexis, 2012 at
p. 218.

[72] Hose v. Chi. Nw. Transp. Co., 70 F.3d 968, 973–974 (8th Cir. 1995)(allowing into
evidence PET and MRI scans).

[73] United States v. Harris, 55 M.J. 433, 438 (App. Armed Forces 2001)("any doubt as to
the general reliability of the video cassette recording technology has gone the way of the BETA
tape.").

[74] *See* State v. Young, 303 A.2d 113, 116 (Me. 1973)(video recordings "are commonly
admitted into evidence as form of visual testimony"); United States v. Beeler, 62 F. Supp. 2d
136, 148 (D.Me. 1999)("the same contours of law that govern the admissibility of . . . audio
recordings and photographs are to be applied to the question of whether . . . videotape is
admissible.").

[75] Carrie Leonetti and Jeremy Bailenson, "High-Tech View: The Use of Immersive
Virtual Environments in Jury Trials," 93 Marq. L. Rev. 1073 (2010) at p. 1087 (citing Paul R.
Rice, *Electronic Evidence: Law and Practice*, 2d ed., American Bar Association, 2008, at p.
357).

[76] Id.

[77] Id. (citing Michael R. Arkfield, Information Technology Primer for Legal Professionals
§ 1.2(a)(2009)).

[78] Jill Witkowski, "Can Juries Really Believe What They See? New Foundation
Requirements for the Authentication of Digitial Images," 10 Wash. U. L. & Policy 267, 271
(2002)("Digital images are easier to manipulate than traditional photographs and digital
manipulation is more difficult to detect.").

[79] Catherine Guthrie and Brittan Mitchell, "The Swinton Six: The Impact of State v.
Swinton on the Authentication of Digital Images," 36 Stetson L. Rev. 661 (2007).

"electronic/digital imaging is a scientifically valid and proven technology for recording, enhancing, and printing images and like conventional silver-halide based photography, it is accepted by professional commercial photographers, law enforcement photographers, and the identification community."[80] The IAI also offers certification in forensic photography and imaging[81] and forensic video.[82] To address concerns about digital alterations and the difficulties in detecting such alterations, forensic imaging experts formed the Scientific Working Group on Imaging Technology (SWGIT) to develop best practices and guidelines for all aspects of forensic still and motion imaging, and for the standards and use of the equipment used in these endeavors.[83] SWGIT ceased operations in May, 2015, but the IAI Forensic Photographic & Imaging Certification Board continues to recognize the SWGIT publications as best practices for certification testing. The Organization of Scientific Area Committees (OSAC) has a subcommittee on Video/Imaging Technology and Analysis focusing on standards and guidelines related to the application of methods and technologies to analyze information related to forensic imagery from a variety of systems.[84]

As digital photography became more prevalent in society, digital images and recordings were presented more frequently in court[85] and are now generally subject to the same evidentiary standards as conventional images.[86] In *United States v. Seifert*, concerning the admission of a digitally-enhanced surveillance tape in an arson prosecution, the court analogized the digital enhancement to conventional images and recordings:

---

[80] The Resolution is available at: http://www.theiai.org/pdf/res97_9.pdf (last accessed August 16, 2016).

[81] Certification requirements and information about the process are available at: http://www.theiai.org/certifications/imaging/index.php (last accessed August 19, 2016).

[82] Certification requirements and a roster of certified video examiners are available at: http://www.theiai.org/certifications/video/index.php (last accessed August 19, 2016).

[83] The standards and guidelines are available at: http://www.theiai.org/certifications/imaging/SWGIT_Guidelines.pdf (last accessed August 16, 2016).

[84] Information on the OSAC subcommittee is available at: https://www.nist.gov/topics/forensic-science/videoimaging-technology-and-analysis-subcommittee (last accessed February 23, 2017).

[85] James H. Rotondo, David B. Broughel and Edgar B. Hatrick, "Digital Images: Don't Blink or You Will Miss Them," 23 Prod. Liab. L & Strategy 3, 3 (March 2005).

[86] *See, e.g.,* Williams v. Hooker, 2008 WL 2120771, *4 (E.D. Mo. 2008)(overruling, in civil rights action against correctional officers arising from attack on plaintiff by another inmate, defendants' objection to admission of videotape that presented the attack at a viewable rate of speed when advanced frame by frame); Almond v. State, 553 S.E.2d 803, 805 (Ga. 2001)(digital photographs authenticated using same standards as conventional photographs: "fair and truthful representations of what they purported to depict"); Macaluso v. Pleskin, 747 A.2d 830, 837 (N.J. Super. App. Div. 2000)(digital x-ray images authenticated by testimony of doctor that the xrays were a "fair and accurate depiction"); United States v. Beeler, 62 F. Supp. 2d 136, 148–150 (D. Me. 1999)(denying motion to suppress enhanced surveillance videotapes, in prosecution for malicious damage of vehicle by explosive materials and related charges, because the enhanced tapes were accurate, authentic, and trustworthy versions of the original surveillance tape). *But see,* State v. Swinton, 847 A.2d 921, 943 (Conn. 2004)(imposing additional authentication requirements on enhanced digital photographs).

Adjustments to brightness or contrast, or enlargement of the image, while arguably a manipulation are in fact no more manipulative than the recording process itself. The image is black and white; the world is not. In the non-digital world, a camera's lens, its aperture, shutter speed, length of exposure, film grade, and development process—all affect the image. Each of these is entirely unremarkable so long as the "image" remains an accurate recording of that which occurred before the camera. If a photographic negative were magnified by lens, and an enlarged image resulted, no one would question the larger picture. Similarly, in the event of a tape recording, no one would comment if the volume were increased to make a recorded conversation more easily heard—again, so long as the volume-increased words were accurately recorded by the recording medium.[87]

3.   USE BY EXPERTS

The most common use of images and recordings by experts is to document and illustrate to the trier of fact the expert's opinions,[88] such as images taken during the analysis to show what the examiner observed.[89] In *Smith v. State*,[90] the appellate court acknowledged the gruesome nature of the photographs taken at the crime scene and during autopsy of the victim's body depicting decomposition, insect

---

[87]   United States v. Seifert, 351 F. Supp.2d 926, 928 (D. Minn. 2005), *aff'd*, 445 F.3d 1043 (8th Cir. 2006).

Digitally enhanced sound recordings have also been subject to the same evidentiary standards as conventional sound recordings. United States v. Calderin-Rodriguez, 244 F.3d 977, 986 (8th Cir. 2001)("[W]e see no distinction between the foundation required for the tape recorder and that for the digital enhancement program, which, from the point of view of the listener, simply improves the quality of the recording. If the capacity for digital enhancement were built into the tape recorder itself, rather than a separate step being required, the admissibility of the resulting tapes would clearly be governed by [the evidentiary standard applied to conventional recordings]. There is nothing in the use of this separate device that should change our analysis.").

[88]   *See, e.g.,* Szeliga v. Gen. Motors Corp., 728 F.2d 566, 568 (1st Cir. 1984)(film admitted to illustrate testimony of manufacturer's expert witness).

[89]   Gonzalez v. State, 2012 Tex. App. LEXIS 455 (Tex. App. Corpus Christi 2012)(autopsy photographs were properly admitted because they illustrated the doctor's testimony concerning injuries observed during examination); Williams v. State, 2009 Tex. App. LEXIS 4201 (Tex. App. Houston 1st Dist. 2009)(photographs of the victim were properly admitted because medical examiner said the photos of the child before and during autopsy would assist him in describing his findings to the jury); Grayson v. State, 2008 Tex. App. LEXIS 2210 (Tex. App. Houston 1st Dist. 2008)(photographs used by the medical examiner and blood pattern examiner to explain the manner of death and the amount of force used by the defendant when hitting the victim with a baseball bat and the absence of any struggle between the victim and defendant); Scarlett v. Ouellette, 948 So.2d 859 (Fla. 3rd DCA 2007)(photographs used by expert as an example of a factitious, self-inflicted injury that supported defense theory the patient's injury was self-inflicted); Douglas v. State, 878 So.2d 1246 (Fla. 2004), *cert. denied*, 543 U.S. 1061 (2005)(autopsy photographs aided expert in explaining the nature of the victim's injuries to the jury); Westry v. Commonwealth, 206 Va. 508, 513, 144 S.E.2d 427, 431 (1965)(photographs illustrated medical testimony).

[90]   28 So.3d 838 (Fla. 2009), *cert. denied*, 564 U.S. 1052 (2011).

activity, and blunt force trauma.[91] The court found that the photographs were relevant to illustrate the doctor's testimony concerning blunt force trauma, repositioning of the body, and outside forces affecting the genitalia which explained the lack of physical evidence (seminal fluid) of a sexual assault.[92] Finding the probative value of the photographs was not outweighed by the prejudicial impact, the court upheld the admission of the photographs.[93]

Experts may also use images or recordings as the bases for their opinions, making the images substantive evidence supporting the expert's testimony.[94] In *Knapp v. State*,[95] photographs taken of the body when it was discovered showing mature maggot activity served as the basis of the expert's opinion as to the time of death. The court held that differences in what the expert perceived in the photos (not noting mature maggot activity during the first review) "went to the weight of his opinion, as tested by cross-examination, and not the admissibility of the photos or of his over all opinion."[96]

§2.08 STATIC RENDERINGS

Static renderings are non-photographic images and two or three dimensional representations or depictions. Common types of static renderings include diagrams, charts, graphs, and models. Static renderings were some of the first demonstrative exhibits presented at trial[97] and continue to be prevalent in cases involving scientific evidence.[98] Although initially admitted only as substantive evidence in specific categories of cases (e.g., land disputes), static renderings were gradually accepted as demonstrative exhibits in all manner of cases with the introduction of conventional photography in the courts.[99] Courts apply the same evidentiary standards to static renderings as to

---

[91]   28 So.3d at 862.

[92]   28 So.3d at 862–863.

[93]   Id.

[94]   State v. Swinton, 847 A.2d 921, 943 (Conn. 2004)(digitally enhanced photographs of bite mark provided basis for forensic odontologist's opinion).

[95]   9 N.E.3d 1274, 1282 (Ind. 2014).

[96]   Id. at 1283. *See also* Green v. K-Mart Corp., 849 So.2d 814, 826–830 (La. App. 2003)(upholding admission of PET-scan based testimony to diagnose prior brain trauma).

[97]   *See* Western & Atl. R.R. v. Stafford, 25 S.E. 656 (Ga. 1896)(diagram of railroad crossing); Fuller v. State, 23 So. 688 (Ala. 1897)(diagram of murder location); Commonwealth v. Hourigan, 12 S.W. 550 (Ky. 1889)(same); County Commissioners v. Wise, 18 A. 31 (Md. 1889)(diagram of accident scene); Pennsylvania Coal. Co. v. Kelly, 40 N.E. 938 (Ill. 1895)(model of a coal bucket that caused injury); People v. Durant, 48 P. 75 (Cal. 1897)(scaled model of church murder scene).

[98]   *See, e.g.*, Taylor v. Progressive Sec. Ins. Co., 33 So. 3d 1081 (La. Ct. App. 3d Cir. 2010), writ denied, 45 So. 3d 1044 (La. 2010)(anatomical model and other static renderings were properly used as demonstrative aids to assist the jury with understanding the expert's testimony).

[99]   Jennifer L. Mnookin, "The Image of Truth: Photographic Evidence and the Power of Analogy," 10 Yale J.L. & Human 1, 63 (1998)("In the 1880s and 1890s, not only were photographs frequently used in the courtroom and made the subject of appeals, but models, maps, and unofficial diagrams also became popular courtroom devices.").

conventional/digital images[100] and experts use the demonstratives to document their results and illustrate their testimony.[101] In *Avula v. State*,[102] the prosecution's expert witness presented a chart from training materials he received concerning the effects alcohol can have on the human body.[103] The expert "had no knowledge about who made the chart, the methodology used in making the chart, or whether the information in the chart had been peer reviewed."[104] The appellate court held that admission of chart as a demonstrative exhibit was not error because the chart was properly authenticated by the expert's testimony that he acquired it during training and it was used to aid the jury in understanding the expert's testimony regarding the increase and decrease in signs of intoxication in relation to blood alcohol levels.[105]

§2.09 ANIMATIONS AND SIMULATIONS

Animations and simulations are visual (and possibly audio) representations based on a witness's testimony (animation) or based on specific data (simulations), which may be offered for use or admission at trial.[106] Experts use animations to explain scientific principles and to assist the jury in understanding the expert's testimony.[107] An animation functions as a visual depiction of the expert's theory about how an accident occurred as opposed to a recreation of the actual event.[108] Unlike animations, simulations are not offered merely to illustrate testimony. To reach an opinion, expert witnesses frequently conduct experiments under controlled conditions to demonstrate or discern the cause of an accident or event. These experiments are sometimes referred to as simulations or reenactments, although the second term is inappropriate because these types of experiments do not involve the participants or the exact conditions from the event. Simulations are offered for more than illustration, but also to prove a fact at issue. By supplying

---

[100] *See* Baker v. State, 177 S.W.3d 113, 123 (Tex. App. Houston Dist. 1 2005)(trial court's discretion to permit use of charts and other demonstrative evidence during trial is well established); Markey v. State, 996 S.W.2d 226, 231 (Tex. Ct. App. 1999)("[C]harts, graphs, maps, diagrams, or other exhibits prepared for courtroom use which clarify or illustrate some fact in issue may, in the trial court's discretion, be admitted into evidence.").

[101] Schuler v. Mid-Central Cardiology, 729 N.E.2d 539, 545–546 (Ill. App. 2000)("risk stratification" chart used to illustrate expert testimony on the evaluation process used with patients).

[102] 2015 Tex. App. LEXIS 937 (Tex. App. Dallas Dist. 5 2015).

[103] 2015 Tex. App. LEXIS at *32.

[104] Id.

[105] 2015 Tex. App. LEXIS at *35.

[106] Fred Galves, "Where the Not-So-Wild Things Are: Computers in the Courtroom, the Federal Rules of Evidence, and the Need for Institutional Reform and More Judicial Acceptance," 13 Harv. J. Law & Tec 161, 208–209 (2000).

[107] *See* Stavrou v. Edward Health Servs. Corp. 2016 Ill. App. 2d. 15002-U, 2016 Ill. App. Unpub. LEXIS 1244 (Ill. App. 2016)(admitting animation of fetus and the flow of oxygenated blood from mother to fetus as explanatory of the general medical issues involved in the case).

[108] Hinkle v. City of Clarksburg, 81 F.3d 416, 425 (4th Cir. 1996).

information to prove a disputed material fact in the case, the simulation functions as substantive evidence.[109]

Although animations and simulations may use sophisticated technology, the same evidentiary standards used for conventional demonstrative exhibits generally apply to the use and admission of animations and simulations.[110] To establish relevance, an animation or simulation must be a "fair and accurate representation of the evidence to which it relates."[111] For animations, this standard is relatively easy to meet. For animations intended to illustrate the expert's opinion, the animation just needs to fairly represent the expert's testimony. "It need not be exact in every detail, but the important elements must be identical or very similar to the scene" as described by the proponent's evidence.[112] Similarly, animations used by experts to depict scientific principles "need not strictly adhere to the facts"[113] of the case and should be sufficiently general to avoid being misinterpreted by the jury as a recreation of the event.[114]

For simulations that recreate the event the "substantial similarity test" can be much more difficult to meet.

> The burden is on the party offering [the simulation] to lay a proper foundation establishing a similarity of circumstances and conditions. Although the conditions of the [simulation] need not be identical to the event at issue, they must be so nearly the same in substantial particulars as to afford a fair comparison in respect to the particular issue to which the test is directed. Further, experimental or demonstrative evidence, like any evidence offered at trial, should be excluded if its probative value is substantially outweighed by the danger of unfair prejudice, confusion of the issues, or misleading the jury.[115]

Commentators have noted the difficulty in meeting the substantial similarity test for simulations: "substantial similarity is a nearly impossible burden to meet because accident recreation is always under

---

[109] *See* Pierce v. State, 718 So.2d 806, 808 (Fla. Dist/ Ct. App. 1997).

[110] *See, e.g.,* Commonwealth v. Serge, 586 Pa. 671, 685, 896 A.2d 1170, 1179 (2006)(computer animation illustrating Commonwealth's theory of the homicide properly admitted after authentication and meeting the requirements of state evidence rules analogous to Federal Rules 401, 402, and 403).

[111] People v. Cauley, 32 P.3d 602, 607 (Colo. App. 2001).

[112] Clark v. Cantrell, 529 S.E.2d 528, 537 (SC 2000). The court does not have to exclude an animation if it is inconsistent with the opposing party's evidence, as long as it "fairly and accurately" portrays the proponent's version of events. Id.

[113] Four Corners Helicopters, Inc. v. Turbomeca, S.A., 979 F.2d 1434, 1442 (10th Cir. 1992).

[114] *See* Muth v. Ford Motor Co., 461 F.3d 557, 566–567 (5th Cir. 2006)(upholding trial court's ruling that the taped experiments were not similar enough to be simulations, yet too closely resembled the disputed accident to be animations presenting abstract principles effectively without misleading the jury).

[115] United States v. Gaskell, 985 F.2d 1056, 1060 (11th Cir. 1993)(internal footnotes, quotations, and citations omitted).

controlled circumstances, which are necessarily absent from the past event."[116]

Fusco v. General Motors Corp.[117] illustrates the difficulty litigants may face with animations and simulations. In *Fusco*, the plaintiff claimed that a defective part broke, causing the accident.[118] The defense unsuccessfully sought to introduce tapes prepared by experts to demonstrate that the part at issue could not have been broken prior to the accident as alleged by the plaintiff.[119] The tapes showed a car with that part disconnected leaving a distinctive marking on the roadway that was not observed in the plaintiff's accident and not leaving the roadway as plaintiff's vehicle had.[120] On appeal, the First Circuit Court of Appeals held that the tapes were properly excluded both as animations of scientific principles and as simulations. As purported animations to demonstrate abstract scientific principles, the conditions on the tape were too specific to the accident at issue and created "a risk of misunderstanding by the jury."[121] However, as purported simulations of the event, the conditions on the tapes were not close enough to the event (controlled conditions, test track with stunt driver, and a disconnected test part instead of the actual broken part) to be relevant.[122]

Additionally, some courts require a computer-generated simulation to meet the evidentiary standard for the admission of scientific evidence.[123] If the simulation involves complex computer analysis, the computer software renders its own "opinion" based on its internal calculations.[124] This standard only applies to the complex computer analysis that cannot be replicated by the expert through standard "on paper" calculations.[125] These simulations depend on the proper

---

[116] Jessica M. Silbey, "Judges as Film Critics: New Approaches to Filmic Evidence," 37 U. Mich. J.L. Reform 493, 525 (2004); Jonathan M. Hoffman, "If the Glove Don't Fit, Update the Glove: The Unplanned Obsolescence of the Substantial Similarity Standard for Experimental Evidence," 86 Neb. L. Rev. 633 (2008).

[117] 11 F.3d 259 (1st Cir. 1993).

[118] 11 F.3d at 260–261.

[119] 11 F.3d at 261.

[120] 11 F.3d at 262.

[121] 11 F.3d at 264.

[122] Id. *See also* Leonard v. Nichols Homeshield, Inc., 557 A.2d 743, 747 (Pa. Super. Ct. 1989)(videotaped experiments to show how much force is required to disengage a latched screen from a window held to be too specific to the facts of the case to be a demonstration of general principles, but not similar enough to the case facts to be admitted as a simulation).

[123] *See* Chapter I, Sections 1.02 and 1.03 for a discussion of the various evidentiary standards applied to scientific evidence.

[124] Tull v. Fed. Express Corp., 197 P.3d 495, 499 (Okla. Civ. App. 2008); Constans v. Choctaw Transp., Inc., 712 So.2d 885, 901 (La. Ct. App. 1997).

[125] "[W]hen the [animation] is used to illustrate an opinion that the expert has arrived at without using the computer, the fact that the visual aid was generated by a computer . . . does not matter because the witness can be questioned and cross-examined concerning the perceptions or opinions to which the witness testified. In that situation, the computer is no more or less than a drafting device." State v. Tollardo, 77 P.3d 1023, 1029 (N.M. App. 2003).

application of scientific principles and must meet the evidentiary standards for scientific evidence.[126]

IV. Resources

§2.10 Expert Services

Most demonstrative exhibits used by experts in presenting scientific evidence are prepared by the expert witness. If additional preparation or assistance is necessary, various companies and organizations specialize in the preparation of demonstrative exhibits, including:

A2L Consulting—Demonstrative Evidence Services Provider: www.a2lc.com

21st Century Forensic Animations—Forensic Animation Firm: www.call21st.com

AI2–3D—Forensic Mapping, Analysis and Visualization: www.ai2-3d.com

Legal Demonstrative Exhibits—Illustration and Animation for Legal Professional: www.legaldemonstrativeexhibits.com

Miller Visualization—Forensic Animation: www.millerviz.com

Prolumina—Litigation Communication: www.prolumina.net

§2.11 Bibliography of Additional Resources

Lori G. Baer and Christopher A. Riley, "Technology in the Courtroom: Computerized Exhibits and How to Present Them," 66 Def. Couns. J. 176 (1999).

Elizabeth L. Browning, "Demonstrative Evidence Created In-House," 35 Houston Lawyer 19 (1998).

Timothy W. Cerniglia, "Computer-Generated Exhibits—Demonstrative, Substantive or Pedagogical—Their Place in Evidence," 18 Am. J. Trial Advoc. 1 (1994).

Mary Quinn Cooper, "The Use of Demonstrative Exhibits at Trial," 34 Tulsa L. Rev. 567 (1999).

A. Tana Kantor, *Winning Your Case with Graphics*, CRC Press, 1999.

Jason M. Lynch and Iris Eytan, "The Importance of Visual Presentation at Trial," 60 Champion 14 (2016).

Steven C. Marks, "The Admissibility and Use of Demonstrative Aids," 32 The Brief 24 (2003).

Edward M. Robinson, *Crime Scene Photography,* 2d ed., Academic Press, 2010.

---

[126] People v. Cauley, 32 P.3d 602, 606–607 (Colo. App. 2001).

Ronald J. Rychlak, "Trial Technique: The Graphic Explanation: Why Less is More" 36 Am. J. Trial Advoc. 111 (2012).

Louis-Georges Schwartz, *Mechanical Witness: A History of Motion Picture Evidence in U.S. Courts,* Oxford University Press, 2009.

John Selbak, "Digital Litigation: The Prejudicial Effects of Computer-Generated Animation in the Courtroom," 9 High Tech L.J. 337 (1994).

Carolyn Smart, "The Computer Must be Right: Computer-Generated Animations, Unfair Prejudice and Commonwealth v. Serge," 26 Temp. J. Sci. Tech. & Envtl. L. 387 (2007).

Edward R. Tufte, *Beautiful Evidence*, Graphics Press, 2006.

Young, Caitlin O., "Employing Virtual Reality Technology at Trial: New Issues Posed by Rapid Technological Advances and Their Effects on Jurors' Search for 'The Truth,' " 93 Tex. L. Rev. 257 (2014).

CHAPTER 3

FINGERPRINT EVIDENCE[1]

I. INTRODUCTION

§3.01 SCOPE OF THE CHAPTER

A fingerprint is an impression of the intricate design of friction skin ridges found on the palmar side of a person's finger or thumb. The same type of friction skin, with tiny ridge configurations, can also be found on the entire palmar surface of the hands and on the plantar surfaces (soles) of the feet in humans and higher primates. There is no physical, physiological, or biological difference between the friction skin on the fingers and that on the palms of the hands and the soles of the feet. The friction skin ridges bear rows of sweat pores, through which perspiration is exuded which flows over the ridges; the perspiration acts as a lubricant, and insures a firmness of grip. Because of this perspiration, and the incidental coating of the skin with other bodily

---

[1]   This chapter was originally authored by Andre A. Moenssens. Andre Moenssens began his study of fingerprints in Belgium in 1950. He is a life member of the International Association of Identification (IAI) and a Distinguished Fellow of the American Academy of Forensic Science (AAFS). He has authored textbooks and written many articles on fingerprints, law, and forensic science.

oils, an impression of the ridge pattern of the finger is left whenever that finger touches a relatively smooth surface.

Fingerprints have been used as seals or in lieu of signatures since antiquity. Fingerprint pattern impressions were studied, typed, and classified by European researchers and scientists in the 1600's.[2] In the late 1850's, a British colonial civil servant in Bengal, India, used handprints on contracts to prevent impersonations. Independently, a Scottish doctor working in Japan became interested in the subject and postulated in 1880 that the skin designs found at crime scenes could be used to identify criminals.[3] The first textbook on the subject was authored by Sir Francis Galton in England in 1892.[4] Individual fingerprint ridge characteristics are still sometimes called "Galton details." Some limited experimental use was made of fingerprint analysis between that time and its official adoption at Scotland Yard soon after the beginning of the twentieth century.

After some isolated experiments on a local level, beginning in 1902, fingerprinting came into widespread use in the United States around 1910. Today, fingerprint identification units are found in law enforcement agencies or in state crime laboratories. Most states also have statewide identification agencies, often part of the Department of Public Safety or the Attorney General's office. The largest collection of fingerprints in the world is housed at the Federal Bureau of Investigation (FBI).

"Fingerprint identification" is a commonly used term for the field that encompasses fingerprint evidence. That term technically does not appropriately describe the discipline. The term fails to accommodate the concept that there is no difference between an identification based on friction skin on the fingers and that which is found on the palms of the hands and the soles of the feet. "Fingerprints" are but a part of what should be more appropriately described as discipline involving "friction

---

[2] Dr. Nehemiah Grew, a Fellow of the Royal Society and the College of Physicians, made a presentation before the Royal Society in London in 1684 on the friction skin and published drawings of ridge patterns. The following year, Dutch scientist Dr. Govard Bidlo, described the skin ridge patterns in his book (in Latin) *Anatomi Humani Corporis.* Anatomy Professor Dr. Marcello Malpighi described, in his 1686 book (in Latin) *De externo tactus organo,* the ridges, spirals and loops in fingerprints. As early as 1788, Dr. J.C.A. Mayer, incorporated a section on fingerprints in which he observed that the skin patterns are never duplicated in two persons, even though they may look physically similar, in his work *Anatomische Kupfertafeln nebst dazu gehörigen Enklörungen.* Groundbreaking research by Dr. Johannes E. Purkinje, a Czech physiologist and biologist working at the University of Breslau, Prussia (now Poland) was published in a thesis titled *Comentatio de examine physiologico organi visus et systematis cutanei* in which the author divided fingerprints into nine pattern types useful for classification and personal identification; this work was translated by Drs. Harold Cummins and Charles Midlo (of Tulane University) and the translation published as "Physiological Examination of the Visual Organ of the Cutaneous System" in 34 AM. J. CRIM. LAW. CRIMINOLOGY 343–356 (1940).

[3] Henry Faulds, "On the Skin—Furrows of the Hand," 22 NATURE 605 (1880). Faulds' publication sparked a life-long controversy between him and Sir William J. Herschel, the British civil servant in India, as to who originated the use of fingerprints for identification.

[4] Sir Francis Galton, *Finger Prints,* 1892. Long out of print, this book was reprinted in 1965 by Da Capo Press (New York) with a new foreword by the late Dr. Harold Cummins of Tulane University. Galton's work was initially inspired by Herschel's earlier efforts.

ridges." Similarly, the term "identification" has generated controversy as challenges have been raised to the scientific validity of conclusions of identity based on comparison techniques involving partial latent prints. For purposes of this chapter, the term "fingerprint evidence" will be used to describe the discipline and "fingerprint examiner" will be used to describe the experts in the field. Fingerprint examiners are primarily responsible for performing examinations on submitted evidence for the presence and/or development of latent prints; comparing detected prints with the prints of known individuals; and providing expert testimony on reported findings in legal proceedings.

This chapter will discuss the general principles underlying the discipline of fingerprint evidence, including classification systems, modern computerized searching systems, and identification of individuals from intentionally collected prints. Concerning latent print analysis, the visualization, comparison methodology, and individualization claims will be briefly described to provide context for the scientific validity challenges that are currently shaping the reporting and presentation of fingerprint evidence in criminal cases. Research on error rates, the qualification of experts, and evidence issues will also be summarized.

§3.02   Terminology

ACE-V: Term to describe the methodology used in the comparison analysis of friction ridge patterns. The initials stand for: Analysis (of unknown and known impressions), Comparison (looking for differences and similarities in ridge features), Evaluation (determining the value or merit of ridge structures), and Verification (the independent examination following A–C–E methodology by another examiner who is trained to competence).

AFIS: Automated Fingerprint Identification System. A computerized storage and retrieval system that electronically compares unknown latent prints to known prints stored in a data base. The computer produces a candidate list of those prints which meet predetermined identifying criteria. A latent print examiner then determines whether a match can be made between the unknown and one of the candidates.

Algorithm: Mathematical routine used in computer processing, e.g., an AFIS matching algorithm establishes the correlation of Level 2 detail between fingerprints.

Anthropometry: System of identification of individuals by measurements of parts of the body, invented by Alphonse Bertillon, but abandoned because of its unwieldiness when fingerprinting became popular.

APIS: Automated Palm Print Identification System. Computerized system for storage, searching, and retrieval of known and latent palm print records based on friction ridge detail.

Arch (Plain): A fingerprint pattern type in which the ridges enter on one side of the impression, and flow, or tend to flow, out the other with a rise or wave in the center.

Arch (Tented): A type of fingerprint pattern that possesses either an angle, an upthrust, or two of the three basic characteristics of the loop.

Bifurcation: The point at which one friction ridge divides into two friction ridges.

Central Pocket Loop: A subclassification of the whorl which has two deltas and at least one ridge making a complete circuit that may be spiral, oval, circular or variant of a circle, and a second ridge recurve either connected to or independent of the first recurve.

Chance Impression: Commonly referred to as a Latent Print (US) or Latent Mark (UK).

Characteristics: Distinctive detail visible in friction ridges. Variously referred to as minutia(e), Galton detail, point, feature, ridge formation, ridge morphology.

Class characteristics: Characteristics used to put patterns into groups or classes, e.g., arches, loops, whorls.

Classification: Alphanumeric formula of finger and palm print patterns used as a guide for filing and searching.

Core: The approximate center of a pattern. There exists an elaborate set of rules in the profession to determine the precise location of the core in various configurations of ridge formations.

Crease: A line or linear depression; grooves at the joints of the phalanges, at the junction of the digits and across the palmar and plantar surfaces that accommodate flexion.

Delta: The point on a ridge at or nearest to the point of divergence of two type lines, and located at or directly in front of the point of divergence.

Dermatoglyphics: A term used by anatomists, biologists, geneticists and medical researchers to describe the study of friction ridge skin for medical or other scientific research.

Discrepancy: A difference in two friction ridge impressions due to different sources of the impressions (exclusion). It is also sometimes referred to as a Dissimilarity.

Dissociated ridges: Disrupted, rather than continuous, ridges; an area of ridge units that did not form into friction ridges.

Distortion: Variances in the reproduction of friction skin caused by pressure, movement, force, contact surface, or other factors.

Dot: An isolated ridge unit whose length approximates its width in size.

Double Loop: A subclass of the whorl group with two separate loop formations containing separate sets of shoulders and two deltas.

Enclosure: A single friction ridge that bifurcates and rejoins after a short course and continues as a single friction ridge.

Exclusion: The determination that two areas of friction ridge impressions did not originate from the same source.

Exemplar: An impression or image of friction ridge skin purposely collected with the knowledge of the subject; a non-latent friction ridge impression.

Extended Feature Set (EFS): Vendor-neutral sets of features that may be used to search the FBI's NGI and databases of state and local agencies with different AFIS vendors; a common method of encoding information from latent print images.

Friction Ridge: A raised portion of the epidermis on the palmar or plantar skin, consisting of one or more connected ridge units of friction ridge skin.

Henry Classification: A system of fingerprint classification named for Sir Edward Henry (1850–1931). It served as the basis for the extended manual system of classification in the United States and in all English speaking countries before automation made it less relevant.

IAFIS: Integrated Automated Fingerprint Identification System. The FBI's national AFIS that was encompasses within the Next Generation Identification system in 2011.

IAI: International Association for Identification.

Individualization: The determination that there is sufficient quantity and quality of detail in agreement to conclude that two friction ridge impressions originated from the same source.

Incipient Ridge: A friction ridge not fully developed that appears shorter and thinner in appearance than fully developed friction ridges.

Latent Print: A generic term for questioned friction ridge detail.

Live-scan: Electronic recording of friction ridges (fingers and/or palms).

Loop: A type of fingerprint pattern in which one or more of the ridges enter on either side of the impression, recurve, touch, or pass an imaginary line drawn from the delta to the core, and terminate or tend to terminate on or toward the same side of the impression from whence such ridge or ridges entered.

Markup: The marked (recorded) latent friction ridge features in an impression.

Minutiae: Features marked on a latent print, including bifurcations, dots, and ridge endings.

Minutiae Ridge Count: The intervening number of ridges between minutiae.

NBIS: NIST Biometric Image Software.

NGI: Next Generation Identification, a multimodal biometric identification system maintained by the FBI.

NIST: National Institute of Standards and Technology.

Pattern Classification: The general shape or pattern of the impression.

Plantar Area: The friction ridge skin on the side and underside of the foot.

Pores: Small openings in the friction ridge allowing for secretion of sweat.

Profile (EFS Profile): Defined groups of friction ridge features, primarily for use in latent friction ridge searches of AFIS systems.

Protrusion: An abrupt increase in ridge width that is not long enough to be called a bifurcation (also known as a spur).

Region of Interest (ROI): A single continuous friction ridge impression.

Ridge Count: The number of ridges intervening between the delta and the core. It is used to subdivide loop and some whorl-type patterns in older classification systems widely used before AFIS.

Ridge Edge Features: Protrusions and indentations at the edges of ridges.

Ridge Ending: The abrupt end of a ridge.

Ridge Flow: The arrangement and direction of adjacent friction ridges.

Ridge Segment (Ridge Path Segment): A section of a ridge that connects two minutiae so each ridge segment starts and stops either where the ridge intersects another ridge path segment (a bifurcation), ends (a ridge ending), or leaves the region of interest.

Simultaneous Prints: A cluster of latent impressions believed to have been impressed at the same time by the fingers or fingers, palms or soles of one individual, only some or none of which impressions contain sufficient quantity and quality of detail to permit individualization independently.

Skeleton (Ridge Tracing or Skeletonized Image): A thinned representation of the ridge structure of a friction skin image in which all pixels are white except for a thinned black skeleton following the midpoint of each ridge.

SWGFAST: Scientific Working Group on Friction Ridge Analysis, Study and Technology.

Verification: Confirmation of an examiner's conclusion by another qualified examiner.

Whorl: A pattern having at least two deltas with a complete recurve in front of each. SWGFAST has accepted definitions for the four subgroups of whorls: plain whorl, central pocket loop whorl, double loop whorls, and accidental whorl.

WSQ: Wavelet Scalar Quantization algorithm for compression of fingerprint imagery.

§3.03 EVIDENTIARY USES

Fingerprint evidence is primarily used for identification of individuals and the association of individuals with locations or items of evidence. In the criminal justice system, fingerprint evidence has been used for over a century "to support public safety throughout the world to identify individuals suspected in criminal and terrorist events, among other uses."[5] In addition to establishing the identity of individuals through the comparison of known prints, fingerprint examiners locate, develop, and compare latent prints to the fingerprint records of known individuals to identify witnesses and possible perpetrators. The comparison of latent prints is the duty for which the fingerprint examiner is widely known and which permeates popular culture through crime scene investigation shows and books.

As a technique for establishing the identity of an individual, fingerprinting is also valuable in civil cases to prevent fraud. Will contests, insurance fraud, wrongful death, personal injury, and medical malpractice actions exemplify some of the civil actions in which fingerprint evidence may be used as a means of identification. Many industries and companies also require fingerprint checks of new employees. All companies engaged in contract work for national defense agencies are typically required, as a condition for obtaining the contract, to submit the fingerprints of their employees, or at least of those directly working on the contract assignment.

Beyond regulatory uses of compelled fingerprinting, friction ridge patterns are used as a biometric in controlling access or for facilitating commercial transactions. With the use of the TouchID on the iPhone 5s in 2013, Apple introduced biometric fingerprint authentication into mainstream society. This type of completely automated fingerprint comparison technology is consistent with the current research focus of the larger fingerprint evidence field. More functions of fingerprint analysis, from collection to comparison, are being integrated into automated computer system for efficiency and increased objectivity.

---

[5] National Commission on Forensic Science, "Directive Recommendation: Automated Fingerprint Information Systems (AFIS) Interoperability," adopted August 11, 2015 (available at: https://www.justice.gov/ncfs/work-products-adopted-commission)(last accessed September 9, 2016).

II. GENERAL PRINCIPLES

§3.04   EXEMPLARS—"TENPRINTS"

The most common use of fingerprint evidence is for the identification of an individual through comparison of known fingerprint impressions ("exemplars'). Traditionally, these fingerprint exemplars have been referred to as "tenprints" because the friction ridge details of all ten fingers are typically recorded. Tenprints are recorded during booking procedures in criminal cases and as part of employment or security checks in civil contexts. These recorded known prints are used for identification, background searches, and comparison with unknown prints. Recording known tenprints is accomplished by inking and rolling the fingertip on a paper fingerprint card or by capturing the details through a live scan device that creates a digital image of the prints.

Fingerprints have been traditionally recorded in the United States on standard 8 x 8-inch fingerprint cards. This is done by rolling the fingers, one by one, over an inked slab, then onto the card. In addition to rolled impressions, the card also has spaces for plain impressions made by pressing down the fingers simultaneously. There are also spaces for plain impressions of thumbs. Hands should be prepared by washing with soap and water or wiping with rubbing alcohol. Excessively moist hands should be dried by wiping with rubbing alcohol; excessively dry hands should be treated with a small amount of hand lotion and any residue wiped off.[6]

---

[6]   *See* https://www.fbi.gov/services/cjis/fingerprints-and-other-biometrics/recording-legible-fingerprints (last accessed September 9, 2016). *See also* Department of Justice, Federal Bureau of Investigation, "Guidelines for Preparation of Fingerprint Cards and Associated Criminal History Information" (available at: https://www.fbi.gov/file-repository/guidelines-for-preparation-of-fingerprint-cards-and-association-criminal-history-information.pdf/view)(last accessed September 9, 2016).

Standard Fingerprint Form FD-258

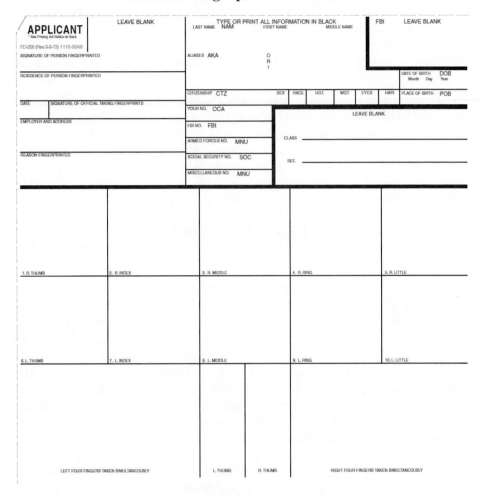

(available at: https://www.fbi.gov/file-repository/
standard-fingerprint-form-fd-258-1.pdf/view)

One of the problems with the older fingerprinting method of inked printing is that dirt, contamination by other materials, or uneven pressure may result in distorted, blurred, or smudged inked prints. Inked impressions also may obliterate fine details of Level 3 features that provide more discriminating power for identification. Newer technologies have improved the legibility of intentionally collected prints. Live-scan, an electronic scanning system, creates a fingerprint image that is projected on a computer screen as if it were an inked impression when a person places their finger on a glass plate and highly sensitive optical equipment photographs the finger.

When law enforcement agencies maintained 10-finger filing systems that were manually operated, a fingerprint card would then be given a classification formula based upon a study of the general types of patterns and their subdivisions. This formula permitted the card to be filed, and subsequently located, among untold thousands of fingerprint records. When a person is again fingerprinted at a later date, a new set of prints is recorded and classified, and in the process of filing this new card according to its formula, the existence of a prior record of fingerprints could be determined.

Departments no longer use manual searching and filing methods, but may still use traditional 8 x 8-inch paper cards. The cards are processed by optical scanning of the individual ridge characteristics that are then retained in a computer storage system. The actual fingerprint card, after such processing, may be filed in the criminal history folder of the arrestee, rather than in a centralized fingerprint collection based on a fingerprint classification system.

§3.05   TRADITIONAL CLASSIFICATION SYSTEMS

1.   PHYSIOLOGY

The practical use of a system of identification and individualization by fingerprints, palmprints, or soleprints derives from three fundamental premises: (1) the friction ridge patterns that begin to develop during fetal life remain unchanged during life, and even after death, until decomposition destroys the ridged skin; (2) the patterns differ from individual to individual, and even from digit to digit, and are never duplicated in their minute details; and (3) although all patterns are distinct in their ridge characteristics, their overall pattern appearances have similarities which permit a systematic classification of the impressions. The third premise was useful only when a manual classification system existed to serve as the primary repository of fingerprint cards filed by a classification formula. Such a system was in wide use before the advent of computerized storage and retrieval systems that have largely done away with the hard-copy traditional fingerprint card collections. Most friction ridge impressions today are captured by inkless methods such as live-scan, which transmit the digitized image of impressions directly into a computer storage bin for further processing.

From childhood to maturity, the friction skin patterns grow and expand in size. As an adult grows old, the finger patterns may shrink in size, but the characteristics used to determine their individuality do not undergo any natural change in relation to one another.[7] Rare cases of mutilation, or the occurrence of some skin disease, such as leprosy, may partially or totally destroy the epidermal ridges. If the destruction is

---

[7]   The rare occurrence of a person born without fingerprints was traced to two related inherited diseases: Naegeli syndrome and dermatopathia pigmentosa reticularis (DPR). See, Handwerk, Brian, "Born Without Fingerprints: Scientists Solve Mystery of Rare Disorder," NATIONAL GEOGRAPHIC NEWS, Sep. 22, 2006.

only partial, it may still be possible to make an identification based on the partial pattern.

The friction skin patterns are formed prenatally through a process of differential growth in the dermis layer of the skin.[8] If the finger is superficially hurt or mutilated to a depth of not more than approximately one millimeter, the injury will reflect itself in the pattern as a temporary scar. Upon healing of the scarred area, however, the pattern will return exactly to its same image as before the injury. If the injury inflicted is more serious and reaches into the dermis layer of the skin to damage the ridge-molding "dermal papillae," a permanent scar will remain after the healing process is completed. Such permanent scars do not affect identification, as long as sufficient undamaged skin remains. They may indeed assist in individualizing a particular person as the maker of an impression if both the record print and the latent impression show the same scar.

Classification and *identification* are two distinct concepts. The old-style manually configured *classification* of a set of fingerprints was traditionally derived by a mathematical formula based upon the types of patterns occurring on the ten fingers of an individual and the various subclassifications and divisions given to these patterns upon the basis of the location, within the patterns, of fixed reference points such as deltas and cores. The traditional classification systems were based on the principle that all fingerprints can be brought within certain general classes of patterns: arches, loops, and whorls, and their subgroups. Thus, the fingerprint cards of multiple individuals may share an identical old-style classification formula allowing them to be grouped for storage.

2. PATTERN TYPES

The traditional classification formula of a set of fingerprints, used until the advent of computerized fingerprint storage and retrieval systems, was assigned on the basis of the preliminary process known as pattern interpretation and blocking out of the set of prints. All fingerprints can be brought within one of three main pattern type groups: arches, loops, and whorls. Arches account for approximately 5% of all fingerprints, loops approximately 60% and whorls 35%.

---

[8]   The process is described in detail in Kasey Wertheim and Alice Maceo, "The Critical Stages of Friction Ridge Pattern Formation," 52 J. FORENSIC IDENT. 35 (2002) and the many other sources cited therein and in the writings of other scientists.

In 2011, the National Institute of Justice (NIJ) published a 16-chapter volume title *The Fingerprint Sourcebook*, in which the chapters are authored by different researchers and specialists in the field. The chapters are extensively annotated with references. As with all NIJ publications, the book can be found at www.nij,gov.

See also, Alice Maceo, "Friction Ridge Skin: Morphogenesis and Overview," IN WILEY ENCYCLOPEDIA OF FORENSIC SCIENCE (Jamieson, A. & Moenssens, A.A., eds.) [3] 1322 (2009, for a full, extensively illustrated discussion of the process of prenatal friction ridge development).

Arches are subdivided into plain arches and tented arches (see Figure 1). Loops are initially subdivided into ulnar and radial loops, depending upon the slant of the loops and the hand on which they appear (see Figure 2); they are further subdivided by a process known as ridge counting. Whorl-type patterns are divided into four subgroups: plain whorls, central pocket loops, double loops, and accidental whorls (see Figure 3); and they may be further subdivided by a process known as ridge tracing.

Figure 1: The pattern on the left is typical of the plain arch; the one on the right of the tented arch type.

Figure 2: Two loop-type patterns with the core and delta locations marked.

Figure 3: The four different whorl-type patterns: upper left, a plain whorl; upper right, a central pocket loop; lower left, a double loop; lower right, an accidental whorl.

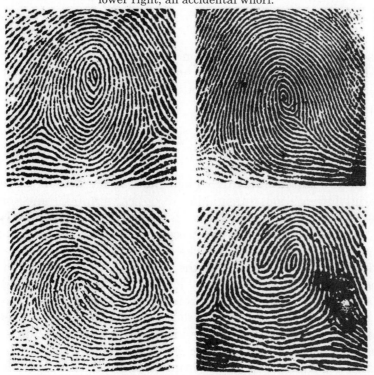

Within all loop and whorl patterns there are also fixed reference points known as deltas. Loops have one delta each. Plain whorls, central pocket loops, and double loops have two deltas, while accidental whorls have at least two deltas but can have more. Another fixed reference point is the core. There are arbitrary rules, set up by the early fingerprint pioneers who devised the classification schemes, and improved upon by later specialists, which the examiner follows to determine the exact location, within a pattern, of the core and delta.

The classification formula of a set of prints in the old-style manually serviced fingerprint collections, can be derived after all the patterns that make up the set have been interpreted and appropriate symbols marked below and above the pattern blocks on the card. The formula is written in the form of an alphanumeric fraction in the modified Henry system of classification with FBI Extensions that was long used in the United States. It was composed of a primary classification, secondary classification, subsecondary, major division, final classification, and key. A typical classification formula with its separate components identified follows here:

Key	Major	Primary	Secondary	Subsecondary	Final
7	I	6	U	IOO	12
	O	18	Ur	OOM	

The traditional classification system has largely fallen into disuse as a way of filing and retrieving sets of fingerprints because of the advances made in the computerized automated fingerprint filing and retrieval systems (AFIS).

§3.06 AUTOMATED FINGERPRINT IDENTIFICATION SYSTEMS

Originally stored on cards which could be mechanically searched, fingerprint information transitioned to optical scanning and computer storage in the 1970's. Automated fingerprint identification systems (AFIS), primarily designed to process tenprints collected through booking and background checks, became standard in police departments in all states and the District of Columbia. In these systems, fingerprint data is no longer stored by the traditional fingerprint formula based on pattern groupings. Instead, fingerprint image data is converted to digital data permitting algorithm searches. For tenprint known exemplars, the images are of sufficient quality and conformity that the features can be extracted for indexing by an automated algorithm. For latent prints, examiners mark the features (e.g., bifurcations, ridge endings) of print within the image file, encoding the data in accordance with the system's specifications to permit indexing and searching. The conversion to digital data permitted faster searches and vastly improved the ability to exchange information among law enforcement agencies.

1. IAFIS/NGI

Since 1924, the FBI has collected, classified, and exchanged fingerprint records for identification purposes with other federal, state, and local law enforcement agencies. The FBI's Integrated Automated Fingerprint Identification System (IAFIS) went online in 1999 and was based primarily on coding for Level 2 Detail (ridge characteristics), though some other visible features were also coded for file searches. IAFIS fully automated the storage, comparison, and exchange of fingerprint data in a digital format. IAFIS provided two major functions in relation to fingerprints: storage of identification prints (generally ten-print card information) and comparison of fingerprint submissions (both through ten-print card information and latent prints).[9] IAFIS eliminated the need to retain paper fingerprint cards and accelerated

---

[9] FBI, "Privacy Impact Assessment Integrated Automated Fingerprint Identification System National Security Enhancements" (available at: https://www.fbi.gov/services/records-management/foipa/privacy-impact-assessments/iafis (last accessed September 7, 2016).

the identification process. The system was built to process slightly over 60,000 ten-prints in a 24-hour period, but hit highs well over 100,000 prints in the same time frame. Some 33,000 additions, changes, or deletions were made in the FBI database of about 52 million individuals on a daily basis by 2006.[10]

To support the FBI and other federal agencies, the National Institute of Standards and Technology (NIST) "conducted fingerprint research, developed fingerprint identification technology and data exchange standards, developed methods for measuring the quality and performance of fingerprint scanners and imaging systems, and produced databases containing a large repository of FBI fingerprint images for public distribution."[11] In 2007, in response to the need of law enforcement and homeland security agencies, NIST developed and released a collection of application programs, utilities, and source code libraries to conduct applied research for the improved automated analysis of fingerprints that is referred to as NIST Biometric Software (NBIS). The software packages included:

> PCASYS—a pattern classification system designed to automatically categorize a fingerprint image as an arch, left or right loop, scar, tented arch, or whorl.

> MINDTCT—a minutiae detection system to locate features in the ridges and furrows of friction skin (approximately 100 minutiae in a typical tenprint.

> NFIQ—fingerprint quality algorithm to rank the quality of the image from 1 (highest) to 5 (lowest).

> BOZORTH3—a fingerprint matching system that uses the MINDTCT detected minutiae to determine if two fingerprints are from the same person, same finger.[12]

Building on IAFIS, the FBI developed the "Next Generation Identification" (NGI) system in 2011. NGI was originally to be the abbreviation for the "Next Generation IAFIS," but that name was deemed to inhibit its potential. Thus, the change to Next Generation Identification. NGI encompassed a multimodal biometric identification system (e.g., fingerprints, facial recognition, iris scans) that permits enhanced searching capabilities and rapid responses. With respect to latent print examinations, NGI contains two groups within the Latent Friction Ridge (LFR) Repository: Friction Ridge Investigative File— containing the known prints associated with an individual, including tenprints and palm prints, and the Unsolved Latent File—containing a

---

[10] Interview with Thomas E. Bush III and Jerome M. Pender, "Planning the structure of NGI: a multimodal, biometric identification system," EVID. TECHNOLOGY MAG., July–Aug. 2006, at 22.

[11] Kenneth Ko, "User's Guide to NIST Biometric Image Software (NBIS)," January 21, 2007, at p. 1 (available at: https://www.nist.gov/node/605221)(last accessed September 12, 2016).

[12] Id. at pp. 3–4.

variety of latent prints searched through the system that remain unidentified.[13]

In February 2011, the first segment of the NGI system was introduced with the Advanced Fingerprint Identification Technology (AFIT) replacing the legacy Automated Fingerprint Identification System (AFIS) segment of the IAFIS. The AFIT enhanced fingerprint and latent processing services, improved system responsiveness, and increased the accuracy of fingerprint matching to 99.6 percent by implementing a new matching algorithm.[14] In August 2011, the Repository for Individuals of Special Concerns (RISC) enabled law enforcement to access selected databases (e.g., sex offenders, outstanding warrants) through a mobile fingerprint scanner.[15] In contrast to the IAFIS system which only permitted latent prints to be searched against the criminal history database, the NGI system enables searches against multiple databases (e.g., criminal history, civil employment and other government mandated collections, and other unidentified latent images). In May 2013, the FBI deployed "Increment 3" of the NGI system to improve the IAFIS services by increasing accuracy, speed, and other functions.[16] At the same time the National Palm Print System (NPPS) was added to provide the same storage and comparison capabilities for palm prints.[17]

2.   INTEROPERABILITY ISSUES

As fingerprint storage and searching functions moved to computer systems, the interoperability of those systems became a critical issue. Different AFIS vendors used different coding systems, requiring the examiner to re-encode each print before searching each AFIS system, making cross-jurisdictional searches time consuming. The lack of interoperability of fingerprint image searching, particularly among individual AFIS units at the state and local level, was addressed in the 2009 NAS Report, advocating for the development of:[18]

    (a)   standards for representing and communicating image and minutiae data among Automated Fingerprint Identification Systems. Common data standards would facilitate the sharing of fingerprint data among law

---

[13]   FBI, "Next Generation Identification (NGI), Latent Best Practices," November 9, 2015, at p. 2 (available at: https://www.fbibiospecs.cjis.gov/Latent/PrintServices)(last accessed September 9, 2016).

[14]   *See* https://www.fbi.gov/services/cjis/fingerprints-and-other-biometrics/ngi.

[15]   Id.

[16]   FBI, "Next Generation Identification (NGI), Latent Best Practices," November 9, 2015, at p. 1 (available at: https://www.fbibiospecs.cjis.gov/Latent/PrintServices)(last accessed September 9, 2016).

[17]   Id.

[18]   Committee on Identifying the Needs of the Forensic Science Community, National Research Council of the National Academies, *Strengthening Forensic Science in the United States: A Path Forward*, The National Academies Press: Washington D.C., 2009. at pp. 269–278.

enforcement agencies at the local, state, federal, and even international levels, which could result in more solved crimes, fewer wrongful identifications, and greater efficiency with respect to fingerprint searches; and

(b) baseline standards—to be used with computer algorithms—to map, record, and recognize features in fingerprint images, and a research agenda for the continued improvement, refinement, and characterization of the accuracy of these algorithms (including quantification of error rates).[19]

As part of the interoperability improvements, the forensic science community first created and advocated for the use of the Extended Feature Set (EFS), a standard method for encoding fingerprint features that can be understood by any AFIS. The FBI and NIST have also established standards and specifications relative to the preservation and exchange of digital fingerprint evidence to enable vendor-neutral AFIS operations. For example, three specifications have been designed to enable AFIS interoperability and to maximize the consistency of marking of friction ridge features among examiners: the Extended Feature Set Profile Specification,[20] the Markup Instructions for Extended Friction Ridge Features,[21] and the Latent Interoperability Transmission Specification.[22] Each of these specifications are based on the ANSI/NIST-ITL standard adopted in 2011 establishing the data format for the exchange of fingerprint and other biometric data.[23] By complying with these standards and specifications, fingerprint examiners have improved the uniformity in their field and maximized

---

[19] Id. at p. 277. *See also* National Commission on Forensic Science, "Directive Recommendation: Automated Fingerprint Information Systems (AFIS) Interoperability," adopted August 11, 2015 (available at: https://www.justice.gov/ncfs/work-products-adopted-commission)(last accessed September 9, 2016).

[20] Melissa K. Taylor et al., National Institute of Standards and Technology, Law Enforcement Standards Office, "Extended Feature Set Profile Specification" (2012)(available at: https://www.nist.gov/node/577986?pub_id=913056)(last accessed September 9, 2016). This document defines the sets of feature to be used in latent friction ridge (fingerprint/palmprint or plantar) AFIS searches.

[21] Melissa K. Taylor et al., National Institute of Standards and Technology, Law Enforcement Standards Office, "Markup Instructions for Extended Friction Ridge Features," NIST Special Publication 1151 (January 2013)(available at: https://www.nist.gov/node/577966?pub_id=913169)(last accessed September 9, 2016). This document specifies a common set of instructions and data annotation guidelines for the recording of EFS latent friction ridge features by latent print examiners.

[22] Melissa K. Taylor et al., National Institute of Standards and Technology, Law Enforcement Standards Office, "Latent Interoperability Transmission Specification" (2013)(available at: https://www.nist.gov/node/577971)(last accessed September 9, 2016). This document completes the procedure by providing definitions for transactions between exchanging agencies.

[23] Kevin C. Mangold, ed. "American National Standards Institute/National Institute of Standards and Technology, Information Technology Laboratory: Data Format for the Interchange of Fingerprint, Facial & Other Biometric Information," 1–2011, NIST Special Publication 500-290, Edition 3 (2015)(available at: https://www.nist.gov/node/1095536)(last accessed September 9, 2016).

their ability to search databases to assist in the identification of individuals and the source association of latent prints.

The FBI and other agencies have also worked to standardize the imaging software and hardware to improve interoperability. The Universal Latent Workstation is an interoperable and interactive software program provided by the FBI at no cost to law enforcement agencies. The program automates many of the procedural steps for the computerized searches of latent prints by uploading a latent print image from a scanner, digital camera, or disk; automatically assessing the quality[24] and enhancing print images; creating a search file; and comparing the latent print with search result files.[25] The software ensures compliance with the WSQ standard. The Wavelet Scalar Quantization (WSQ) fingerprint image compression algorithm is the current standard for the exchange of 500 ppi fingerprint imagery in the criminal justice community.[26] The forensic science community has traditionally captured, processed, and stored friction ridge imagery data in 500 pixels per inch (ppi).[27] The WSQ Gray-Scale Fingerprint Image Compression Specification provides guidance on the encoding and decoding equipment that meet FBI specifications for the acceptable amount of irreversible fidelity loss due to compression.[28] The modern biometric systems are trending towards 1000 ppi, offering greater fidelity to the original print and better representation of Level 3 features, and 1000 ppi may become the new standard in the field.[29]

§3.07 IDENTIFICATION

Features of friction ridge impressions are divided into three levels. Level 1 detail refers to the overall pattern, including ridge flow. Level 1 detail was used to sort prints in the traditional classification system discussed in §3.05 *supra*. Level 2 detail refers to individual friction

---

[24] The software "is not intended to replace the latent print examiner's quality assessment, but is meant to complement that process." Federal Bureau of Investigation, "Universal Latent Workstation LQMetrics User Guide," November 9, 2015, at p. 1 (available at: https://www.fbibiospecs.cjis.gov/Latent/PrintServices)(last accessed September 9, 2016).

[25] Department of Justice, Federal Bureau of Investigation, Criminal Justice Information Services Division, "Universal Latent Workstation," Version 6.6.3 (available at: https://www.fbibiospecs.cjis.gov/Latent/PrintServices)(last accessed September 9, 2016).

[26] *See* https://www.fbibiospecs.cjis.gov/WSQ/Implementations (last accessed September 7, 2016).

[27] The FBI's NGI system only accepts latent images at 500ppi or 1000ppi. See FBI, "Next Generation Identification (NGI), Latent Best Practices," November 9, 2015, at p. 2 (available at: https://www.fbibiospecs.cjis.gov/Latent/PrintServices)(last accessed September 9, 2016).

[28] *See* WSQ Gray-Scale Fingerprint Image Compression Specification," Version 3.1, issued October 2010 (available at: https://www.fbibiospecs.cjis.gov/WSQ/Implementations)(last accessed September 7, 2016). *See also* NIST, "WSQ Certification Procedure" (available at: https://www.nist.gov/programs-projects/wsq-certification-procedure)(last accessed September 7, 2016).

[29] Palm print image sets submitted to the FBI's Next Generation Identification's National Palm Print System must have a scanning resolution of at least 500ppi, and the FBI strongly recommends that the resolution be set at 1000ppi. *See* "A Practical Guide for Palm Print Capture" (available at: https://www.fbibiospecs.cjis.gov/Latent/PrintServices)(last accessed September 9, 2016).

ridge paths and ridge events (ridge ending, bifurcation, and dot). Level 3 detail encompasses ridge structures, such as edge shapes and pores, that are not included in Level 1 or Level 2.

Individualization or *identification*, unlike the classification system which was based on Level 1 pattern information, is concerned largely with a comparison of the individual ridge details of Level 2 and Level 3 features, such as bifurcations, ridge endings, enclosures, ridge dots, ridge width, pore structure, and other minutiae. Before it can be said that two friction ridge impressions are produced by the same friction skin surface, the ridge flow and patterns must of course be of the same pattern type that, for digits, determines its Level 1 detail. That, however, is largely insufficient and meaningless since all fingerprints can be brought within certain general classes of patterns of arches, loops, whorls, and their subgroups. To establish identity, it must be shown that a sufficient number of ridge characteristics are found in the same position and relative frequency, quantitatively and qualitatively, in the same area examined in both friction ridge impressions. Five simple ridge characteristics are illustrated in Figure 4.

Identification through comparison of known tenprints is relatively straight-forward. The known exemplar images are good-quality images and the tenprint cards contain a large amount of individualizing detail. Such known exemplar comparisons are routinely handled through AFIS computer algorithm analysis. Identification through comparison of a latent print to a known print, however, is much more complicated because the quality and appearance of the latent print may be affected by many factors. These factors include the physical conditions of transfer (e.g., pressure and angle of deposition), the medium and substrate (e.g., blood on a porous surface), environmental factors (e.g., moisture), and the methods used for visualization and collection.[30] For latent print identification, this comparison is conducted either wholly or in part by a fingerprint examiner. If the requested examination is for the direct comparison of a latent print to a known print of a particular individual, the analysis is conducted entirely by the fingerprint examiner. If the task is to identify the source of a latent print without an identified potential source, the latent print will be processed through an AFIS containing prints of known individuals to select potential matches. Under typical procedures, the fingerprint examiner must determine whether any of the potential candidates generated by the AFIS search is the source of the latent print. Candidate matches generated by AFIS algorithms are necessarily similar and

---

[30] Sarah J. Fieldhouse, "An Investigation into the Effects of Force Applied During Deposition on Latent Fingermarks and Inked Fingerprints Using a Variable Force Fingerprint Sampler," 60 J. Forensic Sci. 422–427 at 422 (2015). *But see,* H. David Sheets et al., "Distortion in Fingerprints: A Statistical Investigation using Shape Measurement Tools," 59 J. Forensic Sci. 1113–1120 (2014)(although pressure and substrate affect the appearance of the print, they do so in a systematic manner, making the alterations easier to recognize and compensate for in analysis).

distinguishing a true match can be difficult. AFISs are extremely valuable for processing high-volume comparisons, but using the systems also requires fingerprint examiners to routinely distinguish between highly similar prints, increasing the difficulty level and the potential error rate.

Figure 4: In this fingerprint fragment, the individual ridge characteristics have been marked. Points 1, 2, 4 and 5 are ridge endings. Points 8, 10 and 11 are bifurcations. Point 7 is a short ridge. Points 3 and 9 are ridge dots or islands. Point 6 is an enclosure.

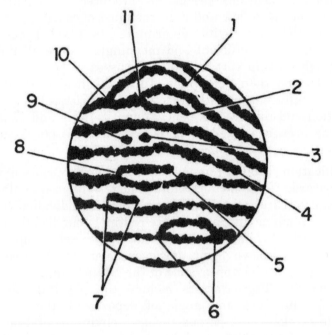

III. LATENT PRINT ANALYSIS

§3.08   VISUALIZATION AND COLLECTION

The friction ridge impression that is accidentally left on a surface is commonly referred to as a "latent print." Latent prints are typically partial or fragmentary and may require additional lights sources, chemicals, or heat to visualize them. Unlike deliberately recorded print impressions documented with ink/paper or digital scanners, the source of a latent print is unknown. It is the duty of the fingerprint examiner to attempt to identify the source of the latent print through comparison with known prints. The theory of latent print identification rests on the premise that friction ridges patterns are unique and unchanging.[31]

---

[31] In addition to research on the development and permanence of friction ridge patterns, examiner observation and empirical data from AFIS databases support the uniqueness premise. *See* Supporting Documentation for Department of Justice Proposed Uniform

Latent prints may be of three varieties:

(1) Plastic print—a visible, long-lasting chance fingerprint impression made in candle wax, tar, clay, oil film, grease, wet paint, or putty;

(2) Patent print—a visible, easily destroyed chance fingerprint impression made in dust, soot, blood, or powder, as well as any other impression resulting from the fingers being covered with foreign matter;

(3) Invisible print—an invisible, easily destroyed chance fingerprint impression resulting from the grease-sweat-dirt coating on the ridges of the friction skin as contact is made with a surface.

There are many methods for developing latent fingerprints on porous and non-porous surfaces. These include the use of powders, lasers, physical developer, small particle reagent, cyanoacrylate esters (superglue fuming), and vacuum metal deposition. Contactless visualization techniques are becoming more important as fingerprints are being collected not just for pattern evidence, but for possible DNA typing as well.[32] Technical books and the professional literature describe the advantages and limitations of older as well as newer latent impression development techniques. The most common development techniques are discussed in the following section,[33] but there are many other techniques available and new techniques are constantly being studied.[34]

Language for Testimony and Reports for the Forensic Latent Print Discipline, at notes 3–7 and accompanying text. (available at: https://www.justice.gov/dag/department-justice-proposed-uniform-language-documents-fiber-footwear-and-tire-treads-general)(last accessed September 14, 2016).

[32] *See* Samuel Nunn, "Touch DNA Collection Versus Firearm Fingerprinting: Comparing Evidence Production and Identification Outcomes," 58 J. Forensic Sci. 601–608 (2013); Li-Chin Tsai et al., "The Influence of Selected Fingerprint Enhancement Techniques on Forensic DNA Typing of Epithelial Cells Deposited on Porous Surfaces," 61 J. Forensic Sci. S221–S225 (2016). *See also* Wei Zeng Low, Bee Ee Khoo, & Ahmad Fahmi Lim bin Abdullah, "Contactless Visualization of Latent Fingerprints on Nonporous Curved Surfaces of Circular Cross Section," 61 J. Forensic Sci. 1093–1099 (2016).

[33] Fingerprint evidence developed through these various techniques has been held admissible. *See, e.g.,* People v. Webb, 6 Cal.4th 494, 24 Cal.Rptr.2d 779, 862 P.2d 779 (1993)(chemical and laser processes); Johnson v. State, 620 So.2d 679 (Ala.Cr.App.1992), *reversed on other grounds,* 620 So.2d 709 (Ala.1993)(ninhydrin process); People v. Eyler, 133 Ill.2d 173, 139 Ill.Dec. 756, 549 N.E.2d 268 (1989), *cert. denied,* 498 U.S. 881 (1990), *rehearing denied,* 498 U.S. 993 (1990)(superglue fuming process).

[34] *See* Stephanie F. Williams et al., "Comparison of the Columnar-Thin-Film and Vacuum-Metal-Deposition Techniques to Develop Sebaceous Fingermarks on Nonporous Substrates," 60 J. Forensic Sci. 295–302 (2015); Glenn Porter et al., "A Novel Method for the Photographic Recovery of Fingermark Impressions from Ammunition Cases Using Digital Imaging," 60 J. Forensic Sci. 418–421 (2015); Stephanie Williams et al., "Columnar-Thin-Film-Assisted Visualization of Depleted Sebaceous Fingermarks on Nonporous Metals and Hard Plastics," 60 J. Forensic Sci. 179–185 (2015); Simon Liu et al., "The Effect of pH on Electrolyte Detection of Fingermarks on Cartridge Cases and Subsequent Microscopic Examination," 60 J. Forensic Sci. 186–192 (2015); Imogen C. Payne, "The Effect of Light Exposure on the

1. POWERS

The oldest and most common method of developing a latent print on a hard, smooth object is by use of a fine powder applied to its surface with a fingerprint brush. The powder adheres to the sweat outlines of the ridges. The color of the fingerprint powder used in the visualization process will vary according to the background surface to provide contrast. Gray and black powders are common but other colors are available. Older powders sometimes spread between the ridges or causes ridges to appear wider, causing an apparent distortion in the print. Newer powders are much finer and permit the visualization of greater detail.

Regular fingerprint powders (titanium dioxide, manganese dioxide, and ferric oxide) are the most consistently used, but many other varieties are available, including magnetic, fluorescent, metallic, and nanopowders. Metallic powders (silver, gold, and gray powder meshed with aluminum and kaolin) remain stable longer and nanometallic powders have greater adhesive properties.[35] In the selection of a fingerprint powder, the type and color of the surface must be considered. The powder should be sufficiently contrasting in color with the surface on which the latent prints were left, affecting the selection of a white, black, gray, or fluorescent powder. Although regular powders do well on nonporous surfaces, magnetic powders perform better on porous surfaces, textured surfaces, and plastics.[36]

2. VAPORS

In the late 1970's and early 1980's, a new fuming method gained widespread acceptance. Some fingerprint technicians had discovered that the ingredients contained in the popular "superglue" product gave off fumes which developed latent fingerprints. From this crude beginning sprang a new developing method, now called the cyanoacrylate fuming process. The cyanoacrylate ester compound reacts with the moisture in perspiration that is left in the ridges of latent impressions and turns them white. The superglue method is often combined with other visualization methods if the white developed print is difficult to analyze on the particular background. Researchers later developed a vapor wand that heats rechargeable cartridges of cyanoacrylate and emits a stream of vapor. The cyanoacrylate fuming

---

Degradation of Latent Fingerprints on Brass Surfaces: The Use of Silver Electroless Deposition as a Visualization Technique," 59 J. Forensic Sci. 1368–1371 (2014).

[35] Ayesha Arshad et al., "Development of Latent Fingermarks on Various Surfaces Using ZnO-SiO$_2$ Nanopowder," 60 J. Forensic Sci. 1182–1187 (2015).

[36] Serkan Gürbüz et al., "A Systematic Study to Understand the Effects of Particle Size Distribution of Magnetic Fingerprint Powders on Surfaces with Various Porosities," 60 J. Forensic Sci. 727–736 (2015).

process can be used in fume hoods, normal fuming chambers, or in outside environments with a vapor wand.[37]

Other vapor methods may be used if the indelible mark or stain left by the superglue method is problematic. Another vapor method used is vacuum metal deposition (VMD). Using VMD, the evidence item is placed in a high-vacuum chamber and then a metal (e.g., copper wire) is heated to boiling. The resulting vapor condenses in a defined layer of thickness over the item. Once the copper is in place, the evidence item is exposed to light of different wavelengths and filters (e.g., near infrared) to reveal the print.

3. CHEMICAL SOLUTIONS

In addition to powders and vapors, latent prints may be developed by chemical solution sprays or immersions. One such long-used method is the silver nitrate spray technique that reacts to the presence of salt (sodium chloride) in the sweat of a latent print. Silver nitrate reacts in the presence of sodium chloride to form silver chloride which is reduced to silver on exposure to ultraviolet light. The ultraviolet light-exposed silver produces a brown image which must be photographed or fixed before it is blackened out by the excess silver nitrate. Other chemical solution spray techniques for detecting prints on paper use reagents like traditional ninhydrin and 1,2-indanedione.[38] The reagent reacts with the amino acids in the sweat of the latent print to form a visible print which can be photographed. Many other reagents have been developed for the visualization of latent fingerprints.[39]

The small particle reagent technique is similar to the powder technique, but uses chemical solution immersion. Iron oxide black or molybderium disulfide powder is suspended in a solution of various chemicals and distilled water. Items for developing are then immersed in a tray containing the suspension. The receptacle is gently agitated for 20–60 seconds, until the fingerprints are developed. This method can be used on objects where the powder technique cannot be applied.

---

[37] Weaver and Clary, "A One-Step Fluorescent Cyanoacrylate Fingerprint Development Technology," 43 J. Forensic Sci. 481 (1993).

[38] Thermal paper, which changes color in response to heat and is used in cash registers and credit card terminals, presents a challenge for latent print development since it tends to change color when exposed to the usual reagents. Heat development, indirect treatment, and adjusting the concentration of the reagents with nonpolar solvents helps to prevent the interfering coloration. See John W. Bond, "Response Assessment of Thermal Papers from Four Continents to Fingerprint Development by Heat," 60 J. Forensic Sci. 1331–1336 (2015); John W. Bond, "A Noninvasive and Speculative Method of Visualizing Latent Fingerprint Deposits on Thermal Paper," 60 J. Forensic Sci. 1034–1039 (2015); Chun-Chieh Chen et al., "Latent Fingerprint Development on Thermal Paper Using Traditional Ninhydrin and 1,2-indanedione," 61 J. Forensic Sci. 219–225 (2016).

[39] See, e.g., J. Almog et al., "5-Methylthio Ninhydrin and Related Compounds—A Novel Class of Fluorogenic Fingerprint Reagents," 37 J. Forensic Sci. 688 (1992).

Results have been obtained on dry, wet, and frost-covered non-porous surfaces.[40]

4. ILLUMINATION

The late 1970's also saw the practical application of the use of laser illumination. Spectroscopists had, for some time, noted that perspiration impressions of fingerprints tend to fluoresce when exposed to laser lighting. From these early observations, a Canadian forensic scientist, B.E. Dalrymple, published a paper advocating the use of the argon-ion laser to illuminate and make visible the compounds contained in palmar sweat that are present in perspiration prints in too small a quantity to become visible with ordinary lighting techniques. This beginning sparked extensive research and experimentation in the use of various laser techniques to make visible latent prints that might not be developed by other means. Now the use of lasers and filtered light sources is widespread. Even if other methods might yield adequate results, the detection of latent fingerprints by their luminescence as revealed in laser lighting is a preferred approach in cases where the resultant staining of most fuming and chemical methods needs to be avoided.[41] Argon-ion lasers, filtered mercury vapor, metal halide, or xenon arc lamps produce fluorescence from residues in latent prints. Infrared filters used with cyanoacrylate fuming also improve the visualization of latent prints on fabrics.[42]

5. COLLECTION

After the print is visualized, it must be collected or documented in some manner to permit further analysis and preservation. This involves photographing or taking a digital image of the prints. If the developed visible print is photographed using a fixed-focus fingerprint camera, the photographic negative of a fingerprint impression will be a correct one-to-one representation of the ridges of the fingerprint. After photographing a powder-developed print, it can then be "lifted"[43] to provide another permanent record. For items that are developed by

---

[40] J. Onstewedder and T. Gamboe, "Small Particle Reagent: Developing Latent Prints on Water-Soaked Firearms and Effect on Firearms Analysis," 34 J Forensic Sci. 321 (1989)(study results revealed small particle reagent analysis yielded better latent impressions than cyanoacrylate ester fuming followed by black powder).

[41] *See* Brian E. Dalrymple *et al.*, "Inherent Fingerprint Luminescence—Detection by Laser," 22 J. FORENSIC SCI. 106 (1977). *See also* E. R. Menzel, "Comparison of Argon-Ion, Copper-Vapor, and Frequency-Doubled Neodymium: Yttrium Aluminum Garnet (ND:YAG) Lasers for Latent Fingerprint Development," 30 J. Forensic Sci. 383 (1985); R. Dalrymple & J. Almopg, "Comparison of Latent Print Detection using Semiconductor Lase and LED Light Sources with Three Chemical Reagents," 62 J. FORENSIC IDENT. 14 (Jan-Feb. 2012).

[42] Emily Sonnex, Matthew J. Almond, and John W. Bond, "Enhancement of Latent Fingerprints on Fabric Using Cyanoacrylate Fuming Method Followed by Infrared Spectral Mapping," 61 J. Forensic Sci. 1100–1106 (2016).

[43] The "lift" may be transparent (a cellphone-like tape) or non-transparent (sticky-surfaced rubber pad).

more non-permanent methods (e.g., visualization by luminescence), the image of the print is the final preservation step.

§3.09 COMPARISON ANALYSIS

By tradition, fingerprint examiners had concentrated on dividing the visible ridge detail in a fingerprint into two categories: class characteristics and individual characteristics. Class characteristics were those shared by many individuals that permitted placing impressions into categories, an especially useful process when classification formulas were calculated manually. These characteristics relied on categorization of impressions as arches, loops, whorls, and their subgroups. Since the sharing of class characteristics only placed impressions into certain groups, it was agreed universally that no individualization was possible on the basis of shared class characteristics only. Individual characteristics included that ridge detail which, upon evaluation, would permit a print belonging to one individual to be differentiated from that individual's other prints as well as from prints of all other people. Individual characteristics were ridge endings, bifurcations, enclosures (double bifurcations), and ridge dots. Other specific ridge features were given additional designations by some earlier researchers and authors.

With the growth of computerized storing of records in AFIS systems that no longer depended on a formula based on class characteristics, but instead relied for storage and searching on the location within an impression of its individual ridge characteristics, the earlier differentiations between characteristics became less descriptive and lost some of their significance. When discovering fragmentary fingerprint detail, it was not always possible to determine a pattern type and thus the "class" to which it belonged. For that reason, the detail that would be characteristic but not necessarily unique to one friction skin exemplar came to be redefined as Level 1 detail. If discernible, the pattern type would be part of this category of detail; if not, what was important was a study of the general ridge flow.

Individual characteristics were further differentiated into two types: those that had been traditionally used to establish uniqueness and were always deemed essential to establishing a match,[44] and those that had not been generally used by the profession because they were not always discernible, but which research had over the years shown to be as persistent as ridge endings and bifurcations. The first category of individual characteristic (composed of ridge endings, bifurcations, and ridge dots) was renamed Level 2 detail. The third category of friction ridge detail, which was not always visible but which had become more readily accessible as technological progress improved the reproduction

---

[44] A conclusion that a match existed between the individual characteristics of two impressions which had been compared had been expressed, in the past, largely by counting the number of matching "points" between two impressions, as was discussed earlier.

of latent and inked impressions, was composed of features related to the ridge morphology of an individual fragment of a friction ridge, such as the pores, ridge edges, and width. These individual ridge characteristics were defined as Level 3 detail.[45]

1. POINT-COUNTING

To compare an unknown latent impression with a fingerprint image of known origin with the aim of determining whether both were made by the same friction skin surface, the examiner considers four different elements: (1) the likeness of the general pattern type, (or, if the type cannot be determined in an incomplete image, whether there exists a general similarity in the flow of the ridges); (2) the qualitative likeness of the friction ridge characteristics; (3) the quantitative likeness of the friction ridge characteristics in a given area of friction skin; and (4) the interrelationships of the characteristics in both impressions. In giving testimony that two or more prints share a common origin, examiners frequently focus on the matching of individual ridge characteristics. Thus, the quantitative aspect of the evaluation was emphasized in the traditional method, which was referred to by some as "point counting."

Latent impressions developed at crime scenes are often blurred or smudged; they may also consist of partially superimposed impressions placed at different times. As long as a sufficiently large area of friction skin that is not blurred, smudged, or rendered useless through superimposition is visible, identity can be established. When using the quantitative method of comparing images, examiners required that a sufficient number of characteristics be found to match in both prints, without unexplained ridge discrepancies. By tradition, though not by empirical studies, many latent print examiners in the United States and elsewhere required a matching of at least eight characteristics in both prints for identity, though most experts preferred at least 10–12 concordances. In England, 14 to 16 matches were long required for court testimony until, in the early part of this century, the profession and the courts abandoned the quantitative method in favor of an approach of weighing quality along with quantity of detail.

2. QUALITATIVE METHOD

Because of criticism leveled against the fingerprint evidence profession for failing to agree on a rule determining the minimum

---

[45] Early AFIS systems had operated essentially on the basis of a comparison of the traditional "individual characteristics" that are now called Level 2 Detail. Newer AFIS systems, such as the NGI system, also rely on Level 3 details. For research discussing Level 3 details, see Alexandre Anthonioz, Nicole Egli, Christophe Champod, Cedric Neumann, Roberto Puch-Solis & Andie Bromage-Griffiths, "Level 3 Details and Their Role in Fingerprint Identification: A Survey among Practitioners," 5 J. FORENSIC IDENT. 562 (2008). The authors subsequently published their research in "Investigation of the Reproducibility of Third-Level Characteristics," 61 J. OF FORENSIC IDENT. 171 (2011). See also, Q. J. Zhao, *et al.*, "Adaptive Fingerprint Pore Modeling and Extraction," *Pattern Recognition*, vol. 43, p. 2833 (2010).

number of ridge characteristics that must match between two impressions before they can be said to be from the same digit, the International Association for Identification (IAI), a professional body composed primarily of fingerprint examiners, created in 1970 a Standardization Committee. The committee consisted of 11 members whose aggregate experience in the identification field amounted to roughly 250 years.[46] The group was charged with several mandates, including the principal mandate to recommend, if feasible, the adoption of a minimum numerical standard for matching characteristics. After a nearly three-year concentrated study, the committee concluded that there existed no valid basis, in the early 1970's, for requiring that a predetermined minimum number of friction ridge characteristics exist in two impressions in order to establish positive identification.

The IAI Standardization Committee concluded: Whether two prints under examination are made by the same digit is a determination that must be made on the basis of the expert's experience and background, taking into account, along with the number of matching characteristics, *other factors such as clarity of the impressions, types of characteristics found and the frequency within which they occur within fingerprint patterns,* the location of the characteristics in relation to the core or delta and other factors. The committee's formal report was unanimously approved by the association's general membership at the 58th annual conference of the IAI in 1973. This approach, relying as much on the quality as on the quantity of visible detail, was later designated as the "holistic approach" of comparing ridge impressions.[47] Using the holistic approach, in order to establish that two impressions were made by the same friction skin matrix, the individual ridge characteristics had to match, quantitatively and qualitatively, with no significant pattern discrepancies.[48]

3. ACE-V METHODOLOGY

By the 1980's, as the jurisprudence for the admission of scientific evidence advanced, some fingerprint examiners had difficulties describing their analytical "method" to judges and jurors. Expert witnesses had been expressing their opinions that a "match" existed,

---

[46] The original author of this chapter (Andre A. Moenssens) was one of the committee members, and also participated in the work and deliberations of the IAI's Standardization II and III special committees of the 1990's and 2000.

[47] The 1973 IAI position rejecting a specific minimum number of matching points was thereafter reaffirmed at an international meeting of fingerprint examiners at Ne'urim, Israel, in 1995, and by subsequent international committees of researchers and professionals.

[48] In comparing latent prints with inked impressions, a number of apparent differences are invariably noted. If these dissimilarities are explainable as having been brought about through ordinary effects, such as pressure distortion, partial blurring, or filling up of ridges through contaminants, they are not considered in the comparison analysis. Should an unexplained discrepancy occur, however, such as the appearance of a clearly defined ridge characteristic in a latent print which does not exist in the inked impression—the difference is considered in the analysis. The inherent subjectivity of these conclusions is one of grounds for the challenge to the reliability of latent print comparison conclusions.

but in essence asked listeners to accept their conclusion at face value. David Ashbaugh was one of the first experts in the English-speaking world to seize on an existing method of analysis (ACE-V) and adapt it to friction ridge examinations. He postulated that if a method resulting in a conclusion that explained the successive steps to be followed to reach a reliable (if not necessarily an accurate) result, more credence would be given to the scientific nature of the process. Ashbaugh and other researchers came to the conclusion that a clear description of the successive steps in the examination process would improve the acceptance of fingerprint comparison analysis as a scientific field by the courts.

ACE-V is an acronym for Analysis, Comparison, Evaluation, and Verification.[49] The first step is Analysis. This step requires a study of the impression for the purpose of determining whether it contains sufficient detail to permit comparison.[50] If the examiner concludes that there is not enough detail visible for comparison, the process is at an end. If the examiner determines that the unknown impression is of a quality that permits analysis and contains a sufficient quantity of Level 2 and/or Level 3 detail, the next step in the process moves to a Comparison of the unknown and known impressions.

In the Comparison stage, the visual examination of two impressions focuses on discovering the extent to which the detail in both impressions is in concordance. It is a laborious process that requires an examiner to follow each ridge line and each visible detail in the unknown and all of the known impressions against which the former must be compared to determine whether they match in their Level 1, Level 2, and Level 3 detail (if the latter is visible). This step also involves exploration of areas of an impression that may be partly smudged, or where the ridges have been subjected to pressure distortion. It is important that the examiner remain objective and noncommittal at this stage to avoid bias or being influenced by the desires of investigating police officers.[51] If, as a result of the comparison

---

[49] The ACE-V methodology is detailed in SWGFAST, "Standard for Examining Friction Ridge Impressions and Resulting Conclusions," March 13, 2013 (available at: http://www. swgfast.org/documents/examinations-conclusions/130427_Examinations-Conclusions_2.0.pdf (last accessed September 12, 2016). *See also* Committee on Identifying the Needs of the Forensic Science Community, National Research Council of the National Academies, *Strengthening Forensic Science in the United States: A Path Forward*, The National Academies Press: Washington D.C., 2009 at pp. 137–142; and Expert Working Group on Human Factors in Latent Print Analysis. *Latent Print Examination and Human Factors: Improving the Practice through a Systems Approach.* U.S. Department of Commerce, National Institute of Standards and Technology. 2012 at pp. 2–9 (available at: https://www.nist.gov/node/577976) (last accessed September 12, 2016).

[50] Ashbaugh describes this stage in his book *Qualitative and Quantitative Friction Ridge Analysis*, 1999, beginning at p. 109. *See also* Christophe Champod, *et al.*, *Fingerprints and Other Ridge Skin Impressions*, 2004, at 15–26 for a description of the ACE-V process; Kasey Wertheim, "Latent Print Sufficiency," in THE DETAIL #162 (weekly online newsletter for latent print examiners), Sept. 2004, archived on www.cplex.com.

[51] It is increasingly recognized that examiner bias is a factor that may influence the accuracy and reliability of the comparison. *See, e.g.,* Itiel E. Dror, et al., "Contextual Information

stage, the examiner concludes that the unknown and known impressions are not produced by the same skin matrix, the process is, again, at an end. If no unexplainable ridge discrepancies have been noted between the two impressions, the examiner has reached the next step in the process.

In the Evaluation stage, the examiner must determine whether the overall available ridge structure visible in both impressions is sufficient to permit the examiner to arrive at an opinion that they were made by the same skin matrix. Three possible conclusions: (1) Exclusion—there are sufficient features in disagreement to conclude that two areas of friction ridge impressions did not originate from the same source; (2) Individualization—there are sufficient features in agreement to conclude that two areas of friction ridge impressions originated from the same source; (3) Inconclusive.[52] After the publication of the 2009 NAS Report discussed *infra*, many law enforcement agencies, including the FBI and the Defense Forensic Science Center (DFSC) of the Department of the Army, modified the language used to express "individualization" to avoid an expression of absolute certainty. The DFSC approved language states that the prints "have corresponding ridge detail" and that [t]he likelihood of observing this amount of correspondence when two impressions are made by different sources is considered extremely low."[53]

Renders Experts Vulnerable to Making Erroneous Identifications," 156 Forensic Sci. Int'l 74 (2006).

[52] *See* notes 55–56 *infra* and accompanying text discussing SWGFAST standards. In a draft standard left pending upon the termination of SWGFAST in 2014, the group proposed:

"Inconclusive is the decision by an examiner that an unknown impression of comparison value cannot be excluded or identified. The reason for each inconclusive conclusion must be documented and reported. Inconclusive conclusions do not apply to impressions determined to be of no value (see section 5.1.1). Reasons for inconclusive may include but are not limited to:

Lack of Comparable Areas (LCA)

This inconclusive conclusion results from a lack of complete and legible known prints. This means comparisons were made to the extent possible, however additional clear and completely recorded exemplars, to include the required anatomical areas, are needed for re-examination.

Lack of Sufficiency for Individualization (LSI)

Corresponding features are observed but not sufficient to individualize. No substantive dissimilar features are observed.

Lack of Sufficiency for Exclusion (LSE)

Dissimilar features are observed but not sufficient to exclude. No substantive correspondence is observed.

There may be other instances where agencies have adopted procedures to report inconclusive conclusions. These are left to the administrative policies and procedures of the individual agency. However, these policies and reporting procedures must be clearly defined by the agency."

See http://www.swgfast.org/documents/examinations-conclusions/130427_Examinations-Conclu sions_2.1.pdf (last accessed September 12, 2016).

[53] Department of Defense, Department of the Army, Defense Forensic Science Center, "Information Paper—SUBJECT: Use of the term "Identification" in Latent Print Technical

The final step in the process involves Verification of the result. Sometimes erroneously referred to as a form of "peer review,"[54] the verification stage requires that the ACE steps be repeated by another examiner of equal or greater competence than the original examiner, working independently, to determine whether the original result is accurate. The verification step is not one that is essential to an examiner's conclusion; it is a quality control step designed to impart greater credibility to the overall process as well as to avoid erroneous individualizations. If this verification is to be "blind" or "double-blind," the evaluator should not be told that the prints have already been examined by someone else. The verifier should also not know that another examiner has already individualized the unknown print, and verification should occur only at the conclusion of all analysis, comparison, and evaluation steps in each case.

§3.10   STANDARDS

In the 1990's members of the forensic science community involved in friction ridge analysis formed the Scientific Working Group on Friction Ridge Analysis, Study and Technology (SWGFAST). The objectives of SWGFAST were:

1.   To establish guidelines and standards for the development and enhancement of friction ridge examiners' knowledge, skills, and abilities.

2.   To discuss and share friction ridge examination methods and protocols.

3.   To encourage and evaluate research and innovative technology related to friction ridge examination.

4.   To establish and disseminate guidelines and standards for quality assurance and quality control.

5.   To cooperate with other national and international organizations in developing standards.

6.   To disseminate SWGFAST studies, guidelines, standards, and findings.[55]

The group worked with support from the FBI and adopted policies and standards for latent and tenprint analysis, including terminology, examination methodology, conclusion language, and many other

---

Reports" CIFS-FSL-LP, November 3, 2015 (available at: http://for-sci-law.blogspot.com/2015/11/marching-toward-improved-latent.html)(last accessed September 12, 2016).

[54] *See, e.g.,* Michele Triplett and L. Cooney, "The Etiology of ACE-V and its Proper Use: An Exploration of the Relationship Between ACE-V and the Scientific Method of Hypothesis Testing," 56 J. FORENSIC IDENT. 345 (2006). See also John "Dusty" D. Clark, "ACE-V—Is It Scientifically Reliable And Accurate?" at www.latent-prints.com.

[55] *See* http://www.swgfast.org/Objectives.htm (last accessed September 12, 2016).

subjects.[56] After the formation on the NIST Organization of Scientific Area Committees (OSAC), SWGFAST ceased operations in 2014. Until new standards are developed and adopted by the OSAC Subcommittee on Friction Ridge Analysis, the SWGFAST voluntary guidelines are generally considered the applicable best practice standards for the field. In addition to the on-going standards development of the OSAC Subcommittee on Friction Ridge Analysis, the FBI has Standard Operating Procedures for its Latent Print Unit that detail each phase of the ACE-V process, required documentation, blind verification procedures, and other areas of the latent print examination.[57]

The Department of Justice has also proposed guidelines for uniform language for testimony and reports for the latent print examination. The proposed standard,[58] still pending adoption as of September 14, 2016, provides:

Identification

1. The examiner may state or imply that an *identification* is the determination that two friction ridge prints originated from the same source because there is sufficient quality and quantity of corresponding information such that the examiner would not expect to see that same arrangement of features repeated in another source. While an *identification* to the absolute exclusion of all others is not supported by research, studies have shown that as more reliable features are found in agreement, it becomes less likely to find that same arrangement of features in a print from another source.

Inconclusive

2. An examiner may state or imply that an *inconclusive* result is the determination that there is insufficient quality and quantity of corresponding information such that the examiner is unable to identify or exclude the source of the print.

---

[56] The "Standard for Examining Friction Ridge Impressions and Resulting Conclusions" contains elaborate descriptions of the process. The Appendix A of the 2013 document consists of the detailed work-flow schematic of the entire Latent Print Process. Although the Appendix A schematic describes the "Latent comparison process, the remainder of the SWGFAST Standard applies to both Latent and Ten-Print Fingerprint operations. See http://www. swgfast.org/documents/examinations-conclusions/130427_Examinations-Conclusions_2.0.pdf (last accessed September 12, 2016).

[57] Supporting Documentation for Department of Justice Proposed Uniform Language for Testimony and Reports for the Forensic Latent Print Discipline at pp. 7–8 and n. 22 (available at: https://www.justice.gov/dag/department-justice-proposed-uniform-language-documents-fiber-footwear-and-tire-treads-general)(last accessed September 14, 2016).

[58] Department of Justice Proposed Uniform Language for Testimony and Reports for the Forensic Latent Print Discipline (available at: https://www.justice.gov/dag/department-justice-proposed-uniform-language-documents-fiber-footwear-and-tire-treads-general)(last accessed September 14, 2016).

Exclusion

3.   An examiner may state or imply that an *exclusion* is the determination that two friction ridge prints did not originate from the same source because there is sufficient quality and quantity of information in disagreement.[59]

The Department of Justice standard specifies that the phrases "exclusion of all other sources," "absolute or numerical certainty," and "zero error rate," are not approved.[60]

§3.11   SCIENTIFIC VALIDITY CHALLENGES

The classic theory of latent print analysis is that identification of an individual by a single latent print is possible because of two premises: (1) uniqueness; and (2) discernibility. Uniqueness is based on the belief that every finger has a unique, unchanging pattern of features and that in the population of the entire world, living and dead, no single fingerprint pattern has ever been, or will be, repeated. Discernibility is based on the belief that a well-trained examiner can determine when an impression displays enough features to distinguish it from an impression of every other finger. In practice, this led to fingerprint examiners testifying that a coincidental match between prints was impossible so a conclusion that an individual's known print matched a latent print meant the individual was the source of the print to the exclusion of all other sources. This classic theory of universal individualization was accepted by examiners and the courts for many years.

In the early 2000's, claims of researchers and commentators that fingerprint evidence lacked underlying validation studies began to echo in the legal community,[61] leading to court challenges to the scientific validity of the latent print comparison.[62] In addition, the traditional claim of infallibility for fingerprint comparison was seriously questioned after a series of high-profile misidentifications, leading to calls for systematic scientific study of the accuracy of fingerprint evidence. As a result, multiple governmental agencies conducting inquiries into the field of forensic science have focused on the presentation of fingerprint evidence.

---

[59] Id. at pp. 1–2.

[60] Id. at p. 2.

[61] *See, e.g.,* Jennifer L. Mnookin, "Fingerprint Evidence in an Age of DNA Profiling," 67 Brooklyn L. Rev. 13–70 (2001); Simon A. Cole, *Suspect Identities.* Cambridge, MA: Harvard University Press (2002); Simon A. Cole, "Is Fingerprinting Identification Valid? Rhetorics of Reliability in Fingerprint Proponents' Discourse," 28(1) Law & Policy 109–135 (2005).

[62] *See* §3.13(1)(b) *infra.*

1.   2009 NATIONAL ACADEMY OF SCIENCES (NAS) REPORT

The 2009 NAS Report[63] made several references to fingerprint evidence and what the NAS Committee viewed as a lack of scientific validity for individualization conclusions in latent print comparison analysis. The report detailed the 2004 misidentification of Brandon Mayfield, a Portland Oregon attorney, in connection with a terrorist attack in Madrid, and the resulting Office of the Inspector General (OIG) report in 2006 as reasons for concern over the reliability of fingerprint evidence.[64] The OIG report noted that the misidentification of the latent print in the Madrid case to Brandon Mayfield:

> "was a watershed event for the FBI laboratory, which has described latent fingerprint identification as the 'gold standard for forensic science.' Many latent fingerprint examiners have previously claimed absolute certainty for their identifications and a zero error rate for their discipline."[65]

The OIG Report concluded that although the latent print had a extraordinarily rare degree of similarity with Brandon Mayfield's print, the misidentification errors occurred in part as a result of procedural violations, contextual bias, and ambiguity in the methodology.[66]

Building on the conclusions in the OIG Report,[67] the NAS Report took issue with each of the premises supporting the universal individualization theory of latent print examination. First, the report noted that:

> [U]niqueness does not guarantee that the prints from two different people are always sufficiently different that they cannot be confused, or that two impressions made by the same finger will also be sufficiently similar to be discerned as coming from the same source. The impression left by any given finger will differ every time, because of inevitable variations in

---

[63] Committee on Identifying the Needs of the Forensic Science Community, National Research Council of the National Academies, *Strengthening Forensic Science in the United States: A Path Forward*, The National Academies Press: Washington D.C., 2009.

[64] Id. at pp. 104–105. Office of the Inspector General, "Special Report: A Review of the FBI's Handling of the Brandon Mayfield Case," March 2006. The unclassified and redacted OIG Report is available at: https://oig.justice.gov/special/s0601/PDF_list.htm (last accessed September 12, 2016)(hereinafter OIG Report).

[65] OIG Report at p. 269.

[66] Id. at p. 271.

[67] The OIG Report included 18 recommendations for the FBI laboratory to improve procedures. In June 2011, the OIG issued a follow up report that found 17 of the 18 recommendations were fully implemented and the remaining recommendation—review of capital cases involving fingerprint evidence—was ongoing. Office of the Inspector General. "A Review of the FBI's Progress in Responding to the Recommendations in the Office of the Inspector General Report on the Fingerprint Misidentification in the Brandon Mayfield Case," Department of Justice: Washington DC (2011)(available at: http://www.justice.gov/oig/special /s1105.pdf)(last accessed September 14, 2016).

pressure, which change the degree of contact between each part of the ridge structure and the impression medium.[68]

Concerning the second premise that a skilled examiner can consistently discriminate between pairs of prints from the same sources and pairs from different sources, the report noted that the field lacked adequate research to prove this premise.[69] The report focused on the subjectivity inherent in the ACE-V methodology for latent print analysis and the resulting opportunity for error:

> [ACE-V] is not specific enough to qualify as a validated method for [conducting friction ridge analysis]. ACE-V does not guard against bias; it is too broad to ensure repeatability and transparency; and does not guarantee that two analysts following it will obtain the same results. For these reasons, merely following the steps of ACE-V does not imply that one is proceeding in a scientific manner or producing reliable results.[70]

The report concluded that: "[h]istorically, friction ridge analysis has served as a valuable tool, both to identify the guilty and to exclude the innocent."[71] However, given the "limited information about the accuracy and reliability of friction ridge analyses," the report concluded that "claims that these analyses have zero error rates are not scientifically plausible."[72]

2. 2012 HUMAN FACTORS REPORT

In December 2008, just prior to the publication of the 2009 NAS Report, the National Institute of Justice Office of Investigative and Forensic Sciences and the NIST Law Enforcement Standards Office convened the Expert Working Group on Human Factors in Latent Print Analysis ("Human Factors Group") to conduct a scientific assessment of the effects of human factors on latent print analysis. The Human Factors Group issued its report in February, 2012.[73] The report noted:

> Courts have accepted latent print evidence for the past century. However, several high-profile cases in the United

---

[68] 2009 NAS Report at p. 144.

[69] Id. After the issuance of the NAS Report, SWGFAST adopted "Standard for the Definition and Measurement of Rates of Errors and Non-Consensus Decisions in Friction Ridge Examination," (first issued March 5, 2012; current version issued November 15, 2012) (available at: http://www.swgfast.org/documents/error/121124_Rates-of-Error_2.0.pdf)(last accessed September 12, 2016). The standard specifically notes it "does not mandate the measurement of rates of error and non-consensus decisions."

[70] 2009 NAS Report at p. 142.

[71] Id.

[72] Id.

[73] Expert Working Group on Human Factors in Latent Print Analysis. *Latent Print Examination and Human Factors: Improving the Practice through a Systems Approach*. U.S. Department of Commerce, National Institute of Standards and Technology. 2012 (available at: https://www.nist.gov/node/577976)(last accessed September 12, 2016)(hereinafter "2012 Human Factors Report").

States and abroad have highlighted the fact that human errors can occur, and litigation and expressions of concern over the evidentiary reliability of latent print examination and other forensic identification procedures has increased in the last decade.[74]

The Human Factors Group was charged with assessing the role of human factors in errors in latent print analysis, evaluating approaches to reduce error, providing guidance on error reduction, and attempting to develop error estimates.[75] The 249-page report is a detailed discussion of the issues that can arise in the analytical process and a thorough analysis of the capabilities and limitations of the latent print examination process. The report also provides an extensive discussion of the challenges and benefits of calculating the prevalence of error in latent print analysis. Ultimately, the report made over 30 recommendations on the following topics: performing ACE-V, reports and testimony, managing the process, training and education, facilities and equipment, and research.

Concerning the theory of universal individualization that troubled the NAS Committee in 2009, the Human Factors Group also concluded: "Because empirical evidence and statistical reasoning do not support a source attribution to the exclusion of all other individuals in the world, latent print examiners should not report or testify, directly or by implication, to a source attribution to the exclusion of all others in the world."[76] They also noted that the fingerprint examiner community, through SWGFAST, had attempted to move away from universal individualization by striking "to the exclusion of all other sources" from its standards. However, the substitute language—"likelihood that the impression was made by another (different) sources is so remote that it is considered a practical impossibility"—was considered equally problematic by some members of the Human Factors Group. Ultimately, the Human Factors Group was unable to agree on recommended language for source-attribution testimony and merely described the alternatives.[77]

3.   2016 PCAST REPORT

In September, 2016, the President's Council of Advisors on Science and Technology (PCAST) approved a report to the President on "Forensic Science in Criminal Courts: Ensuring Scientific Validity of Feature-Comparison Methods" (hereinafter "2016 PCAST Report").[78]

---

[74] 2012 Human Factors Report at p. vi (internal citations omitted)(references to Brandon Mayfield, Stephen Cowans, and Shirley McKie cases).

[75] 2012 Human Factors Report at p. vii.

[76] 2012 Human Factors Report, Recommendation 3.7.

[77] 2012 Human Factors Report at pp. 72–74.

[78] Executive Office of the President, President's Council of Advisors on Science and Technology, "Forensic Science in Criminal Courts: Ensuring Scientific Validity of Feature-Comparison Methods," September 2016 (available at: https://obamawhitehouse.archives.gov/

Like the NAS Report, the 2016 PCAST Report focused on several forensic science disciplines, including latent print analysis. The 2016 PCAST Report acknowledged that "the latent print analysis field has made progress in recognizing the need to perform empirical studies to assess foundational validity and measure reliability."[79] Crediting the FBI, the report summarized a variety of "black-box studies" (designed to measure reliability) and "white-box studies" (designed to understand the factors that influence examiners' decisions) as evidence of progress "to improve latent print analysis as a subjective method."[80] From these studies, PCAST concluded that:

> [L]atent fingerprint analysis is a foundationally valid subjective methodology—albeit with a false positive rate that is substantial and is likely to be higher than expected by many jurors based on longstanding claims about the infallibility of fingerprint analysis.

> Conclusions of a proposed identification may be scientifically valid, provided that they are accompanied by accurate information about limitations on the reliability of the conclusion—specifically, that (1) only two properly designed studies of the foundational validity and accuracy of latent fingerprint analysis have been conducted, (2) these studies found false positive rates that could be as high as 1 error in 306 cases in one study and 1 error in 18 cases in the other, and (3) because the examiners were aware they were being tested, the actual false positive rate in casework may be higher.

> At present, claims of higher accuracy are not warranted or scientifically justified.[81]

Although PCAST concluded that the ACE-V methodology for fingerprint comparison analysis is foundationally valid, they noted several open questions concerning the method's validity as applied: confirmation bias, contextual bias, and proficiency testing. The report concluded:

> From a scientific standpoint, validity as applied requires that an expert: (1) has undergone relevant proficiency testing to test his or her accuracy and reports the results of the proficiency testing; (2) discloses whether he or she documented the features in the latent print in writing before comparing it to the known print; (3) provides a written analysis explaining the selection and comparison of the features; (4) discloses whether, when performing the examination, he or she was aware of any other facts of the case that might influence the

---

blog/2016/09/20/pcast-releases-report-forensic-science-criminal-courts)(last accessed February 24, 2017).

[79]   2016 PCAST Report at p. 87.

[80]   2016 PCAST Report at pp. 87–88, 91–95, 98–100, 102.

[81]   2016 PCAST Report at pp. 101–102.

conclusion; and (5) verifies that the latent print in the case at hand is similar in quality to the range of latent prints considered in the foundational studies.[82]

As the 2016 PCAST Report was in final drafting, a study conducted pursuant to a National Institute of Justice grant was released which called into question the appropriateness of trying to quantify an error rate for the entire field of fingerprint comparison analysis.[83] The study found that "[e]rrors were not distributed randomly across [the samples], but rather, significantly clustered, revealing that difficulty is, to a significant extent, a function of visual aspects of the specific comparison," leading the researchers to conclude:

> [I]t is not especially helpful to seek a field-wide "error rate" for latent fingerprint identification. Instead, as our scientific knowledge of fingerprint identification continues to progress, it will be more useful to seek error rates for different categories of comparisons, based on objective difficulty level.[84]

The study concluded that "[a] more sophisticated understanding of the relationship between error rate and difficulty is, or should be, important for the courts in weighing fingerprint evidence."[85]

In light of the conflicting research, courts may be disinclined to follow the PCAST recommendations concerning informing jurors of specific error rates for the field of fingerprint examination. Given the subjective nature of fingerprint comparison analysis and the lack of validated, objective metrics for the steps in the comparison process, error rate remains an important factor in assessing the appropriate weight to afford comparison conclusions.

IV. TRIAL AIDS

§3.12   EXPERT QUALIFICATIONS

Despite advances in automated processing, comparison fingerprint analysis still requires human examination, so the competence and training of the examiner is a crucial inquiry.[86] Recognizing the need for

---

[82]   2016 PCAST Report at p. 102.

[83]   Jennifer Mnookin et al., "Error Rates for Latent Fingerprinting as a Function of Visual Complexity and Cognitive Difficulty," NIJ Award 2009-DN-BX-K225, Date Received May 2016 (available at: https://www.ncjrs.gov/App/Publications/abstract.aspx?ID=272050)(last accessed September 15, 2016).

[84]   Id. at p. 6.

[85]   Id.

[86]   In a 2016 study, participants with no fingerprint examination training performed approximately at chance levels in making accurate fingerprint comparisons. Jennifer Mnookin et al., "Error Rates for Latent Fingerprinting as a Function of Visual Complexity and Cognitive Difficulty," NIJ Award 2009-DN-BX-K225, Date Received May 2016 (available at: https://www.ncjrs.gov/App/Publications/abstract.aspx?ID=272050)(last accessed September 15, 2016).

expertise in the examination of prints, courts do not allow lay witness testimony on fingerprint identification.[87] The trial judge determines, in the court's discretion, whether a witness is qualified to testify as an expert and such a determination will not be reversed on appeal unless a clear abuse of discretion is shown.[88] In the absence of an attack on the witness's qualifications, the issue is foreclosed on appeal.[89] Some courts deferentially qualify witnesses as experts if their testimony has the potential to assist the court in its fact finding function.[90]

In the early 1970's, the American Academy of Forensic Sciences began a concerted effort to increase professionalization among the practitioners of the forensic sciences. Largely as a result of this impetus, the International Association for Identification (IAI),[91] in 1977, set up a certification board fingerprint examiners. In order to be eligible to take the examination for board certification, the applicant must meet certain academic, technical training and experience criteria. Certification is determined after testing in three areas: a written test covering the technical aspects and the historical development relevant to fingerprint identification; the classification of inked fingerprints and comparison of latent and inked prints; and either oral board testing or presentation of a case for review if the applicant has not yet qualified as an expert in court. The certification is valid for five years, after which time it is necessary to undergo re-credentialing and certification. The process requires 80 hours of continuing education for renewal obtained between the original certification and submitted to the renewal test. It is also provided that if an examiner is shown to have made an erroneous identification after passing the tests, this will automatically cause the certification to be revoked for one year. When the revocation ends, the examiner may again apply for certification upon passing the comprehensive test described in the Latent Print Certification Board's Operations Manual.[92]

In addition to the IAI certification program for fingerprint examiners, competence may be tested and evaluated by the employing

---

[87] McGarry v. State, 82 Tex.Crim.R. 597, 200 S.W. 527 (1918). In 2011, a federal district court in New Mexico, after taking issue with the scientific nature of the ACE-V technique, allow the fingerprint examiner to testify as to his opinion of the source of the prints, but would not allow the examiner to be referred to as "an expert" in front of the jury. United States v. Gutierrez-Castro, 86 Fed. R. Evid. Serv. 319 (D.N.M. 2011).

[88] Davis v. State, 33 Ala.App. 68, 29 So.2d 877 (1947); People v. Flynn, 166 Cal.App.2d 501, 333 P.2d 37 (1958); Green v. Commonwealth, 268 Ky. 475, 105 S.W.2d 585 (1937); People v. Speck, 41 Ill.2d 177, 242 N.E.2d 208 (1968); State v. Tyler, 349 Mo. 167, 159 S.W.2d 777 (1942).

[89] People v. Speck, 41 Ill.2d 177, 242 N.E.2d 208 (1968); State v. Tyler, 349 Mo. 167, 159 S.W.2d 777 (1942).

[90] United States v. Mitchell, 365 F.3d 215, 245 (3d Cir. 2004), cert. denied 543 U.S. 974 (2004).

[91] See www.theiai.org for information on the organization's history, purposes, administration as well as state and international divisions, educational programs, and training opportunities.

[92] For certification requirements, see https://theiai.org/certifications/index.php (last accessed February 24, 2017).

agency as part of their quality control program. Fingerprint evidence units which are part of an accredited laboratory system[93] are required to test the proficiency of examiners.

§3.13 EVIDENCE ISSUES

1. GENERAL ADMISSIBILITY OF FINGERPRINT EVIDENCE

a. Early Court Decisions

In 1911, the Illinois Supreme Court issued the first appellate decision involving fingerprint evidence in *People v. Jennings*.[94] The defendant argued that fingerprint evidence was not admissible under common law rules of evidence and, since there was no Illinois statute authorizing it, the trial court should have refused to permit its introduction. The court held that expert testimony was not limited to classed and specified professions and was admissible where the witness had knowledge or experience not common to the world, and which might aid the court and jury in determining the issues. A few years later, a New Jersey court in *State v. Cerciello*[95] also held that fingerprint evidence, presented by a qualified expert, was admissible.

Most pre-*Daubert* courts held that fingerprint evidence, when relevant[96] and presented by qualified experts, is admissible for the purpose of establishing the identity of an individual defendant.[97] The cases acceptedthe reliability of fingerprint evidence as a means of identification[98] and permitted the admission of fingerprint expert testimony.[99] In 1941, the Texas Court of Criminal Appeals held that

---

[93] The Association of Crime Laboratory Directors—Laboratory Accreditation Board (ASCLD-LAB) has historically provided the accreditation of crime laboratories. In April, 2016, ASCLD-LAB merged with the ANSI-ASQ National Accreditation Board (ANAB) to provide accreditation services for forensic laboratories. *See* http://www.ascld-lab.org/.

[94] 252 Ill. 534, 96 N.E. 1077 (1911).

[95] 86 N.J.L. 309, 90 A. 1112 (1914).

[96] Borum v. United States, 127 U.S.App.D.C. 48, 380 F.2d 595 (1967)(objects on which the fingerprints were found were in a generally accessible area and not probative of the identity of the perpetrator).

[97] *See, e.g.,* Moon v. State, 22 Ariz. 418, 198 P. 288 (1921); People v. Van Cleave, 208 Cal. 295, 280 P. 983 (1929); State v. Chin Lung, 106 Conn. 701, 139 A. 91 (1927); Murphy v. State, 184 Md. 70, 40 A.2d 239 (1944); People v. Roach, 215 N.Y. 592, 109 N.E. 618 (1915); State v. Caddell, 287 N.C. 266, 215 S.E.2d 348 (1975); State v. Viola, 148 Ohio St. 712, 76 N.E.2d 715 (1947), cert. denied 334 U.S. 816 (1948); United States v. Magee, 261 F.2d 609 (7th Cir.1958). David Faigman, *et al.,* in *Modern Scientific Evidence*—Forensics (Student edition), 2006, purports to list all of the cases by federal circuit and state on p. 158, in footnote 9.

[98] *See, e.g.,* People v. Jennings, 252 Ill. 534, 96 N.E. 1077 (1911); Lamble v. State, 96 N.J.L. 231, 114 Atl. 346 (1921); State v. Rogers, 233 N.C. 390, 64 S.E.2d 572 (1951); State v. Bolen, 142 Wash. 653, 254 P. 445 (1927); Piquett v. United States, 81 F.2d 75 (7th Cir.1936), cert. denied 298 U.S. 664 (1936).

[99] People v. Adamson, 27 Cal.2d 478, 165 P.2d 3 (1946), affirmed 332 U.S. 46 (1947), rehearing denied 332 U.S. 784 (1947)(fingerprints are the strongest evidence of identity of a person); Anderson v. State, 120 Ga.App. 147, 169 S.E.2d 629 (1969)(fingerprints serve as the most scientifically accurate method of identifying an individual yet devised); McLain v. State, 198 Miss. 831, 24 So.2d 15 (1945)(fingerprints have been declared unforgeable signatures and the court has confidence in them); Bingle v. State, 144 Tex.Crim.R. 180, 161 S.W.2d 76

since it is so well established that no two fingerprints are alike, henceforth the prosecution would be relieved of the burden of proving this contention, and that the burden of proof to the contrary rests on the accused.[100]

b.   *Post*-Daubert *Decisions*

The first published decision following a major *Daubert* challenge to fingerprinting came in *United States v. Havvard*.[101] The district court rejected the challenge to the admissibility of fingerprint evidence and stated that despite the "fresh and critical look at old habits and beliefs," the evidence satisfied the standards of reliability required by *Daubert/Kumho Tire*.[102] On appeal, the Seventh Circuit Court of Appeals reviewed the *Daubert* criteria and affirmed the district court's ruling, though not always evaluating the evidence in the same manner as had the district judge.[103]

The only case to diverge from the unanimous view on the admissibility of fingerprint evidence was *United States v. Llera Plaza*. By agreement of the parties, the parties submitted the transcript from a *Daubert* hearing in another case[104] for the court's consideration of the defendant's motion to exclude the fingerprint evidence. On January 7, 2002, Judge Pollak of the Eastern District of Pennsylvania, after considering all of the *Daubert* factors, concluded that fingerprinting did not satisfy the reliability criteria of the Supreme Court's opinion and that, while evidence of the practices and methodology as well as the observations of fingerprint experts could be presented, the government's expert testimony on the ultimate issue of whether the defendant's known fingerprints matched a crime scene print would not be admitted at the trial.[105] The government moved for reconsideration and permission to present expert testimony. The court granted the motion and hearings were held on February 25–27, 2002. After consideration of the additional expert testimony presented by both the government and the defense, the court withdrew the earlier ruling and permitted the presentation of expert testimony that the defendant's print and the crime scene impression "matched."[106]

(1942)(fingerprints are the strongest evidence of a person's identity); United States v. Magee, 261 F.2d 609 (7th Cir.1958)(there can be no more reliable evidence of identity than one's own fingerprints); Avent v. Commonwealth, 209 Va. 474, 164 S.E.2d 655 (1968)(fingerprints are an "unforgeable signature").

[100] Grice v. State, 142 Tex.Crim.R. 4, 151 S.W.2d 211 (1941).

[101] 117 F.Supp.2d 848 (S.D.Ind.2000).

[102] 117 F.Supp.2d at 849.

[103] United States v. Havvard, 260 F.3d 597 (7th Cir.2001).

[104] The parties submitted the transcript from the district court proceedings in United States v. Mitchell, 199 F.Supp.2d 262 (E.D. Pa. 2002).

[105] United States v. Llera Plaza, Crim. No. 98-362-10, 11, 12, 2002 U.S. Dist. LEXIS 344 (E.D. Pa. Jan. 7, 2002), *vacated*, 188 F.Supp.2d 549 (E.D. Pa. 2002).

[106] Id.

After *Llera Plaza*, other federal courts[107] and state courts[108] upheld the admissibility of fingerprint evidence, although some courts expressed less deference to the field than others. In *United States v. Mitchell*, the Third Circuit Court of Appeals affirmed the admissibility of fingerprint evidence, but criticized some elements of the comparison analysis, including the lack of standards.[109]

c.   Post–NAS Report Cases

The *Daubert* decision and the NAS Report were seminal events within the legal and forensic science communities. Following the publication of the 2009 NAS Report, admissibility challenges continued the discussion of the underlying methodologies and research supporting the fundamental assumptions of the expert testimony. General challenges to the admissibility of fingerprint evidence focused primarily on the two areas of concern discussed the 2009 NAS Report: the lack of validation studies on the ACE-V methodology and the lack of research to document an error rate of latent print comparisons. Despite the fact that some courts expressed reservations concerning lack of validation and an identifiable error rate,[110] the post–NAS Report court decisions reached the same conclusion as prior courts concerning general challenges to the admission of fingerprint evidence.[111] The courts have upheld the admissibility of fingerprint evidence and noted that any limitations of the methodology are properly addressed in cross-

---

[107] *See* United States v. Vargas, 471 F.3d 255 (1st Cir. 2006); United States v. Estrada, 453 F.3d 1208 (9th Cir. 2006); United States v. Lauder, 409 F.3d 1254 (10th Cir.2005); United States v. Abreu, 406 F.3d 1304 (11th Cir.2005); United States v. Hernandez, 299 F.3d 984 (8th Cir.2002), cert. denied 537 U.S. 1134 (2003); United States v. Rojas-Torres, 66 Fed.Appx. 747 (9th Cir.2003).

[108] Burnett v. State, 815 N.E.2d 201 (Ind. App. 2004); Barber v. State, 2005 WL 1252745— dictum (Ala.Cr.App.2005). *But see* Commonwealth v. Patterson, 445 Mass. 626, 840 N.E.2d 12 (2005)(holding that ACE-V methodology met the *Daubert* standard, but that its application to the analysis of "simultaneous prints" was not generally accepted).

[109] United States v. Mitchell, 365 F.3d 215, 241 (3d Cir.2004), cert. denied 543 U.S. 974 (2004).

[110] *See* United States v. Aman, 748 F. Supp. 2d 531, 542 (E.D. Va. 2010)("In sum, the ACE-V method, although perhaps not worthy of the pedestal on which it has been historically placed, is sufficiently reliable to overcome *Daubert's* bar to admissibility."); United States v. Love, 2011 U.S. Dist. LEXIS 58390, *17–18 (S.D. Cal. 2011)("It is not disputed that the ACE-V method leaves much room for subjective judgment."); United States v. Herrera, 704 F.3d 480, 486–487 (7th Cir. 2013)(equating fingerprint evidence with opinions offered by art experts on whether an unsigned painting was painted by a known painter of another painting and concluding that "[m]atching evidence of the kinds that we've just described, including fingerprint evidence, is less rigorous than the kind of scientific matching involved in DNA evidence," but is admissible evidence). *Cf.* United States v. Council, 777 F. Supp. 2d 1006, 1012 (E.D. Va. 2011)(describing the objections to admissibility as "overstated" and "overblown").

[111] *See* State v. Lizarraga, 191 Wn. App. 530, 364 P.3d 810 (2015), *review denied*, 185 Wn.2d 1022 (2016); United States v. Straker, 800 F.3d 570 (D.C. Cir. 2015); State v. Pigott, 181 Wn. App. 247, 325 P.3d 247 (2014); State v. Dixon, 822 N.W.2d 664, 674–675 (Minn. Ct. App. 2012); United States v. Avitia-Guillen, 680 F.3d 1253 (10th Cir. 2012); Johnston v. State, 27 So.3d 11, *cert. denied*, 562 U.S. 964 (2010); United States v. Rose, 672 F.Supp.2d 723 (D. Md. 2009); United States v. Baines, 573 F.3d 979, 990 (10th Cir. 2009); United States v. Pena, 586 F.3d 105, 110–11 (1st Cir. 2009).

examination.[112] Narrower challenges to specific language in the expert testimony, however, did produce some variation in court decisions. By focusing on the fingerprint examiner's conclusion of universal identification ("to the exclusion of all other sources"), defense counsel in these cases relied on the conclusions of forensic science professional organizations that "absolute certainty" conclusions are not supported by current research.[113] This argument against absolute certainty in testimony has been embraced by some courts.[114]

2.   OTHER FRICTION RIDGE PATTERN EVIDENCE

The friction (papillary) ridges which make up finger impressions also extend over the whole palm of the hand and the soles of the feet. Originally, research conducted on the individuality of papillary ridge characteristics was not confined to an examination of the finger skin; it extended to the skin on the palmar surfaces of the hands and the plantar surfaces of the feet. Barefoot traces, while infrequently occurring in the United States, can be identified in the same manner as fingerprints and palmprints.[115]

The first case where palmprint evidence was in issue is the case of *State v. Kuhl*,[116] decided by the Nevada Supreme Court in 1918. Part of the extensive opinion of the court, in the words of Justice McCarran, reads:

> We have gone at length into the subject of palm print and finger print identification, largely for evolving the indisputable conclusion that there is but one physiological basis by which

[112] *See* United States v. Aman, 748 F. Supp. 2d 531, 541 (E.D. Va. 2010)("the issues defendant raises concerning the ACE-V method are appropriate topics for cross-examination, not grounds for exclusion"); United States v. Love, 2011 U.S. Dist. LEXIS 58390, *30 (S.D. Cal. 2011)("Of course, [the fingerprint examiner] will be subject to cross-examination about her background, methods, analysis, conclusions, and latent fingerprint analysis generally."); United States v. Stone, 2012 U.S. Dist. LEXIS 8973, *14 (E.D. Mich. 2012)("Defendants' criticisms of the ACE-V procedure and concerns about the risks of error such as false positive identifications go to the weight of the evidence and can be explored on cross-examination and/or through presentation of competing evidence."); United States v. Campbell, 2012 U.S. Dist. LEXIS 86799, *17–18 (N.D. Ga. 2012)(same). *But see* United States v. Rivas, 2016 U.S. App. LEXIS 14403 (7th Cir. 2016)(affirming trial court's ruling that questions about the Brandon Mayfield misidentification were not proper during cross-examination concerning the limitations of the ACE-V methodology).

[113] *See, e.g.,* 2012 Human Factors Report at p. 197.

[114] *See* Commonwealth v. Gambora, 457 Mass. 715, 933 N.E.2d 50 (2010)(finding any error in admitting the fingerprint evidence to be harmless, but commenting that "[t]estimony to the effect that latent print matches, or is "individualized" to, a known print, if it is to be offered, should be presented as an opinion, not a fact, and opinions expressing absolute certainty about, or the infallibility of, an "individualization" of a print should be avoided."); United States v. Cerna, 2010 U.S. Dist. LEXIS 144424, *22 (N.D. Ca. 2010)(fingerprint expert not allowed "to testify that her finding of a match is to the exclusion of all other people in the world").

[115] Evans v. State, 39 Ala. App. 404, 103 So.2d 40 (1958), cert. denied 267 Ala. 695, 103 So.2d 44 (1958); People v. Corral, 224 Cal.App.2d 300, 36 Cal.Rptr. 591 (1964); Mincey v. State, 82 Ga.App. 5, 60 S.E.2d 389 (1950); Commonwealth v. Bartolini, 299 Mass. 503, 13 N.E.2d 382 (1938), cert. denied 304 U.S. 565 (1938); State v. Rogers, 233 N.C. 390, 64 S.E.2d 572 (1951).

[116] 42 Nev. 185, 175 P. 190 (1918).

identity is thus established; that the phenomenon by which identity is thus established exists, not only on the bulbs of the finger tips, but is continuous and coexisting on all parts and in all sections and subdivisions of the palmar surface of the human hand.[117]

The same position has been taken repeatedly by all of the courts which have been faced with palmprint evidence. The courts have upheld the admissibility of evidence of identity based on a comparison of palmprint ridge characteristics.[118] Admission has been upheld after *Daubert*[119] and after the 2009 NAS Report.[120]

V. RESOURCES

§3.14 BIBLIOGRAPHY OF ADDITIONAL RESOURCES

1. BOOKS

David R. Ashbaugh, *Qualitative-Quantitative Friction Ridge Analysis: An Introduction to Basic and Advanced Ridgeology*, CRC Press, 1999.

Christophe Champod, *et al., Fingerprints and Other Ridge Skin Impressions*, CRC Press, 2004.

Frederick R. Cherill, *The Fingerprint System at Scotland Yard*, H.M. Stationery Office, 1954.

Simon Cole, *Suspect Identities: A History of Fingerprinting and Criminal Identification*, Harvard University Press, 2001.

James F. Cowger, *Friction Ridge Skin: Comparison and Identification of Fingerprints*, CRC Press, 1992.

David A. Faigman *et al., Modern Scientific Evidence: The Law and Science of Expert Testimony: Fingerprints*, Vol. 5(Ch. 33), West Publishing, 2012.

Federal Bureau of Investigation, *The Science of Fingerprints: Classifications and Uses*, Department of Justice, 1979.

---

[117] 42 Nev. at 190, 175 P. at 194.

[118] State v. Banks, 295 N.C. 399, 245 S.E.2d 743 (1978); Jones v. State, 242 Md. 95, 218 A.2d 7 (1966); Xanthull v. State, 403 S.W.2d 807 (Tex.Cr.App.1966); People v. Atwood, 223 Cal. App. 2d 316, 35 Cal. Rptr. 831 (1963); People v. Les, 267 Mich. 648, 255 N.W. 407 (1934); State v. Reding, 52 Idaho 260, 13 P.2d 253 (1932); State v. Lapan, 101 Vt. 124, 141 A. 686 (1928).State v. Dunn, 161 La. 532, 109 So. 56 (1926), error dismissed 273 U.S. 656 (1927); Sharp v. State, 115 Neb. 737, 214 N.W. 643 (1927).

[119] Barber v. State, 952 So.2d 393 (Ala. Crim. App. 2005)(bloody partial palmprint evidence admissible). United States v. Crisp, 324 F.3d 261 (4th Cir. 2003)(palmprint evidence meets *Daubert* requirements and is admissible just like fingerprint evidence).

[120] State v. Luna, 2013 IL. App. (1st) 072253, 2013 Ill. App. LEXIS 259 (2013)(affirming the admission of palm print evidence under the *Frye* general acceptance standard).

Derek W. Forrest, *Francis Galton: The Life and Work of a Victorian Genius,* Taplinger Pub. Co., 1974.

Francis Galton, *Finger Prints,* 1892(Reprint, William S. Hein & Co., 2003).

Nicholas W. Gilham, *A Life Of Sir Francis Galton,* Oxford University Press, 2001.

Mark Hawthorne, *Fingerprints—Analysis and Understanding,* CRC Press, 2008.

Henry C. Lee and R. E. Gaensslen, ed. *Advances in Fingerprint Technology,* 2d. Ed., CRC Press, 2001.

Davide Maltoni *et al.,* *Handbook of Fingerprint Recognition,* Springer, 2009.

Andre A. Moenssens, *Fingerprints and the Law,* Chilton Book Co., 1969.

Andre A. Moenssens, *Fingerprint Techniques,* Chilton Book Co., 1971.

National Institute of Justice, *The Fingerprint Sourcebook* (2011)(available at: www.nij.gov/pubs-sum/225320.htm (last accessed September 14, 2016).

Nalini Ratha and Ruud Bolle eds., *Automatic Fingerprint Recognition Systems,* Springer-Verlag, 2003.

2. ARTICLES

John Aikenhead, "Friction Ridge Certification Committee (FRCC)," [Canada], IDENTIFICATION CANADA, Vol. 34, 98 (2011).

Joseph Almog and Amnon Gabay, "Chemical Reagents for the Development of Latent Pringerprints, III: Visualization of Latent Fingerprints by Fluorescent Reagents in the Vapor Phase," 25 J. Forensic Sci. 408 (1980).

Joseph Almog and Amnon Gabay, "A Modified Super Glue Technique—The Use of Polycyanoacrylate for Fingerprint Development," 31 J. Forensic Sci. 250 (1986).

Joseph Almog, *et al.,* "Reagents for the Chemical Development of Latent Fingerprints: Synthesis and Properties of Some Ninhydrin Analogues," 27 J. Forensic Sci. 912 (1982).

David R. Ashbaugh, "Ridgeology," 41 J. FORENSIC IDENT.16 (1992).

David R. Ashbaugh, "Incipient Ridges and the Clarity Spectrum," 42 J. FORENSIC IDENT. 106 (1992).

David R. Ashbaugh, "Defined Pattern, Overall Pattern and Unique Pattern," 42 J. FORENSIC IDENT. 503 (1992).

Shaheen Aumeer-Donovan, Chris Lennard and Claude Roux, "Friction Ridge Skin: Fingerprint Detection and Recovery Techniques," in WILEY ENCYCLOPEDIA OF FORENSIC SCIENCE (Jamieson, A. & Moenssens, A.A., eds.) 2009 [3] 1292.

Ann L. Beresford, *et al.*, "Comparative Study of Electrochromeic Enhancement of Latent Fingerprints with Existing Development Techniques," 57 J. FORENSIC SCI. 93 (2012).

Carl W. Bessman, *et al.*, "Comparison of Cyanoacrylate Fuming in a Vacuum Cabinet to a Humidity Fuming Chamber," 55 J. FORENSIC IDENT. 10 (2005).

Thomas A. Busey *et al.*, "Consistency and Variability Among Latent Print Examiners as Revealed by Eye-Tracking Methodologies," 61(1) J. FORENSIC IDENT. 60–91 (2011).

Christophe Champod, "Edmond Locard—Numerical Standard and 'Probable' Identifications," 45 J. FORENSIC IDENT. 136 (1995).

Christophe Champod, "Friction Ridge Examination (Identification): Interpretation of," in WILEY ENCYCLOPEDIA OF FORENSIC SCIENCE (Jamieson, A. & Moenssens, A.A., eds.) 2009 [3] 1277.

David Charleton, Peter A.F. Fraser-Mackenzie, and Itiel E. Dror, "Emotional Experiences and Motivating Factors Associated with Fingerprint Analysis," 55(2) J. Forensic Sci. 385–393 (2010).

J. Dusty Clark, "ACE-V: Is It Scientifically Reliable and Accurate?" 52 J. FORENSIC IDENT. 401 (2002).

Yaron Cohen, *et al.*, "Survivability of Latent Fingerprints—Part I: Adhesion of Latent Fingerprints to Smooth Surfaces," 62 J. Forensic Ident. 47 (2012); and also. "Part II: The Effect of Cleaning Agents on the Survivability of Latent Fingerprints" 62 J. FORENSIC IDENT. 54 (2012).

Simon A. Cole, "Is Fingerprinting Identification Valid? Rhetorics of Reliability in Fingerprint Proponents' Discourse," 28(1) Law & Policy 109–135 (2005).

Brian Dalrymple, *et al.*, "Inherent Fingerprint Luminescence— Detection by Laser," 16 J. FORENSIC SCI. 106 (1976).

John Davis, "Pressure Distortion in Latent Prints," FINGERPR. & IDENT. MAG. (1945) p. 3.

Bogdan Drabarek, *et al.*, "Applying Anti-Stokes Phosphors in Development of Fingerprints on Surfaces Characterized by Strong Luminescence," 62 J. FORENSIC IDENT. 28 (2012).

Itiel E. Dror and David Charleton, "Why Experts Make Errors," 56(4) J. Forensic Ident. 600–616 (2006).

Itiel E. Dror and Jennifer L. Mnookin, "The Use of Technology in Human Expert Domains: Challenges and Risks Arising from the Use of Automated Fingerprint Identification Systems in Forensic Science," 9(1) Law, Probability, & Risk 47–67 (2010).

Ed R. German, "Analog/Digital Image Processing," IDENT. NEWS, Nov. 1983, p. 8.

M. Leanne Gray, "Commentary—Testifying to the Question of 'Points'," 55 J. FORENSIC IDENT. 165 (2005).

Lyn Haber and Ralph N. Haber, "Scientific Validation of Fingerprint Evidence Under *Daubert*," 7 Law, Probability, & Risk 87–109 (2008).

Kerri Huss, John "Dusty" Clark and W. Jerry Chisum, "Which Was First—Fingerprint or Blood," 50 J. FORENSIC IDENT. 344 (2000).

Anthony Iten, "Optimal Temperatures for Latent Print Recovery," FORENSIC MAGAZINE, p. 19 (June-July, 2012).

Anil K. Jain and Sharath Pankanti, "Beyond Fingerprinting," SCIENTIFIC AMERICAN, Sept. 2008, p. 78.

Om Prakosh Jasuja, Gagan Deep Singh and Gurvinder S. Sodhi, "Small Particle Reagents: Development of Fluorescent Variants," 48 SCIENCE AND JUSTICE 141 (2008).

Benjamin J. Jones, *et al.*, "Nanoscale Analysis of the Interaction Between Cyanoacrylate and Vacuum Metal Deposition in the Development of Latent Fingermarks on Low-Density Polyethylene," 57, J. FORENSIC SCI. 196 (2012).

Jonathan J. Koehler, "Fingerprint Error Rates and Proficiency Tests: What They Are and Why They Matter," 59 Hastings L. J. 1077–1100 (2008).

Glenn Langenburg, "Friction Ridge Skin: Comparison and Identification," in WILEY ENCYCLOPEDIA OF FORENSIC SCIENCE (Jamieson, A. & Moenssens, A.A., eds.) 2009 [3] 1282.

Glenn Langenbug, Christophe Champod and Pat Wertheim, "Testing for Potential Contextual Bias Effects During the Verification Stage of the ACE-V Methodology when Conducting Fingerprint Comparisons," 54 J.Forensic Sci. 571–582 (2009).

Tony B. P. Larkin, Nicholas P. Marsh and Patricia M. Larrigan, "Using Liquid Latex to Remove Soot to Facilitate Fingerprint and Bloodstain Examinations: A Case Study," 58 J. FORENSIC IDENT. 540 (2008).

Tony Larkin and Chris Ganniliffe, "Illuminating The Health and Safety of Luminol," 48 Science and Justice 71 (2008).

Simon W. Lewis and Felippo Barni, "Luminol," in WILEY ENCYCLOPEDIA OF FORENSIC SCIENCE (Jamieson, A. & Moenssens, A.A., eds.) 2009 [3] 1645.

Fang Li, "Probability of False Positive with an Innocent Image Processing Routine," 58 J. FORENSIC IDENT. 551 (2008).

Alice Maceo, "The Basis for Uniqueness and Persistence of Scars in the Friction Ridge Skin," FINGERPRINT WHORLD, [31] p. 147 (2005).

Alice V. Maceo, "Friction Ridge Skin: Morphogenesis and Overview," in WILEY ENCYCLOPEDIA OF FORENSIC SCIENCE (Jamieson, A. & Moenssens, A.A., eds.) 2009 [3] 1322.

E. Roland Menzel, *et al.*, "Laser Detection of Latent Fingerprints: Treatment with Glue Containing Cyanoacrylate Ester," 28 J. Forensic Sci. 307 (1983).

E. Roland Menzel and Joseph Almog, "Latent Fingerprint Development by Frequency-Doubled Neodymium: Yttrium Aluminum Garnet (Nd:YAG) Laser: Benzo(f)ninhydrin," 30 J. Forensic Sci. 371 (1985).

Jennifer L. Mnookin, "Fingerprint Evidence in an Age of DNA Profiling," 67 Brooklyn L. Rev. 13–70 (2001).

Jennifer L. Mnookin, "The Validity of Latent Fingerprint Identification: Confessions of a Fingerprinting Moderate," 7 Law, Probability & Risk 127–141 (2008).

Andre A. Moenssens, "Poroscopy—Identification by Pore Structure," FINGERPR. & IDENT. MAG. Jul. 1970, p. 3.

Andre A. Moenssens, "Testifying As A Fingerprint Witness," Fingerpr. & Ident. Mag. Dec. 1972, p. 3. See also the sequel "The Fingerprint Witness in Court," FINGERPR. & IDENT. MAG., April, 1973.

Jaroslaw Moszczynski, Antoni Siejca and Llukasz Ziemnicki, "New System for the Acquisition of Fingerprints by Means of Time-Resolved Luminescence," 58 J. FORENSIC IDENT. 515 (2008).

James Osterburg, "An Inquiry Into the Nature of Proof," 9 J. FORENSIC SCI. 413 (1964).

Mark Page, *et al.*, "Context Effects and Observer Bias (in Forensic Odontology)," 57, J FORENSIC SCI., 108 (2012).

Steven L. Petersen, Shawn L. Naccarato & Gary John, "Enhancing Latent Prints," FORENSIC MAGAZINE, Dec. 2007, p. 31.

Anatastasia V. Petruncio, "A Comparative Study for the Evaluation of Two Solvents for Use in Ninhydrin Processing of Latent Print Evidence," 50 J. FORENSIC IDENT. 462 (2000).

Drew P. Pulsifer *et al.*, "An Objective Fingerprint Quality-Grading System," 231 Forensic Sci. Int'l 204–207 (2013).

Robert Ramatoswski, "A Comparison of Different Physical Developer Systems and Acid Pre-treatments and Their Effects on Developing Latent Prints," 50 J. FORENSIC IDENT. 363 (2000).

Paul Ramsey, "Commentary—Coins in the Pocket: A Simple Explanation of Quantitative-Qualitative Friction Ridge Analysis," 55 J. FORENSIC IDENT. 291 (2005).

Andrew D. Reinholz, "Albumin Development Method to Visualize Friction Ridge Detail on Porous Surfaces," 58 J. FORENSIC IDENT. 524 (2008).

Ander Reitnauer, "Is it a Latent or a Patent? Development of a Latent Print [*in blood*] on Drywall," FINGERPRINT WHORLD, Vol. 37, p. 208 (Oct. 2011).

William C. Sampson and Karen L. Sampson, "Recovery of Latent Prints from Human Skin," 55 J. FORENSIC IDENT. 362 (2005).

Beltrán A. Santamaria, "A New Method for Evaluating Ridge Characteristics," FINGERPR. & IDENT. MAG. Nov. 1955, p. 3.

Bernard Schnetz and Pierre Margot, "Latent Fingerprints, Coloidal Gold and Multimetal Deposition (MMD) Optimisation of the Method," 118 Forensic Sci. Int'l 21 (2001).

Vaughn G. Sears and Tania M. Prizeman, "Enhancement of Fingerprints in Blood—Part 1: The Optimization of Amido Black," 50 J. Forensic Ident. 470 (2000). See also the subsequent installments, in 51 J. Forensic Ident. 28 (2001) and 55 J. FORENSIC IDENT. 741 (2005).

Robert B. Stacey, "Report on the Erroneous Fingerprint Individualization in the Madrid Train Bombing Case," 54 J. FORENSIC IDENT. 706 (2004).

Michael E. Stapleton and Kourosh Nikoui, "Thermal Latent Print Development" EVIDENCE TECHNOLOGY MAGAZINE, p. 20 (Jul-Aug. 2012).

Lyla Thomson, "Latent Print Certification Update," IDENTIFICATION NEWS, p. 13 (April/May 2012).

John I. Thornton, "Modification of Fingerprint Powder with Coumarin 6 Laser Dye," 23 J. FORENSIC SCI. 536 (1978).

Michele Triplett, "Fingerprint Competency," EVIDENCE TECHNOLOGY MAG., March–April 2008, p. 30.

John R. Vanderkolk, "Levels of Quality and Quantity of Detail," 51 J. FORENSIC IDENT. 461 (2001).

C. Wallace-Kunkel, *et al.*, "Evaluation of 5-Methylthiononhydrin for the Detection of Fingermarks on Porous Surfaces and Comparison," 29 IDENT. CANADa 4 (2006).

Stephen P. Wargacki, Linda A. Lewis and Mark D. Dadmun, "Enhancing the Quality of Aged Latent Fingerprints Developed by Superglue Fuming: Loss and Replenishment of Initiator," 53 J. FORENSIC SCI. 1138 (2008).

Wiliam J. Watling, "Using the FFT In Forensic Digital Image Enhancement," 43 J. FORENSIC IDENT. 573 (1993).

David E. Weaver, *et al.*, "Large Scale Cyanoacrylate Fuming," 43 J. FORENSIC IDENT. 135 (1993).

Pat Wertheim, "Detection of Forged and Fabricated Latent Prints," 44 J. FORENSIC IDENT. 652 (1994).

Pat A. Wertheim, "Fingerprint Forgery: A Case Study," IDENTIFICATION NEWS Vol. 38, No. 6, p. 12 (2008).

A. Brian Yamashita, "Use of a Benchtop Desiccator for Vacuum Cyanoacrylate Treatment of Latent Prints," 44 J. FORENSIC IDENT. 149 (1994).

CHAPTER 4

FIREARM AND TOOLMARK EVIDENCE[1]

I.   INTRODUCTION

§4.01   SCOPE OF THE CHAPTER

Unlike fingerprint evidence, which is frequently used in civil and employment identification contexts, firearm evidence and toolmark evidence is predominately used in criminal cases. Firearm and toolmark evidence is a discipline of forensic science that covers two overlapping types of evidence; a firearm is considered a specialized tool. The surfaces of tools, including components of firearms that make contact with ammunition components, generally consist of some type of hard material, such as steel. These surfaces contain random, microscopic irregularities that are produced during the manufacturing process and through subsequent use. These irregularities are considered unique and can be used to distinguish one firearm or tool from another.

Firearm and toolmark comparison is premised on the fundamental physics principle that when a harder object comes in contact with a softer object, the harder object will impart its marks on the softer object.

---

[1]   The Authors gratefully acknowledge the assistance of Lori Schwartzmiller and Todd Reynolds for their contributions to previous versions of this chapter.

147

Therefore, when a tool comes in contact with a softer object or surface, its unique manufacturing and wear marks may be imparted to the object or surface. If the marks from a tool correspond to marks on another object or surface, an association between the tool and the object or surface can be made. Firearm and toolmark comparison analysis is similar to the process used in the other feature pattern disciplines. The comparison process involves the side-by-side examination of the class and individual characteristics of the items to determine whether they could have a common origin.

The comparison analysis methods for firearms and tools are the same, but firearms examination covers many other types of analysis. Firearm examinations involve firearms, ammunition components, serial number restoration, gunshot residue, and other closely related physical evidence. Although the term "ballistics" is often used to refer to the broad field of firearm examination, ballistics is the study of the motion of a projectile, specifically of projectiles discharged from a weapon, and not the examination of the firearm itself.

This chapter will discuss the general principles of firearm and toolmark evidence and focus on the types of examinations typically conducted by examiners, including comparison analysis that is used to link a particular firearm to a shooting event. The scientific validity challenges that have been raised concerning comparison analysis will be discussed as well as the evidence issues that have been raised as a result of those challenges.

§4.02   TERMINOLOGY

Antimony: Metallic element with the chemical symbol of *Sb*, atomic number 51, and atomic weight of 121.75 alloyed with lead to harden the bullet; used in the modern non-corrosive primer compound as an oxidizing agent.

Barrel: Tube that guides the bullet or projectile until it exits the weapon. The barrel may be smooth as in shotguns, or rifled as in rifles and handguns.

Barium: Metallic element with the chemical symbol of *Ba*, atomic number of 56 and atomic weight of 137.34 found in the primer compound in the form of barium nitrate and used as an oxidant.

Bolt: Generally a manual sliding cylindrical unit with an external handle that is used to expend the spent cartridge casing and load a new round into the chamber of a weapon, typically a breech loading rifle.

Bore: Diameter of the barrel; in a rifled firearm, the bore diameter measured from opposing land to opposing land; measurement is expressed in hundredths or thousands of an inch in firearms of American and British manufacture or in millimeters in firearms of other manufacturers.

Breech Block: That portion of a firearm that supports the head of the cartridge in the firing chamber at the moment of discharge that blocks and locks the breech of the firearm before firing.

Caliber: The bore diameter expressed in hundredths or thousands of an inch or in millimeters and measured before the forming or cutting of the rifling grooves. Caliber is used in designating the name of the firearm or cartridge.

Cannelure: (smooth or knurled) Groove or depression rolled into the cartridge case or bullet; sometimes used to hold lubricant or to crimp the end of the cartridge case to hold the bullet at the correct depth in the cartridge.

Cartridge: One unit of ammunition composed of cartridge case, primer, powder and (with or without) a bullet or shot; sometimes referred to as one round of ammunition.

Center Fire: A cartridge and the weapon used to fire such a cartridge, with a primer used in the center of the back of the casing which is fired through use of a firing pin that strikes and detonates the primer. *Contrast* "Rim Fire."

Chamber: Special enlarged area at the breech of a barrel where the cartridge fits and resides after it is loaded and while it is fired. Revolver cylinders are multi-chambered.

Clip: Mechanical device for holding cartridges to speed the loading of a magazine; clips hold the ammunition together, but do not feed the cartridges into the firearm.

Crimping: Compressing of the cartridge case mouth to hold in place the bullet, or a non-bullet propellant holder in the case of a "blank" cartridge.

Ejector: Part of the firearm action that expels or ejects the cartridge case from the firearm after firing, either automatically in the case of automatic or semi-automatic weapons, or when the action is operated by hand as through use of a bolt, lever, slide, or other device for that purpose.

Extractor: Part of the action of the firearm that pulls or withdraws the cartridge case from the firing chamber for ejection.

Firing Pin: Part of the firearm mechanism that strikes the primer of the cartridge (or its rim in the case of rim-fired ammunition) to initiate ignition.

Flash Hole: Aperture through the web of a center fire cartridge case from the primer pocket through which primer flame passes to ignite the powder.

Grain: Standard American unit of weight for bullet weight and weight of powder charge; 7,000 grains to a pound.

Hammer: Part of the firing mechanism that gives impulse to the primer or firing pin. The hammer may be external, in which case it may need to be brought back into firing position prior to use of the weapon, or internal and thus not observable as an aid in determining whether the weapon is ready for firing.

Magazine: Holder for cartridges in a repeating firearm from which cartridges are extracted and chambered.

Rim Fire: A cartridge and the weapon designed to fire such a cartridge in which the primer compound is positioned in the hollow rim of the cartridge case. *Contrast* "Center Fire."

Striker: Firing pin or part of the weapon which strikes the firing pin found in hammerless firearms.

§4.03   EVIDENTIARY USES

Firearm and toolmark evidence is used in a variety of ways in criminal cases.[2] Firearm functionality tests, including trigger pull measurements, may provide information on the likelihood that a firearm discharge was accidental or unintended. Other tests ancillary to the discharge of the firearm, such as gunshot residue analysis, may provide information on the events of the shooting, including relative positions of individuals during the shooting. The most commonly discussed type of firearm evidence, however, involves linking bullets and cartridge cases to an individual firearm. This type of feature pattern comparison analysis has been used in criminal cases since the 1930's.

The comparison analysis used for firearms is also used for the wider category of tools. Toolmarks left at the scene of a crime are typically found in burglary cases and involve all manner of tools. Drills have been matched with the holes bored in a safe.[3] Screwdrivers and crowbars are routinely matched with pry marks on doors,[4] window sashes, and safes. Car tools and tire irons have left their marks on door moldings,[5] and doorknobs,[6] in one case, a tire iron was shown to have been used to puncture the gas tank of a burned automobile containing a corpse.[7] A hammer has been matched with the markings on the spindle of a safe,[8]

---

[2]   Firearms examiners may testify in civil cases, such as wrongful death cases, involving firearms. *See* Economy Premier Assur. Co. v. Welsh, 2016 U.S. Dist. LEXIS 134192 *8 (W.D. Pa. 2016)(" . . . an expert in firearms, examined the weapon and found it to be in good working condition.").

[3]   Starchman v. State, 62 Ark. 538, 36 S.W. 940 (1896).

[4]   State v. Wade, 465 S.W.2d 498 (Mo. 1971); State v. Brown, 291 S.W.2d 615 (Mo. 1956); State v. Eickmeier, 187 Neb. 491, 191 N.W.2d 815 (1971).

[5]   Adcock v. State, 444 P.2d 242 (Okla. Cr. 1968).

[6]   State v. Smith, 156 Conn. 378, 242 A.2d 763 (1968).

[7]   State v. Harris, 241 Or. 224, 405 P.2d 492 (1965)(toolmark evidence countered the defendant's claim that his wife was killed when their car ran off the road and accidentally caught fire).

[8]   State v. Olsen, 212 Or. 191, 317 P.2d 938 (1957).

and a punch with impressions left on a safe's lock pin.[9] Bolt cutters have been connected to a criminal offense when they have been used to gain entry or to disconnect merchandise which is the object of a theft, such as copper tubing.[10] The distinctive marks left by pliers have also been used to associate an individual tool with a crime.[11]

Standards for the field of firearm and toolmark evidence are currently voluntary and promulgated by professional organizations, but recent reform actions in the forensic science community may lead to the adoption of mandatory standards and practices. Since 1969, the Scientific Working Group for Firearm and Toolmarks (SWGGUN) has promoted guidelines for the examination and presentation of evidence of firearm and toolmark examinations. The Scientific Working Group on Gunshot Residue (SWGGSR) has promoted guidelines for the examination and presentation of evidence of gunshot residue examinations. Recently the National Institute of Standards and Technology Organization of Scientific Area Committees (NIST OSAC) formed a subcommittee (Firearms and Toolmark Subcommittee) to focus on standards and guidelines related to the examination of firearm and toolmark evidence, including the comparison of microscopic toolmarks on bullets, cartridge cases, and other ammunition components and may also include firearm function testing, serial number restoration, muzzle-to-object distance determination, tools, and toolmarks.[12] NIST OSAC has also formed a subcommittee (Gunshot Residue Subcommittee) to focus on standards and guidelines related to the analysis of evidence that results from the deposition of or physical transfer of small or minute quantities of gunshot residue.[13] Until standards are promulgated by these two subcommittees, the voluntary guidelines of SWGGUN and SWGGSR remain in effect, but should be considered the minimal standards for competent examination in the field.[14]

---

[9]   State v. Montgomery, 175 Kan. 176, 261 P.2d 1009 (1953).

[10]   Souza v. United States, 304 F.2d 274 (9th Cir.1962). For a case where a stolen coin collection was identified through a record of the mint marks on the coins, *see* Jenkins v. United States, 361 F.2d 615 (10th Cir.1966).

[11]   Mutual Life Ins. Co. of Baltimore, Md. v. Kelly, 49 Ohio App. 319, 197 N.E. 235 (1934).

[12]   *See* https://www.nist.gov/topics/forensic-science/firearms-and-toolmarks-subcommittee.

[13]   *See* https://www.nist.gov/topics/forensic-science/gunshot-residue-subcommittee.

[14]   *See* www.swggun.org and www.swggsr.org for listing of available guidelines.

II. GENERAL PRINCIPLES[15]

§4.04   TYPES OF FIREARMS

1.   RIFLED BARREL

The two types of modern firearms most commonly encountered in criminal cases—handguns and rifles—share the characteristic of a rifled barrel. During the manufacturing process, rifling creates parallel spiral cuts (grooves) and raised ridges (lands) in the inner surface (bore) of a firearm barrel to impart rotary motion, and thus increased stability, of a projectile moving through the barrel. For each model of firearm, the manufacturer establishes "the number of lands and groove, the direction of twist [of the grooves], the angle of twist (pitch), the depth of the grooves, and the width of the lands and grooves."[16]

Handguns and rifles are classified by caliber, which is determined by the diameter of the bore of the barrel. The diameter may be expressed in hundredths or thousandths of an inch, or in millimeters. Therefore, a firearm with a bore diameter of forty-five hundredths of an inch would be a "forty-five" (.45) caliber firearm. Likewise, a firearm possessing a bore diameter of nine millimeters is said to be a nine-millimeter (9 mm) caliber firearm.

a.   Handguns

Commonly encountered handguns are revolvers and semi-automatic pistols. A revolver is distinguished by the presence of a rotating cylinder containing multiple firing chambers, each accommodating a single round of ammunition (cartridge). Revolvers generally have a cylinder with five or six chambers, but can have as many as twelve. The chambers are arranged to revolve on an axis and discharge the shots in succession. Spent cartridges are ejected either by opening the cylinder through a hinge on the side of the weapon, through a release that allows a tilting down of the entire front of the weapon ("break-top;" more characteristic of British revolvers), or (in earlier models) through use of a moveable rod on the side that can be used to push out empty cartridges individually.

---

[15] For a primer on the basics of firearms, ammunition, and the principles of ballistic imaging comparison, *see* National Research Council of the National Academies, Committee of Assess the Feasibility, Accuracy, and Technical Capability of a National Ballistics Database, *Ballistic Imaging,* National Academies Press: Washington, DC (2008).

[16] Federal Research Council, *Reference Manual on Scientific Evidence*, 3d ed., National Academies Press, 2011 at p. 91.

Figure 1: Drawings of a typical revolver (above)
and semi-automatic pistol (below).

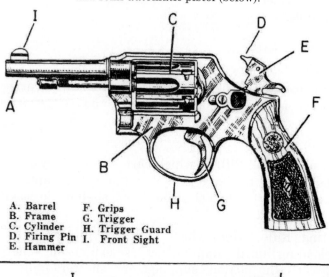

A. Barrel   F. Grips
B. Frame   G. Trigger
C. Cylinder   H. Trigger Guard
D. Firing Pin   I.   Front Sight
E. Hammer

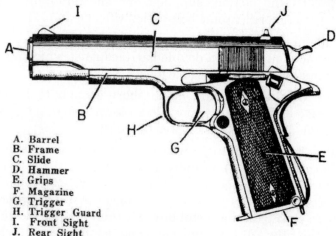

A. Barrel
B. Frame
C. Slide
D. Hammer
E. Grips
F. Magazine
G. Trigger
H. Trigger Guard
I.   Front Sight
J. Rear Sight

While revolvers dominated the handgun market until the late 1970's, their sales have now been superseded by semi-automatic pistols. In a semi-automatic pistol there is no cylinder. The semi-automatic pistol utilizes the powder gas recoil to activate backward movement of the sliding breech block (slide) upon discharge, in the process removing the fired cartridge case from the chamber, and, by its forceful contact with the ejector groove, cocking the hammer in readiness for the next shot; while the spring in the magazine feeds a new round into the chamber of the barrel. When the trigger is again squeezed, the firing pin is driven forward by the hammer, striking the primer of the cartridge which then discharges the round.

The trend in semi-automatics is toward smaller size and double action, as opposed to the single action Colt 1911 designed over a hundred years ago. Newer semi-automatics also are more likely to lack external hammers, lack a safety, and have smaller and very compact designs. Increasingly, polymers and plastics are used in the construction of semi-automatic pistols.

b. Rifles

A rifle is a firearm with a rifled barrel, designed for use with two arms and for firing from the shoulder. Rifles come in a variety of styles including lever action, bolt action, pump, and self (semi-automatic) loaders.

Variations include:

Auto-loading Rifle: Rifle in which part of the energy of the fired shell is used to operate the action to extract and eject the spent shell and then chamber a live shell while cocking for the next shot.

Repeating Rifle: Rifle which will fire repeatedly without reloading until ammunition is exhausted; energy to operate the action supplied by shooter (pump rifle, lever-action rifle, some bolt-action rifles).

Manually Loaded Rifle: Includes single shot rifle, some bolt-action rifles, and double barreled rifles which must be manually reloaded after each shot is fired.

Carbine: Originally a rifle made short enough to be easily carried on horseback, now a loose term applying to a short barreled rifle (18 to 20 inches in length).

Assault Rifle: Military weapon having the following characteristics: (a) an individual weapon with provision to fire from the shoulder (i.e. a buttstock); (b) capable of selective fire; (c) with an intermediate-power cartridge: more power than a pistol but less than a standard rifle or battle rifle; (d) ammunition supplied from a detachable magazine rather than a feed-belt; and (e) a range of at least 300 meters (1000 feet).

c. Class and Individual Characteristics

The manufacturing design of a rifled barrel imparts the class characteristics to the firearm. These include the following caliber and rifling specifications (see Figures 2 and 3):

(1) land and groove diameters

(2) the direction of rifling

(3) the number of lands and grooves

(4) the width of the lands and grooves, and

(5) the degree of the rifling twist.[17]

Figure 2: Manufacturer's specifications for barrel making greatly influence the "class characteristics" left on the bullet after it has been fired through a barrel. *Courtesy: Albert Biasotti, San Jose, Calif.*

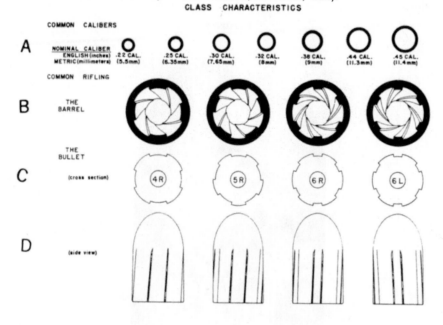

Figure 3: Barrel section showing interior of barrel and bullet. Observe the twist in the grooves and in the projecting interspaces (the lands). Also note the groove and the land impression on the bullet, which has been pushed through the unsectioned portion of the barrel to its present position. *Courtesy: Charles M. Wilson (deceased), Madison, Wis.*

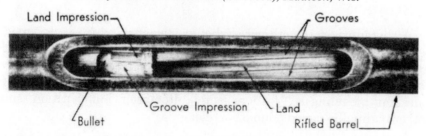

Regardless of the type of instrument used to produce the rifling within a barrel, each barrel inevitably acquires minute marks, called striations or striae, primarily through minor accidental occurrences in the rifling process, but they may also be acquired from the wear and use of the barrel firearm. These minute marks are referred to as individual characteristics. Firearms examiners assume these marks are unique,

---

[17] Id. at p. 92.

although whether empirical research supports this assumption is a subject of debate.[18] When the bullet travels through a rifled barrel the class and individual characteristics are impressed on the bullet. The magnified photograph of a bullet in Figure 4 shows the kind of marks transmitted to the bullet by the structural characteristics of a barrel's interior.

Figure 4

2. SHOTGUN

A shotgun is a smooth-bored shoulder weapon which is designed to fire cartridges with multiple round projectiles or a single solid slug. The term "smooth-bored" means that the inside of the barrel is smooth from end to end rather than being rifled. Shotguns are available in a number of designs including self-loaders (semi-automatic), pump action, single shot, or manually loaded double barreled.

A shotgun may have a choke which is a constriction of the barrel diameter at, or near, the muzzle designed to produce a concentration of shot. Shotguns are available without a choke, or with various chokes including improved cylinder, modified, or full choke. Double-barrel shotguns may have a different choke for each barrel. The degree of choke may be constant or variable. The manufacturer determines whether the choke will be full, improved cylinder, or modified. A variable choke (poly-

---

[18] *See* §4.08 *infra.*

choke) is a device that may be added to the muzzle to allow the shooter to adjust the choke as desired. The influence of the choke on shot pattern becomes increasingly marked the farther the muzzle is from the target. The range of a shotgun is comparatively short, due to the lightness of the shot and lack of stabilization by rifling. However, the cone-like spreading effect of the shot, coupled with the large number of shot, improves the chances of hitting a particular target at moderate range.

The size of large-bore shotguns is expressed by "gauge", which is the term referring to the number of round lead balls of the bore diameter that equal one pound. Thus 12 gauge is the diameter of a round lead ball weighing 1/12th of a pound. The gauge of a shotgun should not be confused with the size or number of the pellets that may be contained in a cartridge fired by a shotgun. The most commonly used gauges are 12 and 16 gauge, with 20 gauge less frequent. A 10 gauge is made but its large size is rare in actual use. The .410 caliber is expressed in hundredths of inches, and used mostly by young people being first introduced to shotguns. The following chart reflects the bore diameter of the more common gauges of shotguns.

Bore Diameter

Gauge No.	Inches	Millimeters
10	.775"	19.68 mm
12	.729"	18.52 mm
16	.662"	16.81 mm
20	.615"	15.62 mm
410	.410"	10.41 mm

§4.05   AMMUNITION COMPONENTS

1. HANDGUNS AND RIFLES

The ammunition unit for a rifled barrel firearm is referred to as a cartridge. A cartridge consists of a projectile, propellant/powder, primer, and a cartridge case. When a firearm is discharged, the firing pin strikes the primer at the base of the cartridge case, igniting the propellant and producing high-pressured gas within the cartridge case, pushing the projectile at opposite end of the cartridge case down the barrel and out of the muzzle of the firearm. When the high-pressured gas is created, it causes the cartridge case to first swell to occupy the chamber of the firearm and then to slam back against the breech face of the firearm.

A bullet, which is shown at the top of the cartridge case in Figure 5, is the projectile propelled by rifled firearms.[19] Bullet diameter is usually somewhat larger than the bore diameter of the weapon from which it is intended to be fired. This is necessary in order to permit the rifling of the barrel to grasp the bullet and impart a spin to it. The caliber of the bullet does not conclusively indicate the caliber of the weapon that fired it, since a slightly smaller caliber bullet may be fired (although with reduced accuracy) through a larger sized barrel.

Figure 5: Rimless bottlenecked centerfire .308 Winchester.

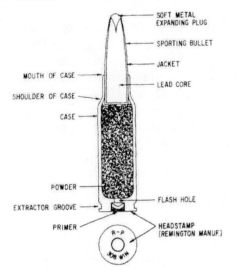

Most bullets are of lead composition hardened with alloys of tin, antimony, and other substances, but are available in several types, including but not limited to:

(1)   Full jacketed non-expanding: the lead core is fully encased with a one-piece metal jacket open only at the base.

(2)   Lead alloy: the lead bullet is unjacketed but is alloyed with other hard metals to increase the bullet hardness.

(3)   Round nose, soft point, expanding or mushrooming bullets: an area of lead is exposed at the tip and a metal jacket covers the base and side of the bullet.

(4)   Open, hollow point, expanding bullet: the base and side of the bullet are enclosed by a one-piece jacket which has been intentionally weakened by nicking near the nose of the

---

[19] Frangibles are an alternative to bullets that do not use a single lead projectile. Examples are cartridges such as the Glaser Safety Slug which is made up of single pellets much like the ammunition used in shotguns. Other frangible bullets are composed of tin, zinc and or copper pieces designed to fire like a bullet but to also disintegrate upon striking a hard body such as a shooting range backboard. This later type is used to avoid toxic lead concentrations at firing ranges. Although usually fired from rifled handguns, the ballistic characteristics of frangible ammunition are similar to projectiles fired by smoothbore shotguns.

bullet. If it is designed to fragment rather than mushroom, the bullet is constructed similarly except that the metal jacketing is thinned to insure maximum fragmentation.

(5) Hollow point bullets of the Hydroshock type: bullets with a sharp ring around the hollowed point, providing not only greater expansion at lower velocities, but also better penetration of slanted automobile windshields which tend to deflect standard round nose bullets.

Modern handguns generally range, in the caliber of ammunition which they are designed to fire, from .22 to .44 magnum. Most modern rifles are designed to fire cartridges between .22 caliber up to .50 caliber or larger. United States military ammunition is usually made to NATO standards and issued in metric sizes such as 5.56 mm and 7.62 mm. Again, many factors contribute to the appropriate application of a particular weapon/cartridge choice, and the options are extensive.

In the past, black powder was the propellant for bullets. Typically composed of 75% potassium nitrate, 10% sulfur, and 15% charcoal, black powder proved unsatisfactory because its combustion produced a great deal of black smoke and resulted in fouling of the inner barrel. A more powerful substance, smokeless powder, was introduced around 1886 and is used in all modern ammunition. It produces a comparatively small amount of smoke and does not markedly foul the firearm. There are two types of smokeless powder: (1) single based smokeless powder, composed of nitrocellulose with additives; and (2) double based powder, composed of nitrocellulose and nitroglycerin with additives.

The primer is the ignition component of a cartridge. The primer is a small charge which is detonated by the crushing blow of the firing pin or hammer. The flame produced by the ignition of the primer ignites the propellant powder. This is the sole purpose of the primer. Primer is of two types: (1) rim fire, and (2) center fire. Rim fire priming involves the positioning of the primer in the fold of the cartridge case rim and over the inner surface of the cartridge head; the primer is ignited when the firing pin strikes the rim. Rim fire cartridge design is commonly found in .22 caliber ammunition. The center fire primer is a small metal cup containing the primer compound. It is placed in the center of the cartridge case in a recess behind the powder charge. When the hammer or firing pin strikes the anvil in the primer, the primer composition between the two is crushed and ignition occurs.

A cartridge case holds the primer, the propellant powder, and the projectile. Together, these components—the case, the primer, the powder and the projectile—form the cartridge. The cartridge case is usually made of brass for use in rifled arms. Cartridge cases have three basic shapes: straight, tapered, and bottlenecked. The head of the case may vary in shape, e.g. being rimmed, semi-rimmed, rimless, rebated rimless, or belted. In ammunition made for semi-automatic pistols the base of the cartridge case is characteristically "rimless." There is only an indented extractor groove running around the circumference immediately above the base. Revolver ammunition is usually rimmed because the design of these weapons requires that the cartridge case be anchored.

The cartridge case from a semi-automatic weapon is more likely to be found at a crime scene than one from a revolver because the semi-automatic immediately ejects all fired cartridge cases while the revolver retains them in the cylinder. The design of the semi-automatic pistol also results in more potentially identifiable marks being imprinted on the cartridge case as it comes in contact with the firing pin, the breech block, the extractor, and the ejector.

2. SHOTGUNS

Shotgun ammunition also contains a projectile, propellant, primer, and case. The propellant and primer are similar to those of rifled firearms. Cases vary slightly in that they are usually plastic or paper instead of metal. The main difference in ammunition between rifled firearms and shotguns is in the projectile. Shotgun projectiles are generally "shot," although an elongated hollow rifled slug may also be fired from a shotgun.

Shot are small spherical pellets used in loading shotgun cartridges. *See* Figure 6. They emerge from the barrel with a typical muzzle velocity of approximately twelve hundred feet per second. Classification of shot is according to numbers, each number indicating a special size. These are measured by diameter and by weight in grains. Shot are typically composed of lead combined with a small percentage of antimony. The weight of the shot in the charge is indicative of the type of cartridge used. However, weight alone is insufficient to establish gauge of the firearm from which it was fired.

Although not a projectile, the wad in a shotgun cartridge is blown out with the fired shot. The wad is a piece of greased felt or plastic between the propellant powder and the shot. The wad acts to seal the bore, to keep gases from escaping, and to protect the projectile from the ignition. An increasing number of manufacturers use a shot collar rather than wads to contain the shot. The collar is a polyethylene sleeve with slits at the side. The shot collar or sleeve typically opens when it reaches approximately 24 inches from the muzzle. The position of the wad or the shot collar when discovered at the crime scene is sometimes useful to the expert in establishing the position and or range of the shotgun at time of discharge. Wads, more than pellets, can sometimes identify the manufacturer of the cartridge and possibly even the specific lot in which it was made.

Figure 6: Centerfire shot shell.

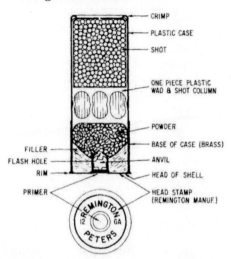

The following charts demonstrate the comparative number of pellets that are contained in different shot sizes as well as the actual diameter of the pellets of the various shot sizes. Notice that for all shot sizes under no. 1, the shot number can be determined by subtracting the diameter of the pellets from 17. Subtracting the shot size from 17 will give the pellet diameter.

Shot Size	Pellets in Charge Weight of Charge in Ounces				
	½	¾	⅞	1	1 ½
9	292	439	512	585	—
8	—	308	359	410	—
7 ½	175	263	—	350	—
6	113	169	197	225	338
5	85	128	149	170	—
4	68	101	118	135	203
2	—	—	—	90	135

Shot Size	Pellet Diameter	
9	.08″	
8	.09″	
7 ½	.095″	
7	.10″	
6	.11″	
5	.12″	
4	.13″	
2	.15″	
1	.16″	
BB	.18″	
00 Buck	.33″	(Buckshot is molded round shot about the size of a pea)

III. FIREARM AND TOOLMARK ANALYSIS

§4.06 ANCILLARY TESTS

1. FUNCTIONAL TESTS[20]

Firearm examiners are often asked to determine the functionality of a submitted firearm, i.e., if the firearm operates in the manner in which the manufacturer designed it.[21] If relevant, accidental discharge and trigger pull analysis may be conducted to assess the firearm's safety system, condition, and factory specification. If an accidental discharge is a possible scenario, firearm examiners will examine the firearm for defects, and if none are discovered, a "drop test" will be performed to determine if there is a possibility the firearm will discharge if dropped. Recommended procedures for a drop test are as follows:

1. Place a one-inch-thick rubber pad onto a solid floor (such as concrete).

---

[20] For detailed technical procedures of functional firearm tests, see North Carolina State Crime Laboratory, Physical Evidence Section—Firearm Unit, "Technical Procedure for Firearm Examination," Version 10, December 11, 2015 (available at: http://www.ncdoj.gov/getdoc/c474e00c-bf9d-47e5-95c3-1330cc974e38/Firearm-Examination.aspx)(last accessed September 30, 2016).

[21] Simple measurements of the firearm may be relevant to the issues in a case. See R.A.F. v. R.A.F., 2016 Pa. Super. LEXIS 540 (September 21, 2016)(examiner testified about the functionality and the shortened length of the shotgun and barrel in prosecution for possession of a sawed-off shotgun).

2.   Place a primed cartridge case in the chamber that will receive the hammer strike.

3.   Cock the firearm.

4.   Disengage the external safety.

5.   Drop the firearm from a height of about three feet onto the pad.

6.   Test all positions of the firearm—top, bottom, left side, right side, rear, and muzzle. (Before each drop, the primed case should be checked for firing pin indentations and the findings recorded.)[22]

Trigger pull analysis is done to determine the amount of force necessary to activate the trigger of the firearm and may be conducted by weights, spring gauge, force gauge, or an automated trigger pull device.[23]

2.   GUNSHOT RESIDUE (GSR)[24]

When a person fires a firearm, a gas of discharge residue and traces left by smoke, dust, and fire escape the firearm. Once this gas condenses, due to the heat and pressure created from the firing, it will form spheroidal-shaped particles that will deposit on the surrounding surfaces, including the skin and clothing of the shooter and other individuals present. This gunshot residue (GSR)[25] consists of partially burnt and unburnt residues of the propellant powder, the primer, and metals from the cartridge. It may deposit on the hands of the shooter or individuals in close proximity to the discharging firearm. GSR may also be found on items along the path of the projectile, depositing detectable residues on the clothing or skin of shooting victims, or on items in close proximity to the discharging firearm. Gunshot residue examination may provide important information concerning the shooting:[26]

---

[22] Kathleen A. Savage & Greg Freed, "Firearm Examiner Training" (available at: http://projects.nfstc.org/firearms/module01/fir_m01.htm)(last accessed September 29, 2016).

[23] SWGGUN Guidelines for Trigger Pull Analysis, November 14, 2006 (available at: www.swggun.org).

[24] The following article contains a comprehensive review of all major aspects of GSR analysis: O. Dalby, D. Butler & J.W. Birkett, "Analysis of Gunshot Residue and Associated Materials," 55(4) J. Forensic Sci. 924–943 (2010).

For an overview of GSR techniques *see* Arie Zeichner, "Firearm Discharge Residue: Analysis of," in WILEY ENCYCLOPEDIA OF FORENSIC SCIENCE, (Jamieson A. & Moenssens A.A., eds) 2009 & online updates.

[25] Other terms are also used, e.g., cartridge discharge residue, firearm discharge residue. See J.S. Wallace and J. McQuillan, "Discharge residues from cartridge-operated industrial tools," 24 J. Forensic Sci. Soc. 495–508 (1984); J. Flynn et al., "Evaluation of X-Ray Micro-Fluorescence Spectrometry for the Elemental Analysis of Firearm Discharge Residues," 97 Forensic Sci. Int'l 21–36 (1998).

[26] Kyla L. Kersh, James M. Childers, Dale Justice & Greg Karim, "Detection of Gunshot Residue on Dark-Colored Clothing Prior to Chemical Analysis," 59 J. Forensic Sci. 754–762 (2014) at p. 755.

(a)   determination of entry and exit wounds;[27]

(b)   estimations of shooting distance;

(c)   establishment of the type of ammunition used;[28]

(d)   the trace of the projectile trajectory;

(e)   relation of the individual to the shooting incident;[29] and,

(f)   incorporation of the above elements into the reconstruction of the [event].

Two of the most commonly conducted examinations—GSR on hands and distance determinations—will be discussed further.

a.   GSR on Hands

In 1933 Theodoro Gonzalez of Mexico announced that he had developed a test to detect the GSR on hands. Gonzalez's test, known as the "paraffin test" (or dermal nitrate test), consisted of making a paraffin cast of one or both of an individual's hands and then treating the inside area of the cast with drops of diphenylamine in a concentrated solution of sulphuric acid. The chemical solution will react by turning dark blue in the presence of nitrates. The theory behind the test was that if a reaction occurred in the form of dark blue pinpoint specks, it was considered evidence of recent gun firing. The limitation of this theory was that similar reactions could result from the presence of other substances containing nitrates. Research established that many people who had never fired a gun but whose profession, occupation, or happenstance brought them in contact with nitrates yielded positive reactions to the test. Among them are photographers, engravers, match workers, and farmers. At the first seminar on scientific aspects of police work conducted by the International Criminal Police (Interpol) in 1963, the participating experts of the several countries unanimously rejected the dermal nitrate test as without value, not only as evidence in court, but even as furnishing workable investigative leads to the police.[30]

---

[27]   GSR from the passage of a bullet will deposit around an entrance hole (bullet wipe)and is an important means of distinguishing bullet entrance holes/wounds from exit holes/wounds. P. Bergman and E. Springer, "Bullet Hole Identification Kit: Case Report," 32(3) J. Forensic Sci. 802–805 (1987).

[28]   Based on the proportions of lead, antimony, and barium present in the GSR, the chemical class of the primer can be determined to assist in differentiating various types of ammunition. Z. Brozek-Mucha and A. Jankowicz, "Evaluation of the Possibility of Differentiation between Various Types of Ammunition by Means of GSR Examination with SEM-EDX Method," 123 Forensic Sci Int'l 39–47 (2001).

[29]   Research supports conclusions that individuals within 3 feet of the shooting are likely to have GSR on their hands while individuals beyond 10 feet from the shooting are not likely to have GSR on their hands. Michael Trimpe, "The Current Status of GSR Examinations," FBI Law Enforcement Bulletin, May 2011, pp. 24–32.

[30]   Note, INTERN. CRIM. POL. REV., Jan. 1964, p. 28. See also Henry W. Turkel and Jerome Lipman, "Unreliability of Dermal Nitrate Test for Gunpowder," 46 J. CRIM. L., CRIMINOL. & P.S. 281 (1955).

Another color test, much more specific than the dermal nitrate test, was suggested by Harrison and Gilroy.[31] Instead of nitrates from gunpowder residue, their test detected the presence of antimony, barium, and lead in primer residues. The Harrison-Gilroy test did not gain wide acceptance among crime laboratories mainly because its detection levels are not sufficiently low to make it adequately sensitive to detect the tenths of a microgram amounts of gunshot residues. The colors developed tend to be unstable and interference has been encountered in the color reactions of the three elements when tested simultaneously.[32] Additionally, the three component particles tested (lead, antimony, and barium) have not been proven to be unique to primer gunshot residue.[33] The production of non-toxic (lead-free) ammunition, which replaces lead in the primer with a wide variety of elements (such as strontium, potassium, silicon, and titanium), has also complicated the chemical analysis of GSR.[34]

Today, scanning electron microscopy/energy-dispersive x-ray spectrometry (SEM/EDS or SEM/EDX)[35] is the most common method used for searching for gunshot primer residues. SEM/EDS is a non-destructive method that provides both morphological information and the chemical composition of individual particles within a sample. The method has the ability to detect primer residues by their distinctive morphology derived from gunshot residues as opposed to other non-firearm related sources for those inorganic elements.[36] SEM/EDS analysis is also a very

---

[31] Harold C. Harrison and Robert Gilroy, "Firearms Discharge Residues," 4 J. FORENSIC SCI. 184 (1959). *But see*, K. S. Pillay, "New Method for the Collection and Analysis of Gunshot Residues as Forensic Evidence," 19 J. FORENSIC SCI. 769 (1974).

[32] John H. Dillon, "A Modified Griess Test: A Chemically Specific Chromophic Test for Nitrite Compounds in Gunshot Residues," 22 A.F.T.E. J. 243 (Oct. 1990).

[33] Michael Trimpe, "The Current Status of GSR Examinations," FBI Law Enforcement Bulletin, May 2011, pp. 24–32.

[34] Seth R. Hogg, Brian C. Hunter and Ruth Waddell Smith, "Elemental Characterization and Discrimination of Nontoxic Ammunition Using Scanning Electron Microscopy with Energy Dispersive X-Ray Analysis and Principal Components Analysis," 61 J. Forensic Sci. 35–42 (2016).

[35] Scanning electron microscopy with energy dispersive x-ray spectrometry uses a focused electron beam scanned over the surface of a sample and measures the energy dispersed by the emitting x-rays. The technique is nondestructive, fast, and useful with small samples. See generally Jan Andrasko and L. C. Maehly, "Detection of Gunshot Residues on Hands by Scanning Electron Microscope," 22 J. FORENSIC SCI. 279 (1977); Kage Shigetoshi *et al.*, "A Simple Method for Detection of Gunshot Residue Particles from Hands, Hair, Face, and Clothing Using Scanning Electron Microscopy/Wavelength Dispersive X-Ray (SEM/WDX)," 46 J. FORENSIC SCI. 830 (2001); Jozef Lebiedzik and David L. Johnson, "Rapid Search and Quantitative Analysis of Gunshot Residue Particles in the SEM," 45 J. FORENSIC SCI. 83 (2000). *See also* A. J. Schwoeble and David L. David, *Current Methods in Forensic Gunshot Residue Analysis*, 2000.

[36] Research has shown environmental sources, such as brake pad linings, fireworks, or paints, can produce particles that resemble characteristic primer GSR. M. Morelato et al., "Screening of Gunshot Residue Using Desorption Electrospray Ionisation-Mass Spectrometry (DESI-MS)," 217 (1–3) Forensic Sci. Int'l 101–106 (2012).

sensitive technique, able to detect a single primer GSR particle among thousands of non-primer GSR particles.[37]

SEM/EDS is like other tests for gunshot residue in that a finding of the trace metals does not necessarily mean that the suspect has fired a gun. The presence of gunshot residue on hands is not an indicator exclusively of the firing of a gun. Merely handling a weapon, being in close proximity to a firing gun,[38] or secondary transfer[39] may result in detectable GSR on a person's hands. Additionally, the persistence of GSR on hands varies greatly, primarily based on the physical activities taking place after the shooting incident. Residue particles may be both removed and transferred through direct action (e.g., washing, wiping, or rubbing hands) and other circumstances (e.g., excessive sweating, weather conditions).[40] The challenges with expert witness testimony concerning gunshot residue derive from the fact that while the examiner can report that the detected particles may have come from a fired weapon, the examiner cannot say how the particles were deposited. The Scientific Working Group for Gunshot Residue (SWGGSR) developed voluntary guidelines for the analysis of primer gunshot residue by SEM/EDS using automated and manual methods.[41] The comprehensive guidelines include recommendations concerning procedures, results interpretation, and expert witness testimony. The guidelines caution that any

[37] Leah Ali, Kyle Brown, Holly Castellano, and Stephanie J. Wetzel, "A Study of the Presence of Gunshot Residue in Pittsburgh Police Stations Using SEM.EDS and LC-MS.MS," 61 J. Forensic Sci. 928–938 (2016) at p. 929 (internal citation omitted).

[38] Research has shown that individuals up to three feet from the side of the shooter will probably have GSR present on their hands. Michael Trimpe, "The Current Status of GSR Examinations," FBI Law Enforcement Bulletin, May 2011, pp. 24–32.

[39] N. Geusens and S. Charles, "A Study of the Potential Risk of Gunshot Residue Transfer from Special Units of the Police to Arrested Suspects," 216 Forensic Sci. Int'l 78–81 (2012); R.E. Bork, S.A. Rochowicz, M. Wong and M.A. Kopina, "Gunshot Residue in Chicago Police Vehicles and Facilities: An Empirical Study," 52(4) J. Forensic Sci. 838–841 (2007); Dean M. Gialamas, E.F. Rhodes, and L.A. Sugarman, "Officers, Their Weapons and Their Hands: An Empirical Study of GSR on the Hands of Non-Shooting Police Officers," 40(6) J. Forensic Sci. 1086–1089 (1995).

[40] Romain Gauriot et al., "Statistical Challenges in the Quantitation of Gunshot Residue Evidence," 58 J. Forensic Sci. 1149–1155 (2013).

[41] SWGGSR, "Guide for Primer Gunshot Residue Analysis by Scanning Electron Microscopy/Energy Dispersive X-Ray Spectrometry," November 29, 2011 (available at: swggsr.org).

See also ASTM E1588-16a "Standard Practice for Gunshot Residue Analysis by Scanning Electron Microscopy/Energy Dispersive X-Ray Spectrometry" (available at: https://www.astm.org/Standards/E1588.htm)(last accessed September 26, 2016). In accordance with the ASTM guideline, for a particle to be described as "characteristic of" primer GSR, the particle must contain lead (Pb), barium (Ba), and antimony (Sb), while possessing the distinctive morphology and within a specified size range. A particle may be described as "consistent with" primer GSR if it contains only two of the three elements, has the distinctive morphology, and meets the size specifications. A particle is described as "commonly associated with" primer GSR when it contains only one of the elements, has the distinctive morphology, and meets the size specifications.

The National Institute of Standards and Technology Organization of Scientific Area Committee has formed a Gunshot Residue Subcommittee to transition the work of the SWGGSR to standards for the forensic science community. Until new standards and guidelines are adopted by the Gunshot Residue Subcommittee, the voluntary SWGGSR guidelines and ASTM Standard remain in effect.

limitations of the conclusions must be described and provide the following examples of acceptable conclusions:

Example: Particles containing barium/antimony, lead/barium, or lead/antimony were found on the lifts from John Doe. Such particles are found in primer residue, but also may originate from other sources.

Example: Primer residue can be deposited on the hands by circumstances such as firing a weapon, handling a weapon, being in the proximity of the discharge of a weapon or coming into contact with an object that has primer residue on it. The examination itself cannot determine the relative likelihood of these listed circumstances.

Example: The presence of primer residue on an item is consistent with that item having been in the vicinity of a firearm when it was discharged or having come in contact with primer residue on another item.

Example: The absence of gunshot residue on a person's hands does not eliminate that person from having discharged a firearm.

Example: The absence of primer residue on the hands is consistent with an individual not having fired a weapon. A negative result could also occur from circumstances such as washing the hands, wiping the hands, wearing gloves, sweating profusely, environmental factors including wind and rain, bloody hands, excessive debris on the sample, normal physical activity within 4 to 6 hours passing between firing and sampling, or the weapon not producing primer residue on the hands when discharged.[42]

b. Distance Determinations

The reconstruction of the shooting incident to differentiate among scenarios of accident, self-defense, suicide, and homicide in a shooting may involve a determination of the distance between the gun muzzle and the victim's clothing or skin. Besides the projectile (shot or bullet), other elements are ejected from the muzzle of the gun at the time of firing. Depending upon the kind of ammunition used, partially burned/unburned powder, soot and/or vaporous lead, nitrite residues, and other particulate metals are ejected a distance consistent with each component's physical properties and with air resistance. The residue pattern observed may indicate the general category of shot involved and may be replicated using the same firearm and ammunition to approximate a muzzle-to-target distance involved in the shooting.

---

[42] SWGGSR, "Guide for Primer Gunshot Residue Analysis by Scanning Electron Microscopy/Energy Dispersive X-Ray Spectrometry," November 29, 2011 at pp. 28–30.

Examination of autopsy photographs/reports or clothing through which a gunshot is suspected to have passed may result in a categorization of the gunshot based on muzzle-to-target distance as: a distant shot, a close range shot, or a contact shot. A distant shot does not deposit residues on the target. Close range shots deposit residues around the area of entry, causing tattooing or stippling. A contact shot displays burns where the weapon's muzzle connected with the surface of the target; very little gunshot residue will be found around the entrance hole, but will be present along the bullet track in the underlying tissues through which it has passed. In some circumstances, the examiner may be able to further approximate the muzzle-to-target distance through additional examination of the actual firearm and similar ammunition.

SWGGUN adopted "Guidelines for Gunshot Residue Distance Determinations" (SWGGUN Gunshot Distance Guidelines) that provide for protocols for such examinations.[43] The guidelines utilize microscopic examination, chemical processing, and distance comparison tests. Microscopic observations consistent with the passage of a bullet are a hole in the item and bullet wipe (a ring of GSR around the perimeter of the hole). Microscopic observations consistent with the discharge of a firearm are: vaporous lead (smoke), particulate lead, unburned gunpowder, and melted/adhering gunpowder. Microscopic observations indicative of a contact shot are: ripping, tearing, burning, singeing, melted synthetic fibers in fabrics, and heavy vaporous lead residues. Further analysis through chemical testing[44] may detect various types of gunshot residues and may produce an observable gunshot residue dispersion pattern.[45] When a suspected gun is obtained, as well as ammunition of the same type and brand as was used to produce the residue, a series of firings can produce test patterns from various distances for comparison purposes. By comparing the distance test patterns with the pattern found on the victim's clothing or on some other object, an examiner may be able to approximate the distance range at which the shot was fired. If no residue is detected, the relevant distance determination may be the "drop off"—the maximum distance from which

---

[43] SWGGUN, "Guidelines for Gunshot Residue Distance Determinations," February 18, 2013 version (available at www.swggun.org).

[44] '[A]ny GSR examination [of elemental composition (such as SEM/EDS)], must be performed prior to chemical testing, because the chemical testing could be destructive." Kyla L. Kersh, James M. Childers, Dale Justice and Greg Karim, "Detection of Gunshot Residue on Dark-Colored Clothing Prior to Chemical Analysis," 59 J. Forensic Sci. 754–762 (2014).

[45] SWGGUN, "Guidelines for Gunshot Residue Distance Determinations," February 18, 2013 version at sections 3.4–3.6.

There are several chemical tests that may be used, including:

[T[he Modified Greiss Test is used to detect the presence of nitrite, the Sodium Rhodizonate Test to detect the presence of lead and the Rubeanic Acid Test to detect the presence of copper, the latter being found in full metal jacket ammunition. All of these tests are based on chemical color reactions.

Monika H. Seltenhammer et al., "Does the Prior Application of the Field Kit Bullet Hole Testing Kit 3 on a Suspected Bullet Hole Bias the Analysis of Atomic Absorption Spectrophotometry," 59 J. Forensic Sci. 1364–1367 (2014) at p. 1364.

residues are discharged from the firearm—to support a conclusion that the firing distance was at least as far as this point.[46]

Several studies have concluded that the distance from the muzzle to the target in shotgun firings can be determined by examining the spread patterns of the pellets. In one such study, using a 12 gauge shotgun with 00 and 0 buckshot, firing tests were made at varying distances while averages and standard deviations of the spread patterns were made. The standard deviation was 50–60 percent for mean values of distance between buckshot and 20–30 percent for mean values of pattern diameter. The study also showed evidence of poor test results when only a few holes of the spread pattern are available.[47] More recent studies have also shown a correlation between the degree of choke and pellet dispersion.[48]

Distance determinations cannot be reduced to a formula or table.[49] Although the cloud of gaseous discharge forms a roughly cone-shaped figure, the spread, shape, and density of the pattern depend on many factors which require, for proper evaluation, extensive experience and experimentation. Different combinations of gun and ammunition influence the pattern at any given distance. Any factor or variable which affects the burning rate and pressure characteristics of gun powders may result in a powder pattern variance. Thus variations in the length of the barrel, the gap between cylinder and barrel, and the fit of the bullet in the barrel may change the pattern even though the weapon tested is of the same make and model as that which produced the evidence pattern. In fact, even ammunition of the same make but of different manufactured lots can produce variations in spread and density of the pattern, even when fired from the same gun. Consequently, evidence of this nature must be introduced with appropriate limitations expressed in the conclusions. SWGGUN guidelines note:

---

[46] Id. at section 3.7.

[47] Alfonsi, et al., "Shooting Distance Estimation for Shots Fired by a Shotgun Loaded with Buckshot Cartridges", 25 Forensic Sci. Int'l 83 (1984). Other studies have developed mathematical formulas to help determine the muzzle to target distance by the dimensions of the spread pattern. Chugh, "Mathematical Analysis of Dispersion of Pellets Fired From a Shot Gun," 32 Forensic Sci. Int'l 93 (1986); Nag & Lahiri, "An Evaluation of Distribution of Pellets Due to Shotgun Discharge," 32 Forensic Sci. Int'l 151 (1986).

[48] M. Mustafa Arslan, Hakan Kar, Bulent Uner and Gursel Cetin, "Firing Distance Estimates with Pellet Dispersion from Shotgun with Various Chokes: An Experimental, Comparative Study," 56 J. FORENSIC SCI. 988–992 (2011).

[49] Mathematical formulations have previously been reported in the effort to give greater quantitative definition to the muzzle to target distance assessment. Deinet & Leszlynski, "Examinations to Determine Close-Range Firing Distances Using a Process Control Computer," 31 Forensic Sci. Int'l 41 (1986). In fact, what actually occurs is only an approximation. A very comprehensive survey of "Methods for the Determination of Shooting Distance" is presented by W. Lichtenberg in 2 FORENSIC SCI. REV. 35 (June 1990). For more recent "improved" approaches, see Baruch Glattstein et al., "Improved Method for Shooting Distance Determination, Part I, Bullet Holes in Clothing Items," 45 J. FORENSIC SCI. 801 (2000), and Baruch Glattstein et al., "Improved Method for Shooting Distance Determination, Part II, Bullet Holes in Objects that Cannot Be Processed in the Laboratory," 45 J. FORENSIC SCI. 1000 (2000).

Gunshot residue distance determinations are a result of residues detected on an item of evidence. The absence of residues is not a basis for expressing a distance determination. The examiner should understand that shooting events are dynamic and must consider the possibility of intervening objects when determining a maximum (drop-off) distance for gunshot residue deposits.[50]

When reproducing residue patterns (powder particles or vaporous lead), it is essential that the suspect firearm and similar ammunition be used for the distance tests to accurately reproduce residue patterns. Factors affecting the pattern of residues include, but are not limited to, ammunition, barrel length, caliber, and powder type/charge.[51]

3. SERIAL NUMBER RESTORATION

The serial number of a firearm can be an important investigative tool. In tracing the manufacture and sale of a firearm, one of the most valuable resources in an investigation can be the National Tracing Center of the Bureau of Alcohol, Tobacco, Firearms and Explosives.[52] The Bureau's capability allows an investigator to trace a weapon directly from the manufacturer to a licensed dealer. In some instances, the National Tracing Center has been used to link the firearm directly to a suspect, while in other instances the tracing information can help identify the firearm as being stolen, leading to the firearm's return to its rightful owner.[53] Investigators sometimes encounter firearms from which the original serial numbers have been obliterated, making tracing the guns more difficult. It is occasionally possible, through various chemical or other techniques, to reveal the number that has been eradicated.[54]

Methods for serial number restoration on metallic firearms include polishing, which can be effective independently, but is more often used in conjunction with other processes; magnetic particle inspection; and chemical etching. Magnetic particle restoration is a non-destructive

---

[50] SWGGUN, "Guidelines for Gunshot Residue Distance Determinations," February 18, 2013 version, at section 3.6.

[51] Id. at section 3.7.1.

[52] For information about the National Tracing Center *see*: https://www.atf.gov/firearms/national-tracing-center (last accessed September 27, 2016).

[53] A good discussion of the Bureau's current tracing abilities can be found in Bureau of Alcohol, Tobacco, Firearms and Explosives, "Firearm Tracing Guide: Tracing Recovered Firearms to Reduce Violent Crime," ATF P 3312.13, March 2012 (available at: https://www.atf.gov/firearms/national-tracing-center)(last accessed September 27, 2016).

[54] *See generally* Nicholas R. Maiden, "Serial Number Restoration: Firearm" in WILEY ENCYCLOPEDIA OF FORENSIC SCIENCE, (Jamieson A. & Moenssens A.A., eds) 2009 & online updates.

Many methods used to obliterate a serial number can severely hamper, or completely frustrate, the recovery of the serial number. One very simple method is overstamping. A counterfeit serial number is restamped over the area in which the filed or ground original serial number was located. If the counterfeit serial numbers are not located directly over the original numbers, recovery of the original numbers is still possible.

technique used prior to chemical processes. The method exploits the fact that the magnetic properties of deformed metal are different from that of the unworked surrounding metal. After polishing the surfaces, a suspension of magnetic particles is applied to the object. It is then magnetized by directly applying a magnetic field (through a horseshoe magnet or an electro-magnetic yoke).[55] If polishing and magnetic processes do not reveal the serial number, chemical etching may be used. The chemical etchant used will depend on the material in question.[56] The etching solution is applied by pipette or cotton swab and rubbed across the area with a cotton swab. If characters become discernible, distilled water may be applied to slow or stop the oxidation process and allow for examination.[57]

§4.07   COMPARISON ANALYSIS

The foundation of firearm and toolmark comparison analysis is premised on the assumption that no two tools should have, or produce, the same microscopic marks that would cause the origin of the marks to be misinterpreted. The comparison analysis relies on human pattern recognition and the subjective assessment of the examiner as to whether the marks are sufficiently distinctive and similar to identify the source. The "uniqueness" of the microscopic marks is supported by studies involving consecutively manufactured tools and firearms.[58] The accuracy of the "human factor" continues to be studied.[59]

Comparison analysis for firearms and toolmarks, like fingerprint analysis, involves side-by-side comparison of class and individual characteristics. Class characteristics are measurable features of a specimen which indicate a restricted group source. For firearms and tools, class characteristics result from design factors, and are therefore determined prior to manufacture. Class characteristics are not sufficient to identify a particular weapon as having fired a specific bullet or cartridge case, though they may permit a rapid classification process for

---

[55] Turley, "Restoration of Stamp Marks on Steel Components by Etching and Magnetic Techniques," 32 J. Forensic Sci. 640 (1987); Wolfer et al., "Application of Magnetic Principles to the Restoration of Serial Numbers," 50 J.CRIM.L.CRIMINOL. & P.S. 519 (1960); Cook, "Obliterated Serial Numbers," 7 A.F.T.E. J. 27 (Mar. 1975); Polk & Giessen, "Metallurgical Aspects of Serial Number Recovery," 7 A.F.T.E. J. 37 (July 1975).

[56] For steel, Fry's Reagent (5g cupric chloride, 60ml water, 30 ml ammonium hydroxide, and 60ml hydrochloric acid) has proven to be the most sensitive and able to restore erased die stamped marks. Annalisa Fortini, Mattia Merlin, Chiara Soffritti, and Gian L. Garagnani, 61 J. For. Science 160–169 (2016).

[57] John Thornton et al., "The Mechanism of the Restoration of Obliterated Serial Numbers by Acid Etching," 16 J. FORENSIC SCI. SOC. 69 (1976). See also Cook, "Chemical Etching Reagents for Serial Number Restoration," 7 A.F.T.E. J. 80 (July 1975).

[58] James E. Hamby, Stephen Norris & Nicholas D.K. Petraco, "Evaluation of GLOCK 9mm Firing Pin Aperture Shear Mark Individuality Based on 1,632 Different Pistols by Traditional Pattern Matching and IBIS Pattern Recognition," 61 J. Forensic Sci. 170–176 (2016).

[59] Tasha P. Smith, G. Andrew Smith and Jeffrey B. Snipes, "A Validation Study of Bullet and Cartridge Case Comparisons Using Samples Representative of Actual Casework," 61 J. Forensic Sci. 939–946 (2016).

screening fired bullets and cartridge cases. A difference in class characteristics may support an exclusion of a firearm or tool as the source. Individual characteristics are imperfections or irregularities produced accidentally during manufacturing or caused by wear or use. Firearms and toolmark examiners use individual characteristics to distinguish a specific weapon or tool from all others in its class.

The Association of Firearm and Tool Mark Examiners, an international organization for practitioners of firearm and toolmark identification, issued the following "Theory of Identification as it Relates to Toolmarks" to detail the scientific foundations of the comparison methodology:

1. The theory of identification as it pertains to the comparison of toolmarks enables opinions of common origin to be made when the unique surface of two toolmarks are in "sufficient agreement."

2. This "sufficient agreement" is related to the significant duplication of random toolmarks as evidence by the correspondence of pattern or combination of patterns of surface contours. Significance is determined by the comparative examination of two or more sets of surface contour patterns comprised of individual peaks, ridges and furrows. Specifically, the relative height or depth, width, curvature and spatial relationship of the individual peaks, ridges and furrows within one set of surface contours are defined and compare to the corresponding features in the second set of surface contours. Agreement is significant when the agreement in individual characteristics exceeds the best agreement demonstrated between toolmarks known to have been produced by different tools and is consistent with agreement demonstrated by toolmarks known to have been produced by the same tool. The statement that "sufficient agreement" exists between two toolmarks means that the agreement of individual characteristics is of a quantity and quality that the likelihood another tool could have made the mark is so remote as to be considered a practical impossibility.

3. Currently the interpretation of individualization/ identification is subjective in nature, founded on scientific principles and based on the examiner's training and experience.[60]

---

[60] Association of Firearm and Tool Mark Examiners, "Theory of Identification as it Relates to Tool Marks: Revised," 43 AFTE J. 287 (2011)(available at: https://afte.org/about-us/what-is-afte/afte-theory-of-identification (last accessed September 28, 2016).

The AFTE Range of Conclusions was developed by the Criteria for Identification Committee and adopted by the Association membership at its annual business meeting in April 1992:

1. Identification

    Agreement of a combination of individual characteristics and all discernible class characteristics where the extent of agreement exceeds that which can occur in the comparison of toolmarks made by different tools and is consistent with the agreement demonstrated by toolmarks known to have been produced by the same tool.

2. Inconclusive

    a. Some agreement of individual characteristics and all discernible class characteristics, but insufficient for an identification.

    b. Agreement of all discernible class characteristics without agreement or disagreement of individual characteristics due to an absence, insufficiency, or lack of reproducibility.

    c. Agreement of all discernible class characteristics and disagreement of individual characteristics, but insufficient for an elimination.

3. Elimination

    Significant disagreement of discernible class characteristics and/or individual characteristics.

4. Unsuitable

    Unsuitable for examination.[61]

SWGGUN has promulgated several guidelines for comparison analysis, including Guidelines for the Standardization of Comparison Documentation, Guidelines: Criteria for Identification, Guidelines for the Documentation of Firearm Examinations, and Guidelines for the Documentation of the Examination of Tools and Toolmarks.[62] In June 2016, the Department of Justice Proposed Uniform Language for Testimony and Reports in a number of forensic science disciplines, however, firearms and toolmark examination was one of the two disciplines specifically unaddressed.[63]

In an effort to develop objective standards and increase the efficiency of firearm analyses, attention in the field of firearm examination is shifting to automated computer imaging systems—Integrated Ballistics

---

[61] https://afte.org/about-us/what-is-afte/afte-range-of-conclusions (last accessed September 28, 2016).

[62] Available at: www.swggun.org.

[63] *See* https://www.federalregister.gov/documents/2016/07/25/2016-17551/notice-of-public-com ment-period-on-proposed-uniform-language-for-testimony-and-reports (last accessed September 30, 2016).

Identification Systems (IBIS).[64] In 1999 the ATF established the National Integrated Ballistic Information Network (NIBIN) to automate Program automates firearm comparison evaluations and provide potential links between unsolved crimes. "NIBIN is the only interstate automated ballistic imaging network in operation in the United States and is available to most major population centers in the United States."[65] Like the automated fingerprint identification systems established to assist with print identifications, the automated ballistics imaging systems "giv[e] firearms examiners the ability to screen virtually unlimited numbers of bullets and cartridge casings for possible matches."[66] Digital images of test-fired or evidence cartridge cases/shotshell casings are entered into the database and searched against earlier entries. The automated system assists, but does not replace, the work of the examiner. The system produces "high confidence candidate" images ("hits") that are referred to a firearms examiner for the final comparison.[67] As of March, 2016, NIBIN has approximately 2.8 million images and has resulted in more than 74,000 "hits" that were confirmed by trained firearm examiners.[68]

1.   BULLETS

When a bullet travels through a rifled barrel, the bearing (exterior) surface of the bullet comes in contact with the interior surface of the barrel and may acquire the class and individual characteristics of the barrel. Since there is no practical way of making a comparison directly between the imperfections and irregularities within a barrel and the reverse impressions on a bullet, the firearm examiner fires a series of test bullets[69] from the suspected weapon and then uses the test bullets instead of the gun barrel for comparison. In order to secure a comparison test bullet without damaging its individual characteristics or distorting

---

[64] *See* Fabiano Riva and Christophe Champod, "Automatic Comparison and Evaluation of Impressions Left by a Firearm on Fired Cartridge Cases," 59 J. Forensic Sci. 637–647 (2014); Yan Yang, Avi Koffman, Gil Hocherman and Lawrence M. Wein, "Using Spatial, Temporal and Evidence-status Data to Improve Ballistic Imaging Performance," 59 J. Forensic Sci. 103–111 (2014). *See also* Brian J. Heard, *Handbook of Firearms and Ballistics,* 2nd ed., Wiley-Blackwell, 2008; David L. Faigman, *et al.,* Modern Scientific Evidence: The Law and Science of Expert Testimony, 2011–2012 ed., West, 2011, Vol. 4, pp. 641–730.

[65] https://www.atf.gov/firearms/national-integrated-ballistic-information-network-nibin.

[66] Richard E. Tontarski and Robert M. Thompson, "Automated Firearms Evidence Comparison: A Forensic Tool in Firearm Identification—An Update," 43 J. Forensic Sci. 641 (1998).

[67] Paul C. Giannelli, Edward J. Imwinkelried and Joseph L. Peterson, "Reference Guide on Forensic Identification Expertise," in *Reference Manual on Scientific Evidence*, 3rd ed., National Academies Press: Washington DC, 2011 at p. 95.

[68] https://www.atf.gov/resource-center/fact-sheet/fact-sheet-national-integrated-ballistic-information-network

Other computer ballistic identification systems are used in other countries. Ilker Kara, "Investigation of Ballistic Evidence through an Automatic Image Analysis and Identification System," 61 J. Forensic Sci. 775–781 (2016).

[69] Test cartridges should reasonably correspond to the essentials of the evidence bullet. Finding the manufacturer of ammunition therefore becomes essential. Ruprecht Nennstiel, "The Determination of the Manufacturer of Ammunition," 31 J. FORENSIC SCI. INT'L 1 (1986).

its shape, the test bullet is fired into a specially constructed box filled with soft material such as cotton waste (a "bullet trap") or water (a "bullet recovery tank").[70] After making a preliminary examination to determine the test bullet's various class characteristics (lands, grooves, etc.), the examiner conducts a microscopic examination of the individual characteristics of both bullets.

The firearm examination uses a binocular comparison microscope,[71] which is essentially two separate microscopes mounted side by side and fitted with a comparison bridge in which there is an arrangement of lenses and prisms that produces a single composite image of objects as they appear in the field of each microscope. The evidence bullet is placed under one microscope and the test bullet under the other. The bullets are mounted horizontally by means of a plastic substance on cylindrical adjustable holders. After the two bullets are mounted in the comparison microscope, the usual practice is for the examiner to scrutinize the entire surface of the evidence bullet at relatively low magnifications for the purpose of locating the most prominent group of striations. Once such marks are located on the evidence bullet, that bullet is permitted to remain stationary. Then the examiner rotates the test bullet in an attempt to find a corresponding area with individual characteristics that match those on the evidence bullet. If what appears to be a match is located, the examiner rotates both bullets simultaneously to determine whether similar coincidences exist on the other portions of the bullets. A careful study of all of the detail on both bullets ultimately contributes to the conclusion as to a common origin. While the binocular comparison microscopy has changed little in the past few decades, advanced digital photography now permits detailed imaging of the comparison through scanning electron microscopy, 2D and 3D laser scanning, and thermal infrared imaging.[72]

Figure 7 illustrates how two bullets fired through the same barrel appear when viewed through the comparison microscope. The photographs show portions of the evidence and test bullets side by side, separated by a fine hairline in each illustration, with characteristics on both bullets in matching positions.

---

[70] Water tanks are popular, but present their own problems, including algae formation and ricochet. For a comprehensive reference on topics covered in this chapter *see* Brian J. Heard, *Handbook of Firearms and Ballistics,* 2nd ed. New York: Wiley-Blackwell, 2008.

[71] The inventor of the comparison microscope is said to be Alexander von Inostranzeff. *See* John Thornton, "Some Historical Notes on the Comparison Microscope," 10 A.F.T.E.J. 71 (Mar. 1978); Beck, "Alexander von Inostranzell and the Technical Development of Optical Comparison Systems," 21 A.F.T.E.J. 317 (Jan. 1989).

[72] Darrell Stein and Jorn Chi Chung Yu, "The Use of Near-Infrared Photography to Image Fired Bullets and Cartridge Cases," 58 J. Forensic Sci. 1330 (2013).

The admission of firearm examiner testimony based on analysis using 3D imaging has been upheld. State v. Foshay, 370 P.3d 618, 239 Ariz. 271 (2016).

Figure 7: A is a photomicrograph showing two bullets in match position at relatively low magnification. B illustrates the match position of only a small portion of the same bullet at higher magnification.

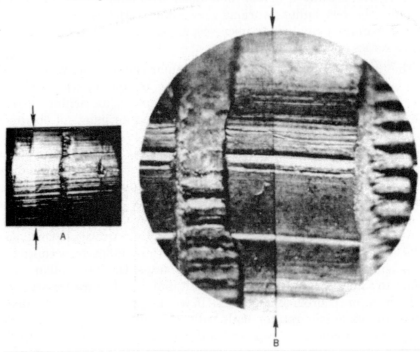

Typically, firearm examiners do not require a predetermined number of points of similarity between the evidence and the test bullets and follow the conclusion guidelines recommended by the AFTE. Additionally, discrepancies in the individual characteristics will not necessarily eliminate the firearm as the source of the bullet. Even if bullets are fired in succession from the same weapon, not all individual characteristics may be identical. There may be some striations caused by powder residues and other surface factors or marks caused outside the barrel from contact or impact. Moreover, there may be other striations on the bullets which have no relationship to the interior of the barrel. For instance, there might be marks on metal-cased bullets due to imperfections on the interior of the sizing die used in the fabrication of the bullet. Obviously, the presence or absence of such marks, whether duplicated or not, must be taken into consideration by the examiner.

2. CARTRIDGE CASES

The combustion of the propellant in a cartridge produces gases which propel the projectile(s) from the cartridge and through the barrel toward the target. Pressure emanating from the expanding gases within the cartridge case is sufficiently violent to force the case against the breech face and the chamber walls. The characteristics thus imprinted on the cartridge case are the basis of identification of a suspect weapon.

Identification of a cartridge case as having been fired in a particular firearm is dependent upon the same principles of probability as govern bullet identification. In many instances the cartridge case is more easily identifiable than the bullet. Recoil pressure of the powder gases forces the brass or nickel cartridge case against the steel breech block or bolt of the firearm with the result that the striation irregularities present on the steel surface are imprinted onto the base and sides of the cartridge case. The striations of the breech face are produced by hand filing of the breech surface.

Also during the manufacturing process, marks are acquired on a gun's firing pin and on its ejector and extractor. The shape of the indentation caused by the firing pin or hammer is a characteristic peculiar to the firearm. It can aid in identifying a particular firearm but is not always conclusive. The firing pin on center fire firearms is customarily rounded. Some exceptions are the rectangular and the "Glock" shaped firing pins which are found on a few center fire firearms. A firing pin, either by static contact or through a sliding action which produces scrape marks, may also leave individual impressions or striations on the cartridge case which may be used to link the ammunition to a firearm.[73] Similarly, the extractor and ejector may leave characteristic marks on the cartridge case.[74]

3. TOOLMARKS

Toolmark comparison uses the same techniques and decision making criteria as that used in firearm examination.[75] The beginning of a toolmark examination is the proper collection and preservation of the initial mark at a scene. Tools or other implements used for cutting metal or for turning or prying objects apart have edges with ridges and hollows created either in the process of manufacture or by wear in the use of the tool.[76] These ridges and hollows often leave impressions or striations on the material to which they are applied. The obvious gross impressions may only indicate the nature of the tool or implement used.

---

[73] G. P. Sharma, "The Importance of Firing Pin Impressions in the Identification of Firearms," 54 J. CRIM. L. CRIMINOL. & P.S. 378 (1963), G. P. Sharma, "Firing Pin Scrape Marks and the Identification of Firearms," 57 J. CRIM. L. CRIMINOL. & P.S. 365 (1966).

[74] Unlike the firing pin impressions, the extractor and ejector marks alone may indicate only that the cartridge was loaded and removed from a particular firearm. Paul C. Giannelli, Edward J. Imwinkelried and Joseph L. Peterson, "Reference Guide on Forensic Identification Expertise," in *Reference Manual on Scientific Evidence*, 3rd ed., National Academies Press: Washington DC, 2011 at p. 95.

[75] As with firearm comparison analysis, the "uniqueness" of toolmark features has been studied through analysis of sequentially manufactured tools, *see* Ryan Spotts and Scott Chumbley, "Objective Analysis of Impressed Chisel Toolmarks," 60 J. Forensic Sci. 1436–1440 (2015), and the field has been integrating objective computer-based algorithms to assist the analysis. Ryan Spotts et al., "Angular Determination of Toolmarks Using a Computer-Generated Virtual Tool," 60 J. Forensic Sci. 878–884 (2015); Ryan Spotts et al., "Optimization of a Statistical Algorithm for Objective Comparison of Toolmarks," 60 J. Forensic Sci. 303–314 (2015).

[76] Nikolai Volkov, Nir Finkelstein, Yehuda Novoselsky and Tsadok Tsach, "Bolt Cutter Blade's Imprint in Toolmarks Examination," 60 J. Forensic Sci. 1589–1593 (2015).

Microscopically discernible marks may also be left which can be of great value in determining whether they were made by a particular tool. The results of comparisons with test marks and evidence marks will be given in the same range and with the same degree of certainty as might be rendered in any other area of opinion testimony.[77]

§4.08   SCIENTIFIC VALIDITY CHALLENGES

1.   2004 NAS REPORT (CABL)

When a firearm is not recovered or the ammunition components recovered have insufficient striations and other markings to permit comparison analysis, different approaches must be taken to attempt to link the evidence to an individual. In the mid-1900's, the Federal Bureau of Investigation (FBI) introduced an analytical technique which came to be known as CABL (compositional analysis of bullet lead) to attempt to link crime scene bullets or bullet fragments with recovered unused ammunition linked to a suspect. The CABL technique involved determining the concentrations of seven elements in the lead bullet alloy of the evidence ammunition and the ammunition linked to a suspect. If the elemental concentrations were statistically indistinguishable, the examiner concluded all of the ammunition came from the same "source." The underlying premise of the technique was that variations within the manufacturing process for each batch of bullets meant that separate batches of bullets were distinguishable. In testimony, FBI examiners stated or implied that the elemental composition of all bullets within a box of ammunition would be statistically indistinguishable from each other, but that different boxes of ammunition would be distinguishable.

In 2004, the National Academy of Science (NAS) released a report that examined the scientific validity of the CABL, *Forensic Analysis: Weighing Bullet Lead Evidence* (2004 NAS Report).[78] The report was intended to address three subjects: analytical method, statistics for comparison, and interpretation issues.[79] In conducting its review, the NAS committee reviewed the bullet manufacturing process and determined that the process did not support conclusions as stated by FBI examiners. In particular, the committee determined that the production methods were neither consistent nor predictable, resulting in bullets from different elemental mixtures being packaged in the same box of ammunition. The report found:

---

[77] The SWGGUN Guidelines on the Criteria for Identification discussed *supra* are applicable to toolmark examination conclusions.

[78] National Research Council of the National Academies, Committee on Scientific Assessment of Bullet Lead Elemental Composition Comparison, *Forensic Analysis: Weighing Bullet Lead Evidence,* National Academies Press: Washington, DC (2004).

[79] Id. at p. 2.

Variations among and within lead bullet manufacturers make any modeling of the general manufacturing process unreliable and potentially misleading in CABL comparisons.[80]

On September 1, 2005, the FBI announced that it had discontinued CABL examinations.[81] The scientific validity of CABL was discredited before it was used beyond the FBI Laboratory. After a spate of post-conviction challenges to the prior admission of such testimony,[82] the technique has not been widely discussed. The 2004 NAS Report, however, was not the last report discussing the scientific validity of aspects of firearms examination.

2.   2008 NAS REPORT

In 2004, the National Institute of Justice asked the National Research Council of the National Academy of Sciences to address the issues raised by computerized ballistic imaging technology. A committee was formed to "assess the feasibility, accuracy and reliability, and technical capability of developing and using a national ballistics database as an aid to criminal investigations."[83] The committee members were primarily from academia with a concentration of experience in statistics, computer science, and public policy. No firearm examiners were on the committee, although a former firearm and toolmark examiner served as a consultant to the committee.[84] The committee published its report, *Ballistics Imaging*, in 2008 (2008 NAS Report).

Although the 2008 NAS Report focused on computer imaging of bullets, a section of the report examined the theory and methodology of firearm identification evidence:

> Underlying the specific tasks with which the committee was charged is the underlying question of whether firearm-related toolmarks are unique: that is, whether a particular set of toolmarks can be shown to come from one weapon to the exclusion of all others.[85]

The 2008 NAS Report cited the committee's review of the research studies on the fundamental assumptions of uniqueness and reproducibility of the individual characteristics that provide the foundation for firearm identification evidence and commented that

---

[80] Id. at p. 5.

[81] *See* https://archives.fbi.gov/archives/news/pressrel/press-releases/fbi-laboratory-announces-discontinuation-of-bullet-lead-examinations (last accessed September 28, 2016).

[82] For scientific and legal analyses relevant to such appeals, *see* David L. Faigman, et al., *Modern Scientific Evidence: The Law and Science of Expert Testimony,* 2011–2012 ed. (West, 2011) at pp. 731–748.

[83] Committee to Assess the Feasibility, Accuracy, and Technical Capability of a National Ballistics Database, National Research Council of the National Academies, *Ballistic Imaging*, The National Academies Press: Washington D.C., 2008 (hereinafter "2008 NAS Report") at p. 2.

[84] Id. at pp. v-vi, xii.

[85] Id. at p. 3.

"[m]ost of these studies are limited in scale and have been conducted by firearms examiners (and examiners in training) in state and local law enforcement laboratories as adjuncts to their regular casework."[86] The 2008 NAS Report concluded that "[t]he validity of the fundamental assumptions of uniqueness and reproducibility of firearm-related toolmarks has not yet been fully demonstrated," but cautioned that "[o]ur review . . . is not—and is not meant to be—a full weighing of evidence for or against the assumptions, but is ample enough to suggest that they are not fully settled, mechanically or empirically."[87] The report went on to address the scientific validity of expressions of absolute certainty by firearm examiners:

> *Conclusions drawn in firearm identification should not be made to imply the presence of a firm statistical basis when none has been demonstrated.* Specifically, [as described *supra*], examiners tend to cast their assessments in bold absolutes, commonly asserting that a match can be made 'to the exclusion of all other firearms in the world.' Such comments cloak an inherently subjective assessment of a match with an extreme probability statement that has no firm grounding and unrealistically implies an error rate of zero.[88]

The Association of Firearm and Tool Mark Examiners (AFTE) responded to the report by emphasizing that the committee was not tasked with investigating the scientific validity of firearm comparison analysis.[89] In response to the report's "tangential" statements regarding the uniqueness of toolmarks, the reproducibility of toolmarks, and the subjectivity of the interpretation of toolmarks, the AFTE asserted that existing research had already addressed any concerns.[90]

3.   2009 NAS REPORT

The National Academy of Science, on February 18, 2009, released its report on strengthening the forensic sciences in the United States.[91] As previously discussed in Chapter 1, the report was critical of several forensic disciplines, including firearm and toolmark comparison evidence. The 2009 NAS Report cited the 2008 NAS Report's conclusions on the fundamental assumptions of uniqueness and reproducibility of

---

[86] Id. at p. 70.

[87] Id. at pp. 81–82.

[88] Id. at p. 82 (emphasis in original).

[89] Response of the Association of Firearm and Tool Mark Examiners to the National Academy of Sciences 2008 Report Assessing the Feasibility, Accuracy, and Technical Capability of a National Ballistics Database, August 20, 2008, 40(3) AFTE J. 234–244 (2008) at pp. 236–237 (available at: https://afte.org/resources/afte-position-documents)(last accessed September 29, 2016).

[90] Id. at pp. 243–244.

[91] Committee on Identifying the Needs of the Forensic Science Community, National Research Council of the National Academies, *Strengthening Forensic Science in the United States: A Path Forward*, The National Academies Press: Washington D.C., 2009. For a discussion of the entire report, *see* Chapter 1.

firearms-related toolmarks.[92] In its summary of the firearm/toolmark discussions, the 2009 NAS Report concluded:

"Toolmark and firearm analysis suffers from the same limitations discussed above for impression evidence. Because not enough is known about the variabilities among individual tools and guns, we are not able to specify how many points of similarity are necessary for a given level of confidence in the result. Sufficient studies have not been done to understand the reliability and repeatability of the methods. The committee agrees that class characteristics are helpful in narrowing the pool of tools that may have left a distinctive mark. Individual patterns from manufacture or from wear might, in some cases, be distinctive enough to suggest one particular source, but additional studies should be performed to make the process of individualization more precise and repeatable.

A fundamental problem with toolmark and firearms analysis is the lack of a precisely defined process. As noted above, AFTE has adopted a theory of identification, but it does not provide a specific protocol.

. . .

This AFTE document, which is the best guidance available for the field of toolmark identification, does not even consider, let alone address, questions regarding variability, reliability, repeatability, or the number of correlations needed to achieve a given degree of confidence.

Although some studies have been performed on the degree of similarity that can be found by marks made by different tools and the variability in marks made by an individual tool, the scientific knowledge base for toolmark and firearm analysis is fairly limited."[93]

SWGGUN responded to the report acknowledging awareness of "the scientific and systemic issues identified in this report for some time," including the "disparity or 'fragmentation' that presently exists in the application of forensic science in general and within the discipline of Firearm and Toolmark Identification specifically."[94] The professional group pledged to improve procedures to enhance the quality and reliability of firearm comparison examinations. The AFTE was not as conciliatory in its response and took issue with many of the report's statements about firearm comparison analysis:

---

[92] 2009 NAS Report at p. 154.

[93] Id. at pp. 154–155.

[94] *See* "SWGGUN Initial Response to the NAS Report" (available at: http://www.swggun.org/index.php?option=com_content&view=article&id=37:responce-to-nas&catid=13:other&Itemid=22)(last accessed September 28, 2016).

In their report, the NAS Committee painted an incomplete and inaccurate portrait of the field of firearm and toolmark identification using a very broad brush, and in doing so did not consider the appropriate scientific principles on which our discipline was founded.

. . .

Justice cannot be served if the results of well-documented firearm and toolmark comparisons are precluded from American courts. Forensic casework performed by trained and competent examiners not only has the potential to identify the responsible firearm used in a crime, but may also quickly exclude a suspected firearm as having any association with a shooting incident.[95]

In support of its response, AFTE cited ongoing research that it said had "the potential to further support the validity and reliability of firearm and toolmark identifications and provide quantitative data to supplement the [existing] empirical research."[96] In 2016, another governmental entity would have the opportunity to review that research as the group reconsidered the scientific validity of firearm comparison evidence.

4.   2016 PCAST REPORT

In September, 2016, the President's Council of Advisors on Science and Technology (PCAST) approved a report to the President on "Forensic Science in Criminal Courts: Ensuring Scientific Validity of Feature-Comparison Methods" (hereinafter "2016 PCAST Report").[97] Like the NAS Report, the 2016 PCAST Report focused on several forensic science disciplines, including firearm comparison analysis. The report took issue with assertion that the AFTE "Theory of Identification" was a scientific theory, describing it as just "a claim that examiners applying a subjective approach can accurately individualize the origin of a toolmark" based on a method that was inherently circular:

It declares that an examiner may state that two toolmarks have a "common origin" when their features are in "sufficient agreement." It then defines "sufficient agreement" as occurring

---

[95] ATFE Committee for the Advancement of the Science of Firearm and Tool Mark Identification, "The Response of the Association of Firearm and Tool Mark Examiners to the February 2009 National Academy of Science Report 'Strengthening Forensic Science in the United States: A Path Forward," 41 ATFE J. 204–208 (2009) at pp. 206–207 (available at: https://afte.org/uploads/documents/position-nas-2009.pdf)(last accessed September 28, 2016).

[96] Id. at p. 207.

[97] Executive Office of the President, President's Council of Advisors on Science and Technology, "Forensic Science in Criminal Courts: Ensuring Scientific Validity of Feature-Comparison Methods," September 2016 (available at: https://obamawhitehouse.archives.gov/blog/2016/09/20/pcast-releases-report-forensic-science-criminal-courts)(last accessed February 27, 2017).

when the examiner considers it a "practical impossibility" that the toolmarks have different origins.[98]

After reviewing the research conducted prior to 2009, PCAST concurred with the 2009 NAS Report conclusion that "sufficient studies have not been done to understand the reliability and reproducibility of the methods."[99] As to research conducted after 2009, PCAST found that only one study was appropriately designed to assess foundational validity and estimate reliability.[100] Ultimately, PCAST concluded:

> PCAST finds that firearm analysis currently falls short of the criteria for foundational validity, because there is only a single appropriately designed study to measure validity and estimate reliability. The scientific criteria for foundational validity require more than one such study, to demonstrate reproducibility.

> Whether firearms analysis should be deemed admissible based on current evidence is a decision that belongs to the courts.

> If firearm analysis is allowed in court, the scientific criteria for validity as applied should be understood to require clearly reporting the error rates seen in appropriately designed black-box studies (estimated at 1 in 66, with a 95 percent confidence limit of 1 in 46, in the one such study to date).[101]

IV. TRIAL AIDS

§4.09   EXPERT QUALIFICATIONS

Evidentiary rules permit qualification of an expert through various means, including but not limited to, training, experience, and the study of the literature relating to a field.[102] Since there are no formal educational degrees to become a firearms examiner, the training and experience of the expert is usually acquired through professional training courses, supplemented by practical work in law enforcement crime laboratories. Usually, years of work, under proper supervision, in comparing and examining weapons and ammunition are required before attaining the degree of proficiency to do comparison analysis. A thorough familiarity with the technical literature, optical equipment including the comparison microscope, standard laboratory measuring techniques, and photography as well as the knowledge of and adherence to the accepted methodology of the profession would also be required. SWGGUN has

---

[98] Id. at p. 60.

[99] Id. at p. 11.

[100] Id at pp. 104–111.

[101] Id. at p. 112.

[102] United States v. Otero, 849 F. Supp.2d 425, 436 (D.N.J. 2012).

adopted minimum qualification guidelines for firearm examiner trainees and existing examiners that require trainees to have a bachelor's degree in a natural/physical science, but permit experience to be considered in lieu of scientific degrees or formal educational background for existing examiners.[103] SWGGUN guidelines recommend completion of a training program and two years of firearm/toolmark casework experience for experienced examiner status. The time spent in the training program may count towards the two year experience requirement.[104]

The most significant relevant professional group is the Association of Firearm and Toolmark Examiners (AFTE),[105] although many experts belong to the Criminalistics Section of the American Academy of Forensic Sciences,[106] and to the International Association for Identification.[107] All of these professional associations require their members to exhibit a certain level of competency for membership and compliance with the organizations' ethics codes. The AFTE offers a certification program in firearm examination, toolmark examination, and GSR examination "[t]o demonstrate to interested parties that successful applicants have met a standard of excellence in knowledge and skill for a qualified examiner as defined by AFTE; and [t]o promote professionalism among firearm and toolmark examiners by establishing certification as a level of accomplishment."[108] As of February 16, 2014, the qualifications to apply for certification require two years of training, three years of paid firearm and toolmark examiner status, and a four-year baccalaureate degree.[109] The certification process requires successful completion of both written and practical examinations.[110] The written examination is administered by the National Forensic Science Technology Center (NFSTC).[111] AFTE maintains a roster of certified members on its website.[112]

Since the overwhelming majority of firearms identification experts in criminal prosecutions testify for the prosecution, the courts have been fairly lenient in qualifying expert witnesses. The courts assume that if the crime laboratories feel the witness is competent to work in the field, the witness ought to qualify as an expert—an assumption that may have

---

[103] SWGGUN, "Minimum Qualifications for Firearm and Toolmark Examiner Trainees," April 20, 2006; SWGGUN, "Minimum Qualifications for Experienced Firearm and Toolmark Examiners," April 20, 2006 (available at www.swggun.org).

[104] SWGGUN, "Minimum Qualifications for Experienced Firearm and Toolmark Examiners," April 20, 2006.

[105] *See* www.afte.org.

[106] *See* www.aafs.org.

[107] *See* www.theiai.org.

[108] https://afte.org/afte-certification/certification-program.

[109] Id.

[110] The written examination is 100 multiple choice questions. Successful completion requires 70% correct responses. Id.

[111] Id.

[112] https://afte.org/afte-certification/certified-member-roster.

some well-founded basis in most of the cases, but not in all.[113] Thus, a state toxicologist was permitted to give an opinion that a weapon required "more than an average pull on the trigger" and that "it would be difficult for it to be fired accidentally."[114]

§4.10   EVIDENCE ISSUES

1.   FIREARM COMPARISON ANALYSIS

a.   *Early Court Decisions*

The first appellate court decision concerning the admissibility of testimony regarding the similarity between fired bullets was a 1879 homicide case in Virginia; however, the case did not involve modern firearm comparison techniques, but the comparison of the weight of the fatal and test bullets fired from the defendant's firearm.[115] The first case involving the comparison of characteristic markings on firearm evidence was the 1902 Massachusetts case of *Commonwealth v. Best*.[116] A test bullet was obtained from the defendant's rifle by "pushing" it through the barrel, after which photographs were taken of that bullet and the fatal bullets for the purpose of comparison. The defendant objected to the admission of the evidence pertaining to their similarity, mainly on the ground that "the conditions of the experiment did not correspond accurately with those at the date of the shooting, that the forces impelling the different bullets were different in kind, that the rifle barrel might be supposed to have rusted more in the little more than a fortnight that had intervened. . . ." To these arguments, the Massachusetts Supreme Court, in an opinion by Oliver Wendell Holmes, Jr., replied:

> "We see no other way in which the jury could have learned so intelligently how that gun barrel would have marked a lead bullet fired through it, a question of much importance to the case. Not only was it the best evidence attainable but the sources of error suggested were trifling. The photographs avowedly were arranged to bring out the likeness in the

---

[113] In Dudley v. State, 480 N.E.2d 881 (Ind. 1985), one of the arresting officers was permitted to give testimony concerning bullet paths and powder burns existing on the car used by the accused, over the objection of the defense that he was not a firearms expert. The Indiana Supreme Court held that the officer, although not a firearms expert, was more knowledgeable than the average juror and, therefore, the trial judge did not abuse his discretion in admitting the opinion.

[114] Boswell v. State, 339 So.2d 151 (Ala.Cr.App.1976).

[115] Dean v. Commonwealth, 73 Va. (32 Gratt.) 912 (1879). The appellate court also upheld the admission of testimony to the effect that of all the guns in the community none were found which had the same bore or which could carry precisely the same ball. Two or three only, out of a large number examined, were even "nearly" of the same bore, so that only they "might have" carried the same type ball as that removed from the body of the deceased, and all of those weapons were accounted for, with the exception of the defendant's weapon.

[116] 180 Mass. 492, 62 N.E. 748 (1902). Between the *Dean* and *Best* cases, three other relatively inconsequential firearms identification cases were decided, which are noted only for their historical interest: State v. Smith, 49 Conn. 376 (1881); People v. Mitchell, 94 Cal. 550, 29 P. 1106 (1892); State v. Hendel, 4 Idaho 88, 35 P. 836 (1894).

marking of the different bullets and were objected to on this further ground. But the jury could correct them by inspection of the originals, if there were other aspects more favorable to the defense."[117]

Holmes' decision was not immediately followed by a flood of case law heralding this new scientific development. In 1923, the Illinois Supreme Court case of *People v. Berkman*[118] went so far as to label as "preposterous" the suggestion that distinctive markings were impressed upon bullets fired from different pistols of the same caliber and make. It was not until the case of *Jack v. Commonwealth*,[119] a Kentucky case decided in 1928, that expert testimony concerning firearms identification began to receive thorough attention by appellate courts. The extended discussion devoted to the subject in that opinion represents the first satisfactory treatment of this comparatively new phase of circumstantial evidence, even though there was a reversal of the trial court's conviction because of other evidentiary deficiencies. A year later, the same court, in *Evans v. Commonwealth*,[120] rendered the first exhaustive opinion treating firearms identification as a science, and sanctioning its use for the purpose of establishing the guilt of the accused. Shortly after these Kentucky cases, firearms identification evidence was readily admitted in an Ohio case, *Burchett v. State*,[121] and in an Illinois case, *People v. Fisher*.[122]

Identification based upon a comparison of breechface imprints, firing pin impressions, and extractor and ejector marks, achieved recognition by the courts concurrent with the identification of bullets. *State v. Clark*,[123] an Oregon case decided in 1921, appears to be the first case approving identification based on markings upon fatal and test cartridge cases.[124] During that same year, a conviction was obtained in *State v. Vuckovich*,[125] a Montana case, partly upon the evidence that "a peculiar crimp" on an empty cartridge case found at the scene of a murder corresponded with a similar mark on shells fired from the defendant's pistol.[126] Cartridge casings were used to supplement the identification of

---

[117] 62 N.E. at 75.

[118] 307 Ill. 492, 139 N.E. 91 (1923).

[119] 222 Ky. 546, 1 S.W.2d 961 (1928).

[120] 230 Ky. 411, 19 S.W.2d 1091 (1929).

[121] 35 Ohio App. 463, 172 N.E. 555 (1930).

[122] 340 Ill. 216, 172 N.E. 743 (1930). The *Fisher* case represents an about-face from the view expressed in *Berkman* in that the court recognized firearms identification as trustworthy.

[123] 99 Or. 629, 196 P. 360 (1921). *See generally* E. LeFevre, "Expert Evidence to Identify Gun From Which Bullet or Cartridge was Fired," 26 A.L.R.2d 892 (1952, 2012).

[124] "A peculiar mark on the brass part of the primer" of the shell was used as the identifying characteristic.

[125] 61 Mont. 480, 203 P. 491 (1921).

[126] Evidence was also introduced to show that "the firing marks made by the lands and grooves of the barrel of the pistol were the same" on both test and fatal bullets. Thus, this appellate decision represents an acceptance of both methods of identification, cartridge cases as well as bullets. The cartridge case matching, however, was based on a class characteristic.

bullets[127] and in some cases provided the sole connection with a particular weapon when a questioned bullet was unavailable[128] or was too mutilated for a comparison.[129] In *Edwards v. State*,[130] breechface markings were the only possible means of identification since the defendant had made a bullet comparison impossible by removing much of the rifling within the barrel by the use of steel wool.[131]

b.   *Post*-Daubert *Decisions*

After *Daubert* and *Kumho Tire*, courts readily admitted, with few exceptions, evidence of firearm examinations. The courts relied upon the wide acceptance of the methodology and permitted firearm examiners to testify without proof of compliance with the other *Daubert* factors.[132] The defense in criminal cases began to mount serious challenges firearm and toolmark comparison evidence in the early-2000's. These early challenges to the reliability of the methodology were largely unsuccessful,[133] but by 2005, legal and forensic science commentators began expressing concerning about the subjective nature of the methodology.[134]

Building on the legal commentary, defense attorneys continued to challenge the underlying methodology and began to focus on the expressions of "absolute certainty" used by firearms examiners. Citing the reported lack of empirical research on the uniqueness the firearm markings, some courts began to restrict the scope of the expert testimony

---

[127] State v. Lane, 72 Ariz. 220, 233 P.2d 437 (1951); State v. Gonzales, 92 Idaho 152, 438 P.2d 897 (1968).

[128] For cases involving shell comparison without bullets, *see* People v. Appleton, 1 Ill.App.3d 9, 272 N.E.2d 397 (1971); Norton v. Commonwealth, 471 S.W.2d 302 (Ky.1971). In State v. Michael, 107 Ariz. 126, 483 P.2d 541 (1971), the trial court was permitted to let an expert testify on the basis of photographs even though the spent casings were lost prior to trial.

[129] In State v. Bayless, 357 N.E.2d 1035 (Ohio 1976), the expert testified that the fatal bullets were so mutilated that he could not determine whether they were fired by the gun taken from the accused, but he could say that the bullets were fired from a gun having characteristics similar to those of a gun obtained from the accused which had physical characteristics like those on bullets in the accused's gun.

[130] 198 Md. 132, 81 A.2d 631 (1951), reargument denied 198 Md. 132, 83 A.2d 578 (1951).

[131] *See also* Dominguez v. State, 445 S.W.2d 729 (Tex.Cr.App.1969); Williams v. State, 169 Tex.Crim.R. 370, 333 S.W.2d 846 (1960).

[132] United States v. Hicks, 389 F.3d 514, 526 (5th Cir. 2004) ("We have not been pointed to a single case in this or any other circuit suggesting that the methodology . . . is unreliable.") See also Al Amin v. State, 278 Ga. 74, 81, 597 S.E.2d 332, 344 (2004); United States v. Foster, 300 F.Supp.2d 375 (D. Md. 2004).

[133] *See, e.g.,* United States v. Cooper, 91 F. Supp.2d 79 (D. DC 2000); United States v. Santiago, 199 F. Supp.2d 101 (S.D. NY 2002); United States v. Foster, 300 F. Supp.2d 375 (D. Md. 2004); United States v. Hicks, 389 F.3d 514 (5th Cir. 2004); Commonwealth v. Whitacre, 878 A.2d 96 (PA Super. Ct. 2005); State v. Anderson, 624 S.E.2d 393 (NC Ct. App. 2006); United States v. Diaz, No. 05-0167, 2007 U.S. Dist. LEXIS 13152, 2007 WL 485967 (ND Cal. Feb. 12, 2007).

[134] *See, e.g.,* David L. Faigman, et al., *Modern Scientific Evidence: The Law and Science of Expert Testimony,* 2011–2012 ed, Eagan, MN: West, 2011, Vol. 4, pp. 1–112 with particular attention to pp. 91–95. *See also* Adina Schwartz, "A Challenge to the Admissibility of Firearms and Toolmark Identifications: *Amicus Brief* Prepared on Behalf of the Defendant in United States v. Kain, Crim. No. 03–573–1 (E.D.Pa.2004)," 4 J. PHILOSOPHY, SCI. & L. 2004.; Adina Schwartz, "A Systemic Challenge to the Reliability and Admissibility of Firearms and Toolmark Identification," 6 COL. SCI. & TECHNOLOGY L.REV. 1 (2005).

to bar identifications "to the exclusion of every other firearm in the world."[135] Additionally, although firearm and toolmark comparison evidence continued to be admitted, several court opinions included critical assessments of the scientific validity of the methods used in firearm comparison analysis:

> "[W]hen liberty hangs in the balance—and, in the case of the defendants facing the death penalty, life itself—the standards should be higher than were met in this case, and than have been imposed across the country. The more courts admit this type of toolmark evidence without requiring more documentation, proficiency testing, or evidence of reliability, the more sloppy practices will endure; we should require more."[136]

c.   *Post–NAS Reports Decisions*

Following the publication of the two NAS Reports, defense attorneys challenging firearm and toolmark comparison evidence had additional supporting material[137] and the admissibility challenges continued.[138] Citing decades of admission, most courts denied the challenges and refused to place any limitations on the testimony.[139] Other courts, while

---

[135] *See* United States v. Green, 405 F. Supp. 2d 104, 109 (D. Mass. 2005); United States v. Diaz, CR05-00167 WHA, 2007 WL 485967 (ND Cal. 2007). *But see* United States v. Natson, 469 F. Supp. 2d 1253, 1261 (MD Ga. 2007) (opinion "to 100% degree of certainty" admitted).

[136] United States v. Green, 405 F. Supp. 2d 104, 109 (D. Mass. 2005). *See also* United States v. Monteiro, 407 F. Supp. 2d 351, 355 (D. Mass. 2006) (finding that "there is no reliable . . . scientific methodology which will currently permit the expert to testify . . . [as to] a 'match' to an absolute certainty, or to an arbitrary degree of statistical certainty," but permitting admission with limited conclusions, noting no federal court has yet deemed firearms comparison evidence inadmissible).

[137] In addition to citing the NAS reports in admissibility challenges, some defendants used the NAS reports during cross-examination of firearm examiners. *See* State v. Harper, 344 Wis.2d 297, 821 N.W.2d 412 (2012) (trial court erroneously precluded admission of the NAS report on cross-examination).

[138] *See generally* United States v. Sebbern, No. 10-CR-87, 2012 U.S. Dist. LEXIS 170576 (E.D.N.Y. Nov. 30, 2012)(collecting cases and describing numerous *Daubert* hearings).

[139] *See, e.g.,* State v. McGraw, 779 S.E.2d 787 (N.C. Ct. App. 2015) ("Defendant has failed to demonstrate that compelling new developments . . . divested the trial court of its discretion to allow [the] expert testimony without limitation"); Northern v. State, 467 S.W.3d 755 (Ark. Ct. App. 2015) ("firearm and toolmark science has been . . . in existence for many years and it is well-recognized and generally accepted science"); United States v. Casey, 928 F. Supp.2d 397, 400 (D. P.R. 2013) ("[T]he Court declines to follow sister courts who have limited expert testimony based upon the 2008 and 2009 NAS reports and, instead, remains faithful to the long-standing tradition of allowing unfettered testimony of qualified ballistics expert.") *See also* Turner v. State, 953 N.E.2d 1039 (Ind. 2011) (firearms identification evidence admitted without limitation); Jones v. United States, 27 A.3d 1130 (DC Ct. App. 2011) (firearm identification evidence admissible, any error in the expression of "absolute certainty" was harmless).

In United States v. Otero, 849 F. Supp.2d 425 (D. NJ 2012),the court directly addressed "the reliability of forensic toolmark examination employed to identify the firearm from which discharged ammunition originated." 849 F. Supp.2d at 427. The defense challenged the individualized identification of the firearm as based on a theory that has not been proven scientifically, citing both NAS Reports. 849 F. Supp.2d at 430. The court held that the evidence met all of the *Daubert* factors for admission while heavily criticizing the qualifications and testimony of the defense expert as "an advocate for a particular position rather than as a dispassionate analyst." 849 F. Supp.2d at 436–437.

rejecting challenges to the entire methodology, criticized the subjectivity of the underlying methodology and the lack of research on the fundamental assumptions of firearms comparison analysis. These courts concluded that some limitations on the firearms examiners' testimony were appropriate.

In *United States v. Glynn*,[140] the court concluded that firearm comparison analysis "lacks the rigor of science [and] suffers from greater uncertainty than many other kinds of forensic evidence."[141] The court barred the examiner from testifying as to absolute certainty of the identification, and permitted the conclusion to be expressed only as "more likely than not" that the firearm had fired the evidentiary bullet.[142] Similarly, in *United States v. Taylor*,[143] after noting the "limitations on the reliability of firearm identification evidence," the court did not permit the examiner to testify that the bullet came from a particular gun to the exclusion of all other guns and limited the examiner's conclusion to "the bullet came from the suspect rifle to within a reasonable degree of certainty in the firearms examination field."[144] In *United States v. Willock*,[145] the court held that the examiner "shall not opine that it is a 'practical impossibility' for a firearm to have fired the cartridges other than the common 'unknown firearm' to which [the examiner] attributes the cartridges ... and [the examiner] shall state his opinions and conclusions without any characterization as to the degree of certainty with which he holds them."[146] After reviewing the limitations imposed in other courts, the court in *United States v. Ashburn*[147] imposed the following restrictions on the firearm examiner testimony:

> [G]iven the extensive record presented in other cases, the court joins in precluding this expert witness from testifying that he is "certain" or "100%" sure of his conclusions that certain items match. Nor can [the expert] testify that a match he identified is to "the exclusion of all other firearms in the world," or that there is a "practical impossibility" that any other gun could have fired the recovered materials. Therefore, the court will limit [the expert] to stating that his conclusions were reached to a "reasonable degree of ballistics certainty" or a "reasonable degree of certainty in the ballistics field."[148]

---

[140] 578 F. Spp. 2d 567 (S.D. N.Y. 2008).

[141] 578 F. Supp. 2d at 574–575.

[142] 578 F. Supp.2d at 568–569, 575.

[143] 663 F. Supp.2d 1170 (D. N.M. 2009), motion denied by, stay denied by, United States v. Taylor, 663 F. Supp.2d 1157 (D.N.M. 2009).

[144] 663 F. Supp.2d at 1180.

[145] 696 F. Supp.2d 536 (D. Md. 2010), overruled in part, 2010 U.S. Dist. LEXIS 35695 (D. Md. 2010).

[146] 696 F. Supp.2d at 546–549.

[147] 88 F. Supp.3d 239 (E.D.N.Y. 2015).

[148] 88 F. Supp.2d at 249.

In response to the continued scrutiny of the scientific validity of comparison methodologies, courts have generally not excluded entire classes of expert testimony, but have refined the approach to such evidence through limitations on the scope of the expert's testimony,[149] more permissive admission of opposing expert testimony,[150] and other requirements. In *Commonwealth v. Heang*,[151] although the court upheld the decision to admit the firearm identification evidence, the appellate court established the following guidelines for the admission of such evidence in future cases in Massachusetts:

> "First, before trial, the examiner must adequately document the findings or observations that support the examiner's ultimate opinion, and . . . this documentary evidence . . . shall be provided in discovery. . . . Second, before an opinion is offered at trial, [the examiner] should explain to the jury the theories and methodologies underlying the field. . . . Third, in absence of special circumstances casting doubt on the reliability of an opinion . . . [the examiner] may present an expert's opinion . . . to a 'reasonable degree of ballistic certainty.'"[152]

The court specifically noted that "[p]hrases that could give the jury an impression of greater certainty, such as 'practical impossibility' and 'absolute certainty,' should be avoided."[153]

As with other areas of forensic science, neither *Daubert* nor the NAS Reports resulted in the widespread exclusion of firearm comparison testimony, but the scope of the testimony has been refined with some courts limiting opinions of certainty. With broader recognition of the subjectivity of firearm comparison evidence, courts are expected to continue addressing assertions that the methodology lacks scientific validity.

2. ANCILLARY TESTS

The first reported case deciding the question of admissibility of the results of gunpowder residue test was *Commonwealth v. Westwood*,[154]

---

[149] In Gardner v. United States, 140 A.3d 1172, 1184 (D.C. Ct. App. 2016), the District of Columbia Court of Appeals held that:

> [I]n this jurisdiction a firearms and toolmark expert may not give an unqualified opinion, or testify with absolute or 100% certainty, that based on ballistics pattern comparison matching a fatal shot was fired from one firearm, to the exclusion of all other firearms.

[150] In State v. Romero, 365 P.3d 358, 360–361 (2016), the Arizona Supreme Court held that the trial court abused its discretion in precluding the defendant from offering expert testimony criticizing the methods used by firearms examiners to match a gun to a crime and the Court of Appeals of Arizona vacated the murder conviction after determining the error was not harmless. 2016 Ariz. App. LEXIS 217 (2016).

[151] 942 N.E.2d 927 (2011).

[152] 942 N.E.2d at 944–945.

[153] 942 N.E.2d at 946.

[154] 324 Pa. 289, 188 A. 304 (1936).

decided in 1936. The Pennsylvania Supreme Court held that the testimony of experts who had administered the dermal nitrate (paraffin) test, and who had concluded that the specks on the paraffin mold taken from defendant's hand were gunpowder residues, was admissible, even though a chemist who testified for the defense stated that the chemical test would give an identical reaction with thirteen other materials, including tooth powder, cigar ashes, cigarette ashes, and different kinds of matches. Despite research questioning the reliability of the paraffin test,[155] the admission of the results of the paraffin test was also upheld in Texas and North Carolina in the 1950's.[156]

The results of gunshot residue testing on hands is now routinely admitted. The negative results of GSR testing have been admitted, even though the limited conclusions that could be drawn from such evidence were obvious. In *McMillan v. State*, the examiner testified that the testing showed no primer residue on the hands of the individual, "which meant that [the individual] did not discharge a firearm, discharged a firearm that did not deposit significant quantities of residue particles on the hands, or washed or wiped his hands after firing a weapon."[157]

Evidence of gunshot residue on clothing and other target surfaces may be admitted into evidence along with tests conducted to show at what distance from the muzzle a target must be in order for the particular weapon in question to deposit similar powder residue and burns.[158] GSR pattern tests should be conducted under conditions sufficiently similar to those present during the questioned discharge.[159] For example, in *State v. Atwood*,[160] the tests were conducted with the same weapon and similar ammunition, and consequently the sheets of blotting paper used in the test were admitted into evidence. When conditions are not sufficiently similar, the GSR test pattern results may be excluded. In *Done v. State*[161] the results were excluded because the sheriff conducted powder-burn tests by nailing a towel to a tree. In *Miller v. State*,[162] test results were barred because of variations in atmospheric conditions, bullet weight, condition of weapons, and ammunition type. In

---

[155] Henry W. Turkel and Jerome Lipman, "Unreliability of Dermal Nitrate Test for Gunpowder," 46 J. CRIM. L. C. & P.S. 281 (1955).

[156] Henson v. State, 159 Tex.Crim.R. 647, 266 S.W.2d 864 (1953); State v. Atwood, 250 N.C. 141, 108 S.E.2d 219 (1959).

[157] McMillan v. State, 2016 Tex. App. LEXIS 7034, *13 (Tex. Ct. App. 5th Dist., July 1, 2016).

[158] Opie v. State, 389 P.2d 684 (Wyo.1964); McPhearson v. State, 271 Ala. 533, 125 So.2d 709 (1960); Straughn v. State, 270 Ala. 229, 121 So.2d 883 (1960); Washington v. State, 269 Ala. 146, 112 So.2d 179 (1959).

[159] State v. Jiles, 258 Iowa 1324, 142 N.W.2d 451 (1966). *See also* State v. Meikle, 60 Conn.App. 802, 761 A.2d 247 (2000).

[160] 250 N.C. 141, 108 S.E.2d 219 (1959).

[161] 202 Miss. 418, 32 So.2d 206 (1947)(defendant claimed his pistol discharged accidentally when it fell from the glove compartment of his automobile).

[162] 250 Ind. 656, 236 N.E.2d 585 (1968)(gun condition was different since the original weapon was unrecovered, ammunition also differed).

Jorgenson v. People,[163] the state failed to show either that the test shot was fired at an angle similar to that of the questioned shot, or that the angle would make little difference with regard to residue deposits. These omissions, coupled with the use of different cloth and different cartridges, led to the inadmissibility of the test results.

Few evidentiary problems have been encountered in the admission of evidence of restored serial numbers on firearms. The restoration techniques are simple and straightforward and, when relevant to triable issues, such expert testimony has been admitted.[164] In *United States v. Adams*,[165] evidence of a firearm's altered serial number was introduced, but no issue appears to have been made of the reliability of evidence of alteration. Similarly, in *Commonwealth v. Toran*, the firearm examiner testified that he was able to restore the original manufacturer's serial number from the revolver without challenge.[166]

3.   TOOLMARK COMPARISON ANALYSIS

The comparison of an object and an impression allegedly made by that same object was admitted as evidence in a criminal case as early as 1879 in *Dean v. Commonwealth*.[167] In that case, the distinct square impression and a "peculiar" notch left on a fence rail, presumably when the defendant rested his weapon in order to fire at the deceased, were found to be probative. By actual experiment "made by some of the witnesses," the defendant's gun, when laid upon the same rail and drawn back, left "a similar square impression and a similar notch made by the small piece of iron which was fastened to the barrel near the muzzle." The lack of expertise on the part of those testifying did not preclude the admission of this evidence. Although the evidence in the *Dean* case was clearly of a conjectural nature and would probably be viewed with skepticism today, the Virginia Supreme Court held it admissible in this first degree murder prosecution.

In *State v. Baldwin*,[168] the value of toolmark examination was demonstrated, along with the need for expert testimony in its support. A panel had been cut out of the door of the house where a crime had been committed. The defendant was a carpenter and when he was arrested he

---

[163] 174 Colo. 144, 482 P.2d 962 (1971). *See also* Rhea v. State, 208 Tenn. 559, 347 S.W.2d 486 (1961)(test results were not admitted because the powder used in the test might have been different from the unidentified powder firing the fatal bullet).

[164] *See, e.g.,* People v. Snow, 21 Ill.App.3d 873, 316 N.E.2d 216 (1974).

[165] 305 F.3d 30 (1st Cir.2002). The issue on appeal was whether the defendant was properly found to have violated the statute prohibiting possession of a firearm from which the manufacturer's serial number had been "removed, obliterated, or altered" within the meaning of 18 USC 922 (k), where of the six digits in the serial number four were "scratched or abraded" so that they were significantly more difficult to read.

[166] The examiner also testified that the "firearm was functional and capable of discharging the type of ammunition for which it was manufactured." Commonwealth v. Toran, 2016 Pa. Super. Unpub. LEXIS 1252, *3–*4 (April 15, 2016).

[167] 73 Va. (32 Gratt.) 912 (1879).

[168] 36 Kan. 1, 12 P. 318 (1886).

had a knife in his possession. The court allowed experts to testify concerning the items of evidence, and said of the witnesses:

> "These men were skilled workers in wood, and their experience enabled them to judge, from the marks and impressions left upon the door by the tool used, whether it had been cut with a knife, chisel, or saw; whether it had been cut by a thick or a thin bladed knife; whether it had been cut by one accustomed to the use of tools; and the marks or traces made upon the wood by the knife would indicate to the trained eye whether it had been cut from the outside or the inside. The manner in which the cutting was done, and the effect of the tools upon the wood, involve skill and experience to judge of, and are not within common experience. . . ."[169]

Courts do not frequently distinguish between firearm comparisons and toolmark examinations, because the same forensic discipline is said to encompass both fields.[170] Courts also analogize toolmark examination to other feature comparison methods, such as fingerprints. The Washington Supreme Court remarked, "The edge on one blade differs from the edge of another blade as the lines on one human hand differ from the lines on another."[171] Certainly, despite the historical judicial acceptance of the general principles on which firearm and toolmark comparison analysis is based, specific applications in individual cases still deserve close scrutiny.

V. RESOURCES

§4.11 BIBLIOGRAPHY OF ADDITIONAL RESOURCES

Christina S. Atwater, Marie E. Durina, and Robert D. Blackledge, "Visualization of Gunshot Residue Patterns on Dark Clothing using the Video Spectral Comparator," 51 J. FORENSIC SCIENCES 1091 (2006).

Yaniv Y. Avisar, *et al.*, "Identification of Firearms Holders by the $[Fe(PDT)_3]^{+2}$ Complex, Qualitative Determination of Iron Transfer to the Hand and its Dependence on Palmar Moisture Levels," 49 J. FORENSIC SCI. 1215 (2004).

---

[169] Id. at 324.

[170] *See* Eliot Springer, "Toolmark Examinations—A Review of Its Development in the Literature," 40 J. Forensic Sci. 964 (1995). See also Al A. Biosotti, "A Statistical Study of the Individual Characteristics of Fired Bullets," 4 J. FORENSIC SCI. 34 (1959); Al A. Biasotti, "The Principles of Evidence Evaluation as Applied to Firearms and Tool Mark Identification," 9 J. FORENSIC SCI. 428 (1964); W. Deinet, "Studies of Models of Striated Marks Generated by Random Processes," 26 J. FORENSIC SCI. 78 (1983); T. Uchiyama, "The Probability of Corresponding Striae in Toolmarks," 24 A.F.T.E.J. 273 (1992).

[171] State v. Clark, 156 Wash. 543, 287 P. 18 (1930).

Anthony A. Braga and Glenn L. Pierce, "Linking Crime Guns: The Impact of Ballistics Imaging Technology on the Productivity of the Boston Police Department's Ballistics Unit," 49 J. FORENSIC SCI. 701 (2004).

Stephen G. Bunch, "Consecutive Matching Striation Criteria: A General Critique," 45 J. FORENSIC SCI. 955 (2000).

Donald E. Carlucci, *Ballistics—Theory and Design of Guns and Ammunition*, CRC PRESS, 2007.

Peter De Forest, *et al.*, "Gunshot Residue Particle Velocity and Deceleration," 49 J. FORENSIC SCI. 1237 (2004).

Jan de Kinder, "Ballistic Fingerprinting Database," 42 SCI. & JUSTICE 197 (2002).

Jan de Kinder, *et al.*, "Reference Ballistic Fingerprint Imaging Database Performance," 140 For. Sci. Int'l 207 (2004).

Gerard Dutton, "Firearms: Bullet and Cartridge Case Identification," in WILEY ENCYCLOPEDIA OF FORENSIC SCIENCE, (Jamieson A. & Moenssens A.A., eds) 2009 & online updates.

Dale Garrison, "Comparison Question: Should Photographic Documentation Be a Standard Operating Procedure for all Firearm and Toolmark Examinations?" EVIDENCE TECHNOLOGY MAGAZINE, Nov.-Dec. 2007, p. 12.

W. George, "Fingerprinting Firearms—Reality or Fantasy," 36 AFTE J. 289 (2004).

Paul C. Giannelli, "Comparative Bullet Lead Analysis—An Update," CRIMINAL JUSTICE, Summer 2008, p. 24.

Baruch Glattstein, *et al.*, "Improved Method for Shooting Distance Estimation, Part I, Bullet Holes in Clothing Items," 45 J. FORENSIC SCI. 801 (2000).

Baruch Glattstein, *et al.*, "Improved Method for Shooting Distance Estimation, Part 2, Bullet Holes in Objects that Cannot be Processed in the Laboratory," 45 J. FORENSIC SCI. 1000 (2000).

Michael G. Haag & Lucien C. Haag, *Shooting Incident Reconstruction*, 2nd ed. Academic Press, 2006.

James E. Hamby, "The History of Firearm and Toolmark Identification," 31 A.F.T.E. J., Summer, 1999.

Mark Hansen, "Bullet Proof," ABA J., Sept. 2004, p. 58.

Brian J. Heard, *Handbook of Firearms and Ballistics: Examining and Interpreting Forensic Evidence,* 2nd ed., Wiley-Blackwell, 2008.

H. W. Hendrick, P. Paradis and R.J. Hornick, *Human Factors Issues in Handgun Safety and Forensics,* CRC Press, 2008.

Kristy G. Hopper and Bruce R. McCord, "A Comparison of Smokeless Powders and Mixtures by Capillary Zone Electrophoresis," 50 J. FORENSIC SCI. 307 (2005).

Edward E. Hueske, *Practical Analysis and Reconstruction of Shooting Incidents*, CRC Press, 2005.

Shigetoshi Kage, *et al.*, "A Simple Method for Detection of Gunshot Residue Particles from Hands, Hair, Face, and Clothing Using Scanning Electron Microscopy/Wavelength Dispersive X-Ray (SEM/WDX)," 46 J. FORENSIC SCI. 830 (2001).

Horst Katterwe, "Toolmarks," in WILEY ENCYCLOPEDIA OF FORENSIC SCIENCE, (Jamieson A. & Moenssens A.A., eds) 2009 & online updates.

Jozef Lebiedzik and David L. Johnson, "Rapid Search and Quantitative Analysis of Gunshot Residue Particles in the SEM," 45 J. FORENSIC SCI. 83 (2000).

Li Ma, *et al.*, "NIST Bullet Signature Measurements System for RM (Reference Material) 8240 Standard Bullets," 49 J. FORENSIC SCI. 649 (2004).

Nicholas Maiden, "Firearms: Scene Investigation," in WILEY ENCYCLOPEDIA OF FORENSIC SCIENCE, (Jamieson A. & Moenssens A.A., eds) 2009 & online updates.

Nicholas Maiden, "Serial Number Restoration," in WILEY ENCYCLOPEDIA OF FORENSIC SCIENCE, (Jamieson A. & Moenssens A.A., eds) 2009 & online updates.

Deborah W. Morton, "A Cut Above—Sharpening the Accuracy of Knife and Saw Mark Analysis," FORENSIC MAG., June–Jul., 2006 p. 8.

Ronald G. Nichols, "Firearm and Toolmark Identification Criteria: A Review of the Literature, Part II," 48 J. FORENSIC SCI. 318 (2003).

Ronald Nichols, "The Scientific Foundations of Firearms and Tool Mark Identification—A Response to Recent Challenges," CAC NEWS, 2d Quarter 2006, p. 8.

Ronald Nichols, "Defending the Scientific Foundations of the Firearms and Tool Mark Identification Discipline: Responding to Recent Challenges," 52 J. FORENSIC SCIENCES 586 (2007).

Zachariah Oommen and Scott M. Pierce, "Lead-Free Primer Residues: A Qualitative Characterization of Winchester WinClean(TM), Remington/UMC Leadless(TM), Federal BallistiClean(TM), and Spear Lawman Clean Fire(TM) Handgun Ammunition," 51 J. FORENSIC SCI. 509 (2006).

Ian K. Pepper and Steve T. Bloomer, "Cartridge Casing Ejection Patterns from Two Types of 9 mm Self-Loading Pistols Can Be Distinguished from Each Other," 56 J. FORENSIC SCI. 721 (2006).

Nicholas Petraco, *Color Atlas of Forensic Toolmark Identification*. Baca Raton: CRC Press, 2011.

R. Ravikumar, *et al.*, "Bullets without Striations—Fired or Unfired?," 56 J. FORENSIC SCI. 730 (2006).

Adina Schwartz, "A Systemic Challenge to the Reliability and Admissibility of Firearms and Toolmark Identification," 6 COLUM. SCI. & TECHN. L.REV. 1 (2005).

James Smyth Wallace, *Chemical Analysis of Firearms, Ammunition, and Gunshot Residue,* CRC Press, 2008.

Tom Warlow, *Firearms, the Law, and Forensic Ballistics,* 3rd ed., CRC Press, 2012.

Arie Zeichner, *et al.*, "Vacuum Collection of Gunpowder Residue from Clothing Worn by Shooting Suspects, and Their Analysis by GC/TEA, IMS, and GC/MS," 48 J. FORENSIC SCI. 961 (2003).

Arie Zeichner, "Firearm Discharge Residue: Analysis Of," in WILEY ENCYCLOPEDIA OF FORENSIC SCIENCE, (Jamieson A. & Moenssens A.A., eds) 2009 & online updates.

Arie Zeichner, "Shooting Distance: Estimation of," in WILEY ENCYCLOPEDIA OF FORENSIC SCIENCE, (Jamieson A. & Moenssens A.A., eds) 2009 & online updates.

CHAPTER 5

FORENSIC DOCUMENT EXAMINATION[1]

I. INTRODUCTION

§5.01 SCOPE OF THE CHAPTER

Since prehistoric men began drawing pictures of animals on cave walls between 20,000 and 35,000 BC,[2] handwriting has been a vital

---

[1] Sections I, II, III and subsections 5.16 and 5.19 of this chapter were authored by Jane A. Lewis, based on prior versions by Andre Moenssens. Jane Lewis is a member of the American Society of Questioned Document Examiners, a Fellow in the American Academy of Forensic Sciences (AAFS) and a Diplomate of the American Board of Forensic Document Examiners (ABFDE). She has written a textbook and articles on forensic document examination.

[2] Donald Jackson, *The Story of Writing*, Taplinger Publishing Co., Inc., 1981.

means of communication. Early writing types included: Cuneiform, Egyptian, Phoenician, Greek, Etruscan, Roman, Gothic Script, Italic Script, Copperplate Handwriting, Calligraphy and modern business handwritings like those taught in the Palmer Method and Zaner-Bloser.[3] Penmanship during the 1800s in the United States commanded interest. Master penmen wrote beautifully and taught students to create lovely writing used in calling cards and letters. In the early days of the profession the title "questioned document examiner" described penmanship teachers. Today the job title is "forensic document examiner" (FDE).

Two early pioneers in the profession were Daniel Ames and Albert S. Osborn. Daniel Ames developed from a skilled penman to an early forerunner in the field of forensic document examination. His textbook, *Ames on Forgery*, in 1901, blazed a trail for future research in the field. Albert S. Osborn (1858–1946) contributed by developing a scientific approach to disputed document cases.[4] His book, *Questioned Documents,* published in 1910, and the Second Edition of the book published in 1929, displayed his methodology in the scientific examination of papers, inks, typewriting, handwriting, hand printing, and signatures. *Questioned Documents* contains illustrations of his instrumentation and numerous court charts. Osborn and his early colleagues began to meet informally at his home to discuss questioned document cases. These meetings lead to the formation of the American Society of Questioned Document Examiners formed in 1942. This organization still exists today and members include many prominent FDEs.[5] Other classical early textbooks in forensic document examination consist of: *The Problem of Proof,* written by Albert S. Osborn, *Suspect Documents,* written by Wilson R. Harrison, and *Evidential Documents,* written by James V.P. Conway. Ordway Hilton helped establish the Questioned Document section in the American Academy of Forensic Sciences in 1946 and also wrote the text book, *Scientific Examination of Questioned Documents.*

The early practitioners sought to distance themselves from graphologists. Graphology seeks to determine character traits from handwriting. Graphology and forensic document examination could not be more different, but confusion surrounds them because they both involve handwriting. FDEs through education, training, and experience learn to make scientific examinations and comparisons of questioned handwriting with known specimens in order to determine the origin or authenticity of the questioned material. The methodology uses analysis, comparison, and evaluation of questioned and known items to arrive at an opinion that can be expressed in a report and demonstrated with

---

[3]   Jane A. Lewis, *Forensic Document Examination Fundamentals and Current Trends,* Academic Press, 2014.

[4]   Id.

[5]   American Society of Questioned Document Examiners (ASQDE): http://www.asqde.org.

illustrative charts of significant features for identification. Graphologists (sometimes called graphoanalysts) analyze a sample of handwriting to reveal personality traits of the writer. The practice of graphology would not normally interest FDEs; it does not try to accomplish the identification and authentication of questioned documents. Unfortunately, correspondence school trained graphologists have begun testifying as experts in FDE without the education, training, and experience required to work as an FDE. Research studies testing graphology used generally for employment purposes as opposed to psychological testing did not validate the practice.[6]

Evidence types encountered by FDEs include: forged checks, threatening letters, loan documents, mortgage documents, medical records, suicide notes, partnership agreements, wills, trusts, change of beneficiary forms for retirement plans and insurance policies, personal guarantees, receipts, letters, applications, graffiti, and tests. This chapter will illustrate in detail a few case examples containing typical questioned document problems. Foundational research in the field,[7] current studies, and an extensive bibliography will conclude this chapter.

§5.02 USE OF DOCUMENT EXAMINATIONS

Civil and criminal cases require forensic document examinations. Many FDEs work in federal laboratories like the FBI, US Secret Service, the Internal Revenue Service National Forensic Laboratory, and the US Postal Service Laboratory. State crime laboratories also employ many FDEs across the country. Another group of government

---

[6] Gershon Ben-Shakhar et al., "Can Graphology Predict Occupational Success? Two Empirical Studies and Some Methodological Ruminations," 71 J. Applied Psychology 645–653 (1986); Efrat Neter and Gershon Ben-Shakhar, "The Predictive Validity of Graphological Inferences: A Meta-Analytic Approach," 10 Personality and Individual Differences 737–745 (1989); Richard J. Klimoski and Anat Rafaeli, "Inferring Personal Qualities through Handwriting Analysis," 56 J. Occupational Psychology 191–202 (1989).

[7] Research supporting the science of forensic document examination grew in amount and quality over the last 25 years. Validation of the individuality of handwriting was accomplished by the research of Dr. Sargur Srihari and others at the University of New York, Buffalo, in the article "Individuality of Handwriting" published in the *Journal of Forensic Sciences.* A computer program was able to identify the 1500 writers in the sample with a confidence level of 98% using only eight handwriting characteristics. Sargur Srihari et al., "Individuality of Handwriting," 47 J. Forensic Sci. 856–872 (2002). This work followed research by Dr. Moshe Kam which validated the skill of professional FDEs. Moshe Kam et al., "Proficiency of Professional Document Examiners in Writer Identification," 39 J. Forensic Sci. 5–14 (1994). Recent research has focused on (i) at what ages do individual handwriting characteristics begin to develop; (ii) at what rate do these individual handwriting characteristics develop; (iii) what are the most common (less unique) individual characteristics that develop and (iv) what are the least common individual (more unique) individual characteristics that develop. *See* Lisa M. Hanson, "Development of Individual Handwriting Characteristics in ~1800 Students: Statistical Analysis and Likelihood Ratios that Emerge Over an Extended Period of Time," NIJ Fundamental Research to Improve Understanding of the Accuracy, Reliability, and Measurement Validity of Forensic Science Disciplines (FY2010); MN Bureau of Criminal Apprehension; DUNS-804886729 (May 15, 2016)(available at: https://www.ncjrs.gov/App/Publications/abstract.aspx?ID=272325)(last accessed December 19, 2016).

laboratories exist at the county and city levels. Cases worked by government FDEs are exclusively criminal cases. Forensic document evidence in criminal matters include: letters in homicide cases, hotel registration forms in terrorism investigations, a check with a simulated signature in a family homicide for financial gain, notes detailing the plan of a suspect to murder and dismember a sex worker, pencil writing in a phone book in a homicide, fabricated release from prison documents, forged checks, threatening letters, altered checks, immigration forms, and tax records.

Numerous FDEs work in the private sector and handle mainly civil cases. These FDEs usually have trained in government laboratories or reputable private laboratories. Certification by the American Board of Forensic Document Examiners (ABFDE) is a credential shared by many competent examiners. Document evidence in civil cases consist of examples like: a simulated signature on a will presented one month after the death of a business partner, anonymous letters in the work place, change of beneficiary forms for a life insurance policy, artist signatures on paintings in question, typewriting on company Board minutes, a will that was presented as an original document when it was a photocopy, partnership agreements, a no compete agreement, mortgage documents, trust documents, personal guarantees, test papers, and loan documents.

The work of FDEs goes beyond the identification of handwriting and handprinting. Other aspects of forgery and fraud detection may involve identifying printing methods in suspect documents, detecting indented writing in order to determine the sequence of pages prepared in a medical record, recovering erasures, enhancing faded writing, detecting watermarks for dating purposes on documents, performing ink analysis in order to determine whether one formula of ink was used to create an entire document, dating documents, distinguishing fluid ink from ballpoint pen ink, detecting alterations, identification of printing, and copying methods. Voluminous research in handwriting and other related document examinations are illustrated in a long list in Section 5.19 at the end of this chapter.

Government forensic document laboratories and private examiners use cutting edge instrumentation to perform their work. The stereoscopic microscope and light source are vital instruments that allow for original ink, photocopy toner, indented writing, inkjet printing, and typewriting to be identified. The laboratory must also have a video spectral comparator (VSC) in order to differentiate visually similar inks composed of different dye formulas. It also visualizes indented writing and reveals obliterated writing and erasures. The VSC has a camera sensitive to the infrared part of electromagnetic spectrum and a series of lights and filters. The electrostatic detection apparatus (ESDA) develops latent indented writings. The laboratories also contain reference libraries for typewriting, printing samples, and other document samples. A library of relevant text books and journals are also part of the laboratory.

The most common requests of FDEs in civil and criminal cases are:

1. Who wrote the questioned document?

2. Can the questioned document be dated?

3. Does the questioned document show evidence of alteration?

According to the SWGDOC Standard for Scope of Work of Forensic Document Examiners:

> *The forensic document examiner makes scientific examinations, comparisons, and analyses of documents in order to: (1) establish genuineness or nongenuineness, or to expose forgery, or to reveal alterations, additions, or deletions, (2) identify or eliminate persons as the source of handwriting, (3) identify or eliminate the source of typewriting or other impression, marks, or relative evidence, and (4) write reports or give testimony, when needed, to aid the users of the examiner's services in understanding the examiner's findings.*[8]

II. GENERAL PRINCIPLES

§5.03 NATURE OF DOCUMENTARY EVIDENCE

A forensic science is the application of science to the law. Forensic document examination is the application of science and analytical techniques to questions concerning documents. What is a document? A broad description is anything that expresses the thoughts of man. Most questioned documents consist of handwriting or hand printing on paper. Other documents commonly received for analysis are: forms printed with black toner, inkjet printed documents, thermal printed receipts, facsimiles, typewritten letters or forms, documents containing rubber stamps and dry seals. Additionally FDEs receive handwriting written on the sides of buildings, cars, mirrors, and restroom stalls. Photographs of graffiti occasionally become case evidence.

The word "questioned" in questioned document examination means that something about the evidence is unsettled. Uncertainty about the origin or history of the documents usually requires comparative examinations to determine the truth. Uncertainty about whether the amount was changed on a check or a signature was erased or scanned and placed on a document with Photoshop also requires the specialized training of an FDE.

---

[8] www.swgdoc.org.

Along with understanding types of evidence in typical questioned document cases, lawyers and investigators should be aware of the need for original documents and special collection and handling procedures. If possible, known specimens collected for comparison purposes should be contemporaneous with the questioned document. Questioned document evidence often requires careful handling to ensure fingerprints are not transferred to the document. Any documents that will be processed for latent prints after the forensic document analysis should be handled with gloves and stored in envelopes.

§5.04   KNOWN SAMPLES FOR COMPARISON

1.   HANDWRITING

In order to determine whether a questioned signature or handwriting is genuine, FDEs rely on known samples for comparison. Known samples are also referred to as known specimens, standards, or exemplars. "Known" means that the samples used for comparison are of established origin. Investigators or attorneys must verify that the standards submitted are indeed written by the person to whom the documents are attributed. Verification of the known standard may be accomplished by speaking with witnesses to the documents preparation; choosing business documents that also bear the signatures of witnesses; cross checking reliable everyday business documents like checks, driver licenses, and tax forms for internal consistency; or asking the writer, relatives, or close business associates of the writer to authenticate the known samples.

Two categories of known standards exist. Request standards require that the suspect or person whose handwriting must be collected for comparison with a questioned document provide a dictated written sample for an investigator or an attorney. An investigator dictates the questioned writing generally using the same text as the questioned document. In the case of signatures, 20–30 repetitions on separate sheets of paper will usually suffice. A handwritten anonymous letter may require 4–5 repetitions of the text of the questioned letter by the writer.

The second category of known standard is called collected standards. These are signatures or handwriting gathered from everyday business to establish the range of natural variation of the particular writer of interest in the case. The text book *Scientific Examination of Questioned Documents, 2nd Edition*,[9] explains the process of collecting known writings extensively.

---

[9]   Edited by Jan Seaman Kelly and Brian S. Lindblom, *Scientific Examination of Questioned Documents*, 2nd Edition, published by CRC Press in 2006, is an update of the Ordway Hilton text from 1982. The text is written by a group of forensic document examiners. Brian S. Lindblom wrote Chapter 12, which addresses handwriting standards in detail on pp. 127–143.

Attorneys and investigators often inquire about potential sources of collected known writing standards. An extensive list was offered by Brian Lindblom in *Scientific Examination of Questioned Documents, 2nd Edition,*[10] and includes all manner of financial records (e.g., checks, signature cards, loan applications), personal documents (e.g., diaries, agendas), legal documents (e.g., affidavits, divorce papers, wills), government documents (e.g., passports, naturalization papers, tax documents), retail materials (e.g., hotel registrations), and employment records (e.g., time sheets, applications).

Standards must closely duplicate the signatures or handwriting found in the questioned documents. If the questioned document is a check, it may be useful to collect cancelled checks as standards. If the questioned document is an anonymous letter, collection of police statements or written correspondence may provide the best specimens for comparison. Like must always be compared with like. For example, the signature "John Jones" cannot be effectively compared to the signature "Laura Neu", since these two signatures only have one letter in common. The "John Jones" signature must be compared to other "John Jones" signatures. Also, cursive writing must be compared with cursive known standards and hand printing with hand printed standards.

Standards should also be contemporaneous with the questioned document. Contemporaneous defined for FDE purposes is within 2–3 years before or after the date of the questioned document. The case evidence will be most useful if known standards are acquired from the same year as the questioned document.

2. TYPEWRITING AND OTHER PRINTED MATERIALS

Although once common in offices, schools, and homes, typewriters exist today in off-the-grid cabins, for artistic effects in communication, and for the occasional address on an envelope. Christopher Latham Sholes of Milwaukee, Wisconsin, USA, receives credit for the invention of the typewriter in 1867 because his invention actually went commercial.[11] Computers, word processors, and printers have taken over and surpassed the typewriter in modern business communications. Printers include inkjet printers, laser printers, thermal printers, dot matrix printers, facsimile, and photocopiers (color and black and white). Business and property documents from the heyday of the typewriter are still in circulation, so the FDE must be prepared to work the occasional typewriting case.

The method to determine the origin or authenticity of a typewritten document follows the principles of analysis, comparison, and evaluation of a handwritten document. Standards produced by a particular

[10] Id. at pp. 131–132.

[11] Wilfred A. Beeching, *Century of the Typewriter*, British Typewriter Museum Publishing, 1974 at p. 28.

typewriter would be compared to the questioned typewriting. The exact text of the questioned document should be typed several times on the known typewriter. Other typewriter examinations may intercompare typewriting within a single document or series of documents in order to determine whether more than one typestyle was used to prepare the document. Also, the make and model of the questioned typewriting may be determined by comparing the questioned typewriting to a reference collection of known typewriting. The typewritten text read and examined from a carbon film typewriter ribbon may be compared to typewriting on a questioned document. Typewriters can through wear and use develop damage to the type bars, elements, or daisy wheels. That wear to the typefaces appears on a document as a defect. A nonprint area on the lower right portion of the loop of the "d" was found on a questioned threatening letter and the typewriter ribbon from a suspect's typewriter.

Extensive, specific standards must be collected when the questioned document is typewritten, produced on a printer, facsimile, or photocopier. Consult with a FDE in order to determine the exact type and amount of standards to collect to suite the specifics of your case. For an extensive treatment of these topics see *Scientific Examination of Questioned Documents, Second Edition, 2006.*[12]

§5.05 COMPARISON OF HANDWRITINGS[13]

Forensic document examination is an applied science. In the handwriting comparison part of the work, FDEs use their education, training, experience, scientific methodology, and instrumentation to answer questions about the origin or authenticity of disputed writings. The principle at the heart of handwriting identification is that each person has a unique combination of handwriting characteristics. FDE observations for more than 100 years and research supporting the individuality of handwriting[14] make handwriting comparison a vital scientific evidence. The individuality of handwriting gained further scientific support from recent research that showed children's

---

[12] *See* note 9 *supra.*

[13] FDEs are trained to treat hand printing and handwriting the same and SWGDOC guidelines do not distinguish between the two, defining a "handwritten item" as "an item bearing something written by hand (for example, cursive writing, hand printing, signatures)." *See* Scientific Working Group for Forensic Document Examination, SWGDOC Standard for the Examination of Handwritten Items, ver. 2013–1 at p. 1 (available at: http://swgdoc.org/index. php/standards/published-standards)(last accessed November 4, 2016). One court has found the application of the same standards to handwriting and hand printing to be problematic given the critical differences that exist between the two. *See* United States v. Johnsted, 30 F. Supp.3d 814, 819 (W.D. Wisc. 2013). A study by Mitchell and Merlino found a high reliability rate of FDEs identifying or excluding the writers of block hand printing and used the same methodology employed in cursive handwriting cases. *See* L. Mitchell and M. Merlino, "A Blind Study on the Reliability of Hand Printing Identification by Forensic Document Examiners," 19 J. Am. Soc. of Quest. Doc. Exam. 25–31 (2016).

[14] Sargur Srihari et al., "Individuality of Handwriting," 47 J. Forensic Sci. 856–872 (2002).

handwriting gained more distinctiveness as children developed and progressed through grade school.[15]

A second principle in the examination of handwriting is that each person has natural variation. People are not writing machines and handwriting is not reproduced with machine-like precision. The act of handwriting involves a combination of visual, muscular, and cognitive processes. No two signatures will be exactly alike. The typical small changes in repeated writing of the same material are referred to as natural variation in handwriting.

A third principle in the examination and comparison of handwriting is that each person, generally, cannot exceed their skill level. A poorly skilled writer will have difficulty simulating the writing of highly skilled writer.

A person who tries to simulate the signature of another person will generally focus on the construction of the letter forms, but FDEs consider many other qualities and features in their examinations. The Scientific Working Group for Forensic Document Examination (SWGDOC) Standard for the Examination of Handwritten Items provides the following list of significant writing features considered by FDEs:

> Among the features to be considered are elements of the writing such as abbreviation; alignment; arrangement, formatting, and positioning; capitalization; connectedness and disconnectedness; cross strokes and dots, diacritics and punctuation; direction of strokes; disguise; embellishments; formation; freedom of execution; handedness; legibility; line quality; method of production; pen hold and pen position; overall pressure and patterns of pressure emphasis; proportion; simplification; size; slant; skill; slant or slope; spacing; speed; initial, connecting, and terminal strokes; system; tremor; type of writing; and range of variation.

> Other features such as lifts, stops and hesitations of the writing instrument; patching and retouching; slow, drawn quality of the line; unnatural tremor; and guide lines of various forms should be evaluated when present.[16]

Albert S. Osborn, considered the father of questioned documents, described the following principles of the identification of handwriting in his 1929 text book *Questioned Documents*:

> One of the first of these principles is that those identifying or differentiating characteristics are of the most force which are

---

[15] Sargur Srihari et al., "Development of Individuality in Children's Handwriting," 61 J. Forensic Sci. 1292–1300 (2016).

[16] SWGDOC Standard for Examination of Handwritten Items, ver. 2013–1 (available at: http://swgdoc.org/index.php/standards/published-standards)(last accessed October 26, 2016).

most divergent from the regular system or national features of a particular handwriting under examination.

The second principle, perhaps more important than the first, is that those repeated characteristics which are inconspicuous should first be sought for and should be given the most weight, for these are likely to be so unconscious that they would not intentionally be omitted when the attempt is made to disguise and would not be successfully copied from the writing of another when simulation is attempted.

A third principle is that ordinary system or national features and elements are not alone sufficient on which to base a judgement on identity of two writings, although these characteristics necessarily have value as evidence of identity, as stated above, if present in sufficient number and in combination with individual qualities and characteristics.

Any character in writing or any writing habit may be modified and individualized by different writers in many different ways and in many varying degrees, and the writing individuality of any particular writer is made up of all these common and uncommon characteristics and habits. As in identifying a person, as we have already seen, it always is the combination of particulars that identifies, and necessarily the more numerous and unusual the various elements and features the more certain the identity.[17]

Handwriting features are useful in identification of questioned documents because handwriting is mainly executed without conscious attention to it, rather as an efficient means of communication. Figure 1 shows a chart from a threatening letter case. The hand printing in question and the counterparts in the known sample illustrate some of the unconscious features that served to identify the writing in the questioned letter. The significant features include misspellings, capitalization characteristics, spacing characteristics, and overwriting.

---

[17] The first edition was published in 1910; the second in 1929, pp. 250–253.

Figure 1: Image of a chart showing questioned hand printing and known hand printing from a suspect in a threatening letter to a witness case.

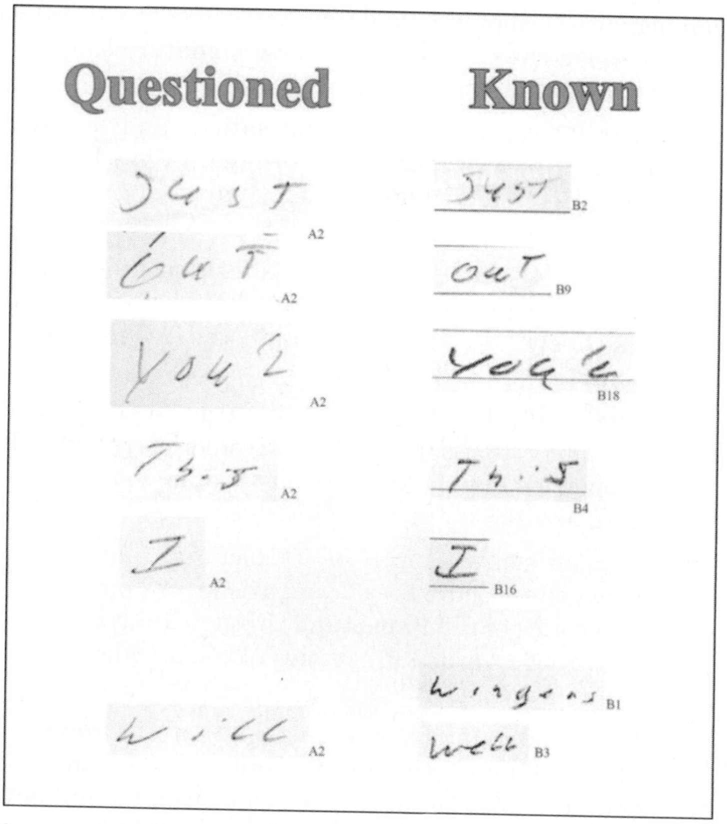

Differences in handwriting comparisons have great importance. Just as a combination of similarities proves who wrote a questioned document, a combination of differences eliminates a person who did not write the questioned writing. A forger may pay greatest attention to execution of the capital letters when simulating another person's handwriting. The lowercase letters often provide a trove of inconspicuous differences in a simulated writing because the forger lacks appreciation for their significance in identification. Line quality in genuine writing is also difficult for a person simulating another's handwriting to accomplish. Natural writing flows smoothly on the page where unnatural writing of a forger contains hesitations, blunt beginning and ending strokes, patching and retouching, and possibly tremor in the line.

In comparing signatures FDEs need to acquire signature standards contemporaneous with the questioned signature and also collect the same type of signature. Formal signatures on wills, trusts, and partnership agreements may differ considerably from informal signatures used in everyday business. If the questioned signature is on a change of beneficiary form, other formal signatures should be collected for comparison specimens. A wide range of signatures should be collected for comparison purposes in a disputed signature case. An extensive sample of 20–30 known signatures from everyday business and formal signatures should help define the range of natural variation of the writer in each case. Additional known signature samples may be required depending on the particular case.

Modern methodology in the examination and comparison of disputed handwriting was described originally by Roy Huber, a Canadian FDE. He referred to it as analysis, comparison, and evaluation (ACE):

> There are three distinct stages in establishing the identity of any person or thing through which the forensic scientist must pass, consciously or otherwise, in the course of his examination:[18]
>
> 1. Analysis. The "unknown" item must be classified according to its properties or characteristics. These properties may be directly observable, measurable, or implied.
>
> 2. Comparison. Stripped of its pictorial effects and its subjective context, a comparison is made of the properties of the item found through analysis with the known of recorded properties of others whose identity is unquestioned.
>
> 3. Evaluation. It is not sufficient that the comparison disclose similarities or dissimilarities in any of the characteristic properties of knowns and unknowns. Each property will have a certain value for identification purposes, determined chiefly by its relative frequency of occurrence. The weight of significance of each must be considered.

The comparison of handwriting by an FDE with proper education, training, and experience provides evidence concerning the source of a disputed signature on a will or an anonymous letter in the work place. The details evaluated in a questioned document case are well beyond the knowledge of the laymen. Consultation with a properly trained FDE will assist in reaching the truth of the matter and may prevent a miscarriage of justice.

§5.06 STANDARDIZATION

Forensic document examiners were early adapters of standards governing their work. The FDE community needed to standardize terminology of conclusions so that FDEs could better understand each other and so that the courts and attorneys who used their services could

---

[18] Royston A. Huber, "Expert Witnesses: In Defense of Expert Witnesses in General and Document Examiners in Particular," 2 Criminal Law Quarterly 274–295 (1959).

also appreciate the exact meaning of the conclusions. In 1990, the Questioned Documents Section of the American Academy of Forensic Sciences and the American Board of Forensic Document Examiners adopted recommended guidelines for terminology in reports and testimony.[19] In formulating the guidelines, the drafters found that, in addition to the three basic conclusions of "identification," "elimination," and "no conclusion," the bulk of the qualified examiners also presented conclusions dealing with six qualified opinions. The drafters established an opinion scale with 9 levels of certainty for expressing conclusions in questioned document cases:

(1) identification (definite conclusion of identity);

(2) strong probability (highly probable, very probable);

(3) probable;

(4) indications (evidence to suggest);

(5) no conclusion (totally inconclusive, indeterminable);

(6) indications did not (a very weak opinion);

(7) probably did not;

(8) strong probability did not; and

(9) elimination.[20]

In particular, the guidelines provided clarity for the conclusions that there were "indications" a subject "may have written" or "may not have written" the questioned document that had caused misunderstanding:

> Indications (evidence to suggest)—A body of writing has few features which are of significance for handwriting comparison purposes, but those features are in agreement with another body of writing.
>
>> Example: There is evidence which indicates (or suggests) that John Doe may have written the questioned material, but the evidence falls far short of that necessary to support a definite conclusion.
>
> Note: this is a very weak opinion, and a report may be misinterpreted to be an identification by some readers if the report simply states, "The evidence indicates that John Doe wrote the questioned material." There should always be additional limiting words or phrases (such as "may have" or "but the evidence is far from conclusive") when this opinion is reported, to ensure that the reader understands that the opinion is weak. . ."[21]

---

[19] Their suggestions were later published. Thomas McAlexander, Jan Beck and Ronald Dick, "The Standardization of Handwriting Opinion Terminology," Letters to the Editor, 36 J. Forensic Sci. 311 (1991).

[20] Id.

[21] Id. at p. 315.

In a further stride toward standardization in forensic document examination, a group of FDEs formed a group called the Technical Working Group for Document Examiners (TWGDOC) in 1997. This group later became the Scientific Working Group for Document Examination (SWGDOC). SWGDOC published standards through the American Society for Testing and Materials International (ASTM).[22] ASTM E1658 Standard Terminology for Expressing Conclusions of Forensic Document Examiners formally established the nine-point opinion scale originally written by McAlexander, Beck, and Dick.[23] In 2012, SWGDOC made their standards available for free through its website and now has published 21 peer-reviewed standards:[24]

Standard for Scope of the Work of Forensic Document Examiners

Standard for Test Methods for Forensic Writing Ink Comparisons

Standard Terminology for Expressing Conclusions of Forensic Document Examiners

Standard for Writing Ink Identification

Terminology Relating to the Examination of Questioned Documents

Standard for Examination of Mechanical Checkwriter Impressions

Standard for Examination of Dry Seal Impressions

Standard for Examination of Fracture Pattern and Paper Fiber Impressions on Single-Strike Film Ribbons and Typed Text

Standard for Physical Match of Paper Cuts, Tears, and Perforations in Forensic Document Examinations

Standard for Examination of Rubber Stamp Impressions

Standard for Examination of Handwritten Items

Standard for Indentation Examinations

Standard for Non-destructive Examination of Paper

Standard Examination of Altered Documents

Standard Minimum Training Requirements for Forensic Document Examiners

Standard for Examination of Documents Produced with Liquid Ink Jet Technology

---

[22] Carl R. McClary, "Chapter 32: Conclusions and Guidelines" in Jan Seaman Kelly & Brian Lindblom eds., *Scientific Examination of Questioned Documents*, 2d ed., CRC Press, 2006 at pp. 167–171.

[23] ASTM International: www.astm.org.

[24] *See* http://swgdoc.org/index.php/standards/published-standards (last accessed November 2, 2016).

Standard for Examination of Documents Produced with Toner Technology

Standard for Examination of Typewritten Items

Standard for Preservation of Charred Documents

Standard for Preservation of Liquid Soaked Documents

Standard for Use of Image Capture and Storage Technology in Forensic Document Examination

The American Society for Testing Materials International (ASTM) continues to offer several active standards applicable to forensic document examination.[25] Standardization also continues to define best practices for the work of FDEs through the work of the National Institute of Standards and Technology (NIST) Organization of Scientific Area Committees (OSAC). The OSAC Forensic Document Examination Subcommittee will focus on standards and guidelines related to the forensic analysis, comparison, and evaluation of documents.[26]

III. FORENSIC DOCUMENT EXAMINATIONS

§5.07 DECIPHERMENT OF INDENTED WRITING, CHARRED DOCUMENTS, AND EVIDENCE OF ALTERATIONS

Instrumentation allows the visualization of latent indented writing, the writing on charred documents, and alterations of documents. Photography and digital imaging techniques, along with other specialized instruments, provide FDEs with support in deciphering evidence and also in demonstrating their findings.[27]

A message written on the top sheet of a legal pad of paper leaves indented impressions on the pages below the top page. Recovered indented writing may become evidence of a crime in a criminal case or reveal a clue about the date of preparation of a document in a civil case. The instrument used by FDEs to visualize indented writing is the Electrostatic Detection Apparatus (ESDA) made by an English company. Other manufacturers also make electrostatic detection

---

[25] *See* www.astm.org.

[26] *See* https://www.nist.gov/topics/forensic-science/forensic-document-examination-sub committee (last accessed November 2, 2016).

[27] *See* Jane A. Lewis, *Forensic Document Examination Fundamentals and Current Trends.* Academic Press, 2014 at Chapter 6: Instrumentation. *See also,* Frank Hicks, Brian S. Lindblom and Robert Gervais, "Chapter 31: Cameras, Scanners, and Image Enhancement," in Jan Seaman Kelly and Brian S. Lindblom eds, *Scientific Examination of Questioned Documents,* 2d ed., CRC Press, 2006 at pp. 359–364; Frank Hicks, Brian S. Lindblom and Robert Gervais, "Chapter 34: Demonstrative Charts," in in Jan Seaman Kelly and Brian S. Lindblom eds, *Scientific Examination of Questioned Documents,* 2d ed., CRC Press, 2006 at pp. 375–382; David Ellen, *Scientific Examination of Documents Methods and Techniques,* 3d ed., CRC Press, 2005 at pp. 155–164.

devices. Research pertaining to ESDA flourished over the last two decades.[28]

Figure 2: Indented writing from a burglary case.

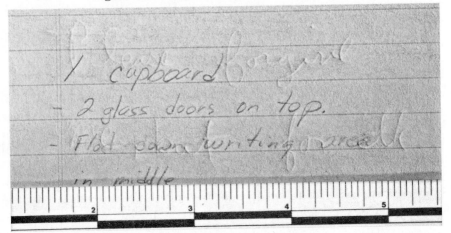

The ESDA process begins with humidifying a questioned document in a humidity chamber. The document is then placed on a metal platen and a vacuum pump secures it to the platen. Transparent imaging film covers the document and is then charged with a corona wand. Cascade developer is poured over the charged imaging film to develop the image of indented material. The image is then secured with transparent fixing film. The ESDA lift is visualized with a white sheet of paper placed behind the ESDA lift. This process was used on a burglary case. A note was left behind at the crime scene that displayed indented writing. See Figure 2. The image shows a portion of the questioned document with oblique lighting to visualize the indented writing on the document. Figure 3 shows an ESDA lift of the document from Figure 2 that reveals the entire text of the developed indented writing.

---

[28] *See* Bonnie L. Beal, "Effects of Water Temperature vs. Time in Humidifying Documents for Electrostatic Detection Apparatus Examination," 5 J. Am. Soc. of Quest. Doc. Exam. 78 (2002); Jerry L. Brown and Gary Licht, "Using the ESDA to Visualize Typewriter Indented Markings," 1 J. Am. Soc. of Quest. Doc. Exam. 113 (1998); Melanie Holt, Alison Sears and Chris Lennard, "Effect of DNA Tape Lifting on the Ability of the ESDA to Recover Latent Indentations in Paper," 1 J. Am. Soc. Of Quest. Doc. Exam. 17 (2014); Jane A. Lewis, "Indentation Examination Enhancement," 2 J. Am. Soc. Of Quest. Doc. Exam. 8 (2005); Kate Savoie, "Development of a Supplemental Technique to Increase Visualization of Handwriting Indentations in Crumpled Documents with the Use of and Electrostatic Detection Device (EDD)," 1 J. Am. Soc. Of Quest. Doc. Exam. 16 (2013).

Figure 3: ESDA lift showing developed indented writing from a burglary case.

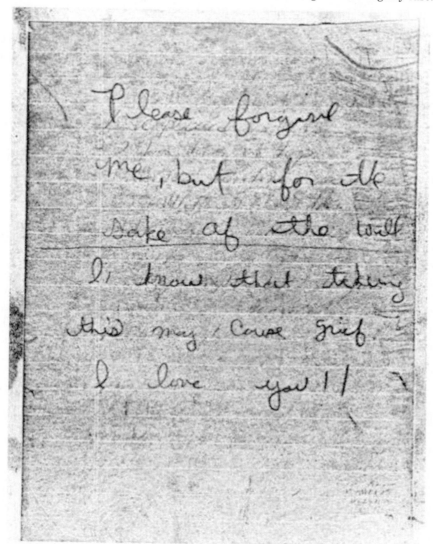

Special handling secures the condition of charred documents. Handwriting on burned documents may be visualized with special photography or image processing, but first the ash fragments must be preserved for analysis. Shallow boxes with cotton to protect the fragile document can be effective. Protection and preservation of charred documents by polyester film encapsulation is another method.[29]

Digital image processing has largely replaced traditional photography in the FDE laboratory. Evidence arriving for examination is typically labeled, photocopied, and scanned on a flatbed scanner.

---

[29] Hector I. Maldonado, "Polyester Film Encapsulation in Charred Document Cases," Presentation at the 46th Annual Meeting of the American Academy of Forensic Sciences, San Antonio, Texas, February 18, 1994.

Images will then be cropped for insertion in a study chart. Digital cameras mounted on a quadrapod and lit with a light source to provide oblique light may be used to capture indented writing on a document. The captured digital images will then be arranged in labeled charts with the program Adobe Photoshop. A handheld digital microscope that displays images on the screen of a laptop computer may also be employed to illustrate subtle pen lifts or blunt beginning and ending strokes of handwriting. Digital cameras mounted on stereo microscopes produce photomicrographs which depict details like striation patterns in an ink line or inkjet printing characteristics. The video spectral comparator (VSC) helps to reveal alterations to documents. It separates visually similar inks that have different formulas with filters and a video camera sensitive to the visual, ultraviolet, and infrared portion of the electromagnetic spectrum. A raised amount on a check can be revealed with the VSC if the inks react differently to lights and filters of the instrument. One ink may absorb infrared light and darken while another ink on the same document may reflect infrared light and lighten or disappear. The VSC is also useful in revealing obliterated writing if the obliteration is a different formula of ink from the ink under the obliterated writing. These techniques are used in medical records cases and alterations of checks or any business documents. The basic technology is described in research by Richards in 1977.[30] Figure 4 shows an altered receipt with two different inks recorded with a VSC.

Figure 4: Alteration of a receipt revealed using the VSC displaying infra-red luminescence. Image from Jim Lee.

30 Gerald B. Richards, "The Application of Electronic Video Techniques to Infrared and Ultraviolet Examinations," 22 J. Forensic Sci. 53–60 (1977).

§5.08   SPECIAL CONSIDERATION IN HANDWRITING COMPARISONS

A distorted questioned signature on a will may not agree with a known writing sample collected only a year prior to the date of the will. Certain circumstances may cause a genuine signature to look unnatural. Illness, the use of the unaccustomed hand, and old age may cause a change in handwriting. FDEs consider these factors and many others in their analysis of questioned documents.

Writing with the unaccustomed or off hand is one method used by forgers to disguise their natural handwriting. This method of disguise may appear in threatening letters written anonymously. Suspects in forged check cases may write with their off hand when giving handwriting samples for comparison purposes. The writing, in most instances, looks unnatural. The off hand lacks the skill and practice of the principle writing hand. The writing will often appear irregular with poor line quality shown in uneven spacing, speed, and rhythm.[31] Since handwriting has visual and cognitive components, off hand writing may still produce individualizing characteristics found in the handwriting from the usual hand. When collecting a handwriting sample from a suspect it is common practice to also collect handwriting written with the unaccustomed hand.

Poor health may change the appearance of signatures and handwriting and is a consideration in the work of FDEs. The question of handwriting and infirmities is a vast subject area that will be briefly addressed here. Research shows that schizophrenia and the drugs used to treat conditions like schizophrenia also have an effect on handwriting.[32] Questions about illness and handwriting generally occur during cases involving signatures on wills, trusts, change of beneficiary forms, and other documents prepared during old age or at the end of life. Illness may affect signatures. Changes to signatures or handwriting from sickness may cause the writing to be less controlled and lack a smooth line quality. The obstacle of a questioned signature executed during illness may be overcome by collecting other known signatures from the same time period as the questioned signature. If no such signature specimens are available from the relevant time period, the FDE may need to acknowledge the limitations of the evidence and arrive at a qualified or no conclusion opinion.[33]

---

[31] *See* Greg Dawson, "Brain Function and Writing with the Unaccustomed Left Hand," 30 J. Forensic Sci. 167 (1985); Linton A. Mohammed et al., "The Dynamic Character of Disguise Behavior for Text-Based, Mixed, and Stylized Signatures," 56 J. Forensic Sci. S136–S141 (2011).

[32] Ilhami Komur et al., "Differences in Handwriting of Schizophrenia Patients and Examination of Change after Treatment," 60 J. Forensic Sci. 1613–1619 (2015).

[33] David Ellen, *Scientific Examination of Documents: Methods and Techniques,* 3d ed., CRC Press, 2005 at pp. 27–41.

Deterioration of handwriting often occurs with advanced age, but not always. Forensic document examiner Jane Lewis's mother supplied a sample of her handwriting (showing the Palmer Method) in 2013, when she was 88 years old. The quality of the handwriting was very good.[34] More often, handwriting changes over time. A recent study examined the effects of gender and age on signature deterioration in older adults found general deterioration with advanced age and more disfluency in men than women.[35]

In advanced age, people may write less or have a family member or aid sign checks, receipts and medical documents for them. The danger of a corrupted known sample must be considered by the FDE when receiving a sample that could contain the handwriting of more than one writer. Intercomparison of a relevant set of known writing specimens will allow the FDE to sort out signatures that fall outside the range of natural variation of the writer and proceed with the proper known signature sample.[36] Other extraneous factors also cause handwriting to change. The choice of writing instrument may affect the writing. The appearance of writing produced with a broad tipped marker, pencil, or ballpoint pen may reveal a wide range of details in the written product. Also, signing a receipt outside on a cold day may inhibit the fluid movement of the hand.

Sufficient contemporaneous known standards will minimize the effect of illness, age and other environmental factors on handwriting. In case preparation, investigators and attorneys must gather original and extensive known writing samples to help answer all possible questions about the evidence in questioned document cases.

§5.09 COMPARISON OF TYPEWRITINGS

Typewritten corporate documents generated from the 1960s through the 1980s were at the center of a dispute over whether one partner willingly transferred shares to another family member. The typewritten documents were either genuine or fabricated later. Forensic document examiners may be asked to determine the answer to questions like this with the help of their knowledge of introductory dates of typewriters, knowledge of types of ribbons, and the introduction date of correction fluid.[37] Extensive typewriter reference

---

[34] Jane A. Lewis, Forensic Document Examination Fundamentals and Current Trends, Academic Press, 2004 at p. 16.

[35] Michael P. Caligiuri et al., "Kinematics of Signature Writing in Healthy Aging," 59 J. Forensic Sci. 1020–1024 (2014).

[36] See Howard C. Rile, Jr., "Chapter 9: Identification of Signatures" in Jan Seaman Kelly and Brian S. Lindblom eds., Scientific Examination of Questioned Documents, 2d ed., CRC Press, 2006 at pp. 75–108.

[37] See Mary W. Kelly, "Chapter 15: Typewriters" in Jan Seaman Kelly & Brian Lindblom eds., Scientific Examination of Questioned Documents, 2d ed., CRC Press, 2006 at pp. 177–190. See also Significant Dates of Modern Typing Methods, by Jan Seaman Kelly, The American Board of Forensic Document Examiners Monograph, 1993.

files and experience working many disputed typewriting cases also contributes to the FDEs' expertise.

Some understanding of the evolution of the typewriter is necessary to appreciate the evidence and process of cases involving typewriting evidence. The fact that Milwaukee, Wisconsin, USA, is the birthplace of the typewriter elicits great civic pride to those of us who live in the town better known for beer and bratwurst. As mentioned in a previous section of this chapter, Christopher Latham Sholes gets the credit for inventing the typewriter because his version went commercial. A plaque at the intersection of 4th and State Street in Milwaukee commemorates this history. See Figure 5. Early Sholes era typewriters live on in a business on Juneau Street in Milwaukee that used to be Christopher Latham Sholes' house. See Figure 6.

Figure 5: Invention of the Typewriter plaque honoring Sholes and colleagues on State Street downtown Milwaukee, Wisconsin, USA.

Figure 6: Remington typewriter at Sholes' house in Milwaukee, Wisconsin, USA.

The Sholes typewriter used a manual type bar mechanism to impress the type letter into a paper. In 1961, IBM introduced a ball element that was referred to as a golf-ball element.[38] This single spherical element replaced the type bars from the early typewriters. All of the characters were contained on a small ball element that was interchangeable with ball elements containing other typestyles. A different typestyle could be accomplished without removing the paper from the typewriter by simply popping out the ball element and replacing it with another. The final evolution of the typing mechanism for typewriters occurred in 1974 with the introduction of the typewheel element or daisy wheel element.[39] The daisy wheel consists of spokes with letters on the end of each spoke arranged around a central hub. Most modern machines still in use today use a daisy wheel element mechanism.

Defects in typewriter printing mechanisms occur from wear and tear on the type bars, ball elements, or daisy wheel elements. They may appear on a typed document as nonprint areas, heavy inking on one side of the letter or letters typed out of horizontal or vertical alignment.

---

[38] *See* Mary W. Kelly, "Chapter 15: Typewriters" in Jan Seaman Kelly & Brian Lindblom eds., *Scientific Examination of Questioned Documents,* 2d ed., CRC Press, 2006 at p. 181.

[39] Id. at pp. 184–186.

Defects become individualizing characteristics that can serve to identify a typed document with a particular typewriter.

Classification systems allow FDEs to search a typewritten document to determine the possible make and model of the typewriter used to generate the questioned document. Present day classification systems evolved from those developed by Ordway Hilton, David Crown, Gerry de la Durantaye, and Richard Totty.[40] Dr. Philip Bouffard's TYPE computerized classification system was presented in a 1992 paper at the AAFS.[41] The source of samples for the TYPE system were from the Haas atlases written in German. The latest evolution of the TYPE system of classification is Win Type, a Windows based format.[42]

Some of the characteristics that serve to identify typed text may include: the particular typewriting mechanism, the pitch or horizontal spacing, the style of type (for example, courier or prestige), the size of the characters, the kind of ribbon, and the correction fluid, tape, or lift off mechanism.[43]

§5.10 WORD PROCESSORS AND COMPUTER-PRODUCED DOCUMENTS

Word processing began in the memory mechanism of a typewriter before moving to word processing programs in personal computers or lap tops with electronic attachments to printers. The output from printers attached to computers largely eliminates the wear characteristics observed in typewriters. Forensic document examiners still examine documents for printing defects and various printing characteristics in order to identify the source of the documents.

Thermal inkjet printers were developed by Hewlett-Packard and Canon in the late 1970s and early 1980s.[44] The mechanism works by using a heated element to force ink droplets onto paper.[45] According to the SWGDOC Standard for Examination of Documents Produced with Liquid Ink Jet Technology, an ink jet printer is a "nonimpact printer in which the characters are formed by projecting droplets of ink onto a

---

[40] Id. at pp. 186–187.

[41] Philip D. Bouffard, "A PC-Based Typewriter Typestyle Classification System Standards," paper presented at the American Academy of Forensic Sciences meeting, New Orleans, LA, 1992.

[42] Karen Nobles, "An Update of the Typestyle Classification Program (TYPE) into Windows Based Format (Win Type)," 13 J. Am. Soc. of Quest. Doc. Exam. 37–42 (2010).

[43] See SWGDOC Standard for Examination of Typewritten Items, ver. 2013–1 (available at: http://swgdoc.org/index.php/standards/published-standards)(last accessed November 1, 2016).

[44] See William J. Flynn, "Chapter 16: The Examination of Computer-Generated Documents," in Jan Seman Kelly & Brian Lindblom eds., Scientific Examination of Questioned Documents, 2d ed., CRC Press, 2006 at pp. 191–218.

[45] Id.

substrate."[46] Epson developed a variation on ink jet technology using a piezoelectric process.[47] SWGDOC Standard for Examination of Documents Produced with Liquid Ink Jet Technology describes the piezoelectric process as "ink jet technology where the electrically stimulated deformation of a crystal causes the expulsion of the droplets from the ink chamber."[48]

Laser/LED or LCD printers produce images with dry toner on paper. The process originated with Chester Carlson, the father of xerography in 1939.[49] Later, the Xerox Company produced a laser printer and began marketing it in 1977.[50] SWGDOC Standard for Examination of Documents Produced with Toner Technology describes a laser printer as a "nonimpact printer that uses a laser light source driven by digital signals to create images on a photoconductor."[51] The light source of a so-called laser printer may not indeed actually be a laser. It could be a Light-Emitting Diode (LED) or a Liquid Crystal Display (LCD) or some other light source.[52]

Other computer-generated printing technologies include: thermal wax printers, dye sublimation printers, mainframe line printers, dot matrix printers, digital offset printers, and many others.[53]

§5.11   COMPARISON OF PRINTED MATTER

If a company stock certificate or an identification document like a passport comes into question, an FDE's training in the recognition of printing processes will help determine a genuine or a counterfeit document. This section will describe five main printing processes used to create commercial documents: letterpress, thermography, gravure, offset lithography, and screen printing.

---

[46] SWGDOC Standard for Examination of Documents Produced with Liquid ink Jet Technology, ver. 2013–1 (available at: http://swgdoc.org/index.php/standards/published-standards)(last accessed November 1, 2016).

[47] *See* William J. Flynn, "Chapter 16: The Examination of Computer-Generated Documents," in Jan Seman Kelly and Brian Lindblom eds., *Scientific Examination of Questioned Documents,* 2d ed., CRC Press, 2006 at pp. 191–218.

[48] SWGDOC Standard for Examination of Documents Produced with Liquid ink Jet Technology, ver. 2013–1 (available at: http://swgdoc.org/index.php/standards/published-standards)(last accessed November 1, 2016). *See also* P. Doherty, "Classification of Ink Jet Printers and Inks," 1 J. Am. Soc. of Quest. Doc. Exam. 88–106 (1998).

[49] William J. Flynn, "Chapter 16: The Examination of Computer-Generated Documents," in Jan Seman Kelly and Brian Lindblom eds., *Scientific Examination of Questioned Documents,* 2d ed., CRC Press, 2006 at pp. 191–218.

[50] Id.

[51] SWGDOC Standard for Examination of Documents Produced with Toner Technology, ver. 2013–1 (available at: http://swgdoc.org/index.php/standards/published-standards)(last accessed November 1, 2016).

[52] William J. Flynn, "Chapter 16: The Examination of Computer-Generated Documents," in Jan Seman Kelly and Brian Lindblom eds., *Scientific Examination of Questioned Documents,* 2d ed., CRC Press, 2006 at pp. 191–218.

[53] Id. *See also* Ian Batterham, *The Office Copying Revolution: History, Identification and Presentation,* National Archives of Australia, 2008.

Letterpress or relief printing is made with metal type, or plates, or photopolymer plates. The image area is above the area not to be printed. The raised area of the type or plate is covered with ink and pressed directly into the paper.[54] This method was used to print newspapers and magazines, but now is more often used for the production of business cards, invitations, greeting cards, and serial numbers on currency. Letterpress printing will exhibit a squeeze-out ring pattern around an individual character when viewed with a microscope.

Thermography appears most often in business cards for the raised feel of the type without the expensive engraved process found in gravure printing. These business cards achieve that feel by printing with letterpress or offset lithography by using a special nondrying ink. The wet ink is then covered with resin powder and heated to produce the raised resinous characters.[55] Documents created with thermography look like a plastic coating over the top of the ink when observed microscopically. They may feel, at first, like engraving, but look completely different under magnification.

Gravure is a type of intaglio printing and requires that the image be etched out of a copper plate. A cylinder moves through a container of ink that fills the etched areas. The excess ink is removed with a doctor blade and the image forms with pressure on the paper from the impression cylinder and plate cylinder.[56] The image formed on the paper in gravure printing is raised. Some feathering of the ink along the path of paper fibers appear under magnification. The printing method produces fine detail, but is expensive. Uses of gravure printing include: newspapers, magazines, postage stamps, business cards, letter head on stationary, fine art reproductions, and currency.

Offset lithography appears most commonly in everyday business documents like: business cards, advertising, greeting cards, labels, posters, packaging, and art work reproductions. Offset lithography prints on one single plane and operates on the principle that water and oil will not mix. Ink is offset from the printing plate to a rubber blanket before printing on paper.[57] The printed image is characterized by a lack of embossing and uniform ink coverage with smooth sharp edges.[58]

---

[54] Michael H. Bruno ed., *Pocket Pal: A Graphic Arts Production Handbook,* International Paper Co., 1992. *See also* Susan Fortunato, "Chapter 23: Conventional Printing Processes," in Jan Seaman Kelly and Brian Lindblom eds., *Scientific Examination of Questioned Documents,* 2d ed., CRC Press, 2006 at pp. 287–293; Gerald La Porte et al., "The Examination of Commercial Printing Defects to Assess Common Origin, Batch Variation, and Error Rate," 55 F. Forensic Sci. 136–140 (2010); Rhett Wiliamson et al., "Characterization of Printing Inks Using DART-Q-TOF-MS and Attenuated Total Reflectance (ATR) FTIR," 61 J. Forensic Sci. 706–714 (2016).

[55] Michael H. Bruno ed., *Pocket Pal: A Graphic Arts Production Handbook,* International Paper Co., 1992.

[56] Id.

[57] Id.

[58] Id.

Screen printing uses a screen made of silk, other fabric, or metal. The image area is a stencil that blocks the non-image area and allows the ink to flow through the stencil area with the help of a rubber squeegee.[59] Screen printing creates images on credit cards, shirts, posters, textiles, mugs, and many other items. Characteristics of screen printing include: thick ink, little embossing, and a jagged edge from the mesh of the screen.

Knowledge of basic commercial and other printing methods help FDEs to distinguish genuine items from counterfeit in a variety of cases through printing method and ink properties analysis. Training in security features normally found in identification documents is also extremely valuable in authenticating this type of evidence.

§5.12   ANALYSIS OF INKS

Ink analysis can provide answers through a variety of techniques to questions concerning when documents were created or endorsed and whether a document was altered after creation. FDEs generally use nondestructive methods to differentiate inks on a single document using a stereoscopic microscope with a fiber optic light source, a video spectral comparator with filters, and a camera sensitive from the ultraviolet through the infrared portions of the electromagnetic spectrum, spectroscopic analysis, and a digital microscope like the Miscope. Consideration of ink line morphology and intersections of ink and other materials used to create a document may also be useful in differentiating and determining the age or history of a document.[60]

Ink chemists follow the nondestructive testing of the FDE with minimally destructive chemical and instrumental testing to provide more information about the chemical composition of inks. This additional testing may serve to differentiate inks on one document, to determine the relative ages of inks on a document, identify the manufacturer of an ink, and determine the introduction date of the ink from samples in an ink reference library. The Internal Revenue Service National Forensic Laboratory and the US Secret Service Laboratory have an extensive ink reference library. Methods to distinguish different inks on the same document in an alteration case of, for example, checks or company share transfer documents, include: thin-layer chromatography,[61] gas chromatography/mass spectrometry

---

[59]   Id.

[60]   Valery N. Aginsky, "Ink Dating—Comparative Examination of Inks on Documents Using Optical and Chemical Methods," 16 J. Am. Soc. of Quest. Doc. Exam. 31–38 (2013); *see also* Jane A. Lewis, "Striation Patterns in New and Used Ballpoint Pens," 6 J. Am. Soc. of Quest. Doc. Exam. 67–71 (2003).

[61]   Jane A. Lewis, "Thin-layer Chromatography of Writing Inks Quality Control Considerations", 41 J. Forensic Sci. 874 (1996); *see also* Om Prakash Jasuja et al., "Examination of Gel Pen Inks Using Physical and Thin Layer Chromatographic Examination", 8 J. Am. Soc. of Quest. Doc. Exam. 83 (2005); Richard L. Brunelle and Kenneth R. Crawford, *Advances in the Forensic Analysis and Dating of Writing Ink,* Charles C. Thomas Pub. Ltd., 2003.

(GC/MS), Fourier Transform Infrared Spectroscopy (FTIR), Raman Spectroscopy, and Time-of-flight secondary ion mass spectrometry (TOF-SIMS).[62] SWGDOC Standard for Test Methods for Forensic Writing Ink Comparison offers a guide for current methods in ink comparison.[63]

Determination of the creation date of a document requires complex analysis and considerations. Inks consist generally of dyes, pigments, resins, volatile components, and other elements. Research over the last 20 years has explored technological advances to determine how old or new an ink is on a paper through analysis of certain ink components. Aginsky has developed two ink aging methods that measure the rate of aging or hardening of resin in ink and the evaporation rate of volatile components in ink as a result of aging.[64] These methods are based on the analysis of 2-phenoxyethanol (PE), a semi-volatile ink ingredient, with Gas Chromatography-Mass Spectrometry-Selective Ion Monitoring (GC-MS-SIM).[65] Recently, Bügler has reported an ink aging technique in which a two-step thermo desorption of PE (first at a low temperature and then at a high temperature) is used instead of a liquid extraction of PE.[66]

Popular writing instruments today are ballpoint pens, fiber tip pens, gel and rollerball pens, and the occasional fountain pen. A brief description of the ink components of each type of pen follows:

Ballpoint Pen Ink—

> The consistency of this ink is thick. It consists of dyes, pigments, organic solvents, resins, lubricants, and other additives to reduce clogging.[67]

---

[62] Brian S. Lindblom, "Chapter 13: Pens and Pencils," in Jan Seaman Kelly and Brian S. Lindblom eds., *Scientific Examination of Questioned Documents*, 2d ed., CRC Press, 2006 at pp. 147–159; *see also* Jihye Lee *et al.*, "TOF-SIMS Analysis of Red Color Inks of Writing and Printing Tools on Questioned Documents," 61 J. Forensic Sci. 815–822 (2016).

[63] SWGDOC Standard for Test Methods for Forensic Writing Ink Comparison, ver. 2013–1 (available at: http://swgdoc.org/index.php/standards/published-standards)(last accessed November 2, 2016). *See also* Richard L. Brunelle, "Inkdating-The State of the Art," 37 J. Forensic Sci. 113–124 (1992)(citations omitted)(The article traces the development of ink dating techniques from the 1930's to 1990); Stephanie Houlgrave, Gerald M. LaPorte and Joseph Stephens, "The Use of Filtered Light for the Evaluation of Writing Inks Analyzed Using Thin Layer Chromatography," 56 J. FORENSIC SCI. 778–782 (2011); Samir Senior, et al., "Characterization and Dating of Blue Ballpoint Pen Inks Using Principal Component Analysis of UV-Vis Absorption Spectra, IR Spectroscopy, and HPTLC," 57 J. FORENSIC SCI. 1087–1093 (2012); Cedric Neumann and Pierre Margot, "Considerations on the ASTM Standards 1789–04 and 1422–05 on the Forensic Examination of Ink," 55 J. FORENSIC SCI. 1304–1310 (2010).

[64] Valery N. Aginsky, "Dating and Characterizing Writing, Stamp Pad and Jet Printer Inks by Gas Chromatography/Mass Spectrometry," 2 Int'l J. Forensic Doc. Exam.103–115 (1996).

[65] Valery N. Aginsky, "Ink Aging Testing—Do Preceding Indentation Examinations Affect Ink Aging Parameters?" 17 J. Am. Soc. Of Quest. Doc. Exam. 49–63 (2014).

[66] Jürgen H. Bügler, Hans Buchner and Anton Dallmayer, "Age Determination of Ballpoint Pen Ink by Thermal Desorption and Gas Chromatography-Mass Spectrometry," 53 J. Forensic Sci. 982–988 (2008).

[67] Richard L. Brunelle and Kenneth R. Crawford, *Advances in the Forensic Analysis and Dating of Writing Ink*, Charles C. Thomas Pub. Ltd., 2003 at p. 31.

Water-based Ink (used in roller ball pens, fountain pens, felt-tip pens, or ink jet printer cartridges)—

The consistency of the ink in these pens is a thin fluid. It contains solvents, binding agents, moist-keeping agents, preservatives, emulsifying agents, pen block preventatives, food dyes, and diluting substances.[68]

Gel Pen Ink—

Gel pen ink has a thick plastic look. Components include pigments, dyes, resins, organic solvents, pseudoplastic imparting agents, semi-synthetic cellulose polymers, pH adjusting agents, lubricants, rust preventatives, and antiseptics.[69]

Understanding the physical, optical, and chemical properties of inks provides key information to determine the history of a document in order to determine its origin or authenticity.

§5.13   EXAMINATION OF PAPERS AND WATERMARKS

Documents like business share transfer agreements or wills may hold clues to their age or history through observations of the paper used to prepare them. If documents are prepared in the normal course of business, the papers are usually consistent in color and size. When a page is substituted in a group of documents it may be differentiated from original pages by optical brighteners, trim lines, weight, or thickness.

Figure 7: Date coded watermark.

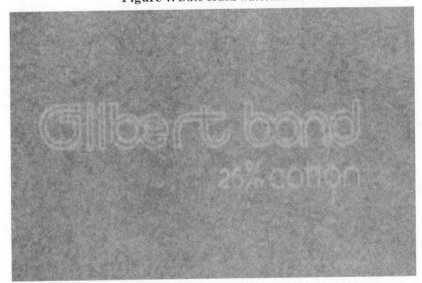

---

[68]   Id at p. 37.
[69]   Id. at pp. 34–35.

Watermarks on paper bear date codes devised by the manufacturer that may serve as an identification mechanism. Figure 7 shows a watermark with a date code of a vertical line beneath the second "o" in "cotton", this watermark was from 1985. Watermarks appear when holding a document to the light as a lighter area or darker area of the paper. They result when a dandy roll with a wire design pushes the paper fibers away to form the image in the wet end of the paper making process. Shaded watermarks are made with a furrow in the screen of the dandy roll to form a slightly darker image in the wet end of the paper making process.[70] Watermarks may be identified and dated by specific date codes and by changes in designs and design features by the manufacturer. Only a few companies manufacture dandy rolls used to create watermarks. Sources of these companies may be found by contacting the Integrated Paper Services Fiber Science Department,[71] and publications like Lockwood-Post Directory of Pulp and Paper Mills.[72] Forgers of watermarks use wax or oils to mimic the transparency of a genuine watermark.[73] False watermarks may be detected by a FDE using a microscope with oblique light or a video spectral comparator (VSC).

Paper is commonly made from cellulose fibers that are cooked with chemicals and water, dried and pressed between rollers, and eventually cut into sheets. Almost anything can be used to make paper. Fibers from silk, wool, or asbestos have been used. Common papermaking materials are hard and soft wood trees, cotton, grasses, and leaf fibers like manila and sisal.[74] Forensic examination of paper to determine the origin or authenticity begins with an analysis of the physical properties of the paper. The size, color, thickness (measured with a micrometer), opacity, fluorescent properties, and watermarks are evaluated by the FDE.[75] The initial physical and optical properties are determined nondestructively. Caution must be exercised in assessing paper brightness since research has shown that occasionally different rolls of paper during the manufacturing process may become combined in a single ream of paper and then different papers in the same ream will exhibit different brightness characteristics.[76] SWGDOC Standard for

---

[70] Susan Fortunato, "Chapter 24: Paper Examinations," in Jan Seaman Kelly and Brian S. Lindblom eds., *Scientific Examination of Questioned Documents*, 2d ed., CRC Press, 2006 at pp. 293–303.

[71] www.integratedpaperservice.com.

[72] Paperloop Publications, *Lockwood-Post's Directory of Pulp and Paper Mills,* Paperloop Publications, San Francisco, published annually. *See* http://www.risiinfo.com/product/lockwood-post/.

[73] Richard L. Brunelle and Robert W. Reed, *Forensic Examination of Ink and Paper,* Charles C. Thomas Pub. Ltd., 1984.

[74] Bertie Lee Browning, *Analysis of Paper*, 2d ed., M. Dekker, 1977.

[75] *See* Richard L. Brunelle and Robert W. Reed, *Forensic Examination of Ink and Paper,* Charles C. Thomas Pub. Ltd., 1984.

[76] James Green, "Reliability of Paper Brightness in Authenticating Documents," 57 J. Forensic Sci. 1003–1007 (2012).

Non-destructive Examination of Paper[77] describes in detail the peer reviewed methods followed by FDEs. Paper fiber analysis is a destructive process in that small sections must be removed from the document and boiled in distilled water to separate the paper into individual fibers. These fibers are placed on glass microscope slides and stained for species analysis.[78] Other additives in papers can be determined with techniques and instrumental analysis used by forensic chemists.

§5.14 EXAMINATION OF CHECKWRITERS

Checkwriters came into existence around 1870.[79] They were intended to prevent alterations of checks by shredding and embossing impressions of the amount of the check and other material into the paper. The design of the different parts of the checkwriter impression areas can be evaluated to identify the manufacturer.[80] Associating a particular checkwriter to a questioned check may be possible through observation of wear related defects from misalignment of the printing elements, damage to pinhole perforations, and random markings from various parts of the machine.[81] Checkwriters impressions seldom appear today in everyday business checks.

§5.15 PHOTOCOPIERS AND FACSIMILES

Photocopiers may be stand-alone machines or multifunction devices that can scan, print, and copy documents. These multifunction devices serve as personal printing presses along with a copier function. Most copiers today use an indirect electrostatic process. Photocopiers have forensic significance in that they impart individual and class characteristics that can be used by a trained FDE to determine whether a document is a copy or an original, the type of printer or copier used to create the document, and whether a questioned document was produced on a particular copier.[82]

In the case of a photocopied anonymous threatening letter in a small office, an FDE will conduct a comparison between samples from one or more office photocopiers and the questioned letter. First, class characteristics of the questioned document will be observed: whether

---

[77] SWGDOC Standard for Non-destructive Examination of Paper, ver. 2013–1 (available at: http://swgdoc.org/index.php/standards/published-standards)(last accessed November 2, 2016).

[78] See Richard L. Brunelle and Robert W. Reed, Forensic Examination of Ink and Paper, Charles C. Thomas Pub. Ltd., 1984.

[79] Thomas Vastrick, "Chapter 21: Checkwriters," in Jan Seaman Kelly and Brian S. Lindblom eds., Scientific Examination of Questioned Documents, 2d ed., CRC Press, 2006 at pp. 269–281.

[80] Id.

[81] Id.

[82] Bonnie L. Beal and Susan E. Morton, "Chapter 17: Photocopiers" in Jan Seaman Kelly & Brian S. Lindblom eds., Scientific Examination of Questioned Documents, 2d ed., CRC Press, 2006 at pp. 217–227.

the document was created by inkjet or toner process (liquid or dry, color), and the presence of roller or gripper marks on the document. Then the same class characteristics of each copier in the office will be observed. If the questioned document is printed in inkjet then the toner copiers can be eliminated from consideration. Toner and inkjet printing have very different microscopic characteristics. Toner in the indirect electrostatic process is raised and shiny while inkjet ink soaks into the paper, is dull in appearance, and has a series of colored dots to form most images. If both the questioned document and one of the known copiers share the same class characteristics, then a search follows for individual characteristics on the questioned document like trash marks that may result from damage, dirt, and debris in the copier parts like the glass platen, photoconductor drum, cover, lens, or fusing rollers. If the same pattern of trash marks appears on the standard documents generated from a known machine, an identification may be possible if the pattern of trash marks is sufficiently complex and individual. Attempts have also been made to classify black toners used in the indirect electrostatic copying process through instrumental methods like Fourier Transform Infrared Spectrometry and X-Ray Fluorescence Spectrometry.[83]

Photocopied evidence submitted in lieu of original documents imposes limitations on the analysis of an FDE. Original evidence should always be submitted when available. If only copies are available, first generation copies are the best choice. High resolution scanned copies may be useful if indeed they are scanned in color or gray scale settings with resolution set at 300 pixels per inch or greater. An example of low resolution copies would be the images of checks that are received from banks along with a monthly statement. Those check images are generally black and white (not gray scale) and have a resolution of 100–200 pixels per inch. Those reproductions may not be of sufficient clarity for a meaningful forensic comparison. Research by Dawson and Lindblom[84] found that FDEs were able to properly evaluate the line quality of photocopied signatures if the photocopies were good quality. The quality of reproductions varies widely. Even with a good quality copy FDEs will face limitations in the examinations. Examination of a copy will not reveal: indented writing, pen type, ink color, most watermarks, subtle ink line morphology like striation patterns in ballpoint pen ink, printing method characteristics, traced signature indentations, and paper fiber disturbances from erasures.

Documents generated from facsimile machines are of interest to FDEs in their work. Facsimile machines, better known as fax machines, allow immediate transfer of printed information through phone lines.

[83] Beata Trzcinski, "Classification of Black Powder Toners on the Basis of Integrated Analytical Information Provided by Fourier Transform Infrared Spectrometry and X-Ray Fluorescence Spectrometry," 51 J. Forensic Sci. 919–924 (2006).

[84] Gregory A. Dawson and Brian S. Lindblom, "An Evaluation of Line Quality in Photocopied Signatures," 38 J. Forensic Sci. 189–194 (1998).

Fax machines owe their existence to Alexander Bain who patented his Bain's Telegraph in 1843.[85] By the late 1940s, fax technology began its use in offices.[86] Faxes increased in office use through the 1990s. Computer scanning and emailing has reduced the use of dedicated fax machines today even though certain industries still use them. They may exist as stand-alone models or function as part of a multi-function machine that also prints, scans, and copies. Printing methods for faxes include: thermal, thermal transfer, ink jet, and laser.[87]

Forensic examination of faxed documents is similar to other printing and copying examinations in that it may be necessary to identify the printing method and make and model of the fax machine. The transmit terminal identifier (TTI) is the identifying information that may include the date, sending telephone number, company name, and page number, that appears across the top edge of a fax, and is generated by the transmitting machine. This information is programmable, so it can be changed. These TTIs can be associated with a particular manufacturer.[88] The receive terminal identifier (RTI) lists identifying information from the receiving fax terminal and usually appears underneath the TTI or along the bottom edge of the page and is generated by the receiving fax machine.[89] A TTI data base exists to assist FDEs to identify the make and model of a particular fax machine.[90]

Alterations of the material on a fax are detectable by forensic examination. Changes in the date may be evident in the lack of proper baseline alignment or the presence of ghosting lines indicating a cut and paste alteration. Differences in pixilation properties of portions of the document will show possible additions of material that did not go through the fax process, but were added later. Also, copies of faxes will lack the sharpness of first generation faxes.[91]

---

[85] Ian Batterham, *The Office Copying Revolution: History, Identification and Presentation,* National Archives of Australia, 2008.

[86] Id.

[87] Brian S. Lindblom, "Chapter 18: Facsimile Machines," in Jan Seaman Kelly and Brian S. Lindblom eds., *Scientific Examination of Questioned Documents,* 2d ed., CRC Press, 2006 at pp. 227–235.

[88] Id.

[89] Id.

[90] Brian S. Lindblom, "Fax Font Project VI TTI Database", Presentation at the American Society of Questioned Document Examiners conference, August 8–13, 2009, Dearborn, Michigan.

[91] Brian S. Lindblom and Robert Gervais, "Chapter 19: Manipulated Photocopies, Faxes, and Computer-Printed Documents," in Jan Seaman Kelly and Brian S. Lindblom eds., *Scientific Examination of Questioned Documents,* 2d ed., CRC Press, 2006 at pp. 235–247.

IV. TRIAL AIDS

§5.16 EXPERT QUALIFICATIONS

College majors in forensic document examination are not available, although a master's degree in Forensic Science with an FDE track is available at Oklahoma State University. General degrees in forensic science are more common among FDEs and most FDEs possess undergraduate or master's degrees in related sciences. Regional and national forensic science organizations generally require a baccalaureate degree as a membership condition.

The American Board of Forensic Document Examiners (ABFDE)[92] certification is a highly desirable credential for FDEs. The purpose is similar to certification boards in other scientific and medical fields.[93] Members of the Questioned Document section of the American Academy of Forensic Sciences (AAFS) and the American Society of Questioned Document Examiners (ASQDE) formed the ABFDE in 1977. A grant from the Department of Justice established the ABFDE with goals to recognize qualified FDEs in government and private laboratories, and promote progress in forensic science.

Minimum qualifications for certification by ABFDE are:

- Baccalaureate degree

- Full-time two-year training program in a laboratory recognized by ABFDE

- Active engagement in forensic document examination

If these minimum qualifications are met, then the candidate must complete a written, practical, and oral examinations to acquire certification. Recertification is required every five years. Points for recertification are gained through research activities, presentation of scientific papers at conferences, and publications. Federal and state laboratories who hire FDEs consistently advertise job announcements that list certification by ABFDE as a desired or required credential. The certification by ABFDE has been cited by several courts as a factor in determining whether the proffered expert is qualified to testify as an expert and what weight should be attributed to the witness's testimony.[94]

---

[92] *See* www.abfde.org.

[93] Certification for questioned document examiners is also offered by the Board of Forensic Document Examiners. *See* http://www.bfde.org/certification.html (last accessed March 1, 2017).

[94] *See, e.g.,* Balimunkwe v. Bank of Am., 2015 U.S. Dist. LEXIS 117980 *37–38, 2015 WL 5167632 (S.D. Ohio 2015)("no indication [the proffered expert] is certified by the ABFDE"); United States v. Revels, 2012 U.S. Dist. LEXIS 65069, *19 (E.D. Tenn. 2012)(The only professional organization in the field of document examination that offers certification is the ABFDE. Neither [the proffered expert] nor his mentor [ ] is an ABFDE member."); Primerica Life Ins. Co. v. Atkinson, 2012 U.S. Dist. LEXIS 173328, *8, 2012 WL 6057888 (W.D. Wash. 2012)("the ABFDE does not have a monopoly on who can and cannot be an expert in federal

The skill of an FDE can be properly evaluated by reviewing his or her education, training, experience, and certification. Training should conform to the SWGDOC Standard for Minimum Training Requirements for Forensic Document Examiners[95] which requires a two year apprenticeship in a forensic science laboratory with a trainer who has also received proper training.

§5.17　HANDWRITING COMPARISON EVIDENCE

At common law, evidence of a comparison of the handwriting on one document with that on another was inadmissible, inasmuch as the only acceptable proof of one's handwriting was deemed to be the testimony of its author.[96] Over the years, however, this rigid view has been abandoned. Today, expert testimony, and lay testimony to some extent, is generally admissible to establish authorship of a questioned writing.

If a lay witness is familiar with the disputed handwriting or signature, he will ordinarily be allowed to testify with respect to authorship.[97] If the witness' familiarity with the purported writer's handwriting was acquired for purposes of the litigation, the writer's testimony should not be allowed.[98] In *Commonwealth v. Ryan*,[99] a lay witness who had worked in the same office with the defendant for more than three years was permitted to testify regarding defendant's handwriting. Lay witness competency to testify depends on the extent of his association with the defendant's handwriting. Thus, where a witness was not particularly familiar with deceased's signature and had seen him write his name perhaps once in the past, the witness would

---

court . . . challenges to [the proffered expert's] qualifications go to the weight of [her] testimony, not its admissibility"); Am. Gen. Life & Accident Ins. Co. v. Ward, 530 F. Supp.2d 1306, 1313 (N.D. Ga. 2008)("the Court finds it significant that [the proffered expert] is not accredited by the American Board of Forensic Document Examiners (the "ABFDE"). The ABFDE is the 'only recognized organization for accrediting forensic document examiners.' Courts have highlighted ABFDE certification and membership as an important factor in determining a document examiner's qualifications.")(citation omitted); Dracz v. Am. Gen. Life Ins. Co., 426 F. Supp.2d 1373, 1379 n. 16 (M.D. Ga. 2006)(noting the importance of ABFDE certification and membership).

[95] *See* www.swgdoc.org.

[96] Rogers v. Ritter, 79 U.S. 317 (1870).

[97] Lay opinion testimony may be an adequate basis under Federal Rule of Evidence 901(b)(1) and (2) to connect a signature or record to a party. *See, e.g.,* United States v. Tipton, 964 F.2d 650 (7th Cir.1992); United States v. Whittington, 783 F.2d 1210 (5th Cir.1986), *cert. denied* 479 U.S. 882 (1986); United States v. Barker, 735 F.2d 1280 (11th Cir.1984), *cert. denied* 469 U.S. 933 (1984); United States v. Mauchlin, 670 F.2d 746 (7th Cir.1982)(prison file documents sufficiently authenticated by a prison official who had seen defendant write on six occasions).

[98] People v. Cepeda, 851 F.2d 1564 (9th Cir.1988).

[99] 355 Mass. 768, 247 N.E.2d 564 (1969). Other laypersons who have been permitted to testify about authenticity of writings include bankers, Stone v. Hubbard, 61 Mass. 595 (1851); post office clerks, State v. Sysinger, 25 S.D. 110, 125 N.W. 879 (1910); and public records custodians, Fenias v. Reichenstein, 124 N.J.L. 196, 11 A.2d 10 (1940).

not be allowed to give his opinion as to the genuineness of a signature in dispute.[100]

Courts and juries have been permitted to make handwriting comparison conclusions as to identity both on the basis of a comparison of handwriting characteristics[101] and on the basis of language use and misspellings in the known and unknown documents.[102] The more common occurrence, however, is for expert testimony on the issue of authorship to be presented. Opinion testimony by a qualified document examiner has been admissible evidence for more than a century and a half in United States courts.[103]

1.   POST-*DAUBERT* CASES

Since the United States Supreme Court's decision in *Daubert v. Merrell Dow Pharmaceuticals*,[104] and *Kumho Tire v. Carmichael*,[105] some courts have required parties proffering document examination evidence to lay an appropriate foundation by establishing the scientific reliability of handwriting comparison analysis before admitting expert opinion evidence based upon it. The first challenges to the admissibility of handwriting analysis arose out of a law review article that had been published four years prior to the *Daubert* decision. The article was titled "Exorcism of Ignorance as a Proxy for Rational Knowledge."[106] The article did not have any immediate impact on litigation after its publication until two of its authors began to testify as experts that handwriting identification was not "scientific" under *Daubert*.

In 1995, the district court in *United States v. Starzecpyzel*[107] held that forensic document examination could not, after *Daubert*, be considered to be based on "scientific knowledge." While the court found that the discipline involved true expertise which could be helpful to the trier of fact and that an expert could testify to the comparisons, the court held that the ultimate opinion that a defendant had or had not authored a questioned document was not admissible.[108] The

---

[100] Noyes v. Noyes, 224 Mass. 125, 112 N.E. 850 (1916).

[101] State v. LeDuc, 306 N.C. 62, 291 S.E.2d 607 (1982).

[102] United States v. Clifford, 704 F.2d 86 (3d Cir. 1983).

[103] For cases permitting expert opinion evidence on handwriting genuineness to be introduced as far back as 1831, 1835, and 1850, *see* Andre A. Moenssens, "Handwriting Identification Evidence in the Post-Daubert World," 66 UMKC L. Rev. 251, 267 (1997).

[104] 509 U.S. 579 (1993).

[105] 526 U.S. 137 (1999). *See* the extensive discussions of *Daubert, Kumho Tire*, and other subsequent decisions in Chapter 1: Scientific Evidence and Expert Testimony.

[106] D. Michael Risinger et al., Exorcism of Ignorance as a Proxy for Rational Knowledge: The Lessons of Handwriting Identification Expertise, 137 U. PA. L.Rev. 731 (1989),. The authors were law professors, two of whom had been induced to write the article as a result of their experiences in defending a notorious New York "madam" as public defenders. None of the authors had ever worked in a document laboratory; the source for their article was a self-directed study of case law and literature.

[107] United States v. Starzecpyzel, 880 F. Supp. 1027 (S.D. NY 1995).

[108] 880 F. Supp. at 1029 ("The problem arises from the likely perception by jurors that FDEs are scientists, which would suggest far greater precision and reliability than was

Starzecpyzel case was followed by a few other district court decisions limiting the scope of handwriting experts' opinions, though the majority of the subsequent cases held not only that the profession meets the *Daubert* requirements, but also that unqualified ultimate opinions on authorship of a disputed writing were admissible.

By the early-2000's, a three-way split of authority on the admission of handwriting comparison analysis had developed.[109] The three-way split has the appellate courts aligning with the majority of trial courts admitting the expert testimony without limitation,[110] a few trial courts excluding expert testimony,[111] and a third group of trial courts permitting the expert testimony but barring individualizing conclusions of authorship.[112]

2. POST–NAS REPORT CASES

Considering the broad criticism leveled against many impression comparison techniques in the 2009 NAS Report,[113] its treatment of forensic document examination was relatively mild. After a brief discussion of the broad field of forensic document examination, the NAS

---

established by the *Daubert* hearing. This perception might arise from several factors, such as the appearance of the words 'scientific' and 'laboratory' in much of the relevant literature, and the overly precise manner in which FDEs describe their level of confidence in their opinions as to whether questioned writings are genuine.").

[109] Federal Judicial Center, *Reference Manual on Scientific Evidence* 3d ed., National Academies Press, 2011 at pp. 89–90.

[110] *See, e.g.,* United States v. Yass, No. 08-40008-JAR, 2008 U.S. Dist. LEXIS 102963, 2008 WL 5377827, at *2 (D. Kan. Dec. 19, 2008)("The Court has reviewed the decisions of the federal appellate courts, including an unpublished Tenth Circuit opinion, which have been unanimous in approving expert testimony in the field of handwriting analysis. . . . [T]he Court finds the process of handwriting analysis sufficiently reliable to satisfy *Daubert* and the Federal Rules of Evidence and declines to depart from the clear majority of courts weighing in on the issue. Moreover, despite the uneven treatment of handwriting experts by district courts, every appellate court to have considered the issue of handwriting testimony has held that the expert's ultimate opinion was admissible); United States v. Prime, 431 F.3d 1147, 1154 (9th Cir. 2005)(district court did not abuse its discretion in admitting testimony from forensic document examiner and noting that '[t]he district court's thorough and careful application of the *Daubert* factors was consistent with all six circuits that have addressed the admissibility of handwriting expert testimony, and determined that it can satisfy the reliability threshold")(collecting cases); United States v. Mooney, 315 F.3d 54, 62–63 (1st Cir. 2002)(district court did not abuse its discretion in allowing handwriting expert to provide opinion that defendant was the author of the letters at issue); United States v. Paul, 175 F.3d 906, 909–911 (11th Cir. 1999)(district court did not abuse its discretion in admitting testimony of handwriting expert). *See also* United States v. Crisp, 324 F.3d 261, 270–271 (4th Cir. 2003); United States v. Sanders, 59 Fed. App.'x 765, 767 (6th Cir. 2003); United States v. Jolivet, 224 F.3d 902, 905–906 (8th Cir. 2000).

[111] *See, e.g.,* United States v. Lewis, 220 F. Supp.2d 548 (S.D. W. Va. 2002).

[112] *See, e.g.,* United States v. Oskowitz, 294 F. Supp.2d 379, 384 (E.D. NY 2003); United States v. Hidalgo, 220 F. Supp.2d 961, 967 (D. Ariz. 2002); United States v. Rutherford, 104 F. Supp.2d 1190, 1192–1194 (D. Neb. 2000).

[113] Committee on Identifying the Needs of the Forensic Science Community, National Research Council of the National Academies, *Strengthening Forensic Science in the United States: A Path Forward,* National Academies Press, 2009, *hereinafter "2009 NAS Report."* The history of the report and its broader conclusions about the state of forensic science practice is discussed in Chapter 1: Scientific Evidence and Expert Testimony.

Report focused on handwriting comparison analysis and concluded with the following assessment:

> The scientific basis for handwriting comparisons needs to be strengthened. Recent studies have increased our understanding of the individuality and consistency of handwriting and computer studies and suggest that there may be a scientific basis for handwriting comparison. . . . [T]he committee agrees that there may be some value in handwriting analysis.[114]

The 2009 NAS Report also briefly discussed ink analyses, but refrained from commenting on its validity because it had not received sufficient input on that topic.[115]

Since post-*Daubert* litigation challenges to handwriting comparison analysis had already questioned the lack of empirical validation discussed in the NAS Report, the NAS Report did not alter the legal landscape significantly. Although some trial courts have rejected handwriting analysis as lacking scientific reliability,[116] the appellate courts and the majority of trial court have upheld the admission of handwriting comparisons and found that any limitations of the discipline are best addressed by thorough cross examination of the expert witness. The 2012 District of Columbia Court of Appeals opinion in *Pettus v. United States* illustrates this position.

In *Pettus v. United States*,[117] the defendant challenged the trial court's admission of expert opinion testimony that he was the author of a note found at the murder scene.[118] Based on the government's concession that "whether handwriting identification meets *Frye's* general acceptance standard" was an open question, the court proceeded to " 'establish the law of the jurisdiction for future cases' involving the admissibility of handwriting identification."[119] The court noted the following two legal principles guiding its determination of the issue:

> [T]he relevant 'community' for purposes of assessing Frye admissibility includes not just forensic scientists (including handwriting experts) but also others 'whose scientific background and training are sufficient to allow them to comprehend and understand the process and form a judgment about it.'

---

[114] 2009 NAS Report at pp. 166–167.

[115] Id. at p. 167.

[116] *See, e.g.,* Almeciga v. Ctr. For Investigative Reporting, Inc., 216 U.S. Dist. LEXIS 60539 (S.D. NY 2016)("finding that handwriting analysis in general is unlikely to meet the admissibility requirements of Federal Rule of Evidence 702, and that, in any event [the proffered expert's] testimony does not meet those standards."); United States v. Johnsted, 30 F. Supp.3d 814, 816 (W.D. Wisc. 2013)("the science or art underlying handwriting analysis falls well short of a reliability threshold when applied to hand printing analysis.").

[117] 37 A.3d 213 (D.C. App. 2012).

[118] 37 A.3d at 216.

[119] 37 A.3d at 217.

[T]he standard of proof for admissibility is a preponderance of the evidence, not more, in part because the party opposing the evidence shown to have met the standard 'may challenge the weight the jury ought to give it.'[120]

Relying on the evidence presented by the government experts concerning the analytical method and standards used in handwriting comparison and studies supporting the performance of expert examiners,[121] the appellate court concluded that the government's evidence:

demonstrated by a preponderance of the evidence that handwriting comparison leading to conclusions of (or against) identification rests on a methodology 'sufficiently established to have gained general acceptance in the particular field in which it belongs.'[122]

The court held that the NAS Report neither represented a different scientific consensus as to handwriting comparison nor implied that handwriting comparison "is based on no 'reliable methodology for making the inquiry.' "[123] The court concluded, however, by reiterating one of the legal principles with which it began its analysis:

[I]t is important—and is reflected in the preponderance of the evidence standard—that appellant was not denied a second opportunity to challenge [the handwriting expert's] opinion, this time before the jury. . . [T]he Supreme Court has reminded us that '[v]igorous cross-examination, presentation of contrary evidence, and careful instruction on the burden of proof are the traditional and appropriate means of attacking shaky but admissible evidence.[124]

§5.18   EVIDENCE OF OTHER FORENSIC DOCUMENT EXAMINATIONS

The relevancy of typewriting identification testimony was recognized as early as 1893.[125] Although the use of typewriters has

---

[120] 37 A.3d at 218.

[121] 37 A.3d at 218–222. The government called Dr. Sargur N. Srihari to testify concerning the research studies supporting the scientific validation of handwriting analysis.

[122] 37 A.3d at 225 (quoting Jones v. United States, 27 A.3d 1130, 1136 (D.C. 2011)).

[123] 37 A.3d at 226, 228.

[124] 37 A.3d at 228. The trial judge had expressed a similar view on the importance of cross-examination:

In consultation with its own experts the defense has fully investigated the points of weakness of the FBI laboratory's approach to handwriting analysis, including its general methodology and the methodology as applied to the case. If the defense counsel exposes those weaknesses to the jury with the same thoroughness and clarity with which it exposed them at the [admissibility] hearing, then in my view there is no reason for any concern that the jury in this case will give undue weight to the FBU document examiner's testimony.

37 A.3d at 229.

[125] Levy v. Rust, 49 A. 1017 (N.J.1893). Apparently, the earliest judicial expression on the point was in a Canadian case in 1886: Scott v. Crerar, 14 Ont.App.Rep. 152 (1886).

diminished greatly, older cases addressed the admission and use of typewriter comparison analysis.[126]

In relatively few cases have reviewing courts addressed the admissibility of expert testimony relating to document examinations dealing with issues other than those relating to the genuineness of handwriting or typewriting. These cases have been sparse, perhaps because these document problems involve issues that are far closer related to scientific and factual explorations and involve examinations that require much less interpretation or subjectivity. Likely, this is the reason why, when it comes to laboratory examinations of documents, there have been few if any *Daubert* challenges.

Different problems are encountered when dealing with more complex examinations or those wherein some controversy in the field still exists, such as certain aspects of ink analyses. In *United States v. Bruno*,[127] the government sought to prove that the ballpoint ink with which one of the defendants had signed a questioned document was of a type which had not been manufactured until May of 1967, and that the document therefore could not have been signed in 1965, the date appearing thereon. The expert testimony was based upon chromatograms made of the ink, a process whereby the ink separates into its component dyes. Considering that the comparison "ink library" of the witness was rather incomplete, and that the expert conceded the existence of a number of variables which might influence the results, the court concluded that "the art in this field of ink identification is not yet sufficiently advanced to be reasonably scientifically certain that an

---

[126] In People v. Risley, 214 N.Y. 75, 108 N.E. 200 (1915), an attorney was prosecuted for offering into evidence as genuine a will while knowing it to have been forged and fraudulently altered by insertion of two typewritten words. Specimens of typewriting made on a machine in the defendant's office two days subsequent to the commission of the alleged offense were held properly admitted as standards of comparison. The expert testified that his experience encompassed examination of some 20,000 typewriters, and that he had never encountered one that was in perfect alignment. He stated that the alignment was the "heart" of the machine, and that the spacing, keys, lever, carriage, and roll center around the alignment. He also stated that a machine could not be manufactured so that the alignment would be perfect.

In State v. Swank, 99 Or. 571, 195 P. 168 (1921) the court recognized the propriety of permitting an expert to testify that in his opinion an authenticated note and a questioned note in a forgery prosecution had been signed by the same individual and also typed on the same typewriter. The reviewing court dwelt on the clarity of the expert testimony, the analytical and convincing manner of his presentation, and the conciseness of the language with which he framed his opinion.

In Lyon v. Oliver, 316 Ill. 292, 147 N.E. 251 (1925), a study of type samples established that a document relating to attorney's fees, purportedly submitted by the attorney as a charge against an estate he represented, was a forgery, by testimony to the effect that the particular typewriter type face used on the document had not been put into use by the manufacturer until several years after the death of the purported writer of the document.

[127] 333 F.Supp. 570 (E.D.Pa.1971).

ink of unknown composition is the same as a known ink."[128] The state of the art has, of course, progressed significantly.[129]

V. RESOURCES

§5.19 BIBLIOGRAPHY OF ADDITIONAL RESOURCES

1. TEXTBOOKS

Daniel T. Ames, *Ames on Forgery*, Ames-Rollison Co., 1901.

Wilfred A. Beeching, *Century of the Typewriter*, St. Martin's Press, 1974.

Herbert L. Blitzer and Jack Jacobia, *Forensic Digital Imaging and Photography*, Academic Press, 2002.

Bertie Lee Browning, *Analysis of Paper*, M. Dekker, 1977.

Richard L. Brunelle and Robert W. Reed, *Forensic Examination of Ink and Paper*, 1984.

James V.P. Conway, *Evidential Documents*, 3d ed., Charles C. Thomas Publisher, Ltd.,1978.

David Ellen, *The Scientific Examination of Documents*, 1989 and 2d ed. 1997.

David Ellen, *Scientific Examination of Documents Methods and Techniques,* 3d ed., CRC Press, 2006.

Wilson R. Harrison, *Suspect Documents: Their Scientific Examination*, Rowman & Littlefield Publishers, 1958.

Gary Herbertson, *Document Examination on the Computer: A Guide for Forensic Document Examiners,* Wideline Pub., 2002.

Ordway Hilton, *The Scientific Examination of Questioned Documents*, CRC Press, 1982.

Roy A. Huber and A.M. Headrick, *Handwriting Identification: Facts and Fundamentals*, CRC Press,1999.

Jan Seaman Kelly, *Forensic Examination of Rubber Stamps: A Practical Guide*, Charles C. Thomas Publisher, Ltd., 2002.

---

[128] Id. *See also* United States v. Wolfson, 297 F.Supp. 881 (S.D.N.Y.1968), affirmed 413 F.2d 804 (2d Cir.1969), rejecting as insufficiently reliable ink analysis by a chemist and examination of watermark evidence.

[129] *See* In re Estate of Lauren G. Angstadt, 2014 Pa. Super. Unpub. LEXIS 3171, *15 (Sup. Ct. Pa. 2014)(both parties presented testimony of expert forensic chemists specializing in questioned documents to discuss the age of the ink found on the 2006 wills. . . . Both experts agreed that after ink is placed on paper, a chemical within the ink called 'phenoxyethanol' evaporates. By measuring the level of phenoxyethanol within the ink, scientists can approximate how long the ink has been on the paper.").

Jan Seaman Kelly and Brian S. Lindblom, eds., *Scientific Examination of Questioned Documents*, 2d ed., CRC Press, 2006.

Justus G. Kirchner, *Thin-Layer Chromatography: 014 (Techniques of Chemistry)*, John Wiley and Sons, Inc., 1978.

Jay Levinson, *Questioned Documents: A Lawyer's Handbook*, Academic Press, 2000.

Jane A. Lewis, *Forensic Document Examination Fundamentals and Current Trends*, Academic Press, 2014.

H.A. Lubs, *The Chemistry of Synthetic Dyes and Pigments*, 1955.

Stephen C. McKasson and Carol A. Richards, *Speaking as an Expert: A Guide for the Identification Sciences from the Laboratory to the Courtroom*, Charles C. Thomas Publisher, Ltd.,1998.

C. Ainsworth Mitchell and T.C. Hepworth, *Inks: Their Composition and Manufacture*, 1904.

Ron N. Morris, *Forensic Handwriting Identification: Fundamental Concepts and Principles*, Academic Press, 2000.

Albert S. Osborn, *Questioned Documents*, 1929.

Albert S. Osborn, *The Problem of Proof,* 1926.

Henry Petroski, *The Pencil: A History of Design and Circumstance*, Alfred A. Knopf. Inc.,1990.

Douglas H. Ubelaker ed., *Forensic Science: Current Issues, Future Directions*, John Wiley and Sons, Ltd., 2013.

2. JOURNAL ARTICLES

Valery N. Aginsky, "Using TLC and GC-MS to Determine Whether Inks Came from the same Manufacturing Batch," 9 J. AM.SOC. OF QUESTIONED DOCUMENT EXAMINERS, 19–27 (2006).

Valery N. Aginsky, "Examination of Paper and Toner in Page Insertion/Substitution Cases Using TLC, GC-MS, and FT-IR Microspectroscopy," 15 J. AM.SOC. OF QUESTIONED DOCUMENT EXAMINERS, 3–15 (2012).

Valery N. Aginsky, "Ink Dating—Comparative Examination of Inks on Documents Using Optical and Chemical Methods," 16 J. AM.SOC. OF QUESTIONED DOCUMENT EXAMINERS, 31–38 (2013).

Valery N. Aginsky, "Ink Age Testing—Do Preceding Indentation Examinations Affect Ink Aging Parameters?" 17 J. AM.SOC. OF QUESTIONED DOCUMENT EXAMINERS, 49–63 (2014).

Y. Akao *et al.*, "Examination of Spur Marks Found on Inkjet-Printed Documents," 58 J. Forensic Sci. 915–923 (2005).

A. Alkahtani, "The Ability of Forensic Handwriting Examiners to Judge the Quality of Signature Simulations in an Unfamiliar Writing System," 13 J. AM. SOC. OF QUEST. DOC. EXAM. 65–69 (2010).

A. Alkahtani and A. Platt, "Relative Difficulty of Freehand Simulation of Four Proportional Elements in Arabic Signatures," 12 J. AM. SOC. OF QUEST. DOC. EXAM. 69–75 (2009).

M. Aloyoni et al., "Deciphering of Counterfeit Traveler's Checks," 13 J. AM. SOC. OF QUEST. DOC. EXAM. 1–7 (2010).

S. Alzaabi and G. Shrfe, "In Situ Analysis of Inks Lines Made by Blue and Black Ballpoint Pens by Reflectance and Luminescence Spectroscopy Using the VSC6000HS," 18 J. AM.SOC. OF QUESTIONED DOCUMENT EXAMINERS, 3–27 (2015).

K. Annunziata Nicolaides, "Using Acceleration/Deceleration Plots in Forensic Analysis of Electronically Captured Signatures," 15 J. AM.SOC. OF QUESTIONED DOCUMENT EXAMINERS, 29–43 (2012).

Leah Balko and John Allison, "The Direct Detection and Identification of Staining Dyes from Security Inks in the Presence of Other Colorants, on Currency and Fabrics, by Laser Desorption Mass Spectrometry," 48 J. FORENSIC SCI. 1172–1178 (2003).

C. Berger et al., "Linking Inkjet Printing to a Common Digital Source Document," 8 J. AM. SOC. OF QUEST. DOC. EXAM. 91–99 (2005).

C. Berger-Karin et al., "Comparison of Natural and Artificial Aging of Ballpoint Inks," 53 J. FORENSIC SCI. 989–992 (2008).

C. Bird et al., "Forensic Document Examiners' Skill in Distinguishing Between Natural and Disguised Handwriting Behaviors," 55 J. FORENSIC SCI. 1291–1295 (2010).

B. Bishop, "Frequency of Selected Hand Printing Characteristics Occurring Within a National Population: the New International Version Bible Across America," 15 J. AM. SOC. OF QUEST. DOC. EXAM. 23–25 (2012).

K. Bojko et al., "An Examination of the Sequence of Intersecting Lines Using Attenuated Reflectance—Fourier Transform Infrared Spectral Imaging," 53 J. FORENSIC SCI. 1458–1467 (2008).

R. Boshir and A. Platt, "The Use of Simple Dimensional Measurements in the Analysis of Simulated Signatures: A Preliminary Study," 15 J. AM. SOC. OF QUEST. DOC. EXAM. 17–21 (2012).

L. Brazeau and M. Gaudreau, "Ballpoint Pen Inks: the Quantitative Analysis of Ink Solvents on Paper by Solid-Phase Microextraction," 52 J. Forensic Sci. 209–215 (2007).

Sharon Brown, et al., "Deciphering Indented Impressions on Plastic," 48 J. FORENSIC SCI. 869 (2003).

Sharon Brown and L. Sin-David, "Diary of an Astronaut: Examination of the Remains of the Late Israeli Astronaut Colonel Ilan Ramon's Crew Notebook Recovered after the Loss of NASA's Space Shuttle Columbia," 52 J. FORENSIC SCI. 731–737 (2007).

Bruce Budowle, *et al.*, "A Perspective on Errors, Bias, and Interpretations in the Forensic Sciences and Direction for Continuing Advancement," 54 J. FORENSIC SCI. 798 (2009).

J. Bulger *et al.*, "Age Determination of Ballpoint Pen ink by thermal Desorption and Gas Chromatography-Mass Spectrometry," 53 J. Forensic Sci. 982–988 (2008).

Antonio A. Cantu, "Ink Analysis," in WILEY ENCYCLOPEDIA OF FORENSIC SCIENCE (Jamieson, A. & Moenssens, A.A., eds.) 2009 [3] 1841.

V. Causin *et al.*, "The Discrimination Potential of Ultraviolet-Visible Spectrophotometry, Thin Layer Chromatography, and Fourier Transform Infrared Spectroscopy for the Forensic Analysis of Black and Blue Ballpoint inks," 52 J. FORENSIC SCI. 1396 (2003).

A. Chaikovsky, *et al.*, "Color Separation of Signature and Stamp Inks to Facilitate Handwriting Examination," 48 J. FORENSIC SCI. 1396–1405 (2003).

N. Cheng *et al.*, "Investigation of Class Characteristics in English Handwriting of Three Main Racial Groups: Chinese, Malay, and Indian in Singapore," 50 J. FORENSIC SCI. 177–184 (2005).

J. Chim *et al.*, "Examination of Counterfeit Banknotes Printed by All-in-One Color Inkjet Printers," 7 J. AM. SOC. OF QUEST. DOC. EXAM. 6976 (2004).

J. deKoeijer *et al.*, "Gelatine Lifting, a Novel Technique for the Examination of Indented Writing," 51 J. FORENSIC SCI. 908–914 (2006).

A. Devlin *et al.*, "Line Direction Determination of Ballpoint Pen Ink Writing," 18 J. AM. SOC. OF QUEST. DOC. EXAM. 29–39 (2015).

T. Dewhurst *et al.*, "Exploring the Significance of Pen Lifts as Predictors of Signature Simulation Behavior," 18 J. AM. SOC. OF QUEST. DOC. EXAM. 3–15 (2015).

Jamie Dunn, *et al.*, "Photodegradation and Laser Desorption Mass Spectrometry for the Characterization of Dyes Used in Red Pen Inks," 48 J. FORENSIC SCI. 652 (2003).

Marie Durina and M. Caligiuri, "The Determination of Authorship from a Homogenous Group of Writers," 12 J. AM. SOC. OF QUEST. DOC. EXAM. 77–90 (2009).

Marie Durina *et al.*, "Do People Always Disguise Their Writing the Same? The Trilogy," 17 J. AM. SOC. OF QUEST. DOC. EXAM. 25–32 (2014).

A. Dyer *et al.*, "Visual Attention and Expertise for Forensic Signature Analysis," 51 J. FORENSIC SCI. 1397–1404 (2006).

A. Dyer *et al.*, "An Insight into Forensic Document Examiner Expertise for Discriminating Between Forged and Disguised Signatures," 53 J. FORENSIC SCI. 1154–1159 (2008).

H. Elliott and L. Stadmeyer, "Stone Paper: An Overview of Its Characteristics and the Impact They Have on Forensic Document Examinations," 15 J. AM. SOC. OF QUEST. DOC. EXAM. 11–29 (2012).

M. Ezcurra et al., "Analysis of Bic Crystal Medium Ballpoint Pen Inks," 12 J. AM. SOC. OF QUEST. DOC. EXAM. 57–68 (2009).

K. Fazio, "The Effects of Constraint on a Signature's Static and Dynamic Features," 18 J. AM. SOC. OF QUEST. DOC. EXAM. 41–56 (2015).

W. Flynn, "Conducting a Forensic Examination of Electronically Captured Signatures, " 15 J. AM. SOC. OF QUEST. DOC. EXAM. 3–10 (2012).

A.B. Giles and A. Giles, "Electrostatic Detection Apparatus Enhancement Using Astronomical Image Stacking and Processing Software," 12 J. AM. SOC. OF QUEST. DOC. EXAM. 19–25 (2009).

J. Green, "Reliability of Paper Brightness in Authenticating Documents," 57 J. FORENSIC SCI. 1003–1007 (2012).

A. Guzowski et al., "Revealing Writing that Has Been Covered Using Correction Tools," 17 J. AM. SOC. OF QUEST. DOC. EXAM. 3–11 (2014).

A. Haddad et al., "Examination of a Collection of Arabic Signatures," 12 J. AM. SOC. OF QUEST. DOC. EXAM. 35–53 (2009).

K. Herlaar et al., "Measuring Magnetic Properties to Discriminate Between Different Laser Printers," 18 J. AM. SOC. OF QUEST. DOC. EXAM. 51–66 (2015).

A.F. Hicks, "The Handwriting Testimony in the Trial of Bruno Richard Hauptmann," 6 J. AM. SOC. OF QUEST. DOC. EXAM. 97–111 (2003).

R. Hofer, "Dating of Ballpoint Pen Ink," 49 J. FORENSIC SCI. 1353–1357 (2004).

S. Houlgrave et al., "The Classification of Inkjet Inks Using Accudart (Direct Analysis in Real Time) Mass Spectrometry—a Preliminary Study," 58 J. FORENSIC SCI. 813–821 (2013).

A. Iqbal et al., "Statistical Evaluation of the Reproducibility and the Influence of Paper on the Analysis of Black Gel Pen Ink Using Laser Desorption Ionization Mass Spectrometry," 15 J. AM. SOC. OF QUEST. DOC. EXAM. 31–40 (2012).

Moshe Kam and Erwin Lin, "Writer Identification Using Hand-Printed and Non-Hand-Printed Questioned Documents," 48 J. FORENSIC SCI. 1391–1395 (2003).

Moshe Kam et al., "Simulation Detection in Handwritten Documents by Forensic Document Examiners," 60 J. FORENSIC SCI. 936–941 (2015).

M. Klein et al., "Quantitative Hyperspectral Imaging Technique for Measuring Material Degradation Effects and Analyzing TLC Plate Traces," 13 J. AM. SOC. OF QUEST. DOC. EXAM. 71–81 (2010).

A. Koenig *et al.*, "Ink Dating Using Thermal Desorption and Gas Chromatography/Mass Spectrometry: Comparison of Results Obtained in Two Laboratories," 60 J. FORENSIC SCI. S152–S161 (2015).

D. Kruger, "The Longpen—the World's First Original Remote Signing Device," 55 J. FORENSIC SCI. 795–800 (2010).

B. Lanners, "Liquid Lead Pencils Revisited," 13 J. AM. SOC. OF QUEST. DOC. EXAM. 51–56 (2011).

G. LaPorte *et al.*, "An Evaluation of Matching Unknown Writing Inks with the United States International in Library," 51 J. FORENSIC SCI. 689–692 (2006).

G. LaPorte *et al.*, "The Examination of Commercial Printing Defects to Access Common Origin, Batch Variation, and Error Rate," 55 J. FORENSIC SCI. 136–140 (2010).

G. LaPorte *et al.*, "The Forensic Analysis of Thermal Transfer Printing," 48 J. FORENSIC SCI. 1163–1171 (2003).

G. LaPorte, "The Use of an Electrostatic Detection Device to Identify Individual and Class Characteristics on Documents Produced by Printers and Copiers—a Preliminary Study," 49 J. FORENSIC SCI. 610–620 (2004).

Jane A. Lewis, "Striation Patterns in New and Used Ballpoint Pens," 6 J. AM. SOC. OF QUEST. DOC. EXAM. 67–71 (2003).

Jane A. Lewis, "Indentation Examination Enhancement," 8 J. AM. SOC. OF QUEST. DOC. EXAM. 65–69 (2005).

Jane A. Lewis, "Minimizing Cognitive Bias in Forensic Document Examination," 19 J. AM. SOC. OF QUEST. DOC. EXAM. 33–36 (2016).

B. Li and P. Xie, "Dating of Iron Ball Ink Using Dissolution-Diffusion Method," 60 J. FORENSIC SCI. 476–481 (2015).

C. Li *et al.*, "Significance of Sequence Strokes in Chinese Handwriting Examination," 52 J. FORENSIC SCI. 467–472 (2007).

C. Li *et al.*, "Individuality of Handwritten Arabic Numerals in Local Population," 50 J. FORENSIC SCI. 185–191 (2005).

G. Licht and E. Murano, "ESDA Effects in Light of Current Discussions," 7 J. AM. SOC. OF QUEST. DOC. EXAM. 7–21 (2004).

S.R. Lines and R. Caradine, "A Study of Business Letter Features," 50 J. FORENSIC SCI. 924–927 (2005).

N. Liu, "The Role of Print Mode Determination for Classification of Inkjet Printers," 16 J. AM. SOC. OF QUEST. DOC. EXAM. 31–42 (2013).

M. Mahajan and S. Arya, "Examination of Writings Concealed by Black Pressure Sensitive Adhesive Tape," 52 J. FORENSIC SCI. 1212–1213 (2007).

R. Marquis *et al.*, "Handwriting Evidence Evaluation Based on the Shape of Characters: Application of Multivariate Likelihood Ratios," 56 J. FORENSIC SCI. S238–S242 (2011).

J.F. Masson, "Scanned Images: How Well Do They Depict the Subtle Features in Handwriting?" 15 J. AM. SOC. OF QUEST. DOC. EXAM. 41–47 (2012).

J.F. Masson, "Computer-Scored Test Answer Marks, aka Bubble Marks: How Individual Are They?" 18 J. AM. SOC. OF QUEST. DOC. EXAM. 57–67 (2015).

William Mazzella and A. Khanmy-Vital, "A Study to Investigate the Evidential Value of Blue Gel Pen Inks," 48 J. FORENSIC SCI. 419–424 (2003).

William Mazzella *et al.*, "Micro-Raman Spectroscopy of Color Inkjet Printed Documents," 9 J. AM. SOC. OF QUEST. DOC. EXAM. 1–8 (2006).

E. McGaw *et al.*, "Characterization of Undigested Particulate Material Following Microwave Digestion of Recycled Document Papers," 54 J. FORENSIC SCI. 1171–1175 (2009).

E. McGaw *et al.*, "Determination of Trace Elemental Concentrations in Document Papers for Forensic Comparison Using Inductively Coupled Plasma-Mass Spectrometry," 54 J. FORENSIC SCI. 1163–1170 (2009).

L. Mitchell and M. Merlino, "A Blind Study on the Reliability of Hand Printing Identification by Forensic Document Examiners," 19 J. AM. SOC. OF QUEST. DOC. EXAM. 25–31 (2016).

Andre A. Moenssens, "Handwriting Identification Evidence in the Post-Daubert World," 66 UMKC L.Rev. 251 (1997).

Linton Mohammed *et al.*, "The Dynamic Character of Disguise Behavior for Text-Based, Mixed, and Stylized Signatures," 56 J. FORENSIC SCI. S136–S141 (2011).

R. Morris and G. Richards, "What is the Basis for a Handwriting Elimination?" 13 J. AM. SOC. OF QUEST. DOC. EXAM. 43–49 (2010).

Cedric Neumann and P. Margot, "Considerations on the ASTM Standards 1789-04 and 1422-05 on the Forensic Examination of Ink," 55 J. FORENSIC SCI. 1304–1310 (2010).

S. Ngan *et al.*, "The Uniqueness of Facsimile Documents Caused by Changes in Character Pixilation," 8 J. AM. SOC. OF QUEST. DOC. EXAM. 17–26 (2005).

L. Ning, "A Study of the Stability and the Utility of Satellite Droplets for Classification of Ink Jet Printers," 14 J. AM. SOC. OF QUEST. DOC. EXAM. 35–45 (2011).

Karen Nobles, "An Update of the Typestyle Classification Program (Type) into a Windows Based Format (WinType)," 13 J. AM. SOC. OF QUEST. DOC. EXAM. 37–42 (2010).

L. Olson, "Indentations Produced by the Document Feeder Mechanisms of Two Black and White Photocopiers," 12 J. AM. SOC. OF QUEST. DOC. EXAM. 1–18 (2009).

R. Brent Ostrum, "Application of Hyperspectral Imaging to Forensic Document Examination Problems," 9 J. AM. SOC. OF QUEST. DOC. EXAM. 85–93 (2006).

R. Brent Ostrum & Tubin Tanaka, "Another Look at Handwriting Movement," 9 J. AM. SOC. OF QUEST. DOC. EXAM. 57–69 (2006).

Joseph L. Parker, "Commentary: Why Forensic Document Examiners' Training Must Be for a Minimum of 24 Months," 8 J. AM. SOC. OF QUEST. DOC. EXAM. 79 (2005).

D. Parrett et al., "Lineup: the Reliability of Examinations Involving Multiple Writers," 6 J. AM. SOC. OF QUEST. DOC. EXAM. 82–84 (2003).

Robert Radley and Brian Lindblom, "Impression/ink Intersection Sequencing—a Comprehensive Overview," 14 J. AM. SOC. OF QUEST. DOC. EXAM. 3–13 (2011).

C. Saunders et al., "Using Automated Comparisons to Quantify Handwriting Individuality," 56 J. FORENSIC SCI. 683–689 (2011).

K. Savoie, "The Frequency of Occurrence of Specific Handwriting Characteristics within a Limited Population," 14 J. AM. SOC. OF QUEST. DOC. EXAM. 15–27 (2011).

Ellen Schuetzner, "A Study of Attempted Simulated Signatures by Teenage Writers," 9 J. AM. SOC. OF QUEST. DOC. EXAM. 95–103 (2006).

S. Senior et al., "Characterization and Dating of Blue Ballpoint Pen inks Using Principal Components Analysis of UV-VIS Absorption Spectra, IR Spectroscopy, and HPTLC," 57 J. FORENSIC SCI. 1087–1093 (2012).

Farrell C. Shiver, "Intersecting Lines," in WILEY ENCYCLOPEDIA OF FORENSIC SCIENCE (Jamieson, A. & Moenssens, A.A., eds.) 2009 [3] 1594.

K. Singer and N. Cox, "Study of Signatures Written Over Extended Periods of Time," 19 J. AM. SOC. OF QUEST. DOC. EXAM. 5–10 (2016).

D. Simmons et al., "The Effects of Constraining Signatures," 14 J. AM. SOC. OF QUEST. DOC. EXAM. 39–50 (2011).

Sargur Srihari et al., "Individuality of Handwriting," 47 J. FORENSIC SCI. 856–872 (2002).

Sargur Srihari et al., "On the Discriminability of the Handwriting of Twins," 53 J. FORENSIC SCI. 43–446 (2008).

Sargur Srihari et al., "Development of Individuality in Children's Handwriting," 61 J. FORENSIC SCI. 1292–1300 (2016).

Shigeru Sugawara, "Comparison of Near Infrared Light Photography and Middle Infrared Light Photography for Deciphering Obliterated Writings," 49 J. FORENSIC SCI. 1349–1352 (2004).

Shigeru Sugawara, "Passport Examination by Polarized Infrared Spectra," 52 J. FORENSIC SCI. 974–977 (2007).

Q. Sun et al., "How Much Can a Forensic Laboratory Do to Discriminate Questioned Ink Entries?" 61 J. FORENSIC SCI. 1116–1121 (2016).

S. Turnbull et al., "Identification of the Class Characteristics in the Handwriting of Polish people Writing English, " 55 J. FORENSIC SCI. 1296–1303 (2010).

Janis Tweedy, "Class Characteristics of Counterfeit Protection System Codes of Color Laser Copiers," 4 J. AM. SOC. OF QUEST. DOC. EXAM. 53 (2001).

Thomas Vastrick, "Admissibility Issues in Forensic Document Examination," 7 J. AM. SOC. OF QUEST. DOC. EXAM. 37–47 (2004).

S. Wang et al., "Examination of the Sequence Between Laser Printing and Rollerball Pen Writing without an Intersecting Stroke," 60 J. FORENSIC SCI. 1594–1600 (2015).

Todd Welch et al., "Fracture Match: A Validation Study of Paper Tears, Part 1," 13 J. AM. SOC. OF QUEST. DOC. EXAM. 15–21 (2010).

C. Weyermann et al., "Differentiation of Blue Ballpoint Pen Inks by Laser Desorption Ionization Mass Spectrometry and High-Performance Thin-Layer Chromatography," 52 J. FORENSIC SCI. 216–220 (2007).

Jeffrey Wilson et al., "Differentiation of Black Gel Inks Using Optical and Chemical Techniques," 49 J. FORENSIC SCI. 364–370 (2004).

CHAPTER 6

FIRE SCENE AND EXPLOSIVES INVESTIGATION[1]

I. INTRODUCTION

§6.01 SCOPE OF THE CHAPTER

This chapter is designed as a primer for the trial attorney or legal scholar on the law and science of fire and explosives analysis, dynamics,

---

[1] The Authors thank Paul Messner; B.A., J.D. for his assistance in updating this Chapter. Paul Messner is a retired Special Agent (FBI—27 years); current Firefighter/EMT/Fire Investigator (Dry Ridge, KY Fire Department—29 years volunteer fire service); and Special Deputy (Grant County, KY Sheriff's Office); AAFS Fellow (Jurisprudence Section); Fire Investigation Technician (International Association of Arson Investigators), and a Special Member of the Alabama State Bar.

The Authors appreciate the assistance of technical researcher Ann C. Smith and legal research assistant Julie Shank in updating previous versions of this chapter. Additionally, the authors gratefully acknowledge the assistance and advice that fire and explosives investigation experts John J. Lentini and Charles R. Midkiff, Jr. provided for an earlier version of this chapter.

and investigation.[2] Although much of the chapter focuses on the criminal aspects of such investigations, materials have also been drawn from the civil side because many of the applicable legal principles are equally relevant in criminal and civil trials, particularly those involving insurance claims. The chapter is subdivided so that the novel terminology of fire and explosion investigation is addressed first, followed by explanations of the rudiments of fire and explosives dynamics. The complex tasks required of the fire investigator are surveyed prefatory to an elaboration of the various forensic laboratory analyses available to support satisfactory investigations of fire and explosions. Finally, the chapter analyzes issues arising from: the use of canines for residue detection; spoliation and destruction of evidence; and the complexities of on-going scientific research that has discredited numerous anecdotal assumptions professed by historical fire investigators which resulted in erroneous criminal convictions and civil judgments and which were, thus, incorporated in older case law.

Forensic laboratory analysis of fire debris and explosive residue is widely recognized as based on solid scientific foundations (primarily chemistry) using accepted and validated instrumentation also used in other fields. However, when seeking to determine the origin and cause of a fire or explosion, the investigator depends on an interpretation of the post-incident burn patterns and damage characteristics. Historically, scientific research regarding fire behavior, burn pattern formation, and damage characteristics was scant. Consequently, fire investigators developed "rules of thumb," based on anecdotes, prior experience, and then-current fire service literature, with which to interpret burn and damage patterns and, in many cases, conclude that a fire had been deliberately set. Eventually, the use of these "rules of thumb" was challenged by investigators and researchers leading to the re-examination of numerous arson convictions across the country and spurring the movement to scientifically validate the field of fire/explosion investigation.

One case came to symbolize the consequences of these "rule of thumb" mythologies. Cameron Todd Willingham was executed for setting the fire that consumed his Corsicana, Texas home and killed his three children on December 23, 1991.[3] Willingham was fighting the fire when neighbors and officials arrived, and they saw a man desperate to

---

[2] Some commentary has noted that although the goals of investigators of both fires and explosions are to scientifically establish the cause and possible responsible parties, the two events are distinguishable based on the statistics that show most fires are accidental and most explosions are not. *See* John J. Lentini, "Fire and Explosion Investigations: Overview," in WILEY ENCYCLOPEDIA OF FORENSIC SCIENCE, (Jamieson A. & Moenssens A.A., eds) 2009 & online updates.

[3] *See* David Grann, "Trial by Fire." *The New Yorker*, September 7, 2009, pp. 42–63 (and subsequent coverage). For related video and text see: http://www.newyorker.com/ magazine/2009/09/07/trial-by-fire (last accessed November 7, 2016). The case also became the basis for the 2011 documentary film *Incendiary: The Willingham Case* by Steve Mims and Joe Bailey, Jr. (available at: http://www.incendiarymovie.com/INCENDIARY/INCENDIARY.html) (last accessed November 7, 2016).

save his children. But, after local arson investigators released word that the fire was "set," assessments of his behavior transformed radically. Willingham was convicted of murder and sentenced to death. Through the persistence of relatives, fire scientists were brought in to re-examine the original fire investigation. These experts concluded that every known myth of arson detection had been used to convict Willingham and that the conclusion of "arson" lacked any scientific basis. Despite these learned opinions, Willingham was executed on February 17, 2004. The case, however, continued to generate examination of the scientific validity of the theoretical assumptions previously used in fire investigation. On April 15, 2011, the Texas Forensic Science Commission issued its report on the case recommending more initial training, continuing education, and proficiency testing for fire investigators and implementing procedures to review old cases.[4] Although Willingham was executed, other wrongfully convicted persons have successfully challenged their convictions based on unreliable arson evidence.[5] As of November, 2016, The National Registry of Exonerations listed 74 persons later exonerated in cases involving arson.[6]

This chapter provides an overview of the terminology, procedures, and methodology of fire and explosives investigation with a caveat that inquiries such as the Willingham investigation and on-going scientific research make this an evolving field. Past court decisions are discussed with the recognition that these cases may have limited precedential value or influence as the legal community addresses the growing body of scientific research and evolving national standards.

§6.02   Terminology

In 1992, the National Fire Protection Association (NFPA) adopted the first *NFPA® 921 Guide for Fire and Explosion Investigations* ("NFPA 921") and which is approved by the American National Standards Institute (ANSI). NFPA 921 is revised every three years. The current 2014 edition became effective on December 2, 2013, on which

---

[4] "Report of the Texas Forensic Science Commission, Willingham/Willis Investigation," April 15, 2011 (available at: http://www.fsc.state.tx.us/documents/FINAL.pdf)(last accessed November 7, 2016). *See also* "Addendum to the April 15, 2011 Report of the Texas Forensic Science Commission, Willingham/Willis Investigation" (available at: http://www.fsc.texas.gov/cases)(last accessed November 7, 2016).

[5] For example, David L. Gavitt was released in June 2012 after 26 years of incarceration for three counts of murder during the commission of arson in Michigan. *See* Gavitt v. Ionia County, 67 F. Supp.3d 838 (E.D. Mich. 2014). *See also* Stephanie Clifford, "3 Men Imprisoned in 1980 Brooklyn Arson Case Are Exonerated," NY Times, December 16, 2015 (available at: http://www.nytimes.com/2015/12/17/nyregion/3-men-imprisoned-in-1980-brooklyn-arson-case-are-exonerated.html?_r=0)(last accessed November 8, 2016); Jonathan Bandler, "William Haughey's Persistence Ends in Exoneration in Putnam 'Arson'," Lohud, The Journal News, May 25, 2016 (available at: http://www.lohud.com/story/news/2016/05/25/william-haugheys-persistence-ends-exoneration-putnam-arson/84903540/)(last accessed November 8, 2016).

[6] *See* The National Registry of Exonerations listing of 74 exonerated persons in arson cases: https://www.law.umich.edu/special/exoneration/Pages/browse.aspx (last accessed November 8, 2016).

date it was approved as an American National Standard.[7] The 2017 edition is due to be released in late 2016. When conducting research, the NFPA 921 edition current at the time of the incident under consideration should be consulted.

NFPA 921[8] provides accepted definitions for common terms in fire and explosion investigations in Chapter 3, Section 3.3. Additional guidance on terminology is provided by the International Association of Fire Chiefs, the International Association of Arson Investigators and the NFPA in International Association of Fire Chiefs, the International Association of Arson Investigators, and the NFPA, *Fire Investigator: Principles and Practice to NFPA 921 and 1033,* Fourth Edition, Jones & Bartlett Learning, 2016 (*hereinafter "IAFC, Fire Investigator 4th ed.).* Other standard texts in the field that provide definitions for commonly used terms are John J. Lentini, *Scientific Protocols for Fire Investigation,* Second Edition, CRC Press, 2013 (*hereinafter "Lentini, Scientific Protocols 2d ed.");* John D. DeHaan and David J. Icove, *Kirk's Fire Investigation,* Seventh Edition, Pearson, 2012 (*hereinafter "DeHaan and Icove, Kirk's Fire Investigation 7th ed."),* and NFPA 1033 *Standard for Professional Qualifications for Fire Investigator,* 2014 Edition. NFPA Standards are revised and issued every five years.[9]

The following definitions are based on the common usage in general scientific literature or in case law. Where applicable, citation to the NFPA 921 definition is included.

Accelerant: A fuel or oxidizer, often an ignitable liquid, intentionally used to initiate a fire or increase the rate of growth or spread of a fire. *See* NFPA 921 §3.3.2. This term should be used carefully as it refers to the ***use*** of a substance as opposed to its chemical nature. As such, the term has legal implications.

Alligatoring: Large, shiny blisters of char (blackened carbonaceous material) on burned material; the presence of which was thought to indicate a fast-moving, rapidly burning fire or the use of accelerants, but currently discredited. *See* DeHaan and Icove, *Kirk's Fire Investigation 7th ed.* at p. 281.

Arc: An electrical discharge (flow of current) across an air gap or through a medium, such as charred insulation, generally producing high temperatures and luminous gases. *See* NFPA 921 §3.3.7.

Area of Origin: A structure, part of a structure, or general geographic location within a fire scene, in which the "point of origin" of a fire or explosion is reasonably believed to be located. *See* NFPA 921 §3.3.11.

---

[7]   *See* www.nfpa.org.

[8]   Guide: "A document that is advisory or informative in nature and that contains only nonmandatory provisions. . .not suitable for adoption into law." *See* NFPA 921, Sec. 3.2.3.

[9]   Standard: A document, the main text of which contains only mandatory provisions using the word "shall" to indicate requirements . . . generally suitable for mandatory reference . . . or for adoption into law. *See* NFPA 921, §3.2.5.

Autoignition: Initiation of combustion by heat without an external spark or flame. *See* NFPA 921 §3.3.14.

Backdraft: An explosion or rapid burning of heated gases resulting from the sudden introduction of air into a confined space where the fire has depleted the available oxygen and the space is heavily charged with smoke and products of incomplete combustion. *See* NFPA 921 §3.3.16.

Bead: A rounded globule of re-solidified metal at the end of the remains of an electrical conductor that was caused by arcing, and is characterized by a sharp line of demarcation between melted and unmelted conductor surfaces. *See* NFPA 921 §3.3.17. In the past, beads were thought to be caused only by arcing. Research has discredited this theory and it has been recommended that the NFPA definition be changed[10]. Beads can form on conductors from flame exposure without the passage of electrical current, however, *the bead's appearance may differ since* "Resolidified copper forms globules that are irregular in shape and size. . .often tapered. . .may be pointed. . .no distinct line of demarcation is present."[11]

Binary explosive: A mixing of two substances to form an explosive. The substances may both be nonexplosive, explosive, or a combination of the two.

Blast Pressure Front Effect: Occurs in an explosion when expanding gases exert pressure on the surrounding atmosphere, rushing away from the point of detonation in a spherical pattern, smashing and shattering objects in its path, diminishing to nothing at a distance. *See* NFPA 921 §3.3. 18.

Booster (or primer): An explosive which provides the detonation link in the explosive train between the detonating device (such as a blasting cap) and the main charge (high explosive).

Brisance: The amount of shattering effect produced by very rapidly detonating thermal decomposition (explosion). Explosives are sometimes rated as to the intensity of their brisance. Plastic explosives and nitroglycerin have high brisance.

Char: Blackened, mainly carbonaceous (containing or composed of carbon) material remaining following the burning of organic materials. *See* NFPA 921 §3.3.28.

Char Depth: The change in surface height of an organic material, such as wood through pyrolitic decomposition and combustion (burning). *See* NFPA 921 §6.2.4 *et seq.*

---

[10] *See* Richard J. Roby and Jamie McAllister, "Forensic Investigation Techniques for Inspecting Electrical Conductors Involved in Fire," July 2012 (available at: https://www.ncjrs.gov/pdffiles1/nij/grants/239052.pdf)(last accessed November 7, 2016).

[11] *See* IAFC, Fire Investigator 4th ed. at pp 131–133.

Combustion: A chemical process of oxidation that occurs at a rate fast enough to produce heat and light in the form of either a glow or flame. *See* NFPA 921 §3.3.34. Oxidation that generates detectable heat and light. *See Kirk's Fire Investigation 7th ed.*

Combustion products: The heat, gases, volatized liquids and solids, ashes, and other particulate matter generated by combustion. *See* NFPA 921 §3.3.35.

Competent Ignition Source: An ignition source that has sufficient energy and is capable of transferring that energy to the fuel long enough to raise the fuel to its ignition temperature. *See* NFPA 921 §3.3.36.

Conflagration: A major fire usually covering a wide area and which has the capacity to cross usual fire barriers such as streets.

Deflagration: Propagation of a combustion zone at a velocity that is less than the speed of sound (1100 ft/sec) in the unreacted medium and can be successfully vented. *See* NFPA 921 §3.3.42 and *Fire Investigator 4th ed.* at p. 448. Deflagrations ordinarily burn faster than open air burning of the material, but slower than a detonation of high explosives.

Detonation: An extremely rapid reaction that generates very high temperatures and an intense pressure/shock wave that produces violently disruptive effects. The combustion zone propagates through the reacting material at supersonic speeds (greater than 1,100 ft/sec) and cannot be successfully vented. *See* NFPA 921 §3.3. 45 and *Fire Investigator 4th ed.* at p. 448.

Drop Down: (Fall Down) The spread of fire by the dropping or falling of burning materials. *See* NFPA 921 §3.3.48.

Entrainment: The process of air or gases being drawn into a fire, plume or jet. *See* NFPA 921 §3.3.52.

Expectation bias: Preconceived determination or premature conclusions as to what the cause of the fire was without having examined or considered all of the relevant data. *See Fire Investigator 4th ed.* at p. 449.

Explosion: The sudden conversion of potential energy (chemical or mechanical) into kinetic energy with the production and release of gases under pressure, or the release of gas under pressure. These gases then do mechanical work, such as moving, changing, or shattering nearby materials. *See* NFPA 921 §3.3.53.

Explosive: Any chemical compound, mixture, or device that functions by explosion. *See* NFPA 921 §3.3.54.

Fire: A rapid oxidation process, which is a chemical reaction resulting in the evolution of light and heat in varying intensities; generally occurs only in the gas phase, requiring decomposition of solids into vapors and char via pyrolysis and heating of liquids to produce ignitable mixtures in air. *See* NFPA 921 §3.3.62 and *Fire Investigator 4th ed.* at p. 23.

Fire Cause: The circumstances, conditions, or agencies that bring together a fuel, ignition source, and oxidizer (such as air or oxygen) resulting in a fire or combustion explosion. *See* NFPA 921 §3.3.64.

Fire Effect: The observable or measurable changes in or on a material as a result of exposure to the fire. *See Fire Investigator 4th ed.* at p. 42.

Fire Patterns: The visible or measurable physical changes, or identifiable shapes formed by a fire effect or group of fire effects. *See* NFPA 921 §3.3.68.

First fuel ignited: That fuel which first sustains combustion beyond the ignition source. *See* NFPA 921 §3.3.73.

Flame: Luminous stream or body of burning gases. *See* NFPA 921 §3.3.74.

Flameover: Ignition and burning of unburned fuel from the originating fire that has accumulated at the ceiling during a compartment fire; not a "flashover." *See* NFPA 921 §3.3.76.

Flame Point: (Fire Point) The lowest temperature of a liquid at which the vapors from it will ignite from a flame and burn *continuously*, usually only a few degrees higher than (or even the same as) the flash point.

Flash Point of a Liquid: The lowest temperature of a liquid at which the liquid gives off vapors at a sufficient rate to support a momentary flame across its surface. *See* NFPA 921 §3.3.82.

Flashback: Ignition of a gas or vapor from a source of ignition back to the fuel source (often seen with flammable liquid containers).

Flashover: A transitional stage in the development of a fire in an enclosed compartment in which all surfaces exposed to thermal radiation reach ignition temperature at or about the same time, causing the rapid spread of the fire throughout the space, resulting in total involvement of the compartment or enclosed space. *See* NFPA 921 §3.3.83.

Fuel Controlled Fire: A fire in which the heat release rate and growth rate are controlled by the characteristics of the fuel, such as quantity and geometry, and in which adequate air for combustion is available. *See* NFPA 921 §3.3.88.

Fuel Load: (fire load) The total amount of combustible contents of a building, space or in a fire area, including interior finish and trim, expressed in heat units or the equivalent weight in wood. *See* NFPA 921 §3.3.87.

Gas Chromatography (GC): A technique for separation of components of a mixture in the vapor state. The sample to be examined is vaporized and carried through a small diameter column by a flowing gas stream. Components of the mixture dissolve in a viscous liquid inside the column and are retained to varying degrees to effect a separation. As a component of the mixture completes its passage through the column, it enters a detector which produces an electrical signal indicating its arrival and quantity. The signals from the detector are recorded on a moving chart to produce a chromatogram. The chart pattern is compared with the patterns of known materials for identification. A very small diameter column, or capillary, improves the component separation and for materials which move slowly through the column, increasing the temperature reduces analysis time.

Glowing combustion: Luminous burning of solid material without a visible flame. *See* NFPA 921 §3.3.91. *See also* "smoldering" below.

Heat Release Rate (HRR): (Burning Rate) The rate at which a substance releases heat energy when burning; measured in watts or kilowatts. *See* NFPA 921 §3.3.99. This is a key property of any fuel contributing to "heat flux" which is the measure of the rate of heat transfer to a surface; measured in kilowatts/meter^2. *See* NFPA §3.3.97.

Ignitable liquid: A liquid or the liquid phase of any material capable of fueling a fire. *See* NFPA 921 §3.3.103. Also referred to as a flammable liquid (flash point below 100°F), a combustible liquid (flash point above 100°F), or, incorrectly from a chemical viewpoint, as an "accelerant."

Ignition Temperature: The minimum temperature at which a substance will ignite under specific test conditions. *See* NFPA 921 §3.3.106.

Low Explosive: An explosive that has a reaction velocity of less than 1,000 meters/second (3000 ft/sec). *See* NFPA 921 §3.3.118.

Low Order Damage: A slow rate of pressure rise or low-force explosion characterized by a pushing or dislodging effect on the confining structure or container and by short missile distances. *See* NFPA 921 §3.3.119.

Mass spectrometry (MS): An analytical method to identify materials based upon production and detection of characteristic molecular fragments. The molecule is vaporized and fragmented in a high energy field. The fragments are separated by velocity or behavior in a magnetic field, detected, and their mass determined. Because the fragments produced under controlled conditions are reproducible, they can be related to the original structure of the molecule.

Overcurrent: Any current in excess of the rated current of equipment or the ampacity of a conductor; it may result from an overload (NFPA 921 §3.3.127), short circuit (§3.3.156), or ground fault (§3.3.93). *See* NFPA 921 §3.3.125.

Overhaul: A firefighting term referring to the process of final extinguishment of the fire; often requiring removal of burned contents, forcible exposure of wall, floor and ceiling void spaces and the application of water to fire debris. *See* NFPA 921 §3.3.126.

Plume: Column of hot gases, flames, and smoke rising above a fire; also called *convection column, thermal updraft,* or *thermal column. See* NFPA 921 §3.3.131.

Point of Origin: The exact physical location within the area of origin where a heat source (competent ignition source) and fuel (first fuel ignited) interact, resulting in a fire or explosion. *See* NFPA 921 §3.3.132.

Pyrolysis: The chemical decomposition of a material into simpler molecular compounds through the action of heat alone; pyrolysis often precedes combustion. *See* NFPA 921 §3.3.139.

Scientific Method: The systematic pursuit of knowledge involving the recognition and definition of a problem; the collection of data through observation and experimentation; analysis of the data; the formulation, evaluation and testing of a hypothesis; and, when possible, the selection of a final hypothesis. See NFPA 921 §3.3.149.

Smoldering: Combustion without flame, usually with incandescence and smoke. See NFPA 921 §3.3.161.

Suppression: The sum of all work done to extinguish a fire, beginning at the time of its discovery. See NFPA 921 §3.3.170.

Spalling: The chipping or pitting of concrete or masonry surfaces from heat or mechanical pressure. *See* NFPA 921 §3.3.163.

Spoliation: Loss, destruction, or material alteration of an object or document that is evidence or potential evidence in a legal proceeding by one who has the responsibility for its preservation. *See* NFPA 921 §3.3.167.

Ventilation: Circulation of air in any space by natural wind or convection or by fans blowing air into or exhausting air out of a building; a firefighting tactic for removing smoke and heat from a structure by opening doors and windows (horizontal ventilation) or by making openings in the roof (vertical ventilation). *See* NFPA 921 §3.3.187.

Ventilation-controlled Fire: A fire in which the heat release rate or growth is controlled by the amount of air available to the fire. *See* NFPA §3.3.188.

Venting: The escape of smoke and heat through openings in a building. *See* NFPA 921 §3.3.189.

§6.03 EVIDENTIARY USES

Fire is a part of life. Our homes and businesses could not meet our needs without fire. Fire supports industrial processes, provides energy, and makes modern life possible. The concern is not with fire, but with fire that is out of control. In 2014, public fire departments in the United States responded to some 1,298,000 fires, of which 345,500 were structure fires in homes, businesses, and other buildings.[12] These fires took 3,280 lives, resulted in 15,700 injuries, and caused approximately $14.3 billion in direct loss.[13] Of those figures, "intentional" home structure fires alone are estimated to have caused 27,400 fires, 310 deaths, 760 injuries, and $441 million in direct property damage.[14] Dwelling structure fires accounted for only 57% of all intentional structure fires, but 87% of civilian fire deaths.[15]

Arson, defined as "any willful or malicious burning or attempting to burn, with or without intent to defraud, a dwelling house, public building, motor vehicle or aircraft, or personal property of another,"[16] is the most recent addition to the FBI's Crime Index, permanently categorized as the eighth Index crime when Congress passed the Anti-Arson Act of 1982. In 2010, law enforcement agencies participating in the Uniform Crime Reporting (UCR) Program reported 56,825 arsons (19.6 arsons offenses for every 100,000 inhabitants).[17]

Improvised explosive devices and similar weapons have long been the scourge of warfare and the tools of terrorists. In 1881, Tsar Alexander II of Russia was torn apart by a bomb thrown at his feet. In Europe near the end of the nineteenth century, anarchists made several bomb throwing attempts on heads of state. In the modern era, explosives have become the stock in trade of violent groups and individuals who claim to have political justification for their terrorist acts. Ted Kaczynski, known as the Unabomber, took his campaign against technology to a national level from the 1970s to the mid-1990s in a series of bombs sent to those whom he believed violated his particular moral code. Kaczynski was finally arrested in 1996 and is

---

[12] The National Fire Protection Association (NFPA) Estimates, Fire Estimates (2015) (available at: http://www.nfpa.org/news-and-research/fire-statistics-and-reports/fire-statistics/fires-in-the-us/overall-fire-problem/number-of-fires-by-type-of-fire)(last accessed November 7, 2016).

[13] Id.

[14] NFPA's Latest Estimates of Intentional Home Structure Fires, August, 2016 (available at: http://www.nfpa.org/news-and-research/fire-statistics-and-reports/fire-statistics/fire-causes/arson-and-juvenile-firesetting/intentional-fires. As noted in cited report: "Intentional" specifically includes "deliberate misuse of heat source or a fire of an incendiary nature.")(last accessed November 7, 2016).

[15] Id.

[16] U.S. Department of Justice—Federal Bureau of Investigation, "Uniform Crime Report: Crime in the United States, 2010—Arson," September 2011 (available at: http://www.fbi.gov/about-us/cjis/ucr/crime-in-the-u.s/2010/crime-in-the-u.s.-2010/property-crime/arsonmain.pdf)(last accessed November 7, 2016).

[17] Id.

serving a life sentence. The first bombing of the New York World Trade Center, in early 1993, awakened the country to the frightening potential of international terrorism in the United States. The tragic bombing of the Murrah Federal Building in Oklahoma City, in 1995, again shattered the public consciousness about relative national safety.[18] The use of planes as incendiary devices, on September 11, 2001, at the New York World Trade Center, the Pentagon in Virginia, and a field in Shanksville, Pennsylvania, killing over 2,500 people, devastated an already disappearing sense of security. The most current national statistics on the problem of explosive use in criminal incidents are provided by the U.S. Bomb Data Center (USBDC), maintained by the Bureau of Alcohol, Tobacco, Firearms and Explosives (ATF) as a national repository for explosives and arson-related incident data. In 2015, the USBDC reported 630 explosion-related incidents, of which 400 were bombings (with 6 church bombings and 6 school bombings) resulting in 8 fatalities and 58 injuries.[19]

In addition to the criminal investigation of intentionally set fires and explosions, the analysis of accidental or negligent fires and explosions are important in civil litigation involving issues of insurance liability, wrongful death, personal injury, worker's compensation, and product liability.[20] The United States Fire Administration (USFA) analyzed data from 2012–2014 and reported that an estimated 243,800 fires occur annually in one- and two-family residential buildings, resulting in 2,110 deaths, 7,950 injuries, and 5.8 billion dollars in property loss.[21] In multifamily buildings, an estimated 108,000 fires occur annually with 410 deaths, 4,125 injuries, and $1.3 billion in

---

[18] The Unabomber cases and the events of the 1990s were by no means the first instances of terror by explosives in the U.S. Others too, motivated less by political concerns than by other interests, have employed explosives for their perfidious purposes. In 1949, Albert Guay and his two accomplices blew a Quebec Airways DC-3 out of the air killing 23 passengers, including Guay's heavily insured wife. In 1955, John Gilbert Graham killed his mother and 43 other passengers on a United Airlines plane out of Denver to repay her for refusing to remain with him during Thanksgiving. George Metesky, the "Mad Bomber" of New York City, put that city under siege in 1956 when his homemade bombs exploded in theaters, subways and other public places, quite fortuitously not killing anyone. His rampage sought vengeance against the firm that had fired him in 1931.

[19] ATF, 2015 Explosives Incident Report (EIR), 9/21/2016, (available at: https://www. atf.gov/rules-and-regulations/docs/report/2015usbdcexplosiveincidentreportpdf/download)(last accessed November 7, 2016).

[20] *See, e.g.,* Maryland Casualty Co. v. Therm-O-Disc, Inc., 137 F.3d 780 (4th Cir. 1998) (dryer fire caused by defective thermometer); Bryte v. American Household, Inc., 429 F.3d 469 (4th Cir. 2005)(fire caused by defective electric throw); Seeley v. Hamilton Beach/ProctorSilex, Inc., 349 F. Supp.2d 381 (N.D. N.Y. 2004); Dieker v. Case Corp., 30 Kan. App. 2d 751, 48 P.3d 5 (2002)(oil combine fire); Cottrell, Inc. v. Williams, 266 Ga. App. 357, 596 S.E.2d 789 (2004) (defective auto transport equipment causing burns); Turner v. Burlington Northern Santa Fe RR. Co., 338 F.3d 1058 (9th Cir. 2003)(range fire destroying a home); Fireman's Fund Insurance Co. v. Canon U.S.A., Inc., 394 F.3d 1054 (8th Cir. 2005)(various legal theories in action for copier causing fire).

[21] Federal Emergency Management Administration, U.S. Fire Administration, "One- and Two-Family Residential Building Fires (2012–2014), 17(2) *Topical Fire Report Series,* June, 2016 (available at: https://www.usfa.fema.gov/downloads/pdf/statistics/v17i2.pdf).

property loss.[22] The leading causes of fires are cooking misadventures, then other unintentional or careless actions, followed by electrical malfunctions.[23]

Investigation is necessary for the analysis of any fire or explosion event to render opinions as to the origin, cause, responsibility, and prevention of such events. Fire and explosion scenes are among the most difficult to process and analyze because of the inherent destructiveness of the event and subsequent rescue, suppression, or recovery efforts. In addition, ignitable liquids and chemical compounds are often so common that their presence at the scene may not be meaningful, making it difficult to distinguish intentional acts from accidental or negligent events. Moreover, investigation is often hampered by the lack of witnesses to the ignition of the fire or the initial detonation of the explosion. It may not be possible to determine whether a crime occurred, much less who might have committed the offense.

Investigation is also hampered when conclusions are drawn that adhere to theories which have been discounted by newer, scientific studies. Investigators at fire scenes sometimes still rely on time honored "principles" or "rules of thumb" that are no longer held to be either conclusive or valid. As the National Academy of Sciences concluded in its 2009 report on forensic science, "[d]espite the paucity of research, some arson investigators continue to make determinations about whether or not a particular fire was set. However . . . many of the rules of thumb that are typically assumed to indicate that an accelerant was used (e.g., "alligatoring" of wood, specific char patterns) have been shown not to be true."[24] Professional organizations of firefighters and fire investigators contributed to the findings in the 2009 NAS Report and have been leading the efforts to compile scientific findings and collaborate with others in setting national standards for investigation.[25]

In 1992, the National Fire Protection Association (NFPA) promulgated the initial *NFPA® 921 Guide for Fire and Explosion Investigations*. While the NFPA is not, in itself, a scientific or policy

---

[22] Federal Emergency Management Administration, U.S. Fire Administration, "Multifamily Residential Building Fires (2012–2014), 17(3) *Topical Fire Report Series*, June, 2016, (available at: https://www.usfa.fema.gov/downloads/pdf/statistics/v17i3.pdf).

[23] Federal Emergency Management Administration, U.S. Fire Administration, "One- and Two-Family Residential Building Fires (2012–2014), 17(2) *Topical Fire Report Series*, June, 2016 (available at: https://www.usfa.fema.gov/downloads/pdf/statistics/v17i2.pdf).

[24] Committee on Identifying the Needs of the Forensic Science Community, National Research Council of the National Academies, *Strengthening Forensic Science in the United States: A Path Forward,* National Academies Press, 2009 (*hereinafter "2009 NAS Report"*) at p. 173.

[25] *See* The National Center for Forensic Science and the Technical/Scientific Working Group for Fire and Explosions, "Fire and Explosion Investigations and Forensic Analyses: Near- and Long-Term Needs Assessment for State and Local Law Enforcement," January 8, 2008 (available at: https://www.ncjrs.gov/pdffiles1/nij/grants/225085.pdf) at p. 2: noting the lack of uniformity in investigative capabilities and the "desire to use more scientific and forensically sound methods."

organization, and claims no enforcement authority, it has a respected history compiling and publishing a wide variety of fire service and fire protection codes and standards. Using a technical committee consensus model, NFPA is in a unique position to advance the profession's scientific validation. NFPA coordinated advancements from throughout the field and helped forge an evolving consensus through a succession of editions culminating in the *NFPA® 921: Guide for Fire & Explosion Investigations, 2014 Edition*.[26] In addition, NFPA created an accompanying *NFPA® 1033: Standard for Professional Qualifications for Fire Investigator* (discussed *infra* at §6.13). Other groups, including the International Association of Fire Chiefs,[27] the International Association of Arson Investigators,[28] and the International Association of Bomb Technicians and Investigators,[29] have contributed to the standardization of the field and promoted research to establish the validity of investigative methodologies. Scientific research is being conducted by academic institutions and by private sector forensic entities. The Technical Working Group for Fire and Explosions (TWGFEX), the National Center for Forensic Science (NCFS), National Institute for Standards and Technology (NIST), the National Institute of Justice (NIJ), and the Bureau of Alcohol, Tobacco, Firearms and Explosives (ATF) have also worked to document best practices for investigating fires and explosions.[30]

This new era of professionalism is grounded not only in the standards of scientific evidence and modern evidentiary law, but also in engineering, chemistry, physics, radiography, and computer modeling to cite but a few related fields. Modern firefighting has moved beyond "put the wet stuff on the red stuff" and requires firefighters to have a firm understanding of: basic fire science; fire behavior in different types of buildings, occupancies, vehicles and the outdoors; building systems (heating, air conditioning, plumbing, elevators, construction techniques); fire suppression systems (water, powder, gaseous); electricity; and fuel gas systems. They must understand the chemistry and physics of fire and explosions; have a solid knowledge of how structures, machinery, and all manner of vehicles are built, powered, and operated; and be familiar with the intricacies of liquid, solid, and gaseous fuels and electrical power transmission and wiring.

---

[26] NFPA 921 Guide for Fire and Explosion Investigations, 2014 Edition has been approved for inclusion on the NIST Organization of Scientific Area Committees (OSAC) for Forensic Science Registry—"a trusted repository of high-quality, science-based standards and guidelines for forensic practice." NFPA 921 was the first guideline so approved for inclusion. *See* https://www.nist.gov/news-events/news/2016/09/fire-and-explosion-investigation-guideline-approved-osac-registry (last accessed November 7, 2016).

[27] IAFC, see www.iafc.org.

[28] IAAI, *see* www.firearson.com.

[29] IABTI, see www.iabti.org.

[30] The TWGFEX webpage provides links and downloadable resources, *see* https://ncfs.ucf.edu/databases/ (last accessed November 7, 2016).

Today, an attorney responsible for any aspect of a case involving a fire or explosion, potential or established, civil or criminal, should have access to the latest editions of, at least, NFPA 921 and NFPA 1033 (available for purchase in either hard copy or electronic formats from NFPA).[31] NFPA 921 *"Guide* for Fire and Explosion Investigations" specifies the *procedures* that *should* be followed to conduct a thorough and competent investigation. Adherence to NFPA 1033 *"Standard* for Fire Investigator Qualifications" is mandatory and its use in qualifying fire investigators as expert witnesses is increasing in frequency.

II. BASICS OF FIRE AND EXPLOSIONS

§6.04   THE FUNDAMENTALS OF FIRE

The mechanisms of fire, combustion, and explosion are complex subjects and their analyses fill countless texts.[32] The following section provides a basic understanding of the principles of ignition and combustion that guide fire investigations.[33] Fire, or combustion, is a rapid oxidation process (a chemical reaction) that produces light and heat of varying intensities along with smoke, toxic gases, and water.[34] Four components are necessary for combustion to occur: an oxidizing agent, a fuel, heat, and an uninhibited chemical chain reaction.[35] Combustion occurs when enough energy (heat) is applied to a combustible fuel (usually an organic compound) in the presence of an oxidizer (oxygen in the atmosphere) in sufficient quantities to initiate a self-sustaining chemical reaction.[36] Once initiated, combustion will continue only so long as the *exothermic* chemical chain reaction produces sufficient heat to generate combustible vapors from the fuel. Elimination or removal of any of these components—fuel, air, heat, or chemical reaction—will extinguish the fire.

Combustion generally occurs in the gaseous state (a solid or liquid fuel must be heated sufficiently to decompose or vaporize the fuel into a combustible gas). A solid must be decomposed by heat to generate the flammable gases needed for flaming combustion. Wood itself does not burn, rather, when it is heated sufficiently, pyrolysis distills off the

---

[31]   Free access to all NFPA codes and standards is available at nfpa.org, however, access is restricted to registered users and the print function has been disabled.

[32]   Useful references include IAFC, *Fire Investigator 4th ed.* at pp. 26–41; David J. Icove and John D. DeHaan, *Forensic Fire Scene Reconstruction*, 2d ed., Pearson Education, Inc. 2009 at pp. 55–100); DeHaan and Icove, *Kirk's Fire Investigation 7th ed.* at pp. 33–64; and John J. Lentini, "Fire: Chemistry of," in Wiley Encyclopedia Of Forensic Science, (Jamieson A. & Moenssens A.A., eds) 2009 & online updates.

[33]   For a detailed discussion, with accompanying diagrams, *see* NFPA 921 Chapter 5 "Basic Fire Science."

[34]   Lentini, *Scientific Protocols 2d ed.* at p. 29.

[35]   IAFC, *Fire Investigator 4th ed.* at pp. 26–28.

[36]   DeHaan and Icove, *Kirk's Fire Investigation 7th ed.* at pp. 33–34.

combustible gases leaving behind "char." Pyrolysis is the process whereby a solid material (such as wood) irreversibly decomposes into simpler molecular compounds solely through heating; producing the flammable gases necessary for combustion. The energy produced by the combustion of this flammable gas-air mixture then radiates back to the material, heating it to continue the pyrolytic action until either the material is consumed or the fire is extinguished.[37] In the presence of sufficient heating, the gases produced by the pyrolysis of wood can auto-ignite.[38]

Fire takes the form of either flaming fire or glowing fire. In a flaming fire, the flame consists of the heat, light, and gaseous products produced by a combustion process where both the fuel and oxidizer are gases; flames can only occur when a gas or vapor is burning.[39] The existence of flames shows that the combustion of a gaseous fuel is taking place. For a flammable gas to ignite, it must be present within its *flammable range,* which varies depending on the composition of the gas. If the concentration is below this range, there is too little fuel for ignition to occur; above this range, there is insufficient oxygen to support combustion.[40] Gases can be ignited by either *piloted* ignition (an arc, spark, flame, or glowing ember) or *auto-ignition*—where the gas-air mixture is heated to a gas-specific (auto-ignition) temperature at which the mixture ignites without a piloted ignition source.[41]

A glowing (smoldering) fire is characterized by the absence of flames while the surface of a solid material is sufficiently hot to be rapidly oxidized directly by oxygen in the air, creating light (incandescence) and heat. An example of glowing fire is a charcoal briquette.[42] The reaction takes place at the surface of the solid, continuing until either the fuel is exhausted, it makes the transition to flaming combustion, or is extinguished.[43] The reaction rate is limited by the surface-to-mass ratio of the fuel and the availability of oxygen. Compared to flaming combustion, smoldering is less efficient and produces more products of incomplete combustion, such as smoke (containing particulates and liquid aerosols) and toxic gases. Combustible solid fuels such as cloth, wood, and paper may smolder when, for example, access to oxygen is limited.[44] If the oxygen supply increases, the reaction rate can increase sufficiently to allow for flaming combustion.

---

[37] Id. at p. 22.

[38] NFPA 921 §5.7.4.3.

[39] Id. at p. 34.

[40] IAFC, *Fire Investigator 4th ed.* at p. 30.

[41] Id. at pp. 28–30.

[42] David J. Icove and John D. DeHaan, *Forensic Fire Scene Reconstruction,* 2d ed., Pearson Education, Inc., 2009 at p. 59.

[43] DeHaan and Icove, *Kirk's Fire Investigation 7th ed.* at pp. 38–40.

[44] Id.

Flaming combustion may transition to smoldering as the fire consumes the available oxygen. Such a smoldering fire is known as a "ventilation-controlled" fire. If a fresh supply of oxygen is introduced, the smoldering fire will likely return to flaming combustion. If the oxygen supply is rapidly increased, by fire department tactics or structural collapse, that transition will also be rapid; potentially causing a "backdraft" explosion.[45]

A liquid must be converted to a gas by either vaporization, evaporation, or mechanical atomization before it can burn with a flame.[46] An important and measurable property of liquid fuels is the flash point, the lowest temperature at which a liquid produces a flammable vapor.[47] Another measurable property of a liquid is its flame point (or fire point), the lowest temperature at which a liquid will produce a flammable vapor sufficient to sustain burning after the ignition source has been removed.[48] Flash points and flame points are useful in determining the relative flammability of one liquid compared to another.[49] Some materials are capable of "self-heating" solely due to exothermic reactions between the material and the surrounding atmosphere."[50] Self-heating and spontaneous combustion (self-ignition)[51] are usually encountered with organic materials such as animal fats and vegetable oils containing highly-reactive polyunsaturated fatty acids or with certain inorganic materials, such as metal powders, capable of rapid oxidation given appropriate conditions.[52] Typical situations involving self-heating materials include: placing inadequately-washed oily laundry items in a clothes dryer, improper storage of oil-based painting materials, and bales of insufficiently-dried agricultural products such as cotton or hay.[53]

---

[45] Id. at p. 41.

[46] Lentini, *Scientific Protocols 2d ed.* at p. 47.

[47] IAFC, *Fire Investigator 4th ed.* at p. 30.

[48] Id.

[49] DeHaan and Icove, *Kirk's Fire Investigation 7th ed.* at pp. 91–94.

[50] NFPA 921 §5.7.4.1.2.1.

[51] "Spontaneous combustion requires certain steps for it to occur. First, the material must be capable of self-heating and must be subjected to conditions where self-heating is elicited. Next, the self-heating must proceed to thermal runaway (i.e., the heat generated exceeds the heat losses to the environment). Thermal runaway, in theory, means a temperature rise so large that stable conditions can no longer exist. In practice, it means that the material will undergo an internal temperature rise (often at or near its middle) on the order of several hundred degrees Celsius. Next, thermal runaway must result in self-sustained smoldering. The opposite of this is a condition where the material chars locally, but fails to establish a propagating smolder front." NFPA 921 §5.7.4.1.3.

So-called Spontaneous Human Combustion is not true spontaneous combustion because it requires a source of heat near the body. It is an extremely rare event, but has been documented. *See* Thierry W. Levi-Faict and Gerald Quatrehomme, "So-called Spontaneous Human Combustion," 56 J. Forensic Sci. 1334–1339 (2011).

[52] IAFC, *Fire Investigator 4th ed.* at pp. 30–31.

[53] Id.

The power of a fire is determined by its heat release rate (HRR),[54] the amount of energy released by the individual fuels being consumed (measured in watts or kilowatts). The materials consumed during a fire are referred to as "fuel items" and when combined or placed in proximity, a "fuel package" is created.[55] HHR is an important property of fire, because it permits predictions of the fire's behavior throughout the course of the fire.[56] "The HRR affects the temperature of the fire, its ability to entrain air, and the identity of the chemical species produced in the fire."[57] Also important to understanding fire behavior is heat flux—the rate at which energy is falling on or flowing through a surface (measured units of power per unit area—kilowatts/meter^2).[58] Another important parameter is the total energy impact—the duration of the heat flux energy transfer (obtained by multiplying the heat flux by time of exposure in seconds).[59]

Fire behaves differently in the confined space of a structure such as a building or a room (a "compartment") than in the open air of outdoor environments.[60] With a compartment fire, the configuration of the space and the location of the fire in the compartment affects the way the fire interacts with its surroundings, including the spread of the fire. The products of combustion will influence the materials within a compartment and the degree of influence will be a function of the materials' characteristics, intensity of the combustion products, and exposure duration.[61] This process creates fire effects—observable and measurable changes in or on a material as a result of a fire.[62] The grouping of fire effects (fire patterns) provides an indication of fire travel, intensity, and/or duration.[63] The primary driver of fire effect creation is the total amount of heat transferred (cumulative heat flux[64]) to the surface of the material over the duration of the fire[65].

---

[54] NFPA 921 §5.6.3.1; DeHaan and Icove, *Kirk's Fire Investigation 7th ed.* at pp. 43–44.

[55] IAFC, *Fire Investigator 4th ed.* at p. 26.

[56] Id. at p. 27.

[57] John J. Lentini, "Fire: Chemistry of," in Wiley Encyclopedia Of Forensic Science, (Jamieson A. & Moenssens A.A., eds) 2009 & online updates, at p. 2. *See also* Lentini, *Scientific Principles 2d. ed.* at p. 24.

[58] Lentini, *Scientific Protocols 2d ed.* at pp. 24–25.

[59] Id. at p. 27.

[60] For a detailed discussion of compartment fire development and phenomena, with accompanying explanatory diagrams *see* NFPA 921 §§5.10–5.12.

[61] Gregory E. Gorbett, William D. Hicks, Andrew T. Tinsley, *Fire Patterns, Analysis with Low Heat Release Initial Fuels*, 64 Fire & Arson Investigator 1, July, 2013, at p. 18. (*hereinafter* "Gorbett, *Fire Patterns*").

[62] NFPA 921 §6.2.1.

[63] Gorbett, *Fire Patterns* at p. 18.

[64] *Heat flux* is a measure of the rate of energy falling on or flowing through a surface. Heat flux is distinct from *heat release rate* which quantifies the energy (in kilowatts) released from a fuel item. Heat flux is the amount of that energy impacting an area of surface— kilowatts/meter^2. *See* Lentini, Scientific Principles 2d ed. at pp. 24–29.

[65] Id.

As a fire develops, a plume is created by the heat column rising from the fire and air being pulled (entrained) into the column. The fire plume and the various heat fluxes generated by it are one of the primary means of damage production in the early stages of a fire.[66] Fire effects generated by this plume (plume-generated patterns) depend on its location in relation to vertical and horizontal surfaces. A plume from a fire away from the walls will create a circular pattern on the ceiling. The plume from a small, early stage fire at the base of a wall will create an "inverted V" or "cone" pattern (∧) on the wall, where the base is the width of the fire and the tip is the top of the developing plume. As that fire plume develops and entrains air, the plume spreads and creates a "V" pattern.[67] The plume continues to develop, eventually intersecting with the ceiling surface and creating a ceiling jet—heat and hot gases flowing along the horizontal surface—and forming a hot gas layer along the ceiling. As the fire progresses, more energy is absorbed by the upper gas layer increasing the heat flux to the ceiling and walls. As the temperature of the gases in the upper layer increases and the duration of influence between these gases and the surfaces (total energy impact) increases, the cumulative heat flux impinging on these surfaces reaches a critical threshold that begins damaging the material and creating fire effects attributable to the hot gas layer.[68]

As the fire and fire plume grow, more energy is absorbed by the upper gas layer and it expands, with the bottom of this layer descending along the walls and causing fire effects as the layer sinks. Even as the upper gas layers absorbs energy, it radiates some of the absorbed energy down towards floor level (radiant heat flux).[69] As the fire progresses, the intensity of the radiation from the upper gas layer upon exposed combustibles in the room increases, driving the surface temperatures of those surfaces higher, producing pyrolitic gases.[70] When the upper gas layer temperature reaches about 1100°F (590°C) all of the combustible surfaces exposed to the upper gas layer radiation ignite nearly-simultaneously. This phenomenon, called "flashover" (or 'full-involvement') transitions the fire from "a fire in a room" to "a room on fire."[71]

Until flashover, the fire is "fuel-controlled"—there is plenty of oxygen, so the size of the fire (the heat release rate) is determined by the amount of fuel. During or after flashover, when all exposed fuel is already ignited, the size of the fire, and the heat release rate, becomes dependent on the availability of oxygen, and is considered "ventilation-controlled."[72] In a ventilation-controlled fire, more complete combustion

---

[66] Gorbett, *Fire Patterns* at p. 18.

[67] IAFC, *Fire Investigator* at pp. 49–51.

[68] Gorbett, *Fire Patterns* at p. 19.

[69] Lentini, *Scientific Protocols 2d ed.* at p. 77.

[70] NFPA 921 §5.10.2.6.

[71] Lentini, *Scientific Protocols 2d ed.* at p. 77.

[72] Id.

occurs at those locations where the fuel/air mixture is adequate, such as near ventilation openings and along air flow paths.[73] Substantial damage (fire effect) is often found directly adjacent or opposite to window and door openings.[74] When interpreting fire patterns in a compartment(s) fire, "ventilation" fire effects may mimic patterns associated with those of a fire origin; resulting in an incorrect origin determination. Proper analysis requires combining available fire patterns research with compartment fire dynamics.[75]

§6.05　THE BASICS OF ELECTRICITY[76]

Electricity is so central to our lives that we tend to use it routinely with minimal thought, but its nature and potential remain poorly understood even within the fire service. In 2014, approximately 23,900 fires in U.S. homes were attributed to electrical malfunctions, causing 325 deaths, 900+ injuries, and $929,400,000 in property losses.[77] Electrical equipment should be considered as an ignition source equally with all other possible sources and not as either a first or last choice. The presence of electrical wiring or equipment at or near the origin of a fire does not necessarily mean that the fire was caused by electrical energy. Often the fire may destroy insulation or cause changes in the appearance of conductors or equipment that can lead to false assumptions. Careful evaluation is warranted.[78]

An oft-used analogy to explain basic electricity concepts is that of water flowing through a pipe. Wider pipes have a larger capacity to carry water, or larger potential carrying capacity. The pressure of the flowing water (lbs/in²) is analogous to "voltage"—the pressure pushing electrons through a conductor. Amperage, or amps, is the rate of electrical conduction through a wire, analogous to the rate of water being forced through the pipe in gallons/minute. Only so much water can flow through a pipe of given diameter at any given time, and, as the speed and pressure increase, the amount of water flowing reaches the pipe's maximum carrying capacity; in electrical terms, this is the conductor's "ampacity" the amount of current that a conductor can safely carry without exceeding its temperature rating. Ampacity is directly related to the type and diameter of the conductor, normally electrical wire. A "watt" is a measure of electrical power (analogous to mechanical horsepower), and is a function of voltage (water pressure) times amperage (water flow rate). The larger the diameter of a pipe, the

---

[73]　Gorbett, *Fire Patterns* at p. 19.

[74]　Id.

[75]　"This type of damage...has been recognized as a major factor by educated fire investigators since 1997." Id.

[76]　*See* NFPA 921 §§9.2–9.8.3.2.

[77]　U.S. Fire Administration; *Fire Estimate Summary: Residential Building Fire Trends*, June, 2016 (available at: https://www.usfa.fema.gov/downloads/pdf/statistics/res_bldg_fire_estimates.pdf)(last accessed November 7, 2016).

[78]　NFPA 921 §9.1.1.

greater the possible flow; the larger the diameter of a conductor (e.g., wire) the more amps it can carry. The diameter of wire is measured by sizes in the American Wire Gauge (AWG). A smaller AWG number correlates to a larger wire diameter.[79]

Electricity creates heat as it flows through a conductor due to resistance (analogous to the friction of water flowing though a pipe). The term "conductor" includes any material through which electrons can flow, such as wires, terminal lugs, bus bars, metal enclosures, human tissue, etc.[80] For reasons of cost efficiency, electricity is distributed at much higher voltages than those used by the end customer.[81] Typically, electricity is transmitted over long distances at 100–1,000 Kv (kilo-volts), is stepped-down at a sub-station to 3–20 Kv and then to 240 volts by either pole-mounted or surface pad-mounted transformers. Heat is produced as electricity flows through this distribution system; then along the *service drop* (or *service lateral* for surface or underground service) to a home; through the usage meter and main service panel into the branch circuits for distribution to switches, receptacles (including wall outlets), and appliances throughout the building.[82] Generally, the higher the resistance, the more heat is produced. In some instances, such as hair dryers or portable electric heaters, this resistance heating is a design feature. In other circumstances, such as a faulty connection at a wall outlet, the heat produced may become a source of ignition.[83] 120/240 volt alternating current single-phase service electrical systems are common in U.S. residential and smaller commercial buildings. A single-phase service consists of three conductors: two line conductors—referred to as the "hot legs"—and a neutral conductor which is grounded near the source transformer outside the building.[84] Larger commercial and industrial buildings use a three-phase service with four conductors: three insulated hot legs and an isolated neutral.[85] Electrical wiring can be intricate, with multiple service panels and sub-panels, even in single family dwellings. A typical residential single-phase service distribution panel has a master disconnect, either a switch or a pair of circuit breakers (one for each "hot leg") fastened together, that cuts off the power to the individual branch circuits. A commercial three-phase system will require three main circuit breakers—one for each of the three "hot legs." This master disconnect must have enough capacity to carry the entire current load of the structure and is rated in amps (e.g., a 100 amp or a 200 amp service).[86] The usage meter reads watts,

---

[79] IAFC, *Fire Investigator 4th ed.* at pp. 116–127.

[80] DeHaan and Icove, *Kirk's Fire Investigation 7th ed.* at p. 402.

[81] Id. at p. 422.

[82] IAFC, *Fire Investigator 4th ed.* at pp. 116–127.

[83] Id. at pp. 127–128.

[84] Id. at p. 119.

[85] Id. at pp. 119–120.

[86] NFPA 921 §9.6.3.2.1.

however, not amps and electricity usage is measured and billed in kilowatt hours.

Modern electrical systems, installed to code and properly maintained, are generally safe; however, problems can arise. A few of these problems are intrinsic to the utility. Power can be lost, but also can flux or surge as the result of switching activity, shifting demand, error, or weather. Excessive power can overload a user's service, damage insulation, or create excessive heat.[87] While whole-house surge protectors are available, they can malfunction, particularly when tripped two or more times without replacement. Also, wiring components can be defective or fail under prolonged use.

The more common problems result from improper use. Residents frequently compromise a properly-wired structure by using an inadequate extension cord between a receptacle and an appliance, or by powering a collection of seemingly small-draw items together on the same extension cord. Either circumstance can overheat the extension cord; for example, drawing a 30 amp current through a 14 gauge wire extension cord rated for only 8 amps.[88] The danger from overloading an extension cord is compounded when the extension cord is run under a rug or other objects that trap the heat being produced by the overload; potentially igniting nearby combustible materials.[89] Something as innocuous as an incandescent or halogen light bulb coming in contact with fabric, a pillow case for example, can start a fire. Moreover, people often try to push the capacity of their electrical system by defeating safety features; inserting pennies behind screw-in fuses was a classic example. Individuals not wishing or able to pay for their power use, as well as persons engaged in illicit marijuana growing activities, have bypassed the meter and the main service panel by installing a "hot tap" before the meter, frequently using inadequate connectors or wiring to connect the service drop or lateral directly to the building's wiring.[90]

Another area of difficulty, which can be traced both to improper installation as well as user error, involves proper grounding. In direct current (DC) electrical systems, such as those in motor vehicles, power is supplied on a single wire and then passes on to a common ground. Proper grounding is necessary to close the circuit and provide current a path through which to flow.[91]

American alternating current (AC) single-phase and three-phase wiring systems also require a proper ground—either to buried metallic

---

[87] An overload—a persistent excessive flow of current—can cause various electrical components to overheat, thereby igniting a fire. IAFC, *Fire Investigator 4th ed.* at p. 117.

[88] Id. at p. 127.

[89] DeHaan and Icove, *Kirk's Fire Investigation 7th ed.* at p. 427.

[90] Victor Massenkoff, *Indoor Marijuana Grow and Butane Hash Oil Fires*, Presentation to the 67th Annual Training Conference, International Association of Arson Investigators, Orlando, Florida, April 28, 2016.

[91] IAFC, *Fire Investigator 4th ed.* at p. 118.

water pipes or to a ground rod. However, unlike with DC circuits, in an AC system, a ground is not needed for current to flow. Rather, grounding an AC electrical system prevents any housing or exposed metal objects in the system from becoming electrically charged.[92] An AC ground is a safety mechanism, providing an alternate path for current to flow should a hot conductor short to a metal object connected to the grounded conductor; the resulting ground-fault current surge should open that circuit's ground-fault protection cutting off current flow.[93]

Roughly analogous to a DC ground is the "neutral" conductor in an AC system. As with the DC ground, the AC "neutral" serves as the return path to the electrical distribution grid for current flowing through the hot legs. However, unlike with the DC ground, current flow is not dependent on an intact "neutral." Current will continue to flow if the "neutral" connection is broken (referred to as an "open" or "floating" neutral), but the voltage between the hot legs will become unstable; varying from zero to 240 volts depending on what loads are on the circuit.[94] Such fluctuations can damage electronics; overload appliances and lighting fixtures; overheat motors; and create over-current conditions in wiring. Also, when the neutral opens, the current normally flowing through it must find an alternative path. Often that path is through the grounding system; resulting in current at fluctuating voltages flowing through ground wiring without over-current protection; potentially, sending current through the metal chassis of an appliance or heating the ground wire and igniting nearby combustibles.[95] It should be noted that an "open" neutral does not need to occur inside a building to affect its wiring. If the neutral is broken on the utility's side of the meter, for example by a tree damaging the neutral conductor at the power pole, the path for current inside the building to return to the electrical grid is still broken and the consequences of an "open" neutral will occur downstream of the break— on the building side of the meter.[96]

Branch circuit breakers (or fuses installed in the main service distribution panel or sub-panels) are the primary structural wiring protection devices to prevent damage due to over-current or over-loading of a circuit. They are, however, designed to interrupt current flow only within specific time/temperature parameters. Consequently, they will respond slowly to a modest over-current and quickly to a major over-current.[97] A circuit breaker likely will not trip in the extension cord misuse example mentioned above because that over-current is specific to that particular small gauge wire, the wire's limited

---

[92] NFPA 921 §9.5.1.1.

[93] Id.

[94] Cameron Novak and Brent Fukuda, "*Open Neutrals—The Point of No Return,*" 64 Fire & Arson Investigator 2 (2013) at pp. 17–19.

[95] Id. at p. 19.

[96] Id.

[97] DeHaan and Icove, *Kirk's Fire Investigation 7th ed.* at p. 418.

ampacity and the relatively minor excess current draw (30 amps on a typical 20 amp residential circuit) occurs over a relatively extended period of time.[98] Circuit breakers can also fail to operate even within their design parameters because of age, condition (corrosion, excessive external temperature), or user abuse.

Additional protection in specialized areas, such as bathrooms, kitchens and bedrooms, is provided by *ground-fault circuit interrupters* (GFCI or GFI) and *arc-fault circuit interrupters* (AFCI). GFCIs (recognizable as a rectangular outlet with "push-to-test" and "reset" buttons) provide protection from electrocution, acting as "shock protection" by reacting to an imbalance between energized conductors ("hot leg") and the neutral conductor. Such an imbalance occurs when the current leaving the GFCI is greater than the returning current, indicating that some or all of the current is flowing along a dangerous pathway—a ground fault.[99] GFCIs are used in primarily in circuits where shock hazards to people are common; for example, near bathroom sinks around which hair dryers, electric razors or curling irons are used and which can deliver potentially fatal current flows through a person. GFCIs installed in the branch circuit provide primarily shock prevention and not fire prevention. However, GFCIs installed remotely in a service panel act as both a conventional circuit breaker for over-current protection and as shock prevention.[100]

Arc-fault circuit interrupters (AFCI), however, are designed to prevent conductor overheating due to arcing (and causing fires) by discriminating between normal current flow and arcing current flow using wave form variations. They function similarly to GFCIs by comparing outgoing and returning current, but use special circuitry to differentiate between normal and unwanted arcing events. Normal arcing events happen when a switch is opened or an energized appliance is unplugged.[101] AFCIs are designed to not trip when such normal arcing occurs, but to interrupt current flow when an arc causes a potentially hazardous increase in current flow and before a fire can start.[102]

Most modern appliances incorporate additional protective devices to prevent harm from thermal, over-current, or short circuit events. These devices include: replaceable fuses, resettable circuit breakers, thermostatic controls, replaceable thermal cutouts (TCOs), motion (tip-over) sensors, metal oxide varisters, and pressure cut-off switches.[103]

---

[98]   IAFC, *Fire Investigator 4th ed.* at p. 123.

[99]   Id.at pp. 123–124.

[100] Id. *See also* NFPA 921 §9.6.3.4.

[101] NFPA 921 §9.6.3.5.

[102] DeHaan and Icove, *Kirk's Fire Investigation 7th ed.* at p. 422.

[103] For a detailed discussion about protective devices, switches and sensors used in consumer appliances *see* IAFC, *Fire Investigator 4th ed.* at pp. 353–363.

There are many more areas of potential problems with electricity, often associated with arcs and sparks (primary ignition sources) caused by poor connections, inadequate wiring or breaks in wiring, or even with the required moving connections in components such as electrical motors. Mechanical abrasions and contamination of wiring components can lead to arcing and short circuits (an improper contact of wires that can result in excessive heat-producing draw).[104] Also, water in GFCI receptacles has been linked to fires.[105]

For ignition to occur from an electrical failure, four conditions must exist: the wiring must be energized; sufficient heat and temperature must be produced; the fuel must be capable of being ignited by electrical energy; and the heat source and first-fuel-ignited must be close enough together for a sufficient time to generate ignitable vapors.[106] Potential sources of electrical ignition include:

- Resistance heating—at poor or corroded connections
- Heat-producing devices—misuse or abuse
- Over-current and over-load—current draw beyond the ampacity of the conductor
- Arcs—high-voltage arcs, lightning strikes, static electrical, parting arcs, arcs through insulation, arcs across contaminated surfaces.[107]

Fire investigator training in electrical science has increased significantly in recent years. This is an area in which official causes of fires were all too often attributed to unsubstantiated assumptions. New fire scene examination techniques now permit more accurate conclusions, and the resources and standards[108] required to make that possible are now being stressed in training.[109]

§6.06   THE CHARACTERISTICS OF AN EXPLOSION

For a fire and explosion investigator, an explosion is "[t]he sudden conversion of potential energy (chemical or mechanical) into kinetic energy with the production and release of gases under pressure, or the release of gas under pressure," which then moves, changes or shatters nearby materials.[110] An explosive is "[a]ny chemical compound, mixture, or device that functions by explosion.[111] An explosion, as that term is used in this chapter, must involve pressurized gas. There are,

---

[104] Id. at pp. 425–450.

[105] DeHaan and Icove, *Kirk's Fire Investigation 7th ed.* at p. 421.

[106] IAFC, *Fire Investigator 4th ed.* at p. 127.

[107] NFPA 921 §9.9.1–§9.9.6.

[108] *See, e.g.,* American Society for Testing and Materials, ASTM D 495: Dielectric Withstand Voltage; ASTM E 2345: Investigation of Electrical Incidents.

[109] *See* DeHaan and Icove, *Kirk's Fire Investigation 7th* ed. at p. 464.

[110] NFPA 921 § 23.1.3.

[111] NFPA 921 §3.3.50; 23.1.1 et seq.

however, two types of explosions: mechanical and chemical. A mechanical explosion, such as a Boiling Liquid Expanding Vapor Explosion (BLEVE), occurs when the pressure inside a container ruptures the container. The pressure increase is caused by a physical reaction, such as over-filling a propane tank or by fire heating a railroad tank car and boiling the liquid inside thereby increasing the interior gas pressure beyond the strength of the container. A mechanical explosion neither originates from a chemical reaction nor changes the chemical composition of the substances involved.[112] A chemical explosion "is one in which an exothermic reaction is the source of the high pressure gas" and the chemical composition of the explosive is changed.[113]

The chemistry of an explosion is similar to that of a fire. Just as is the case with the burning of fuel oil or gasoline, a chemical explosion is predicated on the oxidation of fuel. Fires and explosions are differentiated by the speed of the chemical reaction causing the production and release of gases under pressure. The ignition of a vapor in a closed container that damages the container is an explosion;[114] the same ignition occurring in an open area is not an explosion, but a deflagration (subsonic propagation reaction vs. "detonation," a supersonic reaction wave) because the reaction proceeds slowly enough to be successfully vented, allowing the dissipation of the gases.[115]

The damage from an explosion is typically classified as either *low-order*: resulting from a slow pressure increase and characterized by dislodging or displacement of structural components with large pieces of debris thrown short distances; or *high-order*: occurring from a rapid pressure increase, characterized by shattered structural components with pulverized debris items thrown large distances.[116] Damage characteristics of an explosion are typically divided into four groups: blast overpressure and wave effects; projected fragments (shrapnel) effects; thermal effects; and seismic (ground shock) effects.[117] Blast overpressure and wave effects consist of a positive pressure phase (the outward expansion from the area of origin of gases at high speeds) and a negative pressure phase (from the movement of air rushing to fill the low pressure area left by the outward-moving positive pressure wave). Although damage can occur during both phases, the positive pressure wave is more powerful and causes most of the pressure damage[118].

---

[112] IAFC, *Fire Investigator 4th ed.* at pp. 304–305.; *see also* NFPA 921 §21.1.5.

[113] Id.

[114] For a discussion of the characterization of fragmentation patterns of improvised explosive devices, *see* Dana Bors, Josh Cummins and John Goodpaster, "The Anatomy of a Pipe Bomb Explosion: Measuring the Mass and Velocity Distributions of Container Fragments," 59 J. Forensic Sci. 42–51 (2013).

[115] IAFC, *Fire Investigator 4th ed.* at pp. 306–309; *see also* NFPA 921 §23.1.5.

[116] IAFC, *Fire Investigator 4th ed.* at p. 307.

[117] NFPA 921 §§21.4–21.4.4; *see generally* IAFC, *Fire Investigator 4th ed.* at pp. 304–308.

[118] Id. at p. 306; *see also* NFPA 921 Guide §21.1.5.

Shrapnel, pieces of debris resulting from the blast pressure wave fronts, may cause secondary damage some distance from the origin of the explosion. Thermal effects occur when the explosion ignites nearby combustibles, are common with BLEVES, and may complicate efforts to determine which occurred first—the explosion or the fire. Seismic effects, the transmission of tremors through the ground causing structural damage, occur with larger explosions.[119]

The size of an explosion is often estimated by "scaling" blast parameters and expressing the "TNT equivalency" of the damage. For example, "the explosion caused damage equivalent to 3 pounds of TNT."[120] The physical effects of an explosion vary tremendously and are influenced by the following factors: type and configuration of the fuel; the nature, shape, size, and composition of the containment vessel; items within the vessel; location and magnitude of the ignition sources; venting of the vessel; relative maximum pressure achieved; and the rate of the pressure increase.[121]

An explosive is "[a]ny chemical compound, mixture, or device that functions by explosion."[122] An explosive cannot be self-initiating; it must be caused to explode generally either by heat or by shock. While an explosive can not be self-initiating, it must be self-sustaining, so that its action will continue throughout the entire explosive charge once it has been initiated at any point within it. A vast assemblage of explosives exists. Explosives can be classified in a number of different ways, including by the source of their manufacture or their use. The most widely recognized classification system distinguishes explosives as "low" or "high" based on their reaction velocity.

When an explosive reaction is initiated, the speed of the reaction will vary depending on the explosive used. Although there is no precise line of demarcation, if the reaction occurs at a rate of less than 1000 meters per second (3,280 ft/sec), the explosive is generally described as a *low explosive* which is said to *deflagrate* rather than detonate.[123] If the speed of the reaction is greater than 1000 meters per second (3,280 ft/sec), the explosive is usually termed a *high explosive* which is said to *detonate* rather than deflagrate.[124] Low explosives cannot support a detonation wave. Low explosives can do great damage, but typically will push out in mass; the debris fragments are large and travel a limited distance. High explosives, on the other hand, shatter everything in their way into small pieces that then travel long distances very quickly.[125]

---

[119] IAFC, *Fire Investigator 4th ed.* at pp. 306–308.

[120] For a detailed discussion of scaling and TNT equivalency estimates, *see* Alexander Beveridge, *Forensic Investigations of Explosions*, Second Edition, CRC Press, 2012 at pp. 36–38.

[121] IAFC, *Fire Investigator 4th ed.* at p. 308.

[122] NFPA 921 §23.12.

[123] DeHaan and Icove, *Kirk's Fire Investigation 7th ed.* at p. 507.

[124] Id. at p. 509.

[125] Id.at pp. 513–514.

The low explosives that are commonly involved in criminal enterprises use black or smokeless powders. Black powder, usually combining the oxidizing agent potassium nitrate with much smaller quantities of sulfur and charcoal,[126] can be confined in a pipe or other container and detonated by a fuse or a blasting cap. Smokeless powder may be single base, involving nitrocellulose only, or double base, adding 30 to 40% nitroglycerin to nitrocellulose.[127] Low explosives can also result from the ignition of gaseous fuels in combination with atmospheric oxygen. Natural gas leaks, whether intentional or unintentional, can be low explosives. Other combustible gases can produce a similar explosive effect as long as the gas to air mixture is within the upper and lower explosive limits of the particular gas when ignited. An explosion which leaves no trace of a crater signals an explosion of a gaseous nature. The blowing out of walls on all sides and the equal distribution of explosive forces on all sides are other signs of a gaseous explosion.[128] Similarly, many solids which have poor burning power or none at all in a solid state will explode when diffused into the air as minute, dust-like particles, so long as the right air/particle mixture obtains and ignition occurs. Coal, aluminum, magnesium, grain and flour have this capacity when in the form of dust.

High explosives are those that support a detonation wave and will detonate when initiated by heat or shock.[129] High explosives can be subdivided into those that are so insensitive to heat, friction, and shock that they require initiation by another, more sensitive explosive contained either in a blasting cap, a primer charge or in a fuse-like detonating cord. Such explosives are called secondary explosives and include dynamite,[130] TNT,[131] PETN,[132] and RDX.[133] The primary

---

[126] Alexander Beveridge, *Forensic Investigations of Explosions*, Second Edition, CRC Press, 2012 at pp. 2–3.

[127] Id. at pp. 3–4.

[128] DeHaan and Icove, *Kirk's Fire Investigation 7th ed.* at pp. 490–491.

[129] Id. at p. 509.

[130] Dynamite, derived from the Greek word for power, was first commercially produced by Alfred Nobel, who later established the Nobel Prizes. The composition of dynamite has changed markedly from what it was when produced by Nobel in the late 19th century. Straight dynamite has high brisance. Gelignite is a European generic name for a type of gelatin dynamite, used in underground mining. Gelatin dynamites are much more water resistant than straight dynamite. Blasting gelatin is the most powerful of commercial dynamites.

Dynamite is generally packaged in round cartridges of wax-coated paper or cardboard. Nitroglycerin is sometimes seen to exude through the dynamite cylinder as the dynamite ages. Being an oil, NG can be readily absorbed by the skin and will cause blood vessels to dilate; hence its medicinal use to alleviate angina. *See* Alexander Beveridge, *Forensic Investigations of Explosions*, Second Edition, CRC Press, 2012 at pp. 8–10; DeHaan & Icove, *Kirk's Fire Investigation 7th ed.* at pp. 509–510.

[131] TNT (2, 4, 6-trinitrotoluene) is a nitro compound which is derived from toluene, a petroleum product, which has many legitimate uses. In view of its stability in storage and under varying temperature conditions, it is a widely used military explosive. Moisture does not affect it. Its detonation velocity is about 6900 meters per second, which gives it a high brisance. *See* Alexander Beveridge, *Forensic Investigations of Explosions*, 2d ed., CRC Press, 2012 at p. 5.

explosives are those which initiate the secondary explosive. In this category are lead azide, lead styphnate, silver azide, nitrogen triodide and mercury fulminate. The sensitivity of these explosive charges makes them exceedingly dangerous to use in improvised bombs. Based upon the functions performed by them, the ingredients in multi-component explosives are classed as explosive bases, combustibles, oxygen carriers, antacids and absorbents. Combustibles and oxygen are added to achieve oxygen balance, whereas the explosive base releases heat energy upon detonation by heat or shock. The antacid stabilizes an explosive while in storage and an absorbent absorbs a liquid explosive base.

III. GENERAL ASPECTS OF SCENE INVESTIGATION

§6.07 OVERVIEW

The National Fire Protection Association provides an excellent summary of the purposes of a scene investigation in its 921 guide:

> "The major objective of any fire scene examination is to collect data as required by the scientific method. . .Such data include the patterns produced by the fire. A fire pattern is the visible or measurable physical changes or identifiable shapes formed by a fire effect or group of fire effects. Fire effects are the observable or measurable changes in or on a material as a result of exposure to the fire. The collection of fire scene data requires the recognition and identification of fire effects and fire patterns. The data can also be used for fire pattern analysis (i.e., the process of interpreting fire patterns to determine how the patterns were created). This data and analysis can be used to test hypotheses as to the origin of the fire."[134]

Identifying the origin of a fire or explosion, determining the cause, and properly assigning responsibility (if any) requires a thorough and complete investigation; one that grows more complex as the scale of the fire or explosion increases. An investigation of a small, contained and quickly extinguished fire, for example in a metal wastepaper can, will

---

[132] PETN (Pentaerythritol Tetranitrate). It is used as a priming compound for detonators, as a base charge in blasting caps and as the core for detonating cord, commercially known as Primacord. Id. at pp. 5–6.

[133] RDX (a British acronym for Research Department Explosive or Royal Demolition Explosive), cyclotrimethylene trinitramine, was developed by the British for military uses during World War II. RDX mixed with motor oil and filler/binder materials becomes a plastic puttylike material known in the U.S. military as Composition C-4. This consistency allows C-4 to be molded around an object and therefore becomes more effective for demolition than rigid explosives like TNT. Id. at p. 6.

[134] NFPA 921 §6.1.1.

likely be fairly simple. If that same fire escapes the waste can and grows to involve the entire building, the scope and complexity of the investigation would increase in parallel. Regardless of the size or complexity of an incident, a standardized approach is necessary to obtain consistent and reliable results.[135] The NFPA, fire/explosion investigation organizations and authoritative publications strongly recommend a systematic methodology incorporating the *scientific method*.[136] The scientific method has been described by a commentator as "an iterative process that requires the investigator to work through the steps of the method over and over again; hypothesizing, collecting information, analyzing, testing, reformulating and re-hypothesizing, until a satisfactory end point is reached."[137] The best outcome will be an understanding of pre-fire conditions supported by post-fire artifacts and evidence; however, in the majority of cases the outcome will not be absolute, but probabilistic[138] with conclusions ranging from *unknown*, *possible, probable*, to *a reasonable degree of scientific certainty,* or other terms indicating an investigator's level of confidence.[139]

§6.08   DETERMINING ORIGIN AND CAUSE

In any fire/explosion investigation, correctly identifying the point at which the fire or explosion originated is crucial. In most instances, the cause cannot be determined if an origin cannot be determined.[140] Until the correct origin is identified, a hypothesis about the ignition sequence—how the first-fuel ignited and the ignition source came together—can neither be formulated, tested, nor a cause determined. Consequently, a proper on-scene examination is critical and should include: an initial scene assessment; a safety assessment; interior and exterior examinations; scene reconstruction; fire or debris spread analysis; witness information; and post-scene follow-up.[141] A fire/explosion investigation begins not upon extinguishment, but at the time of discovery. Information about the fire conditions before the arrival of fire service responders may provide leads to the fire's origin, cause, and potentially responsibility. In addition to fighting the fire, suppression firefighters have a role in the fire investigation.[142] Firefighters are trained to recognize indicators of incendiarism: presence of incendiary devices or trailers; the presence of ignitable liquids or containers in the vicinity of the origin; lack of expected

---

[135] IAFC, *Fire Investigator 4th ed.* at p. 256.

[136] (a) Recognize the need; (b) Define the problem; (c) Collect data; (d) Develop a hypothesis; (e) Test the hypothesis; (f) repeat (c),(d),(e) to select validated final hypothesis. *See* IAFC, *Fire Investigator 4th ed.* at p. 257.

[137] Steven J. Avato, "Scientific Methodology Revisited," 64 Fire & Arson Investigator 1 (2013) at p. 39.

[138] Id.

[139] NFPA 921 §4.5 *et seq.*

[140] NFPA 921 §18.1.

[141] IAFC, *Fire Investigator 4th ed.* at p. 256.

[142] NFPA 921 §17.3.5 et seq.

contents; and multiple fires. Additionally, firefighters are responsible for preserving the fire scene and any physical evidence and should avoid causing damage to the fire scene beyond that needed to fully extinguish the fire. In particular, they should employ caution when using hose streams; while searching for fire extension; and when conducting *salvage* and *overhaul*[143] (both operations have the potential to substantially alter the fire scene before it can be examined and documented[144]). Firefighters should also limit access to prevent contamination of the scene.

After verifying legal access to the incident location, a thorough scene examination must be conducted to collect the data with which to effectuate the scientific method. It is crucial that the investigator conduct the investigation without any preconceptions, presumptions, or expectations; any of which could lead the investigator in to the traps of *expectation bias* (premature conclusions or determinations without considering all relevant data), or *confirmation bias* (a failure to test alternative hypotheses or discount hypotheses that contradict data).[145]

There are numerous sources for recommended procedures for conducting systematic, thorough, and comprehensive fire scene examinations, as well as for the overall investigation. Among the more authoritative are: NFPA 921® *Guide for Fire & Explosion Investigations*, 2014 Edition, Chapters 13–26; IAFC, IAAI & NFPA, *Fire Investigator: Principles and Practice to NFPA 921 and 1033*, 4th Edition, Chapters 4–24; DeHaan and Icove, *Kirk's Fire Investigation*, 7th Edition, Chapters 7–17; Lentini, *Scientific Protocols for Fire Investigation*, 2d Edition, Chapters 4, 6, 10. Also available from a variety of sources, including those mentioned above, are forms for documenting various aspects of an examination (field notes, building condition, photo log, evidence recovery/chain of custody, safety assessment, etc.). Computer programs are also used to analyze observational and measurement data with simulation software.[146]

Fire Investigator Principles and Practice to NFPA 921 and 1033, Fourth Edition recommends a systematic approach which includes these major considerations:

---

[143] Salvage: minimizing incidental damage from fire, water, falling debris, or weather during and after the fire, normally by covering or removing contents. Overhaul: locating hidden flames, glowing embers, hot ashes by pulling ceilings, breaching or removing walls, removing contents.

[144] Lentini, *Scientific Protocols 2d ed.* at p. 125.

[145] IAFC, *Fire Investigator 4th ed.* at p. 17.

[146] The Fire Dynamics Simulator (FDS) program was developed by the National Institute of Standards and Technology (NIST) in 2000 and is continuously updated. NIST has also produced a visualization program (Smokeview) to display the output of the FDS program. *See* https://www.nist.gov/services-resources/software/fds-and-smokeview (last accessed November 8, 2016). *See also* Jen-Hao Chi, "Reconstruction of an Inn Fire Scene Using the Fire Dynamics Simulator (FDS) Program," 58 J. Forensic Sci. S227–S234 (2013).

- Safety—including hazard and risk assessments, protective clothing, and respiratory protection.[147]

- Sources of Information—including witness interviews, governmental records, and private sources (e.g., insurance companies).[148]

- Planning—gathering basic information and requesting/coordinating additional resources, specialized personnel, and technical consultants.[149]

- Documentation—use of photography, diagrams/drawings, note-taking, and reports.[150]

- Physical evidence—identifying, preserving, collecting, documenting, transporting, storing, avoiding contamination/spoliation, examination, and testing.[151]

- Origin Determination—using the scientific method while examining and interpreting fire patterns to identify in three dimensions where the fire originated.[152]

- Fire Cause Determination—identifying the circumstances, conditions, or agents that brought the fuel, ignition source, and oxidizer together and the conditions under which the fire was able to start and propagate.[153]

- Classification of Fire Cause—accidental, natural, incendiary, or undetermined.[154]

- Analyzing the Incident for Cause and Responsibility—determining if a person or other entity bears responsibility for the event or sequence of events that caused the fire or explosion by failure analysis and other analytical tools: timelines, system analysis, fault trees, failure mode and effects analysis, mathematical/engineering modeling, fire dynamics analysis.[155]

1. ORIGIN DETERMINATION

The fire patterns that are observed by an investigator represent much of the history of the fire and the investigator must interpret that history to travel back through the development of the fire to its

---

[147] Id. at Chapter 11.
[148] Id. at Chapter 12.
[149] Id. at Chapter 13.
[150] Id. at Chapter 14.
[151] Id. at Chapter 15.
[152] Id. at Chapter 16,
[153] Id. at Chapter 17.
[154] Id. at Chapter 18.
[155] Id. at Chapters 19–20.

origin.[156] Fire patterns have been described in older case law as the "linchpin of all fire investigation" to alert the investigator to the point or area of origin.[157] Fire patterns are subject to misinterpretation, especially in extensively-damaged or complex fire scenes; if the compartment fire has transitioned to "full-involvement"; or if the numerous factors affecting fire effect creation, fire pattern formation, and pattern persistence are poorly understood or not fully considered.[158] With the uncertainty inherent in the interpretation of fire effects, it can be challenging for the fire investigator to determine fire travel, intensity, and duration to locate the area of origin.[159] As the IAFC has correctly noted: "Every fire is different and produces unique fire patterns that must be interpreted. . .The investigator should analyze individual fire patterns within the context of the complexity of all the patterns. . .not rely on solely or too heavily on only one fire pattern. . .[a] pattern analyzed in isolation can lead to an incorrect conclusion."[160]

The following fire effects are likely to be observed at a fire/ explosion scene; the interpretation of which is crucial to identifying the correct fire origin:[161]

- loss of material mass

- charring (carbonaceous material that remains after pyrolysis)

- spalling (cracking, breaking, chipping or cratering of concrete, masonry, rock or brick)

- oxidation (changes in color or texture on metals, rocks or soil)

- color changes (generic, non-oxidation caused)

- melting of materials (an indicator of minimum fire temperature based on known melting points of common materials as aluminum, copper, thermo plastics)

---

[156] An overview of the dynamics of fire effects and fire pattern production is presented in NFPA 921 §§ 6.2—6.3, covering the basic principles of the way the three modes of heat transfer (conduction, convection, and radiation) produce the fire patterns and the nature of the flame, heat, and smoke movement within a structure. *See also* John J. Lentini, "Fire: Dynamics and Pattern Production," in Wiley Encyclopedia Of Forensic Science, (Jamieson A. & Moenssens A.A., eds) 2009 & online updates.

[157] Sandburg-Schiller v. Rosello, 119 Ill.App.3d 318, 74 Ill.Dec. 690, 456 N.E.2d 192 (1983).

[158] Gorbett, *Fire Patterns* at p. 19 ("Some fire investigators often regard the initial plume effects as being destroyed or obscured after. . .full-room involvement. . ."). *See also* Chad D. Camanell and Steven J. Avato, "Fire Origin Pattern Persistence," 67 Fire & Arson Investigator 2 (2016) at pp. 12–21.

[159] Gorbett, *Fire Patterns* at p. 18.

[160] IAFC, *Fire Investigator 4th ed.* at p. 48.

[161] NFPA 921 §§6.2–6.2.17.9; *see also* IAFC, *Fire Investigator 4th ed.* at pp. 42–48.

- thermal expansion and deformation of materials (for example, steel beams and columns begin deforming at 900°F (500°C)

- deposition of smoke on surfaces (deposits of particulates and aerosols in smoke may indicate direction of spread)

- clean burn (a distinct and visible effect on non-combustible surfaces after combustible layers (soot, paint, paper) have burned away)

- calcination (a predictable response by gypsum wall board to heat exposure wherein water has been driven off, leaving behind a physically-distinct, less-dense material)

- window glass (intact, smoke stained, broken, crazed)

- heat shadowing (caused when an object blocks the travel of radiated or convected heat or direct flame to a surface)

- protected area (when an object is in physical contact with another material so as to shield that material from the effects of heat, combustion or deposition)

- victim injuries (bodies exhibit material responses to heat and fire and can provide indications of position, orientation to heat sources).

Fire patterns will be formed from these fire effects depending on how the fire's dynamics influenced the space(s) in which the fire event occurred. Fire pattern formation is affected primarily by: ignition factors; heat release rates; heat flux; total energy impacts; fuel loads; location and orientation of fuel items; configuration of the compartment(s); ventilation openings; airflow; barriers to fire spread; and enhancements to heat and smoke travel.[162]

Fire patterns can be generated by several types of dynamic fire conditions, including:

- plume-generated—interaction between the plume above the fire and surfaces in the compartment.[163]

- ventilation-generated—ventilation through windows, doors, or other openings greatly increases air flow over combustible materials, enhancing fire effect creation.[164]

- hot gas layer-generated—the radiant heat flux from the hot gas layer descending from the ceiling can create damage to the upper surfaces of contents and floor coverings.[165]

---

[162] NFPA 921 §§6.3.1, 6.3.1.1, 6.3.2.1.

[163] Id.

[164] NFPA 921 §6.3.2.2.

[165] NFPA 921 §6.3.2.3.

- full room involvement (flashover) generated—increased damage to all surfaces and contents from the hot gas layer radiant heat flux and additional fuel items ignited by flashover.[166]

- suppression-generated—water and other extinguishing agents can alter or destroy patterns, affect fire spread, and create damage beyond that associated with fire behavior; ventilation tactics can also alter or damage patterns.[167]

Common fire patterns of investigative utility include:

a. "V" Pattern, Cone (∧), Hourglass, "U" Shaped[168]

These are "plume generated" patterns; plumes are formed by the entrainment of air into the hot gas column above the burning fuel item. The location and configuration of a fuel item when first ignited influences plume formation, which in turn affects pattern formation: a circular pattern on the ceiling above the fire, a cone pattern (∧) above a very early fire at the base of the wall, or a "V" pattern above the same fire after growth (development of such a fire may also result in an "hour-glass" shape with the V expanding from the tip of the original cone (∧) pattern instead of subsuming the cone and spreading from the base of the fire).[169]

The fire investigator will attempt to locate the first plume pattern generated by the fire.[170] The angle of the borders of the V pattern are not directly correlated to the speed of fire growth or rate of heat release; that is, a wide V does not indicate a slow fire and a narrow V does not indicate a fast fire.[171] The apex of a "V" pattern is sometimes erroneously assumed to be the point of origin of a fire. A "V" pattern is the result of any fuel item burning at or near a vertical surface. "V" patterns can also be caused by *drop down* (fallen burning materials), a leaking fuel gas orifice or by the presence of a secondary fuel item ignited by the spreading fire; for example, window curtains ignited by radiation from the hot gas layer fall to the base of the wall below a window.[172] A cone pattern (∧) is frequently caused by ignitable liquids burning on the floor,[173] but is equally likely an indication of a fire of short duration or low HRR.[174]

---

[166] NFPA 921 §6.3.2.4.

[167] NFPA 921 §6.3.2.5.

[168] NFPA 921 §6.3.7.1.1.

[169] NFPA 921 §6.3.2.1.

[170] Lentini, *Scientific Protocols 2d ed.* at p. 84.

[171] NFPA 921 §6.3.7.1.2.

[172] Lentini, *Scientific Protocols 2d ed.* at pp. 85–86.

[173] Lentini, *Scientific Protocols 2d ed.* at p. 83, Figure 3.12.

[174] NFPA 921 §§6.3.7.2.1–6.3.7.2.2.

b. Depth of Char

Conclusions drawn solely from the depth and appearance of char are highly suspect. "Alligatoring" (large, shiny blisters of char) was formerly considered to have significance in determining how quickly the fire spread and to indicate the presence of a liquid accelerant. These concepts have been discredited.[175] Depth of char can be a useful tool in evaluating fire spread when properly surveyed. Systematically measuring the relative depth of charring at points on surfaces of similar composition and orientation is useful in determining which portions of that material were exposed longer to a heat source. This may aid the investigator in deducing the direction of fire spread.[176]

c. Calcination of Gypsum Wallboard

A similar depth-measuring technique may be applied to gypsum wall board. Gypsum wallboard reacts to the heat of a fire in a predictable manner; potentially creating lines of demarcation as the covering burns away and as the water content is driven off, causing "calcination"—a change in the color and composition of the gypsum. Systematically measuring the depth of calcination in exposed sheets of gypsum wallboard can indicate the direction of fire spread.[177] As with depth of char, such depth-of-calcination surveys will not correlate to the time of burning.[178]

d. Irregularly Shaped Floor Fire Patterns

It is important to differentiate between fire patterns created by a burning pool of an ignitable liquid and those caused by fire dynamics. A liquid at its flame point temperature is boiling off vapors sufficient to maintain flaming combustion and generating heat which radiates back to the liquid pool. This radiant heat is partly absorbed by the remaining pool of liquid and in part by the adjoining floor surface at the edge of the pool. By absorbing the heat, the remaining liquid protects the surface below it from combustion since the temperature of the liquid cannot exceed its boiling temperature.[179] The pool's edges, however, are not protected, potentially resulting in scorching or other fire effects outlining the protected area. Whether a discernible pattern is generated depends on the composition of the substrate material (carpet, hardwood, tile, linoleum), the depth of the liquid pool and the properties of the ignitable liquid.[180] A shallow pool of a low-boiling point liquid like

---

[175] See NFPA 921 §6.2.4.3; see also IAFC, *Fire Investigator 4th ed.* at p. 43.

[176] See NFPA 921 §§6.2.4.5.

[177] See Gregory E. Gorbett et al., "A New Method for the Characterization of the Degree of Fire Damage in Gypsum Wallboard for Use in Fire Investigations," 60 J. Forensic Sci. S193–S196 (2015).

[178] IAFC, *Fire Investigator 4th ed.* at p. 46.

[179] DeHaan and Icove, *Kirk's Fire Investigation 7th ed.* at pp. 109–111.

[180] Id.

methyl alcohol (150°F, 65°C) will leave few effects on plywood. A deeper pool of a heavy petroleum fuel, such as diesel fuel, can reach boiling temperatures (650°F, 340°C) sufficient to scorch some flooring and, because the edges burn for longer periods, may create *halo, donut, pool-shaped, or irregularly shaped patterns.*[181]

Such outlines, when observed after a fire has been controlled, were formerly referred to as "pour patterns," and were said to be characteristic signatures of an accelerant induced fire.[182] NFPA 921 §6.3.7.8.5 concludes that the term "pour pattern" implies an intentional act and its use should be avoided. Modern fire investigators use the term "irregularly shaped fire pattern" which may, but does not necessarily, indicate the burning of an ignitable liquid. In addition to the fire effects produced by burning ignitable liquids, such "pour patterns" can be produced by the differential burn rates of glue used in the installation of wall-to-wall carpets, full-room involvement, ventilation flow-paths, hot gases, melted plastic, and building collapse[183]. Proper investigation requires sampling of the suspect pattern(s) with the presence (or absence) of ignitable liquids being determined by laboratory analysis.[184]

e. Spalling

Spalling is the chipping, flaking, pitting, or similar erosion of the surface of cement or masonry. In the past, fire investigators routinely asserted that spalling reflected the use of accelerants and that it only occurred because the moisture within the concrete reacted violently to the intense heat produced by the ignition of accelerants at the site of the spall; however, neither assertion is true.[185] Spalling may also occur in areas of mechanical stress, in areas with a significant fuel load of ordinary combustibles (common accelerants burn at roughly the same temperatures as ordinary combustibles) or it may be present before the fire.[186] Additionally, the use of accelerants does not always produce spalling.[187] Most experts would concede that spalling is caused by heat, and therefore, spalling in some type of pattern may be significant. A

---

[181] DeHaan and Icove, *Kirk's Fire Investigation 7th ed.* at pp. 300–302.

[182] *See* John J. Lentini, "Arson Investigation: Misconceptions and Mythology," in Wiley Encyclopedia Of Forensic Science, (Jamieson A. & Moenssens A.A., eds) 2009 & online updates, at pp. 7–8.

[183] IAFC, *Fire Investigator 4th ed.* at p. 50; *see also* NFPA 921 §6.3.7.8.2 *et seq.*

[184] NFPA §6.3.7.8.5. *See* Dana L. Greely, *Sampling Ignitable Liquid Pour Patterns on Carpet*; 64 Fire & Arson Investigator 3, April, 2014; pp. 14–22. Research conducted by Dana L. Greely of the Hamilton County, Ohio Coroner's Laboratory, compared sampling results of kerosene and gasoline pours in circular and linear patterns on carpet over padding squares. Greely reported that in most cases, samples nearer the center of a circular pour returned better results. *See also* IAFC, *Fire Investigator 4th ed.* at p. 246, which recommends sampling the lowest or most insulated parts of the pattern; *see also* NFPA 921 §17.5.4.4.

[185] David J. Icove and John D. DeHaan, *Forensic Fire Scene Reconstruction*, 2d ed., Pearson Education, Inc., 2009 at pp. 131–136.

[186] DeHaan and Icove, *Kirk's Fire Investigation 7th ed.* at pp. 283–284.

[187] IAFC, *Fire Investigator 4th ed.* at p. 46.

trail of spalling on concrete may be just as informative as a trail of burning on carpet or wood. It is the pattern which is important, not the mere existence of spalled concrete.

f. Line of Demarcation

Lines or areas of demarcation are created when flames, heat, or smoke impinge on an object or a surface, producing a border between the more affected and less affected areas.[188] For instance, in a fire where a hot gas layer has formed, but the fire is extinguished before flashover, a border will form on the walls at the lowest edge of the hot gas layer, separating the area affected by the hot gases from that not yet affected. Similarly, a fire moving along a hallway may form a line of demarcation rising from the end where the fire entered the hallway, and burned longer or with greater intensity, towards the as yet unaffected end.[189]

g. Beveling

Beveling is an indicator of fire direction on wood wall studs. Loss of mass is greater closer to the fire. Consequently, the bevel, or sloped portion, will face the fire, as will the slope of the remaining portions of a linear series of wall studs.[190] A similar pattern is encountered with penetrations of a horizontal surface and the direction faced by the beveled edge indicates whether fire burned up or down through the surface.[191]

2. CAUSE DETERMINATION

After the point or area of origin has been sufficiently identified, determination of the cause of the fire can proceed. Cause determination requires identifying the factors necessary for the fire to have occurred, including: the presence of a competent ignition source; the type and form of the first fuel ignited; the oxidizer (usually air); and the ignition sequence. The ignition sequence includes the circumstances, conditions, or agents (such as device failures or human actions) that brought the ignition source and fuel together to allow the fire to occur.[192]

The ignition source will be at or near the point of origin or within the area of origin. The ignition source may or may not be recognizable as such; it may have been altered, destroyed, consumed, moved, or removed.[193] Or, as in the case of an appliance failure, identification of a specific component as the ignition source may require off-scene examination, testing, and analysis involving several interested parties.

---

[188] Id. at p. 50.

[189] DeHaan and Icove, *Kirk's Fire Investigation 7th ed.* at p. 267.

[190] IAFC, *Fire Investigator 4th ed.* at pp. 51–52.

[191] Id.

[192] NFPA 921 §19.1.

[193] Id. at §19.1.3.

In such circumstances, a public sector investigator may have neither the resources or need to identify the exact failure; only that the appliance was a competent ignition source (e.g. capable of and generating heat at time of ignition; able to transmit enough heat to the first fuel for that fuel to reach ignition temperature; and that fuel was heated long enough to have reached ignition temperature).[194] A private sector investigator, however, may need to identify which component(s) failed, and by what failure mode, in order to determine responsibility (among manufacturer, sub-contractors, repair personnel, retailer, etc.) for the damages caused by the failure and subsequent fire.[195]

The first fuel ignited must be able to be ignited by the ignition source and be able to sustain combustion beyond that ignition source. Even if the fuel has an ignition temperature within the range produced by the ignition source, the fuel's configuration may not permit the fuel to absorb enough heat to ignite (thermal inertia).[196] Surface area-to-mass ratio matters. A block of wood and a pile of shavings from the same block of wood ignite at the same temperature. But, the shavings have a much greater surface area to mass ratio than the solid block of wood and reach ignition temperature faster. In all instances, the ignition source must generate sufficient heat long enough for the fuel to reach ignition temperature.[197]

Identifying a competent ignition source, an ignitable fuel, and an oxidizer is insufficient to establish the cause of a fire. Some event or series of events must have occurred to bring these three legs of the fire triangle together to allow the fire to start and continue. The ignition sequence explains what this event(s) or circumstance was and helps determine the cause of the fire.[198]

Using the scientific method, the investigator must collect and analyze data regarding each of the elements of the fire cause—competent ignition source, first fuel ignited, and ignition sequence—developing and testing hypotheses about each element, collecting more data as required, developing and testing new hypotheses until a validated hypothesis identifying the ignition source, first fuel, and ignition sequence is reached.[199]

A problematic cause determination technique is the concept of "negative corpus" wherein an investigator eliminates all accidental or natural causes and concludes, without any independent evidence, that the fire could only have been incendiary. Although the *process of elimination* is essential to the analysis of the fire's cause, concluding that the last remaining hypothesis must be valid because all other

---

[194] IAFC, *Fire Investigator 4th ed.* at pp. 270–271.

[195] Id.

[196] Id.

[197] Id.

[198] Id. *see also* NFPA 921 §19.1.5, §§19.4.4.1–19.4.4.2.1.

[199] NFPA 921 §§19.5–19.6.4.

hypotheses were eliminated, without any positive evidence to support the conclusion, does not comport with the scientific method.[200] A valid hypothesis must be supported by and consistent with the facts derived from observations, physical and other evidence, science, calculations and experiments.[201] Consequently, an identification of an ignition source solely through the elimination of all other ignition sources known or believed to be in the area of origin, without some articulated factual support, should be viewed with skepticism.[202]

The 2011 Edition of NFPA 921 included a section (§18.6.5) "Inappropriate Use of the Process of Elimination" discussing *negative corpus* and concluding that *negative corpus* analysis was inappropriate and should not be used because "any hypothesis formulated for the causal factors (e.g., first fuel, ignition source, and ignition sequence) must be based on facts. . .[s]peculative information cannot be included in the analysis."[203] The 2014 Edition of NFPA 921 omits both §18.6.5 and any discussion of negative corpus, but does permit the use of evidence-based logical inferences in circumstances when no physical evidence of an ignition source is found at or near the fire's origin.[204]

3. CLASSIFICATION OF FIRE CAUSE

Classification of the cause of the fire or explosion may differ depending on the jurisdiction. NFPA 921 uses only the classifications: *accidental, natural, incendiary, or undetermined.*[205] *Determination* of cause and *classification* of cause are distinct. *Determination* of cause identifies the circumstances that brought the fuel, ignition source, and oxidizer together and the sequence of events under which the fire was able to start and propagate.[206] *Classification* of cause is used for assigning responsibility, reporting purposes, or compilation of statistics.[207]

Classifying a fire as *"suspicious"* is not appropriate since the term "suspicion" refers to a level of proof or certainty and not to the cause of an act.[208] Suspicion about the cause, or responsibility for the cause, is not an acceptable level of proof for making a determination of cause; fires for which the level of certainty is either *possible* or *suspected* should be classified as *undetermined.*[209]

---

[200] IAFC, *Fire Investigator 4th ed.* at p. 273.

[201] Id.

[202] Thomas Ost-Prisco, *"Negative Corpus,"* 64 Fire&Arson Investigator 3 (2014) at p. 35.

[203] Id. at p. 34.

[204] NFPA 921 2014 Edition at p. 198; and §19.4.4.3.

[205] NFPA 921 §§20.1–20.1.4.

[206] IAFC, *Fire Investigator 4th ed.* at p. 278.

[207] NFPA 921 §20.1.

[208] NFPA 921 §4.5.1 Two levels of certainty: Probable—more likely than not; Possible—feasible but not demonstrably probable.

[209] NFPA 921 §4.5.2 "If the level of certainty of an opinion is merely "suspected," the opinion does not qualify as an expert opinion. If the level of certainty is only "possible," the

NFPA 921 §§ 20.1–20.1.4 defines acceptable fire classifications as follows:

- Accidental—fires for which the proven cause does not involve an intentional human act to ignite or spread fire into an area where the fire should not be, some deliberately ignited fires can still be accidental—as when a trash fire is spread by a sudden gust of wind.

- Natural—fires caused without direct human intervention or action, such as fires resulting from lightning, earthquake, wind, or flood.

- Incendiary—a fire that is deliberately set with the intent to cause a fire to occur in an area where the fire should not be.

- Undetermined—whenever the cause of a fire cannot be proven to an acceptable level of certainty, the proper classification is undetermined as follows: a) fires that have not yet been investigated, or are under investigation, or have been investigated and have insufficient information to classify further (new information may change the classification; b) failure to identify all elements of a fire cause may not necessitate the undetermined classification, for example, confirming the presence of an accelerant without finding the ignition source may be sufficient for an incendiary classification.[210]

4.   INCENDIARY FIRE INDICATORS

Some fire scene investigators have in the past relied heavily upon a number of fire effects and patterns (so-called accelerant or arson indicators) as circumstantial proof of the incendiary cause of a fire. In the wake of scientific research conducted over the last three decades, very few of these indicators are considered to still have merit.[211] Black smoke was said to result from the burning of an ignitable liquid accelerant, while a blinding white flame was said to be the intense flame of a fire fueled by a "high-temperature accelerant." However, many commonly used items contain hydrocarbons (e.g., plastics, furniture foam, rubber wheels) which emit black smoke when burning. Similarly, the color of a flame is no longer considered an accurate indicator "of what is burning, or the temperature of the flame."[212] Other

---

opinion should be specifically expressed as "possible." Only when the level of certainty is considered "probably," should an opinion be expressed with reasonable certainty."

[210] NFPA 921 §§20.1.1–20.1.4.

[211] *See generally* John J. Lentini, "Arson Investigation: Misconceptions and Mythology," in Wiley Encyclopedia Of Forensic Science, (Jamieson A. & Moenssens A.A., eds) 2009 & online updates. See also Lentini, Scientific Principles, *supra*, Chapter 8 The Mythology of Arson Investigation.

[212] NFPA 921 §5.6.4.1.

indicators observable in the fire debris, such as "alligatoring" or "alligator char," deep charring, crazed glass, "pour patterns" (puddle-shaped patterns on floor coverings), sagged furniture springs and spalling, were erroneously believed to always indicate the use of an accelerant.[213]

Discussed below are several currently-accepted incendiary fire indicators which may provide physical evidence of an incendiary fire cause. Ascertainment of one or more of these incendiary indicators necessitates further investigation, such as sampling for ignitable liquids, before any conclusions regarding an incendiary cause can validated.

a. Multiple Fires

Multiple fires burning simultaneously in different locations on the same premises were once said to be a classic illustration of an incendiary fire. The assumption underlying such a position was that the multiple fires were either separately ignited or were spread to other sites using trailers. In either event, the assumption was that an incendiary act was indicated by multiple fires.

However, multiple or simultaneous fires (or multiple apparent points of origin) can occur from normal fire dynamics spreading fire by: conduction, convection, radiation; flying brands/embers; direct flame impingement; falling flaming materials (drop-down); through shafts, pipe chases, duct work; or through wall, floor, attic spaces.[214] Multiple fires may also be caused by overloaded electrical wiring, utility system failures, lightning, and by the explosion and launching of aerosol cans.[215] Multiple fire areas may also be caused by sustained burning or smoldering during or after suppression or overhaul.[216] The possibility of previous fires at the same premises should be also considered. A full scene examination, including a fire history of the premises, scene reconstruction, fire spread analysis, and a search of undamaged areas for additional, unignited fire *sets*, should be conducted before an investigator can hypothesize that apparent multiple fires were caused by an intentional act.[217]

b. Trailers

Trailers are used to deliberately spread fire from one area to another by linking them together with trails of ignitable liquid or combustible fuels. Thus, one fire will ignite others via the trailers.[218]

---

[213] Lentini, *Scientific Protocols 2d ed.* at pp. 473–474. *See also* discussion regarding expectation bias and confirmation bias in IAFC, *Fire Investigator 4th ed.* at p. 17.

[214] NFPA 921 §24.2.1.2.

[215] Id.

[216] IAFC, *Fire Investigator 4th ed.* at p. 322.

[217] Id.

[218] Id.

Materials used for trailers include: ignitable liquids, paper, straw, and clothing. Typically, trailers leave a discernible pattern along horizontal surfaces, but they may be hidden under fire debris.[219] "Trailer" patterns may be caused by other mechanisms, such as radiant heat flux during flashover, and care must be taken to account for these other factors. Similarly, many common household items are either ignitable liquids (e.g., cleaning fluids) or combustible (e.g., paper, clothing), and their presence at the scene may not be indicative of their use in a trailer. The presence of fuel does not indicate a trailer, but the manner and location in which the fuel was used determines whether a trailer is indicated.[220]

c.   Presence of an Incendiary Device

Incendiary devices consist of a wide range of mechanisms capable of initiating a fire. In many instances, careful examination of the area of origin, especially when no obvious source of ignition can be identified, will locate the remains of an ignition device, along with the fuel used[221] (for example, a fire bomb consisting of an ignitable liquid in a breakable container with a wick). As with trailers, incendiary devices may consist of common materials (e.g., books of matches, cigarettes, candles, altered heating appliances, flammable cleaning fluids) whose presence at the scene may not be unusual, but whose being found in the area of origin justifies further investigation.[222] Fire-setters will use delay devices to allow them to leave the area safely. Common delay devices include candles, cigarettes, and mechanical or electrical timers.[223]

d.   Presence of Ignitable Liquids in Area of Origin

The presence of ignitable liquids, or containers/remains thereof, at or near the area of origin should be fully investigated and samples taken for laboratory analysis.

e.   Other Possible Indicators[224]

A few indicators of a possible incendiary cause need little explanation from an expert for the jury to comprehend their meaning. The removal of a householder's personal effects from the scene of a fire shortly before the fire, although ambiguous, can be read as a sign of an incendiary intent on the part of the homeowner.[225] That a refrigerator in an occupied house which has been burned is found to be empty may be, if not satisfactorily explained, possible evidence of arson.[226] Some

---

[219] Id.

[220] Id at p. 323.

[221] NFPA 921 §24.2.7.

[222] IAFC, *Fire Investigator 4th ed.* at p. 324.

[223] NFPA 921 §24.2.7.2.

[224] IAFC, *Fire Investigator 4th ed.* at p. 323.

[225] People v. Freeman, 135 Cal. App.2d 11, 286 P.2d 565 (1955).

[226] Waters v. State, 174 Ga. App. 916, 331 S.E.2d 893 (1985).

signs such as the stacking of furniture, or finding containers of ignitable liquids in areas where they would not normally be, while not necessarily conclusive, provide some basis for a possible incendiary fire.

Other discoveries by a fire investigator may require the testimony of an expert to enlighten the jury as to their significance if the charge is arson, such as lack of expected fuel load (*e.g.,* too much damage, too little stuff), lack of expected ignition sources, and unusual fuel load or configuration (e.g., stacked furniture). Also in this category are freshly drilled holes in the floors and roof of a burned building which represent evidence of an effort to rapidly spread the fire by providing a ready upward route of travel for the fire.[227] Other potential indicators not directly related to combustion that may be circumstantial indicators of an incendiary fire include: damaging or disabling fire protection systems: obstruction of entries or exits; delaying discovery by covering windows/doors; removal/replacement of contents before the fire; absence of personal items prior to the fire; inappropriate opening of doors/windows; financial stress of owner/occupant; fires at other properties; and over-insurance.[228]

§6.09   Electrical Fire Investigations

A fire may be ignited by electrical means when sufficient electrical energy exists to cause sustained ignition in a particular environment.[229] For example, small areas of overheated wire or small arcs and sparks are of little consequence in the ignition of a solid material with a high ignition temperature, whereas the smallest discernible spark is a serious hazard in a case of a combustible gas or vapor. Ignition by electrical energy may be caused by: resistance heating; excessive current flow (over-current); parting arcs; over-lamping of light fixtures; lamps, heaters or cooking equipment in too close proximity to combustibles; and lack of heat dissipation from energized conductors or equipment.[230]

Resistance heating is encountered whenever electrical current flows through something with high resistance. This resistance may be intentional, as with hair dryers or portable electric heaters, or unintentional, as with a poor or corroded connection at a wall outlet.[231] Even at normal current flows, a poor connection will allow formation of an oxide interface at the point of connection, increasing resistance and

---

[227] Rogers v. State, 161 Tex. Crim. R. 536, 279 S.W.2d 97 (1955).

[228] *See* NFPA 921 §§24.3.1–24.4.7.

[229] "For ignition to be from an electrical source, the following must occur:

(1) The electrical wiring, equipment, or component must have been energized from a building's wiring, an emergency system, a battery, or some other source.

(2) Sufficient heat and temperature to ignite a close combustible material must have been produced by electrical energy at the point of origin by the electrical source."

NFPA 921 §9.9.1.

[230] IAFC, *Fire Investigator 4th ed.* at p. 127.

[231] Id. at p. 128.

producing more heat to create a "hot spot." The hot spot may reach temperatures exceeding 1000°F, enough to ignite nearby combustibles.[232]

The current a conductor should carry is limited so that manageable amounts of heat are generated. When these current flows are persistently exceeded and a conductor is overloaded, the generation of heat becomes a hazard. Over time the temperature of the conductor will rise, the rate of temperature increase depending on the degree of over-current and its duration. Eventually, the heat given off by the conductor will either cause the insulation to fail allowing energized conductors to short and produce arcing or sparking; or heat surrounding materials, potentially to their ignition temperature.[233]

An arc is a high-temperature (potentially several thousand degree) discharge across a gap where the conductor is missing. Arcs are usually a very brief phenomena and are an unlikely ignition source except in the presence of very high surface to mass ratio solids (dust, tissue paper) or ignitable gases. A parting arc is a brief discharge created when the electrical path is opened while energized (light switches may produce parting arcs when the light is turned off, as will pulling an appliance plug from a wall outlet while the appliance is energized).[234]

Utilizing a light bulb of wattage beyond the design limit of a light fixture is known as "over-lamping." Over-lamping may cause ignition for the same reasons that over-current is dangerous—excess current flow creates more heat than can safely be managed and may result in conductor failure or ignition of adjacent combustibles.[235] Heat produced by incandescent or halogen bulbs (even of the correct wattage) is able to ignite combustibles placed on, about, or too closely to the bulb.[236] Placing portable heaters closer than recommended to combustibles or placing combustibles too close to cooking equipment or to fixed, heat-producing appliances (clothes dryers, water heaters, electric stoves/ovens) may also create conditions susceptible to ignition.[237]

When electrical failure is detected at the scene of a fire, it is exceedingly difficult to determine whether it was the cause or result of the fire. When an investigator locates the point of origin of a fire as being adjacent to a heating appliance in an area containing several electrical circuits, it does not necessarily mean that either the appliance or electrical wiring was the source of ignition. Nor can it be assumed that evidence of a short circuit near the fire's point of origin indicates that the short circuit is the cause of the fire. Tracking the location of short circuits in a fire scene can, however, aid in the determination of

---

[232] Id.

[233] Id.

[234] Id. at p. 129.

[235] Id. at p. 127.

[236] Id. at p. 128.

[237] Id. at p. 127.

the point of origin, since once an arc occurs in a circuit, additional downstream arcing is unlikely.[238] Arc mapping or arc surveys are an important part of a fire investigation and require examination of the electrical circuits to locate arcing within the circuit.[239] Electrical conductors should be examined for damage.[240] Evidence of arcing, melting, and severed connections should be documented and evaluated in context with other information, including: location in the room, identification of the branch circuit to which the damaged conductor is connected, and the state of the over-current protection for that branch circuit.[241]

As with the other assumptions previously applied in fire investigation, assumptions regarding indicators of electrical fires have also been discredited through research. For example, the presence of a bead on the end of an electrical conductor was previously thought to indicate exposure to fire while the electrical conductor was energized, supporting a conclusion that the device was a potential source of the fire. Recent research has demonstrated the presence of such beads upon flame exposure only—without the accompanying electrical current.[242] Therefore, the presence of a bead on a wire does not mean that the device was electrically energized at the time of the fire.

§6.10 EXPLOSIONS

Evidence collection procedures for explosive events have the same objectives as a fire scene investigation: determine the origin, establish the fuel and ignition sources, identify the cause, and collect evidence to help determine the responsibility for the event.[243] The initial scene investigation tasks are:[244]

1. Identify whether the incident was an explosion or fire.

2. Determine high- or low-order damage.

3. Identify seated or non-seated explosion.[245]

4. Identify the type of explosion.

5. Identify the potential general fuel type.

---

[238] *See* the discussion of the elucidation of tracking the progress of a fire in a circuit or an appliance through the arcs in John J. Lentini, "Appliance Fires: Determining Responsibilities," 39 Fire & Arson Inv. 52 (June 1989).

[239] NFPA 921 §9.11.7.1. *See generally* IAFC, *Fire Investigator 4th ed.* at p. 129–135.

[240] See NFPA 921 §9.11.1. For examples of this damage and whether such damage could be the cause of a fire, *see* IAFC, *Fire Investigator 4th ed.* at p. 131.

[241] NFPA 921 §§9.11.7.4–9.11.7.5. *See generally* IAFC, *Fire Investigator 4th ed.* at pp. 134–135.

[242] *See* Richard J. Roby and Jamie McAllister, "Forensic Investigation Techniques for Inspecting Electrical Conductors Involved in Fire," July 2012 (available at: https://www.ncjrs.gov/pdffiles1/nij/grants/239052.pdf).

[243] IAFC, *Fire Investigator 4th ed.* at p. 313.

[244] Id.at p. 314.

[245] A seated explosion is characterized by a crater or concentrated area of damage that is roughly circular or spherical. NFPA 921 §23.6.1.

6.   Establish the origin.[246]

7.   Establish the fuel source and explosive type.

8.   Establish the ignition source.[247]

Following the initial assessment, additional steps should be taken to thoroughly document the scene, including damage patterns; collect post-blast debris and possible bomb components[248] for further laboratory analysis; and, evaluate every possible fuel source and ignition source.[249] The physical search for evidence involves (1) swabbing for explosive residues; and (2) the organized search for evidentiary materials through visual searching, sifting, and vacuuming.[250]

Explosions fueled by many explosives, especially high explosives which have high velocity positive pressure phases at detonation, are often easily identified by craters or highly localized areas of great damage.[251] The most commonly encountered explosions are those involving gases or vapors, especially fuel gases or the vapors of ignitable liquids.[252] The explosion damage to structures (low-order and high-order) depends on a number of factors, including "the fuel-to-air ratio, vapor density of the fuel, turbulence effects, volume of the confining space, location and magnitude of the ignition source, venting, and the characteristic strength of the structure."[253] The damage patterns vary widely because of the possibility of secondary explosions and fires.

---

[246] The origin may not be the area with the most damage. NFPA 921 §23.14.3.7.

[247] IAFC, *Fire Investigator 4th ed.* at p. 315; NFPA 921 §23.14.3.8.

[248] Examples of commonly found evidence (in whole or in pieces) include circuitry, bomb power sources, timers, switches, detonators, explosive charge wrapper fragments, and bomb-making equipment. *See* Alexander Beveridge, *Forensic Investigations of Explosions*, 2d ed., CRC Press, 2012 at p. 115.

[249] Protocols must be developed to minimize the opportunity for cross-contamination of evidence samples, a problem repeatedly observed with explosive residue testing. See Filipa Belchior and Stephen P. Andrews, "Evaluation of Cross-contamination of Nylon Bags with Heavy-loaded Gasoline Fire Debris and with Automotive Paint Thinner," J. Forensic Sci. 2016 (available online at: onlinelibrary.wiley.com), USDOJ/OIG Special Report, "The FBI Laboratory One Year Later: A Follow-Up to the Inspector General's April 1997 Report on FBI Laboratory Practices and Alleged Misconduct in Explosives-Related and Other Cases," June 1998 (available at: https://oig.justice.gov/special/9806.htm)(last accessed November 8, 2016).

[250] *See generally* James T. Thurman, "Explosions: Scene Investigation," in Wiley Encyclopedia Of Forensic Science, (Jamieson A. & Moenssens A.A., eds) 2009 & online updates. *See also* James T. Thurman *Practical Bomb Scene Investigation*, 2nd ed., CRC Press, 2011.

[251] NFPA 921 §23.6.2.

[252] NFPA 921 §23.8.

[253] NFPA 921 §23.8.2.

IV. ANALYTICAL METHODS AND INSTRUMENTATION

Laboratory analysis of fire and explosive debris generally involves the detection of residues from accelerants or explosive materials.[254] The analytical methods involve isolating the residue, analyzing the residue molecular components, and identifying the residue through comparison to reference standards.[255] Additionally, the hands of individuals may be swabbed for the detection of residues associated with accelerants or explosive materials.[256] Metallographic analysis through microscopic examination of electrical circuitry may also be conducted.[257] This section will address the most commonly performed analyses of fire and explosive residue detection.

Contamination of evidence with traces of fire or explosive residues is a serious concern in any investigation and careful attention should be paid to protocols and procedures for minimizing possible contamination. Contamination can occur through a variety of means, including cross-scene examination,[258] evidence collection and packaging procedures,[259] and sample handling and storage.[260]

---

[254] See Karlijn D.B. Bezemer et al., "The Potential of Isotope Ratio Mass Spectrometry (IRMS) and Gas Chromatography-IRMS Analysis of Triacetone Trieroxide in Forensic Explosives Investigations," 61 J. Forensic Sci. 1198–1207 (2016).

[255] See generally John J. Lentini, "Fire Debris: Laboratory Analysis of," in Wiley Encyclopedia Of Forensic Science, (Jamieson A. & Moenssens A.A., eds) 2009 & online updates.

[256] See Dan Muller, Aharon Levy and Ran Shelef, "Detection of Gasoline on Arson Suspects' Hands," 206 Forensic Sci. Int'l 150–154 (2011); Isabelle Montani, Stefane Comment and Olivier Delemont, "The Sampling of Ignitable Liquids on Suspects' Hands," 194 Forensic Sci. Int'l 115–124 (2010).

[257] See Jen-Hao Chi, "Metallographic Analysis and Fire Dynamics Simulation for Electrical Fire Scene Reconstruction," 57 J. Forensic Sci. 246–249 (2012).

[258] See Patricia A. Contreras, Stephen S. Houck, William M. Davis and Jorn C.-C. Yu, "Pyrolysis Products of Linear Alkylbenzenes—Implications in Fire Debris Analysis," 58 J. FORENSIC SCI. 210-216 (2013)(noting that some dishwashing liquids result in breakdown products common to ignitable liquids).

[259] See Rafal Borusiewicz, "Comparison of New Ampac Bags and Fire DebrisPAK® Bags as Packaging for Fire Debris Analysis," 57 J. Forensic Sci. 1059–1063 (2012)(noting that the best containers for fire debris should not be exposed to temperatures above 80 degrees C because they emit some volatile compounds that are also the components of some flammable liquids); see also Michiel M. P. Grutters, Judith Dogger, and Jeanet N. Hendrikse, "Performance Testing of the New AMPAV Fire Debris Bag Against Three Other Commercial Fire Debris Bags," 57 J. Forensic Sci. 1290–1298 (2012)(discussing the limitations of other products); Jorge Saiz et al., "Study of Losses of Volatile Compounds from Dynamites. Investigation of Cross-Contamination Between Dynamites Stored in Polyethylene Bags," 211 Forensic Sci. Int'l 27–33 (2011); see also Lisa Schwenk, Evidence Packaging for Fire Debris: Why Vapor-Tight Containers Matter, 64 Fire & Arson Investigator 3, April, 2014. at pp. 24–27 ("Results indicate that if items are not packaged in vapor-tight containers, a full gasoline profile. . .can be observed in as little as one hour on items that did not originally contain gasoline.").

[260] Alexander Beveridge, Forensic Investigations of Explosions, 2d ed., CRC Press, 2012 at pp. 94–95. See also Dee A. Turner and John V. Goodpaster, "The Effect of Microbial Degradation on the Chromatographic Profiles of Tiki Torch Fuel, Lamp Oil, and Turpentine," 56 J. Forensic Sci. 984–987 (2011).

§6.11   ANALYSIS OF FIRE RESIDUES

The importance of laboratory analysis of fire residue has been excellently summarized: "The laboratory analysis of fire debris is the only way to validly determine that an ignitable liquid was used to start a fire, at least in a compartment that has become fully involved. Even when the compartment has not become fully involved. . .the investigator still needs to determine the identity of the ignitable liquid."[261] Confirmation of the presence of accelerants is of major importance in determining the cause of an incendiary fire. Laboratory examination of physical evidence is necessary to test any hypothesis formulated during the on-scene examination of fire patterns, canine hits, witness statements, or other indicators, of a "set" fire.[262] The crime laboratory, of necessity, puts major emphasis upon seeking traces of such ignitable liquids.[263] Residues of ignitable liquids will likely survive a fire, even a fire which totally destroys the premises.[264] Porous substances are ideal absorbents of ignitable liquids. Soil will also retain traces of such liquids.[265]

The purpose of laboratory analysis is to locate the residues of any ignitable liquids, to assess the composition of such liquid, and to trace it to a particular manufacturer or source where possible. The sophistication of current GC/MS technology makes it possible to discriminate between products previously thought to be indistinguishable. This ability does not, however, assure identification of the source; rather, it reduces the number of possibles. Since any mass-produced material starts from different feedstocks in different manufacturing facilities, many factors can affect its components at numerous stages—such as mixing with product already in storage or in distribution channels.[266] Although researchers have recently found ways to discriminate among some gasoline samples to more closely identify a source of gasoline,[267] without extensive sampling and validation of the reproducibility of the patterns detected, identifying a

---

[261] Lentini, *Scientific Protocols 2d ed.* at p. 163.

[262] Approximately 50% of all arson case submissions to crime laboratories involve the detection of ignitable liquids. *See* DeHaan and Icove, *Kirk's Fire Investigation 7th ed.* at p. 562.

[263] Id.at p. 582.

[264] Joseph Nicol, "Recovery of Flammable Liquids from a Burned Structure," 114 Fire Engineering 550 (1961). *See also* NFPA 921 §17.5.4.1.

[265] NFPA §17.5.4.4.

[266] DeHaan and Icove, *Kirk's Fire Investigation 7th ed.* at p. 582.

[267] *See* Syahidah A. Muhammad et al., "Assessing Carbon and Hydrogen Isotpoic Fractionation of Diesel Fuel n-alkanes During Progressive Evaporation," 60 J. Forensic Sci. S56–S65 (2015); Weiying Lu et al., "Ignitable Liquid Identification Using Gas Chromatography/Mass Spectrometry Data by Projected Difference Resolution Mapping and Fuzzy Rule-Building Expert System Classification," 220 Forensic Sci. Int'l 210–218 (2012); Maria Monfreda and Adolfo Gregori, "Differentiation of Unevaporated Gasoline Samples According to Their Brands, by SPME-GC-MS and Multivariate Statistical Analysis," 56 J. Forensic Sci. 372–380 (2011).

manufacturer, facility, or location as the sole source of a sampled ignitable liquid is unlikely.[268]

Laboratories must initially separate the suspected flammable liquid residues from liquid samples, ashes, debris, carpeting, swabs, or other matrix recovered from the fire scene. It is widely recognized that it is the separation technique which determines how small an amount of flammable or combustible liquid residue a laboratory will be able to detect. Problems can be encountered when the substrate itself contains hydrocarbon-based products such as plastics, rubber, and synthetic carpeting. A number of different methods exist for the preparation of debris for laboratory analysis. The ASTM has published several standard methods for separating and concentrating volatile components from a sample of fire debris.[269]

Gas chromatography/mass spectrometry (GC/MS) is the most widely used and accepted analytical technique for determining the presence of flammable or combustible liquid residues in fire debris.[270] Its sensitivity, moderate cost, and relatively uncomplicated operation commend it to laboratories. Gas chromatography operates on a principle of separation resulting from the vaporization of a sample and its being carried through a suitably packed or capillary column of the gas chromatograph by an inert carrier gas, usually helium or nitrogen. The speed of a compound's passage through the column is largely a function of its molecular weight. A detector, generally a flame ionization detector, charts the component peaks on a chromatogram as they emerge from the end of the column. When a mass spectrometer is coupled with a gas chromatograph, measuring the molecular weight of the unknown compound by ionizing it and passing it through a magnetic field, each compound can be identified as it elutes from the chromatographic column.[271] Additional analytical tools, such as infrared

---

[268] DeHaan and Icove, Kirk's *Fire Investigation* 7th ed. at p. 582.

[269] *See* the following ASTM standards: E2154 Standard Practice for Separation and Concentration of Ignitable Liquid Residues from Fire Debris Samples by Passive Headspace Concentration with Solid Phase Microextraction (SPME); E1413 Standard Practice for Separation and Concentration of Ignitable Liquid Residues from Fire Debris Samples by Dynamic Headspace Concentration; E1412 Practice for Separation and Concentration of Ignitable Liquid Residues from Fire Debris Samples by Passive Headspace Concentration; E1388 Standard Practice for Sampling Headspace Vapors from Fire Debris Samples; E1386 Standard Practice for Separation and Concentration of Ignitable Liquid Residues from Fire Debris Samples by Solvent Extraction; E1385 Standard Practice for Separation and Concentration off Ignitable Liquid Residues from Fire Debris Samples by Steam Distillation. *See* http://www.astm.org/.

For a detailed discussion of the various methods, including the capabilities and limitations of each, *see* DeHaan and Icove, *Kirk's Fire Investigation 7th ed.* at pp. 569–573. *See also* Lentini, *Scientific Protocols 2d ed.* at pp. 163–177.

[270] *See* ASTM Standard E1618 Standard Test Method for Ignitable Liquid Residues in Extracts from Fire Debris Samples by Gas Chromatography-Mass Spectrometry. *See also* Lentini, *Scientific Protocols 2d ed.* at pp. 163–177.

[271] *See* Perry Michael Koussiafes, "GCMS for the Arson Investigator," 65 Fire & Arson Investigator 2, (2014) at pp. 30–39, for a discussion about the information GCMS can provide written for "people without a strong science background but with an interest in how the presence of ignitable liquids is determined in fire debris."

spectroscopy, energy dispersive radiography, or high-performance liquid chromatography, and scanning electron microscopy may also be used.[272]

Research has been conducted regarding the survival of blood, bloodstains, and DNA during a fire. Results indicated that all three can survive a fire and provide usable bloodstain pattern, serology and DNA information, as long as the blood was not exposed to temperatures above 800°C.[273]

§6.12 ANALYSIS OF EXPLOSIVE RESIDUES

Laboratory analysis of explosives residues is aimed at identifying the explosive that was used and its manufacturer as well as providing any other clues not immediately observable to the bomb scene investigator. Visual examination of the debris is the first order of business.[274] Laboratory specialists in explosives have a wide array of chemical analytical methods, for which exacting protocols must be followed. Among them are color tests, which are good for tentative field identification, and numerous sensitive and definitive instrumental techniques, including GC/MS, infrared spectroscopy, and other spectroscopic and chromatography methods. TWGFEX has issued *Recommended Guidelines for Forensic Identification of Post-Blast Explosive Residues*[275] that provides recommended practices and suggests the use of multiple techniques for identification. An Appendix to the guidelines provides information on explosives and their post-blast residues.

Various examinations may be appropriate on the same evidence fragment. On metal fragments from a pipe bomb, a number of procedures may be appropriate, such as latent fingerprint examinations, looking for unconsumed particles of explosives or explosive residue to determine the type of main charge, and metallurgical examinations to determine the specific metal used. If biological fluids are found on the debris, such as blood or perspiration, DNA may connect the materials to a possible suspect.[276] Examination of debris through a low power stereomicroscope is an important step. Because of their distinctive morphology, microscopic examination may

---

[272] Ongoing research continues to identify and explore additional methodologies. *See* Ina Fettig et al., "Evaluation of a Headspace Solid-Phase Microextraction Method for the Analysis of Ignitable Liquids in Fire Debris," 59 J. Forensic Sci. 743–749 (2014); Matthew J. Aernecke and David R. Walt, "Detection and Classification Ignitable Liquid Residues Using Fluorescence-Based Vapor-Sensitive Microsphere Array," 55 J. Forensic Sci. 178–184 (2010).

[273] Leanor Bender, Kyle Hoskins, Amy Michaud, Karolyn L. Tontarski, and Tani Watkins, *Chemical Enhancement Techniques of Bloodstain Patterns and DNA Recovery After Fire Exposure*, 63 Fire & Arson Investigator 3, April, 2012, at pp. 10–13.

[274] *See generally* Sarah L. Lancaster, Maurice Marshall and Jimmie C. Oxley, "Explosion Debris: Laboratory Analysis of," in Wiley Encyclopedia Of Forensic Science, (Jamieson A. & Moenssens A.A., eds) 2009 & online updates.

[275] TWGFEX, *Recommended Guidelines for Forensic Identification of Post-Blast Explosive Residues* (available at: http://ncfs.ucf.edu/twgfex/docs/)(last accessed November 7, 2016).

[276] *See* David R. Foran, Michael E. Gehring and Shawn Stallworth, "The Recovery and Analysis of Mitochondrial DNA from Exploded Pipe Bombs," 54 J. Forensic Sci. 90–94 (2009).

reveal black or smokeless powder traces. Other explosive traces require different and possibly more exacting analysis.

After a microscopic study of the debris, extraction may be necessary to separate the explosive residues from the nonexplosive substrate. Acetone is usually sufficient to make most organic high explosives soluble. Cold water is the best medium for the extraction of water soluble inorganic substances like the nitrates and chlorates. The acetone mixture is filtered and permitted to air dry which will reveal the explosive residues. Heating to hasten the drying time is not recommended since it might also cause the explosives' particles to decompose.

Once explosive residues have been successfully removed from the hands for testing, several analytical techniques are available for detection and identification, including gas chromatography with electron capture detection,[277] gas liquid chromatography with thermal energy analyzer detection,[278] and other instrumental methods.[279]

V. TRIAL AIDS

§6.13　EXPERT QUALIFICATIONS

Fire/explosion scene investigators work for both government agencies, including: federal civilian/military investigative entities and fire departments; state fire marshal's offices and state police agencies; county and municipal fire or police departments; and for private sector concerns such as insurance companies, forensic science consultancies, and law firms. Insurance companies have a considerable financial interest in obtaining accurate and reliable fire/explosion origin and cause determinations and the insurance industry underwrites most private sector investigations.[280] In many states, a private sector fire/explosion scene investigator is considered a private investigator, subject to licensing and training requirements.[281]

---

[277] John M. Douse, "Trace Analysis of Explosives in Handswab Extracts Using Amberlite XAD-7 Porous Polymer Beads, Silica Capillary Column Gas Chromatography with Electron-Capture Detection and Thin-Layer Chromatography," 234 J.Chromatogr. 415 (1982). *See* David J. Tranthim-Fryer, "The Application of a Simple and Inexpensive Modified Carbon Wire Adsorption/Solvent Extraction Technique to the Analysis of Accelerants and Volatile Organic Compounds in Arson Debris," 35 J. Forensic Sci. 271 (1990).

[278] John M. Douse, "Trace Analysis of Explosives at the Low Picogram Level Using Silica Capillary Column Gas Chromatography with Thermal Energy Analyser Detection," 256 J. Chromatog. 359 (1983).

[279] *See generally* Alexander Beveridge, *Forensic Investigations of Explosions*, 2d ed. CRC Press, 2012 at pp. 149–152.

[280] Lentini, *Scientific Protocols 2d ed.* at p. 481.

[281] *See, e.g.,* Va. Code § 9.1–138 ("Private investigator" means any individual who engages in the business of, or accepts employment to make, investigations to obtain information on (i) crimes or civil wrongs; (ii) the location, disposition, or recovery of stolen property; (iii) the cause of accidents, fires, damages, or injuries to persons or to property; or (iv) evidence to be

Professional qualification, competency, and investigative standards for fire and explosion investigators have evolved tremendously since 1972, when the National Professional Qualifications Board was created to develop national standards for the fire service. The resulting NFPA®1033 *Professional Qualifications for Fire Inspector, Fire Investigator, Fire Prevention Officer,* was promulgated in 1977.[282]

The current NFPA®1033 *Standard for Professional Qualifications for Fire Investigator,*[283] 2014 Edition requires competency in six duties (scene examination, scene documentation, evidence collection/ preservation, interviewing, post-incident investigation, presentations) and 28 minimum job performance requirements (JPRs) to accomplish those duties, for fire investigators in both public and private sectors.[284] NFPA 1033 also delineates minimum knowledge and continuing education requirements for 16 specific topics.[285] Both NFPA 921 and 1033 incorporate relevant ASTM International®standards[286] with NFPA 921 also incorporating other pertinent NFPA and industry standards publications.[287] Knowledge of NFPA 921 has been recognized as an important factor in assessing expert competence[288] and the reliability of the proffered expert's conclusions.[289]

The National Fire Academy (NFA) has trained thousands of students since 1975, enhancing the abilities of fire and emergency services and allied professionals to deal more effectively with fires and related emergencies. With the assistance of the Bureau of Alcohol,

---

used before any court, board, officer, or investigative committee.) Virginia registration requirements, including 60 hours of training, background check, and non-refundable licensing fees, are detailed on the Virginia Department of Criminal Justice Services website (available at: https://www.dcjs.virginia.gov/licensure-and-regulatory-affairs/private-investigator)(last accessed November 7, 2016).

[282] NFPA 1033, 2014 Edition, at p. 1. Note: NFPA 1033 as a mandatory standard is distinguished from NFPA 921 which is a guide; however, both 921 and 1033 are considered to be authoritative publications in their field and conformance to both is expected. *See* Terry-Dawn Hewitt et al., "Renewed Focus on Industry Standards: The Growing Implications of ASTM Standards for Fire Investigators in the Offing," 65 Fire & Arson Investigator 2 (2014) at p. 24.

[283] Id. at p. 24.

[284] *See* NFPA 1033 §4.2 et seq. Each duty includes several JPRs; each JPR specifies the task to be performed and the requisite knowledge and skills to successfully accomplish the task.

[285] NFPA 1033 was first promulgated in 1977 and required minimal educational requirements—a high school diploma and currency in only three areas.

[286] See NFPA 921 §2.1 et seq.; *see also* NFPA 1033 Annex C §C.1.2.1.

[287] Including those of the: American Boat and Yacht Council (ABYC); American National Standards Institute (ANSI); American Petroleum Institute (API); Underwriters Laboratories (UL); and U.S. Government, among numerous others. See NFPA 921 §2.2 et seq.

[288] *See* Int'l Paper Co. v. Deep S. Equip. Co., 2015 U.S. Dist. LEXIS 35238, *16 (W.D. La. 2015)(testimony of proffered expert barred in part because "he was not knowledgeable about the current version of NFPA 921, which he purported to rely upon to form his opinion.").

[289] *See* Atl. Specialty ins. Co. v. Porter, Inc., 2016 U.S. Dist. LEXIS 145415, *12 (E.D. La. 2016)(proffered expert's report excluded because its theory of causation did "not conform with the Scientific Method as applied to fire causation investigations, as explained by National Fire Protection Association publication 921, Guide for Fire and Explosives Investigations.").

Tobacco, Firearms and Explosives (BATFE, aka ATF), NFA offers training in fire investigation and related topics. Certification programs are offered by the International Association of Arson Investigators (IAAI) and the National Association of Fire Investigators (NAFI), and require an application process, passing of an examination, and continuing education.[290] Both organizations offer fire/explosion-specific training at the international, national and, through chapters, at state and local levels. Additionally, there are numerous academic institutions offering undergraduate and graduate degrees in fire science, fire protection engineering, and related forensic sciences disciplines. The American Board of Criminalistics offers a certification program in fire debris and explosives analysis.[291] The National Center for Forensic Science and the Technical Working Group for Fire and Explosives (TWGFEX) are also heavily involved in the development of professional training for fire and explosives investigators. In 2014, the National Institute of Standards and Testing (NIST) created the Organization of Scientific Area Committees (OSAC) to promulgate *best practices, guidelines and standards* for the forensic science community in general.[292] The designation of a *Fire Scene and Explosives Subcommittee* promises to bring about further advances in fire/explosion scene methodologies and investigative standardization.[293]

Laboratory personnel who test the debris from a fire scene must have the academic and experiential training in chemistry sufficient for the instrumental and chemical tasks they perform. They must, therefore, be skilled in the recognition of the patterns on the chromatograms of gasoline, fuel oil and other flammable liquids which they are called upon to analyze. In effectuating their analysis, they should follow recognized ASTM protocols. Laboratory analysts should have expertise in mass spectrometry, generally used in conjunction with gas chromatography (GC-MS) to further analyze components that were separated during the GC process.

§6.14   EVIDENCE ISSUES

1.   GENERAL ADMISSIBILITY

As in all other areas of expert opinion testimony, the courts have a great deal of latitude in deciding when a fire/explosion investigator is qualified to offer opinion testimony on the origin and cause of a fire or explosion. Courts frequently permit fire marshals who conduct fire

---

[290] *See generally* John J. Lentini, "Fire Investigator: Standardization, Accreditation, and Certification," in Wiley Encyclopedia Of Forensic Science, (Jamieson A. & Moenssens A.A., eds) 2009 & online updates.

[291] *See* http://www.criminalistics.com/certification.html.

[292] NIST, *Plan for the Organization of Scientific Area Committees Roles and Responsibilities* available at: http://www.nist.gov/forensics/osac.cfm.

[293] NIST, *Organization of Scientific Area Committees Roles and Responsibilities*, available at: http://www.nist.gov/forensics/osacroles.cfm.

investigations to testify about their findings and conclusions.[294] The fact that a witness may not have been "certified" by a professional association as an expert may sometimes bar qualifying the person to give expert opinion evidence,[295] but elsewhere such circumstance may be held to not disqualify the person from testifying as an expert.[296] Decisions on whether a person will be permitted to give testimony as an expert are highly dependent on the nature of the precise testimony that is sought to be offered and the issues of a particular case.[297] Even generally qualified experts may be precluded from testifying on one issue but permitted to testify on another issue.[298]

In arson prosecutions, generally, three elements must be proven: a) there has been a burning of property; b) the burning was the result of an intentional act; and c) the act was done with malicious intent (a willful criminal act).[299] The fire investigator's expert opinion regarding the origin, cause and classification of the fire is particularly relevant, although not always admissible. In most jurisdictions an expert can give an opinion on the cause of a fire and the point of its origination whenever the jury is unable to adequately understand the facts or draw inferences from the facts without expert assistance. The majority view is in accord with the Federal Rules of Evidence which allow the opinion testimony of experts if it assists the trier of fact in understanding the evidence or in determining a fact in issue. The cause of fires is generally held to be beyond the scope of ordinary training and knowledge and thus expert testimony is admissible.[300] Expert testimony on the location of the origin of a fire is also generally admissible.[301]

---

[294] *See, e.g.,* Savage v. ScriptoTokai Corp., 266 F.Supp.2d 344 (D. Conn. 2003)(fifteen years as fire fighter, fire inspector, senior inspector, and fire marshal having conducted cause and origin investigations, state certified as a fire inspector, with training at the National Fire Academy, among other qualifications); State v. Hales, 344 N.C. 419, 474 S.E.2d 328 (1996)(fire marshal who previously worked at a community college as fire and rescue training coordinator, a volunteer fire fighter for 27 years, and several hundred classroom hours of fire and arson training, certified as an arson investigator by a state commission on fire and rescue).

[295] *See, e.g.,* Donegal Mutual Insurance Co. v. White Consolidated Industries, Inc., 153 Ohio App.3d 619, 795 N.E.2d 133 (2003)(trial court abused its discretion when it permitted, over objection, the expert testimony of an unlicensed fire inspector as to the cause of the fire).

[296] United States v. Santiago, 202 Fed.Appx. 399 (11th Cir.2006).

[297] *See, e.g.,* Tunnell v. Ford Motor Co., 330 F.Supp.2d 731 (W.D. Va. 2004)(witness with Ph.D. in materials science and engineering and a B.S. degree in electrical engineering permitted to give an opinion grounded "on the prevailing industry standard.").

[298] Ortiz-Semprit v. Coleman Co., Inc., 301 F.Supp.2d 116 (D. Puerto Rico 2004)(safety engineer certified by NFPA as a fire and explosives investigator not permitted to testify as to adequacy of consumer warnings on electric generator).

[299] DeHaan and Icove, *Kirk's Fire Investigation 7th ed.* at p. 659.

[300] *See* Commonwealth v. Nasuti, 385 Pa. 436, 123 A.2d 435 (1956)("Certainly laymen could hardly be expected to have knowledge in regard to various types of fires and the difference in the nature, violence, and intensity of flames resulting from the burning of inflammable liquids or other materials as contrasted with the burning of a wooden counter or chair upholstery.").

Some expert opinions on the cause of a fire have been based on having considered all of the possible causes, and having eliminated all but one cause. In Red Hill Hosiery Mill Inc. v. MagneTek, Inc., 159 N.C.App. 135, 582 S.E.2d 632 (2003), a products liability case against the

Over the past century, the cases that have dealt with the admission of expert testimony regarding fire and explosives evidence have been legion. The relevancy and competency of such evidence has been discussed as it relates to both civil and criminal cases. For that reason, a listing of representative cases in this chapter cannot be exhaustive and is intended to be mainly representative of the courts' attitudes over the years.

Early court decisions allowed such testimony liberally, reflecting the relaxed state of affairs that existed when expert testimony was far from sophisticated and seldom based on sound scientific principles. Modern decisions, especially those after the *Daubert* trilogy cases, tend to be more critical of such testimony and demand that the reliability of challenged opinion evidence be established.[302] Fire investigation was included in *Daubert* scrutiny by *Michigan Millers Mutual Ins. Corp. v. Benfield*.[303] Subsequently, courts have turned to NFPA 921 to evaluate the conduct of fire investigations; by 2014, NFPA 921 had been cited in, at least, 270 U.S. court decisions.[304]

Even so, the wide discretion that has traditionally been accorded judges in deciding the admission of opinion testimony and the qualifications needed to present such evidence continues to produce cases wherein the showing that scientific principles must undergird the experts' opinions are given only lip service. However, in the wake of *Daubert* and the increase in NFPA 921 citations by courts, the trend appears that a fire/explosion investigator's qualifications and methodologies will draw greater objective scrutiny. Specifically, a fire investigator could reasonably be expected to: obtain relevant certifications from IAAI or NAFI; comply with NFPA 1033 knowledge and skill requirements; and demonstrate compliance with industry standards and best practices—including NFPA 921 and 1033, and relevant ASTM and other industry standards.[305]

---

manufacturer of a ballast and light fixture, the expert was held to have properly considered and eliminated all of the possible causes to conclude that the ballast had overheated due to a malfunction within the ballast and caused the fire in the building.

The failure to exclude other possible sources of the fire may result in exclusion of the expert's proffered testimony as unreliable. *See* Bryte v. American Household, Inc., 429 F.3d 469 (4th Cir. 2005).

[301] *See, e.g.,* Galloway v. State, 416 So.2d 1103 (Ala.Cr.App.1982); State v. Garrett, 682 S.W.2d 153 (Mo.App.1984).

[302] In a unanimous decision, the United States Supreme Court, in Weisgram v. Marley Co., 528 U.S. 440 (2000), reversed a jury verdict based upon a post-trial motion by the defense to set the verdict aside because the trial judge abused his discretion by allowing the plaintiff to present experts on the causation of a fire whose opinions were not reliable because they were not based upon sound methodology. Such invalid testimony results in an unreliable opinion.

[303] 140 F.3rd 915 (11th Cir. 1998).

[304] Terry-DawnHewitt & Wayne J. McKenna, IAAI Fire Investigation Standards Committee (FISC), 65 Fire&Arson Investigator (3), January, 2015, at p. 22.

[305] Terry-Dawn Hewitt, Renewed Focus on Industry Standards: The Growing Implications of ASTM Standards for Fire Investigations in the Offing, 65 Fire&Arson Investigator (2), October, 2014, at p. 27.

Fire and explosives science has progressed tremendously in the past two decades. Early case law allowed opinions of woefully unqualified individuals to be introduced regularly on a variety of issues, particularly involving the origin and cause of fires. These opinions frequently amounted to no more than pure speculation, conjecture, or guesswork. As the need for scientific principles to support opinion evidence became more recognized in laboratory services, responsible organizations and institutions initiated procedures and articulated protocols to better provide scientific bases for conclusions drawn by experts from available data. Despite this progress, already alluded to in the first part of this chapter, room for improvement still exists.[306]

2.   CANINE USES AND LIMITATIONS

Many ignitable liquids and some solids have recognizable odors. Ammonia, for example, which arsonists may use to mask the aroma of ignitable liquids, is readily detectable by its odor. The fire investigator's problem comes in attempting to identify the traces of one or more ignitable liquids having been smelled at the fire scene and then, from the smell, to hypothesize one or more causes for the fire.

The olfactory sense is a most unreliable indicator of the cause of a fire or of the specific ignitable liquid consumed in it. Gasoline, kerosene, and other liquid substances have distinctive odors, but the odor of one ignitable liquid can be mistaken for that of another, such as kerosene for paint thinners. The error-prone nature of investigating the cause of a fire through recourse to the sense of smell was revealed in one case[307] during a courtroom demonstration on the cross examination of a firefighter who claimed to have smelled ammonia and chloride of sulfur while he was combating a fire. The defense attorney was permitted to test the firefighter by producing four containers which the witness was asked to smell and identify in turn. The defense attorney had the witness inhale from the ammonia-filled container first. This inhalation momentarily so dulled his sense of smell that the witness was disabled from identifying the contents of the other three containers. While the demonstration was staged to benefit the defense it also disclosed one of many serious flaws in typecasting liquids through the odors they produce.

Canines have olfactory systems that are used today in fire scene investigations. Dogs, and those dogs bred to hunt by scent in particular,

---

[306] In Tamez v. Mack Trucks, Inc., 100 S.W.3d 549 (Tex.App.2003), the reviewing court concluded that the expert's opinion on cause of fire was "not scientific in nature," but that the trial court abused discretion in excluding it under the state Rule 702 because the expert properly identified the underlying facts he relied upon in arriving at his opinion on cause of a truck fire; his testimony was therefore reliable and admissible under the state equivalent rule of FRE 702.

[307] J.A. Gamm, "Defense vs. Offense" or "The Bad Guys vs. The Good Guys," 35 The Fire and Arson Investigator 33, 43 (1984).

have an indisputably superior sense of smell.[308] They can be taught to seek out specific odors, are low to the ground, and can perform a sweep or search of a site for the presence of accelerants or explosives far more quickly than any other known procedure. The courts have broadly supported the use of canines in arson, explosive, and drug cases,[309] despite often strenuous objection.[310]

Hydrocarbon detection canines had their start in the 1980s when the Connecticut State Police started training dogs for that purpose. Even though they are used widely, there have been very few cases in which the use of dogs in arson investigations became an issue. The two following cases are illustrative of the course the courts are following when presented with evidence of alerts by hydrocarbon detection dogs.

In *Fitts v. State*,[311] two hydrocarbon sniffing dogs were used in a search of the premises in which defendant was charged to have set a fire. The "handler," who would later testify at an evidentiary hearing, was employed by the Houston Fire Department and had attended several dog training seminars. In searching the defendant's residence, the handler used two dogs that he had owned for over four years and had trained, with the help of other experts in the field, to detect the presence of hydrocarbons, various narcotics, cadavers, and air scents. By the time of trial, he was able to assert that, in controlled tests, his dogs had alerted correctly 99.9% of the time. When he had used the dogs at 50 fires investigated at the request of law enforcement, 49 of these fires were later determined, either through laboratory testing or by independent verification from witnesses or arson investigators, to have involved an accelerant. While the dogs were not expected to determine whether a particular fire was caused by arson, they alerted when they detected the presence of hydrocarbons by scratching or whining near the location where they detected the scent of a hydrocarbon. He also produced incident reports detailing each search he had conducted at the request of law enforcement agencies. After giving lengthy testimony, during which he was thoroughly cross examined by the defendant, he concluded that there were hydrocarbons present at the fire scene, a conclusion later confirmed by laboratory testing. The reviewing court concluded that the trial court's decision to admit the evidence as reliable under the state rule (identical to FRE 702) and was not an abuse of discretion.

By contrast, in *State v. Webber*,[312] the Rhode Island Supreme Court was confronted with a case where a fire investigator had brought a dog

---

[308] The number of olfactory receptor cells are 4 billion in a bloodhound, compared to just 5 million in a human and 100 million in a rabbit. The surface area of bloodhound olfactory epithelium is 59 sq.in. in comparison to a human's 1.55 sq.in. (10 sq.cm.).

[309] "Trials: 'Suspicious origin' opinion" 10 Am. Jur. Trials 301 (2012).

[310] Ken Lammers, "Canine Sniffs: The Search that Isn't" 1 N.Y.U. J. L. & Liberty 845 (2005).

[311] 982 S.W.2d 175 (Tex. App. 1998).

[312] 716 A.2d 738 (R.I. 1998).

trained to detect the presence of flammable substances that could be used to propagate the spread of fires, to the scene, after a fire had partially destroyed the defendant's home. The fire investigator testified, without objection, that the dog had "alerted" in seven or eight different locations in the house. The defense did object to mention of the alert at the Webber's floor mat, which was later tested by gas chromatography at the University of Rhode Island Crime Laboratory and shown to be negative for the presence of an "accelerant." Various experts concluded the fire was incendiary in nature and defendant was convicted of arson. On appeal, the court held that the use of the dog alert evidence constituted the prejudicial admission of unreliable evidence under its Evidence Rule 702, and that essential foundation testimony was totally absent. Accordingly, the court vacated the conviction and reversed for a new trial. Crucial to its decision was the fact that the state failed to introduce any testimony concerning the dog's training or reliability. The court indicated that dog alert testimony would be admissible upon the laying of proper predicate evidence showing the expertise of the dog's owner, the dog's training, and the degree of accuracy achieved during investigations. No such evidence had been introduced in this case.

The use of accelerant-detection-canines (ADC) should be limited to that of an investigative aid; their alerts do not in themselves constitute criminal proof. The body of scholarly literature to date confirms that even the best ADC cannot discriminate between accelerants and all possible background contaminants or byproducts of pyrolysis.[313] Further, there is scant proof that a dog's olfactory sensitivity is more accurate than state-of-the-art GC/MS instruments used in laboratories.[314]

Scent detection by a trained ADC may be recognized as justification for performing sampling and laboratory analysis, but any argument that the ADC alert in and of itself is "proof" of arson or any other crime should be legally challenged. There is general agreement, in the scientific community, that an *unconfirmed* ADC alert should be considered invalid, unreliable, and entitled to no weight.[315] As has been noted by an experienced fire investigator, "[D]ogs can only tell us where to collect samples, not what the samples contain."[316]

Courts, however, are less uniform in deciding the reliability of such an alert and in ruling on the admissibility of an ADC alert as an indicator of the presence of an ignitable liquid. Among the factors a court should consider when evaluating the reliability of ADC alerts are: initial training and certification of the ADC and handler; continuing

---

[313] Colin C. Murphy, *Admissibility of Unconfirmed Accelerant-Detection-Canine Alert*, Proceedings of the 65th Annual Scientific Meeting, American Academy of Forensic Sciences, 2013, at p. 125.

[314] Id.

[315] Id.

[316] Lentini, *Scientific Protocols 2d ed.* at p. 517.

training of ADC and handler; accurate data regarding the ADC's proficiency—confirmed positive alerts vs. false positive alerts; and continuous proficiency testing to determine the ADC's error rate.[317]

3. Evolving Science

In arson criminal cases as well as in civil cases wherein an insurance company raises an "arson defense" to avoid paying out fire policies, testimony as to sensory perceptions, such as smell or sight, which were believed to indicate arson, were previously held relevant and often dispositive on the issue of whether an incendiary fire occurred. There were many such indicators, such as the color of smoke, crazing of glass, alligatoring effect, depth of char, pour patterns, sagging furniture springs, low burning, holes in floors, V pattern angle, and spalling.[318] Courts generally accepted such evidence even without establishing a foundation as to what different indicators can demonstrate,[319] or after adopting definitions of them which varied from jurisdiction to jurisdiction.[320] The courts were sensitive to the cumulative effect of the presence of numerous incendiary fire indicators, and seemed less likely to question the admissibility of a particular indicator when evidence was available as to many of them.[321]

As a result of advances in fire science debunking these and other myths of fire behavior; extensive, continuing scientific research; the availability of NFPA 921, NFPA 1033, and ASTM and other industry standards to assess the conduct of an investigation and the qualifications of a prospective expert witness; and challenges to the scientific validity of pattern-analysis forensic disciplines, courts have an opportunity to be more discriminating when ruling on the admissibility

---

[317] Joseph J. Maltese & Stephanie Domitrovich, *Who Let the Dogs In? The Admissibility and Scope of Testimony of Dog Handlers*, Proceedings of the 65th Annual Scientific Meeting, AAFS, 2013, at p. 126.

[318] Lentini, *Scientific Protocols 2d ed.* at pp. 473–474.

[319] *See, e.g.*, United States v. Gere, 662 F.2d 1291 (9th Cir. 1981); United States v. Gargotto, 476 F.2d 1009 (6th Cir. 1973).

In State v. DuBose, 617 S.W.2d 509 (Mo. App. 1981), two fire investigators who had conducted separate investigations each testified that multiple fires, inverted cone patterns, and alligatoring, all indicating arson, existed at the burned premises and the appellate court accepted this evidence as establishing the incendiary nature of the fire without inquiring, for example, as to what an "inverted cone pattern" was.

[320] *Compare* People v. Green, 146 Cal. App.3d 369, 194 Cal. Rptr. 128 (1983)(burn patterns indicate the cause of fire) *with* In re Beverly Hills Fire Litigation, 695 F.2d 207 (6th Cir. 1982)(burn patterns are marks indicating the path taken by the fire which enable an expert to pinpoint the location of the origin of the fire).

[321] *See* Zaitchick v. American Motorists Ins. Co., 554 F.Supp. 209 (S.D.N.Y. 1982)(evidence introduced as to burn patterns, odor, black smoke, spalling of concrete); T.D.S. Inc. v. Shelby Mut. Ins. Co., 760 F.2d 1520 (11th Cir. 1985)(observations made of multiple separate fires, pour pattern, burn patterns, spalling of concrete).

In People v. Lippert, 125 Ill.App.3d 489, 80 Ill.Dec. 824, 466 N.E.2d 276 (1984), expert testimony was presented for both the defense and the prosecution as to the cause of the fire. The prosecution offered several arson indicators as evidence of the defendant's guilt, but could not suggest a reasonable motive. The defense presented expert testimony that a furnace was the accidental cause of the fire and the defendant had no motive for murdering his wife.

of fire and explosive expert testimony. It will be up to the attorneys involved in fire or explosion matters to ensure the court has the accurate information it needs to fulfill its gatekeeper function. Attorneys will need to ascertain from the prospective expert fire/explosion witness whether established professional protocols, standards and best practices were followed.[322]

VI. RESOURCES

§6.15   BIBLIOGRAPHY OF ADDITIONAL RESOURCES

1.   EXPLOSIVES

Ken Alibek and Stephen Handelman, *Biohazard*, Randomhouse, 1999 (available at: https://www.nlm.nih.gov/nichsr/esmallpox/biohazard_alibek.pdf).

Alexander Beveridge, ed. *Forensic Investigations of Explosives*, CRC Press, 1998.

T.G. Brodie, *Bombs and Bombing*, Charles C. Thomas Publisher, Ltd., 1996.

Hayley Brown *et al.*, "New Developments in SPME Part 2: Analysis of Ammonium Nitratebased Explosives," 49 J. Forensic Sci. 215 (2004).

Eric J. Buckowsli *et al.*, "From Homeland Defenses to Forensic Laboratories-Fourier Transform Infra-Red (FTIR) Spectroscopy for the Identification of Explosives," Forensic Mag., June-July 2006, p. 15.

Stéphane Calderara, *et al.*, "Organic Explosives Analysis Using On-Column-Ion Trap EI/NICI GC-MS with an External Source," 49 J. Forensic Sci. 1005 (2004).

Sonio Casamento, *et al.*, "Optimization of the Separation of Organic Explosives by Capillary Electrophoresis with Artificial Neural Networks," 48 J. Forensic Sci. 1075 (2003).

Paul Cooper, *Explosives Engineering*, Wiley-VCH, 1996.

Paul Cooper and Stanley R. Kurpwski, *Introduction to the Technology of Explosives*, Wiley-VCH, 1996.

James B. Crippin, *Explosives and Chemical Weapons Identification*, CRC Press, 2006.

Cecelia Crowson *et al.*, "A Survey of High Explosives Traces in Public Places," 41 J. Forensic Sci. 980 (1996).

---

[322] *See* United States v. Aman, 748 F. Supp. 2d 531 (E.D. Va. 2010)(holding that the methodology described in NFPA 921 as sufficiently reliable to support admission).

Hazel Cullum *et al.*, "A Second Survey of High Explosives Traces in Public Places," 49 J. Forensic Sci. 684 (2004).

David De Tata *et al.*, "The Identification of the Emulsion Component of Emulsion Explosives by Liquid Chromatography-Mass Spectrometry," 51 J. Forensic Sci. 303 (2006).

Hank D. Ellison, *Handbook of Chemical and Biological Warfare Agents*, CRC Press, 2000.

Donato Firrao *et al.*, "Metal Objects Mapping After Small Charge Explosion," 51 J. Forensic Sci. 520 (2006).

Alexi Gapeev and Yehuda Yinon, "Application of Spectral Libraries for Characterization of Oxidizers in Post-Blast Residues by Electrospray Mass Spectrometry," 49 J. Forensic Sci. 227 (2004).

Lisa Harvey and Jeffrey W. Harvey, "Reliability of Bloodhounds in Criminal Investigation," 48 J. Forensic Sci. 811 (2003).

David J. Icove and John D. DeHaan, *Forensic Fire Scene Reconstruction*, 2d ed., Pearson Ltd., 2008.

Kenneth L. Kosanke *et al.*, "Characterization of Pyrotechnic Reaction Residue Particles by SEM/EDS," 48 J. Forensic Sci. 531 (2003).

Kenneth L. Kosanke *et al.*, "Pyrotechnic Reaction Residue Particle Analysis," 51 J. Forensic Sci. 296 (2006).

Adrienne Mayor, *Greek Fire, Poison Arrows and Scorpion Bombs: Biological and Chemical Warfare in the Ancient World*, Overlook Books, 2003.

Lou Michel and Dan Herbeck, *American Terrorist: Timothy McVeigh and the Oklahoma City Bombing*, Harper Collins, 2001.

D. Muller *et al.*, "Improved Method for the Detection of TAPT After Explosion," 49 J. Forensic Sci. 935 (2004).

Jimmie Oxley *et al.*, "Quantification and Aging of the Post-Blast Residue of TNT Landmines," 48 J. Forensic Sci. 742 (2003).

Jimmie Oxley *et al.*, "Trends in Explosive Contamination," 48 J. Forensic Sci. 334 (2003).

Henry Schuster and Charles Stone, *Hunting Eric Rudolph*, Berkley Hardcover, 2005.

James T. Thurman, *Practical Bomb Scene Investigation,* 2d ed., CRC Press, 2011.

Xioacoma Xu *et al.*, "Trace Analysis of Peroxide Explosives by High Performance Liquid Chromatography-Atmospheric Pressure Ionization-Tandem Mass Spectrometry (HPLC-APCI-MS/MS) for Forensic Applications," 49 J. Forensic Sci. 1230 (2004).

2.   FIRE INVESTIGATION

Stephen P. Allan and Stuart W. Case, "Survey of Forensic Science Laboratories by the Technical Working Group for Fire and Explosives (TWGFEX)," Forensic Sci. Comm. [FBI], Jan. 2000.

Andrew Armstrong *et al.*, "The Evaluation of the Extent of Transporting of 'Tracking' an Identifiable Ignitable Liquid (Gasoline) Throughout Fire Scenes During the Investigative Process," 49 J. Forensic Sci. 741 (2004).

Vytenis Babrauskas, *Ignition Handbook: Principles and Applications to Fire Safety Engineering, Fire Investigation, Risk Management and Forensic Science*, Fire Science Pub., 2003.

W. Bertsch, G. Holzer and C. Sellers, *Chemical Analysis for the Arson Investigator and Attorney*, Wiley-VCH Verlag GmbH,1993.

Mark E. Byrnes, David A. King and Philip M. Tierno, Jr., *Nuclear, Chemical and Biological Terrorism*, CRC Press, 2003.

Fire Protection Research Foundation, *Recommendations of The Research Advisory Council on Post-Fire Analysis—A White Paper,* 2002.

Glenn S. Frysinger and Richard G. Gaines, "Forensic Analysis of Ignitable Liquids in Fire Debris by Comprehensive Two-Dimensional Gas Chromatography," 47 J. Forensic Sci. 471 (2002).

Kenneth G. Furton *et al.*, "A Novel Method for the Analysis of Gasoline from Fire Debris Using Headspace Solid-Phase Microextraction," 41 J. Forensic Sci. 12 (1996).

Leslie A. Geddes, *Handbook of Electrical Hazards and Accidents*, CRC Press, 1995.

Ashley Harris and John F. Wheeler, "GC-MS of Ignitable Liquids Using Solvent-Desorbed SPME for Automated Analysis," 48 J. Forensic Sci. 41 (2003).

Terry-Dawn Hewitt and Wayne J. McKenna, A Perfect Storm Brewing for Fire Investigators in Court, March 3, 2014 (available at: SSRN: https://ssrn.com/abstract=2381519).

John J. Lentini, *et al.*, "The Petroleumlaced Background," 45 J. Forensic Sci. 968 (2000).

John J. Lentini, "Persistence of Floor Coating Solvents," 46 J. Forensic Sci. 1470 (2001).

John J. Lentini, *Scientific Protocols for Fire Investigation,* 2d ed., CRC Press, 2013.

R. Newman *et al., GC-MS Guide to Ignitable Liquids*, 1998.

Alastair D. Pert *et al.*, "Review of Analytical Techniques for Arson Residues," 51 J. Forensic Sci. 1033 (2006).

Michael E. Sigman and Mary Williams, "Degraded Ignitable Liquids Database: Any Applied Study of Weathering and Bacterial Degradation on the Chromatographic Patterns of ASTM E 1618 Ignitable Liquid Classes", (December, 2016), National Criminal Justice Reference Service (Document Number 250468), www.ncjrs.gov/pdffiles1/nij/grants/250468.pdf.

United States Department of Justice, *A Guide for Explosion and Bombing Scene Investigation*, 2000.

Mary R. Williams *et al.*, "Adsorption Saturation and Chromatographic Distortion Effects on Passive Headspace Sampling with Activated Charcoal in Fire Debris Analysis," 50 J. Forensic Sci. 316 (2005).

3. USEFUL WEBSITES

American Academy of Forensic Sciences, www.aafs.org.

American Board of Criminalistics (ABC), www.criminalistics.com.

American Society for Testing and Materials, www.astm.org.

Bureau of Alcohol, Tobacco, Firearms, and Explosives, www.atf.gov.

CFItrainer.net—online fire/explosion investigation resource.

Federal Bureau of Investigation, www.fbi.gov.

FIRE.GOV—NIST Fire Research Division, www.nist.gov/el/fire-research-division-73300/firegov-fire-service.

International Association of Arson Investigators (IAAI), www.firearson.com.

International Association of Bomb Technicians and Investigators, www.iabti.org.

International Association of Fire Chiefs, www.iafc.org.

International Association of Fire Fighters (AFL-CI), www.iaff.org.

International Association for Fire Safety Science, www.iafss.org.

ModernFireBehavior.com—informational clearinghouse of modern fire behavior research.

National Fire Academy, www.usfa.fema.gov/training/nfa.

National Fire Incident Reporting System (NFIRS), http://nfirs.fema.gov.

National Fire Protection Association (NFPA), www.nfpa.org.

National Institute of Standards and Technology, www.nist.gov.

National Insurance Crime Bureau, www.nicb.org.

Technical/Scientific Working Group for Fire and Explosions, www.ncfs.ucf.edu/twgfex.

U.S. Fire Administration, Federal Emergency Management Agency, Department of Homeland Security, http://www.usfa.dhs.gov.

CHAPTER 7

TRACE EVIDENCE: MATERIALS

I. INTRODUCTION

§7.01 SCOPE OF THE CHAPTER

The term "trace evidence" is a catch-all term that applies to many types of physical evidence that may result from the transfer of small or microscopic quantities of materials.[1] As it is commonly used, trace evidence does not include the types of evidence handled by other specialists, such as DNA, fingerprint evidence, or gunshot residue evidence, even though small or microscopic quantities of physical

---

[1] Three common definitions of trace evidence are: "a very small amount of a substance, often too small to be measured;" "the surviving evidence of a former occurrence or action of some event or agent;" and "the analysis of materials that, because of their size or texture, transfer from one location to another and persist there for some period of time. Microscopy, either directly, or an adjunct to another instrument is involved." James Robertson and Claude Roux, "Trace Evidence: Here Today, Gone Tomorrow?" 50 SCI. & JUST. 18–22 (2010).

evidence may be involved. The examination and interpretation of trace evidence is handled by forensic scientists referred to as "trace evidence examiners," "criminalists," or other specialist labels. There is no one profession or job classification that claims all trace evidence analyses. Recognizing that the examiner of trace evidence may be designated by a variety of job titles, the term "trace examiner" will be used in this chapter for the sake of simplicity.

An expert microscopic or chemical analysis of small objects and particles can serve two primary functions: (1) in criminal cases it may be an investigative aid in the apprehension of an offender or the elimination of an individual as a possible suspect; and (2) in both civil and criminal litigation, it may permit the possible association of a small piece of physical evidence with a particular location, or establish the common origin of several items of trace evidence. In order to establish these connections, evidentiary principles be observed. Care must be taken in the collection of evidence so that it is not contaminated or altered; evidence must be properly marked and identified; the chain of possession must be carefully noted; and the proper analytical techniques must be followed by the trace examiner.

This chapter will discuss the general aspects of trace evidence analysis, the examination methods, common types of trace evidence, and evidentiary issues relevant to trace evidence. Because there is a considerable overlap with the instrumentation and methodology used in analysis of the various types of trace evidence and several different techniques may be used in each examination, these areas will be discussed generally. In the context of this chapter, the items of trace evidence discussed are hair, fibers, paint, and glass. These trace particles are the types of evidence most often analyzed by the typical trace examiner.

§7.02 TERMINOLOGY

Anagen Phase: The stage during which hair grows.

Catagen Phase: The intermediate stage of hair growth, also referred to as the transition phase.

Central Region: In a transverse plane, the area of the hair shaft toward the core area of the shaft.

Chromatography: A category of analytical techniques for the separation of mixtures involving the passing of a mixture dissolved in a "moving" phase through a fixed material phase. Chemical compounds differ in their retention on the fixed material phase and some are held to a greater extent than others. Weakly retained compounds move quickly through the system while those more strongly held move more slowly and complete their passage through the system later. Because of differences in this retention time, effective separation of a mixture into components can be made. Types of chromatography used in the analytical laboratory include gas, thin layer, and high performance liquid chromatography.

Concoidal Lines: Edge characteristics of glass fractures.

Cortex: The interior portion of a hair, containing pigment and other microscopic particles.

Cuticle: The outer layer of scales covering a hair, or the thickened scale or plate at the free end of some epithelial cells.

Distal End: In a longitudinal plane, the end of the hair shaft distant from the root.

Electrophoresis: Electrophoresis is a separation technique based on the differential transportation of charged species in an electric field through a conductive medium. Capillary electrophoresis (CE) separates compounds based on their size-to-charge ratio in the interior of a small capillary filled with an electrolyte. CE is a high speed, high resolution separation process that can be used for qualitative and quantitative analysis. CE uses small sample volumes and is compatible with a variety of detection methods. CE can be used on compounds that cannot be separated by gas chromatography, such as compounds that are thermally liable or nonvolatile.

Fluorescence: Production of light by radiant energy.

Gas Chromatography: A technique for the separation of components of a mixture in the vapor state. The sample to be examined is vaporized and carried through a small diameter column by a flowing gas stream. Components of the mixture dissolve in a viscous liquid inside the column and are retained to varying degrees to effect a separation. As a component of the mixture completes its passage through the column, it enters a detector which produces an electrical signal indicating its arrival and quantity. The signals from the detector are recorded on a moving chart to produce a chromatogram. The chart pattern is compared with the chart patterns of known materials for identification. A very small diameter column, or capillary, improves component separation, and for materials which move slowly through the column, increasing the temperature reduces analysis time.

High-performance liquid chromatography (HLPC): In high performance liquid chromatography the separation occurs through the relative solubility of the substance between the liquid-mobile phase and a stationary phase (usually a molecular layer bonded to a silica support). The sample is injected by a high-pressure pump into the liquid-mobile phase and moves through the column (the stationary phase) where the separation occurs and the components then pass through a detector.

Inductively coupled plasma-mass spectrometry (ICP-MS): Technique for metal analysis using radio frequency energy to detect and quantify metals.

Locard's Exchange Principle: Dr. Edmond Locard (Lyons, France) posited that when two objects are in contact with one another, each will leave traces on the other which may be revealed through microscopic techniques.

Mass Spectrometry: An analytical method to identify materials based upon production and detection of characteristic molecular fragments. The molecule is vaporized and fragmented in a high energy field. The fragments are separated by velocity or behavior in a magnetic field, detected and their mass determined. Because the fragments produced under controlled conditions are reproducible, they can be related to the original structure of the molecule. Combining the separating power of gas or liquid chromatography with the ability of the mass spectrometer to identify a compound provides a powerful tool for the identification of individual components in a mixture and is widely used to confirm preliminary identification of a suspected drug or toxin.

Medial Region: The portion of the hair shaft, in longitudinal plane, intermediate between the proximal and distal ends.

Medulla: The lengthwise core or axial structure of a hair.

Melanin: A pigment found in the hair, skin, and retina.

Peripheral Region: In a transverse plane, the portion of the hair shaft toward the outermost areas of the hair, including the cuticle and the outer areas of the cortex, distant from the medullary region.

Polymer: Any of a number of natural and synthetic compounds composed of usually high molecular weight consisting of up to millions of repeated linked units, each of a relatively simple and light molecule.

Proximal End: In a longitudinal place, the end of the hair shaft nearest the root.

Pyrolysis: The process of inducing chemical changes by heat or burning.

Qualitative Analysis: An analysis to determine the composition of a sample, *i.e.* what materials are present.

Quantitative Analysis: An analysis to determine the relative concentrations of one or more components of a sample.

Refractive Index: The ratio of the speed of light in a vacuum to the speed of light through a transparent medium

Spectrometry/Spectrography: A category of analytical techniques for identification of a chemical compound. Most types involve the measurement of light or other radiation absorbed by or emitted from a sample. The specific wavelengths of radiation absorbed/ emitted are related to the chemical structure of the molecule.

Measurement of the radiation's frequency or wavelength and/or the amount absorbed/emitted is used to identify a particular chemical species or determine the quantity present. Most types are named for the radiation used such as visible, infrared or ultraviolet light or x-ray.

Telogen Phase: The resting or dormant period during which hair does not grow and sheds naturally.

Thin-Layer Chromatography: Analytical separation method using a glass plate with a thin coating of silica gel, cellulose, or alumina as the stationary phase on which the sample is spotted. The plate is placed in a tank containing a small amount of solvent and separation occurs based on the relative affinity of the compounds between the moving phase (the solvent) and the stationary phase (the silica gel). The method is simple, inexpensive and sensitive to extremely low levels of a material in the sample. Spraying of the dried plate with a specific chemical reagent develops a color to aid in identifying the material in a particular spot.

§7.03 EVIDENTIARY USES

Trace evidence analysis was one of the first forensic science disciplines to be used in criminal cases. The first published American court opinion involving trace evidence was the 1882 Wisconsin decision in Knoll v. State,[2] involving a microscopic hair comparison. Trace evidence was also involved in many high profile criminal cases, including the Lindbergh kidnapping,[3] Ted Bundy's prosecution in Florida,[4] the Atlanta child killer case,[5] and the Green River murders.[6]

The identification and comparison of minute particles and objects plays an important role in other types of litigation as well. While the trace evidence analysis discussed in this chapter is presented more frequently in criminal cases, trace evidence analysis has application to civil litigation as well. Recovery and examination of paint and glass particles during a crime or an accident can provide reconstruction information. Trace evidence recovered from a hit-and-run victim can

---

[2] 12 N.W. 369 (Wis. 1882).

[3] The expert, Arthur Koehler, traced part of the wood ladder used to reach the child's second story bedroom from its mill source to a lumberyard near the defendant's home. He also testified that a piece of the ladder came from a floor board in the defendant's attic. *See* Shirley A. Graham, "Anatomy of the Lindbergh Kidnapping," 42 J. FORENSIC SCI. 368 (1977). *See also* Arthur Koehler, "Technique Used in Tracking the Lindbergh Kidnapping Ladder," 27 J. CRIM. L., C. & POL. SCI. 712 (1937).

[4] Edward J. Imwinkelried, "Forensic Hair Analysis: The Case Against the Underemployment of Scientific Evidence," 39 WASH. & LEE L. REV. 41, 43 (1982).

[5] Williams v. State, 251 Ga. 749, 312 S.E.2d 40 (1983)(a prosecution for two of twenty-eight killings of blacks in Atlanta, Georgia; the crux of the case against Williams was the fiber evidence).

[6] Transferred paint particles were used to establish an association between a suspect and the victims. S.G. Ryland and E.M. Suzuki, "Analysis of Paint Evidence" in L. Kobilinsky ed., *Forensic Chemistry Handbook,* Hoboken NJ: Wiley (2012), pp. 131–124.

provide valuable information to identify the vehicle involved in the collision. Similarly, trace evidence recovered from a suspected vehicle can associate it to the hit-and-run victim. The analysis of trace evidence can also be used in product liability cases to assist in the reconstruction of events. Any case for which the determining facts are dependent upon a reconstruction of events or associations between individuals, places, and objects may potentially involve trace evidence analysis.

II. GENERAL ASPECTS OF TRACE ANALYSIS

§7.04 TRANSFER AND PERSISTENCE

The basis for trace evidence analysis is the Locard Exchange Principle: "every contact leaves a trace." With the transfer of evidence (whether a hair, fiber, or other particle) a link can be established between two items. If the evidence persists for a period of time after the contact, it can later be detected and recovered. Transfer and persistence are the fundamental concepts that provide the evidential relevance for trace analysis. If a particle from one item is transferred to another item, the trier of fact can infer that the two items were in direct or indirect contact. For the particle transfer to have any probative value, however, the particle must persist in its new matrix for a sufficient period of time after the contact to enable it to be recovered and analyzed.

The concept of "evidence dynamics" must also be considered in understanding the relevance of trace analysis. The principles of transfer and persistence are neither one-directional nor uniform. The degree of transfer of material is affected by (1) the duration of contact; (2) the strength of the contact; (3) the nature of the trace material; and (4) the nature of the receiving matrix.[7] Transfer of trace evidence can produce secondary (or higher order) transfer as the receiving matrix establishes its own set of contacts.[8] For trace evidence, five factors greatly determine the persistence of trace materials: (1) the amount of material initially transferred; (2) the tenacity of the trace material; (3) the nature of post-contact activity; (4) redistribution/reincorporation mechanisms; and (5) retentive properties of the receiving matrix.[9]

---

[7] Sean D. McDermott, "Trace Evidence: Transfer, Persistence, and Value," in WILEY ENCYCLOPEDIA OF FORENSIC SCIENCE, (Jamieson A. & Moenssens A.A., eds) 2009 & online updates.

[8] J.C. French, R.M. Morgan, P. Baxendell, and P. A. Bell, "Multiple Transfers of Particulates and their Dissemination within Contact Networks," 52 SCI. & JUST. 33–41 (2012).

[9] Id., see also Sean D. McDermott, "Trace Evidence: Transfer, Persistence, and Value," in WILEY ENCYCLOPEDIA OF FORENSIC SCIENCE, (Jamieson A. & Moenssens A.A., eds) 2009 & online updates.

§7.05   EVIDENCE COLLECTION

Criminal investigators need to be extremely careful in collecting trace evidence. Much of trace evidence is barely visible to the naked eye and some trace evidence is only visible with enhanced viewing techniques. In the recovery of trace evidence, the investigators must exercise care so as not to destroy, alter, or contaminate the trace evidence or other evidence that may be of value to other examiners. A fundamental concept in the collection of trace evidence is sampling: "the removal of a part of a substance to assess the materials present in the whole."[10]

The Scientific Working Group for Materials Analysis (SWGMAT)[11] recommended voluntary guidelines for trace evidence recovery designed to preserve the integrity and significance of the trace evidence.[12] The guidelines require proper documentation of the collection process and appropriate safeguards against contamination and loss through sample packaging and security. For collection, the guidelines describe the following techniques: picking (using forceps), lifting (using adhesive tape), scraping (using a spatula), vacuum sweeping, combing, and clipping.[13] "Dislodging," a collection method often used for glass and paint particles on textiles, involves beating the textile from the back with a plastic rod over a sterile surface for recovery.[14] The technique used is determined based on the nature of the evidence, scene considerations, and case circumstances.[15] Sufficient representative known samples

---

[10] Mary Giblin, "Sampling Trace Evidence," in WILEY ENCYCLOPEDIA OF FORENSIC SCIENCE, (Jamieson A. & Moenssens A.A., eds) 2009 & online updates (discussing principles of sampling trace evidence, population determination, sampling plans used for trace evidence, sampling questions, and methods of trace evidence sample recovery).

[11] SWGMAT was formed by the Department of Justice with law enforcement officials to formulate guidelines applicable to the analysis of fibers, glass, paint, hair, and tape. The SWG later added "associate members" from outside law enforcement in addition to "regular" members from law enforcement. The SWG is no longer active, but its work is described by the American Society of Trace Evidence Examiners. *See* http://www.asteetrace.org.

The National Institute of Standards and Technology Organization of Scientific Area Committees has a Materials (Trace) Subcommittee to support the development and promulgation of forensic science consensus documentary standards and guidelines related to the examination and interpretation of physical evidence that may result from the transfer of small or minute quantities of materials. The SWGMAT standards are under review for possible adoption or revision by that subcommittee. *See* https://www.nist.gov/topics/forensic-science/materials-trace-subcommittee (last accessed February 27, 2017).

[12] SWGMAT, "Trace Evidence Recovery Guidelines," January 1998 (available at: https://www.nist.gov/topics/forensic-science/materials-trace-subcommittee)(last accessed February 27, 2017).

[13] Id. at Section 5. *See also* SWGMAT, "Forensic Human Hair Examination Guidelines," April 2005, at Section 7; SWGMAT, "Forensic Fiber Examination Guidelines," April 1999); SWGMAT, "Collection, Handling, and Identification of Glass," July 2004; SWGMAT, "Forensic Paint Analysis and Comparison Guidelines," May 2000, at Section 7 (all available at: https://www.nist.gov/topics/forensic-science/materials-trace-subcommittee)(last   accessed February 27, 2017).

[14] *See* Maurice Olderiks, Martin Baiker, Jill van Velzen and Jaap va der Weerd, "Recovery of Spray Paint Traces from Clothing," 60 J. Forensic Sci. 428–434 (2015).

[15] SWGMAT, "Trace Evidence Recovery Guidelines," January 1998 at Section 5 (available at: https://www.nist.gov/topics/forensic-science/materials-trace-subcommittee).

must be collected to enable comparison with the questioned trace evidence. This process requires collection of sufficient samples to represent all variations within the item.[16]

If the trace evidence will be sectioned for further examination, the examiner may embed the sample in a medium to permit the sectioning. The specimen type and the analysis type should be considered in selecting an embedding medium[17] to avoid interacting with the specimen, to ensure stability, and enable the examiner to obtain cross-sections of the appropriate thickness. Conventional epoxy resins were the standard for many years, but blue-light curing acrylic resins are gaining acceptance. These acrylic resins are cured by exposure to blue light, such as from a high intensity LED flashlight, and do not require pressure, heat, or ultraviolet radiation to cure.[18] With commercially-available kits,[19] acrylic resins provide a simple, cost effective embedding process.

§7.06 INTERPRETATION ISSUES

Although trace evidence analysis has been judicially accepted for over 100 years, it is one of the fields of forensic science where the fundamental limitations have not always been recognized by the courts. The probative value of most common types of trace evidence involve mass-produced materials (e.g., glass, fibers, paint) with little to no individual variability. In the absence of exceptional circumstances, the probative value of most trace evidence is limited to class associations. These limitations were well-recognized in the forensic science community, but some trace examiners and legal advocates made overstatements or exaggerations in some cases concerning the value of the class associations.

Trace evidence was one of the forensic science fields most directly impacted by the 2009 NAS Report.[20] Although the report emphasized that it was not addressing admissibility issues,[21] many of the conclusions of the report concerning the scientific validity of various analytical techniques have resulted in changes in how forensic science evidence is viewed by the courts and practiced by the forensic science community. Of particular relevance to trace evidence analysis was the conclusion that "[a]mong the existing forensic methods, only nuclear DNA analysis has

---

[16] Id. at Section 6.

[17] Ethan Groves and Christopher S. Palenik, "Applications of Blue Light-curing Acrylic Resin to Forensic Sample Preparation and Microtomy," 61 J. Forensic Sci. 489, 489 (2016)(citing M. Wachowiak, "Routine and High-Volume Preparation of Embedded Coating Cross Sections," 50(4) Microscope 147–153 (2002).

[18] Ethan Groves and Christopher S. Palenik, "Applications of Blue Light-curing Acrylic Resin to Forensic Sample Preparation and Microtomy," 61 J. Forensic Sci. 489, 489 (2016).

[19] Tuffleye® is a blue light-curing acrylic resin that was originally adapted by a dentist for fly-tying in the fly fishing community. Id. See also http://www.wetahook.net/page2/page2.html (last accessed August 25, 2016).

[20] National Academies of Science, *Strengthening Forensic Science in the United States: A Path Forward* (National Academies Press, 2009)(*hereinafter "2009 NAS Report"*).

[21] "No judgment is made about past convictions and no view is expressed as to whether courts should reassess cases that have already been tried." Id. at p. 85.

been rigorously shown to have the capacity to consistently, and with a high degree of certainty, demonstrate a connection between an evidentiary sample and a specific individual or source."[22] This finding directly contradicts the position of some trace examiners that comparisons can individualize a trace evidence sample to a single source to the exclusion of all others.

The 2009 NAS Report highly criticized attempts to individualize trace evidence, but did not discount the value of trace evidence analysis of class characteristics to narrow the number of potential contributing sources. For each of the fields specifically discussed, the report recognized that analytical techniques can yield reliable information about class characteristics.[23] Beyond class characteristics, however, the report concluded:

> [T]estimony linking microscopic hair analysis with particular defendants is highly unreliable. In cases where there seems to be a morphological match (based on microscopic examination), it must be confirmed using mtDNA analysis; microscopic studies are of limited probative value. The committee found no scientific support for the use of hair comparisons for individualization in the absence of nuclear DNA. Microscopy and mtDNA analysis can be used in tandem and add to one another's value for classifying a common source, but no studies have been performed to specifically quantify the reliability of their joint use.[24]

> [T]here have been no studies to inform judgments about whether environmentally related changes discerned in particular fibers are distinctive enough to reliably individualize their source, and there have been no studies that characterize either reliability or error rates in the procedures. Thus, a "match" means only that the fibers could have come from the same type of garment, carpet, or furniture; it can provide only class evidence.[25]

> As with fiber evidence, analysis of paints and coatings is based on a solid foundation of chemistry to enable class identification. . . . However, the community has not defined precise criteria for determining whether two samples come from a common source class.[26]

Another conclusion of the report also implicates trace evidence comparisons: that more research needs to be conducted to investigate the effects of observer bias and human error on conclusions from techniques

---

[22] Id. at p. 100.

[23] Id. at p. 157 (hair), 161 (fibers), 168 (paint).

[24] Id. at p. 161.

[25] Id. at p. 163.

[26] Id. at p. 170.

with a subjective component. Trace evidence comparisons that are dependent on "sufficient" commonalities without objective standards for declaring two samples "matching" are highly subjective and may be greatly influenced by observer effects such as contextual bias and suggestion. One of the first studies to document biasing effects involved hair comparison evidence.[27] Much commentary and some research have been offered in the area of observer effects.[28]

The report's recommendation for implementing standard terminology has been embraced in most trace evidence fields, although the terminology is evolving. A professional forum covering trace evidence, the Scientific Working Group for Materials Analysis (SWGMAT), adopted guidelines and standards that recommend specific terms and phrasings for conclusions.[29] Although voluntary, these guidelines do provide a standard framework for the field. SWGMAT recommended guidelines for expert reporting that emphasize providing a written report detailing all relevant sample identification information and essential facts, assumptions, or information relied upon to form the opinions and conclusions expressed in the report, including any limitations in conclusions or opinions.[30] More recently, the National Commission on Forensic Science (NCFS) issued a document concerning the dangers of inconsistent terminology, specifically referencing a case involving hair comparison:

> When terms are not clearly defined, they might not convey their intended meaning. In *Williamson v. Reynolds*, [904 F. Supp. 1529 (E.D. Okla. 1995), rev'd *Williamson v. Ward*, 110 F.3d 1508 (10th Cir. 1997),] for example, an expert testified that hair samples were "consistent microscopically." The question becomes, "what does this term mean?" Does it mean the same as "consistent with?" Without further explanation, which was not provided, the evidence may have little probative value, but the jury may not appreciate this fact. In fact, in *Williamson*, the problem was exacerbated because the expert during the trial went on to explain: "In other words, hairs are not an absolute identification, but they either came from this

---

[27] Larry S. Miller, "Procedural Bias in Forensic Science Examinations of Human Hair," 11 LAW & HUM. BEHAV. 157, 161 (1987)("The findings of the present study raise some concern regarding the amount of unintentional bias among human hair identification examiners . . . A preconceived conclusion that a questioned hair sample and a known hair sample originated from the same individual may influence the examiner's opinion when the samples are similar.").

[28] *See* William C. Thompson, "Interpretation: Observer Effects," in WILEY ENCYCLOPEDIA OF FORENSIC SCIENCE, (Jamieson A. & Moenssens A.A., eds) 2009 & online updates; Itiel E. Dror, "Cognitive Forensics and Experimental Research about Bias in Forensic Casework," 52 SCI. & JUST. 128–130 (2012); Itiel E. Dror, "Letter to the Editor: Expectations, Contextual Information, and Other Cognitive Influences in Forensic Laboratories," 52 SCI. & JUST. 132 (2012); P. Brauner, "Letter to the Editor: RE. Subjectivity and Bias in Forensic DNA Mixture Interpretation," 52 SCI. & JUST. 131 (2012).

[29] *See* http://www.asteetrace.org/WebPages.cfm?action=viewCat&BIZ_UNL_id=41559.

[30] SWGMAT, "Expert Reporting Guideline," January 2009.

individual or there is—could be another individual somewhere in the world that would have the same characteristics to their hair." This phrasing suggests that very few people in the world would have "consistent" hair—erroneous.

This example highlights the problem with terminology that overstates the value of the information in the context of testimony. When examiners are trying to explain their findings but do not have clear and concise terminology upon which to rely, there is a temptation to try to clarify, which can lead to redefining the term, sometimes overstating the conclusion and creating even more confusion.[31]

In September, 2016, the President's Council of Advisors on Science and Technology (PCAST) approved a report to the President on "Forensic Science in Criminal Courts: Ensuring Scientific Validity of Feature-Comparison Methods" (hereinafter "2016 PCAST Report").[32] Like the NAS Report, the 2016 PCAST Report focused on several forensic science disciplines, including hair comparison analysis. Unlike the NAS, PCAST specifically sought to address questions of scientific validity, both foundational validity and validity as applied. Concerning hair analysis, PCAST did not conduct a comprehensive review of the discipline, but did review the studies relied upon by the Department of Justice as support for the conclusion that "microscopic hair comparison has been demonstrated to be a valid and reliable scientific methodology."[33] PCAST concluded that "based on their methodology and results, the papers described in the DOJ supporting document do not provide a scientific basis for concluding that microscopic hair examination is a valid and reliable process."[34] Contrary to the DOJ position that appropriate estimates of accuracy are unnecessary for

---

[31] National Commission on Forensic Science, "Inconsistent Terminology" (adopted April 30, 2015), at pp. 4–5 (internal citations omitted)(available at: https://www.justice.gov/ncfs/work-products-adopted-commission)(last accessed August 25, 2016).

A 2015 joint review by the FBI and the Innocence Project concerning hair examination testimony found that examiners made erroneous statements in over 90% of cases. These errors overstated the probative value of the comparison analysis. See https://www.fbi.gov/news/press rel/press-releases/fbi-testimony-on-microscopic-hair-analysis-contained-errors-in-at-least-90-percent-of-cases-in-ongoing-review (last accessed September 20, 2016). For more information on the ongoing review project, see https://www.fbi.gov/services/laboratory/scientific-analysis/fbidoj-microscopic-hair-comparison-analysis-review (last accessed September 20, 2016).

[32] Executive Office of the President, President's Council of Advisors on Science and Technology, "Forensic Science in Criminal Courts: Ensuring Scientific Validity of Feature-Comparison Methods," September 2016 (available at: https://obamawhitehouse.archives.gov/blog/2016/09/20/pcast-releases-report-forensic-science-criminal-courts)(last accessed February 27, 2017).

[33] DOJ included this conclusion in a draft standard submitted for public comment. See Department of Justice Proposed Uniform Language for Testimony and Reports for Forensic Hair Examination Discipline and Supporting Documentation for Department of Justice Proposed Uniform Language for Testimony and Reports for the Forensic Hair Examination Discipline (available at: https://www.justice.gov/dag/proposed-uniform-language-documents-anthropology-explosive-chemistry-explosive-devices-geology)(last accessed September 20, 2016).

[34] 2016 PCAST Report at p. 120.

conclusions that hair samples are "similar—or even indistinguishable," PCAST found these conclusions "scientifically meaningless [with] no probative value, and considerable potential for prejudicial impact."[35]

In addition to the criticisms in the 2009 NAS Report and the 2016 PCAST Report, trace evidence expert testimony has been implicated in several wrongful convictions of individuals later exonerated by DNA testing. A study of 200 DNA exonerations found that expert testimony on hair evidence was involved in 34 cases, soil comparison testimony in 5 cases, and fiber comparison testimony in 1 case.[36] Additional studies also suggested that flawed scientific testimony contributed to wrongful convictions.[37] In April, 2012, the Washington Post ran a series of articles reporting on hundreds of cases where hair and fiber comparison testimony may have falsely implicated the innocent.[38]

Against that backdrop, the field of trace evidence has continued to evolve and remains an integral part of criminal investigations and civil litigation to support claims of association and to help the trier of fact answer questions of "what happened." The field continues to need additional research and, as with all forensic science disciplines, benefits greatly from standardization efforts and improved training for practitioners.

III. INSTRUMENTATION AND ANALYTICAL METHODS

§7.07 MICROSCOPY

Perhaps the most basic and oldest instrument in the examination of physical evidence is the microscope. There are many different types of microscopes. Among those frequently used by trace examiners are: stereomicroscopes, polarizing microscopes, and comparison microscopes.

A stereomicroscope is two compound microscopes[39] which are aligned side-by-side to provide a stereoscopic image. In the hands of the trained

---

[35] 2016 PCAST Report at p. 121.

[36] Brandon L. Garrett, "Judging Innocence," 108 COLUM. L. REV. 55, 81 (2008). This does not necessarily mean the testimony was erroneous, but the public perception has clearly been that the evidence was misused.

[37] See Brandon L. Garrett and Peter J. Neufled, "Invalid Forensic Science Testimony and Wrongful Convictions," 95 VA. L. REV. 1, 34–84 (2009); Paul C. Giannelli, "Wrongful Convictions and Forensic Science: The Need to Regulate Crime Labs," 86 N.C. L. REV. 163, 165–170, 172–207 (2007).

[38] See, e.g., Spencer S. Hsu, "Convicted Defendants Left Uninformed of Forensic Flaws Found by Justice Dept.," Washington Post, April 16, 2012 (available at: http://www.washingtonpost.com/local/crime/convicted-defendants-left-uninformed-of-forensic-flaws-found-by-justice-dept/2012/04/16/gIQAWTcgMT_story.html)(last accessed February 27, 2017).

[39] A compound microscope has more than one lens so that the image magnified by one lens can be magnified by another lens. Today, the term microscope generally refers to a compound microscope with one lens referred to as the objective lens and the other lens referred to as the eyepiece. See James Robertson, "Microscopy: Low Power," in WILEY

analyst, this instrument affords a magnified image of the object exactly as it appears in nature, the three dimensions of length, breadth, and depth being visible. It is employed in the examination of bulk items such as clothing and weapons, and also minute items such as glass, hairs, fibers, paint, soil and other trace materials. One of the best uses of the instrument is to extract and isolate minute particles that may be present on a larger item and to separate debris into separate constituents.

A second important instrument at the disposal of the trace examiner is the polarized light microscope. This unit is equipped with two polarizing elements positioned in the optical path of the microscope and allows for the study of specimens in very exact detail with respect to their physical and chemical properties. The assignment of mathematical values to the results of these examinations and tests makes this instrument extremely valuable in the analysis of trace evidence.[40]

The comparison microscope is another widely used and valuable instrument. This microscope actually consists of two microscopes with identical optical systems, matched objectives and eyepieces and identical light sources of equal intensity. The two microscopes are connected by an optical bridge.[41] One specimen is placed on the stage of one microscope, and a second specimen placed on the other microscope stage. When these specimens are observed through the optical bridge they appear side by side as if both specimens were in one field. This instrument is used mainly in the comparison of morphological characteristics. To the trace examiner, it is extremely valuable in the comparison of hairs and fibers.

The phase contrast, interference, and dark field microscopes are also available to the trace examiner. These instruments, through the use of special objectives, condensers, and illuminators, diffract certain rays of light coming through the objective, improving the resolving power of the microscope and thereby exhibiting greater detail of the object being examined. The use of these instruments is usually resorted to in the examination of certain types of specimens or to search for characteristics that will not be revealed in great detail by the ordinary bright field microscope.

Forms of microscopy routinely used by trace examiners include fluorescence microscopy, UV-vis microspectrophotometry, and scanning electron microscopy. Analysis by fluorescence by reflected or incident light, also referred to as epifluorescene, uses energy stimulation of the sample (through ion, x-ray, electron, or photon radiation or chemical reactions) to generate luminescence that can be measured to assist in the

---

ENCYCLOPEDIA OF FORENSIC SCIENCE, (Jamieson A. & Moenssens A.A., eds) 2009 & online updates.

   [40] *See* Thomas J. Hopen and Malcolm Davis, "Microscopy: Light Microscopes," in WILEY ENCYCLOPEDIA OF FORENSIC SCIENCE, (Jamieson A. & Moenssens A.A., eds) 2009 & online updates.

   [41] *See* James Robertson, "Microscopy: High Power," in WILEY ENCYCLOPEDIA OF FORENSIC SCIENCE, (Jamieson A. & Moenssens A.A., eds) 2009 & online updates.

identification of the sample components.[42] Ultraviolet-visible microspectrophotometry (UV-Vis) uses absorption or reflection in the ultraviolet of visible light range to distinguish components. Scanning electron microscopy (SEM) uses electrons to overcome the optical limits of light and permits the visualization of very small objects. When combined with energy-dispersive x-ray spectroscopy, SEM-EDX allows the measurement of the emitted x-ray wavelengths for elemental analysis.[43]

§7.08 CHEMICAL ANALYSIS[44]

Microcrystalline tests involve treatment of a suspect material with a specific chemical reagent to produce crystals of characteristic color or shape. The crystals are examined under a microscope using either ordinary or polarized light. Microcrystalline tests can be used to help identify the elements in a sample. The test benefits include ease of use, minimal equipment costs (glass slides and drops of the appropriate reagent), and readily observable crystal structures that can be distinguished by the trained analyst. Limitations include the narrow time window in which the probative crystal structures can be observed, the use of a relatively large sample (several milligrams), and the need for careful imaging or a second procedure to obtain confirmation of the results from a second analyst.

Similar to crystal tests are chemical spot tests or solvent tests in which a reagent or solvent is added to a small amount of the suspect material. The chemical spot test reactions observed may be development of a particular color with a single reagent or observation of a series of colors or other changes occurring as different reagents are added. Reactions for solvent tests include softening, swelling, curling, dissolution, fluorescence, and color changes. Spot and solvent tests are used primarily as screening or presumptive tests. For definitive identification, the identity of the material is confirmed by other methods.

§7.09 CHROMATOGRAPHY

1. HIGH PERFORMANCE LIQUID CHROMATOGRAPHY AND THIN LAYER CHROMATOGRAPHY

Liquid chromatography describes a category of analytical techniques for the separation of mixtures involving the passing of a mixture dissolved in a "moving" phase through a fixed material phase.

---

[42] *See* Thomas J. Hopen and Malcolm Davis, "Microscopy: Light Microscopes," in WILEY ENCYCLOPEDIA OF FORENSIC SCIENCE, (Jamieson A. & Moenssens A.A., eds) 2009 & online updates.

[43] *See* Aita Khanmy-Vital, "Microscopy: Scanning Electron Microscopy," in WILEY ENCYCLOPEDIA OF FORENSIC SCIENCE, (Jamieson A. & Moenssens A.A., eds) 2009 & online updates.

[44] *See generally* William M. Schneck, "Microchemistry," in WILEY ENCYCLOPEDIA OF FORENSIC SCIENCE, (Jamieson A. & Moenssens A.A., eds) 2009 & online updates.

Chemical compounds differ in their retention on the fixed material phase and some are held to a greater extent than others. Weakly retained compounds move quickly through the system while those more strongly held move more slowly and complete their passage through the system later. Because of differences in this retention time, effective separation of a mixture into components can be made. Types of chromatography used in the analytical laboratory include high performance liquid chromatography (HLPC) and thin layer chromatography (TLC).

HPLC is a separation and comparison technique that provides preliminary identification of analytes and sample components and can be used as a quantitation method. Because HPLC is non-destructive, samples can be recovered for additional testing. Limitations include the necessity for appropriate standards with each set of samples, high purity solvents, and pre-test equilibration time. The possibility of sample carry-over also requires constant monitoring and implementation of rigorous quality control measures.

TLC is a rapid separation and comparison technique that provides preliminary data on the identity of an analyte and the presence of additional sample components based on differences in retention factors (Rf). The retention factor of the compound is calculated as the distance traveled divided by the distance traveled by the developing solvent. TLC may be used as a preparative method and, if non-destructive detection methods are used, TLC may be combined with other methods for greater selectivity. TLC is one of the most widely used separation techniques due in part to its simplicity and low cost. Detection of the compounds can be made by fluorescence or spray reagents, such as FPN reagent (ferric chloride/perchloric acid/nitric acid), Marquis reagent (formaldehyde and concentrated sulfuric acid), and Mandelin's reagent (ammonium vanadate in sulfuric acid).

The benefits of TLC include the option to run multiple samples simultaneously, easy visualization of results, and increased selectivity from the use of specific eluents. Limitations are the moderate level of discrimination, the need to match standard and sample concentrations, and different pattern development from salt forms of certain compounds.

2. GAS CHROMATOGRAPHY

Gas chromatography (GC) is a technique for separation of components of a mixture in the vapor state. The sample to be examined is vaporized and carried through a small diameter column by a flowing gas stream. Components of the mixture dissolve in a viscous liquid inside the column and are retained to varying degrees to effect a separation. As a component of the mixture completes its passage through the column, it enters a detector which produces an electrical signal indicating its arrival and quantity. The signals from the detector are recorded on a moving chart to produce a chromatogram. The chart pattern is compared with the chart patterns of known materials for identification. A very small diameter column, or capillary, improves component separation. For materials which move slowly through the capillary column, increasing the temperature will reduce analysis time.

The technique can be used as a screening tool or to prepare samples for more discriminating techniques. Because detector response is proportional to sample concentration, GC can be used as a quantitative method. Although very specific, different compounds may have the same retention time, so this method may be combined with other analytical methods to be more discriminating. Limitations also include the inability to identify salts (which are dissociated during the injection process) and nonvolatile compounds.

GC is frequently combined with various detectors for greater selectivity. Gas chromatography mass spectrometry (GC/MS) is frequently used to identify unknown compounds, because of the high specificity and sensitivity and the available of a library of spectra for comparison with a large range of compounds. GC may also be combined with pyrolysis (PGC) which is a destructive technique that uses heat to decompose organic components for analysis.

§7.10 SPECTROMETRY

Trace examination also uses mass spectrometry, infrared spectrometry, x-ray spectrometry, raman spectrometry, inductively coupled plasma-optical emission spectrophotometry, and inductively coupled plasma-mass spectrometry. Spectroscopy is a category of analytical techniques for identification of a chemical compound. Most types involve the measurement of light or other radiation absorbed by or emitted from a sample. The specific wavelengths of radiation absorbed/emitted are related to the chemical structure of the molecule. Measurement of the radiation's frequency or wavelength and/or the amount absorbed/emitted is used to identify a particular chemical species or determine the quantity present.

1. MASS SPECTROMETRY

Mass spectrometry (MS) is an analytical method to identify materials based upon production and detection of characteristic molecular fragments. The molecule is vaporized and fragmented in a high energy field. The fragments are separated by velocity or behavior in a magnetic field, detected, and their mass determined. Because the fragments produced under controlled conditions are reproducible, they can be related to the original structure of the molecule. Combining the separating power of gas or liquid chromatography with the ability of the mass spectrometer to identify a compound provides a powerful tool for the identification of individual components in a mixture.

2. INFRARED SPECTROMETRY[45]

Infrared spectrometry (IR) involves the measurement of light or other radiation absorbed by or emitted from a sample. The specific wavelengths of radiation absorbed/emitted are related to the chemical structure of the molecule. Measurement of the radiation's frequency or wavelength and/or the amount absorbed/emitted is used to identify a particular chemical species or determine the quantity present. Infrared spectroscopy (IR) has very high discriminating power. Fourier transform infrared (FTIR) spectrometers, which use smaller samples than traditional IR instruments, are common in most laboratories. In addition to a high discriminatory power, benefits of using IR include sample recovery for additional qualitative and quantitative testing. Limitations include the need to address volatility, heat, and pressure effects to avoid chemical composition changes during analysis.

3. X-RAY SPECTROMETRY

Scanning electron microscopy with energy dispersive x-ray spectrometry uses a focused electron beam scanned over the surface of a sample and measures the energy dispersed by the emitting x-rays. The technique is nondestructive, fast, and useful with small samples.

X-ray fluorescence spectrometry measures the x-rays emitted from a sample following excitation by an x-ray source. The energies of the detected x-rays are used to identify the elements present and the intensities of the x-ray peaks can be used to quantify the concentration of the element in the sample. The technique is nondestructive, fast, needs minimal sample preparation, but requires matrix-based standards for accurate results.

The x-ray diffractometry (XRD) technique utilizes x-rays passing through a crystallized substance and interacting with the electrons in the atoms. When the x-ray photons collide with electrons, some photons from the incident beam will be deflected away from the original direction of travel (diffraction). In crystals, the atoms are arranged in a regularized structure and the diffracted waves consist of sharp interference maxima (peaks) with the same symmetry as the distribution of atoms. The peaks in an x-ray diffraction pattern correlate to the interatomic distances. Measuring the diffraction pattern allows the analyst to deduce the distribution of atoms in a substance.

4. RAMAN SPECTROSCOPY

Raman spectroscopy, a form of vibrational spectroscopy, measures the spectra of scattered radiation, giving much the same information as IR; however, a specific electronic transition (one that is "Raman active")

---

[45] *See generally* K. Paul Kirkbride, "Microscopy: FTIR" in WILEY ENCYCLOPEDIA OF FORENSIC SCIENCE, (Jamieson A. & Moenssens A.A., eds) 2009 & online updates.

must be used. A sample is illuminated with a laser beam. The laser light interacts with molecular vibrations resulting in the energy of the laser photons being shifted up or down. The resulting light is collected with a lens and sent to a detector. The shift in energy gives information about the vibrational modes in the system.

Although Raman spectroscopy has the benefits that it requires little or no sample preparation before analysis, can be conducted rapidly, and produces information through nondestructive testing, the technique has a lower discriminating power. Traditional Raman spectroscopy also produces a relatively weak signal that may be obscured by fluorescence. The discriminating ability of Raman spectroscopy varies depending on the fiber type, color, and the laser wavelength used.[46] Studies have shown that Raman spectroscopy provides complementary information for traditional analytical methods (microscopy and chemical methods) to provide further discriminating information for the analysis of fibers.[47] Raman spectroscopy is also useful for paint comparison. In vehicle cases where the suspected vehicle is unknown, the method may provide sufficient information to identify the color and make of the vehicle.[48]

5. INDUCTIVELY COUPLED PLASMA METHODS

In inductively coupled plasma-optical emission spectrophotometry (ICP-OES) an electrical discharge is initiated in a flowing stream of inert gas and sustained in a radio frequency field. The sample is introduced into the resulting plasma causing atomization, ionization, and excitation of the atoms in the sample. As the atoms move to lower excited states, they emit light at characteristic wavelengths which can be dispersed with a spectrophotometer into a spectrum with measurable intensities. The spectrum can be compared to standards for identification of the elements present and the measured intensities can used to quantify the relative concentration of the element present in the sample.

Inductively coupled plasma can also be paired with mass spectrometry (ICP-MS) as an analytical method for lower detection limits and greater sensitivity (but poorer precision) that ICP-OES.[49]

---

[46] Patrick Buzzini and Genevieve Massonnet, "The Discrimination of Colored Acrylic, Cotton, and Wool Textile Fibers Using Micro-Raman Spectroscopy. Part 1: *In situ* Detection and Characterization of Dyes," 58 J. Forensic Sci. 1593–1600 (2013).

[47] Patrick Buzzini and Genevieve Massonnet, "The Analysis of Colored Acrylic, Cotton, and Wool Textile Fibers Using Micro-Raman Spectroscopy. Part 2: Comparison with Traditional Methods of Fiber Examination," 60 J. Forensic Sci. 712–720 (2015); Laurence C. Abbott, Stephen N. Batchelor, John R. Lindsay-Smith and John N. Moore, "Resonance Raman and UV-Visible Spectroscopy of Black Dyes on Textiles," 200 Forensic Sci. Int'l 54–63 (2010).

[48] Janina Zieba-Palus and Beata Trzcinska, "Application of Infrared and Raman Spectroscopy in Paint Trace Examination," 58 J. Forensic Sci. 1359–1363 (2013).

[49] LA—ICP-OES has proven useful in the elemental analysis of glass. Emily R. Schenk and Jose R. Almirall, "Elemental Analysis of Glass by Laser Ablation Inductively Coupled

IV. COMMON TRACE EVIDENCE

§7.11   HAIR

1.   THE NATURE OF HAIR

Hair is indigenous to the mammalian species. Hair grows from the hair follicle located in the skin. The root or bulb of the hair is embedded in the follicle. As the hair cells harden, they are extruded from the follicle with the results that the hair grows outward from the root end. The growth rate of human hair is about one-half inch every thirty days, although considerable variation may be noted. Hardening of the hair cells results from the influx of the inert protein keratin. Hair structure resembles somewhat the scales of fish, with overlapping scales giving it the appearance of a spiral. An important feature of hair is that it retains its structural characteristics for extremely long periods. The cuticle layer imparts this resistance to chemical decomposition and stability.[50]

Microscopic hair examination may be used for associative and investigative purposes and to assist in crime scene reconstruction;[51] however, microscopic hair analysis does not identify a hair as coming from a particular individual.[52] Arguably, the most that can be stated is that a questioned hair is consistent with a hair sample of known origin in all microscopic characteristics.[53] DNA analysis, discussed in Chapter 14 *supra*, must be conducted on hairs to reach more definitive conclusions concerning identity.[54]

Plasma Optical Emission Spectrometry (LA-ICP-OES)," 217 FORENSIC SCI. INT'L 222–228 (2012).

[50] *See generally* James Robertson, "Hair: Microscopic Analysis," in WILEY ENCYCLOPEDIA OF FORENSIC SCIENCE, (Jamieson A. & Moenssens A.A., eds) 2009 & online updates.

[51] For a detailed discussion of the scientific basis for microscopic hair comparison and analysis, *see* Cary T. Oein, "Forensic Hair Comparison: Background Information for Interpretation," 11(2) FORENSIC SCI. COMM. April 2009 (available at: http://www.fbi.gov/about-us/lab/forensic-science-communications/fsc/april2009/review/2009_04_review02.htm/) (last accessed December 13, 2016).

[52] SWGMAT, "Forensic Human Hair Examination Guidelines," April 2005, at Sections 1 and 6 (available at: https://www.nist.gov/topics/forensic-science/materials-trace-subcommittee) (last accessed February 27, 2017).

[53] The National Commission on Forensic Science, however, has suggested this terminology ("consistent with") may be misleading and has called on the forensic science community to consider using more clarifying language to avoid overstating or exaggerating the probative value of the conclusions. *See* National Commission on Forensic Science, "Inconsistent Terminology," adopted April 30, 2015 (available at: https://www.justice.gov/ncfs/work-products-adopted-commission)(last accessed August 25, 2016).

[54] DNA has come to play an important role in hair studies and analysis. It is understood that microscopic hair comparisons cannot state whether a given hair came from a particular individual. However, if a hair of unknown origin that is being examined possesses its root, nuclear DNA analysis is able to compare it with known specimens to determine whether a positive match exists. Even when the root of a hair is not present, it may still be possible to link

Among the issues that the trace examiner seeks to resolve are:

1.   Is the questioned particle hair?

2.   If so, from what species does the hair belong?

3.   If human, from what part of the body did it come?

To determine if a specimen is mammalian hair or vegetable fiber, the trace examiner may examine the specimen microscopically. Hair is recognized by the presence of a root (when present) embedded in the hair follicle, and a shaft. External mammalian hair consists of three layers: (1) the surface cuticle composed of transparent pigment-free overlapping scales pointing toward the tip end of the hair; (2) the cortex or cornified shaft surrounding the medulla and containing some color pigment granules of melanin; and (3) the medulla or core which contains cellular debris and some pigments. Synthetic hairs or other fibers do not possess these three elements. In the absence of melanin granules, hair is white or gray. The color and distribution of these granules are important for identification purposes. There are two principal types of mammalian hair, namely short, fine fuzz, and long stiff strands which are commonly known as down and guard hairs, respectively.

Once the specimen is determined to be a hair, the next determination is the species of origin.[55] Human hair has certain microscopically observable characteristics which permit differentiation from hair of other mammals:

- A medullary index, the relation between the diameter of the medulla and the whole hair, can be used to identify species origin from medullary diameter. A low index is indicative of human origin, because the medullary layer of the hair in cross section is narrower in man and a few other mammals (such as the horse and the monkey) than in other mammals.

- The cortex layer of the human hair contains most of the pigment granules while in other mammals pigmentation is found primarily in the medulla.

- In human hair, the cuticle scales overlap smoothly, while in other mammalian species they protrude in a rough serrated form.

- A squared-off end from cutting may suggest human origin.

---

the hair with a high degree of statistical probability to that of a known person by examining the mitochondrial DNA. Jacon C. Kolowski et al., "A Comparison Study of Hair Examination Methodologies," 49 J. FORENSIC SCI. 1253 (2004).

[55] It may be difficult to differentiate between animals of different species by hair microscopic comparison. *See generally* Silvana R. Tridico, "Hair: Animal," in WILEY ENCYCLOPEDIA OF FORENSIC SCIENCE, (Jamieson A. & Moenssens A.A., eds) 2009 & online updates.

- Human hair tapers gradually to a point; animal hair comes to a point abruptly.

If the hair is determined to be human, the trace examiner may try to determine the body area or origin, generally distinguishing between scalp, body, and pubic hair. Head (scalp) hair is ordinarily more uniform in diameter size and has a more even pigment distribution than hair from other body parts. Pubic hairs are wiry and have more constrictions and twists than other hairs. They ordinarily have unevenly distributed pigments and continuously broad medullas. They also may vary in diameter along the shaft. Hairs from the chest or back appear immature. They vary in thickness along the shaft, having fine and gradual tip ends. In other respects they are somewhat like scalp hairs, although they may look like immature pubic hairs as well. Hairs from the legs and arms are shorter, less coarse, and contain less pigment generally.

2.   EXAMINATION METHODS[56]

A hair is first observed by the traditional microscopic method. This microscopic analysis affords an opportunity to look for the presence of foreign matter, such as blood and fibers, and to document the microscopic characteristics of the hair. Microscopic characteristics exhibited within a human hair can be grouped into two categories—general and individual. Both categories are important in the actual comparison process. The following subcategories describe general characteristics:

1.   Color (hue, pigmentation, variation)

2.   Structure (form, diameter, cross-sectional shape, cortex, medullation, shaft aberration)

3.   Cuticular traits (scales, thickness, margins, sequence, weathering)

4.   Acquired characteristics (proximal ends, distal ends)

5.   Length

Individual characteristics differ from general characteristics in that they occur infrequently. Individual characteristics include:

1.   Artificial coloration

2.   Abnormalities

3.   Uncommon structural conditions

4.   An unusual value for a particular general characteristic

5.   Artifacts

Through the proper use of various microscopes and their accessories, the hair is studied for the distinguishing features outlined in the preceding paragraphs. Cuticular scale type is determined while the hair

---

[56] Detailed examination procedures are discussed in SWGMAT, "Forensic Human Hair Examination Guidelines," April 2005, at Section 11.

is either mounted dry or in a transparent cast; the examination is made by placing a drop of tinted varnish or collodion on a microscope slide to form a film on which the hair is placed. After the film is dry, the hair can be lifted off and a cast of the cuticular scale outlines will remain. The medulla and cortex are examined either in a mounting medium, oil, or balsam. If the hair is densely pigmented, it may have to be bleached to render the characteristics visible.

Microscopic examination may reveal whether the hair was cut recently and whether it was forcefully removed. Since hair tapers to a fine point, due to brushing, combing, or even naturally; a square appearance will suggest it has been recently cut. If the root end is present, it can be often determined whether the hair has fallen out naturally, or was pulled out. The naturally fallen hair has a clean bulb formation at the root end; if it was pulled forcibly it will usually have a portion of the sheath clinging to the bulb, which may also appear mutilated.

Microscopic hair comparison techniques remain useful in that the technique is fast, inexpensive, non-destructive, and can easily be used to screen and rule out large quantities of hair evidence before the costlier and more time consuming DNA analysis is done.

---

§7.12 FIBERS

1. THE NATURE OF FIBERS

Fibers, as evidence, are usually found in the same places where hairs are discovered.[57] They may adhere to objects or be embedded in them.[58] Their presence at a given location may be accidental through normal shedding[59] or they may have been pulled out in a struggle. They may simply have been transferred from one surface to another through ordinary, non-violent physical contact. Fibers of value to the trace examiner may be found in a victim's hands, under the fingernails, and in

---

[57] The persistence of fibers is also similar. *See* Ray Palmer and Hilary J. Burch, "The Population, Transfer, and Persistence of Fibres on the Skin of Living Subjects," 49 SCI. & JUST. 259–264 (2009)(no fibers retained after 24 hours of normal activity).

[58] Fabric recovered from a stolen auto was compared with the jacket and shirt of the defendant and was found to be identical in color, weave, and fiber content. *See* Tomolillo v. State, 4 Md.App. 711, 245 A.2d 94 (1968) In another case, blue fibers found under the murder victim's fingernails were determined to be identical in appearance to threads taken from the overalls of the defendant. State v. Johnson, 37 N.M. 280, 21 P.2d 813 (1933) In Nixon v. State, 204 Md. 475, 105 A.2d 243 (1954), the murder weapon was "identified" by the presence of fibers from the victim's shirt. Traces of clothing left on automobiles can be of importance in vehicular homicides and assaults such as in Hunter v. State, 468 S.W.2d 96 (Tex.Cr.App.1971) where the blouse of the victim was matched with a swatch of cloth snagged on the defendant's car.

[59] Shedding potential varies with the fabric type, the texture, the yarn type, and the nature and number of different fiber types involved. *See* K. DeWael, L. Lepot, K. Lunstroot and F. Gason, "Evaluation of the Shedding Potential of Textile Materials," 50 SCI. & JUST. 192–194 (2010).

or on other parts of the body or clothing.[60] They may also be found in or on motor vehicles (for example, the trunk of a car in a kidnaping or murder case, or underneath a hit-and-run vehicle); on weapons such as knives, clubs, firearms, or on fired bullets that have penetrated clothing.[61] They may also be located embedded in blood, tissue, semen, or other body substances.

Generally speaking, fibers fall into four broad class categories: animal, vegetable, mineral, and synthetics. In the first class are wool, silk, camel's hair, and furs. Vegetable fibers include cotton, linen, hemp, sisal, jute. Mineral fibers can be, among others, asbestos, glass wool, or fiber glass, materials commonly used in insulation. Among the synthetic fibers are many different types of polymers. All of these possess certain characteristics recognizable by the trained trace examiner.[62]

Most natural textile fibers rarely present any problems of identification, particularly cotton and wool. They are examined microscopically and chemically, and their characteristics compared with those of known standards. The most common natural textile fiber material is probably cotton. It is easily recognizable microscopically because its soft and short fibers resemble a flat, spirally twisted, or corkscrew appearing band. Linen fibers resemble those of cotton, but are smoother; they also show numerous cross bands. Linen fibers can be either bleached or unbleached. Jute fibers are coarse and stiff and, when viewed microscopically, display marked differences from, for example, linen. Hemp, another vegetable fiber, resembles somewhat unbleached linen, but is even lighter in appearance. Other vegetable fibers, too, exhibit quite characteristic differences when viewed under magnifications of over 300X. Even at lower magnifications, differences

---

[60] *See* R. Palmer and G. Polwarth, "The Persistence of Fibres on Skin in an Outdoor Deposition Crime Scene Scenario," 51 SCI. & JUST. 187–189 (2011)(majority of fibers lost in first two days, but fibers were not completely lost, even after 12 days in a controlled outdoor experience with pig carcasses).

[61] The most famous fiber case is Williams v. State, 251 Ga. 749, 312 S.E.2d 40 (1983), a prosecution for two of twenty-eight killings of blacks in Atlanta, Georgia. The crux of the case against Williams was the fiber evidence, which was challenged as unreliable by the defense on appeal. The appellate court affirmed the conviction, settling the reliability issue in a one sentence finding that it was for the trial court to determine whether a given scientific principle or technique is competent evidence.

[62] *See generally* Kornelia Nehse, "Examination of Fibers and Textiles," in WILEY ENCYCLOPEDIA OF FORENSIC SCIENCE, (Jamieson A. & Moenssens A.A., eds) 2009 & online updates.

The manufacturing process itself may also produce artifacts which assist in the association of a fiber to a particular fabric. *See* Kris DeWael, Christian Baes, Laurent Lepot and Frabrice Gason, "On the Frequency of Occurrence of a Peculiar Polyester Fibre Type Found in Blue Demin Textiles," 51 SCI. & JUST. 154–162 (2011).

Examiners must also consider the effects of laundering process in assessing color differences in fibers. *See* Jolanta Was-Gubala, "The Kinetics of Colour Change in Textiles and Fibres Treated with Detergent Solutions Part I—Colour Perception and Fluorescence Microscopy Analysis," 49 SCI. & JUST. 165–169 (2009); Jolanta Was-Gubala and Edyta Grzesiak, "The Kinetics of Colour Change in Textiles and Fibres Treated with Detergent Solutions Part I—Spectrophotometric Measurements," 50 SCI. & JUST. 55–58 (2010).

are noticeable, as can be observed in the nine photomicrographs in Figure 1.

The difference between vegetable and animal fibers is easily established, since animal fibers used in the textile industry have medullas and show cuticular cells. Natural silk fibers are composed, chemically, of two proteins and are ordinarily spun from 5 cocoon threads, although some fibers are spun from as few as 3 or as many as 8. Animal and vegetable fibers can also be distinguished through the burning test. When animal fibers are withdrawn from a flame, they will continue to burn for a short time only, while emitting an odor that is characteristic of sulphur. The fibers will also have a swollen appearance at the ends. Vegetable fibers, on the other hand, will continue to burn quite easily after they are withdrawn from the flame. The smell emitted will resemble that of burned wood; also, the burned ends of the fibers will appear sharp. The flame test cannot be utilized when only one or a few fibers are available, since it results in at least a partial destruction of the evidence. Chemical tests of great variety also result, to a certain extent, in a degradation of the evidence.

Figure 1. Photomicrographs of various types of natural fibers. All photographs are longitudinal views. Top row, left to right, the specimens are wool, silk, and cotton. Second row, they are mohair, camel hair, and Tussah silk. Bottom row, they are flax, jute, and kapok.

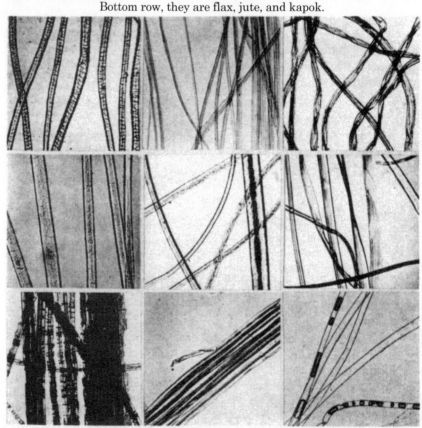

Because of the tremendous increase in the use of synthetic fibers since 1935, when rayon, the first man-made regenerative fiber was produced, the modern methods of fiber identification have largely centered on synthetic fibers. They are used in clothing, upholstered furnishings, decorations, and carpeting. Carpeting is the source of one of the most commonly recovered fibers. Carpet fibers are easily shed, transferred, and recovered, making them a common tool for trying to associate people and places. The benefits of synthetic fibers are that they are commonly encountered, easily recovered, and remarkably stable.[63] The limitation on their probative value, however, is that they are generally uniform and differentiation between sources is difficult. Without data concerning the prevalence of a particular fiber in a relevant community, it is difficult to assess the probative value of a positive association between a recovered fiber and a suspected source.

2. EXAMINATION METHODS

"[M]ethods for the forensic analysis of fibers are well developed, including national consensus guidelines for morphology, optical properties, composition, and dyes/pigmentation."[64] In an examination of most fibers, the first step would be to distinguish natural from synthetic fibers, and, among the synthetic ones, those characteristics that are sought to be determined by the criminalist include color, surface appearance, cross-sectional shape and diameter, fluorescence, and type. For many of the fiber examinations, the mainstay of the forensic laboratory is the microscope, including the stereomicroscope, comparison microscope, and a compound polarized light microscope.[65] A variety of methods in addition to comparison microscopy are used in the analysis of fibers, including polarized light microscopy, fluorescence microscopy, microspectrophometry, infrared spectroscopy, and chromatography.[66] The dyestuffs used for coloration of fibers can also be analyzed for comparison purposes. Thin-layer chromatography, visible absorption spectroscopy, and dichroism measurements of optical light microscopy

---

[63] In a recent study of manufactured fibers, aside from complete degradation in certain environments, the fibers studied showed no changes in optical properties, infrared spectra, solubility, or melting points after 6 months of environmental exposure. Kelly M. Brinsko, Sebastian Sparenga and Meggan King, "The Effects of Environmental Exposure on the Optical, Physical, and Chemical Properties of Manufactured Fibers of Natural Origin," 61 J. Forensic Sci. 1215–1227 (2016).

[64] Andrew Bowen and David Stoney, "A New Method for the Removal and Analysis of Small Particles Adhering to Carpet Fiber Surfaces," 58 J. Forensic Sci. 789, 790 (2013)(citing SWGMAT guidelines and M. Grieve and J. Robertson, *Forensic Examination of Fibers*, 2d ed. (London UK: Taylor and Francis, Ltd., 1999).

[65] *See* Michael C. Grieve, "The Role of Fibers in Forensic Science Examinations," 28 J. Forensic Sci. 877 (1983).

[66] *See* ASTM E2228-10: Standard Guide for Microscopic Examination of Textile Fibers, ASTM E2225-10: Standard Guide for Forensic Examination of Fabrics and Cordage, ASTM E2224-10: Standard Guide for Forensic Analysis by Infrared Spectroscopy, ASTM E2227-13: Standard Guide for Forensic Examination of Non-reactive dyes in textile fibers by Thin-Layer Chromatography)(available at: https://www.nist.gov/topics/forensic-science/materials-trace-sub committee)(last accessed February 27, 2017).

are among the tools used to examine dyed fibers.[67] SWGMAT guidelines and ASTM International Standards provide detailed discussions of each methodology, including procedures, advantages, and limitations.[68]

Absent a fracture match ("jigsaw puzzle") between the fiber and a source, the fiber examination will reach the limited conclusions of: dissimilar, inconclusive, or similar.[69] Thus, an association between a fiber and a suspected source only permits determining a possible origin. Research is being conducted to determine whether small particles adhering to fibers, particularly carpet fibers, might provide an independent means to test the hypothesis of common origin to permit more definitive conclusions.[70] This type of particle analysis is referred to as particle combination analysis, where complex combinations of particles are examined for possible common source attribution.[71]

§7.13   PAINT

1.   THE NATURE OF PAINT

Paint may be removed from an object, transferred onto an object, or both removed from and transferred to the object. Paint is recovered as

---

[67]   *See generally* A. W. Hartshorne and D. K. Laing, "Microspectrofluorimetry of Fluorescent Dyes and Brighteners on Single Textile Fibers: Part 1—Fluorescence Emission Spectra," 51 Forensic Sci. Int'l 203 (1991); A. W. Hartshorne and D. K. Laing, "Microspectrofluorimetry of Fluorescent Dyes and Brighteners on Single Textile Fibers: Part 2—Colour Measurements," 51 Forensic Sci. Int'l 221 (1991); A. W. Hartshorne and D. K. Laing, "Microspectrofluorimetry of Fluorescent Dyes and Brighteners on Single Textile Fibers: Part 3—Fluorescence Decay Phenomena," 51 Forensic Sci. Int'l 239 (1991); Min Huang, et al., "Forensic Identification of Dyes Extracted from Textile Fibers by Liquid Chromatography Mass Spectrometry (LC-MS)," 49 J. FORENSIC SCI. 238 (2004); Kenneth G. Wiggins et al., "The Importance of Thin Layer Chromatography in the Analysis of Reactive Dyes Released from Wool Fibers," 41 J. FORENSIC SCI. 1042 (1996); K. DeWael and T. Vanden Driessche, "Dichroism Measurements in Forensic Fibre Examination Part 1—Dyed Polyester Fibres," 51 SCI. & JUST. 57–67 (2011); K. DeWael and T. Vanden Driessche, "Dichroism Measurements in Forensic Fibre Examination Part 2—Dyed Polyamide Wool and Silk Fibres," 51 SCI. & JUST. 163–172 (2011); K. DeWael and T. Vanden Driessche, "Dichroism Measurements in Forensic Fibre Examination Part 3—Dyed Cotton and Viscose Fibres," 51 SCI. & JUST. 173–186 (2011); K. DeWael and T. Vanden Driessche, "Dichroism Measurements in Forensic Fibre Examination Part 4—Dyed Acrylic and Acetate Fibres," 52 SCI. & JUST. 81–89 (2012).

[68]   Id. *See also* Note 66.

[69]   "If questioned fibers are associated with known fibers, the questioned fibers either originated from the known textile or from another source, which not only is composed of fibers of the exact type and color but also from a fabric that had to be available to contribute those fibers through direct or indirect contact." SWGMAT, "Forensic Fiber Examination Guidelines," April 1999 at Chapter 1, Section 5.5.

If the fibers are indistinguishable using the above methods, proposed Department of Justice guidelines provide that it can be concluded that "the fibers are consistent with originating from the same item, or another item comprised of fibers that exhibit the same microscopic characteristics and optical properties." If the fibers are distinguishable in any way, it can be concluded that "the fibers are not consistent with originating from the same item. Supporting Documentation for Department of Justice Proposed Uniform Language for Testimony and Reports for the Forensic Textile Fiber Discipline at p. 5 (available at: https://www.justice.gov/dag/department-justice-proposed-uniform-language-documents-fiber-footwear-and-tire-treads-general)(last accessed September 20, 2016).

[70]   *See* Andrew Bowen and David Stoney, "A New Method for the Removal and Analysis of Small Particles Adhering to Carpet Fiber Surfaces," 58 J. Forensic Sci. 789 (2013).

[71]   Id.

evidence in various incidents such as hit-and-run accidents, burglary scenes, or homicides. As with other trace materials, microscopic bits of paint may be carried away from the scene of a crime on the clothes,[72] shoes, or tools of a criminal offender. By analyzing paint chips or fragments, the trace examiner may be able to establish their type and possible origin to associate individuals, scenes, and items.

The purpose of paint is to provide a covering over another surface. To achieve that result, a liquid or semi-liquid substance, such as oil, in which color pigments have been suspended, is used. Paint consists of a pigment in a resinous binder (polymer) reduced by a solvent (water or oil) with one of more additives to provide gloss, viscosity, or other properties. All of these substances possess characteristics that can be detected and isolated.[73]

Paints may be classified by color based on the pigment used. White pigments are calcium carbonate (the least expensive), zinc oxide, lead basic carbonate, lead basic sulfate, titanium dioxide, silica, barium sulfate, and zinc sulfide mixed with barium sulfate. Black pigments usually are amorphous carbon (lamp black), bone black, ivory black (one of the most expensive), graphite, or asphalt. The most common pigments for other colors are:

Yellow: hydrated ferric oxide with clay (ochres), lead monoxide, lead chromate, zinc chromate, arsenic trisulfide, cadmium sulfide, cadmium lithopones, and gamboge.

Brown: hydrated ferric oxide and manganese dioxide with clay minerals (the yellow-brown forms are called siennas, the red-brown ones umbers), or Vandyke brown.

Red: ferric oxide, trilead tetroxide, and antimony trisulfide.

Green: chromic oxide, copper basic carbonate, copper basic arsenite, or copper acetoarsenite.

Blue: iron ferroferricyanide, sodium aluminosilicosulfide (ultramarine), cobalt aluminate, or copper basic carbonate (azurite).

Considering paints from the viewpoint of their suspension medium, paints fall basically into three groups: (1) drying oil types; (2) solvent types; and (3) synthetic emulsion types. Among the drying oil types of paint are most enamels and exterior building paints. They harden after application by means of autocatalytic polymerization of unsaturated fatty acids in drying oils such as linseed, tung, and other vegetable oils. In the

---

[72] *See* Rachel Moore, Delia Kingsbury, Joanna Bunford and Valerie Tucker, "A Survey of Paint Flakes on the Clothing of Person Suspected of Involvement in Crime," 52 SCI. & JUST. 96–101 (2012)(72% of garments submitted for casework examination bore one or more paint flakes).

[73] *See generally* John McCullough, "Paint" and Genevieve Massonnett and Florence Monnard, "Paint: Interpretation," in WILEY ENCYCLOPEDIA OF FORENSIC SCIENCE, (Jamieson A. & Moenssens A.A., eds) 2009 & online updates.

solvent or spirit types (spirit varnishes and lacquers), drying is achieved by evaporation of an organic solvent. The synthetic emulsion types contain a polyvinyl acetate, with or without additives, emulsified in water.

2.   EXAMINATION METHODS

The main focus of paint examination, like other trace examination methods, is searching for differences between the evidence samples and the reference samples. Because of the wide variability in physical and chemical characteristics in paint samples from the same source, however, the trace examiner must assess the significance of the observed differences. A conclusion that the paint samples could have a common source is supported by the absence of significant differences and the strength of that conclusion is determined by the type and number of similar characteristics. SWGMAT guidelines state that the definitive conclusion that two paint samples do have common source is possible only with a physical fracture match between samples ("jigsaw puzzle" fit),[74] but research has indicated that using multivariate statistical analysis of spectra collected from infrared or raman spectrometry allows objective comparisons and increases the potential for discriminating paint to a particular manufacturer.[75]

Because of the tremendous variety of different paints, there are many different methods for the identification and comparison of paint samples by physical and chemical features. The physical characteristics include color, layer sequence and thickness, surface features, contaminants, and wear effects. The chemical characteristics include pigments, polymers, and additives. The analytical methods used to distinguish these characteristics can be roughly classified into physical and microscopic examinations, chemical solubility tests, and instrumental analysis.[76] The National Institute of Standards and Technology Organization of Scientific Area Committees is considering the adoption of an OSAC guideline on forensic paint analysis and comparison based on ASTM: E1610-14, which notes that:

> Forensic paint analyses and comparisons are typically distinguished by sample size that precludes the application of

---

[74] *See* SWGMAT, "Forensic Paint Analysis and Comparison Guidelines," May 2000, at Section 5.2. *See also* Department of Justice Proposed Uniform Language for Testimony and Reports for the Forensic Paints and Polymers Discipline (available at: https://www.justice.gov/dag/proposed-uniform-language-documents-anthropology-explosive-chemistry-explosive-devices-geology)(last accessed September 20, 2016).

[75] *See* Cyril Muehlethaler, Genevieve Massonnnet and Pierre Esseiva, "The Application of Chemometrics on Infrared and Raman Spectra as a Tool for the Forensic Analysis of Paints," 209 FORENSIC SCI. INT'L 173–182 (2011). Comparison analysis and discrimination of architectural paint samples using multiple analytical techniques permitted differentiation of all non-same source samples. Diane M. Wright, Maureen J. Bradley and Andria Hobbs Mehlretter, "Analysis and Discrimination of Architectural Paint Samples Via a Population Study," 209 FORENSIC SCI. INT'L 86–95 (2011).

[76] *See* SWGMAT, "Forensic Paint Analysis and Comparison Guidelines," May 2000, at Section 5.1.

many standard industrial paint analysis procedures or protocols. The forensic paint examiner must address concerns such as the issues of a case or investigation, sample size, complexity and condition, environmental effects, and collection methods. These factors require that the forensic paint examiner choose test methods, sample preparation schemes, test sequence, and degree of sample alteration and consumption that are suitable to each specific case.[77]

SWGMAT and ASTM guidelines recommend a scheme for forensic paint examinations that encompasses a variety of useful techniques for discriminating paint pigments, polymers, and additives. The specific techniques to be used will be restricted by sample size and type. Following microscopic examination[78] of physical characteristics, instrumental analysis using infrared spectrometry (FTIR),[79] pyrolsysis gas chromatography (PGC), scanning electron microscopy-energy dispersive x-ray analysis (SEM-EDS),[80] x-ray fluorescence (XRF), and x-ray diffraction may be conducted to identify and compare pigment, polymer, and additives in the paint sample.[81] Raman spectroscopy may also be used to detect the main pigments.[82] Destructive solvent/microchemical tests may also be used to discriminate differing pigment and polymer compositions that are otherwise visually similar.[83]

For the analysis of the possible origins of motor vehicle paint, SWGMAT guidelines recommend using microscopy methods to first

---

[77] ASTM International, ASTM E1610-14 Standard Guide for Forensic Paint Analysis and Comparison, Section 1.1 (available at: https://www.nist.gov/topics/forensic-science/materials-trace-subcommittee)(last accessed February 27, 2017).

NIST OSAC is also considering adopting ASTM E2937-13 Standard Guide for Using Infrared Spectroscopy in Forensic Paint Examinations, as an OSAC Guideline. See http://www.nist.gov/forensics/osac/status-of-other-standards-and-guidelines-recommended-for-inclusion-on-the-osac-registries.cfm (last accessed August 29, 2016).

[78] *See* ASTM E2808-11: Standard Guide for Microspectrophotometry and Color Measurement in Forensic Paint Analysis, (available at: https://www.nist.gov/topics/forensic-science/materials-trace-subcommittee)(last accessed February 27, 2017).

[79] *See* ASTM E2937-13: Standard Guide for Using Infrared Spectroscopy in Forensic Paint Examinations, (available at: https://www.nist.gov/topics/forensic-science/materials-trace-subcommittee)(last accessed February 27, 2017).

[80] *See* ASTM E2809-13: Standard Guide for Using Scanning Electron Microscopy/X-ray Spectrometry in Forensic Paint Examinations, (available at: https://www.nist.gov/topics/forensic-science/materials-trace-subcommittee)(last accessed February 27, 2017).

[81] Id. *See also* SWGMAT, "Forensic Paint Analysis and Comparison Guidelines," May 2000, at Sections 8.3, 8.10 through 9.5 and Figure 1.

Research has also shown that Isotope Ratio Mass Spectrometry (IRMS) may be useful in discriminating white architectural paints. *See* N. Farmer, W. Meier-Augenstein and D. Lucy, "Stable Isotope Analysis of White Paints and Likelihood Ratios," 49 SCI. & JUST. 114–119 (2009).

[82] Raman spectroscopy is also useful when the evidence sample is small and does not represent the entire morphology of the whole paint coat. Janina Zieba-Palus and Beata Trzcinska, "Application of Infrared and Raman Spectroscopy in Paint Trace Examination," 58 J. Forensic Sci. 1359–1363 (2013).

[83] *See* SWGMAT, "Forensic Paint Analysis and Comparison Guidelines," May 2000, at Section 8.38.

determine if the paint is from the original equipment manufacturer (OEM). If the paint is not OEM, only the color can be provided and no further analysis conducted. If the paint is OEM, the analytical techniques used in conducting a paint comparison examination can be used to determine the physical and chemical characteristics of the topcoats and undercoats to provide data for searching in databases of known values.[84]

§7.14   GLASS

1.   THE NATURE OF GLASS

Glass is technically defined as "[t]he inorganic product of fusion which has cooled to a rigid condition without crystallizing."[85] Glass is defined by its atomic structure. "In contrast to crystalline solids, which have an ordered internal arrangement of atoms, the internal structure of glass consists of a network of atoms lacking long-range symmetry."[86] Because the viscosity that characterizes liquids is not present, the material is rigid and appears solid. The different components and the variety of manufacturing methods used to make glass result in physical and chemical differences that can be used to differentiate one item of glass from another.

Common window glass contains mostly silica sand, with soda ash, lime, and soda. Plate glass, on the other hand, contains, in addition to silica sand, soda ash, salt cake, limestone, and a small quantity of charcoal. The composition of glass may be altered considerably to produce special types and colors of glass. The constituent elements are heated in a furnace until the whole mass is fused. After the gases have been allowed to escape, the liquid is withdrawn and worked while still in a heated form, by blowing, molding, or rolling.[87]

The physical and chemical properties of glass fragments recovered may be compared with those of broken glass at the scene and a determination thereby made as to whether the fragments came from that source.[88] In some instances the breaking of glass may be the result of an intentional act; in others, the result of an accidental occurrence. An illustration of the former is the breaking of the window of an automobile

---

[84]   Id. at Section 8.4 and Figure 2 (flowchart of examination methods).

[85]   ASTM International, Standard C162-05, "Standard Terminology of Glass and Glass Products," 2010.

[86]   Maureen C. Bottrell, "Forensic Glass Comparison: Background Information Used in Data Interpretation," 11–2 FORENSIC SCI. COMM. April 2009 (available at: http://www.fbi.gov/about-us/lab/forensic-science-communications/fsc/april2009/review/2009_04_review01.htm/) (last accessed February 27, 2017).

[87]   On the nature of glass, its variability, and its evidential value, see Tina J. Lovelock, "Glass, in WILEY ENCYCLOPEDIA OF FORENSIC SCIENCE, (Jamieson A. & Moenssens A.A., eds) 2009 & online updates. See also James Michael Curran et al., Forensic Interpretation of Glass Evidence, 2000.

[88]   Wheeler v. State, 255 Ind. 395, 264 N.E.2d 600 (1970)(glass splinter in soles of defendant's shoes matched with the broken lens of the victim's eyeglasses).

or a building to steal something within it. An accidental breaking of a glass object, such as a glass bottle or drinking glass, may occur in the course of a struggle. In either situation, glass fragments may become embedded in clothing.[89] Fragments may even become lodged in the implement used in an intentional breaking. Criminal prosecutions involving breaking and entering or the use of a motor vehicle[90] and civil cases resulting from automobile accident investigations scenes are the situations which most frequently call for analysis of glass particles.

An expert in glass comparisons can render a positive opinion that two or more pieces of glass had a single source, to the exclusion of all other sources, only where a mechanical fit (jigsaw puzzle) has been made.[91] The examiner might also be able to state, positively, that the pieces could *not* have had a common source. Beyond these two possible opinions, the expert frames an opinion only in terms of association to a group but never to a single source.[92]

2.   EXAMINATION METHODS

Unlike other trace evidence such as hair and fibers, associations based on glass evidence can be established through physical matches of the fragments or from the physical properties of glass. Absent a physical fracture match between glass fragments,[93] however, the examiner cannot conclude that a particular glass fragment originated from a particular

---

[89]   *See* Moreno v. People, 156 Colo. 503, 400 P.2d 899 (1965)(glass fragments from a location resembled pieces removed from defendant's shoes); State v. Menard, 331 S.W.2d 521 (Mo.1960)(glass fragment from scene similar to fragments found in the defendant's clothes). *See also*, State v. Spring, 48 Wis.2d 333, 179 N.W.2d 841 (1970)(glass particles found on the defendant's boots were compared to glass present near footprints at the crime scene).

Glass may also be retained in the pockets of a garment and later migrate to the surface, which can present interpretation difficulties as to the significance of glass on the surface of a garment. *See* S. O'Sullivan. T. Geddes, and T.J. Lovelock, "The Migration of Fragments of Glass from the Pockets to the Surfaces of Clothing," 208 FORENSIC SCI. INT'L 149–155 (2011).

[90]   Rolls v. State, 35 Ala.App. 283, 46 So.2d 8 (1950)(glass collected at the scene of the accident and the glass removed from the damaged headlight of the suspect's automobile were of the same origin).

[91]   Maureen C. Bottrell, "Forensic Glass Comparison: Background Information Used in Data Interpretation," 11 Forensic Science Communications, April 2009 (available at: https://www2.fbi.gov/hq/lab/fsc/current/review/2009_04_review01.htm)(last accessed February 27, 2017); *see also* SWGMAT, "Introduction to Forensic Glass Examination," July 2004, Section 5.3.

[92]   Id. Although not endorsed by the Scientific Working Group for Materials Analysis, some commentators have advocated for the utilization of statistical analysis (i.e., likelihood ratios) to help the trace examiner's assessment of the significance of the trace analysis of the glass samples. *See* James M. Curran and Tacha N. Hicks, "Glass Evidence: Bayesian Approach to," in WILEY ENCYCLOPEDIA OF FORENSIC SCIENCE, (Jamieson A. & Moenssens A.A., eds) 2009 & online updates; Margaret Irwin, "Transfer of Glass Fragments When Bottles and Drinking Glasses Are Broken," 51 SCI. & JUST. 16–18 (2011)(using likelihood ratio analysis to evaluate the significance of glass fragments present on a suspect's clothing as to whether the suspect broke the bottle or did not break the bottle).

[93]   In the event pieces of evidence glass can be fitted together by a mechanical fit, the examiner can make a conclusion of a single source to the exclusion of all other sources. SWGMAT, "Introduction to Forensic Glass Examination," July 2004, Section 5.3.

source based solely on the properties of the glass.[94] When examining the physical properties of glass, the objective is to compare glass samples to determine if they can be differentiated using their physical, optical, or chemical properties (for example, color, refractive index (RI), density, or elemental composition). If the samples are distinguishable in any of these observed and measured properties, it may be concluded that they did not originate from the same source of broken glass. If the samples are indistinguishable in all of these observed and measured properties, the possibility that they originated from the same source of glass cannot be eliminated.

The initial examination of glass measures color, fluorescence, surface features, curvature, and thickness to determine whether the glass fragments are from different sources. These properties can be used to exclude glass fragments as originating from a single source.[95] If the glass fragments are larger than two to three millimeters, a measurement of glass density[96] can be made by placing the glass sample into suspension in a liquid solution.[97] Density measurements also can be used to exclude glass fragments as originating from a single source.[98]

Another determination in the examination of glass is the measurement of the refractive index (RI) of the sample. Refractive index is the measure of the speed at which light travels through a transparent medium compared to the speed of light traveling in a vacuum and how the wavelength of the light in that medium differs from its wavelength in a vacuum. The RI of glass is dependent upon the elemental composition and the manufacturing process (the heating and cooling events that created the glass), which is referred to as the "thermal history." If two glass items have the same elemental composition but a different thermal history, the glass items will have different RI values. Similarly, items having the same thermal history but different elemental composition will have different RI values. However, since RI is dependent upon these two independent factors, it is possible for two items with different elemental compositions and different thermal histories to have the same RI value.[99]

---

[94] *See* Department of Justice Proposed Uniform Language for Testimony and Reports for the Forensic Glass Discipline (available at: https://www.justice.gov/dag/department-justice-proposed-uniform-language-documents-fiber-footwear-and-tire-treads-general)(last accessed September 20, 2016).

[95] Maureen C. Bottrell, "Forensic Glass Comparison: Background Information Used in Data Interpretation," 11 Forensic Science Communications, April 2009 (available at: https://www2.fbi.gov/hq/lab/fsc/current/review/2009_04_review01.htm)(last accessed February 27, 2017); SWGMAT, "Initial Examinations of Glass," July 2004, Section 8.1.

[96] Density varies with changes in composition and thermal history and is closely correlated with refractive index so little additional discrimination is achieved by measuring both density and refractive index. SWGMAT, "Glass Density Determination, July 2004, Section 5.1.

[97] Id. at Section 4.

[98] Id. at Section 8.4.

[99] Crystal Munger, Kris M. Gates and Christopher Hamburg, "Determining the Refractive Index Variation within Panes of Vehicle Windshield Glass," 59 J. Forensic Sci. 1351–1357 (2014).

The RI of the glass fragments is first determined microscopically using the Emmons Double Variation or Automated Glass Refractive Measurement.[100] RI may also be measured microscopically using Dispersion Staining and Becke Line immersion methods in which the fragment is immersed in a refractive index liquid, and the difference between the refractive index of the glass fragment relative to the liquid is measured.[101] RI measurements may be used to exclude glass fragments as originating from a single source.[102] Any conclusions, however, should take into consideration the RI variation within samples.[103]

In addition to measuring RI of the glass fragments, a trace examiner may use annealing to classify the sample as being tempered or annealed glass. Annealing is the removal of the internal stresses in glass fragments by the application of heat above the transformation range of the glass and then slowly cooling it.[104] After annealing, the refractive index is measured and the magnitude of the change in the refractive index indicates whether the glass is tempered or annealed.[105] The method may also be useful in indicating from which category of glass (e.g., container, window, or automobile) the fragment originated.[106] Annealing alters the original sample and cannot be used on very small fragments.

The use of an elemental analysis method to determine the major, minor, and trace elements present in glass fragments may yield high discrimination among sources of glass.[107] Elemental analysis of glass can

---

[100] For a description of these two methods, *see* Maureen C. Bottrell, "Forensic Glass Comparison: Background Information Used in Data Interpretation," 11 Forensic Science Communications, April 2009 (available at: https://www2.fbi.gov/hq/lab/fsc/current/review/2009 _04_review01.htm)(last accessed February 27, 2017); SWGMAT, "Glass Refractive Index Determination," July 2004, Sections 7.1 and 7.2 Detailed descriptions are also found in Association of Analytical Chemists Method 973.65 "Emmons Double Variation" and American Society for Testing and Materials Standard E1967: Standard Test method for the Automated Determination of Refractive Index of Glass Samples Using Oil Immersion Method and a Phase-Contrast Microscope."

[101] Maureen C. Bottrell, "Forensic Glass Comparison: Background Information Used in Data Interpretation," 11 Forensic Science Communications, April 2009 (available at: https:// www2.fbi.gov/hq/lab/fsc/current/review/2009_04_review01.htm)(last accessed February 27, 2017); SWGMAT, "Glass Refractive Index Determination," July 2004, Section 7.3.

[102] Id. at Section 8.7.

[103] Crystal Munger, Kris M. Gates and Christopher Hamburg, "Determining the Refractive Index Variation within Panes of Vehicle Windshield Glass," 59 J. Forensic Sci. 1351–1357 (2014); A.W.N. Newton, "An Investigation into the Variability of the Refractive Index of Glass: Part II—The Effect of Debris Contamination," 204 FORENSIC SCI. INT'L 182–185 (2011).

[104] K.P. Rushton, S.A. Coulson, A.W.N. Newton, and J.M. Curran, "The Effect of Annealing on Variation of Glass Refractive Index," 209 FORENSIC SCI. INT'L 102–107 (2011).

[105] A change of more than $+1 \times 10^{-3}$ indicates tempered glass; a change of less than $+8 \times 10^{-4}$ indicates annealed glass. SWGMAT, "Glass Refractive Index Determination," July 2004, Section 7.4.2.4.

[106] David Lucy and Grzegorz Zadora, "Mixed Effects Modelling for Glass Category Estimation from Glass Refractive Indices," 212 FORENSIC SCI. INT'L 189–197 (2011).

[107] Emily R. Schenk and Jose R. Almirall, "Elemental Analysis of Glass by Laser Ablation Inductively Coupled Plasma Optical Emission Spectrometry (LA-ICP-OES)," 217 FORENSIC SCI. INT'L 222–228 (2012).

be used to measure the absolute or relative concentrations of major, minor, and trace elements ranging in mass from grams to less than one microgram.[108] Analytical techniques currently used include scanning electron microscopy-energy dispersive x-ray spectrometry (SEM-EDS), X-ray fluorescence spectrometry, inductively coupled plasma-optical emission spectrometry (ICP-OES) and inductively coupled plasma-mass spectrometry (ICP-MS).[109] The trace examiner may test for concentrations of the following elements: magnesium (Mg), aluminum (Al), iron (Fe), titanium (Ti), manganese (Mn), rubidium (Rb), strontium (Sr), zirconium (Zr), barium (Ba), lanthanum (La), cerium (Ce), neodymium (Nd), samarium (Sm), and lead (Pb).[110]

V. TRIAL AIDS

§7.15   EXPERT QUALIFICATIONS

In the examination of physical evidence, the trace examiner must, of necessity, be an expert in the analytical methods used. The use of proper optics, illuminators, filters, and the correct preparation of specimens for examination are essential if the desired results are to be obtained. In addition, the witness also must be shown to be a competent expert.[111] A police officer's testimony that pieces of cloth or fabric and a jacket were of the same material was held inadmissible because the officer had not been shown to be competent to give opinion testimony as an expert.[112]

Because of the great diversity of backgrounds from which forensic scientists in these sometimes disparate fields are drawn, it is difficult to define precise educational backgrounds which are required for competency in a given area of trace evidence analysis. However, certification is available for the broader field of criminalistics through the

---

[108] SWGMAT, "Elemental Analysis of Glass," July 2004, Section 1.1.

[109] Id. at Sections 7.1 through 7.4.

[110] NIST OSAC has recommended the adoption of the following ASTM documents as OSAC Standards:

  (e) ASTM: E2330-12 Standard Test Method for Determination of Concentrations of Elements in Glass Samples Using Inductively Coupled Plasma Mass Spectrometry (ICP-MS) for Forensic Comparisons.

  (f) ASTM: E2926-13 Standard Test Method for Forensic Comparison of Glass Using Micro X-ray Fluorescence (μ-XRF) Spectrometry.

See https://www.nist.gov/topics/forensic-science/status-other-standards-and-guidelines-recommended-inclusion-osac-registries (last accessed February 27, 2017).

[111] A witness who had attended various universities, had studied and later lectured on forensic microanalysis, including the identification of paint and glass, and who had made over two thousand prior analyses similar to the one involved in the trial, was deemed competent as an expert in forensic microanalysis: People v. Green, 28 Ill.2d 286, 192 N.E.2d 398 (1963).

Similarly, an employee of the FBI for nine years, having received B.S. and M.S. degrees, trained at the FBI for one year, and thereafter having conducted over 1,000 examinations of hairs and fibers, was properly qualified as an expert in State v. Wallace, 181 Conn. 237, 435 A.2d 20 (1980).

[112] People v. Patno, 13 A.D.2d 870, 215 N.Y.S.2d 309 (1961).

American Board of Criminalistics (ABC). To be eligible for certification status (fellow or diplomate status), the applicant must possess a minimum of an earned baccalaureate degree, or its equivalent, in a natural science or an appropriately related field from an accredited institution and a minimum of two years full-time experience (including on-the-job training) and be actively working in Criminalistics.[113] The ABC has two specialty certification tests in trace evidence: (1) Hairs and Fibers; and, (2) Paints and Polymers. The tests are structured with 60% general questions and 40% specialty questions among the 220 multiple choice questions (of which only 200 are scored and 20 serve as pilot questions for future examinations).[114] Glass, soil, and other trace evidence analysis are not currently covered by the ABC fellow certification process. ABC also maintains a list of certified examiners on its website.[115]

§7.16 EVIDENCE ISSUES

1. GENERAL ADMISSIBILITY

Prior to *Daubert*, courts were extremely deferential to trace evidence and almost uniformly admitted hair[116] and other trace evidence comparison testimony.[117] Courts became slightly more circumspect in dealing with opinions based on hair comparison and statistically based estimates of the probabilities of error after the *Daubert* trilogy decisions. A 1995 court was the first to apply the *Daubert* criteria to hair analysis evidence, pointing to the scarcity of scientific studies supporting the reliability of hair comparisons: "unsuccessful in its attempts to locate any indication that expert hair comparison testimony meets any of the requirements [of *Daubert*]."[118] That decision was followed in short order by an Indiana decision, *McGrew v. State*, which upheld the admission of hair comparison testimony under state evidentiary standards of

---

[113] http://www.criminalistics.com/certification-requirements.html.

[114] http://www.criminalistics.com/faqs.html.

[115] www.criminalistics.com.

[116] *See, e.g.* United States v. Brady, 595 F.2d 359 (6th Cir.1979), cert. denied 444 U.S. 862 (1979); State v. Kersting, 50 Or.App. 461, 623 P.2d 1095 (1981); People v. Schultz, 99 Ill.App.3d 762, 55 Ill.Dec. 94, 425 N.E.2d 1267 (1981); State v. Clayton, 646 P.2d 723 (Utah 1982); State v. Carlson, 267 N.W.2d 170 (Minn.1978); People v. Columbo, 118 Ill.App.3d 882, 74 Ill.Dec. 304, 455 N.E.2d 733 (1983); People v. Pride, 3 Cal.4th 195, 10 Cal.Rptr.2d 636, 833 P.2d 643 (1992). *But see* State v. Faircloth, 99 N.C.App. 685, 394 S.E.2d 198 (1990)(comparative hair microscopy not sufficiently accepted as reliable evidence to positively identify a person).

[117] Fibers: *See, e.g.,* State v. Hall, 297 N.W.2d 80 (Iowa 1980); Commonwealth v. Bartolini, 299 Mass. 503, 13 N.E.2d 382 (1938), cert. denied 304 U.S. 565 (1938); People v. Smith, 142 Cal.App.2d 287, 298 P.2d 540 (1956); Maxwell v. State, 236 Ark. 694, 370 S.W.2d 113 (1963).

Glass: People v. Frisby, 160 Ill.App.3d 19, 111 Ill.Dec. 700, 512 N.E.2d 1337, 1349 (1987); Hicks v. State, 544 N.E.2d 500, 504 (Ind.1989); Johnson v. State, 612 So.2d 1288, 1301 (Ala.Cr.App.1992); Johnson v. Nagle, 58 F.Supp.2d 1303 (N.D.Ala.1999).

[118] Williamson v. Reynolds, 904 F.Supp. 1529, 1554 (E.D.Okla.1995) rev'd on this issue sub nom. Williamson v. Ward, 110 F.3d 1508, 1523 (10th Cir.1997). Although the Tenth Circuit upheld habeas relief, the circuit court ruled that the district court committed error by applying the wrong evidentiary standard in the habeas proceeding (due process fundamental fairness standard applies in habeas; not *Daubert* standard).

"reliability."[119] Although a commentator opined in 1996 that "[i]f the purveyors of this dubious science cannot do a better job of validating hair analysis than they have done so far, forensic hair comparison analysis should be excluded altogether from criminal trials,"[120] the overwhelming majority of courts continued to give deference to the admission of hair and other trace comparison testimony.[121]

Since the publication of the 2009 NAS Report, the field of trace evidence comparison has received more scrutiny in the courts. For example, in *United States v. Zajac*,[122] the defense challenged as unreliable the trace expert's testimony that "white adhesive" residue found on materials at the bomb scene was "consistent with" and "could have come from the same source as" a tube of Gorilla Glue in the defendant's home. The court detailed the microscopic and analytical tests that were conducted and found that the tests were sufficient for the expert "to opine on the visual, chemical, and elemental consistency between the adhesives on the Salt Lake City device and those found at Zajac's home." The court also found, however, that the expert's conclusion that the material "could have come from the same source" was not admissible because there was an undue risk of prejudice that the jury would overvalue this testimony from "an expert in polymers" without fully considering that "it is just as likely the adhesives came from a different source."

The presentation of trace evidence testimony, however, has been impacted from events occurring outside the courtroom. On November 9, 2012, the FBI, the Innocence Project, and the National Association of Criminal Defense Lawyers (NACDL) entered into a Memorandum of Understanding (MOU) on the nature and limitations of microscopic hair examinations. The Memorandum stated that trace examiner may "offer an opinion that a known individual can either be included or excluded as a source of a questioned hair collected at a crime scene [but] the size of the pool of people who could be included as a possible source of [the] specific hair is unknown."[123] Voluntary guidelines and standards

---

[119] 673 N.E.2d 787 (Ind.App.1996), vacated, 683 N.E.2d 592 (Ind.), aff'd in part & rev'd in part, 682 N.E.2d 1289 (Ind. 1997), affirming the trial court ruling on admission of the evidence.

[120] Clive A. Stafford Smith and Patrick A. Goodman, "Forensic Hair Comparison Analysis: Nineteenth Century Science of Twentieth Century Snake Oil?," 27 COLUM. HUM. RTS. L. REV. 227, 231 (1996).

[121] *See, e.g.,* Thompson v. State, 395 Md. 240, 909 A.2d 1035 (2006)(microscopic pubic hair comparison properly admitted); State v. McDonald, 180 N.C. App. 693, 639 S.E.2d 142 (2006)(fiber comparison evidence properly admitted); People v. Prieto, 124 P.3d 842 (Colo.App.2005)(fiber analysis properly admitted); United States v. Santiago, 156 F.Supp.2d 145 (D. Puerto Rico 2001)("upon independent research . . ." that the principles and procedures underlying hair and fiber evidence are overwhelmingly accepted and reliable, and that courts which have excluded hair evidence are rare while courts that have been receptive to hair analysis comprise a large body of law); Johnson v. State, 521 So.2d 1006 (Ala. Ct. Crim. App. 1986)(admission of testimony that glass imbedded in the nose of a bullet "matched, with no measurable discrepancies" in RI values the broken window glass at the scene).

[122] 2010 U.S. Dist. LEXIS 92350 (Central Div. Utah, 2010).

[123] Commonwealth v. Perrot, 2016 Mass. Super. LEXIS 3, *71–72 (2016).

generated by the forensic science community have recognized similar limitations for other types of trace evidence.[124]

2.   PROBABILITY ESTIMATES AND STATISTICS

While there is no microscopic technique that can positively identify a crime scene hair as having come from a specific individual, experts testifying to microscopic hair comparisons sometimes made a probabilistic assessment as to the likelihood of this occurrence. SWGMAT guidelines clearly state: "Probabilities and population statistics should not be used to interpret microscopical hair comparisons."[125] However, in the past, some examiners couched their opinion in the form of a statistical likelihood that was so high as to suggest, to the scientifically illiterate juror, judge, and/or lawyer, that the possibility of error is statistically insignificant.

In the 1970's, Canadian studies by B. D. Gaudette were published and were used to support testimony that a number of characteristics in hair can make the hair specimens of people significantly different.[126] These studies induced some hair examiners to make estimates that were extremely impressive to the non-scientist, estimates of 1 in 4,500 for scalp hair and 1 in 800 for pubic hair that the same characteristics would be found to match in hairs of different individuals. The problem with using these statistics was that, while they suggested the likelihood of a near positive match between the crime scene hair and the hairs known to have come from the defendant, this was not what the statistics meant:[127]

> "The hair studies described . . . represent an attempt to provide an objective basis for opinions regarding the confidence level of hair individualization. Unfortunately, the bias in the experimental design and the failure to relate probabilities to the questions posed generated probability estimates that were irrelevant to hair individualization. Furthermore, the errors in

---

[124] *See* ASTM and SWGMAT guidelines discussed *supra*.

[125] SWGMAT, "Forensic Human Hair Examination Guidelines," April 2005, at Section 14.

Researchers are investigating various methods for assessing the objective numerical significance of microscopic hair observations. *See* Elizabeth Brooks, Bruce Comber, Ian McNaught, and James Robertson, "Digital Imaging and Image Analysis Applied to Numerical Applications in Forensic Hair Examination," 51 SCI. & JUST. 28–37 (2011).

[126] The leading studies were described in the following sequence of articles: B. D. Gaudette and E. S. Keeping, "An Attempt at Determining Probabilities in Human Scalp Hair Comparison," 19 J. FORENSIC SCI. 499 (1974); B. D. Gaudette, "Probabilities and Human Pubic Hair Comparisons," 21 J. FORENSIC SCI. 514 (1976); B. D. Gaudette, "Some Further Thoughts on Probabilities and Human Hair Comparisons," 23 J. FORENSIC SCI. 758 (1978).

The studies were extensively criticized. *See* P. Barnett and R.R. Ogle, "Probabilities and Human Hair Comparison," 27 J. Forensic Sci. 272 (1982); Hoffman, "Statistical Evaluation of the Evidential Value of Human Hairs Possibly Coming from Multiple Sources," 36 J. Forensic Sci. 1053 (1991).

[127] Vigorously challenging the use of statistical estimates in litigation, *see* Leonard Jaffee, "Of Probativity and Probability: Statistics, Scientific Evidence, and the Calculus of Chance at Trial," 46 U. PITTSBURGH L.REV. 925 (1985), concluding that probability evidence is irrelevant and incompetent and distorts the fact finding process. *See also* E. Callen, "A Brief Word on the Statistical Evidence Debate," 66 Tul. L.Rev. 1405 (1992).

the derivation introduced a problem to the administration of justice greater than that which the experiments attempted to solve. . . ."[128]

As might be expected, even the early courts were divided on whether evidence of probabilistic estimates ought to be admissible in hair comparison cases. Some courts held that the jury able to understand such evidence and give it its due weight—a conclusion that is subject to some doubt in light of unscientific polls taken of jurors' understanding of expert testimony—while others held that such evidence ought not to be admitted.

In *State v. Clayton*,[129] the defendant argued that the probability of hair matches was too speculative for jury consideration. The Utah high court rejected this argument, but the exact nature of the statistical testimony of the hair expert was not given in the opinion. Similarly, in *People v. DiGiacomo*,[130] the defendant unsuccessfully challenged the admission of the expert's testimony that there was only a 1 in 4500 chance that the hair from the victim's car did not belong to defendant. The exact basis for this opinion was not referred to in the decision, but it is obvious that the expert witness used the Gaudette statistics. The Seventh Circuit Court of Appeals upheld the admission of the Gaudette statistics by an Illinois state court, even though the jury had apparently been confused by the probability evidence.[131]

The leading case rejecting the admissibility of statistical testimony in hair comparisons is *State v. Carlson*.[132] In *Carlson,* an analyst from the Minnesota state crime laboratory testified that defendant's pubic hairs matched two pubic hairs found stuck to the victim in all 15 categories of microscopic comparison and Gaudette himself stated that, based on his own studies, there was a 1 in 800 chance that the pubic hairs found stuck to the victim were not the defendant's, and a 1 in 4,500 chance that the foreign head hairs were not the defendant's. On appeal the defendant argued, in part, that it is improper to allow evidence in a criminal trial to be expressed statistically, and the Minnesota Supreme Court agreed: "Testimony expressing opinions or conclusions in terms of statistical probabilities can make the uncertain seem all but proven, and suggest, by quantification, satisfaction of the requirement that guilt be established 'beyond a reasonable doubt.' "[133]

---

[128] P. Barnett and R.R. Ogle, "Probabilities and Human Hair Comparison," 27 J. Forensic Sci. 272 (1982).

[129] 646 P.2d 723 (Utah 1982).

[130] 71 Ill.App.3d 56, 27 Ill.Dec. 232, 388 N.E.2d 1281 (1979); see also People v. Rainge, 112 Ill.App.3d 396, 445 N.E.2d 535 (1983).

[131] During the deliberations, the jury had submitted a note to the judge asking if the hair sample conclusively established that defendant was present in the victim's car. The trial judge refused to answer the question. United States ex rel. DiGiacomo v. Franzen, 680 F.2d 515 (7th Cir.1982)(per curiam).

[132] 267 N.W.2d 170 (Minn.1978).

[133] In United States v. Massey, 594 F.2d 676 (8th Cir.1979), the expert stated that in his own experience he had examined approximately 2,000 cases and in only one or two instances

Absent the scientific studies to quantify the relative pools of possible sources, statistical testimony as to any trace evidence is likely to be excluded and the improper admission of such testimony may be grounds for a new trial. The 2012 MOU between the FBI, the Innocence Project, and NACDL concluded that "probabilities to a particular inclusion of someone as a source of a hair of unknown origin cannot be scientifically supported [and statements of] rareness implicitly suggesting probability could not be squared with the limits of science."[134] In *Commonwealth v. Perrot*, the Massachusetts Superior Court at Hampden granted a new trial for a 1922 rape conviction based on the "new consensus of the limitations and nature of hair analysis evidence" reflected in the 2012 MOU.[135]

VI. RESOURCES

§7.17   BIBLIOGRAPHY OF ADDITIONAL RESOURCES

1.   GENERAL ANALYTICAL PROCEDURES

Colin Aitken and Franco Taroni, *Statistics and the Evaluation of Evidence for Forensic Scientists*, 2d ed., John Wiley & Sons, 2004.

Jihad Rene Albani, *Principles and Applications of Fluorescence Spectroscopy*, John Wiley & Sons, 2007.

Imran Ali and Hassan Y. Aboul-Enein, *Instrumental Methods in Metal Ion Speciation*, CRC Press, 2006.

Robert D. Blackledge, "The Increasingly Diverse and Challenging Discipline of Trace-Evidence Analysis," EVIDENCE TECHNOLOGY MAG., Nov.–Dec. 2008, p. 15.

M. J. Bogusz ed., *Forensic Science, Handbook of Analytical Separations*, Elsevier Science, 2008.

Richard G. Brereton, *Applied Chemometrics for Scientists*, John Wiley & Sons, 2007.

"was he ever unable to make identification." In addition, the witness referred to the Gaudette study which concluded that there is a one in 4,500 chance of mismatching hair samples when matched in the manner used by this expert. In summation the prosecutor claimed that the expert had stated that out of 2,000 or 2,500 examinations only in 3 to 5 instances was he "unable to distinguish the hair from two different people." The prosecutor also made the following statement: "A handful—3 to 5 out of 2,000—that's better than 99.44 percent; it's better than Ivory soap, if you remember the commercial. It's very convincing."

In reversing the defendant's conviction and ordering a new trial, the *Massey* court stated that the prosecutor had used "misleading mathematical odds" and had "infused in the minds of the jury the confusion in identifying the hair with identifying the perpetrator of the crime."

[134] Commonwealth v. Perrot, 2016 Mass. Super. LEXIS 3, *72 (2016).

[135] 2016 Mass. Super. LEXIS at *105.

Chhabil Dass, *Fundamentals of Contemporary Mass Spectrometry*, John Wiley & Sons, 2006.

Peter R. Griffiths, James A. DeHaseth and James D. Winefordner, *Fourier Transform Infrared Spectrometry*, 2d ed., John Wiley & Sons, 2007.

Eli Grushka and Nelu Grinberg, eds., *Advances in Chromatography*, CRC Press, 2016.

Teresa Kowalska and Joseph Sherma, *Preparative Layer Chromatography*, CRC Press, 2006.

Jorg P. Kutter and Yolanda Fintschenko, eds., *Separation Methods in Microanalytical Systems*, CRC Press, 2006.

Gillian McMahon, *Analytical Instrumentation: A Guide to Laboratory, Portable and Miniaturized Instruments*, John Wiley & Sons, 2008.

J. Throck Watson and O. David Sparkman, *Introduction to Mass Spectrometry: Instrumentation, Applications, and Strategies for Data Interpretation*, 4th ed., John Wiley & Sons, 2007.

2.   HAIRS

Lori E. Baker, *et al.*, "A Silica-Based Mitochondrial DNA Extraction Method Applied to Forensic Hair Shafts and Teeth," 42 J. FORENSIC SCI. 126 (2001).

Bruce A. Brenner Jr., *et al.*, "Characterization of Surface Organic Components of Human Hair by On-Line Supercritical Fluid Extraction—Gas Chromatography/Mass Spectrometry," 48 J. FORENSIC SCI. 554 (2003).

John V. Goodpaster, *et al.*, "Evaluation of Extraction Techniques for the Forensic Analysis of Human Scalp Hair Using GC-MS," 48 J. FORENSIC SCI. 299 (2003).

Max M. Houck, "Review of Hair ID," 38 J. FORENSIC SCI. 1439 (2003).

Ivan M. Kempson, "A Method for the Longitudinal Sectioning of Single Hair Samples," 47 J. FORENSIC SCI. 889 (2002).

Jason C. Kolowski, *et al.*, "A Comparison Study of Hair Examination Methodologies," 49 J. FORENSIC SCI. 1253 (2004).

Robert R. Ogle Jr. and Michelle J. Fox, *Atlas of Human Hair—Microscopic Characteristics*, CRCPress, 1998.

Joseph T. Tafaro, "The Use of Microscopic Postmortem Changes in Anagen Hair Roots to Associate Questioned Hairs With Known Hairs and Reconstruct Events in Two Murder Cases," 45 J. FORENSIC SCI. 495 (2000).

3. FIBERS

W. Bruschweiler and M. Grieve, "A Study of the Random Distribution of a Red Acrylic Target Fibre," 37 Science & Justice 85 (1997).

Nicola J. Clayson and Kenneth G. Wiggins, "Microfibers—A Forensic Perspective," 42 J. FORENSIC SCI. 842 (1997).

Liling Cho, et al., "A New Method for Fiber Comparison Using Polarized Infrared Microspectroscopy," 44 J. FORENSIC SCI. 275 (1999).

Liling Cho, et al., "Forensic Classification of Polyester Fibers by Infrared Dichroic Ratio Pattern Recognition," 44 J. FORENSIC SCI. (1999).

Kris De Wael, Fabrice G. Gason and Christiaan A. V. Baes, "Selection of an Adhesive Tape Suitable for Forensic Fiber Sampling," 53 J. FORENSIC SCIENCES 168 (2008).

ENFSI-European Fibres Group, Manuel of Best Practice for Fibre Examinations in Forensic Science, 2000.

Katherine Flynn, et al., "Forensic Analysis of Biocomponent Fibers Using Infrared Chemical Imaging," 51 J. FORENSIC SCI. 586 (2006).

Nicola J. Grayson, "Microfibers—A Forensic Perspective," 42 J. FORENSIC SCI. 842 (1997).

Michael C. Grieve, "The Evidential Value of Black Cotton Fibres," 41 Science & Justice 245 (2001).

Michael C. Grieve and Kenneth G. Wiggins, "Fibres Under Fire: Suggestions for Improving Their Use to Provide Forensic Evidence," 46 J. FORENSIC SCI. 67 (2001).

A. W. Hartshorne and D. K. Laing, "Microspectrofluorimetry of Fluorescent Dyes and Brighteners on Single Textile Fibers: Part 1—Fluorescence Emission Spectra," 51 Forensic Sci. Int'l 203 (1991).

A. W. Hartshorne and D. K. Laing, "Microspectrofluorimetry of Fluorescent Dyes and Brighteners on Single Textile Fibers: Part 2—Colour Measurements," 51 Forensic Sci. Int'l 221 (1991).

A. W. Hartshorne and D. K. Laing, "Microspectrofluorimetry of Fluorescent Dyes and Brighteners on Single Textile Fibers: Part 3—Fluorescence Decay Phenomena," 51 Forensic Sci. Int'l 239 (1991).

Max M. Houck and Bruce Budowle, "Correlation of Microscopic and Mitochondrial DNA Hair Comparisons," 47 J. FORENSIC SCI. 964 (2001).

Max M. Houck, "Inter-Comparison of Unrelated Fiber Evidence," 135 Forensic Sci. Int'l 146 (2003).

Min Huang, et al., "Forensic Identification of Dyes Extracted from Textile Fibers by Liquid Chromatography Mass Spectrometry (LC-MS)," 49 J. FORENSIC SCI. 238 (2004).

Imelda P. Keen, et al., "Characterization of Fibers by Raman Microprobe Spectroscopy," 43 J. FORENSIC SCI. 82 (1998).

Robert D. Koons, "Comparison of Individual Carpet Fibers Using Energy Dispersive X-Ray Fluorescence," 41 J. FORENSIC SCI. 199 (1996).

Menachem Lewin ed., *Handbook of Fiber Chemistry*, 3rd ed., CRC Press, 2006.

Ray Palmer and Vongai Chinherende, "A Target Fibres Study Using Cinema and Car Seats as Recipient Items," 41 J. FORENSIC SCI. 802 (1996).

Ray Palmer, "The Retention and Recovery of Transferred Fibers Following the Washing of Recipient Clothing," 43 J. FORENSIC SCI. 502 (1998).

Ray Palmer, William Hutchinson and Verity Fryer, "The Discrimination of (Non-Denim) Blue Cotton," 49 Science & Justice 12 (2009).

Gisela Skopp, *et al.*, "Experimental Investigations on Hair Fibers as Diffusion Bridges and Opiates as Solutes in Solutions," 41 J. FORENSIC SCI. 117 (1996).

Scott F. Stoeffler, "A Flowchart System for the Identification of Common Synthetic Fibers by Polarized Light Microscopy," 41 J. FORENSIC SCI. 297 (1996).

Jolanta Was, *et al.*, "The Use of FTIR Microspectroscopy for the Identification of Thermally Changes Fibers," 41 J. FORENSIC SCI. 1005 (1996).

Kenneth G. Wiggins, *et al.*, "The Importance of Thin Layer Chromatography in the Analysis of Reactive Dyes Released from Wool Fibers," 41 J. FORENSIC SCI. 1042 (1996).

4. PAINT, GLASS, AND OTHER PHYSICAL EVIDENCE

Werner R. Bernhard, "Paint and Tape: Collection and Storage of Microtraces of Paint in Adhesive Tape," 45 J. FORENSIC SCI. 1312 (2000).

Brian Caddy, ed. *Forensic Examination of Glass and Paint: Analysis and Interpretation*, CRC Press, 2001.

James M. Curran, Tacha Natalie Hicks and John S. Buckleton, *Forensic Interpretation of Glass Evidence*, CRC Press, 2000.

Yun-Seng Giang, *et al.*, "Identification of Tiny and Tin Smears of Automotive Paint Following A Traffic Accident," 47 J. FORENSIC SCI. 625 (2002).

Robert D. Koons and JoAnn Buscaglia, "Interpretation of Glass Composition Measurements: The Effects of Match Criteria on Discrimination Capability," 47 J. FORENSIC SCI. 505 (2002).

Kristin A. Kopchick and Christopher R. Bommarito, "Color Analysis of Apparently Achromatic Automotive Paints by Visible Microspectrophotometry," 51 J. FORENSIC SCI. 340 (2006).

Shirly Montero, *et al.*, "Elemental Analysis of Glass Fragments by ICP-MS As Evidence of Association: Analysis of a Case," 48 J. FORENSIC SCI. 1101 (2003).

Scott Ryland, *et al.*, "Discrimination of 1990s Original Automotive Paint Systems," 42 J. FORENSIC SCI. 31 (2001).

Edward M. Suzuki and Martin X. McDermot, "Infrared Spectra of U.S. Automotive Original Finishes," 51 J. FORENSIC SCI. 532 (2006).

Edward M. Suzuki and Mike Carrabba, "In Situ Identification and Analysis of Automotive Paint Pigments During Line Segment Excitation Raman Spectroscopy: Inorganic Pigments," 46 J. FORENSIC SCI. 1053 (2001).

CHAPTER 8

VEHICLE INVESTIGATIONS[1]

I. INTRODUCTION

§8.01 SCOPE OF THE CHAPTER

Vehicles are an ubiquitous part of American society and scientific evidence involving vehicles is frequently involved in litigation, both civil and criminal. Two types of scientific evidence involved in vehicle investigations will be discussed in this chapter: speed detection and accident reconstruction. Both types of evidence may be used in civil and criminal cases to support various claims of liability, including personal injury, wrongful death, and minor or serious criminal charges. Law enforcement officers are frequently used as both fact and expert witnesses to present evidence of vehicle investigations, but privately retained experts are also used, particularly with complex accident reconstruction scenes.

---

[1] The Authors gratefully acknowledge the valuable assistance given by Betty R. Fitterman and Thomas L. Bohan who contributed to the previous versions of portions of this chapter.

Although courts have found the observation and testimony of lay witnesses sufficient to establish speed of a vehicle without the benefit of any scientific tools or expert training,[2] this chapter deals with the more technical and scientific methods used to determine speed. These methods include radar, laser device, and photo speed enforcement. The capabilities and limitations of these methods as well as evidentiary issues regarding speed estimations will be discussed.

In addition to scientific evidence of speed, the chapter will discuss the analysis of motor vehicle collisions[3] to determine the circumstances of the collision. The term "accident reconstruction" will be used in this chapter, but the analysis is often referred to by many different labels (*e.g.*, motor vehicle accident reconstruction, automobile accident reconstruction, traffic crash investigation and reconstruction, vehicular accident reconstruction, crash analysis, collision reconstruction). The objective of an accident reconstruction expert is to determine, based on the physical evidence and witness statements, how the motor vehicle collision or crash occurred.[4] Some commentators have described accident reconstruction as more art than science;[5] however, it is more accurate to say the field is a combination of science and technical knowledge. The "science" of the field derives from the basic principles of physics and mathematics, while the "technical" aspects of the field encompass engineering and computer applications. This chapter provides an overview of the process, methodology, and underlying scientific principles of accident reconstruction analysis to reach conclusions about how and why a motor vehicle accident occurred. The qualifications of experts and the admissibility of accident reconstruction evidence in civil and criminal litigation are also addressed.

---

[2] *See* Greenway v. Commonwealth, 254 Va. 147, 152, 487 S.E.2d 224, 227 (1997)(*quoting* Moore v. Lewis, 201 Va. 522, 525, 111 S.E.2d 788, 790 (1960)("An estimate of the speed at which an automobile was moving at a given time is generally viewed as a matter of common observation rather than expert opinion, and it is accordingly well settled that any person of ordinary experience, ability, and intelligence having the means or opportunity of observation, whether an expert or nonexpert, and without proof of further qualification may express an opinion as to how fast an automobile which came under his observation was going at a particular time. The fact that the witness had not owned or operated an automobile does not preclude him from so testifying. Speed of an automobile is not a matter of exclusive knowledge or skill, but anyone with a knowledge of time and distance is a competent witness to give an estimate; the opportunity and extent of observation goes to the weight of the testimony.")

[3] Although motor vehicle crashes may be intentional (for example, in cases of murder or suicide), the overwhelming majority of crashes are unintentional ("accidents"). This chapter will refer to "accident reconstruction," but the same reconstruction principles and methodologies also apply to intentional crashes.

[4] Thomas C. Christensen and Laura L. Liptai, "Reconstruction: Accident," in WILEY ENCYCLOPEDIA OF FORENSIC SCIENCE, (Jamieson A. & Moenssens A.A., eds) 2009 & online updates.

[5] Donald J. Van Kirk, *Vehicular Accident Investigation and Reconstruction,* CRC Press LLC, 2001 at p. xi.

§8.02 TERMINOLOGY

Acceleration: Rate of change of translational or angular velocity with respect to time.

Acceleration mark: Mark left by a tire spinning about its axle while slipping on the road surface. Unlike skid marks, which start out light and then darken, acceleration marks begin dark and then become light.

Accelerometer: Device that measures and records, usually by electrical means, the acceleration of any object to which it is affixed.

Angular momentum: Refers to the rotation of an object about an axis and equals the body's moment of inertia (q.v.) about that axis multiplied by the rate of that rotation, the latter usually referred to as the object's angular velocity.

Angular velocity: The rate at which an object rotates about an axis, having dimensions of angular displacement per unit time.

Coefficient of friction: A measure of the frictional force resisting the sliding of one surface across a second surface; when applicable it is the frictional force divided by the force pressing the two surfaces together.

CRASH3: Calspan Reconstruction of Accident Speeds on the Highway, Version 3; a computer accident reconstruction program for estimating crash severity.

Delta-V: The change in velocity of the center of mass of a vehicle during the 25–100 ms period of maximum engagement during a crash.

Dynamic crush: The maximum deformation of a vehicle's surfaces during the course of a crash, as distinguished from residual crush, the deformation that remains following the crash.

Groove: Long, narrow gouge in a road surface caused by a motor vehicle crash.

Inertia: Physical property of a body that underlies that body's resistance to a change in velocity. It is the basis of Newton's Laws stating that a body will remain at rest or continue to move at a constant velocity unless acted on by an external force, that is, a push or pull exerted from outside the body.

Kinetic energy: The energy of a body due to its motion alone.

Linear momentum: The momentum a body possesses as a result of its translational (as opposed to rotational movement), equal to the body's mass multiplied by its velocity.

Pitch: The change in a vehicle's orientation associated with the vehicle rotating about its pitch axis; the pitch axis extends horizontally through a vehicle's two sides, passing through the vehicle's center of mass.

Roll: The change in a vehicle's orientation associated with the vehicle rotating about its roll axis; the roll axis extends horizontally through a vehicle from its front to its rear, passing through the vehicle's center of mass.

Scrape: Mark on a surface that is wider than it is deep.

Scratch: Linear mark on a surface lacking appreciable depth.

Scuffmarks: Short tire marks on a road surface lacking the specific characteristics of skid marks (q.v.), acceleration marks (supra), or yaw marks (q.v.).

Skid mark: Mark on road made by a skidding tire, that is, a tire on a wheel that has ceased rotating as the result of braking as a vehicle slides to a stop.

Speed: Time rate of change of position, otherwise stated as the distance traveled per unit time.

Translational Velocity: Rate of change of displacement with both a magnitude and direction. The magnitude of velocity is also referred to as speed. Velocity is speed with a defined direction.

Yaw: The rotation of a vehicle about its yaw axis; the yaw axis passes vertically through the vehicle's center of mass.

Yaw mark: A curved mark with lateral striations caused by a tire that is rotating and turning at the same time, typically on a vehicle that is rounding a curved trajectory at high speed. The angle of the lateral striations is dependent on the speed of the vehicle.

§8.03 EVIDENTIARY USES

Speed is one factor generally considered to increase the likelihood and severity of vehicle collisions. The National Highway Traffic Safety Administration (NHTSA) estimates that the economic cost to society of speeding-related crashes is $52 billion per year.[6] As such, speeding receives considerable attention from communities, safety organizations, and law enforcement. According to NHTSA, speed contributed to 28 percent of all fatal crashes in 2014, costing 9,262 lives.[7] Law enforcement plays a role in promoting safety on roadways concerning the factor over which it has the most control: driver behavior, and responds with an arsenal of methods to detect and document excessive speeding for use in eventual prosecution.

In 2014, the number of motor vehicle crashes reported to law enforcement agencies in the United States exceeded 6 million. Over

---

[6] U.S. Department of Transportation, NHTSA, *Quick Facts 2014*, DOT HS 812 234 (March 2016) at p. 6 (available at: https://crashstats.nhtsa.dot.gov/Api/Public/ViewPublication/812234)(last accessed October 19, 2016).

[7] U.S. Department of Transportation, NHTSA, *Traffic Safety Facts 2014 Data*, DOT HS 812 265 (April 2016)(available at: https://crashstats.nhtsa.dot.gov/Api/Public/ViewPublication/812265)(last accessed October 19, 2016).

32,000 people (vehicle occupants, motorcyclists, and non-occupants) were killed as a result of motor vehicle crashes in 2014, an average of 90 people killed per day. In addition to the loss of life, over 2.3 million people were injured and the total societal harm, including economic and quality of life losses, was estimated to be in excess of $836 billion.[8] With such an impact on life and property, motor vehicle crashes frequently result in questions about civil and criminal liability.[9] Criminal cases arising from traffic crashes include prosecutions for murder and manslaughter as well as for assault and aggravated assault. Underlying many prosecutions is a charge of impaired driving. Civil cases involve wrongful death or personal injury actions against drivers and vehicle manufacturers. The latter can also be targets of products liability and negligent manufacture actions. In deciding whether someone is criminally or civilly liable for a traffic crash, the trier of fact must first determine the details of the crash, including the factors that caused it.

In some motor vehicle crash cases, it is only through the use of an accident reconstruction expert that a judge or jury can even begin to understand how and why the accident occurred. An accident reconstruction expert may be able to determine the speed of the vehicles, the identity of the driver, and the relative positioning of vehicle, as well as possible human factors implicated in the crash (including the driver's reaction and perception). Reconstruction techniques are useful when there are no eyewitnesses and essential when there are (because eyewitness testimony is both remarkably unreliable and remarkably convincing to lay jurors). It is this need for expert testimony in accident cases that has spawned the specialized field of accident reconstruction.

The accident reconstruction process has been described as "putting the pieces of the puzzle back together to compose the original image."[10] The accident investigation expert will attempt to reconstruct the behavior of the vehicles both prior to and during the accident. The starting point is their behavior immediately post-impact, as the vehicles are moving to rest. This is done by means of deductions, inductions, and inferences concerning the physical evidence found at the scene of the incident and the physical attributes of the vehicles and the roadway (or other scene). The relevant physical evidence includes, but is not limited to, marks on the roadway, trace evidence collected at the scene and from the vehicles, and resulting impact damage to the vehicles, people, and structures. By properly piecing together and interpreting these bits

---

[8] U.S. Department of Transportation, NHTSA, *Quick Facts 2014*, DOT HS 812 234 (March 2016)(available at: https://crashstats.nhtsa.dot.gov/Api/Public/ViewPublication/812234)(last accessed October 19, 2016).

[9] Accident reconstruction analysis is also important to federal and state agencies, insurance companies, vehicle manufacturers, and consumer advocacy groups for improving motorist safety.

[10] Thomas C. Christensen and Laura L. Liptai, "Reconstruction: Accident," in WILEY ENCYCLOPEDIA OF FORENSIC SCIENCE, (Jamieson A. & Moenssens A.A., eds) 2009 & online updates.

of evidence, the accident reconstruction expert strives to provide an accurate post-incident description of how and why the accident occurred.

II. EXTERNAL SPEED MEASUREMENT

§8.04   STANDARDS

Technological methods used to measure speed include mobile and stationary radar, laser devices, and photo speed enforcement. The NHTSA has provided guidelines for the appropriate use of such technologies:

> Selection of speed enforcement equipment should relate to the road type where it is used. Hand-held radar is sufficient for residential areas and other relatively low volume locations. Laser devices are often more useful for arterial roads where speeds and volume may be higher and pinpointing an individual vehicle is more difficult. Mobile radar devices, including single and dual antenna units, are effective for use on higher speed roads in urban and suburban areas. Automated Speed Enforcement has been found to be effective on local and arterial roads in urban and suburban areas.[11]

To provide uniform specifications and to ensure public trust in the accuracy and reliability of speed measuring devices, the Enforcement Technology Program of the International Association of Chiefs of Police (IACP) determines which products meet NHTSA performance standards for speed measurement devices and publishes a Conforming Product List (CPL).[12] Manufacturers voluntarily submit their products for review to be included on this list and the products are evaluated for their conformance with the NHTSA standards for "Down-the-Road Radar Module,"[13] "Across-the-Road Radar Module,"[14] and laser[15] speed

---

[11] U.S. Department of Transportation, NHTSA, *Speed Enforcement Program Guidelines,* DOT HS 810 915 (March 2008), p. 17.

[12] International Association of Chiefs of Police, Enforcement Technology Program, *Conforming Product List, Speed Measuring Devices,* September 30, 2016 (available at: http://www.theiacp.org/portals/0/documents/pdfs/combined-cpl.pdf)(last accessed November 8, 2016).

[13] U.S. Department of Transportation, NHTSA, *Speed-Measuring Device Specifications: Down-the-Road Radar Module,* DOT HS 812 266 (April 2016). These specifications apply "to radar speed-measuring devices that transmit unmodulated continuous-wave (CW) microwave energy, monitor the reflected signal from moving vehicles within the microwave beam, and process the Doppler shift of the reflected signal to display the speed of the vehicle that is being tracked, and if applicable, the speed of the patrol vehicle." Id. at p. 1–1.

[14] U.S. Department of Transportation, NHTSA, *Speed-Measuring Device Performance Specifications: Across-the-Road Radar Module,"* DOT HS 810 845 (October 2007). These specifications apply to stationary, automated, across-the-road radar devices "that transmit an unmodulated continuous wave (CW) microwave beam across the roadway, monitor the signals reflected from moving vehicles crossing the microwave beam, process the Doppler shifts of the reflected signals for the vehicle speeds, and may automatically record images of those vehicles which exceed a preset speed." Id. at p. 1–1.

measuring devices. Meeting the standards established by the NHTSA and being listed on the IACP CPL does not mean units necessarily comply with local and state regulations. Most states also require a state agency to approve certain devices for use by law enforcement and additionally require certification of the devices on a prescribed schedule.[16]

§8.05 AUTOMATED SPEED ENFORCEMENT (ASE)

Automated Speed Enforcement (ASE), also known as photo speed enforcement, is a somewhat controversial speed measurement method used in a number of jurisdictions to photograph violations of speed limits. The excessive speed is recognized by a speed measuring device, which triggers a camera or cameras to record electronic images of the vehicle. Citations or notices are issued to the registered vehicle owner. As of November, 2016, this type of speed monitoring is used in 143 communities in 12 states, the District of Columbia and the US Virgin Islands.[17]

Because of the many considerations involved in using automated speed enforcement, it is considered a supplemental tool and not a primary means of speed control for jurisdictions. Positive aspects of using ASE include efficient use of resources, high rate of detection, accuracy, and safety because the operation does not involve pulling motorists to the side of the road. Negative issues associated with ASE are many, some of which are privacy concerns, suspicious attitudes toward the financial motives of jurisdictions, fairness of citing only the registered owner of the car, and time lag between detection and citation—thus providing no immediate inducement to slow down.[18]

Speed enforcement through ASE may be conducted with or without the presence of law enforcement, from a fixed position or mobile based camera, with or without warning, site specific or jurisdiction wide, with one camera or more, photos taken of the driver or not, and the unit may actually be working or just appear to be in operation. States and

---

[15] U.S. Department of Transportation, NHTSA, *LIDAR Speed-Measuring Device Performance Specifications,* DOT HS 809–811 (March 2013). These specification apply to laser speed-measuring devices and systems that transmit coherent infra-red light pulses, measure the time of flight for the pulses reflected from moving vehicles, then calculate and display or output the speed of the target vehicle, and may automatically record images of those vehicles which exceed a preset speed." Id. at p. 1.

[16] *See* Va. Code § 46.2–882 (". . . . The Division of Purchases and Supply, pursuant to § 2.2–1112, shall determine the proper equipment used to determine the speed of motor vehicles and shall advise the respective law-enforcement officials of the same. Police chiefs and sheriffs shall ensure that all such equipment and devices purchased on or after July 1, 1986, meet or exceed the standards established by the Division.")

[17] *See* http://www.ghsa.org/html/stateinfo/laws/auto_enforce.html (last accessed November 8, 2016) and http://www.iihs.org/iihs/topics/laws/automated_enforcement (last accessed November 8, 2016).

[18] U.S. Department of Transportation, NHTSA, "Speed Enforcement Camera Systems, Operational Guidelines," DOT HS 810 916 (March 2008).

communities that approve the use of this method decide which variables are appropriate and legal in their jurisdiction.[19]

In ASE zones where cameras are stationary, they are positioned to take images of the license plates and sometimes of the drivers of vehicles that pass a preset value established by localities. The speed of the vehicle can be determined by radar, laser sensors, in-pavement sensors or reflective light. The threshold speed that triggers the camera to take a photograph is generally considerably higher than the posted limit to leave less potential for arguments of instrument inaccuracy and to limit legal action to more flagrant offenses. Different thresholds can be set for different types of vehicles with some systems that can detect the length of the vehicle. For example, trucks can be given less leeway and have a lower speed threshold to trigger the camera and a consequent violation. Once the photo system is triggered by a vehicle meeting the threshold speed level, digital photos of the vehicle's license are taken and merged with the speed information. The photos can be taken once or over two or more points.

Automated license plate recognition technology can be used for spend enforcement to take images at two different points and measuring the time from point to point. The algorithmic system finds, manipulates, reads, and converts images on the license plates for ready analysis and is a constantly-updated and widely-used tool that has many adaptations for law enforcement and businesses. It involves a complex series of operations that can accommodate shape, color, character, and other varieties in plate images, even at very fast speeds. Photo systems include very fast shutter (1/1000 sec) illumination able to capture photos in all conditions and minimized glare. Infrared illuminators can be used for viewing license plates at any time of day in any kind of weather. One camera can capture the images of several lanes of traffic and license plates. The ever-developing capacity of automated license plate recognitions and its growing use exponentially increases the capacity of law enforcement to monitor traffic and individual vehicles, including for speed measurement.

Law enforcement generally reviews the photos and certifies that the cameras and speed detectors were operating properly. A time limit is usually established by which the notice or citation is sent to the owner or renter of the registered vehicle. The citation is based on law enforcement's inspection of the photos. Some systems make images available online and these can be accessed by entering the citation number, such as in Washington, D.C. Safeguards are taken to limit use of the images to the process of adjudicating the speeding violation. Citations may explain the procedures to challenge the citation for those

---

[19] The Governors Highway Safety Association maintains a listing of state laws, with links, concerning speed and red light enforcement cameras (available at: http://www.ghsa.org/html/stateinfo/laws/auto_enforce.html)(last accessed November 8, 2016).

vehicle owners or renters who claim not to have been driving the vehicle at the time of the infraction.

Testing protocol includes assuring proper positioning of the camera, initiating an internal test for sequencing of the system including internal timing, determining that the threshold speed is set on the radar, activating the tuning fork to the specifications, and other indicators.

§8.06   RADAR

1.   GENERAL PRINCIPLES

The radar speed detector is probably the most common instrumental speed detection device currently used. Contemporary units were developed as an offshoot of military radar utilized during World War II to measure the height, speed and distance of various objects. The word "RADAR" is an acronym for RAdio Detection And Ranging, and is applied to both the technique and the equipment used. The core of a radar unit consists of a transmitter and a receiver of radio waves, coupled to a specially designed voltmeter calibrated on a scale in mile-per-hour equivalents, and an optional graph recorder. The transmitter sends out a cone-shaped stream of radio wave crests continuously in the direction the radar unit is pointed. The number of wave crests is constant, being the frequency of the radio wave. When the beam strikes an object, some of the beam is reflected back to the receiver part of the radar device. The reflection is called the "echo." If the object is stationary, the frequency of the echo is identical to the frequency of the original transmitter beam. If the object is moving toward or away from the transmitter, the echo has a different frequency and the change in frequency varies directly with the speed of the moving object off which the echo is reflected. This change in frequency is part of an effect that Christian J. Doppler called attention to in 1842.

The Doppler Effect is an apparent change in the frequency of a vibration which occurs when there is relative motion between the source of the vibration and the receiver of the vibration. The Doppler Effect is particularly suitable for measuring the speed of motor vehicles. When a car is moving along a road toward a radar speed measuring device, it runs into wave crests emitted by the radar unit that it would not have run into until the next microsecond had it been standing still. To the car, the frequency of the transmitter seems to be higher than it actually is. In reflecting these waves toward the receiver of the radar device, the car becomes a moving source of waves of this slightly higher frequency. The receiver picks up the waves of the transmitter and the waves sent back by the car, thus forming a "beat" wave similar to the one produced by striking two piano keys simultaneously. By means of a simple formula calculated within the machine, the difference in the frequencies of the beat wave is determined to be directly proportional to the velocity of the car. The velocity is recorded in mile-per-hour equivalents on the radar window for the control officer's evaluation and record.

Today's radar can be operated in several different modes to detect speeders. These modes include stationary or mobile, target approaching or target going away. Many models change automatically from mode to mode. Mobile radar considers two different speeds, that of the officer's car and the speed of closing or distancing between the target and the patrol vehicle to calculate the target vehicle speed. Refinements to this process in newer models bring about even greater confidence in speed measurement. One of these is Vehicle Speed Sensing (VSS), a digital signal processing, which is attached to the transmission or axle and sends speed information to the speedometer, cruise control, and other computers. This system is in all late model vehicles. These advanced radar units tap into the VSS to monitor the patrol car speed. With this technology, the "shadowing" phenomenon that plagued earlier models is virtually eliminated. Shadowing refers to an incorrect radar reading of the speed of the patrol vehicle. Normally, this measure is taken by using the reflection of the road surface as background. If the patrol radio is behind a large vehicle such as a tractor-trailer, the radio may interpret that vehicle's speed as the background to determine the patrol car speed. With VSS, the patrol car is able to find the correct background to use the radar to measure it instead of the large vehicle's speed. Radar still measures the patrol car speed as is the practice in settled case law, but it does not erroneously choose the wrong ground speed. Radar units that connect to the patrol unit's on-board diagnostics center through the data port or digital signal processing offer the same interference free calculation.[20]

Many radar units now have more than two windows displaying additional information, greatly expanding the capabilities and accuracy of identifying speeders. Two-window units read the closest or strongest vehicle. The strongest vehicle is determined by a number of factors including distance, vehicle size and composition, and the terrain, such as having curves or hills which block the radar cone. With fastest technology, the unit is able to distinguish between the fastest and the strongest signal, and unit displays the speed of the fastest vehicle in the cone. These three-window units display the patrol vehicle speed, the strongest vehicle speed and the fastest vehicle speed. Officers are trained how to visually recognize the fastest vehicle and estimate its speed. This estimate factored with fastest technology gives a relatively unassailable judgment of which vehicle is speeding, particularly when combined with the capability of some models to register the distance of the fastest vehicle.

---

[20] Geoffrey Gluckman, "Tracking Vehicle Speed," Law Enforcement Technology, September 2004.

Some patrol vehicles are equipped with four display windows. In this arrangement, the windows indicate target, mode, lock, and patrol speed so that the officer knows which direction the radar is reading in both stationary and moving modes. For example, the Ranger EZ lists in its specifications the window display configuration as "Left Window: Target Speed/Strongest Signal; Middle Window: Fastest Speed/Choice of Locked Fastest or Locked Strongest Target; Right Window: Patrol Speed; Mode Window: A Fourth Window (between the Middle and Right Speed Display Windows) simulates the antenna signal direction in relation to the patrol car: Front Antenna: Approaching, Opposite Direction or Moving in the Same Direction, Rear Antenna: Receding Opposite Direction or Approaching in the Same Direction." Promotional materials also state that the model detects the range of the fastest vehicle and the strongest vehicle and differentiates them.[21]

2. FACTORS AFFECTING RELIABILITY

The science underlying radar speed measurement devices are validated principles of physics. As with any device operated by human beings, either technical problems or human error, or both, may result in an erroneous determination of the true speed of a targeted vehicle. New models eliminate many of the technical problems formerly associated with radar, as with the previously mentioned Vehicle Speed Sensing technology. However, any factor that impacts the propagation of radio waves at or near the frequencies used by the radar unit can affect speed measurements.

a. Distinguishing Targets

Radar is beamed as a cone and measures an object's reflectivity, position, and speed. For vehicles, these values correspond to biggest, closest and fastest. The cone-shaped radar pattern transmission rapidly embraces a broad area. With a beam of nine to 25 degrees, most units can cover up to eight lanes of traffic at a relatively short range. In those units, within this cone-shaped beam, only one speed will be displayed, though any metallic object can return echoes to the set. Ordinarily, if the suspect vehicle is the only moving target, the reading can be fairly accurate, but if many vehicles are in the cone, the process is much more difficult. This inability to designate which specific vehicular unit is speeding is true of stationary units as well as with mobile radar.

b. Angle Error

Assuming proper targeting and vehicle identification, a properly maintained and functioning radar unit will produce an accurate reading of the speed of the target vehicle if the transmitting unit is either

---

[21] *See* Ranger EZ Ranging Traffic Radar System Datasheet (available at http://www.mph industries.com/pdfs/Ranger%20Datasheet%202-page%20101014%202.pdf)(last accessed November 8, 2016).

directly in front or directly behind the target. This scenario rarely occurs on the highway and there is nearly always a difference between the angle of the radar beam's path and the path of the target vehicle. This difference may result in an error that either favors the target vehicle or overestimates the speed of it. To take into account this directional difference, speed can be determined by use of a mathematical cosine formula.

A related problem occurs when the radar waves are bounced back off a metallic billboard or other highly reflective surface. Under those circumstances, the unit may calculate the patrol speed as being less than it actually is. This will automatically increase the reported speed of the target vehicle above its actual speed. The possibility of angle error is one that should be carefully considered.

c. Radio Frequency Interference (RFI)

RFI can affect the reliability of radar readings. GPS, mobile data computers, automated transmissions, and cell phones in patrol cars can increase the potential for RFI. Manufacturers have responded by digitizing antennas receiving the Doppler signal and added shielded cables to protect the system from such interference.

Outside the patrol car, the presence of electrical transmission wires, especially high-voltage lines, can produce interference that results in "ghost" readings or other effects that distort the accuracy of the radar reading, as can the presence of other transmitters in the area, such as airport surveillance radar. Other sources of interference, such as other police or Citizens Band radio signals, neon lights, garage door openers, and other sources of microwave radiation may produce interference.

When operating hand-held equipment, if the radar antenna is inadvertently directed toward a mechanical device within the patrol car, such as the whirring blades of the heater or cooling fan, a "panning error" may be induced. This may also occur when the antenna is pointed toward the control head or other electronic equipment, such as the vehicle's radios, or even a radar unit operated within the same vicinity by another officer. Though less likely to occur when radar is used in a stationary mode, panning error can occur when the officer fails to adjust the set in order to diminish or eliminate the interference. A different form of panning error occurs when a hand-held unit is swung around by the officer using it to follow a car passing by. In such a case, the speed of the motion of the hand-held antenna is added to the speed of the target vehicle to produce a higher readout than the vehicle's actual speed.[22]

---

[22] Joseph G. Trichter and Joseph Patterson, "Police Radar 1980: Has the Black Box Lost Its Magic?" 11 ST. MARY'S L. J. 829, 848 (1980).

3. REQUIRED TESTING OF EQUIPMENT

The radar speed-measuring device is also subject to error if it is not sufficiently tested to ensure accuracy. This is very important because many courts hold that untested radar equipment readings standing alone are insufficient to convict for speeding. The proper testing requirements vary with the equipment used and with the requirements imposed by the states. Most states require approval of the unit by state officials and periodic testing, as often as once every thirty days or as infrequently as once a year.

NHTSA details the following tests to determine if Down-the-Road radar modules meet their standards: labeling, tuning fork calibration, radar device tuning fork test, microwave transmission, environment extremes, low supply voltage operation, Doppler audio, speed monitor alert, power surge test, speed display, conducted electromagnetic interference, radiated electromagnetic interference, and speed accuracy field operation, and common output protocol.[23] NHTSA lists the following testing requirements for Across the Road units: tuning fork calibration, microwave transmission, environmental tests, low supply voltage tests, Doppler audio (if applicable), power surge, speed display, internal circuit test., signal processing, conducted electromagnetic interference, radiated electromagnetic interference, speed accuracy: field operation, and vehicle determination: field operation.[24]

The internal tests must be performed by an electronics technician and involve checking the oscillation input of the device. An extremely small variation in this input can produce a significant error in the speed reading. Based on the proposition that an oscillation variation of .1% produces a speed error of two miles per hour, it can readily be seen that an error in oscillation of a mere one percent produces a speed error of 20 miles per hour, an error that would most assuredly render the device useless as a means of enforcing speed laws.

Field-testing the radar device is a necessary verification of accurate operation. Several tests are generally used for this purpose. One is to run a vehicle with a calibrated speedometer past the radar unit and compare the speedometer reading in the "drive through" vehicle with the reading obtained on the radar unit. Another commonly used test of accuracy requires the use of an external tuning fork. Since the unit measures the Doppler Effect, which is in turn a measurement of reflected frequency of vibration, any given frequency corresponds to a given speed as it would be recorded in the speedometer. Tuning forks are available that are calibrated in almost all speeds from 15 mph to 100 mph in multiples of 5 mph. By holding several different tuning forks in front of the speedometer and observing whether the recorded

---

[23] U.S. Department of Transportation, NHTSA, *Speed-measuring Device Specifications: Down-the-Road Radar Module*, DOT HS 812 266 (April 2016) at pp. 2-1 to 2-10.

[24] U.S. Department of Transportation, NHTSA, *Speed-measuring Device Performance Specifications: Across-the-Road Radar Module*, DOT HS 810 845 (October 2007) at pp. 2-1 to 2-8.

speed corresponds with that for which each tuning fork was designed, the field accuracy of the radar unit may be established. A number of states have made such a testing procedure mandatory before and after use.[25]

§8.07   LASER SPEED-MEASURING DEVICES

Another technology used to measure speed is an adaptation of laser technology. Admired for its pin-point accuracy in locating targets in the Gulf War, this adaptation of laser aiming devices to the detection of speeders has been steadily increasing in use. According to estimates, laser devices made up 30 percent of the speed enforcement electronics market in 2006, up from 10 percent in 2004.[26]

"Laser" is an acronym for Light Amplification by Stimulated Emission of Radiation. Unlike the electromagnetic radiation generated by radar units, lasers use light energy instead. As a result of the pioneering work of scientists Schawlow, Townes, and Maiman, a host of solid state and other types of lasers have been developed.[27] Laser techniques have seen many applications in everyday life beyond the military uses, such as in printing processes, in compact disc players, in surgical instruments, in holography, in communications, and even at grocery store check-out stands. Laser speed measuring devices are also known as LIDAR for LIght Detection And Ranging.

The laser beam is produced when a material within a cavity that is partially mirrored is stimulated by electrical or light energy. As the material becomes stimulated, a chain reaction begins, wherein the energy emitted by the material itself further excites the material. When the energy generated is of a sufficient intensity, it passes through the mirror as a narrow, straight, and intense beam of monochromatic and coherent light.[28] Its application to the detection of speeders on the highway relies on invisible light waves that are emitted at frequencies which allow the laser beam to be focused onto a very narrow target.

The greatest advantage LIDAR has over radar, with its difficulties in target selection when multiple targets are present, is the narrow band-width of laser that theoretically permits an officer to select a target out of a cluster of targets. "LIDAR devices are usually hand held, similar to hand-held radar. When using LIDAR, the officer focuses on one vehicle at a time, producing evidence that can be more precisely

---

[25]   Kenneth A. Vercammen, "How to Win When Your Client Has a Speeding Ticket," 20 BARRISTER 47, 48 (Spring, 1993).

[26]   Lisa Solomon, "LIDAR: The Speed Enforcement Weapon of Choice," OFFICER.COM, November 12, 2006 (available at: http://www.officer.com/article/10250592/lidar-the-speed-enforcement-weapon-of-choice)(last accessed November 8, 2016).

[27]   On the pioneering work with Masers and Lasers, see the topic "Maser," in Van Nostrands' *Scientific Encyclopedia*, 4th ed., 1968, at pp. 1081–1085.

[28]   U.S. Department of Transportation, NHTSA, "Law Enforcement Bulletin; Laser Speed Measurement Devices," Feb. 9, 1993. *See also*, "Shedding Some Light On Lasers," R.A.D.A.R. REPORTER (June, 1992).

associated with a specific vehicle than with radar. LIDAR is not vulnerable to radio interference, is not detectable by radar detectors, and is not easily detected by LIDAR detectors."[29]

§8.08   Other Methods of Speed Measurement

VASCAR is an acronym for Visual Average Speed Computer And Record. It originated as a relatively simple device patented in 1958 in West Virginia by Arthur N. Marshall. The original device was purely mechanical and allowed for the measurement by a pursuit vehicle of the distance traveled by a suspect vehicle by simply having the pursuit vehicle travel the same distance while the device measured that distance. At the same time, a stopwatch measured the time it took the suspect vehicle to travel the known distance. The device offered a crude improvement on the conventional speedometer-odometer combination but left much to be desired. The officer still had to compute the speed of the suspect vehicle using time-distance information obtained from the device and the stopwatch, and he was forced to observe two instruments while attempting to watch the suspect vehicle at the same time.

When the Federal Sign and Signal Corporation assumed manufacturing and marketing responsibility in 1967, VASCAR quickly developed into a sophisticated and highly refined electronic digital computer. Acceptance and use of the device grew tremendously. VASCAR was at one time widely used, but its popularity waned as radar guns became more sophisticated and laser speed detection devices were developed. VASCAR is particularly suited for open road conditions and is not as appropriate for congested traffic areas.

VASCAR operates on the simple and scientifically proven formula that average velocity equals the distance traveled divided by the time taken to travel that distance, or, as expressed in a formula: $AV = D/T$. In patrol cars, the system is linked with the Vehicle Speed Sensor and a combined computer/control module to perform calculations and retain data. The system allows for manual tracking, if reference marks are used. On VASCAR Plus, the control module has two switches, one for time input, the other for distance, along with a small three-digit speed display window and thumbwheels for manual distance inputs. The Tracker, manufactured by Kustom Signals with a newer design, has three windows and a mini-toggle switch for manual distance input.[30]

ENRADD is an acronym for Electronic Non Radar Detection Device, used primarily in Pennsylvania. In that state, radar is permitted only for use by the State Police, not local law enforcement

---

[29] U.S. Department of Transportation, NHTSA, "Speed Enforcement Program Guidelines," DOT HS 810 915 (March 2008) at p. 18. (available at: http://www.nlelp.org/wp-content/uploads/2014/05/NHTSASpeedEnforcementProgramGuidelines.pdf)(last accessed February 27, 2017).

[30] *See also* www.kustomsignals.com.

agencies.[31] Local agencies, therefore, have resorted to VASCAR and ENRADD as common speed detection equipment. With ENRADD, two small metal half square shaped bars are placed on the shoulders of the road about three feet apart. The first set of bars has two transmitters and the second has two receivers. Infrared beams of light are sent from the transmitters to the receivers. The device calculates the amount of time it takes for a vehicle to pass determines its speed. A nearby police car receives a signal on an ENRADD monitor which displays the speed if it exceeds a threshold set by the officer. This speed is generally much greater than the speed limit so as not to trigger minor violations. The equipment must be tested every 60 days to ensure accuracy and has a built in test which runs prior to every use. Negative aspects include the set-up process which requires aligning the transmitter and receiver bars on the roadway shoulders. This is time consuming, can be dangerous for the officer, and the crown of the roadway can interfere with the alignment of the bars. The units are unsuitable for hilly or mountainous terrain and in inclement weather. Also, error codes on the equipment do happen, often as a result of two vehicles passing through the system at the same time.[32]

Although not used for citing drivers for speeding, external measurements of speed through closed circuit television (CCTV) images are sometimes used in accident reconstruction work. For example, if a vehicle is recorded by several CCTV cameras prior to a collision, investigators may seek to determine how fast the vehicle was driving before the collision through two moments captured on the CCTV recordings—either through two cameras on the same system or two images recorded with the same camera. By estimating the travelled distance of the vehicle between the two images and the time elapsed, estimation of the velocity is straightforward, but quantifying the measurement uncertainty is more complicated.[33]

III. ACCIDENT RECONSTRUCTION

§8.09   EVIDENCE COLLECTION

1.   SCENE EVIDENCE

In order for an accident reconstruction expert to formulate a description of how the accident occurred, as much background

---

[31]   75 PA. CONS. STAT. § 3368. At this time Pennsylvania is the only state that restricts radar to State Police (although attempts to permit local law enforcement agencies to use radar, and for the state as a whole to adopt more diverse methods of speed detection are perennially introduced and stopped at the legislature).

[32]   *See* www.ENRADD.com.

[33]   *See* Bart Hoogeboom & Ivo Alberink, "Measurement Uncertainty When Estimating the Velocity of an Allegedly Speeding Vehicle," 55 J. Forensic Sci. 1347–1351.

information and physical evidence must be gathered as possible. The quantity and quality of the information and evidence recovered will determine the conclusions the accident reconstruction expert can validly reach and the limitations of those conclusions.[34] The evidence collection stage is vital in constructing a complete and accurate description of how the accident occurred.

Background information includes the types of vehicles involved, the environment in which the vehicles were being operated, and the human factors of the drivers prior to the accident. In gathering information on the vehicles involved in an accident, the reconstruction expert will want to have the specific design information on the model and make of the vehicles involved (including weight and dimensions). The environmental factors include weather conditions (i.e., rain, fog or snow), the physical surroundings of the accident scene, and the actual roadway conditions. Human factors, or the conditions of both drivers, are also significant in accident reconstruction. Intoxication, impairment, or distraction, will affect a driver's ability to perceive and react and may be factors in determining how the accident occurred. The drivers' driving experience, emotional status, physical deficiencies, and familiarity with the vehicle, road and surroundings also need to be evaluated for impact on the driver's perception-response times.[35]

Physical evidence may include photography or videography of the scene to document damage to the roadway or other structures, the resting place of the vehicles, debris patterns, and any marks or defects in the roadway from the accident. Examination of injuries to occupants or other involved persons may also be necessary to identify wound patterns or trauma that can help in reconstruction,[36] and accident reconstruction experts may consult with other experts, such as pathologists and anthropologists, to interpret injury patterns.[37] Trace

---

[34] Some commentators regard "accident investigation" as a separate field from "accident reconstruction," noting the differences in focus and personnel involved. *See* Raymond M. Brach and R. Matthew Brach, *Vehicle Accident Analysis and Reconstruction Methods*, SAE International, 2005 at p. xiii. Because accident reconstruction analysis is dependent on the quality and quantity of the evidence collected, the two fields will be discussed together in this Chapter.

[35] In reconstruction analysis, experts apply generally accepted recommended driver response times because research has shown that too many variables affect individual response time to make an individualized assessment reliable. The generally accepted recommended response time for a reasonably clear hazard in a normal situation is 1.5 seconds. Research has indicated that 85–95% of drivers will respond within that time. Thomas C. Christensen and Laura L. Liptai, "Reconstruction: Accident," in Wiley Encyclopedia Of Forensic Science, (Jamieson A. & Moenssens A.A., eds) 2009 & online updates.

[36] Using biomedical engineering methodology, trauma causation conclusions can assist in the reconstruction by providing such information as the positions of the occupants in the car, the possible speed of the vehicle at collision based on the degree of force needed to cause the trauma, whether the occupants were using restraint devices, and whether the injuries were caused by the initial collision or a secondary event. For a discussion of the biomedical engineering principles that can assist in determining trauma causation *see* Laura L. Liptai, "Trauma Causation: Analysis of Automotive," in Wiley Encyclopedia Of Forensic Science, (Jamieson A. & Moenssens A.A., eds) 2009 & online updates.

[37] *See* Ashley E. Kendall, Julie M. Fleischman and Laura C. Fulginiti, "Traumatic Injury Pattern Analysis in a Light Rail Transit Death: A Retrospective Case Study," 60 J. Forensic

evidence, such as debris or vehicle parts and transfer evidence, should be collected from the scene. The accident reconstruction expert must examine the vehicles for damage, including to the interior of the vehicle, which will be relevant to occupant placement and injury causation.[38] The vehicle should be examined for trace evidence, damage to the tires,[39] and post-manufacturing modifications or mechanical problems that may have contributed to the accident. Increasingly, physical evidence recovery also means collecting and analyzing data from computer systems, sensors, and safety modules within the vehicle.

2.   EVENT DATA RECORDERS

An Event Data Recorder (EDR),[40] sometimes referred to as a "black box" because of similarities to airline flight data recorders, records information related to a vehicle crash.[41] Information collected by EDRs can aid crash investigations by identifying system failures and sources of injuries, resulting in improved vehicle safety.[42]

Motor vehicle manufacturers initially incorporated their recording devices into the airbag controller systems because these systems already featured sensors and memory devices that contained crash data.[43] The development of the airbag sensor systems by General Motors Corporation hailed the arrival of today's increasingly sophisticated EDR technology. GM began recording airbag status and crash severity data in 1974.[44] Since then the National Highway Traffic Safety Administration (NHTSA) and the National Transportation Safety Board (NTSB) have substantially facilitated the development of event data recorders, but have not yet required the installation of EDRs

---

Sci. 764–769 (anthropologists' assessment of severe grinding abrasion of the lower appendage); Michael D. Freeman, Anders Eriksson and Wendy Leith, "Injury Pattern as an indication of Seat Belt Failure in Ejected Vehicle Occupants," 59 J. Forensic Sci. 1271–1274 (pathologist's assistance in assessing an anatomic injury pattern).

[38] Donald J. Van Kirk, *Vehicular Accident Investigation and Reconstruction,* CRC Press, 2001, at pp. 141–180, 237–259.

[39] Tires may reveal tread defects from a skid, blowouts, cuts, or other damage. For a discussion of the evidentiary significance of tires, *see* id. at pp. 131–132.

[40] The technology is also sometimes referred to as a Crash Data Recorder (CDR).

[41] The technology can be used in many different devices, but in this chapter EDR will be used to describe a device installed in motor vehicle to record vehicle data for a brief period of time (seconds) before, during, and immediately after a crash.

[42] For additional information regarding the development and use of EDRs see National Highway Traffic Safety Administration (NHTSA) Event Data Recorder Research Web site available at: https://www.nhtsa.gov/research-data/event-data-recorder (last accessed November 8, 2016).

[43] See Holly A. Adams, "Airbags," in WILEY ENCYCLOPEDIA OF FORENSIC SCIENCE, (Jamieson A. & Moenssens A.A., eds) 2009 & online updates.

[44] Karl A. Menninger, II, "Data and Voice Recorders in Airplanes, Motor Vehicles and Trains," 84 Am. Jur. Proof of Facts 3d 1 (2006). General Motors (GM) installed the first airbags in regular production models in 1974 and referred to the embedded event data recorder as a Sensing Diagnostic Module (SDM).

in new motor vehicles.[45] By 2005, General Motors, Ford, Isuzu, Mazda, Mitsubishi, Subaru, and Suzuki were all voluntarily equipping their vehicles with EDRs, according to NHTSA.[46] Most new passenger vehicles now have EDRs, although the quantity and type of information recorded is dependent upon the manufacturer of the vehicle and the manufacturer of the airbag systems.[47]

The NHTSA has issued standards related to EDRs installed in light duty vehicles, including the minimum set of specified data elements to be required in EDR fitted in Model Year 2013,[48] and beginning with the 2011 model year, automakers are required to disclose in the owner's manual if a vehicle has been equipped with an EDR.[49]

In the early years of EDR technology, downloading of data was available only through the proprietary recorder manufacturer, but with the introduction of the commercial crash data retrieval systems (CDR systems), the data from EDRs installed in most vehicles can be more widely accessed. Other systems and vehicle manufacturers offer

---

[45] *See generally* National Highway Traffic Safety Administration (NHTSA) Event Data Recorder Research Web site available at: https://www.nhtsa.gov/research-data/event-data-recorder (last accessed November 8, 2016).

[46] National Highway Traffic Safety Administration. 2006. Final regulatory evaluation—event data recorders. Table III-1: Estimate of the number of EDRs in light vehicles with a GVWR of 3,855 kilograms (8,500 pounds) or less. July 2006. p. 111–12. Washington, DC: US Department of Transportation.

[47] *See* http://www.crashdataservices.net/Vehicles.html.

[48] For Model Year 2013 motor vehicles equipped with EDRs, the EDR must minimally record the following information:

1.1	Change in forward speed
2.1	Maximum change in forward speed
3.1	Time from beginning of crash at which the maximum change in forward crash speed occurs
4.1	Vehicle speed
5.1	Percentage of engine throttle, percentage full (how far the accelerator pedal was pressed)
6.1	Brake action
7.1	Ignition cycle (number of power cycles applied to the EDR) at the time of the crash
8.1	Ignition cycle (number of power cycles applied to the EDR) when the EDR data were downloaded
9.1	Driver safety belt use
10.1	Frontal airbag warning lamp on/off
11.1	Driver frontal airbag deployment time
12.1	Right front passenger frontal airbag deployment time
13.1	Number of crash events
14.1	Time between first two crash events, if applicable
15.1	Whether or not EDR completed recording

Office of the Federal Register. 2006. National Highway Traffic Safety Administration—Final rule. Docket no. NHTSA-2006-25666; 49 CFR Part 563 Event data recorders. Federal Register, vol. 71, no. 166, pp. 50998–51048. Washington, DC: National Archives and Records Administration.

[49] Id.

downloads of stored data, often through video links to TV monitors or through Internet connections.

Although there was initially some debate over ownership of the EDR data, federal regulations and state legislation now clearly provide that the car owner or lessee owns the EDR information.[50] In 2004, California passed the first law requiring that manufacturers of new vehicles include information about the presence of a recording device in the owner's manual of all vehicles sold or leased in the state.[51] The statute also defines the circumstances under which recorded data may be retrieved.

EDRs based on the airbag sensor systems used in passenger vehicles are firmly affixed under a vehicle's dashboard, seat, or console. Within its housing, the system "senses" acceleration or deceleration just as an occupant in a vehicle feels the force exerted on him or her by the seat back when a vehicle accelerates and the retarding force exerted by the seat belt when a vehicle decelerates.[52] If a decelerating force is great enough to move the sensor across a predetermined threshold, an electrical switch coupled to the sensor closes, and the electrical output is used in combination with data received from another sensor or sensors to determine if the air bag should be deployed.[53] Successive generations of sensor systems have become more sophisticated with the addition of accelerometers, microprocessors, and computer algorithms to make deployments decisions.[54] As the sensor systems became more sophisticated and relied on more information in making deployment decisions, the amount of information recorded has also increased.[55] As EDR devices become more advanced, accident reconstruction experts are utilizing the data in various ways. A vehicle's change in velocity, designated by delta-V, is utilized to signify crash severity. Delta-V is used

---

[50] For a detailed analysis of the state statutes *see* Jim Harris, *Event Data Recorders—State Statutes and Legal Consideration,* 18 ACCIDENT RECONSTRUCTION J., Jan.-Feb. 2008 at 50. *See also* "Privacy of Data from Event Data Recorders: State Statutes" on the National Conference of State Legislatures website (available at: http://www.ncsl.org/research/telecommunications-and-information-technology/privacy-of-data-from-event-data-recorders.aspx)(last accessed November 8, 2016).

[51] Cal. Vehicle Code Sec. 9951.

[52] *Forensic Accident Investigation: Motor Vehicles,* (Thomas L. Bohan & Arthur C. Damask, eds. Supp. 2006), at 122–123. Also note that it is the rate of *change* in the vehicle's speed during a crash that is the relevant factor, not the vehicle's actual speed at the time of impact. Id. at 126, n. 16.

[53] Id. Thus an airbag located in front of a driver or passenger is not designed to fire unless a decelerating event such as a front end crash is detected. In vehicles equipped with side-impact or other "multi-axis response" airbags, multiple sensors are used. Id. at 125, nn. 14–15.

[54] *See* Holly A. Adams, "Airbags," in WILEY ENCYCLOPEDIA OF FORENSIC SCIENCE, (Jamieson A. & Moenssens A.A., eds) 2009 & online updates.

[55] For a detailed discussion of the evolution of EDR technology and how government agencies, legislatures, courts, and insurance companies have approached EDR data, *see* John Buhrman, "Riding with Little Brother: Striking a Better Balance Between the Benefits of Automobile Event Data Recorders and Their Drawbacks," 17 Cornell J. L. & Pub. Pol'y 201 (2007). A history of EDR usage and development is available: Rusty Haight, "An Abbreviated History of CDR Technology," COLLISION MAGAZINE, Vol. 5, Issue 1 (Spring 2010).

in many calculations in accident reconstruction analysis and in estimating occupant injury in crashes.[56]

As with any recording system, if the system works properly it can provide detailed and useful information. However, EDRs can be impacted by the collision itself or circumstances in the collision may impact the ability of the EDR to properly record the data. For example, if the vehicle vaults upon impact, the EDR may record an inaccurately high speed.[57] EDR data should be recovered and considered like other evidence collected for accident reconstruction analysis. The EDR does not provide the explanation for what happened. The EDR merely provides data that can be used, along with other evidence collected, by the expert in reaching conclusions about what happened.

§8.10   PRINCIPLES

Applying fundamental principles of physics, mathematical analysis, and engineering concepts, the accident reconstruction expert applies theory to the physical evidence to provide an explanation for what occurred. The accuracy and extent of the conclusions reached is dependent upon the quantity and quality of the physical evidence recovered. The analysis is equally dependent upon the expert's understanding and accuracy in applying the underlying theories. A detailed discussion of the underlying physics, engineering, and mathematical concepts implicated by accident reconstruction would consume multiple texts.[58] However, an overview of the process can be provided through a brief explanation of the fundamental laws of physics involved and a discussion of the physical evidence frequently used in accident reconstruction.

The basic scientific principles underlying accident reconstruction include the basic laws of physics: conservation of momentum, energy, and angular (or rotational) momentum. Conservation of momentum is the physics principle that states: absent external forces (what is also referred to as an "isolated system"), the total of the momentum of objects in the system is the same before and after a collision. In other words, the sum of the momentum of two vehicles before a collision will equal the sum of the momentum of the vehicles after the collision; any momentum lost from one vehicle will be gained by the other vehicle.[59] Conservation of energy holds that energy in a system remains constant,

---

[56] *See* Section 8.14(2) *infra* for resources detailing calculations commonly employed in accident reconstruction analysis.

[57] Alan J. Watts, *Accident Reconstruction Science 4th ed.,* Lawyers & Judges Publishing, Inc., 2011 at pp. 327–328.

[58] Recommended texts include: Alan J. Watts, *Accident Reconstruction Science 4th ed.,* Lawyers & Judges Publishing, Inc., 2011; Harold Frank and Darren Franck, *Mathematical Methods for Accident Reconstruction,* CRC Press, 2010; Raymond M. Brach and R. Matthew Brach, *Vehicle Accident Analysis and Reconstruction Methods,* SAE International, 2005.

[59] For a detailed discussion of the conservation of momentum and derivative concepts used in accident reconstruction, *see* Raymond M. Brach and R. Matthew Brach, *Vehicle Accident Analysis and Reconstruction Methods,* SAE International, 2005 at pp. 103–128.

although it may change form. The principle of conservation of energy is necessary for relating the damage to a vehicle to the speeds involved in the collision.[60] Similarly, the angular momentum of an isolated system remains constant in magnitude and direction. If one part of the system is given an angular momentum in a given direction, then some other part or parts of the system must have an angular momentum of the same magnitude in the opposite direction. The principle of the conservation of angular momentum is important for analyzing collisions involving rotation.[61]

Application of theory (based in part on these fundamental principles of physics) to the collected evidence will (if sufficient evidence is available) permit the accident reconstruction expert to reach such conclusions as vehicle speed prior to impact, angles of impact, principal direction of force, occupant kinetics, and potential trauma. The application of theory to evidence allows the accident reconstruction expert to reach conclusions about how and why the collision occurred.

Some of the commonly encountered physical evidence used by accident reconstruction experts includes tire marks, impact damage to the roadway, and impact damage to the vehicle. Many more factors may be relevant and the accident reconstruction expert must be open to considering all factors in the reconstruction.[62]

1.   TIRE MARKS

The friction between the tires and a driving surface may result in tire marks that can be used in accident reconstruction analysis for postulating the vehicle speed, direction of travel, and deceleration or acceleration forces.[63] Four types of tire marks that have historically been used are tire imprints, skid marks, acceleration marks, and yaw marks. The first mark (tire imprint) is created just from the tires rolling over the driving surface and shows the course and position of a vehicle.[64] The three remaining marks are created because the entire

---

[60] *See generally* Thomas C. Christensen and Laura L. Liptai, "Reconstruction: Accident," in WILEY ENCYCLOPEDIA OF FORENSIC SCIENCE, (Jamieson A. & Moenssens A.A., eds) 2009 & online updates.

[61] For a detailed (and practical) discussion of angular momentum, *see* Alan J. Watts, *Accident Reconstruction Science* 4th ed., Lawyers & Judges Publishing, Inc., 2011 at pp. 148–153.

[62] *See, e.g.,* Chan-Seoung Park et al., "Wind-Drag Estimation in a Traffic Accident Involving a Motor Scooter and a Tractor-Trailer," 57 J. Forensic Sci. 1108–1113 (2012).

[63] For a full discussion of various tire marks (with explanatory photographs), *see* R.W. Rivers, *Evidence in Traffic Crash Investigation and Reconstruction* (Springfield, IL: Charles C. Thomas Publisher, Ltd. 2006) at pp. 112–130.

Research into the utility of collecting residues for association with specific tire manufacturers has demonstrated difficulties with lack of homogeneity in the tires and the lack of repeatability in test samples. *See* Garry Sarkissian, "The Analysis of Tire Rubber Traces Collected After Braking Incidents Using Pyrolysis-Gas Chromatography/Mass Spectrometry," 52 J. FORENSIC SCI. 1050–1056 (2007).

[64] A tire imprint may also provide details of the tire tread and its physical characteristics.

surface of the tire is not always moving at the same speed, resulting in residue from the tire being deposited on the driving surface.

Skid marks are created when a rotating tire locks up and the tire slides over the driving surface. Skid marks are generally straight and show parallel striations from the tire tread.[65] Rubber particles are torn off the tire and the tire's temperature may increase anywhere from 200 degrees to one thousand degrees Fahrenheit depending on the composition of the tire. Natural rubber stays the coolest while synthetic rubber increases the most in temperature during skids. If the temperature becomes sufficiently high from friction, the tire literally melts. Skid marks may show, among other things, the speed,[66] course, and position of the vehicle and braking coordination between wheels. Skid marks are measured from the terminal point backward. The marks created by the front wheels must be distinguished from those created by the rear wheels. Also, each tire mark must be measured separately as all four wheels may not lock at the same time; the length of the skid mark is the average length of the marks of all four wheels. Usually the rear wheels are slightly misaligned from those of the front wheels, but if there is a perfect overlap, the wheelbase of the vehicle is used to determine front and rear wheel marks.

Skid marks are distinguished from tire imprints in several ways: (1) tire imprints show the tire tread, whereas skid marks appear slick and smooth; (2) tire imprints are uniform in intensity and in degree, whereas skid marks are likely to be darker or more prominent at their beginnings and ends; (3) the appearance of "stipples" is highly characteristic of tire imprints; such stipples are made when a tire, rolling through a viscous substance like oil or slime, pulls up little points of the sticky material as it passes through; (4) splatters of bits or mud on each side of the tire are also characteristic of tire imprints because a rolling tire creates these marks by squirting wet substances from its treads as they press down on the roadbed, whereas sliding tires do not squirt the substance out but splash it to each side.

Skips in skid marks must be distinguished from gaps between successive skid marks. Skips are created when the skidding vehicle hits a bump or hole in the road and starts bouncing. The initial skid in such a case is sometimes more than a yard long. Skips are included in the measurement of a skid mark because the tires incur increased resistance when they spring up and come back down, which compensates for the lack of friction while they are in the air. Gaps in skid marks are longer than skips. Gaps usually result from releasing or

---

[65] A skid mark may result from a tire sliding sideways (without rotation), but it will not exhibit the parallel striations. Alan J. Watts, *Accident Reconstruction Science* 4th ed., Lawyers & Judges Publishing, Inc., 2011 at p. 351.

[66] For a discussion of how skid marks are used in calculating speed with the specific mathematical formulas used, *see* Thomas C. Christensen and Laura L. Liptai, "Reconstruction: Accident," in WILEY ENCYCLOPEDIA OF FORENSIC SCIENCE, (Jamieson A. & Moenssens A.A., eds) 2009 & online updates.

pumping the brakes. Gap marks should be measured and the marks treated separately.

The utility of skid marks in calculating the speed of the automobile has diminished with the advent of the anti-lock braking system (ABS) installed in most automobiles. Unlike older braking systems in which the brakes would "lock up" the wheels during a sudden, hard braking situation, anti-lock brakes are designed to prevent such locking up. Instead of the braking calipers locking around the brake disc—which causes the brakes to lock and the vehicle to skid—anti-locking braking calipers pulsate many times per second to avoid locking up and skidding.

Skid marks start out light, then darken, and usually end abruptly. Acceleration marks appear in the reverse; they start out dark and then lighten and disappear. Acceleration marks are created when the tire, rotated by the axle, accelerates suddenly. The outside of the tire moves faster than the center of the tire (which is being held by the coefficient of friction to the roadway) and leaves a mark on the roadway until the outside surface is moving at the same speed as the center surface.

What appears to be a curved skid mark may, in fact, be a yaw mark. A tire creates a yaw mark as it tries to rotate in one direction while sliding in another. The striations or force lines in skid marks are parallel with the mark. The striations in a yaw mark are oblique to the mark. Yaw mark width and the number and angle of the striations are dependent upon vehicle speed.[67] Yaw marks indicate the vehicle made a sudden turn at a relatively high speed. This can suggest an avoidance maneuver of a potential hazard, or if a turn precedes yaw marks it may indicate a loss of driver control (such as in a rollover). The speed at the beginning of the maneuver is referred to as critical speed and may be calculated from the yaw mark. Critical Speed Yaw (CSY) analysis is a technique reconstruction experts use to determine a vehicle's speed.[68] The expert determines the speed by measuring the radius of the path of the turning vehicle and then analyzes the lateral acceleration to road friction.[69]

Certain factors unrelated to the accident may affect tire marks. After an accident has occurred, drivers of oncoming cars may not see the scene of the accident until they are very close. This sudden

---

[67] Donald J. Van Kirk, *Vehicular Accident Investigation and Reconstruction* (Boca Raton, FL: CRC Press, 2001) at p. 75.

[68] For a discussion of CYS and the mathematical formulas involved, *see* Alan J. Watts, *Accident Reconstruction Science* (Tucson, AZ: Lawyers & Judges Publishing, Inc., 4th ed. 2011) at pp. 353–354.

[69] Wade Bartlett and William Wright, *Summary of 56 Recent Critical Speed Yaw Analysis Tests including ABS and Electronic Stability Control on Pavement, Gravel, and Grass*, 18 ACCIDENT RECONSTRUCTION J., May–June 2008, at 29.

For a detailed discussion of the use of yaw marks in speed calculations and the associated uncertainty estimations, see Raymond M. Brach and R. Matthew Brach, *Vehicle Accident Analysis and Reconstruction Methods* (Warrendale, PA: SAE International, 2005) at pp. 51–64.

discovery may force them to apply their brakes, creating road surface marks which may obliterate those made by the vehicle or vehicles involved in the accident. All skid marks and other road surface marks will eventually be worn away by traffic. Also, weather conditions such as rain, snow, and wind wash off or blow away tire marks under varying conditions. Some road surface marks are visible because they contain particles with moisture in them. When the sun dries up these particles, the marks start to disappear. Other factors such as road repair work right after the accident or sweeping the area to remove broken glass and debris will affect the road surface marks.

2.   IMPACT DAMAGE TO THE ROADWAY

Scratches are made by damaged solid parts of the vehicle other than the tires when they cut into, press into, or slide along the paved surface. They indicate the course of movement of the vehicle, ordinarily after impact; they also may indicate the position of the vehicle when the impact occurred. Scratches may also indicate that a vehicle overturned, because vehicles sliding along on their side or top leave distinctive scratches made by their trim, bumpers, door handles, and other protruding parts: they often contain minuscule samples of paint from the vehicle which can be compared with paint samples of a known origin; and they may show the force and direction of impact. Scratches made before a collision, indicating that a part or parts of the vehicle broke down, may show the cause of the accident. Wheel rim scratches occurring before the collision point may show that a flat tire or blow-out caused the accident.

Gouges are like scratches, but are deeper and wider. Rather than merely tearing or separating road surface materials, gouges chip chunks out of it. They often appear at the collision point in a head-on accident, indicating that the colliding vehicles dug in with great force in meeting. Groove gouges are made by bolts or other similar elongated vehicle parts which dig into the surface and scoop out parts of it. If the groove curves or appears in a wavy line, it may indicate that the vehicle was starting to spin at the time. Chop gouges are made when broad sharp edges of parts such as cross frame members or transmission housing hit the pavement while moving. The chop gouge is usually followed by a broad rubber scratch running in the direction of vehicle movement.[70]

When vehicle wheels roll in snow, mud, moist soil, or clay, ruts are made. Furrows are similar to ruts, but differ in that furrows are made by sliding wheels or other vehicle parts. They often are a continuation of skid marks after the vehicle left the pavement. Holes, which may be found at the end of ruts, furrows, skid marks, or scuffs, are made when

---

[70] Scrapes, scratches, grooves, chips, gouges, chops, and holes are described in depth (with accompanying photographs in R.W. Rivers, *Evidence in Traffic Crash Investigation and Reconstruction* (Springfield, IL: Charles C. Thomas Publisher, Ltd. 2006) at pp. 107–109.

vehicle wheels or parts move sideways and scoop out broad pits in the earth. They are usually a foot or so in depth and one to two feet wide. They tend to show a pivotal point on which a vehicle started to spin or began to roll over.

3.   IMPACT DAMAGE TO THE VEHICLE

In addition to inspection of the vehicle for defects and possible malfunctioning parts, the accident reconstruction expert will examine the vehicle for damage related to the collision.[71] Damage to the vehicle can be used in determining the principle direction of force and for reconstructing the sequence of impacts or events. Of particular importance to the accident reconstruction expert will be the degree of crush damage to the vehicle and any resulting metal folds from the collision.

"Crush" refers to changes in the external dimensions of a vehicle and is used as a measure of the severity of a crash and can be correlated to the speed of the vehicle in certain circumstances.[72] For crashes resulting in significant vehicle damage, measurements of crush damage are made using standard techniques derived from a measuring protocol published by the Society of Automotive Engineers in 1988.[73] The measurements are used in mathematical equations to calculate the square inch area of damage and to derive the amount of energy it took to create the crush damage.[74]

The direction of the metal folds in the body of the vehicle will indicate the direction of impact (i.e., front to rear folds indicate a frontal impact), and multiple directional folds will indicate multiple impacts and may suggest the order of the impacts.[75]

---

[71] Relevant impact damage may included small changes to the vehicle, including needle marks on the speedometer as an indication of speed at the time of the collision. *See* Daiquin Tao et al., "The Experimental and Case Study of Needle Marks on the Speedometer as the Physical Evidence for the Collision Speed Analysis," 57 J. Forensic Sci. 772–777 (2012).

[72] For detailed discussion of crush measurement and use in accident reconstruction, *see* Alan J. Watts, *Accident Reconstruction Science* (Tucson, AZ: Lawyers & Judges Publishing, Inc., 4th ed. 2011) at pp. 226–230; Raymond M. Brach and R. Matthew Brach, *Vehicle Accident Analysis and Reconstruction Methods* (Warrendale, PA: SAE International, 2005) at pp. 153–164.

For a comparison of equations for estimating vehicle speed in frontal impacts with narrow objects such as poles and trees based upon maximum residual frontal crush *see* Joseph N. Colfone et al., *A Comparison of Equations for Estimating Speed Based on Maximum Static Deformation for Frontal Narrow-Object Impacts*, 17 ACCIDENT RECONSTRUCTION J., Nov.-Dec. 2007, at 19.

[73] Nicholas Tumbas and Russell Smith, "Measuring Protocol for Quantifying Vehicle Damage from an Energy Basis Point of View," SAE Technical Paper 880072, 1988, doi:10.4271/880072.

[74] Thomas C. Christensen and Laura L. Liptai, "Reconstruction: Accident," in WILEY ENCYCLOPEDIA OF FORENSIC SCIENCE, (Jamieson A. & Moenssens A.A., eds) 2009 & online updates.

[75] For a detailed discussion of the evidentiary significance of metal folds and explanatory pictures, *see* Donald J. Van Kirk, *Vehicular Accident Investigation and Reconstruction* (Boca Raton, FL: CRC Press, 2001) at pp. 109–120.

Examination of light bulbs and filaments in vehicles can provide information to answer critical questions concerning whether the lights were in use during the collision.[76]

4. OTHER TRACE EVIDENCE

Debris left by the accident, and rust, paint, or small vehicle parts, vehicle fluids, solid or liquid cargo, blood, and other trace evidence may indicate a number of things to the trained expert other than the path of the vehicle. Trace evidence is very important when the identities of the vehicles or drivers involved in the collision are unknown. Trace biological evidence can be used to link an individual to a vehicle (including a particular occupant position in the vehicle) or to establish a link between a person and a vehicle.[77] Similarly, paint recovered from an accident scene can be used to suggest a link between a vehicle and a scene or to exclude the vehicle as a possible participant.[78]

§8.11 METHODOLOGY

Current accident reconstruction makes extensive use of computer spreadsheets and modeling programs. The programs are important labor-saving devices and permit multiple simultaneous calculations while utilizing national databases of vehicle specifications and standardized variables. The accuracy of the results of the program, however, is dependent upon the expert's understanding of the capabilities and limitations of the program as well as proper data entry. The computer programs should not be viewed as "black boxes of truth" that simply produce the correct answer in each case analysis. Because of the varied circumstances of traffic crashes,[79] no one program is suitable for every crash, and using any program with an appreciation of

---

[76] Examination can answer two issues: whether the filament was energized at the time the glass housing broke and whether the filament was energized at the time of the filament's rupture. It is important to remember that the glass housing break or the filament rupture *may* have occurred at the time of the collision, but may have been a separate event. *See* Eric Stauffer, "Light Bulbs and Filaments: Examination of," in WILEY ENCYCLOPEDIA OF FORENSIC SCIENCE, (Jamieson A. & Moenssens A.A., eds) 2009 & online updates; *see also* Eric Stauffer, "Interpretation of Automotive Light Bulb Examination Results: An Intriguing Case," 52 J. FORENSIC SCI. 119–124 (2006).

[77] Air bag deployment releases residue from the gas generation system which can associate a person with the vehicle at the time of the collision. *See* Robert E. Berk, "Automated SEM/EDS Analysis of Airbag Residue. I. Particle Identification," 54 J. FORENSIC SCI. 60–68 (2009).

[78] The discriminating power of paint comparison is limited by frequency of the paint type in the population as well as the quality of the samples collected. *See* Genevieve Massonnet and Florence Monnard, "Paint: Interpretation," in WILEY ENCYCLOPEDIA OF FORENSIC SCIENCE, (Jamieson A. & Moenssens A.A., eds) 2009 & online updates.

[79] Commentators have noted that "Each accident reconstruction is unique as no two accidents are the same." Raymond M. Brach and R. Matthew Brach, *Vehicle Accident Analysis and Reconstruction Methods* (Warrendale, PA: SAE International, 2005) at p. xiv.

its limitations is essential to achieving scientifically reliable conclusions.[80]

One of the first computer programs providing a simplified mathematical analysis of motor vehicle accidents was CRASH, developed by the federal government in the 1970's.[81] The program was developed to provide a standardized and objective method of interpreting the physical evidence from a collision scene to estimate crash severity. The third version of the program, CRASH3, is still frequently used.[82] CRASH3 computes delta-v from known vehicle stiffness parameters and damage measurements on the vehicles involved in a collision. The program essentially computes the energy required to produce the measured vehicle damage and the calculated speed changes associated with the loss of energy indicated by the damage. The program also incorporates the conservation of momentum principle to calculate the trajectory (path) of the vehicles using the impact and rest positions recorded at the scene. These two calculations should be consistent if sufficient data is available for both calculations.

CRASH3 employs several assumptions which limit its utility to a discrete subset of collisions. Because the program assumes driver control ceases at impact, the program is not useful in cases where the driver has active steering after a moderate impact. The program also assumes that at some point two vehicles in a collision will reach a common velocity, which is not applicable to side-swipe incidents. The two-dimensional analysis of the program also excludes use in rollovers, curb mountings, or steep inclines. Similarly, the accuracy of the program is affected by non-uniform friction surfaces in a collision incident (i.e., asphalt, then gravel, then grass). The program also assumes uniform crush stiffness for the entire vehicle and uses standardized vehicle specifications (such as vehicle length and widths) that will affect the precision of the calculations.[83]

In addition to computer programs, accident reconstruction experts sometime rely on experiments to explain how an accident occurred, generally limited to low-speed collisions for obvious cost and safety reasons. Experiments can actually *show* what happened, as opposed to just describing the crash, but the accuracy of the experiment is

---

[80] "Always use physics and engineering to crosscheck a [computer program] before accepting its answer." Alan J. Watts, *Accident Reconstruction Science* (Tucson, AZ: Lawyers & Judges Publishing, Inc., 4th ed. 2011) at p. 77.

[81] A. L. Turner, "A Review of Crash Severity Assessment Programs Applied to Retrospective Real-World Accident Studies," Transport Research Laboratory, Paper Number 98-06-O-09 (available at: http://www-nrd.nhtsa.dot.gov/pdf/Esv/esv16/98S6O09.PDF)(last accessed on May 1, 2012).

[82] Many different programs are available, both through the NHTSA (see: http://www.nhtsa.gov/Research/Databases-and-Software) and private venders (see: http://www.vcrashusa.com).

[83] Crash3 Technical Manual, U.S. Department of Transportation, National Highway Traffic Safety Administration, National Center for Statistics and Analysis, Accident Investigation Division (1986)(available at: http://www.mchenrysoftware.com/crash3.pdf)(last accessed November 10, 2016) at pp. 1.6–1.9.

dependent upon correctly replicating the variables of the crash and the resulting damage. Because repeated tests are often necessary to replicate the exact damage, experiments can be prohibitively expensive.[84]

Because accident reconstruction analysis often begins well after a collision, direct measurements of scene and vehicle features may be limited. Experts frequently rely on photographs for the reconstruction analysis. Photogrammetry is the process of using photographs (or video) to obtain quantitative dimensional information about the physical objects depicted. The methodology can be used to quantify roadway observations like tire marks, crush damage (if the vehicle is no longer available), and to estimate speed from surveillance video.[85] Several different photogrammetry methods are used in accident reconstruction, including some that base measurements off single photographs and others which use a series of photographs involving two or more camera positions with variable separation distance from the object being measured.[86]

A very important concept in accident reconstruction analysis that was frequently overlooked or minimized in the past is the estimation of uncertainty in the measurements and conclusions. Uncertainty acknowledges limitations of knowledge and the inability to account for every influencing factor in an analysis. The estimation of uncertainty in an analysis is necessary to measure the "meaningfulness" of a result to provide a basis for evaluating the weight to be attributed to the result in making decisions.[87] For accident reconstruction, uncertainty in measurements and estimations of sources of error should be expressed in all conclusions.[88]

§8.12 MOTORCYCLE, BICYCLE, AND PEDESTRIAN ISSUES

Vehicle collisions with pedestrians, motorcycles, and bicyclists apply the same underlying fundamental scientific principles, but necessarily involve different reconstruction issues. Evidence collection involves the same examination of the scene, vehicle, and any injured

---

[84] See Alan J. Watts, *Accident Reconstruction Science* (Tucson, AZ: Lawyers & Judges Publishing, Inc., 4th ed. 2011) at pp. 144–146.

[85] Bart Hoogeboom and Ivo Alberink, "Measurement Uncertainty When Estimating the Velocity of an Allegedly Speeding Vehicles from Images," 55 J. FORENSIC SCI. 1347–1351 (2010).

[86] See Raymond M. Brach and R. Matthew Brach, *Vehicle Accident Analysis and Reconstruction Methods* (Warrendale, PA: SAE International, 2005) at pp. 179–214 (providing a detailed overview of the various methods, equations, capabilities and limitations of photogrammetry); Harold Franck and Darren Franck, *Mathematical Methods for Accident Reconstruction*, CRC Press, 2010, at pp. 52–58 (discussion and diagrams explaining the methods).

[87] See Raymond M. Brach and Patrick F. Dunn, *Uncertainty Analysis for Forensic Science*, Lawyers & Judges Publishing Company, Inc., 2009.

[88] For a detailed discussion of specific uncertainty measurements encountered in accident reconstruction, see Raymond M. Brach and R. Matthew Brach, *Vehicle Accident Analysis and Reconstruction Methods*, SAE International, 2005 at pp. 1–12.

parties, but important considerations are: location and pattern of vehicle deformation, type and location of trauma, impact and rest positions for the vehicle and the pedestrian, bicycle, or motorcycle, and markings on the roadway/ground.[89] Other relevant information may include the visibility in the area and the pre-impact behavior of the pedestrian or cyclist.

Pedestrian-vehicle collisions (and bicyclist-vehicle collisions) are usually categorized according to the type of impact and the post-impact motion of the pedestrian: forward projection, wrap, carry, roof vault, and fender vault.[90] These types take into account the differences in post-impact dynamics depending on whether the pedestrian is struck below center mass (which generally results in motion to the rear of the car with a possible "vault" over the vehicle) or above center mass (which generally results in forward motion and a possible run over situation).[91]

Reconstruction analysis is generally limited to determining vehicle speed and the pedestrian-vehicle interaction dynamics. In pedestrian-vehicle collisions, in the absence of EDR data or skid marks for estimating speed of the vehicle[92] prior to collision, accident reconstruction experts will rely on impact location and the post-impact trajectory of the pedestrian to estimate impact velocity.[93] Speed measurement points may need to be estimated from scene debris (i.e. shoes) and witness statements.[94] For interaction dynamic determinations, accident reconstruction experts typically rely on computer modeling or simulation programs.[95]

For motorcycle-vehicle collisions, similar evidence collection considerations apply in detecting and documenting impact damage to

---

[89] Raymond M. Brach and R. Matthew Brach, *Vehicle Accident Analysis and Reconstruction Methods*, SAE International, 2005 at p. 165.

[90] Id.

[91] Harold Franck and Darren Franck, *Mathematical Methods for Accident Reconstruction*, CRC Press, 2010 at pp. 169–170.

[92] If the speed of the pedestrian is an issue, in some cases the part of the body which impacted the vehicle may be useful in calculating pedestrian speed. *See* Harold Franck and Darren Franck, *Mathematical Methods for Accident Reconstruction*, CRC Press, 2010 at pp. 172–173.

[93] Thomas C. Christensen and Laura L. Liptai, "Reconstruction: Accident," in WILEY ENCYCLOPEDIA OF FORENSIC SCIENCE, (Jamieson A. & Moenssens A.A., eds) 2009 & online updates.

Equations used in calculating the vehicle speed in these cases are detailed in Raymond M. Brach and R. Matthew Brach, *Vehicle Accident Analysis and Reconstruction Methods,* SAE International, 2005 at pp. 167–177; and Harold Franck and Darren Franck, *Mathematical Methods for Accident Reconstruction,* CRC Press, 2010 at pp. 170–171. *See also* Tiefang Zou et al., "Two Simple Formulas for Evaluating the Lower Bound of the Impact Velocity in Vehicle-pedestrian Accidents," 61 J. Forensic Sci. 959–965 (2016).

[94] *See* Donald J. Van Kirk, *Vehicular Accident Investigation and Reconstruction*, CRC Press, 2001 at p. 320 (discussion of the utility of witness statements).

[95] Two common programs are "MADYMO" and "PC-Crash Pedestrian Model." *See* J. van Wijk, J. Wismans, J. Maltha and L. Wittebrood, "MADYMO Pedestrian Simulations," International Congress and Exposition, Paper 830060, SAE International, Warrendale, PA, 1983; and A. Moser, H. Steffan, H. Hoschopf and G. Kasanicky, "Validation of the PC-Crash Pedestrian Model," Paper 2000-01-0847, SAE International, Warrendale, PA 2000.

the roadway, the motorcycle, and the injuries to the rider(s). Reconstruction experts generally rely on standardized methods for determining the velocity at which the motorcycle struck, or was struck by, a vehicle.[96]

IV. TRIAL AIDS

§8.13   EXPERT QUALIFICATIONS

1.   EXTERNAL SPEED MEASUREMENT

Evidence of external speed measurements is almost always presented through law enforcement officers who participate in a speed enforcement program. Proof that an officer is qualified to use a speed detection device, which is usually accomplished through testimony that the officer has completed adequate training in the use of the device, plays a significant role in determining whether the evidence obtained by any such device is admissible in a speeding case or sufficient to sustain a speeding conviction.[97] "Proper training helps ensure that the officer's testimony and the measurement device's readings meet the standards of evidence and thus are sufficient proof of speeding to sustain a conviction for the offense. . . . Training on the use of speed measurement equipment includes the theory of how the instrument works, operating procedures, legal considerations, and field exercises."[98] The NHTSA Speed Measuring Device Operator Training Program is used by law enforcement agencies and specialized training, course materials, and other resources are available from: State police academies, IACP, National Sheriffs' Association, International Association of Directors of Law Enforcement Standards and Training— courses institutionalized in the States as Police Officer Standards and Training (P.O.S.T.), and NHTSA Enforcement and Justice Services Division.

---

[96]   These standard equations are discussed extensively in Donald J. Van Kirk, *Vehicular Accident Investigation and Reconstruction,* CRC Press, 2001 at pp. 306–312.

[97]   See, e.g., State v. Brown, 344 S.C. 302, 543 S.E.2d 568 (Ct. App. 2001)(upholding magistrate's admission of radar reading into evidence where officer testified, *inter alia,* "she was trained in the operation of moving radar at the [CJA]"); State v. Williamson, 166 P.3d 387, 390 (Idaho Ct. App. 2007)(in speeding prosecution where state seeks to introduce radar or laser evidence, state must prove, *inter alia,* "the officer was qualified to operate the device"); 8 Am. Jur. 2d Automobiles§ 981 (stating a radar reading is generally sufficient to sustain a speeding conviction if the prosecution shows, *inter alia,* "[t]he officer operating the device was adequately trained in its use"); Thomas J. Goger, Annotation, *Proof, by Radar or Other Mechanical or Electronic Devices, of Violation of Speed Regulations,* 47 A.L.R.3d 882 ("It is generally recognized that proper operation of a radar device is a prerequisite to a speeding conviction based on evidence obtained by use of the device. . . . An issue closely related . . . involves the qualifications required of the police officer manning the radar equipment.").

[98]   U.S. Department of Transportation, NHTSA, "Speed Enforcement Program Guidelines," DOT HS 810 915 (March 2008) at p. 20. (available at: http://www.nlelp.org/wp-content/uploads/2014/05/NHTSASpeedEnforcementProgramGuidelines.pdf)(last accessed February 27, 2017).

The amount of training for speed enforcement varies considerably among agencies; 40 hours or more each on radar or LIDAR is not uncommon.[99] In some jurisdictions, training documentation must be available for presentation in court and formal reevaluation is conducted on an annual basis for each type of equipment.[100]

2.   ACCIDENT RECONSTRUCTION

Accident reconstruction analysis is not a field requiring licensing or certification and the backgrounds of those who hold themselves out as experts in the field vary widely. Some experts are police officers with a high school diploma; others are engineers with a doctorate degree. Because there is no required educational background, formal licensing, or mandatory certification, the individual background and experience of the expert should be thoroughly assessed.

There are numerous training centers and programs for accident reconstruction experts, with long-standing facilities at the Center for Public Safety (formerly the Traffic Institute) at Northwestern University, the Institute of Police Technology and Management (IPTM) at the University of North Florida, the Texas Law Enforcement and Security Training Division (LESTD) at Texas A & M University, and the Transportation Research Institute at the University of Michigan.

International, national and state professional associations to which accident reconstruction experts may belong, and through which they may receive additional continuing education, are numerous. The most widely-recognized associations have representatives on the board of directors of the Accreditation Commission for Traffic Accident Reconstruction (ACTAR).[101] Most of these associations also maintain expert directory searchable databases on their websites.[102]

In the late 1990's, ACTAR was created by accident reconstruction organizations and professional associations to implement minimum training and competency standards in the field. ACTAR provides for the

---

[99] In Michigan, the Office of Highway Safety Planning partnered with the Commission on Law Enforcement Standards to establish formal standards for speed measurement operators and instructors (available at: http://www.michigan.gov/mcoles/0,4607,7-229-41626_47372---,00.html)(last accessed November 9, 2016).

[100] *See, e.g.,* North Carolina Administrative Code Section 9B.0200 Minimum Standards for Criminal Justice Schools and Criminal Justice Training Programs or Courses of Instruction; Section 9B.0300 Minimum Standards for Criminal Justice Instructors; Section 9B.0400 Minimum Standards for Completion of Training; Section 9C.0300 Certification of Criminal Justice Officers; and Section 9C.0600 Equipment and Procedures.

[101] A listing of the associations is available on the ACTAR website at: https://actar.org/about/organizations (last accessed November 10, 2016).

[102] *See* https://actar.org/directory (last accessed November 10, 2016), http://www.iaars.org/wp-content/uploads/2016/05/IAARS-Member-Directory.pdf (International Association of Accident Reconstruction Specialists)(last accessed November 10. 2016); http://napars.org (National Association of Professional Accident Reconstruction Specialists)(last accessed November 10, 2016).

voluntary certification[103] of accident reconstruction experts and currently has certified more than 1250 experts throughout the United States, Canada, Australia, Singapore, and the United Arab Emirates. To become certified an individual must apply to the commission and meet minimum standards of education and experience, which are evaluated by a committee. Then the applicant must complete a written Theory examination of 75 questions (true-false, multiple choice, and problem solving) and a Practical, or Case Study, examination with a staged collision.[104] Once certified, in order to maintain that status, the reconstruction expert must obtain 80 continuing educational units (CEUs) every five years and must abide by ACTAR's code of ethics. Individuals may waive the CEU requirement by successfully retaking the complete ACTAR exam.

Additional resources, including links to organizations, forums, publications, training courses, and expert directories, are available on the website of the Accident Reconstruction Communication Network (The ARC Network) at www.accidentreconstruction.com.

Because the field of accident reconstruction does not have formal requirements, courts have relied upon training and experience to determine whether an individual may testify as an expert in the field.[105]

§8.14 EVIDENCE ISSUES

1. EXTERNAL SPEED MEASUREMENT

The courts have accepted, as proof of the speed of a moving motor vehicle, non-scientific evidence of a variety of types. It has been stated that the excessive speed of an automobile can be established by the visual observations of lay witnesses.[106] This type of opinion may be viewed as a matter of common observation, not calling for a witness

---

[103] Although ACTAR uses the term "accreditation," the term "certification" will be used here because the process concerns individual competency (certification), not facility competency (accreditation).

[104] *See* https://actar.org/accreditation/exam (last accessed November 10, 2016).

[105] *See* Commonwealth v. Bowser, 425 Pa. Super. 24, 624 A.2d 125 (1993)(trooper qualified based on advanced training in the field, had performed six reconstructions and was a member of the National Association of Professional Accident Reconstruction Specialists); Mathieu v. Schnitzer, 559 So.2d 1244 (Fla.Dist.Ct.App.1990)(court concluded the witness' years of experience in investigating the causes of accidents were sufficient to qualify her as an expert in accident reconstruction); Favia v. Ford Motor Co. 381 Ill.App.3d 809, 320 Ill.Dec. 113, 886 N.E.2d 1182 (2008)(One expert had worked in law enforcement since 1991, had studied accident investigation at the Indiana Law Enforcement Academy, and had investigated approximately 75 crashes annually; second expert began his law enforcement career as a road deputy in 1976, had attended 80 hours of crash investigation school, and had 40 hours of advanced technical crash investigation); *see also* Rosado v. Deters, 5 F.3d 119 (5th Cir.1993)(witness not qualified as an expert because proffered witness had last qualified as an accident reconstructionist almost thirty years before, had taken no refresher courses, and admitted he could not independently establish the physical and mathematical basis for his opinion).

[106] *See, e.g.,* Hastings v. Serleto, 61 Cal.App.2d 672, 143 P.2d 956 (1943); Horton v. State, 119 Ga.App. 43, 166 S.E.2d 47 (1969); Heacox v. Polce, 392 Pa. 415, 141 A.2d 229 (1958).

endowed with expert qualifications. Courts have also permitted individuals with some qualifications not ordinarily had by the common man to make precise estimates of speed based upon sound.[107] Other courts have not been willing to permit the introduction of such evidence, however, where the witnesses lacked special experimental qualifications to judge speed by auditory perception only.[108] Sometimes, courts have admitted testimony which used the less definite terms of "fast," "very fast," or "at a high rate of speed," based on sound alone, but again, there is no uniformity among the jurisdictions and the cases appear to be decided pretty much on an *ad hoc* basis, depending on a totality of the facts and circumstances of a particular case. Courts have also differed on whether a police officer's visual observation of speeding is sufficient, absent detection device results, to support a conviction for speeding or to provide probable cause for a traffic stop.[109]

When radar evidence was first sought to be introduced,[110] the courts required that technical testimony be offered to demonstrate the scientific principle underlying the technique of detecting the speed of motor vehicles by radar.[111] Courts have since taken judicial notice of the fact that radar is a reliable means of measuring speed.[112] This does not mean new devices are exempt from judicial review of reliability, if a challenge is raised to the admissibility of the device results. In *City of Seattle v. Peterson*,[113] the court said that the accuracy of a particular model of radar unit is not a proper subject of judicial notice. Therefore,

---

[107] Kuhn v. Stepheson, 87 Ind. App. 157, 161 N.E. 384 (1928)(an automobile mechanic with twelve years' experience in his trade was permitted to state that a car was going 45 miles per hour based on the sound of the motor only, since he had not seen the vehicle as it passed by). *See also* Pierson v. Frederickson, 102 N.J. Super. 156, 245 A.2d 524 (1968).

[108] Challinor v. Axton, 246 Ky. 76, 54 S.W.2d 600 (1932); Bernardini v. Salas, 84 Nev. 702, 448 P.2d 43 (1968); Meade v. Meade, 206 Va. 823, 147 S.E.2d 171 (1966).

[109] In State v. Hall, 269 Neb. 228, 691 N.W.2d 518 (2005), the court stressed that an officer's visual observation of the speed of a vehicle needed to be corroborated by the use of a radio microwave, mechanical, or electronic speed measuring device. But an officer's estimate of speed was found to support a conviction of speeding in In re B.D.S., 269 Ga. App. 89, 603 S.E.2d 488 (2004).

See U.S. v. Sowards, 690 F.3d 583 (4th Cir. 2012)(where cocaine was found in vehicle during traffic stop initiated based on visual speed estimate, suppression was warranted under the Fourth Amendment because officer lacked probable cause to initiate a traffic stop for speeding based exclusively on his uncorroborated and unsupported belief that defendant was traveling 75 mph in a 70-mph zone); State v. Petzoldt, 803 N.W.2d 128 (Iowa Ct. App. 2011)(where a police officer believed that defendant was speeding but made no estimate as to how fast the vehicle was traveling or how much over the posted speed limit the pickup was traveling, where the officer's visual estimate of speed was not confirmed by any other means of corroboration such as radar or pacing, and where the officer observed no other traffic infractions or other driving anomalies, the officer lacked probable cause to stop defendant for speeding).

[110] For an excellent overview of scientific and legal issues in the context of jurisdiction-by-jurisdictional review see Thomas J. Goger, "Proof, by radar or other mechanical or electronic devices, of violation of speed regulations," 47 A.L.R.3d 822 (1973, 2012).

[111] *See* People v. Torpey, 204 Misc. 1023, 128 N.Y.S.2d 864 (1953)

[112] *See, e.g.,* Everight v. City of Little Rock, 230 Ark. 695, 326 S.W.2d 796 (1959); State v. Tomanelli, 153 Conn. 365, 216 A.2d 625 (1966); State v. Dantonio, 18 N.J. 570, 115 A.2d 35 (1955); People v. Magri, 3 N.Y.2d 562, 170 N.Y.S.2d 335, 147 N.E.2d 728 (1958)

[113] 39 Wash. App. 524, 693 P.2d 757 (1985)

in the absence of evidence that shows the unit utilized in the case has been determined to be reliable, readings from the device will not to be admitted. The court added that if "the validity of a scientific principle is a prerequisite to its admission into evidence, then consistency requires that evidence of the ability of a machine to employ that scientific principle reliably must also precede admission of the machine's results into evidence."[114]

Some states also have passed statutes that provide for the admissibility of radar evidence without requiring expert testimony. These statutes, in effect, make the evidence of speed obtained through radar devices prima facie evidence of actual vehicle speed, subject to a showing of the proper operation and testing of the instrument and subject to having a qualified operator.[115] Many states also regulate radar speed detection by statute in a wide variety of ways.[116]

Although evidence of a radar unit reading is now generally allowed into evidence, a proper foundation for its admission must be laid. In a jurisdiction which has not judicially noted the accuracy of the underlying scientific principles, this would require: (1) a showing, by expert testimony, on how the apparatus is constructed, functions and operates; (2) a showing that the operator of the device had the requisite training; (3) that the apparatus had been properly calibrated, checked and tested after it was set up at a site; (4) that the operator had observed the speed of defendant's car on the apparatus as it broke the radar beam; and (5) that the operator could positively identify the defendant's car as the one which was responsible for the speed

---

[114] 39 Wash. App. at 527; 693 P.2d at 758; *see also,* State v. Doria, 135 Vt. 341, 376 A.2d 751 (1977).

[115] *See* Va. Code § 46.2–882.

[116] *See, e.g.,* N.C.Gen.Stat. § 8–50.2(a)(admitting radar evidence only as corroborating the opinion of the officer as to the speed of a vehicle based on visual observation); 75 PA. CONS. STAT. 3368 (prohibiting use of radar to issue citations for speeding in speed zones unless the violation is in excess of six mph over the posted speed limit and prohibiting use of radar by anyone not a state police officer).

See also Fla.Stat.Ann. Title 13 § 316.1906(2):

"(2) Evidence of the speed of a vehicle measured by any radar speed-measuring device shall be inadmissible in any proceeding with respect to an alleged violation of provisions of law regulating the lawful speed of vehicles, unless such evidence of speed is obtained by an officer who:

(a) Has satisfactorily completed the radar training course established by the Criminal Justice Standards and Training Commission pursuant to s. 943.17(1)(b).

(b) Has made an independent visual determination that the vehicle is operating in excess of the applicable speed limit.

(c) Has written a citation based on evidence obtained from radar when conditions permit the clear assignment of speed to a single vehicle.

(d) Is using radar which has no automatic speed locks and no audio alarms, unless disconnected or deactivated.

(e) Is operating radar with audio Doppler engaged.

(f) Is using a radar unit which meets the minimum design criteria for such units established by the Department of Highway Safety and Motor Vehicles."

reading.[117] Where the court has taken judicial notice of the scientific principles underlying speed detection by radar, the first step may be omitted, but all of the remaining steps must be shown.[118] "Judicial notice does not extend to the accuracy or efficiency of any given instrument designed to employ the principle. Whether the instrument itself is accurate and is accurately operated must necessarily be demonstrated to the satisfaction of the trier [of fact]."[119]

Testing of the unit is an essential prerequisite if the radar unit reading is the only evidence of speeding. In *State v. Gerdes*,[120] the Minnesota Supreme Court held that a speeding conviction cannot be predicated solely upon evidence of speed derived from a radar device which had not been subjected to external testing, whether by use of a reliably calibrated tuning fork, or by an actual test run with a police car.[121] Some courts have held that external testing with a tuning fork alone is insufficient, and that additional proof of accuracy is required,[122] but this added proof would appear to be unnecessary with the models currently in use. Of course, some courts have held that a reading from an untested radar device, or from an untested speedometer, is admissible but not sufficient in itself to support a conviction; the deficiency can be overcome by the observations about the speed of the vehicle by the trained police officer who is shown to have experience in judging speed.

Because of the less frequent use of the VASCAR device, there are fewer significant court cases deciding the legal requirements of its evidentiary use. Testimony of speeding based on VASCAR readings has been admitted in over a dozen states, usually after the foundation for admissibility was laid by testimony from the manufacturer on the workings of the VASCAR device and its scientific reliability.

In *State v. Schmiede*,[123] the trial court found that VASCAR units were scientifically accurate and held that testimony based upon it is admissible provided it is shown that the unit was checked for proper

---

[117] Lattarulo v. State, 261 Ga. 124, 401 S.E.2d 516 (1991)(RADAR as a technique for measuring speed and its admissibility as scientific evidence is widely accepted in Georgia and other states); Maysonet v. State, 91 S.W.3d 365 (Tex.App.2002)(while RADAR is a familiar concept and based on proven scientific theories, the state still must show that its operator had followed accepted procedures).

[118] State v. Graham, 322 S.W.2d 188 (Mo.App.1959); People v. Skupien, 33 Misc.2d 908, 227 N.Y.S.2d 165 (Cty.Ct.1962); Farmer v. Commonwealth, 205 Va. 609, 139 S.E.2d 40 (1964). See also, Sweeny v. Commonwealth, 211 Va. 668, 179 S.E.2d 509 (1971).

[119] State v. Tomanelli, 153 Conn. 365, 371, 216 A.2d 625, 629 (1966).

[120] 291 Minn. 353, 191 N.W.2d 428 (1971).

[121] *See also* Hardaway v. State, 207 Ga. App. 150, 427 S.E.2d 527 (1993); Brooker v. State, 206 Ga. App. 563, 426 S.E.2d 39 (1992).

[122] *See, e.g.,* City of Ballwin v. Collins, 534 S.W.2d 280 (Mo.App.1976); Cromer v. State, 374 S.W.2d 884 (Tex.Crim.App.1964); Biesser v. Town of Holland, 208 Va. 167, 156 S.E.2d 792 (1967); *but see* Honeycutt v. Commonwealth, 408 S.W.2d 421 (Ky.1966)(accuracy of the RADAR may be established by tuning fork alone); People v. Stankovich, 119 Ill.App.2d 187, 255 N.E.2d 461 (1970)(same).

[123] 118 N.J.Super. 576, 289 A.2d 281 (1972); *see also* State v. Finkle, 128 N.J. Super. 199, 319 A.2d 733 (1974).

calibration, and the operator trained in its use. In this case, the state trooper operating the unit had received one day's training in its use and had then employed it for one month under the supervision of a qualified supervisor who administered a series of 30 tests to the witness which he passed with the greatest deviation being 7/10th of a mile and the average being .229 miles. It is interesting to note that the court, prior to issuing its ruling on admissibility, went out on the road with the trooper to permit him to demonstrate his familiarity with the VASCAR unit's operating principles and calibration.

Contrast the laying of the foundation in the *Schmiede* case with that in *People v. Leatherbarrow*,[124] where no testimony was offered concerning the theory and operation of the unit or of the scientific facts and principles upon which it was founded. The two police officers who testified to a reading of 94.3 miles per hour in a 55 mph speed zone had not proffered an opinion on the device's reliability, nor had it been shown that they possessed sufficient familiarity with its operation to allow such an opinion. Consequently, the county court reversed the conviction of speeding, even though the court, based on its own research, believed the unit was undoubtedly an accurate speed measuring device. Since the operating principles and the accuracy of VASCAR were, at that time, not yet widely known, the court felt that proof of accuracy and reliability was necessary.

Because the technique simply amounts to a method of timing the speed of a vehicle over a known distance, the principle is unassailable, and judicial notice was not long in coming. Thus, barely two years after the *Schmiede* case, the New Jersey Superior Court took judicial notice of the scientific reliability of VASCAR in *State v. Finkle*.[125] While VASCAR still is used less frequently than radar, its use is sanctioned by statute in several states, either explicitly or by implication.[126] Courts seem to have had little difficulty in admitting evidence based on VASCAR speed measurements, provided the operator was properly qualified and the instrument tested.[127]

California courts have found VASCAR to be, in essence, a speed trap operation. In *People v. Johnson*,[128] the appellant contended that a

---

[124] 69 Misc.2d 563, 330 N.Y.S.2d 676 (1972).

[125] 128 N.J. Super. 199, 319 A.2d 733 (1974); City of St. Louis v. Martin, 548 S.W.2d 622, 623 (Mo.App.1977)("key to demonstrating VASCAR accuracy was proof of proper testing").

[126] *See, e.g.,* N.C. Gen. Stat. § 8–50.2(a): "The results of the use of radio, microwave, laser, *or other speed-measuring instruments* shall be admissible . . ." (emphasis added).

[127] *See, e.g.,* State v. Lomack, 238 Neb. 537, 471 N.W.2d 441 (1991)(VASCAR evidence admissible, but no effective objections were made to either testing of the unit or the officer's qualifications); State v. Reynolds, 133 Wis.2d 474, 394 N.W.2d 920 (App.1986)(conviction on basis of VASCAR speed measurement admissible despite mathematical errors by operator); State v. Dobrofsky, 146 Wis.2d 866, 431 N.W.2d 327 (App.1988)(VASCAR enjoys presumptive accuracy; Commonwealth v. Smolow, 364 Pa. Super. 20, 527 A.2d 131 (1987)(VASCAR evidence admissible); *but see* Commonwealth v. Martorano, 387 Pa. Super. 151, 563 A.2d 1229 (1989)(no proper foundation of compliance with statutory requirements for VASCAR evidence, and officer's uncorroborated testimony as to vehicle speed insufficient for conviction).

[128] 29 Cal. App. 3d Supp. 1, 105 Cal. Rptr. 212 (Super. Ct. 1972).

VASCAR speed reading used in the trial court hearing was not admissible because it was a violation of California's rather rigorous speed trap law. The appellate court agreed and reversed the conviction because the law specifically defined a speed trap as "a particular section of a highway measured as to distance and with boundaries marked, designated or otherwise determined in order that the speed of a vehicle may be calculated by securing the time it takes the vehicle to travel the known distance."[129] The appellate court concluded that VASCAR essentially operates in that manner.

Appellate decisions have generally permitted evidence of the speed of a motorist as measured by a laser speed detection device to be admitted provided a proper foundation is laid,[130] although some courts have taken judicial notice of the reliability of laser speed measurements under modern reliability standards for admission of expert evidence.[131] In *State v. Ali*,[132] the appeals court drew, by analogy, upon the radar cases, to hold that "so long as there is adequate evidence that a laser-based speed-measuring device used to support a conviction has been tested for accuracy and their officers using the device have been trained in its use, a district court may take judicial notice of the device's general reliability."[133] Other states have followed with their own process and reached a general conclusion of LIDAR reliability.[134]

Constitutional and procedural issues rather than sufficiency of evidence have been the major legal challenges to automated traffic enforcement results in the courts. Objections on the basis of the right to privacy, freedom of association, illegal search and seizure, due process, and the equal protection doctrine have been largely settled in favor of the use of ASE.[135] Not all decisions, though, have favored the

---

[129] Id.

[130] State v. Hall, 269 Neb. 228, 691 N.W.2d 518 (2005)(trial court may admit laser speed findings as permitted by statute but such admission is discretionary and "the trial court may require further evidence if it doubts the underlying technology"); State v. Branch, 243 Ore. App. 309, 259 P.3d (Ore. Ct. App. 2011)(LIDAR admissible as reliable scientific evidence).

[131] State v. Green, 417 N.J. Super. 190, 9 A.3d 172 (N.J. Sup. Ct. 2010)(although laser speed detectors (LIDAR) generally are widely accepted in the relevant scientific communities as a means to measure speed, the Stalker LIDAR device has not been established as scientifically reliable in New Jersey. As a consequence, it may not be used in the trial courts as proof of speed until its accuracy has been established at least through the minimal type of testing used to establish the scientific reliability of the LTI Marksman 20–20).

[132] 679 N.W.2d 359 (Minn. App. 2004).

[133] State v. Thompson, 168 Ohio Misc. 2d 3, 966 N.E.2d 320 (Muni. Ct. 2012)(To convict a person for a speeding violation, the state must prove and the record must show (1) expert testimony of the construction of the device and its method of operation in determining the speed of the approaching vehicle, (2) evidence that the device is in proper working order, and (3) evidence that the officer using the device is qualified for its use by training and experience).

[134] District of Columbia v. Chatilovicz, No. 2006-CTF-2633-DC super Ct June 12, 2008; *but see* Hall v. State, 297 S.W.3d 294 (Tex. Crim. App. 2009)(LIDAR reliability not established).

[135] Bevis v. New Orleans, 686 F.3d 277 (5th Cir. 2012)(ordinance imposed civil rather than criminal penalties because (1) the ordinance repeatedly described the fine as a civil penalty, and (2) the fact that some of the conduct that violated the ordinance would also be punishable as a crime, if done with the requisite mental state, was not enough to overcome

systems,[136] thereby resulting in subsequent ordinances addressing those concerns. Evidentiary questions in ASE primarily revolve around the science of the photo-radar, authentication of the photos, and the chain of custody.

2.   EVENT DATA RECORDERS/SENSOR INFORMATION

The reliability of information downloaded from vehicle event data recorders and introduced as scientific evidence faced challenges in the courts in the past. In 2002, an Illinois state appellate court provided the first detailed analysis of admissibility of EDR evidence under the *Frye* standard.[137] In *Bachman v. General Motors Corp.*, the plaintiff alleged that the airbag Sensing and Diagnostic Module (SDM) erroneously interpreted objects striking the car's floor pan as a deployment event. When the airbag unexpectedly deployed, the plaintiff lost control of the car and crashed. Before the trial, the plaintiff moved to exclude all recorded data evidence as inadmissible under *Frye*. Engineers, including the project manager who designed and developed the SDM installed in the plaintiff's Cavalier, testified that the automobile industry and NHTSA held crash event data as generally accurate and reliable. GM admitted that it had investigated reports that the SDMs in some Cavaliers had interpreted impacts from small objects striking the floor pan as deployment events. GM recalibrated the deployment threshold, and maintained that the recalibration and, in particular, the initial problem had no effect on the accuracy of the data that the SDM recorded. The appellate court agreed with the trial court, holding that downloaded SDM data met the standards for admissibility under the *Frye* test.[138]

---

legislative intent. That conclusion disposed of plaintiffs' contention that the ordinance violated the Ex Post Facto Clause, which applied only to criminal sanctions. The ordinance supplied constitutionally adequate process because (1) the maximum fine was a relatively minor amount, (2) requiring a driver to file a civil action in order to challenge the outcome of the initial hearing did not deprive a driver of due process, (3) no fundamental interest was involved, and (4) the city's interest was to reduce the risk of road accidents); Dixon v. District of Columbia, 753 F. Supp. 2d 6 (D.C. Dist. Ct. 2010)(equal protection claim denied); Agomo v. Fenty, 916 A.2d 181 (D.C. Ct. App. 2007)(trial court's grant of summary judgment to the District of Columbia on a Fifth Amendment challenge by a vehicle owner and a leasing corporation to an automated traffic enforcement system was affirmed because the owner's and the corporation's due process rights were not violated by the system).

[136] State v. Kuhlman, 722 N.W.2d 1 (Minn. Ct. App. 2006)(Minneapolis photo-enforcement ordinance conflicted with the Minnesota Highway Traffic Regulation Act because the ordinance was inconsistent with the Act's uniformity requirement and changed the burden of proof provided by Minn. Stat. § 169.06, subd. 4 (2004); the Minneapolis ordinance was invalid under Minn. Stat. § 169.022 (2004)).

[137] Bachman v. General Motors Corp., 332 Ill.App.3d 760, 267 Ill.Dec. 125, 776 N.E.2d 262, 283 (2002). The Illinois appellate court considered the issue of SDM data admissibility as a case of first impression. Id. at 282. In deciding the issue, the court followed the standard for the admissibility of scientific evidence as outlined in Frye v. United States, 293 F. 1013, 1014 (D.C.Cir.1923). The *Frye* court ruled that scientific evidence is admissible if the underlying methodology or scientific principles is "sufficiently established to have gained general acceptance in the particular field in which it belongs." Id.

[138] Id. at 283.

Since the Illinois appellate court decision in *Bachman*, other courts have found the EDR evidence to be reliable and admissible.[139] EDR evidence is frequently used in both criminal and civil cases,[140] and the failure to preserve or examine the EDR data can be an issue at trial.[141]

3.   RECONSTRUCTION EVIDENCE

Accident reconstruction expert testimony is generally admissible throughout the United States;[142] however, some jurisdictions limit the scope of expert testimony and permit lay witnesses to give opinion testimony in certain areas that impact accident reconstruction analysis. The restrictions on expert testimony derive from adherence to the common law restriction on the scope of expert testimony.[143] In most common law jurisdictions, experts are adduced as witnesses to assist the trier of fact (judge or jury) in areas outside their common knowledge.[144] In federal courts, which must follow Federal Rule of Evidence 702, and in the state courts that have adopted a similar rule, the codified admissibility standard is a more liberal formulation of the subject matter requirement and requires only that the expert testimony "assist the trier of fact."[145]

---

[139] *See, e.g.,* Commonwealth v. Zimmerman, 70 Mass. App. Ct. 357, 873 N.E.2d 1215 (2007); State v. Shabazz, 400 N.J. Super. 203, 946 A.2d 626 (2005); Matos v. State, 899 So.2d 403, 407 (Fla.Dist.Ct.App.2005); People v. Slade (Sup. Ct. Nassau Co., N.Y.2005); In re Detention of Erbe, 344 Ill.App.3d 350, 279 Ill.Dec. 295, 800 N.E.2d 137, 150 (2003); People v. Reynolds, 193 Misc.2d 697, 749 N.Y.S.2d 687 (N.Y.2002).

[140] *See, e.g.,* Commonwealth v. Safka, 141 A.3d 1239 (Pa. 2016); Ferguson v. Nat'l Freight, Inc. 2016 U.S. LEXIS 37487 (W.D. Va. 2016).

[141] Cook v. Tarbert Logging, Inc., 190 Wn. App. 448, 360 P. 3d 855 (2015).

[142] Courts have noted that accident reconstruction utilizes the basic laws of physics. *See, e.g.,* Giard v. Darby, 360 F.Supp.2d 229, 236 (D. Mass 2005)(engineering background and experience of accident reconstruction "enabled him to apply basic physics to form his opinions in the case at bar"); Fowler v. Bauman, 663 So. 2d 438, 440 (La. App. 1995)(trial court properly admitted testimony of accident reconstruction expert because testimony "was based on accident reconstruction principles which have been widely accepted by courts for many years" and his "opinions were based on 'the law of physics and engineering,' which we find is 'generally accepted in the scientific community.' ").

Even with the recognition that the field of accident reconstruction is scientifically reliable, the courts still assess whether the individual expert's testimony is reliable. *See* Smith v. BMW N. Am., Inc., 308 F.3d 913, 921 (8th Cir. 2002)(accident reconstruction expert's testimony about principal direction of force admissible); Morton Int'l v. Gillespie, 39 S.W.3d 651, 655 (Tex. App. 2001)(mechanical engineer's testimony as to air bag deployment reliable). *But see* Sigler v. Am. Honda Motor Co., 532 F.3d 469, 479 (6th Cir. 2008)(mechanic's testimony on accident reconstruction ruled unreliable); Volkswagen of Am., Inc. v. Ramirez, 159 S.W.3d 897, 906 (Tex. 2004)(accident reconstruction expert's opinion unreliable).

[143] Admissibility standards and the applicable rules of evidence are discussed extensively in Chapter 1.

[144] Bond v. Commonwealth, 226 Va. 534, 311 S.E.2d 769 (1984)(when the evidence, exclusive of expert testimony, is sufficient to enable a jury of laymen to reach an intelligent conclusion, expert testimony is inadmissible).

[145] Federal Rule of Evidence 702; State v. Chapple, 135 Ariz. 281, 292–293, 600 P.2d 1208, 1219–1220 (1983)(the standard in Rule 702 "is not whether the jury could reach some conclusion in absence of the expert evidence, but whether the jury is qualified without such testimony to determine intelligently and to the best possible degree the particular issue without enlightenment from those having a specialized understanding of the subject.")(internal citations omitted); Hampton v. State, 588 N.E.2d 555, 558 (Ind. App.

In most applications the two standards result in similar rulings. One exception is the field of accident reconstruction testimony. In jurisdictions which use the more restrictive "outside common knowledge" admissibility standard,[146] like the Commonwealth of Virginia, the courts have limited accident reconstruction expert testimony to descriptions of "tire marks, skid marks, or cuts which he observed on the pavement at or near the place of an automobile accident, [as well as damage to the vehicles], but the inference to be drawn from such testimony is 'solely [within] the province of the jury."[147]

The testimony of an accident reconstruction expert is properly admissible, even if there is eyewitness testimony,[148] where it is necessary to rely on the expert's knowledge and the application of principles of physics, engineering, and other sciences beyond the knowledge of the average juror. In *Rios v. Navistar International Transportation Corp.*,[149] the operator of a tractor brought an action against the manufacturer of the tractor for injuries sustained when the tractor rolled over his leg. The appellate court affirmed the trial court's holding for the manufacturer, stating that the trial court did not abuse its discretion in admitting accident reconstruction testimony. The court stated that such testimony would not be allowed in a product liability action where available physical evidence or eyewitness testimony would be sufficient for the jury to draw its own conclusion. However, it may be allowed in addition to eyewitness testimony when matters in the case involve scientific principles beyond the understanding of the jury and the expert testimony will assist the jury in understanding those principles. The court reiterated the holding in *Augenstein v. Pulley*,[150] in which the court stated that the availability of eyewitness testimony should be considered as merely one factor in determining whether the expert's testimony will aid the fact finder in arriving at a just result.

1992)("Portions of the [expert testimony] were beyond the common knowledge and experience of the average lay person, but portions of it were also inherently understandable.").

Although FRE 702 states the standard for the admissibility of expert testimony, the additional FRE 403 probative value weighing test that applies to all evidence must also be satisfied for the admission of expert testimony: "Although relevant, evidence may be excluded if its probative value is substantially outweighed by the danger of unfair prejudice, confusion of the issues, or misleading the jury, or considerations of undue delay, waste of time, or needless presentation of cumulative evidence."

[146] The restrictive admissibility standard is similar to the "ultimate issue doctrine" that bars expert testimony on the ultimate issue in the case because that would invade the province of the jury. *See* Notes 157–158 *infra* and accompanying text.

[147] Venable v. Stockner, 200 Va. 900, 905, 108 S.E.2d 380, 383–384 (1959)(*quoting* Richardson v. Lovvorn, 1900 Va. 688, 693, 101 S.E.2d 511, 514 (1958)).

[148] Expert testimony concerning accident reconstruction is also admissible to challenge or support the credibility of the eyewitnesses. *See* Bowling v. United States, 740 F. Supp. 2d 1240, 1258 (D. Kan. 2010)(accident reconstruction testimony concerning the location of the accident admissible even though "where the accident occurred is not germane to anything other than the credibility of the parties and witnesses.").

[149] 200 Ill.App.3d 526, 146 Ill.Dec. 289, 558 N.E.2d 252 (1990).

[150] 191 Ill.App.3d 664, 138 Ill.Dec. 724, 547 N.E.2d 1345 (1989).

The court believed that the expert's testimony was valuable in assisting the jury and understanding the defendant's theory of the case and was therefore admissible.

A court may properly restrict an accident reconstruction expert's testimony to the circumstances of the accident and exclude testimony unrelated to the expert's knowledge of accident reconstruction.[151] If an expert's opinion is based on neither personal knowledge[152] nor observation, there is no factual basis and therefore an improper foundation for his opinion.[153] Expert testimony may also be excluded if the witness failed to account for differences between the accident and his simulation of the accident,[154] failed to account for the conditions as they were at the time of the accident in the reconstruction,[155] or involved non-validated theories.[156]

Another issue regarding the scope of the admissibility of scientific evidence is the ultimate issue doctrine. The rationale for the doctrine is that the expert should not be permitted to invade the province of the jury. Rule 704, Federal Rules of Evidence, has rejected the ultimate issue rule: "Testimony in the form of opinion or inference otherwise admissible is not objectionable because it embraces an ultimate issue to be decided by the trier of fact." A majority of states have abandoned the ultimate issue doctrine. Most jurisdictions now allow experts to testify to ultimate issues (like negligence or whether a collision was "an accident"), leaving it to the jury to decide how much weight to give the expert's opinion on the ultimate issue.[157] A minority of states still follow the ultimate issue doctrine.[158]

---

[151] Crawford v. Koloniaris, 199 A.D.2d 235, 605 N.Y.S.2d 718 (1993)(holding no foundation laid for testimony regarding standard procedures for police on pulling speeding motorist off highways; as well, it was within the ability and experience of the jury to determine whether the state trooper was negligent in pulling motorist over).

[152] In Commonwealth v. Addy, 79 Mass. App. Ct. 835, 838, 950 N.E.2d 883, 887 (2011), the defendant argued that the expert testimony should have been excluded because it was based in large part on the expert's observations at the scene and did not "utiliz[e] scientific methods, analysis, or mathematical calculations in forming his opinion." The appellate court held that the defendant failed to prove why such devices were needed and found that the failure to perform certain tests only went to the weight of the testimony, not its admissibility.

[153] Wallach v. Board of Education of Prince George's County, 99 Md.App. 386, 637 A.2d 859 (1994).

[154] See Kirk v. Union Pacific Railroad, 514 N.W.2d 734 (Iowa Ct. App.1994).

[155] See Dulin v. Maher, 200 A.D.2d 707, 607 N.Y.S.2d 67 (1994).

[156] See Chapman v. Maytag Corp., 297 F.3d 682, 688 (7th Cir. 2002)(expert's testimony about his "resistive short" theory in product case unreliable); Smith v. Yang. 829 N.E.2d 624, 629 (Ind. App. 2005)(accident reconstruction expert's "faked-left-syndrome" theory unreliable); Moore v. Harley-Davidson Motor Co Group, 158 Wn. App. 407, 241 P.3d 808 (Ct. App. 2010)(expert's "metal spatter" theory novel and unreliable).

[157] See Denham v. Holmes, 60 So. 3d 773 (Miss. 2011)(noting that the Court allows, where appropriate, an accident reconstruction expert to opine as to ultimate conclusions regarding causation, but finding the particular expert's testimony unreliable).

[158] The Commonwealth of Virginia is one jurisdiction which still bars expert testimony on the ultimate issue in criminal cases. Zelanak v. Commonwealth, 25 Va. App. 295, 299, 487 S.E.2d 873, 875 (1997); Llamera v. Commonwealth, 243 Va. 262, 264, 414 S.E.2d 597, 598 (1992) See also State v. Ellington, 253 P.3d 727, 740–741 (Idaho 2011)(finding that the expert's testimony that the collision was "not an accident" and "intentional" was inadmissible).

Jurisdictions that admit expert testimony on the ultimate issue of fact do not permit all such testimony without limit. In *McKenzie v. Supervalue Incorporated*,[159] a motorist brought a personal injury action against a tractor-trailer driver and his employer after the motorist skidded into the trailer while the truck's driver was attempting a turn. The jury found in favor of the defendants, and on appeal, the plaintiff claimed that the trial court erred in admitting testimony from an accident reconstructionist as testimony on the ultimate issue that invaded the province of the jury. At trial, the expert stated that the accident "would not have happened" if the plaintiff had been "keeping a proper look out and operating his vehicle under control at a safe speed."[160] The appellate court explained that the Mississippi Rules of Evidence 704 essentially abolished the prohibition against testimony by experts on the "ultimate issue" solely on the grounds that it usurps the role of the jury. However, the court noted that Rule 704 does not result in the admission of all opinions because under Mississippi Rules of Evidence 701 and 702, expert opinions are admissible only if they are helpful for the triers of fact in the determination of the case.

V. Resources

§8.15 Bibliography of Additional Resources

1. Speeding

Valerie Alvord, "Motorists Race to Court to Challenge RedBLight Cameras," USA Today, Jul. 6, 2001.

Robert R Blackbun and Daniel T. Gilbert, Photographic Enforcement of Traffic Laws, 1995.

Dorothy J. Glancy, "Privacy On the Open Road," 30 Ohio N.U.L.Rev. 295 (2004).

Thomas J. Goger, Anno., Proof by Radar or Other Mechanical or Electronic Devices, of Violation of Speed Regulations, 47 A.L.R.3d 822 (1973 & supp.).

M. Goodson, "Technical Shortcomings of Doppler Traffic Radar," 30 J. Forensic Sci. 1186 (1985).

Mark G. Milone, "Biometric Surveillance: Searching For Identity," 57 Bus. Lawyer 497 (2001).

---

[159] 883 So.2d 1188 (Miss.App.Ct.2004). Compare to *Bowman v. Pennington*, 2007 WL 437782 (D.Kan.2007). The court granted defendant's request to exclude sections of the investigating officer's report that addressed the cause and contributing factors of the accident. The court stated this was for the jury to determine because it went to the ultimate issue of who was legally responsible for the accident.

[160] Id. at 1190.

Lisa S. Morris, "Photo Radar: Friend Or Foe?" 61 UMKC L.Rev. 805 (1993).

Steven T. Naumchick, "Review of Selected 1998 California Legislation: Transportation and Motor Vehicles: Stop! Photographic Enforcement of Red Lights," 30 McGeorge L.Rev. 846 (1999).

Hon. Robert J. Steigmann, "Applying the Frye Standard to Expert Testimony: A Guide for Lawyers and Judges," 92 Ill. Bar J. 363 (2004).

Lior Jacob Strahilevitz, " 'How's My Driving?' For Everyone (And Everything?)," 81 N.Y.U.L.Rev. 1699 (2006).

2.   RECONSTRUCTION

ACCIDENT INVESTIGATION QUARTERLY and ACCIDENT RECONSTRUCTION J. (Bimonthly journal)(both edited by Victor Craig (301) 843–1371).

Michael Allison, "Cement Truck v. Pedestrian: A Case Study," 18 ACCIDENT RECONSTRUCTION J., Mar.-Apr. 2008.

Andrew Askland, "The Double Edged Sword that is the Event Data Recorder," 25 Temp. J. Sci. Tech. & Envtl. L. 1 (2006).

Joseph E. Badger, "Reconstruction of Traffic Accidents," 9 Am.Jur.3d Proof of Facts 115 (2006).

Wade Bartlett and William Wright, "Summary of 56 Recent Critical Speed Yaw Analysis Tests Including ABS and Electronic Stability Control on Pavement, Gravel, and Grass," 18 ACCIDENT RECONSTRUCTION J., May–June 2008.

Thomas L. Bohan and Arthur C. Damask, eds., *Forensic Accident Investigation: Motor Vehicles*, Lexis Law Pub., 2006.

Thomas L. Bohan, *Crashes and Collapses,* Facts on File, Inc., 2009.

Raymond M. Brach and R. Matthew Brach, *Vehicle Analysis and Reconstruction Methods,* SAE International, 2005.

John Fiske Brown, Kenneth S. Obenski and Thomas R. Osborn, *Forensic Engineering Reconstruction of Accidents, 2d ed.,* Charles C. Thomas Pub., Ltd., 2002.

Michael Chi and Jafar Vossoughi, "Engineering Aspect of Automobile Accident Reconstruction Using Computer Simulation," 30 J. Forensic Sci. 814 (1985).

Larry Coben, "Investigating Automotive Accidents," TRIAL, March 1994.

Joseph N. Colfone *et al.,* "A Comparison of Equations for Estimating Speed Based on Maximum Static Deformation for Frontal Narrow-Object Impacts," 17 ACCIDENT RECONSTRUCTION J., Nov.–Dec. 2007.

John Daily, Nathan Shigemura and Jeremy Daily, *Fundamentals of Traffic Crash Reconstruction,* Institute of Police Technology and Management, 2004.

Mark Erickson and Wilson C. Hayes, *Drag Factor Attenuation for Rotating Vehicles*, 18 ACCIDENT RECONSTRUCTION J., May–June 2008.

Harold Franck and Darren Franck, *Mathematical Methods for Accident Reconstruction*, CRC Press, 2010.

Jascha Hoffman, "The Science of Reconstructing Car Accidents," 2004 AUG. LEGAL AFF. 6 (August 2004).

Mark Kimsey, "Speed Calculation From a Video Tape," 18 ACCIDENT RECONSTRUCTION J., July–Aug. 2008 at 23.

John B. Kwasnoski, "Constructing Hypotheticals in Motor Vehicle Homicide Cases," THE CHAMPION, November 1992, at 6.

J. E. Macy, "Admissibility of Opinion Evidence As To The Cause of An Accident or Occurrence," 38 A.L.R. 2d 13, at ' 20.

Elaine McArdle, " 'Black Box' Ruling Could Transform Auto Crash Litigation," LAWYERS WEEKLY USA, May 29, 2000, at B3.

Karl A. Menninger, II, "Data and Voice Recorders in Airplanes, Motor Vehicles and Trains," 84 Am.Jur. POF 3d 1 (2006).

Mortimer N. Moore, "A *Daubert* Challenge to Accident Reconstruction," 50 FEB. R.I. B.J. 11 (2002).

Patrick R. Mueller, "Every Time You Brake, Every Turn You Make—I'll Be Watching You: Protecting Driver Privacy in Event Data Recorder Information," 2006 Wis. L. Rev. 135 (2006).

Gerald D. Murphy, "Accident Reconstruction Section 1.7," *Massachusetts Continuing Legal Education Handbook* (2003).

R. W. Rivers, *Evidence in Traffic Crash Investigation and Reconstruction*, Charles C Thomas Publisher Ltd, 2006.

C. Gregory Russell, *Equations and Formulas for the Traffic Accident Investigator and Reconstructionist 2d ed.*, Lawyers & Judges Pub. Co. Inc., 2006.

Kevin Schlosser, " 'Black Box' Evidence," 2005 N.Y.L.J. 16 (2005).

Carian Simms and Denis Wood, *Pedestrian and Cyclist Impact: A Biomechanical Perspective*, Springer Science + Business Media, BV, 2009.

Donald J. Van Kirk, *Vehicular Accident Investigation and Reconstruction*, CRC Press, 2001.

Donald J. Van Kirk, "A Scientific Approach to Documenting Evidence for Accident Reconstruction," 29 J. FORENSIC SCI. 806 (1984).

Alan J. Watts, *Accident Reconstruction Science*, Lawyers & Judges Publishing Co. Inc., 2011.

CHAPTER 9

DIGITAL FORENSICS[1]

I. INTRODUCTION

§9.01 SCOPE OF THE CHAPTER

Digital communication and processing is ubiquitous. People have not only desktop and laptop computers, but smartphones and tablets that provide communication services and store vast amounts of data including contact information, still and motion pictures, and Global Positioning System (GPS) data used in location services. All of these personal devices can be linked together and their contents synchronized. This personal network can also be linked, through network cables or wirelessly, to the Internet. Cloud services have gained market influence by providing a host of services, including storage, infrastructure, and software.[2] All of these capabilities are used by the government and the private sector. Manufacturing processes, national and international finance, and the

---

[1]   The Authors thank the following subject matter experts for their assistance with this chapter: Douglas S. Lacey, BEK TEK LLC; Breck McDaniel, Cellular Evidence Services, LLC; and Mark M. Pollitt, Ph.D., Digital Evidence Professional Services, Inc.

[2]   Examples of software as a service include Office 365 and Google Apps where the software used is cloud-based, not located on the individual device.

operation of electrical grids, nuclear reactors, water supply systems, as well as all forms of communication and transportation, are monitored and controlled through digital systems typically operating at least in part in cyberspace.[3]

Digital evidence will be used in this Chapter to refer to any information of probative value that is stored or transmitted in binary form,[4] and includes information in audio files, video recordings, and digital images.[5] Transmission may be through wires, but also through fiber optic cable, or by satellite, radio, microwave, or other medium. Storage may be on magnetic or optical disks, but also on other storage media such as non-volatile random access memory (NVRAM), non-volatile solid state storage medium (flash) devices, magnetic tape, or on other retention devices. "The analysis of digital evidence deals with the gathering, processing, and interpreting digital evidence, such as electronic documents, lists of phone numbers and call logs, records of a device's location at a given time, e-mails, photographs, and more."[6]

Computer forensics has been defined as "the use of specialized techniques for recovery, authentication and analysis of electronic data when an investigation or litigation involves issues relating to reconstruction of computer usage, examination of residual data, authentication of data by technical analysis or explanation of technical features of data and computer usage."[7] When the examination extends beyond computers to cellphones, smartphones, and other digital devices, the term "digital forensics" is used. Broadly defined, digital forensics is "the identification, collection, preservation, analysis, and reporting of digital evidence"[8] and "a branch of forensic science focusing on the recovery and investigation of raw data residing in electronic or digital

---

[3] Cyberspace has been defined as "the interdependent network of information technology infrastructures that includes the Internet, telecommunications networks, computer systems, embedded processors, and controllers in critical industries." National Security Presidential Directive 54/Homeland Security Presidential Directive 23 (NSPD-54/HSPD 23). See also Executive Office of the President of the United States, "Cyberspace Policy Review: Assuring a Trusted and Resilient Information and Communications Infrastructure," May 8, 2009.

[4] Scientific Working Group on Digital Evidence, "SWGDE Digital and Multimedia Evidence Glossary," Version 3.0 (Approved June 23, 2016) at p. 7 (available at: https://www.swgde.org/documents/Current%20Documents/SWGDE%20Digital%20and%20Multimedia%20Evidence%20Glossary)(last accessed November 14, 2016) Digital information generally is encoded in bits which are the zeros and ones we associate with computer data, where the bits in turn make up bytes that represent recognizable numbers, letters, or other symbols.

[5] *See* NIST, Digital Evidence at: https://www.nist.gov/property-fieldsection/digital-evidence (last accessed November 14, 2016).

[6] Committee on Identifying the Needs of the Forensic Science Community, National Research Council of the National Academies, *Strengthening Forensic Science in the United States: A Path Forward*, The National Academies Press: Washington D.C., 2009 at p. 179.

[7] The Sedona Conference, *The Sedona Conference® Glossary: E-Discovery & Digital Information Management*, 4th ed., 2014 at p. 7 (available at: https://thesedonaconference.org/publication/sedona-conference%C2%AE-glossary-e-discovery-digital-information-management-fourth-edition)(last accessed November 21, 2016).

[8] Kim-Kwang Raymond Choo & Ali Dehghantanha, *Contemporary Digital Forensic Investigations of Cloud and Mobile Applications*, Elsevier, Inc. 2017 at p. 1.

devices."[9] Digital forensics requires specialized expertise to go beyond normal data collection and preservation techniques used by consumers or system support personnel. A digital forensic examiner locates, identifies, collects, analyzes, and examines data, while preserving the integrity and maintaining a strict chain of custody of information discovered.

This chapter will discuss digital forensics and the specific issues involved in the acquisition, analysis, and presentation of evidence recovered in such investigations. The use of digital evidence as demonstrative exhibits and digital evidence derived from different forensic examination methods are covered in other chapters. Because the digital device technology is one of the fastest evolving fields, the technical aspects of digital forensics will only be discussed in broad terms and other textbooks and sources should be consulted for detailed technical information. The need to secure and preserve data for investigation and analysis will be discussed as well as forensic tools and techniques and applicable professional standards. The unique challenges of mobile device investigation and investigation tools of intercepting devices and location data will be summarized. As trial aids, the chapter will briefly discuss expert qualifications, the use of digital forensic examiners in pretrial discovery of electronically stored information, and the admissibility of evidence derived from digitial forensic examinations. The constitutional protections implicated in digitial investigations are discussed in depth, as these issues now dominate the legal landscape.

§9.02 TERMINOLOGY

The following terms are among those commonly encountered in digital forensic investigations. More complete listings of terminology are found in the Scientific Working Group on Digital Evidence, *SWGDE Digital & Multimedia Evidence Glossary,*[10] the National Institute of Standards and Technology, *Guidelines on Mobile Digital Forensics,*[11]

---

[9] Heather Mahalik, Satish Bommisetty & Rohit Tamma, *Practical Mobile Forensics*, 2d ed., Packt Publishing, 2016 at p. 9.

The Scientific Working Group on Digital Evidence defines digital forensics as "the process used to acquire, preserve, analyze, and report on electronically stored information using scientific methods that are demonstrably reliable." *SWGDE Digital and Multimedia (Digital Forensics) as a Forensic Science Discipline*, Ver. 2.0 (September 5, 2014) at p. 3 (available at: https://www.swgde.org/documents)(last accessed November 30, 2016).

[10] Scientific Working Group on Digital Evidence, *SWGDE Digital & Multimedia Evidence Glossary*, Ver. 3.0, June 23, 2016 (available at: https://www.swgde.org/documents)(last accessed November 30, 2016).

[11] Rick Ayers, Sam Brothers, and Wayne Jansen, *Guidelines on Mobile Device Forensics*, National Institute of Standards and Technology Special Publication 800-101r1 Natl. Inst. Stand. Technol. Spec. Publ. 800-101 Revision 1, 87 pages (May 2014)(available at: http://nvl pubs.nist.gov/nistpubs/SpecialPublications/NIST.SP.800-101r1.pdf)(last accessed November 29, 2016).

and the Sedona Conference, *The Sedona Conference® Glossary: E-Discovery & Digital Information Management.*[12]

Acquisition: A process by which digital evidence is duplicated, copied, or imaged.

Analysis: The examination of acquired data for its significance and probative value to the case.

Architecture: Hardware, software, or a combination of both that make up the digital system, device, or network.

Authentication Mechanism: Hardware or software-based mechanisms that force users to prove their identity before accessing data on a device.

Bit: The smallest unit of computer data, a binary digit, either 0 or 1.

Byte: A basic measurement of computer data; eight bits.

Bluetooth: A wireless protocol that allows two similarly equipped devices to communicate with each other within a short distance (e.g., 30 ft.).

Brute Force Password Attack: A method of accessing an obstructed device by attempting multiple combinations of numeric/alphanumeric passwords.

Closed Source Operating System: Source code for an operating system is not publicly available.

Cookie: Text file containing tracking information (date, time) downloaded to a computer or mobile device when a website is accessed

Deleted File: A file that has been logically, but not necessarily physically, erased from the operating system, perhaps to eliminate potentially incriminating evidence. Deleting files does not always necessarily eliminate the possibility of recovering all or part of the original data.

Encryption: Any procedure used in cryptography to convert plain text into cipher text to prevent anyone but the intended recipient from reading that data.

Examination: A technical review that makes the evidence visible and suitable for analysis; as well as tests performed on the evidence to determine the presence or absence of specific data.

Extraction: A process of exporting data from a source

Extranet: An intranet (see *supra*) that is shared with selected outside parties, such as vendors, suppliers, clients, and business partners.

---

[12] The Sedona Conference, *The Sedona Conference® Glossary: E-Discovery & Digital Information Management*, 4th ed., 2014 at p. 7 (available at: https://thesedonaconference.org/publication/sedona-conference%C2%AE-glossary-e-discovery-digital-information-management-fourth-edition)(last accessed November 21, 2016).

Forensic Copy: A bit-for-bit reproduction of the information contained on an electronic device or associated media, whose validity and integrity has been verified using an accepted algorithm. An exact copy of an entire physical digital storage media; also called a physical acquisition copy, mirror image, bit image, bit-stream image, or cloned image.

Global Positioning System (GPS): A system for determining position by comparing radio signals from several satellites.

Hardware Driver: Applications responsible for establishing communication between hardware and software programs.

Hashing: The process of using a mathematical algorithm against data to produce a numeric value that is representative of that data.

HyperText Transfer Protocol (HTTP): A standard method for communication between clients and Web servers.

Intranet: A private computer network established using Internet protocols and network connectivity to create a private version of the Internet only available within a particular organization, agency, or company.

Jailbreak: Bypassing security restrictions on a digital device to take full control of the operating system. The most common reason to jailbreak a digital device is to load unapproved apps, but it can aid in forensic examinations

Metadata: Information about an electronic file that is either embedded in the file itself (application metadata) or associated with the file in the application or system (system metadata) that reflects the generation, handling, transfer, and storage of the file. Metadata varies depending on the type of file, in addition to file designation, creation and edit dates, authorship, and comments, typical word processing documents also include hidden codes of formatting.

Multimedia Messaging Service (MMS): An accepted standard for messaging that lets users send and receive messages formatted with text, graphics, photographs, audio, and video clips.

Non-volatile Memory: Memory that keeps its content without constant power.

Operating system (OS): The software platform on the digital device on which all other programs and applications run.

Short Message Service (SMS): A cellular network facility that allows users to send and receive short text messages of alphanumeric characters on their handset. The original SMS were limited to 140 characters using 8 bits per character, but the more widely used concatenated SMS (also known as a Protocol Data Unit (PDU) mode SMS) provides 160 characters by using 7 bits per character.

Volatile Memory: Memory that loses its content when power is turned off or lost.

Write Blocker: Software or hardware device that stops specific communication from a computer to a digital storage media to allow investigators to examine the storage media while preventing data writes from occurring on the media.

Write Protection: Hardware or software methods of preventing data from being written to a disk or other medium.

§9.03 EVIDENTIARY USES

While there are national laws and policies in place to protect essential digital infrastructure,[13] some people do not think the existing laws and policies are sufficient to address the ever-evolving cybersecurity threats.[14] The law of digital evidence and cybercrime often lags far behind the technical and operational realities. Further complicating the legal framework is the fact that technical issues presented by digital forensics are among the most challenging in scientific evidence, and lawyers and judges often lack the understanding of how the technology functions. These factors have had a profound effect in the application of the law to digital evidence in civil and criminal cases causing changes in civil liability, rules of discovery, and the prosecution and defense of criminal cases. In criminal cases, the prevalence of the Internet in current crimes has made the technology and use of mobile phones, tablets, and other digital devices the focus of developing Fourth Amendment law. Existing Fourth Amendment concepts such as expectation of privacy, particularity, and plain view are evolving to adapt to the way technology is used with, and information is stored in, digital devices.

---

[13] For example, in late 2012, President Obama issued Presidential Policy Directive (PPD) 20 which reportedly established a broad and strict set of standards to guide the operations of federal agencies in confronting threats in cyberspace and superseding National Security Directive 38 issued in 2004 and complementing NSPD-54/Homeland Security Presidential Directive (HSPD)-23 on "Cybersecurity Policy" of January 8, 2008; National Security Directive (NSD)-42 on "National Policy for the Security of National Security Telecommunications and Information Systems" of July 5, 1990; and PPD-8 on "National Preparedness" of March 30, 2011. On February 12, 2013, President Obama issued Executive Order 13636 on Improving Critical Infrastructure Cybersecurity.

In December 2014, Congress passed five major legislative proposals designed to enhance U.S. cybersecurity: The National Cybersecurity Protection Act of 2014; The Federal Information Security Modernization Act of 2014; The Cybersecurity Workforce Assessment Act; The Homeland Security Workforce Assessment Act; and The Cybersecurity Enhancement Act of 2014.

On July 26, 2016, President Obama issued PPD 41 on United States Cyber Incident Coordination (available at: http://fas.org/irp/offdocs/ppd/ppd-41.html)(last accessed November 14, 2016).

[14] *See, e.g.,* Matthew Y. Chang, "Note: Mobile Banking: The Best Hope for Cyber Security Development," 2016 U. Ill. L. Rev. 1191 (2016); Lawrence J. Trautman, "Article: Cybersecurity: What About U.S. Policy?" 2015 U. Ill. J.L. Tech. & Pol'y 341 (2015); Robert Gyenes, "A Voluntary Cybersecurity Framework is Unworkable—Government Must Crack the Whip," 14 PGH. J. Tech. L. & Pol'y 293 (2014).

Evidence derived from digital forensic investigations can be involved in civil or criminal cases because the technological explosion of digital devices means that more communications, commerce, and other transactions use digital devices. Information stored on digital devices can provide evidence of a person's actions or state of mind, liability, relationships, or other issues relevant in civil cases. For criminal cases, crimes may be planned, and even executed, digitally. Crimes ranging from fraud, to identity theft, to child pornography, to terrorism are committed or aided through digital information. Criminals obtain unauthorized access to data in banking, healthcare, retail, and other computer systems for theft, terrorism, intimidation, or mischief. Predators arrange meetings with their victims, exchange child pornography, and spy on targets from the convenience and privacy of their electronic havens. Digital storage media and devices are "the most commonly encountered in criminal and counterintelligence matters, but laboratories have been asked to examine such items as scuba dive watches in death investigations and black boxes in aircraft mishaps."[15]

The explosion of smartphones and other mobile media has led to significant changes in the way digital evidence is relevant to civil and criminal investigations. In the past, digital devices (primarily computers) were the instrumentality or target of the crime through theft and fraud cases and the devices were analyzed accordingly. With the proliferation of smartphones, more everyday commerce and social interaction occurs through digital devices. These digital devices have become vast repositories for evidence both of the direct commission of crimes and of corroborative or contradictory evidence of events and an individual's intent. "[By] the end of each day, hundreds of megabytes of data may have been generated about where individuals have been, how fast they got there, to whom they spoke, and even what was said."[16] The digital information found on mobile devices and the ways that it can be relevant in civil and criminal cases is expected to have a tremendous impact on litigation.

II. TOOLS AND TECHNIQUES

§9.04 INVESTIGATION FRAMEWORK

The specific processes and procedures for a digital forensic examination will vary in detail depending on the digital media being examined, the tools and techniques used, and the data sought. The processes and procedures, however, can be broadly described in four

---

[15] Committee on Identifying the Needs of the Forensic Science Community, National Research Council of the National Academies, *Strengthening Forensic Science in the United States: A Path Forward*, The National Academies Press: Washington D.C., 2009 at p. 179.

[16] Id.

steps: preservation, acquisition, examination and analysis, and reporting.[17] Although different organizations and agencies use different labels for the steps of the investigation framework, the actions of the steps are consistently described:[18]

Preservation (also known as seizure): The process of securely maintaining custody of property without altering or changing the contents of data that reside on devices and removable media. This step involves the search, recognition, documentation, and collection of digital evidence.[19]

Acquisition (also known as extraction or collection): The process of exporting the digital data from the device. This step may use many different methods and may use software and hardware devices to acquire the data.

Examination and Analysis: Reviewing the digital data recovered and translating it into a useable form. This step may involve automated tools targeted to the type of data implicated in the investigation (*e.g.*, images, documents, Internet activity logs).

Reporting (also known as presentation): Documenting the results of the examination to inform others as to the data recovered.

§9.05 MOBILE DEVICE FORENSICS

Mobile devices, particularly smartphones, have proliferated exponentially in the last decade.[20] For 2017, the number of smartphone users in the United States is expected to reach 222.9 million, with the number of smartphone users worldwide to exceed 2 billion.[21] These mobile devices are used for voice calls and exchanging text messages, and for smartphones, the vast services available through the Internet. Increasingly popular mobile voice over Internet (VoIP) applications, such as Skype, WhatsApp, and Viber, allow the exchange of video,

---

[17] *See* Rick Ayers, Sam Brothers, and Wayne Jansen, *Guidelines on Mobile Device Forensics*, National Institute of Standards and Technology Special Publication 800-101r1 Natl. Inst. Stand. Technol. Spec. Publ. 800-101 Revision 1, 87 pages (May 2014)(*hereinafter "NIST, Guidelines on Mobile Device Forensics")* at pp. 27–55 (available at: http://nvlpubs.nist.gov/nistpubs/SpecialPublications/NIST.SP.800-101r1.pdf)(last accessed November 29, 2016).

[18] *See* Lee Reiber, *Mobile Forensic Investigations: A Guide to Evidence Collection, Analysis, and Presentation*, McGraw Hill Education, 2016 (*hereinafter "Reiber, Mobile Forensic Investigations")* at pp. 27–28 (describing the procedures of the International Association of Computer Investigative Specialists (IACIS) and the International Society of Forensic Computer Examiners (ISFCE)); Heather Mahalik, Staish Bommisetty & Rohit Tamma, *Practical Mobile Forensics*, 2d ed., Packt Publishing, 2016 at p. 9 (listing seizure, acquisition, and examination/analysis).

[19] NIST, *Guidelines on Mobile Device Forensics* at p. 27.

[20] For a brief history of the mobile device, *see* Reiber, *Mobile Forensic Investigations* at pp. 3–7.

[21] *See* https://www.statista.com/statistics/201182/forecast-of-smartphone-users-in-the-us/ (last accessed November 23, 2016).

audio, and images in addition to traditional calls and texts.[22] The use of mobile devices allows these communication services at a much lower cost than traditional communication techniques, but presents challenges for digital forensic examinations. Additional potential evidence may be located within the myriad of mobile applications on mobile devices, including financial records, location information, and communications, but recovering such evidence also presents challenges. A non-exclusive list of common data on mobile devices includes:[23]

- Address Book
- Call History
- SMS (text messages)
- MMS (media files)
- E-mail
- Web browser history
- Photos
- Videos
- Music
- Documents
- Calendar
- Network communications (contains GPS locations)
- Maps
- Social networking data
- Deleted data

The nature of mobile devices, with a wide range of proprietary hardware, encryption, and strict user identification features, makes access to the information on mobile devices more complicated than traditional computer forensics. Additionally, the constant evolution of both mobile device technology and cellular network characteristics requires equally-evolving recovery tools and techniques.[24] To address these challenges, the digital forensic community is focusing more attention on mobile digital forensics and it is one of the fastest growing fields. "Mobile device forensics is the science of recovering digital evidence from a mobile device under forensically sound conditions using accepted methods [and] is an evolving specialty in the field of digital forensics."[25] At the core of mobile digital forensics is the recognition that communicating with mobile devices requires specialized software

---

[22] *See* T. Dargahi, A. Dehghantanha & M. Conti, "Forensic Analysis of Android Mobile VoIP Apps," in Kim-Kwang Raymond Choo and Ali Dehghantanha, eds. *Contemporary Digital Forensic Investigations of Cloud and Mobile Applications*, Elsevier, Inc., 2017 at pp. 7–20.

[23] *See* Heather Mahalik, Staish Bommisetty & Rohit Tamma, *Practical Mobile Forensics*, 2d ed., Packt Publishing, 2016 at pp. 24–25.

[24] Id. at p. 7.

[25] NIST, *Guidelines on Mobile Device Forensics* at p. III.

tools designed to recover and analyze specific digital data on mobile devices.[26] Because mobile devices store data in a variety of locations, several different types of software tools may be used on one device.[27]

The National Institute of Standards and Technology (NIST) provides guidelines for mobile device forensics discussing the procedures for the preservation, acquisition, examination, analysis, and reporting of digital evidence.[28] The guidelines are a "compilation of best practices within the discipline and references have been taken from existing forensic guidelines. . . . [with the purpose] to inform readers of the various technologies involved and potential ways to approach them from a forensic point of view."[29] As discussed in the NIST guidelines, the forensic investigation framework for mobile devices is the same used in other digital forensics. Experts have noted that: "To be successful in the discipline of mobile device forensics, the examiner must understand that the process from seizure to analysis is no different from. . .a computer forensic examination."[30] Mobile device characteristics, however, require additional considerations, particularly in the preservation of evidence. These characteristics, sometimes referred to as challenges, include: hardware differences, wider variety of operating systems, platform security features, dynamic nature of digital evidence on mobile devices, remote access features, and the incredible variety of applications available to users.[31]

Incorrect procedures in securing and handling a mobile device may result in the destruction of digital data. A mobile device, like a cellphone, is an "active" device because it is attached to several networks that allow outside communication which may interfere with the physical collection and extraction of data.[32] Many mobile devices offer the ability to perform either a remote lock or remote wipe[33] by simply sending a command (e.g., text message) to the mobile device, so

---

[26] Reiber, *Mobile Forensic Investigations* at p. 10.

[27] Id.

[28] NIST, *Guidelines on Mobile Device Forensics.*

[29] Id. at p. 1.

A comprehensive discussion on the nature of digital evidence on mobile devices, along with a complete guide on forensic techniques to handle, preserve, extract, and analyze evidence from mobile devices is also provided in E. Casey and B. Turnbull, "Digital Evidence on Mobile Devices," in Eoghan Casey, ed. *Digital Evidence and Computer Crime: Forensic Science, Computers, and the Internet,* 3rd ed., Academic Press, 2011.

[30] Reiber, *Mobile Forensic Investigations* at p. 43.

[31] *See* Heather Mahalik, Staish Bommisetty & Rohit Tamma, *Practical Mobile Forensics,* 2d ed., Packt Publishing, 2016 at pp. 11–12.

[32] Id. at p. 65.

[33] Remote wiping was also an issue in a civil lawsuit alleging violations of the Federal Computer Fraud and Abuse Act. A recently resigned employee was accused of using the remote wiping feature on a work-issued smartphone to erase valuable corporate contacts and information. See Samantha Joseph, "Salesman Accused of Using iPhone Feature to Delete Company's Confidential Data," The Connecticut Law Tribune, November 29, 2016 (available at: http://www.ctlawtribune.com/id=1202773410075/Salesman-Accused-of-Using-iPhone-Feature-to-Delete-Companys-Confidential-Data?mcode=0&curindex=0)(last accessed November 30, 2016).

disabling the cellular network connectivity and isolating the device from all radio networks (e.g. WiFi, cellular, and Bluetooth) are important. Cellular network isolation techniques include cellular isolation network cards, shielded containers, disabling service through the network provider, and jamming/spoofing devices. The three basic methods for isolating the mobile device from radio networks are enabling "airplane mode," turning the device off, and placing the device in a shielded container. The limitations of each isolation method must be considered before implementation, including whether authentication codes or resets will be activated by any disruptions in network connectivity.[34]

§9.06 RECOVERY AND ANALYSIS TOOLS

Digital forensic examinations often require specialized tools (software and hardware) for the recovery and analysis of the data. These specialized tools, however, are not uniform and vary greatly in their capabilities, limitations, and specifications. Tools may vary in the recovering and reporting of the data, the decoding and translation of recovered data, and the ability to recover all relevant data.[35] The type of digital device involved and the type of data to be recovered generally determine what tools will be appropriate in an investigation. NIST has been a leader in digital forensics and maintains several resources to provide a foundation for toolmakers to improve tools and for users to make informed choices:

> The National Software Reference Library is a regularly updated archive of known, traceable software applications collected by NIST. [NIST] generate[s] digital signatures from all files in that archive and release[s] them in a quarterly Reference Data Set (RDS). When a law enforcement organization seizes a computer or mobile device as part of a criminal investigation, they can use the RDS to quickly identify the known files on that device. This reduces the effort required to determine which files are important as evidence and which are not.[36]

> The Computer Forensic Tool Testing program establishes a methodology for testing computer forensic software tools by developing general tool specifications, test procedures, test criteria, test sets, and test hardware. The results help toolmakers to improve their products, allows users to make informed choices about which tools to use, and provides

---

[34] NIST, *Guidelines on Mobile Device Forensics* at pp. 29–30; *see also* Reiber, *Mobile Forensic Investigations* at pp. 54–56.

[35] Reiber, *Mobile Forensic Investigations* at pp. 3–7. *See also* NIST, *Guidelines on Mobile Device Forensics* at p. 25.

[36] https://www.nist.gov/topics/digital-multimedia-evidence (last accessed November 29, 2016).

information to all interested parties on the capabilities of various computer tools used in forensic investigations.[37]

The NIST Cloud Computing Forensic Science Program aims to improve the accuracy, reliability, scientific validity, and usefulness of cloud forensic science. In support of this project, NIST has established the Cloud Computing Forensic Science Public Working Group to perform research and identify gaps in technology, standards and measurements; to address various challenges in cloud forensics; and to develop a cloud forensics reference architecture.[38]

An important publication from NIST, the Computer Forensics Tool Testing Handbook,[39] provides the results of the Computer Forensics Tool Testing (CFTI) program. The CFTI tests digital forensic software tools to determine their performance of core forensic functions such as imaging drives and extracting information from mobile devices. The handbook provides a summary of the performance of each tool tested, a link to the detailed report of the testing, and any vendor information. To maintain confidence in the results of a forensic examination, experts have noted that the examiner "must be confident in the tools that are being used to perform the data collection and examination."[40]

1. MOBILE DEVICE FORENSIC TOOLS

The forensic tools for mobile devices are considerably different from those for computers. Although the majority of mobile device operating systems are open source, mobile devices with the same operating system may vary widely in their implementation, creating significant challenges for mobile forensic tool manufacturers and examiners. Tools include commercial and open source (free) software that may be classified as "forensic" or "non-forensic." Forensic tools are designed to acquire data without altering content and to calculate integrity hashes for the acquired data. Non-forensic tools may allow unrestricted two-way flow of information and omit data integrity hash functions. The range of devices for which the tools operate vary with platforms, operating system, and architecture. Tool manufacturers must continually update their tools as the underlying device and software manufacturers issue new products and update existing products. The task is formidable and tool manufacturers may lag significantly behind the device marketplace.

---

[37] https://www.nist.gov/topics/digital-multimedia-evidence (last accessed November 29, 2016).

[38] https://www.nist.gov/topics/digital-multimedia-evidence (last accessed November 29, 2016).

[39] National Institute of Standards and Technology, National Institute of Justice, *Computer Forensic Tool Testing Handbook*, Rev. August 6, 2015 (available at: http://www.cftt. nist.gov/CFTT-Booklet-08112015.pdf)(last accessed November 29, 2016).

[40] Reiber, *Mobile Forensic Investigations* at p. 116.

a. Extraction Methods

Tools also vary in the methods used to extract data, from recording information off of the screen to using a high powered microscope to physically examine the state of the gates within memory. NIST produced a tool classification system for comparing the different methods of extraction used by the various available tools:[41]

Level One: Manual Extraction

A manual extraction method involves viewing the data content stored on a mobile device through the manual manipulation of the buttons, keyboard, or touchscreen to view the contents of the mobile device. Information discovered may be recorded using an external digital camera.

Benefits: Ease of use and cost efficient

Limitations: Deleted information cannot be recovered; time consuming; data on the device may be inadvertently modified, deleted, or overwritten as a result of the examination; a broken/missing LCD screen or a damaged/missing keyboard interface may prohibit manual extraction.

Level Two: Logical Extraction

Logical extraction involves the connection between a mobile device and a forensic workstation (computer). Logical extraction tools send a series of commands over the established connection from the computer to the mobile device. The mobile device responds by sending data to the computer for reporting purposes.

Benefits:

Limitations: Different connection types may result in data being modified or different amounts or types of data being extracted.

Level Three: Hex Dumping and JTAG[42]

Hex dumping, the more commonly used method by tools at this level, involves uploading a modified boot loader (or other software) into a protected area of memory (e.g., RAM) on the device through a flasher box connected to the mobile device's data port and the forensic workstation. Flasher boxes are small devices originally designed to

---

[41] NIST, *Guidelines on Mobile Device Forensics* at pp. 17–20. *See also* Heather Mahalik, Staish Bommisetty & Rohit Tamma, *Practical Mobile Forensics*, 2d ed., Packt Publishing, 2016 at pp. 21–23.

[42] *See* Scientific Working Group on Digital Evidence, *SWGDE Best Practices for Examining Mobile Phones Using JTAG*, Ver. 1 (September 29, 2015)(available at: https://www.swgde.org/documents)(last accessed November 30, 2016).

service or upgrade mobile devices, The flasher box aides the examiner by communicating with the mobile device using diagnostic protocols to communicate with the memory chip. A series of commands is sent from the flasher box to the mobile device to place it in a diagnostic mode. Once in diagnostic mode, the flasher box captures all (or sections) of flash memory and sends it to the forensic workstation.

Benefits: Access to more raw data; many flasher box software packages provide the added functionality of recovering passwords from mobile device memory.

Limitations: Requires a reboot, so user identification features (passwords) that are activated may prevent recovery; data is recovered in encrypted form; flasher boxes are complicated, difficult to use, and may not have access to all areas of memory.

Joint Test Action Group (JTAG) defines a common test interface for processor, memory, and other semiconductor chips. Forensic examiners can communicate with a JTAG-compliant component by utilizing special purpose standalone programmer devices to probe defined test points. This method involves attaching a cable (or wiring harness) from a workstation to the mobile device's JTAG interface and accessing memory via the device's microprocessor to push data from the mobile device to the computer.

Benefits: Possible avenue for acquiring data from locked or damaged devices.

Limitations: Invasive, as access to the connections frequently require that the examiner dismantle some (or most) of a mobile device to obtain access to establish the wiring connections; requires extensive training.

Level Four: Chip-Off[43]

Chip-Off methods involve acquisition of data contained within a device by removing the device's flash memory chip from the printed circuit board and directly reading the data on the chip through a chip reader.

Benefits: Provides examiners with the ability to create a binary image of the removed chip; this type of acquisition is the most closely related to the physical imaging a hard disk drive as in traditional computer forensics.

---

[43] *See* Scientific Working Group on Digital Evidence, *SWGDE Best Practices for Chip-Off,* Ver. 1.0 (February 8, 2016)(available at: https://www.swgde.org/documents)(last accessed November 30, 2016).

Limitations: Extensive training is required in order to successfully perform extractions at this level;[44] risk of causing physical damage to the chip during the removal process; the chip reader appropriate to the chip must be used.

Level Five: Micro Read

A Micro Read involves recording the physical observation of the gates on a NAND or NOR chip with the use of an electron microscope. No know US law enforcement agencies perform data acquisitions at this level.

Benefits: Access to raw data; does not alter the data

Limitations: Extremely difficult and requires a team of experts, proper equipment, time and in-depth knowledge of proprietary information; no commercially available Micro Read tools.

The Scientific Working Group on Digital Evidence (SWGDE) uses a similar structure to describe the level of extraction and analysis, noting that each level has its own corresponding skillset.[45]

b. Examination and Analysis

Because of the prevalence of proprietary case file formats in mobile devices, the forensic tool used for extraction of specific data will also typically be the one used for examination and analysis of that data. Different tools, however, may be necessary to extract, examine, and analyze data in other locations (directories or applications) on the same device. Data storage points for mobile devices include internal and

---

[44] SWGDE recommends training on the following topics, at a minimum:

(a) digital forensic procedures and evidence handling;

(b) basic electronics concepts, theory, and troubleshooting;

(c) repairing and disassembling devices;

(d) identification of flash memory and memory controller chips;

(e) differences in chip packages;

(f) familiarity with rework stations and processes;

(g) procedures for removing chips;

(h) reballing or preparing chips to be read;

(i) soldering and desoldering techniques;

(j) procedures for reading chips with a flash programmer.

Scientific Working Group on Digital Evidence, *SWGDE Best Practices for Chip-Off*, Ver. 1.0 (February 8, 2016) at p. 5 (available at: https://www.swgde.org/documents)(last accessed November 30, 2016).

[45] SWGDE uses seven levels: (1) Manual; (2) Logical; (3) File System; (4) Physical (Non-Invasive); (5) Physical (Invasive); (6) Chip-Off; and (7) MicroRead. Scientific Working Group on Digital Evidence, SWGDE Best Practices for Mobile Phone Forensics, Ver. 2.0 (February 11, 2013) at pp. 7–8 (available at: https://www.swgde.org/documents)(last accessed November 30, 2016).

File System extraction collects "the files and folders that the device uses to populate applications, system configurations, and user configurations along with user storage areas." Reiber, *Mobile Digital Forensic Investigations* at p. 121.

external media storage cards, built-in applications, user-loaded applications, and backups.[46] Each of these data point may require a different tool and technique for data extraction. Using multiple tools will not only allow the recovery of additional data the initial tool did not support, but will also allow verification of data the initial tool recovered.[47]

c. *Obstructed Devices*

In mobile device forensics, examiners are often confronted with obstructed devices: mobile devices that require successful authentication using a password or some other means to obtain access to data on the device. Content encryption capabilities (through password locks and encrypted memory cards) are offered as a standard feature in many mobile devices. These capabilities provide the user with additional means to protect data and make the recovery of such data more complex. The methods for recovering data from obstructed devices are categorized as: software-based, hardware-based, and investigative (e.g., ask the user, look for documents containing the password, ask the service provider or manufacturer).[48] The utility of a particular method is device dependent, and other than the investigative method of obtaining the password from the user, no method is universally successful.

2. FORENSIC HASHING

For digital forensic examinations, it is important to maintain the integrity of the original data source being acquired and also that of the extracted data. "Preserving integrity not only maintains credibility from a legal perspective, but it also allows any subsequent investigation to use the same baseline for replicating the analysis."[49] To maintain the original data source, the examiner may use a tool to block or otherwise eliminate write requests to the device containing the data. To maintain the integrity of the recovered data, examiners use forensic hash validation. A forensic hash computes a cryptographically strong, non-reversible value over the acquired data—essentially a mathematical fingerprint of the data.[50] Any changes to the data would result in a new hash value inconsistent with the original hash value. By comparing the hash value of the post-examination data with the hash value of the original data, the examiner can establish that no changes were made to the data, that the integrity of the data has been maintained.

Hash values and the integrity of the data recovered from mobile devices must be considered differently than the traditional computer

---

[46] Reiber, *Mobile Forensic Investigations* at pp. 14–19.

[47] Id. at p. 13.

[48] NIST, *Guidelines on Mobile Device Forensics* at pp. 24–25.

[49] Id. at p. 26.

[50] Reiber, Mobile Forensic Investigations at p. 29.

forensic examination. Mobile devices are not mass storage devices and write blockers cannot be used to prevent alteration of the data on the mobile device. Additionally, when connected to a computer for extraction or examination, the mobile device makes changes to communicate to the computer (through a driver). Mobile devices also make changes through their constant action and continuous updates (e.g., the device clock or location information). Back-to-back acquisitions of a mobile device will be different and will produce different hash values. However, the hash values computed over selected data items, such as individual files or directories, should remain consistent.[51]

§9.07 STANDARDS

In 1998, the FBI formed the Scientific Working Group on Digital Evidence (SWGDE) to "brin[g] together organizations actively engaged in the field of digital and multimedia evidence to foster communication and cooperation as well as to ensure quality and consistency in the forensic community."[52] Formed with multiple federal, state, and local law enforcement agency members, the group focuses primarily on the practice of digital evidence in the laboratory setting, but promotes best practice standards and guidelines that are useful to field practice.[53] The American Society of Crime Laboratory Directors Laboratory Accreditation Board (ASCLD-LAB), which merged with ANAB in April 2016, implemented a set of standards for accreditation based on the SWGDE standards and compliance with international standards such as ISO 17025 and ENFSI 2003.[54] The guidelines, recommendations, and best practice documents from SWGDE cover the wide range of digital and multimedia investigations, including:

> SWGDE Best Practices for Computer Forensics, Version 3.1 (September 5, 2014)

> SWGDE Best Practices for Mobile Phone Forensics, Version 2.0 (February 11, 2013)

> SWGDE Core Competencies for Mobile Phone Forensics, Version 1.0 (February 11, 2013)

> SWGDE Recommended Guidelines for Validation Testing, Version 2.0 (September 5, 2014)

> SWGDE Proficiency Test Guidelines, Version 1.0 (September 29, 2015)

---

[51] NIST, Guidelines on Mobile Device Forensics at p. 26. See also Reiber, Mobile Forensic Investigations at p. 29.

[52] *See* https://www.swgde.org.

[53] Mark M. Pollitt, "Who is SWGDE and what is the history?" January 22, 2003 (available at: https://www.swgde.org/pdf/2003-01-22%20SWGDE%20History.pdf)(last accessed November 15, 2016).

[54] For more information see http://www.enfsi.eu/ which also provides access to a Forensic Information Technology (FIT) best practices guide.

SWGDE Image Processing Guidelines, Version 1.0 (February 8, 2016)

SWGDE Best Practices for Collection of Damaged Mobile Devices, Version 1.1 (February 8, 2016)

SWGDE Digital Image Compression and File Formats Guidelines, Version 1.0 (June 23, 2016)

SWGDE Best Practices for Digital Audio Authentication, Version 1 (June 23, 2016)

The National Institute of Standards and Technology (NIST) also has a range of guidelines available, including the NIST *Guidelines on Mobile Device Forensics*, and other resources for digital forensics.[55] NIST has also supported the Organization of Scientific Area Committees (OSAC), including the Digital/Multimedia Committee appointed in September 2014.[56] The purpose of the OSAC is to "facilitate the development and promulgation of consensus-based documentary standards and guidelines for forensic science, promoting standards and guidelines that are fit-for-purpose and based on sound scientific principles, promoting the use of OSAC standards and guidelines by accreditation and certification bodies, and establishing and maintaining working relationships with other similar organizations."[57] The Digital/Multimedia Committee is expected to build on the documents promulgated by SWGDE and other professional organizations.

III. COMMONLY RECOVERED INFORMATION

§9.08   COMMUNICATIONS[58]

Wiretaps are the interception of actual communication over a medium such a telephone wire or its wireless counterpart including cell phones and smartphones. Through a wiretap, a listener can hear exactly what the individuals placing and receiving the call can hear. Wiretaps are heavily regulated. Most wiretaps are conducted by states, with only about a quarter by the federal government. While wiretaps can be conducted on VoIP,[59] satellite, or microwave communications, most wiretaps are still conducted on conventional voice phone

---

[55]   https://www.nist.gov/topics/digital-multimedia-evidence.

[56]   https://www.nist.gov/topics/forensic-science/digitalmultimedia-scientific-area-committee.

[57]   https://www.nist.gov/topics/forensic-science/about-osac.

[58]   A brief overview of these topics is contained in Jeff Strange, "A Primer on Wiretaps, Pen Registers, and Trap and Trace Devices," Texas District & County Attorneys Association 39(4) *The Prosecutor* 39 (July-August 2009)(available at: http://www.tdcaa.com/node/4813.) While law varies by jurisdiction, this article presents a comprehensive overview, operational details, and several useful case studies of wide applicability.

[59]   *See* https://www.fcc.gov/consumers/guides/voice-over-internet-protocol-voip.

connections, text messages, and Internet Protocol (IP) activity. Laws vary by jurisdiction, and the process itself is expensive. Different jurisdictions use wiretaps for different purposes, but the most frequent applications outside of international security are in drug trafficking investigations.

A trap and trace represents the real-time reporting of the incoming addressing, routing, signaling information of electronic communications. Practically speaking, this information identifies the incoming phone numbers, IP addresses, and email addresses communicating with electronic communications accounts. This addressing, routing, and signaling information does not provide any of the contents (i.e., the content of a text message, email, and/or phone call), but simply provides the dates, times, and incoming identifiers for phone numbers, IP addresses, and email addresses sending information to a target under real-time surveillance. This addressing, routing, and signaling information is analogous to the outside of an envelope where the address, return address, postage stamp, and even the dimensions/weight of the envelope may be recorded, but the contents of the envelope (i.e., the contents of a written letter) are not revealed.

A pen register represents the same information as a trap and trace, except pen registers reveal to law enforcement, in real time, the outgoing addressing, routing, signaling, dialed digits of electronic communications transactions. Collectively, traps and traces and pen registers are often known as CALEA delivery. The CALEA acronym represents the federal Communications Assistance to Law Enforcement Act (CALEA) requiring electronic communications providers to have the capabilities to pull this data out of their networks and to deliver this data, in real time, to law enforcement.[60] CALEA delivery is federally mandated and applies to all electronic communications providers who provide electronic communications services for profit, including those who do not directly charge the customer for providing the service (i.e., free email services such as Gmail) but nonetheless, provide services for commercial reasons. As a result, any provider of any type of phone service (landline, cellular, VoIP/via smartphone application, etc.) as well as any Internet Service Provider (ISP), email provider, and even smartphone applications/websites that provide private communications capabilities, are all required to be CALEA compliant. Even if carriers are never required to do so, they are legally required to have the capability to do so and may be fined, according to statute, $10,000 a day, for non-compliance in addition to other potential sanctions.

---

[60] When conducting pen registers/traps and traces on cellular devices, the cellular providers are unable to filter out location data (discussed in Section §9.09 *supra*). As a result, the cell site and sector information is automatically provided to law enforcement and justification for the location data is typically included in modern pen register/trap and trace requests for cellular devices/activity.

§9.09 LOCATION DATA

1. PHYSICAL DEVICE DATA

a. *Historical Data*

Cellular telephones, and other cellular devices such as tablet computers (i.e., iPads), mobile hotspots, etc., have various types of location data associated with their use stored within the physical devices themselves and cell phone companies will typically retain a large amount of location-based data. The devices are able to estimate their locations through embedded Global Positioning System (GPS) chips,[61] ubiquitous Wi-Fi networks, and Bluetooth devices. These methods have limitations that can impact accuracy, but modern cellular devices can accurately determine their locations the majority of the time, especially in urban and near-urban areas. When a cell phone determines its location through any method, this information is stored inside the cell phone for at least some period of time that varies based upon numerous factors. Once appropriate authority to seize/search a device for location data is obtained, location data may be extracted. While one can look manually through some cell phones as a typical user and obtain useful location data (e.g., by pressing buttons/soft buttons), a competent digital forensics examiner can extract this location-based data stored physically on cellular devices through more advanced methods.

b. *Real-Time Data*

A method of obtaining real-time location data directly from a digital device involves the use of cell site simulators. These devices simulate cell towers by emitting signals that cause the cellular devices in the area to transmit information back to the simulator device.[62] "This technology, commonly called the StingRay, the most well-known brand name of a family of surveillance devices more generally known as 'IMSI catchers,' is used by law enforcement agencies to obtain, directly and in real time, unique device identifiers and detailed location information of cellular phones—data that it would otherwise be unable to obtain without the assistance of a wireless carrier."[63] Since the cell site

---

[61] GPS location methods require the device to have an unobstructed view of the sky to access multiple satellites. As a result, GPS will not work with cellular devices unless the devices are located outside, near-outside (near a window), or in a structure with a very thin roof (*e.g.,* a tent).

[62] *See* Department of Justice Policy Guidance: Use of Cell-Site Simulator Technology, at p. 2 (available at: https://www.justice.gov/opa/file/767321/download)(last accessed November 18, 2016).

[63] State v. Andrews, 227 Md. App. 350, 379 (2016) (citation and emphasis omitted). One model of the device is manufactured by Harris Corporation and sold under the name "StingRay." Cell site simulators are also called Hailstorm, KingFish, IMSI catcher, triggerfish, or digital analyzer. C. Justin Brown & Kasha M. Leese, "StingRay Devices Usher in a New Fourth Amendment Battleground," The Champion, June 2015 at pp. 12–20.

simulator does not obtain or download any location information from the cellular device or its applications, it does not act as a GPS locator.

As of November 2016, at least 68 law enforcement agencies in 23 states and the District of Columbia have the cell site simulators.[64] Although law enforcement agencies typically use the devices to target surveillance of a particular individual, the device collects information from all cell phones in the range of its signal, including from phones of individuals not under surveillance.[65] Cell site simulators have the ability to interfere with and intercept communications from cellphones and other wireless devices,[66] but the simulators used by the Department of Justice must be configured as pen registers so they do not collect the contents of any communications, in accordance with 18 U.S.C. § 3127(3), and do not provide subscriber account information.[67]

2.   NETWORK DATA

a.   *Historical Data*

In addition to data on physical devices, all of the major and most of the minor cell phone companies maintain various types of location data on cellular device activity on their networks. The beginning cell site sector and the ending cell site sector are recorded in the normal course of business by the companies. Additionally, at least one major company (AT&T), can provide interim, or intermediate, cell sites and sectors used by a cell phone during phone calls so that all cell sites/sectors used during a phone call are reported, not just the beginning and ending.

The information captured by the cell site simulator includes the cell phone's electronic serial number ("ESN") or international mobile subscriber identification ("IMSI").

[64] *See* American Civil Liberties Union, StingRay Tracking Devices: Who's Got Them (available at: https://www.aclu.org/map/stingray-tracking-devices-whos-got-them)(last accessed November 17, 2016).

[65] "By impersonating a cellular network base station, a StingRay—a surveillance device that can be carried by hand, installed in a vehicle, or even mounted on a drone—tricks all nearby phones and other mobile devices into identifying themselves (by revealing their unique serial numbers) just as they would register with genuine base stations in the immediate vicinity. As each phone in the area identifies itself, the StingRay can determine the location from which the signal came." State v. Andrews, 227 Md. App. 350, 379 (2016).

If law enforcement does not know the particular device associated with an individual, the cell site simulator can be used to identify the device. "By gathering identifying signals from many cell phones in proximity [to the target's physical presence], and then gathering new samples from other locations where the [target] is present at other times, a law enforcement officer can narrow the list of identified cell phones to those that match the [target's] location and eliminate the many that do not appear to follow the [target] from one place to another . . . to deduce the phone numbers which may belong to the [target]." United States v. Tutis, 2016 U.S. Dist. LEXIS 145196, *15 (D. N.J. 2016). *See also* Department of Justice Policy Guidance: Use of Cell-Site Simulator Technology, at p. 1 (available at: https://www.justice.gov/opa/file/767321/download)(last accessed November 18, 2016).

[66] *See* Electronic Privacy Information Center, Epic v. FBI—StingRay/Cell Site Simulator at: http://epic.org/foia/fbi/stingray/ (last accessed November 18, 2016).

[67] *See* Department of Justice Policy Guidance: Use of Cell-Site Simulator Technology, at p. 2 (available at: https://www.justice.gov/opa/file/767321/download)(last accessed November 18, 2016).

The major companies maintain this data for various amounts of times typically ranging from one year to several years.

This data allows a competent analyst to determine the precise location of the cellular system antennas used by a cellular device during phone calls, text messages, and Internet usage. After the cell site and sector is determined for each activity, a competent analyst can estimate optimal coverage for each cell site sectors used by the cellular device, and using triangulation,[68] produce a reliable estimate of the area in which the device was located at certain dates and times. This detailed information also typically allows a competent analyst to determine the directionality of any movement of the user from the identified cellular antennas that the cellular device accessed at the beginning and ending of the activity.

In addition to historical cell site and sector information, there may also be other historical location data available from various companies. Such data is often not considered to be maintained in the normal course of business by the cellular companies, but nonetheless, is often available. This data, such as ranging data and historical precise location data [known as Network Element Location System (NELOS) data with AT&T] may also be available for various periods of time historically. Ranging data usually provides the distance from the antenna, within the noted cell site and sector, for phone calls, text messages, and Internet activity on companies such as Sprint and Verizon Wireless. This additional location-based data may be retained for only a few days or up to a year or more.[69]

b. Real-Time Data

Cellular companies and all electronic communications providers, such as Internet Service Providers (ISPs) and email providers, are required to have the capability to provide law enforcement certain real-time information. These providers are required by federal law to be able to conduct traps and traces, pen registers, and electronic communications intercepts ("wiretaps").[70]

---

[68] Triangulation (or "multilateration") determines the location of a cell phone in relation to its servicing base station(s) of towers. If there is only one base station within range of the cell phone, it will estimate the location by direction and signal strength. The cell phone need not be in use, but must at least be on and thus "roaming" or staying in touch with its source of service, and the service is always working to know how the cell phone can best be reached in the event that another caller is trying to reach the cell phone in question.

[69] The availability of all historical data varies by company and no current regulations or laws require cellular companies to retain historical location-based data. But, if the companies possess the data and/or the ability to produce this data, they can be compelled with the appropriate legal process to release the information.

[70] For pen registers/traps and traces (CALEA deliveries), the services provide must retain location data in standardized form. In addition to the normal addressing, routing, and signaling information, with cell phones the providers must also provide the beginning cell site and sector, and the ending cell site and sector of all phone calls. They must also provide the cell site and sector for all other electronic communication events under surveillance such as

Several of the major cell phone companies can also provide law enforcement with an additional forms of real-time geolocation-based surveillances. One real-time surveillance method, commonly referred to as geolocates or geolocations and sometimes broadly referred to as "pings," uses cell tower triangulation. The cellular service provider sends electronic signals (pings) from multiple separate cell towers to a particular cellular device. Upon contacting the device, the pings force the device to send a responsive signal. By measuring the delay between responsive signals received by each tower, the service provider can provide an estimated latitude and longitude point of the device. This triangulation process is invisible to the user of the cellular device, except for the additional battery power usage. Sprint maintains a website for law enforcement (the "L-site") to obtain real-time or contemporaneous longitudinal and latitudinal information linked to GoogleMaps that is updated every fifteen minutes twenty-four hours a day.[71]

Another technique for cellular service providers to collect precise location information is GPS location. Similar to the cell tower triangulation method, the service provider can send an electronic signal (a GPS ping) to the cellular device to direct the device to transmit its GPS location data back to the service provider.[72] This process is also undetectable to the user of the device except for battery usage.

IV. TRIAL AIDS

§9.10   EXPERT QUALIFICATIONS

In the past, computer forensics suffered from a lack of credentialing standards, adequate certifying sources, and inconsistent training standards.[73] In 2009, the National Academy of Sciences report, *Strengthening Forensic Science in the United States: A Path Forward,* noted:

> Digital evidence has undergone a rapid maturation process. This discipline did not start in forensic laboratories. Instead, computers taken as evidence were studied by police officers and detectives who had some interest or expertise in computers. Over the past 10 years, this process has become more routine

---

the addressing, routing, and signaling information (i.e., not content) of text messages [short message service (SMSs)] and Internet data transactions (i.e., the IP addresses to and from).

[71]   United States v. Harris, 2016 U.S. Dist. LEXIS 102731, *6–8 (M.D. Fla. 2016).

[72]   In re Application of U.S. for an Order Authorizing Disclosure of Location Info. of a Specified Wireless Tel., 849 F. Supp.2d 526, 532–533 (D. Md. 2011).

[73]   For a historical overview *see* Eoghan Casey, ed., *Digital Evidence and Computer Crime,* 3rd ed. Waltham, MA: Elsevier, 2011, pp. 10–14. For a list of some of the existing certifications *see*: http://certification.about.com/cs/securitycerts/a/compforensics.htm.

and subject to the rigors and expectations of other fields of forensic science. There holdover challenges remain: (1) the digital evidence community does not have an agreed certification program or list of qualifications for digital forensic examiners; (2) some agencies still treat the examination of digital evidence as an investigative rather than a forensic activity; and (3) there is wide variability in and uncertainty about the education, experience, and training of those practicing this discipline.[74]

In response to the 2009 NAS Report's comments on the problems in digital evidence credentialing, a Council of Digital Forensic Specialists (CDFS) was formed to establish core standards.[75] Other groups, such as the International Association of Computer Investigative Specialists (IACIS)[76] and the International Society of Forensic Computer Examiners® (ISFCE),[77] built on those efforts and have active certification programs. The IACIS Certified Forensic Computer Examiner (CFCE) certification program is "based on a series of core competencies in the field of computer/digital forensics"[78] and has two phases:

1. Peer review phase—Candidates complete four scenario based problems guided by a forensic professional through a mentored process whereby candidates are able to submit reports or assessment documents after completing each practical exercise

2. Certification Phase—an independent exercise wherein the candidate must complete a practical exercise and written final examination. Upon successful completion, the candidate will be awarded the Certified Forensic Computer Examiner (CFCE) certification.[79]

Members must satisfy recertification requirements every three years, including successful proficiency test completion. IACIS maintains a directory of certified members on its website.[80] The IACIS offers a specific certification for mobile device examiners. The IACIS Certified Mobile Device Examiner (CMDE) program has two components: a written examination and a practical exam:

> The IACIS CMDE is a tool agnostic assessment in the practical application of fundamental mobile device and digital forensic

---

[74] Committee on Identifying the Needs of the Forensic Science Community, National Research Council of the National Academies, *Strengthening Forensic Science in the United States: A Path Forward*, The National Academies Press: Washington D.C., 2009 at p. 181.

[75] *See* http://www.cdfs.org/.

[76] *See* www.iacis.com.

[77] *See* www.isfce.com.

[78] http://www.iacis.com/certifications/overview.

[79] Id. The IACIS is accredited by the Forensic Specialties Accreditation Board. See http://thefsab.org/accredited.htm.

[80] http://www.iacis.com/certifications/directorycfce.

concepts in the examination and analysis of various smartphone mobile device operating systems and file systems. Candidates must obtain a minimum score of 80% on the exam to pass. Candidates who achieve a passing score will be allowed to proceed onto the practical exam.[81]

The ISFCE certification program requires candidates to complete one of its authorized training programs, possess a minimum of 18 months of professional experience in conducting digital examinations, or have a documented self-study in digital forensics before starting the certification process.[82] That certification process requires completion of an online test and examination of, and reporting on, three pieces of media.[83] The ISFCE also maintains a directory of certified members.[84]

To address the inconsistencies in training, SWGDE issued *SWGDE/SWGIT Guidelines & Recommendations for Training in Digital & Multimedia Evidence*, but as noted in the document's preface:

> There are many topics to include in forensic digital and multimedia training. There are also many vehicles to provide training, such as in-service and out-service training and distance learning. . . .It should be recognized that some agencies might choose to provide training other than what is recommended in this section. In such circumstances, those agencies should demonstrate and document that the training selected is adequate to meet their anticipated needs.[85]

The guidelines provide topical areas for training for four job categories: (1) Manager/Commander/Supervisor; (2) Examiner/Analyst; (3) Technician; and, (4) First Responder.[86] The ASTM E2678, *Standard Guide for Education and Training in Computer Forensics*[87] describes qualifications for a career in computer forensics, structures for degree programs and certificate programs, and the training and continuing education of practitioners.

§9.11   PRETRIAL DISCOVERY OF ELECTRONICALLY STORED INFORMATION

Discovery is the process of identifying and producing evidence in legal actions. Discovery is generally conducted in pretrial proceedings,

---

[81]   https://iacis1-public.sharepoint.com/Pages/CMDE.aspx.

[82]   http://www.isfce.com/requirements.htm.

[83]   http://www.isfce.com/competencies.htm.

[84]   http://www.isfce.com/ccelist.htm.

[85]   Scientific Working Group on Digital Evidence, *SWGDE/SWGIT Guidelines & Recommendations for Training in Digital & Multimedia Evidence,* Ver. 2.0 (January 15, 2010) at p. 2 (available at: https://www.swgde.org/documents)(last accessed November 30, 2016).

[86]   Id. at p. 5.

[87]   https://www.astm.org/Standards/E2678.htm.

but is a continuing obligation so production may occur at any time.[88] Information that is stored on computers, file servers, mobile devices, in the cloud, or on a variety of other platforms is referred to as "electronically stored information," or "ESI."[89] The discovery of ESI can be conducted by the parties or counsel without the use of a digital expert, simply by accessing and copying the data on individual devices for production. The assistance of a digital expert may be useful, however, where the amount of data involved is large. In complex cases, the amount of data turned over in discovery can exceed several terabytes.[90] Additionally, expert assistance may be required when:

- Relevant ESI has been deleted, but may be recoverable
- Evidence of tampering of ESI is relevant
- ESI usage activity and patterns are relevant
- Necessary to authenticate a digital file as accurate
- Technical issues make data collection difficult[91]

A mere suspicion that relevant ESI may have been deleted, altered, or tampered is not sufficient to justify a court order that a digital forensic examination be conducted in discovery.[92] Allegations of certain factual circumstances, such as the use of company computers to transfer proprietary secrets, may cause a court to order a forensic examination of relevant digital devices.[93]

§9.12 ADMISSIBILITY

Digital evidence is now involved in virtually every case, whether through emails, text messages, digital images, computer-generated animations or a host of other formats. The December 1, 2011 amendments to the Federal Rules of Evidence specifically recognized

---

[88] Federal Rule of Civil Procedure 26 and Federal Rule of Criminal Procedure 16 govern discovery in the federal courts.

[89] For general information on the discovery of ESI, *see* Barbara J. Rothstein, Ronald J. Hedges & Elizabeth C. Wiggins, *Managing Discovery of Electronic Information: A Pocket Guide for Judges.* Federal Judicial Center, 2007 (available at: http://www.fjc.gov/public/pdf.nsf/lookup/eldscpkt2d_eb.pdf/$file/eldscpkt2d_eb.pdf). *See also* Michele C. S. Lange & Kristin M. Nimsger, *Electronic Evidence and Discovery: What Every Lawyer Should Know Now,* 2nd ed. Chicago: American Bar Association, 2009. For a helpful ongoing resource see the eDiscovery Reading Room at: http://www.ediscoveryreadingroom.com/?p=125.

[90] In United States v. Budovsky, a prosecution in the Southern District of New York, news reports stated that discovery included over 52 terabytes of data. *See* Bloomberg News, "Liberty Reserve Founder Denies Running Black Market Bank, October 14, 2014 (available at: http://www.bloomberg.com/news/articles/2014-10-14/liberty-reserve-founder-denies-running-black-market-bank)(last accessed November 17, 2016).

[91] *See* Shira A. Schendlin and The Sedona Conference®, *Electronic Discovery and Digital Evidence in a Nutshell,* 2d ed. West Academic Publishing, 2016 at pp. 23, 147.

Evidence of tampering also may be relevant in criminal prosecutions if police interrogation tapes are altered or video surveillance tapes are edited. See Doug Carner, "Evidence Forensics—Exposing Tampered Recordings," The Champion January/February 2015 at pp. 44–50.

[92] *See* John B. v. Goetz, 531 F.3d 448 (6th Cir. 2008).

[93] *See* Ameriwood Indus. v. Liberman, et al., (E.D. Mo. 2006).

the potential admissibility and use of digital evidence. Rule 101(b)(6) provides that "a reference to any kind of written material or any other medium includes electronically stored information." Digital evidence is admissible subject to the same rules as paper or hardcopy evidence of the same type: the evidence must be reliable, probative, and authentic.

Evidence derived from digital forensic examinations (e.g., recovered emails, text messages, GPS location data, digital images) is subject to the same evidentiary standards, including the rules concerning expert testimony. To admit evidence recovered during a digital forensics examination, the party may be required to prove that the evidence was prepared in a scientifically reliable manner and that the methods used meet the applicable evidentiary admissibility standards (e.g., *Daubert* or *Frye*). For example, in *United States v. Chiaradio*,[94] the digital forensic examiner used an enhanced peer-to-peer file sharing program ("EP2P") customized by the FBI to assist in the location of individuals suspected of downloading child pornography. The defendant challenged the admissibility of the results of the program because the source code of the program was undisclosed.[95] Following a Daubert hearing, the court acknowledged that the software had not been independently tested (i.e., subject to peer review), but concluded that the forensic examiner's testimony was admissible because the EP2P technology had never produced a false positive association and its results could be independently verified through other means (which had been demonstrated to the defense).[96]

§9.13 CONSTITUTIONAL PROTECTIONS

1. FIRST AMENDMENT

The Privacy Protection Act ("PPA"), 42 U.S.C. § 2000aa through 2000aa12, pertains to conduct by governmental employees in connection with the investigation or prosecution of criminal offenses from searching for or seizing "any work product materials possessed by a person reasonably believed to have a purpose to disseminate to the public a newspaper, book, broadcast, or other similar form of communication."[97] It was enacted to protect the First Amendment rights to freedom of speech and press by affording a civil right of action against governmental actors in certain limited circumstances.[98] The

[94] 684 F.3d 265 (1st Cir. 2012).

[95] 684 F.3d at 276.

[96] 684 F.3d at 277–278.

[97] 42 U.S.C. § 2000aa(a).

[98] S.H.A.R.K. v. Metro Parks Serving Summit County, 499 F.3d 553, 567 (6th Cir. 2007) (The PPA is intended to "protect innocent third parties in possession of documents and papers from governmental intrusion which would unnecessarily subject their files and papers to a search and seizure."); Makas v. New York State Dep't of Motor Vehicles, 1998 U.S. Dist. LEXIS 3840, *3 (N.D.N.Y. 1998)("The PPA specifically provides that persons aggrieved under the PPA shall have a civil cause of action against the United States, against a State which has waived its sovereign immunity, or against any other governmental unit.").

largest limitations on the application of the PPA is that it does not apply to those who are suspected of committing a crime[99] and does not apply to the actions of private citizens.[100]

Federal law enforcement searches that implicate the PPA must be pre-approved by a Deputy Assistant Attorney General of the Criminal Division. The Computer Crime and Intellectual Property Section serves as the contact point for all federal law enforcement searches involving computers.[101]

2. FOURTH AMENDMENT

The Fourth Amendment to the United States Constitution, made applicable to the states by the Fourteenth Amendment,[102] provides:

> The right of the people to be secure in their persons, houses, papers, and effects, against unreasonable searches and seizures, shall not be violated, and no warrants shall issue, but upon probable cause, supported by oath or affirmation, and particularly describing the place to be searched, and the persons or things to be seized.[103]

The first clause of the amendment protects individuals against unreasonable searches and seizures,[104] and the second clause requires that warrants be particular and supported by probable cause.[105] The collection and use of digital information by law enforcement[106] in criminal investigations is subject to these Fourth Amendment protections.[107] From 2010 to 2014, the United States Supreme Court

---

[99] The PPA does not apply where "there is probable cause to believe that a person possessing such materials has committed or is committing the criminal offense to which the materials relate," and specifically excludes searches where the offense "involves the production, possession, receipt, mailing, sale, distribution, shipment, or transportation of child pornography, the sexual exploitation of children, or the sale or purchase of children. . . .". 42 U.S.C. § 2000aa(a)(1)&(b)(1) See also United States v. Mittelman, 999 F.2d 440, 443 (9th Cir. 1993) (the PPA "does not apply to criminal suspects").

[100] Canning v. Hofmann, 2015 U.S. Dist. LEXIS 148345, *9–*10 (N.D.N.Y. 2015).

[101] For further details on 42 U.S.C. § 2000aa and handling other situations that may involve privileged documents *see* Criminal Division, U.S. Department of Justice, *Searching & Seizing Computers and Obtaining Electronic Evidence in Criminal Investigations,* 3rd ed. (2009) at pp. 58–65. (available at: https://www.justice.gov/sites/default/files/criminal-ccips/legacy/2015/01/14/ssmanual2009.pdf.).

[102] Mapp v. Ohio, 367 U.S. 643, 655 (1961).

[103] U.S. Const. amend. IV.

[104] *See* Katz v. United States, 389 U.S. 347, 359 (1967) ("Wherever a man may be, he is entitled to know that he will remain free from unreasonable searches and seizures").

[105] *See* Payton v. New York, 445 U.S. 573, 584 (1980).

[106] The Fourth Amendment only concerns governmental action. Searches by private citizens do not implicate the Fourth Amendment. In United States v. Grimes, 244 F.3d 375 (5th Cir. 2001), a private citizen who was not working with law enforcement searched the defendant's computer and discovered incriminating information. The information was turned over to law enforcement and used in the prosecution against the defendant.

[107] *See generally* Criminal Division, U.S. Department of Justice, *Searching & Seizing Computers and Obtaining Electronic Evidence in Criminal Investigations,* 3rd ed. (2009)(available at: https://www.justice.gov/sites/default/files/criminal-ccips/legacy/2015/01/14/ssmanual2009.pdf.).

issued three opinions addressing the Fourth Amendment protection of the reasonable expectation of privacy with respect to digital data: *City of Ontario v. Quon*,[108] *United States v. Jones*,[109] and *Riley v. California*.[110] Using these cases to address whether a search warrant was necessary to seize digital information, the Court's reasoning was very fact specific and revealed the concern that rapid technological changes make clear legal doctrines in this area difficult. Subsequent lower court decisions show that attorneys and judges are grappling with how to deal with the particularity requirement and the application of the plain view doctrine to data seizures and searches.

a.   Warrant Requirement

In *City of Ontario v. Quon*, a police officer filed suit against his employer alleging a violation of his Fourth Amendment rights when his text messages on an employer-supplied pager were reviewed by the employer without obtaining a search warrant. The Court assumed *arguendo* that Quon had a reasonable expectation of privacy, the review of the text messages was a search, and the same privacy principles that apply to physical employee spaces also apply to digital data spaces.[111] Even with these assumptions, the Court held that the warrantless search of the test messages was reasonable because it was motivated by a work-related purpose and was not excessive in scope.[112] The Court noted that the review of the text messages "was not nearly as intrusive as a search of his personal e-mail account or pager, or a wiretap on his home phone, would have been."[113]

The monitoring and collection of location tracking data for 28 days from a GPS device attached by law enforcement to the undercarriage of the defendant's car in *United States v. Jones* raised Fourth Amendment issues. The Court unanimously affirmed the Court of Appeals for the District of Columbia Circuit's holding that the electronic surveillance over a period of 28 days was a search and that the admission of evidence obtained by the warrantless[114] use of the GPS device violated

---

[108] 560 U.S. 749 (2010).

[109] 565 U.S. 400 (2012).

[110] 134 S.Ct. 2473 (2014).

[111] 560 U.S. at 748.

The Court noted that issue of privacy expectations are particularly malleable with communication technology:

> Cell phone and text message communications are so pervasive that some persons may consider them to be essential means or necessary instruments for self-expression, even self-identification. That might strengthen the case for an expectation of privacy. On the other hand, the ubiquity of those devices has made them generally affordable, so one could counter that employees who need cell phones or similar devices for personal matters can purchase and pay for their own.

560 U.S. at 760.

[112] 560 U.S. at 748.

[113] 560 U.S. at 762–763.

[114] Law enforcement obtained a warrant to place the GPS device on the vehicle in the District of Columbia within 10 days, but actually attached the device on the 11th day in

the Fourth Amendment.[115] Although the majority opinion focused on the physical trespass of attaching the device to the vehicle, Justice Sotomayor addressed the invasion of privacy from the collection of the location data:

> GPS monitoring generates a precise, comprehensive record of a person's public movements that reflects a wealth of detail about her familial, political, professional, religious, and sexual associations. The government can store such records and efficiently mine them for information years into the future. And because GPS monitoring is cheap in comparison to conventional surveillance techniques and, by design, proceeds surreptitiously, it evades the ordinary checks that constrain abusive law enforcement practices: "limited police resources and community hostility." Awareness that the government may be watching chills associational and expressive freedoms. And the government's unrestrained power to assemble data that reveal private aspects of identity is susceptible to abuse. The net result is that GPS monitoring—by making available at a relatively low cost such a substantial quantum of intimate information about any person whom the government, in its unfettered discretion, chooses to track—may "alter the relationship between citizen and government in a way that is inimical to democratic society."[116]

Justice Alito, concurring only in the judgment, found the appropriate inquiry to be "whether the respondent's reasonable expectations of privacy were violated by the long-term monitoring of the movements of the vehicle he drove."[117] He noted that the majority's reasoning focusing on the physical attachment to the vehicle "will present particularly vexing problems in cases involving surveillance that is carried out by making electronic, as opposed to physical, contact with the item to be tracked."[118]

The third decision from the United States Supreme Court was issued in 2014. In *Riley v. California*, the Supreme Court held that the defendants' cell phones were unlawfully searched upon their arrests since the arresting officers generally could not, without a warrant, search digital information on the cell phones seized from the defendants as incident to the defendants' arrests which did not pose a threat to the officers. Recognizing the immense storage capacity of a cell phone, the Court held that obtaining this data without a search warrant would

---

Maryland. The government conceded that the attachment was outside the scope of the warrant and argued that a warrant was not required. 565 U.S. at 402–403.

[115] 565 U.S. at 404.

[116] 565 U.S. at 415–416 (internal citations omitted).

[117] 565 U.S. at 419.

[118] 565 U.S. at 426.

violate the Fourth Amendment protection against unreasonable search and seizure:

> The storage capacity of cell phones has several interrelated consequences for privacy. First, a cell phone collects in one place many distinct types of information—an address, a note, a prescription, a bank statement, a video—that reveal much more in combination than any isolated record. Second, a cell phone's capacity allows even just one type of information to convey far more than previously possible. The sum of an individual's private life can be reconstructed through a thousand photographs labeled with dates, locations, and descriptions; the same cannot be said of a photograph or two of loved ones tucked into a wallet. Third, the data on a phone can date back to the purchase of the phone, or even earlier. A person might carry in his pocket a slip of paper reminding him to call Mr. Jones; he would not carry a record of all his communications with Mr. Jones for the past several months, as would routinely be kept on a phone. Finally, there is an element of pervasiveness that characterizes cell phones but not physical records. Prior to the digital age, people did not typically carry a cache of sensitive personal information with them as they went about their day. Now it is the person who is not carrying a cell phone, with all that it contains, who is the exception.[119]

Following this Supreme Court trilogy of cases, district courts have addressed expectations of privacy in digital information. In *United States v. DiTomasso*,[120] the court addressed the defendant's expectation of privacy in emails and online chats that provided evidence of the possession of child pornography. Law enforcement obtained the information from the internet service providers (ISP). Although the court held that the defendant had an expectation of privacy in his communications,[121] the court denied the motion to suppress the evidence. With respect to communications disclosed by one ISP, the court held that the defendant had consented to the search because the company's terms of use warned the defendant that the company would monitor the communications for illegal activity and would permit law enforcement access to the communications as needed.[122] The communications disclosed by the second ISP were not implicated by the terms of use, but the court found that the ISP was not acting as an agent of law enforcement when it reviewed the communications.[123]

---

[119] 134 S.Ct. at 2489–2490.
[120] 56 F. Supp.3d 584 (S.D.N.Y. 2014).
[121] 56 F. Supp.3d at 594–595.
[122] 56 F. Supp.3d at 597.
[123] 56 F. Supp.3d at 597–598.

b.   Particularity Requirement

If law enforcement does obtain a warrant for the search of a digital device for digital information, whether the specific data seized is within the scope of the warrant may be an issue. To comply with the Fourth Amendment, a search warrant must describe the place to be searched and the things to be seized with particularity.[124] The purpose of the particularity requirement is to prevent general searches[125] and prevent "exploratory rummaging in a person's belongings."[126] The need to prevent general exploratory searches is especially acute in digital evidence cases because digital devices and electronic media storage "intermingle data, making them difficult to retrieve without a thorough understanding of the filing and classification systems used—something that can often only be determined by closely analyzing the data."[127] Based on these concerns, some courts have rejected applications for warrants for all digital data associated with a particular email or online account[128] or contained on a particular digital device.[129] One court noted:

> Here, the warrant describes only certain emails that are to be seized—and the government has only established probable cause for those emails. Yet it seeks to seize all e-mails by having them "disclosed" by [the email host]. This is unconstitutional because "[t]he government simply has not shown probable cause to search the contents of all emails ever sent to or from the account."[130]

Other courts held that search warrants for the entire contents of digital devices and email/online accounts are not general warrants,"[131] even where only a portion of the data may be responsive to the warrant allegations.[132] These courts have reasoned that relatively broad

---

[124] United States v. SDI Future Health, Inc. 568 F.3d 684, 702–703 (9th Cir. 2009).

[125] Maryland v. Garrison, 480 U.S. 79, 84 (1987).

[126] Andreson v. Maryland, 427 U.S. 463, 480 (1976).

[127] United States v. Comprehensive Drug Testing, Inc., 621 F.3d 1162, 1175 (9th Cir. 2010) (en banc)(per curiam).

[128] *See, e.g.,* In the Matter of the Search of Information Associated with [redacted]@mac.com that is Stored at Premises Controlled by Apple, Inc., 13 F. Supp.3d 145 (D.D.C. 2014); In the Matter of Applications for Search Warrants for Information Associated with Target Email Accounts/Skype Accounts, 2013 U.S. Dist. LEXIS 123129 (D. Kan. 2013).

[129] *See, e.g.,* In re Search of Apple iPhone, 31 F. Supp.3d 159 (D.D.C. 2014); In re Nextel Cellular Telephone, 2014 U.S. Dist. LEXIS 88215 (D. Kan. 2014); In the Matter of the Search of ODYS LOOX Plus Tablet, 28 F. Supp.3d 40 (D.D.C. 2014); In re U.S.'s Application For A Search Warrant To Seize and Search Electronic Devices From Edward Cunnius, 770 F. Supp.2d 1138, 1139 (W.D. Wash. 2011).

[130] In the Matter of the Search of Information Associated with [redacted]@mac.com that is Stored at Premises Controlled by Apple, Inc., 13 F. Supp.3d 145 (D.D.C. 2014)(quoting In re Search of Target Email Address, 2012 U.S. Dist. LEXIS 138465 (D. Kan. 2012)).

[131] United States v. Deppish, 994 F. Supp.2d 1211 (D. Kan. 2014)(search of full content of specified email account is not a "general search").

[132] *See* United States v. Flores, 802 F.3d 1028, 1044–1045 (9th Cir. 2015)(affirming denial of motion to suppress search of all 11,000 pages of Facebook data where only approximately 100 pages were responsive to the warrant); In re A Warrant for All Content & Other Info.

seizures of digital data are accepted and a necessary reality because "[t]here is no way to be sure exactly what an electronic file contains without somehow examining its contents"[133] and digital concealment efforts take many forms, "such as hiding images in text documents, or the simple expedient of changing the names and extensions of files to disguise their content from the casual observer."[134]

To avoid searching beyond the scope of the warrant and to address concerns about the potential for searching nonresponsive data, law enforcement may use the digitial forensic examination to separate the data into responsive and non-responsive data before review by investigators.[135]

c. *Plain View Doctrine*

The difficulty with searching digital data and devices, as opposed to physical containers, is that "[t]here is no way to be sure exactly what an electronic file contains without somehow examining its contents—either by opening and looking, using specialized forensic software, keyword searching or some other technique."[136] For this reason, "over-seizing is an inherent part of the electronic search process. . .and this will be far more common than in the days of paper records."[137] The Ninth Circuit Court of Appeals has cautioned its courts to use "greater vigilance" in reviewing applications for search warrants of electronic data so "[t]he process of segregating electronic data that is seizable from that which [does] not become a vehicle for the government to gain access to data which it has no probable cause to collect."[138] Efforts to establish "minimizing procedures" concerning the government's handling and

---

Associated with the Email Account xxxxxxx@Gmail.com Maintained at Premises Controlled by Google, Inc., 33 F. Supp.3d 386, 392–396 (S.D.N.Y. 2014)(permitting search of all emails in an account); United States v. Taylor, 764 F. Supp.2d 230, 232, 237 (D. Me. 2011) (upholding search of "all information associated with an identified Microsoft Hotmail account"); United States v. Grimmett, 439 F.3d 1263, 1269 (10th Cir. 2006)(upholding search of entire computer); United States v. Bach, 310 F.3d 1063, 1065 (8th Cir. 2002)(upholding seizure of "all of the information" from defendant's email account); United States v. Hay, 231 F.3d 630, 637 (9th Cir. 2000)(upholding search of entire "computer system").

[133] United States v. Comprehensive Drug Testing, Inc., 621 F.3d 1162, 1176 (9th Cir. 2010)(en banc)(per curiam). *See also* United States v. Graziano, 558 F. Supp.2d 304, 317 (E.D.N.Y. 2008)(courts have afforded law enforcement "leeway in searching computers for incriminating evidence within the scope of materials specified in the warrant")(citations omitted); United States v. Schesso, 730 F.3d 1040, 1046 (9th Cir. 2013)(the challenge of "searching for digital data that was not limited to a specific known file or set of files" and the inability to know "which or how many illicit files there might be or where they might be stored, or of describing the items to be seized in a more precise manner" justified seizure of "entire computer system and associated digital storage devices").

[134] United States v. Taylor, 163 F. Supp.3d 816, 820 (D. Or. 2016)(internal quotations and citations omitted).

[135] Shira A. Schendlin and The Sedona Conference®, *Electronic Discovery and Digital Evidence in a Nutshell*, 2d ed. West Academic Publishing, 2016 at pp. 371–372.

[136] United States v. Comprehensive Drug Testing, Inc., 621 F.3d 1162, 1176 (9th Cir. 2010)(en banc)(per curiam).

[137] 621 F.3d at 1177.

[138] Id.

retention of digital information by requiring third parties to cull the information and imposing destruction of non-responsive material have largely been rejected.[139]

Despite the concern from some courts that data searches are too intrusive and evade the particularity restrictions of the Fourth Amendment, the courts have generally embraced the theory that data discovered accidentally during the forensic examination of a digital device is subject to the "plain view" doctrine, particularly where the accidentally discovered evidence concerns child pornography.[140] For the plain view doctrine to apply, (1) the officer must be lawfully in the place where the seized item was in plain view; (2) the item's incriminating nature was "immediately apparent"; and (3) the officer must have had a "lawful right of access to the object itself."[141]

If the incriminating nature of the data is not "immediately apparent" and only reveals itself after the passage of time or additional investigation, the plain view doctrine will not apply. In *United States v. Ganias*,[142] the government seized computer information pursuant to a

---

[139] Judge Kozinski attempted to provide handling and retention conditions as guidance for magistrates in cases where investigators seek to search digital data in United States v. Comprehensive Drug Testing, Inc., 621 F.3d 1162, 1178–1180 (9th Cir. 2010), however, his proposals have not been embraced by the courts. *See* United States v. Mann, 592 F.3d 779, 785 (7th Cir. 2010)(finding the attempt "efficient but overbroad"); United States v. Burgess, 576 F.3d 1078, 1094 (10th Cir. 2009)(despite efforts to establish search protocols to limit "overseizures," "there may be no practical substitute for actually looking in many (perhaps all) folders and sometimes at the documents contained within those folders"). *See also* United States v. Richards, 659 F.3d 527, 539–540 (6th Cir. 2011); United States v. Stabile, 633 F.3d 219, 239–240 and n. 13 (3d Cir. 2011).

One legal commentator has argued that such restrictions imposed at the time the search warrant is approved are constitutionally impermissible, are not actually enforced in suppression proceedings, and are ineffective in protecting Fourth Amendment rights. *See* Orin S. Kerr, "Ex Ante Regulation of Computer Search and Seizure," 96 Va. L. Rev. 1241 (2010). But see Paul Ohm, "Massive Hard Drives, General Warrants, and the Power of Magistrate Judges," 97 Va. L. Rev. In Brief 1 (2011)(arguing such restrictions may be necessary).

In In re Search Warrant, 193 Vt. 51, 71 A.3d 1158 (2012), a Vermont state magistrate issued a search warrant that contained certain restrictions on the search protocol that law enforcement was to follow in conducting the digital data search on a computer. The Vermont Supreme Court upheld the restrictions as within the magistrate's authority, but did not rule on whether such restrictions were required by the Fourth Amendment. 193 Vt. at 64–65. *See also* Preventive Med. Assocs., Inc. v. Commonwealth, 465 Mass. 810, 823 (2013)(search protocol for a warrant imposed because there was a serious risk that the electronic information sought would contain privileged communications); In re Search of Info. Associated with the Facebook Account Identified by the Username Aaron.Alexis, 21 F. Supp.3d 1 (D.D.C. 2013)(magistrate's modifications of the search warrant included requiring production only of information about Alexis's account and the content of messages that he sent, and records of communications—but not the content of communications—between third parties and Alexis).

[140] United States v. Taylor, 163 F. Supp.3d 816, 820 (D. Or. 2016)(holding that plain-view doctrine applies to child pornography discovered during lawful search of a computer or digital device); United States v. Williams, 592 F.3d 511, 521 (4th Cir. 2010); United States v. Wong, 334 F.3d 831, 838 (9th Cir. 2003)(same). *See also* United States v. Giberson, 527 F.3d 882, 890 (9th Cir. 2008)(search for fake ID photographs allowed agent to search all images and photographs, and child pornography discovered in the search was admissible under plain-view doctrine).

[141] Horton v. California, 496 U.S. 128, 136–137 (1990); *see also* United States v. Antrim, 389 F.3d 276, 283 (1st Cir. 2004).

[142] 755 F.3d 125 (2d Cir. 2014).

November 2003 warrant.[143] Personal financial records of the defendant that were not within the scope of the warrant were segregated from the responsive information by December 2004, but were not purged or deleted.[144] In 2006, after additional investigation, the government expanded its investigation to include possible tax violations by the defendant, viewed the personal financial records, and recognized the incriminating nature of the records.[145] The Second Circuit Court of Appeals held that the Fourth Amendment does not permit officials "executing a warrant for the seizure of particular data on a computer to seize and indefinitely retain every file on that computer for use in future criminal prosecutions."[146] "Without some independent basis for its retention of those documents [from 2004 to 2006], the Government clearly violated Ganias's Fourth Amendment rights by retaining the files for a prolonged period of time and then using them in a future criminal investigation."[147]

d. Location Data

i. Network Data

Law enforcement access to certain wireless subscriber information is covered by the Stored Communications Act (SCA), 18 U.S.C. § 2703. The covered information is listed in subsection (c)(2):

> A provider of electronic communication service . . . shall disclose to a governmental entity the—
>
> (A) name;
>
> (B) address;
>
> (C) local and long distance telephone connection records, or records of session times and durations;
>
> (D) length of service (including start date) and types of service utilized;
>
> (E) telephone or instrument number or other subscriber number or identity, including any temporarily assigned network address; and
>
> (F) means and source of payment for such service (including any credit card or bank account number), of a subscriber to or customer of such service when the governmental entity uses an administrative subpoena authorized by a Federal or State statute or a Federal or

---

143 755 F.3d at 128.

144 755 F.3d at 129.

145 755 F.3d at 129–130.

146 755 F.3d at 137.

147 755 F.3d at 138.

State grand jury or trial subpoena or any means available under paragraph (1).[148]

Cell site location data is not specifically covered by the SCA, and courts have split on whether network location data is protected by the Fourth Amendment. Notwithstanding a 1999 federal statute declaring that call location records belong to the customer,[149] some courts have held that cell site records are ordinary business records of the provider in which the customer has no reasonable expectation of privacy so the Fourth Amendment warrant requirement does not apply and the government may obtain the data through court order pursuant to the SCA.[150] Other courts have held that as a constitutional matter, cell site records are protected by the Fourth Amendment, and therefore a warrant based on probable cause or a judicial order complying with the Fourth Amendment probable cause and particularity requirements is required to obtain them.[151]

Under the SCA, the government will usually request the information as to a particular target, but some courts have approved government applications for "cell tower dumps," the records for all wireless devices using a specific tower at a specific time.[152] Because this type of request is not for location data directly, but for subscriber information (name and phone numbers of the subscribers using a tower at a specific time), courts have reasoned that this information is specifically covered by the SCA as a business record of the network provider in which the customer has no expectation of privacy.[153]

ii. Cell Site Simulators

Law enforcement use of cell site simulators to obtain real-time location data is also a current litigation issue and courts have split on

---

[148] 18 U.S.C. § 2703(c)(2).

[149] Wireless Communication and Public Safety Act 47 U.S.C. § 222(f)(1) (call location records belong to the customer as "customer proprietary network information," and cannot be used, disclosed or accessed "without the express prior authorization of the customer.").

[150] See, e.g., In re Application of the United States for Historical Cell Site Data, 724 F.3d 600 (5th Cir. 2013).

The standard for obtaining an order under the SCA is less than probable cause. See, e.g., In re Application of the United States of America for an Order Pursuant to 18 U.S.C. § 2703(d), 707 F.3d 283, 287 (4th Cir. 2013)("This is essentially a reasonable suspicion standard."); United States v. Davis, 785 F.3d 498, 505 (11th Cir. 2015)("[§ 2703(d)'s] statutory standard is less than the probable cause standard for a search warrant"); In re Application of the U.S. for an Order Directing a Provider of Elec. Commc'n Serv. To Disclose Records to Gov't, 620 F.3d 304, 315 (3d Cir. 2010) (§ 2703(d) standard is "less stringent than probable cause.").

[151] See, e.g., United States v. Harris, 2016 U.S. Dist. LEXIS 102731 (M.D. Fla. 2016)(discussing real-time location data maintained on Sprint's "L-site" website for law enforcement).

[152] See, e.g., In re Cell Tower Records Under 18 U.S.C. § 2703(D), 90 F. Supp.3d 673 (S.D. Tex. 2015); In the Matter of Application For an Order to Disclose Cell Tower Log Information, 42 F. Supp.3d 511 (S.D.N.Y. 2014).

[153] In re Cell Tower Records Under 18 U.S.C. § 2703(D), 90 F. Supp.3d 673, 676 (S.D. Tex. 2015).

whether a pen register/trap & trace order is sufficient to obtain the information or whether a search warrant is required. In *State v. Andrews*,[154] the Court of Special Appeals of Maryland held that:

> [P]eople have a reasonable expectation that their cell phones will not be used as real-time tracking devices by law enforcement, and—recognizing that the Fourth Amendment protects people and not simply areas—that people have an objectively reasonable expectation of privacy in real-time cell phone location information. Thus, we hold that the use of a cell site simulator requires a valid search warrant, or an order satisfying the constitutional requisites of a warrant, unless an established exception to the warrant requirement applies.[155]

How the device is used may be determinative of whether a search warrant or judicial authorization is issued. A federal district court in the Southern District of Texas denied the government's application to authorize the use of a StingRay under the Pen/Trap Statute, 18 U.S.C. § 3123(b)(1) to determine the number of cell phone used by a suspected drug dealer.[156] The court held that the statute was not intended to be used to discover the phone number of a target phone because the statute requires that a pen/trap order must specify in advance "the number or other identifier" of the target phone.[157] A federal magistrate in Arizona authorized the use of the StingRay by judicial order where the cell site simulator was used to track the location of a particular cell phone.[158] The government conceded in the district court that the Fourth Amendment's probable cause standard applied, but argued that the judicial order under the Pen-Trap Statute was appropriate. The district court agreed because this use of a cell site simulator easily satisfied the definition the broad definition of a "tracking device" under 18 U.S.C. § 3117(b).[159]

Pursuant to guidance policy, the Department of Justice requires agents to obtain a search warrant prior to the use of cell site simulators, except in exigent or exceptional circumstances with court approval.[160] Even where a search warrant or judicial order is issued, the court may impose conditions on the handling and retention of non-target, third party information.[161]

---

[154] 227 Md. App. 350, 134 A.3d 324 (2016).

[155] 227 Md. App. at 355, 134 A.3d at 327.

[156] In re Application for an Order Authorizing the Installation and Use of a Pen Register and Trap and Trace Device, 890 F. Supp.2d 747 (S.D. Tex. 2012).

[157] 890 F. Supp.2d at 751.

[158] United States v. Rigmaiden, 844 F. Supp.2d 982, 995 (D. Ariz. 2012).

[159] "[T]he term 'tracking device' means an electronic or mechanical device which permits the tracking of the movement of a person or object." 18 U.S.C. § 3117(b).

[160] *See* Department of Justice Policy Guidance: Use of Cell-Site Simulator Technology, at p. 3 (available at: https://www.justice.gov/opa/file/767321/download)(last accessed November 18, 2016).

[161] *See, e.g.,* In re United States, 2015 U.S. Dist. LEXIS 151811 (N.D. Ill. 2015).

3.   FIFTH AMENDMENT

The Fifth Amendment to the United States Constitution provides in part that no person "shall be compelled in any criminal case to be a witness against himself."[162] "[A] person may be required to produce specific documents even though they contain incriminating assertions of fact or belief because the creation of those documents was not 'compelled' within the meaning of the privilege [against self-incrimination]."[163] The act of production of documents, however, may be protected in two situations: (1) if the existence and location of the documents are unknown to law enforcement; and (2) if the production is necessary to authenticate the documents.[164]

Under a narrow set of circumstances, generally involving encryption, the Fifth Amendment privilege against self-incrimination may be involved in digital forensic cases. Three elements must be present: (1) there must be governmental compulsion, which usually takes the form of a subpoena or court order; (2) the compulsion must seek "testimony" as opposed to physical evidence; and (3) such testimony would be incriminating.[165]

On December 16, 2006, when Sebastien Boucher crossed into Vermont from Canada, a customs agent noticed files on his laptop computer that suggested child pornography.[166] When asked to make the files visible, Boucher opened the Z drive and the agent viewed several videos and images appearing to contain child pornography.[167] The agent arrested Boucher, seized the laptop and shut it down.[168] During the digital forensic examination, law enforcement realized the Z drive was encrypted.[169] When subpoenaed to provide the encryption key, Boucher moved to quash the subpoena as a violation of his Fifth Amendment right against self-incrimination because the encryption key was not in document form and only existed in his personal memory.[170] The federal magistrate court granted his motion.[171] The government appealed to the district court arguing that the subpoena was not for the password to the encrypted drive, but for Boucher to produce an uncrypted version of the

---

[162] "No person shall be held to answer for a capital, or otherwise infamous crime, unless on a presentment or indictment of a grand jury, except in cases arising in the land or naval forces, or in the militia, when in actual service in time of war, or public danger; nor shall any person be subject for the same offense to be twice in jeopardy of life or limb, nor shall be compelled in any criminal case to be witness against himself, nor be deprived of life, liberty, or property without due process of law; nor shall private property be taken for public use without just compensation." U.S. Const. Amend. V.

[163] 530 U.S. at 35–36.

[164] 530 U.S. at 36.

[165] Hubbell v. United States, 530 U.S. 27 (2000).

[166] In re Grand Jury Subpoena (Boucher) 2009 U.S. Dist. LEXIS 13006, *4 (D. Vt. 2009).

[167] 2009 U.S. LEXIS at *5.

[168] Id.

[169] Id.

[170] 2009 U.S. LEXIS at *6.

[171] In re Grand Jury Subpoena (Boucher), 2007 U.S. Dist. LEXIS 87951 (D. Vt. 2007).

drive to the grand jury. The district court held that because the government knew of the existence and location of the drive and its files, and because the act of producing an unencrypted version of the drive was not necessary for authentication, Boucher could be compelled to provide an unencrypted version of the drive.[172]

In *Commonwealth v. Baust*,[173] the Circuit Court of the City of Virginia Beach held that a person cannot be compelled to reveal the passcode of his iPhone, but could be compelled to unlock the phone with his fingerprint.[174] The court followed long-standing precedent that "there is a significant difference between the use of compulsion to extort communications from a defendant and compelling a person to engage in conduct that may be incriminating."[175] "[T]he privilege offers no protection against compulsion to submit to fingerprinting, photography, or measurements, to write or speak for identification, to appear in court, to stand, to assume a stance, to walk, or to make a particular gesture."[176]

In 2015, following the holdings in *Boucher* and *Baust*, the Superior Court of Maine in Cumberland County was asked to order a defendant to insert the passcodes into two cell phones so the State could gain access to the phones' contents.[177] The court held that the passcode was testimonial and the state could not establish that the production of the passcode would "add little or nothing to the sum total of the [State]'s information."[178] The state had absolutely no knowledge of what information was on the phones.[179] The court held:

> Based on the facts and circumstances of this particular case, given the dearth of preexisting knowledge possessed by the State, the court finds that the foregone conclusion exception does not apply in these circumstances, and accordingly finds that compelling Defendant to divulge the contents of his mind—either by compelling him to surrender the passcodes or compelling him to himself open the phones—would violated his privilege against self-incrimination protected by the Federal and Maine Constitutions.[180]

In *United States v. Holland*,[181] law enforcement discovered child pornography images on an encrypted drive after obtaining the password

---

[172] In re Grand Jury Subpoena (Boucher) 2009 U.S. Dist. LEXIS 13006, *8–*10 (D. Vt. 2009).

[173] 89 Va. Cir. 267, 2014 Va. Cir. LEXIS 93 (City of Va. Beach, 2014).

[174] 89 Va. Cir. at 271.

[175] Hubbell, 530 U.S. at 35.

[176] United States v. Wade, 388 U.S. 218, 223 (1967).

[177] State v. Trant, 2015 Me. Super. LEXIS 272 (Cumberland Cty Sup. Ct. 2015).

[178] 2015 Me. Super. LEXIS at *8.

[179] 2015 Me. Super. LEXIS at *9.

[180] 2015 Me. Super. LEXIS at *9–10.

[181] 2016 U.S. Dist. LEXIS 143074 (D. S.C. 2016).

from the defendant during interrogation.[182] The defendant moved to suppress his statements, including the password, because they were obtained in violation of his right to counsel under the Fifth Amendment during interrogation.[183] The court held that the continued interrogation after the defendant invoked his right to counsel was in violation of the Fifth Amendment and suppressed his statements.[184] The scope of the suppression order, however, did not extend to the child pornography images.[185]

V. RESOURCES

§9.14   BIBLIOGRAPHY OF ADDITIONAL RESOURCES

Rick Ayers, Sam Brothers and Wayne Jansen, *Guidelines on Mobile Device Forensics.* NIST Special Publication 800-101, May 2014 (available at: http://nvlpubs.nist.gov/nistpubs/SpecialPublications/ NIST.SP.800-101r1.pdf).

Marjie T. Britz, *Computer Forensics and Cyber Crime: An Introduction,* 3d ed., Prentice Hall, 2012.

Eoghan Casey, ed. *Digital Evidence and Computer Crime,* 3d ed., Elsevier, 2011.

Kim-Kwang Raymond Choo and Ali Dehghantanha, eds., *Contemporary Digital Forensic Investigations of Cloud and Mobile Applications,* Elsevier, Inc., 2017.

Department of Justice, *Electronic Surveillance Manual,* June 2005 (available at: http://www.justice.gov/criminal/foia/docs/elec-sur-manual.pdf).

Aaron Edens, *Cell Phone Investigations: Search Warrants, Cell Sites and Evidence Recovery,* Police Publishing, 2014.

Hanni M. Fakhoury, "Digital Searches After Riley v. California," The Champion, March 2015 at pp. 36–40.

Sanjay Goel, ed. *Digital Forensics and Cyber Crime: First International ICST Conference, ICDF2C 2009.,* Springer, 2010.

Jim Harper, "Litigating the Fourth Amendment After Jones," The Champion, January/February 2013 at pp. 20–28.

Heather Mahalik, Satish Bommisetty and Rohit Tamma, *Practical Mobile Forensics,* 2d ed., Packt Publishing, 2016.

---

[182] 2016 U.S. Dist. LEXIS at *1–2.

[183] 2016 U.S. Dist. LEXIS at *2.

[184] Id.

[185] 2016 U.S. Dist. LEXIS at *12.

David R. Matthews, *Electronically Stored Information: The Complete Guide to Management, Understanding, Acquisition, Storage, Search, and Retrieval,* 2d ed., CRC Press, 2016.

Stephanie K. Pell and Christopher Soghoian, "A Lot More Than a Pen Register, and Less Than a Wiretap: What the StingRay Teaches Us About How Congress Should Approach Reform of Law Enforcement Surveillance Technology," 16 Yale L.J. & Tec. 134 (2013–2014).

Prosecuting Computer Crimes. Computer Crime and Intellectual Property Section, Criminal Division, United States Department of Justice, 2010 (available at: https://www.justice.gov/sites/default/files/criminal-ccips/legacy/2015/01/14/ccmanual.pdf).

Lee Reiber, *Mobile Forensic Investigations: A Guide to Evidence Collection, Analysis, and Presentation*, McGraw Hill Education, 2016.

Caitlin E. Rice, "Police in My Pocket: The Need for Fourth Amendment Protection for Cellular Telephone Tracking," The Champion, November/December 2014 at pp. 36–47, 62–63.

Barbara J. Rothstein, Ronald J. Hedges and Elizabeth C. Wiggins *Managing Discovery of Electronic Information: A Pocket Guide for Judges.* Federal Judicial Center, 2007 (available at: http://www.fjc.gov/public/pdf.nsf/lookup/eldscpkt.pdf/$file/eldscpkt.pdf).

Shira A. Scheindlin, The Sedona Conference, *Electronic Discovery and Digital Evidence in a Nutshell*, 2d ed. West Academic Publishing, 2016.

Marcia G. Shein, "Cybercrime and the Fourth Amendment," The Champion, July 2016 at pp. 36–44.

Michael G. Solomon, K. Rudolph, Ed Tittel, Neil Broom and Diana Barrett, *Computer Forensics Jumpstart,* 2nd ed., John Wiley and Sons, 2011.

Searching & Seizing Computers and Obtaining Electronic Evidence in Criminal Investigations, 3rd ed. Criminal Division, U.S. Department of Justice, 2009 (available at: https://www.justice.gov/sites/default/files/criminal-ccips/legacy/2015/01/14/ssmanual2009.pdf).

Soutfiane Tahiri, *Mastering Mobile Forensics*, Packt Publishing, 2016.

U.S. Department of Justice, National Institute of Justice, *Electronic Crime Scene Investigations: A Guide for First Responders,* 2009. (available at: www.ncjrs.gov/pdffiles1/nij/227050.pdf.).

CHAPTER 10

FORENSIC ANTHROPOLOGY[1]

I. INTRODUCTION

§10.01 SCOPE OF THE CHAPTER

Anthropology is the "study of humans" and generally is divided into four areas of study: socio-cultural anthropology (the examination of social patterns and practices across cultures), archaeology (the examination of past humans and cultures through analysis of material remains), linguistic anthropology (the study of the influence and reflection of language on culture), and physical or biological anthropology (the study of biological influences on human variation).[2] The fourth area—physical

---

[1]   The Authors thank the following subject matter experts for their assistance with this chapter: Laura C. Fulginiti, PhD, D-ABFA, Forensic Anthropologist, Office of the Medical Examiner, Maricopa County; and Katelyn Bolhofner, MA, PhD Candidate, Arizona State University, School for Human Evolution and Social Change.

[2]   *See* American Anthropological Association website: www.aaanet.org/about/Whatis Anthropology.cfm (last accessed August 9, 2016).

anthropology—provides the basis for the field of forensic anthropology.[3] Forensic anthropology is broadly defined as "the application of the science of physical or biological anthropology to the legal process."[4] Forensic anthropologists primarily apply the techniques of osteology (the study of bones) and skeletal identification to problems of legal and public concern.[5] Currently, forensic anthropologists are involved in both personal identification and the assessment of trauma and pathologic conditions in bone, as well as providing information regarding the postmortem interval. Many large metropolitan medical examiner offices in the United States either employ forensic anthropologists on a full or part time basis, or use them routinely as expert consultants.

One of the main functions performed by a forensic anthropologist is the examination of human remains to establish identity, including estimations of sex, age at death, ancestry, and the stature of the individual. In the last 20 years, the field of forensic anthropology has undergone a paradigm shift, broadening the scientific scope of the field beyond the biological profile of the remains to "the physical and forensic context" in which the remains are recovered.[6] Additional questions that may be answered by a forensic anthropological examination include the estimated postmortem interval; whether the body suffered trauma before death, at the time of death, or after death; what types of trauma were suffered; and whether the decedent suffered from any nutritional deficiencies or disease processes that may affect bone.

Like many areas of forensic science, forensic anthropology currently lacks regulatory oversight and mandatory national standards.[7] Professional groups are working to develop standard protocols for the common fields of inquiry in forensic anthropology, but these standards are not mandatory. The National Institute of Standards and Technology (NIST) has developed the Organization of Scientific Area Committees (OSAC), one of which pertains specifically to anthropology. This group is tasked with creating "Best Practices" for the discipline of forensic anthropology.[8] They are building on the standards and guidelines

---

[3] Debra A. Komar and Jane E. Buikstra. *Forensic Anthropology: Contemporary Theory and Practice,* (New York, NY: Oxford University Press, 2008).

[4] *See* American Board of Forensic Anthropology website: www.theabfa.org (last accessed August 9, 2016).

[5] Ellis R. Kerley, "Recent Developments in Forensic Anthropology," 21 Y.B. PHY. ANTHRO. 160 (1978).

[6] Clifford Boyd and Donna C. Boyd, "Theory and the Scientific Basis for Forensic Anthropology," 56 J. Forensic Sci. 1407–1415 (2011) at p. 1407 (*quoting* D.C. Dirkmaat, L.L. Cabo, S.D. Ousley and S.A. Symes, "New Perspectives in Forensic Anthropology," 51YEARBOOK PHYS. ANTHROPOL. 33–52 (2008) AT P. 47).

[7] The standards referenced in this Chapter are the standards developed by the Scientific Working Group for Forensic Anthropology (SWGANTH). These standards are voluntary and forensic anthropologists are not required to adhere to these standards. *See* Angi M. Christensen and Christian M. Crowder, "Evidentiary Standards for Forensic Anthropology," 54 J. FORENSIC SCI. 1211–1216 (2009)(discussing the lack of professional standards).

[8] *See* The OSAC Anthropology Subcommittee website for more information: https://www.nist.gov/topics/forensic-science/anthropology-subcommittee (last accessed February 21, 2017).

produced by the Scientific Working Group for Anthropology (SWGANTH) cited in this chapter and available online.[9] Once NIST-OSAC standards are developed they will be submitted to a Standards Development Organization (SDO) such as the Academy Standards Board (ASB) of the American Academy of Forensic Sciences.[10] Similarly, certification in forensic anthropology from the American Board of Forensic Anthropology (ABFA) is preferred and may become the standard in Forensic Anthropology, but it is not currently mandatory. The field does benefit, however, from strong ties to academia[11] and collaborative efforts with other scientists that provide foundational support for research and the expanding databases containing necessary biometric information. Much of the current research in forensic anthropology involves validation of methods and standardization of the discipline, and can be found by reviewing recent years of the Proceedings of the American Academy of Forensic Sciences.[12]

This chapter provides an overview of the evidentiary value of forensic anthropological analysis, the determinations made by forensic anthropologists in examining unknown remains and assessing bone trauma, and the methods most commonly used in making those determinations. Unlike other areas of forensic science that are strictly laboratory-based, forensic anthropologists frequently examine suspected skeletal remains in the field. Recovery efforts can benefit greatly from their participation, which maximizes the evidentiary value and minimizes the alteration and contamination of the recovered material. This on-scene involvement is particularly important for the recovery of mass disaster victims and in multiple-victim situations. The specific procedures for on-scene recovery are not discussed in this chapter, but principles and techniques of forensic archaeology are generally implicated in the recovery of buried materials.[13]

§10.02 Terminology

The following terms are used in this Chapter or are commonly used in forensic anthropology investigation reports.

Alveolar bone: Bone structure in the mandible or maxilla (jaws) that contains the alveoli (sockets) of the teeth; dental alveoli.

Antemortem: Prior to death.

---

[9] See The Scientific Working Group for Forensic Anthropology (SWGANTH): www.swganth.org (last accessed August 23, 2016).

[10] See AAFS Academy Standards Board: http://asb.aafs.org (last accessed February 28, 2017).

[11] "The academic roots of forensic anthropology extend back over a century to the general field of human anatomy and reflect a great deal of collective experience, research, and testing." Douglas H. Ubelaker, "Issues in the Global Applications of Methodology in Forensic Anthropology," 53 J. Forensic Sci. 606–607 (2008).

[12] See http://www.aafs.org/resources/proceedings/ (last accessed August 23, 2016).

[13] See John Hunter, "Archaeology," in Wiley Encyclopedia Of Forensic Science, (Jamieson A. & Moenssens A.A., eds) 2009 & online updates.

Bone cells: Includes osteoblasts, osteocytes, osteoclasts, and osteoprogenitor cells.

Compact bone: The outer cortical layer of bone consisting of periosteum, endosteum, and Haversian systems.

Endosteum: The tissue lining the medullary cavity of bone.

Haversian canal: Canal (space) in compact bone containing blood and lymph vessels and nerves (named after 18th century English anatomist Clopton Havers).

Haversian systems: Tubular cellular structures in bone that appear circular in cross section; caused by the remodeling of parallel layers that are deposited in a concentric fashion to the cross-sectional axis of the bone.

Histology: The examination of the minute structure, composition, and function of tissues; microscopic examination of tissue samples.

Long bone: Larger bone that consists of a shaft (also called a "diaphysis") and two ends (also referred to as "epiphyses"); the femur (upper leg), humerus (upper arm), radius and ulna (lower arm), tibia and fibula (lower leg).

Macroscopic: Visible to the unaided eye or without a microscope.

Microscopic: Visible only with the aid of a microscope or other technology.

Osseous Traumata: Antemortem or perimortem injury to bones.

Osteology: The scientific study of bones.

Osteon: The basic unit of structure of compact bone, comprising a Haversian canal (space) and its concentrically arranged lamellae (bony plates).

Pelvis: Bowl-shaped bony structure bounded on the sides by the two bones commonly referred to as the hips and in the back by the sacrum (triangular bone just below the lumbar vertebrae) and the coccyx (small bone below the sacrum—the "tail bone").

Perimortem: Around the time of death; either immediately prior to death, at the time of death, or immediately after death.

Periosteum: Specialized connective tissue covering all bones; in adults, consists of two layers that are not sharply defined (external layer with dense connective tissue containing blood vessels; internal layer with loosely arranged collagenous bundles with spindle-shaped connective tissue cells and thin elastic fibers).

Postmortem: After death.

Postmortem interval: Time since death; the time between death and the discovery of the remains ("PMI").

Short bones: Smaller bones that consist of a shaft and two ends, such as the metacarpals (hand bones) and metatarsals (foot bones).

Skull: The cranium (comprised of the frontal, occipital, sphenoid, parietals (2), zygomatics (2), nasals (2), maxillae (2), lacrimals (2), temporals (2), palatines (2), nasal conchae (2), vomer and ethmoid) and the mandible.

Suture: Type of fibrous joint in which opposed surfaces are closely united; the line of junction between two bones, usually in the skull.

Taphonomy: The study of the process of decay and decomposition.

Trabecular bone: Spongy bone that surrounds marrow spaces and makes up the main portion of a bone; cancellous bone.

Vertebrae: Segments of the spinal column: cervical vertebrae (7), thoracic vertebrae (12), lumbar vertebrae (5), sacral vertebrae (5) (fused to form the sacrum), and coccygeal vertebrae (4) (fused to form the coccyx).

§10.03 EVIDENTIARY USES

Forensic anthropological evidence may be relevant in any case in which the identity of human remains is an issue, and in cases where trauma to the bony structures is evaluated, including criminal cases, infant death cases, and suspected elder abuse cases.[14] The services of forensic anthropologists mainly have been used in three general areas: (1) medicolegal death investigations, including acts of terrorism; (2) noncriminal events resulting in multiple deaths, *e.g.*, arising from natural disasters; and (3) human rights violation investigations, *e.g.*, war crimes and genocide.[15] Forensic anthropology is also occasionally used to answer questions concerning living persons, to compare identifications to photographic or video images, to provide age estimations of individuals depicted in photographic images in cases of alleged child pornography,[16] and to assess age in immigration matters.[17]

Forensic anthropologists may be involved in civil cases where the identification of the remains is in question. For the purpose of recovering the proceeds of life insurance policies, the identification of the insured as deceased is fundamental. Regardless of whether the insured died from

---

[14] In some criminal cases, the individual identity of the remains may not be an issue, but the age of the remains may be, such as cases under the Archeological Resources Protection Act (16 U.S.C. § 470ee(a)). *See* United States v. Lynch, 233 F.3d 1139 (9th Cir. 2000). The age of the remains and ancestry are also relevant in cases under the Native American Graves Protection and Repatriation Act (25 U.S.C. § 3001 *et seq.*). *See* Bonnichsen *et al.* v. United States *et al.*, 367 F.3d 864 (9th Cir. 2004).

[15] *See* Patrick Randolph-Quinney, Xanthe Mallett and Sue Black, "Anthropology," in WILEY ENCYCLOPEDIA OF FORENSIC SCIENCE, (Jamieson A. & Moenssens A.A., eds) 2009 & online updates.

[16] *See* Cristina Cattaneo, "Forensic Anthropology: Developments of a Classical Discipline in the New Millennium," 165 FORENSIC SCI. 185 (2007); A. Schmeling et al., "Age Estimation," 165 FORENSIC SCI. INT'L 178 (2008).

[17] *See* US Immigration and Customs Enforcement Memorandum on Age Determination Procedures for Custody Decisions, August 20, 2004. (available at www.ice.gov/doclib/foia/dro_policy_memos/agedeterminationproceduresforcustodydecisionsaug202004.pdf)(last accessed August 9, 2016).

accidental, homicidal, suicidal, or natural causes or even from an undetermined event, the fact of death is of overarching importance to the beneficiaries' recovery on a life insurance policy.[18] Forensic anthropologists also have testified in product liability cases[19] and in cases regarding contested exhumations of historically significant persons.[20]

Mass disasters resulting from acts of terrorism, catastrophic weather events, or similar multiple casualty events can produce difficult identification issues for which forensic anthropological assistance is essential.[21] The identification of casualties of war is another form of mass fatality event where strong biological profiles are critical. Key considerations in these types of large scale events are locating the scene, establishing a mortuary for recovered remains, collecting personal information on suspected victims, and scientifically identifying the remains.[22] With commingled and cremated remains, careful recovery and documentation of the original condition of the remains has proven extremely important in making accurate and timely identifications.[23]

Forensic anthropology has become increasingly essential in the investigation of violations of human rights laws and war crimes. The protection of human rights is a concern for anthropologists and professional organizations have provided assistance and support for the investigation of suspected human rights violations (*e.g.*, war crimes, genocide, human trafficking).[24] Unlike traditional criminal cases, these violations are generally committed on foreign soil with the support of a particular government or regime, and often result in mass graves with commingled remains.[25] Forensic anthropological assistance is used to establish not only the individual identities of the victims, but also the

---

[18] *See* Roberts v. Wabash Life Ins. Co., 410 N.E.2d 1377 (Ind. Ct. App. 1980).

[19] Brooks v. Beech Aircraft Corporation, 120 N.M. 372, 902 P.2d 54 (1995) ("crashworthiness" of a particular shoulder harness).

[20] Exhumation of Lewis, 999 F.Supp. 1066 (MD Tenn. 1998); Bonnichsen v. U.S. Depart. of the Army, 969 F.Supp. 614 (D. Or. 1997).

[21] *See* Doug H. Ubelaker et al., "The Role of Forensic Anthropology in the Recovery and Analysis of Branch Davidian Compound Victims: Recovery Procedures and Characteristics of the Victims," 40 J. Forensic Sci. 335–340 (1995); Soren Blau, S. Robertson and M. Johnstone, "Disaster Victim Identification: New Applications for Postmortem Computed Tomography," 53 J. FORENSIC SCI. 956–961 (2008).

[22] Soren Blau and Christopher A. Briggs, "The Role of Forensic Anthropology in Disaster Victim Identification (DVI)," 205 FOR. SCI. INT'L 29–35 (2011)(discussing the DVI following bushfires in Australia, 2009).

[23] Dae-Kyoon Parl et al., "The Role of Forensic Anthropology in the Examination of the Daegu Subway Disaster (2003, Korea)," 54 J. FORENSIC SCI. 513–518 (2009).

[24] *See generally* Committee for Human Rights, American Anthropological Association, *Declaration on Anthropology and Human Rights*, available at: http://humanrights.american anthro.org/1999-statement-on-human-rights/ (last accessed August 9, 2016).

[25] *See* Simun Andelinovic et al., "Twelve-year Experience in Identification of Skeletal Remains from Mass Graves," 46 CROATIA MED. J. 530 (2005); Marija Djuric et al., "Identification of Victims from Two Mass-Graves in Serbia: A Critical Evaluation of Classical Markers of Identity," 172 FORENSIC SCI. INT'L. 125 (2007); Marija Djuric and Hugh Tuller, "Keeping the Pieces Together: Comparison of Mass Grave Excavation Methodology," 156 Forensic Sci. Int'l. 192 (2006).

collective or group identity of the victims to support allegations of human rights violations or genocide.[26]

In 1948, the United Nations General Assembly formally adopted the Universal Declaration of Human Rights, which sets forth "freedoms considered essential to humankind." These freedoms involve the right to religion, nationality, expression, opinion, work, rest, health, and education. They also include the right to be free from torture, unfair prosecution, arbitrary detention, exile, discrimination, and slavery.[27] Although this document does not carry the force of law, subsequent international attempts have been made to strengthen the Declaration.[28] In 1948, the United Nations General Assembly also defined genocide as:

> "[A]ny of the following acts committed with intent to destroy, in whole or part, a national, ethnical, racial or religious group, as such:
>
> (a) Killing members of the group;
>
> (b) Causing serious bodily injury or mental harm to members of the group;
>
> (c) Deliberately inflicting on the group conditions of life calculated to bring about its physical destruction in whole or part;
>
> (d) Imposing measures intended to prevent births within the group;
>
> (e) Forcibly transferring children of the group to another group."[29]

The collective identity of the victims (civilians or soldiers, members of an ethnic group, women of child-bearing age, etc.) can be critical evidence of the intent to target a particular group to support charges of genocide.[30]

---

[26] Erin H. Kimmerle, Richard L. Jantz, Lyle W. Konigsberg and Jose Pablo Baraybar, "Skeletal Estimation and Identification in American and East European Populations," 53 J. FORENSIC SCI. 524–532 (2008). *See also* Erin H. Kimmerle and Richard J. Lantz, "Variation as Evidence: Introduction to a Symposium on International Human Identification," 53 J. FORENSIC SCI. 521–523 (2008)(noting that the identity of the victims—rather than the perpetrator—is primarily at issue in human rights cases).

[27] Debra A. Komar and Jane E. Buikstra. *Forensic Anthropology: Contemporary Theory and Practice,* Oxford University Press, 2008.

[28] For a discussion of International Humanitarian Law, *see* H. McKelvie and B. Loff, "Human Rights, Controls, and Principles," in Jason Payne-James et al., eds, *Encyclopedia of Forensic and Legal Medicine,* Vol. 2, Elvesier Ltd., 2005, at pp. 538-546 (available for purchase at: http://www.sciencedirect.com)(last accessed February 28, 2017).

[29] Article II of the *Convention on the Prevention and Punishment of the Crime of Genocide (*Adopted by Resolution 260(III)A of the U.N. General Assembly on 9 December 1948, effective 12 January 1951).

[30] Erin H. Kimmerle and Richard L. Jantz, "Variation as Evidence: Introduction to a Symposium on International Human Identification," 53 J. FORENSIC SCI. 521–523 (2008).

II. IDENTIFICATION

§10.04 PROCESS OF IDENTIFICATION: IN GENERAL

A forensic anthropological examination begins with three fundamental determinations:

1.   Whether the material is bone;

2.   Whether the bone is human;

3.   Whether the bone is forensically significant.

The criteria for the third determination (forensic significance) depend upon the circumstances of the inquiry. For death investigations that may involve criminal activity, the remains may be forensically significant as long as a purported suspect may be alive. In other circumstances, such as investigations of violations of the Archeological Resources Protection Act, only much older remains would be forensically significant.[31] In general, remains which are from a person dead for more than fifty years at the time of discovery may not be the subject of a state death investigation and responsibility for the remains may be transferred to the state archaeologist.[32]

In making the determination of the age of the remains, two methodologies are widely accepted: contextual indicators and carbon dating (radiocarbon analysis). Carbon dating, also known as C14 dating, is useful for determining whether the remains are more than 50 years old, but must take into account both the age at death of the individual and the type of tissue analyzed. Alternatively, the forensic anthropologist can use taphonomic or contextual indicators (cemetery remains, site formation processes, environmental conditions, etc.) and gross examination of the condition of the bone to establish forensic significance.

Once the material is identified as human bone[33] and of forensic significance, the forensic anthropologist begins the process of identifying the remains through the development of a biological profile. After skeletal preparation,[34] the determination of the minimum number of individuals (MNI),[35] and the resolution of commingled human remains,[36]

---

[31] *See* Note 14 *supra.*

[32] Louisiana Unmarked Human Burial Sites Preservation Act (La. R.S. § 8:671–681). In some states this figure may extend to one hundred years. *See* Colo. Rev. Stat. § 24–80–1303(2)(a).

[33] In some cases, such as illegal hunting, animal smuggling, or animal cruelty cases, non-human bones may be of forensic significance. Forensic anthropology, however, focuses on human remains. *See* Scientific Working Group for Forensic Anthropology, "Determination of Medicolegal Significance from Suspected Osseous and Dental Remains," issued 05/25/2011 (available at www.swganth.org).

[34] *See* Scientific Working Group for Forensic Anthropology, "Skeletal Sampling and Preparation," issued 05/25/2011 (available at www.swganth.org); Todd W. Fenton, Walter H. Birkby, and Jered Corelison, "A Fast and Safe Non-Bleaching Method for Forensic Skeletal Preparation", 48 J. FORENSIC SCI. 1 (2003).

[35] Debra A. Komar and Jane E. Buikstra. *Forensic Anthropology: Contemporary Theory and Practice,* Oxford University Press, 2008.

the skeletal material is examined to estimate four basic biological criteria:[37]

1. The sex of the individual;
2. The age of the individual at death;
3. The ancestry of the individual;
4. The stature of the individual during life.

Standard methods and associated confidence intervals for each of these categories of analysis have been developed and tested by statistical analysis of the features of large numbers of skeletons of known identities. These collections of documented skeletons provide important biometric data for use by forensic anthropologists. The Terry collection, housed at the Smithsonian Institution in Washington, D.C, consists of 1728 specimens of known age, sex, ethnic origin, cause of death, and pathological conditions.[38] The Terry collection is fairly evenly distributed between the sexes, but overwhelmingly White or Black in race with only five Asiatic males (no Asiatic females) and one specimen of unknown origin.[39] Another commonly utilized collection is the larger Hamann-Todd collection at the Cleveland Museum of Natural History, which has over 3000 human specimens.[40] The primary drawback associated with the Terry and Hamann-Todd collections is that both collections are based on specimens collected from 1850 to 1900.[41] Skeletal changes within the human population over the past 100 to 150 years have thus lessened the applicability of these older samples. The shifting demographics of the American population have also rendered these collections unrepresentative of the current population, especially in terms of ancestry.[42]

More recent collections include the Maxwell Museum at the University of New Mexico, based on donated bodies, and the Hartnett-Fulginiti collection, a more limited sample of 600 associated pubic

---

[36] *See* Scientific Working Group for Forensic Anthropology, "Resolving Commingled Human Remains," issued 01/22/2013 (available at www.swganth.org).

[37] *See* Patrick Randolph-Quinney, Xanthe Mallett and Sue Black, "Anthropology," in WILEY ENCYCLOPEDIA OF FORENSIC SCIENCE, (Jamieson A. & Moenssens A.A., eds) 2009 & online updates.

[38] Robert J. Terry Anatomical Skeletal Collection, Department of Anthropology, National Museum of Natural History, Smithsonian Institution. *See* http://anthropology.si.edu/cm/terry.htm (last accessed August 9, 2016).

[39] Id.

[40] Hamann-Todd Human Osteological Collection, Cleveland Museum of Natural History, *See* https://www.cmnh.org/phys-anthro/collection-database (last accessed August 9, 2016).

[41] *See* David R. Hunt and John Albanese, "History and Demographic Composition of the Robert J. Terry Anatomical Collection," 127 AM. J. PHYS. ANTHRO. 406 (2005); Stephen D. Ousley and Richard L. Jantz, "The Forensic Data Bank: Documenting Skeletal Trends in the United States," in Kathleen J. Reichs ed., *Forensic Osteology: Advances in the Identification of Human Remains*, 2d ed., 1998 at p. 441.

[42] *See* M. Katherine Spradley et al., "Demographic Change and Forensic Identification: Problems in Metric Identification of Hispanic Skeletons," 53 J. FORENSIC SCI. 21–28 (2008).

symphyses and sternal rib ends from a known autopsy sample.[43] The William M. Bass Forensic Skeletal Collection at the University of Tennessee, Knoxville, is another modern sample that is increasingly used by forensic anthropologists, nationally and internationally.[44] Although smaller than the Terry and Hamann-Todd collections (the Bass collection currently has over 1600 individuals), the Bass collection was started in 1981 to build a collection for research purposes, including skeletal biometric data.[45] For cases in the United States, this collection provides superior modern population data for analysis and comparison.

The University of Tennessee also maintains the Forensic Anthropology Data Bank, started in 1986 to collect demographic and skeletal information from modern forensic anthropology cases, including 3D coordinate data from some cases.[46] The Bass collection has a predominantly American European and African ancestry demographic profile; however, the Forensic Anthropology Data Bank contains information from approximately 290 Hispanic skeletons, making it more representative of the current US population.[47] An additional benefit of the Forensic Anthropology Data Bank is its provision of the database for *FORDISC* 3.0,[48] making sex, ancestry, and stature estimation criteria available in an easily accessible format.

After the primary biological profile is determined, the forensic anthropologist will examine secondary traits to assist in the individualization of the remains. Secondary traits may include body modifications; surgical interventions; evidence of trauma, including healing or healed fractures; and macroscopic or microscopic lesions, indicative of chronic disease or malnutrition.

1. BONE

The first determination for the forensic anthropologist is whether the material is bone. Typically, skeletal material is readily identified through the observation of trabecular bone, vascular components, or

---

[43] *See* https://www.unm.edu/~maxwell/ (last accessed August 23, 2016); Kristen M. Hartnett, "A re-evaluation and revision of pubic symphysis and fourth rib aging techniques," PhD dissertation, School of Human Evolution and Social Change. Arizona State University, Tempe, 2007.

[44] William M. Bass Forensic and Donated Skeletal Collection, University of Tennessee, Knoxville. See http://web.utk.edu/~fac/facilities.html (last accessed August 9, 2016).

[45] Id.

[46] Forensic Anthropology Data Bank. *See* https://fac.utk.edu/background/ (last accessed August 9, 2016).

[47] M. Katherine Spradley, Richard L. Jantz, Alan Robinson and Fredy Peccerelli, "Demographic Change and Forensic Identification: Problems in Metric Identification of Hispanic Skeletons," 53 J. FORENSIC SCI. 21–28 (2008).

[48] *FORDISC* 3.0, created by Stephen D. Ousley and Richard L. Jantz, is an interactive computer program for comparing skeletal measurements to database profiles to help forensic anthropologists with classifications. *FORDISC* 3.0 Personal Computer Forensic Discriminant Functions. *See* https://secure.touchnet.com/C21610_ustores/web/store_main.jsp?STOREID= 15&SINGLESTORE=true (last accessed August 9, 2016).

osteological landmarks.[49] In additional to gross examination, other methodologies for classifying material as bone include microscopic techniques and elemental techniques.[50]

Skeletal material has distinctive, microscopically observable characteristics. Osteons, cylindrical and oriented perpendicular to the long axis of the bone, are the structural component of dense bone. Each osteon has a Haversian canal (vascular structure) and is surrounded by the concentric lamellar bone. Spongy (trabecular) bone is less dense and lacks osteons and Haversian canals.[51] Microscopic examination to determine whether the material is bone involves identifying these distinctive structures. These structures, particularly osteons, are identifiable even after extensive burning[52] or decomposition.

Elemental techniques, such as scanning electron microscopy/energy dispersive x-ray spectroscopy (SEM/EDS), analyze the chemical composition of the suspected bone.[53] This chemical composition is then compared to known reference samples,[54] such as the entries stored in the Spectral Library for Identification and Classification (SLICE), maintained at the FBI laboratory in Washington, D.C.[55] Researchers often focus on the calcium to phosphoros ratio because non-skeletal material rarely has the same ratios of these two substances as skeletal material.[56]

2. HUMAN BONE

If the material is determined to be bone, the forensic anthropologist then must assess whether it is human.[57] Non-human bones may be forensically significant in some cases, such as poaching, but other experts such as forensic biologists are the primary investigators in those types of

---

[49] *See* Scientific Working Group for Forensic Anthropology, "Determination of Medicolegal Significance from Suspected Osseous and Dental Remains," issued 05/25/2011 (available at www.swganth.org).

[50] Id.

[51] For more information on the microscopic structures of bone, *see* Gary A. Thibodeau and Kevin T. Patton, *Anatomy & Physiology,* 6th ed., Elvesier Ltd., 2007.

[52] Bruce Bradtmiller and Jane E. Buikstra, "Effects of Burning on Human Bone Microstructure: A Preliminary Study," 29 J. FORENSIC SCI. 537 (1984); Tim Thompson, "Recent Advances in the Study of Burned Bone and Their Implications for Forensic Anthropology," 146 SUPPL. FORENSIC SCI. INT'L S203 (2004). *See also* F. Dedouit, et al., "Virtual Anthropology and Forensic Identification: Report of One Case," 173 FORENSIC SCI. INT'L 182 (2007) and T.J. Thompson & J.A. Chudek, "A Novel Approach to the Visualisation of Heat-Induced Structural Change in Bone," 47 Science & Justice 99 (2007).

[53] Douglas H. Ubelaker, et al., "The Use of SEM/EDS Analysis to Distinguish Dental and Osseous Tissues from Other Materials," 47 J. FORENSIC SCI. 940 (2002).

[54] *See* Scientific Working Group for Forensic Anthropology, "Determination of Medicolegal Significance from Suspected Osseous and Dental Remains," issued 05/25/2011 (available at www.swganth.org).

[55] Douglas H. Ubelaker et al., "The Use of SEM/EDS Analysis to Distinguish Dental and Osseous Tissues from Other Materials," 47 J. FORENSIC SCI. 940 (2002).

[56] Id.

[57] Murray K. Marks, "William M. Bass and the Development of Forensic Anthropology in Tennessee," 40 J. Forensic Sci. 729 (1995)(30% of non-human bones identified as human by non-experts).

cases. Where complete bones in good condition are recovered, the anthropologist can determine the species as human from the morphology.[58] If the bone fragments are sufficiently large, they can be compared to collections of different types of animal bones to see if they are consistent with any other animal.[59] If the remains are difficult to identify due to significant alteration by trauma, fire, or other environmental effects, DNA analysis may be used to determine whether the bone is human.[60] If DNA analysis is unavailable or inconclusive,[61] histological procedures and immunoassays can be used to determine the species.

---

[58] Recent research suggests that metric assessments, in the absence of morphological markers, may be useful in differentiating human from non-human remains. Bree Saulsman, Charles E. Oxnard and Daniel Franklin, "Long Bone Morphometrics for Human from Non-human Discrimination," 202 FORENSIC SCI. INT'L 110.e1–110.e5 (2010).

[59] Collections of animal skeletons are available for comparison at most museums of natural history. For more information, see Elisabeth Schmid, *Atlas of Animal Bones for Prehistorians, Archaeologists, and Quaternary Geologists,* Elsevier Publishing Co., 1972.

[60] E.A. Guglich, P.J. Wilson and B.N. White, "Forensic Application of Repetitive DNA Markers to the Species Identification of Animal Tissue," 39 J. Forensic Sci. 353–361 (1994). For more information about DNA analysis, see Chapter 17: Determining Individuality by DNA.

If the bone is not human, DNA testing may also reveal the species of origin of the animal. See Sue Coticone and Heather Walsh-Haney, Abstract for the American Academy of Forensic Sciences Annual Meeting (2007); S. A. Miller, et al., "A Simple Salting Out Procedure for Extracting DNA from Human Nucleated Cells," 16 Nucl. Acids. Res. 1215 (1988); C. Bellis, et al., "A Molecular Genetic Approach for Forensic Animal Species Identification," 134 Forensic Sci. Int'l 99 (2003); and C. Cattaneo, et al., "Determining the Human Origin of Fragments of Burnt Bone: A Comparative Study of Histological, Immunological and DNA Techniques," 102 Forensic Sci. Int'l 181 (1999).

[61] DNA may be very difficult to extract from charred or very dry bone. Cristina Cattaneo and Davide Porta, "Species Determination of Osseous Remains," in WILEY ENCYCLOPEDIA OF FORENSIC SCIENCE, (Jamieson A. & Moenssens A.A., eds) 2009 & online updates, p. 4. *See also* B. G. Brogdon, Marcella H. Sorg and Kerriann Marden, "Fingering a Murderer: A Successful Anthropological and Radiological Collaboration," 55 J. FORENSIC SCI. 248–250 (2010). DNA analysis may also be unavailable or prohibitively expensive in many parts of the world. Jose Pablo Baraybar, "When DNA Is Not Available, Can We Still Identify People? Recommendations for Best Practice," 53 J. FORENSIC SCI. 533–540 (2008).

Figure 1: The human skeleton with the principal bones identified.
Douglas H. Ubelaker, *Human Skeletal Remains: Excavation,*
Analysis, Interpretation, Second Edition (1989).

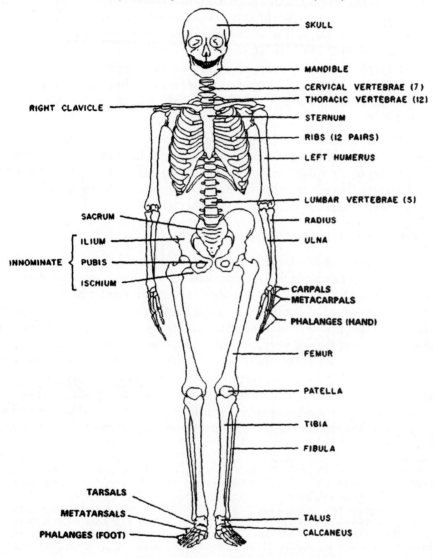

If the bone is too fragmented for gross identification or too small for
conclusive species determination, a thin section of the cortical bone can
be examined under a microscope.[62] Caution is needed, though, as the
irregular distribution of osteons typically considered indicative of human

---

[62] For a detailed discussion of histological methods, *see* M.L. Hillier and L.S. Bell,
"Differentiating Human Bone from Animal Bone: A Review of Histological Methods," 52 J.
FORENSIC SCI. 249–263 (2007).

bone is also found in some animals.[63] Further, while plexiform (fibrolamellar) bone is characteristic of animal bones, it is occasionally present in fetal human remains.[64] Differentiation between species may also involve measurements of the diameters of Haversian systems and Haversian canals, as well as Haversian system density, to determine if the measurements are consistent with human measurement ranges.[65] Ultimately, the positive determination of human origin microscopically is not always possible, but it may be possible to exclude a bone as not of human origin based on comparison of osteon configuration, and metric parameters.[66]

With extraction of species-specific proteins from the remains, immunoassays[67] can be used to distinguish human bone.[68] Protein radioimmunoassay (pRIA) may be used to distinguish human from non-human bones based on the antibody response.[69] More sophisticated enzyme-linked immunoassays may also be used.[70]

3. ESTIMATION OF POSTMORTEM INTERVAL

The estimation of the postmortem interval (PMI) is an important determination, particularly in criminal cases. This determination is different from the "age of the remains" determination, which is used to establish the forensic significance of the remains. The estimation of the PMI estimation can be a narrow time range, but is often a wider range based on the number of variables affecting the estimate. The PMI may assist in the identification of the remains through a search of the records of persons missing in the determined time range or otherwise provide information relevant to establishing the time of death to aid the investigation. The most important method of estimating the time since death is the observation of the extent of decomposition of the soft tissue

---

[63] *See* Scientific Working Group for Forensic Anthropology, "Determination of Medicolegal Significance from Suspected Osseous and Dental Remains," issued 05/25/2011, p. 3 (available at www.swganth.org).

[64] In plexiform bone, osteons are packed tightly with no bone between them, while in human bone, osteons are scattered in an evenly spaced manner with bone between them. *See* Douglas H. Ubelaker, *Human Skeletal Remains: Excavation, Analysis, Interpretation,* 3d ed., Taraxacum, 1999 at p. 51; *See also* Dawn Mullhorn and Douglas H. Ubelaker, "Differences in Osteon Banding between Human and Nonhuman Bone," 46 J. FORENSIC SCI. 220 (2001).

[65] M.L. Hillier and L.S. Bell, "Differentiating Human Bone from Animal Bone: A Review of Histological Methods," 52 J. FORENSIC SCI. 249–263 (2007).

[66] Id.

[67] For a discussion of immunoassay methodologies, *see* Chapter 14: Forensic Biology and DNA Analysis.

[68] *See* Patrick Randolph-Quinney, Xanthe Mallett and Sue Black, "Anthropology," in WILEY ENCYCLOPEDIA OF FORENSIC SCIENCE, (Jamieson A. & Moenssens A.A., eds) 2009 & online updates.

[69] *See* Scientific Working Group for Forensic Anthropology, "Determination of Medicolegal Significance from Suspected Osseous and Dental Remains," issued 05/25/2011, p. 3 (available at www.swganth.org).

[70] Cristina Cattaneo and Davide Porta, "Species Determination of Osseous Remains," in WILEY ENCYCLOPEDIA OF FORENSIC SCIENCE, (Jamieson A. & Moenssens A.A., eds) 2009 & online updates.

and the estimation of the amount of time necessary for the body to decompose to that extent. Estimating the PMI from early soft tissue changes from decomposition is the role of the forensic pathologist.[71] The determination of PMI based on more extensive decomposition, mummification, skeletonization or the development of adipocere falls within the purview of the forensic anthropologist. Decomposition begins upon death and continues until the body is completely skeletonized. Skeletonization rates are affected by temperature, humidity, insect activity, animal activity, circumstances of the death, and location. A detailed understanding of the local climate, active carnivores, and insect populations in the area, and the microenvironment at the site of recovery are crucial when estimating the postmortem interval in specific cases.

During warmer temperatures, near or complete skeletonization may occur in two to four weeks, while cold temperatures may completely arrest decomposition. Fluctuating temperatures make specific determination of time since death extremely difficult.[72] Higher humidity is correlated with higher levels of insect activity, and therefore an increased rate of decomposition.[73] In dry environments, such as the desert, soft tissue can become mummified and remain intact after thousands of years.

Carnivores and rodents will eat flesh and bone and carry bones away, accelerating the rate of decomposition.[74] In remains that have sustained trauma with penetrating wounds, insects and carnivores are attracted to the open wounds and their activities will accelerate decomposition in those areas.[75] For completely or partially skeletonized remains, it may be extremely difficult to determine the PMI interval, even in ranges of years, because of the influence and variability of environmental factors.[76] For this reason, forensic anthropologists focus on the context of the skeletal remains, emphasizing the surrounding observations to make PMI estimations.[77]

---

[71] *See also* Scientific Working Group for Forensic Anthropology, "Taphonomic Observations in the Postmortem Interval", issued 06/12/2003 (available at www.swganth.org).

[72] Estimations for the PMI are further complicated by the variety of temperatures encountered within a relatively small geographic area. Gretchen R. Dabbs, "Caution! All Data Are Not Created Equal: The Hazards of Using National Weather Service Data for Calculating Accumulated Degree Days," 202 FOR. SCI. INT'L E49–E52 (2010).

[73] *See* Alison Galloway et al., "Decay Rates of Human Remains in an Arid Environment," 34 J. Forensic Sci. 607 (1989).

[74] *See* William D. Haglund, "Contribution of Rodents to Postmortem Artifacts of Bone and Soft Tissue," 37 J. Forensic Sci. 1459 (1992).

[75] Stanley Rhine and James E. Dawson, "Estimation of Time Since Death in the Southwestern United States," in Kathleen J. Reichs ed., *Forensic Osteology: Advances in the Identification of Human Remains*, 2d ed., Charles C. Thomas Publisher, 1998 at p. 154.

[76] Cristina Cattaneo and Daniele Gibelli, "Postmortem Interval: Anthropology," in WILEY ENCYCLOPEDIA OF FORENSIC SCIENCE, (Jamieson A. & Moenssens A.A., eds) 2009 & online updates.

[77] *See also* Scientific Working Group for Forensic Anthropology, "Taphonomic Observations in the Postmortem Interval", issued 06/12/2003 (available at www.swganth.org).

§10.05 SEX

Estimation of the sex of the remains is usually the first step in the construction of a biological profile, as other estimates involved generally use methodologies that are sex-differentiated. Skeletal sex estimation is based on visual examination of sexually dimorphic features[78] or metric assessment of sexually dimorphic bones.[79] Determination of sex in sub-adults is more difficult because primary and secondary sexual characteristics have not become fixed. As such, most sub-adults appear feminized (female) before puberty. Professional standards advise against making sex assessments for fetal, infant, or under 12 year-old child skeletal remains based on the lack of valid sex assessment techniques.[80] For older adolescents, the onset of puberty may enable the use of adult sex assessment techniques.

If the entire skeleton is recovered, the estimation of sex using a combination of gross morphological examination and metric assessment is considered nearly one hundred percent accurate. Unfortunately, the recovery of a full skeleton is not always possible in some forensic situations. If the skull and pelvis are complete, a visual assessment or a combination of methods achieves a reported 98% accuracy, the pelvis alone or the pelvis and long bones a reported 95% accuracy, the skull alone a reported 90% accuracy, the skull and long bones a reported 90–95% accuracy, and the long bones alone a reported 80–90% accuracy.[81] These accuracy rates, however, should be considered optimal research rates (with controlled populations), as population differences, age, and pathological and taphonomic changes can affect the accuracy of the estimate.[82]

1. GROSS MORPHOLOGY: PELVIS

The most sexually dimorphic feature of the skeleton, and therefore the bony structure from which the most accurate determination of sex

[78] Jane E. Buikstra and Douglas H. Ubelaker, *Standards for Data Collection from Human Skeletal Remains: Proceedings of a Seminar at the Field Museum of Natural History,* Arkansas Archeological Survey (1994).

[79] Humans display a pattern of morphological differences between males and females (sexual dimorphism). The primary sexual features include pelvic morphology. Secondary sexual features include size and shape differences in the form and robusticity of the skeletons (males generally exhibit greater stature and body weight). Patrick Randolph-Quinney, Xanthe Mallett and Sue Black, "Anthropology," in WILEY ENCYCLOPEDIA OF FORENSIC SCIENCE, (Jamieson A. & Moenssens A.A., eds) 2009 & online updates.

[80] *See* Scientific Working Group for Forensic Anthropology, "Sex Assessment," issued 06/03/2010, p. 3 (available at www.swganth.org).

[81] Wilton M. Krogman and M. Yasar Iscan, *The Human Skeleton in Forensic Medicine,* 2d ed. (Charles C. Thomas Pub. Ltd. 1986) at p. 259; S. Mays and M. Cox, "Sex Determination in Skeletal Remains," in *Human Osteology in Archaeology,* (S. Mays and M. Cox eds) Greenwich Medical Media, London 2000, pp. 117–130.; P.L. Walker, "Sexing Skulls Using Discriminant Function Analysis of Visually Assessed Traits," 136 AMER. J. OF PHYS. ANTHROP. 39–50 (2008).

[82] Patrick Randolph-Quinney, Xanthe Mallett and Sue Black, "Anthropology," in WILEY ENCYCLOPEDIA OF FORENSIC SCIENCE, (Jamieson A. & Moenssens A.A., eds) 2009 & online updates.

can be made, is the pelvis. The adult female pelvis is relatively broad compared to its height, with an expanded outlet compared to the taller, more narrow male pelvis.[83] Features of the adult pelvis that are the most sexually dimorphic include the sciatic notch, the attributes of the subpubic region, and the morphology of the auricular region.[84] (*See* Figure 2 and Table 1.)

Figure 2: The human pelvis with features used to determine sex identified. Douglas H. Ubelaker, *Human Skeletal Remains: Excavation, Analysis, Interpretation*, Second Edition, 53 (1989).

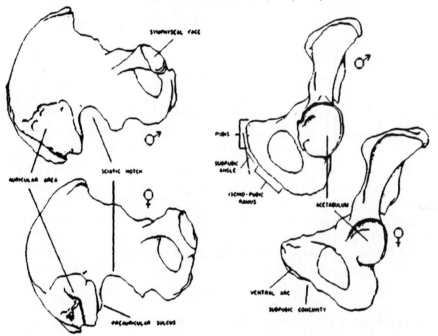

[83] Jane E. Buikstra and Douglas H. Ubelaker, *Standards for Data Collection from Human Skeletal Remains: Proceedings of a Seminar at the Field Museum of Natural History,* Arkansas Archeological Survey (1994).

[84] T. Phenice, "A Newly Developed Visual Method of Sexing in the Os Pubis," 30 Amer J Phys Anthro 297–301 (1969).

Table 1: Sex Determination*

Morphological Feature	Male	Female
Sciatic Notch	Narrow	Wide
Subpubic Angle	More Acute	More Obtuse
Auricular Area	Smooth	Rough
Pre-Auricular Sulcus	Absent	Present
Ventral Arc	Absent	Present
Pubis	Shorter	Longer
Subpubic Concavity	Absent/Slight	Large

* Derived from Ubelaker, D.H., Human Skeletal Remains: Excavation, Analysis, Interpretation 53–54, (1989).

The assignment of sex based on morphological features of the pelvic bones is very reliable for adults even when some of the features to be studied are not found or are too fragmented for analysis. Age (adult) does not appear to impact the precision of this analysis.[85] Accuracy of sex assessments based on the entire pelvis is reported between 95% and 98%.[86] Several researchers have tested the precision of the Phenice-triad (ventral arc, subpubic concavity, ischiopubic crest) characters resulting in varying degrees of accuracy from approximately 66% to 96.5%.[87] One study which used only one characteristic of the pelvis, the ventral arc, as a determinant of sex reported achieving an accuracy of 96%.[88]

2. GROSS MORPHOLOGY: OTHER BONES

In the absence of the pelvis, gross morphological features of other skeletal material can be examined. While sex related differences have been described for the sternal ends of the ribs and for the thyroid cartilage, features of the cranium and long bones are among those traits

---

[85] Tracy Rogers and Shelley Saunders, "Accuracy of Sex Determination Using Morphological Traits of the Human Pelvis," 39 J. Forensic Sci. 1047 (1995).

[86] Cristina Cattaneo and Davide Porta, "Sex Determination of Remains," in WILEY ENCYCLOPEDIA OF FORENSIC SCIENCE, (Jamieson A. & Moenssens A.A., eds) 2009 & online updates.

[87] Douglas H. Ubelaker and Crystal Volk, "A Test of the Phenice Method for the Estimation of Sex," 47 J. FORENSIC SCI. 19 (2002); Susan MacLaughlin and Margaret Bruce, "The Accuracy of Sex Identification in European Skeletal Remains Using the Phenice Characters," 35 J. Forensic Sci. 1384, 1389 (1990).

[88] Leslie Sutherland and Judy M. Suchey, "Use of the Ventral Arc in Pubic Sex Determination," 36 J. Forensic Sci. 501, 510 (1991). For additional statistics see Marija Djuric, et al., "The Reliability of Sex Determination of Skeletons from Forensic Context in the Balkans," 147 Forensic Sci. Int'l 159 (2005). See also K.R. Nagesh, "Sexual Dimorphism of Acetabulum-Pubis Index in South-Indian Population," 9 LEG. MED. 305 (2007).

(other than the pelvis) considered most reliable for sex estimation.[89] The male cranium is generally larger and more robust than the female cranium.[90] Generally the facial features, such as the supraorbital ridge and the mandible, are more prominent in males than in females. Muscle attachments of the cranium typically are more developed in males than in females, especially in the nuchal region at the back of the cranium, where the neck and shoulder muscles attach. A bony muscle attachment on the skull just below the opening for the ear canal, called the mastoid process, is more prominent in males than in females.[91] Muscle attachments on the long bones, which reflect increased muscle mass, are typically more robust and pronounced in males. However, these comparisons are generalizations as human populations show great variation in the degree of robusticity indicative of sexual dimorphism. Depending on the skeletal elements available for analysis, gross morphological examination can be a relatively subjective method of determining the sex of an individual. In cases where the condition of the remains or ambiguous morphological features make sex determination based on gross morphology difficult, metric assessments may be used in making sex determinations.[92]

3. METRIC ASSESSMENT

Several mathematical means for determining the sex of skeletal remains have been devised. These methods consist of measuring specific morphological features, such as the head of the femur, the length of the ischium and the pubis, or certain features of the cranium and comparing these measurements to those of skeletons of known sex, resulting in a male or female determination. Many researchers use the *FORDISC* 3.0 for classifying adults by ancestry and sex using a combination of standard measurements.[93]

While metric assessment of sex is useful in contexts where morphological estimation is difficult, recent research has indicated that the specific measurements available can greatly affect the accuracy of the

---

[89] *See* Jane E. Buikstra and Douglas H. Ubelaker, *Standards for Data Collection from Human Skeletal Remains: Proceedings of a Seminar at the Field Museum of Natural History,* Spiral-Bound, Fig. 4, (Arkansas Archeological Survey 1994)(illustrating visible differences in male and female facial and cranial characteristics). *See also* Erin H. Kimmerle, et al., "Sexual Dimorphism in America: Geometric Morphometric Analysis of the Craniofacial Region," 53 J. FORENSIC SCI. 54 (2008).

[90] Cristina Cattaneo and Davide Porta, "Sex Determination of Remains," in WILEY ENCYCLOPEDIA OF FORENSIC SCIENCE, (Jamieson A. & Moenssens A.A., eds) 2009 & online updates.

[91] Jane E. Buikstra and Douglas H. Ubelaker, *Standards for Data Collection from Human Skeletal Remains: Proceedings of a Seminar at the Field Museum of Natural History,* Arkansas Archeological Survey (1994).

[92] P.L. Walker, "Sexing Skulls Using Discriminant Function Analysis of Visually Assessed Traits," 136 AMER. J. OF PHYS. ANTHROP. 39–50 (2008).

[93] *FORDISC* 3.0, created by Stephen D. Ousley and Richard L. Jantz, is an interactive computer program for comparing skeletal measurements to database profiles to help forensic anthropologists with classifications. *FORDISC* 3.0 Personal Computer Forensic Discriminant Functions.

sex determination. For example, cranial morphological variability makes *FORDISC* a relatively unreliable tool for making sex determinations from cranial measurements alone.[94]

§10.06 AGE AT DEATH

The aging process has three phases: growth and development, equilibrium, and senescence.[95] Due to individual variation, both in genetics and in environmental influences (diet, stress, activity), the timing of these phases can result in a divergence of "skeletal age" from chronological age.[96] Chronological age is the number of years lived since birth while skeletal or biological age is determined by physiological factors during development of degeneration. Since forensic anthropologists analyze features that reflect skeletal age, these age at death determinations involve correlations with observations in individuals of known age,[97] and databases of known aged individuals are essential for these correlations. The age at death determinations are not exact and are stated in ranges that may increase later in life after the moderately predictable growth and development phase has passed.[98] This increase in error rates is known as the "Trajectory Effect."[99]

Forensic anthropological methods for determining age at death focus on two types of age-related changes: formative changes (such as epiphyseal closure rates and dental eruption) and degenerative changes (such as the degree of osteoarthritis).[100] A variety of methods are used to estimate age at death. Professional standards require these methods to be based on age indicators that meet four criteria: "1) morphological changes proceed unidirectionally with age; 2) features have a high correlation with chronological age; 3) changes occur roughly at the same age in all individuals (at least within a distinguishable subgroup); and 4) the characteristics are measured or classified with known intra- and inter-observer error rates."[101] There are many methods available for

---

[94] Pierre Guyomarc'h and Jaroslav Bruzek, "Accuracy and Reliability in Sex Determination from Skulls: A Comparison of *Fordisc* 3.0 and the Discriminant Function Analysis," 208 FORENSIC SCI. INT'L 180.e1–180.e6 (2011).

[95] Patrick Randolph-Quinney, Xanthe Mallett and Sue Black, "Anthropology," in WILEY ENCYCLOPEDIA OF FORENSIC SCIENCE, (Jamieson A. & Moenssens A.A., eds) 2009 & online updates.

[96] Id.

[97] *See* Scientific Working Group for Forensic Anthropology, "Age Assessment," issued 06/03/2010, p. 1 (available at www.swganth.org).

[98] Patrick Randolph-Quinney, Xanthe Mallett and Sue Black, "Anthropology," in WILEY ENCYCLOPEDIA OF FORENSIC SCIENCE, (Jamieson A. & Moenssens A.A., eds) 2009 & online updates.

[99] S.P. Nawrocki, "The Nature and Sources of Error in Estimation of Age at Death from the Human Skeleton," in K.E. Lantham and M. Finnegan (eds), *Age Estimation of the Human Skeleton,* Charles C. Thomas Publisher, 2010.

[100] Debra A. Komar and Jane E. Buikstra. *Forensic Anthropology: Contemporary Theory and Practice,* Oxford University Press, 2008.

[101] *See* Scientific Working Group for Forensic Anthropology, "Sex Assessment," issued 06/03/2010, p. 2 (available at www.swganth.org).

estimating age at death, but no single method has 100% accuracy. All methods for estimating age at death have two sources of error: (1) variation in the individual; and (2) population variations.[102]

Forensic anthropological methods used to determine age at death differ for sub-adults and adults. The techniques for sub-adults are based on changes in bone related to growth (formative changes), while the methods used for adults are based on changes due to degeneration of the bone. In the case of a sub-adult, the distinctive features of the teeth and long bones (bones of the arms and legs) are primarily used to estimate age at death.[103] For adults, the most reliable methods use late fusing epiphyses that persist into the twenties, morphological changes to specific joint surfaces such as the pubic symphysis and auricular surface of the pelvis and sternal rib ends, microscopic features of the long bones, or a combination of those features. Other methods of determining age at death, such as degree of fusion of the cranial sutures[104] or of the maxillary sutures of the hard palate[105] or osteoarthritic changes in the joints may be used in conjunction with the foregoing methods. However, these additional methods are not considered reliable enough to be used alone.[106] If the skull is the only skeletal element submitted for examination, a limited age estimate reported in decades based on cranial suture closure and in the general categories of child, adolescent, young, middle aged, or old adult in the case of maxillary suture closure may be assigned.[107]

Age estimations depend greatly on the skeletal elements available and the degree of taphonomic damage.[108] Environmental conditions can change the appearance of the pertinent macroscopic and even microscopic characteristics of bone (such as porosity). In order to obtain the best assurance of an accurate estimate of the age at death, the maximum number of methods should be used. The age ranges estimated by

---

[102] Debra A. Komar and Jane E. Buikstra. *Forensic Anthropology: Contemporary Theory and Practice,* Oxford University Press, 2008.

[103] Richard O. Pfau and Paul Sciulli, "A Method for Establishing the Age of Sub-Adults," 39 J. Forensic Sci. 165 (1994).

[104] *See* Jane E. Buikstra and Douglas H. Ubelaker, *Standards for Data Collection from Human Skeletal Remains: Proceedings of a Seminar at the Field Museum of Natural History,* Spiral-Bound, pp. 32–38 (Arkansas Archeological Survey 1994)(describing the methods for age determinations based on rate of cranial suture closure).

[105] Robert Mann, et al., "Maxillary Suture Obliteration: Aging the Human Skeleton Based on Intact or Fragmentary Maxilla," 32 J. Forensic Sci. 148 (1987); Kathy Gruspier and Grant Mullen, "Maxillary Suture Obliteration: A Test of the Mann Method," 36 J. Forensic Sci. 512 (1991); Robert Mann, et al., "Maxillary Suture Obliteration: A Visual Method for Estimating Skeletal Age," 36 J. Forensic Sci. 781 (1991).

[106] Jamie Ginter, "A Test of the Effectiveness of the Revised Maxillary Suture Obliteration Method in Estimating Adult Age at Death," 50 J. FORENSIC SCI. 1303 (2005). *See also* Israel Hershkovitz, et al., "Why do We Fail in Aging the Skull from the Sagittal Suture?," 103 AM. J. PHYS. ANTHRO. 393 (1997).

[107] Robert Mann, et al., "Maxillary Suture Obliteration: A Visual Method for Estimating Skeletal Age," 36 J. Forensic Sci. 781 at 790 (1991).

[108] Daniel Franklin, "Forensic Age Estimation in Human Skeletal Remains: Current Concepts and Future Directions," 12 LEGAL MEDICINE 1–7 (2010).

different methods should be integrated (not averaged) appropriately so that the narrowest, most accurate age range can be achieved. No one method should be used as the single criterion for judging the skeletal age in forensic cases.[109]

1. SUB-ADULTS

Dental eruption, epiphyseal closure rates, and skeletal measurement methods are the primary means used to estimate age in sub-adult skeletal remains.[110] One of the most accurate methods of determining age at death in sub-adults (of sufficient age)[111] depends upon an assessment of the degree of completeness in the formation of tooth roots and the degree of eruption of deciduous (baby, temporary) teeth.[112] Tooth formation, tooth eruption, and deciduous teeth root resorption generally occur at predictable ages within a population absent rare diseases or disorders. Standardized data are reported in charts that have been devised that show the progression of formation, eruption, and resorption for many different populations.[113] Most charts separate males and females because the rate differs between them. Charts separating the sexes have a smaller range of error.[114]

---

[109] S. Saunders, et al., "A Test of Several Methods of Skeletal Age Estimation Using a Documented Archaeological Sample," 25 CAN. SOC. FORENSIC SCI. J. 97, 116 (1992); C. Owen Lovejoy, et al., "Test of the Multifactorial Aging Method Using Skeletons with Known Ages-at-death from the Grant Collection," 91 AM. J. PHYS. ANTHRO. 287 (1993); Virginia Galera, et al., "Comparison of Macroscopic Cranial Methods of Age Estimation Applied to Skeletons from the Terry Collection," 43 J. FORENSIC SCI. 933 (1998).

[110] Daniel Franklin, "Forensic Age Estimation in Human Skeletal Remains: Current Concepts and Future Directions," 12 LEGAL MEDICINE 1–7 (2010).

[111] For fetal or infant remains where accurate assessment of dental development is not possible, professional standards advocate using long bone measurements, assessment of the development of the ilium and the petrous portion of the temporal bone, and the maturation of other skeletal elements. See Scientific Working Group for Forensic Anthropology, "Sex Assessment," issued 06/03/2010, p. 3 (available at www.swganth.org).

See also Michael W. Warren, "Radiographic Determination of Developmental Age in Fetuses and Stillborns," 44 J. FORENSIC SCI. 708 (1999). Another method of determining a fetal/newborn age involves the vertebral column. F. Kosa and C. Castellana, "New Forensic Anthropological Approachment for the Age Determination of Human Fetal Skeletons on the Base of Morphometry of Vertebral Column," 147 SUPP. FORENSIC SCI. INT'L S69 (2005).

[112] *See* Helena Ranta, et al., "Reliability and Validity of Eight Dental Age Estimation Methods for Adults," 48 J. FORENSIC SCI. 149 (2003), and Niels Lynnerup, et al., "Evaluation of Post-Mortem Estimated Dental Age Versus Real Age: A Retrospective 21-Year Survey," 159 SUPP. FORENSIC SCI. INT'L 1 S84 (2006); H.M. Liversidge and Theya Molleson, "Developing Permanent Tooth Length as an Estimate of Age," 44 J. FORENSIC SCI. 917 (1999). Anthropologists have also proposed a new, related technique involving mandibular measurements of sub-adults. D. Franklin and A. Cardini, "Mandibular Morphology As an Indicator of Human Subadult Age: Interlandmark Approaches," 52 J. FORENSIC SCI. 1015 (2008).

[113] Michele Muller-Bolla et al., "Age Estimation from Teeth in Children and Adolescents," 48 J. FORENSIC SCI. 140 (2003); Bruno Foti *et al.*, "New Forensic Approach to Age Determination in Children Based on Tooth Eruption," 132 FORENSIC SCI. INT'L. 49 (2003); Aurora Valenzuela, et al., "Multiple Regression Models for Age Estimation by Assessment of Morphologic Dental Changes According to Teeth Source," 23 AM. J. FORENSIC MED. PATH. 386 (2004).

[114] A. A. El-Nofely, "Dental Aging for Egyptian and Other Middle Eastern Children," 22 CAN. SOC. FORENSIC SCI. J. 130 (1989).

To estimate age by dental features, radiographs are obtained from the maxilla and mandible. Each tooth is examined to determine presence and degree of formation of the crown and root. The degree of resorption of the roots of the deciduous teeth is also examined in older sub-adults who are losing these teeth. The results of these examinations are compared to the charts of known individuals from the appropriate reference populations to determine an accurate age. Research suggests that conventional measurement methods are equal to or superior to computer-assisted measurement methods.[115]

Using the same developmental theory, age at death estimations for sub-adults who are still growing may be made by taking radiographs of the long bones to assess fusion at the epiphyses. If the long bones are unavailable, the technique may also be used with other bones.[116] Each long bone consists of the diaphysis (the long shaft of the bone) and the epiphysis (the ends of the bone). During growth, the diaphysis and epiphysis gradually fuse together at the metaphysis (the growth plate). Growth stops when union of the epiphysis and the diaphysis is complete. Several skeletal components do not complete growth until the second or third decade, making this method applicable to young adults.[117] The timing and sequence of epiphyseal union vary among individuals, particularly between the sexes, as females exhibit complete union at earlier ages than males. With several years between initial and final closure, the degree of closure must be evaluated carefully and the age at death interval adjusted accordingly. While direct observation of the skeletal element can be performed, radiographic assessment is more accurate for determining the degree of fusion. In order to obtain the most accurate age estimate, the degree of fusion should be assessed for multiple skeletal elements per individual.

2. ADULTS

Age at death estimation methods for adults (except for young adults who have not completed the growth and development phase) generally rely on degenerative changes that occur with age. The primary methods for estimating age at death in adults are based on either the observation of morphological changes or the application of histomorphometry.[118] The forensic anthropology methods, macroscopic and microscopic, typically result in large range estimates for age (10–15

---

[115] Kristin M. Kolltveit, et al., "Methods of Measuring Morphological Parameters in Dental Radiographs. Comparison Between Image Analysis and Manual Measurements," 94 Forensic Sci. Int'l 87 (1998).

[116] *See* S. Serinelli, V. Panetta, P. Pasqualetti and D. Marchetti, "Accuracy of Three Age Determination X-Ray Methods on the Left Hand-Wrist: A Systematic Review and Meta-Analysis," 13 LEGAL MEDICINE 120–133 (2011).

[117] Patrick Randolph-Quinney, Xanthe Mallett and Sue Black, "Anthropology," in WILEY ENCYCLOPEDIA OF FORENSIC SCIENCE, (Jamieson A. & Moenssens A.A., eds) 2009 & online updates.

[118] Daniel Franklin, "Forensic Age Estimation in Human Skeletal Remains: Current Concepts and Future Directions," 12 LEGAL MEDICINE 1–7 (2010).

years).[119] Morphological techniques are the primary method for age estimations in adults and involve analysis of the degree of degeneration at articulations of the pubic symphysis, osteochondral surface of the fourth rib, and the auricular and acetabular surfaces of the *os coxae*.[120]

a.   Gross Morphology

i.   Pubic Symphysis

The most widely used methods involve the examination of the pubic symphysis. The pubic symphysis is located at the center of the pelvic girdle where the left and right pubic bones join. The left and right pubic bones have a small amount of cartilage between them that allows for a small amount of movement between the bones. (See Figures 3 and 4.) The area examined is that which is revealed when the pubic bones are separated and the cartilage is removed. The appearance of this area changes in a predictable manner as a person ages, although there is more variability in females. A phase number and a corresponding age range are assigned to the individual based on the morphology of the pubic symphysis and the relative characteristics of different parts of the surface.

The changes in the pubic symphysis and their relationship to the aging of individuals were first documented by Todd in 1920 using ten phases.[121] In 1955, Brooks modified Todd's method, changing some of the morphological patterns for some ages and shifting the ages assigned to the different phases.[122] McKern and Stewart proposed a method in 1957 which utilized only three components of the pubic symphysis in the determination of age.[123] In the late 1980's, Suchey and Brooks introduced a technique including six phases describing morphological changes and their corresponding ages.[124] The Suchey and Brooks technique was

---

[119] Cristina Cattaneo, "Anthropology: Age Determination of Remains," in WILEY ENCYCLOPEDIA OF FORENSIC SCIENCE, (Jamieson A. & Moenssens A.A., eds) 2009 & online updates.

[120] Id. ("The rationale behind [the selection of] these anatomical sites is that they are articulations, which are equally stressed for all individuals, regardless of activity. Thus, they should reveal a degree of degeneration, which should be proportional only to the age and thus standardizable for aging procedures.").

Research using age estimations from teeth has also shown reliability and intra-population stability. Stefanio De Luca, Josefina Bautista, Inmaculada Aleman and Roberto Cameriere, "Age-at-Death Estimation by Pulp/Tooth Area Ratio in Canines: Study of 20th-Century Mexican Sample of Prisoners to Test Cameriere's Method," 56 J. FORENSIC SCI. 1302–1309 (2011).

[121] T. Wingate Todd, "Age Changes in the Pubic Bone I. The Male White Pubic," 3 AM. J. PHYS. ANTHRO. 467 (1920).

[122] Sheilagh T. Brooks, "Skeletal Age at Death: Reliability of Cranial and Pubic Age Indicators," 13 AM. J. PHYS. ANTHRO. 567 (1955).

[123] Thomas W. McKern and Thomas D. Stewart, "Skeletal Age Changes in Young American Males: Analyzed from the Standpoint of Age Identification," 24 AM. ANTIQUITY 198 (1958).

[124] Sheilagh T. Brooks and Judy M. Suchey, "Skeletal Age Determination Based on the Os Pubis: A Comparison of the Acsadi-Nemeskeri and Suchey-Brooks Methods," 5 HUMAN EVOL. 227 (1990).

updated and a phase seven was introduced in a study by Hartnett and Fulginiti using known pubic symphysis taken from a modern autopsy sample.[125] The Hartnett-Fulginiti study emphasized bone quality as a major factor for the later phases.[126, 127]

Figure 3: The human pelvis, anterior view. Pubic symphysis identified. William M. Bass, *Human Osteology: A Laboratory and Field Manual,* Third Edition, 186 (1987).

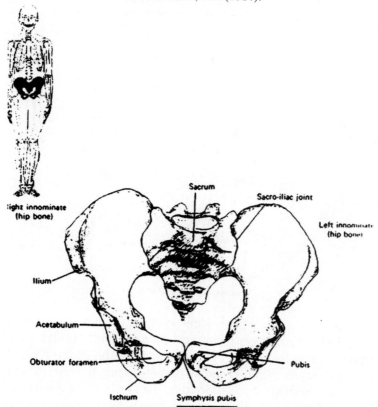

Changes in the pubic symphysis are sexually dimorphic so the older methods separated guidelines for males and females.[128] The Suchey and Brooks six phase technique defines the phases by characteristics found in both males and females in the same progression; however, the age range assigned to each of these phases is different for males and females. For example, a pubic symphysis from a male classified as phase III under

---

[125] *See* Kristen M. Hartnett, "A re-evaluation and revision of pubic symphysis and fourth rib aging techniques," PhD dissertation, School of Human Evolution and Social Change. Arizona State University, Tempe, 2007.

[126] Kristen M. Hartnett, "Analysis of age-at-death estimation using data from a new, modern autopsy sample—part I: pubic bone," 55 J. Forensic Sci. 1145–1151 (2010).

[127] Kristen M. Hartnett, "Analysis of age-at-death estimation using data from a new, modern autopsy sample—part II: sternal end of the fourth rib," 55 J. Forensic Sci. 1152–1156 (2010).

[128] Judy M. Suchey, "Problems in the Aging of Females Using the Os Pubis," 51 AM. J. PHYS. ANTHRO. 467 (1979).

this method would be aged within a range of 21 years to 46 years, while a female would be aged from 21 years to 53 years.[129] The Hartnett-Fulginiti method separates males and females and offers specific criteria for each sex with different age ranges.[130]

Figure 4: View of the face of the pubic symphysis, used in the estimation of age. William M. Bass, *Human Osteology: A Laboratory and Field Manual*, Third Edition, 186 (1987).

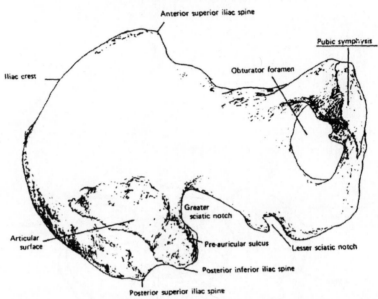

Age-related changes in the pubic symphysis may also be affected by ancestry, particularly in younger age ranges. Thus, under the Suchey-Brooks progression formula, if the ancestry of the individual is known, the pubic symphysis is assigned a phase (using the six phases of the Suchey-Brooks method), and compared to a statistical table to determine the age range for the specific ancestry. Some researchers have proposed population specific estimates.[131] Additional research suggests the application of digital imaging and radiological techniques to pubic

---

[129] Sheilagh T. Brooks and Judy M. Suchey, "Skeletal Age Determination Based on the Os Pubis: A Comparison of the Acsadi-Nemeskeri and Suchey-Brooks Methods," 5 HUMAN EVOL. 227, 233 (1990). Recent researchers have suggested a modification of the phases, *see* G.E. Burge, "Pubic Bone Age Estimation in Adult Women," 53 J. FORENSIC SCI. 569 (2008)(suggesting "the need for a new phase, phase VII, that follows the Suchey-Brooks phase VI").

[130] *See* Kristen M. Hartnett, "A re-evaluation and revision of pubic symphysis and fourth rib aging techniques," PhD dissertation, School of Human Evolution and Social Change. Arizona State University, Tempe, 2007.

[131] *See, e.g.,* E.H. Kimmerle, L.W. Konigsberg, R.L. Jantz, and J.P.Baraybar, "Analysis of age-at-death estimation through the use of pubic symphyseal data," 53 J. Forensic Sci. 558–568 (2008); X. Chen, Z. Zhang, and L. Tao, "Determination of male age at death in Chinese Han population: using quantitative variables statistical analysis from pubic bones," 175 Forensic Sci. Int. 36–43 (2008).

symphysis analysis.[132] For example, in 2014 Wink demonstrated that CT scans of the pelvis are adequate for creating 3D images of the pubic symphysis.[133]

ii.   Auricular Surface

The auricular surface of the ilium, like the pubic symphysis, is an important feature of the *os coxa* which changes over time.[134] The auricular ("ear-shaped") surface is the articulation joint with the sacrum and has a fairly high survival rate, which increases its forensic significance.[135] Originally a method for estimating age from changes to the auricular surface was developed on a large archaeological sample.[136] These scientists divided morphological changes describing the surface into eight distinct age-correlated phases. Buckberry and Chamberlain revised the phase method into a component based system that eliminated retroauricular activity from consideration and instead emphasized transverse organization of the striae, surface texture, microporosity, macroporosity, and apical changes.[137] The methods for estimating age from the auricular surface have been tested and criticized as difficult to apply, in part because of the lack of comparative materials. "The amount of degenerative change in the auricular surface is not dependent upon race or sex in any given age category. However, the rate of degenerative change is too variable to be used as a single criterion for the estimation of age; the range of estimation is simply too large for forensic science purposes."[138] More recent efforts have attempted to evaluate the effects of obesity on the auricular surface aging and the use

---

[132] *See* Myra Sitchon & Robert Hoppa, "Assessing Age-related Morphology of the Pubic Symphysis from Digital Images Versus Direct Observation," 50 J. FORENSIC SCI. 791 (2005); Norbert Telmon, et al., "Application of the Suchey-Brooks Method to Three-Dimensional Imaging of the Pubic Symphysis," 50 J. FORENSIC SCI. 507 (2005).

[133] A.E. Wink, "Pubic symphyseal age estimation from three-dimensional reconstructions of pelvic CT scans of live individuals," 59 J. Forensic Sci. 696–702 (2014).

[134] C. Owen Lovejoy, et al., "Chronological Metamorphosis of the Auricular Surface of the Ilium: A New Method for the Determination of Adult Skeletal Age at Death," 68 AM. J. PHYS. ANTHRO.15 (1985); *See also* Daniel Osborne, et al., "Reconsidering the Auricular Surface as an Indicator of Age at Death," 49 J. FORENSIC SCI. 905 (2004)(concluding that "auricular surface performs as well as any other single skeletal indicator of adult age"); Yuriko Igarashi, et al., "New Method for Estimation of Adult Skeletal Age at Death from the Morphology of the Auricular Surface of the Ilium," 128 AM. J. PHYS. ANTHRO. 324 (2005); Clotilde Rouge-Maillart, et al., "The Determination of Male Adult Age at Death by Central and Posterior Coxal Analysis: A Preliminary Study," 49 J. FORENSIC SCI. 208 (2004).

[135] Jo L. Buckberry and Andrew Chamberlain, "New Method for Estimation of Adult Skeletal Age at Death from the Morphology of the Auricular Surface of the Ilium," 119 AM. J. PHYS. ANTHRO. 324 (2002)(noting "the higher survival rates of the auricular surface compared with the pubic symphysis").

[136] C.O. Lovejoy, et al., "Chronological metamorphosis of the auricular surface of the ilium: a new method for the determination of adult skeletal age at death," 68 Am. J. Phys. Anthropol. 15–28 (1985).

[137] J.L. Buckberry and A.T. Chamberlain, "Age estimation from the auricular surface of the ilium: a revised method," 119 Am. J. Phys. Anthropol. 231–239 (2002).

[138] Katherine Murray and Tracy Murray, "A Test of the Auricular Surface Aging Technique," 36 J. Forensic Sci. 1162 (1991).

of CT scans for evaluating this feature.[139] The auricular surface, in spite of criticism, continues to be used to estimate age at death in unknown human remains.

iii. Sternal Ends of Ribs

The sternal ends of the ribs—the ends of the ribs that articulate with the costal cartilage in the front of the body—also change in a predictable manner as a person ages. Iscan, Loth, and Wright first introduced a method of determining age from the ends of the ribs in 1984 and have continually updated their system.[140] The theory underlying this approach is the same as the theory supporting the estimate of age from the changes in the pubic symphysis. The morphological features of the rib that are examined are the amount of billowing or depth and shape of pitting of the articular surface, the appearance of the rim around the articular surface, the quality of the bone, and the presence or absence of bony projections. This method has been applied to a range of populations.[141]

The sternal rib end is assigned to a phase based on its morphology. Each phase is representative of a range of ages. The analysis of the morphological features is complex, but in general a deep pit, an irregular rim end, and poor quality of the bone are indicators of an older individual. The morphological features characteristic of each phase and the consequent age range assigned to each phase are different for males and females, with males more likely to ossify along the margins of the rib cartilage and females more likely to ossify outward from the rib end and through the center of the rib cartilage.[142]

Hartnett and Fulginiti assessed over 600 sets of known sternal rib ends and provided an update to Iscan et al. that included a seventh phase

---

[139] *See* P. Barrier et al., "Age at death estimation using multislice computed tomography reconstructions of the posterior pelvis," 54 J. Forensic Sci. 773–778 (2009). O. Ferrant et al., "Age at death estimation of adult males using coxal bone and CT scan: a preliminary study," 186 Forensic Sci. Int. 14–21 (2009). D.J. Wescott and J.L. Drew, "Effect of obesity on the reliability of age-at-death indicators of the pelvis," 156 Am. J. Phys. Anthropol. 595–605 (2015).

[140] M. Yasar Iscan, et al., "Age Estimation from the Rib by Phase Analysis: White Males," 29 J. Forensic Sci. 1094 (1984); M. Yasar Iscan, et al., "Age Estimation from the Rib by Phase Analysis: White Females," 30 J. Forensic Sci. 853 (1985); M. Yasar Iscan and Susan R. Loth, "Determination of Age from the Sternal Rib in White Males: A Test of the Phase Method," 31 J. Forensic Sci. 122 (1986); M. Yasar Iscan and Susan R. Loth, "Determination of Age from the Sternal Rib in White Females: A Test of the Phase Method," 31 J. Forensic Sci. 990 (1986); Susan R. Loth, et al., "Intercostal Variation at the Sternal End of the Rib," 65 Forensic Sci. Int'l 135 (1994); Cassady Yoder, et al., "Examination of Variation in Sternal Rib End Morphology Relevant to Age Assessment," 46 J. FORENSIC SCI. 223 (2001).

[141] *See* M. Yasar Iscan, et al., "Age Assessment by Rib Phase Analysis in Turks," 98 Forensic Sci. Int'l 47 (1998); M. Yasar Iscan, et al., "Racial Variation in the Sternal Extremity of the Rib and Its Effect on Age Determination," 32 J. Forensic Sci. 452 (1987).

[142] Jane E. Buikstra and Douglas H. Ubelaker, *Standards for Data Collection from Human Skeletal Remains: Proceedings of a Seminar at the Field Museum of Natural History*, Spiral-Bound, Fig. 4, (Arkansas Archeological Survey 1994).

for both males and females.[143] Bone quality again played a significant role in their phase system. Berg included a seventh phase for females in his 2008 publication as well.[144]

b.   Transition Analysis

In order to address some of the statistical uncertainties that arise in the estimation of age at death in adult skeletal remains, particularly for adults older than 50 years of age, Boldsen and colleagues developed a method for combining skeletal age indicators mathematically to produce statistical likelihood estimates of age at death with associated confidence intervals.[145] Referred to as "Transition Analysis" because it relies upon estimated age of transition between age phases, this method utilizes Bayesian probability statistics and observations of characteristics of the pubic symphysis, auricular surface, and cranial suture closure together in order to help account for variability in the aging process.[146] A probability density function is used to calculate mean age at transition for skeletal traits. While transition analysis offers solutions to several age-estimation issues (e.g. age-mimicry, large ranges in older adults, inaccurate representation of estimate uncertainty), required assumptions about the associated reference sample and scoring techniques must be considered in evaluation of the method.[147]

c.   Histomorphometric Methods

Determination of age at death in adults can also be achieved through the microscopic examination of histomorphic structures of bones. The microscopic method of determining age using long bones, first devised by Kerley in 1965,[148] has been reviewed and updated several times.[149] The

---

[143] Kristen M. Hartnett, "Analysis of age-at-death estimation using data from a new, modern autopsy sample—part II: sternal end of the fourth rib," 55 J. Forensic Sci. 1152–1156 (2010).

[144] G.E. Berg, "Pubic bone age estimation in adult women," 53 J. Forensic Sci. 569–577 (2008).

[145] J.L. Boldsen, G.R. Milner, L.W. Konigsberg and J.W. Wood, "Transition Analyses: A New Method for Estimating Age from Skeletal Samples," in R.D. Hoppa and J.W. Vaupel, eds., *Paleodemography: Age Distributions from Skeletal Samples,* Cambridge University Press, 2002, at pp. 73–106.

[146] Boldsen et al. (2002) have published a statistical package for use in transition analysis, ADBOU, available from http://math.mercyhurst.edu/~sousley/Software/. Instructions for performing transition analysis using the R statistical package is available from Dr. Lyle Konigsberg's website (link available at http://www.anthro.illinois.edu/people/lylek).

[147] For further discussion, *see* L.W. Konigsberg, N.P. Herrmann, D.J. Wescott, and E.H. Kimmerle, "Estimation and Evidence in Forensic Anthropology: Age-at-Death. 53 J. FORENSIC SCI. 541–557 (2008).

[148] Ellis Kerley, "The Microscopic Determination of Age in Human Bone," 23 AM. J. PHYS. ANTHRO. 149 (1965).

[149] I.J. Singh and D.L. Gunberg, "Estimation of Age at Death in Human Males from Quantitative Histology of Bone Fragments." 33 AM. J. PHYS. ANTHRO. 373 (1970); Ellis R. Kerley and Douglas H. Ubelaker "Revisions in the Microscopic Method of Estimating Age at Death in Human Cortical Bone," 49 AM. J. PHYS. ANTHRO. 545 (1978); Mary F. Ericksen, "Histologic Estimation of Age at Death Using the Anterior Cortex of the Femur," 84 AM. J. PHYS. ANTHRO.

method involves taking a thin section of the femur, tibia, and fibula and microscopically examining it in four small circular areas (the diameter being approximately 1.62mm)[150] from the outer section of the bone. The number of primary osteons (formed when the surrounding bone was formed), secondary osteons (formed when the bone is remodeled), osteon fragments (results from remodeling), and the percentage of compact lamellar bone (evenly spaced bands of bone that are parallel to each other and appear as long, parallel fibers under the microscope) present in the sample are calculated. The numbers are used in regression equations that determine the age at death of the individual. This method has been used with fragmented bones, even if the entire cross section is not present, and does not appear dependent on age, sex, or ancestry.[151] Other factors, however, such as population differences, nutrition, disease, and socioeconomic status, have been shown to influence the rate of bone turnover and the accuracy of histomorphometric methods.[152]

Other histomorphometric methods for determining adult age involve analysis of the teeth[153] and measured bone density.[154]

§10.07 ANCESTRY

The determination of ancestry is one of the more problematic assessments for forensic anthropologists.[155] As race is not a biological construct, some anthropologists reject the position that modern humans

---

171 (1991); Douglas H. Ubelaker, "The Evolving Role of the Microscope in Forensic Anthropology," in Kathleen J. Reichs ed., *Forensic Osteology Advances in the Identification of Human Remains*, 2d ed., Charles C. Thomas Publisher,1998, at p. 514; Niels Lynnerup, et al., "Intra- and Inter-observer Variation in Histological Criteria Used in Age at Death Determination Based on Femoral Cortical Bone," 91 Forensic Sci. Int'l 219 (1998); Christian M. Crowder, et al., "Variation in Cortical Bone Histology Within the Human Femur and Its Impact on Estimating Age at Death," 132 AM. J. PHYS. ANTHRO. 80 (2006); Niels Lynnerup, et al., "Assessment of Age at Death by Microscopy: Unbiased Quantification of Secondary Osteons in Femoral Cross Sections," 159 SUPPL. 1 FORENSIC SCI. INT'L S100 (2006).

150 Samuel. D. Stout and Sarah J. Gehlert, "Effects of Field Size When Using Kerley's Histological Method for Determination of Age at Death," 58 AM. J. PHYS. ANTHRO. 123, 125 (1982).

151 *See* Samuel. D. Stout, et al., "Population-specific Histological Age-estimating Method: A Model for Known African-American and European-American Skeletal Remains," 47 J. FORENSIC SCI. 12 (2002)(addressing variations caused by ancestral differences).

152 N. Keough, E.N. L'Abbe and M. Steyn, "The Evaluation of Age-Related Histomorphometric Variables in a Cadaver Sample of Lower Socioeconomic Status: Implications for Estimating Age at Death," 191 FORENSIC SCI. INT'L 114.e1–114.e6 (2009).

153 P. Kagerer and G. Grupe, "On the Validity of Individual Age-at-death Diagnosis by Incremental Line Counts in Human Dental Cementum," 59 ANTHRO. ANZEIGER 331 (2001); R. Jankauskas, et al., "Incremental Lines of Dental Cementum in Biological Age Estimation," 52 HOMO. 59 (2001). *See also* G. González-Colmenares, at al., "Age Estimation by a Dental Method: A Comparison of Lamendin's and Prince & Ubelaker's Technique," 52 J. FORENSIC SCI. 1156 (2008).

154 Rafael Fernandez Castillo and Maria del Carmen Lopez Ruiz, "Assessment of Age and Sex by Means of DXA Bone Densitometry: Application in Forensic Anthropology," 209 FORENSIC SCI. INT'L 53–58 (2011).

155 Patrick Randolph-Quinney, Xanthe Mallett and Sue Black, "Anthropology," in WILEY ENCYCLOPEDIA OF FORENSIC SCIENCE, (Jamieson A. & Moenssens A.A., eds) 2009 & online updates.

can be subdivided clearly based on ancestral origin.[156] However, due to histories of reproductively and geographically separated populations, modern humans do exhibit some traits that display regional population differences.[157] The global population trend toward progressive genetic integration makes it increasingly difficult to estimate ancestry, but anthropological observations can suggest an affiliation with a particular major ancestral group. Ancestry may be categorized broadly as European, African, and Asian, which typically includes individuals from Native American and Inuit ancestry.[158] Like the estimation of sex, the estimation of ancestry from skeletal material is based on either gross morphological examination or mathematical analysis of different measurements of morphological features.[159] The most reliable indicator of ancestry is the skull.[160]

1.   GROSS MORPHOLOGY

The morphological features examined in the bones of the skull that may be used in estimates of ancestry are summarized in the attached chart. (*See* Table 2.)

---

[156] *See* Norm J. Sauer, "Forensic Anthropology and the Concept of Race: If Races Don't Exist, Why Are Forensic anthropologists So Good at Identifying Them?," 34 SOCIAL SCI. AND MED. 107–111 (1992).

[157] S.D. Ousley and R.L. Jantz, "Social Races and Human Populations: Why Forensic anthropologists are Good at Identifying Races," 34 AM. J. PHYS. ANTHRO. Annual Meeting Issue, 121.

[158] Cristina Cattaneo, "Anthropology: Ancestry and Stature Determination," in WILEY ENCYCLOPEDIA OF FORENSIC SCIENCE, (Jamieson A. & Moenssens A.A., eds) 2009 & online updates. Others use an additional category of Australoid (Australian Aborigines, Pacific Islanders, Fijians, and Papuans). Patrick Randolph-Quinney, Xanthe Mallett and Sue Black, "Anthropology," in WILEY ENCYCLOPEDIA OF FORENSIC SCIENCE, (Jamieson A. & Moenssens A.A., eds) 2009 & online updates.

[159] *See* Scientific Working Group for Forensic Anthropology, "Ancestry Assessment," issued 06/12/2013 (available at www.swganth.org).

[160] Patrick Randolph-Quinney, Xanthe Mallett and Sue Black, "Anthropology," in WILEY ENCYCLOPEDIA OF FORENSIC SCIENCE, (Jamieson A. & Moenssens A.A., eds) 2009 & online updates.

Table 2: Ancestry Determination *

Morphological Feature	European	African	Asian
Zygomatic Bones	Retreating (No Projection)	Little Projection	Marked Projection
Eye Orbits	Triangular	Rectangular	Circular
Nasal Aperture Shape Lower Margin	Narrow Nasal Sill	Wide Nasal Guttering	Moderate Slightly Pointed
Palate	Narrow	Broad	Moderate
Alveolar process of maxilla	Flat	Prognathous	Flat

* Derived from Douglas H. Ubelaker, *Human Skeletal Remains: Excavation, Analysis, Interpretation* Second Edition 119, (1989), and William M. Bass, *Human Osteology: A Laboratory and Field Manual* Third Edition, 83–88, (1987).

Examination of the relative curvature of the femur as a method of ancestry estimation has been shown reliable for Americans of African and European descent and Native Americans, but unreliable for other populations.[161] Marked femoral curvature is more likely to be Native American populations, lack of curvature is seen in African populations, and medium curvature may be noted in European populations. However, there is considerable overlap between ancestral groups (*i.e.,* there is greater variability within an ancestral group than between groups) and the trait can be difficult to assess without comparative samples.

2.   METRIC ASSESSMENT

Nonmetric assessments of ancestry based on "trait lists" have been criticized as too subjective and inherently biased;[162] therefore, metric assessments increasingly are used in assessing ancestry.[163] Metric assessments of the pelvis[164] and other postcranial bones[165] have been

---

[161] B. Miles Gilbert, "Anterior Femoral Curvature: Its Probable Basis and Utility as a Criterion of Racial Assessment," 45 AM. J. PHYS. ANTHRO. 601, 604 (1976); Daniel Wescott, "Population Variation in Femur Subtrochanteric Shape," 50 J. FORENSIC SCI. 286 (2005).

[162] Cris E. Hughes et al., "A Simulation for Exploring the Effects of the 'Trait List' Method's Subjectivity on Consistency and Accuracy in Ancestry Estimations," 56 J. FORENSIC SCI. 1094–1106 (2011).

[163] Sabrina B. Sholts et al., "Identification of Group Affinity from Cross-sectional Contours of the Human Midfacial Skeleton Using Digital Morphometrics and3D Laser Scanning Technology," 56 J. FORENSIC SCI. 333–338 (2011).

[164] *See* Susan R. Loth, et al., "Metric Assessment of Race from the Pelvis in South Africans," 127 Forensic Sci. Int'l 104 (2002); M. Yasar Iscan and Timothy S. Cotton, "The Effect of Age on the Determination of Race from the Pelvis," 14 J. HUM. EVOL. 275, 281 (1985).

[165] James Taylor, et al., "Metropolitan Forensic Anthropology Team (MFAT) Studies in Identification: 1. Race and Sex Assessment by Discriminant Function Analysis of the Postcranial Skeleton," 29 J. Forensic Sci. 798 (1984); Trenton Holliday and Anthony Falsetti, "A New Method

used, but cranial measurement remains the most common technique for estimating ancestry. Giles and Elliot introduced a method that uses measurement of the skull for estimating ancestry in 1962.[166] Currently anthropologists rely upon information from the Howells database,[167] which draws from globally distributed archaeological samples, or from *FORDISC* 3.0, which expands upon the Giles and Elliot data. Regardless of the method used, the limitations of the data upon which *FORDISC* is based must be taken into consideration and recognition made that reference samples often represent a mix of groups.[168]

§10.08 STATURE

The estimation of stature from skeletal remains is possible because of the relationship between skeletal dimensions and height. Until recently, the primary methods for stature estimation used by forensic anthropologists have been based on regression equations developed from collections of known individuals.[169] These equations use long bone lengths to produce estimates of stature, and were formulated with consideration of sex and ancestry differences.[170] The relationship between length and living stature is more reliable for some bones than others, and the more long bones that are able to be measured, the more accurate the estimation of stature during life.

The Complete Skeleton Method (also referred to as the Fully Method) is an alternative approach to the estimation of stature. This method uses aggregated axial and appendicular measurements of a suite of skeletal elements (the cranium, vertebral column from cervical 2 to lumbar 5, the first sacral vertebra, femur, tibia, talus, and calcaneus) to produce an estimate of stature.[171] The measurements are totaled and a soft tissue "correction" is added for the final stature interval, which is considered a slightly more accurate measure of stature than that

---

for Discriminating African-American from European-American Skeletons Using Postcranial Osteometrics Reflective of Body Shape," 44 J. FORENSIC SCI. 926 (1999).

[166] Eugene Giles and Orville Elliot, "Race Identification from Cranial Measurements," 7 J. FORENSIC SCI. 147 (1962).

[167] W.W. Howells, "Who's who in skulls: ethnic identification of crania from measurements," 82 *Papers of the Peabody Museum*, (1995), Peabody Museum of Archaeology and Ethnology, Harvard University, Cambridge, MA.

[168] Debra A. Komar and Jane E. Buikstra. *Forensic Anthropology: Contemporary Theory and Practice,* (New York, NY: Oxford University Press, 2008).

[169] *See* M. Trotter, "Estimation of Stature from Intact Long Bones", In T.D. Stewart (ed) *Personal Identification in Mass Disasters* (Smithsonian, 1970); *also* M. Trotter and G.C. Gleser, "A Re-evaluation of estimation of stature based on measurements of stature taken during life and of long bones after death," 16 AM. J. PHYS. ANTHRO. 79 (1958).

[170] *See* Scientific Working Group for Forensic Anthropology, "Stature Estimation," 08/02/2012, available at www.swganth.org.

[171] Patrick Randolph-Quinney, Xanthe Mallett and Sue Black, "Anthropology," in WILEY ENCYCLOPEDIA OF FORENSIC SCIENCE, (Jamieson A. & Moenssens A.A., eds) 2009 & online updates.

produced by a regression equation.[172] However, because all of the listed skeletal elements must be present and measurable for a calculation, the practical use of this method is limited.[173] Directions for the appropriate measurement method are available in the scientific literature and the "help" files of *FORDISC*.[174]

If no intact long bones are recovered, methods for the estimation of stature using fragmentary limb bones may be employed.[175] The Steele and McKern method for estimating stature from long bone fragments includes data for several different fragments on each long bone.[176] Using these measurements, the length of the long bone can be extrapolated, and the stature estimated using the length of the long bone. If the necessary anatomical landmarks are difficult to locate on the fragmentary bones, three easily located measurements on the femur (the vertical diameter of the femur head, the proximal femur breadth, and the posterior height of the fibular condyle),[177] and five measurements of the lateral and medial condyles of the tibia and their articular surfaces may be used.[178]

If no long bones are recovered, certain non-limb bones may be used to produce a stature estimate.[179] For example, second metacarpal lengths have been reported as reliable in stature approximations.[180]

§10.09 INDIVIDUALIZATION OF HUMAN BONE

There are two forms of identification in the medicolegal investigation of death: scientific and circumstantial. Scientific methods include DNA, fingerprint and dental/medical radiograph comparison. The biological profile produced by examining the skeleton (age, sex, ancestry, and stature) provides a starting place for identification by narrowing the potential pool of possible matches. The primary profile, however, is rarely sufficient to positively identify the human remains. Every individual exhibits unique skeletal characteristics that can be added to a basic biological assessment in order to make scientific identification more

---

[172] *See* Scientific Working Group for Forensic Anthropology, "Stature Estimation," issued 08/02/2012 (available at www.swganth.org).

[173] Id.

[174] P.M. Moore-Jansen, Stephen D. Ousley and Richard L. Jantz, "Data Collection Procedures for Forensic Skeletal Material," *Report of Investigations* No. 48 (Knoxville, TN: University of Tennessee, 1994).

[175] *See* Scientific Working Group for Forensic Anthropology, "Stature Estimation," 08/02/2012, available at www.swganth.org.

[176] *See* Kenneth Jacobs, "Estimating Femur and Tibia Length from Fragmentary Bones: An Evaluation of Steele's (1970) Method Using a Prehistoric European Sample," 89 AM. J. PHYS. ANTHRO. 333 (1992).

[177] Tal Simmons, "Stature Estimation from Fragmentary Femora: A Revision of the Steele Method," 35 J. Forensic Sci. 628, 633, 635 (1990).

[178] Thomas Holland, "Estimation of Adult Stature from Fragmentary Tibias," 37 J. Forensic Sci. 1223 (1992).

[179] *See* Scientific Working Group for Forensic Anthropology, "Stature Estimation," issued 08/02/2012 (available at www.swganth.org).

[180] Lea Meadows and Richard L. Jantz, "Estimation of Stature from Metacarpal Lengths," 37 J. Forensic Sci. 147 (1992).

likely. Pathologic conditions such as healed fractures, arthritic changes, or surgical interventions (*e.g.*, surgical pins, screws or plates), anomalous conditions (normal variants) such as a sternal foramen, extra vertebrae or a septal aperture, or congenital conditions like spina bifida occulta all contribute to a unique profile that narrows the list of potential matches. These individual skeletal features, when added to the basic skeletal evaluation, may provide the initial lead to identification which can then be confirmed by scientific methods such as DNA profile matches, fingerprint comparison, and dental or medical radiograph comparison.[181]

For forensic anthropology, professional standards list comparative radiography and comparison of surgical implants as the methods which may result in a positive identification.[182] Comparative radiography[183] involves comparing antemortem and postmortem radiographs for consistencies and inconsistencies in: "bone morphology; trabecular patterns; orientation and placement of foreign materials, including bullets, shrapnel, surgical implements; skeletal anomalies, pathological conditions, and trauma including heal fractures, surgical intervention, enteric accretions; skull features, including paranasal sinuses, sella turcica, cranial sutures, mandibular canal; dental features, including morphology, restorations, pathologies, missing teeth."[184] Surgical implants often have serial numbers or manufacturer information that may be linked with an individual.[185]

1.   COMPARATIVE RADIOLOGY

A number of skeletal structures show tremendous variation between individuals and may assist in identification if antemortem radiographs are available for comparison. Proposed professional standards include the following as typical areas for comparison: "trabecular lattice patterns within individual bones or regions of bones; distinctive areas of bone lucency and density; cranial sinus shapes and patterns; pathological features . . .; size, location, and contours of features (e.g., spines, processes, tubercles, sutures, foramina)."[186] Certain areas of the skeleton,

---

[181] Patrick Randolph-Quinney, Xanthe Mallett and Sue Black, "Anthropology," in WILEY ENCYCLOPEDIA OF FORENSIC SCIENCE, (Jamieson A. & Moenssens A.A., eds) 2009 & online updates.

[182] *See* Scientific Working Group for Forensic Anthropology, "Personal Identification," issued 06/03/2010, p. 2 (available at www.swganth.org).

[183] When using areas of variability to identify skeletal remains, the radiograph of the skeletal material and the ante-mortem radiographs "should match in sufficient detail to conclude that they are from the same individual with no unexplainable differences." Id.

[184] Id.

[185] Even if the surgical implants cannot be traced to a specific individual, it may help limit the number of potential candidates for identification purpose, if, for example, it can be traced to a specific hospital or provide a time frame for implantation. Id. p. 3.

See also Rebecca J. Wilson, Jonathan D. Bethard and Elizabeth A. DiGangi, "The Use of Orthopedic Surgical Devices for Forensic Identification," 56 J. FORENSIC SCI. 460–469 (2011) (discussing the practical limitations of the use of surgical devices for identification).

[186] *See* Scientific Working Group for Forensic Anthropology, "Identifying and Describing pathological Conditions, Lesions and Anomalies," issued 08/01/2012 (available at www.swganth.org).

such as the frontal sinuses, the mastoid sinus and arterial patterns on the skull,[187] the scapula,[188] and the abdomen and pelvis,[189] have been found sufficiently variable to allow for a positive identification of an individual. Other proposed methods also suggest comparative analysis based on lumbar spines, bony details of the cranium, chest structures, vertebral features, hand bones, and foot and ankle bones.[190]

Comparative radiology may be used to compare additional secondary characteristics, such as surgical interventions (staples or wiring) and pathological conditions (including congenital abnormalities and healed fractures).[191]

In the event that a scientific identification cannot be made, circumstantial means may be employed. Clothing, jewelry, and consistencies in the basic skeletal profile are commonly used to make a circumstantial identification. In addition, if the facial skeleton is intact, a comparison can be made by superimposing the skull onto a photograph. This method is not considered to be sufficient for identification.[192] Reconstruction of the soft tissue of the face, facial approximation, or a 2D rendition may be an additional consideration, but also are not generally accepted as a means of personal identification.[193]

2.   SKULL-PHOTO SUPERIMPOSITION

If the entire skull or sizeable portions of the skull are found, a photographic or video superimposition can be performed, involving the

---

[187] Stanley Rhine and Kris Sperry, "Radiographic Identification by Mastoid Sinus and Arterial Pattern," 36 J. Forensic Sci. 272 (1991); Nigel Kirk et al., "Skeletal Identification Using the Frontal Sinus Region: A Retrospective Study of 39 Cases," 47 J. FORENSIC SCI. 318 (2002); Angi Christensen, "The Impact of Daubert: Implications for Testimony and Research in Forensic Anthropology (and the Use of Frontal Sinuses in Personal Identification)," 49 J. FORENSIC SCI. 427 (2004); Roberto Cameriere et al., "Frontal Sinuses for Identification: Quality of Classifications, Possible Error and Potential Corrections," 50 J. FORENSIC SCI. 770 (2005); Angi Christensen, "Testing the Reliability of Frontal Sinuses in Positive Identification," 50 J. FORENSIC SCI. 18 (2005); Victoria A. Smith, Angi M. Christensen, and Sarah W. Myers, "The Reliability of Visually Comparing Small Frontal Sinuses," 55 J. FORENSIC SCI. 1413–1415 (2010).

[188] Douglas H. Ubelaker, "Positive Identification of American Indian Skeletal Remains from Radiographic Comparison," 35 J. Forensic Sci. 466 (1990).

[189] Robert W. Mann and Douglas W. Owsley, "Positive Personal Identity of Skeletonized Remains Using Abdominal and Pelvic Radiographs," 37 J. Forensic Sci. 332 (1992).

[190] See Aurora Valenzuela, "Radiographic Comparison of the Lumbar Spine for Positive Identification of Human Remains. A Case Report," 18 AM. J. FORENSIC MED. & PATH. 215 (1997); Deborah Smith et al., "Identification of Human Skeletal Remains by Comparison of Bony Details of the Cranium Using Computerized Tomographic (CT) Scans," 47 J. FORENSIC SCI. 937 (2002); Carrie Kuehn et al., "Validation of Chest X-ray Comparisons for Unknown Decedent Identification," 47 J. FORENSIC SCI. 725 (2002); T. Kahana et al., "Personal Identification Based on Radiographic Vertebral Features," 23 AM. J. FORENSIC MED. & PATH. 36 (2002); Michael Koot et al., "Radiographic Human Identification Using Bones of the Hand: A Validation Study," 50 J. FORENSIC SCI. 263 (2005).

[191] Patrick Randolph-Quinney, Xanthe Mallett and Sue Black, "Anthropology," in WILEY ENCYCLOPEDIA OF FORENSIC SCIENCE, (Jamieson A. & Moenssens A.A., eds) 2009 & online updates.

[192] See Scientific Working Group for Forensic Anthropology, "Personal Identification," issued 06/03/2010, pp. 3–4 (available at www.swganth.org).

[193] Id. at p. 5.

superimposition of a photograph of the presumed individual onto the skull or partial skull.[194] Comparisons are made between the structures visible in the photograph and the skeleton. Shared structures must be evaluated for commonality in the population; differences should be evaluated to determine if they are based on chronological factors or variances in the medium, or are truly distinguishing structures. If there is significant congruence, the identification is supported.[195] However, if there is not significant agreement, identification is not supported.[196]

3.   FACIAL APPROXIMATION

Facial approximation (also referred to as facial reconstruction, craniofacial reconstruction, facial reproduction, or facial depiction)[197] also requires that the entire skull or large portions of it be in good shape. The traditional method involves the actual three-dimensional reconstruction in clay of the soft tissues (fatty tissue, muscle, and skin) of the face. Developments in digital imaging have led to the creation of computer assisted three dimensional facial reconstructions and databases to assist in reconstructions.[198] This technique uses software to generate the reconstruction, which can then be distributed for identification purposes. 2D drawings are created using the same techniques. The thickness of soft tissue in different areas of the face differs based upon sex, age, and

---

[194] *See* Scientific Working Group for Forensic Anthropology, "Personal Identification," issued 06/03/2010, p. 4 (available at www.swganth.org).

[195] *See* P. T. Jayaprakas et al., "Cranio-facial Morphanalysis: A New Method for Enhancing Reliability While Identifying Skulls by Photo Superimposition," 117 Forensic Sci. Int'l 121 (2001)("reliability of identification achieved has been shown to be 91%.").

[196] An exclusion can lead to an identification. *See* Todd W. Fenton, Amber N. Heard and Norman J. Sauer, "Skull-Photo Superimposition and Border Deaths: Identification Through Exclusion and the Failure to Exclude," 53 J. FORENSIC SCI. 34–40 (2008).

[197] For an overview of this subject, *see* Caroline Wilkinson, *Forensic Facial Reconstruction,* Cambridge University Press, 2004; G. Quatrehomme et al., "Assessment of the Accuracy of Three-Dimensional Manual Craniofacial Reconstruction: A Series of 25 Controlled Cases," 121 INT'L J. LEG. MED. 469 (2007); Cristina Cattaneo and Davide Porta, "Facial Reconstruction," in WILEY ENCYCLOPEDIA OF FORENSIC SCIENCE, (Jamieson A. & Moenssens A.A., eds) 2009 & online updates.

[198] For more literature on this subject, *see* Dirk Vandermeulen, et al., "Computerized Craniofacial Reconstruction Using CT-derived Implicit Surface Representations," 159 SUPP. 1 FORENSIC SCI. INT'L S164 (2006); Peter Claes, et al., "Craniofacial Reconstruction Using a Combined Statistical Model of Face Shape and Soft Tissue Depths: Methodology and Validation," 159 SUPP. 1 FORENSIC SCI. INT'L S147 (2006); De Sven de Greef and Guy Willems, "Three-dimensional Cranio-facial Reconstruction in Forensic Identification: Latest Progress and New Tendencies in the 21st Century," 50 J. FORENSIC SCI. 12 (2005); Akihiko Nakasima, et al., "Three-dimensional Computer-generated Head Model Reconstructed from Cephalograms, Facial Photographs, and Dental Cast Models," 127 AM. J. ORTHO. DENT. ORTHOP. 282 (2005). P. Claes, et al., "Craniofacial Reconstruction Using a Combined Statistical Model of Face Shape and Soft Tissue Depths: Methodology and Validation," 159 FORENSIC SCI. INT'L SUPPL. S147 (2006); W.D. Turner, et al., "A Novel Method of Automated Skull Registration for Forensic Facial Approximation," 154 Forensic Sci. Int'l 149 (2005). *See also* Francoise Tilotta et al., "Construction and Analysis of Head CT-Scan Database for Craniofacial Reconstruction," 191 FORENSIC SCI. INT'L 112.E1–112.E12 (2009).

ancestry.[199] For that reason, the sex and ancestry of the individual must be determined before the facial approximation can begin.

Facial approximation is not an accepted method of personal identification,[200] but can assist in making a presumptive identification and should be used for investigative purposes only.[201]

III. TRAUMA

§10.10 TYPES OF TRAUMA

Trauma is a physical injury caused by an external force. Trauma to bone is categorized according to its source, such as gunshot wounds, blunt force trauma, including blunt neck trauma from strangulation, and sharp force trauma, including cut marks from dismemberment. Trauma may be detectable from the skeletal remains even when there has been extreme destruction of the body. Such trauma may be discerned and analyzed through visual observation or, due to technological advances, via three dimensional reconstructions of skulls and other skeletal structures created with computer software and radiological equipment.[202]

When there is evidence of trauma in skeletal remains, the forensic anthropologist may assist the investigation by providing information through the determinations of (1) the time of the trauma, and (2) the mechanism that produced the trauma.[203] The forensic anthropologist also may be called to testify as to their findings in cases involving bone trauma.

When evaluating alterations to bone, whether they be injury or damage, the forensic anthropologist will categorize them as: antemortem (before death), perimortem (around the time of death), or postmortem

---

[199] Shelley Smith and Peter Buschang, "Midsagittal Facial Tissue Thicknesses of Children and Adolescents from the Montreal Growth Study," 46 J. FORENSIC SCI. 1294 (2001); Matthew Williamson, et al., "Variation in Midfacial Tissue Thickness of African-American Children," 47 J. FORENSIC SCI. 25 (2002); S. de Greef, et al., "Large-Scale In-Vivo Caucasian Facial Soft Tissue Thickness Database for Craniofacial Reconstruction," 159 FORENSIC SCI. INT'L SUPPL. S126 (2006); J.M. Starbuck and R.E. Ward, "The Affect of Tissue Depth Variation on Craniofacial Reconstructions," 172 FORENSIC SCI. INT'L 130 (2007).

[200] See Scientific Working Group for Forensic Anthropology, "Personal Identification," issued 06/03/2010, p. 5 (available at www.swganth.org).

[201] See Scientific Working Group for Forensic Anthropology, "Facial Approximation," issued 05/253/2011, p. 2 (available at www.swganth.org).

[202] See Nicholas V. Passalacqua and Christopher W. Rainwater, *Skeletal Trauma Analysis. Case Studies in Context*, (Wiley & Sons, 2015); Michael J. Thali et al., "Into the Decomposed Body: Forensic Digital Autopsy Using Multislice-Computed Tomography," 134 Forensic Sci. Int'l 109 (2003); J. C. Myers, et al., "Three-dimensional (3-D) Imaging in Post-mortem Examinations: Elucidation and Identification of Cranial and Facial Fractures in Victims of Homicide Utilizing 3-D Computerized Imaging Reconstruction Techniques," 113 INT'L J. LEG. MED. 33 (1999).

[203] See Scientific Working Group for Forensic Anthropology, "Trauma Analysis," issued 05/27/2011, p. 1 (available at www.swganth.org).

(after death).[204] All three may be forensically significant. Antemortem trauma can be used to assist in the personal identification of the remains or in demonstrating a pattern of abuse. Perimortem trauma can help the pathologist determine the cause and manner of death. Postmortem damage or alteration can provide details of what happened to the body after death, which may help establish the postmortem interval and the types of implements used (in dismemberment or other physical changes to the remains). In assessing the trauma to determine the time injury was inflicted, forensic anthropologists will visually, microscopically, and radiographically inspect the remains.[205]

The hallmark of antemortem bone trauma is healing. Signs of healing are absent in perimortem injury and in postmortem alterations. The healing is a physiological response to the injury, and bone will show signs of thickening and bony proliferation with rounded edges. The degree and timing of the healing will vary among individuals and in bones in the same individual depending on four main factors: the severity of the fracture (severe damage or misaligned bone fragments will have delayed or incomplete healing), the vascularity of the area (blood is needed to transport the cellular elements of healing), the stability of the area (movement will impede healing), and the health of the individual (infection, increased age, poor nutrition, and chronic reinjury will decrease healing rates). Visible bone changes that occur during healing are present in ideal circumstances within two weeks following a fracture and remain visible for years, except in very young children whose bones may remodel.[206]

Postmortem alteration can be distinguished from antemortem trauma by the lack of any signs of healing. Fracture patterns can be used to distinguish postmortem damage and perimortem trauma based on the different patterns resulting from the fracture of wet (perimortem) and dry (postmortem) bone. Fracture patterns, however, are also the product of the type of force applied, so there are no absolutes in distinguishing time of trauma by fracture pattern.[207] Generally, the edges of postmortem fractures will be sharp, splintered, and without any bent edges.[208]

---

[204] Not all forensic anthropologists will classify postmortem injuries as "trauma" and will instead refer to these events as taphonomic alternations. Id. at p. 2.

[205] See Scientific Working Group for Forensic Anthropology, "Trauma Analysis," issued 05/27/2011, p. 2 (available at www.swganth.org).

[206] Vicki L. Wedel and Alison Galloway, eds, *Broken Bones: Anthropological Analysis of Blunt Force Trauma, Second Edition*, Charles C. Thomas Publisher, 2014.

[207] Douglas H. Ubelaker and B. Adams, "Differentiation of Perimortem and Postmortem Trauma using Taphonomic Indicators," 40 J. FORENSIC SCI. (1995) 3:509–512.

[208] "A bone will break when it cannot absorb all of the traumatic energy. Bone is weakest in tension and strongest in compression. A tensile failure of bone can occur under bending when the surface of the outside of the bow in a long bone undergoes elongation resulting in a transverse fracture. A long bone subjected to torsion can fail in a spiral fracture." Bruce P. Wheatley, "Perimortem of Postmortem Bone Fractures? An Experimental Study of Fracture Patterns in Deer Femora," 53 J. FORENSIC SCI. 69–72, at p. 69 (2008).

Thermal changes to the bone can be produced by exposure to high temperatures, electricity, or flame.[209] Heat exposure can result in color change, delamination, extensive fracturing, shrinkage, charring, and calcinations in skeletal remains.[210] Notation of aberrant patterns or positions may provide information about the circumstances of the death.[211]

§10.11 GUNSHOT

The analysis of gunshot wounds which either penetrate (enter without exiting) or perforate (enter and exit) bone can be informative.[212] When gunshot wounds are identified on skeletal remains, the main issues for the forensic anthropologist concern the distinction between entrance and exit wounds, the sequence when more than one has left marks on bone, and the directionality of the trajectories.[213]

In the case of high velocity gunshot wounds to the cranial vault, the entrance wound in bone typically is a circular wound with internal beveling and clean margins.[214] The typical exit wound can be irregular and usually exhibits an external bevel around the defect, Entrance and exit wounds created by a low velocity gunshot wound more closely resemble each other, and both wounds may be circular.[215] If the beveling characteristics are obvious and discretely different from each other, they may be used alone to distinguish between entrance and exit wounds. However, if they are not, the fractures in the skull around the defects

---

[209] *See* Scientific Working Group for Forensic Anthropology, "Trauma Analysis," issued 05/27/2011, p. 6 (available at www.swganth.org).

[210] Douglas H. Ubelaker, "The Forensic Evaluation of Burned Skeletal Remains: A Synthesis", 183 FORENSIC SCI. INT. 1–5 (2009).

[211] Id. *See also* Christopher W. Schmidt and Steven A. Symes, *The Analysis of Burned Human Remains,* 2d ed., Academic Press, 2015.

[212] For an overview of what happens when bullets strike osteological material, *see* Hugh E. Berryman and Steven A. Symes, "Recognizing Gunshot and Blunt Cranial Trauma through Fracture Interpretation," in Kathleen J. Reichs ed., *Forensic Osteology: Advances in the Identification of Human Remains*, 2d ed., Charles C. Thomas Publisher, 1998, at p. 333. *See also* Gerald Quatrehomme and M. Yasar İscan, "Characteristics of Gunshot Wounds in the Skull," 44 J. FORENSIC SCI. 568 (1999); N.R. Langley, "An Anthropological Analysis of Gunshot Wounds to the Chest," 52 J. FORENSIC SCI. 532 (2007).

[213] Shotgun wounds produce different marks on bone depending on the size of the pellets, the muzzle-to-target distance, and degree of injury. Debra A. Komar and Jane E. Buikstra. *Forensic Anthropology: Contemporary Theory and Practice,* Oxford University Press, 2008.

[214] "The ability to estimate caliber from entrance and exit wounds is a matter of considerable debate within forensic pathology (*see, e.g.* A.H. Ross, "Caliber estimation from cranial entrance defect measurements," 41 J. FORENSIC SCI. 629–633 (1996).) . . . Because of the viscoelastic nature of bone, projectiles may produce defects in bones that are significantly smaller than their diameters," Debra A. Komar and Jane E. Buikstra, *Forensic Anthropology: Contemporary Theory and Practice,* Oxford University Press, 2008, at p. 181.

Identification of bullet caliber from measurement of the entrance wound defect is considered an "unacceptable practice." *See* Scientific Working Group for Forensic Anthropology, "Trauma Analysis," issued 05/27/2011, p. 6 (available at www.swganth.org).

[215] Hugh E. Berryman and Steven A. Symes, "Recognizing Gunshot and Blunt Cranial Trauma through Fracture Interpretation," in Kathleen J. Reichs ed., *Forensic Osteology: Advances in the Identification of Human Remains*, 2d ed., Charles C. Thomas Publisher, 1998, at p. 347.

may reveal the origin of the defect.[216] The sequence of gunshot wounds to the skull may be revealed in the examination of intersecting fractures associated with defects caused by a projectile.[217] In the absence of an exit wound, or in cases of multiple gunshot traumas to bone, the beveling of the entrance defect may be used to indicate the direction of fire. If the beveled entrance area is round, the bullet likely entered the entered the bone at a right angle. Otherwise, the elongated portion of the bevel indicates the direction of fire.[218]

§10.12 BLUNT FORCE

Blunt force trauma is defined as injury produced by the impact of a blunt object, such as a hammer, baseball bat, fist, or motor vehicle, or by impact of a body against a blunt surface (*e.g.*, a fall).[219] Skeletal response to blunt force impact depends on both the intrinsic features of the bone and the extrinsic factors of the implement and incident.[220] Assessment of blunt force trauma includes examination and documentation of the location of fractures, fracture patterns and complexity, the sequence of impacts, if relevant, and any impression at the impact site.[221]

In the description of blunt force trauma, fracture complexity may be described as either linear, referring to a single fracture line, or comminuted, referring to a crushing fracture or multiple extending fracture lines.[222] Injuries due to blunt force trauma may be described as having resulted from a single event, or from multiple traumatic events, and not all fracture lines are complete. Incomplete, or "greenstick", fractures are the result of a bone sustaining a force without breaking.[223] The direction of force relative to the body can be estimated by considering the viscoelastic nature of bone. That is, bone is stronger under compression than tension and the bone will fail first on the side of tension, with fractures progressing toward the side of compression.[224] In motor vehicle accidents involving pedestrians, the fracture patterns can

---

[216] *See* Gina O. Hart, "Fracture Pattern Interpretation in the Skull: Differentiating Blunt Force from Ballistics Trauma Using Concentric Fractures," 50 J. FORENSIC SCI. 1276 (2005); Todd W. Fenton *et al.*, "Symmetrical Fracturing of the Skull from Midline Contact Gunshot Wounds: Reconstruction of Individual Death Histories from Skeletonized Human Remains," 50 J. FORENSIC SCI. 274 (2005).

[217] J. Stanley Rhine and Bryan K. Curran, "Multiple Gunshot Wounds of the Head: An Anthropological View," 35 J. Forensic Sci. 1236, 1243 (1990).

[218] Id.

[219] *See* Scientific Working Group for Forensic Anthropology, "Trauma Analysis," issued 05/27/2011, p. 7 (available at www.swganth.org).

[220] O.E. Smith, E.E. Pope, and S.A. Symes. "Look until you see: identification of trauma in skeletal material," in D.W. Steadman (ed.), *Hard Evidence: Case Studies in Forensic Anthropology,* Pearson Education, 2008.

[221] Vicki L. Wedel and Alison Galloway, eds. *Broken Bones: Anthropological Analysis of Blunt Force Trauma,* 2d ed., Charles C. Thomas Publisher, 2014.

[222] Debra A. Komar and Jane E. Buikstra. *Forensic Anthropology: Contemporary Theory and Practice,* Oxford University Press, 2008.

[223] Id.

[224] Vicki L. Wedel and Alison Galloway, eds. *Broken Bones: Anthropological Analysis of Blunt Force Trauma,* 2d ed., Charles C. Thomas Publisher, 2014.

be used to determine the direction of force, particularly in the long bones of the legs.

In cases where blunt force trauma has resulted from multiple blows or injuries, the forensic anthropologist may estimate the number and sequence of events. The points of impact must be determined and patterns of radiating and concentric fractures from this point identified. Because fractures terminate when they intersect with existing fracture lines, the sequence of impacts may be determined.[225] In some instances, patterned injuries can occur that identify the type of wounding instrument.[226]

Blunt force trauma to the neck resulting from compression, whether from an instrument, a ligature, or manual strangulation, can also result in fractures to the cartilage and bones of this region. Both complete and incomplete fractures can occur in the hyoid bone and the thyroid cartilage due to blunt force trauma.[227]

Infant deaths are often the result of single, or repetitive blunt force injuries. Forensic anthropologists may be asked to describe and interpret these fractures and provide timeframes for when the injury occurred.[228] Recognition of disease or nutritional deficiencies in these cases is imperative in the differential diagnosis of non-inflicted trauma. Similarly, the forensic anthropologist may be asked to opine about repetitive injuries in cases of alleged elder abuse.[229]

§10.13 SHARP FORCE

Sharp force injury in bone is usually described as incised defects. Incised injuries in bone can be V-shaped with clean margins when inflicted with a tapered edge. Implements with one sharp edge and one blunt edge can leave square shaped edges at one end of the incised injury. Serrated blades mark in a characteristic manner. Chopping implements can exhibit both blunt and incised marks in the bone depending on the weight of the implement. Chopping injuries can result in multiple fragments rather than single incised injuries.[230] Dismemberment injuries in bone vary depending on the power source. Manual saw blades tend to produce irregular striae and more bone

---

[225] Id. *See also* Scientific Working Group for Forensic Anthropology, "Trauma Analysis," issued 05/27/2011, p. 7 (available at www.swganth.org).

[226] *See* Werner U. Spitz, "The Road Traffic Victim," *Medicolegal Investigation*, 4th ed., Charles C. Thomas Publisher, 2006, at p. 528.

[227] Debra A. Komar and Jane E. Buikstra. *Forensic Anthropology: Contemporary Theory and Practice*, Oxford University Press, 2008.

[228] *See* J.C. Love, S.M. Derrick, and J.M Wiersema, *Skeletal Atlas of Child Abuse* Springer, 2011.

[229] Id.

[230] *See* Debra A. Komar and Jane E. Buikstra. *Forensic Anthropology: Contemporary Theory and Practice*, Oxford University Press, 2008.

fragments. Mechanized saw blades can produce more regular striae and cleaner margins.[231]

IV. TRIAL AIDS

§10.14 EXPERT QUALIFICATIONS

Forensic anthropology is an anthropology subspecialty and requires additional training beyond the typical four years of college or university. Following graduation from college, most forensic anthropologists pursue at least a Master's degree and many obtain a Doctorate degree in physical anthropology with specialized training in forensic anthropology.[232] Many colleges and universities offer graduate degrees in physical anthropology but few offer a forensic doctoral track and the application process is highly competitive.[233] After completing graduate education and specialized training, the anthropologist may become certified in forensic anthropology. Standardization of credentials is currently being reviewed in response to the National Academy of Standards report issued in 2009.[234]

Forensic anthropology certification is a voluntary process in the United States. While certification is not currently required, a PhD and board certification are strongly encouraged within the field as a means of ensuring educational and practical competency in forensic anthropology. Many practitioners are actively working to promote standardization of credentials in forensic anthropology. The non-profit Forensic Specialties Accreditation Board[235] has accredited the American Board of Forensic Anthropology (ABFA) to administer certification of forensic anthropologists. Certification through the ABFA requires three years of post-doctoral degree experience in forensic anthropology, successful review by the ABFA of three cases files reflecting the applicant's work, successful completion of a multiple choice

---

[231] For a more detailed discussion of sharp force trauma, see Kathleen J. Reichs, "Postmortem Dismemberment: Recovery, Analysis and Interpretation," in Kathleen J. Reichs ed., *Forensic Osteology: Advances in the Identification of Human Remains*, 2d ed., Charles C. Thomas Publisher, 1998 at p. 353; Joshua H. Humphrey and Dale L. Hutchinson "Macroscopic Characteristics of Hacking Trauma," 46 J. FORENSIC SCI. 228 (2001); Dale L. Hutchinson et al., "Microscopic Characteristics of Hacking Trauma," 46 J. FORENSIC SCI. 234 (2001). P. A. Saville, S. V. Hainsworth and G. N. Rutty, "Cutting Crime: The Analysis of the 'Uniqueness' of Saw Marks on Bone," 121 INT'L. J. LEG. MED. 349 (2007).

[232] SWGANTH standards establish 3 levels of forensic anthropologists with Forensic anthropologist III able to independently conduct forensic anthropological analyses and issue reports. That level requires a PhD and certification by the ABFA. Scientific Working Group for Forensic Anthropology, "Qualifications," issued 06/02/2010, pp. 2–3 (available at www. swganth.org).

[233] The American Association of Physical Anthropology maintains a listing of graduate programs on its website: www.physanth.org.

[234] See http://www.nap.edu/catalog/12589/strengthening-forensic-science-in-the-united-states-a-path-forward.

[235] See http://thefsab.org.

examination, and successful completion of a practical examination.[236] Membership in the American Academy of Forensic Sciences Physical Anthropology Section requires application, adherence to ethical standards, and an ongoing record of activities in forensic science. Additionally the American Anthropological Association (AAA) and the American Association of Physical Anthropologists (AAPA) are professional organizations that offer education, training, meetings, and publications to practitioners.[237]

§10.15 EVIDENCE ISSUES

Forensic anthropologists routinely testify as experts in court. Their testimony can be subpoenaed by prosecution, defense, or civil litigators depending on the matter at hand. Many forensic anthropologists are consulted by medical examiner or coroner offices and their reports may be used by prosecution in the development of their case. Similarly, civil litigators consult with forensic anthropologists in cases arising out of negligence and other similar torts. Criminal defense attorneys are becoming more accustomed to the appearance of forensic anthropology testimony. In *Ibar v. State*,[238] the Supreme Court of Florida held that defense counsel was ineffective for failing to consult a forensic anthropologist to explain the physical differences between the defendant and the individual on the surveillance camera video of the murder.[239]

When forensic anthropologists are called to testify, their qualifications and the status of forensic anthropology as an accepted scientific discipline are, in most cases, assumed without the necessity for argument or proof. In *State v. Klindt*[240] the defense did challenge the reliability of the field of forensic anthropology, but did not challenge the qualifications of the expert. The Iowa Supreme Court agreed with the trial court that "forensic anthropology is a recognized scientific discipline ... used in identifying burned and dismembered crash victims and to determine the time, cause, and manner of death of decomposed victims of homicides."[241]

Courts are also willing to recognize that, due to their training and experience, anthropologists are skilled in a number of other scientific disciplines, such as radiology and odontology. These subjects are necessarily related to the performance of the anthropologist's primary tasks in the analysis of skeletal remains. Most forensic anthropology

---

[236] American Board of Forensic Anthropology, ABFA Manual; ABFA Guidelines for Case File Submission (available at www.theabfa.org).

[237] American Anthropological Association: www.aaanet.org; American Association of Physical Anthropologists: www.physanth.org.

[238] 190 So.3d 1012 (Fla. 2016).

[239] 190 So.3d at 1021.

[240] 389 N.W.2d 670 (Iowa 1986). *See also* State v. Miller, 429 N.W.2d 26, 39 (S.D.1988).

[241] Klindt, 389 N.W.2d at 673.

programs include training in radiography and odontology and therefore the competence of an anthropologist includes the ability to read radiographs or to make assessments regarding the dentition and to make scientific identification. Courts have generally given forensic anthropologists latitude to present their opinions on such matters.[242] Determining cause and manner of death is not within the purview of the forensic anthropologist. However, when a pathologist declares neck trauma to be the cause of a death, an anthropologist's finding of a fractured hyoid bone gives added credence to the pathologist's judgment.[243] Anthropologists have also been allowed to give in-court approximations about the length the time that has elapsed between the death of an individual and the discovery of his or her remains.[244]

Forensic anthropologists have been permitted to testify as to differences or similarities between individuals and perpetrators of crimes observed in video surveillance or photographs.[245] While forensic anthropologists may be asked to opine about a wide variety of issues, including biological profile, postmortem interval, scientific identification of the decedent, and scene recovery techniques, the most common testimony involves describing osseous traumata as it relates to the pathologist's determination of cause of death.

V. RESOURCES

§10.16 BIBLIOGRAPHY OF ADDITIONAL RESOURCES

Soren Blau and Douglas H. Ubelaker (eds.), *Handbook of Forensic Anthropology and Archaeology, Reprint Edition,* Left Coast Press, 2011.

Steven N. Byers, *Introduction to Forensic Anthropology: A Textbook,* 4th ed., Prentice Hall, 2010.

Angi M. Christensen, Nicholas V. Passalacqua and Eric J. Bartelink, *Forensic Anthropology: Current Methods and Practice.* Elsevier, 2013.

Dennis Dirkmaat ed., *A Companion to Forensic Anthropology,* , Wiley-Blackwell, 2012.

Tosha L. Dupras, John J. Schultz, Sandra M. Wheeler and Lana J. Williams, *Forensic Recovery of Human Remains, Archaeological Approaches,* 2d ed., CRC Press, 2016.

---

[242] State v. Goodman, 643 S.W.2d 375 (Tenn. Crim. App. 1982); State v. Hartman, 703 S.W.2d 106 (Tenn. 1985).

[243] State v. Crowley, 475 So.2d 783 (La. Ct. App. 1985).

[244] Gore v. Secretary for Dept. of Corrections, 492 F.3d 1273 (11th Cir. 2007).

[245] Penalver v. State, 926 So.2d 1118 (Fla. 2006).

Diane L. France, *Human and Nonhuman Bone Identification—A Color Atlas*, CRC Press, 2008.

M. Yasar Iscan, "Progress in Forensic Anthropology: The 20th Century," 98 Forensic Sci. Int'l 1 (1998).

M. Yasar Iscan, "Global Forensic Anthropology in the 21st Century," 117 Forensic Sci. Int'l 1 (2001).

M. Anne Katzenberg & Shelley R. Saunders, eds., *Biological Anthropology of the Human Skeleton*, 2d ed., Wiley-Liss, 2008.

Evan W. Matshes, *et al.*, *Human Osteology and Skeletal Radiology: An Atlas and Guide*, CRC Press, 2004.

Marc Oxenham, *Forensic Approaches to Death, Disaster and Abuse*, Australian Academic Press, 2008.

James Pokines and Steven A. Symes eds., *Manual of Forensic Taphonomy*, CRC Press, 2013.

Ann H. Ross and Suzanne M. Abel, eds., *The Juvenile Skeleton in Forensic Abuse Investigations*, Humana Press, 2011.

Aurore Schmitt, E. Cunha and J. Pinheiro, *Forensic Anthropology and Medicine: Complementary Science from Recovery to Cause of Death*, Humana Press, 2006.

Thomas D. Stewart, *Essentials of Forensic Anthropology*, Charles C. Thomas Publisher, 1979.

Mark Tibbett and David O. Carter, *Soil Analysis in Forensic Taphonomy: Chemical and Biological Effects of Buried Human Remains*, CRRC Press, 2008.

Michael W. Warren, Heather A. Walsh-Haney, and Laurel Freas *The Forensic Anthropology Laboratory*, CRC Press, 2008.

Tim D. White and Pieter A. Folkens, *The Human Bone Manual*, Academic Press, 2005.

CHAPTER 11

FORENSIC ODONTOLOGY

I. INTRODUCTION

§11.01 SCOPE OF THE CHAPTER

Forensic odontology, or forensic dentistry, is broadly defined as the application of dental science to questions of law. Forensic odontologists gather, examine, and interpret dental and related evidence[1] to address legal issues including identification, causation, and reconstruction of events.

Forensic odontology has five major areas of application: (1) dental malpractice and negligence; (2) analysis of dental features to provide an age estimation for an individual or to contribute to the biological profile of unidentified human remains; (3) identification of human remains through comparison with antemortem dental records and radiographs; (4) analysis of suspected trauma; and controversially, (5) bite mark comparison. This chapter describes the principles, techniques, and limitations involved in the final three areas of application: dental identification of human remains, analysis of suspected trauma, and bite

---

[1] Christopher J. Plourd, "Science, the Law, and Forensic Identification," in David R. Senn and Paul G. Stimson, eds., *Forensic Dentistry*, 2d ed., CRC Press, 2010 at p. 4.

mark comparison.[2] The qualifications of the expert and evidence issues in forensic odontology are also discussed.

Dental evidence may be used to provide information concerning issues in criminal and civil cases, including questions involving identity, causation, and the reconstruction of events.[3] Forensic odontologists may provide opinion testimony on the identity of human remains,[4] the extent and manner of injury to dental features, the presence of suspected human bite marks, and possibility of a correlation between the dentition of an individual and a suspected human bite mark. It is this final category of testimony that has generated considerable controversy in the scientific and legal communities.

Forensic odontology, like many areas of forensic science, is currently working on establishing regulatory oversight and mandatory national standards.[5] The National Institute of Standards and Technology has established an Odontology Subcommittee in the Crime Scene/Death Investigation Organization of Scientific Area Committee to establish standards for forensic odontology.[6] The Odontology Subcommittee will transition the guidelines developed by the Scientific Working Group on Disaster Victim Identification (SWGDVI) and draft any new standards and guidelines needed for the practice of forensic odontology.

Although not mandatory beyond their membership, professional organizations have developed best practices and guidelines for some applications of forensic odontology. The American Board of Forensic Odontology (ABFO) has guidelines for various areas of forensic odontology published in its *Diplomates Reference Manual*.[7] The International Organization for Forensic Odonto-Stomatology has guidelines for many topics, including general considerations in quality assurance, single-case identification, identification in mass disasters, age estimation, tooth marks (bite mark) analysis and comparison,

---

[2] Age estimations based on dental features are discussed in Chapter 10 Forensic Anthropology.

[3] Forensic odontologists are also sometimes asked to assist in archaeological examinations. *See* Emilio Nuzzolese and Matteo Borrini, "Forensic Approach to an Archaeological Casework of 'Vampire' Skeletal Remains in Venice: Odontological and Anthropological Prospectus," 55 J. FORENSIC SCI. 1634–1637 (2010).

[4] The odontology information may also be used as a preliminary screening step to support disinternment requests for further identification procedures. *See* Calvin Y. Shiroma, "A Comparison of Dental Chartings Performed at the Joint POW/MIA Accounting Command Central Identification Laboratory and the Kokura Central Identification Unit on Remains Identified from the Korean War," 61 J. Forensic Sci. 59–67 (2016).

[5] States provide oversight of the practice of dentistry through licensing requirements; however, there is currently no separate state or national regulation of forensic odontology. The practice of dentistry is generally defined as the treatment of dental issues and does not necessarily cover the practice areas of forensic odontology. *See* Va. Code § 54.1–2700 *et seq.* ("Dentistry means the evaluation, diagnosis, prevention, and treatment, through surgical, nonsurgical or related procedures, of diseases, disorders, and conditions of the oral cavity and the maxillofacial, adjacent and associated structures and their impact on the human body.").

[6] *See* https://www.nist.gov/topics/forensic-science/odontology-subcommittee (last accessed February 28, 2017).

[7] American Board of Forensic Odontology, *Diplomates Reference Manual*, March 2017 edition (available at: https://abfo.org/resources/abfo-manual/)(last accessed February 28, 2017).

dental injuries, and reporting.[8] The American Dental Association publishes a national forensics data standard for the submission of supporting documentation from the dentist or dentists who treated the patient to assist forensic odontologists in establishing positive identification of human remains.[9]

Similarly, certification in forensic odontology is available from the ABFO,[10] but is not mandatory beyond the membership of ABFO and is not required for working as a forensic odonotology expert. The field benefits from strong ties to academia and collaborative efforts with dental practitioners and scientists that provide foundational research support.

§11.02 TERMINOLOGY

The following terms are used in this Chapter or are commonly used in forensic odontology investigation reports.

Abscess: An infection of a tooth, soft tissue or bone.

Abutment: The teeth on either side of a missing tooth.

Adhesive Dentistry: Contemporary term for dental restorations that involve "bonding" of composite resin or porcelain fillings to natural teeth.

Alveolar Bone: The jawbone that anchors the roots of teeth.

Amalgam: Restorative material for posterior teeth, commonly known as "silver fillings," consisting of an alloy of mercury, silver, tin, copper, and zinc. This makes a plastic mass that can be fitted into a tooth cavity and will harden in a short time.

Antemortem Record: Dental records taken prior to the individual's death consisting of charts, X-rays and dental casts.

Anterior Teeth: Teeth readily visible in the center of the mouth, including the central and lateral incisors and the cuspids.

Bicuspid: Also called premolars; tooth adjacent to the cuspid. An adult has eight bicuspids.

Bonding: Adhesive dental restoration technique; a tooth-colored composite resin to repair and/or change the color or shape of a tooth.

Bridge: Stationary dental prosthesis (appliance) fixed to teeth adjacent to a space; replaces one or more missing teeth, cemented or bonded to supporting teeth or implants adjacent to the space.

---

[8] *See* http://www.iofos.eu/Quality_assurance2.html (last accessed February 28, 2017).

[9] ANSI/ADA Specification No. 1058 for Forensic Dental Data Set (available for purchase at: http://ebusiness.ada.org/productcatalog/findproduct.aspx#q=forensic&sort=relevancy)(last accessed July 11, 2016).

[10] A sample ABFO Certification test is available at: https://www.orainc.com/testing (last accessed July 11, 2016).

Buccal: One of the five surfaces of a tooth, the surface of the posterior teeth on the side toward the cheek.

Cap: Common term for dental crown.

Caries: Decay of the teeth, produced by acid dissolution of the calcium salts which make up most of the teeth.

Cast: Reproduction of structures made by pouring plaster or stone into a mold.

Cross Bite: An abnormal relation of one or more teeth of one arch to the opposing tooth or teeth of the other arch, caused by deviation of tooth position or abnormal jaw position.

Crown: The portion of the tooth that is visible above the gum.

Cuspid: Also called canine. Tooth adjacent to the incisors and primarily used for cutting and tearing. An adult has four cuspids; they are at the corner of the mouth, the third tooth from the midline on both sides. The shape is frequently pointed and peglike.

Deciduous Dentition: Baby or "milk" teeth which begin to erupt from the gums when a child reaches the age of seven months. Deciduous dentition consists of 20 teeth only, 10 in each jaw, five in each of the right and left quadrants. In each quadrant there are two incisors, one cuspid, and two molars.

Dental Implant: A cylinder surgically placed in the bone of the upper or lower jaw to provide support for a dental restoration or appliance.

Dentin: Inner layer of tooth structure, immediately under the surface enamel.

Dentition: A set of teeth of an individual. Humans acquire two sets of teeth during their lifetime, the first acquired during childhood (deciduous or primary dentition), the second set which replaces the first set one by one as the jaw grows (the permanent or secondary dentition). There are four different types of teeth: incisors, cuspids (canines), bicuspids (premolars) and molars. An adult dentition comprises 32 teeth. Each tooth has five surfaces: occlusal, mesial, distal, buccal, and lingual.

Denture: Upper and lower false teeth. *See* Prosthesis.

Diastema: Space between teeth.

Distal: Tooth surface in direct contact with the adjacent tooth on the side away from the midline of the jaw (abbreviation "D").

Enamel: The outer surface of a tooth and the most resistant and hardest substance of the body.

Endodontia: Branch of dentistry concerned with diseases of the dental pulp and removal of the dental pulp, the nerve and other tissue of the pulp cavity.

Eruption: Process of teeth protruding through the gums.

Exodontia: Practice of dental extractions.

Freeway Space: Distance between the upper and lower teeth with the lower jaw in rest position.

Full Denture: Removable dental prosthesis (appliance) replacing all upper or lower teeth.

Impaction: Partial or completely unexposed tooth that is wedged against another tooth, bone, or soft tissue, precluding the eruption process.

Implant: Artificial device replacing tooth root; may anchor an artificial tooth, bridge, or denture.

Impression: Mold made of the teeth and soft tissues.

Incisor: Tooth primarily used for biting and cutting and placed in the center of the mouth. An adult has eight incisors, two in each quadrant of the mouth. The upper central incisor is the largest tooth; the lateral incisors are a little smaller. The lower incisors are smaller than either the upper central or lateral incisors.

Interproximal: Surfaces of adjoining teeth.

Lingual: The surface of a tooth facing toward the inside of the mouth (abbreviation "L").

Malocclusion: "Bad bite" or misalignment of the upper and lower teeth.

Mandible: Lower jaw, which is movable.

Maxilla: Upper jaw, which is stationary.

Mesial: Tooth surface which is in direct contact with an adjacent tooth on the side facing the midline of the jaw (abbreviation "M").

Model: *See* Cast.

Molar: The teeth farthest back in the mouth. An adult has three molars in each quadrant of the mouth, or a total of 12. Their primary use is to grind and smash food.

Occlusal: Tooth surface which contacts the opposing tooth when the jaws are closed (in occlusion)(abbreviations "O").

Occlusion: Closure; the relationship of the upper and lower teeth upon closure.

Open Bite: A malocclusion in which the teeth do not close or come together in the front of the mouth.

Orthodontics: Dental specialty that treats misalignment of teeth.

Overbite: Vertical overlapping of the upper teeth over the lower.

Overjet: Horizontal projection of the upper teeth beyond the lower.

Palate: The roof of the mouth, consisting of a hard bony forward part (the hard palate) and a soft fleshy back part (the soft palate).

Partial Denture: Removable dental prosthesis (appliance) replacing one or more natural teeth.

Perikymata: Wavelike features found in the surface enamel of teeth. They result from the incremental deposits of enamel during tooth crown development. They undergo changes due to age, location of tooth in mouth and oral habits.

Permanent Teeth: Thirty-two adult teeth (usually) in a complete dentition.

Posterior Teeth: The teeth in the back of the mouth, all bicuspids and molars.

Postmortem Record: Dental record obtained by charting the dentition, extractions and restorations of a dead body.

Prosthodontist: Dental specialist skilled in restoring or replacing teeth with fixed or removable prosthesis (appliance), maintaining proper occlusion.

Pulp: Material occupying a cavity located inside the teeth comprised of nerves, lymph, blood vessels and fibrous tissue.

Prosthesis: Artificial teeth which may either be fixed or removable. Fixed prosthesis could be a bridge consisting of a device used to span a gap in the dentition. A removable prosthesis is either a complete or a partial set of false teeth. The partial denture would attach to remaining teeth by clasps and hooks.

Restoration: Replacement of portion of a damaged tooth.

Root: Tooth structure that connects the tooth to the jaw.

Root Canal: The procedure of removing the pulp from a tooth and filling the space with some substance. Since this work is then covered by a restoration, it can only be discovered through x-rays.

Rugae: Ridges or folds as those on the palate.

Tooth: Hard white structure in mouth used primarily for mastication of food; a tooth is comprised of a crown (the functional part that is visible above the gum) and one or more roots (the unseen portion that attaches the tooth to the jaw).

Unerupted tooth: A tooth that has not pushed through the gum and assumed its correct position in the dental arch.

Wisdom teeth: Third (last) molars that usually erupt between ages 18–25.

An extensive online glossary of dental clinical and administrative terms is provided by the American Dental Association.[11]

§11.03 EVIDENTIARY USES

Teeth are an extremely useful individualization tool because they are one of the elements of the human body most resistant to destructive

---

[11] Available at: http://www.ada.org/en/publications/cdt/glossary-of-dental-clinical-and-administrative-ter (last accessed July 11, 2016).

forces of decomposition, fire, water, and other environmental factors.[12] DNA can be extracted from almost all dental material, but the pulp of the teeth provides the greatest quantity of DNA material for DNA typing identification.[13] Additionally, teeth and other dental structures are particularized to the individual through anatomical, pathological, and therapeutic features.[14]

Dental evidence has considerable importance in civil and criminal cases. The majority of forensic odontology examination concerns identification of individuals through the comparison of antemortem dental records of missing persons with dental features of unidentified human remains. In some states, the law requires consultation with a dentist in cases of unidentified human remains[15] and the retention of dental features for a prescribed period of time following identification.[16]

Bodies sometimes cannot be identified by the traditional means of (1) visual recognition, (2) DNA typing, or (3) fingerprint comparison. The utility of visual recognition and fingerprint comparison are quickly impacted by decomposition; difficulties with DNA recovery increase as decomposition progresses. Natural disasters, terrorist strikes, human rights violations, and other cases with multiple victims often lead to the recovery of commingled, fragmented, and badly decomposed human remains where the victims cannot be identified through the traditional means. In these cases and any criminal or civil case in which human remains are not readily identifiable, forensic odontologists can use dental identification techniques to assist in the identification of the remains and to provide information concerning any trauma inflicted on the dental remains. The success of dental identification is dependent, however, on

---

[12] High temperatures can make teeth fragile and subject to fracture, altering the physical appearance of teeth. However, dental materials, such as dental resins, are extremely resistant to heat and can survive cremation sufficiently to allow identification of the brand or brand group. *See* Mary A. Bush, Raymond G. Miller, Ann L. Norrlander, and Peter J. Bush, "Analytical Survey of Restorative Resins by SEM/EDS and XRF: Databases for Forensic Purposes," 53 J. FORENSIC SCI. 419–425 (2008).

[13] Vilma Pinchi et al., "Techniques of Dental DNA Extraction: Some Operative Experiences," 204 FORENSIC SCI. INT'L 111–114 (2011).

[14] Cristina Cattaneo and Danilo De Angelis, "Odontology," in WILEY ENCYCLOPEDIA OF FORENSIC SCIENCE, (Jamieson A. & Moenssens A.A., eds) 2009 & online updates.

[15] *See, e.g.,* Cal. Gov't. Code § 27521 ("(b) A postmortem examination or autopsy shall include, but shall not be limited to, the following procedures: . . . (2) A dental examination consisting of dental charts and dental X-rays of the deceased person's teeth, which may be conducted on the body or human remains by a qualified dentist as determined by the coroner."); Nev. Rev. Stat. Ann. 480.500 ("1. When a coroner is unable to establish the identity of a dead body by means other than by dental records, the coroner shall have a dental examination of the body made by a dentist. The dentist shall prepare a record of his or her findings and forward it to the coroner, who shall enter the information into the computer for the National Crime Information Center."). *But see* La. Rev. Stat. § 13–5713 (requiring dental examination by a "dentist or forensic anthropologist or forensic pathologist").

[16] *See* Cal. Gov't Code 27521 (e) "The body of an unidentified deceased person may not be cremated or buried until the jaws (maxilla and mandible with teeth), or other bone sample if the jaws are not available, and other tissue samples are retained for future possible use. . . . The coroner, medical examiner, or other agency responsible for a postmortem examination or autopsy shall retain the jaws and other tissue samples for one year after a positive identification is made, and no civil or criminal challenges are pending, or indefinitely.").

the accuracy and completeness of both the postmortem data and the antemortem records. The inadequacy of antemortem data and the need for proper training of disaster recovery personnel was evident in difficulties experts had in identifying the victims through dental examination following the 2004 South Asian tsunami.[17]

In other cases, the identity of human remains is not an issue, but the possible mechanism of dental trauma is an issue. Particularly in cases of suspected child abuse, whether an injury to dental features could have occurred accidentally or intentionally may be a determinative factor in assessing liability. As mandatory child abuse reporters, dentists are required to assess injuries for possible reporting.[18] Abuse may result in injuries to dental features such as bruises, burns, lacerations, fractured or displaced teeth, or fractured jaw features.[19] Meticulous observation and documentation of such injuries may provide important information for determining the timing, nature, and manner of the injuries. Forensic odontologists may be called to testify in both civil and criminal cases concerning dental injuries.[20]

The identification of a suspected human bite mark may also be an issue in some cases. Forensic odontologists may conduct an examination to determine if the mark is a human bite mark. If DNA analysis is unavailable, the forensic odontologist may be asked for an opinion on the source of the bite mark through comparison of an individual's dental features with the bite mark. Although dental identification constitutes the majority of the work of forensic odontologists, it is the examination of human bite marks that has generated the most controversy and garnered the attention of the courts.[21] Media coverage of exonerations through DNA analysis of evidence in cases of individuals wrongfully convicted in part on bite mark analysis has eroded public confidence in the reliability of bite mark comparison evidence.[22] The controversy is reflected in the following observations of the National Academy of Sciences in 2009:

---

[17] *See* Jules A. Kieser, Wayne Laing and Peter Herbison, "Lessons Learned from Large-scale Comparative Dental Analysis Following the South Asian Tsunami of 2004," 51 J. FORENSIC SCI. 109–112 (2006).

[18] *See* Va. Code § 63.2–1509.

[19] American Academy of Pediatrics Committee on Child Abuse and Neglect and the American Academy of Pediatric Dentistry, "Guideline on Oral and Dental Aspects of Child Abuse and Neglect," Reaffirmed 2010 (available at: http://www.aapd.org/media/policies_guidelines/g_childabuse.pdf)(last accessed July 13, 2016).

[20] *See, e.g.,* McBeath v. State, 739 So.2d 451 (Miss. Ct. App. 1999)(dentist testified as to the extent of oral injuries to the child victim, including the need for a root canal in the future for an infection in a cracked tooth); King v. Illinois Nat'l Ins. Co., 782 So.2d 1104 (La. Ct. App. 2001)(dentist testified as to the extent of oral injuries and the need for future treatment as the result of motor vehicle accident).

[21] Robert E. Barsley, "Odontology as a Forensic Science, the North American Experience," 201 FORENSIC SCI. INT'L. 5–7 (2011).

[22] *See* Radley Balko, "How the Flawed 'Science' of Bite Mark Analysis Has Sent Innocent People to Prison," Washington Post, February 13, 2015 (available at: https://www.washingtonpost.com/news/the-watch/wp/2015/02/13/how-the-flawed-science-of-bite-mark-analysis-has-sent-innocent-people-to-jail/)(last accessed July 13, 2016); "Editorial: Taking the Bite out of Unreliable Evidence," Free Lance-Star, April 15, 2016 (available at: http://www.fredericks

"Although the methods of the collection of bite mark evidence are relatively noncontroversial, there is considerable dispute about the value and reliability of the collected data for interpretation. Some key areas of dispute include the accuracy of human skin as a reliable registration material for bite marks, the uniqueness of human dentition, the techniques used for analysis, and the role of examiner bias. . . . Although the majority of forensic odontologists are satisfied that bite marks can demonstrate sufficient detail for positive identification, no scientific studies support this assessment, and no large population studies have been conducted. In numerous instances, experts diverge widely in their evaluations of the same bite mark evidence, which has led to questioning of the value and scientific objectivity of such evidence. . . . The committee received no evidence of an existing scientific basis for identifying an individual to the exclusion of all others."[23]

Bite mark evidence has been admitted in court for decades to link an individual to a particular bite mark.[24] However, the willingness of courts to admit bite mark evidence may change as scientific research has challenged the reliability of bite mark identifications of individuals.

II. IDENTIFICATION

§11.04 THEORY

For identification purposes, anything different (varying from the normal trait or structure) is an important tool for differentiating one person from another. For forensic odontologists, the search for differences focuses on dental structures and appearances. Although distinguishing differences can be found in many features of the oral cavity,[25] most identification investigations focus on the teeth. Teeth and dental restorations are some of the most durable structures in the body. They

---

burg.com/opinion/editorials/editorial-taking-the-bite-out-of-unreliable-evidence/article_e3d875 fb-029e-5f17-819a-97cb248fdfb7.html)(last accessed July 13, 2016). *See also* National Research Council of the National Academies and federal Judicial Center, *Reference Manual on Scientific Evidence,* 3d ed. National Academies Press, 2011 at pp. 109–110 (discussing several exonerations in bite mark cases).

[23] National Academies of Science, *Strengthening Forensic Science in the United States: A Path Forward,* National Academies Press, 2009 (*hereinafter "2009 NAS Report"*) at p. 176 and accompanying citations.

[24] *See* E.H. Dinkel, "The Use of Bite Mark Evidence as an Investigative Aid," 19 J. FORENSIC SCI. 535 (1973); *see also* §11.10(2) *infra.*

[25] *See* Paul M. Jibi, Keshav K. Gautam, Nadig Basappa and Orekondi S. Raju, "Morphological Pattern of Palatal Rugae in the Children of Davangere," 56 J. FORENSIC SCI. 1192–1197 (2011)(studying variations in the folds of tissue in anterior part of the roof of the mouth—the palatal rugae); *see also* D. Shukla et al., "Establishing the Reliability of Palatal Rugae Pattern in Individual Identification (Following Orthodontic Treatment)", 29 J. FORENSIC ODONTOSTOMATOL. 20–29 (2011)(same).

are highly resistant to destruction, decomposition, and mutilation.[26] Therefore, it is frequently possible to discover both the teeth and restorations of a victim among the remains, even when the rest of the body has been totally destroyed.

Each adult human has five anatomic surfaces on as many as 32 teeth for a total of 160 surfaces.[27] Teeth also have individual characteristics caused by wear patterns, spacing, fillings and restorations, positioning, and other features that will distinguish one person's dental profile from another. Although an individual's dental features change throughout their life (through cavities, filings, implants, wear, etc.), the features do not change significantly after death through decomposition. Therefore, dentists have theorized that given sufficient data, no two mouths will have identical characteristics[28] and this uniqueness survives death.[29]

While the premise of individuality of human dentition for bite mark comparison is debatable,[30] it has long been accepted that overall dental features and structures can provide sufficient individualizing detail to permit positive identification.[31] "According to one court, 'it cannot be seriously disputed that a dental structure may constitute a means of identifying a deceased person . . . where there is some dental record of that person with which the structure may be compared.' "[32]

---

[26] Teeth are not immune from destructive forces. As the dental investigations following the 2009 Victorian bushfires demonstrated, dental features may suffer damage from collapsing buildings and intensive prolonged heat exposure which resulted in "dislodgement of teeth from sockets, loss of tooth crowns from roots, disruption of anatomical location of teeth and damage to bony features." Russell Lain et al., "Comparative Dental Anatomy in Disaster Victim Identification: Lessons from the 2009 Victorian Bushfires,"205 FORENSIC SCI. INT'L. 36–39 (2011).

Dental implants, however, can survive fire and can be useful for identification. See Danilo De Angelis and Cristina Cattaneo, "Implant Bone Integration Importance in Forensic Identification," 60 J. Forensic Sci. 505–508 (2015).

[27] National Research Council of the National Academies and federal Judicial Center, Reference Manual on Scientific Evidence, 3d ed., National Academies Press, 2011 at p. 104.

[28] R.L.R. Tinoco et al., "Dental Anomalies and Their Value in Human Identification: A Case Report," 28 J. FORENSIC ODONTOSTOMATOL. 39–43 (2010).

[29] Identical twins have been shown to have different dentition. Reidar F. Sognnaes et al., "Computer Comparison of Bitemark Patterns in Identical Twins," 105 J. AM. DENTAL ASS'N 449 (1982). Recent research, however, has questioned prior studies purportedly establishing uniqueness and databases have been established to collect data to calculate the frequencies of dental profiles similar to DNA typing frequencies. See H. David Sheets et al., "Dental Shape Match Rates in Selected and Orthodontically Treated Populations in New York State: A Two-Dimensional Study," 56 J. FORENSIC SCI. 621–626 (2011).

[30] See Mary J. Bush, Peter J. Bush and H. David Sheets, "Statistical Evidence for the Similarity of the Human Dentition," 56 J. FORENSIC SCI. 118–123 (2011).

[31] Bruce A Schrader and David R. Senn, "Scope of Forensic Odontology," in David R. Senn and Paul G. Stimson, eds., Forensic Dentistry, 2d ed., CRC Press, 2010 at p. 26; and Anthony R. Cardoza, "Forensic Dentistry Investigation Protocols," in C. Michael Bowers ed., Forensic Dental Evidence: An Investigator's Handbook, 2d ed., Academic Press, 2011 at p. 74.

[32] National Research Council of the National Academies and federal Judicial Center, Reference Manual on Scientific Evidence, 3d ed., National Academies Press, 2011 at p. 105 (quoting People v. Mattox, 237 N.E.2d 845, 846 (Ill. App. Ct. 1968)).

Identification by dental information is not a modern concept. During the Revolutionary War, Dr. Joseph Warren, who was a prominent physician and a general in George Washington's army, had a young Boston dentist construct a silver-ivory dental bridge for him. Later, General Warren made use of the dentist's services for a totally different task; he sent the young dentist—Paul Revere—around the countryside to warn the people of the impending approach of the British. After the war was over, Paul Revere used the silver-ivory dental bridge to identify General Warren as one of the casualties of the Battle of Bunker Hill buried in an unmarked grave.[33]

The earliest recorded court case in which dental evidence was used to prove the identity of human remains in a criminal case in the United States was a Massachusetts case in which a Harvard Medical School professor was accused of the 1849 murder of Dr. George Parkman.[34] The dismembered remains of the victim were identified by his dentist, Dr. Nathan Keep. Dr. Keep examined the recovered charred teeth and identified pieces of porcelain denture as the dentures he constructed for Dr. Parkman in 1846. The court found the identification of the dental remains as sufficient to establish the identity of Dr. Parkman as the deceased.[35]

Dental identification also played an important role in the identification of the bodies of Adolf Hitler and Eva Braun during World War II[36] and in the identification of the exhumed body of Lee Harvey Oswald.[37] There have been other dramatic events in which many individuals were identified through an examination of their teeth or dentures, including the 1944 Barnum and Bailey circus fire in Connecticut; the 1949 Noronic Steamship fire in Toronto, Canada; the 1987 sinking of the Herald of Free Enterprise in Belgian waters; the 1993 bombing at the World Trade Center in New York City; the 1993 Branch Davidian siege in Waco, Texas; the September 11, 2001 terrorist attack on the World Trade Center; the 2004 South Asian Tsunami;[38] and the 2005 terrorist bus bombings in London.

---

[33] D. Ben Tesdahl, "Bite Mark Evidence: Making an Impression in Court," 1989 Army Law. 13.

[34] Commonwealth v. Webster, 59 Mass. (5 Cush.) 295 (1850).

[35] For more information on the history of forensic odontology, *see* Paula C. Brumit and Paul G. Stimson, "History of Forensic Dentistry," in David R. Senn and Paul G. Stimson, eds., *Forensic Dentistry*, 2d ed., CRC Press, 2010 at pp. 11–24; Marie Svoboda, C. Michael Bowers, Michel Perrier and Scott Swank, "Historical Dental Investigations," in C. Michael Bowers ed., *Forensic Dental Evidence: An Investigator's Handbook*, 2d ed., Academic Press, 2011 at pp. 1–28.

[36] Reidar F. Sognnaes, "Eva Braun Hitler's Odontological Identification—A Forensic Enigma?" 19 J. FORENSIC SCI. 215 (1974).

[37] Linda E. Norton, James A. Cottone, Irvin M. Sopher & Vincent J.M. DiMaio, "The Exhumation and Identification of Lee Harvey Oswald," 29 J. Forensic Sci. 19 (1984).

[38] The utility of dental identifications following the tsunami were limited in Thailand by deficiencies in training of the volunteers who collected postmortem data and reporting errors in the antemortem records provided by family practitioners. Jules A. Kieser, Wayne Laing and Peter Herbison, "Lessons Learned from Large-scale Comparative Dental Analysis Following the South Asian Tsunami of 2004," 51 J. FORENSIC SCI. 109–112 (2006).

§11.05 TECHNIQUES

Modern routine dental identifications compare the dental data from the unidentified corpse with documented dental information (dental records, models, and x-rays) of the individual suspected to be the deceased.[39] The comparison of the characteristics of dental features is usually accomplished by examining both the antemortem radiographs of the suspected individual and postmortem radiographs of the unidentified human remains. The comparison of antemortem and postmortem radiographs may be assisted by computer imaging and measurement software.[40] If the features match to a sufficient degree and there are no unexplainable differences, it may be possible to establish identity. If there are differences which cannot be explained by the passage of time between radiographs, perimortem and postmortem trauma, or differences in radiographic alignment and conditions,[41] the suspected individual can be excluded as the deceased.[42] An overall error rate for dental identifications has not been established, but recent studies suggest an accuracy rate of approximately 85%.[43]

The American Board of Forensic Odontology (ABFO) guidelines provide a non-exclusive list of dental features that may be useful in

---

[39] "Body Identification Guidelines," in *ABFO Diplomates Reference Manual*, Section III: Policies, Procedures, Guidelines & Standards, March 2017 edition, (available at: https://abfo.org/resources/abfo-manual/)(last accessed February 28, 2017).

[40] *See* Diane J. Flint et al., "Computer-aided Dental Identification: An Objective Method for Assessment of Radiographic Image Similarity," 54 J. FORENSIC SCI. 177–184 (2009).

[41] "[C]are should be exercised when using dental treatment radiographs for direct comparison against postmortem radiographs as there are distortion and angulation factors that need to be considered." John W. Berketa, Robert S. Hirsch, Denice Higgins and Helen James, "Radiographic Recognition of Dental Implants as an Aid to Identifying the Deceased," 55 J. FORENSIC SCI. 66–70, at 66 (2010).

[42] For a detailed explanation of forensic dental identification procedures, including postmortem charting forms and a sample written report, *see* Anthony R. Cardoza, "Forensic Dentistry Investigation Protocols," in C. Michael Bowers ed., *Forensic Dental Evidence: An Investigator's Handbook*, 2d ed., Academic Press, 2011 at pp. 73–92.

For a discussion of recent technological and scientific advances and how they can assist in dental identification, *see* Michael P. Tabor and Bruce A Schrader, "Forensic Dental Identification," in David R. Senn and Paul G. Stimson, eds., *Forensic Dentistry*, 2d ed., CRC Press, 2010 at pp. 178–181.

[43] Dirk T. van der Meer et al., "Root Morphology and Anatomical Patterns in Forensic Dental Identification: A Comparison of Computer-Aided Identification with Traditional Forensic Dental Identification," 55 J. FORENSIC SCI. 1499–1503 (2010)(dental identifications solely based on root morphology and anatomical patterns using ABFO guidelines produced a mean accuracy rate for identification of 86% for forensic odontologists and 85% for digital imaging software comparisons); I.A. Pretty, R.J. Pretty, B.R. Rothwell and D. Sweet, "The Reliability of Digitized Radiographs for Dental Identification: A Web-Based Study," 48 J. FORENSIC SCI. 1325–1330 (2003)(web-based comparison of radiographs from actual forensic identification cases produced overall mean accuracy of 85.5%).

An interesting study was conducted assessing the accuracy rates of trained forensic odontologists and dental students in making identifications based on radiographic comparisons. None of the odontologists produced a false positive identification, but half of the students did. The students used more postmortem images in making their identifications, but spent less time per image than the odontologists. A. Wenzel, A. Richards and J. Heidmann, "Matching Simulated Antemortem and Postmortem Dental Radiographs from Human Skull by Dental Students and Experts: Testing Skills for Pattern Recognition," 28 J. FORENSIC ODONTOSTOMATOL. 5–12 (2010).

identification.[44] In addition to dental features, the modern identification process may involve the radiographic recognition of dental implants. Dental implants are components that are placed within the jaw bones to provide support for dental prostheses and the materials currently used survive destructive forces like fire.[45] Manufacturers frequently etch batch numbers on their prosthetic devices.[46] Recent advances with implant recognition software and batch numbers contribute to the dental identification by the forensic odontologist.[47]

Forensic odontologists may also use dental computer systems that record information regarding restored dental surfaces, physical descriptors, and pathological and anthropologic findings to rank possible matches to assist in identifying remains.[48] WinID3 is the most commonly used conventional coding and sorting algorithms used in the United States for the identification of human remains by dental features.[49]

After comparison of the antemortem and postmortem materials, the ABFO guidelines recommend four possible conclusions:

(A) Positive Identification: The antemortem and post mortem data match in sufficient detail to establish that they are the same individual [and] there are no irreconcilable discrepancies.

(B) Possible Identification: The antemortem and postmortem data have consistent features but, due to the quality of either the postmortem remains or the antemortem evidence, it is not possible to positively establish dental identification.

(C) Insufficient Evidence: The available information is insufficient to form the basis for a conclusion.

(D) Exclusion: The antemortem and postmortem data are clearly inconsistent.[50]

---

[44] Body Identification Guidelines," in *ABFO Diplomates Reference Manual*, Section III: Policies, Procedures, Guidelines & Standards, March 2017 edition, (available at: https://abfo. org/resources/abfo-manual/)(last accessed February 28, 2017).

[45] Joseph D. Bonavilla, Mary A. Bush, Peter J. Bush, and Eugene A. Pantera, "Identification of Incinerated Root Canal Filling Materials After Exposure to High Heat Incineration," 53 J. FORENSIC SCI. 412–418 (2008).

[46] *See* J. Berketa, H. James and V. Marino, "Survival of Batch Numbers Within Dental Implants Following Incineration as an Aid to Identification," 28 J. FORENSIC ODONTOSTOMATOL. 1–4 (2010) and J. Berketa, H. James and V. Marino, "Dental Implant Changes Following Incineration," 201 FORENSIC SCI. INT'L 50–54 (2011).

[47] T.K. Deepalakshmi and Manoj Prabhakar, "Role of Dental Implants in Forensic Identification," 6(2) J. FORENSIC DENT. SCI. 145–147 (2014).

[48] *See* Bradley J. Adams and Kenneth W. Aschheim, "Computerized Dental Comparison: A Critical Review of Dental Coding and Ranking Algorithms Used in Victim Identification," 61 J. Forensic Sci. 76–86 (2016).

[49] WinID3 can be downloaded free at http://abfo.org/winid/ (last accessed July 11, 2016).

[50] Body Identification Guidelines," in *ABFO Diplomates Reference Manual*, Section III: Policies, Procedures, Guidelines & Standards, March 2017 edition (available at: https://abfo. org/resources/abfo-manual/)(last accessed February 28, 2017).

The ABFO guidelines also permit identification by exclusion in certain circumstances, such as a closed population of missing individuals.[51]

§11.06 LIMITATIONS

Limitations in dental identification generally involve the quality of the antemortem records[52] or the postmortem state of the remains.[53] Antemortem records, particularly older records, may be incomplete or have charting errors, and some individuals have no antemortem dental record. Most states have laws or regulations requiring the retention of patient information for a period of time, usually 3–10 years.[54] Problems are sometimes encountered in obtaining suitable postmortem radiographs for comparison with antemortem records. It may be necessary to take a number of radiographs of varying densities. If the dentist is confronted with a skeleton, she may have to separate the skull from the body to be able to take the proper radiographs. Intact but decomposed bodies are dealt with differently and at times jaw resection (removal of the dental apparatus) is recommended.[55]

The lack of dental features in the individual can also be a complicating factor; for individuals who have lost all or most of their teeth (endentulous individuals), positive identification through forensic odontological examination can be extremely challenging.[56] If the individual had dentures and they are recovered, identification is sometimes possible.[57] Dentures often contain the manufacturer's markings, just as the individual teeth that make up the denture may

---

[51] Id.

[52] AR Al-Azir, J. Harford, and H. James, "Awareness of Forensic Odontology Among Dentists in Australia: Are They Keeping Forensically Valuable Dental Records?" 61 Australian Dental Journal 102–108 (2016)(recommending improvements in recording and retaining dental information to maximize accuracy and adequacy of dental records).

[53] Jules A. Kieser, Wayne Laing and Peter Herbison, "Lessons Learned from Large-scale Comparative Dental Analysis Following the South Asian Tsunami of 2004," 51 J. FORENSIC SCI. 109–112 (2006); Russell Lain et al., "Comparative Dental Anatomy in Disaster Victim Identification: Lessons from the 2009 Victorian Bushfires,"205 FORENSIC SCI. INT'L. 36–39 (2011).

Forensic odontologists are working to develop standards and training to improve the process of dental identifications following mass disasters. See Harry K. Zohn et al., "The Odontology Victim Identification Skill Assessment System," 55 J. FORENSIC SCI. 788791 (2010).

[54] See, e.g., Fla. Admin. Code R. 61 FS 17.005 (dentists must maintain written dental records for four years after the patient is last examined or treated); Maryland Health-General Code § 4–403 (dentists must retain records for five years after the record is made or, if the patient is a minor, three years after the date of maturity); MCL 333.16644 (Michigan dentists must retain records for not less than 10 years after the last date of treatment); 18 VAC 60–20–15 (dental patient records must be maintained for at least three years following the most recent date of service).

[55] Guidelines for the collection and preservation of postmortem dental evidence are available, see "Body Identification Guidelines," in ABFO Diplomates Reference Manual, Section III: Policies, Procedures, Guidelines & Standards, March 2017 edition (available at: https://abfo.org/resources/abfo-manual/)(last accessed February 28, 2017).

[56] See Raymond Richmond and Iain A. Pretty, "Identification of the Edentulous Individual: An Investigation into the Accuracy of Radiographic Identifications," 55 J. FORENSIC SCI. 984–987 (2010).

[57] See Rogers v. State, 256 Ga. 139, 344 S.E.2d 644 (1986).

have specific mold numbers corresponding to their shape and color shade numbers.

III. TRAUMA ANALYSIS

§11.07 DENTAL TRAUMA

Trauma is a physical injury caused by an external force. Forensic odontologists may be asked to examine an individual (living or deceased) for evidence of trauma to facial/dental structures such as dental root fractures, alveolar fractures, jaw fractures, tears in the frenulum, palatal petechiae, bruises, and burns. Untreated trauma may result in other signs such as pulpal necrosis, malocclusion.[58] Facial/dental trauma is often found in cases involving domestic violence, child abuse, elder abuse, and human rights violations.[59]

Forensic odontologists are sometimes asked to assist in determinations of how dental trauma occurred or whether such trauma was inflicted accidentally or intentionally.[60] In making such determinations, investigators will compare the physical injuries with the version of events provided and variances or discrepancies will suggest the circumstances under which the trauma occurred.[61] Other physical traits about the injuries, such as location, laterality, pattern, and number of injuries, may assist in distinguishing the source and manner of injury.[62] In *Dunlap v. Woods*,[63] the forensic odontologist was asked to examine the defendant's broken tooth to determine whether such an injury could have occurred, as the defendant alleged to support his claim of self-defense, from a blow by the victim. Based on the location of the broken tooth (back molar), the force necessary to knock out such a tooth, and no visible injury to the corresponding side of the defendant's face, the forensic odontologist concluded the injury was more likely caused by the defendant biting down on something hard and not a blow during a fight.[64]

---

[58] Helena Soomer Lincoln and Michael J. Lincoln, "Role of the Odontologist in the Investigation of Domestic Violence, Neglect of the Vulnerable, and Institutional Violence and Torture," 201 FORENSIC SCI. INT'L. 68–73 (2010).

[59] *See* Id. (Over 75% of abuse victims have injuries to the head, face, mouth, and neck and so dentists are often the first responders.").

[60] John McDowell, "Recognizing, Documenting, and Analyzing Physical Evidence in Abuse Cases," in C. Michael Bowers ed., *Forensic Dental Evidence: An Investigator's Handbook*, 2d ed., Academic Press, 2011 at pp. 225–241.

[61] Id. at 226. *See also* John D. McDowell, "Abuse: The Role of Forensic Dentists," in David R. Senn and Paul G. Stimson, eds., *Forensic Dentistry*, 2d ed., CRC Press, 2010 at pp. 369–378.

[62] Helena Soomer Lincoln and Michael J. Lincoln, "Role of the Odontologist in the Investigation of Domestic Violence, Neglect of the Vulnerable, and Institutional Violence and Torture," 201 FORENSIC SCI. INT'L. 68–73 (2010).

[63] 2016 U.S. Dist LEXIS 53311 (ED Mich. April 21, 2016).

[64] Id. at *7.

Distinguishing antemortem trauma from postmortem effects in dental tissue following fires may not be possible.[65]

§11.08 IDENTIFICATION OF BITE MARKS

A particular form of trauma of interest to forensic odontologists is the trauma inflicted by a human bite. The bite mark is a reactive response generated by the injured skin.[66] Although current ABFO Guidelines note "[t]he meaning of [the term bite mark] is clear and there is no need for the ABFO to endorse a particular form,"[67] the guidelines do contain the following definition of bite mark: "A physical alteration in a medium caused by the contact of teeth[;] [a] representative pattern left in an object or tissue by the dental structures of an animal or human."[68] A bite mark may be caused by "a human biting another human, by an animal biting a human, or by either biting an object."[69] For purposes of discussion, this section will focus on human bite marks on other humans, but many of the principles and limitations are applicable to the other types of bite marks.

As with identification of the source of the bite mark (discussed *infra*), the best method for determining whether a mark is a human bite mark is from DNA collected at the site of injury which is foreign to the victim (the person on whom the bite mark was inflicted), and therefore is from the saliva of the biter.[70] In the absence of DNA, a bite mark may be difficult to recognize, especially if the mark is partial or without the complete complement of front teeth.[71] The ABFO guidelines provide the following list of component injuries that may be observed in bite marks: "Abrasions (scrapes), contusions (bruises), lacerations (tears), ecchymosis, petechiae, avulsion, indentations (depressions), erythema (redness) and punctures."[72] Features indicative of bite marks in skin include ovoid/elliptical patterns, interrupted abrasions, and continuous bruises.[73]

---

[65] *See* Miranda N. Campbell and Scott I. Fairgrieve, "Differentiation of Traumatic and Heat-Induced Dental Tissue Fractures via SEM Analysis," 56 J. FORENSIC SCI. 715–719 (2011).

[66] Mark L. Bernstein, "Nature of Bitemarks," in Robert B.J. Dorion, ed., *Bitemark Evidence*, CRC Press, 2005 at p. 61.

[67] "ABFO Bitemark Methodology Standards and Guidelines" in *ABFO Diplomates Reference Manual*, Section III: Policies, Procedures, Guidelines & Standards, March 2017 edition (available at: https://abfo.org/resources/abfo-manual/)(last accessed February 28, 2017) at p. 94.

[68] Id. at p. 101.

[69] David R. Senn and Richard R. Souviron, "Bitemarks," in David R. Senn and Paul G. Stimson, eds., *Forensic Dentistry*, 2d ed., CRC Press, 2010 at p. 333.

[70] *See* C. Michael Bowers, "Recognition, Documentation, Evidence Collection, and Interpretation of Bitemark Evidence," in C. Michael Bowers ed., *Forensic Dental Evidence: An Investigator's Handbook*, 2d ed., Academic Press, 2011 at pp. 94, 98–99.

[71] Id. at 100.

[72] "ABFO Bitemark Terminology Guidelines" in *ABFO Diplomates Reference Manual*, Section III: Policies, Procedures, Guidelines & Standards, March 2017 edition, at p. 100.

[73] C. Michael Bowers, "Recognition, Documentation, Evidence Collection, and Interpretation of Bitemark Evidence," in C. Michael Bowers ed., *Forensic Dental Evidence: An Investigator's Handbook*, 2d ed., Academic Press, 2011 at pp. 104–105.

The difficulties in examining bite marks and evaluating their worth for identification purposes are many and varied. It is critical that a pathologist performing an autopsy or a physician examining a victim correctly recognizes soft tissue pattern injuries resulting from human bites. Forensic pathologists and odontologists have misidentified other pattern injuries, abrasions, and insect bites as bite marks.[74] To conclude that an injury is a bite mark, ABFO guidelines recommend that the following criteria be met: "pattern demonstrates class and/or individual characteristics of human teeth."[75] Class characteristics are further defined as features that "distinguish a bitemark from other patterned injuries" with an example provided of "four approximating linear or rectangular contusions" as a class characteristic of human incisors.[76] An individual characteristic is defined as "a feature, trait, or pattern that represents an individual variation rather than an expected finding within a defined group" with two categories: arch characteristics (tooth arrangement) and dental characteristics (individual tooth variation).[77] Based on the class and individual characteristics, ABFO guidelines recommend three possible conclusions: human bitemark, not a human bitemark, or inconclusive.[78]

Age estimation of a human bite mark has been described as "neither a scientific nor an accurate process."[79]

§11.09 Bite Mark Comparisons

1. Theory

The identification of the source of a human bite mark can be made using DNA typing technology on the salivary DNA left behind by the biter.[80] In the absence of DNA, forensic odontologists may examine the features of the bite mark for comparison with the dental features of a

---

[74] *See, e.g.*, Kris Sperry & Homer R. Campbell, "An Elliptical Incised Wound of the Breast Misinterpreted as a Bite Injury," 35 J. Forensic Sci. 1226 (1990). *See also* C. Michael Bowers, "Recognition, Documentation, Evidence Collection, and Interpretation of Bitemark Evidence," in C. Michael Bowers ed., *Forensic Dental Evidence: An Investigator's Handbook*, 2d ed., Academic Press, 2011 at pp. 105–106 (describing postmortem effects and a knife injury that have been mistaken for human bite marks); Robert B.J. Dorion and Richard R. Souviron, "Patterns, Lesions, and Trauma-Mimicking Bitemarks" in Robert B.J. Dorion ed., *Bitemark Evidence: A Color Atlas and Text*," 2d ed., CRC Press, 2011 at pp. 283–299 (discussing postmortem effects and other injuries that have been mistaken for human bite marks).

[75] "ABFO Bitemark Terminology Guidelines" in *ABFO Diplomates Reference Manual*, Section III: Policies, Procedures, Guidelines & Standards, March 2017 edition, at p. 102.

[76] Id. at p. 100.

[77] Id.

[78] Id. at p. 102.

[79] C. Michael Bowers, "Recognition, Documentation, Evidence Collection, and Interpretation of Bitemark Evidence," in C. Michael Bowers ed., *Forensic Dental Evidence: An Investigator's Handbook*, 2d ed., Academic Press, 2011 at p. 108.

[80] June Kenna et al., "The Recovery and Persistence of Salivary DNA on Human Skin," 56 J. Forensic Sci. 170–175 (2011).

particular individual. This area of forensic odontology is very controversial.[81]

Biting is "a dynamic procedure that involves three moving systems with three-dimensional characteristics: the maxilla and mandible of the biter, the skin, and the movement of the person bitten."[82] Additional factors affecting the appearance of a bite mark are the pressure of the bite, where on the body the bite is located, and individual variations in the skin of the person bitten. The principles on which bite mark comparison has been premised are that human dentition is unique and that sufficient individualizing characteristics are reflected in a human bite mark to permit conclusions about the identity of the biter.[83] These principles, however, have come under considerable attack from the legal and scientific communities as DNA typing has demonstrated the inaccuracy of bite mark comparisons in the cases of individuals wrongfully convicted or arrested.[84]

Of the first principle on which bite mark comparisons have been premised—uniqueness of human dentition—researchers have disproven older statistical studies[85] and most forensic odontologists will agree that although an individual's overall dental structure may be unique, "the *degree* to which a given *individual's* dentition is unique will vary."[86] Some scientific commentators have argued that uniqueness is actually irrelevant and that the central focus should be on determining the quantification of match probabilities.[87] The second principle—that individualizing dentition features will reliably transfer through a human bite to human skin—is a prominent source of controversy and continuing study.[88]

---

[81] Guy Willems, John Clement and David Sweet, "Editorial, Forensic Odontology Special Issue—September 2010" 201 FORENSIC SCI. INT'L. 1–2 (2010)("The one area where controversy still exists in our discipline relates to the analysis of bite mark and other patterned injuries and whether our current analytical approaches will stand up to scrutiny in a well-informed adversarial system of justice. Recent cases of very delayed exonerations on DNA evidence from the USA would indicate that, in some quarters at least, we have a problem.").

[82] Ana Molina and Stella Martin-de-las-Heras, "Accuracy of 3D Scanners in Tooth Mark Analysis," 60 J. Forensic Sci. S222–S226 (2015).

[83] C. Michael Bowers and Ian A. Pretty, "Expert Disagreement in Bitemark Casework," 54 J. FORENSIC SCI. 915–918 (2009).

[84] *See* Notes 156–162 *infra* and accompanying text.

[85] Mary A. Bush, Peter J. Bush and H. David Sheets, "Statistical Evidence for the Similarity of the Human Dentition," 56 J. FORENSIC SCI. 118–123 (2011).

[86] C. Michael Bowers and Ian A. Pretty, "Expert Disagreement in Bitemark Casework," 54 J. FORENSIC SCI. 915–918 (2009). *See also* Iain A. Pretty, "Resolving Issues in Bitemark Analysis," in Robert B.J. Dorion ed., *Bitemark Evidence: A Color Atlas and Text,"* 2d ed., CRC Press, 2011 at pp. 608–612(summarizing the current state of research on uniqueness).

[87] Mark Page, Jane Taylor and Matt Blenkin, "Uniqueness in the Forensic Identification Sciences—Fact or Fiction?," 206 FORENSIC SCI. INT'L. 12–18 (2011)("The reality is that uniqueness is impossible to prove, and is not anywhere near as relevant as some may claim; mistakes and misidentifications are not made because someone has an identical [dental profile] to someone else in the world. They are made because of guesswork, poor performance, lack of standards, bias and observer error.").

[88] C. Michael Bowers and Ian A. Pretty, "Expert Disagreement in Bitemark Casework," 54 J. FORENSIC SCI. 915–918 (2009). *See also* Iain A. Pretty, "Resolving Issues in Bitemark

2. TECHNIQUES

Techniques of comparison analysis of bite marks have included overlays, test bites, photo and dental cast comparisons, transillumination of tissue, superimposition histology, microscopy, and computer enhancement and/or digitization. The methods are mentioned in the ABFO Guidelines[89] and discussed in great detail in other texts.[90] Analysis has also been done by direct comparison of photographs[91] or comparison of photographs with models.[92] In addition to photographs and models of the bite marks of the suspected biter, examiners collect dental evidence exemplars for comparison from dental history records, photography, extraoral and intraoral examinations, impressions, and casts.[93]

The physical characteristics of a bite mark that are analyzed by the forensic odontologist have been described as follows:[94]

> "The general arch size and shape are the first characteristics considered. If there is a discrepancy, the suspect can be eliminated. The analysis continues in the absence of a discrepancy. . . . Dominant features of the dentition are inspected first for discordance with the bitemark. Explanations for discordance (while asserting a bite's identification) cannot be scientifically proven and should be considered bias."

3. LIMITATIONS

The limitations of bite mark comparison were described in the 2009 NAS Report and have been summarized as follows:

1. The uniqueness of the human dentition has not been scientifically established.

2. Transfer of a pattern, if unique, to skin has not been established.

Analysis," in Robert B.J. Dorion ed., *Bitemark Evidence: A Color Atlas and Text,"* 2d ed., CRC Press, 2011 at pp. 601–606 (summarizing the current state of research on human skin as a bite registration material).

[89] "ABFO Bitemark Methodology Standards and Guidelines" in *ABFO Diplomates Reference Manual*, Section III: Policies, Procedures, Guidelines & Standards, March 2017 edition, at p. 99.

[90] John Curtis Dailey, "Methods of Comparison," in Robert B.J. Dorion ed., *Bitemark Evidence: A Color Atlas and Text,"* 2d ed., CRC Press, 2011.

[91] Michelle McClure, "Odontology: Bite Marks as Evidence in Criminal Trials," 11 Santa Clara Computer & High Tech. L.J. 269 (July 1995).

[92] Norman D. Sperber, "Forensic Odontology," Scientific and Expert Evidence 721, 744–47 (Edward J. Imwinkelreid, ed., 1981).

[93] L. Thomas Johnson, "The Suspect," in Robert B.J. Dorion ed., *Bitemark Evidence: A Color Atlas and Text,"* 2d ed., CRC Press, 2011 at pp. 463–406.

[94] C. Michael Bowers, "Recognition, Documentation, Evidence Collection, and Interpretation of Bitemark Evidence," in C. Michael Bowers ed., *Forensic Dental Evidence: An Investigator's Handbook*, 2d ed., Academic Press, 2011 at pp. 124–125.

    a.   Ability to analyze and interpret scope of distortion in skin has not been demonstrated.

    b.   Effect of distortion on comparison techniques has not been quantified.

3.   Accuracy of the skin as registration material has not been established.

4.   Standard for evidentiary value has not been established.

5.   Effect of healing process is not understood.

6.   No large population studies have been performed.

7.   Rarely are comparisons made between the bite mark and a number of models.[95]

Apart from the limitations concerning the theory of uniqueness and deficiencies in standards and protocols, the limitations concern the specific properties of skin. A bite mark is not an exact representation of the teeth that caused its impression. To understand this, one must consider the bite dynamics and its effects on the impression made by the teeth. The lower jaw (mandible) is movable and delivers the bite force against the upper jaw (maxilla) which is stationary. The upper teeth hold the substance which is being bitten as the lower teeth approach for the purpose of cutting the substance. When referring to bite marks in skin, this would mean that the skin is curved between the upper and lower teeth but as the lower jaw moves up to cut the tissue, the skin is stretched away from its normal curvature between the teeth. It will be considerably out of shape when the force is actually inflicted that causes the skin to be pinched between the upper and lower teeth. In this whole process, the skin itself has not been stationary, because it tends to slip along the upper teeth until they catch hold when the bite occurs.

The degree of distortion in a bite mark varies significantly based on "skin tension lines, anatomical location, underlying tissue structure, movement during and after bitemark infliction, and clothing among other factors."[96] The distortion can affect the degree to which individual dentition features are transferred to human skin, and therefore, the comparison of the bite mark to an individual's dental features. Efforts to account for the distortion through bite mark profiling and arbitrary distortion compensation have been proven ineffectual because the distortional ranges are non-uniform both between bites as well as within each bite.[97]

---

[95] Mary A. Bush and Peter J. Bush, "Current Context of Bitemark Analysis and Research," in Robert B.J. Dorion ed., *Bitemark Evidence: A Color Atlas and Text,*" 2d ed., CRC Press, 2011 at p. 305.

[96] Raymond G. Miller, Peter J. Bush, Robert B.J. Dorion and Mary A. Bush, "Uniqueness of the Dentition as Impressed in Human Skin: A Cadaver Model," 54 J. FORENSIC SCI. 909–914 (2009).

[97] Mary A. Bush, Howard I. Cooper and Robert B.J. Dorion, "Inquiry into the Scientific Basis for Bitemark Profiling and Arbitrary Distortion Compensation," 55 J. FORENSIC SCI. 976–983 (2010).

Another serious criticism of bite mark analytical methods concerns the degree of subjectivity of the process and the sources of potentially biasing influences.[98] Context effects surrounding bite mark analysis include the violent nature of the case (typically rape, murder, or other serious violent assault) and on-going working relationships with law enforcement. Other biasing effects include contrast effects ("seeing" similarities because looking for similarities) and overconfidence (over-estimating ability on routinely performed tasks).[99] Suggestions have been made for minimizing the effects of bias, but current professional guidelines have not adopted these suggestions.

The ABFO has adopted the following standard[100] for "Bitemark Terminology" that limits the conclusions that can be stated for bite mark comparisons:

1. Terms assuring unconditional identification of a perpetrator, or identification "without doubt", are not sanctioned as a final conclusions (sic) in an open population case.

2. Terms used in a different manner from the guidelines should be explained in the body of a report or in testimony.

3. All forensic odontologists certified by the American Board of Forensic Odonotology are responsible for being familiar with the standards set forth in this document.[101]

Similarly, the ABFO has adopted the following guidelines for terms used to relate a suspect's dentition to a bitemark:

A. Excluded as Having Made the Bitemark

B. Not Excluded as Having Made the Bitemark

C. Inconclusive[102]

4. POST-2009 NAS REPORT RESEARCH

To improve the reliability of bite mark comparisons, researchers worked on methods to quantify match probabilities,[103] to make

---

[98] Mark Page, Jane Taylor, and Matt Blenkin, "Context Effects and Observer Bias—Implications for Forensic Odontology," 57 J. FORENSIC SCI. 108–112 (2012).

[99] Id.

[100] ABFO Standards have more impact on professionals than ABFO Guidelines. Standards are "[a] model to be followed. . . compulsory minimum level of practice . . . more restrictive than guidelines; more enforceable." "Definitions of Guidelines, Standards and Policies," *ABFO Diplomates Reference Manual*, Section III: Policies, Procedures, Guidelines & Standards, March 2017 edition at p. 92.

[101] "ABFO Bitemark Methodology Standards and Guidelines," *ABFO Diplomates Reference Manual*, Section III: Policies, Procedures, Guidelines & Standards, March 2017 edition at p. 94.

[102] Id. at p. 102.

[103] *See* Mihran Tuceryan et al., "A Framework for Estimating Probability of a Match in Forensic Bite Mark Identification," 56 J. FORENSIC SCI. S83–S89 (2011).

morphometric comparisons by three-dimensional analysis of biting mechanisms,[104] to improve evidence collections procedures,[105] to use computer-assisted morphometric assessments,[106] to statistically assess the range of distortion in bite marks,[107] to assess the utility of affine transformations in matching bite marks,[108] and to assess context effects and observer bias in bite mark analysis.[109] However, the research conducted after the release of the 2009 NAS Report did little to quell the controversy surrounding the use of bite mark comparison for identification. Studies demonstrated wide variability in methods, reasoning, and terminology leading to inconsistencies in identifying bite marks from other pattern injuries.[110] Studies disputed the assumptions underlying bite mark comparison: the uniqueness of human dentition,[111] the ability of human skin to accurately record variations in dentition,[112] and the ability of ABFO-certified forensic odontologists to distinguish injuries as human bite marks.[113]

---

[104] *See* Ana Molina and Stella Martin-de-las-Heras, "Accuracy of 3D Scanners in Tooth Mark Analysis," 60 J. FORENSIC SCI. S222–S226 (2015).

[105] Sylvain Desranleau and Robert B.J. Dorion, "Bite Marks: Physical Properties of Ring Adhesion to Skin—Phase 1," 56 J. FORENSIC SCI. S214–S219 (2011); Sylvain Desranleau and Robert B.J. Dorion, "Bite Marks: Physical Properties of Ring Adhesion to Skin—Phase 2," 57 J. FORENSIC SCI. 201–205 (2012).

[106] Valeria Santoro, Piercarlo Lozito, Antonio De Donno and Francesco Introna, "Experimental Study of Bite Mark Injuries by Digital Analysis," 56 J. FORENSIC SCI. 224–228 (2011).

[107] Mary A. Bush, Peter J. Bush and H. David Sheets, "A Study of Multiple Bitemarks Inflicted in Human Skin by a Single Dentition Using Geometric Morphometric Analysis," 211 FORENSIC SCI. INT'L. 1–8 (2011).

[108] Gerrit Stols and Herman Bernitz, "Reconstruction of Deformed Bite Marks Using Affine Transformations," 55 J. FORENSIC SCI. 784–787 (2010); Herman Bernitz and Gerrit Stols, "The Application of Affine Transformations in Matching Distorted Forensic Samples with a Common Origin," 201 Forensic Sci. Int'l. 56–58 (2010); H. David Sheets and Mary A. Bush, "Mathematical Matching of a Dentition to Bitemarks: Use and Evaluation of Affine Methods," 207 FORENSIC SCI. INT'L. 111–118 (2011).

[109] Mark Page et al., "Context Effects and Observer Bias—Implications for Forensic Odontology," 57 J. FORENSIC SCI. 108–112 (2012); *see also* S. I. Avon, C. Victor, J.T. Mayhall and R.E. Wood, "Error Rates in Bite Mark Analysis in an In Vivo Animal Model," 201 FORENSIC SCI. INT'L. 45–55 (2010).

[110] Mark Page et al, "Expert Interpretation of Bitemark Injuries—A Contemporary Qualitative Study," 58 J. FORENSIC SCI. 664–672 (2013).

[111] Mary A. Bush, Peter J. Bush, and H. David Sheets, "Statistical Evidence for the Similarity of the Human Dentition," 56 J. FORENSIC SCI. 118–123 (2011); H. David Sheets et al, "Dental Shape Match Rates in Selected and Orthodontically Treated Populations in New York State: A Two Dimensional Study," 56 J. FORENSIC SCI. 621–626 (2011); Mary A. Bush, Peter J. Bush and H. David Sheets, "Similarity and Match Rates of the Human Dentition in 3 Dimensions: Relevance to Bitemark Analysis," 125 INT'L J. LEGAL MED. 779–784 (2011).

[112] Mary A. Bush, Peter J. Bush, and H. David Sheets, "A Study of Multiple Bitemarks Inflicted in Human Skin by a Single Dentition Using Geometric Morphometric Analysis," 211 FORENSIC SCI. INT'L 1–8 (2011); Mary A. Bush et al., "The Response of Skin to Applied Stress: Investigation of Bitemark Distortion in a Cadaver Model," 55 J. FORENSIC SCI. 71–76 (2010); Mary A. Bush, Howard I. Cooper and Robert B.J. Dorion, "Inquiry into the Scientific Basis for Bitemark Profiling and Arbitrary Distortion Compensation," 55 J. FORENSIC SCI. 976–983 (2010); Raymond G. Miller, Peter J. Bush, Robert B.J. Dorion, and Mary A. Bush, "Uniqueness of the Dentition as Impressed in Human Skin: A Cadaver Model," 54 J. FORENSIC SCI. 909–914 (2009).

[113] Iain Pretty and Adam Freeman, "Construct Validity Bitemark Assessments Using the ABFO Decision Tree," 2015 (presentation available at: http://online.wsj.com/public/resources/documents/ConstructValidBMdecisiontreePRETTYFREEMAN.pdf (last accessed July 13,

5.   2016 REPORTS

Despite efforts of the professional organizations to conduct research and standardize analytical methods, the criticism of bite mark identification evidence intensified after the 2009 NAS Report. In July 2015, the assistant director of the White House Office of Science and Technology Policy called bite mark comparison one of "the kinds of methods that have to be eradicated from forensic science."[114] In April, 2016, the Texas Forensic Science Commission released its report on the bite mark comparison evidence in the case of Steven Mark Chaney that concluded by recommending that bite mark comparison analysis be barred from admission in criminal cases in Texas.[115]

After collecting and reviewing the existing scientific literature and data, including requesting input from the ABFO membership and other recognized forensic odontologists, and holding three meetings with prominent forensic odontologists and bite mark comparison critics, the Texas Forensic Science Commission Bite Mark Investigation Panel recommended that bite mark comparison evidence not be admitted in Texas criminal cases "unless and until the following are established:"[116]

1. Criteria for identifying when a patterned injury constitutes a human bitemark.

2. Criteria for identifying when a human bitemark was made by an adult versus a child.

3. Rigorous and appropriately validated proficiency testing using the above criteria.

4. A collaborative plan for case review including a multidisciplinary team of forensic odontologists and attorneys.

In addition to accepting the recommendation of the panel, the Commission made two observations that "should be universally accepted among forensic odontologists and stakeholders in the broader criminal justice community":[117]

2016); see also Radley Balko, "A Bite Mark Matching Advocacy Group Just Conducted a Study that Discredits Bite Mark Evidence," Washington Post, April 8, 2015 (available at: https://www.washingtonpost.com/news/the-watch/wp/2015/04/08/a-bite-mark-matching-advocacy-group-just-conducted-a-study-that-discredits-bite-mark-evidence/)(last accessed July 14, 2016).

[114] Radley Balko, "A High-Ranking Obama Official Just called for the "Eradication" of Bite Mark Evidence," Washington Post, July 22, 2015 (available at: https://www.washingtonpost.com/news/the-watch/wp/2015/07/22/a-high-ranking-obama-official-just-called-for-the-eradication-of-bite-mark-evidence/)(last accessed July 12, 2016).

[115] Texas Forensic Science Commission, "Forensic Bitemark Comparison Complaint Filed by National Innocence Project on Behalf of Steven Mark Chaney—Final Report," April 12, 2016 (available at: http://www.fsc.texas.gov/sites/default/files/FinalBiteMarkReport.pdf)(last accessed July 12, 2016).

[116] Id. at pp. 15–16.

[117] Id. at pp. 11–12.

First, there is no scientific basis for stating that a particular patterned injury can be associated to an individual's dentition.

Second, there is no scientific basis for assigning probability or statistical weight to an association, regardless of whether such probability or weight is expressed numerically (e.g., 1 in a million) or using some form of verbal scale (e.g., highly likely/unlikely).

The Commission concluded that "the overwhelming majority of existing research does not support the contention that bitemark comparison can be performed reliably and accurately from examiner to examiner due to the subjective nature of the analysis."[118]

In September, 2016, the President's Council of Advisors on Science and Technology (PCAST) approved a report to the President on "Forensic Science in Criminal Courts: Ensuring Scientific Validity of Feature-Comparison Methods" (hereinafter "2016 PCAST Report).[119] Like the NAS Report, the 2016 PCAST Report focused on several forensic science disciplines, including bite mark comparison analysis. The report detailed the research conducted since the 2009 NAS Report and emphasized the studies showing disagreement among bitemark examiners on even the basic question of whether an injury was a human bite mark at all.[120] After review of the empirical research, PCAST found:

> [B]itemark analysis does not meet the scientific standards for foundational validity, and is far from meeting such standards. To the contrary, available scientific evidence strongly suggests that examiners cannot consistently agree on whether an injury is a human bitemark and cannot identify the source of [a] bitemark with reasonable accuracy.[121]

In response to statements from practitioners that the exclusion of bitemark evidence could hamper prosecution efforts, PCAST cautioned that, if that concern is appropriate, the correct solution would be to attempt to develop a scientifically valid method. In conclusion, PCAST expressed the opinion that the likelihood of developing a scientifically

---

[118] Id. at p. 12.

[119] Executive Office of the President, President's Council of Advisors on Science and Technology, "Forensic Science in Criminal Courts: Ensuring Scientific Validity of Feature-Comparison Methods," September 2016 (available at: https://obamawhitehouse.archives.gov/blog/2016/09/20/pcast-releases-report-forensic-science-criminal-courts)(last accessed February 28, 2017).

[120] 2016 PCAST Report at p. 84 (citing a presentation by Adam Freeman and Iain Pretty "Construct Validity of Bitemark Assessment Using the ABFO Decision Tree," at the 2016 Annual Meeting of the American Academy of Forensic Sciences, see http://online.wsj.com/public/resources/documents/ConstructValidBMdecisiontreePRETTYFREEMAN.pdf)(last accessed September 16, 2016).

[121] 2016 PCAST Report at p. 87.

valid method to be so low that significant resources should not be expended on such an effort.[122]

Given the current state of research, the comparison analysis of purported human bite marks to implicate suspects is extremely controversial and such evidence in any individual case should be carefully scrutinized for any appropriate evidentiary challenge.

IV. TRIAL AIDS

§11.10 EXPERT QUALIFICATIONS

Forensic odontology is a dentistry subspecialty and requires additional training beyond the typical four years of college or university. Following graduation from college, forensic odontologists pursue a dentistry degree (D.D.S.: Doctor of Dental Surgery or D.M.D.: Doctor of Dental Medicine) with specialized training in forensic odontology. After completing the required education and training and licensure in dentistry, the dentist may become certified in forensic odontology through a professional organization.

Forensic odontology certification is a voluntary process in the United States. While dental licensing is necessary for practice in a particular state, licensing establishes a minimum competency requirement and does not represent specialization in any area of dentistry. Certification in forensic odontology, while not required, is highly encouraged as a means of ensuring educational and practical competency in the field. The non-profit Forensic Specialties Accreditation Board[123] has accredited the American Board of Forensic Odontology (ABFO) to administer certification of forensic odontologists.[124] Certification through the ABFO requires a DDS, DMD or equivalent dental degree from an accredited institution; attendance at 4 annual meetings of a national forensic or forensic dental organization; participation in 2 annual programs, two-year affiliation with a medical examiner/coroner agency, law enforcement agency, insurance agency, federal dental service or mass disaster team; observation of 5 complete autopsies; performance of 32 forensic dental cases, including four bite mark cases; ABFO successful review of casework; evidence of forensic dental activity; and successful completion of a written, practical and oral examination.[125] Certification can be denied, suspended, or revoked for a misstatement or misrepresentation

---

[122] Id.

[123] *See* www.thefsab.org.

[124] American Board of Forensic Odontology website: www.abfo.org (last accessed July 13, 2016).

[125] "Qualifications and Requirements for Certification," *ABFO Diplomates Reference Manual*, Section III: P.olicies, Procedures, Guidelines & Standards, March 2017 edition, at pp. 63–70.

in the application, misleading or false statements in sworn testimony, conviction of a felony or crime of moral turpitude, ineligibility for certification, conduct contrary to the purposes of the ABFO, failure to recertify every five years, and nonpayment of fees owed to the ABFO.[126] As of July, 2016, over 100 individuals maintain certification as diplomates in forensic odontology by the ABFO.[127]

Membership in the American Academy of Forensic Sciences Odontology Section requires application, adherence to ethical standards, and an ongoing record of activities in forensic science. As of July 13, 2016, the AAFS Odontology Section had 395 members.[128] Additionally the American Dental Association (ADA)[129] and the American Society of Forensic Odontology (ASFO)[130] are professional organizations that offer education, training, meetings, and publications to practitioners.

Unlike many other scientific specialties in the forensic sciences, forensic odontologists tend to be available to all who seek their professional assistance. Rarely are forensic odontologists full-time employees of law enforcement laboratories. The main national accreditation bodies[131] do not offer accreditation in bite mark comparison. Sometimes there is an affiliation with the office of a medical examiner but more commonly these experts are positioned in the academic departments of universities or in private practice in the various states. As a consequence forensic odontologists are generally available to both the prosecution and the defense in criminal cases and to both sides in civil litigation.

§11.11 EVIDENCE ISSUES

1. GENERAL ADMISSIBILITY

As early as 1931, the Illinois Supreme Court was confronted with testimony concerning dental identification in the case of *People v. Greenspawn*.[132] There, the defendant was prosecuted for passing a forged paper. He attempted to prove his alibi through the testimony of an X-ray technician that X-rays of his teeth were taken by the technician at the precise time the crime was supposed to have been committed and that thereafter the defendant had taken these X-rays to his dentist who

---

[126] Id. at p. 71.

[127] The ABFO maintains a listing, with contact links, of all members in good standing on its website: http://www.abfo.org/wp-content/uploads/2013/02/ABFO-Diplomate-Information-revised-9-29-2015.pdf (last accessed July 13, 2016).

[128] Link to AAFS section statistics available at: www.aafs.org/about-aafs/section (last accessed July 13, 2016).

[129] American Dental Association website: www.ada.org.

[130] American Society of Forensic Odontology website: www.asfo.org.

[131] E.g., American Society of Crime Laboratory Directors/Laboratory Accreditation Board (ASCLD/LAB), ANSI-ASQ National Accreditation Board (ANAB), and American Association for Laboratory Accreditation (A2LA).

[132] 346 Ill. 484, 179 N.E. 98 (1931).

proceeded to extract three teeth. The X-rays were offered in evidence, along with the testimony of the dentist who offered to identify them as being of the defendant's teeth. The trial court excluded much of the testimony but the Illinois Supreme Court reversed the conviction, holding that the dental identification evidence should have been admitted.

Other courts also recognized the value of dental identification. For example, in *Fields v. State*,[133] a murder prosecution in a case in which the victim was burned beyond recognition, dental identification was admitted. In *Wooley v. People*,[134] the court admitted testimony by a dentist who had compared the dental records of a patient with the teeth of a corpse and had positively identified the corpse as his former patient. The Illinois Appellate Court, in *People v. Mattox*, recognized that dental structure constitutes a valid means of identifying a deceased person who is otherwise unrecognizable when there is a dental record of that person with which the structure may be compared: 'it cannot be seriously disputed that a dental structure may constitute a means of identifying a deceased person . . . where there is some dental record of that person with which the structure may be compared.' "[135]

2. BITE MARK IDENTIFICATION EVIDENCE

In dealing with the admissibility of bite mark evidence, until recently, the courts had been remarkably unanimous in upholding testimony of dentists to the effect that a bite mark found on a victim of a crime had been produced by the defendant's teeth. The first case involving bite mark comparison analysis was *People v. Marx*.[136] The California Appellate Court held that "we do not believe that under all the circumstances of this case the standard of 'general acceptance in the field,' is determinative of admissibility."[137] The appellate court made this determination despite the fact that its own supreme court has repeatedly held "general acceptance" to be the standard for the admission of novel scientific evidence.[138] Apart from whether the appellate court correctly followed state law, bite mark comparison evidence was admitted for the first time.[139]

In *People v. Milone*,[140] the Illinois Appellate Court was also faced with the issue of bite mark evidence. Unlike *Marx*, the claim that the *Milone* bite marks were in any way unique or unusual was disputed. The Illinois court held the bite mark comparison evidence met the *Frye* case's "general acceptance" test, finding "concept of identifying a suspect by

---

[133] 322 P.2d 431 (Okla. Crim. App. 1958).

[134] 148 Colo. 392, 367 P.2d 903 (1961).

[135] People v. Mattox, 237 N.E.2d 845, 846 (Ill. App. Ct. 1968).

[136] 54 Cal.App.3d 100, 126 Cal.Rptr. 350 (1975).

[137] People v. Marx, 54 Cal.App.3d 100, 126 Cal.Rptr. 350, 355 (1975).

[138] See, e.g., Huntingdon v. Crowley, 64 Cal.2d 647, 51 Cal.Rptr. 254, 414 P.2d 382 (1966).

[139] The case is discussed in: Gerald L. Vale, et al., "Unusual Three-Dimensional Bite Mark Evidence in a Homicide Case," 21 J. FORENSIC SCI. 642 (1976).

[140] 43 Ill.App.3d 385, 2 Ill.Dec. 63, 356 N.E.2d 1350 (1976).

matching his dentition to a bite mark found at the scene of a crime. . .a logical extension of the accepted principle that each person's dentition is unique."

In the years since the *Marx* and *Milone* decisions, other courts followed suit, and challenges to admissibility were unsuccessful,[141] even though in the early years there had been no general acceptance of standards for comparison of bite marks.[142] This did not stop courts from finding, on the testimony in the record of experts who were proponents of the evidence, that such a general acceptance had already been conferred,[143] or that general acceptance was not necessary as long as the testimony was based on "established scientific methods,"[144] or, like in *Marx,* permitting such testimony as an exception to the stricter general acceptance test.[145] Other cases held bite mark evidence admissible because courts in other states had done so.[146]

Prior to the 2009 NAS Report discussing the deficient scientific record on the validity/reliability of bite mark identification, more than thirty-five jurisdictions had admitted bite mark evidence.[147] In the various cases, experts expressed their opinions that the bite mark on the victim was "consistent with" those which would be made by the defendant's teeth,[148] that the identification was "highly probable,"[149] or that "with reasonable dental certainty [the defendant made the bite mark]"[150] or "with reasonable medical certainty, [the defendant] caused

---

[141] *See* State v. Hodgson, 512 N.W.2d 95 (Minn. 1994); Seivewright v. State, 7 P.3d 24 (Wyo. 2000).

[142] Doyle v. State, 159 Tex.Crim. 310, 263 S.W.2d 779 (1954).

[143] State v. Sager, 600 S.W.2d 541 (Mo. Ct. App. 1980), *cert. denied* 450 U.S. 910 (1981)(disagreement among experts went only to the weight and not admissibility); State v. Kleypas, 602 S.W.2d 863 (Mo.Ct.App.1980); People v. Middleton, 54 N.Y.2d 42, 444 N.Y.S.2d 581, 429 N.E.2d 100 (1981); Bundy v. State, 455 So.2d 330 (Fla. 1984).

[144] State v. Temple, 302 N.C. 1, 273 S.E.2d 273 (1981).

[145] State v. Jones, 273 S.C. 723, 259 S.E.2d 120 (1979); State v. Peoples, 227 Kan. 127, 605 P.2d 135 (1980).

[146] Kennedy v. State, 640 P.2d 971 (Okla. Crim. App. 1982)("Bite-mark comparison has received evidentiary acceptance in all eight of the jurisdictions in which its admission was sought."); Seivewright v. State, 7 P.3d 24 (Wyo. 2000)(citing prior decisions as a basis for not requiring a *Daubert* hearing).

[147] *See, e.g.,* State v. Tankersley, 211 Ariz. 323, 121 P.3d 829 (2005); Meadows v. Commonwealth, 178 S.W.3d 527 (Ky. Ct. App. 2005); Garrison v. State, 103 P.3d 590 (Okla. Crim. App. 2004); Mataya v. Kingston, 371 F.3d 353 (7th Cir. 2004); Ege v. Yukins, 380 F.Supp.2d 852 (E.D. Mich. 2005).

[148] Bludsworth v. State, 98 Nev. 289, 646 P.2d 558 (1982)(expert testified that the mother did not make the bite mark and that the stepfather's dentition was "consistent with the mark.").

Some experts expressed even stronger opinions. *See* People v. Middleton, 54 N.Y.2d 42, 444 N.Y.S.2d 581, 429 N.E.2d 100 (1981)(expert said the possibility of someone else's having the same individual characteristics that were represented in the defendant's dentition to be "astronomical.").

[149] People v. Slone, 76 Cal.App.3d 611, 143 Cal.Rptr. 61 (1978)(expert also testified it was "very highly improbable" that some individual other than defendant had inflicted the bite).

[150] Bradford v. State, 460 So.2d 926, 929 (Fla. Ct. App. 1984)("to a reasonable degree of dental certainty and/or probability"); Bundy v. State, 455 So.2d 330, 337 (Fla. 1984), *cert. denied,* 476 U.S. 1109 (1986)("to a high degree of reliability"); Louisiana v. Vital, 505 So.2d 1006, 1008 (La. Ct. App. 1987)("within a reasonable forensic or medical certainty that (defendant's) teeth

the bite marks."[151] In *State v. Timmendequas*,[152] the case that resulted in the establishment of "Megan's Law",[153] the state's forensic odontologist testified that a bite mark found on the defendant "was inflicted" by the victim. The defendant alleged that the expert's testimony was plain error due to the scientific unreliability of bite mark analysis. The court relied on the holdings of other courts finding bite mark evidence admissible and noted that no court had rejected bite mark evidence as unreliable.[154] With the recognized superior identification power of DNA analysis, bite mark identification evidence has diminished, but no court has yet held that such testimony is inadmissible.[155]

Despite the unanimous court approval of bite mark identification, the field suffered credibility problems through the widely-reported exonerations of at least 14 defendants convicted on erroneous bite mark testimony.[156] Ray Krone was twice convicted of murder in Arizona largely on the basis of a disputed bite mark left through the victim's tank top into her left breast. The mark had been identified by the State's dental expert as having been made by Krone.[157] After serving 10 years and facing the death penalty, saliva in the bite mark on the tank top was re-tested for DNA. The test determined that Krone's DNA did not match the DNA recovered in the area of the bite mark. A search of the national database identified Kenneth Phillips. Phillips had lived near the victim and was later convicted of another sex crime. Krone was exonerated and released on April 8, 2002.[158]

Several defendants who were the subject of the appellate cases upholding the admission of bite mark testimony were also later

---

would have been able to make that bite mark"); Draper v. Adams, 215 F.3d 1325 (6th Cir. 2000)("90% plus certain").

[151] Harward v. Commonwealth, 5 Va. App. 468, 472, 364 S.E.2d 511, 513 (1988).

[152] 161 N.J. 515, 737 A.2d 55 (1999).

[153] On May 17, 1996, President Clinton signed Megan's Law requiring states to register individuals convicted of sex crimes against children, and requiring states to make registered sex offenders' private and personal information available to the public. (H.R. 2137, P.L. 104–145).

[154] State v. Timmendequas, 161 N.J. 515, 737 A.2d 55, 114 (1999).

[155] Although in the cases since 2009, consistent with the revised ABFO guidelines, forensic odontologists do not identify a particular individual as the source of a bite mark, but merely opine that the individual "cannot be excluded as having made the bite mark." American Board of Forensic Odontology, Inc., Diplomates Reference Manual, Bitemark Methodology Standards and Guidelines, p. 103 (March 2016). See also Coronado v. State, 384 S.W.3d 919 (Tex. Ct. App. 2012).

[156] In addition to the list of 14 wrongful convictions detailed by the Innocence Project in 2015, Keith Allen Harward was exonerated in April, 2016. See Complaint Letter from the Innocence Project, July 22, 2015, Exhibit D contained as Exhibit I of the Texas Forensic Science Commission, "Forensic Bitemark Comparison Complaint Filed by National Innocence Project on Behalf of Steven Mark Chaney—Final Report," April 12, 2016 p. 867–872 (available at: http://www.fsc.texas.gov/sites/default/files/FinalBiteMarkReport.pdf)(last accessed July 12, 2016) and note 162 *infra* and accompanying text discussing Keith Allen Harward's case.

[157] State v. Krone, 182 Ariz. 319, 897 P.2d 621 (1995).

[158] Dennis Wagner, *et al.*, "DNA Frees Arizona Inmate After 10 Years in Prison," THE ARIZONA REPUBLIC, April 9, 2002 (available at: http://www.truthinjustice.org/krone.htm (last accessed September 20, 2016).

exonerated with DNA evidence. In approving the admission of bite mark evidence, the Wisconsin appellate court in *State v. Stinson* concluded:

> [B]ite mark identification evidence presented by an expert witness can be a valuable aid to the jury un understanding and interpreting evidence in a criminal case. The bite mark evidence presented in the case enabled the jury to see the comparisons being made by the experts. By looking directly at the physical evidence used, the models and the photos, the jury was able to judge for itself whether Stinson's teeth did in fact match the bite marks found on the victim's body.[159]

After 23 years of wrongful incarceration, Stinson was finally released following exoneration by DNA testing.[160] Similarly, Keith Harward was exonerated by DNA analysis in 2016 following 33 years of wrongful conviction.[161] In 1985 and 1988, Harward challenged the admission of the bite mark evidence as insufficiently reliable to be a scientifically recognized procedure, but the Virginia appellate courts denied those challenges.[162]

The field of bite mark identification also suffered from the exposure of the fraudulent techniques of one of its most prominent proponents. Mississippi dentist Michael West testified in 72 trials between 1988 and 2002 as a bite mark identification expert, mostly for prosecutors in the southern United States.[163] West had an uncanny ability to see things that his colleagues could not and this ability often led to conviction. West frequently told defense attorneys in court that his bite mark identification error rate was "something less than my savior, Jesus Christ."[164] West also used what he called the "West Phenomenon," a method he invented which involves yellow goggles and a blue laser. Using the "West Phenomenon," he claimed that he could identify bite marks, scratches, and other tissue imperfections on a corpse that were invisible to everyone else, including other bite mark experts. Many

---

[159] State v. Stinson, 397 N.W.2d 136, 140 (Wisc. App. 1986).

[160] Stinson v. City of Milwaukee, 2013 U.S. Dist. LEXIS 140654 (E.D. Wisc. 2013). Stinson has sued the forensic odontologists who testified against him. A panel of the Seventh Circuit Court of Appeals granted the odontologists qualified immunity, Stinson v. Gauger, 799 F.3d 833 (7th Cir. 2015), but that decision was vacated, and as of July 13, 2016, the case is pending decision by the entire court.

[161] Louis Llovio and Frank Green, "After 33 Years, Keith Allen Harward Walks Out of a Virginia Prison a Free Man," Richmond Times Dispatch, April 8, 2016 (available at: http://www.richmond.com/news/local/crime/article_4c8094e7-a230-54ba-b912-901de1e03a45.html)(last accessed July 12, 2016).

[162] *See* Harward v. Commonwealth, 229 Va. 363, 330 S.E.2d 89 (1985)(reversing capital murder conviction on other grounds); Harward v. Commonwealth, 5 Va. App. 468, 364 S.E.2d 511 (1988)(upholding first degree murder conviction on retrial).

[163] Jim Fisher, *Forensics Under Fire: Are Bad Science and Dueling Experts Corrupting Criminal Justice?* (2008).

[164] Mark Hanson, "Out of the Blue," 82 ABA J. 50 (1996).

convictions in cases involving Dr. West have been reversed after his testimony and methods were discredited.[165]

3.   MISCELLANEOUS ISSUES

Bite marks have been introduced to show aggravating circumstances for death penalty purposes.[166] They have also been admitted to show a defendant's state of mind,[167] and as evidence of unfitness of a parent in a child custody matter.[168]

At times courts have allowed experts to testify well beyond what many in the field would state an odontologist is competent to opine. An example is *Commonwealth v. Henry*[169] in which the court held the dentist was qualified to testify that bite marks on the victim's body were attacking or sadistic in nature since he had done research in categorizing human bite marks as "fighting, "sadistic," or "sexually oriented."

Defendants convicted in part on bite mark analysis but later exonerated through DNA analysis have brought civil claims against the forensic odontologists. In *Starks v. Waukegan*,[170] the exonerated defendant argued that the forensic odontologists' opinions at trial were "riddled with so many errors as to amount to a due process violation."[171] Citing the 2009 NAS Report and peer-reviewed article published since the report, the court found "[t]here appears to be little, if any, scientifically valid data to support the accuracy of bite mark comparison, and the data that does exist is damning."[172] Noting that bite mark testimony would likely no longer be admissible in federal court under the *Daubert* standard, the court still dismissed the civil claims because there was no evidence the forensic odontologists "deliberately falsified their analysis or hid exculpatory results, . . . as opposed to merely forming them incompetently."[173]

---

[165] *See* Caleb Bedillion, "Women Taste Freedom After Convictions Vacated," Daily Leader, June 29, 2012; Radley Balko, "Video Shows Controversial Forensic Specialist Michael West Fabricating Bite Marks," Huffington Post, September 1, 2011 (available at: http://www.huffingtonpost.com/entry/michael-west-fabricating-bite-marks_n_944228)(last accessed July 14, 2016).

[166] Commonwealth v. Edwards, 521 Pa. 134, 555 A.2d 818 (1989).

[167] People v. Stanciel, 225 Ill.App.3d 1082, 168 Ill.Dec. 157, 589 N.E.2d 557 (1991)(that he intended to do great bodily harm to a three-year-old decedent when he bit her).

[168] In re Rimer v. Rimer, 395 N.W.2d 390 (Minn. Ct. App. 1986).

[169] 524 Pa. 135, 569 A.2d 929 (1990).

[170] 123 F.Supp.3d 1036 (ND Ill. 2015).

[171] Id. at 1050.

[172] Id. at 1051.

[173] Id. at 1054–1055.

V. RESOURCES

§11.12 BIBLIOGRAPHY OF ADDITIONAL RESOURCES

Radley Balko, "The Path Forward on Bite Mark matching—and the Rearview Mirror," Washington Post, February 20, 2015 (available at: https://www.washingtonpost.com/news/the-watch/wp/2015/02/20/the-path-forward-on-bite-mark-matching-and-the-rearview-mirror/)(last accessed July 14, 2016).

Radley Balko, "Attack of the Bite Mark Matchers," Washington Post, February 18, 2015 (available at: https://www.washingtonpost.com/news/the-watch/wp/2015/02/18/attack-of-the-bite-mark-matchers-2/)(last accessed July 14, 2016).

Radley Balko, "It Literally Started with a Witch Hunt: A History of Bite Mark Evidence," Washington Post, February 17, 2015 (available at: https://www.washingtonpost.com/news/the-watch/wp/2015/02/17/it-literally-started-with-a-witch-hunt-a-history-of-bite-mark-evidence/)(last accessed July 14, 2016).

Genie Bang, "Factors of Importance in Dental Identification," 1 FORENSIC SCI. 91 (1972).

Joseph C. Barbenel and John H. Evans, "Bite Marks in Skin—Mechanical Factors," 14 J. FORENSIC SCI. SOC. 235 (1974).

Herman Bernitz, Johanna H. Owen, Willie F.P. van Heerden and Tore Solheim, "An Integrated Technique for the Analysis of Skin Bite Marks," 53 J. FORENSIC SCIENCES 194 (2008).

Mark L. Bernstein, "Two Bite Mark Cases with Inadequate Scale References," 30 J. Forensic Sci. 958 (1985).

Bureau of Legal Dentistry (website: http://www.boldlab.ubc.ca)(last accessed July 14, 2016).

Jeffrey P. Carpenter, "Dental Identification of Plane Crash Victims," 51 J. N.C. DENTAL SOC. 9 (1968).

Christina Cataneo and Danilo De Angelis, "Odontology" in WILEY ENCYCLOPEDIA OF FORENSIC SCIENCE (Jamieson, A. & Moenssens, A.A., eds.) 2009 and online updates.

James A. Cottone and S. Miles Standish, Outline of Forensic Dentistry (1982).

Robert B.J. Dorion, ed, Bitemark Evidence, CRC Press, 2005.

Forensic Dentistry Online (website: http://forensicdentistryonline.com) (last accessed July 14, 2016).

Paul C. Giannelli, "Bite Mark Evidence," CRIM. JUSTICE, Spring 2007, p. 42.

Judy Jakush, "Forensic Dentistry," 119 J. AM. DENTAL ASS'N 355 (1989).

Terrence F. Kiely, *Forensic Evidence: Science and the Criminal Law*, 2nd ed., CRC Press, 2005.

Jules Kieser *et al.*, "Bitemarks: Presentation, Analysis, and Evidential Reliability," in *Forensic Pathology Reviews,* Volume 3 (2005).

Jules Kieser *et al.*, " The Uniqueness of the Human Anterior Dentition: A Geometric Morphometric Analysis," 52 J. Forensic Sci. 671–677 (2007).

Roland F. Kouble and Geoffrey T. Craig, "A Survey of the Incidence of Missing Anterior Teeth: Potential Value in Bite Mark Analysis," 47 Science and Justice 19 (2007).

Persephone Lewin, *Bite to Byte: The Story of Injury Analysis*, Parrel Press, 2006.

Virginia Lynch, "Bite Mark Injuries," in *Forensic Nursing* (2005).

Evan Matshes and Emma Lew, "Forensic Odontology" in David Dolinak, Evan Matshes and Emma Lew, eds., *Forensic Pathology: Principles and Practice*, Academic Press, 2005.

Michael J. Saks, "Merlin and Solomon: Lessons from the Law's Formative Encounters with Forensic Identification Science," 49 Hastings L.J. 1069 (1998).

David Senn and Paul Stimson, *Forensic Dentistry* 2d ed., CRC Press, 2010.

William E. Silver and Richard R. Souviron, *Dental Autopsy,* CRC Press, 2009.

Michael N. Sobel, "Forensic Odontology," in Cyril H. Wecht and John T. Rago, eds., *Forensic Science and Law: Investigative Applications in Criminal, Civil and Family Justice,* CRC Press, 2005.

Helena Soomer, "Forensic Odontology: Teeth and Their Secrets," in Ashraf Mozayani and Carla Noziglia, eds., *The Forensic Laboratory Handbook: Procedures and Practice,* Springer, 2005.

Pamela Zarkowski, "Bite Mark Evidence: Its Worth in the Eyes of the Expert," 1 J. L. & ETHICS DENTISTRY (1988).

CHAPTER 12

FORENSIC PATHOLOGY[1]

I. INTRODUCTION

§12.01 SCOPE OF THE CHAPTER

A forensic pathologist is a physician (MD or DO) trained in anatomical pathology, with subspecialty training in forensic pathology.[2] The forensic pathologist determines the cause of death.[3] Death investigations are performed by a diverse array of professionals and the

---

[1]   The Authors thank the following subject matter expert for his assistance with this chapter: Andrew M. Baker, MD, Chief Medical Examiner, Hennepin County Medical Examiner's Office, Minneapolis, MN.

[2]   The National Association of Medical Examiners, the professional organization of forensic pathologists in the United States, defines a forensic pathologist as "A physician who is certified in forensic pathology by the American Board of Pathology or who, prior to 2006, has completed a training program in forensic pathology that is accredited by the Accreditation Council on Graduate Medical Education or its international equivalent or has been officially "qualified for examination" in forensic pathology by the American Board of Pathology".

[3]   Manner of death is certified by relevant medicolegal authority (the medical examiner or coroner).

degree of training, including medical training, can vary widely. Coroners and medical examiners, the individuals authorized by law to conduct death investigations for the government, may or may not be "pathologists" or "forensic pathologists." In discussing the scientific methodologies utilized and the factual determinations made by individuals performing death investigations, the terms "forensic pathologist" and "pathologist" will be used for convenience—not to denote that such specialized training is required or always encountered.

Forensic pathologists answer, at a minimum, a number of cause and effect questions in both civil and criminal cases. Forensic pathologists specialize in determining the cause and manner of death in cases involving sudden, unexpected, suspicious, or violent deaths, but many state statutes require death investigations in a broader category of cases. Among the functions of the forensic pathologist are:

(1) To establish the identity of the deceased;

(2) To establish the cause of death, either as due to natural causes or violence, including the additive effect of trauma and natural disease;

(3) If the cause of death involved injury, to infer the mechanism of injury;

(4) To classify the manner of death: natural, accident, suicide, homicide, or undetermined;

(5) To estimate the time of death; and

(6) To evaluate the significance of the presence or absence of medications or drugs in the body.

The breadth of death investigations and the myriad of circumstances involved in such investigations require the forensic pathologist to have at least a familiarity with a variety of other science disciplines, such as anthropology, toxicology, weapon mechanics, and entomology. Forensic pathologists work in a variety of employment settings, including state, local, and federal government facilities; private medical groups; hospitals; and universities.

This chapter discusses death investigations and the role of the forensic pathologist in both criminal and civil justice systems. This chapter will discuss the legal authority that establishes the death investigation systems in the United States, the determinations made by forensic pathologists in fulfilling the duties of death investigations, and common evidentiary issues encountered in cases involving forensic pathology.

§12.02 TERMINOLOGY

The following terms are used in this Chapter or are commonly used in death investigation reports.

Algor mortis: Cooling of the body after death.

Antemortem: Before death.

Anterior: Front.

Asphyxia: Lack of oxygen.

Autopsy: External and internal examination of a body to determine the cause and manner of death.

Cause of death: The disease or injury that leads to death.

Caudal: Away from the head; lower (*see also* "Inferior").

Contusion: Bruise.

Coroner: A public official charged with conducting death investigations and certifying deaths in some jurisdictions. Depending on the law of the jurisdiction, the coroner may or may not be trained in medicine.

Cyanosis: Blue discoloration of the skin and mucous membranes due to excessive concentration of reduced hemoglobin in blood (deficient oxygen in the blood).

Cranial: Toward the head end of body; upper (*see also* "Superior").

Distal: Away from or farthest from the trunk or the point of origin of a part.

Dorsal: Back (*see also* "Posterior").

Entomology: The study of insects.

Forensic pathologist: A physician trained in the medical specialty of pathology and the subspecialty of forensic pathology (the examination of persons who die suddenly, unexpectedly, or violently).

Hemorrhage: Bleeding, the escape of blood from the vessels. Small hemorrhages are classified according to size as petechiae (very small), purpura (up to 1 centimeter), and ecchymoses (larger). The space-occupying accumulation of blood within an organ or tissue is a "hematoma."

Histology: Microscopic examination of tissue samples.

Hypoxia: Reduction of oxygen.

Inferior: Away from the head; lower (*see also* "Caudal").

Lateral: Away from the midline of body.

Livor mortis: The settling of blood after death; also "lividity" and "hypostasis."

Manner of death: The circumstances surrounding a death; generally classified as natural, accident, suicide, homicide, or undetermined.

Medial: Toward the midline of the body (*see also* "Mesial").

Medical examiner: A trained physician charged with conducting death investigations. Depending on the law of the jurisdiction, the medical examiner may or may not be trained in pathology.

Mesial: Toward the midline of the body (*see also* "Medial").

Pathologist: A physician trained in the medical specialty of pathology (the diagnosis of disease and causes of death).

Petechiae: Pinpoint, nonraised, round, purple-red spots caused by intradermal (within the skin) or submucous (beneath the mucous membrane) hemorrhage.

Posterior: Back (*see also* "Dorsal").

Postmortem: After death.

Proximal: Toward or nearest the trunk or the point of origin of a part.

Putrefaction: Decomposition, often with the production of foul-smelling compounds.

Rigor mortis: Stiffening of the muscles after death.

Sagittal: A lengthwise plane running from front to back; divides the body or any of its parts into right and left.

Superior: Toward the head end of body; upper (*see also* "Cranial").

Ventral: Front.

Wounds:

Penetrating: one that enters, but does not exit, the body or an organ or other bodily part.

Perforating: one that enters and exits (passing completely through) the body or an organ or other bodily part.

§12.03 EVIDENTIARY USES

Whether a death in the United States will be investigated by the government is determined by state law. If a formal death investigation occurs, the designated governmental authority will issue a report detailing the findings of the death investigation. Even if the death is not formally investigated by the designated governmental authority, a death certificate will be recorded.

Required by each state for every human death occurring within the state,[4] a death certificate is the only recognized legal proof of death in many contexts, including for estate settlement, tax determinations, and

---

[4] *See, e.g.,* 16 Del. C. § 3123: "A certificate of death for each death which occurs in this State shall be filed with the Office of Vital Statistics . . .";

O.R.S. § 432.133: "A report of death for each death that occurs in this state must be submitted to the county registrar of the county in which the death occurred or to the Center for Health Statistics, or as otherwise directed by the State Registrar of the Center for Health Statistics . . ."; Va. Code § 32.1–263: "A death certificate . . . shall be filed for each death which occurs in this Commonwealth with the registrar of the district in which the death occurred . . ."

insurance purposes. The death certificate requires identification of the deceased and a description of the cause of death and the manner of death. Although the exact requirements of a death certificate are determined by state law, most states have adopted the U.S. Standard Death Certificate, issued by the National Center for Health Statistics

U.S. STANDARD CERTIFICATE OF DEATH

LOCAL FILE NO.   STATE FILE NO.

1. DECEDENT'S LEGAL NAME (Include AKA's if any) (First, Middle, Last) | 2. SEX | 3. SOCIAL SECURITY NUMBER

4a. AGE-Last Birthday (Years) | 4b. UNDER 1 YEAR — Months, Days | 4c. UNDER 1 DAY — Hours, Minutes | 5. DATE OF BIRTH (Mo/Day/Yr) | 6. BIRTHPLACE (City and State or Foreign Country)

7a. RESIDENCE-STATE | 7b. COUNTY | 7c. CITY OR TOWN

7d. STREET AND NUMBER | 7e. APT. NO. | 7f. ZIP CODE | 7g. INSIDE CITY LIMITS? ☐ Yes ☐ No

8. EVER IN US ARMED FORCES? ☐ Yes ☐ No | 9. MARITAL STATUS AT TIME OF DEATH ☐ Married ☐ Married, but separated ☐ Widowed ☐ Divorced ☐ Never Married ☐ Unknown | 10. SURVIVING SPOUSE'S NAME (if wife, give name prior to first marriage)

11. FATHER'S NAME (First, Middle, Last) | 12. MOTHER'S NAME PRIOR TO FIRST MARRIAGE (First, Middle, Last)

13a. INFORMANT'S NAME | 13b. RELATIONSHIP TO DECEDENT | 13c. MAILING ADDRESS (Street and Number, City, State, Zip Code)

14. PLACE OF DEATH (Check only one: see instructions)

IF DEATH OCCURRED IN A HOSPITAL: ☐ Inpatient ☐ Emergency Room/Outpatient ☐ Dead on Arrival | IF DEATH OCCURRED SOMEWHERE OTHER THAN A HOSPITAL: ☐ Hospice facility ☐ Nursing home/Long term care facility ☐ Decedent's home ☐ Other (Specify):

15. FACILITY NAME (If not institution, give street & number) | 16. CITY OR TOWN , STATE, AND ZIP CODE | 17. COUNTY OF DEATH

18. METHOD OF DISPOSITION: ☐ Burial ☐ Cremation ☐ Donation ☐ Entombment ☐ Removal from State ☐ Other (Specify): | 19. PLACE OF DISPOSITION (Name of cemetery, crematory, other place)

20. LOCATION-CITY, TOWN, AND STATE | 21. NAME AND COMPLETE ADDRESS OF FUNERAL FACILITY

22. SIGNATURE OF FUNERAL SERVICE LICENSEE OR OTHER AGENT | 23. LICENSE NUMBER (Of Licensee)

ITEMS 24-28 MUST BE COMPLETED BY PERSON WHO PRONOUNCES OR CERTIFIES DEATH | 24. DATE PRONOUNCED DEAD (Mo/Day/Yr) | 25. TIME PRONOUNCED DEAD

26. SIGNATURE OF PERSON PRONOUNCING DEATH (Only when applicable) | 27. LICENSE NUMBER | 28. DATE SIGNED (Mo/Day/Yr)

29. ACTUAL OR PRESUMED DATE OF DEATH (Mo/Day/Yr) (Spell Month) | 30. ACTUAL OR PRESUMED TIME OF DEATH | 31. WAS MEDICAL EXAMINER OR CORONER CONTACTED? ☐ Yes ☐ No

CAUSE OF DEATH (See instructions and examples)

Approximate interval: Onset to death

32. PART I. Enter the chain of events—diseases, injuries, or complications—that directly caused the death. DO NOT enter terminal events such as cardiac arrest, respiratory arrest, or ventricular fibrillation without showing the etiology. DO NOT ABBREVIATE. Enter only one cause on a line. Add additional lines if necessary.

IMMEDIATE CAUSE (Final disease or condition resulting in death) ——→ a. _____ Due to (or as a consequence of):

Sequentially list conditions, if any, leading to the cause listed on line a. Enter the UNDERLYING CAUSE (disease or injury that initiated the events resulting in death) LAST — b. _____ Due to (or as a consequence of):

c. _____ Due to (or as a consequence of):

d. _____

PART II. Enter other significant conditions contributing to death but not resulting in the underlying cause given in PART I | 33. WAS AN AUTOPSY PERFORMED? ☐ Yes ☐ No | 34. WERE AUTOPSY FINDINGS AVAILABLE TO COMPLETE THE CAUSE OF DEATH? ☐ Yes ☐ No

35. DID TOBACCO USE CONTRIBUTE TO DEATH? ☐ Yes ☐ Probably ☐ No ☐ Unknown | 36. IF FEMALE: ☐ Not pregnant within past year ☐ Pregnant at time of death ☐ Not pregnant, but pregnant within 42 days of death ☐ Not pregnant, but pregnant 43 days to 1 year before death ☐ Unknown if pregnant within the past year | 37. MANNER OF DEATH ☐ Natural ☐ Homicide ☐ Accident ☐ Pending Investigation ☐ Suicide ☐ Could not be determined

38. DATE OF INJURY (Mo/Day/Yr) (Spell Month) | 39. TIME OF INJURY | 40. PLACE OF INJURY (e.g., Decedent's home; construction site; restaurant; wooded area) | 41. INJURY AT WORK? ☐ Yes ☐ No

42. LOCATION OF INJURY: State: | City or Town: | Street & Number: | Apartment No.: | Zip Code:

43. DESCRIBE HOW INJURY OCCURRED: | 44. IF TRANSPORTATION INJURY, SPECIFY: ☐ Driver/Operator ☐ Passenger ☐ Pedestrian ☐ Other (Specify)

45. CERTIFIER (Check only one):
☐ Certifying physician-To the best of my knowledge, death occurred due to the cause(s) and manner stated.
☐ Pronouncing & Certifying physician-To the best of my knowledge, death occurred at the time, date, and place, and due to the cause(s) and manner stated.
☐ Medical Examiner/Coroner-On the basis of examination, and/or investigation, in my opinion, death occurred at the time, date, and place, and due to the cause(s) and manner stated.

Signature of certifier: _____

46. NAME, ADDRESS, AND ZIP CODE OF PERSON COMPLETING CAUSE OF DEATH (Item 32)

47. TITLE OF CERTIFIER | 48. LICENSE NUMBER | 49. DATE CERTIFIED (Mo/Day/Yr) | 50. FOR REGISTRAR ONLY- DATE FILED (Mo/Day/Yr)

51. DECEDENT'S EDUCATION-Check the box that best describes the highest degree or level of school completed at the time of death.
☐ 8th grade or less
☐ 9th - 12th grade; no diploma
☐ High school graduate or GED completed
☐ Some college credit, but no degree
☐ Associate degree (e.g., AA, AS)
☐ Bachelor's degree (e.g., BA, AB, BS)
☐ Master's degree (e.g., MA, MS, MEng, MEd, MSW, MBA)
☐ Doctorate (e.g., PhD, EdD) or Professional degree (e.g., MD, DDS, DVM, LLB, JD)

52. DECEDENT OF HISPANIC ORIGIN? Check the box that best describes whether the decedent is Spanish/Hispanic/Latino. Check the "No" box if decedent is not Spanish/Hispanic/Latino.
☐ No, not Spanish/Hispanic/Latino
☐ Yes, Mexican, Mexican American, Chicano
☐ Yes, Puerto Rican
☐ Yes, Cuban
☐ Yes, other Spanish/Hispanic/Latino (Specify) _____

53. DECEDENT'S RACE (Check one or more races to indicate what the decedent considered himself or herself to be)
☐ White
☐ Black or African American
☐ American Indian or Alaska Native (Name of the enrolled or principal tribe) _____
☐ Asian Indian
☐ Chinese
☐ Filipino
☐ Japanese
☐ Korean
☐ Vietnamese
☐ Other Asian (Specify)_____
☐ Native Hawaiian
☐ Guamanian or Chamorro
☐ Samoan
☐ Other Pacific Islander (Specify)_____
☐ Other (Specify)_____

54. DECEDENT'S USUAL OCCUPATION (Indicate type of work done during most of working life. DO NOT USE RETIRED).

55. KIND OF BUSINESS/INDUSTRY

(Left margin labels: NAME OF DECEDENT — For use by physician or institution; To Be Completed/Verified By: FUNERAL DIRECTOR; To Be Completed By: MEDICAL CERTIFIER; To Be Completed By: FUNERAL DIRECTOR)

(NCHS) of the Centers for Disease Control and Prevention (CDC), which complies with the International Classification of Diseases of the World Health Organization.[5]

The most important provisions of the death certificate are the identification of the deceased and the cause and manner of death determinations. The identification of the deceased is necessary for relatives and heirs to secure death benefits, inheritances, and to settle estates. In Part I of the standard form, the cause of death is listed, and in Part II any other significant conditions contributing to death are listed and the manner of death is indicated.[6] The cause and manner of death determinations are often essential to civil and criminal litigation involving the death of the individual.

In addition to cause and manner determinations required for the completion of a death certificate, coroners or medical examiners will conduct death investigations of suspicious deaths or deaths otherwise required by law to be investigated. The death investigation may include examining the scene of death (or injury), reading medical records, reviewing law enforcement reports, and/or performing an autopsy to determined the cause and manner of death. The results of death investigations by forensic pathologists may be used in criminal prosecutions. Death investigations also provide information to aid in civil litigation, such as malpractice, personal injury, wrongful death, and insurance claims. Public safety interests are also furthered by the investigation of deaths to identify public health and occupational hazards or to assist prevention strategies.

In a criminal prosecution, the burden is on the state to prove that the death was the result of a criminal act, requiring proof of both the cause of death and the manner of death.[7] These are frequently proven through the expert testimony of the forensic pathologist. In many civil actions, such as for wrongful death or in toxic tort cases, the cause of death and the manner of death determinations are essential to proving causation for liability and may be used in determining damages. Forensic pathologists are also called to testify in other litigation where their background and experience can assist the parties in providing relevant testimony about causation and other issues in the cases.

---

[5]   U.S. Standard Certificates of Live Birth and Death were last revised in 2003 and are available at: http://www.cdc.gov/nchs/nvss/vital_certificate_revisions.htm (last accessed August 31, 2016).

[6]   Causes of death (immediate and underlying) are discussed in §12.09 *infra*.

[7]   The state must establish, as part of the corpus delicti of homicide, that death occurred by a criminal agency. 41 C.J.S. Homicide § 312(d)(1).

II. Authority

§12.04 Statutory/Constitutional Establishment

In the United States, every state has a death investigation system established by state statutory law or by state constitution. The death investigation systems vary from state to state, with some systems operated statewide (centralized or decentralized) and others operated by locality. For example, Alaska has a medical examiner system statewide[8] and South Carolina has a mixed coroner/medical examiner system that operates by county.[9]

The state death investigation systems also differ in their structure, with some states using coroner systems (*e.g.*, Nevada[10]), some states using medical examiner systems (*e.g.*, Virginia[11]), and some states employing a mixture of both systems (*e.g.*, Kentucky[12]). A major difference between coroners and medical examiners arises from the manner of their selection: coroners are generally elected and medical examiners are generally appointed.

The credentials and training requirements of personnel within the systems also vary widely. For example, Alaska requires the state medical examiner, deputy medical examiners, and individuals conducting autopsies to be physicians.[13] In South Carolina, prior to March 1, 2011, coroners were only required to have a high school diploma or its equivalent. Effective March 1, 2011, South Carolina also requires elected coroners to have at least one of the following:

(a) have at least three years of experience in death investigation with a law enforcement agency, coroner, or medical examiner agency;

(b) have a two-year associate degree and two years of experience in death investigation with a law enforcement agency, coroner, or medical examiner agency;

(c) have a four-year baccalaureate degree and one year of experience in death investigation with a law enforcement agency, coroner, or medical examiner agency;

(d) be a law enforcement officer, as defined by Section 23–23–10(E)(1), who is certified by the South Carolina Law

---

[8]   *See* AK Stat. § 12.65.015 (2015).

[9]   *See* S.C. Const. Art. V, § 24; S.C. Code of Laws § 17–5–5 through § 17–5–610.

[10]   *See* Nev. Rev. Stat. § 244.163 and § 259.010.

[11]   *See* Va. Code § 32.1–283.

[12]   *See* Ky. Rev. Stat. § 72.210 ("In enacting legislation establishing an Office of the Kentucky State Medical Examiner for the Commonwealth of Kentucky, it is not the intention of the General Assembly to abolish or interfere with the coroner in his role as a constitutionally elected peace officer. It is the intention of the General Assembly for the office to aid, assist, and complement the coroner in the performance of his duties by providing medical assistance to him in determining causes of death.").

[13]   *See* AK Stat. § 12.65.051(b) and (d)(2015).

Enforcement Training Council with a minimum of two years of experience;

(e) have completed a recognized forensic science degree or certification program or be enrolled in a recognized forensic science degree or certification program to be completed within one year of being elected to the office of coroner;

(f) be a medical doctor; or

(g) have a bachelor of science degree in nursing.[14]

However, South Carolina medical examiners, who may be employed to conduct autopsies by counties of a certain population size, are required to be skilled physicians or pathologists.[15] West Virginia requires the chief medical examiner to "be a physician licensed to practice medicine or osteopathic medicine in the state of West Virginia, who is a diplomat of the American board of pathology in forensic pathology, and who has experience in forensic medicine."[16]

The states also differ in which deaths are required to be investigated,[17] although most states require investigations in the following cases:

- Suspected homicides or suicides;

- Accidents;

- Unexplained, unusual or sudden deaths; and

- Deaths involving motor vehicles.

There is no federal oversight of death investigators or facilities used in death investigations. Voluntary accreditation of facilities and systems can be obtained from two professional organizations: the National Association of Medical Examiners (NAME)[18] and the International Association of Coroners and Medical Examiners (IAC&ME).[19] Individual certification of pathologists and forensic pathologists is not mandated by federal law.[20]

There are also no required national standards or guidelines for conducting death investigations. Model guidelines covering some aspects of death investigations have been issued by federal and state agencies and professional organizations. In 1954, the National Conference of Commissioners on Uniform State Laws published the Model Post-Mortem Examinations Act to provide a model for the establishment of medical examiner-based death investigation systems,

---

[14] S.C. Code of Laws § 17–5–130.

[15] S.C. Code of Laws § 17–5–230.

[16] W.Va. Code § 61–12–3(c).

[17] *Compare* Va. Code § 32.1–283 *and* Or. Rev. State. § 146.090.

[18] *See* www.thename.org.

[19] *See* www.theiacme.com.

[20] Certification of forensic pathologist is discussed in §12.14 *infra*.

but only about half of the states have enacted similar legislation.[21] The CDC published guidelines for investigation of sudden, unexplained infant deaths in 2007.[22] The National Institute of Justice published "Death Investigation: A Guide for the Scene Investigator" in 1999[23] and updated in 2011.[24] The New Mexico Office of the Medical Investigator has also published Scene Investigator Guidelines.[25] The most comprehensive standards addressing the professional aspects of autopsy performance are maintained by NAME.[26]

§12.05 DEATH INVESTIGATION SYSTEMS

1. CORONER

In the United States, ten states vest the authority to conduct official death investigations exclusively with the coroner, which is usually an elected position authorized by state statute or constitution to oversee the death investigation system for a particular jurisdiction. Some states have provisions that provide counties with the option of supplementing the coroner system with an appointed medical examiner system to conduct the scientific inquiries of death investigations.[27]

The position of coroner was inherited from England during colonial days. The office of "crowner" (later changed to "coroner") was established to protect the financial interests of the governing monarch in death investigations.[28] At the time the United States was founded, the coroner in England would conduct an inquest, using an unbiased jury, to determine as an "independent legal investigator" the manner of a "sudden, violent, unnatural or unexpected death."[29]

The position of coroner, as an elected official, has been widely criticized as permitting scientific determinations by undertrained or untrained individuals subject to political pressures. The position,

[21] National Academies of Science, *Strengthening Forensic Science in the United States: A Path Forward* (National Academies Press, 2009)(*hereinafter "2009 NAS Report"*) at p. 242.

[22] Centers for Disease Control and Prevention, *Infant Death Investigation: Guidelines for the Scene Investigator*, available at http://www.cdc.gov/sids/trainingmaterial.htm.

[23] US Department of Justice, National Institute of Justice, *Death Investigation: A Guide for the Scene Investigator*, November, 1999.

[24] *See* http://www.nij.gov/topics/law-enforcement/investigations/crime-scene/guides/death-investigation/pages/welcome.aspx (last accessed August 31, 2016).

[25] New Mexico Office of the Medical Investigator, University of New Mexico, Health Sciences Center, *Scene Investigator's Guidelines*, 2002.

[26] National Association of Medical Examiners, *Forensic Autopsy Performance Standards*, prepared and adopted 2005, amended 2006, 2011, 2012, 2014, and 2015 (available at: www.thename.org)(last accessed August 1, 2016).

[27] *See, e.g.,* S.C. Code of Law § 17–5–220 *et seq.*

[28] For a discussion of the historical development of the office of coroner in England and the United States, *see* 2009 NAS Report at pp. 241–243.

[29] W. David S. McLay, *Clinical Forensic Medicine*, 2d ed., Greenwich Medical Media,1996.

however, has been resilient and resistant to abolition.[30] Advantages of the coroner system include autonomy, with the coroner theoretically answerable only to the will of the electorate, and the ability to best reflect the community's needs and values. Disadvantages include the above-mentioned lack of required skill and possible conflicts of interest where the coroner also serves in additional capacities (such as sheriff or justice of the peace). The most crippling disadvantages, however, may be in the fragmentation and the limitation of resources inherent in a small-locality based system: coroners serve in 2050 of the 3145 county-equivalent jurisdictions in the U.S.[31] Regional or statewide systems permit governments to implement standardization, utilize large-scale efficiencies, and provide oversight to address fraud and waste.

2. MEDICAL EXAMINER

The introduction of the first medical examiner system in the United States occurred in Massachusetts in 1877 and required that the person in charge of death be a physician. In 1914, New York City established the first medical examiner's office in which the chief medical examiner had to be a pathologist, a physician with special training in the performance of autopsies.

Twenty-one states (and the District of Columbia) have replaced the coroner system with the medical examiner system, either statewide, by county, or by district. Another nineteen states have a mix of coroner and medical examiner systems. Unlike the coroner, the medical examiner is an appointed position and usually has more stringent training and educational requirements, including the certification in forensic pathology, which is required in some jurisdictions.[32] Some states have central offices with statewide jurisdiction, and other states have regional or local deputy examiners who may function under the direction of the state medical examiner or may operate independently.

The customary duties of the medical examiner are to perform autopsies and microscopic tissue examinations, to record all remarkable findings in detail, and to order any appropriate chemical, toxicological, serological, or microbiological analyses. The medical examiner acts as the case coordinator for the evidence collection and medical assessments in a death investigation. The best medical examiners are usually experienced forensic pathologists with sufficient training to provide scientific testimony comprehensibly in a legal context.

---

[30] Not to be overlooked is the fact that abolishing the office of coroner would require a considerable change in state laws. This is especially true in states where the office is established by state constitution since the process of constitutional amendment can be burdensome. *See, e.g.,* S.C. Const. Art. XVI, § 1.

[31] Randy H. Hanzlick, "A perspective of medicolegal death investigation in the United States: 2013," 4(1) Academic Forensic Pathology 2–9 (2014).

[32] *See* W.Va. Code § 61–12–3.

§12.06 REFORM

In February 2009, the National Research Council of the National Academy of Sciences discussed the challenges and deficiencies of death investigation systems in its report concerning the need to strengthen forensic science in the United States. The report's Chapter 9 is titled "Medical Examiners and Coroner Systems: Current and Future Needs."[33]

After a lengthy exploration of the current state of both medical examiner systems and coroner systems in the United States, the National Academy of Sciences reiterated calls for the abolition of the coroner system and elevation of the practice of forensic pathology in the criminal justice system with the following recommendation:[34]

Recommendation 11:

To improve medicolegal death investigation:

    (a)   Congress should authorize and appropriate incentive funds to the National Institute of Forensic Science (NIFS) for allocation to states and jurisdictions to establish medical examiner systems, with the goal of replacing and eventually eliminating existing coroner systems. Funds are needed to build regional medical examiner offices, secure necessary equipment, improve administration, and ensure the education, training, and staffing of medical examiner offices. Funding could also be used to help current medical examiner systems modernize their facilities to meet current Centers for Disease Control and Prevention—recommended autopsy safety requirements.

    (b)   Congress should appropriate resources to the National Institutes of Health (NIH) and NIFS, jointly, to support research, education, and training in forensic pathology. NIH, with NIFS participation, or NIFS in collaboration with content experts, should establish a study section to establish goals, to review and evaluate proposals in these areas, and to allocate funding for collaborative research to be conducted by medical examiner offices and medical universities. In addition, funding, in the form of medical student loan forgiveness and/or fellowship support, should be made available to pathology residents who choose forensic pathology as their specialty.

    (c)   NIFS, in collaboration with NIH, the National Association of Medical Examiners, the American

---

[33] 2009 NAS Report at pp. 241–268.

[34] 2009 NAS Report at pp. 267–268.

Board of Medicolegal Death Investigators, and other appropriate professional organizations, should establish a Scientific Working Group (SWG) for forensic pathology and medicolegal death investigation. The SWG should develop and promote standards for best practices, administration, staffing, education, training, and continuing education for competent death scene investigations and postmortem examinations. Best practices should include the utilization of new technologies such as laboratory testing for the molecular basis of diseases and the implementation of specialized imaging techniques.

(d) All medical examiner offices should be accredited pursuant to NIFS-endorsed standards within a timeframe to be established by NIFS.

(e) All federal funding should be restricted to accredited offices that meet NIFS-endorsed standards or that demonstrate significant and measurable progress in achieving accreditation within prescribed deadlines.

(f) All medicolegal autopsies should be performed or supervised by a board certified forensic pathologist. This requirement should take effect within a timeframe to be established by NIFS, following consultation with governing state institutions.

Professional organizations, such as NAME, IAC&ME, the College of American Pathologists (CAP), the American Board of Pathology, and the American Board of Medicolegal Death Investigators remain the primary sources of oversight and support for accreditation and certification of death investigators and facilities.[35]

III. POSTMORTEM DETERMINATIONS

§12.07 AUTOPSY

In making cause and manner of death determinations, the forensic pathologist generally relies on an autopsy—the external and internal examination of a body after death[36] using microscopy, laboratory

---

[35] *See* National Association of Medical Examiners: www.thename.org; International Association of Coroners and Medical Examiners: www.theiacme.com; College of American Pathologists: www.cap.org; American Board of Pathology: www.abpath.org; American Board of Medicolegal Death Investigators: www.abmdi.org.

[36] Autopsies pursuant to governmental authority are generally conducted shortly after death and prior to embalming or burial. Embalming prior to a postmortem examination can affect external and internal observations through artifacts and contamination of the organs and tissues. Although autopsies within 24 hours of death provide the most information,

analysis, and anatomical examination. Some professional organizations recommend performance of an autopsy for every death to contribute critical medical knowledge to the understanding of disease and mechanisms of death as well as providing information for legal investigations (both criminal and civil).[37] The autopsy rate in the United States, however, has steadily decreased: the percentage of deaths for which an autopsy was performed decreased by more than 50% between 1972 and 2007 to a total rate of just 8.5%.[38] Limited resources, religious objections, improved diagnostic technologies used pre-death, and the end of autopsy requirements for hospital accreditation are often cited for the declining number of autopsies performed each year.

Prior to conducting the autopsy, the forensic pathologist should assess all available information to "(1) direct the performance of the forensic autopsy, (2) answer specific questions unique to the circumstances of the case, (3) document evidence, the initial external appearance of the body, and its clothing and property items, and (4) correlate alterations in these items with injury patterns on the body."[39] The purposes of an autopsy are to confirm clinical findings; to provide additional information relative to the identity of the deceased and the cause, manner, and time of death; to uncover conditions not readily apparent upon external observation; and to obtain any samples necessary for ancillary investigations.[40] Examination is typically done in an autopsy room of a hospital or at the morgue, although in some rural areas funeral homes may be used. Autopsies usually take several hours or more to perform, depending on the complexity of the case, with documentation and additional testing results delaying the final report for 6–8 weeks.

At the autopsy the pathologist examines the body of the deceased externally and internally for signs of injury. A search is also made for the presence of natural diseases, e.g., heart disease or lung disease, in the circulatory, respiratory, nervous, and alimentary systems. Disease

---

autopsies on decomposed or exhumed bodies can still provide vital information on the cause and manner of death.

If not done prior to burial, exhumation of a body for postmortem examination is generally allowed when the next of kin gives permission or by court order upon a showing of sufficient cause. *See* Va. Code § 32.1–286.

[37] For a discussion of the history of autopsies, *see* Pekka J. Saukko and Stefan Pollak, "Autopsy," in WILEY ENCYCLOPEDIA OF FORENSIC SCIENCE, (Jamieson A. & Moenssens A.A., eds) 2009 & online updates.

[38] Donna L. Hoyert, "The Changing Profile of Autopsied Deaths in the United States, 1972–2007," NCHS Data Brief, No. 67, August 2011 (available at: http://www.cdc.gov/nchs/data/databriefs/db67.pdf)(last accessed August 31, 2016).

[39] National Association of Medical Examiners, *Forensic Autopsy Performance Standards*, prepared and adopted 2005, amended 2006, 2011, 2012, 2014, and 2015 (available at: www.thename.org)(last accessed August 1, 2016).

[40] Pekka J. Saukko and Stefan Pollak, "Autopsy," in WILEY ENCYCLOPEDIA OF FORENSIC SCIENCE, (Jamieson A. & Moenssens A.A., eds) 2009 & online updates.

may be caused by the presence of hereditary, congenital, infectious, cancerous, metabolic, or toxic abnormalities. The pathologist must be able to distinguish between structural changes produced by trauma and those produced by disease processes. The basic techniques of an autopsy include full external and internal examination with dissection and inspection of the body cavities and, if warranted, histological examination.[41] Increasingly, various imaging techniques (such as plain-film radiography, computed tomography (CT), and even magnetic resonance imaging (MRI)) are also used.[42]

Radiographic imaging assists death investigations through the diagnosis of the cause of death and assisting in the reconstruction of the circumstances surrounding the death.[43] In firearms cases, imaging can locate foreign material, such as bullets or bullet fragments, in the body; aid in establishing the direction of fire; and indicate bullet embolism (when the bullet enters one part of body and travels within the bloodstream to another area of the body). *See* Figures 1A and 1B. Radiographic imaging techniques can be helpful in investigation of deaths caused by stab wounds to identify any embedded weapon parts and to demonstrate the break pattern of the weapon. In pediatric deaths, radiographic imaging is done to detect signs of child abuse by the evaluation of acute or healing bony injuries. Radiographic imaging techniques should always be performed when death may involve explosive devices, since fragments of that device may have entered the body.

A typical autopsy report will include a general description of the deceased (sex, age, hair and eye color, race, frame, deformities, stature, musculature, scars, tattoos); indications relative to a determination of time of death (discussed *infra*); an external examination of the head, trunk, extremities, and genitalia; an examination of external wounds; a description of the internal course of such wounds; and an internal

---

[41] Histological examination is left to the discretion of the pathologist in the two most common U.S. model protocols for forensic autopsies. *See* B.B. Randall, Marcella F. Fierro, and R.C. Froede, "Practice Guidelines for Forensic Pathology," 122 ARCH. PATHOL. LAB. MED. 1056–1064 (1998)(discussing proposed "Standards for the Practice of Forensic Pathology" of the Forensic Pathology Committee, College of American Pathologists); National Association of Medical Examiners, "Forensic Autopsy Performance Standards," 27 AM. J. FORENSIC MED. PATHOL. 200–225 (2006).

Some within the forensic community have advocated for greater and routine use of histological examination. *See* Geoffroy L. de la Grandmaison, Philippe Charlier, and Michel Durigon, "Usefulness of Systematic Histological Examination in Routine Forensic Autopsy," 55 J. FORENSIC SCI. 85–88 (2010); Stefano Bacci, Beatrice DeFraia, Paolo Romagnoli, and Aurelio Bonelli, "Advantage of Affinity Histochemistry Combined with Histology to Investigate Death Causes: Indications from Sample Cases," 56 J. FORENSIC SCI. 1620–1625 (2011).

For a detailed discussion of microscopy and histopathology, *see* Pekka J. Saukko and Stefan Pollak, "Histology," in WILEY ENCYCLOPEDIA OF FORENSIC SCIENCE, (Jamieson A. & Moenssens A.A., eds) 2009 & online updates.

[42] Pekka J. Saukko and Stefan Pollak, "Autopsy," in WILEY ENCYCLOPEDIA OF FORENSIC SCIENCE, (Jamieson A. & Moenssens A.A., eds) 2009 & online updates.

[43] *See* Mark D. Viner, "Radiology," in WILEY ENCYCLOPEDIA OF FORENSIC SCIENCE, (Jamieson A. & Moenssens A.A., eds) 2009 & online updates.

examination of the organ systems (heart and great vessels, lungs, liver, spleen, pancreas, kidneys, stomach and its contents, intestines, reproductive organs, neck, and central nervous system). Biological materials and collected trace evidence may be submitted for additional forensic examination, such as toxicological analysis and DNA typing.[44] A complete sample autopsy report in a homicide case is found in §12.16 *infra*.

Figure 1A: Radiography of gunshot wound: The skull shows a bullet pathway traveling back to front and slightly upward, with the main projectile fragment lodged in the forehead.

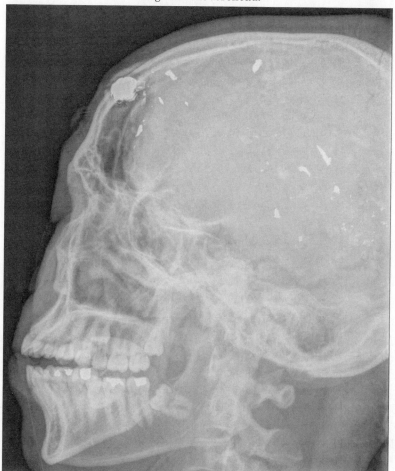

In addition to the physical autopsy, a review of the medical records of the decedent, and statements from relevant witnesses as to the decedent's state of mind, can be very helpful. For example, a multiple gunshot wound death is usually homicide, but can be suicide in rare cases.[45] The pathologist considers information from sources in addition

---

[44] For a discussion of swabbing techniques for collection of trace evidence, *see* Louise McKenna, "Biological Swabs," in WILEY ENCYCLOPEDIA OF FORENSIC SCIENCE, (Jamieson A. & Moenssens A.A., eds) 2009 & online updates.

[45] *See* Note 94 *infra*.

to the physical autopsy to evaluate the decedent's intention at the time of death. This data may assist the pathologist in piecing together the circumstances surrounding the death. Other relevant information may include life history, psychiatric and psychological data, communication information, and financial information.[46]

Figure 1B: Radiography of gunshot wound: A bullet in the right side of the chest.

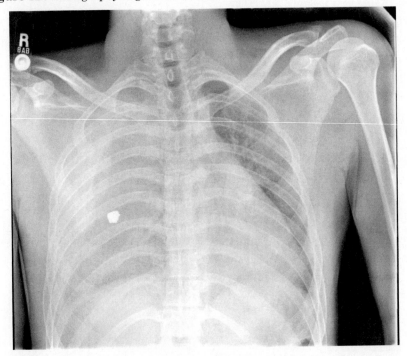

§12.08 IDENTITY OF THE DECEASED

Methods of identification are determined by the circumstances of the case, including the state of the remains and the availability of recorded identification information. Methods can include viewing the remains; comparison of dentition, fingerprints, or radiographs; and, DNA typing analysis to compare the DNA profile obtained from the remains to a known DNA profile of the deceased, to a known biological sample of the suspected deceased (such as from a toothbrush or hairbrush), or to samples from relatives.

In the case where a body is badly decomposed, charred, or dismembered, and no presumptive identification is available, a forensic pathologist may be able to formulate a general description of the victim through the postmortem examination. The description furnishes the predicate for an inferential identification of the deceased. The condition

---

[46] Appropriate fact gathering is important to the medical examiner in confirming the manner of death. This fact gathering of information and its analysis with the physical facts of a death scene has sometimes been wrongly referred as a psychological autopsy (discussed *infra*).

of the joints, the presence of arthritic disease, the condition of teeth, the degree of ossification in bone endings, and the cranial sutures are helpful in determining approximate age. A physical anthropologist may be utilized as a consultant and expert witness to estimate sex, approximate age, and race from human skeletal remains[47] to provide leads for presumptive identifications.

Although there are four federal databases maintained by the Federal Bureau of Identification that can be used to assist in providing identification of deceased persons,[48] there is no mandate requiring the submission of unidentified decedent information, and access to these databases is limited to specific officials and agencies. Another federal database, however, is widely accessible and has provided successful identifications where other methods have failed. The National Missing and Unidentified Persons System (NamUs) is a free online database for missing persons reports and unidentified decedent records that can be searched by death investigators and the general public to attempt to identity unknown decedents. The Unidentified Persons Database contains information from forensic pathologists; the Missing Person Database contains information supplied by anyone (verified by NamUs). When new information is entered into either database, the information is automatically cross-matched between databases to search for similarities. Successful identifications have been made in cases dating as far back as 1987 through the cross-matching feature, law enforcement research, and even citizen research.[49]

§12.09 CAUSE OF DEATH

The cause of death can be the basis for assessing both civil and criminal liability, and can be one of the most controversial determinations made by a forensic pathologist. Writing cause of death statements can be challenging where there are multiple contributing conditions or insufficient information. The goal is to report a complete sequence of conditions that explains why the person died.

The cause of death is the trauma, disease, or combination of conditions that terminated the person's life. When reporting on the cause of death, pathologists determine the immediate cause and any additional causes of death. The immediate cause of death is the factor contributing to the death that is most proximate to it. Other causes of death are the traumas or diseases that remotely contributed to the series of pathogenic factors leading to the person's death.

The following is an example of how the cause of death might be reported:

---

[47] *See* Chapter 10: Forensic Anthropology.

[48] Integrated Automated Fingerprint Identification System (IAFIS); National Instant Criminal Background Check System (NICS); National Crime Information Center (NCIC); and the Uniform Crime Reporting National Incident-Based Reporting System (UCR/NIBRS).

[49] *See* www.namus.gov.

An automobile driver suffers a myocardial infarction (heart attack), loses control of his car and dies from a subdural hematoma due to the head trauma sustained in the accident. The "subdural hematoma due to the blunt force head trauma as a consequence of a car accident" is the immediate cause of death while the "myocardial infarction" is a condition contributing to death.[50]

§12.10 MANNER OF DEATH

Death investigation systems that use the United States Standard Certificate of Death have the following possible alternatives for the manner of death: natural, accident, suicide, homicide, and undetermined.

When the cause of death is solely disease, the manner of death is natural, unless the disease was initiated by another person. If the death is caused solely by injury, an injury that aggravates a pre-existing condition, an injury that leads to a natural condition which then proves fatal, or an injury that precedes or follows a natural condition that the person might have otherwise survived, the death is unnatural and the manner of death will be identified as accident, suicide, or homicide.

Suicides occur when a person intentionally inflicts fatal injury on himself or herself.[51] Accidental deaths occur when a person unintentionally, and without criminal negligence, inflicts fatal injury on themselves or others. Common examples of accidental deaths include falls, unintended drug overdoses, and most traffic fatalities. The manner of death is homicide if the death is the result of the actions of another and was not accidental. A homicide is not necessarily unlawful.[52] For example, a justifiable or excusable homicide would not be a criminal homicide. The decision whether to charge a homicide as a crime is made within the criminal justice system.

The forensic pathologist may identify the manner of death as undetermined when the circumstances leading to the death cannot be ascertained. For example, if the cause of death is poisoning, but the pathologist cannot establish how the decedent came to ingest the lethal substance, the manner of death would likely be labeled "undetermined." The pathologist would need more information about the circumstances

---

[50] *See* "Writing Cause of Death Statements—Basic Principles" available at www.thename.org. (https://netforum.avectra.com/public/temp/ClientImages/NAME/76bc59b3-9464-4ca8-8b2a-1f0624b22f99.pdf)(last accessed August 31, 2016).

[51] A current controversy exists as to whether "suicide" as a manner of death is limited to self-inflicted injuries or whether suicide can occur through the forced intervention of another person, such as "suicide by cop" situations where a person intentionally provokes the use of lethal force by a police officer. *See* Amber R. Neitzel and James R. Gill, "Death Certification of 'Suicide by Cop,'" 56 J. FORENSIC SCI. 1657–1660 (2011); E.F. Wilson *et al.,* "Homicide or Suicide: The Killing of Suicidal Persons by Law Enforcement Officers," 43 J. FORENSIC SCI. 46–52 (1998).

[52] *See* Black's Law Dictionary 739 (7th ed. 1999)("The legal term for killing a [person], whether lawfully or unlawfully is 'homicide.' There is no crime of 'homicide.' ").

leading to the death to determine whether the decedent knowingly ingested the poison, accidentally ingested the poison, or was intentionally given the poison by another person.

§12.11 TIME OF DEATH

All standard death certificates require a statement as to date and time of death, or date and time the body was found. A time of death determination has the most relevance in cases of suspected homicide. In a homicide case where the identity of the perpetrator is an issue, law enforcement uses the time of death determination to identify individuals who may have had access to the decedent around the time of death.

A pathologist's opinion as to time of death based on postmortem examination of the decedent is always an estimate of an interval during which death might have occurred. In reaching an opinion on the time of death, a pathologist will rely upon a number of assumptions drawn from sequential relationships involving known or postulated acts by the decedent and secondary observations at postmortem examination. Because no single method of estimating time of death has been demonstrated to produce a precise and accurate time, the pathologist generally relies on a combination of methods.[53] Methods for estimating time of death focus on two different types of observations: antemortem changes and postmortem factors.

Antemortem changes include wound age estimation and estimations from gastric content processing; these changes normally provide only rough estimates of time of death.[54] The inspection of stomach contents is part of every postmortem examination since it may provide information as to the cause of death as well as the time of death. A variety of factors can affect gastric emptying, so time of death estimates based on it are of corroborative value only and must be stated with extreme caution.[55] The stomach usually empties 90% of its contents from two to four hours following the last meal, and the intestine usually does so from 10 to 12 hours after the last meal was eaten. This guide is only general and may not be correct if the individual was sick or under great stress for a period of several hours following the eating of the last meal. Digestion also continues after death as putrefaction takes its course. Therefore, the best use of

---

[53] For a detailed discussion of time of death estimation methods, *see* Burkhard Madea, "Time of Death Determinations," in WILEY ENCYCLOPEDIA OF FORENSIC SCIENCE, (Jamieson A. & Moenssens A.A., eds) 2009 & online updates.

[54] Id.

[55] M. Horowitz, "Gastric Emptying-Forensic Implications of Current Concepts," 25 MED., SCI. & L. 3 (1985). Courts have admitted time of death estimations based on stomach contents. *See* State v. Origer, 418 N.W.2d 368 (Iowa App.1987).

stomach contents for time purposes is to support or refute a time of death based on witness statements.[56]

The major postmortem factors involved in a determination of time of death include:

(1) Early postmortem interval:

    a.   Livor mortis: the color of death;

    b.   Rigor mortis: the stiffening of death;

    c.   Algor mortis: the cooling of death; and

    d.   Other factors: *e.g.,* corneal clouding, potassium level in the vitreous humor.

(2) Late postmortem interval:

    a.   Putrefaction;

    b.   Insect activity.

Each of the above factors in time of death determinations will be discussed in more detail to reveal its contributions and drawbacks in estimating the time of death.[57]

1. EARLY POSTMORTEM INTERVAL

The early postmortem interval includes the period of time up to 48 hours after death. Livor, rigor, and algor mortis all occur during this time interval. Other factors present in the first 48 hours can also be used to determine the approximate time of death.

a. Livor Mortis: The Color of Death

Livor mortis is also known as lividity and hypostasis. When red blood cells stop circulating, they sink due to the force of gravity to the lowest (dependent) portions of the body in relation to the earth's surface. The upper portions of the body pale as they are drained of blood. As the term lividity indicates, the lower surfaces of the body consequently assume a discoloration ranging from standard purple-red to cherry-red (in deaths from carbon monoxide poisoning, hypothermia, and acute cyanide poisoning). Subsequently, as putrefaction begins, the lividity undergoes a color change to green and then brown as the blood diffuses from the vessels into the tissues.

The livor of the down side of a body may be disrupted by blanched areas. These pale patches of skin are caused by the failure of blood to flow into those areas where the vessels were compressed by the weight

---

[56] *See* F. A. Jaffe, "Stomach Contents and Time of Death: Reexamination of a Persistent Question," 10 AM.J. OF FOR.MED. & PATH. 37 (1989); Suzuki, "Experimental Food Studies on the Presumption of the Time After Food Intake From Stomach Contents," 35 Forensic Sci. Int'l 83 (1987).

[57] For a detailed discussion of these factors, *see* Burkhard Madea, "Death: Time of," in WILEY ENCYCLOPEDIA OF FORENSIC SCIENCE, (Jamieson A. & Moenssens A.A., eds) 2009 & online updates.

of the body on its reclining surface. Blanched areas sometimes show a patterned livor distribution that may reflect a ligature impression or the surface where the body lay when livor mortis began. An impression from a surface may indicate that a body was moved after death.

The onset of livor mortis is variable, but generally becomes noticeable 30 minutes to 3 hours after death. The time of onset of lividity is subject to a number of variables. For example, an anemic person would characteristically develop livor more slowly than a normal person. The degree of lividity will decrease in instances of substantial blood loss from trauma. The livor becomes "fixed" when the pressure exerted on the capillary walls cause them to rupture so that the blood is no longer in the vessels. This occurs from 6 to 24 hours after death. If lividity is blanched out by finger pressure, it means the person has been dead less than approximately 12 hours.

Livor mortis can occasionally be difficult to distinguish from contusions to skin. In recently deceased persons, the pathologist can tell the difference by several factors. Livor tends to be of a uniform color, while a bruise may take on varying shades. Livor usually has a linear margin, while contusions occur in all shapes. Livor also can be distinguished from a bruise by its tendency to blanch from the skin when pressure is applied; a bruise does not do so. However, once the livor becomes fixed, its color cannot be blanched by finger pressure. The distinction is further complicated once decomposition begins because the blood from ruptured vessels tends to form pools where blood has settled previously.

Postmortem movement of a body from one place or position to another may be an issue in a suspected homicide. If livor has not become fixed when the body is moved, the blood will again flow with gravity, and new areas of livor will appear on the body surfaces then closest to the earth. The subsequent livor may be inconsistent with the initial livor. Pathologists use this observation in deciding whether a corpse has been moved from the original death scene to the place where it is found.

b. Rigor Mortis: The Stiffening of Death

The order and speed of rigor mortis can be highly variable, but generally two hours after death there is detectable stiffening of the involuntary and voluntary muscles, followed by the stiffening of the body at the joints which is first noticeable in the facial joints. This is due to the fact that the small muscles and their joints become noticeably involved first.[58] This stiffening, rigor as it is commonly termed, typically becomes fully established in about 12 hours after death. It disappears in order of appearance after about 36 hours.

---

[58] I. Gordon, H.A. Shapiro and S.D. Berson, *Forensic Medicine: A Guide to Principles,* 3d edd., Churchill Livingstone, 1988 at p. 30.

Heat hastens the onset of rigor mortis and causes it to be more pronounced. Cold has the effect of delaying the onset of rigor. Rigor mortis may also appear quicker in situations of violence where the victim has exerted muscular activity immediately prior to death, e.g., electrocution, fights, and struggles.[59] Other variables which indirectly affect the time range of rigor mortis are the state of the deceased's nutrition, preexisting disease or debilitation, high fever at the time of death, movement of atmospheric air, amount of clothing worn, and age. For example, rigor is often of short duration in infants and sickly adults.

Estimating time of death from the degree of rigor is an uncertain science.[60] Using rigor to determine the position of a body at the time of death is more certain. When rigor mortis is fully developed, the joints of the body become fixed dependent upon the position of the body at the onset of stiffening. If the body is moved after the onset of rigor, examination of the rigor will indicate the change in position unless the rigor mortis was broken down by force. In such a case, the stiffening of the joint will not recur and the muscle will be torn.

A phenomenon known as cadaveric spasm or instantaneous rigor adds another note of uncertainty to the variable onset of rigor mortis. It is characterized by instantaneous rigidity of the whole body or an appendage such as the hand gripping a weapon or a clump of the assailant's hair or clothing. Instant rigor may suggest the manner and cause of death. For example, certain poisons like strychnine may cause instant rigor. A cadaveric spasm during which the decedent grabbed a piece of soap in the bathtub or some vegetation in a lake suggests the person was alive when submerged and likely drowned. Natural death involving sudden, intense pain may also cause instant rigor.[61] Experts believe instantaneous rigor is linked to emotion and violent muscular exertion since the essential physiochemical changes are the same as found in ordinary rigor mortis but at a greatly accelerated pace and exaggerated degree.

c.   Algor Mortis: The Cooling of Death

The decrease in body temperature is highly dependent on the variables of the ambient atmosphere. If there are only a few degrees difference between the environmental and body temperature, heat loss is meaningless in determining time of death. While not precise, heat

---

[59] It is believed that heat accelerates the depletion of adenosine phosphates (including adenosine triphosphate) in muscle tissue; however, the correlation of adenosine phosphate levels and the onset and development of rigor has not been extensively studied. Hong Huang et al., "Determination of Adenosine Phosphates in Rat Gastrocnemius at Various Postmortem Intervals Using High Performance Liquid Chromatography," 55 J. FORENSIC SCI. 1362–1366 (2010).

[60] Courts have allowed expert testimony as to the approximate time of death based on rigor observations. See United States v. Kennedy, 890 F.2d 1056 (9th Cir. 1989).

[61] Cyril J. Polson, et al., The Essentials of Forensic Medicine, 4th ed., Pergamon Printing, 1985, at p. 18.

loss from the standard body temperature can be a useful tool in estimating time of death in cases where death occurred within eight to twelve hours prior to examination and there has been no refrigeration of the body.[62]

Cooling depends on the temperature of the environs surrounding the body and on the clothing, ventilation, and degree of body fat, size, and age of the deceased. The head and hands of a clothed body cool first. Clothing causes heat retention, as do obesity and size. Disease that causes an increase of body temperature (fever) will influence the rate of cooling. The body begins cooling quicker from a higher temperature than a normal one. Deaths that occur with the body having been in convulsions or seizures prior to death will also have a higher initial body temperature than normal.

Normal body temperature is 98.6 degrees Fahrenheit, although this does vary throughout the day. There is no hard and fast rule as to the exact progression of heat loss that bodies will display. Generally, a clothed adult will reach environmental temperature in an average room temperature environment in approximately 20 to 30 hours. One rough approximation is that the body suffers 1½ degrees F of heat loss per hour for the first 12 hours after death and 1 degree F for the next 12–18 hours until reaching environmental atmospheric temperature. The following formula has also been used to measure heat loss:

$$\frac{98.6\ F\ -\ \text{Rectal Temperature}}{1.5\ F\ \text{per hour (in hours)}} = \text{Postmortem interval}$$

d.   Other Factors

The most common signs of death, such as stoppage of the heart and respiration and pallor of the skin, are not useful to pathologists in fixing the postmortem interval. Another external observation, the clouding of the eyes, may be useful in determining time of death. The external surface of the eyeball begins to show a film as soon as ten minutes after death. Cloudiness of the cornea appears in 12 to 24 hours postmortem, depending on variables such as humidity, temperature and position of the eyelids. Its onset is much quicker when the eyelids are open. The cornea is completely opaque by 48 to 72 hours.

Two chemical methods are sometimes used to estimate time of death: the potassium and sodium levels in the fluid of the eye (vitreous humor) and the metabolite 3-methoxytyramine (3-MT) level in the putamen of the brain.[63] When both methods are properly performed

---

[62]   Khalil S. Wardak and Stephen J. Cina, "Algor Mortis: An Erroneous Measurement Following Postmortem Refrigeration," 56 J. FORENSIC SCI. 1219–1221 (2011).

[63]   Kusum D. Jashnani, Smita A. Kale, and Asha B. Rupani, "Vitreous Humor: Biochemical Constituents in Estimation of Postmortem Interval," 55 J. FORENSIC SCI. 1523–1527 (2010); John I. Coe, "Vitreous Potassium as a Measure of the Postmortem Interval: An Historical Review and Critical Evaluation," 42 Forensic Sci. Int'l 201, 209 (1989); D.L. Sparks

with controls accounting for cause of death and temperature factors, the post-mortem interval can be estimated up to approximately 8 hours.

2.   LATE POSTMORTEM INTERVAL

a.   *Putrefaction*

Putrefaction by decomposition of a body exposed to the air in mild weather begins soon after death and is apparent in some corpses 24 to 72 hours after death. Its onset is characterized by a green discoloration of the skin of the flanks and abdomen. Anaerobic bacteria, microorganisms from the intestinal tract and wounds, enter the blood vessels and tissues through the walls of the intestines and from the air. It is the gas formed by the bacteria that gives the body a bloated aspect, beginning with a swelling of the abdominal area. The action of putrefying bacteria is largely dependent on access to free oxygen. Thus, a body submerged in water or buried in soil will putrefy more slowly than one exposed directly to the air, since air contains higher levels of free oxygen. The generally accepted approximation for degree of decomposition is that one week in air is equivalent to two weeks in water and eight weeks in soil. There is also a direct correlation between the decay rate and the depth of burial—the deeper the burial, the slower the rate of decomposition.[64]

The rate of decomposition increases with higher temperatures. In hot, humid climates decomposition may be apparent as early as two or three hours after death. Conversely, cold weather retards decomposition.[65] Other variables such as the action of predatory animals, the amount of clothing, and insect activity can also affect the rate of decomposition. The presence of certain chemicals may also alter the rate. For example, arsenic in the tissues and kerosene-soaked skin both delay decomposition.

Decomposition of the body in water or wet soil may result in the formation of a waxy, yellow-white substance from decomposed fat beneath the skin. This substance, adipocere, may aid an expert in estimating the approximate length of time a body had been in water.

---

et al., "Comparison of Chemical Methods for Determining Postmortem Interval," 34 J. Forensic Sci. 197 (1989).

[64] W. C. Rodriguez, "Decomposition of Buried Bodies and Methods That May Aid Their Location," 30 J. Forensic Sci. 3 (1985).

[65] For more information on how temperature affects decomposition, see the controlled study by M.S. Micozzi, "Experimental Study of Postmortem Change Under Field Conditions: Effects of Freezing, Thawing, and Mechanical Injury," 31 J. Forensic Sci. 953 (July 1986) and see generally, A. Galloway et al., "Decay Rates of Human Remains in an Arid Environment," 34 J. Forensic Sci. 607 (1989).

b. *Insect Activity*

When an estimate of time of death is required on a body discovered more than several days postmortem, entomological data is invaluable.[66] Estimations of time of death based on insect activity are based on the knowledge of entomological succession (the predictable and sequential colonization of specific insects over time), fly life cycle and development, and thermal requirements for stage development of carrion-feeding flies.[67] Insects such as flies may lay eggs in the mucous membranes of eyes, mouth and nose, or in wounds within a matter of several hours after death. The entomological opinion concerning minimum time of death is based on knowledge of the length of gestation of the larval and pupal stages of insect development when compared to those found in the body. It is generally believed that maggots can completely destroy the soft tissues in four to six weeks during the summer.

A major problem in accurate estimation of time of death from entomological data is that insect larval development is greatly affected by temperature and by any factor affecting access to the body.[68] Two computer programs have been developed that are capable of modeling development of the insect species present in a local area. In tests of the model, the estimates generated have agreed well with those made based on other information.[69] A study using the green bottlefly (Lucilia sericata) compared their growth cycle in the field versus the laboratory under artificial conditions set to mimic the field. The results showed no difference in the lifecycles of both groups. Thus, if the microclimatic conditions in which the larvae developed on a corpse are known, those conditions can be recreated in a lab to determine a reliable time of death index.[70]

§ 12.12 CRIMINAL CASES

The causes of death commonly encountered in criminal cases are discussed below. The forensic pathological findings that can assist in determining the manner of death in these cases are also discussed.[71]

---

[66] For a detailed discussion of entomology, *see* Richard W. Merritt and M. Eric Benbow, "Entomology," in WILEY ENCYCLOPEDIA OF FORENSIC SCIENCE, (Jamieson A. & Moenssens A.A., eds) 2009 & online updates.

[67] Id. Additionally, the presence of non-indigenous insects may indicate the body was moved from another locale and dumped.

[68] Jutta Bachmann and Tal Simmons, "The Influence of Preburial Insect Access on the Decomposition Rate," 55 J. FORENSIC SCI. 893–900 (2010).

[69] H. Williams, "A Model for the Aging of Fly Larvae in Forensic Entomology," 25 FORENSIC SCI. INT'L 91 (1984).

[70] F. Introna et al., "Time Since Death Definition by Experimental Reproduction of Lucilia Sericata Cycles in Growth Cabinet," 34 J. Forensic Sci. 478 (March 1989).

[71] Although common findings associated with particular manner of death determinations are discussed, forensic pathologists should avoid rigid application of any informal "rules" about such findings. Cases can frequently present extraordinary circumstances that defy these "rules." *See* Stojan Petkovic, Miljen Maletin, and Maja Durendic-Brenesel, "Complex Suicide: An Unusual Case with Six Methods Applied," 56 J. FORENSIC SCI. 1368–1372

1. ASPHYXIA (ANOXIA AND HYPOXIA)

Asphyxia in forensic usage denotes deaths from an acute cerebral deprivation of oxygen (total deprivation—anoxia; partial deprivation—hypoxia).[72] Asphyxia is technically not a cause of death, but a mechanism of death, and the cause of death is the cause of the asphyxia (i.e., strangulation, drowning).[73] The classification of asphyxia and the use of various subtypes have not been uniform among pathologists, therefore, "labels" for cause and manner of death determinations in asphyxia cases should be examined carefully.[74]

The common denominator in all of these types of deaths is the insufficient amount of oxygen reaching the brain and other essential tissues or organs of the body. There are many ways in which this can be accomplished: (a) by a decrease in the capability of the tissues to utilize oxygen, such as in cyanide poisoning; (b) by a reduced capability of the blood to carry oxygen to the tissues, such as in carbon monoxide poisoning, or in instances of acute decrease in the amount of blood, such as with massive hemorrhage; (c) in instances where the blood does not circulate rapidly enough to keep up with the demands of the brain and other tissues, such as in shock; (d) from breathing air which contains an insufficient amount of oxygen to sustain life; (e) from a mechanical interference with the passage of air into the respiratory tract, such as in smothering or drowning, and in some instances manual strangulation and hanging; and (f) by cutting off the circulation to or from the brain by pressure, as in manual or ligature strangulation and in most instances of hanging.

Petechial hemorrhages,[75] occurring as small, pinpoint, dark red spots on the skin (especially of the face) and mucous membranes (especially the conjunctiva of the eye and in the mouth), occur in some asphyxial deaths (particularly those deaths involving pressure applied to the neck). These spots are caused by the rupture of small blood vessels called capillaries that bleed into the tissues; they may be confused by some observers with Tardieu spots, which are postmortem phenomena resulting from the rupture of tiny capillaries on the skin due to the settling of red blood cells after death due to gravity.

(2011)(discussing a suicide in which there were six different types of self-inflicted injuries, including screwdriver stab wounds to the head that were the cause of death).

[72] Asphyxia may also be present in natural deaths. Raffaele Giorgetti, Roberto Bellero, Luciano Giacomelli, and Adriano Tagliabracci, "Morphometric Investigation of Death by Asphyxia," 54 J. FORENSIC SCI. 672–675 (2009).

[73] Michael Pollanen, "Asphyxia," in WILEY ENCYCLOPEDIA OF FORENSIC SCIENCE, (Jamieson A. & Moenssens A.A., eds) 2009 & online updates.

[74] Anny Sauvageau and Elie Boghossian, "Classification of Asphyxia: The Need for Standardization," 55 J. FORENSIC SCI. 1259–1267 (2010).

[75] It was once believed that petechiae were caused by the asphyxia, but it is now generally accepted that the petechial hemorrhages are caused by the increased jugular venous pressure that frequently occurs in asphyxia cases. See S.F. Ely and C.S. Hirsch, "Asphyxial Deaths and Petechiae: A Review," 45 J. FORENSIC SCI. 1274–1277 (2000).

There are three common types of traumatic death by asphyxia, any one of which may involve criminal conduct: strangulation, drowning, and smothering.

a. Strangulation

Strangulation may be homicidal, suicidal, or accidental.[76] Strangulation may be manual or by ligature.[77] Death from strangulation by obstruction of blood flow to the brain is typical of hangings. Intense congestion, venous engorgement, and cyanosis are present above the rope or ligature in partial suspension hangings, as the weight pressure exerted on the neck allows for arterial blood flow to the head. The victim dies of strangulation as a result of noose pressure on the neck exerted by body weight (*see* Figure 2). Full suspension hanging usually results in an absence of facial congestion and petechiae, as the pressure on the neck blocks all blood flow into or out of the head (*see* Figure 3). Accidental strangulation by hanging is often associated with sexual asphyxia (autoerotic death).[78]

Strangulation by hanging and strangulation by ligature can be differentiated by looking at the grooved imprint ("furrow") in the neck. The hanging ligature furrow cants upwards; the homicidal furrow is horizontal. *See* Figures 2, 3 and 4A and 4B. Other typical pathological findings include throat-skeleton fractures with hemorrhaging of the soft tissues, congestive hemorrhaging in the conjunctiva (mucous membrane covering the front of the eye and the inside of the eyelids), and buccal mucosa (mucous membrane on the inside of the cheek).[79]

---

[76] For a full explanation of the physics of asphyxial deaths by strangulation and the anatomic structures of the neck, *see* M.L. Taff and L.R. Boglioli, "Strangulation: A Conceptual Approach for Courtroom Presentation," 10(3) AM.J.FOR.MED. & PATH. 216 (1989).

Expert testimony that the cause of death was anoxia due to strangulation is routinely admitted. *See* Commonwealth v. Lanoue, 392 Mass. 583, 467 N.E.2d 159 (1984); McKinstry v. State, 264 Ind. 29, 338 N.E.2d 636 (1975); Commonwealth v. Pettie, 363 Mass. 836, 298 N.E.2d 836 (1973).

[77] Manual strangulation may be homicidal, suicidal, or accidental. Strangulation by constriction is accomplished by the use of a ligature which is twisted around the neck and tightened by some means other than body weight (see Figures 2, 3, and 4A and 4B).

[78] *See generally* James L. Knoll, IV and Michael M. Baden, "Autoerotic Deaths," in WILEY ENCYCLOPEDIA OF FORENSIC SCIENCE, (Jamieson A. & Moenssens A.A., eds) 2009 & online updates.

Victims of autoerotic death tend to be predominantly young and male. *See* Roger W. Byard and Calle Winskog, "Autoerotic Death: Incidence and Age of Victims—A Population-based Study," 57 J. FORENSIC SCI. 129–131 (2012).

In determining the manner of death in suspected autoerotic death cases, pathologists will look for signs of previous sublethal asphyxia episodes. *See* Roger W. Byard et al, "Could Intra-alveolar Hemosiderin Deposition in Adults be Used as a Marker for Previous Asphyxial Episodes in Cases of Autoerotic Death?" 56 J. FORENSIC SCI. 627–629 (2011).

[79] Slobodan Nikolic, Vladimir Zivkovic, Dragon Babic, and Fehim Jukovic, "Cervical Soft Tissue Emphysema in Hanging—A Prospective Autopsy Study," 57 J. FORENSIC SCI. 132–135 (2012).

Figures 2A and 2B: Asphyxia by hanging. Suicide. The weight of the body against the rope ligature causes the furrow to cant upwards above the Adam's apple (thyroid cartilage) and toward the knot (left). Note the facial congestion and petechiae of the eyes and eyelids (right).

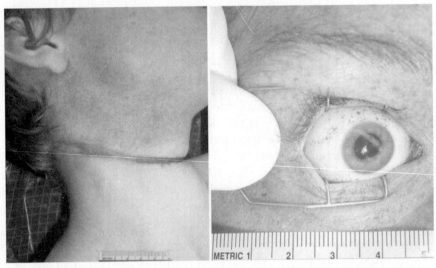

Figure 3: Asphyxia by hanging. Suicide. In a full suspension hanging, the weight of the body collapses the arteries and veins of the neck so that no blood is pumped into the head and cyanosis and petechiae do not develop.

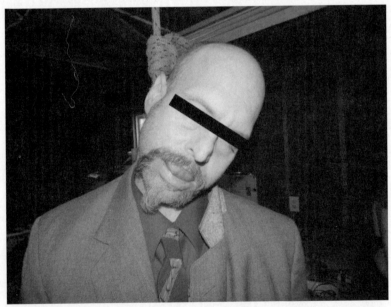

Figures 4A and 4B: Asphyxia by ligature strangulation. Homicide. The rope was pulled tight from behind causing a circumferential horizontal ligature abrasion below the Adam's apple. Note the petechiae above the ligature mark.

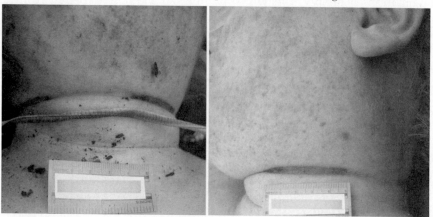

Fingernail marks on the neck may be a sign of manual strangulation, as well as defensive wounds reflecting attempts to remove constriction (see Figure 5).

Figure 5: Asphyxia by manual strangulation. Homicide. Abrasions and fingernail marks on the neck.

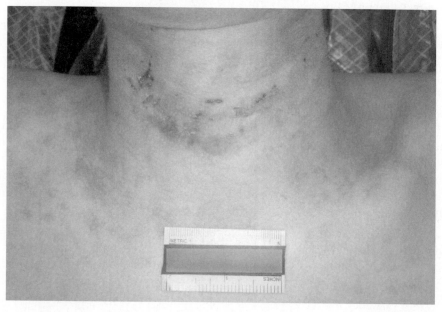

b.   *Drowning*

Drowning results from submersion or partial submersion in a fluid medium. A classic drowning has five stages.[80] The first stage is the surprise stage where the person is stunned and may involuntarily

---

[80] For discussion of a non-classic drowning, *see* Giovanni Cecchetto *et al.*, "Fatal Drowning Accident and Undiagnosed Hydrocephalus," 55 J. FORENSIC SCI. 826–829 (2010).

inhale some water. The second stage occurs when the person attempts to hold their breath while struggling to reach air. In the third stage, the person inhales deeply and white or pinkish foam is expelled from the mouth and nose. Often, the person's mouth and eyes are open during the drowning. A fourth stage of respiratory arrest follows in which there is no thoracic movement and the pupils dilate. The final (fifth) stage involves three to four quick respiratory movements.

The inhalation of water or other liquid into the air passages as the result of submersion or partial submersion causes choking, which in turn results in the formation of mucus in the throat and windpipe. This foamy mucus passes into the lungs and disrupts the air passages. Thus, drowning is a form of choking in that death results from an obstruction in the throat.

The postmortem signs of drowning include pale color of the body, edema (fluid filling) of the lungs, foam in and about the mouth and nostrils (*see* Figure 6), aspirated marine life, and water in the stomach. Not all of these signs are necessarily present in any single drowning victim. Similarly, these signs may also be present in circumstances other than drowning. For example, edema of the lungs and foam about the mouth and nostrils can occur from an opioid drug overdose or congestive heart failure.

On occasion (approximately 20% of the cases of drowning), a victim will die of asphyxia due to submersion in water without inhaling a significant amount beyond the larynx. The inhalation of a small amount of very cold water or other liquid into the air passage as a result of submersion or aspiration while drinking may result in spasm of the larynx and immediate obstruction of the passage of air into the lungs. Under these conditions, the more classical alterations within the body associated with regurgitation and swallowing of large quantities of water may not occur. Hence, the expression "dry drowning" in which the lungs are relatively dry and the stomach free of fluid, in contrast with the more frequently encountered "wet drowning" with evidence of fluid inhalation and swallowing.

There are no specific pathologic findings or diagnostic tests for drowning. The determination is based upon evaluation of the results of the investigation, autopsy, chemical studies, and toxicological examinations, as well as the exclusion of other possible causes of death. An internal examination is necessary to rule out other causes of death before a pathologist determines drowning is the cause of death. In an internal examination in a classic drowning, the lungs will be distended and contain water fluid.[81] While not exclusive to drowning, blood in the mastoid air cells of the middle ear may also be indicative of drowning.[82]

Figure 6: The classic oronasal "foam cone" often seen in (but not exclusively in) drowning deaths.

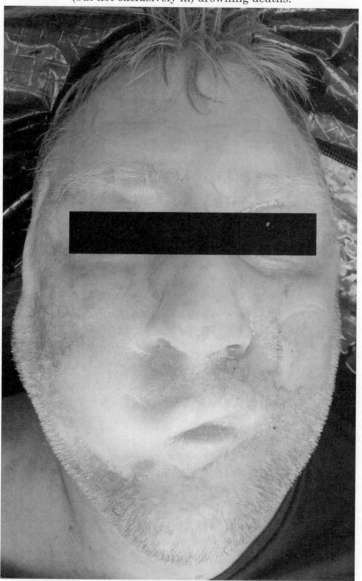

---

[81] *See* D.J. Sptz, "Investigation of Bodies in Water," in Spitz and Fisher's Medicolegal Investigation of death (W.U. Spitz and D.J. Spitz, eds), Charles C. Thomas, Springfield, IL (4th ed. 2006), pp. 846–881.

[82] M.H.A. Piette and E.A. De Letter, "Drowning: Still a Difficult Autopsy Diagnosis," 163 Forensic Sci. Int'l 1–9 (2006).

Petechial and neck hemorrhage may also be attributable to drowning, although this is a controversial conclusion. *See* Russell T. Alexander and Jeffrey M. Jentzen, "Neck and Scleral Hemorrhage in Drowning," 56 J. FORENSIC SCI. 522–525 (2011).

c.   Smothering / Suffocation

Smothering occurs when the external openings of the air passages, the nostrils and the mouth, are closed by an obstructing object with resulting suffocation.[83] Postmortem examination may reveal a general discoloration associated with the accumulation of fluid or edema. There may be small or faintly discernible contusions or lacerations on the inner aspects of the lips. Petechial hemorrhages may be seen. If a soft object has been used to obstruct the external orifices of the air passages, the body itself may disclose no visible signs of trauma.

2.   WOUNDS

The examining pathologist may be asked to supply more information about wounds than just whether the wound was the cause of death, including a description of the instrument inflicting the wound, the time of infliction, and other factors to assist in a reconstruction of events leading to the death.

Alterations of wounds may occur as a result of therapeutic actions on the part of the treating physician. Incisions may be made through the wounds, drainage tubes may be inserted through the wounds, and the wounds may have been altered through surgical intervention to such an extent that their original appearance is completely lost.[84]

a.   Gunshots and Wound Ballistics

The pathologist studies the gunshot wound to determine the extent and course of the wound, whether it was mortal, whether it could have been self-inflicted, and whether it was inflicted before or after death. Evidence recovered by the pathologist may be used to determine the nature of the weapon and projectile used, and the distance (range) and direction of fire. In some cases the relative position of the victim and the shooter may be estimated, although extreme care must be exercised in stating opinions on this issue because of the vast number of variables involved in positioning.

Care must be exercised in recovering foreign objects from the body. Metal forceps and probes can alter or add to striations on a bullet that a firearms examiner might use to associate a particular firearm. Bullets removed from bodies and crime scenes should be carefully examined before being cleaned or otherwise handled to avoid altering or destroying valuable evidence.

---

[83] Suffocation may also be the result of suicide. *See* M.J. Bullock and D. Diniz, "Suffocation Using Plastic Bags: A Retrospective Study of Suicides in Ontario, Canada," 45 J. FORENSIC SCI. 608–613 (2000).

[84] Testimony from an expert as to the entry and exit wounds of a gunshot victim may be excluded if such an alteration of the body occurs as to distort the examination, e.g., where cotton was stuffed into the wounds prior to expert's examination: Roberts v. State, 70 Tex.Crim.R. 297, 156 S.W. 651 (1913).

Figure 7: Gunpowder residue and gasses follow behind the bullet exiting from the muzzle of the gun and may travel a distance of 12 to 18 inches, spreading in cone-like fashion, depending on the weapon and the ammunition. Test firings assist in determining the distance the muzzle was from the victim at the moment of discharge.

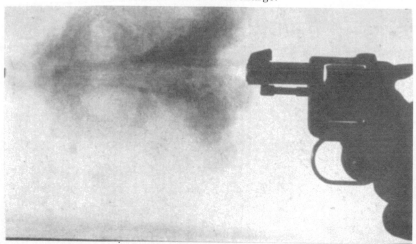

The pathologist conducting a death investigation in a case involving gunshot wounds must be knowledgeable concerning the rudiments of firearm identification and the science of ballistics (*see* Figure 7). The pathologist must also be aware of the variables that may affect wound appearances and trace evidence recovery, such as the position and movement of the body, the clothing, and blood traces. For example, a single layer of clothing may completely remove the secondary effects of a very short-range gunshot wound such as powder stippling (tattooing) or soot deposit (*see* Figure 8). Thus, if the clothes were removed from the victim and discarded prior to examination, the appearance of the bullet wound may mislead the pathologist.

The pathologist should also be familiar with the various characteristics of wounds from improvised or homemade firearms.[85] Homemade firearms are made from a variety of materials and in a wide range of calibers.[86] Their barrels, which are frequently short, and their use of loose fitting ammunition create pressure normally below that of equivalent commercial firearms. Powder may be observed in firings from up to three meters, and the partially burned grains will be larger than normal. In the firing of improvised shotguns, the pellet pattern may resemble that of a conventional firearm at greater range. A

---

[85] Clare H. Cunliffe and J. Scott Denton, "An Atypical Gunshot Wound from a Home-Made Zip Gun—The Value of a Thorough Scene Investigation," 53 J. FORENSIC SCI. 216–644 (2008).

[86] Brian Linert, Janis Regnier, Barrett W. Doyle, and Joseph A. Prahlow, "Suicidal Shotgun Wound Employing a Shotgun Barrel, A shotgun Shell, and a BB," 55 J. FORENSIC SCI. 546–548 (2010).

combination of wide shot pattern spread and a strong powder pattern may also indicate the use of an improvised firearm.[87]

Figure 8: Gunshot perforation of clothing. This circular entrance perforation has a ring of dark staining, known as "bullet wipe," indicating that this is an entrance wound.

b.   Bullet Wounds

Locations and appearances of entrance and exit bullet wounds are frequently important to assist in determining the firearm used, the relative positioning of the firearm, and to reconstruct the events leading to the death.[88]

i.   Entrance/Exit Wounds

The appearance of an entrance wound will vary according to the type of weapon, the ammunition, the area of the body affected, and the distance of the weapon from the body of the victim. The bullet as it strikes the skin is moving forward at high speed and is also rotating on its axis as a result of the spin imparted to it by the rifling of lands and grooves in the barrel. At the point of entry, the bullet pushes the skin in and perforates the skin through indentation and stretch. The size of the

---

[87]   J.K. Modi et al., "Improvised Firearms Versus Regular Firearms," 26 Forensic Sci. Int'l 199 (1984).

[88]   For a recent extensive discussion of the topic of bullet wounds, liberally illustrated by color photography, *see* Stefan Pollak and Pekka J. Sauko, "Gunshot Wounds," in WILEY ENCYCLOPEDIA OF FORENSIC SCIENCE, (Jamieson A. & Moenssens A.A., eds) 2009 & online updates.

entrance wound may correspond roughly to the caliber of the bullet, but it is not a direct indication of bullet size. After the bullet has passed through the skin, the hole it leaves in the skin may become smaller in diameter than when the bullet was passing through. In contact wounds, the explosive action of powder gases may result in a large gaping wound.

The exit wound will not display soot deposition, powder stippling, or (with rare exceptions) a marginal abrasion collar. The size of the exit wound will depend on the weapon type, ammunition, type of bullet, and the path of the bullet. The bullet may continue to spin on its axis, tumble end over end, or wobble (yaw). A tumbling or yawing bullet will cause more tearing at the exit than an axis spin.

The bullet may also strike bone and fragment, thereby diminishing its velocity and causing a lacerating effect in the exit wound. Bone splinters produced by the bullet may also contribute to the lacerating effect of the exit wound. Thus, if the bullet encounters resistance within the body, its form may be altered, with a consequent enlargement of the exit wound into a stellate or jagged form.

If the bullet passes on its axis through the soft tissues of the body unobstructed by bone, the exit wound may be small, with the edges of the skin surrounding it turned out. If the bullet has fragmented, there may be multiple exit wounds. If the skin is supported in the area where the bullet exits, the wound may very closely resemble a wound of entrance because the exiting bullet causes the surrounding skin to be abraded from rubbing against the firm surface. This abrasion ring is similar to entrance wounds where the incoming bullet rubs against the margins of the perforated skin causing the characteristic abrasion collar. The exit abrasion ring may occur when the area of exit is in contact with an unyielding surface such as a floor or wall, or when the area is covered by tight fitting clothing such as a belt or bra strap. This type of supported wound is sometimes termed a "shored" wound, and the area of abrasion is often irregular, lopsided, or disproportionately large.[89]

Several types of handgun rounds are designed to provide greater stopping power than conventional ammunition or to meet specialized needs (i.e. fragmentation or expansion). Because of their unique design, some of these projectiles expend their energy in the target faster than conventional ammunition and can cause much greater wound damage,[90] while others are designed to have a more concentrated impact.[91]

---

[89] P.E. Besant-Matthews, "Examinations and Interpretations of Rifled Firearm Injuries," in J.K. Mason & B.N. Purdue, eds., *The Pathology of Trauma*, Arnold, London (3rd ed. 2000); *see also* S. Dixon, Characteristics of Shored Exit Wounds, 26 J. Forensic Sci. 691 (1981).

[90] B. Gern, "Wounding Effects of Unconventional Ammunition," 10 FORENSIC SCI. DIGEST 13 (1984).

[91] Craig L. Nelson and David C. Winston, "A New Type of Shotgun Ammunition Produces Unique Wound Characteristics," 52 J. FORENSIC SCI. 195–198 (2007).

ii.   Contact, Intermediate, and Distant Range Wounds

A contact entrance wound results from the placement of the muzzle of the firearm in contact with the victim at the time it was fired. *See* Figure 9. An intermediate range wound is defined as a wound surrounded by discrete powder stippling, and generally considered as one in which the muzzle was held from one inch to approximately three feet from the point of entry at the time of discharge. A distant range (also called "indeterminate" range) wound occurs at any distance greater than intermediate range (generally greater than three feet).

Figure 9: Hard contact gunshot wound of right side of head. Suicide. Note the patterned muzzle stamp imprint and the large entrance perforation with a marginal tear caused by expanding gases under the skin when the weapon was discharged.

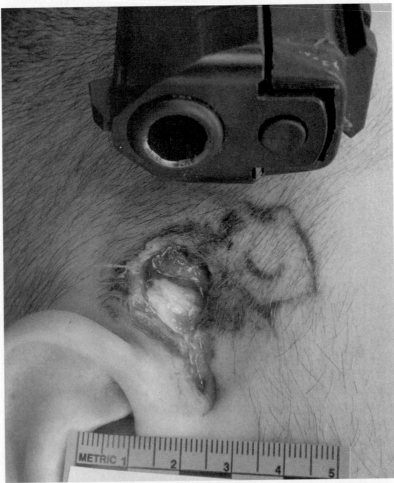

Depending on the variable types of firearms and ammunition used, there are several general characteristics that may appear in contact or near contact wounds on bare skin. These peculiarities aid the pathologist in determining the range and direction of fire:

a.   A scorching of hairs and skin results from flame discharge and hot powder gases in very close shots. The degree of scorching varies according to the surface of the target, the type of powder, the pressure of the gases, and the distance from firearm to impact surface.

b.   Soot staining (sometimes called smudging or fouling) of the skin results from powder smoke or powder gases. *See* Figure 10. Soot staining is found internally if a muzzle is in direct contact with skin, and externally in the case of a near contact shot. Soot staining may be wiped from the skin with a damp cloth. If this is done, the wound may mislead the pathologist who speculates as to the range of fire.

Figure 10: Near contact gunshot wound, homicide. Note the soot staining on the skin surrounding the defect.

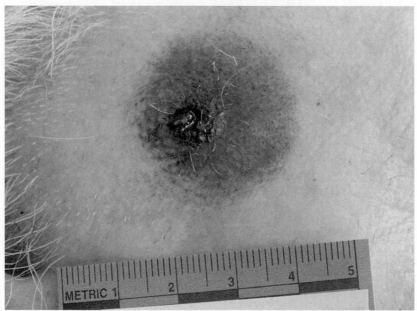

c.   Tattooing or stippling of the epidermal layer of skin with embedded grains of burned or partially burned powder occurs in intermediate range wounds (*see* Figure 11). Unburned *smokeless* powder tattoos the skin. Unburned *black* powder only smudges the skin. Powder tattooing cannot be rubbed off. Scanning Electron Microscopy (SEM) of the dermal surface of tattooing from powder burns may reveal that these particles remain trapped in the basement membrane despite mechanical separation of the epidermis and a thorough washing of the area. This suggests that gunshot residue particles may be identified even on skin in an advanced state of decomposition.[92] The proportion of unburned powder depends on the barrel length, type of powder, and gas pressure.

Figure 11: Intermediate range wound, homicide. Note the dense powder stippling (tattooing) around the entrance, with powder grains visible in some of the stipple marks.

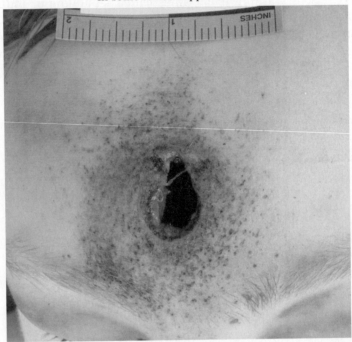

d.   An abrasion collar of the skin around the entrance defect occurs as the bullet punches its way through the skin, rubbing off the outer layer of skin as it passes through (*see* Figure 12).

---

[92]   C. Torre et al., "New Observation on Cutaneous Firearm Wounds," 7 AM.J.FOR.MED. & PATH. 3 (1986).

Figure 12: Entrance gunshot wound, homicide. Note the abrasion collar (outer layer of skin rubbed from wound edges) ringing the wound.

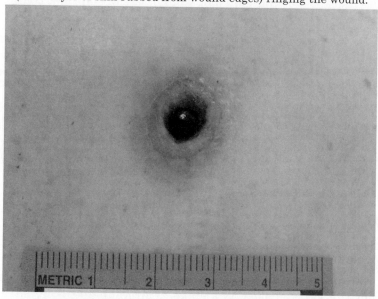

e.   A gaping or star-shaped ("stellate") contact entrance wound may be caused by the force of gases tearing the skin, especially when there is bone directly under the skin. This occurrence is most common in contact gunshot wounds of the head (*see* Figure 13).

Figure 13: Entrance gunshot wound, suicide. The gaping, stellate lacerations result from the gas exiting the weapon and tearing the skin from underneath.

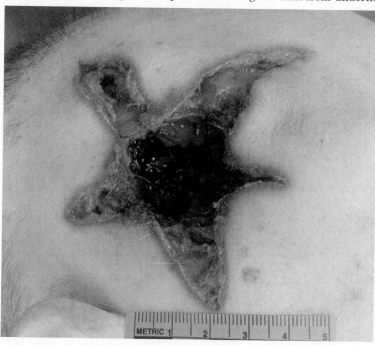

The overwhelming majority of suicidal gunshot wounds are contact range.[93] Cases of multiple gunshot wound suicides are not common but do occur.[94]

A distant range wound refers to the discharging firearm being far enough from the point of entry so that no soot staining or powder stippling can be seen.[95] This distance—depending upon the nature of the powder, cartridge, and weapon—is usually more than three feet. The distance at which a shot was fired cannot be determined by examination of a distant range wound. Many forensic pathologists prefer the term "indeterminate range," rather than distant range, for such wounds, since clothing or an intermediary target (such as drywall or a window), could filter out the soot and powder and make a closer range shot appear "distant."

c.   *Shotgun Wounds*

Shotguns produce soot staining and powder stippling of the skin, as described above for contact and intermediate range wounds from handguns and rifles. *See* Figure 14. A shotgun held within one or two feet from the skin surface will make a large, single hole. At greater distances, its progressively expanding pattern of shot will result in multiple pellet wounds. *See* Figure 15. Within a distance of four or five yards, wadding pads or plastic sleeve collars used to contain the shot may be propelled into the wound. At somewhat longer ranges the individual wads may not penetrate the skin but may leave rather typical appearing "wad marks" on the skin. The presence of wads or

---

[93] For an analysis of entrance wound sites in gunshot suicides see, J. Eisele et al., "Sites of Suicidal Gunshot Wounds," 26 J. Forensic Sci. 480 (1981).

A common theory has been that people who commit suicide do not shoot through their clothing, but rather push it aside to place the barrel next to bare skin. This common theory has not been supported by the empirical evidence. *See* Petr Hejna and Miroslav Safr, "Shooting Through Clothing in Firearm Suicides," 55 J. FORENSIC SCI. 652–654 (2010).

[94] *See, e.g.*, Anastasia E. Kastanaki, Elena F. Kranioti, Pavlos N. Theodorakis, and Manolis Michalodimitrakis, "An Unusual Suicide Inside a Grave with Two Gunshot Wounds to the Head—The Psychological Approach," 54 J. FORENSIC SCI. 404–407 (2009); G. Kury, J. Weiner, and J. Duval, "Multiple Self-inflicted Gunshot Wounds to the Head: Report of a Case and Review of the Literature," 21(1) AM. J. FORENSIC MED. PATHOL. 32–35 (2000). *See also*, C.S. Hirsch & Lester Adelson, "A Suicidal Gunshot Wound of the Back," 21 J. FORENSIC SCI. 659 (1976). *Cf.* Bartram v. State, 33 Md.App. 115, 364 A.2d 1119 (1976), *aff'd*, 280 Md. 616, 374 A.2d 1144 (1977)(defendant claimed decedent committed suicide but pathologist testified that the third shot could not have been fired by the victim).

[95] For a detailed discussion of classification of entrance wounds based on range from muzzle to target (shooting distance), *see* Stefan Pollak and Pekka J. Sauko, "Gunshot Wounds," in WILEY ENCYCLOPEDIA OF FORENSIC SCIENCE, (Jamieson A. & Moenssens A.A., eds) 2009 & online updates. *See also* Arie Zeichner, "Shooting Distance: Estimation of," in WILEY ENCYCLOPEDIA OF FORENSIC SCIENCE, (Jamieson A. & Moenssens A.A., eds) 2009 & online updates.

In State v. Massey, 242 Kan. 252, 747 P.2d 802 (1987), there were no powder burns at the entrance wound on the decedent's head. No lab tests were performed on the bedspread which covered the decedent and contained what appeared to be bullet holes in it. Without such evidence, the absence of powder burns could be explained as either a distant bullet wound (which supported the defendant's accidental discharge defense) or a bullet wound inflicted with the bedspread between the gun and the decedent's head.

sleeves combined with a charting of the uniform cone-like shot patterns by test firing the suspect weapon or a facsimile under similar conditions as prevailed at the time of the homicide provides a good estimation of shotgun distance.[96]

Figure 14: Contact entrance wound from a shotgun.

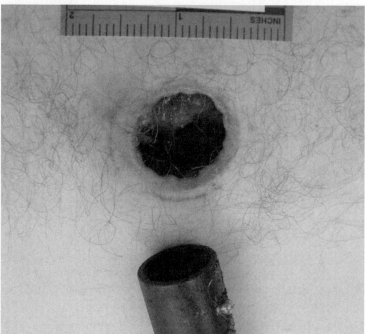

The shot dispersal pattern should be measured on the skin of a shotgun wound victim. Radiographs are not helpful in assessing range of fire because the shot pellets disperse widely and unpredictably after perforating the skin, even at close range. Estimation of range of fire is less accurate as the distance between the gun muzzle and the target increases, especially if only some of the pellets strike the target surface.

Shotgun injuries may exhibit wide variability, and careful examination is necessary to avoid misinterpretation of shotgun wounds. In extreme cases, a contact wound to the temple may result in the injection of large amounts of gas into the skull that causes a large gas blowout wound between the eyes. Such blowouts can be mistaken for entry wounds if the pathologist is not aware of this unusual shotgun injury.[97] In another case, what was initially thought to be two shotgun charges from different ranges was actually the result of an unusual intermediate target. A "dust cover" consisting of a shotgun casing had been inserted into the muzzle of the shotgun. This intermediate target

---

[96] In Miller v. State, 250 Ind. 656, 236 N.E.2d 585 (1968), a shot range experiment did not sufficiently replicate the conditions to support admissibility.

[97] G.C. Johnson, "Unusual Shotgun Injury-Gas Blowout of Anterior Head Region," 6 Am.J.For.Med. & Path. 3 (1985).

actually became part of the projectile and produced the unusual defects.[98]

Figure 15: Shotgun wound of the back with wide dispersion of pellets.

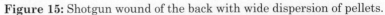

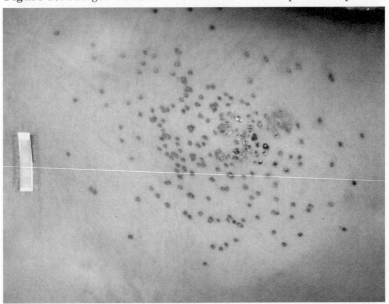

Some of the significant factors in evaluating shotgun wounds to determine whether death resulted from suicide, homicide, or accident include the gauge and choke of the weapon, the size and number of pellets within the shell fired (*see* Figure 16), and the proximity of the muzzle to the victim.

Figure 16: Evidence recovered from the autopsy of a shotgun wound. Homicide. The shot cup is on the left, pellets are in the middle, and wadding is on the right.

---

[98] R.C. Challener & S.B. Rosenberg, "An Unusual Shotgun Injury Pattern Produced by an Intermediate Target," 7 Am.J.For.Med. & Path. 3 (1986).

d.   Incised Cuts, Stab Wounds, and Chop Wounds

The cause of death in cases of cuts, stabbing, or chop wounds is usually internal or external hemorrhage from a vital vessel or a vital organ.[99] Incised wounds can be homicidal, suicidal, or (rarely) accidental.[100]

An incised wound (cut) is linear—its length on the skin surface is greater than its depth in the body. The edges are typically clean-cut, sharp, and even. The nature of an incised cut wound varies with the instrument used;[101] the manner in which the instrument was used; the type, length, and sharpness of the blade; and the area in which the wound is inflicted. *See* Figure 17. What appears to be a clean-cut wound in an area of skin backed by bone (such as the skull, elbow, or knee) may actually be the result of a dull edge or a blunt instrument producing lacerations.

Stab wounds are deeper in the body than they are long on the skin surface. The nature of the stab wound varies with the instrument used, the manner in which it was used, and the length and sharpness of the blade. *See* Figures 18 and 19. Examination of the corners of the stab wound may suggest the nature of the instrument: a weapon on which both edges are sharpened may produce a stab wound in which both ends are sharply incised, while a weapon which is sharpened on one side only may result in a wound with one end squared. Whether a given wound gapes or closes will depend somewhat on whether the stab wound was cut at right angles to the elastic fibers of the dermal skin or whether it was cut along the line of the fibers.

---

[99] For a detailed discussion of sharp injury wounds with color photographs, see Stefan Pollak and Pekka J. Saukko, "Wounds: Sharp Injury," in WILEY ENCYCLOPEDIA OF FORENSIC SCIENCE, (Jamieson A. & Moenssens A.A., eds) 2009 & online updates.

[100] Serafettin Demirci, Kamil Hakan Dogan, and Gursel Gunaydin, "Throat-Cutting of Accidental Origin," 53 J. FORENSIC SCI. 965–967 (2008).

[101] Stab-cut dimensions in clothing do not accurately disclose knife blade widths. P.A. Costello and M.E. Lawton, "Do Stab-Cuts Reflect the Weapon Which Made Them?," 30 J. FORENSIC SCI. SOC. 89 (1990).

Figure 17: Homicidal stab wounds of the neck. All of stab wounds were all made by the same knife, but have different shapes depending on how the weapon was wielded, the movement of the assailant, the movement of the victim, and the angle in which underlying elastic tissue fibers were cut.

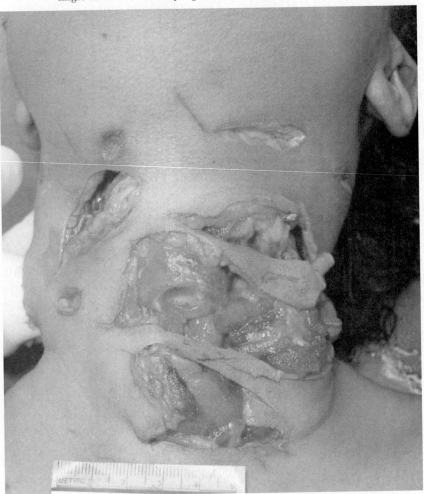

Figure 18: Gaping stab wound (left) and reapproximation of the cut margins with clear tape (right). Reapproximation better documents the wound size, and in this example suggests that the knife was single-edged.

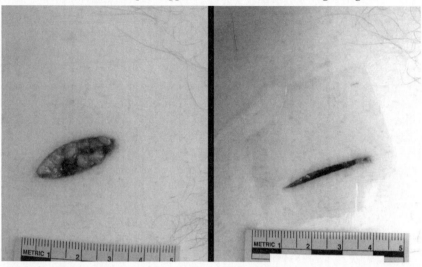

Figure 19: The patterned injury associated with the multiple stab wounds in this homicide victim suggest that the knife was serrated.

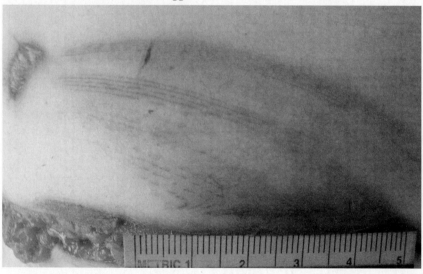

In cases of stab wounds a pathologist may be queried on the depth of the wounds to prove or disprove their consistency with the suspected weapon used. Depth cannot be determined merely by an observation of the size of the wound on the skin or the amount of bleeding. The nature of the soft tissues in the thorax and abdomen, their degree of stretching and displacement, and the degree of compression accompanying stabbing makes it difficult, if not impossible, to accurately determine the length of a weapon by measurement of the track of the wound at autopsy, except in extreme circumstances.

Chop wounds, typically inflicted by an axe, cleaver, hatchet, or machete, are rarely suicidal. Although the interpretation of such wounds is generally governed by the above considerations, the duller edges of such instruments can produce injuries with features (such as marginal abrasions or tissue bridges) usually associated with blunt trauma.

As with other types of wounds, a key issue for the pathologist's determination in cases of cutting and stabbing is whether the wound is the result of homicide or suicide. A pathologist is often asked whether the deceased could have produced the injuries that caused death and whether there were any body signs of a struggle. The presence of numerous cuts on the decedent's hands may be suggestive of "defensive" injuries incurred during an attempt to ward off an attacker. *See* Figure 20.

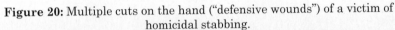

Figure 20: Multiple cuts on the hand ("defensive wounds") of a victim of homicidal stabbing.

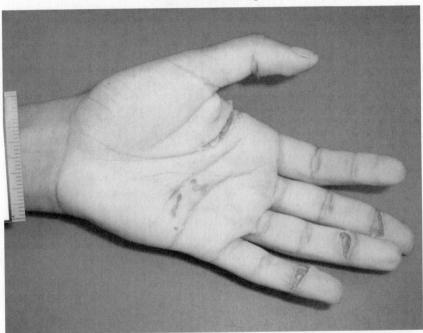

In cases of suicide by sharp instrument "hesitation marks" may be present.[102] *See* Figure 21. Hesitation marks are superficial cuts inflicted prior to the individual gaining the courage to make the fatal slash or plunge. Suicidal wounds, however, can be inflicted in the absence of hesitation marks.[103] The direction of the cut and whether the victim

---

[102] P. Vanezis and L.E. West, "Tentative Injuries in Self-Stabbing," 21 FORENSIC SCI. INT'L 89–94 (1992).

[103] For examples of suicidal stab cases where there were no hesitation marks, *see* Iain West, "Single Suicidal Stab Wounds A Study of Three Cases," 21 Med. Sci. & Law 198 (1981).

was right or left handed may be factors that enter into an expert's opinion as to whether death was by the victim's own hand.

Figure 21: Hesitation wounds.

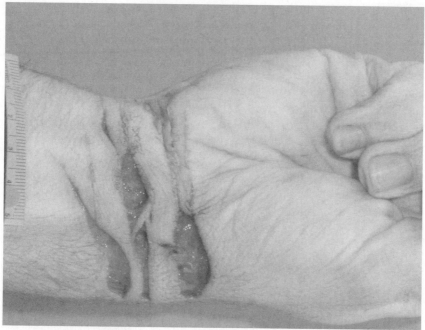

e.   *Blunt Force Trauma*

Blunt force wounds result from something blunt striking the body, or the body striking something blunt, and occur in a variety of circumstances such as falls, punches or kicks, motor vehicle crashes, or being struck with a blunt item. Blunt force injuries are classified as contusions (bruises), abrasions, lacerations, fractures, or rupture of vital organs. The discrimination of injuries caused by falls or accidental impact from injuries caused by homicidal force is a common, and sometimes challenging, problem for forensic pathologists.

Contusions commonly reflect an antemortem event because blood circulation is considered necessary for their formation.[104] Differentiation can be made of a contusion from early livor mortis since pressure will not dispel a contusion. Several recent studies have shown that it is virtually impossible to determine by color alone the length of time a contusion has been present.[105]

---

[104] For a discussion of contusion patterns, *see* Henry J. Carson, "Patterns of Ecchymoses Caused by Manner of Death and Collateral Injuries Sustained in Bruising Incidents: Decedent Injuries, Profiles, Comparisons, and Clinicopathologic Significance," 55 J. FORENSIC SCI. 1534–1542 (2010).

[105] For a detailed discussion of blunt force injuries with color photographs, *see* Stefan Pollak and Pekka J. Saukko, "Blunt Force Trauma," in WILEY ENCYCLOPEDIA OF FORENSIC SCIENCE, (Jamieson A. & Moenssens A.A., eds) 2009 & online updates.

Fatal injuries involving blunt force trauma to the head frequently occur.[106] Contusions to the cerebral tissue have patterns that are of great importance in cases of alleged homicide (*see* Figures 22, 23, 24, and 25). If the moving head strikes a fixed object, as with a fall, then the cerebral contusions resulting from this trauma will be more severe on the point of the brain that is opposite from the site of impact (contrecoup). If the fixed head is struck by a moving object, as with a blow from a weapon, the cerebral damage will be more severe beneath the area of impact (coup). The identification of coup and contrecoup contusions can be used for reconstructing the direction of the impacting force, for estimating its relative magnitude, and for determining whether the head was struck by an object or whether it struck an object in a fall. *See* Figure 26.

Figure 22: Homicidal blunt force trauma inflicted by a hammer showing typical abrasions and a star-like laceration (left), overlying a concentric depressed skull fracture (right).

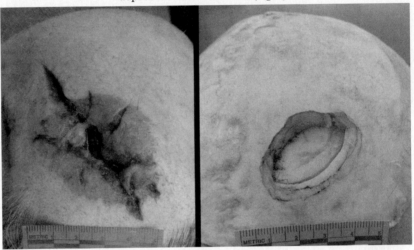

Fatal blunt force injuries to the head involving intracranial hemorrhage are of four types: (a) epidural; (b) subdural; (c) subarachnoid; and (d) within the brain (intracerebral).

Epidural bleeding involves a tearing or rupture of an artery, traversing between the layers of the dura mater firmly adherent to the inner surface of the skull cap. The arterial injury is usually a consequence of displacement of one of the margins of a fractured skull. Death results from compression of the brain by the blood clot so formed.

---

[106] Sudden death may also result from an otherwise non-fatal blow to the head, although it is not common and frequently occurs in conjunction with alcohol consumption or "second impact syndrome" in sports. Abigail E. Veevers, William Lawler, and Guy N. Rutty, "Walk and Die: An Unusual Presentation of Head Injury," 54 J. FORENSIC SCI. 1466–1469 (2009).

Figure 23: Blunt force trauma to the scalp resulting in a laceration surrounded by an abrasion. The bridges of tissue in the depths of the laceration distinguish this form of blunt trauma from a sharp force injury.

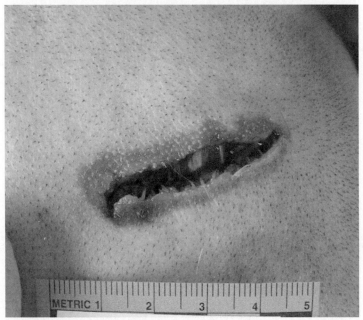

Subdural hemorrhage, the most common form of traumatic blunt force injury causing death, usually involves bleeding from a ruptured vein leading from the dura mater to the underlying brain. Death from a subdural hematoma (blood clot) formed from a torn vessel may occur quickly, or several days or even weeks after the traumatic event.

Due to the fact that extradural bleeding, because of its arterial origin, occurs more briskly than subdural hemorrhage, the duration of life following the infliction of the injury will also vary considerably. The lucid interval refers to the interval between the infliction of the injury and the onset of definite symptoms due to the bleeding in both extradural and subdural hemorrhages. The lucid interval is much longer in a subdural hemorrhage than in the extradural hemorrhage.

Subarachnoid hemorrhage is bleeding beneath the thin, transparent, outer covering of the brain itself, into an artificial space that does not exist until so created by the bleeding (*see* Figure 25).

Figure 24: Battered child with numerous contusions visible when the scalp is reflected at autopsy.

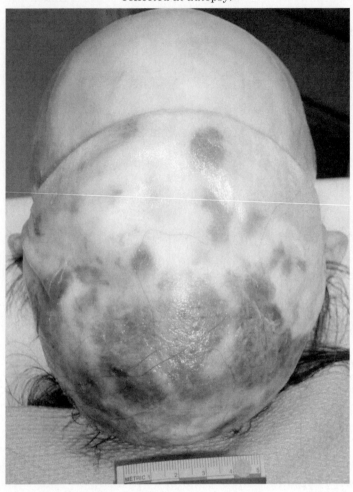

Figure 25: Subarachnoid hemorrhage is occasionally due to trauma when there is a blow to the neck that causes tearing of a cerebral artery. The vertebral artery is most vulnerable as it enters the cranial cavity from the cervical spine. This victim was kicked in the side of the neck tearing the vertebral artery, causing immediate loss of consciousness.

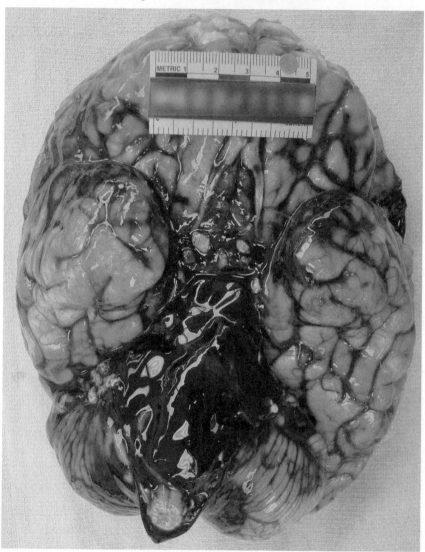

Figure 26: Contrecoup contusions. This decedent fell on the back of his head, but the most significant contusions (contrecoup contusions—arrows) are on the frontal lobes of the brain.

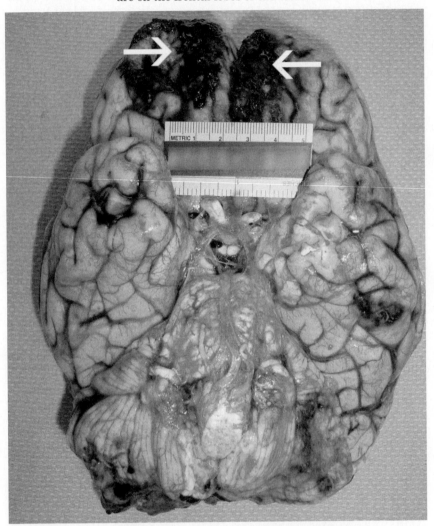

Deep brain hemorrhage occurs within the substance of the brain, and is usually the result of natural disease processes (such as hypertension or arteriovenous malformations) or the use of illicit stimulants such as cocaine or methamphetamine. Deep brain hemorrhage is not usually the result of trauma.

Resuscitative measures may cause injuries and artifacts that the pathologist must differentiate from fatal trauma. These include chest wall injuries and rib fractures from CPR, facial and oral injuries from airway management and intubations, and surgical incisions for chest tubes and other emergent interventions.

3.   POISONS AND BURNS

Although the presence of some observable characteristics of a deceased body might suggest poisoning, toxicological and histopathological analysis must be done for confirmation.[107] Some observable characteristics that the forensic pathologist might note concern skin color, gastric contents, odor, and alterations in the skin around the mouth. The presence of cherry-red lividity on a body should lead a pathologist to consider death by carbon monoxide poisoning.[108] Poisoning by sodium or potassium cyanide also produces a bright red or brick color of livor in the body. Such a death is associated with the odor of bitter almonds emanating from the body and its organs; however, about 50% of people cannot smell that odor. Additionally, the odor of bitter almonds may also attend the body of one dead of nitrobenzene poisoning. Corrosion of the skin around the mouth may indicate death by drinking acid or alkali. Brown "coffee ground"-like vomitus is also characteristic of acid poisoning.

Burns may be caused by heat, chemicals, or electricity.[109] The manner of death may be suicide, accident, or homicide.[110] Fire victims are usually found in a "pugilistic" position with clenched fists or bent arms, similar to the pose of a boxer. This phenomenon is caused by the heating of protein in muscle cells that causes contraction.[111]

Pathologists may uncover a homicide in which an attempt was made to simulate accidental death by burning the body. Smoke contains carbon monoxide. Therefore, if carbon monoxide is lacking from the victim's blood, death probably occurred prior to the fire. Minor (sublethal) concentrations of cyanide may be found in the blood of burn victims. The cyanide is the product of combustion of plastics, wool, and certain synthetic fabrics. Therefore, the mere presence of cyanide in the blood of a burn victim exposed to burning plastics and synthetics does not indicate that he was poisoned with cyanide prior to the beginning of the fire.[112]

---

[107] For a discussion of the histopathological findings associated with botulism poisoning, *see* Kelly G. Devers and Jeffrey S. Nine, "Autopsy Findings in Botulism Toxin Poisoning," 55 J. FORENSIC SCI. 1649–1651 (2010).

[108] *See* Frank R. Dutra, "Physiological Principle of Carbon Monoxide Poisoning," 54 J.CRIM.L., C. & P.S. 513 (1963).

[109] Differentiation of injuries caused by thermal burns, abrasions, and electrocution skin injuries can sometime be difficult. Elif Akyildiz, Ibrahim Uzun, Akif Inanici, and Huseyin Baloglu, "Computerized Image Analysis in Differentiation of Skin Lesions Caused by Electrocution, Flame Burns, and Abrasions," 54 J. FORENSIC SCI. 1419–1422 (2009).

[110] William F. Zaloga and Kim A. Collins, "Pediatric Homicides Related to Burn Injury: A Retrospective Review at the Medical University of South Carolina," 51 J. FORENSIC SCI. 396–399 (2006).

[111] For a detailed discussion of burn injuries with color photographs, *see* Michael Bohnert, "Injury: Burns, Scalds, and Chemical," in WILEY ENCYCLOPEDIA OF FORENSIC SCIENCE, (Jamieson A. & Moenssens A.A., eds) 2009 & online updates.

[112] *See,* Thomas E. Noguchi et al., "Significance of Cyanide in Medicolegal Investigations Involving Fires," 9 AM.J.FOR.MED. & PATH. 304 (1988).

§12.13 CIVIL CASES

The forensic pathology report regarding cause and manner of death is not only used in criminal proceedings. The pathologist is also often called to testify as an expert witness in civil proceedings. Although many civil cases require the testimony of a pathologist, three categories are featured here: workplace environmental injuries, accidental traffic injuries, and medical malpractice.

1. WORKPLACE AND ENVIRONMENTAL INJURIES

The autopsy is an effective tool for recognizing new disorders due to occupational or environmental influences, and forensic pathological investigations involve areas of public health, industrial safety, environmental hazards, and occupational disease.[113] State medical examiners and coroners diagnose many natural deaths each year due to trauma and diseases associated with the workplace and the environment.[114] For example, pneumoconiosis and mesothelioma are two environmental conditions that may be investigated by a forensic pathologist. Pneumoconiosis is an environmental pathology caused by inhaling minute airborne particulates. When the solid matter is inhaled, it produces reactions in the body that result in various debilitating conditions. The most common historical pneumoconiosis affects coal miners. This condition, Black Lung Disease, is prevalent enough that Congress enacted the Black Lung Benefits Act.[115] Mesothelioma, a fatal cancer of the lining of the lung or abdominal cavity,[116] is a type of tumor that has been found almost exclusively in people who have been exposed to asbestos. Most cases are diagnosed 30 years or more after the first exposure to asbestos.[117] Asbestos was widely used for years as a fireproofing agent and an insulator; it is

---

[113] Cyril H. Wecht and John T. Rago, eds., *Forensic Science and Law: Investigative Applications in Criminal, Civil, and Family Justice,* CRC Press, 2005.

[114] *See* Giovanni Cecchetto et al, "Machinery-Related Deaths: Relevance of Workplace Investigation and Antemortem Radiological Data in Reconstructing the Fatality," 55 J. FORENSIC SCI. 845–848 (2010).

[115] Black Lung Benefits Act, 30 U.S.C. § 901 et seq. The Act requires coal operators to compensate certain miners and their survivors for death or disability due to black lung disease caused by employment in coal mines. See Usery v. Turner Elkhorn mining Co., 428 U.S. 1 (1976); Dir. v. Greenwich Collieries, 512 U.S. 267 (1994). See, Amax Coal Company v. Director, Department of Labor, 993 F.2d 600 (7th Cir.1993), in which pathologists disagreed whether the decedent had suffered from the disease.

Similarly, the Longshore and Harbor Workers' Compensation Act (33 U.S.C. § 901 et seq.) provides for the payment of compensation, medical care, and vocational rehabilitation services to workers disabled from injuries on the job and on navigable waters of the United States, or in adjoining loading or repair facilities. The covered "injury" includes occupational diseases, hearing loss, and illnesses arising out of the employment.

[116] Norfolk & Western R. Co. v. Ayers, 538 U.S. 135, 142 (2003).

[117] *See* Agency for Toxic Substances & Disease Registry, www.atsdr.cdc.gov/asbestos/asbestos/health_effects.

found in many buildings, including schools and hospitals.[118] The estimates of asbestos-related death vary, but average around 900 deaths per year.[119] Asbestos-related litigation has increased and expanded to include recovery for mental anguish resulting from the fear of developing cancer by railroad workers suffering from actionable injury asbestosis by work-related exposure to asbestos.[120]

An environmental pathogen of current concern to forensic pathologists is lead poisoning. For children aged 1–5, the CDC recommends blood lead levels lower than 10 micrograms of lead per deciliter of blood.[121] Exposure to lead most often occurs from lead-based paint or through drinking water traveling through lead-based pipes, as was recently discovered in Flint, Michigan. Until 1980, lead-based paint was widely used in homes, public buildings, and as a coating for steel structures. Lead-based pipes in homes may connect to municipal water systems.[122] In deaths where lead poisoning is implicated, the pathologist seeks to determine if the cause of death was chronic or acute lead poisoning. In cases of acute poisoning, the pathologist will often find renal damage, arteriolar degeneration, and areas of renal-sclerosis and lead lines in the bones.[123]

Another area of environmental pathology involves radiation injuries. Everyone is exposed to natural and man-made sources of radiation. Natural sources include radiation from outer space (such as solar radiation), radiation from the earth (such as radon gas[124]), and naturally-occurring radioactive minerals (such as uranium). Man-made radiation includes x-rays, nuclear power plant produced radioactive substances, other industrial radiation sources, and aboveground electric lines. Pathologists can help determine if lesions and increased density or eburnation of the bone (conversion of the bone into an ivory-like mass) are related to radiation exposure.[125] This information can be used to encourage the reduction of radiation hazards and is helpful in

---

[118] Asbestosis, chronic and progressive inflammation of the lungs, is another condition relating to asbestos exposure that has resulted in litigation. *See* Brown & Root, Inc. v. Sain, 162 F.3d 813, 817 (4th Cir. 1998).

[119] See www.ewg.org/asbestos/facts/fact1.php.

[120] Norfolk & Western Ry. v. Ayers, 538 U.S. 135 (2003).

[121] There is no "safe" blood lead level, but the CDC has established the threshold level of public safety intervention at ≥10μ/dL. CDC, "Preventing Lead Poisoning in Young Children," August, 2005.

[122] In Washington, DC, approximately 23,000 homes have lead-based water service pipes. See http://www.cdc.gov/nceh/lead/leadinwater/ (last accessed August 31, 2016).

[123] Cyril H. Wecht and John T. Rago, eds., *Forensic Science and Law: Investigative Applications in Criminal, Civil, and Family Justice,* CRC Press, 2005.

[124] Radon is a radioactive gas that seeps up from the earth and can be released through concrete, tile, or brick. Radon is estimated to cause about 21,000 lung cancer deaths per year, according to the Environmental Protection Agency (EPA), 2003 Assessment of Risks from Radon in Homes (EPA 402–R–03–003).

[125] Cyril H. Wecht and John T. Rago, eds., *Forensic Science and Law: Investigative Applications in Criminal, Civil, and Family Justice,* CRC Press, 2005,

litigation where an injured party seeks compensation for radiation-induced trauma or disease.

2.   TRAFFIC FATALITIES

The pathologist's examination may be essential in establishing what happened in traffic fatalities.[126] The forensic pathologist may be asked to determine from the injuries sustained whether the decedent was the driver, a passenger, a pedestrian, or a person who suffered a non-vehicular death on the side of the road. Other areas of inquiry include toxicological conditions, speed estimations, point of impact determinations, and positional findings.[127] Obviously, the accuracy of these determinations and findings is dependent on the ability to ascertain the environmental variables such as road, weather, and equipment conditions.

Certain injuries can point to the decedent as the driver at the time of impact.[128] The most obvious evidence is a circular impression on the skin of the chest, which is caused by the steering wheel.[129] Such impact often causes fracturing of the sternum and ribs with compression of the chest and lacerations of the lungs. It may also cause injury to the liver, pancreas, and surrounding vessels.[130] The driver may also sustain a skull fracture when striking the roof or windshield. One or both feet on the brake may indicate the driver anticipated the accident, whereas a foot on the accelerator may suggest the crash was unexpected or intentional. The driver and other front seat occupants may sustain fractures of the ankles different from the leg fractures suffered by a pedestrian.

In contrast, a passenger in the right front seat (unless protected by an airbag) will sustain face, chest, abdomen, and knee injuries due to being thrust against any combination of the following: windshield, roof, dashboard, glove compartment, and floorboard. Horizontal bruising of the lower abdomen and across the chest indicates the use of a seat belt and the directionality of the chest bruising may indicate whether the decedent was the passenger (from right to left) or the driver (left to right). Both factors are important to note in the autopsy report for consideration of comparative or contributory negligence.

---

[126] Laura L. Liptai, "Trauma Causation: Analysis of Automotive," in WILEY ENCYCLOPEDIA OF FORENSIC SCIENCE, (Jamieson A. & Moenssens A.A., eds) 2009 & online updates.

[127] Pathologists may also be asked to identify risk factors and prevention strategies. Sarah L. Lathrop, Travis B. Dick, and Kurt B. Nolte, "Fatal Wrong-way Collisions on New Mexico's Interstate Highways, 1990–2004," 55 J. FORENSIC SCI. 432–437 (2010).

[128] See State v. Knight, 36 So.3d 1163 (La. Ct. of App. 2010)(pathologist testified that the pattern of injuries on defendant indicated he was the driver during the accident).

[129] Although airbags prevent impact of the wheel, airbags have also been responsible for burns and trauma during rapid deployment. See Pasquale Mastroroberto, Guilio Di Mizio, Federica Colosimo, and Pietrantonio, "Occlusion of Left and Right Coronary Arteries and Coronary Sinus Following Blunt Chest Trauma," 56 J. FORENSIC SCI. 1349–1351 (2011).

[130] G.M. Weisz, et al., "Injury to the Driver," 14 J. TRAUMA 212 (1974).

Motorcycle injuries differ from automobile injuries largely in degree of injury and the fact that the driver may sustain injuries from collisions with secondary objects such as trees, lampposts, or guardrails.[131] While there are no steering wheel impact injuries, more massive fractures of the skull (where no helmet is worn) and extremities may be present. If the driver anticipates the crash and decides to take it "lying down," he will suffer massive abrasions from the sliding stop on the pavement. The pathologist should examine and retain the helmet in all motorcycle deaths since there may be future litigation regarding whether the individual was wearing a helmet and whether the headgear measured up to protective standards for impact resistance.

Pedestrians killed in roadway accidents fall into three distinct categories. The first is the person walking along the side of the road in the same direction as the flow of traffic. Such a person will sustain bumper fractures when struck by a car. A bumper fracture is a fracture found in the lower third of the pedestrian's legs, which is due to the force of the bumper of the automobile. If lower on the legs than the height of the bumper, the motorist can be said to have been braking at the moment of impact. The pedestrian may be knocked out of their shoes. When hit, the pedestrian may cartwheel up and back which will cause a severely arched spine and head strike on the hood, windshield, or roof of the car. How the pedestrian hits the car depends on a number of variables including the speed and design of the car. The spinal arching can result in fracture-dislocations of the thoracic and/or lumbar spine while the impact of the head can produce a skull fracture.

The second category of pedestrian is the person walking along the side of the road facing oncoming traffic. Such a person will sustain similar injuries to the above-discussed pedestrian. However, since this pedestrian may react to the oncoming collision, the bumper fractures may be replaced with evidence of high speed impact higher up on the body and more extensive fractures in the extremities from attempting to jump up or out of the way.

The third type of pedestrian is the person struck while attempting to cross the street. This pedestrian may also sustain injuries, but since the impact will probably be from the side, there is less likely to be extensive skull injuries or other effects from the cartwheel motion experienced by the other two types of pedestrians. This pedestrian is less likely to be thrown up and back, but more likely to be run over by the wheels of the vehicle. Runover injuries are compressed injuries that are generally distinguishable from other impact pattern injuries. In such cases, a tire pattern is often found on the skin or clothing, and the

---

[131] Francesco Brandimarti et al., "Massive Lesions Owing to Motorcyclist Impact Against Guardrail Posts: Analysis of Two Cases and Safety Considerations," 56 J. FORENSIC SCI. 544–546 (2011).

pathologist should carefully measure and photograph it for later comparison and testimony.

In addition to the injuries themselves, pathologists can gather other evidence that could have great importance in future litigation. Whether the deceased is a driver, passenger, or pedestrian, the pathologist should do a toxicological study for blood alcohol, carbon monoxide, and drug levels. These findings could evidence the circumstances leading to the accident, and in some jurisdictions, may support a contributory negligence defense. A postmortem radiograph of the decedent's body may reveal the presence of parts of the accident-causing vehicle, which can later be matched and used to identify the vehicle. Also, the victim's clothing may contain fragments of paint, glass, or other material that can be used to help investigators identify the automobile involved in the accident.[132]

3. MEDICAL MALPRACTICE

Forensic pathologists are often used to diagnose injuries due to medical negligence.[133] When a patient dies in a hospital, the hospital pathologist may perform an autopsy with the permission of the decedent's family. In some jurisdictions, the medical examiner/coroner will review the death instead of the hospital pathologist. This is often done to avoid a possible conflict of interest. The patient's medical record, prescriptions, course of treatment, and any surgical procedures will be reviewed. The purpose of this retrospective is similar to the death investigations in suspected criminal cases in that the cause and manner of death must be determined. The reviewing pathologist may be called upon to testify in litigation related to the death.

Any death associated with a procedure or medication prescribed by a doctor should be investigated to determine if the procedure or medication caused the death, and whether the death resulted from medical negligence. The testimony of a pathologist as to whether the death is due to a pre-existing condition or the medical treatment itself will be key evidence in a potential medical malpractice action and in any hearing by the state medical licensing board. In some cases, the forensic pathologist may have to review the record to make sure that the minimum amount of required care was offered.[134] If the physician refused to or failed to provide necessary treatment for a patient, the

---

[132] *See* Chapter 7 Trace Evidence: Materials.

[133] *See generally* Burkhead Madea, "Medical Malpractice," in WILEY ENCYCLOPEDIA OF FORENSIC SCIENCE, (Jamieson A. & Moenssens A.A., eds) 2009 & online updates.

[134] Statutes and administrative regulations may contain terms that impose liability and which may cause some confusion because the term may not meet the medical definition. *See, e.g.,* Feltner v. Lamar Adver., Inc., 83 F.Appx. 101 (6th Cir. 2003(the statutory definition of "permanent total disability" under the Tennessee Workers Compensation Act is not the same as the medical definition); Endorf v. Bohlender, 995 P.2d 896 (Kan. Ct. App. 2000)(statutory phrase "clinical practice" intended to meet the medical definition); Coleman v. Workers' Comp. Appeal Bd. (Ind. Hosp.), 842 A.2d 349 (Pa. 2004)(term "physical examination" implied common usage, not the medical definition).

physician may be guilty of medical negligence. The forensic pathology findings are fundamental in determining whether the doctor acted according to the standards prescribed for the customary practice of the profession or was negligent in the care of the decedent.

Although medical examiners may be involved in the investigation of medical negligence claims, medical examiners and their staff generally have immunity from tort liability for their negligent acts in the performance of their duties.[135] The retention of human remains has resulted in next-of-kin litigation against government pathologists pursuant to 42 U.S.C. § 1983 under a theory of deprivation of property without due process, but has generally failed to result in liability for government-authorized medical examiners and coroners.[136]

IV. TRIAL AIDS

§12.14 EXPERT QUALIFICATIONS

Forensic pathology is a medical subspecialty and requires additional training beyond the typical four years of medical school. Following graduation from medical school, physicians must receive an additional three to four years of training in anatomical (or combined anatomical and clinical) pathology before entering an additional year of forensic pathology training known as a fellowship.[137] As of 2015, there were 39 such programs in the United States.[138] After completing the required training, the physician may become certified as a forensic pathologist.

Medical specialty certification, including in pathology or forensic pathology, is a voluntary process in the United States. While medical licensing is necessary for medical practice in a particular state, licensing establishes a minimum competency requirement and does not represent specialization in any area of medicine. Pathology is a

---

[135] In LeBlanc v. Commonwealth, 457 Mass. 94, 927 N.E.2d 1017 (2010), parents sued for negligence in the death investigation of their infant son, seeking compensation for exhumation, DNA testing, and emotional distress resulting from identification errors in the autopsy. The court found that the medical examiner and the state were immune from suit by statutory authority.

[136] Albrecht v. Treon, 617 F.3d 890 (6th Cir. 2010)(based on Ohio law which does not recognize a next-of-kin's property interest in decedent remains, no cause of action under 42 U.S.C. § 1983); In re: Certified Question (Waeschle v. Oakland County Medical Examiner), 488 Mich. 1, 3–4 (2010)(responding to certified question of law from the United States District Court for the Eastern District of Michigan, Michigan Supreme Court found no property interest for next-of-kin in decedent remains removed pursuant to lawful death investigation).

[137] The Forensic Pathology Residency Programs are accredited by the Accreditation Council for Graduate Medical Education (ACGME), the organization responsible for accrediting over 8700 residency programs in 26 specialties and 130 subspecialties. Specific requirements for the programs are available at www.acgme.org.

[138] See Kimberly Collins, "The future of the forensic pathology workforce" 5(4) Acad. Forensic Pathol. 526–533 (2015).

recognized medical practice specialty of the non-profit American Board of Medical Specialties (ABMS). This Board certifies twenty four specialties through its member boards and numerous additional subspecialties as recognized areas of expert practice.

The ABMS is the recognized organization for this purpose for many medical specialties. The American Board of Pathology is a member board of the American Board of Medical Specialties. As such it administers the examinations for forensic pathology, clinical pathology, anatomic pathology, and other pathology subspecialties. Certification through the American Board of Pathology requires successful completion of both a written and a practical exam; recertification is now required every 10 years.[139] In 2006, the ABMS adopted a Maintenance of Certification (MOC) for all specialties that also requires continuing education and adherence to national standards.[140]

The Accreditation Council for Continuing Medical Education (ACCME) identifies and promotes standards for continuing education for physicians.[141] Continuing education programs in forensic pathology are offered by numerous professional organizations, including NAME, the American Academy of Forensic Sciences (AAFS), the College of American Pathologists (CAP), and the American Society for Clinical Pathologists (ASCP).

In addition to individual certification, a forensic pathologist conducting autopsies should work in an accredited facility. Accreditation, like certification, is a voluntary process in the United States. Both the National Association of Medical Examiners (NAME) and the International Association of Coroners and Medical Examiners (IAC&ME) offer peer-review, voluntary inspection and accreditation programs for death investigation facilities and systems.[142]

In addition to forensic pathologists on staff in government-authorized medical examiner/coroner units, private practice forensic pathologists and facilities are available. CAP and NAME both maintain lists of board-certified pathologists and facilities available for private consulting and investigation.

§12.15 EVIDENCE ISSUES

1.   GENERAL ADMISSIBILITY

The field of pathology, as a specialty of medicine, is one in which expert testimony is entirely appropriate, since the jury cannot be expected to have any familiarity with its procedures and the meaning of

---

[139] www.abpath.org.

[140] *See* www.certificationmatters.org.

[141] www.accme.org.

[142] NAME Inspection and Accreditation documents are provided on the NAME website: www.thename.org; IAC&ME Accreditation requirements and applications are available on the IAC&ME website: www.theiacme.com.

its findings.[143] For example, expert medical testimony has been admitted to prove that death occurred by poisoning,[144] strangulation,[145] and asphyxiation.[146] However, if the expert is asked to testify as to an "ultimate issue," some courts have expressed concern and imposed limitations to avoid invading the province of the jury.[147]

Cause of death is not always a straightforward conclusion, even for forensic pathologists. In *State v. Plude*,[148] the emergency room physician concluded the decedent drowned, either from pulmonary edema or from toilet bowl submersion, and made no determination on manner of death; the medical examiner concluded the decedent drowned from pulmonary edema due to reduced blood circulation caused by the presence of drugs in the body and concluded the manner of death was suicide or accidental overdose; and the pathologist who performed the autopsy determined the cause of death was "drug intoxication probably abetted by drowning" and that manner of death was either suicide or homicide. The appellate court reversed the conviction and remanded for a new trial because a fourth expert witness had lied about his credentials.

a. Expertise

In the past, courts have held that any properly qualified expert may express an opinion on the cause of death,[149] requiring only that the medical expert be a physician or have experience in death investigation.[150] More recent cases, however, have required not only

---

[143] Stringer v. Commonwealth, 956 S.W.2d 883, 889–890 (Ky. 1997)("[Jurors] usually do need the assistance of a medical expert in determining the cause of a physical condition in order to understand the ultimate fact in issue.").

[144] State v. Buck, 88 Kan. 114, 127 P. 631 (1912); Byrd v. State, 243 Ind. 452, 185 N.E.2d 422 (1962); Hand v. State, 77 Tex.Crim.R. 623, 179 S.W. 1155 (App.1915).

[145] Landrigan v. Trujillo, 623 F.3d 1253 (9th Cir, 2010)(expert medical testimony established that ligature strangulation was the cause of death); People v. Lowe, 184 Colo. 182, 519 P.2d 344 (1974); Commonwealth v. Tallon, 478 Pa. 468, 387 A.2d 77 (1978).

[146] Stroble v. California, 343 U.S. 181 (1952)(autopsy revealed that the immediate cause of death was asphyxia due to strangulation); State v. Mondaine, 655 S.W.2d 540 (Mo.App.1983); Schultz v. State, 82 Wis.2d 737, 264 N.W.2d 245 (1978). See Anno., 66 A.L.R.2d 1082 (1959).

[147] *See* Clark v. Arizona, 548 U.S. 735, 777 (2006)("When . . . 'ultimate issue' questions are formulated by the law and put to the expert witness who must then say 'yea' or 'nay,' then the expert witness is required to make a leap in logic. . . . These impermissible leaps in logic made by expert witnesses confuse the jury. . . .").

[148] 310 Wis.2d 28, 750 N.W.2d 42 (2008).

[149] *See* Barber v. State, 628 S.W.2d 104 (Tex.App. 1981), cert. denied Barber v. Texas, 459 U.S. 874 (1982); State v. Carter, 217 La. 547, 46 So.2d 897 (1950); Commonwealth v. Juvenile (No. 1), 365 Mass. 421, 313 N.E.2d 120 (1974).

[150] Cobb v. State, 50 Ala.App. 707, 282 So.2d 327 (1973)(doctor who was not licensed to practice medicine permitted to testify as to cause of death); State v. Melvin, 390 A.2d 1024 (Me.1978)(lack of certification in forensic pathology not a bar to admissibility). Funeral directors and non-physician coroners have been permitted to testify as to the cause of death: Tracy v. Cottrell ex rel. Cottrell, 206 W.Va. 363, 524 S.E.2d 879 (1999)(undertaker); Stout v. State, 460 S.W.2d 911 (Tex.Cr.App.1970)(Justice of the Peace acting as coroner); see also State v. Howard, 274 N.C. 186, 162 S.E.2d 495 (1968); Jackson v. State, 412 So.2d 302 (Ala.Cr.App.1982); Neal v. State, 386 So.2d 718 (Miss.1980).

specialty certification, but training and experience in narrow areas of inquiry specific to the circumstances of the case, such as pediatric pathology.[151]

Similar to the past expansive view on qualifications to provide cause of death determinations, the courts have also provided wide latitude to the pathologist in providing expert testimony on an array of death-related issues, such as manner of death,[152] time of death,[153] ballistics,[154] relative positioning,[155] whether the decedent was forced to have sex,[156] whether the injuries were intentional,[157] and the degree of pain the decedent would have felt.[158] However, courts have drawn the line on speculative testimony, such as whether a bullet wound indicates the trigger of a firearm was pulled by one or two people.[159]

A few courts have limited manner of death testimony to avoid invading the province of the jury in deciding whether a crime was committed.[160] Most courts, however, permit expert testimony on

---

See also Massie v. State of Md., 349 Md. 834, 709 A.2d 1316 (1998)(forensic chemist allowed to testify as to time of death); Jackson v. State, 454 S.W.2d 733 (Tex.Crim.App.1970)(deputy sheriff allowed to testify as to cause of death).

[151] Kyser v. Diane Harrison, 908 So.2d 914 (Ala. 2005)(board certification in anatomic and forensic pathology, experience as a state medical examiner, and prior experience as death-scene investigator insufficient to testify that an infant died of asphyxiation).

See also Hawkins v. State, 933 So.2d 1186 (Fla. Ct. of App. 2006)(medical examiner's opinion that victim died of recent silicone injection was inadmissible because the medical examiner had no experience as to the migration rate of silicone in the body); Wilson v. City of Chicago, 6 F.3d 1233, 1239 (7th Cir. 1993)(testimony of pathologist excluded because "an expert on postmortems" is not an "expert on the effects of electroshock treatments on human body and psyche.").

[152] Durr v. Cordray, 602 F.3d 731 (6th Cir. 2010)(deputy coroner allowed to testify that the manner of death was homicidal violence); Baraka v. Commonwealth, 194 S.W.3d 313 (Ky. 2006)(medical examiner testified that the cause of death was heart attack and the manner of death was homicide due to stress during physical altercation). *See also* State v. Langley, 354 N.W.2d 389 (Minn.1984) and Fridovich v. State, 489 So.2d 143 (Fla.App.1986).

[153] State v. Pridgen, 313 N.C. 80, 326 S.E.2d 618 (1985).

[154] State v. Spears, 70 N.C.App. 747, 321 S.E.2d 13 (1984).

[155] People v. Britz, 128 Ill.App.3d 29, 83 Ill.Dec. 639, 470 N.E.2d 1059 (1984)(pathologist gave opinion that wound was consistent with a scenario in which deceased was kneeling and the assailant was standing).

[156] State v. Tolliver, 11 So.3d 584 (La. Ct. of App. 2009)(associate medical examiner testified that the blunt-force injuries were caused by struggle or restraint and evidenced forced sex).

[157] State v. Unger, 278 Mich. App. 210 (2008)(medical examiner allowed to testify that the victim did not die from head injuries sustained upon impact with the pavement, but had drowned after being dragged or moved into Lower Herring Lake); Harris v. State, 489 So.2d 688 (Ala.Cr.App.1986); State v. Knowles, 598 So.2d 430 (La.App.1992).

[158] Minor v. State, 914 So.2d 372 (Ala. Ct. of Crim. App. 2004).

[159] Edmonds v. State, 955 So.2d 787 (Miss. 2007)("While Dr. Hayne is qualified to proffer expert opinions in forensic pathology, a court should not give such an expert carte blanche to proffer any opinion he chooses.").

[160] *See* State v. Bradford, 618 N.W.2d 782 (Minn.2000); State v. Jamerson, 153 N.J. 318, 708 A.2d 1183, 1194–1195 (N.J. 1998)(forensic pathologist could not render an opinion that vehicular collision was a homicide as opposed to an accident because pathologist was no more competent than the jury to determine cause of vehicle collision); Medlock v. State, 263 Ga. 246, 430 S.E.2d 754, 756–757 (Ga. 1993)(Where an expert's findings as to cause of death "would have permitted the jury to find the death-causing injury either accidental or intentional . . . it

manner of death and describe the term "homicide" as neutral.[161] Courts do not always clearly delineate between cause of death and manner of death testimony.[162] In some jurisdictions the medical expert need not testify as to cause of death beyond a reasonable doubt.[163] The degree of certainty may be "probable" or "likely."[164] Qualifications of this nature do not render the evidence too uncertain for court purposes.[165]

b.   Gunshot Wounds

In the area of gunshot wounds, medical expert testimony may be directed toward a broad variety of conclusions, such as the nature of the weapon used, the number of wounds inflicted, wound location, the trajectory of the bullets through the body, the distance and direction of the fire, as well as the nature and extent of the wound.[166] In *Tolston v. State*,[167] medical witness testimony as to the nature of the projectile used was held proper. In *Ward v. State*,[168] testimony regarding the location of gunshot wounds met with approval. In *Watson v. State*,[169] the court allowed the expert in forensic pathology to offer an opinion relating to the gunshot wounds of a decedent because it found that how gunshot wounds are sustained is inherent in the specialty of forensic pathology. In *Bell v. State*,[170] the court affirmed the conviction and held that the forensic pathologist could testify as to the position of the victim's hands being in front of his face when he received the gunshot wounds. In *Taylor v. State*,[171] the court allowed an expert pathologist to testify as to the relative positions of the shooters. In *People v. Mayfield*,[172] the court permitted a forensic pathologist to testify as to

---

would [be] impermissible for the expert to state his opinion that homicide was the cause of death.").

[161] *See* State v. Scott, 206 W.Va. 158, 522 S.E.2d 626, 632 (W.Va. 1999)("homicide can be committed without criminal intent and without criminal consequences[,] . . . the term . . . is neutral [and] . . . pronounces no judgment on its moral or legal quality.").

[162] *See* Ingram v. Stovall, 368 Fed. Appx. 662 (6th Cir. 2010)(medical examiner testified that the victim "died from ligature strangulation and that the cause of death was homicide").

[163] Commonwealth v. Floyd, 499 Pa. 316, 453 A.2d 326 (1982).

[164] Sharpe v. United States, 230 F.R.D. 452, 460 (E.D. Va. 2005)("It is not enough for the plaintiff's expert to testify that the defendant's negligence might or may have caused the injury on which the plaintiff bases her claim. The expert must establish that the defendant's negligence was 'more likely' or 'more probably' the cause of the plaintiff's injury . . .").

[165] People v. Solomon, 49 Cal.4th 792, 815, 234 P.3d 501, 519, 112 Cal. Rptr.3d 244, 265 (2010)(Pathologists could not determine the precise cause of death, but found that asphyxiation was a possible cause of death; however, "the pathologists' testimony provided a 'reasonable foundation' for [jury's] inference of premeditation and deliberation.").

[166] State v. Clark, 171 W.Va. 74, 297 S.E.2d 849 (1982).

[167] 93 Tex.Crim.R. 493, 248 S.W. 50 (App.1922).

[168] 427 S.W.2d 876 (Tex.Cr.App.1968). *See also* Bryant v. State, 539 S.W.2d 816 (Tenn.Cr.App.1976).

[169] 816 So.2d 1029 (Miss.App.2002).

[170] 725 So.2d 836 (Miss.1998).

[171] 710 N.E.2d 921 (Ind.1999).

[172] 14 Cal.4th 668, 60 Cal.Rptr.2d 1, 928 P.2d 485 (1997).

whether gunpowder stippling or tattooing would be present in a hypothetical situation.

c. Psychological Autopsy

One area that the courts have been reluctant to admit expert testimony is the so-called psychological autopsy. The term was coined in 1977 when the Los Angeles Medical Examiner's Office began using a novel procedure to investigate suicide cases described in Shneidman, E. (1977), "The Psychological Autopsy," in L. Gottschalk et. al. (Eds.) *Guide to the Investigation & Reporting of Drug Abuse Deaths.* Using this method, experts offer an opinion on the decedent's state of mind after considering the decedent's circumstances, medical history, where the decedent's body was found, and interviewing family members and others.[173] Psychological autopsy testimony focused on the specific decedent's intent is different from expert testimony concerning general factors that indicate an individual may be suicidal or other factors used in determining manner of death. Testimony about suicidal factors has been admitted,[174] as has testimony concerning other factors in determining manner of death.[175]

2. DISCLOSURE OF HEALTH RECORDS

Most states classify full autopsy reports and information gained during a death investigation by the designated state death investigator to be confidential and restrict public access to all but cause and manner of death findings.[176] In other states the autopsy report is considered a public document, which may be released in whole or in part, depending upon the timing of the release, the status of an active criminal investigation, or the particularities of the law of the individual state.[177] The personal information protected by the decedent's privacy interest may be redacted. In most death investigations, the public interest should outweigh the need for secrecy.[178]

---

[173] *See* 24 Am. J. Crim. L., "Psychological Autopsies; Do They Belong in the Courtroom?" (1996); J. Ogloff & R. Otto, "Psychological Autopsy: Clinical and Legal Perspectives," 37 ST. LOUIS UNIV.L.J. 607, 644 (1993). See also State v. Guthrie, 627 N.W.2d 401 (2001)(psychological autopsy evidence that wife would not commit suicide was inadmissible); Bethley v. Keller Constr., 836 So.2d 397 (La.App.2002)(expert testimony that job made decedent suicidal inadmissible in worker's compensation matter).

[174] *See* U.S. v. St. Jean, 45 M.J 435 (U.S. Armed Forces 1996).

[175] *See* State v. Wilson, 248 P.3d 315 (N.M. 2010)(forensic pathologist permitted to testify that cause of death was consistent with smothering determined in part on information in police report and defendant's inconsistent statements).

[176] *See, e.g.,* Va. Code § 32.1–283.4.

[177] Penn Jersey Advance, Inc. v. Grim, 962 A.2d 632 (Pa. 2009)(autopsy reports are public records). The newly-enacted "Right to Know Law" in Pennsylvania (65 P.S. § 67.310.1) exempts certain records from disclosure if protected by other state or federal law. The court did not address whether federal medical records confidentiality laws (such as HIPAA) would protect autopsies from disclosure.

[178] *See* Ken Shuttleworth and Southern New Jersey Newspapers, Inc. v. The City of Camden; the Police Department of Camden; the Custodian of Records for the Police

It should be noted that the medical examiner should not be hampered by the federal privacy law known as HIPAA (The Health Insurance Portability and Accountability Act of 1996)[179] in obtaining any and all information relevant to a criminal investigation. The relevant section of the law is entitled "Disclosures for Law Enforcement Purposes § 164.512(f)."

3.   CONTROVERSIAL ISSUES

Although the diagnosis "shaken baby syndrome" (SBS) has been accepted since the 1970's, the term "abusive head trauma" (AHT) has become more widely used in recent years. The National Center on Shaken Baby Syndrome, an advocacy group, estimates that there are about 1300 cases a year of severe or fatal head trauma from SBS or AHT.[180] SBS was initially described in the 1970s by radiologists to explain babies who developed traumatic subdural hemorrhages, brain swelling, and retinal hemorrhages in the backs of the eye without clinical evidence of a force impacting the head. Proponents of SBS have asserted over many years that the presence of a certain triad of symptoms (subdural hematoma, retinal hemorrhages, and brain swelling), or even just the presence of retinal hemorrhages in a young child is distinctly characteristic of the child having been violently shaken. According to the theory, such violent shaking results in the immediate loss of consciousness precedent to death. In this way, the SBS theory is used both to establish that a crime occurred, the homicide of a child by violent shaking, and to identify the criminal agent as the last person to have control of the child before the child's loss of consciousness. Recently, some experts have recognized the controversy about the scientific validity of the SBS diagnosis and use "abusive head trauma" or "abusive head injury" as a more general term for inflicted injury.[181]

Some physicists, biomechanical engineers, and neurologists who investigated the theorized mechanism of injury, however, have asserted (1) that no scientific studies support the SBS theory and (2) that those studies that have been done establish that shaking alone cannot cause the symptoms associated with the SBS triad.[182] Furthermore, some

---

Department of the City of Camden; the Medical Examiner of the County of Camden; and the State of New Jersey, 258 N.J.Super. 573, 610 A.2d 903 (App.Div.1992).

[179] Act Aug 21, 1996, P.L. 104–191.

[180] *See* http://www.dontshake.org/learn-more (last accessed August 31, 2016).

[181] *See* Commonwealth v. Epps, 474 Mass. 743, 53 N.E.3d 1247 (2016)(expert testified that a "significant minority" of pediatricians and child abuse specialists recognize that the science behind SBS is questionable and instead adopt the term "abusive head trauma" or "abusive head injury" as a more general term for inflicted injury).

[182] New findings from a series of autopsies promise to further complicate the debate by finding that the SBS theory that head or brain trauma causes the death is flawed, but that shaking alone can cause death by damaging the nerves in the neck which regulate breathing in babies. Evan Matshes *et al.*, "Shaken Infants Die of Neck Trauma, Not of Brain Trauma," 1(1) ACAD. FORENSIC PATH. 82–91 (2011).

medical personnel have reported lucid intervals prior to death in infants displaying the triad, thus bringing into question the key element by which the SBS adherents claim to be able to identify the perpetrator. At present, the proponents of SBS and the opponents of SBS are engaged in an increasingly bitter dispute.[183] Both groups contain respected physicians, highly placed in the medical establishment. Norman Guthkelch, the pediatric neurosurgeon who is credited with first observing the syndrome, has recently expressed concerns over the use of the diagnosis.[184] In 2015, the Washington Post published a series of articles on the SBS diagnosis and efforts to reverse convictions based on the diagnosis.[185]

Although SBS is accepted as a diagnosis by a majority of physicians[186] and convictions continue to be based on SBS evidence,[187] some courts have reversed convictions or granted new trials based on new research challenging the scientific validity of the diagnosis.[188] In 2016, the Massachusetts Supreme Court noted that "[t]here is a heated debate in the medical community as to whether a violent shaking of a baby alone can generate enough force to cause the triad of symptoms of traumatic brain injury, and as to whether these symptoms can sometimes be caused by a short accidental fall."[189]

---

[183] For a detailed discussion of SBS and the conflicting assertions, *see* Waney Squier, "Shaken Baby Syndrome," in WILEY ENCYCLOPEDIA OF FORENSIC SCIENCE, (Jamieson A. & Moenssens A.A., eds) 2009 & online updates; *see also* Deborah Tuerkheimer, "Science-Dependent Prosecution and the Problem of Epistemic Contingency: A Study of Shaken Baby Syndrome," 62:3 Ala. L. Rev. 513–569 (2011).

[184] *See* Joseph Shapiro, "Rethinking Shaken Baby Syndrome," National Public Radio, June 29, 2011 (available at: www.npr.org/2011/06/29/137471992/rethinking-shaken-baby-syndrome)(last accessed June 25, 2012).

[185] See https://www.washingtonpost.com/graphics/investigations/shaken-baby-syndrome/ (last accessed August 31, 2016).

[186] *See* Sandeep K. Narang, Cynthia Estrada, Sraha Greenberg & Daniel Lindberh, "Acceptance of Shaken Baby Syndrome and Abusive Head Trauma as Medical Diagnoses," Journal of Pediatrics (July 2016). See also Ann & Robert H. Lurie's Children Hospital of Chicago, "Shaken baby syndrome accepted as diagnosis by majority of physicians," ScienceDaily, 22 July 2016 (available at: https://www.sciencedaily.com/releases/2016/07/160722092934.htm)(last accessed August 31, 2016).

[187] *See, e.g.,* State v. Simpson, 186 So.3d 195 (La. App. 2 Cir. 2016); State v. Olbricht, 23 Neb. App. 607 (2016); Perdue v. State, 298 Ga. 841, 785 S.E.2d 291 (2016); Edward v. Commonwealth, 65 Vap. App. 655, 779 S.E.2d 858 (2015); *see also* People v. Thomas, 46 Misc.3d 945, 998 N.Y.S.2d 590 (2014)(denying motion for *Frye* hearing because New York case law recognizes SBS/AHT as being generally accepted in the relevant scientific community, but noting that "there has been a shift in mainstream medical opinion" and "there are now competing medical opinions").

[188] *See, e.g.,* In re Pers. Restraint of Fero, 192 Wn. App. 138, 367 P.3d 588 (Wash. Ct. App. 2016)(evidence that the medical community's additional research and acceptance that multiple conditions can mimic "the symptoms of what used to be classified as 'shaken baby syndrome') warranted grant of new trial); Commonwealth v. Epps, 474 Mass. 743, 53 N.E.3d 1247 (2016) (new trial warranted where defense attorney was ineffective for failing to consult with an expert on scientific validity of SBS diagnosis). But see Gimenez v. Ochoa, 821 F.3d 1136 (9th Cir. 2016)(finding that new research does not repudiate SBS, but reveals only "a vigorous debate about its validity within the scientific community).

[189] Commonwealth v. Millien, 474 Mass. 417, 418, 50 N.E.3d 808, 809 (2016).

A second type of controversial child death, sudden infant death syndrome (SIDS), occurs when the forensic pathologist cannot identify the mechanism of death. SIDS is also known as crib death, or cot death, and is defined by the CDC as "the sudden death of an infant less than 1 year of age that cannot be explained after a thorough investigation is conducted, including a complete autopsy, examination of the death scene, and a review of the clinical history."[190] The CDC estimates there are approximately 3,500 sudden unexpected infant deaths each year, and in 2014, 1,500 of those deaths were due to SIDS. in 2014.[191] Although the rate of SIDS has declined significantly since the early 1990's, this decrease has been due to the advances in identifying other causes of death in sudden infant death cases, such as suffocation. Many states have laws that regulate the protocols for autopsies of suspected SIDS cases, require reporting, and implement special training in SIDS for medical responders and caretakers.[192] There is controversy among forensic pathologists and pediatricians in this country as to whether more than two SIDS deaths in a family should be considered indicative of homicide.[193]

§12.16 EXAMPLE EXCERPTS OF A TYPICAL AUTOPSY REPORT

The following excerpts are from a homicide case report and illustrate the type of information that will be contained in a report from a complete and competently performed autopsy.

---

[190] See http://www.cdc.gov/sids/aboutsuidandsids.htm (last accessed August 31, 2016).

[191] See http://www.cdc.gov/SIDS/index.htm (last accessed August 31, 2016).

[192] See National Conference of State Legislatures, Sudden Infant Death Syndrome (SIDS) at http://www.ncsl.org/research/health/sudden-infant-death-syndrome-laws.aspx (last accessed August 31, 2016).

[193] See Wilson v. State, 136 Md.App. 27, 764 A.2d 284 (2000).

MEDICAL EXAMINER'S OFFICE
AUTOPSY REPORT

ME NO.: 15-

MEDICAL RECORDS NO.:

CASE TITLE: GUNSHOT WOUND OF THE HEAD

DECEASED: SEX: M AGE:

DATE AND HOUR OF DEATH: ; 9:32 p.m.

DATE AND HOUR OF AUTOPSY: ; 8:40 a.m.

PATHOLOGIST:

FINAL DIAGNOSES:

 -year-old man who was shot by another person; taken to
  Medical Center ( ), where he later died

I. Gunshot wound of the head, penetrating, intermediate range of
  fire

  A. Entrance just lateral to left eye

  B. Pathway through bony structures of left cheek/orbit (left
    zygomatic bone and orbital bones), orbital contents, bones
    of left anterior cranial fossa, left frontal lobe of the
    brain, optic chiasm and optic nerves, midbrain, and right
    occipital lobe of the brain

  C. Associated findings

    1. Multiple skull fractures (with associated subgaleal
      and periosteal hemorrhage)

    2. Diffuse subdural and subarachnoid hemorrhage, with
      right convexity subdural hemorrhage collection
      (approximately 50 mL)

    3. Cerebral edema with cerebellar tonsillar softening

    4. Proptosis and drying of collapsed left globe

  D. Projectile recovered from right occipital lobe of brain;
    additional metal fragment recovered from left temporalis
    muscle

Page 2

E.   Direction: front to back, slightly left to right, and
     slightly upward

II. Other significant injuries not identified

III. No natural diseases identified

IV. Toxicology

     A.   Blood ethanol (performed by ▓▓▓ on specimen collected
          ▓▓▓▓▓▓▓ at 01:18): 0.093 g/dL

     B.   Blood drug and THC screen (performed on ▓▓▓ specimen
          collected ▓▓▓▓▓▓▓ at 01:18): THC positive by immunoassay;
          immunoassay and mass spectrometry otherwise negative

     C.   Blood phencyclidine (PCP) (performed on ▓▓▓ specimen
          collected ▓▓▓▓▓▓ at 01:18): none detected by GC/MS

     D.   Blood LSD (lysergic acid diethylamide) trace analysis:
          (performed on ▓▓▓ specimen collected ▓▓▓▓▓▓ at 01:18,
          ▓▓▓ Labs): none detected

     E.   Blood cannabinoids panel: (performed on ▓▓▓ specimen
          collected 11/15/15 at 01:18, ▓▓▓ Labs):

          1.   11-Hydroxy Delta-9 THC: 1.0 ng/mL

          2.   Delta-9 Carboxy THC: 43 ng/mL

          3.   Delta-9 THC: 2.6 ng/mL

_____   _____
Chief Medical Examiner   Reviewing Pathologist

Page 3

ADDITIONAL PERSONNEL PRESENT AT AUTOPSY:

- Special Agent [redacted], [redacted] Bureau of Criminal Apprehension
- Special Agent [redacted], Federal Bureau of Investigation

IDENTIFICATION:

Positive identification is made by comparison of antemortem and postmortem fingerprints ([redacted] Bureau of Criminal Apprehension).

EXTERNAL EXAMINATION:

The body is that of a normally developed, adequately nourished appearing, 70 inch long, 168-pound male whose appearance is consistent with the reported age of [redacted] years. Lividity is posterior and dependent, and blanches with very firm pressure. Rigor mortis is beginning to develop in all of the extremities. The protected parts of the body are still slightly palpably warm.

The scalp is covered with long, black hair tightly coiled into dreadlocks. The right iris is brown, and the pupil is round. There are no right-sided bulbar or palpebral conjunctival petechiae. Assessment of the left eye and periorbital tissues is limited by injury (further described below). The external auditory canals are free of blood. The ears are unremarkable. Abundant bloody fluid emanates from the nares. The nares are otherwise patent. The lips are atraumatic (except for medical intervention described below). The nose, right maxilla, and mandible are palpably stable. The teeth appear intact, are native, and are in good repair. A black mustache and goatee style beard are on the face.

The neck is straight, and the trachea is midline. The chest is symmetric. Prominent, hypopigmented stretch striae are on both anterior axillary lines, extending onto the lateral pectoral regions and onto the anterior aspects of each arm. A pair of vertically oriented, 5.5 and 7 cm long co-linear scars is on the left side of the chest extending onto the left epigastrium. The abdomen is flat. A 3 cm long, hyperpigmented scar is on the far right side of the abdomen. The genitalia are those of a normal adult male. The testes are descended and free of masses. Pubic hair is present in a normal distribution. The back, buttocks, and anus are unremarkable.

Page 4

The upper and lower extremities are symmetric and without
clubbing or edema. The nails of the hands are trimmed very
short and are focally dirty, but are otherwise unremarkable.
Approximately thirteen round and linear hyperpigmented scars,
ranging from less than 0.5 cm diameter to 3.5 cm long, are
scattered across the lateral surface of the right arm, over the
posterior right elbow, and on the posterolateral right forearm.
A faint, 0.6 cm long, linear scar is on the dorsum of the right
wrist. A 3 cm long faint, obliquely oriented scar is on the
anterior right wrist. Multiple 0.2 to 0.7 cm maximum dimension
oval and linear scars are scattered across the dorsum of the
right hand, primarily over the metacarpal-phalangeal joints.
Approximately eleven oval to linear scars, ranging from 0.2 cm
maximum dimension to 4 cm long, are scattered across the lateral
aspect of the left arm and over the left elbow. Five macular,
hyperpigmented, oval scars ranging from 0.3 cm to 1.5 cm maximum
dimension are scattered over the posterior and medial left
wrist. Patchy, nondescript scars are scattered over and around
both knees, more pronounced on the right. The nails of the toes
are unremarkable.

TATTOOS:

- A 14 cm maximum dimension monochromatic blue tattoo of an
  animal head-like figure with associated scroll work is on
  the anterior right forearm.
- A 17 cm maximum dimension monochromatic blue tattoo that
  appears to be an outline of the state of ▮▮▮▮▮▮ is on
  the anterior left forearm.

MEDICAL INTERVENTION:

- Hospital bracelets (2), right wrist
- Intravascular catheter, anterolateral right forearm
- Intravascular catheter, right antecubital fossa
- Urinary bladder catheter with attached tubing and
  collection bag
- Hospital tag, right 2nd toe
- Intravascular catheter, dorsolateral left forearm
- Intra-arterial vascular catheter, left radial artery
- Triple-lumen intravascular catheter, left subclavian
- Gauze and medical tape covering the left eye and cheek
- Electrocardiographic lead, left shoulder
- Dried, curvilinear orange abrasion (2.5 cm long) over the
  distal sternum, suggestive of cardiopulmonary resuscitation

- Linear, dried brown abrasion (2.5 cm long) extending from the left corner of the mouth and in direct continuity with a faint, 8 cm long line along the left side of the jawline, suggestive of a strap for an endotracheal tube
- Linear, dried brown abrasion (1.5 cm long) extending from the right corner of the mouth, suggestive of a strap for an endotracheal tube
- Healing, focally dried black and scabbed abrasion (1.5 cm maximum dimension) on the lateral aspect (cutaneous and mucosal surfaces) of the right side of the lower lip, consistent with oral endotracheal intubation

RADIOGRAPHS:

Review of the decedent's antemortem CT scan demonstrates a main projectile in the right side of the cranial vault in the region of the right occipital lobe; numerous minute metal fragments project in and around a fractured left orbit.

EVIDENCE OF INJURY:

GUNSHOT WOUND OF THE HEAD:

Just lateral to the left eye, 5 inches below the top of the head, 3¼ inches from the anterior midline (nasal bridge), and 3¼ inches from the left external auditory meatus, is an entrance gunshot wound. The central, circular, 0.9 cm diameter defect is circumferentially surrounded by a 0.1 cm wide pink abrasion collar. Radiating microtears (0.2-0.3 cm long) extend from the defect edges in the 8, 11, 12, 1, and 2 o'clock directions. The defect is centered within an 8 x 8 cm area of powder stippling of the skin that extends from the left cheek onto the inferior left forehead and from the left zygomatic prominence to the upper and lower lids of the left eye.

The left globe is collapsed and proptic due to extensive injury of the orbital bones with injury to, and swelling of, the orbital contents. There is dark red-black drying of the exposed sclera and conjunctiva.

The wound pathway continues through the bony structures of the left cheek/orbit (left zygomatic bone and orbital bones), the left orbital contents, the bony structures of the left anterior cranial fossa, the left frontal lobe of the brain, the optic chiasm and optic nerves, the midbrain, and the right occipital lobe of the brain.

Page 6

The wound pathway through the brain is pulpified and hemorrhagic, containing multiple pieces of fragmented bone. A thin, diffuse layer of subarachnoid and subdural hemorrhage coats the cerebral convexities and base of the brain. Approximately 50 mL of loosely clotted subdural hemorrhage is over the right cerebral convexity. The cerebral hemispheres are diffusely swollen, with flattening of the gyri, narrowing of the sulci, and compression of the lateral ventricles. The cerebellar tonsils are swollen, softened, and tightly apposed to the brainstem.

There is a comminuted, complex, eggshell fracture of all of the left anterior cranial fossa and medial right anterior cranial fossa bony structures, extending into the lesser sphenoid wing and medial aspect of the greater sphenoid wing on the left. The fracturing of the left anterior cranial fossa radiates into a 5 cm long linear fracture of the right side of the frontal bone, a 7 cm long linear fracture of the left parietal bone, and a 3 cm long linear fracture of the petrous ridge of the left temporal bone. A separate, hemorrhagic, 1 cm maximum dimension aggregate of hairline fractures is in the orbital roof of the right anterior cranial fossa. Four localized 0.4 to 0.7 cm maximum dimension foci (two right and two left) of hemorrhagic hairline fractures are in the squamous portion of each temporal bone, just anterior to the petrous ridges. There is multifocal hemorrhage in the frontal, superior, and right lateral scalp, confined to the periosteum and subgaleal connective tissue and in areas overlying or in continuity with the aforementioned bony injuries; incisions of these areas show no subcutaneous hemorrhage in tissue superficial to the aponeurosis of the scalp. All layers of the scalp are widely hemorrhagic and swollen on the left, in association with the gunshot wound and the related left anterior cranial fossa fractures. There is periorbital ecchymosis (5 cm maximum dimension) of the right eye.

Recovered from the right occipital lobe of the brain, just right of the sagittal midline, is a 2.7 cm maximum dimension copper- and lead-colored projectile. A 0.5 cm maximum dimension lead-colored metal fragment is recovered from the left temporalis muscle.

The overall wound direction, relative to standard anatomic position, is front to back, slightly left to right, and slightly upward.

OTHER INJURIES:

• A pair of obliquely oriented, linear, 3 and 1 cm long dried scratches is on the lateral aspect of the right arm.

• A 1.5 cm long, obliquely oriented, dried linear scratch is on the lateral aspect of the distal left forearm.

• A discontinuous line of vertically oriented scratches, 2.5 cm maximum dimension, is just left of the midline of the upper back.

SOFT TISSUE DISSECTIONS:

BACK: An incision is carried down the midline of the posterior neck and back to the right and left buttocks. Subcutaneous dissection of the neck, shoulders, back, flanks, and buttocks demonstrates no occult contusions.

WRISTS: The anterior aspect of each distal forearm and wrist is vertically incised. Circumferential subcutaneous dissection demonstrates no occult contusions, or other injuries suggestive of restraint. Localized hemorrhage is encountered over the left radial artery, consistent with documented medical intervention. Two cutaneous macular scars on the posterior aspect of the left wrist are also incised, confirming absence of contusions.

INTERNAL EXAMINATION:

HEAD: The brain weighs 1210 g. Coronal sections through uninjured parts of the brain demonstrate sharp demarcation between white and gray matter, without hemorrhage or contusive injury. The atlanto-occipital joint is stable.

NECK: The anterior strap muscles of the neck are homogeneous and red-brown, without hemorrhage. The thyroid cartilage and hyoid are intact. The larynx is lined by intact white mucosa. The thyroid is symmetric and red-brown, without cystic or nodular change. The tongue is free of bite marks, hemorrhage, or other injuries.

Page 8

BODY CAVITIES: The ribs, sternum, and vertebral bodies are visibly and palpably intact. A measured 150 mL straw-colored fluid is in each pleural cavity, and a measured 100 mL straw-colored fluid is in the peritoneal cavity. The organs occupy their usual anatomic positions.

RESPIRATORY SYSTEM: The right and left lungs weigh 1080 and 1010 g, respectively. The external surfaces are smooth and deep red-purple. The pulmonary parenchyma is diffusely congested, edematous, and virtually airless. No mass lesions or areas of consolidation are present. The pulmonary vascular tree is free of thromboemboli. The tracheobronchial tree is free of blood, edema fluid, or foreign material.

CARDIOVASCULAR SYSTEM: The 345 g heart is contained in an intact pericardial sac. The epicardial surface is smooth, with minimal fat investment. The coronary arteries are present in a normal distribution, with a right-dominant pattern. Cross sections of the vessels show no atherosclerotic stenoses and no occlusions. The myocardium is homogeneous, red-brown, and firm. The valve leaflets are thin and mobile. The walls of the left and right ventricles are 1.3 and 0.4 cm thick, respectively. The endocardium is smooth and glistening. The aorta gives rise to three intact and patent arch vessels. The renal and mesenteric vessels are unremarkable.

LIVER AND BILIARY SYSTEM: The 1415 g liver has an intact, smooth capsule and a sharp anterior border. The parenchyma is tan-brown and congested, with the usual lobular architecture. No mass lesions or other abnormalities are seen. The gallbladder contains a minute amount of green-black bile and no stones. The mucosal surface is green and velvety. The extrahepatic biliary tree is patent.

SPLEEN: The 160 g spleen has a smooth, intact, red-purple capsule. The parenchyma is maroon and congested.

PANCREAS: The pancreas is firm and yellow-tan, with the usual lobular architecture. No mass lesions or other abnormalities are seen.

ADRENALS: The right and left adrenal glands are symmetric, with bright yellow cortices and gray medullae. No masses or areas of hemorrhage are identified.

GENITOURINARY SYSTEM: The right and left kidneys weigh 140 and 175 g, respectively. Except for rare, minute, focally sunken scars on the left renal cortex, the external surfaces are intact and smooth. The cut surfaces are red-tan and congested, with uniformly thick cortices and sharp corticomedullary junctions. The pelves are unremarkable and the ureters are normal in course and caliber. White and focally hemorrhagic (catheter-related) bladder mucosa overlies an intact bladder wall. The bladder is empty. The prostate is normal in size, with lobular, yellow-tan parenchyma. The seminal vesicles are unremarkable. The testes are free of mass lesions, contusions, or other abnormalities.

GASTROINTESTINAL TRACT: The esophagus is intact and lined by smooth, gray-white mucosa. The stomach contains approximately 300 cc of watery green fluid with numerous multicolored fragments of food-like particulate matter. The gastric wall is intact. The duodenum, loops of small bowel, and colon are unremarkable. The appendix is present.

ADDITIONAL PROCEDURES:

- Documentary photographs are taken.
- Specimens retained for toxicologic testing: vitreous fluid (right eye), femoral blood, urine (from urinary bladder catheter collection bag), liver, and gastric contents.
- Representative tissue biopsies are submitted in formalin for microscopic examination.
- The dissected organs are returned to the body.
- Fingernail clippings are placed in labeled, sealed envelopes.
- Pulled head hairs are placed in a labeled, sealed envelope.
- The recovered projectile and metal fragment are photographed and placed in labeled, sealed envelopes.

MICROSCOPIC EXAMINATION:

BRAIN (1-3): Sections of midbrain, cerebral cortex, and cerebellum are examined. Multiple areas of parenchymal hemorrhage and disruption, consistent with mechanical trauma, are observed; these are particularly prevalent in the midbrain. Hypoxic-ischemic changes are readily observed in many of the Purkinje cells in the cerebellum. No neoplastic or inflammatory changes are seen.

PANCREAS (4): No significant pathologic abnormality.

Page 10

LUNG (4):	Congestion and scattered foci of anthracotic pigment deposition; no significant pathologic abnormality.
HEART (5):	Cross sections of right and left ventricular myocardium show the expected microscopic architecture, without necrosis, inflammation, or scarring.
ADRENAL (6):	No significant pathologic abnormality.
LIVER (6):	Congestion; no significant pathologic abnormality.
SPLEEN (6):	No significant pathologic abnormality.
THYROID (7):	No significant pathologic abnormality.
KIDNEY (7):	No significant pathologic abnormality.

V. RESOURCES

§12.17 BIBLIOGRAPHY OF ADDITIONAL RESOURCES

Elizabeth Abraham, Margaret Cox and David Quincey, "Pigmentation: Postmortem Iris Color Change in the Eyes of *Sus scrofaI,*" 53 J. Forensic Sci. 626 (2008).

Lester Adelson, *The Pathology of Homicide,* Charles C. Thomas Publisher, 1974.

Anil Aggrawal, *Forensic and Medico-Legal Aspects of Sexual Crimes and Unusual Sexual Practices*, CRC Press, 2009.

William Bernet and Neelanjan Ray, "Child Sexual Abuse," in Wiley Encyclopedia of Forensic Science (Jamieson, A. & Moenssens, A.A., eds.) 2009 & online updates.

Jochen Beyer, "Poisons: Detection of Naturally Occurring Poisons," in Wiley Encyclopedia of Forensic Science (Jamieson, A. & Moenssens, A.A., eds.) 2009 & online updates.

Sue Black & Lucina Hackman, "Disaster Victim Identification," in Wiley Encyclopedia of Forensic Science (Jamieson, A. & Moenssens, A.A., eds.) 2009 & online updates.

Thomas L. Bohan, *Crashes and Collapses,* Facts on File, Inc. 2009.

Michael Bohnert, "Injury: Burns, Scalds, and Chemical," in Wiley Encyclopedia of Forensic Science (Jamieson, A. & Moenssens, A.A., eds.) 2009 & online updates.

Cristina Cattaneo, Davide Porta and Danilo De Angelis, "Identification of Human Remains," in Wiley Encyclopedia of Forensic Science (Jamieson, A. & Moenssens, A.A., eds.) 2009 & online updates.

Melissa Connor, "Mass Grave Investigation," in Wiley Encyclopedia of Forensic Science (Jamieson, A. & Moenssens, A.A., eds.) 2009 & online updates.

Dominick J. DiMaio and Vincent J. M. DiMaio, *Forensic Pathology,* 2d ed., CRC Press, 2001.

Vincent J. M. DiMaio and Suzanna E. Dana, *Handbook of Forensic Pathology*, 2d ed., CRC Press, 2007.

Vincent J. M. DiMaio, *Gunshot Wounds: Practical Aspects of Firearms, Ballistics, and Forensic Techniques*, 3d ed., CRC Press, 2015.

David Dolinak, *et al., Forensic Pathology: Principles and Practice,* Elsevier Academic Press, 2005.

A.C. Duhaime, C.W. Christian, L.B. Rorke, and R.A. Zimmerman, "Nonaccidental head injury in infants—the "shaken-baby-syndrome," 338(25) N Eng J Med 1822–1829 (1998).

Anders F. Eriksson & Mats G. Ostrom, "Traffic Fatalities," M in Wiley Encyclopedia of Forensic Science (Jamieson, A. & Moenssens, A.A., eds.) 2009 & online updates.

Abdullah Fatteh, *Medicolegal Investigation of Gunshot Wounds,* Lippincott, Williams and Wilkins,1976; revised 2000.

Russell S. Fisher & Charles S. Petty, *A Handbook of Forensic Pathology for Non-Forensic Pathologists,* National Institute of Law Enforcement and Criminal Justice, US Department of Justice, 1977.

Dorothy E. Gennard, *Forensic Entomology: An Introduction*, 2d ed., Wiley, 2012.

Robert P. Granacher, Jr., *Traumatic Brain Injury*, 2007.

Randy Hanzlick, *Death Investigation: Systems and Procedures*, 2007.

Perry Hookman, *Medical Malpractice Expert Witnessing*, 2007.

J.M. Jentzen, *Death Investigation in America. Coroners, Medical Examiners, and the Pursuit of Medical Certainty* (Cambridge MA and London, UK: Harvard Press, 2009).

Bernard Knight, *Forensic Pathology*, 2d. ed. 1996.

Jan E. Leestma, *Forensic Neuropathology,* 1988.

J.K. Mason & B.N. Purdue, eds., *The Pathology of Trauma,* (3rd ed.) 2000.

J.K. Mason, *Forensic Medicine, An Illustrated Reference,* 1993.

Burkhard Madea. Estimation of the Time Since Death, 3rd ed., 2015.

Gregory Murrey & Donald Starzinski, *The Forensic Evaluation of Traumatic Brain Injury*, 2007.

Frank H. Netter, *Atlas of Human Anatomy*, 4th ed. 2006.

Charles O'Hara, *Fundamentals of Criminal Investigation,* (7th ed.) 2003.

Bobbi Jo O'Neal, *Investigating Infant Deaths*, 2007.

James Phillips, *Forensic Science and the Expert Witness,* 1985.

Vernon D. Plueckhahn, *Ethics, Legal Medicine, and Forensic Pathology,* (2nd ed.) 2001.

C.J. Polson, D.J. Gee & B. Knight, *The Essentials of Forensic Medicine,* (4th ed.) 1985.

J. Prahlow, *Forensic Pathology for Police, Death Investigators, Attorneys, and Forensic Scientists* (New York, NY: Springer Science+Business Media, LLC, 2010).

Pekka Saukko & Bernard Knight, *Knight's Forensic Pathology*, 4th ed., 2015.

Simpson's Forensic Medicine, (12th ed.) 2003.

W.U. Spitz and D.J. Spitz, *Spitz and Fisher's Medicolegal Investigation of Death: Guidelines for the Application of Pathology to Crime Investigation,* 4th Ed. (Springfield, IL: Charles C. Thomas Publisher, 2006).

Stefan Timmermans, *Postmortem: How Medical Examiners Explain Suspicious Deaths*, 2006.

Scott A. Wagner, *Death Scene Investigation*, 2008.

Jon Waltz & Fred E. Inbau, *Medical Jurisprudence,* 1971.

Tomio Watanabe, *Atlas of Legal Medicine,* (3rd ed.) 1975.

Cyril H. Wecht, *Forensic Sciences,* 5 vols., 1999 (with annual supplements).

Cyril H. Wecht, *Microscopic Diagnosis in Forensic Pathology,* 1980.

CHAPTER 13

FORENSIC TOXICOLOGY[1]

I. INTRODUCTION

§13.01 SCOPE OF THE CHAPTER

Forensic toxicology covers a broad range of investigation, including poisoning, drug and alcohol screening, and the detection of toxins in the environment and consumer products. Forensic toxicology is a subspecialty within the broader field of Analytical Chemistry and the same scientific principles underlie the techniques used by the analytical chemist and the forensic toxicologist. The analytical chemist conducts examinations on a variety of materials and for purposes ranging from product quality control to the identification of substances in debris from a terrorist attack. The focus of the forensic toxicologist is the detection and identification of foreign chemicals in the body or in materials originating from living organisms. Particular emphasis is placed on substances considered toxic or potentially hazardous to living organisms. Because these toxins may be present only at very low levels, the forensic toxicologist and the analytical chemist routinely use the same sensitive analytical instruments.

---

[1] The Authors thank the following subject matter expert for her assistance with this chapter: Ruth E. Winecker, Ph.D. F-ABFT, Chief Toxicologist, Division of Public Health, Office of the Chief Medical Examiner, North Carolina Department of Health and Human Services, Clinical Assistant Professor, UNC-SOM-Dept. of Pathology and Laboratory Medicine.

Clinical toxicology shares the same focus on biological material as forensic toxicology, and the two fields also frequently use the same analytical equipment. However, the end uses of the results (diagnostic purposes v. use in the justice system) impose different considerations on the two fields. The rigor of admissibility standards and burdens of proof in the justice system often impose additional requirements on the forensic toxicologist that counteract the frequent necessity for rapid diagnostic information in the clinical laboratory setting.

The evidentiary uses, methodologies, and legal issues related to toxicological investigations, including alcohol intoxication, will be described in this chapter. This chapter will review the effects of alcohol on the body and the mind, with emphasis on the absorption and elimination principles that provide the foundation for expert conclusions about alcohol concentration in bodily specimens in living persons.[2] Expert qualifications and evidence issues specific to forensic toxicology are also covered.

§13.02 TERMINOLOGY

Absorption/Adsorption: Absorption refers to one material taken up by another and held within the absorbing material. Adsorption refers to a liquid or gas taken up by a solid but held only on the surface of the solid material.

Alcohol: An organic compound in which a hydroxyl functional group is bonded to the carbon atom, including methyl, propyl, isopropyl, butyl, and others, in addition to ethyl alcohol. The term "alcohol" is commonly used to refer to only ethyl alcohol (also known as ethanol or grain alcohol).

Alcohol Concentration: Alcohol in a volume of breath or blood or other biological specimen.

Aldehydes: A class of compounds produced from oxidation of alcohols. . Examples of aldehydes include formaldehyde (a methanol metabolite and ingredient of embalming fluid) and acetaldehyde (an ethanol metabolite).

Alkaloids: A group of complex compounds of vegetable origin containing nitrogen. Many are toxic to humans and most are colorless, crystalline solids with a bitter taste.

Antibody/Antigen: An antibody, also known as an immunoglobulin, is a large Y-shaped protein produced by the immune system to identify and neutralize foreign objects. The antibody bonds with a specific part of the foreign material (the antigen).

---

[2] Postmortem alcohol analysis offers a wider variety of sample collection options (*e.g.*, vitreous humor) and different challenges (*e.g.*, postmortem alcohol production through putrefaction and bacterial contamination). Post-mortem alcohol analysis is discussed in Chapter 12 Forensic Pathology.

Atomic Absorption Spectrometry: An analytical technique primarily used to measure metals in a sample. The sample in solution is vaporized and compounds in the sample decomposed into free atoms. These atoms absorb light at wavelengths characteristic of a particular element. From the amount of light absorbed at a selected wavelength, the concentration of the element in the sample is determined.

Benzodiazepines: Psychoactive drug with a core chemical structure of a benzene ring fused with a diazepine ring which produces sedation in low doses, reduces anxiety in moderate doses, and has hypnotic effects in higher doses. Benzodiazepines are among the most commonly prescribed central nervous system depressants in the United States.

Blood Alcohol Concentration (BAC): The alcohol in a volume of blood, typically expressed in grams of alcohol per deciliter (100 milliliters) of blood.

Boiling Point: The temperature at which the vapor pressure of a liquid is equal to the pressure of the surroundings.

Breath Alcohol Concentration (BrAC): The alcohol in a volume of breath, typically expressed in grams of alcohol per 210 liters of breath.

Chromatography: A category of analytical techniques for the separation of mixtures involving the passing of a mixture dissolved in a "moving" phase through a fixed material phase. Chemical compounds differ in their retention on the fixed material phase and some are held to a greater extent than others. Weakly retained compounds move quickly through the system while those more strongly held move more slowly and complete their passage through the system later. Because of differences in this retention time, effective separation of a mixture into components can be made. Types of chromatography used in the analytical laboratory include column, gas, paper, and thin-layer chromatography.

Column Chromatography: A technique for the separation of a mixture in which a solution is passed through a column containing a solid adsorbent (commonly referred to as stationary phase). Certain components in the mixture are retained by the solid while others pass through with the solvent. The ability of the technique to effect efficient separation can be enhanced by careful solvent selection or by changing the composition of the stationary phase of the column. This technique is often referred to as liquid chromatography.

Concentration: The quantity of a given compound or target analyte in a mixture or solution. It may be expressed as percent by volume weight by volume, parts per million or in chemical terms such as molarity (number of moles of solute dissolved in one liter of solution).

Derivative: A substance extracted or produced from another. One natural derivative is morphine from opium. In toxicology, derivatives of a compound are often chemically prepared to obtain another compound more easily detected by an analytical technique.

Detection: Indication of the presence of a substance in the material being examined. Detection, however, does not prove that the material has been uniquely identified.

Detection Limit: The minimum concentration of a material capable of reliable detection with an analytical system. It is usually determined from the ratio of the analytical signal to the background noise in the system. Detection limits should be demonstrated for all assays/analytes.

Electrochemical Sensor: Testing device in which alcohol in a breath sample undergoes a chemical oxidation reaction when in contact with the Authors: This URL does not lead to a working page. Please update link.platinum plate or disk within the sensor. The magnitude of the electrical response (current) is proportional to the amount of alcohol present. Also called "fuel cell" sensor or technology.

Enzyme: A protein that initiates or facilitates a biochemical reaction. Although the enzyme participates, on completion of the reaction it remains unchanged.

Gas Chromatography: A technique for separation of components of a mixture in the vapor state. The sample to be examined is vaporized and carried through a small diameter column by a flowing gas stream. Components of the mixture dissolve in a viscous liquid or solid inside the column and are retained to varying degrees to effect a separation. As a component of the mixture completes its passage through the column, it enters a detector which produces an electrical signal indicating its arrival and quantity. A very small diameter column, or capillary, improves component separation. Increasing the temperature or gas flow reduces analysis time, but will result in decreased resolution between analytes of interest.

Identification: Identification of a substance means that its chemical structure has been verified.

Infrared sensor: Testing device in which alcohol in a breath sample is measured by passing a narrow band of infrared light through a chamber containing the breath sample. The alcohol concentration in the breath sample is measured by the amount of infrared light absorbed. The magnitude of the difference in the light introduced and the light detected is proportional to the alcohol present.

Ketones: A class of compounds formed by oxidation of alcohols. Volatile ketones are common components of paint removers or industrial solvents and toxic at high levels. Ketones are produced in the body when fat is used as the main fuel source. This can occur during weight loss or in certain disease states such as diabetic keto-acidosis. One of these ketones, acetone, under specific conditions can be reduced in the body to isopropanol. This ketone "metabolite" can cause false positives with electrochemical oxidation alcohol detection devices.

Mass Spectrometry: An analytical method used to identify materials based upon production and detection of characteristic molecular fragments. The molecule is vaporized and fragmented in a high-energy field. The fragments are separated by velocity or behavior in a magnetic field, detected, and their mass determined. Because the fragments produced under controlled conditions are reproducible, they can be related to the original structure of the molecule. Combining the separating power of gas or liquid chromatography with the ability of the mass spectrometer to identify a compound provides a powerful tool for the identification of the individual components in a mixture and is widely used to confirm preliminary identification of a suspected drug or toxin.

Melting Point: The temperature at which liquid and solid forms of a material are in equilibrium. The melting point is the temperature at which a solid begins to change into a liquid at atmospheric pressure.

Metabolite: The products of the biochemical processes used by the body to degrade and eliminate substances from the body.

Molecular Structure: The exact sequence and arrangement of the atoms within the molecule of a chemical compound.

Molecule: The smallest unit of a substance which exhibits the properties of that substance. Further reduction of the molecule of a substance will produce a new substance or atoms comprising the original composition of the substance. For example, reduction of a water molecule will produce hydrogen and oxygen, neither of which exhibits the properties of water.

Organophosphates: A group of organic compounds containing phosphorus, many of which are highly toxic. Originally produced as chemical warfare agents, some are now used as potent insecticides and occasionally encountered in poisonings.

Qualitative Analysis: An analysis to determine the composition of a sample, i.e. what materials are present.

Quantitative Analysis: An analysis to determine the concentration of one or more components of a sample.

Selectivity: The ability of an analytical technique to discriminate between similar materials in the sample. Selectivity is essential to avoid "false positives" and obtain reliable analytical results.

Sensitivity: The minimum amount of a component capable of reliably being detected by the analytical system.

Spectrometry: A category of analytical techniques for identification of a chemical compound. Most types involve the measurement of light or other radiation absorbed by or emitted from a sample. The specific wavelengths of radiation absorbed/emitted are related to the chemical structure of the molecule. Measurement of the radiation's frequency or wavelength and/or the amount absorbed/emitted is used to identify a particular chemical species or determine the quantity present. Most types are named for the radiation used such as visible, infrared or ultraviolet light, or x-ray.

Thin-Layer Chromatography: Analytical separation method superior to paper chromatography. A glass plate with a thin coating of silica gel, cellulose, or alumina is the stationary phase on which the sample is spotted. The plate is placed in a tank containing a small amount of solvent and developed. The analytes separate into distinct spots as they move up the plate. After the solvent has moved a predetermined distance, the paper is removed and dried. The distance each spot has moved is used to tentatively identify the material. Spraying of the dried plate with a specific chemical reagent develops a color to aid in identifying the material in a particular spot.

§13.03 EVIDENTIARY USES

Forensic toxicology is widely used to detect alcohol or drugs in suspected impaired drivers, employee screening, competitive sports testing, and suspected victims of drug-facilitated sexual assaults.[3] The choice of testing specimen will be determined by the scope of the inquiry and any regulations applicable to the inquiry. Mere usage of alcohol and drugs can be detected through presence in hair and urine specimens. If the relevant question, however, is the involvement of the substance in a specific action of the subject (*i.e.*, driving under the influence), blood, breath, and oral fluid specimens are more appropriate to properly calculate relative concentrations and estimate the period of exposure.[4]

Forensic toxicology is also used in criminal and civil investigations to determine the cause and manner of death or injury. These tests detect the presence of alcohol, drugs, and toxins in biological material to establish what role these substances may have played in the death or injury. The investigations include homicides, suicides, accidental deaths or poisonings, product tampering, toxic torts, and other environmental contamination.

---

[3]   The exploitation of incapacitated persons and the drugging of persons to incapacitate them were not new phenomenon, but the surreptitious drugging of persons to sexually assault them gained attention as a distinct crime scenario in the mid-1990's. Alcohol, cannabinoids, and benzodiazepines are the most commonly used substances in the drug-facilitated sexual assaults. Marc A. LeBeau and Ashraf Mozayani eds., *Drug-Facilitated Sexual Assault*, Academic Press, 2001 at pp. 21, 100.

[4]   Peter Felgate, "Toxicology: Initial Testing," in WILEY ENCYCLOPEDIA OF FORENSIC SCIENCE, (Jamieson A. & Moenssens A.A., eds) 2009 & online updates.

1. DRUG-USE TESTING

Drug-use testing involves the detection of specific regulated or banned substances in the body.[5] These tests are routinely used in private and public employment, intramural and competitive sports, parole and probation supervision, and increasingly in child custody matters. The testing may be conducted as a condition of employment, prior to participation in an activity, on a random basis during employment or participation, or based on suspicion following an allegation or accident.[6] Drug-use testing analyzes biological material for the presence of drugs or drug metabolites. These drug metabolites are excreted by the body in urine, and can also be found in blood, sweat, oral fluid, and hair shafts.

One of the largest drug-use testing programs is managed by the Substance Abuse and Mental Health Services Administration (SAMHSA), which regulates the drug-use testing of federal government employees and contractors conducted pursuant to the Drug-Free Workplace Act. SAMHSA maintains comprehensive regulations of every aspect of the drug-use testing process from sample collection to reporting.[7] For example, the SAMHSA guidelines require the collection of urine specimens for testing, limit routine testing to specific substances (required testing for marijuana and cocaine; authorized testing for amphetamines, opiates, and phencyclidine),[8] and require the use of certified laboratories. Although SAMHSA guidelines are limited to drug testing services provided to specified federal agencies, many private employers choose to follow the guidelines or require the use of the same certified laboratories.[9] The guidelines are also frequently cited as evidence of industry standards.[10]

Another oversight program is operated by the College of American Pathologists (CAP) to oversee quality assurance, testing proficiency,

---

[5]   Although this section will focus on the detection of substances in humans, drug-use testing is also used to enforce regulations in animal sports as well. *See* The International Agreement on Breeding, Racing, and Wagering published by the International Federal of Horseracing Authorities (IFHA). January 2016 (available at: http://www.horseracingintfed.com) (last accessed June 14, 2016).

[6]   The Forensic Toxicology Council, *Briefing: What is Forensic Toxicology?*, August 2010 (available at www.swgtox.org)(last accessed June 14, 2016).

[7]   *See* SAMHSA Mandatory Guidelines for Federal Workplace Drug Testing Programs 73 FR 71858 (Nov. 25, 2008)(*hereinafter* "SAMHSA Guidelines")(available at: http://www.samhsa. gov/laws-regulations-guidelines/substance-use-regulations-mandates#workplace)(last accessed June 14, 2016).

[8]   The use of oral fluid for testing and an expansion of the testing for specific drugs (oxycodone, hydrocodone, oxymorphone, hydromorphone) is likely to be authorized in the next SAMHSA published guidelines but for now testing for additional drugs is permitted in an individual case only for reasonable suspicion, post-accident, or unsafe practice testing. SAMHSA Guidelines, Section 3.2.

[9]   *See* Mayfield v. NASCAR, 713 F. Supp.2d 527 (W.D. NC 2010). The certifying agency is actually the Department of Health and Human Services. SAMHSA Guidelines, Subpart I, Section 9.1. *See also* Barry Levine, *Principles of Forensic Toxicology* 40 (2003).

[10]   *See* Landon v. County of Orange *et al.*, 2009 U.S. Dist. LEXIS 64927 (S.D. NY 2009).

and accreditation of laboratories conducting drug testing programs.[11] The program covers the accreditation of laboratories that perform non-medical purpose testing of biological material for drugs of abuse.

To be scientifically valid, drug testing should follow a two-step process.[12] The first is an initial screening test which eliminates samples where the results are negative, indicating an exclusion. Samples with positive screening results indicate possible substance concentrations at or above the designated threshold level. Such positive specimens should then be subjected to a confirmatory drug test.

There are two types of widely used initial screening tests (discussed in detail in Section II "Analytical Methods" *infra*): chromatographic techniques and immunoassays. The most common tests are immunoassays because of the low cost and broad applications to analyze different types of drugs.[13] However, owing to a surge in the abuse of new and novel psychoactive substances, immunoassays are increasingly being supplemented with chromatographic screening techniques due to a lack of commercial assays targeting these new drugs of abuse. The initial screening test techniques are very sensitive to minimize "false negatives" (test results which indicate that no drugs or metabolites were found, even though the drugs or metabolites are present in the biological sample), but because they are only presumptive evidence, a confirmatory drug test must be used for scientific specificity.

Confirmatory testing is usually done with a combination of chromatographic separation and spectrometric identification techniques (discussed in detail in Section II "Analytical Methods" *infra*). It is unacceptable for a confirmatory technique to be a second immunoassay test. Instead, the technique should exploit a completely different technology and be specific for the drug(s) being confirmed. This in turn minimizes "false positives" (test results which indicate that drugs or metabolites were found, even though the drugs or metabolites are not present in the biological sample).

Laboratories should have policies and procedures that minimize the risk of reporting false negatives and false positives and many of these practices are specified in laboratory certification programs. Some examples of these quality assurance measures are: specimen validity testing to detect adulterated or substituted specimens; separate sections of the laboratory for aliquoting, screening, and confirmation

---

[11] *See* CAP Standards for Drug Testing Laboratory Accreditation, 2009 Edition, available at: http://www.cap.org/apps/docs/laboratory_accreditation/forensic_urine.pdf.

[12] Warren D. Hamilton, "Drug Testing: Urine," in WILEY ENCYCLOPEDIA OF FORENSIC SCIENCE, (Jamieson A. & Moenssens A.A., eds) 2009 & online updates.

[13] SAMHSA Guidelines require the initial drug test to be an immunoassay test. A second test may be done using a different method to rule out cross-reactivity, but the initial test must be an immunoassay. SAMHSA Guidelines, Section 11.10.

testing; engineering controls to prevent inadvertent sample switching; and quality control and training programs.

Although not permitted under SAMHSA, with the technical advancements in drug testing technology, employers can perform onsite urine drug screening, removing the need for approximately 95% of the samples to be sent to the laboratory by excluding samples with negative screening results from further testing.[14] Onsite drug screening can be performed rapidly and at a low cost. Any samples that test positive on the screening test are sent to laboratories for confirmatory tests. A positive result on a drug-use test does not necessarily indicate a person's impairment. Although some metabolites may have little physiological activity, some metabolites have equal or greater physiological activity than the drug that was consumed. Drug-use testing that detects inactive metabolites in urine does not measure the psychoactive ingredient in the substance. Nor is urine the correct specimen to determine impairment since the time that a drug was used cannot be established from urine concentrations.[15] Most drugs can be found in urine for several days or weeks after use depending on the type of drug used and the length of time the drug was used.[16] Marijuana metabolites may be found in urine for 2–4 days after smoking for a casual user, but the average detection window for a chronic user increases to 21 days.[17] As the following table[18] indicates, drug metabolites can be detected in urine from one day to several weeks following exposure:

Substances	Approximate Duration of Detection
Amphetamines	2 days
Barbiturates	1 to 7 days
Benzodiazepines	3 days
Cocaine metabolites	2 to 3 days
Methadone	3 to 7 days

---

[14] Warren D. Hamilton, "Drug Testing: Urine," in WILEY ENCYCLOPEDIA OF FORENSIC SCIENCE, (Jamieson A. & Moenssens A.A., eds) 2009 & online updates.

[15] R. Sam Niedbala et al., "Detection of Marijuana Use by Oral Fluid and Urine Analysis Following Single Dose Administration of Smoked and Oral Marijuana," 25 J. ANAL. TOX. 289 (July/Aug. 2001).

[16] Gary T. Marx, "Seeing Hazily (But Not Darkly) Through the Lens: Some Recent Empirical Studies of Surveillance Technologies," 30 Law & Soc. Inquiry 339, 385 (2005).

[17] Warren D. Hamilton, "Drug Testing: Urine," in WILEY ENCYCLOPEDIA OF FORENSIC SCIENCE, (Jamieson A. & Moenssens A.A., eds) 2009 & online updates; Paul Gahlinger, *Illegal Drugs: A Complete Guide to Their History, Chemistry, Use and Abuse* 333 (2001).

[18] K. Wolff et al., "A Review of Biological Indicators of Illicit Drug Use, Practical Considerations and Clinical Usefulness," 94 ADDICTION 1279 (Sept. 1999).

Codeine	2 days
PCP, single use	7 to 14 days
Heavy use	30 days
Cannibinoids single use	3 days
moderate use (4 times/week)	5 days
heavy smoker (daily)	10 days
chronic heavy smoker	21 days

Although the actual effects of most drugs last for a few hours, they are detectable for much longer, and any correlations between a positive drug-use test and the degree of impairment are impossible.[19] In addition, it cannot be determined through urinalysis whether a particular subject is a chronic or occasional user.[20] In order to determine whether a person is a chronic user of a particular drug, multiple urinalyses must be conducted over time, or an alternative matrix (such as hair) must be tested.

As hair grows it absorbs drugs and their metabolites into the hair shaft while the hair is being formed in the follicle and through external processes such as sweat/sebum excretion onto the hair shaft. The exact mechanism of absorption is unknown, but it is generally thought that drugs enter through the blood during hair formation, from sweat, and from the external environment.[21] As the hair shaft grows, it forms a roughly longitudinal record of the compounds it has absorbed, including illicit substances. The drugs and metabolites appear in detectable levels about a week after ingestion or possible exposure. Hairs are collected by pulling or cutting. Testing is done through chromatographic and spectrometry procedures. Positive results can be obtained through the use of a single strand of hair, but a larger sample (between 40 and 50 hairs) is preferred.[22] Scalp hair is most commonly used, but any body hair can be utilized.[23] After collection of the hair sample, the sample is

---

[19] Tee L. Guidotti et al., *Occupational Health Services: A Practical Approach*, 2d ed., Routledge (2012).

[20] Kurt M. Dubowski, "The Role of Scientists in Litigation Involving Drug-use Testing," 34 Clin. Chem. 788 (1988).

[21] Pascal Kintz, "Hair: Toxicology," in WILEY ENCYCLOPEDIA OF FORENSIC SCIENCE, (Jamieson A. & Moenssens A.A., eds) 2009 & online updates.

[22] Baumgartner, "Hair Analysis for Drugs of Abuse: Solving the Problems of Urinalysis," testimony before Subcommittee on Human Resources, House Comm. on Post Office and Civil Service, U.S. House of Representatives (May 20, 1987).

[23] F. Musshof et al., "Results of Hair Analyses for Drugs of Abuse and Comparison with Selfreports and Urine Tests," 156 For. Sci. Int'l 118 (Jan. 2006).

washed in order to remove any possible external contaminants.[24] Newer studies have demonstrated the potential of washing to cause hair contaminated with target analytes to move from the outside of the hair shaft to the inside. Specialized mass spectrometry imaging analysis has the potential to differentiate between hair that is positive from external contamination and hair positive from ingestion of a target substance.[25]

Several features which distinguish hair testing from bodily fluid testing make hair testing an attractive option for drug-use testing. Hair testing provides a longer time window within which substances can be detected and short periods of nonuse will not significantly alter the results. This factor makes retesting a fruitful option. Hair testing is less intrusive than bodily fluid testing; it simply requires the snipping of a small section of hair from the scalp. Taking blood requires an invasive procedure and urine specimen collection requires close, personal observation to prevent adulteration of the sample. Intentional alteration of the sample is much less likely in hair testing, and although it is possible to damage the hair and reduce the drug concentration,[26] the damage is generally not sufficient to avoid positive results from the sensitive tests. Additionally, hair samples are not as labile as urine samples; they are more chemically and physically stable than urine specimens.[27] This makes the hair sample less subject to destruction during collection, storage and shipment to and from testing sites.

There is a significant amount of scientific writing on the subject of hair analysis and while much of it supports the reliability and acceptance of hair testing in the field of forensic toxicology for the identification of drug use,[28] there remain significant issues that are as yet unresolved including hair color bias (dark hair has been shown to absorb more drug than blonde hair), misinterpretation of timing of drug

---

[24] Barry Levine Ph.D., *Principles of Forensic Toxicology*, 2d ed., American Association for Clincial Chemistry, 2003 at p. 42.

[25] E. Cuypers et al., "Consequences of Decontamination Procedures in Forensic Hair Analysis Using Metal-Assisted Secondary Ion Mass Spectrometry Analysis, " 88 Anal Chem. 3091 (2016).

[26] C. Jurado, P. Kintz, M. Menéndez, M. Repetto, "Influence of the Cosmetic Treatment of Hair on Drug Testing," 110 INT'L J. LEGAL MED. 159 (1997). The study showed that the damage to the hair from the cosmetic treatment of bleach or dye reduced the drug concentration between 40 and 60 percent.

[27] R.L. Dupont and W.A. Baumgartner, "Drug Testing by Urine and Hair Analysis: Complementary Features and Scientific Issues," 70 For. Sci. Int'l 63 (1995).

[28] *See, e.g.*, Welch, et al., "Two New Standard Reference Materials for The Determination of Drugs of Abuse in Human Hair," 376 J. ANAL. BIOANAL. CHEM. (2003); Y. Nakahara and R. Kikura, "Hair Analysis for Drugs of Abuse XIII. Effect of Structural Factors on Incorporation of Drugs into Hair: the Incorporation Rates of Amphetamine Analogs," 70 ARCHIVES TOX. 841 (1996); K.W. Phinney and L.C. Sander, "Liquid Chromatographic Method for the Determination of Enantiomeric Composition of Amphetamine and Methamphetamine in Hair Samples," 378 ANAL. BIOANAL. CHEM. 144 (2004); M. Wada and K. Nakishima, "Hair Analysis: An Excellent Tool for Confirmation of Drug Abuse," 385 ANAL. BIOANAL. CHEM. (2006); T. Mieczkowski, et al., "Using Hair Analysis, Urinalysis, and Selfreports to Estimate Drug Use in a Sample of Detained Juveniles," 33 SUBST. USE MISUSE 1547 (1998)(study compared results of hair analysis with urinalysis and determined that hair analysis provided more accurate detection rates).

ingestion, and the problem of external contamination. As such, the FBI toxicology program suspended analysis of hair for cocaine except for those involving children in 2009 and SAMHSA announced that it would not pursue the addition of hair as an authorized specimen.[29]

2.   HUMAN PERFORMANCE TOXICOLOGY

Drug-use testing focuses on the presence of a drug or its metabolites. Human performance toxicology focuses on the effects of drugs and alcohol on human behavior relevant to legal questions concerning impairment, such as competency, diminished capacity, and intoxication.[30] Investigations which involve human performance toxicology include impaired driving, drug-facilitated sexual assaults, and other drug facilitated violent crimes. The testing methods in human performance toxicology are designed to determine the time of consumption and the concentration of a drug to assess the impairment of the individual relative to the time an activity occurred. Generally, blood[31] and urine[32] samples are tested, but oral fluid and hair are increasingly used.

As with drug-use testing, human performance toxicology uses initial screening tests followed by confirmatory testing. However, for drug-use testing, detection is the goal and the only relevant concentration question is whether the drug is present above the value used to establish and report a specimen as positive (the "cutoff level").[33] For human performance testing, however, concentration levels of the drugs are relevant to the determination of impairment or intoxication

---

[29] *See, e.g.,* E Cuypers et al., "Consequences of Decontamination Procedures in Forensic Hair Analysis Using Metal-Assisted Secondary Ion Mass Spectrometry Analysis, " 88 Anal Chem. 3091 (2016); SAMHSA Mandatory Guidelines for Federal Workplace Drug Testing Programs 73 FR 71858 (Nov. 25, 2008); M LeBeau et al., "Considerations on the Utility of Hair Analysis for Cocaine, " 33 J.Anal Toxicol.343 (2009); Stout et al., External Contamination of Hair with Cocaine: Evaluation of External Cocaine Contamination and Development of Performance-Testing Materials' " 30 J. Anal. Toxicol. 490 (2006); Kamata et al., "Time-Course Mass Spectrometry Imaging for Depicting Drug Incorporation into Hair, " 87 Anal Chem, 5476 (2015).

[30] What constitutes legal impairment or intoxication is determined by statute or case law. Although scientific evidence bears on the question, the determination is ultimately made by the trier of fact. For driving offenses, some jurisdictions have adopted "per se" legislation correlating impairment/intoxication to a specific concentration level of drugs in the body; other jurisdictions require proof of "impairment." *See generally* J.M. Walsh, J.J. De Gier, A.S. Christophersen and A.G. Verstraete, "Drugs and Driving," TRAFFIC INJURY PREVENTION 5, 241–253 (2004). All jurisdictions now have "per se" driving statutes concerning alcohol concentration.

[31] Blood generally correlates best to recent drug use and impairment, so it is considered the best specimen for human performance toxicology. *See* Elke Raes & Alain Verstraete, "Drug-Impaired Driving," in WILEY ENCYCLOPEDIA OF FORENSIC SCIENCE, (Jamieson A. & Moenssens A.A., eds) 2009 & online updates.

[32] Urine is the most frequently collected specimen in cases of drug-facilitated sexual assault. Since drugs and metabolites are concentrated in urine specimens, probative results may be obtained for urine specimens collected up to 96 hours after the alleged drug exposure. Marc A. LeBeau, "Drug-Facilitated Sexual Assault," in WILEY ENCYCLOPEDIA OF FORENSIC SCIENCE, (Jamieson A. & Moenssens A.A., eds) 2009 & online updates.

[33] Cutoff levels are also used to determine whether a specimen has been adulterated, substituted, or should be considered invalid. SAMHSA Guidelines, Sections 1.5, 3.4–3.8.

and the confirmatory testing by mass spectral analysis is also used to measure concentration (mass spectrometry is discussed in Section II "Analytical Methods" *infra*).

Particularly in drugged driving detection, data from testing laboratories is critical to research in public safety. To facilitate consistent data from testing laboratories regarding drugs linked to driving impairment and the potential development of evidence-based public policy, a set of recommendations for minimum testing requirements has been published.[34] Laboratories performing this type of testing may show adherence to industry standards by seeking accreditation. Participating in toxicology proficiency testing (PT) programs such as the ones administered by the CAP are a must for laboratories conducting human performance testing. Recognizing that PT programs are not one size fit all, the CAP has released a new PT program to address the unique challenges of drug facilitated crime cases.[35]

3.   CAUSE AND MANNER OF DEATH OR INJURY

Although most toxicological examinations are conducted in alcohol or drug-related screening and incidents, toxicology plays an important role in other cases for determination of cause and manner of death or injury. The forensic toxicologist is concerned with the detection and characterization of poisons or toxins exhibiting adverse physiological effects. A toxin is any material which when introduced, directly or indirectly into a living system, exerts an effect which may ultimately be life-threatening to the organism. This intentionally broad definition covers not only common drugs of abuse[36] and classic poisons, detection of which is often considered the principal task of the toxicologist,[37] but many other less well known, but equally hazardous materials. Among these are toxic gases such as carbon monoxide and hydrogen cyanide, industrial solvents and refrigerants, heavy metals, and pesticides. Toxic materials may be ingested, inhaled, or absorbed through the skin and

---

[34] Barry K. Logan et al., "Recommendations for Toxicological Investigation of Drug-Impaired Driving and Motor Vehicle Fatalities, " 37 J. Anal. Toxicol. 552 (2013).

[35] College of American Pathologists 2016 Surveys Catalog (available at http://www.cap.org)(last accessed November 5, 2016).

[36] Alcohol is the most prevalent of the misused substances and benzodiazepines are the second; both are frequently detected in a range of forensic cases. Olaf H. Drummer, "Benzodiazepines," in WILEY ENCYCLOPEDIA OF FORENSIC SCIENCE, (Jamieson A. & Moenssens A.A., eds) 2009 & online updates.

[37] Since the 1840 trial of Marie Lafarge for murdering her husband with arsenic, the discovery of murder by poisoning has been "ultimate duty of forensic toxicologists." Erikki Vuori & Ilkka Ojanpera, "Toxicology: Forensic Applications of," in WILEY ENCYCLOPEDIA OF FORENSIC SCIENCE, (Jamieson A. & Moenssens A.A., eds) 2009 & online updates. Although arsenic poisoning is not encountered as frequently as in the 1800's and 1900's, arsenic detection is still important in forensic toxicology. *See* Kathleen F. Gensheimer et al., "Arsenic Poisoning Caused by Intentional Contamination of Coffee at a Church Gathering—A Epidemiological Approach to a Forensic Investigation," 55 J. FORENSIC SCI. 1116–1119 (2010); Gilles Tournel et al., "Acute Arsenic Poisoning: Clinical, Toxicological, Histopathological, and Forensic Features," 56(S1) J. FORENSIC SCI. S275–S279 (2010).

may enter the body in a single massive dose (acute poisoning) or gradually through repeated exposure (chronic poisoning). A series of nonlethal exposures over time results in chronic poisoning and may go undetected in the absence of suspicion that the victim's illness or death is not the result of disease or natural causes. With prescription or over-the-counter (OTC) medications, questions may arise involving adverse reactions, improper prescribing by the physician, suspected error by the pharmacist, or excessive use by the patient.

While blood is the most commonly examined body fluid for detection of toxins, others such as urine, stomach contents,[38] and vitreous humor are also useful. Tissue from body organs such as the brain or liver[39] offers advantages in certain situations[40] and, in bodies in an advanced stage of decomposition, hair, bone, or nail samples may provide otherwise unobtainable information.[41] Because suitable samples may be difficult to obtain after an autopsy or extensive medical treatment, these samples should be collected during treatment or before autopsy. Another reason for obtaining samples as soon as possible is to avoid potential loss of evidential value with time or as a result of chemical interaction. For example, cyanide traces in the body may be destroyed by embalming fluid containing formaldehyde.[42] In fatalities, blood should always be obtained, preferably from multiple sites. Peripheral sites, such as the femoral vein (thigh), are preferred for quantitative analysis; and more central sites, such as subclavian veins and aorta blood, are used for screening purposes. Multiple site collection is preferred to assess specimen validity and the extent of pre-

---

[38] H.M. Stevens, "The Detection of Some Nondrug Poisons in Simulated Stomach Contents by Diffusion into Various Colour Reagents," 26 J.FORENSIC SCI.SOC. 137 (1986); Giovanna Tassoni, Claudio Cacaci, Massimiliana Zampi & Rino Froldi, "Bile Analysis in Heroin Overdose," 52 J. FORENSIC SCI. 1405–1407 (2007); Johan Duflou, Shane Drake & Jennifer Easson, "Morphine Concentrations in Stomach Contents of Intravenous Opioid Overdose Deaths," 54 J. FORENSIC SCI. 1181–1184 (2009).

[39] Olaf H. Drummer & J. Gerostamoulos, "Postmortem Drug Analysis: Analytical and Toxicological Aspects", 24 THE DRUG MONIT. 199 (2002); Graham R. Jones, "Toxicology: Analysis," in WILEY ENCYCLOPEDIA OF FORENSIC SCIENCE, (Jamieson A. & Moenssens A.A., eds) 2009 & online updates.

[40] The highly toxic protein ricin, extracted from the castor bean, has a history of use for medicinal and criminal purposes and is determinable at extremely low levels in tissue extracts. A.G. Leith, et al., "Quantitation of Ricin Toxin Using a Highly Sensitive Avidin/Biotin Enzyme-Linked Immunosorbent Assay," 28 J. FORENSIC SCI. SOC. 227 (1988); G.D. Griffiths, et al., "Identification and Quantification of Ricin Toxin in Animal Tissues Using ELISA", 26 J. FORENSIC SCI. 349 (1986).

Brain tissue may be used to detect and estimate concentration levels for drugs and/or metabolites that are more stable in the brain than in blood (e.g., cocaine, heroin/6-acetylmorphine). Graham R. Jones, "Toxicology: Analysis," in WILEY ENCYCLOPEDIA OF FORENSIC SCIENCE, (Jamieson A. & Moenssens A.A., eds) 2009 & online updates.

[41] These specimens are useful for obtaining evidence of the presence of a toxin, but concentration levels may not be determinable. Wing-Chi Cheng, "Postmortem Toxicology: Laboratory Analysis," in WILEY ENCYCLOPEDIA OF FORENSIC SCIENCE, (Jamieson A. & Moenssens A.A., eds) 2009 & online updates.

[42] See generally Gisela Skopp, "Postmortem Toxicology: Artifacts," in WILEY ENCYCLOPEDIA OF FORENSIC SCIENCE, (Jamieson A. & Moenssens A.A., eds) 2009 & online updates; Gisela Skopp, "Preanalytic Aspects of Postmortem Toxicology. 142 Forensic Science International 75 (2004).

analytic artifacts.[43] Care must be taken when collecting the specimen to visually identify the vessel and specimens collected via external stick (*e.g.,* thoracic puncture, subclavian) should be avoided if they are to be used for quantitative analysis.[44] For toxicological examination, the collected samples should be stored in tightly sealed containers at low temperatures, and apart from blood samples, preservation chemicals are not needed.[45] Blood samples are often preserved with sodium fluoride or an equivalent to suppress postmortem artifacts such as the production of alcohol and the hydrolysis of some drugs.[46]

As a toxicological sample, urine offers some advantages over blood, but levels of a toxin or its metabolites in urine are difficult to relate to earlier levels in the body.[47] Stomach contents provide a rapid route to detection of ingested toxins and are often available from pumping or lavage in suspected poisoning cases. In postmortem sample collection, particularly when the postmortem interval is greater than several days, vitreous humor is an excellent sample medium, being more resistant to contamination and bacterial action than blood. Liver samples are specifically used to resolve difficult cases by assessing the extent of postmortem redistribution and can assist in manner of death determination in cases where there is little difference between normal and overdose postmortem blood concentrations.[48]

Based on their chemical composition, toxins are classifiable as organic or inorganic. Inorganic poisons may be placed into subclasses such as metallic poisons (lead, mercury, barium, or thallium), nonmetallic poisons (cyanide or iodine), and corrosives (acids and alkalis). Organic poisons include: volatile organic poisons (alcohols, acetone, benzene), alkaloids (many drugs, strychnine), and nonalkaloidal poisons (rodenticides, and carbamate, halogenated, or organophosphate insecticides). Gaseous poisons may be organic or inorganic (phosgene, carbon monoxide, carbon dioxide, chlorine, hydrogen sulfide). Metallic poisons do not disappear with decomposition and may be detected in remains long after death. Arsenic, for example,

---

[43] F.E. Barnhart, H.J. Bonnell and K.M. Rossum, "Postmortem Drug Redistribution," 13(2) For. Sci. Reviews 102–109 (2001).

[44] Dinis-Oliveira et al., "Collection of Biological Samples in Forensic Toxicology," 20 Toxicology Mechanisms and Methods 363 (2010).

[45] Wing-Chi Cheng, "Postmortem Toxicology: Laboratory Analysis," in WILEY ENCYCLOPEDIA OF FORENSIC SCIENCE, (Jamieson A. & Moenssens A.A., eds) 2009 & online updates.

[46] Gisela Skopp, "Preanalytical Aspects in Post-mortem Toxicology," 142 (2–3) FOR. SCI. INT'L 75–100 (2004); Nunziata Barbera et al., "Evaluation of the Role of Toxicological Data in Discriminating Between H_2S Femoral Blood Concentration Secondary to Lethal Poisoning and Endogenous H_2S Putrefactive Production," 62 J. Forensic Sci. 392-394 (2017).

[47] John C. Lindon, et al., "Contemporary Issues in Toxicology: The Role of Metabonomics in Toxicology and its Evaluation by the COMET Project," 187 TOX. & APPLIED PHARM. 137 (2003).

[48] See Alphonse Poklis, "Analytical/Forensic Toxicology," in Curtis D. Klaassen ed., *Casarett & Doull's Toxicology: The Basic Science of Poisons,* 5th ed., Mcgraw-Hill, 1996; I McIntyre, "Liver and Peripheral Blood Concentration ratio (L/P) as a Marker for Postmortem Drug Redistribution: a Literature Review" 10 Forensic Sci Med Pathol. 91 (2014).

has been detected in the hair and nails of aged remains such as the hair of the Emperor Napoleon.[49] An acute dose of arsenic may be detected in tissue samples; however, episodic arsenic poisoning may best be detected in the hair. By examining sections taken along the length of the hair, episodic ingestion of nonlethal doses over a period of time can be demonstrated.[50] Similarly, heavy metals such as mercury present in the environment may be detectable in hair or in the bodies of insect larvae feeding on the body.[51] Lead poisoning is particularly destructive in children, who can experience irreversible brain damage.[52] The exposure may arise from lead based paints in old buildings, drinking water, or other environmental sources. Lead is readily detected in blood using atomic absorption analysis. If drinking water is considered as a potential source of heavy metal poisoning, analysis of the water can provide valuable information.[53]

Carbon monoxide (CO), when inhaled, combines with the hemoglobin in the blood to form a stable compound and deprive the body of oxygen. Outside of fire deaths, carbon monoxide poisoning may be suspected from a cherry red color of the body. Analysis of a blood sample readily detects it and permits an estimate of its concentration. Although homicides from CO have occurred, most such fatalities are results of accident or suicide. The best-known sources of CO are building fires and automotive exhaust, but poorly vented stoves, banked fires, and malfunctioning heaters are also potential causes of CO poisoning.

A wide range of readily available materials have the potential to be toxic at sufficiently high levels. In the workplace, potentially toxic materials may include petroleum products, industrial solvents, paint thinners, degreasers, pesticides, and toxic gases. In the home, ordinary products including pesticides, drain cleaners, mothballs, detergents,

---

[49] Hairs taken from Napoleon after his death were tested by the Toxicology Crime Laboratory of the United States Federal Bureau of Investigation and showed toxic levels of arsenic. Ben Weider & John Harry, "Activation Analyses of Authenticated Hairs of Napoleon Bonaparte Confirm Arsenic Poisoning," 20 AM. J. FORENSIC MED. & PATHOL. 378 (1999).

[50] Agency for Toxic Substances and Disease Registry, *Hair Analysis Panel Discussion: Exploring the State of the Science*, (2001)(http://www.atsdr.cdc.gov/HAC/hair_analysis/hairanalysisappC.pdf)(sections of hair from several individuals suspected of having been poisoned demonstrated murder by prolonged chronic exposure to arsenic). Flameless atomic absorption spectrometry also offers sufficient sensitivity for the sectional analysis of hair to determine levels and times of exposure to arsenic. Robert D. Koons and Charles A. Peters, "Axial Distribution of Arsenic in Individual Human Hairs by Solid Sampling Graphite Furnace AAS," 18 J. ANAL. TOXICOL. 36 (1994).

[51] Annamaria Leccese, "Insects as Forensic Indicators: Methodological Aspects," 5 Anil Aggrawai's Internet Jounral of Forensic Medicine and Toxicology 26–32 (2004)(available at: https://www.ncjrs.gov/App/publications/Abstract.aspx?id=206227)(last accessed March 2, 2017); Pekka Nuorteva, "Sarcosaprophagous Insects as Forensic Indicators" in: Tedeschi et al., eds. *Forensic Medicine: Vol. II Physical Trauma,* W.B. Saunders Co., 1977, at p. 1072.

[52] Friends of the Earth, Inc. v. Gaston Cooper Recycling Corp. 204 F.3d 149, 157 (4th Cir. 2000).

[53] Schmelzel, Karpova and Dulude, "Simultaneous Determination of Copper and Lead in Drinking Waters by Graphite Furnace Atomic Absorption Spectrometry" 2 SPECTROSCOPIST 12 (1993); *see also,* Bano v. Union Carbide Corp., 361 F.3d 696 (2d Cir. 2004).

weed killers, and paint removers have been involved in suicidal or accidental death or injury.[54] Over-the-counter medications[55] and herbal medicines[56] may also be involved in death or injury. Even hospitals may be the source of toxins; surgical anesthetics and muscle relaxants[57] have also been involved in deaths by accident, suicide, or homicide.

The rapid growth in the area of new or novel psychoactive substances is not only causing an increased number of injuries and deaths, but is also hampering the laboratories' ability to detect and quantify the substances.[58] These drugs, also known as "legal highs" are designed specifically to evade drug legislation and the use and abuse of these substances has risen dramatically in the last decade. Based on their actions these drugs can be classified into five categories: stimulants (mimics the effects of methamphetamine and MDMA), synthetic cannabinoids (mimics the effects of marijuana), hallucinogens (mimics the effects of PCP, LSD and Ketamine), benzodiazepines (mimics the effects of diazepam), and opioids (mimics the effects of heroin). The main challenges the laboratory faces with these drugs is that screening tests, such as immunoassays, are not effective at detecting these substances; reference standards are often not available; and there is limited published information available on the concentrations associated with acute toxicity after use of these drugs.[59]

---

[54] Rebecca A. Hamilton & Barbara C. Wolf, "Accidental Boric Acid Poisoning Following Ingestion of Household Pesticide," 52 J.FORENSIC SCI. 706–708 (2007); D.M. Reith et al., "Childhood poisoning in Queensland: An analysis of presentation and admission rates," 37 J. PEDIATRICS CHILD HEALTH 1440 (2001); K. Sperry & R. Pfalzgraf, "Fatal Ethanol Intoxication from Household Products Not Intended for Ingestion" 35 J. Forensic Sci. 1138–1142 (1990).

[55] The use of OTC cold medications with toddlers and infants came under scrutiny following the reports of a series of studies and death investigations that ultimately resulted in the 2008 Public Health Advisory of the United States Food and Drug Administration that OTC cough and cold products not be used for infants and children under 2 years of age. William E. Wingert, Lisa A. Mundy, Gary L. Collins & Edward S. Chmara, "Possible Role of Pseudoephedrine and Other Over-The-Counter Cold Medications in the Deaths of Very Young Children," 52 J. FORENSIC SCI. 487–490 (2007).

[56] Heavy metals and organic toxins are frequently included as essential ingredients in certain herbal remedies and the concentrations may be potentially lethal. Roger W. Byard, "A Review of the Potential Forensic Significance of Traditional Herbal Medicines," 55 J. FORENSIC SCI. 89–92 (2010).

[57] Amit Verma, et al., "Succinylcholine Induced Hyperkalemia and Cardiac Arrest: Death Related to an EEG Study," 16 J. CLINICAL NEUROPHYSIOLOGY 46 (1999).

The muscle relaxant succinylcholine chloride was identified as the cause of death in the landmark *Coppolino* case; Coppolino v. State, 223 So.2d 68 (Fla.App.1968). Similarly, curare, or its active ingredient dtubocurarine, was suspected in the alleged murders of surgical patients in a New Jersey hospital. Lawrence H. Hall & Roland F. Hirsch, "Detection of Curare in the Jascalevich Murder Trial" 51 ANAL. CHEM. 812A (1979). In 1981, twelve patients in the Intensive Care Unit of a California hospital suffered seizures and died. Tissue analyses showed high levels of lidocaine and a male nurse was convicted of the homicides. People v. Diaz, 3 Cal.4th 495, 11 Cal.Rptr.2d 353, 834 P.2d 1171 (1992). In an action against a hospital, chemical analysis of residue in a cup inadvertently left on the patient's meal tray identified it as bleach. Lewis v. St. Frances Cabrini Hosp., 556 So.2d 970 (La.App.3d Cir.1990).

[58] Barbara Potocka-Banas et al., "Fatal Intoxication with α-PVP, a Synthetic Cathinone Derivative," 62 J. Forensic Sci. 553–556 (2017).

[59] *See* CCENDU Bulletin: Novel Synthetic Opioids in Counterfeit Pharmaceuticals and Other Illicit Street Drugs. June 2016 (available at http://www.ccsa.ca/Resource%20Library/ CCSA-CCENDU-Novel-Synthetic-Opioids-Bulletin-2016-en.pdf)(last accessed 07-Nov-2016);

Another source of potentially hazardous materials is environmental contamination. Contamination of the soil or water by improper waste disposal, runoff of toxic chemicals, and chemical spills poses a problem which may not be identified or rectified for years. Among better known examples are: pesticide waste contamination of the Love Canal area near Buffalo, N.Y.; Kepone contamination of the Shenandoah River and Times Beach, Missouri; and the 1989 Exxon Valdez crude oil spill off the Alaskan coast. In each of these, contamination resulted in illness, death, or economic losses—and protracted litigation.[60] Similarly, hazards posed by improper disposal of polychlorinated biphenyls (PCBs) used as insulators in electrical transformers have given rise to extensive litigation. Major concerns have also been raised about potential health hazards from residual coal tar at abandoned sites of lighting gas plants and soil and groundwater contamination from explosives disposal at military munitions plants and decommissioned military installations worldwide. The British Petroleum Deepwater Horizon 86-day oil spill off the coast of the United States in the Gulf of Mexico resulted in extensive cleanup efforts and litigation.[61] Environmental contamination cases may also involve the discharge of hazardous materials into the atmosphere. Examples include solvents from chemical or paint production, cyanide containing waste from ore processing or electroplating, metals such as lead or selenium from smelting operations, and mercury released from chemical plants. Environmental contamination cases require careful forensic investigation for many reasons, including the difficulties occasioned by the delayed examination of exposed individuals when adverse effects of contamination develop only long after exposure.[62]

Toxins in foods are another potential source of illness or death from environmental causes. In addition to toxins from improper packaging or spoilage of food such as botulism, another source of toxins is contaminated shellfish. These natural toxins are produced from intake by shellfish such as mussels of certain diatoms. Consumption of contaminated shellfish can result in severe and long lasting neurological effects.[63] Although several states have programs to monitor these toxins in commercial shellfish, the effects of shellfish poisoning

---

Zawilska et al., "Next generation of novel psychoactive substances on the horizon—A complex problem to face," 157 Drug and Alcohol Dependence 1 (2015).

[60] *See* Exxon Shipping Co., et al. v. Baker, et al., 554 U.S. 471 (2008).

[61] In Re: Oil Spill by the Oil Rig "Deepwater Horizon" in the Gulf of Mexico, on April 20, 2010, 2:10md02179-CJB-SS, U.S. Dist. Ct. E.D. of LA (New Orleans)(consolidating thousands of cases).

[62] Douglas W. Cross, "Environmental Science," in WILEY ENCYCLOPEDIA OF FORENSIC SCIENCE, (Jamieson A. & Moenssens A.A., eds) 2009 & online updates.

[63] David H. Green et al., "Phylogenetic and functional diversity of the cultivable bacterial community associated with the paralytic shellfish poisoning dinoflagellate Gymnodinium catenatum" 47 FEMS MICROBIOL. ECOL. 345 (2004); C. Garcia, "Paralytic Shellfish Poisoning: PostMortem Analysis of Tissue and Body Fluid Samples from Human Victims in the Patagonia Fjords," 43 TOXICOL. 149 (2004).

could result in civil litigation. Product tampering, such as the much-publicized cyanide in Tylenol cases, can also lead to involvement of the forensic toxicologist in both civil and criminal cases.[64]

When effects on individuals from toxin exposure are alleged, forensic toxicological examinations are essential. With the wide variety of materials having the potential for serious injury or death, the challenge facing the toxicologist is formidable. The forensic toxicologist must be skilled in the use of the myriad of analytical techniques for detection and identification of any of thousands of materials capable of causing death or illness, whether through accident or design. Laboratories performing this testing should be accredited by a program that assesses not only the technical proficiency of the laboratory, but also whether the scope of testing offered is sufficient to analyze the variety of toxins that may be suspected.

4.   ALCOHOL INTOXICATION

Alcohol, specifically ethyl alcohol or ethanol (CH_3CH_2OH), which is the pharmacologically active ingredient in alcoholic beverages, is the world's most prevalent recreational drug.[65] The wide spread consumption of alcohol combined with its effects on the body and the mind result in alcohol being involved in many incidents that end up in the civil and criminal justice systems. Scientific analysis of bodily specimens for the detection and quantification of alcohol is often encountered in a variety of litigation matters ranging from alcohol-related crimes to traffic accidents or work injuries. Alcohol use can also be relevant to probation revocation proceedings,[66] custody matters, and employment proceedings.

Alcohol-impaired driving is a particular area of legislative and law enforcement concern. In 2014, there were over 9,967 fatalities in the United States from crashes involving drivers with alcohol impairment, approximately 31% of all total traffic fatalities.[67] Alcohol-impaired motor vehicle crashes cost more than an estimated $44 billion annually.[68] Addressing the problems of alcohol-impaired driving to reduce fatalities, injuries, and the associated economic losses are the focus of several national groups, including Mothers Against Drunk Driving (MADD) and

---

[64] An overview of chemical tampering is illustrated by several significant cases. *See* Barry K. Logan, "Product Tampering Crime: A Review" 38 J. Forensic Sci. 918 (1993); Barry K. Logan, et al., "Poisonings Associated with Cyanide in Over the Counter Cold Medication in Washington State" 38 J. Forensic Sci. 472 (1993).

[65] *See generally* Alan W. Jones, "Alcohol" and "Alcohol: Analysis" in WILEY ENCYCLOPEDIA OF FORENSIC SCIENCE, (Jamieson A. & Moenssens A.A., eds) 2009 & online updates. *See also* Alan W. Jones and Anita Holmgren, "Age and Gender Differences in Blood-Alcohol Concentration in Apprehended Drivers in Relation to the Amounts of Alcohol Consumed," 188 FORENSIC SCI. INT'L 40–45 (2009).

[66] *See* Mogg v. State, 918 N.E.2d 750 (Ind. Ct. App. 2009).

[67] National Center for Statistics and Analysis. (2015, December). *Alcohol-impaired driving: 2014 data.* (Traffic Safety Facts. DOT HS 812 231). Washington, DC: National Highway Traffic Safety Administration (available at: http://www-nrd.nhtsa.dot.gov/Pubs/812231.pdf)(last accessed June 13, 2016).

[68] Id.

Remove Intoxicated Drivers (RID). In response to legislative efforts by these and other groups, the federal government and state legislatures have enacted many statutes designed to deter and punish alcohol-impaired driving. The majority of these statutes are predicated upon the detection of alcohol impairment in drivers through scientific testing. There are over 1.1 million impaired driving arrests each year in the United States.[69] As a result, alcohol testing through the detection and interpretation of an individual's blood alcohol level or concentration is the most frequently conducted forensic science analysis in the United States.

II. ANALYTICAL METHODS

§ 13.04 ISOLATION TECHNIQUES

For biological specimens, an isolation process must be performed before instrumental analysis to extract the toxins from the matrix and to remove any material that may interfere with the analysis. Isolation procedures can involve the use of liquid-liquid extraction (LLE) solvents, such as butyl chloride to remove codeine from blood or hexane to remove tetrahydrocannabinol (THC, the active substance in marijuana) from blood. Other isolation techniques commonly used in forensic toxicology are solid supported liquid extraction (SLE), solid-phase extraction (SPE) and solid-phase microextraction (SPME). In LLE, the toxin of interest is separated into one of two immiscible phases using extraction solvents and by manipulating the pH of the liquids to encourage the toxin to move out of the aqueous matrix (blood, urine) into an organic solvent (butyl chloride, chloroform). LLE is a common isolation technique for postmortem samples because of the wide concentration range that can be efficiently extracted, the large number of target analytes that can be extracted by a single procedure, and because the sample does not need pretreatment. Postmortem conditions of blood and tissue may cause complications. In SPE, the sample must be pretreated (usually protein precipitation and centrifugation). The sample is then diluted into a buffer with a predetermined pH and applied to commercially-made cartridges that are bonded with silica. The extraction occurs through adsorption of the toxin of interest onto the solid phase (silica). Wash steps remove interferences and an elution step removes the toxin from the solid phase for further analysis. SPE is

---

[69] Federal Bureau of Investigation, "Crime in the United States: 2014)(available at: https://www.fbi.gov/about-us/cjis/ucr/crime-in-the-u.s/2014/crime-in-the-u.s.-2014/tables/table-29)(last accessed June 13, 2016) Impaired driving is reportedly the most frequently committed crime in the United States. *See* Substance Abuse and Mental Health Services Administration, Results from the 2013 National Survey on Drug Use and Health: Summary of National Findings. Rockville, MD: Substance Abuse and Mental Health Services Administration, 2014. (available at: http://www.samhsa.gov/data/sites/default/files/NSDUHresultsPDFWHTML2013/Web/NSDUHresults2013.pdf)(last accessed June 13, 2016).

widely used for urine drug analyses. In SPME, fibers that selectively retain the substance of interest are used to perform the isolation.

For all laboratory methods, proper validation and quality control mechanisms are essential to obtaining reliable and accurate results. Quality control measures include the use of internal standards, reference compounds, and routine proficiency testing.[70] For postmortem analysis, care must be taken to account for postmortem factors that may affect the interpretation of the results of toxicological analysis of biological material: postmortem changes in blood composition, degradation and formation of drugs during decomposition, and artifacts introduced through storage (including in formaldehyde) and embalming.[71]

§13.05 IDENTIFICATION TECHNIQUES

A wide range of laboratory methods are used by the forensic toxicologist to answer medicolegal questions. The questions posed involve the detection of a drug or toxic material, the determination of the quantity present, and whether the materials identified could arise as a result of environmental exposure or represent intentional administration. The usual practice in forensic toxicological investigation[72] is to screen for a wide array of organic toxins (drugs and poisons). If a toxin is detected, further confirmatory testing is completed, and if necessary, quantitative testing is done to determine the amount of the toxin present. In general, a positive identification of the toxin is made based on at least two analyses, preferably involving different analytical methods.

Immunoassays are used in forensic toxicology primarily to screen biological specimens for the presence of drugs. Immunoassays are based on the binding of antibodies and antigens. The drug is detected by its ability to displace or block the binding of a fixed amount of the labeled drug molecule present in the reagent. Immunoassays are useful in screening large numbers of samples, but will only give an indication of the drug or drug group present and the results must be confirmed with more specific techniques.

The two types of immunoassays are:

a.   homogeneous immunoassays—which measure the optical change—through UV absorption, fluorescence, or chemiluminescence—between the antibody bound drug from the unbound drug (EIA: enzyme immunoassay; EMIT—enzyme multiplied immunoassay; CEDIA: cloned

---

[70] For a detailed discussion of quality control systems see Robert J. Flanagan & Robin Whelpton, "Quality Systems: Toxicology," in WILEY ENCYCLOPEDIA OF FORENSIC SCIENCE, (Jamieson A. & Moenssens A.A., eds) 2009 & online updates.

[71] Gisela Skopp, "Postmortem Toxicology: Artifacts, in WILEY ENCYCLOPEDIA OF FORENSIC SCIENCE, (Jamieson A. & Moenssens A.A., eds) 2009 & online updates.

[72] Alcohol screening frequently occurs before any other drug screening.

enzyme donor immunoassay; FPIA: fluorescence polarization immunoassay;

b. heterogeneous immunoassays—which separates the antibody bound drug and the unbound drug before measurement (ELISA—enzyme-linked immunosorbent assay; RIA—radioimmunoassay; chemiluminescence immunoassays).

Homogeneous immunoassays are widely used because of the following advantages:[73] they test for a wide spectrum of substances and their metabolites; produce quick results; are relatively inexpensive tests to conduct; and can be administered by personnel who lack specialized technological training. In addition, the tests are highly sensitive, detecting low levels of drugs or their metabolites.

Heterogeneous immunoassays have the advantage of a wash step that removes material that may interfere with the signal measurement (such as other compounds in the blood or in highly concentrated urine) and obviates the need for sample extraction before running the immunoassay. These immunoassays also have a much lower level of detection, meaning they can detect smaller amounts of the suspected drug in the samples.[74] Radioimmunoassay (RIA) tests are useful for a wide spectrum of substances, but only measure one substance at a time and are more expensive to run. The RIA test is the standard test for drug testing of hair and is used to test for cocaine, opiates, methamphetamine, phencyclidine (PCP), and marijuana.[75]

Chromatography is primarily a technique to separate the individual components of a complex mixture. In gas chromatography (GC), the separation of substances occurs through the relative solubility between the moving gas phase (usually helium or hydrogen) and a micro-liquid layer bonded to a silica support. When combined with specific detectors or spectrometric analysis, identification of the separated material can be made. Flame ionization detectors (FID) are nonspecific and respond to any organic compounds that pass through the detectors. Nitrogen and phosphorous detectors (NPD) detect only compounds containing nitrogen and phosphorous and are useful in testing for common drugs of abuse. Most volatile poisons, pesticides and gases can be detected in the blood by using headspace sampling (the gas

---

[73] Frederick P. Smith, *Handbook of Forensic Drug Analysis*, Academic Press, 2004 at p. 19.

[74] Detailed discussions of the immunoassay types and the sample preparation stages for immunoassays are found in Peter Felgate, "Toxicology: Initial Testing," in WILEY ENCYCLOPEDIA OF FORENSIC SCIENCE, (Jamieson A. & Moenssens A.A., eds) 2009 & online updates.

[75] Michael T. Flannary et al., "The Use of Hair Analysis to Test Children for Exposure to Methamphetamine," 10 Mich. St. U. J. Med. & L. 143, n. 260 (2006).

space above the liquid in the sample vial) and gas chromatographic analysis.[76]

Other types of chromatography include thin layer and high performance liquid, both of which are simple and relatively sensitive for the detection of drugs and poisons. Thin layer chromatography (TLC) separates substances by the relative solubility (selective partitioning) in solvents (moving through capillary action) and affinity for the support matrix.[77] In high performance liquid chromatography (HPLC) the separation occurs through the relative solubility of the substance between the liquid-mobile phase and a stationary phase (usually a molecular layer bonded to a silica support). The sample is injected by a high-pressure pump into the liquid-mobile phase and moves through the column (the stationary phase) where the separation occurs and the components pass through a detector.

Spectrometric tests provide definitive identification of a material by measurement of the absorption or emission of light or another form of radiation. For a particular chemical element or compound, absorption or emission of radiation occurs at specific wavelengths depending on the structure of the molecule. For example, using infrared (IR) spectroscopy, the recorded pattern of absorption of infrared light (IR spectrum) of an alkaloid such as strychnine definitively identifies the compound if it is pure. IR spectra are less useful for identification of components in a mixture but may be used to determine the concentration of one component. By measuring the absorption at a wavelength characteristic of one material, such as alcohol, in the mixture, its concentration can be determined. Ultraviolet spectra are regularly used for quantitation of components, such as one drug in a formulation containing several compounds. Atomic absorption spectrometry is useful for the determination of species, principally metals, present at levels of only a few parts per million in a sample. X-ray diffraction (XRD) is a technique for the identification of compounds based upon the characteristic scattering of X-rays by the crystal structure of the compound. XRD is useful for the identification of compounds in an unknown mixture. Other spectrometric methods involve use of microwaves or gamma rays for detection and identification of elements or compounds. Gamma ray spectrometry is

---

[76] Barry K. Logan, "Analysis of Alcohol and Other Volatiles," GAS CHROMATOGRAPHY IN FORENSIC SCIENCE 87 (1992); P.J. Streete et al., "Detection and Identification of Volatile Substances by Headspace Gas Chromatography to Aid the Diagnosis of Acute Poisoning" 117 ANALYST 1111 (1992); R.L. Fitzgerald, et al., "Fatality Due to Recreational Use of Chlorodifluoromethane and Chloropentafluoroethane" 38 J. FORENSIC SCI. 476 (1993).

[77] Suicide by ingestion of a carbamate pesticide was demonstrated through measurement of the blood cholinesterase activity and the pesticide identified in blood and gastric contents by thin layer chromatography. K.E. Ferslew, A.N. Hagardorn and W.F. McCormick, "Poisoning from Oral Ingestion of Carbofuran (Furadan 4F), a Cholinesterase-Inhibiting Carbamate Insecticide, and its Effects on Cholinesterase Activity in Various Biological Fluids" 37 J. Forensic Sci. 337 (1992).

used in Neutron Activation Analysis to determine a variety of elements at parts-per-million levels or below.

For definitive identification of compounds, such as drugs, mass spectrometry (MS) is both sensitive and specific, and widely used in toxicological examinations. MS has the ability to provide structural information on the tested substance and retention time matching to authentic standards, providing excellent discriminatory power. In MS, a substance is bombarded with high energy electrons (or small ionized particles) in a high vacuum to create charged particles (ions). The ions are separated by their molecular weight-to-charge ratio and counted by an ion detector. A graph of the detected ions and their relative abundance (a mass spectra) is generated that can be compared to the mass spectra of authenticated samples. In order to meaningfully compare the two spectra the samples must be run under the same conditions, so the functionality of the equipment and the operating conditions must be carefully monitored. The concentration of a specific molecule in a specimen, necessary for human performance toxicology testing, is measured by running a number of known concentration standards to produce a calibration curve to compare to the spectra of the unknown specimen and calculate the relative concentration.[78]

The use of tandem mass spectrometry (MS/MS) is a major technique to confirm the presence of toxins and drugs. In this technique, one or more ions derived through the initial MS are further fragmented and analyzed by a second detector, generating derivative spectra that are more discriminating, allowing the detection of even lower levels of the substances. High resolution mass spectrometry (HRMS) is a powerful technique that affords assignment of an analytes mass out to many decimal places. This provides a high degree of discrimination and is a powerful tool in identification of unknown compounds which has become increasingly important as laboratories try to keep pace with the development of new and novel psychoactive substances.

III. ALCOHOL INVESTIGATIONS

§13.06 GENERAL PRINCIPLES

1.   ALCOHOL IN THE HUMAN BODY[79]

There are a number of different alcohols, *e.g.,* wood alcohol (methyl), rubbing alcohol (isopropyl), and consumable alcohol (ethyl). Ethyl alcohol

---

[78] Warren D. Hamilton, "Drug Testing: Urine," in WILEY ENCYCLOPEDIA OF FORENSIC SCIENCE, (Jamieson A. & Moenssens A.A., eds) 2009 & online updates.

[79] *See generally* Alan W. Jones, "Alcohol" and "Alcohol: Analysis" in WILEY ENCYCLOPEDIA OF FORENSIC SCIENCE, (Jamieson A. & Moenssens A.A., eds) 2009 & online updates.

is the alcoholic ingredient contained in alcoholic beverages. The term "alcohol" will be used throughout this chapter to refer to consumable alcohol. Alcohol is volatile, with a low boiling point, colorless, and practically odorless.[80] Trace amounts of alcohol are produced naturally by the body ("endogenous alcohol") through carbohydrate fermentation or other biochemical reactions, but the amount is normally so low that it is without forensic significance.[81]

When ingested alcohol reaches the stomach, it remains unchanged and undigested. Only a small percentage of alcohol is absorbed into the bloodstream through membranes in the stomach. Alcohol is absorbed throughout the gastrointestinal tract, but absorption occurs much faster in the upper part of the small intestine after passing through the stomach. It is only at this point that the bulk of the alcohol begins to be absorbed into the bloodstream at a fairly constant rate, but the degree and rate of absorption of alcohol is governed by several factors, such as the quantity of alcohol ingested and whether the alcohol was consumed with a meal. Alcohol consumed on an empty stomach will pass into the intestinal tract fairly rapidly and will have a faster absorption rate than alcohol taken with or after a meal. Some foods, such as fatty and oily substances, sugar, and milk, are among the substances that, if still in the stomach in whole or in part at the time alcohol is being ingested, may significantly delay absorption into the blood stream. Carbohydrates in beer delay absorption, which is why the alcohol in beer will be absorbed less rapidly than a like concentration of alcohol in water. After eating, the maximum blood alcohol concentration after ingestion of ethanol may not occur until 30 to 150 minutes later. As long as a person is still in the absorptive period, arterial blood containing alcohol that has been freshly absorbed from the digestive system is slightly higher in alcohol concentration than venous blood. The two will tend to equalize, however, in the post-absorptive stage.

Absorbed alcohol does not undergo chemical change; it remains alcohol until it is metabolized in the liver. Alcohol will be found in blood, urine, and other body fluids such as perspiration, spinal fluid, saliva, and tears. It is in the deep lung tissue that the alcohol is exchanged from the blood into the air (breath). When absorbed alcohol passes into the liver, the majority of the alcohol (90–98%) is eliminated from the body by oxidative metabolism. A small portion (less than 0.2%) undergoes nonoxidative (conjugation) reactions to form the metabolites ethyl

---

[80] Breath odor of a person who has been drinking alcohol in its usual available forms is actually the odor of the other ingredients inserted into the beverage, and this varies from one beverage to another. It is precisely because alcohol itself is odorless, that police officers are taught to say on the witness stand that upon approaching the driver of a vehicle they "detected the odor associated with consumed alcoholic beverages about his person."

[81] In healthy individuals, the concentration of endogenous alcohol in the blood is so very low that it is barely detectable (approximately 0.5 mg/L). Even in diabetic individuals, the level is approximately 2 mg/L (0.0002g/100 ml). *See* M. Simic et al, "Endogenous Ethanol Production in Patients with Diabetes Mellitus as a Medicolegal Problem," 216 FORENSIC SCI. INT'L 97–100 (2012).

glucuronide (EtG) and ethyl sulfate (EtS). The remaining alcohol (2–10%) will be excreted unchanged in urine, sweat, and breath.[82] The higher the concentration of alcohol in the blood, the higher the relative proportion of alcohol excreted in the urine, sweat, and breath. The rate of elimination varies from person to person, but it is reasonably constant according to body size. The average 150-pound man can eliminate 1/3 ounce of pure alcohol per hour.[83]

While in the bloodstream, alcohol is distributed throughout the body in a constant proportional relationship to the water content of the various tissues. For example, the alcohol concentration in urine bears approximately the same relationship to the alcohol concentration of the blood as the water content of the urine bears to the water content of the blood. Urine and blood plasma[84] have higher water contents than whole blood and will have higher alcohol concentrations. Because the distribution of alcohol between plasma and whole blood (or between urine and whole blood) follows the distribution of water, the water concentration ratio can be used as a conversion factor for calculating blood alcohol concentration from these other bodily specimens. The conversion factor (also known as the "partition ratio") commonly used for plasma/whole blood is 1.16:1 and for urine/whole blood is 1.33:1.[85]

Concerning the effects of alcohol on the body, it is important to understand that it is not the amount of alcohol consumed that governs the degree of impairment but rather the amount of alcohol that is absorbed into the blood and carried to the central nervous system.[86] Alcohol acts as a depressant to the responses of the central nervous system (the brain, spinal cord, and spinal nerves). The alcohol rich blood courses over the brain through the vascular system, imparting a depressing effect to the brain tissue until the alcohol disappears from the blood. Its primary blunting effect in low concentrations occurs in the cerebral areas of the brain which control the higher functions, causing

---

[82] Alan W. Jones, "Evidence-based Survey of the Elimination Rates of Ethanol from Blood with Applications in Forensic Casework," 200 FORENSIC SCI. INT'L 1–20 (2010).

[83] Beer ferments to an alcohol concentration of approximately 3 to 6 percent. A 12-ounce bottle of 3% beer contains about 1/3 ounce of alcohol; 4% beer would contain 1/2 ounce of alcohol. Wine ferments to an alcohol concentration of 12 to 14 percent; however, some wines have alcohol added to increase concentration up to 20%. Alcohol percentages of "hard" liquor can be determined by dividing the "proof" by 2, for example "100-proof" whiskey contains 50% alcohol.

[84] For discussion of plasma (or serum)/whole blood distribution of water and alcohol concentration, see Alan W. Jones, "Biomarkers of Recent Drinking, Retrograde Extrapolation of Blood-Alcohol Concentration and Plasma-to-Blood Distribution Ratio in a Case of Driving Under the Influence of Alcohol," 18 J. FORENSIC & LEGAL MED. 213–216 (2011).

[85] See Alan W. Jones, "Alcohol" and "Alcohol: Analysis" in WILEY ENCYCLOPEDIA OF FORENSIC SCIENCE, (Jamieson A. & Moenssens A.A., eds) 2009 & online updates.

The conversion factor used in the analysis may be prescribed by law. See Cal. Code Regs., tit. 17, § 1220.4(e)(setting the partition ratio for urine/blood as 1.3).

[86] Measured blood alcohol concentration in an individual "gives an indication about the quantity of alcohol absorbed and distributed in all body fluids at the time the blood sample was taken." Alan W. Jones and Anita Holmgren, "Age and Gender Differences in Blood-Alcohol Concentration in Apprehended Drivers in Relation to the Amounts of Alcohol Consumed," 188 FORENSIC SCI. INT'L 40–45, at 41 (2009).

reductions in judgment, response to stimuli, and impulse control. At higher concentrations, blood alcohol causes a noticeable loss of muscular control with a lengthening of reaction time, confusion, and disturbance of sensory perception such as hearing and vision. Deteriorations in motor functions occur as a result of the weakened effectiveness of nerve impulse transmissions. At even higher concentration, stupor approaching paralysis results. Finally, at maximal sub-lethal concentration, the individual lapses into unconsciousness with depression of reflexes and impairment of circulation.

Manifestations of alcoholic influence are not uniform. Different responses to similar alcohol consumption result from (1) less alcohol going into the bloodstream because of different consumption tolerances of absorption, distribution, and elimination; and (2) the constitutional tolerance involving a variable susceptibility to alcohol in the nerve cell. At certain blood alcohol concentrations, however, everyone is impaired to a significant degree.

2.   GENERAL ASPECTS OF TESTING FOR ALCOHOL CONCENTRATION

Since impairment of a person's faculties is, in a general sense, proportional to the blood alcohol concentration (BAC), BAC is used as the scientific determinant of whether an individual is "intoxicated" or "under the influence" of alcohol. Because drawing blood is invasive and requires some medical training, the use of other bodily specimens is preferred. Alcohol concentration in another bodily specimen can be converted to a blood alcohol concentration because of the standard proportionality between the water content in blood and the water content in the other bodily specimens.

Of the other bodily specimen tests, the simplest and most socially acceptable one, which has been accepted by the courts as scientifically valid as well, is the test of a specimen of breath. Expelled "deep lung" or "alveolar" air will reflect with a reasonable degree of accuracy a breath alcohol concentration proportional to blood alcohol concentration. Although the partition ratio varies[87] between individuals and within the same individual depending on various factors such as temperature, blood alcohol concentration (BAC) is approximately 2100 times breath alcohol

---

[87] The size of this variance between BrAC and BAC in individuals has been the subject of scientific debate. In a study that was conducted in 2011, the researchers concluded that the study "confirmed a high degree of correlation between BAC and BrAC." Dena H. Jaffe et al., "Variability in the Blood/Breath Alcohol Ratio and Implications for Evidentiary Purposes," 58 J. Forensic Sci. 1233–1237 (2013). This conclusion was criticized, however, for relying on the mean of all test results that were measured at several times after alcohol consumption even though the data indicated "significant overall [and sometime substantial] variability existed between BrAC and BAC measurements obtained from any given individual." Okorie Okorocha, "Commentary on Jaffe DH, Siman-Tov M, Gopher A, Pelef K. Variability in the blood/breath alcohol ratio and implications for evidentiary purposes," 58 J. Forensic Sci. 1405 (2013). In other words, although BrAC and BAC may be strongly correlated in general, in any particular individual the variance between breath test readings and blood alcohol concentration may be large—either over or under estimating BAC.

concentration (BrAC), so the conversion factor commonly used in forensic analysis is 2100:1 (BAC = BrAC x 2100).[88]

One of the principal values of the tests for alcohol is the means afforded for ascertaining whether a person's questionable conduct may be attributed to alcohol, or whether it may be the result of some other nonalcohol factor, *e.g.,* medical conditions causing impaired motor skills or judgment. The scientific determinations from alcohol testing of bodily specimens are (a) whether alcohol is present in a tested person's system at the time of the test, and (b) the approximate percentage of alcohol present at that time in terms of blood volume content.

Based on a common equation (Widmark's equation), an individual's blood alcohol concentration can be extrapolated to an alcoholic content (or the amount of alcohol consumed) during a preceding period—for example, thirty minutes or one or more hours prior to that time. Retrograde extrapolation[89] of BAC "is a mathematical analysis in which a known blood alcohol test result is used to determine what an individual's blood alcohol level would have been at a specified earlier time. The analysis determines the prior blood alcohol level on the basis of (1) the time elapsed between the occurrence of the specified earlier event (e.g., a vehicle crash) and the known blood test, and (2) the rate of elimination of alcohol from the subject's blood during the time between the event and the test."[90] Using an application of the average rates of absorption and elimination of alcohol from the body, the expert will provide an estimate of the person's BAC at the relevant time. Although illegal *per se* statutes (see Section 13.10(1) *infra*) have limited the relevance of retrograde extrapolation evidence in alcohol impaired driving cases,[91]

---

[88] Like the partition ratio used for urine/blood alcohol concentration conversions, the blood/breath ratio is frequently established by state code or regulation. *See* Va. Code § 18.2–266 and Va. Admin. Code, title 6, § 40–20–10 (" 'Blood alcohol concentration' means percent by weight of alcohol in a person's blood based upon grams of alcohol per 100 milliliters of blood or grams of alcohol per 210 liters of breath.")

[89] Retrograde extrapolation of blood alcohol concentration is a complex scientific evaluation that is impacted by a number of variables. *See* Alan W. Jones, "Alcohol" in WILEY ENCYCLOPEDIA OF FORENSIC SCIENCE, (Jamieson A. & Moenssens A.A., eds) 2009 & online updates. For a detailed discussion of the uncertainty associated with retrograde extrapolation, *see* Rod G. Gullberg, "Estimating the Uncertainty Associated with Widmark's Equation as Commonly Applied in Forensic Toxicology," 172 FORENSIC SCI. INT'L 33–39 (2007). For a discussion of variables affecting the calculation, *see* David W. Sadler and Joanna Fox, "Intra-Individual and Inter-Individual Variation in Breath Alcohol Pharmacokinetics: The Effects of Food on Absorption," 51 SCI. & JUSTICE 3–9 (2011).

While some courts allow retrograde extrapolation as evidence, expert testimony may be necessary to establish its reliability and admissibility. *See* People v. Barham, 337 Ill.App.3d 1121, 272 Ill.Dec. 993, 788 N.E.2d 297 (2003).

[90] State v. Cook, 362 N.C. 285, 288, 661 S.E.2d 874, 876 (2008).

[91] The methodology is also used in drug impaired driving cases and other contexts. *See* People v. Jimenez, 242 Cal. App. 4th, 197 Cal. Rptr. 3d 1 (2015)(using drug half-life, expert testified that the blood concentration of methamphetamine would not have changed significantly over a period of an hour).

several courts have discussed the issue and reached inconsistent admissibility determinations.[92]

§13.07 INSTRUMENTATION AND METHODS

1.   BLOOD TESTING

Blood alcohol analysis has traditionally been regarded as the "gold standard" quantitative method to determine a person's alcohol impairment level, but it is invasive, time-consuming, and expensive.[93] Three types of methods may be used to detect and quantify alcohol in blood: (1) chemical methods; (2) biochemical methods; or (3) gas chromatographic methods. Currently, the most scientifically accepted method for the analysis of blood alcohol concentration is headspace gas chromatography with a flame ionization detector after dilution of the blood specimen with aqueous n-propanol as the internal standard.[94]

Chromatography is a technique to separate the individual components of a complex mixture. Alcohol can be detected in the blood by using headspace sampling (the gas space above the liquid in the sample vial) and gas chromatographic analysis.[95] In gas chromatography (GC),[96] the separation of substances occurs through the relative solubility between the moving gas phase (usually helium or hydrogen) and a micro-liquid layer bonded to a silica support (the chromatographic column). The column is maintained at a precisely controlled temperature which is a key parameter in the effective separation of the sample components. The alcohols and other volatile substances in the sample are encouraged to form an equilibrium

---

[92] *See* State v. Green, 707 S.E.2d 715 (N.C. Ct. App. 2011)(affirming admission of retrograde extrapolation expert testimony); United States v. Tsosie, 791 F.Supp.2d 1099 (Dist. N.M. 2011)(admitting retrograde extrapolation); Mata v. State, 46 S.W.3d 902, 916 (Tx. Crim. App. 2001)(reversing trial court's admission of expert testimony regarding retrograde extrapolation, highlighting numerous concerns about the expert's analysis including mathematical errors and inconsistent statements, but noting that "the science of retrograde extrapolation can be reliable in a given case"); Smith v. City of Tuscaloosa, 601 So.2d 1136, 1140 (Ala. Crim. App. 1992)(citing sources critical of retrograde extrapolation, but concluding that "the issue of whether any expert should be allowed to testify to a defendant's blood-alcohol content based upon the application of the process of retrograde extrapolation has not been presented or preserved for review").

[93] Since it is the alcohol in arterial blood that impacts the brain, the arterial blood (blood from a radial artery) concentration, as opposed to venous blood (from a cubital vein) concentration is actually the most relevant measure of alcohol impairment. *See* D. Grubb, *et al.*, "Breath Alcohol Analysis Incorporating Standardization of Water Vapour is as Precise as Blood Alcohol Analysis," 216 FORENSIC SCI. INT'L 88–91 (2012).

Collection of arterial blood in living persons is impractical, so venous blood is routinely used.

[94] Alan W. Jones, "Evidence-based Survey of the Elimination Rates of Ethanol from Blood with Applications in Forensic Casework," 200 FORENSIC SCI. INT'L 1–20 (2010), *see also* Alan W. Jones and J. Schuberth, "Computer-aided Headspace Gas Chromatography Applied to Blood-Alcohol Analysis: Important of Online Process Control," 34 J. FORENSIC SCI. 1116–1127 (1989).

[95] Barry K. Logan, "Analysis of Alcohol and Other Volatiles," GAS CHROMATOGRAPHY IN FORENSIC SCIENCE 87 (1992).

[96] Gas chromatography is also discussed in Chapter 15: Controlled Substance Analysis.

between the headspace and liquid in the vial by incubation of the vial in an oven, the headspace is sampled and then mixed with the mobile gas phase through the column. During the passage through the column, the sample components separate between the gas phase and the stationary phase depending on the component's physical and chemical properties. The relative affinity for either the moving phase or the stationary phase determines how fast the components will move through the column (the "retention time"). When combined with specific detectors or spectrometric analysis, identification of the separated material can be made based on their retention times. Flame ionization detectors (FID) are used in the analysis of alcohol in blood specimens to detect and quantify the blood alcohol concentration. The carrier gas and the substances exit the column and enter the burning flame to produce ions and electrons that pass between an anode and cathode (positive and negative poles) and the flowing current is measured, producing a chromatogram which can be used for the qualitative and quantitative analysis of the components.[97]

The possible contaminating effects of swabbing the skin with a disinfecting alcohol immediately prior to collecting a blood sample have been experimentally tested on many occasions and have been found to be non-existent or negligible.[98]

2. BREATH TESTS

As previously stated, of the various chemical tests for alcoholic intoxication, the preferred testing method, considered in the context of practicability, uses breath specimens. Breath tests that measure the presence and quantity of alcohol in a person's breath (and by conversion—in a person's blood) may be used in probable cause determinations, as evidence at trial of a person's BrAC or BAC level, and for enforcing alcohol restrictions.

Breath tests for alcoholic intoxication are based upon the premise that breath specimens are saturated with alcohol vapor at the temperature of the normal respiratory tract. The exchange of the alcohol that is in blood into the breath occurs in the alveolar sacs (deep lung tissue) in the lungs. Alcohol breath tests are an indirect means of establishing blood alcohol content, and an analytical method that has additional influencing factors than the blood analysis for alcohol content.[99] There is, of course, much less alcohol that is transferred to the

---

[97] *See* Alan W. Jones, "Alcohol: Analysis" in WILEY ENCYCLOPEDIA OF FORENSIC SCIENCE, (Jamieson A. & Moenssens A.A., eds) 2009 & online updates.

[98] *See, e.g.,* K. W. Ryder and M.R. Glick, "The Effect of Skin Cleansing Agents on Ethanol Results Measured with the Du Pont Automatic Clinical Analyzer," 31 J. FORENSIC SCI. 574–579 (1986); Alan W. Jones and J. Schuberth, "Computer Aided Headspace Gas Chromatography Applied to Blood-Alcohol Analysis: Importance of Online Process Control," 34 J. FORENSIC SCI. 1116–1127 (1989).

[99] One factor that must be considered in breath alcohol analysis is the presence of alcohol dissolved in the mucous surfaces of the mouth from a recent drink, burping, or other gastro esophageal reflexes ("mouth alcohol") which will artificially inflate the breath alcohol level out of

breath than is in the blood. The rate, or proportion, of alcohol in blood to alcohol in breath, is known as the partition rate. Since 1950, it has been generally accepted that the ratio is approximately 1 to 2,100.[100] Although there continues to be much debate about the applicability of this ratio,[101] the legal issue has been obviated by statutes which base liability on the breath alcohol measurement directly.[102]

An important aspect of breath testing is the calibration and standardization of the testing devices. In 1973, the NHTSA published Standards for Devices to Measure Breath Alcohol Content, and in 1974 NHTSA first issued a list of qualified breath testing devices that met the standards. In 1984, NHTSA converted the standards to model specifications and published a "Conforming Products List" (CPL) of devices meeting the model specifications. Since then the NHTSA has periodically updated the specifications and updated the CPL after testing all commercially available devices against the specifications.[103]

The analytical capabilities of breath testing devices have been extensively researched and the current generation of breath testing devices have demonstrated reliability and minimized interfering effects.[104] The accuracy and precision of the testing devices must be

---

proportion to the BAC. To control for residual mouth alcohol, breath alcohol testing should involve an observation period of 15–20 minutes (in which the subject does not drink or experience the gastro esophageal effects) to avoid the risk of mouth alcohol contamination. *See* Alan W. Jones, "Alcohol: Analysis" in WILEY ENCYCLOPEDIA OF FORENSIC SCIENCE, (Jamieson A. & Moenssens A.A., eds) 2009 & online updates. The 15 minute observation or deprivation period has been confirmed to be sufficient to dissipate mouth alcohol by experimental studies. See Kari Sterling, "The Rate of Dissipation of Mouth Alcohol in Alcohol Positive Subjects," 57 J. FORENSIC SCI. 802–805 (2012).

See People v. Bonutti, 212 Ill.2d 182, 288 Ill.Dec. 131, 817 N.E.2d 489 (2004)(results of the defendant's breath alcohol test suppressed where the defendant proved that he experienced a silent gastro esophageal reflux) See also Helen W. Gunnarrson, "DUI: The Acid Reflux Defense," ILL. LAW J., 12 (Vol. 92, Nov. 2004).

[100] R. N. Harger et al., "The Partition Ratio of Alcohol Between Air and Water, Urine and Blood: Estimation and Identification of Alcohol in Those Liquids from Analysis of Air Calibrated with Them," 183 J. BIOLOGICAL CHEM. 197 (1950); H. R. Harger et al., "Estimation of the Level of Blood Alcohol from the Analysis of Breath," 36 J. LAB. CLIN. MED. 306 (1950).

The National Highway Traffic Safety Administration has formulated specifications for breath testing equipment which define BAC to be the "Blood alcohol concentration, expressed in percent weight by volume (% w/v) based upon grams of alcohol per cubic centimeters of blood or per 210 liters of breath . . ." \49 FR 48857. Similarly, the Committee on Alcohol and Other Drugs, National Safety Council, specifies that 1-to-2,100 is the accurate ratio to determine BAC from breath tests. 49 FR 48855.

[101] *See, e.g.,* Michael P. Hlastala, "Paradigm Shift for the Alcohol Breath Test," 55 J. FORENSIC SCI. 451–456 (2010); James G. Wigmore, "Commentary on: Paradigm Shift for the Alcohol Breath Test," 56 J. FORENSIC SCI. 266–267 (2011).

[102] *See* Va. Code § 18.2–266.

[103] The updated listing of Approved Evidential Breath Testing Devices is available online at: https://www.transportation.gov/odapc/approved-evidential-breath-testing-devices (last accessed November 8, 2016).

[104] *See* Michele Glinn, Felix Adatsi and Perry Curtis, "Comparison of the Analytical Capabilities of the BAC Datamaster and Datamaster DMT Forensic Breath Testing Devices," 56 J. FORENSIC SCI. 1632–1638 (2011)(noting no evidential effects from objects in the mouth, mouth alcohol, acetone, and radiofrequency interference); Rong-Jen Hwang et al., "Measurement of Uncertainty for Aqueous Ethanol Wet-Bath Simulator Solutions Used with

ensured, not only through performance capabilities of the instrument, but also through the periodic calibration and maintenance of the instrument during use.[105] Calibration uses samples of known alcohol concentration to ensure that the instrument produces the accurate measurement. Failure to regularly calibrate the instrument can lead to incorrect results, as the District of Columbia admitted in 2010 when it removed all breathalyzers from service in its jurisdiction.[106]

Most jurisdictions require breath testing devices to be approved by a governmental agency for the results to be admissible as evidence in impaired driving prosecutions.[107] The requirement may depend on NHTSA approval or additional agency approval within the jurisdiction. For example, the Commonwealth of Virginia requires breath testing devices to be approved by the Department of Forensic Science from the NHTSA Conforming Products List and for the Department to periodically publish the list of approved devices.[108]

a. Preliminary Breath Tests

"Preliminary breath testing" devices (PBTs), sometimes referred to as "roadside screening devices," are one means of establishing probable cause for an impaired driving arrest. PBTs are portable devices (usually handheld and slightly larger than a cellphone) that detect the presence of consumable alcohol in a driver's breath. The PBT displays either a numerical BrAC value or an indication (*e.g.,* a colored light) that a specified level has been exceeded. PBTs are given prior to arrest for impaired driving and most jurisdictions have statutes limiting admission of the results in impaired driving cases to determinations of probable cause to make an arrest for impaired driving.[109] These statutory

---

Evidential Breath Testing Instruments," 60 J. Forensic Sci. 1359–1363 (2016)(studying the measurement of uncertainty for the calibration solutions for breath testing equipment).

[105] Rod G. Gullberg, "Methodology and Quality Assurance in Forensic Breath Alcohol Testing," 12 FORENSIC SCI. REV. 49–68 (2000).

[106] The possibility that incorrect BrAC results had been used in support of impaired driving criminal convictions also resulted in civil litigation against the District of Columbia and officials involved. *See* Jones v. District of Columbia, et al., 2011 D.C. Super. LEXIS 9 (Superior Ct. of DC 2011).

[107] *See, e.g.,* Va. Code 18.2–268.9 (A): "To be capable of being considered valid as evidence in a prosecution under § 18.2–266, 18.2–266.1, or subsection B of § 18.2–272, or a similar ordinance, chemical analysis of a person's breath shall be performed by an individual possessing a valid license to conduct such tests, with a type of equipment and in accordance with methods approved by the Department."

[108] *See* Va. Admin. Code, title 6, § 40–20–80 (requiring VA DFS approval)(approved breath test devices and approved preliminary breath test devices listing available at: http://www.dfs.virginia .gov/laboratory-forensic-services/breath-alcohol/approved-devices/)(last accessed November 8, 2016).

[109] *See* Va. Code § 18.2–267:
"A. Any person who is suspected of a violation of § 18.2–266, 18.2–266.1, subsection B of § 18.2–272, or a similar ordinance shall be entitled, if such equipment is available, to have his breath analyzed to determine the probable alcoholic content of his blood. The person shall also be entitled, upon request, to observe the process of analysis and to see the blood-alcohol reading on the equipment used to perform the breath test. His breath may be analyzed by any police officer of the Commonwealth, or of any

restrictions, however, do not apply to the admission of the results in other contexts, such as civil cases.[110]

PBTs generally rely on electrochemical (fuel cell) sensors to enable alcohol-specific testing in a relatively small sensor unit. These PBT devices require a person to blow in a disposable plastic tube connected to the device for the collection and measurement of the breath sample. The breath sample enters a chamber fitted with an electrode (platinum disk) and an acidic electrolyte solution (such as phosphoric acid). The alcohol is converted through oxidation to acetic acid producing a number of electrons (a current) that is proportional to the concentration of the alcohol that is present in the sample.[111] The advantage of the fuel cell technology is its specificity for alcohol; the disadvantage is the lack of a mouth-alcohol detector, necessitating control measures such as the 15-minute observation period and duplicate testing.[112]

Common devices include the AlcoSensor (Intoximeters, Inc.), LifeLoc (manufactured by LifeLoc, Inc.), and Alcotest (manufactured by Draeger Safety Diagnostics, Inc.). Some of these devices are calibrated at a particular BrAC, such as .05% or .10%. Most devices give a "passfail" reading in the sense that the indicator response is either below or over a

---

county, city or town, or by any member of a sheriff's department in the normal discharge of his duties.

. . . .

C. Any person who has been stopped by a police officer of the Commonwealth, or of any county, city or town, or by any member of a sheriff's department and is suspected by such officer to be guilty of an offense listed in subsection A, shall have the right to refuse to permit his breath to be so analyzed, and his failure to permit such analysis shall not be evidence in any prosecution for an offense listed in subsection A.

D. Whenever the breath sample analysis indicates that alcohol is present in the person's blood, the officer may charge the person with a violation of an offense listed in subsection A. The person so charged shall then be subject to the provisions of §§ 18.2–268.1 through 18.2–268.12, or of a similar ordinance.

E. The results of the breath analysis shall not be admitted into evidence in any prosecution for an offense listed in subsection A, the purpose of this section being to permit a preliminary analysis of the alcoholic content of the blood of a person suspected of having committed an offense listed in subsection A."

In absence of statutory provisions concerning the use of PBTs, courts have split on whether the results are admissible to establish probable cause. *See* United States v. Iron Cloud, 171 F.3d 587, 590–591 (8th Cir. 1999)(PBTs may be used in probable cause determinations); Thompson v. State Dep't of Licensing, 138 Wn.2d 783, 982 P.2d 601, 603 n. 1 (Wash. 1999) (PBT results inadmissible to establish probable cause).

The statutory restrictions on the use of PBTs may only limit the prosecution's use of the results, and may not prevent the defense from introducing the results. *See* Fischer v. Ozaukee County Cir. Ct., 741 F.Supp.2d 944 (E.D. Wisc. 2010)(PBT results admitted to support defense expert's retrograde extrapolation opinion that the defendant's BAC was below .08% at the time of driving).

[110] *See* Rutledge v. NCL (Bahamas), Ltd., 464 Fed.Appx. 825 (11th Cir. 2012)(admitting the results of a "breath test screening" device that indicated BrAC exceeding .08% by color change as relevant to the issue of contributory negligence in a personal injury case).

[111] Robert J. Leonard, "Evaluation of the Analytical Performance of a Fuel Cell Breath Alcohol Testing Instrument: A Seven-Year Comprehensive Study," 57 J. FORENSIC SCI. 1614–1620 (2012).

[112] Id.

calibrated setting, however, some devices give a numerical BrAC reading. Research comparing readings of two PBT's (the Alco-Sensor III and the Alco-Sensor FST) to evidential BrAC test results (from the Datamaster instrument) found the PBT readings to be statistically accurate in predicting the subsequent evidential BrAC results.[113]

b.   *Evidentiary Breath Tests*

Most evidential breath testing devices incorporate infrared spectrometry (IR) to increase the specificity of the analysis. Like the fuel cell technology of the PBTs, IR analysis requires the subject to make a continuous forced exhalation to provide deep lung air into a sample chamber. Analysis of the sample is done by measuring the absorption of infrared radiation. Ethanol molecules absorb radiation at specific wavelengths (3.4 and 9.5 µm). The amount of radiation absorbed is proportional to the alcohol concentration in the breath sample. IR technology also employs a slope detector to help monitor the breath-alcohol exhalation profile to distinguish the deep lung alveolar air.[114] The advantage of IR technology is its ability to make continuous measurements during the course of the sample delivery to ensure sampling of the deep lung air to avoid residual mouth alcohol effects;[115] the disadvantages are the maintenance costs of regular calibration to address the relative instability of the IR sensors.[116]

The United States Department of Transportation maintains a list of "Approved Evidential Breath Testing Devices" on its website.[117] The approved devices meet the standards of the NHTSA and comply with detailed specifications in documenting results. Details of the specifications of the various testing devices are usually provided on the manufacturer's website.[118]

---

[113] The study noted that only highly trained and experienced officers were used to conduct the PBT testing. Nayak L. Polissar et al., "The Accuracy of Handheld Pre-Arrest Breath Test Instruments as a Preidctor of Evidential Breath Alcohol Test Results," 60 J. Forensic Sci. 482–487 (2015). *See also* Robert L. Leonard, "Evaluation of the Analytical Performance of a Fuel Cell Breath Alcohol Testing Instrument: A Seven Year Comprehensive Study," 57 J. Forensic Sci. 1614–1620 (2012).

[114] Alan W. Jones, "Alcohol: Analysis" in WILEY ENCYCLOPEDIA OF FORENSIC SCIENCE, (Jamieson A. & Moenssens A.A., eds) 2009 & online updates.

The slope detector helps to avoid the risk of contamination of the measurement by residual mouth alcohol. The 15–20 minute observational period prior to testing, however, is still recommended even with devices utilizing the slope detectors.

[115] Mouth alcohol effects are generally counteracted by a required minimum observation period (usually 15-20 minutes) before testing. *See* Kari Sterling, "The Rate of Dissipation of Mouth Alcohol in Alcohol Positive Subjects," 57 J. Forensic Sci. 802–805 (2012).

[116] Dariusz Zuba, "Accuracy and Reliability of Breath Alcohol Testing by Handheld Electrochemical Analysers" 178 FORENSIC SCI. INT'L e29–e33 (2008).

[117] *See*   https://www.transportation.gov/odapc/approved-evidential-breath-testing-devices (last accessed November 8, 2016).

[118] For example, product information on the Intox EC/IR II is available at: http://www.intox.com/p-562-intox-ecir-ii.aspx (last accessed June 16, 2016). Detailed descriptions of the Intox EC/IR II instrument and discussions of the procedures involved in evidential breath testing are provided in the Virginia Department of Forensic Science "Breath Alcohol Training Manual" (April 25, 2016) and "Breath Alcohol Procedures Manual" (February 26, 2016)

3.   OTHER BODILY SPECIMENS

Alcohol in the body can be measured through any bodily specimens that contain water.[119] Blood and breath are overwhelmingly the specimens most commonly used, but urine and perspiration may also be used. Implied consent statutes in many states provide for chemical testing of urine in addition to blood or breath analysis,[120] and perspiration alcohol testing is sometimes used to monitor compliance with court restrictions on alcohol use.

Alcohol concentration in urine can be measured through the same three methods typically used to detect and quantify alcohol in a blood specimen: (1) chemical methods; (2) biochemical methods; or (3) gas chromatographic methods. As with blood analysis, the most scientifically accepted method for the analysis of urine alcohol concentration is headspace gas chromatography with a flame ionization detector after dilution of the specimen with aqueous n-propanol as the internal standard.[121]

Urine contains about 1.3 times as much water as blood, and therefore, 1.3 times as much alcohol. Alcohol concentration from urine specimens can be converted to BAC by virtue of this known relationship between the water content of urine as compared to water content of blood. Urine alcohol concentration, when converted, yields the average blood alcohol concentration during the time the urine was accumulating in the bladder.[122] To pin it down to a specific time, the researchers advise that the bladder be emptied and that a test specimen be collected 30 minutes later. The results of a urine test may be affected by the bladder condition before or after the consumption of alcohol. If alcohol is consumed with a full bladder the tests would inaccurately underestimate the degree of blood alcohol content. Conversely, if the individual consumed alcohol with an empty bladder some time prior to the test and had not voided himself recently, the results could easily overestimate the amount of alcohol in the blood at the time of the test.[123]

(available at: http://www.dfs.virginia.gov/laboratory-forensic-services/breath-alcohol/publications-and-resources/)(last accessed June 21, 2016).

[119] Alan W. Jones, "Alcohol: Analysis" in WILEY ENCYCLOPEDIA OF FORENSIC SCIENCE, (Jamieson A. & Moenssens A.A., eds) 2009 & online updates.

[120] See, e.g., Ala. Code § 32–5–192(a); Ariz. Code § 28–1321(A); Conn. Gen. Stat. § 14–227(b)(a); Ga. Code § 40–5–55(a).

[121] For a detailed, step-by-step description of GC analysis of alcohol in bodily specimens, see Alan W. Jones, "Alcohol: Analysis" in WILEY ENCYCLOPEDIA OF FORENSIC SCIENCE, (Jamieson A. & Moenssens A.A., eds) 2009 & online updates.

[122] See People v. Acevedo, 93 Cal.App.4th 757, 113 Cal.Rptr.2d 437 (2001)(defendant entitled to challenge the appropriateness of the "partition ratio" used in the conversion of urine alcohol concentration to blood alcohol concentration).

[123] Using urine tests in conjunction with a blood test can be helpful in disproving claims of post-driving drinking based on the completeness of the absorption and distribution of alcohol in the body fluids. See Alan W. Jones and Fredrik C. Kugelberg, "Relationship Between Blood and Urine Alcohol Concentrations in Apprehended Drivers Who Claimed Consumption of

Urine is commonly used for the detection of the metabolites of alcohol consumption (ethyl glucuronide and ethyl sulfate) in abstinence monitoring programs because the analysis has high sensitivity and specificity (it can detect the consumption of very small amounts of alcohol).[124]

Unlike urine specimen testing, which poses collection issues and requires laboratory analysis, alcohol concentration analysis through sweat is noninvasive, rapid, and much more amenable to monitoring situations. Secure Continuous Remote Alcohol Monitor (SCRAM) bracelets (or more accurately "anklets" since the devices are attached to the lower leg or ankle) measure concentrations of transdermal alcohol— alcohol perspired through a person's skin as perspiration.[125] Transdermal alcohol concentration (TAC) rises and falls on a curve approximately two hours behind the blood alcohol concentration curve consistent with the difference in the rate of absorption of alcohol in the blood and the rate of expiration of alcohol through the skin. The SCRAM device uses a fuel cell to detect alcohol in the vapor from the skin drawn into the collection chamber of the device. The fuel cell technology is similar to the technology used in breath alcohol testing devices discussed *supra*. The device electronically transmits data to a monitoring service and an alert is provided to the supervising entity (probation, court services, etc.) if a positive reading is detected. The device does not record a specific quantitative alcohol concentration, but generally does provide a qualitative assessment of quantity consumed (small, moderate, or large amounts). Research concerning the reliability of the devices has been funded by the manufacturer and the NHTSA.[126] Results from the devices have been admitted to demonstrate alcohol consumption in probation proceedings.[127]

Alcohol After Driving With and Without Supporting Evidence," 194 FORENSIC SCI. INT'L 97–102 (2010).

[124] *See* Annette Thierauf et al., "Urine Tested Positive for Ethyl Glucuronide and Ethyl Sulphate After the Consumption of 'Non-Alcoholic' Beer," 202 FORENSIC SCI. INT'L 82–85 (2010). Hair can also be used to test for longer periods of abstinence than urine. See Ronald Agius, Thomas Nadulski, Hans-Gerhard Kahl and Bertin Dufaux, "Ethyl Glucuronide in Hair—A Highly Effective Test for the Monitoring of Alcohol Consumption," 218 FORENSIC SCI. INT'L 10–14 (2012).

[125] SCRAM bracelets are manufactured by Alcohol Monitoring Systems, Inc. The most recent model of the device is SCRAM CAM. For detailed product information, see http://www.alcoholmonitoring.com/ (last accessed June 21, 2016).

[126] "Evaluating Transdermal Alcohol Measuring Devices," National Highway Traffic Safety Administration, November, 2007. (available at: https://www.scramsystems.com/images/uploads/general/research/evaluating-transdermal-alcohol-measuring-devices.pdf)(last accessed June 21, 2016).

[127] Mogg v. State, 918 N.E.2d 750 (Ct. App. Ind. 2009).

IV. TRIAL AIDS

§13.08 EXPERT QUALIFICATIONS

The determination of whether a witness is qualified to give opinion testimony will be left to the "sound discretion" of the trial court.[128] This determination will not be overturned absent a showing of abuse of this discretion.[129] While either formal study or sufficient practical experience ordinarily suffices to qualify one as an expert in a particular subject area, in the area of forensic toxicology, some formal education in a related science is generally present.[130] Relevant fields of study could include: chemistry, biochemistry, toxicology, serology, hematology, or pharmacology, depending upon the material at issue.

With increasing use and weight being put on forensic evidence, the U.S. Department of Justice's Office of Justice Programs developed a set guidelines called the "Education and Training in Forensic Science: A Guide for Forensic Science Laboratories, Educational Institutions, and Students." The guide is designed to help universities develop forensic science programs that will train forensic scientists to fulfill their role in the criminal justice community.[131] For forensic toxicology, the Scientific Working Group for Forensic Toxicology (SWGTOX),[132] issued detailed standards for laboratory personnel and breath alcohol personnel delineating the "minimum requirements for educational qualifications, training, competency, experience, continuing education, and professional development, and certification for laboratory personnel and breath alcohol personnel.[133] Adopted in 2014, the SWGTOX guidelines will remain effective until updated by the National Institute of

---

[128] U.S. v. Garza, 448 F.3d 294 (5th Cir.2006); U.S. v. Middlebrook, 141 Fed.Appx. 834 (11th Cir.2005); Redi Roast Products, Inc. v. Burnham, 531 So.2d 664 (Ala.Civ.App.1988); Cody v. Louisville & Nashville R. Co., 535 So.2d 82 (Ala.1988); Mathis v. Glover, 714 S.W.2d 222 (Mo.App.1986).

[129] In Stuart v. Director of Revenue, 761 S.W.2d 234 (Mo.App.1988), the trial court was found to have abused its discretion in rejecting the testimony of a police officer trained in the operation of the breathalyzer.

[130] *But see* State v. Wakefield, 781 S.E.2d 222 (W.Va. 2015)(former police officer allowed to testify as an expert in GHB intoxication based on her work experience with drug facilitated sexual assaults).

[131] U.S. Department of Justice, National Institute of Justice, *Education and Training in Forensic Science: A Guide for Forensic Science Laboratories, Educational Institutions, and Students* (2004)(available at: https://www.ncjrs.gov/pdffiles1/nij/203099.pdf)(last accessed March 2, 2017).

[132] SWGTOX was a voluntary association of experts in the field working to develop and disseminate consensus standards for the practice of forensic toxicology. The organization was supported through the National Institute of Justice until the National Institute of Standards and Technology created the Organization of Scientific Area Committees (OSAC). Forensic toxicology standards are being addressed by the Toxicology Subcommittee of the Chemistry/Instrumental Analysis Committee.

[133] Scientific Working Group for Forensic Toxicology (SWGTOX) Standard for Laboratory Personnel, SWGTOX Doc 006, Revision 1, October 9, 2014; Scientific Working Group for Forensic Toxicology (SWGTOX) Standard for Breath Alcohol Personnel, SWGTOX Doc 005, Revision 1, October 9, 2014. These standards are available at: www.swgtox.org (last accessed June 20, 2016).

Standards and Technology Organization of Scientific Area Committees (NIST OSAC), Chemical/Instrumental Analysis Committee, Toxicology Subcommittee.[134]

It is desirable for the attorney to contact practitioners in a specialty field and inquire as to the specialized knowledge and training required to function effectively in the area. Although the field of forensic toxicology is essentially a subspecialty within analytical chemistry, the proposed expert should have acquired, through experience and specialized training, a working familiarity with relevant aspects of biology, pharmacology, and physiology.

Although certification or licensing[135] is generally not a legal requirement for court qualification as an expert, some states do require certification or licensing as conditions of employment or testimony.[136] The National Academy of Science has recommended establishing mandatory certification of all forensic scientists[137] and on June 21, 2016, the National Commission on Forensic Sciences issued for public comment a draft document calling for certification of all forensic science practitioners within five years of adoption of the document.[138] Certification has been available for toxicologists since 1975 through the American Board of Forensic Toxicology. Certification is available for two levels: Fellow and Diplomate. Both levels have education and experience requirements and successful completion of a comprehensive written examination on the principles and practice of analytical toxicology. Certification may be suspended or revoked pursuant to the organization's guidelines and standards.[139]

The qualifications of expert witnesses in alcohol intoxication prosecutions vary widely, depending on the specific testimony offered and encompassing the broad discretion courts have in qualifying expert witnesses. For breath test operators, courts rarely require formal academic degrees,[140] applying the principle reflected in the following

[134] See https://www.nist.gov/topics/forensic-science/toxicology-subcommittee.

[135] Jones v. Jones, 117 Idaho 621, 790 P.2d 914 (1990). Some states do require forensic science testing to be conducted by an accredited laboratory to be admissible in criminal proceedings. See Art. 38.35 Texas Code of Criminal Procedure: Forensic Analysis of Evidence; Admissibility; Sec. 411.0205 Texas Government Code.

[136] See Tex. Code Crim. Proc. Art 38.01 § 4–a(b)(effective January 1, 2019)(making licensing by the Texas Forensic Science Commission mandatory for forensic science practitioners in the state crime laboratories that are subject to mandatory accreditation).

[137] Recommendation 1(b), National Academy of Science, Strengthening Forensic Science in the United States: A Path Forward, National Academies Press, 2009.

[138] See Agenda for Meeting June 20–21, 2016 (available: https://www.justice.gov/ncfs/file/865141/download)(last accessed June 21, 2016). The subcommittee draft document is available at: https://www.justice.gov/ncfs/file/864991/download (last accessed June 20, 2016).

[139] Information concerning certification requirements and general information about ABFT is available at: www.abft.org.

[140] The SWGTOX standards also do not impose educational requirements on breath test operators, who are considered fact witnesses by SWGTOX. Associate or bachelor's degrees are considered the minimum for technicians, analysts, toxicologists, and technical directors of the breath alcohol programs. See Scientific Working Group for Forensic Toxicology (SWGTOX)

case excerpt: "As pertains to the sufficiency of an expert's qualifications, we discern no qualitative difference between credentials based on formal, academic training and those acquired through practical experience."[141] As with any expert testimony, the expert's qualification with respect to the particular issue that is the subject of the testimony is the determining factor.[142] It is necessary, however, that the witness received proper training in the usage of any breath test measuring devices and the conditions under which the test should be conducted. Courts will consider whether the testing has been conducted in conformity with prescribed procedures mandated by the relevant statute or the regulations established by the jurisdiction's designated agency.

In many jurisdictions only those persons who have passed state-required training are considered qualified to testify in court regarding breathalyzer test results. The permit issued by the state readily satisfies the court that the witness is qualified.[143] Of course, competence in administering the test cannot save its admission if it is established that the operator falsified breathalyzer results. Thus, in New Jersey, an undercover officer posing as a motorist caught a breathalyzer operator falsifying test results and extorting money from DUI arrestees. Thereafter, the Supreme Court of New Jersey held that persons convicted of drunken driving offenses on the basis of tests administered by the same officer were entitled to new trials, at which the state would have the burden of demonstrating that its BAC test evidence is free from the taint of the officer's misconduct.[144]

In criminal cases, toxicologists and related specialists are readily available to the prosecution as federal, state, or local crime laboratory personnel. In addition, such specialists are also available in governmental agencies such as the coroner or medical examiner's offices, government run medical facilities, and public health services. For the defense in a criminal case or the attorney in a civil action, unlike many other specialty areas of forensic science, expert assistance in these areas is widely available. Hospitals, clinics or private clinical laboratories are potential sources of assistance for toxicology examinations, and private analytical laboratories can provide chemical

---

Standard for Breath Alcohol Personnel, SWGTOX Doc 005, Revision 1, October 9, 2014, Appendix A, p. 15 (available at: www.swgtox.org)(last accessed June 20, 2016).

[141] Howerton v. Arai Helmet, Ltd., 358 N.C. 440, 462, 597 S.E.2d 674, 688 (2004).

[142] *See* City of South Milwaukee v. Hart, 337 Wis.2d 430, 805 N.W.2d 736 (Wis. Ct. App. 2011)(excluding proposed expert witness who was a chemist with training and certification in the alcohol-testing field because she had "no education, training, or experience in assessing periodontal disease *and* whether alcohol could or would be retained in the mouth as a result.").

[143] As to whether the state-issued permit establishes the witness's qualifications, *compare* State v. Batiste, 327 So.2d 420 (La.1976) and State v. Jones, 316 So.2d 100 (La.1975)(test results inadmissible unless operator physically produces official certification of a valid permit because official certificate is best evidence of operator's qualifications), *with* Davis v. State, 541 P.2d 1352 (Okl.Crim.App.1975)(testimony of operator that he possessed a valid permit is sufficient without introducing permit).

[144] State v. Gookins, 135 N.J. 42, 637 A.2d 1255 (1994).

analyses. These laboratories may also be able to provide expert testimony if required.

Other potential sources of expert assistance include national or regional societies in forensic science or the particular scientific discipline required. The American Academy of Forensic Sciences has a Toxicology Section with many recognized authorities experienced in expert testimony and who perform private work. Regional forensic societies such as the Mid Atlantic, Northwest, Southern or Midwest Associations of Forensic Science, and the California Association of Criminalists may suggest sources of expert assistance. Subject area societies such as the Society of Forensic Toxicology (SOFT) can also provide guidance to potential experts.

§13.09 EVIDENCE ISSUES—FORENSIC TOXICOLOGY IN GENERAL

The admissibility of toxicological test results and testimony are governed by the general guidelines for admissibility of expert testimony of the relevant jurisdiction (discussed in Chapter 1). Toxicologists are frequently allowed to testify to the effects of particular substances on the body even though they are not pharmacologists or medical doctors.[145] Similarly, a medical examiner, qualified as an expert, was permitted to testify to the results of a toxicology report even though he did not personally perform the tests.[146] Physicians are generally considered qualified to testify to physiological effects, even in the absence of personal experience and relying solely on published information.[147] Generally, in cases involving the reliability and methodology of forensic toxicology tests, courts have required expert testimony from toxicologists or similarly qualified witnesses.[148] Courts

---

[145] Ph.D. microbiologist and professor in a university medical school who had done research on Toxic Shock Syndrome permitted to testify to diagnosis and cause even though not a medical doctor. Baroldy v. Ortho Pharmaceutical Corp., 157 Ariz. 574, 760 P.2d 574 (1988). Biochemist, professor of biochemistry and immunology can testify regarding causal connection between flu vaccine and recipients' disease. Wyeth Laboratories v. Fortenberry, 530 So.2d 688 (Miss.1988). Ph.D. biochemist qualified as expert in pulmonary biochemistry and could testify to physiological effects of phosgene gas even though some of his testimony comprised medical opinion. Walls v. Olin Corp., Inc., 533 So.2d 1375 (La.App.3 Cir.1988). Testimony of toxicologist to effects of dibromochloropropane. Loudermill v. Dow Chemical, 863 F.2d 566 (8th Cir.1988); Toxicologist to intoxication in automobile accident. May v. Strecker, 453 N.W.2d 549 (Minn.App.1990); Biochemist to link PCB exposure with colon cancer. Rubanick v. Witco Chemical Corp., 242 N.J.Super. 36, 576 A.2d 4 (App.Div.1990), remanded to reconsider in light of new standard, 125 N.J. 421, 593 A.2d 733 (1991).

[146] Ellis v. Phillips, 2005 WL 1637826 (S.D.N.Y.2005), Commonwealth v. Gilliard, 300 Pa.Super. 469, 446 A.2d 951 (1982).

[147] U.S. v. Frazier, the court points out that physicians are not experts in every field and may not have experience in the particular field of medicine in question but have a general level of common knowledge and that "it would be ideal to have a citation to some medical publication." 387 F.3d 1244 (11th Cir.2004).

[148] Ruiz-Troche v. Pepsi Cola of Puerto Rico Bottling Co., 161 F.3d 77, 83–85 (1st Cir 1998)(pharmacologist could testify concerning the amount of drugs a driver consumed and the amount of the consumption through interpretation of toxicology results of driver's biological material specimens).

have restricted other experts, such as an expert in metallurgy, from testifying concerned the toxicity of elements and the capacity of those elements to be absorbed by humans because the expert was not a toxicologist, and therefore, "lacked the necessary medical knowledge and training."[149]

The Federal Judicial Center's Reference Manual on Scientific Evidence explains that "no single academic degree, research specialty, or career path qualifies an individual as an expert in toxicology [because toxicology is a] heterogenous field . . . [but] a proposed expert should be able to demonstrate an understanding of the discipline of toxicology, including statistics, toxicological research methods, and disease processes."[150] The manual also lists the following "indicia of expertise" to be considered on questions of admissibility and weights of the evidence: (1) an advanced degree in toxicology, pharmacology or related field; (2) board certification and membership in relevant professional organizations; and (3) quality and number of peer-reviewed articles, services on scientific advisory panels, and university appointments.[151]

Blood and urine drug testing has been deemed a reliable and accurate measure of drug use by a majority of courts. Immunoassay results are often accepted by courts as evidence of drug use in state parole, probation, and inmate good-time credit cases, even when a GC/MS confirmatory test has not been conducted.[152] Revocations of supervised release in federal court, however, are required by statute to have confirmation by GC/MS.[153]

The testing of hair for the use of narcotics has become an acceptable practice, although analytical methods have been treated differently by courts. In *United States v. Cravens*,[154] the Court noted the scientific reliability of hair analysis by GC/MS for testing for contraband drugs under *Daubert*. In *Cravens,* the Court noted that "forensic acceptability of hair testing relies on the same science, an immunoassay and gas chromatography/mass spectrometry (GC/MS) analysis, as tests for drugs in other body fluids and tissues."[155] Drug

---

[149] Jones v. Lincoln Electric Company, 188 F.3d 709, 723–724 (7th Cir. 1999), cert. denied, 529 U.S. 1067 (2000); *see also* Cooper v. Laboratory Corp. of Amer. Holdings, Inc., 150 F.3d 376, 380 (4th Cir. 1998)(results of urine alcohol testing properly excluded where witness was not a toxicologist and only had general knowledge of chemistry).

[150] Federal Judicial Center's Reference Manual on Scientific Evidence, §II at 415–416, 2d ed. (2000).

[151] Id. at 415–418.

[152] Louis v. Dep't of Corr. Servs. Of Neb., 437 F.3d 697 (8th Cir. 2006).

[153] 18 U.S.C. § 3583(d), provides, in pertinent part: "A drug test confirmation shall be a urine drug test confirmed using gas chromatography/mass spectrometry techniques or such test as the Director of the Administrative Office of the United States Courts after consultation with the Secretary of Health and Human Services may determine to be of equivalent accuracy."

[154] 56 M.J. 370 (United States Armed Forces 2002).

[155] 56 M.J. at 373.

analysis of hair by immunoassays alone, however, has not been uniformly accepted by the courts.[156]

In worker's compensation cases, courts have used hair-testing results indicating the presence of marijuana metabolites as evidence of the presence of marijuana to invoke a statutory presumption that an injury was substantially caused by the use of illegal drugs.[157]

In any scientific discipline, the validation of testing methodologies, adherence to professional standards, and the implementation of quality control systems are essential to obtaining reliable results. Forensic toxicology benefits from the various certification, guidelines, and standards that have been developed by government agencies (such as SAMHSA) and professional organizations (such as CAP, SOFT, ABFT, and AAFS). Adherence and proper implementation of these guidelines and standards should be verified for each case.

Even under optimal conditions, laboratory analysis involves a degree of uncertainty and there can be interpretation difficulties in forensic toxicology cases. Cross-reactivity of non-illegal substances in drug-use and human performance testing, such as codeine or poppy seeds with immunoassay tests for morphine consistent with heroin use, can complicate interpretation of results and may require additional testing.[158] Urinalysis drug tests detect metabolites of the substances rather than the substances themselves. As a result, screening tests sometimes incorrectly identify metabolites created by legal substances or human enzymes, such as the artificial production of the heroin metabolite (6-acetylmorphine) when aspirin and morphine are taken together as the metabolite of an illicit substance.[159]

The limitations of the specific testing methodology and the quality of the testing must also be considered to avoid false interpretations. An example of erroneous results from poor quality testing and from cross-reactivity of substances is the case of Patricia Stallings who was wrongfully accused of poisoning her son when toxicological results misidentified ethylene glycol (present in antifreeze) instead of another compound naturally produced by her son's metabolic disease.[160] Due diligence requires that attorneys understand the reliability factors and

---

[156] *Compare* Nevada Employ. Sec. Dep't v. Holmes, 112 Nev. 275, 914 P.2d 611 (Nev. 1996)(RIA hair analysis showing presence of cocaine substantial evidence to support employment termination); In re Adoption of Baby Boy L, 157 Misc.2d 353, 596 N.Y.S.2d 997 (N.Y. Fam Ct. 1993)(RIA results admissible) *with* United States v. Foote, 898 F.2d 659, 665 (8th Cir. 1990)(radioimmunoassay analysis of hair "intrusive" and "unreliable" in nature).

[157] Jackson v. Smith Blair, Inc., 210 Ark. App. 691 (2010); Waldrip v. Graco Corp., 101 Ark. App. 101, 270 S.W.3d 891 (2008).

[158] Warren D. Hamilton, "Drug Testing: Urine," in WILEY ENCYCLOPEDIA OF FORENSIC SCIENCE, (Jamieson A. & Moenssens A.A., eds) 2009 & online updates.

[159] *See*: Mark A. Rothstein, "Workplace Drug Testing: A Case Study in the Misapplication of Technology," 5 Harv. J.L. & Tech. 65, 74 (1991); Naso-Kasper et al., "In Vitro Formation of Acetylmorphine from Morphine and Aspirin in Postmortem Gastric Contents and Deionized Water," 37 J. Anal. Toxicol. 500 (2015).

[160] A summary of the case is available at www.justicedenied.org/patriciastallings.htm.

limitations of all forensic toxicology results that may be used as evidence.[161]

§13.10 EVIDENCE ISSUES—ALCOHOL INVESTIGATIONS

1. STATUTES

The available scientific literature regarding the various alcohol concentration testing methods is voluminous, and it is not feasible in a portion of any text to do more than discuss some of the basics of testing in understandable terminology to cover the relevant scientific principles and test procedures.[162] The legal aspects of the evidentiary value of the testing, however, are rather straightforward.[163]

All 50 states, the District of Columbia, Puerto Rico, and the federal government have enacted laws criminalizing performing certain conduct either with a certain blood alcohol concentration or while "under the influence" of alcohol.[164] The laws primarily focus on the operation of motor vehicles[165] and the results of the alcohol testing are either determinative of guilt or probative of the defendant's guilt or innocence. Statutes concerning impaired driving fall into two general categories: general "under the influence" statutes and illegal *per se* statutes.

---

[161] Attorneys should obtain and review all laboratory documentation necessary for an independent review, including the laboratory operational manuals, validation records, proficiency test results, accreditation and certification records, audit documentation, case intake and control records, quality control procedures, and any documentation related to the case samples, reference compounds, and reagents.

[162] At the conclusion of this Chapter there is an extensive bibliography of additional resources.

[163] The actual statutes involved, however, are frequently complex with detailed procedural requirements. Although common concepts are discussed in this Chapter, the practitioner must consult the specific statutes and case law in the relevant jurisdiction.

[164] Most states also have laws that prohibit driving while impaired by drugs other than alcohol, but the statutes vary greatly. Although many of the toxicological concepts of alcohol and drug testing of bodily fluids specimens are similar, the most commonly used testing for alcohol (breath analysis) is inapplicable to other drugs.

[165] Similar statutes may cover the operation of other transportation devices, such as watercraft or aircraft. *See* Va. Code § 29.1–738(B):

No person shall operate any watercraft, as defined in § 29.1712, or motorboat which is underway (i) while such person has a blood alcohol concentration at or greater than the blood alcohol concentration at which it is unlawful to drive or operate a motor vehicle as provided in § 18.2–266 as indicated by a chemical test administered in accordance with § 29.1738.2, (ii) while such person is under the influence of alcohol, (iii) while such person is under the influence of any narcotic drug or any other self-administered intoxicant or drug of whatsoever nature, or any combination of such drugs, to a degree which impairs his ability to operate the watercraft or motorboat safely, (iv) while such person is under the combined influence of alcohol and any drug or drugs to a degree which impairs his ability to operate the watercraft or motorboat safely, or (v) while such person has a blood concentration of any of the following substances at a level that is equal to or greater than: (a) 0.02 milligrams of cocaine per liter of blood, (b) 0.1 milligrams of methamphetamine per liter of blood, (c) 0.01 milligrams of phencyclidine per liter of blood, or (d) 0.1 milligrams of 3,4-methylenedioxymethamphetamine per liter of blood.

See also 18 U.S.C. § 342 (prohibiting an individual from "operat[ing] or direct[ing] the operation of a common carrier while under the influence of alcohol. . . .").

General "under the influence" statutes (also known as "driving under the influence" or "driving while intoxicated" statutes) may define "under the influence" by statute or by case law.[166] An example of a state that utilizes a statutory definition is Delaware,[167] which defines "under the influence" to mean that "the person is, because of alcohol or drugs or a combination of both, less able than the person would ordinarily have been, either mentally or physically, to exercise clear judgment, sufficient physical control, or due care in the driving of a vehicle."[168]

Illegal *per se* statutes do not require evidence of impairment or intoxication; the BAC or BrAC test result is the basis for conviction. In response to anti-impaired driving legislative efforts, as of 2005 the District of Columbia, Puerto Rico, and all 50 states, have illegal *per se* statutes making it illegal to operate a motor vehicle with a blood alcohol concentration of .08 g/dl or the equivalent BrAC.[169] Some states have also enacted illegal *per se* laws that make the time of the testing (not just the time of the operation of the motor vehicle) an additional relevant time period for the specified BAC or BrAC level.[170] All states have also enacted "zero tolerance" illegal *per se* statutes with .02 BAC or BrAC levels for drivers 18–21 years old.[171]

---

[166] *See* Ala. Code § 32–5A-191: "(a) A person shall not drive or be in actual physical control of any vehicle while . . . (2) Under the influence of alcohol".

The Alabama Supreme Court has defined "under the influence of alcohol" as meaning "having consumed such an amount of alcohol as to affect his ability to operate a vehicle in a safe manner." Ex Parte Buckner, 549 So.2d 451, 454 (Ala. 1989).

[167] Del. Code Title 21 § 4177(a)(1): "No person shall drive a vehicle . . . when the person is under the influence of alcohol."

[168] Del Code Title 21 § 4177(c)(5).

[169] Most states also maintain a general statute in addition to the illegal *per se* statute. See Va. Code § 18.2–266: "It shall be unlawful for any person to drive or operate any motor vehicle, engine or train (i) while such person has a blood alcohol concentration of 0.08 percent or more by weight by volume or 0.08 grams or more per 210 liters of breath as indicated by a chemical test administered as provided in this article, (ii) while such person is under the influence of alcohol, (iii) while such person is under the influence of any narcotic drug or any other self-administered intoxicant or drug of whatsoever nature, or any combination of such drugs, to a degree which impairs his ability to drive or operate any motor vehicle, engine or train safely, (iv) while such person is under the combined influence of alcohol and any drug or drugs to a degree which impairs his ability to drive or operate any motor vehicle, engine or train safely, or (v) while such person has a blood concentration of any of the following substances at a level that is equal to or greater than: (a) 0.02 milligrams of cocaine per liter of blood, (b) 0.1 milligrams of methamphetamine per liter of blood, (c) 0.01 milligrams of phencyclidine per liter of blood, or (d) 0.1 milligrams of 3,4-methylenedioxymethamphetamine per liter of blood. A charge alleging a violation of this section shall support a conviction under clauses (i), (ii), (iii), (iv), or (v)."

[170] *See* Utah Code 41–6a-502(1)(a): "A person may not operate or be in actual physical control of a vehicle within this state if the person . . . has sufficient alcohol in the person's body that a subsequent chemical test shows that the person has a blood or breath alcohol concentration of .08 grams or greater at the time of the test . . ." As the Utah Court of Appeals recently held: "Subsection (1)(a) plainly does not require the State to establish that a person had a BAC of .08 or greater at the time he or she operated or controlled a vehicle. . . . Defendant's BAC at the time he operated his motorcycle was irrelevant to whether Defendant had the requisite BAC for conviction under subsection (1)(a), it was not a fact in issue. . . ." State v. Manwaring, 2011 UT App 443, P34–P36, 268 P.3d 201, 209–210 (Utah Ct. App. 2011).

[171] "Countermeasures That Work: A Highway Safety Countermeasure Guide for State Highway Safety Offices," US Department of Transportation, National Highway Traffic Safety

In addition to the statutes criminalizing alcohol-impaired driving, most states have imposed administrative license revocation or suspension statutes triggered by a specified BAC or BrAC concentration.[172] As of December 2014, 49 states and the District of Columbia also have statutes imposing higher or additional penalties for drivers with specified higher BAC or BrAC levels (as defined by the individual state, but typically 0.15 or 0.20 BAC).[173]

To compel cooperation with alcohol testing by suspected impaired drivers, all states have enacted implied consent laws. Implied consent laws deem a person to have consented to alcohol/drug testing if arrested for an impaired driving offense.[174] If the person refuses the testing,

---

Administration (8th ed. 2015) at p. 1–59 (available at: http://www.ghsa.org/resources/counter measures2015)(last accessed November 8, 2016).

See Va. Code § 18.2–266.1(A) "It shall be unlawful for any person under the age of 21 to operate any motor vehicle after illegally consuming alcohol. Any such person with a blood alcohol concentration of 0.02 percent or more by weight by volume or 0.02 grams or more per 210 liters of breath but less than 0.08 by weight by volume or less than 0.08 grams per 210 liters of breath as indicated by a chemical test administered as provided in this article shall be in violation of this section."

[172] As of December 31, 2014, 42 states and the District of Columbia administrative license revocation or suspension statutes. US Department of Transportation, National Highway Traffic Safety Administration, "Digest of Impaired Driving and Selected Beverage Control Laws," (29th Ed. April 2016) at p. xviii (available at: https://www.nhtsa.gov/document/digest-impaired-driving-and-selected-beverage-control-laws-twenty-ninth-edition)(last accessed June 21, 2016). The suspension/revocation periods range from 7 days to 1 year. *See* Va. Code § 46.2–391.2 (7 day mandatory suspension); Ga. Stat. 40–5–67.1 (up to one year, 30 days mandatory).

In Mackay v. Montrym, 443 U.S. 1 (1979), the United States Supreme Court held that the right of due process is not violated if a driver's license is suspended prior to an administrative hearing, as long as provisions are made for a swift post-suspension hearing.

[173] US Department of Transportation, National Highway Traffic Safety Administration, "Countermeasures That Work: A Highway Safety Countermeasure Guide for State Highway Safety Offices," (8th ed. 2015) at p. 1–14 (available at: http://www.ghsa.org/resources/countermeasures2015)(last accessed June 21, 2016).

See also Va. Code § 18.2–270(A): "Except as otherwise provided herein, any person violating any provision of § 18.2–266 shall be guilty of a Class 1 misdemeanor with a mandatory minimum fine of $250. If the person's blood alcohol level as indicated by the chemical test administered as provided in this article or by any other scientifically reliable chemical test performed on whole blood under circumstances reliably establishing the identity of the person who is the source of the blood and the accuracy of the results (i) was at least 0.15, but not more than 0.20, he shall be confined in jail for an additional mandatory minimum period of five days or, (ii) if the level was more than 0.20, for an additional mandatory minimum period of 10 days." OR ST. (Oregon) § 813.010(6)(d)(minimum $2000 fine for BAC of 0.15 or greater).

[174] *See* Va. Code § 18.2–268.2:

A. Any person, whether licensed by Virginia or not, who operates a motor vehicle upon a highway, as defined in § 46.2–100, in the Commonwealth shall be deemed thereby, as a condition of such operation, to have consented to have samples of his blood, breath, or both blood and breath taken for a chemical test to determine the alcohol, drug, or both alcohol and drug content of his blood, if he is arrested for violation of § 18.2–266, 18.2–266.1, or subsection B of § 18.2–272 or of a similar ordinance within three hours of the alleged offense.

B. Any person so arrested for a violation of clause (i) or (ii) of § 18.2–266 or both, § 18.2–2661.2 or subsection B of § 18.2–272 or of a similar ordinance shall submit to a breath test. If the breath test is unavailable or the person is physically unable to submit to the breath test, a blood test shall be given. The accused shall, prior to administration of the test, be advised by the person administering the test that he has the right to observe the process of analysis and to see the blood-alcohol reading

their driving privileges may be revoked or suspended, they may incur civil penalties, or in some states, the refusal may constitute a separate criminal offense.[175] The fact of the refusal may also be admissible in criminal impaired driving prosecutions and civil cases.

It is well settled that the Fifth Amendment self-incrimination privilege is limited to testimonial compulsion and is inapplicable to the procurement of physical evidence such as blood, urine, or breath specimens.[176] The due process clause of that Amendment has applicability with regard to such evidence only the police resort to collection procedures that offend "a sense of justice," or, stated another way, procedures that are "shocking to the conscience" of the courts.[177]

In *Schmerber v. California*,[178] the Supreme Court held that the Fourth Amendment did not bar the warrantless collection of a blood sample upon an arrest for DUI following an accident. Courts differed on whether *Schmerber* was expressly limited to the "special facts" of the exigency of the accident requiring medical treatment,[179] or whether the natural dissipation of alcohol in the blood constitutes the exigency permitting the warrantless collection of a bodily specimen upon arrest.[180]

---

on the equipment used to perform the breath test. If the equipment automatically produces a written printout of the breath test result, the printout, or a copy, shall be given to the accused.

C. A person, after having been arrested for a violation of clause (iii), (iv), or (v) of § 18.2–266 or § 18.2–266.1 or subsection B of § 18.2–272 or of a similar ordinance, may be required to submit to a blood test to determine the drug or both drug and alcohol content of his blood. When a person, after having been arrested for a violation of § 18.2–266 (i) or (ii) or both, submits to a breath test in accordance with subsection B or refuses to take or is incapable of taking such a breath test, he may be required to submit to tests to determine the drug or both drug and alcohol content of his blood if the law-enforcement officer has reasonable cause to believe the person was driving under the influence of any drug or combination of drugs, or the combined influence of alcohol and drugs.

[175] As of 2013, 18 states criminalized the refusal to take a BAC or BrAC test following an arrest for impaired driving. "Countermeasures That Work: A Highway Safety Countermeasure Guide for State Highway Safety Offices," US Department of Transportation, National Highway Traffic Safety Administration (8th ed. 2015) at p. 1–18 (available at: http://www.ghsa.org/resources/countermeasures2015)(last accessed November 8, 2016).

In Birchfield v. North Dakota, 136 S.Ct. 2160 (2016), the Supreme Court held that motorists may be criminally punished for refusing to submit to a warrantless breath test, but not for a warrantless blood test.

Some states provide for civil penalties for a first offense and criminal penalties for subsequent offenses. *See* Va. Code § 18.2–268.3.

[176] Schmerber v. California, 384 U.S. 757 (1966); South Dakota v. Neville, 459 U.S. 553 (1983).

[177] *See* Rochin v. California, 342 U.S. 165 (1952)(stomach pump used by physician in a hospital at request of police, but over the arrestee's protest, to secure narcotic capsules swallowed by arrestee was found by the Court to offend a sense of justice).

[178] Schmerber, 384 U.S. at 766–772 (after an arrest upon probable cause for impaired driving, the procurement of a blood specimen in a reasonable manner—i.e., by a physician using accepted medical procedures—does not constitute a Fourth Amendment violation).

[179] *See* State v. Rodriguez, 156 P.3d 771 (Utah 2007); State v. Johnson, 744 N.W.2d 340 (Iowa 2008).

[180] *See* State v. Bohling, 494 N.W.2d 399 (Wisc. 1993); State v. Faust, 682 N.W.2d 371 (Wisc. 2004); State v. Shriner, 751 N.W.2d 538 (Minn. 2008); State v. Netland, 762 N.W.2d 202

On April 17, 2013, the Supreme Court decided *Missouri v. McNeely*[181] to address the question,[182] but the holding was narrowly focused on whether drunk driving in every case provides an exigency that negates the warrant requirement for collection of a blood sample. On that narrow issue, the Supreme Court held that the interest in combating drunk driving does not justify departing from the warrant requirement without a showing of exigent circumstances that make securing a warrant impractical in the specific case. On June 23, 2016, the Supreme Court addressed broader issues in *Birchfield v. North Dakota* and held that (1) the Fourth Amendment permits warrantless breath tests incident to arrests for drunk driving, but not warrantless blood tests; and (2) motorists may not be criminally punished for refusing to submit to a warrantless blood test based on legally implied consent to submit to them.[183]

McNeely and *Birchfield* did not address the other important holding of *Schmerber*: that the Sixth Amendment right to counsel does not apply to the taking of physical evidence from the body of the accused. Therefore, there is no federal constitutional right to the presence of an attorney at the taking of a breath or blood sample.[184]

Other criminal actions related to impaired driving offenses, such as vehicular homicide or maiming, may incorporate the illegal *per se* BAC or BrAC levels used in the impaired driving statutes.[185]

2.   GENERAL ADMISSIBILITY OF TESTING RESULTS

Although witness testimony concerning observations of impairment is admissible,[186] most intoxication prosecutions rely on the results of

---

(Minn. 2009); State v. Milligan, 748 P.2d 130 (Ore. 1988); State v. Machuca, 227 P.3d 729 (Ore. 2010).

[181] 133 S.Ct. 1552 (2013).

[182] The implications of the 5–4 decision are complicated by the fact that there were four opinions—a majority, two separate opinions supporting the result, and one dissenting opinion—that limit any broad implications of the reasoning of the majority opinion.

[183] 136 S.Ct. 2160 (2016).

[184] State law may, however, provide such a right, either by statute or state constitutional provision. *See* Sites v. State, 300 Md. 702, 481 A.2d (1984); Brosan v. Cochran, 307 Md. 662, 516 A.2d 970 (1986)("[T]he decision whether to submit to the State test is of the most fundamental importance in determining the ultimate resolution of the suspect's case.").

In Vermont, a state statute permitting a motorist to consult with an attorney prior to deciding whether to submit to a DUI test, provided the consultation take place within 30 minutes from the initial attempt to contact counsel, was held to limit unfairly a suspect's right to counsel if, despite repeated attempts, the public defender could not be located within the 30-minute time limit. State v. Garvey, 157 Vt. 105, 595 A.2d 267 (1991).

[185] *See, e.g.*, Oregon Rev. Stat. § 163–118. See also Va. Code § 18.2–51.4(A): "Any person who, as a result of driving while intoxicated in violation of § 18.2–266 or any local ordinance substantially similar thereto in a manner so gross, wanton and culpable as to show a reckless disregard for human life, unintentionally causes the serious bodily injury of another person resulting in permanent and significant physical impairment shall be guilty of a Class 6 felony."

chemical tests. These results, whether from blood, urine, or breath testing, are generally admissible. Blood testing and urine testing are considered standard forensic toxicological testing and alcohol breath test results have been generally recognized as reliable since at least the 1970's.[187] Courts have held that "the reliability of the methodology, that is, the scientific technique by which [breath testing devices] measure breath alcohol content, is well-established."[188]

With the reliability of the general methodology firmly established, admission of the testing results is determined by the reliability of the testing results. "[R]eliability concerns are addressed by requiring the proponent to show that the machine and its functions are reliable, that it was correctly adjusted or calibrated, and that the data ... put into the machine was accurate. ... In other words, a foundation must be established for the information through authentication."[189] The proper foundation for the admission of the testing results may include proof that: "(1) the type of device in question is accepted as reliable and as suitable for generating the sort of data offered in evidence, (2) the specific device in question was in good working order at the time it generated the data in questions, and (3) the individual that operated the device was competent to do so."[190] Many jurisdictions establish by statute the admission requirements for breath testing results[191] and prohibit attacks

---

[186] "A lay witness is competent to testify whether or not in his opinion a person was drunk or sober on a given occasion on which he observed him." State v. Strickland, 321 N.C. 31, 37, 361 S.E.2d 882, 885 (1987)(citation omitted).

[187] *See* California v. Trombetta, 467 U.S. 479, 489 (1984)(recognizing the breath testing device in question had "passed accuracy requirements established by the [NHTSA]" and had been reviewed and certified by the state); United States v. Brannon, 146 F.3d 1194, 1196 (9th Cir. 1998)("Twenty-five years ago breathalyzers were certified as accurate by the National Highway Traffic Safety Administration of the Department of Transportation. Their methodology is well-known and unchallenged."); United States v. Reid, 929 F.2d 990, 994 (4th Cir. 1991)("The best means of obtaining evidence of the breath alcohol content, and the least intrusive way of testing, is the breathalyzer test.").

[188] United States v. Hamblen-Baird, 266 F.R.D. 38 (Dist. Of Mass. 2010)(citing United States v. Daras, 164 F.3d 626 (4th Cir. 1998)(per curiam)(table)(unpublished)).

See also United States v. Smith, 776 F.2d 892, 898 (10th Cir. 1985)("The technique of testing breath samples for blood alcohol content has general acceptance in the scientific community").

[189] United States v. Washington 498 F.3d 225, 231 (4th Cir. 2007), cert. denied, 129 S.Ct. 2856 (2009).

[190] 31 Charles A. Wright and Victor J. Gold, Federal Practice and Procedure, § 7114, at 152 (2000)(footnotes omitted).

[191] *See* Va. Code § 18.2–268.9 (Assurance of breath-test validity; use of breath-test results as evidence):

A. To be capable of being considered valid as evidence in a prosecution under § 18.2–266, 18.2–266.1, or subsection B of § 18.2–272, or a similar ordinance, chemical analysis of a person's breath shall be performed by an individual possessing a valid license to conduct such tests, with a type of equipment and in accordance with methods approved by the Department.

B. The Department shall establish a training program for all individuals who are to administer the breath tests. Upon a person's successful completion of the training program, the Department may license him to conduct breath-test analyses. Such license shall identify the specific types of breath test equipment upon which the individual has successfully completed training. Any individual conducting a breath

on the general reliability of breath testing machines approved pursuant to statutory procedures, but permit expert testimony to "attack the reliability of the specific testing procedure and the qualifications of the operator."[192] Distinctions are made by the courts as to whether the statutory or regulatory procedures are mandatory or discretionary when deciding whether the failure to follow the procedures renders the testing results inadmissible.[193]

Based on testing results, some parties to litigation will attempt to introduce expert testimony concerning what the individual's BAC was at a time prior to the administration of the test (for example, at the actual time the individual was observed driving). "Retrograde extrapolation is a mathematical analysis in which a known blood alcohol test result is used to determine what an individual's blood alcohol level would have been at a specified earlier time. The analysis determines the prior blood alcohol level on the bases of (1) the time elapsed between the occurrence of the specified earlier event (e.g., a vehicle crash) and the known blood test, and (2) the rate of elimination of alcohol from the subject's blood during the time between the event and the test."[194] Using an application of the average rates of absorption and elimination of alcohol from the body, the expert will provide an estimate of the person's BAC at the relevant time. Although illegal *per*

---

test under the provisions of § 18.2–268.2 shall issue a certificate which will indicate that the test was conducted in accordance with the Department's specifications, the name of the accused, that prior to administration of the test the accused was advised of his right to observe the process and see the blood alcohol reading on the equipment used to perform the breath test, the date and time the sample was taken from the accused, the sample's alcohol content, and the name of the person who examined the sample. This certificate, when attested by the individual conducting the breath test on equipment maintained by the Department, shall be admissible in any court as evidence of the facts therein stated and of the results of such analysis (i) in any criminal proceeding, provided that the requirements of subsection A of § 19.2–187.1 have been satisfied and the accused has not objected to the admission of the certificate pursuant to subsection B of § 19.2–187.1, or (ii) in any civil proceeding. Any such certificate of analysis purporting to be signed by a person authorized by the Department shall be admissible in evidence without proof of seal or signature of the person whose name is signed to it. A copy of the certificate shall be promptly delivered to the accused. Copies of Department records relating to any breath test conducted pursuant to this section shall be admissible provided such copies are authenticated as true copies either by the custodian thereof or by the person to whom the custodian reports.

The officer making the arrest, or anyone with him at the time of the arrest, or anyone participating in the arrest of the accused, if otherwise qualified to conduct such test as provided by this section, may administer the breath test and analyze the results.

[192] State v. Vega, 12 Ohio St.3d 185, 465 N.E.2d 1303, 1307 (Ohio 1984).

[193] *See* Wheeler v. Idaho Trans. Dept., 148 Idaho 378, 223 P.3d 761 (Id. Ct. App. 2009)(failure to change the calibration solution within approximately 100 calibration checks was not mandatory and breath testing results admissible); People v. Clairmont, 961 N.E.2d 914, 356 Ill. Dec. 525 (Ill. Ct. App. 2011)(failure to check breath testing device "at least once every 62 days" mandatory and failure to check the device in a timely manner makes the testing results inadmissible); State v. Richard, 2011 Ohio App. 6631, 2011 Ohio App. LEXIS 5494 (Oh. Ct. App. 1st Dist. 2011)(failure to follow recommended second 20 minutes waiting period for second sample did not render test results inadmissible).

[194] State v. Cook, 362 N.C. 285, 288, 661 S.E.2d 874, 876 (2008).

se statutes have limited the relevance of retrograde extrapolation evidence, it remains a controversial issue on which courts have reached inconsistent admissibility determinations.[195]

3.   MISCELLANEOUS ISSUES

a.   *Preservation*

Although methods are available for the preservation of additional specimens of blood, urine, or breath,[196] the courts have generally not required the preservation of such evidence absent a statutory requirement.[197] The United States Supreme Court has held that any duty the states may have to preserve evidence is limited to evidence that possesses an exculpatory value that is apparent before its destruction and that is unobtainable by the defendant by other reasonable means.[198] In the case of breath samples saved for defense use, they would almost always confirm the results obtained by the state, and any inaccuracies in the state's results could be shown by other means, such as cross-examination or independent tests obtained by the defendant after taking the state's chemical test. Thus, even if the police use a device that saves a breath sample they have *no constitutional duty* to retain it and make it available to the defendant.

b.   *Source Codes*

In an effort to attack the reliability of breath testing devices, some litigants have sought to obtain the "source code" of the machines. The source code contains the computer commands that control the breath testing device as it isolates the breath sample, tests the sample, and uses the test results to calculate the subject's breath or blood alcohol level. The theory advanced for the request for production of the source code is that if given access to the code, an expert could review the code for errors in the commands which could cause the machines to produce inaccurate results. Of the appellate courts that have directly addressed

---

[195] *See* State v. Green, 707 S.E.2d 715 (N.C. Ct. App. 2011)(affirming admission of retrograde extrapolation expert testimony); United States v. Tsosie, 791 F.Supp.2d 1099 (Dist. N.M. 2011)(admitting retrograde extrapolation); Mata v. State, 46 S.W.3d 902, 916 (Tx. Crim. App. 2001)(reversing trial court's admission of expert testimony regarding retrograde extrapolation, highlighting numerous concerns about the expert's analysis including mathematical errors and inconsistent statements, but noting that "the science of retrograde extrapolation can be reliable in a given case"); Smith v. City of Tuscaloosa, 601 So.2d 1136, 1140 (Ala. Crim. App. 1992)(citing sources critical of retrograde extrapolation, but concluding that "the issue of whether any expert should be allowed to testify to a defendant's blood-alcohol content based upon the application of the process of retrograde extrapolation has not been presented or preserved for review").

[196] *See* Bruce E. Goldberger, Yale H. Caplan & J. Robert Zettl, "A Long-Term Field Experience With Breath Ethanol Collection Employing Silica Gel," 10 J. ANALYTICAL TOX. 194 (1986).

[197] *See* State v. Shutt, 116 N.H. 495, 363 A.2d 406 (1976); State v. Teare, 135 N.J.Super. 19, 342 A.2d 556 (1975). *See also,* Lauderdale v. State, 548 P.2d 376, 379–80 (Alaska 1976); People v. Godbout, 42 Ill.App.3d 1001, 1 Ill.Dec. 583, 356 N.E.2d 865 (1976).

[198] California v. Trombetta, 467 U.S. 479 (1984).

the issue, all have upheld the denial of the requests for access to the source codes.[199]

c.   Certificates

Some breath testing devices produce certificates with each breath test reading, including a certificate that the machine has been approved for used by the relevant authority, a certificate that the instrument was calibrated and found to be in compliance with applicable standards, and the testing results for the individual supplying the sample. In some jurisdictions, the certificates for approved use and calibration are provided by the authorizing agency that approves and maintains the machines. Defendants have challenged the admission of the certificates on the grounds that the certificates are testimonial, and therefore, a live witness must be available for cross-examination pursuant to confrontation clause as interpreted in *Melendez-Diaz v. Massachusetts.*[200] All state appellate courts deciding the issue have found that such certificates are not testimonial.[201]

V.   RESOURCES

§13.11 BIBLIOGRAPHY OF ADDITIONAL RESOURCES

1.   FORENSIC TOXICOLOGY

I.M. Abdullat *et al.,* "The Use of Serial Measurement of Plasma Cholinesterase in the Management of Acute Poisoning with Organophosphates and Carbamates," 162 FORENSIC SCI. INT'L 126–130 (2006).

American Board of Forensic Toxicology: www.abft.org.

Jacquelyn E. Baker and Amanda J. Jenkins, "Screening for Cocaine Metabolite Fails to Detect an Intoxication," 29 AM. J. FORENSIC MED. PATHOLOGY 141 (2008).

Edward J. Cone *et al.,* "Urine Drug Testing of Chronic Pain Patients: Licit and Illicit Drug Patterns," 32 J. ANALYTICAL TOXICOLOGY 530 (2008).

---

[199] *See* Commonwealth v. House, 295 S.W.3d 825 (Ky. 2009); State v. Bastos, 985 So.2d 37 (Fla. Ct. App. 2008).

[200] 557 U.S. 305 (2009).

[201] *See, e.g.,* Commonwealth v. Zeininger, 459 Mass. 775, 947 N.E.2d 1060 (Mass. 2011), Ramirez v. State, 928 N.E.2d 214, 220 (Ind. 2010); State v. Bergin, 231 Ore. App. 36, 217 P.3d 1087, 1089–1090 (Or. Ct. App. 2009); Commonwealth v. Dyarman, 2011 PA Super. 245, 33 A.3d 104 (Pa. Super. Ct. 2011).

The certificates, however, may still be inadmissible under other rules of evidence, such as the failure to establish foundational requirements for the admission of the certificate as a routine business record. *See* United States v. Foster, 2011 U.S. Dist. LEXIS 130716 (W.D. Va. 2011).

Baselt Cravey, *Introduction to Forensic Toxicology*, Biomedical Publications, 1981.

A. Furey *et al.*, "Strategies to Avoid the Mis-identification of Anatoxina Using Mass Spectrometry in the Forensic Investigation of Acute Neurotoxic Poisoning," 1082 J. CHROMATOG. 91–97 (2005).

A. Gunn, *Essential Forensic Biology*, 2d ed., CRC Press, 2009.

Virginia Hill *et al.,* "Hair Analysis for Cocaine: Factors in Laboratory Contamination Studies and Their Relevance to Proficiency Sample Preparation and Hair Testing," 176 FORENSIC SCI. INT'L 23 (2008).

Marilyn A. Huestis *et al.,* "Excretion of 9-tetrahydrocannabinol in Sweat," 174 FORENSIC SCI. INT'L 173 (2008).

Jickells, *Clarke's Analytical Forensic Toxicology* (2008).

Subbarao V. Kala *et al.,* "Validation Analysis of Amphetamines, Opiates, Phencyclidine, Cocaine and Benzoylecqonine in Oral Fluids by Liquid Chromatography-Tandem Mass Spectrometry," 32 J. ANALYTICAL TOXICOLOGY 605 (2008).

Steven B. Karch, *Workplace Drug Testing* (2008).

L. Labat *et al.*, "A Fatal Case of Mercuric Cyanide Poisoning," 143 FORENSIC SCI. INT'L 215–217 (2004).

B. Levine, *Principles of Forensic Toxicology,* 2nd ed., 2003.

J. Lv *et al.*, "A Micro-Chemiluminescence Determination of Cyanide in Whole Blood," 148 Forensic Sci. Int'l 15 (2005).

M. Lynch, *Forensic Toxicology* (2006).

H.H. Maurer, "Advances in Analytical Toxicology: the Current Role of Liquid Chromatography-Mass Spectrometry in Drug Quantification in Blood and Oral fluid," 381 J.ANAL. & BIOANAL. CHEM. 110–118 (2005).

H.H. Maurer, "Multianalyte Procedures for Screening for and Quantification of Drugs in Blood, Plasma, or Serum by Liquid Chromatographysingle Stage or Tandem Mass Spectrometry (LC–MS or LC–MS/MS) Relevant to Clinical and Forensic Toxicology," 38 CLIN BIOCHEM. 310–318 (2005).

Christine Moore, "Hair in Toxicology: An Important Bio-Monitor by Tobin DJ," 51 J. FORENSIC SCI. 954 (2006).

Richard Saferstein, *Criminalistics* (9th ed.) 2006.

Tania A. Sasaki, "Forensic Toxicology Widens Net for Drugs of Abuse— The Rise of LC/MS/MS for Toxicology Testing," FORENSIC MAGAZINE, Oct.–Nov. 2007, p. 20.

C. Saudan *et al.*, "Detection of Exogenous GHB in Blood by Gas Chromatography-Combustion-Isotope Ratio Mass Spectrometry: Implications in Postmortem Toxicology," 29 J. ANAL. TOXICOL. 777 (2005).

Harald Schutz *et al.*, "Immunoassays for Drug Screening in Urine: Chances, Challenges, and Pitfalls," 2 FORENSIC SCI. MED. & PATHOL. 75 (2006).

Scientific Working Group for Forensic Toxicology: www.swgtox.org.

Diaa M. Shakleya *et al.*, "Case Report: Trace Evidence of Trans-Phenylpropene as a Marker of Smoked Methamphetamine," 32 J. ANALYTICAL TOXICOLOGY 705 (2008).

B.E. Smink *et al.*, "The Relation Between the Blood Benzodiazepine Concentration and Performance in Suspected Impaired Drivers," 15 J. FORENSIC AND LEGAL MED. 483 (2008).

Society of Forensic Toxicologists/American Academy of Forensic Sciences,Forensic Toxicology Laboratory Guidelines, 2006 Version—available at: http://www.soft-tox.org/files/Guidelines_2006_Final.pdf.

Lolita Tsanaclis and John F.C. Wicks, "Differentiation Between Drug Use and Environmental Contamination When Testing for Drugs in Hair," 176 FORENSIC SCI. INT'L 19 (2008).

Kei Zaitsu *et al.*, "Determination of a Newly Encountered Designer Drug 'p-methoxyethylamphetamine' and Its Metabolites in Human Urine and Blood," 177 Forensic Sci. Int'l 77 (2008).

D. Zeng *et al.*, "Determination of Tetramethylenedisulfotetramine in Human Urine with Gas-Chromatograph-Flame Thermionic Detection Coupling with Direct Immersed Solid-Phased Micro-Extraction," 159 Forensic Sci. Int'l 168 (2006).

2.   ALCOHOL INVESTIGATIONS

Eugene R. Bertolli, Constantine J. Forkiotis, R. Robert Pannone and Hazel Dawkins, "A Behavioral Optometry/Vision Science Perspective on the Horizontal Gaze Nystagmus Exam for DUI Enforcement," THE FORENSIC EXAMINER, Spring 2007, p. 26.

James L. Booker and Kathryn Renfroe, "The Effects of Gastroesophageal Reflux Disease on Forensic Breath Alcohol Testing," 60 J. Forensic Sci. 1516–1522 (2015).

A. Dasgupta, *Alcohol and Its Biomarkers*, Elsevier, 2015.

Richard A. Deitrich and V. Gene Erwin, eds., *Pharmacological Effects of Ethanol on the Nervous System*, CRC Press, 1995.

Chancey C. Fessler, Frederich A. Tulleners, David G. Howitt and John R. Richards, "Determination of mouth alcohol using the Draeger Evidential Portable Alcohol System," 48 Science and Justice 16 (2007).

Patrick N. Friel, Barry K. Logan and John Baer, "An Evaluation of the Reliability of Widmark Calculations Based on Breath Alcohol Measurements," 40 J. Forensic Sci. 91 (1994).

James C. Garriott, ed., *Medical-Legal Aspects of Alcohol*, 4th ed., Lawyers & Judges Publishing, 2003.

Georgia Koukiou and Vassilis Anastassopoulos, "Drunk Person Screening using Eye Thermal Signatures," 61 J. Forensic Sci. 259–264 (2016).

M.J. Lewis, "Blood Alcohol: The Concentration—Time Curve and Retrospective Estimation of Level," 26 J. FORENSIC SCI. SOC 95 (1986).

Teri L. Martin *et al.*, "A Review of Alcohol-Impaired Driving: The Role of Blood Alcohol Concentration and Complexity of the Driving Task," 58 J. Forensic Sci. 1238–1250 (2013).

Paul L. Olson, Robert Dewar and Eugene Farber, *Forensic Aspects of Driver Perception and Response*, 3d ed., Lawyers & Judges Publishing, 2010.

Steven J. Rubenzer and Scott B. Stevenson, "Horizontal Gaze Nystagmus: A Review of Vision Science and Application Issues," 55 J. Forensic Sci. 394–409 (2010).

Ted Vosk *et al.*, "The Measurand Problem in Breath Alcohol Testing," 59 J. Forensic Sci. 811-815 (2014).

Ronald R. Watson, ed., *Alcohol, Drugs of Abuse, and Immune Functions*, CRC Press, 1995.

Websites:

Governors Highway Safety Association: www.ghsa.org

Insurance Institute for Highway Safety: www.iihs.org

Mothers Against Drunk Driving: www.madd.org

National Highway Traffic Safety Administration: www.nhtsa.gov

National Safety Council: www.nsc.org

Traffic Injury Research Foundation: www.tirf.ca

CHAPTER 14

FORENSIC BIOLOGY AND DNA ANALYSIS[1]

I. INTRODUCTION

§14.01 SCOPE OF THE CHAPTER

In the resolution of factual disputes, an analysis of biological material often contributes crucial evidence determining what happened and who might have been involved. This chapter will provide an overview of the investigations of blood and other biological material using forensic

---

[1] The Authors thank the following subject matter expert for her assistance with this chapter: Lucy A. Davis, LDH Consultants.

biology and will provide guidance in using or challenging the results of such examinations. This chapter will also examine the structure of DNA and the forensic techniques employed for analyzing it, including the currently-used typing processes, the probability statistics used in assessing the evidentiary weight of the results, and the legal issues involved in the presentation of DNA testimony.

In criminal investigations, especially in homicides and other violent crimes, the physical evidence commonly includes blood and other bodily fluids. The detection of blood and biological material is a valuable tool in criminal investigations to provide information concerning what happened and who may have been involved. In sexual assault offenses, the principal biological material of interest is seminal fluid and/or sperm cells ejaculated by a male perpetrator, although saliva and other biological materials may be informative as well. When sexual assault is alleged, detection of seminal fluid is often helpful in demonstrating that a sexual contact occurred. Such detection is particularly valuable where the alleged victim is a young child or incapacitated person who may be unable to provide testimony concerning the alleged assault.

When the issues in a case concern identification of the contributor of biological material, the principal method for identification is DNA analysis. Deoxyribonucleic acid (DNA), the basis of the human genetic code, not only creates the traits that make each human unique but also provides the basis for a method of identification. Forensic DNA analysis is the comparison of a person's DNA type, also known as the DNA profile, with an evidentiary sample to determine whether the person's profile matches that of the evidentiary sample such that the person could have contributed the sample. In the case of kinship analysis, DNA profiles are compared to determine whether there is a genetic relationship between individuals.

DNA analysis, called "DNA fingerprinting" by the early pioneers in forensic research, has become the "gold standard" in forensic science by which other methods of forensic science analysis are measured.[2] In its 2009 report on forensic science, the National Academy of Sciences largely exempted DNA analysis from its criticism of the forensic science fields, and recognized the power of DNA analysis "to consistently, and with a high degree of certainty, demonstrate a connection between evidence and a specific individual or source."[3] In summarizing the current state of forensic DNA analysis, the report provided:

> DNA analysis is scientifically sound for several reasons: (1) there are biological explanations for individual-specific findings; (2) the 13 STR loci used to compare DNA samples were selected so that the chance of two different people matching on

[2] David E. Newton, *DNA Evidence and Forensic Science*, Infobase Publishing, 2008 at p. 41.

[3] National Academies of Science, *Strengthening Forensic Science in the United States: A Path Forward*, National Academies Press, 2009 (*hereinafter* "NAS Report") at p. 7.

all of them would be extremely small; (3) the probabilities of false positives have been explored and quantified in some settings (even if only approximately); (4) the laboratory procedures are well specified and subject to validation and proficiency testing; and (5) there are clear and repeatable standards for analysis, interpretation, and reporting.[4]

The report did acknowledge, however, that "errors do occasionally occur [when] interpretational ambiguities occur [or when] samples are inappropriately processed and/or contaminated."[5] The 2016 PCAST Report echoed the NAS Report findings of foundational validity and reliability for DNA analysis of single-source samples and simple mixtures, but as discussed in §14.14 *infra*, PCAST expressed concerns about complex mixture analysis.[6]

§14.02 TERMINOLOGY

Adenine (A): One of the four nucleotides of the DNA molecule, pairs with thymine.

Allele: Used in forensic DNA typing to refer to the individual DNA fragment sequence at a specific region on a chromosome.

Allelic Drop-in: A DNA PCR artifact that can be produced during analysis resulting in an additional allele not present in the original sample.

Allelic Drop-out: When an allele in the sample does not give a detectable signal.

American Society of Crime Laboratory Directors Laboratory Accreditation Board (ASCLD/LAB): A not-for-profit corporation specializing in the accreditation of public and private crime laboratories. Merged with ANSI-ASQ National Accreditation Board (ANAB).

Amplification: The process of reproducing multiple copies of a region of DNA.

Amylase: An enzyme that breaks down starches into sugar. Amylase is found in high concentrations in human saliva, but is also present in other body fluids.

ANSI-ASQ National Accreditation Board (ANAB): A not-for-profit corporation specializing in the accreditation of public and private crime laboratories.

Autosome: Non-sex chromosome, numbered 1 to 22 according to size.

---

[4]　Id. at p. 133.

[5]　2009 NAS Report at p. 132.

[6]　Executive Office of the President, President's Council of Advisors on Science and Technology, "Forensic Science in Criminal Courts: Ensuring Scientific Validity of Feature-Comparison Methods," September 2016 (hereinafter "2016 PCAST Report") at p. 75 (available at: https://obamawhitehouse.archives.gov/blog/2016/09/20/pcast-releases-report-forensic-science-criminal-courts)(last accessed March 3, 2017).

Base pair: Used as a unit of measurement of DNA and refers to one pair of nucleotides on the DNA molecule (AT or GC).

Capillary Electrophoresis (CE): An analytical method for separating DNA fragments according to their length or mass. Electrophoresis is a separation technique based on the differential transportation of charged species in an electric field through a conductive medium. Capillary electrophoresis separates compounds based on their size-to-charge ratio in the interior of a small capillary filled with a polymer, with the smaller DNA fragments moving through the capillary at a faster rate than longer fragments. Tagging the DNA fragments with a fluorescent dye permits detection based on retention time and quantification based on intensity of the fluorescence. An electropherogram is a graph of the intensity of the fluorescence over time (measured as a peak).

Cell: The basic structure of a living organism that contains the DNA in the nucleus and cytoplasm held within a membrane.

Chromosome: A physical structure in the nucleus of a cell that is the DNA molecule.

CODIS: Combined DNA Index System is a computer database administered by the FBI that coordinates DNA profile information from evidentiary DNA samples and persons either arrested or convicted of specific crimes. DNA profiles from individual laboratories (Local DNA Index System, LDIS) will be uploaded to a central state database. Those samples will then be compared to DNA samples maintained in the state offender databases (State DNA Index System, SDIS) and each other. The state will then upload both their evidentiary and offender DNA profiles to a federal centralized database to be searched at the national level (National DNA Index System, NDIS).

Cytosine (C): One of the four nucleotides of the DNA molecule, pairs with guanine.

Degradation: The breaking or fragmentation of the DNA molecule by chemical or physical means.

Differential Amplification: The selection of one target region or locus over another during the polymerase chain reaction. Differential amplification can occur between two alleles within a single locus if one allele has a mutation within the primer binding site causing that allele to be copied less efficiently.

Epithelial cells: Skin cells, vaginal cells or other cells normally found on an inner or outer body surface such as the dermis or mucous membranes.

Gel electrophoresis: An analytical method for separating DNA fragments according to their size, generally used in Restriction Fragment Length Polymorphism (RFLP) typing. Electrophoresis is a separation technique based on the differential transportation of charged particles in an electric field through a conductive medium. Gel electrophoresis separates compounds based on their size-to-charge ratio in a gel with the smaller DNA fragments moving farther in the gel than longer fragments.

Genome: The complete set of chromosomes present in a cell. In humans, over 3 billion nucleotide base pairs make up the genome.

Grouping: Classification of blood by type depending on specific sets of antigens or proteins on the cell membranes. The most commonly referred to blood groups are the ABH grouping system. The A, B, AB and H (formerly known as O) blood types are named for the presence of their antigens on the red blood cells which react with a specific antibody (anti-sera).

Guanine (G): One of the four nucleotides of the DNA molecule, pairs with cytosine.

Hemoglobin: An iron containing protein in the red blood cells which carries oxygen throughout the body. Hemoglobin is a combination of protein molecules and heme. Heme consists of an atom of iron surrounded by heterocyclic organic ring.

Heterozygous: Having two different alleles at a locus.

Homozygous: Having two copies of the same allele at a locus.

Locus: A specific region on a chromosome. Plural is loci.

Luminol: (5-amino-2,3-dihydrophthalazine-1,4-dione   or   3-aminophthalhydrazide): The chemical used to detect traces of blood.

Mitochondria: Physical structure within nucleated cells, but outside of the nucleus of the cell, used for the energy production reactions in the cell. Mitochondria contain their own DNA (mtDNA) that is a circular molecule inherited directly from the mother.

Monoclonal antibodies: Antibodies that are created in a laboratory by identical immune cells that are clones (the same as) of the parent cell. Monoclonal antibodies are specific to the antigen used to create it and may not bind with slightly different forms of the same antigen.

Multiplex System: A test providing for the simultaneous amplification of multiple DNA locations.

Nucleotide: The chemical component of nucleic acid. It is made up of a five carbon sugar, at least one phosphate group and one of the four chemical bases—adenine, thymine, guanine and cytosine. These are referred to as the building blocks of DNA.

Plasma: The colorless liquid portion of the blood remaining after the red and white blood cells are removed but still containing the clotting factors. Plasma is principally water and represents about 55 percent of the blood composition.

Preferential amplification: The unequal amplification of the two alleles present at a heterozygote locus due to a structural difference in the DNA fragments.

Polyclonal antibodies: Antibodies routinely produced by B-lymphocytes in response to an antigen resulting in a diverse range of immunoglobulins that are specific to that antigen.

Polymerase Chain Reaction (PCR): An enzymatic process used to make copies of a specific region of DNA. The process involves repetitive cycles of denaturation (separating) of the DNA strands, the addition of primers to target the specific sequence of interest, and the addition of DNA polymerase to copy the targeted strands to create new strands.

Polymorphism: The presence of more than one allele at a locus in a population.

Restriction Fragment Length Polymorphism (RFLP) Analysis: Detection and analysis of individual variations in the length of DNA fragments produced by digesting DNA with a restriction enzyme that cuts double-stranded DNA at specific base-pair sequences. The fragments are then subjected to gel electrophoresis. Radioactive or chemiluminescence probes are attached to the DNA fragments to allow visualization of the specific DNA fragments in the sample. An autorad is the x-ray print showing the relative positions of the DNA fragments on the gel.

Semen: The male reproductive fluid discharged from the penis during ejaculation, containing seminal fluid (an organic fluid consisting of proteins and other chemical compounds) and cellular components including spermatozoa (sperm), leukocytes (white cells) and epithelial cells.

Serology: The detection, classification, and study of various biological fluids such as blood, semen, and saliva.

Serum: The portion of the blood plasma remaining after the clotting factors and cells are removed when the blood clots.

Short Tandem Repeats (STR): A short repetitive sequence of base pairs. The sequences are usually 2–8 base pairs in length and repeated between 2 and 20 times. Also referred to as "microsatellite" DNA. In most forensic STR loci the repetitive sequence is 4 base pairs in length.

Spermatozoon (sperm): The reproductive cell of the male. Plural is spermatozoa.

Stutter: An artifact of the PCR process due to slippage of the polymerase during amplification. The slippage most often produces a DNA fragment one repeat unit shorter than the primary allele (minus 4).

Stutter may also result in a DNA fragment that is one repeat larger (plus 4) or 2 repeats smaller (minus 8) than the primary allele.

Thymine (T): One of the four nucleotides (bases) of the DNA molecule, pairs with adenine.

Variable Number Tandem Repeat (VNTR): A large repetitive sequence of base pairs. The sequences are usually 20–100 base pairs in length and repeated up to 100 times in the fragment. Also referred to as "minisatellite." RFLP techniques are used to identify VNTR DNA fragments.

§14.03 EVIDENTIARY USES

1. FORENSIC BIOLOGY

In addition to its use for toxicological examinations, blood is commonly used as a source of proof in crimes of violence. Although DNA typing is used to associate a stain to an individual, it may be important to criminal investigations to identify the biological stain. Blood may be found on the surface of the body, on clothing, under the fingernails, at the scene on floors, rugs, furniture, weapons, sink or bathtub, waste containers, or in an automobile. In instances where traces of blood are detected, they may indicate the location of a violent crime or that a bloody body was moved through the area. Other biological materials examined in civil and criminal cases are spermatozoa (sperm), seminal fluid, perspiration, saliva, and tissue (epithelial cells).

Blood is a slightly alkaline fluid which circulates through the vascular system carrying nourishment and oxygen to all parts of the body and transporting waste products to be excreted. Blood represents about 8% of total body weight and has an average volume of 5–5½ liters in adult humans. The fluid portion of the blood is called plasma. Red cells (erythrocytes), white cells (leukocytes and lymphocytes) and platelets (thrombocytes) are suspended in the plasma. The red cells are bi-concave, circular disks with thick edges. They contain hemoglobin which carries oxygen and gives blood its red appearance. Red cells do not have a nucleus, therefore do not have nuclear DNA. The red cell also does not contain mitochondria which means they cannot be used in DNA typing systems. The white cells are round, amoebic masses of protoplasm and are responsible for immune reactions. White cells contain both a nucleus and mitochondria and are the primary cells of blood used for DNA typing. Platelets, oval, circular cell fragments, are present in the plasma that help with the clotting process but they do not contain nuclear DNA. The ratio of red to white cells is typically about 1000 to 1. Detection and identification of blood is normally the result of reactions of the hemoglobin in the red cells with the test reagent.

The value of blood evidence depends on its recognition, collection, and proper preservation during initial evidence processing. Liquid blood is readily putrefied during which its evidentiary value can be lost. Dried bloodstains are generally stable and suitable for DNA testing after many years but is only stable for standard grouping tests for up to 6 months. When liquid blood is recovered, it should be preserved or refrigerated. Alternatively, blood can be left on the object on which it was located, dried in air, and packaged in a porous container for shipment to the laboratory.

Before the use of DNA analysis, forensic biologists (commonly referred to as "serologists") would conduct extensive testing of a sample using multiple blood grouping tests, encompassing testing of enzymes and proteins and antibody profiling, to report or testify that the questioned sample could have originated from a particular individual. Based on data for the occurrence of various blood factors in the general population, or preferably, in a segment thereof, the probability of a sample being included in a group having the same combination of blood types was calculated. In addition, the size of this group relative to the general population was estimated. For example, the serologist may have concluded that a given combination of blood types may occur in only one individual in 100,000. Despite the inability of the serologist to definitively link blood to an individual through blood group typing, exclusions were made with confidence. If the individual's blood differs in any of several successfully typed grouping systems, he or she cannot be the source of the questioned blood or bloodstain.[7]

Blood characterization and type determination is based primarily on antigen-antibody reactions with the most widely used antigen systems being ABH, MN, Rh and Gm. Enzyme grouping systems, protein polymorphisms and, in some instances, identification of antibodies provide additional information for individualization of a blood sample or stain. While a person's ABH type may be known related to medical blood typing, forensic laboratories no longer have the ability or proper reagents to test for this blood group either on liquid or dried stains. A few private laboratories do maintain the appropriate reagents to conduct blood typing and the enzyme grouping systems analysis.

Although DNA analysis is now used for the identification of potential contributors of blood samples, samples can be analyzed for other information. Analysis can be performed to provide information in response to the following questions:

    (1)   Is the sample under examination blood?

    (2)   If blood, is it human or another animal species?

    (3)   If animal, from what species did it originate?

---

    [7]   A more comprehensive and annotated treatment of the identification of Human Blood Types (with 111 references) is provided in D.S. Court, "Blood Grouping," in WILEY ENCYCLOPEDIA OF FORENSIC SCIENCE, (Jamieson A. & Moenssens A.A., eds) 2009 & online updates.

The most commonly encountered biological fluid in criminal sexual assault cases is semen. Semen is seminal fluid that contains spermatozoa (sperm). In addition to providing evidence of sexual contact, semen can be used for identification purposes through DNA typing. Seminal fluid and sperm are frequently detected in sexual assault cases but may also be recovered from the body or clothing of victims in homicides. They may also be important evidence in the investigation of accidental autoerotic deaths and have even been found at the scenes of arson and burglaries.

The identification of oral fluid or saliva stains may be important in the investigation of criminal incidents and could have utility in civil cases as well. For example, a cigarette butt, chewing gum or handkerchiefs (used as a gag) left at a crime scene may have saliva stains present and sufficient DNA may be collected for identification. Saliva has also been collected by swabbing the area of bite marks in assault cases for use in the identification of the assailant. DNA typing of stains on postage stamps or the glued flap portion of an envelope could be used to demonstrate that an individual may have stamped and sealed an envelope at issue.

Other biological material may also contain sufficient DNA to permit typing analysis. Recovered items of clothing which may contain skin cells or hairs deposited through perspiration or transfer are routinely submitted for DNA analysis in both violent and property crime cases.

2. DNA ANALYSIS

When DNA analysis first appeared in the forensic science community,[8] many individuals predicted that it would have a major impact in criminal cases, and to a lesser, but still significant degree, in civil cases. High expectations were rampant. A state trial judge wrote an opinion pronouncing DNA analysis the "single greatest advance in the 'search for truth,' and the goal of convicting the guilty and acquitting the innocent, since the advent of cross-examination."[9] The coined term "DNA fingerprinting" reflected the confidence of its promoters that DNA analysis would gain widespread confidence, utility, and acceptance by forensic scientists, criminal justice professionals, judges, and the public.

---

[8]   The first use of DNA analysis in a criminal case occurred in 1986–1987 involving the murders of two young girls in Leicestershire in England. The DNA analysis first excluded Richard Buckland, who had been arrested and held in custody for three months in connection with one of the murders, and then implicated Colin Pitchfork, who subsequently pleaded guilty to both murders. The case has been extensively discussed in news articles, legal commentary, and books. *See* Ian Cobain, "Killer Breakthrough—the Day DNA Evidence First Nailed a Murdered," The Guardian, June 7, 2016 (available at: https://www.theguardian.com/uk-news/2016/jun/07/killer-dna-evidence-genetic-profiling-criminal-investigation?CMP=Share_AndroidApp_Tweet)(last accessed June 7, 2016); Joseph Wambaugh, *The Blooding*, Bantam: New York, NY (1989).

[9]   People v. Wesley, 140 Misc.2d 306, 533 N.Y.S.2d 643 (1988).

In many ways, DNA analysis has fulfilled expectations concerning its evidentiary power. "Nationwide there have been a multitude of reported cases in which law enforcement agencies have used [DNA evidence] to solve crimes where the identification of the perpetrator was in question."[10] In addition to providing evidence leading to prosecutions, DNA analysis is routinely used to exclude potential suspects during investigations.[11] Identification of a common perpetrator in serial crimes frequently uses DNA evidence.[12] DNA evidence alone can support convictions[13] and also has led to exonerations—even when the other evidence against the defendant has been described as "overwhelming."[14] The United States Supreme Court has recognized that:

> While of course many criminal trials proceed without any forensic and scientific testing at all, there is no technology comparable to DNA testing for matching tissues when such evidence is at issue.[15]

Since its first use in the late 1980's, DNA analysis has become widely accepted, and to some extent expected, in the justice system. Although the exact scientific bases and analysis process may be unknown to the public, DNA analysis is part of the public lexicon. The concept of using DNA analysis to associate a person with a crime scene or to establish paternity has been incorporated in popular television shows and is now commonly accepted.

Although not specifically addressed in this chapter, the identification of non-human DNA is becoming increasingly useful in forensic investigations, as highly polymorphic DNA markers become readily

---

[10] Commonwealth v. Conway, 14 A.3d 101, 113 n. 14 (Pa. Super. Ct. 2011).

[11] Brandon L. Garrett, "Claiming Innocence," 92 MINN. L. REV. 1629, 1652–1653 (2008) (In Virginia, it has been reported that "DNA analysis eliminates twenty-five to thirty percent of suspects in police investigations.").

[12] In September, 2014, authorities were able to link a 2005 rape case in Fairfax County, Virginia, to the abduction and murder of a college student from Charlottesville, Virginia and to the murder of another college student whose body was recovered in Albemarle County, Virginia in 2009. *See* T. Rees Shapiron and Justin Jouvenal, "Jesse Matthew Pleads Guilty in Slayings of College Students," Washington Post, March 2, 2016 (available at: https://www.washingtonpost.com/local/public-safety/jesse-matthew-to-appear-in-court-for-plea-agreement-hearing/2016/03/01/f6b7093a-dfd8-11e5-846c-10191d1fc4ec_story.html)(last accessed June 7, 2016).

[13] *See, e.g.,* State v. Abdelmalik, 273 S.W.3d 61, 66 (Mo. Ct. App. 2008)(DNA material found in a location, quantity, and type inconsistent with casual contact and "there is a one in one quintillion likelihood that someone else was the source of the material," the DNA evidence alone is sufficient to support the conviction); State v. Tommes, 191 S.W.3d 122, 131 (Tenn. Crim. App. 2005) (DNA evidence alone sufficient to convict where probability of a random match ranges from 1 in 5 billion to 1 in 185 billion); Roberson v. State, 16 S.W.3d 156, 170 (Tex. App. 2000)("the testimony of even one DNA expert that there is genetic match between the semen recovered from the victim of a rape and the blood of the defendant . . . is legally sufficient to support a guilty verdict.").

[14] Rodney Uphoff, "Convicting the Innocent: Aberration or Systemic Problem?" 2006 WIS. L. REV. 739, 778 (2006)(describing the 2000 DNA exoneration of Larry Youngblood, who "[c]ontrary to the 'overwhelming evidence' . . . was, in fact, innocent") DNA testing alone does not always prove a prisoner innocent. *See* House v. Bell, 547 U.S. 518, 540–548 (2006)(other incriminating evidence and an alternative explanation for the DNA result).

[15] District Attorney's Office for Third Judicial Dist. v. Osborne, 557 U.S. 52, 62 (2009).

available for a wide range of plant and animal species.[16] For example, scientists were able to analyze and identify the DNA of dried leaves found in the suspect's car and compare it to the DNA of the same tree species that were growing near a shallow grave where the victims were found.[17] DNA analysis of marijuana plants has been used to identify the geographic sources of seized drugs.[18] The prevalence of pets (in 55% of American households) and the high transfer/persistence of animal hair[19] have made the identification of an individual pet useful in associating people to one another or to a particular scene.[20] It is expected that non-human DNA forensic evidence will continue to be used by both the prosecution and the defense in criminal cases.[21]

In the civil context, DNA analysis is one of the primary methods used for determinations of genetic identity. DNA analysis may be involved in paternity cases to establish the obligation of child support,[22] in government entitlement cases to determine the right to receive benefits such as social security, in immigration cases to determine if children are the true offspring of legal residents, in proof-of-death, mass disaster, and missing persons cases to establish the true identity of the deceased.[23] While traditional serological tests and other forensic examinations, such as dental, skeletal, and fingerprint comparisons, can contribute significantly to resolving identity issues in these cases, DNA analysis is frequently used because of its high specificity and utility when other means of identification are unavailable, insufficient, or

---

[16] *See* Heather Miller Coyle, *Nonhuman DNA Typing: Theory and Casework Applications* (2007), Kathleen J. Craft et al., "Application of Plant DNA Markers in Forensic Botany: Genetic Comparison of Quercus Evidence Leaves to Crime Scene Trees Using Microsatellites," 165 FORENSIC SCI. INT'L. 64 (2007); Pierre Taberlet et al., "Power and Limitations of the Chloroplast trnL (UAA) Intron for Plant DNA Barcoding," 35 Nucleic Acids Research 14 (2007); Cheng-Lung Lee et al., "DNA Analysis of Digested Tomato Seeds in Stomach Contents," 27 AM. J. FORENSIC MED. & PATHOLOGY 121 (2006).

[17] Kathleen J. Craft et al., "Application of Plant DNA Markers in Forensic Botany: Genetic Comparison of Quercus Evidence Leaves to Crime Scene Trees Using Microsatellites," 165 FORENSIC SCI. INT'L. 64 (2007); see also State v. Bogan, 183 Ariz. 506, 905 P.2d 515 (Ariz. Ct. App. 1995)(plant DNA admissible in murder case).

[18] Shannon L. Datwyler and George D. Weiblen, "Genetic Variation in Hemp and Marijuana (Cannabis sativa L.) According to Amplified Fragment Length Polymorphisms," 51 J. FORENSIC SCI. 371 (2006); Prapatsorn Tipparat et al., "Characteristics of Cannabinoids Composition of Cannabis Plants Grown in Northern Thailand and its Forensic Application," 215 FORENSIC SCI. INT'L 164–170 (2012).

[19] Marilyn Menotti-Raymond et al., "A Population Genetic Database of Cat Breeds Developed in Coordination with a Domestic Cat STR Multiplex," 53 J. FORENSIC SCI. 596–600 (2012).

[20] *See* Commonwealth v. Treiber, 582 Pa. 646, 874 A.2d 26 (2005)(DNA from dog hair admissible in arson/murder case).

[21] A. Linacre et al., "ISFG: Recommendations Regarding the Use of Non-Human(Animal) DNA in Forensic Genetic Investigations," 5 FORENSIC SCI. INT'L: GENETICS 501–505 (2011).

[22] In re Estate of Gaynor, 13 Misc.3d 331, 818 N.Y.S.2d 747 (Sur. Ct. 2006).

[23] Shannon Odelberg et al., "Establishing Paternity Using Minisatellite DNA Probes When the Putative Father is Unavailable for Testing," 33 J. Forensic Sci. 921 (1988); Mitchell Holland et al., "Mitochondrial DNA Sequence Analysis of Human Skeletal Remains: Identification of Remains from The Vietnam War," 38 J. Forensic Sci. 542 (1993).

inconclusive.[24] Successful analyses of the remains from large-scale national disasters have expanded the parameter of DNA forensic applications.[25]

II. INVESTIGATION OF BIOLOGICAL MATERIAL PRINCIPLES

§14.04 STANDARDS

Although not mandatory, guidelines for the collection and serological examination of biological evidence were adopted on January 15, 2015, by the Scientific Working Group on DNA Analysis Methods (SWGDAM).[26] SWGDAM, discussed in Section 17.12 *infra*, is influential in the field of DNA analysis and the new guidelines are expected to be widely adopted or consulted by federal and state laboratories. As explained by SWGDAM, "the identification and characterization of biological fluids on evidentiary items . . . is often a precursor to DNA examinations . . ., [t]herefore the quality and integrity of the serological testing process is critical for the success of subsequent DNA analysis."[27] Guidelines on the collection and processing of biological evidence are also available from the Technical Working Group on Biological Evidence Preservation.[28]

§14.05 DETECTION AND IDENTIFICATION OF BLOOD

Blood may be readily apparent at a crime scene. Bloodstains on dark surfaces, in small quantities, or where a scene has been altered to conceal evidence, may be harder to detect. Alternate light sources (ALS), ultraviolet (UV) light, and bright white lights disclose many stains on dark surfaces. Luminol or similar commercially produced solutions like Bluestar® which undergo reactions that produce light in

---

[24] *See* William Haglund et al., "Identification of Decomposed Human Remains by Deoxyribonucleic Acid (DNA) Profiling," 35 J. Forensic Sci. 724 (1990). *See* Henry Lee et al., "Genetic Markers in Human Bone: 1. Deoxyribonucleic Acid (DNA) Analysis," 36 J. Forensic Sci. 320, 321 (1991); Manfred Hochmeister et al, "Analysis of Deoxyribonucleic Acid (DNA) Extracted from Compact Bone from Human Remains," 36 J. Forensic Sci. 1649 (1991); Brion Smith et al., "A Systematic Approach to the Sampling of Dental DNA," 38 J. Forensic Sci. 1194 (1993); Ted Schwartz et al., "Characterization of Deoxyribonucleic Acid (DNA) Obtained from Teeth Subjected to Various Environmental Conditions," 36 J. Forensic Sci. 979 (1991).

[25] Leslie G. Biesecker et al., "Epidemiology: DNA Identifications After the 9/11 World Trade Center Attack," 310 SCIENCE 1122 (2005).

[26] Scientific Working Group on DNA Analysis Methods, *SWGDAM Guidelines for the Collection and Serological Examination of Biological Evidence*, approved January 15, 2015 (available at: www.swgdam.org).

[27] Id. at p. 2.

[28] Technical Working Group on Biological Evidence Preservation: National Institute of Standards and Technology, *NISTIR 7928 The Biological Evidence Preservation Handbook: Best Practices for Evidence Handlers*, April 2013 (available at: https://www.nist.gov/publications/biological-evidence-preservation-handbook-best-practices-evidence-handlers).

the presence of blood are often used to reveal trace bloodstains not apparent to the naked eye.

These products are highly sensitive and do not interfere with subsequent DNA testing.[29] Although hydrochlorite-containing bleaches and cleaning products also react with luminol, studies of chemical additives in luminol solutions and air-drying suspected cleaned areas have shown that the interfering effects can be mitigated.[30] Luminol and similar solutions do have limitations in addition to cross-reactivity to non-blood substances. These products require darkness or near darkness to visualize the chemiluminescence. The reactions fade quickly, so documentary photography can be challenging. Luminol is considered a potential carcinogen and safety protocols must be utilized.[31]

When a stain is submitted for examination as blood, it should first be identified using presumptive tests. A presumptive test is a screening test that indicates that a biological fluid (e.g., blood) may be present, but a positive result does not constitute definitive identification of the biological fluid and a negative result only indicates that the biological fluid was not detected. Color reaction tests are the most widely used method for the presumptive identification of blood. They are based on the activity of hemoglobin as a catalyst to promote peroxide oxidation of compounds in the reagent, producing a characteristic color. The chemicals used are colorless in a reduced ionic state, but turn color rapidly when exposed to an oxidant (e.g., hydrogen peroxide) in the presence of a catalyst (in blood, "heme"). The color is produced as a result of the peroxidase activity of blood. Color tests are quick and easy to perform. A dry, sterile cotton swab is moistened with distilled water and rubbed against the suspected blood stain.[32] A drop of the testing reagent is added to the swab.[33] An immediate color change indicates the presence of strong oxidants and the results will be deemed inconclusive.

---

[29] L.J. Blum, Philippe Esperanca and Stephanie Rocquefelte, "A New High-Performance Reagent and Procedure for Latent Bloodstain Detection Based on Luminol Chemiluminescence," 39(3) CAN. SOC FORENSIC SCI. J. 81–100 (2006); Shanan S. Tode, Nigel Watson and Niamh Nic Daeid, "Evaluation of Six Presumptive Tests for Blood, Their Specificity, Sensitivity, and Effect on High Molecular-Weight DNA," 52 J. FORENSIC SCI. SOC. 102–109 (2007).

[30] Erina J.M. Kent, Douglas A. Elliott and Gordon M. Miskelly, "Inhibition of Bleach-Induced Luminol Chemiluminescence," 48 J. FORENSIC SCI. 64–67 (2003); Jonathan I. Creamer et al., "Attempted Cleaning of Bloodstains and Its Effect on the Forensic Luminol Test," 20 LUMINESCENCE 411–413 (2005).

Studies have also shown that blue denim, a common clothing material, also does not significantly interfere with luminol emission even in dilutions of 1:1000. Caitlyn Middlestead and John Thornton, "Sensitivity of the Luminol Test with Blue Denim," 55 J. FORENSIC SCI. 1340–1342 (2010).

[31] Commercially-produced alternatives to luminal do not appear to carry the same safety risks. Lisa Dilbeck, "Use of BlueStar Forensic In Lieu of Luminol at Crime Scenes," 56(5) J.FORENSIC IDENT. 706–720 (2006).

[32] In the alternative, a small cutting of the stain may be placed in a small test tube, on a micro filter plate, or on filter paper and moistened with distilled water.

[33] Some laboratory protocols call for the addition of a drop of ethanol before the addition of the reagent.

If there is no color change, a drop of hydrogen peroxide is added to the swab. A color change in less than 10 seconds after the addition of hydrogen peroxide is a positive presumptive indication for blood. When testing stains on certain materials, the possibility of an interfering reaction with the substrate material must be considered. For example, plant peroxidases, leather, and suede items containing tannins may cause a positive result in the absence of blood. For definitive identification, multiple screening tests may be used if they are based on different chemical principles if the limits of one test are not the same limitations as the other.[34] Quality assurance systems require the reagent to be tested before use against a positive control (known blood stain) and a negative control (swab moistened with distilled water) to ensure the reagent is working properly.

Several color tests are:

(1) Tetramethylbenzidine (TMB) test: This reagent has replaced the carcinogenic benzidine for use in blood identification. Solutions of TMB are more difficult to prepare than those of benzidine and somewhat less sensitive to traces of blood but generally exhibit the same behavior as benzidine.[35] Treatment of the suspected blood with TMB yields a blue or green color indicative of blood. A variety of materials including horse-radish, some vegetables, and citrus juices interfere with the test.

(2) Phenolphthalein test: The test is sensitive, producing a pink to deep rose color in the presence of blood. Interference can be caused by alkalis, copper, nickel, potassium ferrocyanide, and sodium cobaltinitrate.

(3) Leucomalachite Green test: This test is considered less sensitive than phenolphthalein, producing a green color in the presence of blood. False positives may be caused by rust, lead oxide, potato juice, and permanganates.

For adequate assurance that a substance is blood, the principal tests should be used in combination. Many laboratories use both the Phenolphthalein and Tetremethylbenzidine test procedures. A positive reaction with each test reduces the potential for errors attributable to false positives. The use of color tests directly on a stain should be avoided because the reagents may introduce contamination in subsequent DNA typing. Although color tests are not specific for blood, positive results permit the analyst to conclude that "blood may be

---

[34] SOFT/AAFS Forensic Toxicology Laboratory Guidelines, 2006 version, § 8.2. Supporting Documentation for Department of Justice Proposed Uniform Language for Testimony and Reports for the Forensic Examination of Serology.

[35] For a discussion of the value of TMB as a presumptive test for blood, *see* Joanna L. Webb, Johnathan I. Creamer & Terence I. Quickenden, "A comparison of the presumptive luminol test for blood with four non-chemiluminescent forensic techniques," 21 LUMINESCENCE 214–220 (2006).

present." Negative results on a combination of the tests permit the analyst to conclude "no blood was detected." Inconsistent results on a combination of tests should be reported as "inconclusive" or "no determination can be made regarding the presence or absence of blood."[36]

If conducted with care, crystal tests using a microscopic evaluation are sensitive indicators of blood. Rust or other contaminants in the sample may interfere with crystal tests and the tests are less sensitive than color tests. Two of the most common crystal tests are:

(1) Takayama (Hemochromogen Crystals) test: In the presence of an alkaline solution, a reducing sugar and pyridine, hemoglobin forms a characteristic pink, rhomboid shaped crystals of hemochromogen

(2) Teichmann (Hematin Crystals) test: A portion of the stain is treated with saline to release the hemoglobin, dried and glacial acetic acid added. On evaporation, in the presence of hemoglobin, brownish-red, rhombic crystals of hemin are formed singly, in rosettes or clusters.

Crystal tests are considered confirmatory tests for the presence of blood, but are not specific for human blood. Many laboratories will conduct DNA analysis without conducting the confirmatory test to prevent excessive consumption of the evidence. The primers used in DNA typing analysis will only react with human and upper primate (e.g., chimpanzee) DNA. The presence of upper primates is easily ruled out in most criminal cases, so the DNA testing results will be used as support for the conclusion of the presence of human blood.

Other confirmatory tests for the identification of human blood are immunoassays. A precipitin test may be used but is considered too labor intensive in modern forensic laboratories. An extract of the stain is layered above anti-human serum in a small tube or placed in an agarose plate. If the sample is of human origin, it will react with antibodies in the antiserum and form a cloudy ring or line at the interface of the two liquids. Commercially available lateral flow immunoassays specific for human blood contain labeled anti-human hemoglobin antibodies which react with human hemoglobin (hHb). These tests are similar to common pregnancy tests where the extract of the stain is placed in a plastic cassette. Monoclonal anti-human hemoglobin antibodies tagged with a dye are impregnated on a membrane within the cassette. As the extract flows across the membrane, hemoglobin in the extract will bind with these antibodies. At a specific location on the membrane (identified as the "T" or test line), polyclonal antibodies react with hemoglobin to produce a pink line. The monoclonal anti-human hemoglobin antibodies not bound to

---

[36] Department of Justice Proposed Uniform Language for Testimony and Reports for the Forensic Examination of Serology.

hemoglobin will continue to flow down the membrane and bind to a different antibody at the "C" or control line used as a quality control measure to demonstrate that the test cassette is working properly. While these tests are designed to be specific for human hemoglobin, cross-reaction has been seen with other animals such as ferrets. Reporting of these test results are usually coupled with the disclaimer that positive results may be seen with other animal bloods.

§14.06 SEMINAL FLUID AND SPERM CELLS

Seminal fluid is a mixture of secretions of the glands along the genital tract, the prostatic fluid secreted by the prostate gland, and the sperm from the testes. The fluid consists of a highly proteinaceous serum rich in choline and seminal acid phosphatase. The head of the spermatozoa (sperm cell) is oval shaped and the flagellate tail is 10 to 12 times the length of the head. During sexual intercourse, the sexually mature male may ejaculate seminal fluid containing sperm cells. The first portion of the ejaculate consists primarily of the excretion of the bulbo-urethral glands and prostatic fluid, with relatively few sperm cells. The mid-portion of the ejaculate contains the majority of the sperm cells and the final portion is primarily seminal vesicle secretion with relatively few sperm cells.

The sperm present in the seminal fluid is the primary source of DNA. While the DNA in an individual sperm cell is haploid (only one chromosome of each pair in the genome), the collection of multiple cells allow for generation of the complete DNA profile of the male. The normal sperm count runs between 70–150 million per milliliter, comprising roughly 10% of the total volume of the ejaculate. Some males exhibit naturally low sperm counts and less than 20 million per milliliter is considered indicative of male infertility (oligospermic). Males with successful vasectomies are azoospermic with a sperm count essentially zero. While spermatozoa will be undetectable in a vasectomized individual samples, DNA testing on epithelial and white cells and the identification of seminal fluid protein and enzymes will still be possible. If a condom is used during the assault, semen may be undetectable on the victim, but the condom itself can be tested for both the male seminal fluid and the victim's DNA.

In alleged sexual assault cases, a Sexual Assault Examination Kit (SAEK) may be collected from the complaining witness during a medical examination. A similar kit may be collect from an identified suspect within 48 hours of the alleged assault. The SAEK is for the collection of biological material, including saliva, blood, semen, skin cells and hair. Swabs are taken from the person's vaginal cavity, cervix, genitalia, anus, mouth, and under the fingernails. Previously liquid blood samples and pulled head and pubic hairs were taken for typing and microscopic comparison purposes. A liquid blood sample may be collected for comparison, but buccal swabs are now considered the preferred reference sample to use for DNA typing.

Sperm cells and/or seminal stains may also be found on clothing or at the scene. Alternative light sources may be used to detect semen stains, which fluoresce under ultraviolet light. The detection of trace amounts of sperm on the clothing of members sharing the same household may be of limited value and studies have also demonstrated transfer through routine laundering.[37] The presence of intact sperm cells is the best indicator of recent sexual contact. Sperm cells may remain intact (motile) for 8–10 hours after ejaculation in a living human female, and slightly longer in a dead body.[38] Nonmotile sperm have been detected for periods up to seventeen days,[39] but the normal window for detection of sperm in a living person is 72 hours and occasionally up to 96 hours.[40]

The minuscule size of the sperm cells (1/5000th inch) requires examination of the specimen under a microscope. In a dried stain the tail on the sperm cell will become brittle and often detaches from the sperm. In the absence of the complete sperm cell (head, connecting piece and tail) positive identification is more difficult and may require the use of stains to better visualize the sample or specialized polarization microscopic techniques. Three different approaches may be used for the microscopic identification of sperm cells: (1) Interference-Phase microscopy; (2) stained slides; and (3) Phase-Contrast microscopy. The most common method is the stained slide using hematoxylin and eosin or nuclear fast red and picroindigocarmine (the "Christmas Tree stain"). The sperm cells from different species of mammals vary in their microscopic appearance therefore the microscopic identification of the human sperm cell morphology is considered a confirmatory test.

Microscopic examination of extracts of a seminal stain may not reveal the presence of spermatozoa. Seminal fluid can be detected with immunoassays that use monoclonal antibodies specific for either prostate specific antigen (PSA or p30) or semenogelin (proteins highly specific to seminal fluid).[41] It is possible to detect prostatic acid

---

[37] E. Kafarowski, A.M. Lyon and M.M. Sloan, "The Retention and Transfer of Spermatozoa in Clothing by Machine Washing," 29 CAN. SOC. FORENSIC SCI. J. 7–11 (1996).

[38] People v. Cordova, 62 Cal. 4th 104, 113, 358 P.3d 518, 527, 194 Cal. Rptr. 3d 40, 51 (2015) (testimony of Criminalist David Stockwell, Contra Costa County crime laboratory).

[39] J. Poirer, "Care of the Female Adolescent Rape Victim," 18 PEDIATRIC EMERGENCY CARE 53 (2002).

[40] Dale L. Laux, "Biological Stains," in in WILEY ENCYCLOPEDIA OF FORENSIC SCIENCE, (Jamieson A. & Moenssens A.A., eds) 2009 & online updates.

[41] PSA has also been detected, in low concentrations in female urine and breast milk. Proper extraction methods can distinguish these fluids from seminal fluid which has a high concentration of PSA. Dale L. Laux and Sarah E. Custis, "Forensic Detection of Semen III. Detection of PSA Using Membrane Based Tests: Sensitivity Issues with Regards to the Presence of PSA in Other Body Fluids," 19 Midwestern Association of Forensic Sciences Newsletter 33–39 (2004). Semenogelin has only been detected in seminal fluid. I. Sato et al, "Rapid Detection of Semenogelin By One-Step Immunochromatographic Assay for Semen Identification," 287 J. IMMUNOLOGICAL METHODS 137–145 (2004).

phosphatase, an enzyme of the seminal fluid of humans or higher primates. Acid phosphatase (AP) is secreted by the prostate gland located just above the urethra. Its concentration in semen is about 400 times that in any other bodily fluid. The acid phosphatase test results in a color reaction when seminal fluid is treated with a series of reagents. One of the most widely used is an acidic solution of sodium alphanaphthylphosphate and Fast Blue Dye which produces a purple color in the presence of semen. Other reagents may produce different color reactions. The procedure can be conducted in the same manner as swabbing an isolated area to conduct a color tests for blood and the test can be conducted on larger items. This process is called "AP Mapping" and a large sheet of filter paper is laid on the item and saturated with distilled water. The filter paper is then pressed onto the item to transfer any fluid from the item to the paper. The reagents are then sprayed onto the filter paper to determine the location of a stain. As time passes, the ability of a stain or deposit to react with the test reagent generally decreases, although with specimens stored at room temperature, positive tests have been obtained up to 6–8 months.

A number of organisms and biological fluids contain acid phosphatase including bacteria; human milk, liver, urine and kidney; red blood cells; snake toxins; rice bran; sweet almonds; cauliflower; brussel sprouts; clover; bindweed; turnips; raisins; mango; ginger; figs and dates. In tests, the relatively high percentage of acid phosphatase in seminal fluid causes a rapid and permanent development of color. A reaction time of less than 30 seconds is normally considered indicative of semen. Some substances such as cauliflower; however, are reported to produce a color reaction as vivid as that from semen. Another form of acid phosphatase is also found in vaginal secretions, vaginal acid phosphatase, but can be discriminated from prostatic acid phosphatase by a specialized form of electrophoresis known as isoelectric focusing.[42]

Several other tests for semen have the potential for identification of seminal fluid in the absence of spermatozoa. One of these is for a protein designated p30 found in semen and is not present in other bodily fluids. Using immunological or electrophoric techniques, detection of p30 can provide a definitive identification of semen representing a significant improvement over the presumptive test for prostatic acid phosphatase.[43] A lateral flow immunoassay test similar to

---

[42] D. Patzelt, "History of Forensic Serology and Molecular Genetics in the Sphere of Activity of the German Society for Forensic Medicine," 144 Forensic Sci. Int'l. 185 (2004); I. Sato et al., "A Dot–Blot–Immunoassay for Semen Identification Using a Polyclonal Antibody Against Semenogelin, A Powerful Seminal Marker," 122 Forensic Sci. Int'l. 27 (2001); For a general discussion of Isoelectric Focusing see: R. Westermeier, *Electrophoresis in Practice: A Guide to Methods and Applications of DNA and Protein Separations* (2005).

[43] B. Levine et al., "Use of Prostate Specific Antigen in the Identification of Semen in Postmortem Cases," 25 AM. J. FORENSIC MED. & PATHOL. 288 (2004); N.A. Stubbings and P.J. Newall, "An Evaluation of Gamma–Glutamyl Transpeptidase (GGT) and p30 Determinations for the Identification of Semen on Postcoital Vaginal Swabs" 30 J.Forensic Sci. 604 (1985); F.M. Poyntz and P.D. Martin, "Comparison of p30 and Acid Phosphatase Levels in Post-coital Vaginal Swabs from Donor and Casework Studies" 24 FORENSIC SCI.INT. 17 (1984); L.

the test for human blood is available for seminal fluid identification. These tests use monoclonal antibodies specific for the semenogelin or p30 proteins. Immunoassay[44] and monoclonal antibodies[45] are considered confirmatory tests for identification of seminal stains.

Ultraviolet (UV) light examination can be useful in screening of large surfaces such as a bedsheet, rugs or crime scenes for seminal stains. Choline in a seminal stain will fluoresce white or blue-white under UV light. The fluorescence is not specific for semen because a number of other materials also fluoresce under UV and not all semen stains will fluoresce due to a breakdown of the choline in the sample. Many commercial laundry detergents now contain fluorescent brighteners which strongly fluoresce under UV light. The major concern with using UV light to locate semen stains is that UV light will degrade DNA and excessive exposure will decrease the ability to achieve a full DNA profile.

Other light sources (Alternate Light Sources, ALS) such as lasers and high intensity quartz lamps are routinely used for the detection of body secretions such as semen, saliva, and perspiration.[46] These light sources emit specific wavelengths of light within the ultra-violet spectrum. The body fluid will absorb the light and then emit light at a slightly different wavelength. By wearing googles that are specific for the emitted wavelength, the analyst can better visualize the specific fluoresce from the biological fluid. Both UV and ALS examinations are considered searching techniques only and are not used as the basis for identification of a biological fluid. Raman spectroscopic examination can also be used for the identification of biological fluids.[47] This method could be considered a non-destructive, confirmatory identification of the biological fluid.

§14.07 OTHER BIOLOGICAL MATERIAL

Oral fluid (also referred to as saliva) is a complex fluid containing water, enzymes, glycoprotein, buccal (cheek) epithelial and glandular cells that are naturally sloughed from the lining of the mouth. DNA

Kamenev, et al. "An Enzyme Immunoassay for ProstateBSpecific p30 Antigen Detection in the Postcoital Vaginal Tract" ibid. 29 J.FORENSIC SCI. 233 (1989); E.D. Johnson and T.M. Kotowski, "Detection of Prostate Specific Antigen by ELISA" 38 J.Forensic Sci. 250 (1993).

[44] M. Bauer and D. Patzelt, "Protamine mRNA as Molecular Marker for Spermatozoa in Semen Stains," 117 INT'L J. LEGAL MED. 175 (2003).

[45] I. Sato et al., "A Sandwich Enzyme-linked Immunosorbent Assay for ABO Blood Typing of Semen by Using Anti-p 84 Monoclonal Antibody as a Marker of Blood Group Substance in Semen," 45 J. FORENSIC SCI. 795 (2000).

[46] M.J. Auvdel, "Comparison of Laser and Ultraviolet Techniques Used in the Detection of Body Secretions," 32 J.Forensic Sci. 326 (1987); M.J. Auvdel, "Comparison of Laser and High Intensity Quartz Arc Tubes in the Detection of Body Secretions," 33 J.Forensic Sci. 929 (1988).

[47] K. Virkler and I.K. Lednev, "Analysis of body fluids for forensic purposes: From laboratory testing to non-destructive rapid confirmatory identification at a crime scene" 188 For.Sci.Int.1 (2009).

testing is conducted on the cellular material (epithelial and white cells) rather than the oral fluid. Saliva stains are frequently recovered in criminal cases, especially sexual assault cases, on skin[48] or clothing. As with semen, alternative light sources can be used to detect saliva stains. Once detected, the saliva stains can be documented and cut from the item or collected with dry, sterile swabs.

No definitive tests are available for identifying saliva. There are several tests for the alpha-amylase enzyme that is found in high concentrations in saliva. The enzyme is also found in lower concentrations in other body fluids.[49] Most tests are based on the ability of amylase to hydrolyze starch molecules. A radial diffusion assay can be utilized with an agarose gel containing starch and iodine. Iodine in the presence of starch will appear bright blue. The sample is placed in a well cut into the agarose. If amylase is present, a clearing of the agarose will occur as the amylase hydrolyzes the starch.

Kits are available commercially based on the same principle as the starch-iodine reaction. Phadebas® Amylase Test uses a starch polymer coupled with a soluble dye. The dye is released into solution as the amylase hydrolyzes the starch. This procedure may be performed on either individual cuttings or using a "mapping" technique similar to the acid phosphatase mapping. A lateral flow immunoassay test is also available to detect human salivary alpha-amylase using monoclonal antibodies.

Perspiration (sweat) is excreted onto the surface of the skin to regulate body temperature. DNA evidence may be collected from the skin cells in perspiration stains but may also be found as cell-free nucleic acids.[50] Suitable items for testing include handkerchiefs, bandannas, headbands, or a shirt stained under the arms or around the collar. The inside band of a hat or cap, the waist band of undershorts, undershirts, t-shirts or "tank tops" are also potentially attractive for testing if these are left at the crime scene. There are no specific tests to identify the fluid of perspiration.

In addition to its wide use as a specimen for drug testing, the detection of urine at a scene may be supportive of statements or reconstruction of the sequence of events. Although a stain may visually appear to be urine, most assessments are based on the smell associated with the presence of uric acid and urea. Presumptive tests for urine rely on detection of the various components of urine: uric acid, urea, and

---

[48] In studies, full DNA profiles have been obtained from oral fluid on skin up to 96 hours after transfer. June Kenna *et al.,* "The Recovery and Persistence of Salivary DNA on Human Skin," 56 J.FORENSIC SCI. 170–175 (2011).

[49] Amylase can be detected in other human biological material, such as semen and feces, and in bacteria, but the concentration of amylase in saliva are 1000 times the concentration in other body fluids. M.J.Auvdel, "Amylase Levels in Semen and Saliva Stains," 31 J.Forensic Sci. 426–431 (1986).

[50] I. Quinones and B. Daniel, "Cell free DNA as a component of forensic evidence recovered from touched surfaces", For.Sci.International-Genetics 6 (2012) 26–30.

creatinine. The common test for creatinine is the Jaffe test color test: a drop of sodium hydroxide followed by concentrated picric acid in the presence of creatinine forms an intense orange color.[51] Other approaches have been applied to the identification of urine stains including radioimmunoassay for urinary proteins, radial gel diffusion for urea, and immunological techniques.[52] A lateral flow immunoassay test similar to the test for human blood, semen, and saliva is available for urine identification also. It tests for the presence of Tamm-Horsfall (THP) glycoprotein (uromodulin), which is the most abundant protein present in urine.[53] DNA sufficient for typing analysis may be obtained from the urothelial cells (derived from the ureter, bladder, and renal pelvis mucosa) found in urine.

Other biological material may be collected for DNA analysis. In criminal cases, recovered tissue, as for example, skin from under the fingernails, can be analyzed to detect DNA foreign to the individual. Teeth are durable and survive accidents and decomposition. When recovered, the dental pulp inside the tooth may be typed for DNA. Hair is another material which may be encountered at a crime scene, and it can be typed if the root portion is available.[54] Mitochondrial DNA testing is routinely used in the analysis of teeth, hair, as well as bones.

Fecal material may be present at crime scenes. While tests for urobilinogen and urobilin products of bilirubin metabolism have been used for identification,[55] forensic laboratories do not routinely analyze an evidence sample. DNA testing can be conducted on a sample of the material, but the best source of DNA is swabbing from the outer surface.

III. GENERAL PRINCIPLES OF DNA ANALYSIS

§14.08 THE ORIGIN OF DNA TECHNOLOGIES

Current DNA analytical technologies are the result of modern biochemical research that began in the early nineteenth century with the development of powerful light microscopes and techniques for fixing and staining living tissues. These advances allowed scientists to see into the cell, the basic unit of living material. Scientists learned the relationship of the individual cell to that of the organism, to how life reproduces itself,

---

[51] Dale L.Laux, "Biological Stains," in WILEY ENCYCLOPEDIA OF FORENSIC SCIENCE, (Jamieson A. & Moenssens A.A., eds) 2009 & online updates.

[52] Tomoko Akutsu et al., "Evaluation of Tamm-Horsfall Protein and Uroplakin III for Forensic Identification of Urine," 55 J.FORENSIC SCI. 742–746 (2010).

[53] Rapid Stain Identification of Urine (RSID™-Urine) [package insert] Hillside, IL: Independent Forensics (June 2011).

[54] V. Yuasa et al., "Esterase D Phenotyping of Bloodstains and Hair Roots by Low Voltage Isoelectric Focusing" 28 Forensic Sci.Int'l 63 (1985); A. Tahir and B. Welch, "Simultaneous Typing of Erythrocyte Acid Phosphatase, Adenyl Kinase and Adenosine Desaminase in Human Hair Root Sheaths" 26 J.FORENSIC SCI.SOC. 335 (1986).

[55] Stuart H. James, Jon J. Nordby and Suzanne Bell, eds. *Forensic Science: An Introduction to Scientific and Investigative Techniques,* 4th ed., CRC Press, 2014.

and to the particular characteristics of the species. From this foundational knowledge, scientists discovered that every cell results from the growth and splitting of a parent cell into two daughter cells, and that all cells, except red blood cells, have a nucleus.

By the 1860s, chromosomes were identified as rod-like bodies within the nucleus, individual chromosomes within a cell were distinguished by size and shape, and the number of chromosomes per cell was found to be constant. In 1865, the Austrian monk Gregor Mendel crossed peas, proving that traits like color and shape are controlled by hereditary factors—genes—the basis of genetic inheritance. In 1869, Swiss scientist Friedrich Miescher discovered DNA within the cell's nucleus. By 1901, genetic and chromosomal theorems established that chromosomes were the carriers of all hereditary characteristics. In the 1920s, the location of DNA was narrowed to the chromosomes within the nucleus, and by 1944, DNA was generally accepted as the basic genetic material.

In April 1953, American scientist James Watson and British scientist Francis Crick, working together at Cambridge University, announced their discovery of the double-helix structure of DNA.[56] Through this breakthrough, they were able to diagram two chains of nucleotides running in opposite directions, held together as base pairs by hydrogen bonds. The discovery of the DNA structure by Watson and Crick is recognized as one of the major scientific events of the twentieth century.[57] It caused an explosion in biochemistry that has transformed the science and created new fields of research. The application of biotechnology to forensic identification is merely one aspect of its vast biological, medical, and genetic implications.

After the discovery by Watson and Crick, additional research led to the isolation of the first restriction enzyme used to cut DNA strands at specific sites. These enzymes, together with other developments in DNA technologies, led to powerful methods for sequencing DNA, enabling specific portions of the separated DNA strands to be examined. These advances permit the individual variations, or polymorphisms, of DNA to be studied directly.[58] In 1983 the next major scientific breakthrough in DNA testing was done by Kary Mullis with the development of the Polymerase Chain Reaction (PCR) technique.[59] PCR technology allows the scientist to make billions of copies of limited DNA samples and focus their testing to specific locations on the DNA chain.

---

[56] James Watson and Francis Crick, "Molecular Structure of Nucleic Acids: A Structure for Deoxyribose Nucleic Acid," NATURE 4356 (1953).

[57] For a general tribute to the discoveries of Watson and Crick, see "Fifty Years of the DNA Double Helix (1953–2003)," Science Photo Gallery, available at http://www.sciencephoto gallery.co.uk/articles/DNA_50yearsArticle.php.

[58] Committee on DNA Technology in Forensic Science, Board on Biology, Commission on Life Sciences, National Research Council, DNA Technology in Forensic Science, National Academies Press: Washington DC, 1992, (hereinafter "NRC 1992 Report") at p. 32.

[59] R.K. Saiki, et.al. Primer-Directed Enzymatic Amplification of DNA with a Thermostable DNA Polymerase; Science, Vol. 239; pp. 487–492.

§14.09 Introduction to the Structure of DNA[60]

Deoxyribonucleic acid (DNA) is the molecule that contains an individual's genetic information. The DNA molecule is composed of a phosphate, a sugar, and nucleotides. The four types of nucleotides, also known as "bases," are: adenine (A), cytosine (C), guanine (G), or thymine (T). The two strands of the double helix DNA structure are complementary, meaning that two single strands are held together by hydrogen bonds connecting opposite and complementary bases. This is called base pairing. The base adenine (A) always bonds to the base thymine (T), and the base guanine (G) always bonds to the base cytosine (C). Base pairing results in a double helix DNA structure having the appearance of a twisted ladder, where the rungs are the hydrogen bonds of the base pairs, and the side supports are the sugar and phosphate groups.

Most human DNA—and the DNA analyzed with the most common forensic analytical method—is contained within chromosomes. Within each nucleated cell of the human body other than sex cells (sperm cell in the male and egg cells in the female) are twenty-three pairs of chromosomes, one set of each pair having come from the mother and the other set from the father. Forty-four of these chromosomes are "autosomes" (numbered 1 to 22 in descending order of size) and two are "sex chromosomes" (X or Y) that code for a person's gender for a total of 46 chromosomes. The sex cells contain only 22 autosomes and one sex chromosome for a total of 23 chromosomes.

A complete set of chromosomes is called the genome, which encompasses the total genetic make-up of an individual and is comprised of a sequence of A, T, G and C nucleotides totaling more than 3 billion base pairs. An estimated 99.9% of the genome is identical for all humans. The remaining 0.1% (approximately 3 million base pairs) varies among individuals and is what distinguishes an individual from every other person (except an identical twin). DNA material in chromosomes is composed of either "coding" or "non-coding" regions. Coding regions (genes) generate proteins; non-coding regions do not.

The most common current DNA typing methodologies are based on the non-coding regions (loci) on the chromosomes where the base pair sequence varies between individuals. The loci are designated by their location on a specific chromosome or within a specific gene and contain additional identifying information for the marker. For example, the locus name "D5S818" refers to **DNA** chromosome **5**, a **s**ingle copy sequence, at the **818**th locus identified on chromosome 5. The locus TH01 refers to the

---

[60] *See generally* David H. Kaye and George Sensabaugh, "Reference Guide on DNA Identification Evidence," in *Reference Manual on Scientific Evidence*, 3rd ed., National Academies Press: Washington DC, 2011 at pp. 129–210; Committee on DNA Forensic Science: An Update, Commission on DNA Forensic Science: An Update, National Research Council, *The Evaluation of Forensic DNA Evidence*, National Academies Press: Washington DC, 1996, (*hereinafter "NRC 1996 Report"*) at pp. 11–14, 60–65.

human **t**yrosine **h**ydroxylase gene and the repeat region contained in the **1st** intron of the gene.[61]

Each variation of base pair sequence at a locus is called an "allele." If an individual has two copies of the same allele at a locus, the locus is homozygous. If an individual has two different alleles at a locus, the locus is heterozygous. For the analysis of nuclear DNA, the allele is designated by the number of repeats of the sequence present (i.e., 11, 12 etc.). The DNA profile derived from nuclear DNA is reported as numbers identifying the allele types detected at specific loci. For example, a profile might look like:

D5S818   11, 13—heterozygote

TH01   5, 5—homozygote

§14.10 SOURCES OF DNA

With the exception of red blood cells, every cell in the human body contains DNA. Within a blood sample, DNA is located within the nucleated white cells. The sequence of the base pairs in the DNA molecule is the same, regardless of its source (e.g., skin, hair, bone, semen). In the early days of DNA analysis, the analytical technology required a relatively large amount of DNA, so testing was primarily conducted on blood stains, semen stains containing spermatozoa, and sexual assault examination kits (SAEK) containing swabs from suspected sexual assaults.

Technological advances have dramatically decreased the amount of DNA necessary and successful analysis is now conducted on touch samples. Testing specific to the Y chromosome (Y-STR) increased the successful typing of semen in absence of spermatozoa by analyzing the epithelial material present. Additional testing methods using non-nuclear DNA have also expanded the potential sample sources. Routinely collected samples now include not only blood and semen stains, but also hairs, teeth, bone, feces,[62] dandruff, plant material, insects,[63] saliva, and swabs[64] from surfaces that may contain sweat, nasal, and vaginal secretions containing epithelial cells.[65]

---

[61] John M. Butler, *Forensic DNA Typing: Biology, Technology, and Genetics of STR Markers*, 2d ed., Elsevier Press, 2005 at pp. 22–24.

[62] *See* D.J. Johnson, L.R. Martin and K.A. Roberts, "STR-typing of Human DNA from Human Fecal Matter Using the Qiagen Qiaamp® Stool Mini Kit," 50 J. FORENSIC SCI. 802–808 (2005).

[63] *See* R. Zehner, J. Amendt and R. Krettek, "STR Typing of Human DNA from Fly Larvae Fed on Decomposing Bodies," 49 J. FORENSIC SCI. 337–340 (2004).

[64] Cotton swabs are commonly used to collect biological material and have been shown to be effective in maximizing DNA recovery during extraction in forensic cases. Robert J. Brownlow, Kathryn E. Dagnall and Carole E. Ames, "A Comparison of DNA Collection and Retrieval from Two Swab Types (Cotton and Nylon Flocked Swab) When Processed Using Three QIAGEN Extraction Methods," 57 J. Forensic Sci. 713–717 (2012).

[65] Sally-Ann Harbison, "DNA: Sources of," in WILEY ENCYCLOPEDIA OF FORENSIC SCIENCE, (Jamieson A. & Moenssens A.A., eds) 2009 & online updates.

Although the keratin structure of the fingernail itself does not contain DNA, any epithelial cells adhering to the nail may be typed.[66] Fingernails are also potential evidence sources in physical assault cases where biological evidence (blood, semen, saliva, skin or other epithelial cells) may have collected underneath the fingernails.[67]

§14.11 THE FUNDAMENTALS OF DNA ANALYSIS

The DNA structure is ideally suited for forensic analysis because (1) it is the same everywhere in an individual; the same DNA molecule exists in all nucleated cells in the human body: tissues, fluids, organs, and other biological materials; (2) it is inherited from an individual's parents; familial relationships can provide information on the source of a given DNA profile; and (3) it varies from person to person; it is polymorphic.[68] These characteristics make DNA a readily available, somewhat predictable, and highly individualizing type of evidence. Polymorphic loci that differ among individuals are found throughout the non-coding regions of human DNA.[69] For forensic analysis, the variation between individuals makes discrimination and identification possible.

The variations in the DNA sequence can result from several types of mutations. The two forms of genetic polymorphisms are either length or sequence differences. The most common type of DNA analysis utilizes length polymorphisms created by insertion/deletion mutations. These mutations occur in regions of repetitive DNA sequences that result in a variation in the number of units of DNA material arranged in tandem. The human genome is made up 50% repetitive DNA. The repeat unit of these DNA sites can vary from 2 base repeat units to hundreds of bases in each repeated sequence. Variable Numbers of Tandem Repeats (VNTR) are DNA nucleotide sequences typically consisting of 500–10,000 base pairs, composed of repeating sequences of base pairs, usually 15 to 100 base pairs in length. The exact number of repeats varies by allele type, so different alleles can be identified by the length of the VNTR. VNTR also have a high mutation rate, resulting in a large number of different alleles in the population.[70] Short tandem repeats (STR) are repetitive units of DNA with between 2 to 8 base units in length and are most commonly used in forensics today.

---

[66] Id.

[67] *See* Bublil Nurit et al., "Evaluating the Prevalence of DNA Mixtures Found in Fingernail Samples from Victims and Suspects in Homicide Cases," 5 FORENSIC SCI. INT'L: GENETICS 532–537 (2011); Nicola Flanagan and Colin McAlister, "The Transfer and Persistence of DNA Under the Fingernails Following Digital Penetration of the Vagina," 5 FORENSIC SCI. INT'L: GENETICS 479–483 (2011); Melinda Matte, et al., "Prevalence and Persistence of Foreign DNA Beneath Fingernails," 6 FORENSIC SCI. INT'L: GENETICS 236–243 (2012).

[68] *See* Simon J. Walsh, "DNA," in WILEY ENCYCLOPEDIA OF FORENSIC SCIENCE, (Jamieson A. & Moenssens A.A., eds) 2009 & online updates.

[69] John M. Butler, *Forensic DNA Typing: Biology, Technology, and Genetics of STR Markers*, 2d ed., Elsevier Press, 2005 at p. 22.

[70] NRC 1996 Report at pp. 14, 65.

1.   OLDER METHOD (RFLP)

VNTR are useful for DNA analysis only if they can be detected and isolated. This can be done by extracting the DNA from the cellular material and cutting the DNA strand into smaller fragments. This protocol uses restriction enzymes that cut the DNA strand at specific locations of base sequences and produces fragments of variable lengths depending on the number of base pairs in the fragment. By separating (usually through gel electrophoresis) and measuring these fragments, the allele type at specific loci can be determined using radiation or chemiluminescence techniques to develop a DNA profile. This technique is called Restriction Fragment Length Polymorphism (RFLP).[71] This method was the first method used in forensic DNA testing in 1986, but it is now obsolete[72] and only conducted by some private laboratories.

2.   SHORT TANDEM REPEATS (STR)

Currently, DNA analysis is conducted using DNA amplification technology called polymerase chain reaction (PCR). PCR, first developed in 1985,[73] has advantages over RFLP technology and quickly gained widespread acceptance in the forensic community. Polymerase chain reaction selectively amplifies, or duplicates, targeted loci of the sample of DNA by replicating the process by which DNA naturally duplicates itself. The primary advantage of the PCR amplification is that smaller samples of biological material can be analyzed. For this reason, PCR analysis is highly useful for the analysis of limited and degraded samples of DNA, where a significant proportion of the DNA is broken down and only very small fragments are available for analysis. The smaller sample amount required for PCR testing also increase the potential availability of DNA from the original sample for subsequent testing by other laboratories.

With the discovery and implementation of STR analysis processes came the potential for improvement of PCR procedures. Laboratory analysis, using capillary electrophoresis, automated fluorescent tagging, and small amounts of template DNA, facilitate a combination gender and identity determination.[74] Multiplexing of numerous STR loci significantly increases the discrimination power of the DNA analysis.

---

[71] John M. Butler, *Forensic DNA Typing: Biology, Technology, and Genetics of STR Markers*, 2d ed., Elsevier Press, 2005 at p. 3.

[72] For more detailed discussion of RFLP analysis and accompanying technical issues, *see* NRC 1996 Report at pp. 65–69; NRC 1992 Report at pp. 36–40, 56–63.

[73] George Sensabaugh and Cecilia Von Beroldingen, "The Polymerase Chain Reaction: Application to the Analysis of Biological Evidence," *Forensic DNA Technology*, 63 (Mark A. Farley & James J. Harrington, eds., 1991).

[74] Gayveline Calacal et al., "Identification of Exhumed Remains of Fire Tragedy Victims Using Conventional Methods And Autosomal/Y-Chromosomal Short Tandem Repeat DNA Profiling," 26 AM. J. FORENSIC MED. PATHOL. 285 (2005).

IV. CURRENT DNA ANALYSIS METHODOLOGY[75]

§14.12 STANDARDS

Unlike many fields of forensic science, DNA analysis does have established standards that are widely followed. The DNA Identification Act of 1994, 42 U.S.C. § 14132, required the formation of a board to address quality control and other issues relevant to forensic DNA typing. The DNA Advisory Board (DAB) was formed in 1995 to draft standards to be adopted by the Federal Bureau of Investigations (FBI). The FBI issued the "Quality Assurance Standards (QAS) for Forensic DNA Testing Laboratories" in 1998 and the "Quality Assurance Standards for Convicted Offender DNA Databasing Laboratories" in 1999. Both sets of standards were revised in 2009, and further revisions became effective September 1, 2011.[76] Compliance with the standards is mandatory for all DNA laboratories that are federally operated, receive federal funds, or participate in the Combined DNA Indexing System (CODIS) database program (discussed in Section 17.19(3) *infra*).[77] When the DNA Advisory Board statutory time period expired, the DNA Identification Act charged the Scientific Working Group on DNA Analysis Methods (SWGDAM)[78] with the responsibility for recommending additional quality assurance standards, and revisions as necessary. SWGDAM is a group of approximately 50 scientists from federal, state, and local forensic DNA laboratories in the United States and Canada. The Chairman of SWGDAM is selected and serves at the pleasure of the FBI Director. SWGDAM members are appointed by the Chairman based upon recommendations from a Membership Committee. During biannual meetings, the group develop voluntary guidelines and recommendations on virtually all aspects of DNA analysis, including training, validation procedures, mitochondrial DNA interpretation, Y-STR interpretation, and mixed DNA sample STR interpretation.[79] Anyone handling cases involving DNA analysis should consult the SWGDAM website (www.swgdam.org) regularly and review all SWGDAM documents and Quality Assurance Standards documents posted on the site.

---

[75] For a discussion of older analytical techniques, *see* NRC 1996 Report at pp. 65–73.

[76] FBI, "Quality Assurance Standards for Forensic DNA Testing Laboratories" (available at: https://www.fbi.gov/file-repository/quality-assurance-standards-for-forensic-dna-testing-laboratories .pdf/view)(last accessed March 3, 2017).

[77] 42 U.S.C. § 14132(b)(1): "the index described in subsection (a) shall include only information on DNA identification records and DNA analyses that are—(1) based on analyses performed by or on behalf of a criminal justice agency in accordance with publicly available standards that satisfy or exceed the guidelines for a quality assurance program for DNA analysis, issued by the Director of the Federal Bureau of Investigation under section 210303."

[78] *See* http://www.swgdam.org/.

[79] Id.

§14.13 BASIC STR ANALYSIS STEPS[80]

1.   EXTRACTION

The first step in any DNA analysis is to remove the DNA from the host material (the matrix), whether it is a blood sample, semen stain, hair fragment, or other biological material. The DNA must be released from other cellular material for analysis. Extraction, although not a highly complex or technologically sophisticated process, is a critical phase of DNA analysis because it is the stage most susceptible to the occurrence of laboratory-induced contamination of the samples.[81] Quality assurance standards and laboratory protocols for this stage must be carefully planned and strictly followed.

Commonly used extraction methods are organic extraction, chelex extraction, and solid-phase extraction.[82] Although the methods differ in components and actions, the purpose is to separate the DNA from the other cellular material, generally through chemical action or heat, and to isolate the DNA for analysis. Differential extraction, a modified version of extraction, is used to separate sperm cells and epithelial cells that are primarily the female contribution and is especially useful in sexual assault cases. The exact extraction and isolation method used depends on the matrix and frequently utilizes commercially available kits[83] and automated equipment.[84]

The next step is DNA quantitation to determine how much DNA is present to ensure the appropriate DNA concentration for the subsequent amplification step. The commercially produced amplification kits (discussed *infra*) are optimized to produce reliable DNA profiles in a specific range of DNA concentrations. Using too much or too little DNA in the amplification stage can lead to stochastic (randomly generated) errors in the analysis process.[85] Quantification of evidence samples is required by the FBI Quality Assurance Standards to prevent using excessive amounts of the sample.[86]

---

[80] For a detailed information on the STR process and informational resources, see the National Institute of Standards and Technology Short Tandem Repeat DNA Internet Database at: http://www.cstl.nist.gov/biotech/strbase/index.htm (last accessed June 9, 2016).

[81] Eleanor A.M. Graham, "DNA: An Overview," in WILEY ENCYCLOPEDIA OF FORENSIC SCIENCE, (Jamieson A. & Moenssens A.A., eds) 2009 & online updates.

[82] John M. Butler, *Forensic DNA Typing: Biology, Technology, and Genetics of STR Markers*, 2d ed., Elsevier Press, 2005 at pp. 42–49.

[83] *E.g.*, DNA IQ™, manufactured by Promega (www.promega.com) and QIAamp®, manufactured by Qiagen (www.qiagen.com).

[84] *E.g.*, Biomek® NX^P Automation Workstation manufactured by Beckman Coulter, Inc. (www.beckmancoulter.com).

[85] Eleanor A.M. Graham, "DNA: An Overview," in WILEY ENCYCLOPEDIA OF FORENSIC SCIENCE, (Jamieson A. & Moenssens A.A., eds) 2009 & online updates.

[86] FBI, "Quality Assurance Standards for Forensic DNA Testing Laboratories" at Standard 9.4 (available at: https://www.fbi.gov/file-repository/quality-assurance-standards-for-forensic-dna-testing-laboratories.pdf/view)(last accessed March 3, 2017).

2. AMPLIFICATION

Current forensic DNA typing by PCR analysis utilizes commercially available amplification kits containing primers, reaction mix, and polymerase.[87] PCR amplification is analogous to the process by which cells naturally replicate their DNA. The double stranded segment of DNA is separated (denatured) into two separate strands by heating in a thermal cycler.[88] Each denatured DNA strand provides a template for the manufacture of a new strand—identical to the former complementary strand. The temperature is then lowered so primers—short DNA segments designed to bind with the template at a specific locus—are added to the template to target the specific genetic locations for replication. An enzyme (polymerase) then facilitates the addition of bases to the targeted regions to create the new, complimentary strand of DNA at the targeted region. Each DNA strand is copied with each temperature cycle. This process is repeated a number of times (usually 28 cycles) to exponentially increase the number of copies of the targeted region of DNA.

In practice, laboratories simultaneously target multiple regions by using multiple primers in a single reaction. This process—multiplexing—increases the speed of the analysis and allows for a higher discrimination probability using a small amount of sample. For many years, the most commonly used kits typed 16 loci, but laboratories are moving to 24-loci multiplexing systems to comply with the FBI decision to expand the core loci for CODIS from 13 to 20 loci in January, 2017.[89]

3. SEPARATION—CAPILLARY ELECTROPHORESIS

After the DNA fragments are amplified, the fragments must be sorted by size. The sorting is accomplished by using capillary electrophoresis (CE). Electrophoresis is a separation technique based on the differential transportation of charged molecules in an electric field through a conductive or sieving medium. Capillary electrophoresis separates compounds based on their size-to-charge ratio in the interior of a small capillary (a very thin tube) filled with polymer.

---

[87] *E.g.*, GlobalFiler™ PCR Amplification System manufactured by Applied Biosystems or PowerPlex® 16 System manufactured by Promega.

[88] *E.g.*, GeneAmp® 9700 PCR Thermal Cycler, manufactured by Thermo Fisher Scientific Applied Biosystems.

[89] In 2015, the FBI announced the expansion of the 13-core loci that had been used since 1997. The expansion provides greater discrimination potential for identification and enhanced kinship analysis used in missing person cases. The new loci have been used in databases worldwide so the expansion also permits greater international cooperation for law enforcement. Effective January, 2017, the core loci for CODIS will be: CSF1PO, D3S1358, D5S818, D7S820, D8S1179, D13S317, D16S539, D18S51, D21S11, FGA, THO1, TPOX, vWA and new loci: D1S1656, D2S441, D2S1338, D10S1248, D12S391, D19S433, D22S1045. *See* Federal Bureau of Investigation, "Planned Process and Timeline for Implementation of Additional CODIS Core Loci" (available at: https://www.fbi.gov/services/laboratory/biometric-analysis/codis#Planned-Process%20and%20Timeline%20for%20Implementation%20of%20Additional%20CODIS%20Core%20Loci)(last accessed March 3, 2017).

In DNA analysis using CE, the amplified DNA is inserted into a capillary that is subjected to an electrical current. The DNA fragment moves through the capillary at a rate proportional to its size—smaller DNA fragments move faster than larger DNA fragments. Once a DNA fragment reaches the end of the capillary, it passes a laser light. This excites the fluorescent dye tag incorporated by the primers during the amplification process and causes the dye to fluoresce. A camera captures and measures the emitted light, which is reproduced in the corresponding dye color in an electropherogram. It takes approximately 30 minutes for the entire amplified DNA product to move through the CE system.

Some fragments from different loci will be similar in size. To discriminate between fragments of similar size from different loci, different dye colors are used. When the fragments pass through the laser light, the different dye colors will be recorded as well as the time it took for the fragment to move through the capillary. The time it takes the fragment to move through the capillary represents the length of the fragment. The length of the fragment along with the color of the dye indicates the allele type and the corresponding locus.

4. DETECTION AND INTERPRETATION

By measuring the time it takes the fragment to move through the capillary system and registering the color associated with the fragment, the allele and corresponding locus are determined. By measuring the amount of light emitted by the fluorescent tags, the amount of DNA present can also be estimated. The data generated by the CE process is analyzed by computer software that produces a graph of peaks with locations corresponding to alleles at specific loci. By comparing the peaks to allelic ladders, the DNA profile of the sample can be determined. The peak height (the relative fluorescent units captured by the camera) corresponds to the amount of DNA present and is useful in major/minor contributor assessments where a mixture of two or more contributors is present in the evidentiary DNA sample.

§14.14 INTERPRETATION ISSUES

The evidentiary weight of DNA evidence can be extremely high, so the scientific integrity of the DNA analysis is critical. The validity of DNA analysis, the ability to achieve correct results, is paramount. Reliability, the ability to reproduce correct test results by applying a protocol, is also important. The standardization of DNA analysis in the United States has been advanced through the adherence to the national quality assurances standards, the implementation of recommended protocols, and the use of commercially-produced amplification kits, analytical instrumentation, and software. As a result of the standardization, the analysis and interpretation of single-contributor and simple mixture DNA samples is generally recognized as producing straight-forward, scientifically-sound results.[90]

Errors can occur in the process, however, which affect the interpretation of results, whether from sample mishandling, contamination, misinterpretation, and misreporting of results.[91] The 2016 PCAST Report recommended:

> Because errors due to human failures will dominate the chance of coincidental matches, the scientific criteria for validity as applied require that an expert (1) should have undergone rigorous and relevant proficiency testing to demonstrate their ability to reliably apply the method, (2) should routinely disclose in reports and testimony whether, when performing the examination, he or she was aware of any facts of the case that might influence the conclusion, and (3) should disclose, upon request, all information about quality testing and quality issues in his or her laboratory.[92]

Additionally, complex mixtures (more than two contributors or where the major/minor contributors cannot be easily determined) and low concentration samples (touch) complicate the interpretation of the results.

1. QUALITY ASSURANCE

There are several generally recognized sources of potential contamination of DNA samples which are important to recognize because of the sensitivity of PCR to very small amounts of DNA. These sources include contamination from law enforcement officers and laboratory handling, carry-over of DNA from one analysis to another analysis, and biological and non-biological substances. To protect against contamination, laboratories should store evidence in sealed containers that demonstrate a detectable alteration if the seal is broken and maintain strict quality control measures designed to prevent contamination when handling and processing the samples.[93]

One preventable source of contamination is the improper handling of the sample in the laboratory itself. Contamination of the subject sample may come from a transfer between samples or from the laboratory technician doing the work. Appropriate controls are necessary quality assurance measures to help detect contamination within the laboratory. A negative amplification control (also known as an amplification blank

---

[90] *See* 2016 PCAST Report at pp. 73–75; Eleanor A.M. Graham, "DNA: An Overview," in WILEY ENCYCLOPEDIA OF FORENSIC SCIENCE, (Jamieson A. & Moenssens A.A., eds) 2009 & online updates; National Academies of Science, *Strengthening Forensic Science in the United States: A Path Forward*, National Academies Press: Washington, DC (2009) at pp. 7, 130–133.

[91] 2016 PCAST Report at p. 73.

[92] 2016 PCAST Report at p. 75.

[93] For a discussion of evidence handling issues, *see* David H. Kaye and George Sensabaugh, "Reference Guide on DNA Identification Evidence," in *Reference Manual on Scientific Evidence*, 3rd ed., National Academies Press: Washington DC, 2011 at pp. 156–159.

control) consists of only the amplification reagents without the addition of sample DNA and is used to detect DNA contamination of the amplification reagents. Reagent blank controls (consisting of all reagents used in the testing process without any sample) are used to detect DNA contamination of the analytical reagents. In addition to negative controls to detect possible contamination, each analysis should also contain a positive control. A positive control (also known as a positive amplification control) is an analytical control sample (generally commercially available) that is used to determine if the analytical process performed properly. Some laboratories may also use a positive extraction control that consists of a biological sample (blood or saliva) with a known DNA profile that is processed with evidentiary samples.

Validation studies with the methods and equipment used by the laboratory are also necessary to ensure that any variables in the analytical process are known. With the amplification kits, laboratories must be aware of the possibility of differential or preferential amplification of certain alleles. In a perfectly amplified sample, the peak heights of each allele of a heterozygous locus should be equal; each allele should amplify at the same rate. If, however, one allele is preferentially amplified or differentially amplified, there will be an imbalance[94] in the peak heights that may lead to misinterpretation in cases of possible mixtures.[95]

2.   ARTIFACTS V. GENETIC FACTS

When too much DNA is subjected to amplification and subsequently analyzed, artifacts such as pull up, signal spikes, and excessive stutter may occur. Pull up occurs when the detection capabilities of the CE camera is exceed due to an excessive amount of DNA. The software cannot adequately separate the different fluorescent colors, creating small "pull up" peaks in other fluorescent dye colors.

Signal spikes usually occur at the same location in more than one fluorescent dye color and are characterized by a very narrow width. The signal spike does not result from an actual DNA fragment, but from fluctuations in the voltage or air bubbles in the capillary equipment. The interpretation software can be programmed to detect spikes.

Stutter peaks occur due to slippage of the polymerase during DNA amplification. In autosomal STR typing, stutter peaks are most commonly one repeat unit shorter than the true allele peak (i.e., 4 nucleotides smaller than the true allele peak for the tetranucleotide repeats) and routinely referred to as "minus 4". A stutter peak may also appear as multiples of the repeat unit (e.g., 8 nucleotides for tetranucleotide repeats) or may be larger than the true allele peak size

---

[94] Eleanor A.M. Graham, "DNA: An Overview," in WILEY ENCYCLOPEDIA OF FORENSIC SCIENCE, (Jamieson A. & Moenssens A.A., eds) 2009 & online updates.

[95] SWGDAM, "Interpretation Guidelines for Autosomal STR Typing By Forensic DNA Testing Laboratories," *supra* note 78.

(+4 stutter). To help distinguish stutter peaks from true peaks, the software used by the laboratory is programmed to filter out or remove "stutter" peaks that are less than a certain percentage of the next peak (assumed to be the true allele peak) at the locus. This percentage is called the "stutter ratio." The stutter ratio is determined through validation studies at the laboratory or the kit developer and is typically less than 15%.[96] If there is excessive DNA in the sample, the amount of stutter detected may exceed the pre-programmed filter range causing the stutter to be identified as an allele.

The verification of artifact v. true allele can be made by using one or more of the following: re-injection, re-amplification, and review of the data. Stutter and pull-up is reproducible unless the sample is re-amplified using a lower concentration of DNA. Spikes are not reproducible and a re-injection of the sample should not have the same spike.

3. ALLELIC DROPOUT V. GENETIC EXCLUSION

There may be occasions when the DNA profile from the same individual may appear different from one analysis to another because of a missing allele. The phenomena of allelic dropout may be caused by several factors. The analyst must be aware of these factors in order to differentiate an apparent difference in profiles because of allelic dropout from those which are actual genetic differences. Allelic dropout, which is frequently caused by insufficient DNA, can also be caused by degraded DNA and variances in the analysis process.[97]

4. COMPLEX MIXTURE ANALYSIS

In some cases, the DNA analysis may involve biological evidence containing DNA from more than one person in a single sample. For example, in vaginal swabs taken from a woman following a suspected sexual assault by a male perpetrator, the swabs may contain both female and male DNA. The process of differential extraction may be used to separate the sperm fraction of the male contributor from the remaining cellular DNA. However, sometimes the sperm and cellular components cannot be separated completely through differential extraction, making interpretation of the two separate profiles difficult.[98]

Male DNA may be analyzed separately from any female DNA in a mixture amplifying genetic loci only located on the male Y chromosome or Y-STR. This method is similar to analysis of autosomal STR and is especially effective for isolating and identifying a male contributor when

---

[96] Id.

[97] Torben Tvedebrink et al., "Allelic Drop-out Probabilities Estimated by Logistic Regression—Further Considerations and Practical Implementation," 6 FORENSIC SCI. INT'L: GENETICS 263–267 (2012).

[98] Nicoletta Cerri et al., "Mixed Stains from Sexual Assault Cases: Autosomal or Y-Chromosome Short Tandem Repeats?" 44 CROATIAN MED. J. 289 (2003).

there is an excessive amount of female DNA in the mixture. Other mixtures present more difficulty for the analyst in circumstances where Y-STR analysis is unavailable or uninformative, such as mixtures from multiple male contributors or mixtures from multiple female contributors.

In some two person mixtures, the results can be separated into distinct profiles through peak height associations (a "major contributor" and a "minor contributor"). In other mixtures, however, the distinction between major and minor contributors is not easily made and the possibility of stutter and allelic drop-out makes interpretation of the results challenging. The potential for misinterpretation of peak height ratios could lead in some cases to the failure to detect a potential contributor or the failure to properly exclude a potential contributor.[99] For example, the analysis of the major contributor sample may produce stutter that is the same height/peak area as a potential minor contributor's true allele in the mixture, so peaks in stutter position may be (1) the minor contributor's true allele; (2) the minor contributor's true allele plus stutter from the major contributor's profile; or (3) stutter from the major contributor's profile. If allelic drop-out is a possibility with a mixture, the determination that must be made by the analyst is whether the locus is truly homozygous or heterozygous with an allele failing to be detected.

The identification of an individual in complex mixtures (more than two individuals) has been described as "challenging"[100] and the best methodology for doing so is the subject of continuing research.[101] Although the laboratory process is the same as for single source samples, the interpretation of complex mixture profiles is inherently difficult because of allelic drop out, overlapping alleles, artifacts, and peak height imbalances. Interpretation methods using the Combined Probability of Inclusion (CPI), discussed in §14.15(3) *infra*, have received substantial criticism for lack of scientific validity.[102]

§14.15 PROBABILITIES AND STATISTICS

Current DNA typing methods do not examine the entire human genome, but only develop a profile of the DNA by determining the allele types present at certain specified loci. These profiles (based on thousands of base pairs out of the billions of base pairs that constitute an individual's genetic composition) are not assumed to be unique.

---

[99] Michelle Alvarez, Jane Juusola, and Jack Ballantyne, "An mRNA and DNA Co-Isolation Method for Forensic Casework Samples," 335 ANALYTICAL BIOCHEMISTRY 289 (2004).

[100] Lev Voskoboinik and Ariel Darvasi, "Forensic Identification of an Individual in Complex Mixtures," 5 FORENSIC SCI. INT'L: GENETICS 428–435 (2011).

[101] The National Institute of Standards and Technology research project on DNA mixture analysis has collected over 15 years of data. *See* http://www.nist.gov/mml/bmd/genetics/dna_mixture_interpretation.cfm (last accessed June 10, 2016).

[102] 2016 PCAST Report at pp. 75–83.

> [W]hile the results of [current DNA typing] can be interpreted to exclude the possibility that [a particular individual committed the offense], they may never be the basis for excluding the possibility that any, random 'someone other than the suspect' committed the [offense]. This is because DNA profiles are probability based. . . .[103]

Since DNA profiles developed by current forensic DNA typing techniques are not assumed to be unique, accompanying statistics usually are presented to assist the jury in assessing the evidentiary value of the DNA evidence.[104] "[E]vidence of a DNA match is made more probative when it is introduced in conjunction with statistical evidence that expresses the significance of the match."[105] Without accompanying statistics that in some way assess the rarity of the profile, the jury cannot accurately assess the significance of the consistency between an individual's profile and the profile from the evidence sample.

The current SWGDAM guidelines recommend using one of three possible statistical methods for representing the significance of matches in STR results. Each method is to be used separately. "It is not appropriate to calculate a composite statistic using multiple formulae for a multi-locus profile. For example, the CPI and RMP cannot be multiplied across the loci in the statistical analysis of an individual DNA profile because they rely on different fundamental assumptions about the number of contributors to the mixture."[106]

1. RARITY STATISTIC/RANDOM MATCH PROBABILITY (RMP)

Generally, the accompanying statistics involve addressing the "coincidence factor"—i.e., what is the chance that the individual's DNA profile might coincidentally match the evidence profile?

> A determination that the DNA profile of an evidentiary sample matches the profile of a suspect establishes that the two profiles are consistent, but the determination would be of little significance if the evidentiary profile also matched that of many or most other human beings. The evidentiary weight of the match with the suspect is therefore inversely dependent upon the statistical probability of a similar match with the

---

[103] Crews v. Johnson, 702 F. Supp.2d 618, (W.D. Va. 2010) This also demonstrates what is referred to as the "prosecutor's fallacy" discussed *infra*.

[104] *See* §14.15(2) *infra* discussing "source attribution" testimony that relies on statistical calculations, but does not present the statistics to the jury, only the conclusion that an individual is a source of the evidentiary sample.

[105] United States v. Jenkins, 887 A.2d 1013, 1016 (D.C. 2005).

[106] Scientific Working Group on DNA Analysis Methods, *SWGDAM, Interpretation Guidelines for Autosomal STR Typing By Forensic DNA Testing Laboratories*, January 14, 2010, at Standard 4.6.2. (available at: www.swgdam.org).

profile of a person drawn at random from the relevant population.[107]

This statistic, commonly referred to as the "random match probability" (RMP), is the probability that a randomly selected, unrelated individual in the relevant population would have a particular DNA profile. The RMP expresses the rarity of the particular DNA profile in the population and determines the coincidence factor—what is the probability that a random person would coincidentally match the evidence profile.[108] The probability can be calculated according to the relevant broad ethnic or racial population (Caucasian, African-American, Hispanic). When associated with an evidence comparison it is not appropriate to report the statistic related to the perpetrator's ethnic background because that is considered to bias the statistic to the perpetrator and not allow for the assumption that another person of a different ethnic background may be involved. However, courts have recognized that "as the science underlying DNA comparisons continues to improve, the practical significance of the different racial frequencies diminishes."[109]

The RMP is generated using the product rule.[110] To derive the RMP for a single source profile, the individual population frequency (how often the allele type is found in the population) of each allele in a profile are multiplied together. The population frequencies are derived from published data, such as the FBI Allelic Frequency Tables,[111] or large

---

[107] People v. Venegas, 954 P.2d 525, 548–549 (Cal. 1998); see also United States v. Jenkins, 887 A.2d 1013, 1016 (D.C. 2005).

[108] Crews v. Johnson, 702 F. Supp.2d 618, 637 n. 18 (W.D. Va. 2010); United States v. Chischilly, 30 F.3d 1144, 1155 n. 14 (9th Cir. 1994); United States v. Davis, 602 F. Supp. 2d 658, 674 n. 19 (D. Md. 2009); United States v. Jenkins, 887 A.2d 1013, 1018 n. 6 (D.C. 2005).

[109] People v. Wilson, 38 Cal. App. 4th 1237, 1248, 136 P.3d 864, 871, 45 Cal. Rptr.3d 73 81 (2006)(internal citation omitted); see also Jonathan Kahn, "Race, Genes, and Justice: A Call to Reform the Presentation of Forensic DNA Evidence in Criminal Trials," 74 Brooklyn L. Rev. 325 (2009).

[110] The product rule is based on the principle that if two events are independent of each other, the probability of each event occurring can be multiplied to give the probability of the two events occurring together. See United States v. Jenkins, 887 A.2d 1013, 1018 n. 6 (D.C. 2005).

[111] On May 11, 2015, the FBI issued a CODIS bulletin to all National DNA Index System (NDIS) participating laboratories notifying them that there were errors in the original DNA database data published in 1999 and 2001. The FBI provided the corrected allele tables and stated, "[e]mpirical testing described in this publication supports that any discrepancy between profile probabilities calculated using the original and corrected data is expected to be less than a factor of two in a full profile." FBI (2015, June 16). Amended 1999/2001 FBI STR Population Datasets, June 16, 2015 (available at: https://www.fbi.gov/file-repository/amended-fbi-str-final-6-16-15.pdf/view)(last accessed December 6, 2016). The magnitude of the errors was not great (the magnitude of the change in frequencies ranged from 0.000012 to 0.018) and no prosecutions or convictions appear to have been affected by the errors. See Erratum, 60 (4) J. Forensic Sci. 1114 (2015).

Forensic laboratories accredited by ASCLD/LAB were notified June 15, 2015, that they were expected to "take any appropriate action in accordance with accreditation requirements" and "[i]n any laboratory affected by the FBI announcement, accredited or not, the ASCLD/LAB Board of Directors stands firm that laboratory management has an ethical obligation, in consultation with the appropriate legal authorities, to consider the impact of this matter and, if deemed applicable and appropriate, to design and take corrective action."

internal databases, such as the database maintained by the Virginia Department of Forensic Science.[112] Two common misconceptions about the RMP are referred to as the "prosecutor's fallacy" and the "defense attorney's fallacy."[113] The United States Supreme Court has explained: "The prosecutor's fallacy is the assumption that the random match probability is the same as the probability that the defendant is not the source of the DNA sample. . . . [I]f a juror is told the probability a member of the general population would share the same DNA is 1 in 10,000 (random match probability) and he takes that to mean there is only a 1 in 10,000 chance that someone other than the defendant is the source of the DNA found at the crime scene (source probability), then he has succumbed to the prosecutor's fallacy."[114] The defendant's fallacy is to use the RMP probability to calculate the number of other people who are "equally likely to have left the sample" (which ignores other evidence presented at trial) and thus to calculate the odds that the defendant is innocent.[115]

2. LIKELIHOOD RATIO[116]

The likelihood ratio is used as a measure of the probative value of evidence. To calculate the likelihood ratio, the conditional probability of an observation given that one hypothesis is true is divided by the conditional probability of the observation given an alternative hypothesis. The likelihood ratio of two probabilities of the same event (E) under different hypotheses (H_1 and H_2) is written as: $LR = (E{:}H_1 \,/\, E{:}H_2)$.

For forensic DNA analysis, the likelihood ratio compares the competing hypotheses of (1) the source of the evidence sample is the person whose DNA was typed and found to match; and (2) the source of the evidence sample is a randomly selected person unrelated to that person. In most cases, this calculated statistic will be the reciprocal of the

---

ASCLD/LAB (2015, June 15). Notification from the ASCLD/LAB Board of Directors to Laboratories and Interested Parties Concerning Amendments to the 1999 and 2001 FBI STR Population Data, June 15, 2015 (available at: http://www.ascld-lab.org/wp-content/uploads /2015/06/150615-ASCLD_LAB-Statement_RE-FBI-Pop-Data.pdf)(last accessed December 6, 2016).

[112] *See* http://www.dfs.virginia.gov/about-dfs/dna-databank-statistics/ (last accessed December 6, 2016).

[113] *See* William C. Thompson and Edward L. Schumann, "Interpretation of Statistical Evidence in Criminal Trials: The Prosecutor's Fallacy and the Defense Attorney's Fallacy, 11 L. & HUM. BEHAV. 167 (1987).

See also David H. Kaye and George Sensabaugh, "Reference Guide on DNA Identification Evidence," in *Reference Manual on Scientific Evidence*, 3rd ed., National Academies Press: Washington DC, 2011 at pp. 168–170 and accompanying notes.

[114] McDaniel v. Brown, 558 U.S. 120, 127–128 (2010); *see also* NRC 1996 Report at p. 133.

[115] People v. Cua, 191 Cal. App. 4th 582, 600, 119 Cal. Rptr. 3d 391, 407 (Ct. App. 2011).

[116] *See generally* David H. Kaye and George Sensabaugh, "Reference Guide on DNA Identification Evidence," in *Reference Manual on Scientific Evidence*, 3rd ed., National Academies Press: Washington DC, 2011 at pp. 172–173.

rarity statistic (RMP).[117] In other cases, where the designation of alleles is complicated by multiple contributors, artifacts (such as stutter) and the possibility of allelic drop-out, the likelihood ratio becomes much more complicated as these variables are taken into account.[118]

3. COMBINED PROBABILITY OF INCLUSION (CPI) AND COMBINED PROBABILITY OF EXCLUSION (CPE)

The CPI statistic is used only for mixtures. The statistical method may be used on all potential alleles identified for minor contributor profiles or for indistinguishable mixtures. For multiple major contributors to a mixture, the statistical method can be used, but only based on alleles that can be paired through consistent relative peak heights.

The CPI is the product of the individual locus PIs (PI for a locus is the squared sum of the allele frequencies) and the CPE is (1 – the CPI):

PI = (allele 1 frequency + allele 2 frequency)^2

CPI = (PI at locus 1) x (PI at locus 2) . . . etc.

CPE = 1 – CPI

The statistical method is discussed with examples in the SWGDAM Interpretation Guidelines.[119] The method has come under some criticism for the variability in results obtained from different laboratories in two studies in 2010 and 2013. The 2010 study, conducted by a cognitive neuroscientist and a biologist, involved DNA data from a gang rape case sent to 17 expert analysts in accredited laboratories in North America. Only one analyst returned the same results as the analyst in the case (that the defendant could not be excluded); four analysts said the results were inconclusive; and the twelve remaining analysts said the results excluded the defendant who had been convicted.[120] The 2013 study, conducted by the National Institute of Standards and Technology (NIST), involved a case with a four-person mixture on an item of evidence. Of the 108 laboratories participating in the study, 73 falsely included a suspect that was not in the four-person mixture. One of the conclusions of the NIST study was that "CPI is often being used as a substitute for interpretation, and has the risk of including a non-contributor."[121] After

---

[117] See Committee on DNA Forensic Science: An Update, Commission on DNA Forensic Science: An Update, National Research Council, *The Evaluation of Forensic DNA Evidence*, National Academies Press: Washington DC, 1996, at p. 128.

[118] See P. Gill et al., "DNA Commission on the International Society of Forensic Genetics: Recommendations on the Interpretation of Mixtures," 160 Forensic Sci. Int'l 90–101 (2006).

[119] Scientific Working Group on DNA Analysis Methods, *SWGDAM Interpretation Guidelines for Autosomal STR Typing By Forensic DNA Testing Laboratories*, January 14, 2010, pp. 18–19 (available at: www.swgdam.org).

[120] Itiel E. Dror and Greg Hampikian, "Subjectivity and Bias in Forensic DNA Mixture Interpretation," 51 Science and Justice 204–208 (2011).

[121] Michael Coble, "Interpretation Errors Detected in a NIST Interlaboratory Study on DNA Mixture Interpretation in the US (MIX13)," Presentation at the International Forensic Science Symposium, July 20–24, 2015, Washington DC, at Slide 37 (available at: http://www.

reviewing the relevant research, including the 2010 and 2013 studies, the 2016 PCAST Report found that:

> DNA analysis of complex mixtures based on CPI-based approaches has been an inadequately specified, subjective method that has the potential to lead to erroneous results. As such, it is not foundationally valid.[122]

PCAST recommended the rapid transition to probabilistic genotyping software applications (*see* §14.19(6) *infra*) for the interpretation of complex mixtures.[123]

On August 31, 2016, experts proposed a set of rules for the use of the CPI statistic in an effort to standardize the application of the CPI.[124] The proposed rules are being evaluated by DNA examiners and may be implemented in the future.

§14.16 OTHER DNA ANALYSIS TECHNIQUES

1. Y-STRs

A related process analyzes only the Y chromosome short tandem repeats (Y-STR), which permits examination of the male-specific portion of biological evidence. As with autosomal STR, the alleles for Y-STR loci are differentiated by the number of copies of the repeat sequence contained within the amplified region. Y-STR testing is conducted using the same amplification procedures and detection instrumentation described for autosomal STR testing. Commercially available amplification kits specific to Y-STR typing are used and the same analytical software used for autosomal STR analysis can be used. The Y-STR profile from an individual is termed a haplotype, not a genotype as with autosomal STR, because there is only one allele at each locus.[125] The Y-STR are polymorphic among unrelated males and are inherited through the paternal line with little change through generations (all fathers and sons in a genealogical relationship will share a common Y-STR profile). "While the mutational process, drift and social factors continuously diversify the actual stock of Y chromosomes within a given

---

nist.gov/director/upload/interpretation_errors_detected_in_a_NIST_interlab_study_on_DNA_mixture_interpretation_in_the_US_MIX13-coble-crim1.pdf)(last accessed August 29, 2016).

[122] 2016 PCAST Report at p. 82.

[123] Id.

[124] Frederick R. Bieber et al., "Evaluation of Forensic DNA Mixture Evidence Protocol for Evaluation, Interpretation, and Statistical Calculations Using the Combined Probability of Inclusion," 17:125 BMC Genetics 2016 (available at: https://bmcgenet.biomedcentral.com/articles/10.1186/s12863-016-0429-7)(last accessed September 20, 2016).

[125] John M. Butler, *Forensic DNA Typing: Biology, Technology, and Genetics of STR Markers*, 2d ed., Elsevier Press, 2005 at p. 201.

population, the underlying relatedness is not erased and visible in the clustering of haplotypes of common descent."[126]

While is it possible to discriminate between DNA samples from unrelated male contributors, Y-STR analysis also helps identify paternally-related males. Y-STR are commonly used to identify the male component of DNA mixtures with a large female DNA concentration, such as in sexual assault cases from intimate collection swabs or for fingernail swabs collected from female victims who may have collected DNA from male assailants under their nail. Y-STR testing is also used to reconstruct paternal relationships among male individuals and is useful in familial DNA searches.[127]

Y-STR data interpretation differs from autosomal testing in the statistical methods used to assess evidentiary significance to the results. While population specific allele frequency information is available for the commonly typed Y-STR loci, this information is not used in statistical calculations for assessing the significance of a match. All the Y-STR genetic loci are on the same chromosome (the male Y chromosome), the loci are considered "linked" because they are inherited together. The entire Y chromosome haplotype is treated as a single locus in statistical calculations therefore commonly used statistical methods for autosomal STR results cannot be utilized. The Y-STR haplotype frequencies[128] are estimated using the counting method—how frequently the profile is observed in a population database. The profile probability statistic (p) equals the number of times the profile is observed in the database (x) divided by the number of profiles in the database (n). The University of Central Florida retains the US National Y-STR Database that now comprises of greater than 29,000 haplotypes.[129]

In 2014, SWGDAM issued new guidelines for Y-STR analysis that affected both match probability statistics and conclusions in cases involving mixtures.[130] The guidelines emphasized that the "profile probability is not the same as the match probability, which addresses the question of a match between the evidentiary and reference samples [if] the reference donor is not the source of the evidentiary sample."[131] SWGDAM endorsed a match probability equation based on the

[126] Sascha Willuweit et al., "Y-STR Frequency Surveying Method: A Critical Reappraisal," 5 FORENSIC SCI. INT'L: GENETICS 84–90 (2011) at p. 84.

[127] Familial DNA searches are discussed in §14.19(3)(c) infra.

[128] A publicly available database for estimating the haplotype frequency is maintained by the National Center for Forensic Science. The database is located at: http://usystrdatabase.org.

[129] US Forensic Y Chromosome Short Tandem Repeats Database. Ge, J., Budowle, B., Planz, J.V., Eisenberg, A.J., Ballantyne, J. and Chakraborty, R. Legal Medicine 12 289–295 (2010). and Databases. (2015, September 20). Retrieved August 12, 2016, from https://ncfs.ucf.edu/databases/.

[130] Scientific Working Group on DNA Analytical Methods, SWGDAM Interpretation Guidelines for Y-Chromosome STR Typing by Forensic DNA Laboratories, approved January 9, 2014 (available at: www.swgdam.org).

[131] Id. at p. 10.

conservative formula described by the National Research Council in 1996 for DNA analysis.[132]

If a mixture of Y-STR profiles cannot be discerned as major contributor and a minor contributor, the results may be used for exclusionary purposes. The reporting of inclusionary results of indistinguishable mixtures is not endorsed by SWGDAM because the group could not reach a consensus on the appropriate statistical approach for estimating the occurrence of the haplotype combination in the population.[133]

2. MITOCHONDRIAL DNA (MTDNA)

Mitochondrial DNA (mtDNA) is different from autosomal and Y-STR DNA in its size, variability, and method of inheritance, all of which impact its forensic applications. Mitochondrial DNA is found in the mitochondria, the energy producing centers of the cells. The mitochondrial genome is 16,569 base pairs in length, is circular, and consists of coding regions and a noncoding hypervariable control region.[134] Approximately 500 complete copies of the mtDNA genome are contained within each cell.[135] Thus, when the evidentiary sample contains only limited quantities of autosomal DNA or the DNA is degraded, as in such tissues as bone, teeth, and hair, there is a greater chance of recovering mtDNA than nuclear DNA.[136] Mitochondrial DNA has also been used to identify the remains of individuals exposed to extreme environmental conditions for many years.

The mutation rate observed in mtDNA is approximately 10 times that of nuclear DNA which gives rise to the distinguishing polymorphisms. These polymorphisms are not length changes like STR, they are single nucleotide polymorphisms (SNP) resulting in a difference in the DNA sequence. Although nuclear DNA remains the same in each cell of an individual, most people are "heteroplasmic" with respect to their mtDNA, meaning they have more than one mtDNA genome.[137] The mtDNA sequence can differ between tissue types and

---

[132] Id. at p. 13; Committee on DNA Forensic Science: An Update, Commission on DNA Forensic Science: An Update, National Research Council, *The Evaluation of Forensic DNA Evidence*, National Academies Press: Washington DC, 1996.

[133] Scientific Working Group on DNA Analytical Methods, *SWGDAM Interpretation Guidelines for Y-Chromosome STR Typing by Forensic DNA Laboratories*, approved January 9, 2014 (available at: www.swgdam.org) at p. 8.

[134] Mitchell Holland et al., "Mitochondrial DNA Sequence Analysis of Human Skeletal Remains: Identification of Remains from The Vietnam War," 38 J. Forensic Sci. 542 (1993).

[135] John M. Butler, *Forensic DNA Typing: Biology, Technology, and Genetics of STR Markers*, 2d ed., Elsevier Press, 2005 at p. 242.

[136] Mitchell Holland et al., "Mitochondrial DNA Sequence Analysis of Human Skeletal Remains: Identification of Remains from The Vietnam War," 38 J. Forensic Sci. 542 (1993), at p. 543. *See also* Mark Wilson et al., "Guidelines for the Use of Mitochondrial DNA Sequencing in Forensic Science," 20 CRIME LAB. DIG. 68 (1993).

[137] *See* Terry Melton, "Mitochondrial DNA Heteroplasmy," 16 FORENSIC SCI. REV. 1–20 (2004).

even within the same tissue type,[138] but typically occurs only at one position in the sequence analyzed in forensic typing. To differentiate heteroplasmy in a single contributor from a mixture sample, laboratories are encouraged to verify suspected heteroplasmy with a second extraction of the sample.

Mitochondrial DNA is inherited from mother to child. Thus, the mtDNA is identical for siblings and all their maternal relatives, barring any mutation. Consequently, maternal relatives can provide reference samples for direct comparison to a questioned mtDNA type, a helpful advantage in missing persons cases. In criminal cases, however, the utility of mtDNA is limited by the inability to differentiate between maternally related individuals. Most courts have recognized that the decreased discriminating power of mtDNA analysis makes it a tool more useful for exclusion than in identifying the source of a biological sample.[139]

The analytical methods of mtDNA analysis are similar to autosomal STR analysis with PCR amplification, separation by capillary electrophoresis, detection by fluorescent primer tags, and interpretation assisted by commercial software. MtDNA analysis differs, however, in number of necessary amplification stages (with some mtDNA analysis requiring more amplification stages), in methods used to distinguish different profiles, and in the population statistics reported with the results. The electrophoresis of the amplified DNA is slightly different due to the need to determine the differences in the sequence rather than length, therefore single base pair resolution is required. MtDNA mixed sequences are not commonly interpreted.

MtDNA sequencing requires multiple overlapping regions of the mtDNA genome to be amplified and sequenced. Commercially available software[140] is used to edit and assemble these sequences to produce a contiguous sequence that can then be compared between evidentiary and reference samples in evaluating the similarities or differences between the mtDNA sequences. To report a profile, the analysis of mtDNA looks at two regions of the mtDNA genome that are highly variable: Hypervariable Region I (HVI—positions 16024–16365) and Hypervariable Region II (HVII—positions 73–340), which together encompass approximately 610 base pairs.[141] An individual's haplotype

---

[138] *See* John Buckleton, Simon Walsh and Sally-Ann Harbison, "Nonautosomal Forensic Markers," in John Buckleton, Christopher M. Triggs and Simon J. Walsh, eds. *Forensic DNA Evidence Interpretation,* CRC Press, 2005 at p. 304.

[139] *See* Vaughn v. State, 646 S.E.2d 212, 214 (Ga. 2007)("mtDNA is more applicable for exclusionary, rather than identification, purposes"; Wagner v. State, 864 A.2d 1037, 1045 (Md. App. 2005)("MtDNA analysis provides significantly less ability to discriminate among possible donors than does nuclear DNA analysis and has been said to be a test more of exclusion than of identification."); State v. Scott, 33 S.W.3d 746, 756 (Tenn. 2000)("mtDNA typing has been said to be a test more of exclusion than one of identification.").

[140] Such as Sequencher™ software from Gene Codes Corporation (http://genecodes.com).

[141] Mitchell M. Holland and Thomas J. Parsons, "Mitochondrial DNA Sequence Analysis: Validation and Use for Forensic Casework, 11 FORENSIC SCI. REV. 21 (1999).

mtDNA profile (mitotype) is a list of the differences between the sequences observed in those regions and those in a reference sequence known as the revised Cambridge Reference Sequence (rCRS).[142]

The FBI maintains a database consisting of mitotypes generated by forensic DNA typing laboratories and their contractors.[143] A computer program (Popstats), supplied by the FBI and contained within the Combined DNA Index System software (CODIS), is used to search casework mitotypes against the database to provide frequency estimates. The database search result provides the number of database profiles that match the mitotype, as well as the number of profiles in the database that differ by up to five positions. The mitotype profile frequency will then be calculated using the counting method. On July 18, 2013, SWGDAM approved guidelines for mtDNA analysis that note a lack of consensus on the appropriate statistical approach for calculating match probability statistics for mtDNA comparisons.[144]

3.   MINISTR

MiniSTR (also known as "reduced-size STR-amplicons") is a methodology that may be used on degraded DNA samples to discover typing information that may not be detected in conventional STR analysis. MiniSTR analysis follows the same analytical method as STR analysis but targets smaller portions on the STR locus for amplification to enhance recovery of information. Although the use of miniSTR methodology began in 1994, the first commercially available testing kit (Applied Biosystems, Inc. MiniFiler™ kit was not issued until March 2007.[145] The genetic loci in the MiniFiler kit overlap with conventional STR kits. An additional benefit in using miniSTR analysis in conjunction with conventional methodologies can be seen with degraded DNA samples. The longer STR fragments can be lost with the larger multiplex STR kits, but the shorter miniprimers will help identify them.

4.   EMERGING TECHNOLOGIES

Although the analysis techniques of forensic DNA testing has remained stagnant for 20 years, emerging technologies are rapidly being developed to provide quicker results and more information. These techniques focuses on expanding the capabilities of the laboratory and the information that biological evidence can provide.

---

[142] Access to the rCRS is available at: http://www.mitomap.org.

[143] The database has been criticized for being insufficiently representative. See Frederika A. Kaestle et al., "Database Limitations on the Evidentiary Value of Forensic Mitochondrial DNA Evidence," 43 Am. Crim. L. Rev. 53 (2006).

[144] Scientific Working Group on DNA Analytical Methods, *"SWGDAM Interpretation Guidelines for Mitochondrial DNA Analysis by Forensic DNA Testing Laboratories,"* July 18, 2013, at p. 17 (available at: www.swgdam.org).

[145] For detailed information on miniSTR's and extensive resources, *see* http://www.cstl. nist.gov/biotech/strbase/miniSTR.htm (last accessed June 9, 2016).

Rapid DNA testing uses a fully automated DNA analyzer to conduct DNA analysis of the core CODIS genetic loci in 2 hours or less. The FBI has approved the technology for testing of reference samples for inclusion in the CODIS database (discussed in §14.19(3) *infra*) when used by an accredited laboratory. In December 2014, the FBI published *The Addendum to the Quality Assurance Standards for DNA Databasing Laboratories performing Rapid DNA Analysis and Modified Rapid DNA Analysis Using a Rapid DNA Instrument (Rapid QAS Addendum)*.[146] Compliance with these standards is required for reference DNA profiles generated by Rapid DNA testing from a participating laboratory to be uploaded to the national database. The *Rapid DNA Act of 2015* is legislation currently being discussed in Congress to allow non-participating laboratories to integrate their Rapid DNA results to the national database. Reference samples collected and processed by non-forensic scientists at booking facilities or jails through Rapid DNA testing would allow a search of the database prior to the arrestee's release from custody. The technology may also be used to evaluate evidence samples for suitability for additional analysis or private database searching.

Multiple laboratories working on The Human Genome Project took 13 years to sequence the entire human genome.[147] Massively parallel sequencing (MPS) or next generation (NexGen) technologies allow the scientist to simultaneously sequence thousands of sections of the human genome in 24 hours. While the initial analysis steps (extraction and quantification) are the same as that used with capillary electrophoresis, the PCR step is replaced with an amplification method that copies the majority of the DNA in a sample and not just the specific sites of interest. Rather than performing electrophoric analyses, a "chip" binds each DNA fragment generated then determines the sequence of the DNA bases of that fragment. Computer software then creates a "library" of the DNA sequences in the sample by matching overlapping sequences identified.[148] The MPS allows the analyst to identify single nucleotide polymorphisms (SNP) and sequence the STR of forensic interest. This technology can analyze autosomal STR, Y-STR, SNP, and mtDNA in the single sample, allowing the use of all of the information in the genome of the evidence sample.[149] The MPS can provide phenotypic and ancestry SNP data that can be used to predict the individual's ethnicity and outward appearance such as eye color.[150]

---

[146] https://www.fbi.gov/services/laboratory/biometric-analysis/codis/rapid-dna-analysis.

[147] J.C. Venter, et.al. *The Sequence of the Human Genome;* Sci. 15 Feb 2001:1304–1351.

[148] D.G. Hert, C.P. Frediake and A.E. Barron. Advantages and limitation of next-generation sequencing technologies: A comparison of electrophoresis and non-electrophoresis methods. Electrophoresis (2008), 29, 4618–4323.

[149] D.R. Shorts. (Feb.29, 2016) Massively Parallel Sequencing for Forensic DNA Analysis. [Web log post]. Promega Connections: http://www.promegaconnections.com/massively-parallel-sequencing-for-forensic-dna-analysis/.

[150] M. Eduardoff et al, "Inter-laboratory evaluation of SNP-based forensic identification by massively parallel sequencing using the Ion PGM™," 18 Forensic Sci. International:

These new technologies are rapidly gaining acceptance among forensic scientists. The Arizona Department of Public Safety forensic laboratories are currently using Rapid DNA testing conducted by trained law enforcement officers to generate investigative leads.[151] MPS for phenotyping and ancestry determination has been conducted by private laboratories since 2015[152] and public laboratories are beginning the research and validations required for implementing them in their testing procedures. As these new technologies are adopted by forensic laboratories, additional judicial review will be required to evaluate their general acceptance.

V. TRIAL AIDS

§14.17 EXPERT QUALIFICATIONS

The determination of whether a witness is qualified to give opinion testimony will be left to the "sound discretion" of the trial court.[153] This determination will not be overturned absent a showing of abuse of this discretion.[154] While either formal study or sufficient practical experience ordinarily suffices to qualify one as an expert in a particular subject area, in the areas of chemistry or biology some formal education in a related science should be required. For forensic biology, relevant fields of study are: biochemistry, biology, microbiology, molecular biology or genetics, depending upon the material at issue. Where the results of testing are contested in a case, this formal study should be supplemented by practical laboratory experience in the specialty area. It should be recognized that in some instances, these requirements may tend to exclude as experts college teachers or professors who, though

---

Genetics 33–48 (2015); M.Kayser, "Forensic DNA Phenotyping: Predicting human appearance from crime scene material for investigative purposes," 17 Forensic Sci. International: Genetics 110–121 (2015).

[151] Revolutionary DNA Testing Instruments Now Available to DPS Detectives. (2014, May 13). Retrieved August 10, 2016, from http://www.azdps.gov/media/news/View/?p=477.

[152] V. Greenwood. "How Science Is Putting a New Face on Crime Solving", *National Geographic* July 2016 print.

[153] U.S. v. Garza, 448 F.3d 294 (5th Cir.2006); U.S. v. Middlebrook, 141 Fed.Appx. 834 (11th Cir.2005); Redi Roast Products, Inc. v. Burnham, 531 So.2d 664 (Ala.Civ.App.1988); Cody v. Louisville & Nashville R. Co., 535 So.2d 82 (Ala.1988); Mathis v. Glover, 714 S.W.2d 222 (Mo.App.1986).

[154] State v. Fry, 138 N.M. 700, 126 P.3d 516 (2005). The expert also told the court that blood spatter analysis was based in physics and mathematics and was not mere speculation. The trial court recognized blood spatter analysis as a discipline recognized by the state in prior cases and allowed two blood spatter experts to testify. The Supreme Court of New Mexico agreed with the trial court decision in allowing the blood pattern expert testimony and found that there was no abuse of discretion; Mathews v. Chrysler Realty Corp., 627 S.W.2d 314 (Mo.App.1982). In Stuart v. Director of Revenue, 761 S.W.2d 234 (Mo.App.1988), the trial court was found to have abused its discretion in rejecting the testimony of a police officer trained in the operation of the breathalyzer.

familiar with the field through study, lack practical experience in laboratory methods or procedures.

The complete analysis of a DNA sample involves the same scientific disciplines. However, judicial acceptance of DNA evidence and the standardization of the analysis make the need for specialized knowledge in all of these areas unnecessary to establish the admissibility of DNA typing results.[155] Although an extensive scientific background may not be required for admission of results from routine DNA analytical procedures, foundational knowledge may be explored on cross-examination,[156] and is extremely useful in conveying technical information to the jury in a comprehensible manner. Aside from practicing DNA laboratory analysts, academic experts sometimes provide testimony on subject areas in DNA analysis, particularly statistical issues.[157]

Unlike other fields of forensic science, DNA typing has mandatory standards that establish minimal qualifications for employees working in laboratories receiving federal grant funding, those placing DNA profiles in the national database, and by the forensic accreditation bodies.[158] The quality assurance standards promulgated by the FBI impose educational, training, proficiency testing, and continuing education requirements for analysts and supervisors in DNA laboratories.[159] Generally, a technical leader (an employee accountable for the technical operations of the laboratory) must have a master's degree in biology, chemistry, or a forensic science related area with successful completion of 12 credit hours of coursework in biochemistry, genetics, molecular biology, and statistics or population genetics. The technical leader must also have a minimum of three years of experience in a forensic human DNA testing laboratory. Analysts must have bachelor degrees and successful completion of college coursework in biochemistry, genetics, and molecular biology with training in statistics. The analyst must also have a minimum of six months of forensic DNA laboratory experience.

---

[155] David H. Kaye and George Sensabaugh, "Reference Guide on DNA Identification Evidence," in *Reference Manual on Scientific Evidence*, 3rd ed., National Academies Press: Washington DC, 2011 at p. 134.

[156] *See* Roberson v. State, 16 S.W.3d 156, 168 (Tex. Crim. App. 2000).

[157] Academic experts may not have familiarity with specific forensic DNA typing issues, however, and these limitations have been noted by some courts. *See* State v. Copeland, 922 P.2d 1304, 1318 n. 5 (Wash. 1996) (commenting that the statistical expert "was also unfamiliar with publications in the area," including studies by "a leading expert in the field" whom the statistical expert referred to as "a 'guy in a lab somewhere' ").

[158] Federal law also requires DNA laboratories participating in the CODIS program, discussed in Section 17.15(3) *infra*, to be accredited and undergo external audits once every two years. 42 U.S.C. § 14132(b)(2).

[159] FBI, "Quality Assurance Standards for Forensic DNA Testing Laboratories" (available at: https://www.fbi.gov/file-repository/quality-assurance-standards-for-forensic-dna-testing-lab oratories.pdf/view)(last accessed March 3, 2017); FBI, "Quality Assurance Standards for DNA Databasing Laboratories," (available at: https://www.fbi.gov/file-repository/quality-assurance-standards-for-dna-databasing-laboratories.pdf/view)(last accessed March 3, 2017).

Courts have held that formal study in the field alone may qualify one as an expert even though the individual lacks experience in the field.[160] A second "gray area" in qualification as an expert is the skilled technician, who although lacking extensive formal study, has combined experience and training in the subject matter.[161] Emerging areas of technology, where few formal educational programs exist, also pose problems; however, this is less severe in forensic biology than in other areas of scientific forensic investigation. With increasing use and weight being put on forensic evidence, the U.S. Department of Justice's Office of Justice Programs developed a set guidelines called the "Education and Training in Forensic Science: A Guide for Forensic Science Laboratories, Educational Institutions, and Students." The guide is designed to help universities develop forensic science programs that will train forensic scientists to fulfill their role in the criminal justice community.[162]

Although certification or licensing[163] is not a legal requirement for court qualification as an expert, practitioners in the forensic sciences recognize the need for programs to ensure that those purporting to be experts in a particular specialty possess the requisite skills and education of that specialty. The National Academy of Sciences has recommended establishing mandatory certification of all forensic scientists.[164] Certification is available in molecular biology through the American Board of Criminalistics (ABC). To be eligible for certification, the applicant must possess a minimum of an earned baccalaureate degree, or its equivalent, in a natural science or an appropriately related field from an accredited institution and a minimum of two years of full-time experience (including on-the-job training) and be actively working in the field.[165] The certification test is structured with 60% general questions and 40% specialty questions among the 220 multiple choice questions (of which only 200 are scored and 20 serve as pilot

---

[160] Riggle v. State, 585 P.2d 1382 (Okl.Crim.1978), a recent graduate of a school of osteopathic medicine, not yet licensed as a medical doctor, was permitted to testify to cause of death despite the lack of practical experience. In Darling v. Reid, 534 So.2d 255 (Ala.1988), an objection to a professor of medicine who had never practiced and was not board certified went only to weight of testimony and was not grounds for disqualification as expert. Accord: Lavespere v. Niagara Machine & Tool Works, Inc., 910 F.2d 167 (5th Cir.1990).

[161] A public health investigator without medical training or science degree but with 8 years of experience involving sexually transmitted diseases could testify as expert to probability of transmission of gonorrhea from rape victim to defendant. Davis v. United States, 865 F.2d 164 (8th Cir.1988).

[162] U.S. Department of Justice, National Institute of Justice, *Education and Training in Forensic Science: A Guide for Forensic Science Laboratories, Educational Institutions, and Students,* 2004 (available at: http://fepac-edu.org/sites/default/files/NIJReport.pdf)(last accessed March 3, 2017).

[163] Jones v. Jones, 117 Idaho 621, 790 P.2d 914 (1990). Some states do require forensic science testing to be conducted by an accredited laboratory to be admissible in criminal proceedings. *See* Art. 38.35 Texas Code of Criminal Procedure: Forensic Analysis of Evidence; Admissibility; Sec. 411.0205 Texas Government Code.

[164] Recommendation 1(b), National Academy of Sciences, *Strengthening Forensic Science in the United States: A Path Forward,* National Academies Press, 2009.

[165] http://www.criminalistics.com/certification-requirements.html.

questions for future examinations).[166] ABC also maintains a list of certified examiners on its website.[167]

In criminal cases, forensic biologists and related specialists are readily available to the prosecution as federal, state, or local crime laboratory personnel. In addition, such specialists are also available in governmental agencies such as the coroner or medical examiner's offices, government run medical facilities, and public health services. For the defense in a criminal case or the attorney in a civil action, unlike many other specialty areas of forensic science, expert assistance in these areas is widely available. Hospitals, clinics, or private clinical laboratories are potential sources of assistance for either toxicology or serological examinations, and private analytical laboratories can provide additional analyses. These laboratories may also be able to provide expert testimony if required.

Other potential sources of expert assistance include national or regional societies in forensic science or the particular scientific discipline required. The American Academy of Forensic Sciences has sections in Criminalistics and Pathology/Biology with many recognized authorities experienced in expert testimony and who perform private work. Regional forensic societies such as the Mid-Atlantic, Northwest, Southern or Midwest Associations of Forensic Science and the California Association of Criminalists may suggest sources of expert assistance.

§14.18 EVIDENCE ISSUES—ANALYSIS OF BLOOD AND OTHER BIOLOGICAL MATERIAL

Verdicts in many homicides and sexual assaults have been based in large part on testimony of experts that a stain was identified as blood and on the typing of that blood. Blood stained articles discovered at a crime scene are generally admissible in evidence if they aid in providing information about the crime to the jury. Although in some instances, bloodstained items have been admitted at trial without verification that the stain was blood or with only a statement that the stain appeared to be blood as in Miller v. Pate,[168] this is fraught with danger and expert testing should be required to verify the composition of a stain. The results of color, crystal, and immunological tests for identifying blood have received little challenge to their admissibility.[169] However, following the exoneration of Gregory Taylor, proceedings of the North Carolina Innocence Inquiry Commission, and a subsequent independent audit, issues have been raised concerning potentially misleading

---

[166] http://www.criminalistics.com/faqs.html.

[167] www.criminalistics.com.

[168] 386 U.S. 1 (1967).

[169] *See* United States v. Williams, 213 U.S. Dist. LEXIS 120884 (D. Hawaii 2013) (discussing presumptive phenolphthalein blood testing and admitting the confirmatory Takayama test).

laboratory reports indicating the presence of blood despite negative results from additional confirmatory testing.[170]

Blood evidence examinations frequently involve small amounts of material such as stains on clothing, droplets on a weapon, and smears on a wall or floor. Luminol testing had been found admissible as generally accepted within the scientific community.[171] However, significant opportunities exist for contamination of the sample with materials such as dirt, grease, and various chemicals. Cross-examination should cover the possibility of a contaminant causing reactions in the absence of human blood. Exposure to contaminants can destroy blood or severely restrict the validity of conclusions drawn from its examination. Putrefaction of blood poses special problems in identification and characterization, and may give rise to inconclusive results, even as to identification of the sample as blood or determination of species.

The amount of the sample available may limit the extent to which testing is performed; however, with current technology, even tiny spots can be subjected to considerable testing. If destructive testing is conducted, consumption of the entire sample leaves none available for testing by the opposing party and this issue should be raised. Even if unsuccessful as a challenge to the admissibility of the evidence,[172] the trier of fact will be made aware that the defense had no opportunity to independently assess the validity of the results of the prosecution's tests.[173] With the small samples common with blood evidence, chain-of-custody becomes an important issue. Counsel should extensively scrutinize the collection, preservation and handling of blood evidence to ensure that no possibility of contamination or sample misidentification exists. A former chief crime scene investigator in Nebraska's most populous county was convicted in 2011 for planting blood evidence in a 2006 murder investigation.[174]

---

[170] *See* Independent Review of SBI Forensic Laboratory—available at: http://www.ncdoj. gov/News-and-Alerts/News-Releases-and-Advisories/Press-Releases/An-Independent-Review-of-the-SBI-Forensic-Laborato.aspx; The North Carolina Innocence Inquiry Commission Report to the 2011–12 Long Session of the General Assembly of North Carolina and the State Judicial Council, March 1, 2011—available at: http://www.innocencecommission-nc.gov/Forms/pdf/gar/ 2010AnnualReport(sent to GeneralAssemblyin 2011).pdf.

[171] People v. Cumbee, 366 Ill. App. 3d 476, 851 N.E.2d 934 (2006).

[172] Arizona v. Youngblood, 488 U.S. 51 (1988).

[173] Since the Supreme Court decision in Youngblood, federal and state courts alike have concluded that the *Due Process Clause* places no constraints on the good faith consumptive or destructive testing of evidence by the prosecution." People v. Wartena, 156 P.3d 469, 475 (Colo. 2007); *see also,* Carlson v. Minnesota, 945 F.2d 1026, 1029 (8th Cir. 1991); United States v. Stevens, 935 F.2d 1380, 1387 (3d Cir. 1991); Garrett v. Lynaugh, 842 F.2d 113, 116 (5th Cir. 1988).

[174] The case has also resulted in at least two civil actions: Matthew Livers v. Earl Schenck, *et al.*, Case No. 8:08CV107 (US Dist. Ct. Nebraska), and Nicholas Sampson v. Inv. William Lambert, *et al.*, Case No. 8:07CV155 (US Dist. Ct. Nebraska).

§14.19 EVIDENCE ISSUES—DNA ANALYSIS

1. GENERAL ADMISSIBILITY

The journey of DNA analysis over the scientific and legal landscape, from its beginning as a novel scientific technique to a forensic methodology worthy of judicial notice, has not been without incident and has proven an excellent subject for debating evidentiary standards. Regardless of the particular standard applied, however, courts have now universally agreed that the underlying theory and techniques currently used for DNA analysis are valid and reliable.[175] No court has rejected DNA analysis on the basis that it is not generally accepted by the scientific community.[176] Similarly, PCR-based DNA analysis has been adjudicated admissible evidence.[177] Even those courts that ultimately rejected the DNA evidence in the case recognized the general acceptance of the underlying theory and technique.[178]

The Federal Judicial Center's Reference Manual on Scientific Evidence contains an excellent overview of the cases from the 1990s and early 2000s addressing the admission of DNA evidence that demonstrate the evolution of the challenges to admissibility.[179] "[I]n little more than a decade, forensic DNA typing made the transition from a novel set of methods for identification to a relatively mature and well-studied forensic technology."[180]The current state of the judicial assessment of the scientific acceptance of DNA testing is well summarized in *Commonwealth v. Bizanowicz:*

---

[175] Springfield v. State, 860 P.2d 435, 442 (Wyo.1993); United States v. Martinez, 3 F.3d 1191, 1194 (8th Cir.1993), *cert. denied* 510 U.S. 1062 (1994); Rockne P. Harmon, "General Admissibility Considerations for DNA Analysis Evidence: Let's Learn from the Past and Let the Scientists Decide This Time Around," *Forensic DNA Technology*, 168 (Mark A. Farley & James J. Harrington, eds. 1991).

[176] *See, e.g.,* State v. Cauthron, 120 Wash.2d 879, 846 P.2d 502, 511 (1993).

[177] *See, e.g.,* United States v. Wright, 215 F.3d 1020, 1027 (9th Cir. 2000), *cert. denied,* 531 U.S. 969 (2000); United States v. Hicks, 103 F.3d 837, 846–847 (9th Cir. 1996); United States v. Beasley, 102 F.3d 1440, 1448 (8th Cir. 1996), *cert. denied,* 520 U.S. 1246 (1997)(taking judicial notice of general reliability of PCR testing); United States v. Shea, 957 F. Supp. 331, 338–339 (D.N.H. 1997); United States v. Ewell, 252 F. Supp. 2d 104, 106 (D.N.J. 2003) (looking specifically at PCR/STR testing and listing twelve state appellate court cases finding PCR/STR DNA testing to be scientifically reliable); United States v. Cuff, 37 F. Supp. 2d 279, 282 (S.D.N.Y. 1999); United States v. Gaines, 979 F. Supp. 1429, 1433–34 & n. 4 (S.D.Fla. 1997) (collecting at least twenty state appellate court cases finding PCR DNA testing to be scientifically reliable); United States v. Trala, 162 F. Supp. 2d 336, 350–351 (D.Del. 2001) (looking specifically at PCR/STR testing); United States v. Lowe, 954 F. Supp. 401, 416–17, 420–21 (D. Mass. 1997) (collecting approximately twenty state appellate court cases finding that PCR testing methodology comports with *Daubert*).

[178] Commonwealth v. Curnin, 409 Mass. 218, 565 N.E.2d 440 (1991); State v. Schwartz, 447 N.W.2d 422 (Minn.1989); State v. Woodall, 182 W.Va. 15, 385 S.W.2d 253 (1989); People v. Castro, 144 Misc.2d 956, 545 N.Y.S.2d 985 (1989).

[179] David H. Kaye and George Sensabaugh, "Reference Guide on DNA Identification Evidence," in *Reference Manual on Scientific Evidence*, 3rd ed., National Academies Press: Washington DC, 2011 at pp. 132–134.

[180] Id. at p. 134.

[T]he use of [PCR-STR analysis] is generally accepted within the scientific community. There is no scientific debate over the methodology by which such DNA matches are obtained or their validity.[181]

Courts have also admitted the results of mtDNA analysis, rejecting arguments that the methods do not meet the admissibility standards of *Daubert*, that the possibility of heteroplasmy renders the results unreliable, and that the population statistics are too limited.[182] Y-STR testing results have also been admitted.[183]

2.   STATISTICS

Most courts adhere to the rule that tests results showing a DNA match are not admissible without statistical evidence of the likelihood of that match occurring.[184] The statistical probability of finding a DNA profile in the general population is a critical step in DNA analysis.[185] This position is supported by legal commentators who argue that the admissibility of DNA evidence depends upon having scientifically valid statistical assessments of the significance of the match.[186] In *People v. Pike*,[187] the court considered the admission of expert testimony of a 50% probability of inclusion. After a thorough discussion of probability statistical calculations for DNA analysis,[188] the court concluded that admission of the 50% probability of inclusion was error because it was irrelevant, as it did not tend to make the issue of the defendant's identification more likely than not.[189]

---

[181] 459 Mass. 400, 407, 945 N.E.2d 356, 362 (2011)(internal citations omitted).

[182] *See* People v. Sutherland, 860 N.E.2d 178, 271–272 (Ill. 2006); Wagner v. State, 864 A.2d 1037, 1043–1049 (Md. Ct. Spec. App. 2005); United States v. Beverly, 369 F.3d 516, 531 (6th Cir. 2004); United States v. Coleman, 202 F. Supp.2d 962, 967 (E.D. Mo. 2002), aff'd 349 F.3d 1077 (8th Cir. 2003); State v. Pappas, 776 A.2d 1091, 1095 (Conn. 2001).

[183] *See, e.g.,* Curtis v. State, 205 S.W.3d 656, 660–661 (Tex. Ct. App. 2006); Shabazz v. State, 592 S.E.2d 876, 879 (Ga. Ct. App. 2004).

[184] *See, e.g.,* Commonwealth v. Mattei, 455 Mass. 840, 851–855, 920 N.E.2d 845 (2010); Nelson v. State, 628 A.2d 69, 76 (Del. 1993); State v. Williams, 574 N.W.2d 293, 298 (Iowa 1998).

[185] People v. Miller, 173 Ill.2d 167, 185, 670 N.E.2d 721, 219 Ill. Dec. 43 (1996) ("For a [DNA] match to be meaningful, a statistical analysis is required. The statistical analysis determines the frequency in which a match would occur in a database population.").

[186] *See, e.g.,* David L. Faigman, et al., 4 Modern Scientific Evidence: The Law and Science of Expert Testimony, 30:14 (2005–2006 ed); Kenneth S. Brown et al., 1 McCormick on Evidence § 210 (6th ed. 2006). Committee on DNA Technology in Forensic Science, *et al.*, DNA Technology in Forensic Science 74 (1992)("To say that two patterns match, without providing any scientifically valid estimate (or, at least, an upper bound) of the frequency with which such matches might occur by chance, is meaningless.").

[187] People v. Pike, 2016 IL App (1st) 122626, 2016 Ill. App. LEXIS 32 (App. Ct of IL, 1st Dist., 3rd Div., January 27, 2016).

[188] The court noted that the statistic was not a random match probability, but a "probability of inclusion . . . the probability that any person chosen at random in the population would also be included as a contributor to the mixed DNA profile from the gun . . ." Id at *P70.

[189] Id. at *P77.

a.   Source Attribution

A few courts and commentators have expressed approval of "source attribution" expert testimony that—based on statistics demonstrating the extreme rarity of the profile—the evidentiary sample was left by a particular individual.[190] Challenges to the testimony assert (1) the RMP analysis does not take into account the possibility of relatives in the population; (2) the testimony does not take into account the possibility of laboratory error; and (3) population frequencies do not directly address the rarity of a DNA profile in all subpopulations and racial groups.[191]

Source attribution testimony is usually phrased with some qualification, such as "assuming a population of unrelated individuals."[192] Discussed in the 1996 National Research Council report,[193] source attribution statements have gained acceptance as technological advances have increased the number of loci routinely tested, leading to extremely rare profile probabilities. In *Osborne*, the United States Supreme Court recognized the discriminating power of DNA:

> Modern DNA testing can provide powerful new evidence unlike anything known before. Since its first use in criminal investigations in the mid-1980s, there have been several major advances in DNA technology. It is now often possible to determine whether a biological tissue matches a suspect with near certainty.[194]

Courts have held that there is "no categorical prohibition . . . on source attribution-expression by an otherwise qualified expert of an opinion that the quantitative and qualitative correspondence between an evidentiary sample and a known sample from a defendant establishes identity to a reasonable scientific certainty."[195] Recognizing this, the courts have concluded that any "battle of experts" over the validity of source attribution testimony is for the jury to resolve.[196] Whether such testimony is appropriate is clearly dependent on the underlying rarity statistic calculated for the match. As demonstrated in *United States v. Davis*, within one case there may be DNA profiles requiring accompanying statistics to contextualize the significance of the "consistency" in the profiles, but there may be other DNA profiles with

---

[190] *See* People v. Cua, 191 Cal. App. 4th 582, 600, 119 Cal. Rptr. 3d 391, 407 (Ct. App. 2011). *See also* Young v. State, 879 A.2d 44 (Md. 2005)(admitting expert report concluding that the defendant was the "source" of the evidentiary DNA without any accompanying statistics).

[191] United States v. Williams, 213 U.D. Dist. LEXIS 120884 (D. Hawaii 2013).

[192] People v. Cordova, 62 Cal.4th 104, 130, 358 P.3d 518, 538, 194 Cal. Rptr.3d 40, 64 (2015).

[193] NRC 1996 Report at p. 161.

[194] District Attorney's Office for Third Judicial Dist. v. Osborne, 557 U.S. 52, 62 (2009).

[195] People v. Cua, 191 Cal. App. 4th 582, 600, 119 Cal. Rptr. 3d 391, 407 (Ct. App. 2011).

[196] *See* United States v. McCluskey, 954 F.Supp.2d 1224 (D.N.M. 2013).

results at a sufficient number of loci to have rarity statistics so low (e.g., 1 in 300 billion) that source attribution testimony is appropriate.[197]

In *People v. Cordova*, the defendant challenged the source attribution testimony as committing the "prosecutor's fallacy."[198] The court held that the expert's testimony "had nothing to do with the prosecutor's fallacy," because the expert was merely presenting his opinion that given the "astronomical odds against any other person on earth having the same DNA profile," the "defendant was the source of the evidence samples to a reasonable scientific certainty" and was not opining on the defendant's guilt. The court concluded "[d]oing so was not fallacious."[199]

b. Cold Hits

In 2002, the U.S. Department of Justice, by way of the National Commission on the Future of DNA Evidence, published a series of guidelines for the collection, analysis, and efficient management of DNA samples, case logs, and investigation processes to assist law enforcement agencies in using DNA technology to solve "cold" cases, cases in which other investigative leads had been exhausted.[200] The report was in response to the successful use of DNA database comparisons to generate new investigative leads in "cold" cases in the 1990's. In the decade since the release of the report, the use DNA database comparisons has become routine and numerous prosecutions have used evidence derived from hits to DNA database profiles.

One of the first "cold hits," identifying a recidivist in 1993, solved the rape of a sixty-three year old woman. Forensic examiners compared a DNA profile developed from a seminal fluid stain found on the victim's clothing to the DNA profiles in the state of Virginia's DNA database. The hit to the database profile resulted in the arrest of a suspect and he was subsequently convicted at trial.[201]

Subsequent cases have affirmed the use of database comparisons and the evidentiary value of these "cold hits." For example, in one California case, the court denied a motion to suppress DNA evidence showing a "cold hit" match.[202] In another similar case, with evidence of ethnic description to the contrary, the court held that DNA evidence of a match was admissible.[203] A case in Maryland affirmed the admission of

---

[197] 602 F. Supp.2d 658, 680–684 (D. Md. 2005).

[198] *See* §14.15(1) *supra*.

[199] 62 Cal. 4th 104, 131–132, 358 P.3d 518, 539, 194 Ca. Rptr.3d 40, 65 (2015).

[200] U.S. Department of Justice, "Using DNA to Solve Cold Cases," July, 2002 (available at: https://www.ncjrs.gov/pdffiles1/nij/194197.pdf)(last accessed June 10, 2016).

[201] Carlos Sanchez, "Woman, 64, Describes Rape," WASHINGTON POST, D4 (1993). *See also* State v. Bloom, 516 N.W.2d 159 (Minn.1994)(opinion details the process used by the examiner to discover potential suspects through database comparison and to confirm the contributor of the semen).

[202] People v. Johnson, 139 Cal.App.4th 1135, 43 Cal.Rptr.3d 587 (2006).

[203] People v. Wilson, 38 Cal.4th 1237, 45 Cal.Rptr.3d 73, 136 P.3d 864 (2006).

DNA evidence, absent any statistical accompanying facts, holding that the DNA match and expert testimony were sufficient evidence to affirm the previous court's conviction.[204] Similar cases have held that DNA evidence alone was sufficient to convict the suspect of rape or other sexual assault, absent any other corroborating evidence.[205]

Although the courts have uniformly admitted the evidence derived from DNA database comparisons,[206] there has been a lack of consensus in the scientific community and in the courts about the appropriate statistical weight to be attributed to a DNA match derived from a database search, also known as a "database trawl." The controversy stems from a disagreement over whether the probability statistic should take into account the database trawl search process that generated the hit and lead to the identification of the defendant. One side of the debate argues for a modified statistic in cases of database trawls.[207] There are four methods that have been suggested for presenting the statistical weight of a database hit: random match probability (discussed in §14.15(1) *supra*), separate loci set probability, database match probability, and the Bayesian method.

The separate loci set probability was the method described in the 1992 National Research Council report on DNA. This method requires searching the database with a profile based on one set of loci and then confirming the match between an individual's DNA and the evidence sample using a profile based on a different set of loci. The random match probability is calculated only from the second set of loci—not the set of loci used to search the database.[208] This method has been criticized as unnecessarily restrictive and difficult to implement. The method is not widely endorsed in the forensic science community.[209]

---

[204] Young v. State, 388 Md. 99, 879 A.2d 44 (2005); *see also* Jackson v. State, 92 Md. App. 304, 608 A.2d 782 (1992), cert. denied 328 Md. 238, 614 A.2d 84 (The State is not required to offer additional evidence where the DNA testing has been legislatively determined to be reliable and generally admissible, and where standard procedures and equipment were utilized in the conducting of the DNA analysis).

[205] State v. Toomes, 191 S.W.3d 122 (Tenn.Crim.App.2005); Molina v. Commonwealth, 272 Va. 666, 636 S.E.2d 470 (2006)(DNA evidence was sufficient to support a conviction of forcible sodomy); Derr v. State, 434 Md. 88, 131–132, 73 A.3d 254, 280 (2013) (DNA database match which lead to confirmation testing that Derr's DNA matched the evidence sufficient to support conviction despite inconsistent composite sketch witness description).

[206] Courts have also permitted the use of evidence derived from the improper inclusion of the defendant's sample in the DNA database. *See* People v. Robinson, 47 Cal. 4th 1104, 1119, 224 P.3d 55, 64–65, 104 Cal. Rptr.3d 727, 738 (2010)(even if nonconsensual DNA collection violated the Fourth Amendment, law enforcement errors that lead to the collection would not trigger the exclusionary rule); United States v. Davis, 657 F. Supp.2d 630, 663–667 (D. MD 2009)(inclusion of DNA profile in database violated the Fourth Amendment but did not require exclusion of the evidence).

[207] Charles Taylor and Paul Colman, "Correspondence: Forensics: Experts Disagree on Statistics from DNA Trawls," 464 *Nature* 1266–1267 (April 29, 2010).

[208] Committee on DNA Forensic Science, Commission on DNA Forensic Science, National Research Council, *DNA Technology in Forensic Science*, National Academies Press: Washington, DC, 1992 at p. 124.

[209] United States v. Jenkins, 887 A.2d 1013, 1022 n. 17 (D.C. 2005).

Four years later, a different method (the database match probability) was proposed in the 1996 National Research Council report on DNA. This method calculates the odds of finding a match in the database by multiplying the RMP by the number of relevant profiles in the database (for example, if the evidence sample is from a male, only the number of male profiles in the database would be used in the calculation).[210]

The fourth method, the Bayesian method, is different from the other methods in that it does not attempt to address how rare a profile is in the population or in a particular database. Instead, this method focuses on "the probability that the person identified through the cold hit is the actual source of the DNA in light of the fact that a known quantity of potential suspects was eliminated through the database search."[211] The probability statistic generated by this method becomes higher as the size of the database increases because it takes into account that all of the other individuals whose profiles are contained in the database were considered and eliminated as possible contributors of the evidentiary sample.

The courts addressing challenges to the various statistical methods have considered each of the methods scientifically valid: "there is no controversy in the relevant scientific community as to the accuracy of the various formulas."[212] Courts addressing the issue have specifically ruled on the admissibility of the random match probability, but have not barred the admission of any of the different calculations[213] and have recognized that multiple statistics may be admissible in the appropriate case:

> The conclusion that statistics derived from the product rule are admissible in a cold hit case does not mean that they are the *only* statistics that are relevant and admissible. The database match probability statistic might *also* be admissible.[214]

---

[210] Committee on DNA Forensic Science: An Update, Commission on DNA Forensic Science: An Update, National Research Council, *The Evaluation of Forensic DNA Evidence*, National Academies Press: Washington, DC, 1996 at pp. 133–135.

[211] United States v. Jenkins, 887 A.2d 1016, 1022–1023 (D.C. 2005).

[212] Id. at 1022.

[213] The Court in *Davis* did limit the government to presenting the statistical calculation produced by the product rule as "an expression of the rarity of the profile, but not as an expression of the random match probability." United States v. Davis, 602 F. Spp. 2d 658, 677(D. Md. 2009).

Although the federal habeas court in Crews was highly critical of the RMP statistic as "incomplete, if not entirely misleading" in cold hit cases, the admissibility issue was not before the court. Crews v. Johnson, 702 F. Supp.2d 618, 639 (W.D. Va. 2010).

[214] *See* People v. Nelson, 43 Cal.4th 1242, 1267 n. 3, 185 P.3d 49, 66 n. 3, 78 Cal. Rptr. 69, 90 n. 3, *cert. denied,* Nelson v. California, 555 U.S. 926 (2008). *See also* United States v. Jenkins, 887 A.2d 1013, 1022–1023; United States v. Davis, 602 F. Spp. 2d 658, 675–677 (D. Md. 2009).

Given the scientific debate over the appropriate statistical weight to be attributed to database hits, the courts will continue to deal with this issue.[215]

3. DNA DATABASES[216]

a. Constitutionality

The collection of a DNA sample pursuant to a search warrant based upon probable cause is governed by the same constitutional provisions and laws as other biological evidence.[217] In the absence of a warrant and probable cause, DNA may still be collected from an individual for purposes of maintaining a DNA database. Every state has enacted DNA database legislation allowing for the forensic collection and storage of DNA from certain classes of individuals based on qualifying criteria. The National Conference of State Legislatures maintains a database of the authorizing legislation on its website, including a state-by-state listing of the relevant DNA database laws.[218]

The qualifying criteria for requiring the submission of a DNA sample for inclusion in a state or federal database are based on convictions for specified offenses or, in some jurisdictions, an arrest for certain qualifying offenses. The statutory schemes vary greatly between the states, but all 50 states and the federal government require that convicted felony sex offenders provide DNA samples and 48 states and the federal government require all convicted adult felons to provide DNA samples to the state's database. A majority of states also require juveniles convicted or adjudicated guilty of a qualifying offense to provide DNA samples for the database. What crimes constitute "sex offenses" and "felonies" are defined by each state. At least 42 states also include some misdemeanor sex offenses as qualifying offenses requiring database submissions. As of June, 2016, 30 states and the federal government also authorize the collection of a DNA sample from arrestees charged with certain qualifying offenses.[219]

To implement a standardized system of database coordination, the federal 1994 DNA Identification Act, 42 U.S.C. § 14131 *et seq.*, granted the FBI the authority to establish a national DNA database to be used for

[215] *See* Simon J. Walsh and John S. Buckleton, "DNA Databases and Evidentiary Issues," in WILEY ENCYCLOPEDIA OF FORENSIC SCIENCE, (Jamieson A. & Moenssens A.A., eds) 2009 & online updates.

[216] Databases maintained by government agencies are discussed in this section. Databases are also maintained by private companies, typically involving medical or ancestry research. Although law enforcement agencies have searched private DNA databases for investigation purposes, the courts have not yet ruled on any issues associated with such searches. See "Law enforcement investigators seek out private DNA databases," Associated Press, March 26, 2016 (available at: http://mashable.com/2016/03/26/law-enforcement-dna-databases#KmLtOGytDPqo (last accessed August 24, 2016).

[217] *See* Schmerber v. California, 384 U.S. 757 (1996).

[218] *See* http://www.ncsl.org/issues-research/justice/dna-laws-database.aspx (last accessed June 9, 2016).

[219] *See, e.g.,* Va. Code § 19.2–310.2:1.

law enforcement purposes. The FBI created the Combined DNA Index System (CODIS)[220] to coordinate federal and state DNA database collections. The National DNA Index System (NDIS) is part of CODIS and contains the DNA profiles collected by participating federal, state, and local law criminal justice agencies in multiple databases, including the Convicted Offender/Arrestee Database, the Forensic Index, and the Missing Person Database.[221] As of April, 2016, NDIS contained over 12 million convicted offender/arrestee profiles and almost 700,000 evidence profiles from unsolved cases (Forensic Index).[222] Participation in CODIS is restricted to criminal justice agency laboratories that comply with specific quality assurance standards, accreditation requirements, and regular external audits.[223] DNA profiles generated through STR technology at the 13 core CODIS loci (as of January, 2017, the core loci number expands to 20) may be uploaded to the database.[224] Y-STR and mtDNA data can be searched in the Missing Person Database, but cannot be searched against the Convicted Offender/Arrestee database or the Forensic Index.

The purpose of a DNA database is to catalog DNA profiles for future comparison with crime scene samples. Such databases provide investigative leads in cases; act as a deterrent to recidivism;[225] and "[e]qually important, the DNA samples [may] help to exculpate individuals who are serving sentences of imprisonment for crimes they did not commit."[226] Databases give law enforcement officials the ability to make a computerized search for a presumptive match between an evidence DNA profile and a database profile and courts have readily accepted the use of database comparative analysis in the investigation of crimes.[227] The FBI has reported that, as of April 2016, CODIS aided in

---

[220] CODIS is the generic term used to describe the FBI's support programs for criminal justice DNA databases as well as the software used to operate the databases. See *Frequently Asked Questions (FAQs) on the CODIS Program and the National DNA Index System* (available at: https://www.fbi.gov/services/laboratory/biometric-analysis/codis/codis-and-ndis-fact-sheet)(last accessed March 3, 2017).

[221] Id.; 42 U.S.C. § 14132(b)(1).

[222] *CODIS-NDIS Statistics* at http://www.fbi.gov/about-us/lab/codis/ndis-statistics (last accessed June 9, 2016).

[223] 42 U.S.C. 14132(b). The current quality assurance standards are available at: www.swgdam.org.

[224] The 13 core loci are: CSF1PO, FGA, THO1, TPOX, vWA, D3S1358, D5S818, D7S820, D8S1179, D13S317, D16S539, D18S51, D21S11. For forensic samples, results must be generated at 10 loci for submission and searching. *Frequently Asked Questions (FAQs) on the CODIS Program and the National DNA Index System* (available at: http://www.fbi.gov/about-us/lab/codis/codis-and-ndis-fact-sheet)(last accessed June 9, 2016).

[225] Jones v. Murray, 962 F.2d 302, 311 (4th Cir. 1992); see also United States v. Kincade, 379 F.3d 813, 840 (9th Cir. 2004)(Gould, J., concurring).

[226] State v. Scarborough, 201 S.E.3d 607, 621 (Tenn. 2006)(*quoting* United States v. Sczubelek, 402 F.3d 175, 185 (3d Cir. 2005)).

[227] *See, e.g.,* Commonwealth v. Mollett, 2010 PA Super 153, 5 A.3d 291, 296 (Pa. Super. 2010); Shane v. Commonwealth, 243 S.W.3d 336 (Ky. 2007), People v. Buie, 285 Mich. App. 401, 775 N.W.2d 817 (Mich. App. 2009); State v. McMilian, 295 S.W.3d 537 (Mo. App. 2009).

over 316,000 investigations nationwide.[228] On a state level, the Virginia Department of Forensic Science had over 400,000 samples and had reported over 10,000 "hits" to the DNA database as of June, 2016.[229]

Despite the legitimate governmental objectives and the reported success in identifying perpetrators, many legal commentators see DNA database collection laws as causing serious constitutional violations, threatening the privacy and security of the individual, and leading to genetic redlining. Appellate courts addressing the constitutional challenges have overwhelmingly upheld federal and state DNA database collection statutes as applied to convicted offenders,[230] and in June, 2013 the United States Supreme Court upheld the constitutionality of the statutes authorizing arrestee DNA sampling.[231]

b.   Defense Access

An evolving issue concerns non-law enforcement access to the databases. Access to state databases are controlled by state law and some states have specifically provided for defense access in certain circumstances. For example, in Tennessee the Post-Conviction DNA Analysis Act of 2001, Tenn. Code Ann § 40–30–303 et seq., "was designed to permit access to a DNA database if a positive match between a profile developed from crime scene DNA and a profile contained within a database would create a reasonable probability that a petitioner would not have been prosecuted or convicted if exculpatory results from DNA analysis had been previously obtained or that the results would have rendered the petitioner's verdict or sentence more favorable."[232] Other states, such as Pennsylvania, have found that DNA testing laws implicitly grant defense access to databases "for the purpose of determining the person responsible for the crime in question."[233]

Access beyond an individual state's database, however, requires access to NDIS and its coordinated databases. Federal law restricts general access to NDIS to criminal justice agencies for law enforcement purposes. The law makes an exception for research and quality control purposes "if personally identifiable information in removed."[234] This exception has been interpreted by the FBI as limited to research by participating NDIS criminal justices agencies, a limitation challenged

[228] See https://www.fbi.gov/services/laboratory/biometric-analysis/codis/ndis-statistics (last accessed March 3, 2017).

[229] See http://www.dfs.virginia.gov/about-dfs/dna-databank-statistics/ (last accessed June 9, 2016).

[230] See Jones v. Murray, 962 F.2d 302 (4th Cir.1992), cert. denied 506 U.S. 977 (1992); State v. Olivas, 122 Wash.2d 73, 856 P.2d 1076 (1993).

[231] Maryland v. King, 133 S.Ct. 1958 (2013)(cheek swab and DNA analysis on arrestees, like fingerprinting and photographing, was a legitimate booking procedure that was reasonable under the Fourth Amendment).

[232] Powers v. State, 343 S.E.3d 36, 60 (Tenn. 2011).

[233] Commonwealth v. Conway, 2011 Pa. Super. 7, 14 A.3d 101, 112 (Pa. Super. Ct. 2011).

[234] 42 U.S.C. § 14132(b)(3)(D).

by academic scholars as blocking legitimate research needs.[235] With respect to defense access, the law specifically permits criminal defendants "access to samples and analyses performed in connection with the case in which such defendant is charged."[236] Some criminal defendants have sought additional access, including requesting that additional searches be performed in their case.

In 2008, Juan Rivera obtained an order from the Circuit Court of Lake County, Illinois, directing the FBI to compare an unknown DNA profile from his criminal case with the NDIS database. When the FBI refused, Rivera sought review of the FBI's refusal under the Administrative Procedures Act, 5 U.S.C. §§ 701–706 from the United States District Court in the Northern District of Illinois.[237] Juan Rivera was scheduled to be tried for a third time in the 1992 rape and murder of an 11 year-old girl. The first conviction had been overturned for legal errors at trial and the second conviction was overturned after DNA analysis excluded Rivera as the contributor of the semen in the victim. The true contributor of the semen remained unidentified, however, and Rivera sought an order directing the FBI to run the profile through its database to hopefully identify that man. The FBI refused to conduct the search because it was not requested by a law enforcement agency and because the DNA analysis was not conducted by a participating criminal justice laboratory. By order dated February 2, 2009, the United States District Court found the FBI's refusal to be unreasonable and ordered the FBI to conduct the comparison.[238] The search did not produce a match. Rivera was convicted a third time, but the Illinois appellate court reversed the conviction, referencing the DNA evidence exclusion and finding the evidence was insufficient to support conviction.[239] The prosecution decided not to proceed with a fourth trial and Juan Rivera was released on January 6, 2012 after 20 years of incarceration.[240]

During federal habeas proceedings challenging his Ohio convictions and death sentence, Timothy L. Coleman sought comparison of a DNA

---

[235] *See* David H. Kaye, "Trawling DNA Databases for Partial Matches: What Is the FBI Afraid Of?" 19 CORNELL J. L. & PUBLIC POLICY 145–171 (2009); Dan E. Krane et al., "Time for DNA Disclosure," 326 SCIENCE 1631–1632 (2009); Linda Geddes, "Editorial: Unreliable Evidence? Time to Open Up DNA Databases," 2742 NEW SCIENTIST (January 6, 2010); *but see* Bruce Budowle, F. Samuel Baechtel and Ranajit Chakaborty, "Partial Matches in Heterogeneous Offender Databases Do Not Call Into Question the Validity of Random Match Probability Calculations," 123 INT. J. LEGAL MED. 59–63 (2009)(asserting that the CODIS database is not an appropriate tool for assessing statistical assumptions used in DNA match probability calculations).

[236] 42 U.S.C. § 14132(b)(3)(C).

[237] Juan A. Rivera v. Robert S. Mueller, Case No. 08C6185, U.S. Dist. Ct, N. Dist. Of Ill., E. Div., Judge Rebecca R. Pallmeyer.

[238] Order of Rebecca R. Pallmeyer, February 2, 2009, in Juan A. Rivera v. Robert S. Mueller, Case No. 08C6185, U.S. Dist. Ct, N. Dist. Of Ill., E. Div., Judge Rebecca R. Pallmeyer.

[239] People v. Rivera, 2011 Il. App. 2d 091060 (December 9, 2011).

[240] Dan Hinkel, Ruth Fuller and Lisa Black, "Rivera Freed After Lake County Prosecutors Stop Seeking Retrial in Girl's 1992 Slaying," *Chicago Tribune*, January 7, 2012.

profile developed on evidentiary items against profiles in the state and national databases.[241] The evidentiary profile had been developed during testing by a private, non-accredited laboratory, so in January, 2008, the court ordered the Ohio Bureau of Criminal Investigation (BCI) to "adopt" the other laboratory's results or conduct retesting to enable the evidentiary profiles to be compared against the state and national databases.[242] On March 21, 2011, the Ohio BCI notified the court that the profiles had been compared against the state database and a request for a search against the national database had been denied by the FBI because the evidentiary profile did not meet the CODIS minimum loci requirements. Coleman sought an additional order from the court requiring the comparison of the 7-loci evidentiary results against the national database, but the court denied the motion finding that Coleman failed to produce any evidence that the FBI responded "inappropriately" to the request.[243]

In 2006, following a database hit to an evidence sample in a rape case occurring almost 20 years earlier, Norman Bruce Derr sought information from the FBI on the number of "coincidental and unexplained matches" in the CODIS database.[244] On appeal, the Maryland appellate court noted that Derr was "essentially requesting . . . that the FBI conduct a research project," and that there was no evidence that the database had coincidental matches. The court concluded that the defendant had no constitutional right to require the state to create potentially exculpatory information or "to search CODIS for potentially helpful information."[245]

c.   Familial DNA and Partial Match Searches

The use of DNA typing to aid in identifying familial relationships is widely accepted and utilized in civil and criminal paternity cases, missing persons cases, and in mass disaster victim identifications. The use of the same principles to assist in identifying a criminal perpetrator through searching DNA databases for potential close-degree familial matches, however, has generated considerable controversy. For proponents of the technique, known as familial searching, it is just another investigative tool to provide leads to identify the source of DNA evidence. For opponents, however, the civil liberty infringements outweigh any efficacy of the technique.[246]

---

[241] Coleman v. Bradshaw, United States District Court, Southern District of Ohio, Eastern Division, Case No. 3:03CV299.

[242] Id. Order entered January 22, 2008, Magistrate Judge Mark R. Abel.

[243] Id. Order entered May 19, 2011, Magistrate Judge Michael R. Merz.

[244] Derr v. State, 434 Md. 88, 122, 73 A.3d 254, 274 (Ct. App. 2013).

[245] 434 Md. at 124–127, 73 A.3d at 275–277.

[246] G. Naik, "The Gene Police," The Wall Street Journal (February 28, 2008); S. Pope, et al., "More for the same? Enhancing the Investigative Potential of Forensic DNA Databases," 2 FORENSIC SCI. INT'L: GENETICS 458–459 (2009); M. Rothstein and M. Talbott, "The Expanding Use of DNA in Law Enforcement: What Role for Privacy? 34 J. LAW, MED. & ETHICS 153–164 (2006); E. Haimes, "Social and Ethical Issues in the Use of Familial Searching in Forensic

In familial searching, a partial genetic profile match between a database profile and a crime scene sample is used to assist in identifying potential genetic relatives of the source of the crime scene sample.[247] Further investigation is then used to identify whether anyone genetically related to the selected database profiles may be the source of the crime scene sample. Once potential relatives are identified, additional Y-STR DNA testing may be used if the evidence profile and the database profiles are male to confirm a genetic relationship.[248] The technique garnered attention with the identification, arrest, and conviction of the "Grim Sleeper" in California based in part on familial searching of the state's database which produced a lead through the defendant's son.[249]

Familial searches are similar to partial ("moderate stringency") match searches. With a partial match "hit," all alleles present in both the evidence sample profile and the database profile must match, but each profile may contain additional alleles. For example, the following two profiles would be considered to be a partial match:[250]

Locus	Forensic Unknown	Candidate Offender	Match Stringency
D8S1179	13	13, 14	Moderate
D21S11	28, 31.2	28, 31.2	High
D7S820	12	10, 12	Moderate
CSF1PO	10, 12	10	Moderate
D3S1358	15, 17	15, 17	High
TH01	8	7, 8	Moderate

Investigations: Insights from Family and Kinship Studies," 34 J. LAW, MED. & ETHICS 263–276 (2006); H. Greely et al., "Family Ties: The Use of DNA Offender Databases to Catch Offenders' K," 34 J. LAW, MED. & ETHICS 248–262 (2006).

[247] The exact searching method can be by shared alleles, by kinship assessments, or a combination of the two methods. See Jianye Ge, et al., "Comparisons of Familial DNA Database Searching Strategies," 56 J. FORENSIC SCI. 1448–1456 (2011).

[248] Joyce Kim, et al., "Policy Implications for Familial Searching," 2 INVESTIGATIVE GENETICS 22 (2011).

[249] James Queally and Marisa Gerber, "Jurors Vote for Death Sentence for 'Grim Sleeper' Serial Killer," LA Times, June 6, 2016 (available at: http://www.latimes.com/local/lanow/la-me-ln-grim-sleeper-death-verdict-20160606-snap-story.html)(last accessed June 7, 2016); Jennifer Steinhauer, "'Grim Sleeper' Arrest Fans Debate on DNA Use," NY Times, July 8, 2010 (available at: http://www.nytimes.com/2010/07/09/us/09sleeper.html?_r=0)(last accessed June 8, 2016); see also Steven P. Myers et al., "Searching for First-Degree Familial Relationships in California's Offender DNA Database: Validation of a Likelihood Ratio-Based Approach," 5 FORENSIC SCI. INT'L: GENETICS 493–500 (2011).

[250] SWGDAM Recommendations to the FBI Director on the "Interim Plan for the Release of Information in the Event of a 'Partial Match' at NDIS," October 2009 (available at: www.swgdam.org).

D13S317	9, 12	9	Moderate
D16S539	11, 12	12	Moderate
VWA	17	15, 17	Moderate
TPOX	8, 11	8	Moderate
D18S51	24	16, 24	Moderate
D5S818	9, 12	12	Moderate
FGA	24, 25	24, 25	High

The FBI has expressly distinguished the partial matches that it permits in CODIS searching from familial searches:

> [A] moderate stringency search is an effective means of searching forensic profiles from crime scene evidence that may contain DNA from more than one individual (a forensic mixture), forensic DNA that is partially degraded or to accommodate the use of different DNA typing kits by different laboratories. This should not be confused with attempting to search for similar but not matching profiles already stored within the National DNA database—a type of database searching that the FBI does not conduct.[251]

However, the distinction between familial searching and partial matches appears to be more one of "intent" than of result:

> A partial match . . . is the spontaneous product of a routine database search where a candidate offender profile is not identical to the forensic profile but because of a similarity in the number of alleles shared . . . the offender may be a close biological relative of the source of the forensic profile. Familial searching is an intentional or deliberate search of the database conducted after a routine search for the purpose of potentially identifying close biological relatives of the unknown forensic sample associated with the crime scene profile.[252]

Although the FBI does not conduct familial searches (at least intentionally), Arkansas, California, Colorado, Florida, Michigan, Texas, Utah, Virginia, Wisconsin, and Wyoming expressly permit familial searches in their state databases.[253] Maryland and the District

---

[251] See *Frequently Asked Questions (FAQs) on the CODIS Program and the National DNA Index System* (available at: https://www.fbi.gov/services/laboratory/biometric-analysis/codis/codis-and-ndis-fact-sheet#Partial-Matches%20and%20Familial%20Searches)(last accessed March 3, 2017).

[252] Id.

[253] Copies of the familial search policy for Virginia is available at: http://www.dfs.virginia.gov/laboratory-forensic-services/biology/familial-searches/ (last accessed June 10, 2016).

of Columbia expressly forbid familial and partial match searches.[254] The remaining states have a mixture of policies concerning fortuitous partial matches and deliberate (familial) searching.[255]

4.　POST-CONVICTION DNA TESTING

DNA analysis, from its earliest days, has been used to exclude people as contributors and to exonerate the wrongfully convicted. In 1989, Gary Dotson and David Vasquez were exonerated through DNA testing in Illinois and Virginia respectively. Since then, innocence projects have been established nationwide.[256] In addition, law school projects and clinics provide experience and exposure to the exoneration process through innocence projects.[257] By June, 2012, 292 convicted offenders in 35 states and the District of Columbia have been exonerated through DNA testing, including 17 people who had been sentenced to death.[258]

In 1996, the National Institute of Justice released a document describing the process of using DNA evidence to exonerate convicted offenders.[259] In 1999, an additional report on responding to requests for post-conviction DNA testing was issued.[260] Even as DNA evidence was used to support claims of innocence, convicted offenders frequently lacked access to the evidence and the legal remedies for challenging years-old convictions. The "lack of available remedies in the state or federal courts" for convicted offenders led governments to enact legislation affording post-conviction access to DNA testing.[261] The first statutes were enacted in 1999 (Illinois and New York), and by 2016 every state has a specific statute concerning access to post-conviction DNA testing.[262] The statutory schemes vary greatly and advocates for the wrongfully

---

[254] *See* D.C. CODE § 22–4151(b); MD. CODE ANN., PUB. SAFETY § 2–506(d).

[255] *See* Natalie Ram, "Fortuity and Forensic Familial Identification, 63 Stan. L. Rev. 751 (2011).

[256] The Justice Project, Campaign for Criminal Justice Reform, *available at* http://www.the justiceproject.org; Wrongly Convicted Database Index, *available at* http://forejustice.org/db/ innocents.html; Justice Denied Magazine: The Magazine for the Wrongly Convicted, *available at* http://www.justicedenied.org; Truth in Justice website, *available at* http://truthinjustice.org; Michael and Becky Pardue, *Freeing the Innocent: How We Did It* (2001).

[257] Georgann Eubanks, "Overturning Wrongful Convictions," 88 DUKE MAGAZINE (2002).

[258] The Innocence Project maintains a database of all DNA exonerations, including case profiles, on its website (available at: http://www.innocenceproject.org)(last accessed March 3, 2017).

[259] Edward Connors, Thomas Lundregan, Neal Miller and Tom McEwen, *Convicted by Juries, Exonerated by Science: Case Studies in the Use of DNA Evidence to Establish Innocence After Trial*, National Institute of Justice, U.S. Department of Justice (1996)(available at: http:// www.ncjrs.gov/pdffiles/dnaevid.pdf)(last accessed June 10, 2016).

[260] National Commission on the Future of DNA Evidence, *Postconviction DNA Testing: Recommendations for Handling Requests,* National Institute of Justice, U.S. Department of Justice (1999)(available at: https://www.ncjrs.gov/pdffiles1/nij/177626.pdf)(last accessed June 10, 2016).

[261] Brandon L. Garrett, "Claiming Innocence," 92 Minn. L. Rev. 1629, 1673 (2008).

[262] A state by state listing of all forensic science laws, including post-conviction testing statutes, is maintained by the National Conference of State Legislatures (available at: http:// www.ncsl.org/research/civil-and-criminal-justice/dna-laws-database.aspx)(last accessed June 10, 2016).

convicted argue that some laws are too restrictive and lack adequate safeguards for the preservation of evidence.[263]

Whatever the deficiencies in the post-conviction testing statutes, convicted defendants have limited legal remedies beyond these statutory schemes. In *District Attorney's Office for Third Judicial Dist. v. Osborne*,[264] the United States Supreme Court held that when other post-conviction remedies that might allow a convicted offender to obtain DNA evidence for additional testing have not been pursued, constitutional substantive due process does not provide for a free-standing right to DNA testing. In *Skinner v. Switzer*,[265] however, the Court held that where a state court has refused to order the DNA testing under the relevant post-conviction testing statute, the convicted offender may challenge that ruling in habeas proceedings or present a civil rights claim for the DNA testing in an action under 42 U.S.C. § 1983. Access to DNA testing varies from jurisdiction to jurisdiction, based on the differences in statutory schemes and differences in the prosecutorial position on DNA testing.

5. LOW COPY NUMBER/HIGH SENSITIVITY ANALYSIS

Through rigorous validation studies, the optimum levels of DNA for STR testing with frequently used amplification kits have been determined and most manufacturers recommend using samples 0.5 to 2.0 nanograms and 26 to 32 cycles with their amplification kits.[266] Procedures for typing smaller samples, generally involving additional amplification cycles, have been studied[267] and used in some cases with a variety of results. The typing of these small amounts of DNA is generally referred to as Low Copy Number (LCN) testing, "high sensitivity" analysis or "enhanced detection methods".[268] LCN or high sensitivity analysis generally refers to DNA tests done on small amounts of DNA that are well below the "stochastic threshold," meaning the minimum amount of DNA that is necessary to avoid having random processes dominate or manifest in the DNA testing

---

[263] Sherida Hibbard, "Comment: To Test or Not to Test?: Problems with Post-Conviction Relief in Texas," 13 TEX. ADMIN. L.J. 121 (2010).

[264] 557 U.S. 52 (2009).

[265] 131 S.Ct. 1289 (2011).

[266] Maura Barisin, *et al.*, "Developmental Validation of the Quantifiler® Duo DNA Quantification Kit for Simultaneous Quantification of Total Human and Human Male DNA and Detection of PCR Inhibitors in Biological Samples," 54 J. FORENSIC SCI. 305–319 (2009); Scientific Working Group on DNA Analysis Methods, *SWGDAM Guidelines for STR Enhanced Detection Methods*, October 6, 2014, p. 2 (available at: www.swgdam.org).

[267] Other procedures have also been studied. *See, e.g.*, John Buckleton and Peter Gill, "Low Copy Number," in John Buckleton, Christopher M. Triggs and Simon J. Walsh, eds. *Forensic DNA Evidence Interpretation*, CRC Press: Boca Raton, FL (2005) at pp. 275–297.

[268] Although the term "Low Template DNA" has also been used, this term has a variety of uses. *See* Jo-Anne Bright, Peter Gill and John Buckleton, "Composite Profiles in DNA Analysis," 6 FORENSIC SCI. INT'L: GENETICS 317–321 (2012)(defining LtDNA as "any profile where drop-out is possible regardless of the way in which the sample has been amplified or visualised" and LCN as using a particular 34-cycle amplification procedure).

results. The scientific community has not settled on an exact quantity denoting the stochastic threshold, with values varying from below 0.5 nanograms to below 0.125 nanograms.[269] Artifacts such as stutter, peak height imbalance, allelic drop-in and allelic drop-out are exaggerated with testing amounts below the stochastic threshold.[270] LCN analysis typically involves DNA amounts less than 200 or 100 picograms and uses a protocol of amplification of 31 to 34 cycles. The increased amplification procedure creates more DNA for testing, but also increases the effects of artifacts in the results. "The potential for DNA typing inaccuracies, irreproducibility due to stochastic effects, allelic drop-in, contamination risks, and interpretational difficulties, are notable concerns that any laboratory considering [LCN analysis] should contemplate and evaluate."[271] While SWGDAM has not offered an opinion of the viability of LCN testing, on October 6, 2014, they did issue the SWGDAM Guidelines for STR Enhanced Detection Methods.[272]

The cases involving the use of results from LCN analysis are limited to a few states where the process is used. The New York Office of the Chief Medical Examiner is the only government facility currently using LCN DNA analysis, but several private and academic laboratories also use the process. As of June, 2016, only New York and New Mexico,[273] had published decisions discussing the admissibility of LCN analysis.[274] In the cases where the court has addressed the admissibility of the LCN procedures, the results have been mixed, particularly in New York. A federal court in New York, applying a *Daubert* standard, admitted the LCN results.[275] Two New York state trial courts, applying a *Frye* standard, split on the issue of admissibility of LCN results and the state appellate courts have not yet addressed the issue.[276]

---

[269] United States v. Davis, 602 F. Supp.2d 658, 668(D. Md. 2009).

[270] Hannah Kelly, et al., "The Interpretation of Low Level DNA Mixtures," 6 FORENSIC SCI. INT'L: GENETICS 191–197 (2011).

[271] Scientific Working Group on DNA Analysis Methods, *SWGDAM Guidelines for STR Enhanced Detection Methods*, October 6, 2014, p. 2 (available at: www.swgdam.org).

[272] Guidelines for STR Enhanced Detection Methods. (2014, Oct. 6). Retrieved August 11, 2016, from http://www.swgdam.org/.

[273] United States v. McCluskey, 954 F. Supp.2d 1224 (D. N. Mex. 2013) (excluding LCN results).

[274] Other jurisdictions have discussed the issue only in passing to note that the case did not involve LCN DNA. *See, e.g.,* United State Davis, 602 F. Supp.2d 658 (D. Md. 2009). See also State v. Bigger, 227 Ariz. 196, 208, 254 P.3d 1142, 1154 (Ariz. Ct. App. 2011)("We leave for another case the determination of whether there is a generally accepted method for achieving probability statistics from DNA templates significantly smaller than those observed here, or where analysts seek to interpret results below a laboratory's established minimum RFU threshold."); United States v. Sleugh, 2015 U.S. Dist. LEXIS 82877 (D. ND. Cal.)(June 22, 2015)(finding that the defendant failed to prove the amount of DNA tested had any effect on the methodology used or the results).

[275] United States v. Morgan, 53 F. Supp.3d 732 (D. SD. NY 2014)(LCN DNA results admissible under standards set forth in *Daubert* and FRE 702).

[276] Compare People v. Collins, 49 Misc.3d 595 (Sup. Ct. King Co. 2015)(holding high sensitivity analysis is not generally accepted in the relevant scientific community, and

6.   SOFTWARE PROGRAMS

Although the FBI's Quality Assurance Standards for Forensic DNA Testing Laboratories[277] requires human interpretation and review for the interpretation of DNA analysis results, computer programs have been routinely used to assist with the interpretation and calculation of probability statistics. With single-source or non-complex mixture cases subjected to conventional STR testing, the use of such programs has generated little controversy because the software results can be compared to non-assisted conclusions. However, new programs developed to assist with interpretation of LCN and complex mixture analysis have been controversial. Termed "probabilistic genotyping systems" these programs (whether software or a combination of hardware and software) use "analytical and statistical functions that entail complex formulae and algorithms."[278] There are approximately eight different probabilistic genotyping programs on the market as of August 2016, and the two most commonly used are TrueAllele® by Cybergenetics and STRmix™ out of New Zealand.[279] On June 15, 2015, SWGDAM issued Guidelines for the Validation of Probabilistic Genotyping Systems.[280] The 2016 PCAST Report found that probabilistic genotyping programs are a "promising approach."[281]

A few courts have addressed challenges to testimony based on the use of these probabilistic genotyping systems,[282] resulting in conflicting holdings as to admissibility. In *People v. Debraux*, a New York trial court ruled on the admissibility of results from the Forensic Statistical Tool (FST), "a mathematical computer software program developed and used by the Forensic Biology Unit of the New York City Office of the Chief Medical Examiner (OCME) to calculate a likelihood ratio that [the defendant's DNA is part of the complex DNA mixture] found on

---

therefore, inadmissible under the *Frye* standard); and People v. Garcia, 39 Misc.3d 482, 963 N.Y.S.2d 517 (Sup. Ct. Bronx Co 2013)(LCN DNA analysis is "generally accepted" and admissible) and People v. Megnath, 27 Misc.3d 405 (NY Sup. Ct. Queens Co. 2010)(Hanophy, J.)(upholding the use of LCN/high sensitivity analysis).

[277] *See* Section 17.12 *supra*.

[278] Scientific Working Group on DNA Methods, *SWGDAM Guidelines for Validation of Probabilistic Genotyping Systems*, approved June 15, 2015 (available at: www.swgdam.org).

[279] For information on TrueAllele® see www.cybgen.com. For information on STRmix™ see http://strmix.esr.cri.nz/. *See also* S.J. Cooper, C.E. McGovern, J.-A. Bright, D. Taylor and J.S. Buckleton, "Investigating a common approach to DNA profile interpretation using probabilistic software," 16 Forensic Sci. Int'l: Genetics 121–131 (2015).

[280] Guidelines for the Validation of Probabilistic Genotyping Systems. (2015, June 6). Retrieved August 11, 2016, from http://www.swgdam.org/.

[281] 2016 PCAST Report at p. 82. The report further noted that "[a]t present, published evidence supports the foundational validity of analysis, with some programs, of DNA mixtures of 3 individuals in which the minor contributor constitutes at least 20 percent of the intact DNA in the mixture and in which the DNA amount exceeds the minimum required level for the method."

[282] *See* People v. Wakefield, 47 Mics.3d 850,9 N.Y.S.3d 540 (Sup. Ct. Schenectady Co, 2015)(admitting the results of Cybergenetics TrueAllele® Casework).

crime scene evidence."[283] The court noted that other trial courts in New York had conducted extensive *Frye* admissibility hearings on the FST and had reached divergent conclusions.[284] Focusing on the FST's approach to accounting for stochastic effects in its probability computations, the court found that the calculation of likelihood ratios and the Bayesian mathematical principles were generally accepted. The court found that any variability in the calculations from FST's approach to the stochastic effects was more akin to "the calculation of a margin of error of the test results" and went to the weight of the evidence, not the admissibility.[285] In *People v. Hillary*, another New York trial court found that STRmix™ generally met the Frye admissibility standard of general acceptance, but that the specific results of the analysis in the case were inadmissible because it failed to properly account for allelic drop-out (the absence of the defendant's alleles at some loci) in the statistic.[286]

Other challenges to the software have focused on obtaining the "source code," the computer code that determines how the software will process information. As of June, 2016, in published decisions courts have denied access to the source code, deeming it proprietary software and access was unnecessary to evaluate the results.[287] As these programs survive challenge, they gain wider acceptance and use in laboratories.[288]

VI. RESOURCES

§14.20 BIBLIOGRAPHY OF ADDITIONAL RESOURCES

1.   FORENSIC BIOLOGY

Jarrah R. Myers and William K. Adkins, "Comparison of Modern Techniques for Saliva Screening," 53 J.FORENSIC SCI. 862–867 (2008).

---

[283] 50 Misc.3d 247, 21 N.Y.S.3d 535 (Sup. Ct. NY Co. 2015).

[284] See People v. Rodriquez, Ind. No. 54712009 (Sup. Ct. New York Co. Oct. 24, 2013 (Carrithers, J.)(FST generally accepted in the scientific community and admissible); People v. Collins, 49 Misc. 3d 595, 15 NYS3d 564 (Sup. Ct. Kings Co. July 2, 2015) (Dwyer, J.)(FST not generally accepted in the scientific community and is not admissible).

[285] People v. Debraux, 50 Misc.3d 247, 255–256, 21 N.Y.S.3d 535, 542 (Sup. Ct. New York Co. 2015).

[286] Decision and Order on DNA Analysis Admissibility, People v. Oral Nicholas Hillary, County Court of St. Lawrence County, issued August 26, 2016.

[287] *See* People v. Carter, 2016 N.Y. Misc. LEXIS 166 (Sup. Ct. Queens Co. January 12, 2016); see also Commonwealth v. Foley, 38 A.3d 882 (Sup. Ct. PA 2009)("scientists can validate the reliability of a computerized process even if the 'source code' underlying that process is not available to the public.").

[288] Virginia uses TrueAllele® for mixture interpretation and had issued over 200 reports using the system by October, 2015. See Vince S. Donoghue, Chair, Forensic Science Board, Annual Forensic Science Report, dated October 30, 2015, p. 3 (available at: http://leg2.state.va.us/dls/h&sdocs.nsf/By+Year/RD3502015/$file/RD350.pdf)(last accessed March 3, 2017).

Hiroaki Nakanishi *et al.,* "A Simple Identification Method of Saliva by Detecting *Streptococcus Salivarius* Using Loop-Mediated Isothermal Amplification," 56 (S1) J.FORENSIC SCI. S158–S161 (2011).

Jessica V. Norris *et al.,* "Expedited, Chemically Enhanced Sperm Cell Recovery from Cotton Swabs for Rape Kit Analysis," 52 J.FORENSIC SCI. 800–805 (2007).

Joanne L. Simons and Sue K. Vintiner, "Effects of Histological Staining on Analysis of Human DNA from Archived Slides," 56(S1) J.FORENSIC SCI. S223–S228 (2011).

Jessica C. Voorhees *et al.* "Enhanced Elution of Sperm from Cotton Swabs Via Enzymatic Digestion for Rape Kit Analysis," 51 J. FORENSIC SCI. 574 (2006).

2.   DNA ANALYSIS

a.   *Articles and Journals*

Michael Booth, "Court Sustains Constitutionality of Mandatory DNA Sampling Statute," N.J.L.J. (January 24, 2007).

B. Michael Dann *et al.,* "Can Jury Trial Innovations Improve Juror Understanding of DNA Evidence?," 90 Judicature 152 (2007).

Susan E. Davis, "Buried in DNA: Despite Hype about Using DNA to Break Unsolved Crimes, Cold Case Units Face Slow Going," 27 CAL. LAW. 13 (2007).

Troy Duster, "Explaining Differential Trust of DNA Forensic Technology: Grounded Assessment or Inexplicable Paranoia," 34 J.L. Med. & Ethics 293 (2006).

Kirsten Edwards, "Cold Hit Complacency: the Dangers of DNA Databases Re-Examined," 18 Current Issues Crim. Just. 92 (2006).

Sepideh Esmaili, "Searching for a Needle in a Haystack: the Constitutionality of Police DNA Dragnets," 82 Chi.-Kent L. Rev. 495 (2007).

Paul C. Giannelli, "Forensic Science: Under the Microscope," 34 Ohio N.U.L. Rev. 315 (2008).

Paul C. Giannelli, "Science for Judges VII: Evaluating Evidence of Causation & Forensic Laboratories: Current Issues & Standards: Regulating Crime Laboratories: The Impact of DNA Evidence," 15 J.L. & Pol'y 59 (2007).

Henry T. Greely *et al.,* "Family Ties: The Use of DNA Offender Databases to Catch Offenders' Kin," 34 J.L. Med. & Ethics 248 (2006).

Mark Hamblett, "Circuit Approves Taking DNA Samples from Nonviolent Felons on Probation," N.Y. L.J. (April 6, 2007).

Mark Hansen, "DNA Poised to Show Its Civil Side," ABA JOURNAL, Mar. 2008, p. 18.

Joshua Hillel Hubner, "Blinded by Science: Does the General Acceptance of Forensic DNA Evidence Warrant a More Streamlined Approach to Admissibility," 18 U. Fla. J.L. & Pub. Pol'y 93 (2007).

Vesna Jaksic, " 'Abandoned DNA' triggers new debate over privacy" NAT'L L.J. 2007 WL 1506551 (2007).

Tonja Jacobi and Gwendolyn Carroll, "Acknowledging Guilt: Forcing Self-Identification in Post-conviction DNA Testing," 102 Nw. U.L. Rev. 263 (2008).

Elizabeth E. Joh, "Reclaiming 'Abandoned' DNA: the 4th Amendment and Genetic Privacy," 100 Nw. U. L. Rev. 857 (2006).

Frederika A. Kaestle *et al.*, "Database Limitations on the Evidentiary Value of Forensic Mitochondrial DNA Evidence," 43 Am. Crim. L. Rev. 53 (2006).

David H. Kaye, "Who Needs Special Needs? On the Constitutionality of Collecting DNA and Other Biometric Data from Arrestees," 34 J.L. Med. & Ethics 188 (2006).

David H. Kaye, "The Science of DNA Identification: from the Laboratory to the Courtroom (and Beyond)," 8 Minn. J. L. Sci. & Tech. 409 (2007).

Michael E. Kleinert, "Improving the Quality of Justice: the Innocence Protection Act of 2004 Ensures Post-conviction DNA Testing, Better Legal Representation, and Increased Compensation for the Wrongfully Imprisoned," 44 Brandeis L.J. 491 (2006).

Tracey Maclin, "Is Obtaining an Arrestee's DNA a Valid Special Needs Search under the 4th Amendment? What Should (and Will) the Supreme Court Do," 34 J.L. Med. & Ethics 165 (2006).

Paul M. Monteleoni, "DNA Databases, Universality, and the Fourth Amendment," 82 N.Y.U. L. Rev. 247 (2007).

Thomas J. Moyer, Chief Justice, "Biotechnology and the Bar: A Response to the Growing Divide Between Science and the Legal Environment," 22 Berkeley Tech. L.J. 671 (2007).

Matthew J. Mueller, "Handling Claims of Actual Innocence: Rejecting Federal Habeas Corpus As the Best Avenue for Addressing Claims of Innocence Based on DNA Evidence," 56 Cath. U. L. Rev. 227 (2006).

Erin Murphy, "The New Forensics: Criminal Justice, False Certainty, and the 2nd Generation of Scientific Evidence," 95 Cal. L. Rev. 721 (2007).

David R. Paoletti *et al.*, "Assessing the Implications for Close Relatives in the Event of Similar but Nonmatching DNA Profiles," 46 Jurimetrics J.L. Sci. & Tech. 161 (2006).

Julie Rikelman, "Justifying Forcible DNA Testing Schemes under the Special Needs Exception to the 4th Amendment: A Dangerous Precedent," 59 Baylor L. Rev. 41 (2007).

Tania Simoncelli and Barry Steinhardt, "California's Proposition 69: a Dangerous Precedent for Criminal DNA Databases," 34 J.L. Med. & Ethics 199 (2006).

Julie A. Singer *et al.*, "The Impact of DNA and Other Technology on the Criminal Justice System: Improvements and Complications," 17 Alb. L.J. Sci. & Tech. 87 (2007).

Deborah Sulzbach, "DNA Shall Prevail: Postconviction DNA Evidence: an Annotated Bibliography," 25 Legal Reference Serv. Q. 39 (2006).

Katie L. Swango *et al.*, "A Quantitative PCR Assay for the Assessment of DNA Degradation in Forensic Samples," 158 Forensic Sci. Int'l 14 (2006).

Robert Tanner, "DNA Taken from Those Arrested More Frequently," 152 CHI. DAILY L. BULL. 1 (2006).

Robin Williams and Paul Johnson, "Inclusiveness, Effectiveness and Intrusiveness: Issues in the Developing Uses of DNA Profiling in Support of Criminal Investigations," 34 J.L. Med. & Ethics 234 (2006).

b.   *Books*

ABA Standards for Criminal Justice: DNA Evidence, 3d ed., American Bar Association, 2007.

John M. Butler, *Advanced Topics in Forensic DNA Typing: Methodology*, Elsevier Academic Press, 2012.

John M. Butler, *Advanced Topics in Forensic DNA Typing: Interpretation*, Elsevier Academic Press, 2015.

David H. Kaye, *The Double Helix and the Law of Evidence,* Harvard University Press, 2010.

Thomas J. McClintock, *Forensic DNA Analysis: a Laboratory Manual,* CRC Press, 2008.

National Research Council Committee on DNA Forensic Science: *An Update, The Evaluation of Forensic DNA Evidence*, National Academies Press, 1996.

National Research Council Committee on DNA Technology in Forensic Science, *DNA Technology in Forensic Science*, National Academies Press, 1992.

David E. Newton, *DNA Evidence and Forensic Science,* Facts on File, 2008.

Victor W. Weedn & R. E. Gaensslen, *Handbook of Forensic DNA Typing,* CRC Press, 2007.

Robin Williams and Paul Johnson, *Genetic Policing: The Use of DNA in Criminal Investigations,* Willian, 2008.

CHAPTER 15

CONTROLLED SUBSTANCES ANALYSIS[1]

I.   INTRODUCTION

§15.01 SCOPE OF THE CHAPTER

The term "controlled substance" is used to refer to any substance for which the manufacturing, possession, and distribution are regulated by state or federal law. Under federal law, "controlled substance" means

---

[1] The Authors thank the following subject matter expert for his assistance with this chapter: Joseph P. Bono, MA, D-ABC. Mr. Bono previously served as a forensic scientist for the Drug Enforcement Administration and as Laboratory Director for the United States Secret Service. He served on the Scientific Working Group for the Analysis of Seized Drugs (SWGDRUG) and as Chairman of the Virginia Forensic Sciences Board. He is a Past President of the American Academy of Forensic Science and a former adjunct professor in the Forensic and Investigative Sciences Program at Indiana University-Purdue University.

"a drug or other substance, or immediate precursor, included in schedule I, II, III, IV, or V of [21 U.S.C. § 812]."[2] A substance that has been found to have a potential for abuse/addiction is included in the federal schedules I-V according to:

(1)   Its actual or relative potential for abuse.

(2)   Scientific evidence of its pharmacological effect, if known.

(3)   The state of current scientific knowledge regarding the drug or other substance.

(4)   Its history and current pattern of abuse.

(5)   The scope, duration, and significance of abuse.

(6)   What, if any, risk there is to the public health.

(7)   Its psychic or physiological dependence liability.

(8)   Whether the substance is an immediate precursor of a substance already controlled. . . .[3]

Controlled substances are both "street drugs" (e.g., heroin, cocaine, marijuana, methamphetamine) and prescription drugs (e.g., oxycodone, codeine, methadone).

Drug use testing and the toxicological analysis of biological material for controlled substances are addressed in Chapter 13. This chapter deals with the analysis and cases involving seizure controlled substances—before consumption and use. Seized controlled substances ("seized drugs") are involved in the prosecution of possession, trafficking, and manufacturing offenses. As with the toxicological analysis of biological materials, seized drug analysis requires strict adherence to proper evidence handling protocols and analytical procedures. Method validation is also a critical issue in the analysis of seized drugs.

This chapter focuses on seized drug analysis for criminal investigations and prosecutions. The methods and technology discussed, however, are also used in civil and regulatory investigations such as product infringement and the screening of prescription medications to detect contamination or dilution. The drugs of abuse most commonly encountered in criminal prosecutions will be discussed as well as the statutory control of drugs and other substances. Evidence issues, including admissibility of seized drug analysis, chain of custody, quality control, and quantitation will also be discussed.

§15.02 TERMINOLOGY

The following terms are used in this chapter or are commonly encountered in seized drug analysis. Additional terms are defined in the Scientific Working Group for the Analysis of Seized Drugs, "Annex A:

---

[2]   21 U.S.C. § 802(6).

[3]   21 U.S.C. § 811(c).

SWGDRUG Glossary of Terms and Definitions" in *SWGDRUG's Recommendations*, Version 7.1, June 9, 2016.[4]

Alkaloid: An organic base of a chemical makeup which allows it to unite with acids to form salts; its basic molecular structural constituent is the pyridine ring of 5 carbon atoms and one nitrogen atom; basic nitrogen is present in synthetic or plant alkaloids.

Analyte: The substance being detected.

Catalyst: A substance that initiates or alters the rate of a chemical reaction, but does not enter into the reaction.

Certified Reference Material (CRM): reference material characterized for one or more specified properties that is accompanied by a certificate that provides the value of the specified properties, the associated uncertainty, and a statement of metrological traceability.

Detection Limit: The lowest concentration of an analyte in a sample that can be detected, but not necessarily quantified.

Diastereoisomers/Diasteromers: Stereoisomers of a compound that have different configurations at one or more stereocenters, but are not mirror images of each other.

Electrolyte: A substance that dissociates into ions when fused or in solution, thus becoming capable of conducting electricity; an ionic solution.

Enantiomers: A pair of stereoisomers of a compound that have different configurations at all stereocenters; and therefore, are mirror images of each other.

False negative: A test result indicating a substance is not present when that substance is actually present in a mixture in an amount above the detection limit or when there is an interfering compound present which masks a compound which is actually present in the mixture.

False positive: A test result indicating the presence of a substance when that substance is not actually present or is present in an amount below the detection limit.

Measurement Uncertainty: Parameter associated with a measurement result that characterizes the dispersion of values that could reasonably be attributed to the particular quantity being measured.

Phonon: A quantum of energy or quasiparticle associated with a compressional wave such as sound or a vibration of a crystal lattice.

---

[4]   Available at: http://www.swgdrug.org/approved.htm (last accessed December 8, 2016).

Qualitative Analysis: Identification or classification of an analyte based on chemical or physical properties.

Quantitative Analysis: Measurement of the amount or concentration of an analyte; expressed in numerical terms with an estimate of measurement uncertainty.

Quantitation Limit: The lowest concentration of an analyte that may be measured with accepted precision and accuracy.

Reagent: A chemical used to react with another substance, often to confirm the presence or absence of the other substance.

Sensitivity: The smallest amount of substance in a sample that can accurately be measured by the technique—also referred to as the quantitation limit.

Specificity: The ability of the technique to measure or detect only what it is intended to measure or detect; also referred to as discriminating power or degree of discrimination.

Stereoisomers: Isomeric molecules that have the same molecular formula and atom-to-atom connections, but have nonsuperimposable shapes because they differ in three-dimensional orientation.

Uncorrelated Techniques: Techniques that will yield uncorrelated results; techniques that use different fundamental mechanisms for analysis.

Validation: The process of performing a set of experiments that reliably estimates the efficacy, reliability, and reproducibility of an analytical method. The goal of validation is to establish evidence demonstrating that a method is capable of successfully performing as intended and to identify the limitations of the method.

§15.03 EVIDENTIARY USES

Controlled substance prosecutions constitute a large portion of criminal cases handled in both federal and state courts and drug control efforts involve huge expenditures by federal, state, and local governments. In 2015, the highest number of arrests in the United States were for drug abuse violations (1,488,707 arrests).[5] In 2010, the federal government spent over $15 billion to reduce drug use and availability.[6] State and local governments spend at least $25 billion annually in drug-related arrests, prosecutions, and incarcerations.[7] Controlled substances have a wide impact on society from overdose

---

[5] *See* https://ucr.fbi.gov/crime-in-the-u.s/2015/crime-in-the-u.s.-2015/persons-arrested/persons-arrested (last accessed March 3, 2017).

[6] National Drug Control Strategy, FY 2010 Budget Summary, May 2009, available at: http://www.whitehousedrugpolicy.gov/publications/policy/10budget/fy10budget.pdf (last accessed March 3, 2017).

[7] Jeffrey A. Miron & Katherine Waldock, "The Budgetary Impact of Drug Prohibition," Cato Institute, 2010, p. 5.

deaths to child neglect. Opioid overdose deaths surged in 2015; more people died from heroin-related causes than from gun homicides.[8] The manufacture, importation, distribution, and possession of these substances is a major concern for both federal and state governments:

> State, local, and federal law enforcement reporting indicates that gangs in the United States continue to expand, develop, and grow more sophisticated in their criminal enterprises. The National Gang Intelligence Center (NGIC) assesses that the US gang composition is approximately 88 percent street gang members, 9.5 percent prison gang members, and 2.5 percent outlaw motorcycle gang (OMG) members. There are approximately 1.4 million active street, prison, and OMG gang members comprising more than 33,000 gangs in the United States. Though gangs are involved in a multitude of criminal activities, street-level drug trafficking and distribution continues to be their main source of revenue, and they commit violent crimes, such as robbery, assault, threats, and intimidation, in furtherance of those ends.[9]

In 2015, over 27% of all cases reported to the United States Sentencing Commission involved drug trafficking offenses, and almost all of the cases involved either powder cocaine, crack cocaine, methamphetamine, marijuana, heroin, or Oxycodone®.[10] Of the estimated 1.5 million prisoners in state and federal custody on December 31, 2014, 50% of federal inmates and 16% of state prisoners were convicted for drug offenses.[11] Seized drug analysis is necessarily involved in the criminal prosecutions of the possession, distribution, and manufacturing of controlled substances. Although some controlled substance prosecutions are "historical" cases in which the proof of the criminal act (commonly the distribution or manufacturing of controlled substances) is presented through the testimony of cooperating witnesses, most drug prosecutions depend upon the scientific analysis of seized substances to prove the involvement of controlled substances. Seized drug analysis may also be used in civil investigations or proceedings involving patent infringement, counterfeit or adulterated

---

[8] Christopher Ingram, "Heroin deaths surpass gun homicides for the first time, CDC data shows," Washington Post, December 8, 2016 (available at: https://www.washingtonpost.com/news/wonk/wp/2016/12/08/heroin-deaths-surpass-gun-homicides-for-the-first-time-cdc-data-show/?postshare=8861481302772928&tid=ss_tw&utm_term=.63c8d6be7a43)(last accessed December 9, 2016).

[9] United States Department of Justice, Drug Enforcement Administration, *2015 National Drug Threat Assessment Summary*, DEA-DCT-DIR-008-16, October 2015 at p. iv (available at: https://www.dea.gov/resource-center/statistics.shtml)(last accessed December 6, 2016).

[10] United States Sentencing Commission, *Quick Facts: Drug Trafficking Offenses,* May 2016 (available at: http://www.ussc.gov/sites/default/files/pdf/research-and-publications/quick-facts/Quick_Facts_Drug_Trafficking_2015.pdf)(last accessed December 6, 2016).

[11] *See* E. Ann Carson, Bureau of Justice Statistics, *Prisoners in 2014*, NCJ 248955, September 17, 2015 (available at: https://www.bjs.gov/index.cfm?ty=pbdetail&iid=5387)(last accessed December 6, 2016).

prescription medications, and monitoring of drug-production facilities for contamination and dilution.

Many of the analytical methods used in seized drug analysis are used in other areas of inquiry, particularly serological and toxicological analysis, and much of the equipment and instrumentation is shared within these areas. Quality assurance and evidence integrity issues are critical in all of these areas and both the propriety of the analytical method and the competency of the analyst should be considered in reviewing analytical results.

II. ANALYTICAL METHODS

§15.04 TYPES OF ANALYSIS

1. QUALITATIVE ANALYSIS

The qualitative analysis of substances refers to the process of identifying the presence of a particular drug or class of drugs in a submitted sample based on chemical or physical properties. Accepted protocols require the combination of analytical methods to identify a seized drug. (*See* Section 15.05 *infra*) The correct identification of a controlled substance depends on the use of an analytical scheme based on properly validated analytical methods and the competence of the analyst.[12]

Steps that may be used to conduct qualitative analysis of an unknown substance include: physical assessment/macroscopic examination (visual observations, particularly for pharmaceutical markings and in the analysis of marijuana), sample preparation, establishing instrumentation parameters (including software settings), testing pursuant to an appropriate analytical scheme, and calculations. For suspected marijuana plant material or residue, microscopic examination is also conducted as part of the physical assessment. In conducting identification analysis, test results must be "positive" to establish the identification of a controlled substance.[13] In the analysis of seized drugs, the impact of any possible interference from other substances encountered in seized drugs must be considered. Seized drugs frequently have cutting agents in the forms of adulterants, diluents, impurities, contaminants, and manufacturing by-products

---

[12] ASTM E2329–14: "Standard Practice for Identification of Seized Drugs," ASTM Int'l, 2014 at p. 1 (available for purchase at: https://www.astm.org/Standards/E2329.htm)(last accessed December 8, 2016).

[13] "While 'negative' test results provide useful information for ruling out the presence of a particular drug or drug class, these results have no value toward establishing the forensic identification of a drug." SWGDRUG Recommendations Part III B, "Methods of Analysis/Drug Identification," Version 7.1, June 9, 2016 at p. 16 (available at: http://www.swgdrug.org/approved.htm)(last accessed December 8, 2016).

that can interfere with qualitative analysis. The ASTM and SWGDRUG standards (discussed *infra*) have noted that, unlike quantitative analysis, an appropriate analytical scheme effectively results in minimizing to zero the possibility of an improper chemical identification of a substance in a qualitative analysis.[14] As noted in Section 15.05 *infra*, this position is controversial and may change.[15]

As with all forensic examinations, documentation of the analysis sufficient to permit independent review must be maintained be available upon by request to anyone who has a legal right to such documents.[16]

2. QUANTITATIVE ANALYSIS

The type of quantitation determination to be made in criminal and civil cases involving the analysis of seized drugs depends on the legal issues involved. Typically, the numerical values reported are the weight (conventional mass) of the submitted sample or the purity (concentration) of a controlled substance in the submitted sample. The legal issue in some cases may be the amount of the controlled substance excluding cutting agents, by products, or additional substances. In other circumstances, the weight attributed to the controlled substances specifically includes the entire weight of any mixture or substance containing a detectable amount of the controlled substance.[17]

Steps that may be used to conduct quantitative analysis include determination of sample size (by weight measurement, volume measurement, or item count), sample preparation, establishing instrument parameters (including software setting), testing, and calculations (including the measurement of uncertainty associated with the results). For quantitation analysis that relies upon sampling, calculations must take into account the sampling method and any limitations of the analysis must be noted. Uncertainty associated with quantitation analysis is typically expressed in numerical terms and "characterizes the dispersion of the values that could reasonably be attributed to the particular quantity subject to measurement."[18] Many laboratories in conforming to accreditation standards are using a "confidence interval" to objectively and statistically determine the true value in a numerical measurement associated with an analytical

---

[14] Id. at p. 50; *see also* ASTM E2329–14: "Standard Practice for Identification of Seized Drugs," ASTM Int'l, 2014 at p. 1.

[15] *See* notes 24–26 *infra* and accompanying text.

[16] ASTM E2327–15e1: "Standard Practice for Quality Assurance of Laboratories Performing Seized-Drug Analysis," ASTM Int'l, 2015, 12.1.1, p. 3.

[17] *See* United States Sentencing Commission, Guidelines Manual § 2D1.1, Note A (Nov. 1, 2016).

[18] SWGDRUG Recommendations Part III B, "Methods of Analysis/Drug Identification," Version 7.1, June 9, 2016 at p. 50 (available at: http://www.swgdrug.org/approved.htm)(last accessed December 8, 2016).

scheme involving the quantitative measurements in a controlled substance analysis.

§15.05 STANDARDS

The field of seized drug analysis in the United States currently relies on two primary sources for professional standards: ASTM International (formerly American Society for Testing and Materials)(ASTM) and the Scientific Working Group for Seized Drug Analysis (SWGDRUG).[19] The main standard promulgated by ASTM for seized drug analysis is "ASTM E2329-14: Standard Practice for Identification of Seized Drugs."[20] The standard is used by forensic laboratories as a protocol for testing seized drug evidence to determine if drugs of abuse such as cocaine or heroin are present. ASTM produces several other standards relevant to seized drug analysis, including:[21]

- E1968-11: Standard Guide for Microcrystal Testing in Forensic Analysis of Cocaine;

- E1969-11: Standard Guide for Microcrystal Testing in the Forensic Analysis of Methamphetamine and Amphetamine

- E2125-11: Standard Guide for Microcrystal Testing in Forensic Analysis of Phencyclidine and Its Analogues

- E2327-15e1: Standard of Practice for Quality Assurance of Laboratories Performing Seized-Drug Analysis

- E2548-16: Standard for Sampling Seized Drugs for Qualitative and Quantitative Analysis

- E2549-14: Standard Practice for Validation of Seized-Drug Methods

- E2764-11: Standard Practice for Uncertainty Assessment in the Context of Seized-Drug Analysis

SWGDRUG, originally named the Technical Working Group for the Analysis of Seized Drugs, was collaboratively formed by the United States Drug Enforcement Agency and Office of National Drug Control Policy in 1997.[22] SWGDRUG provides recommendations for the analysis

---

[19] The European Network of Forensic Science Institutes (ENFSI) has also promulgated standards relevant to seized drug analysis and these standards are sometimes referenced or used by organizations and agencies in the United States. ENFSI was founded in 1995 with the purpose of improving the mutual exchange of information in the field of forensic science in Europe. Different forensic expertizes are dealt by 17 different Expert Working Groups. ENFSI has been recognized as the monopoly organization in the field of forensic science by the European Commission. *See* http://enfsi.eu (last accessed December 9, 2016).

[20] ASTM E2329-14: "Standard Practice for Identification of Seized Drugs," ASTM Int'l, 2014 (available for purchase at: https://www.astm.org/Standards/E2329.htm)(last accessed December 8, 2016).

[21] All ASTM Standards are available for purchase at: https://www.astm.org/Standard /standards-and-publications.html.

[22] *See* www.swgdrug.org.

of seized drugs, including standard procedures, a code of ethics, and education and training requirements for analysts. The main document produced by SWGDRUG is the Scientific Working Group for the Analysis of Seized Drugs, "SWGDRUG Recommendations."[23]

The National Institute of Standards and Technology (NIST) Organization of Scientific Area Committees (OSAC) formed a Seized Drug Subcommittee to promulgate standards for the analysis of controlled substances. The development of forensic science standards and guidelines is transitioning from the Scientific Working Groups (SWGs) and ASTM to the OSAC. The existing SWGDRUG documents and the ASTM standards will remain in effect until updated documents are disseminated by the OSAC, SWGDRUG, or ASTM.[24] On Jan. 11, 2016, the OSAC Forensic Science Standards Board (FSSB) voted to elevate ASTM Standard E2329-14 "Standard Practice for Identification of Seized Drugs" to the OSAC Registry of Approved Standards. This is the first standard posted to the registry, and the posting was not without controversy. Members of the FSSB and others within NIST objected to the following sentencing in ASTM E2329-14:

> It is expected that in the absence of unforeseen error, an appropriate analytical scheme effectively results in no uncertainty in reported identifications.

The objection to the phrase "effectively results in no uncertainty" as inappropriate for a scientific analysis since "based on accepted scientific protocols, no measurement, qualitative or quantitative, should be characterized as without the risk of error or uncertainty."[25] NIST, OSAC, and ASTM agreed to work together on new language that conveys clear meaning of the phrase and they expected to have a revision within six months.[26] As of December 2016, the updated language has not been added to the current document on the registry.

In addition to the professional standards, each laboratory will have its own procedures for handling seized drug analysis. The laboratory will have general quality control manuals and manuals for specific discipline testing procedures, such as controlled substance analysis.[27] The specific discipline manuals will describe procedures for the

---

[23] Scientific Working Group for the Analysis of Seized Drugs, SWGDRUG Recommendations," Version 7.1, June 9, 2016 (available at: http://www.swgdrug.org/approved.htm)(last accessed December 8, 2016).

[24] *See* https://www.nist.gov/topics/forensic-science/seized-drugs-subcommittee (last accessed December 6, 2016).

[25] NIST Statement on ASTM Standard E2329-14," March 17, 2016 (available at: https://www.nist.gov/news-events/news/2016/03/nist-statement-astm-standard-e2329-14)(last accessed December 8, 2016).

[26] "Joint OSAC FSSB and NIST Statement on ASTM E2329-14," July 15, 2016 (available at: https://www.nist.gov/news-events/news/2016/07/joint-osac-fssb-and-nist-statement-astm-e2329-14)(last accessed December 8, 2016).

[27] The Virginia Department of Forensic Science is an example of an accredited laboratory that maintains copies of its manuals and procedures on their public website. *See* http://www.dfs.virginia.gov/documentation-publications/manuals/#DX (last accessed December 9, 2016).

analytical methods used by the laboratory and methodologies for the different types of controlled substances commonly analyzed. The manual should also provide procedures for estimating the uncertainty in the analysis. For accredited laboratories, these procedures are audited to ensure compliance with national and international standards.[28]

§15.06 COMMONLY USED ANALYTICAL METHODS

The forensic drug analyst frequently deals with substances whose identity is unknown and which may be present in a questioned sample in quantities bordering on the threshold of analytical recognition. In most instances the chemical tests are made directly on the sample suspected to be contraband.

The following general types of qualitative tests are used in determining the identity of a suspected controlled substance:

(1) Physical tests

(2) Crystal tests

(3) Color tests

(4) Immunoassays

(5) Chromatographic tests

(6) Spectrometric tests

As with toxicological analysis, presumptive tests for controlled substance analysis must be used in conjunction with confirmatory tests[29] for identification of a controlled substance.

Standards promulgated by ASTM International SWGDRUG categorize techniques for the analysis of seized drugs into three groups (Category A through C) based on their potential discriminating power. Category A techniques are the most potentially discriminating (having the highest degree of specificity) and include infrared spectroscopy, mass spectrometry, nuclear magnetic resonance spectroscopy, Raman spectroscopy, and x-ray diffractometry. Category B techniques have moderate discriminating power and include capillary electrophoresis; ion mobility spectrometry; microcrystalline tests; gas, liquid, and thin layer chromatography, and pharmaceutical identifiers. Category C techniques are the least potentially discriminating and include color tests, immunoassays, ultraviolet and fluorescence spectroscopy, and melting point.[30] Industry standards require the use of multiple

---

[28] *See* http://www.ascld-lab.org (last accessed December 9, 2016).

[29] The term "confirmatory test" is used in the chapter to conform with the industry practice. These tests technically "identify" the controlled substance; they do not "confirm" the results of the presumptive or screening tests because those preliminary tests do not establish the identity of the substance.

[30] ASTM E2329–14: "Standard Practice for Identification of Seized Drugs," ASTM Int'l, 2014, page 2; Scientific Working Group for the Analysis of Seized Drugs, SWGDRUG

uncorrelated techniques in specified schemes for identification results;[31] for example:

> "When a validated Category A technique [is used], at least one other technique (from either Category A, B or C) shall be used.
>
> When a Category A technique is not used, at least three different validated techniques shall be employed. Two of the three techniques shall be based on uncorrelated techniques from Category B."[32]

In developing an analytical scheme, professional standards require the scheme to demonstrate the identification of the specific controlled substance present, preclude unexplained false positives, and minimize false negatives.[33] If the analytical scheme has limitations, the limitations should be disclosed in the final result.

1.   Examples of Category "A" Tests

a.   Infrared Spectroscopy (IR)

Spectroscopy is a category of analytical techniques for identification of a chemical compound. Most types involve the measurement of light or other radiation absorbed by or emitted from a sample. The specific wavelengths of radiation absorbed/emitted are related to the chemical structure of the molecule. Measurement of the radiation's frequency or wavelength and/or the amount absorbed/emitted is used to identify a particular chemical species or determine the quantity present. Infrared spectroscopy (IR) uses infrared radiation to yield structural information about the chemical structure of a substance, giving it very high discriminating power. IR can distinguish between diastereoisomers (such as pseudoephedrine and ephedrine) and between free base and salts (cocaine base and cocaine HCL), but cannot distinguish between enantiomers. Fourier transform infrared (FTIR) spectrometers, which use smaller samples than traditional IR instruments, are common in most laboratories.[34] A technique of sample analysis used in FTIR is "attenuated total reflection" (ATR) allows the samples to be examined

---

Recommendations Part III B, "Methods of Analysis/Drug Identification," Version 7.1, June 9, 2016 at p. 14.

[31] ASTM E2329–14: "Standard Practice for Identification of Seized Drugs," ASTM Int'l, 2014; SWGDRUG Recommendations Part III B, "Methods of Analysis/Drug Identification," Version 7.1, June 9, 2016.

[32] SWGDRUG Recommendations Part III B, "Methods of Analysis/Drug Identification," Version 7.1, June 9, 2016 at p. 15; *See also* ASTM E2329–14: "Standard Practice for Identification of Seized Drugs," ASTM Int'l, 2014, 5.1.1 and 5.1.2, p. 1.

[33] ASTM E2329–14: "Standard Practice for Identification of Seized Drugs," ASTM Int'l, 2014, 5.1.10, p. 2; SWGDRUG Recommendations Part III B, "Methods of Analysis/Drug Identification," Version 7.1, June 9, 2016 at p. 16.

[34] Heesun Chung *et al.,* "Drug Analysis," in Wiley Encyclopedia Of Forensic Science, (Jamieson A. & Moenssens A.A., eds) 2009 & online updates.

directly in the solid or liquid state without further preparation, drastically reducing the overall examination time.

In addition to a high discriminatory power, benefits of using IR include sample recovery for additional qualitative and quantitative testing. Limitations include the need to address volatility, heat, and pressure effects to avoid chemical composition changes during analysis. All forms of infrared spectroscopy in the forensic identification of seized drugs require samples which are relatively pure. Interfering substances in the form of adulterants or diluents can and usually do prevent an valid spectral analysis and identification of a compound of interest.

b. *Mass Spectrometry (MS)*

Mass spectrometry (MS) is an analytical method to identify materials based upon production and detection of characteristic molecular fragments. The molecule is vaporized and fragmented in a high energy field. The fragments are separated by velocity or behavior in a magnetic field, detected and their mass determined. Because the fragments produced under controlled conditions are reproducible, they can be related to the original structure of the molecule. Combining the separating power of gas or liquid chromatography with the ability of the mass spectrometer in most cases to identify a compound to the exclusion of other compounds provides a powerful tool for the identification of individual components in a mixture and is widely used to confirm the identification of a suspected drug or toxin that has been preliminarily identified by other analytical methods.

As with IR, MS can distinguish between diastereoisomers, but not enantiomers. MS, however, cannot identify salt forms or distinguish between free base and salts. Samples may be recovered for further analysis, including quantitation.

c. *Nuclear Magnetic Resonance Spectroscopy (NMR)*

The absorption of electromagnetic radiation by magnetic atomic nuclei provides the basis for NMR. All nuclei with odd mass numbers and nuclei with odd atomic number (with some exceptions) have magnetic properties. Absorption of energy occurs when the nuclei are in the strong magnetic field of the NMR equipment. The spectrum is developed by changing the magnetic field at a uniform rate and measuring the values of the frequency of absorption. Specific structural information of the analyzed compound may be obtained from the spectra of several nuclei (for example, hydrogen-1 or carbon-13).

Benefits of NMR include the ability to differentiate enantiomers, sample recovery for further analysis, analysis of thermally unstable drugs without decomposition, and simultaneous identification and quantitation. Because concentration ranges vary greatly depending on a number of factors, the technique is not recommended for analysis of residue. Complex mixtures may not produce easily resolved signals, making quantitation difficult.

d.   Raman Spectroscopy

Raman spectroscopy, a form of vibrational spectroscopy, measures the spectra of scattered radiation, giving much the same information as IR; however, a specific electronic transition (one that is "Raman active") must be used. A sample is illuminated with a laser beam. The laser light interacts with molecular vibrations resulting in the energy of the laser photons being shifted up or down. The resulting light is collected with a lens and sent to a detector. The shift in energy gives information about the vibrational modes in the system. Unlike IR with which liquid solutions will have strong interference from the water absorption bands, Raman spectroscopy can be used with aqueous solutions. Spectra can also be obtained through glass containers and other packaging. The method, which produces results in seconds, is more rapid than chromatographic methods, which produce results in minutes.

Raman spectroscopy requires little or no sample preparation before analysis and produces information-rich spectra through nondestructive testing, but it requires a fairly concentrated sample (it is not recommended for analysis of residue). The instrumentation may be difficult to calibrate and validate. Traditional Raman spectroscopy also produces a relatively weak signal that may be obscured by fluorescence. Surface-enhanced Raman scattering is more sensitive and is being studied for use in trace identification.[35]

Raman spectroscopy has been used for the identification of illicit drugs,[36] but quantitative analysis using the technique has been limited by the variation of adulterants commonly found in street drugs.[37]

e.   X-ray Diffractometry

The x-ray diffractometry (XRD) technique uses x-rays passing through a crystallized substance and interacting with the electrons in the atoms. When the x-ray photons collide with electrons, some photons from the incident beam will be deflected away from the direction where they originally travel (diffraction). In crystals, the atoms are arranged in a regularized structure and the diffracted waves will consist of sharp interference maxima (peaks) with the same symmetry as the distribution of atoms. The peaks in the x-ray diffraction pattern correlate to the interatomic distances. Measuring the diffraction

---

[35]   Vinesh Rana et al., "Surface-enhanced Raman Spectroscopy for Trace Identification of Controlled Substances: Morphine, Codeine, and Hydrocodone," 56 J. FORENSIC SCI. 200–207 (2011).

[36]   *See* Alan Ryder, "Classification of Narcotics in Solid Mixtures Using Principal Component Analysis and Raman Spectroscopy," 47 J. FORENSIC SCI. 275–284 (2002).

[37]   Erja Katainen et al., "Quantification of the Amphetamine Content in Seized Street Samples by Raman Spectroscopy," 52 J. FORENSIC SCI. 88–92 (2007).

pattern allows the analyst to deduce the distribution of atoms in a substance.

XRD is a nondestructive technique that works well with small and large samples. The technique has been referred to as the "last resort" technique in criminal cases for its ability to distinguish between elements and their oxides and to discriminate mixtures.[38]

2.   EXAMPLES OF CATEGORY "B" TESTS

a.   Capillary Electrophoresis (CE)

Electrophoresis is a separation technique based on the differential transportation of charged species in an electric field through a conductive medium. Capillary electrophoresis (CE) separates compounds based on their size-to-charge ratio in the interior of a small capillary filled with an electrolyte. CE is a high speed, high resolution separation process that can be used for qualitative and quantitative analysis. CE uses small sample volumes and is compatible with a variety of detection methods. CE can be used on compounds that cannot be separated by gas chromatography, such as compounds that are thermally liable or nonvolatile.

b.   Gas Chromatography (GC)

Gas chromatography is a technique for separation of components of a mixture in the vapor state. The sample to be examined is vaporized and carried through a small diameter column by a flowing gas stream. Components of the mixture dissolve in a viscous liquid inside the column and are retained to varying degrees to effect a separation. As a component of the mixture completes its passage through the column, it enters a detector which produces an electrical signal indicating its arrival and quantity. The signals from the detector are recorded on a moving chart to produce a chromatogram. The chart pattern is compared with the chart patterns of known materials for identification. A very small diameter column, or capillary, improves component separation and for materials which move slowly through the column, increasing the temperature or the flow rate of the carrier gas reduces analysis time. However, changing any parameters in GC analysis must be done carefully to preclude other occurrences detrimental to an identification of an analytical scheme.

The technique can be used as a screening tool or to prepare samples for more discriminating techniques. Because detector response is proportional to sample concentration, GC can be used as a quantitative method. Benefits of GC include the ability to differentiate enantiomers. Although very specific, different compounds may have the same retention time, so this method is not as discriminating as

---

[38] Werner Kugler, "X-Ray Diffraction Analysis in the Forensic Science: The Last Resort in Many Criminal Cases," 46 JCPDS—International Centre for Diffraction Data 1–16 (2003).

Category A tests. Limitations also include the inability to identify salts (which are dissociated during the injection process) and nonvolatile compounds.

GC is frequently combined with various detectors for greater selectivity. The gas chromatograph combined with a mass selective detector (MSD) is one of the most common types of analytical methods for identifying seized drugs. GC/MS is the term most often used to designate this analytical protocol. In short, the different components of the sample are separated and then in most cases, but not all, are individually identifiable. Gas chromatography mass spectrometry (GC/MS) is the routine method for the identification of most drugs, because of the high specificity and sensitivity and the available of a library of spectra for comparison with a large range of compounds.[39]

The gas chromatograph can be combined with a Flame Ionization Detector (instead of an MSD) and is referred to as a GC/FID. The GC/FID results yield a "retention time" (RT) which measures the amount of time required under specific operating parameters for a sample to be vaporized in the injection port of the GC, flow through the column, and finally pass through the flame ionization detector. This retention time is not unique to an individual substance; two substances can have the same or very similar retention times. The RT generated through the GC/FID constitutes another piece of analytical data available to the analyst to formulate a conclusion regarding the identification of a substance.

In recent years GC has been combined with other instrumentation functioning as detectors which enable an analyst to separate and provide information on the individual components of a seized drug sample. For instance, GC has been combined with a FTIR (GC/FTIR) detector. The resulting spectrum from GC/FTIR is generated by the same science of first vaporizing the sample, separating by GC the individual components of the sample, and then detecting those individual components by FTIR. The characteristics of the vapor state FTIR spectrum are usually not as sharp as solid state sample spectrum, but sometimes the spectrum will have enough information to enable an identification. Otherwise, the GC/FTIR spectrum provides additional analytical information.

c. Ion Mobility Spectrometry (IMS)

IMS characterizes chemical substances by measurement of their gas-phase ion mobility. The relatively small size, quick response time, and sensitivity of the instrumentation permit the technique to be used as a presumptive test to screen drugs in the field. The technique, however, is destructive and cannot specifically identify a compound.

---

[39] Heesun Chung *et al.,* "Drug Analysis," in WILEY ENCYCLOPEDIA OF FORENSIC SCIENCE, (Jamieson A. & Moenssens A.A., eds) 2009 & online updates.

Other limitations include vulnerability to temperature fluctuations and other atmospheric conditions and relatively narrow effective concentration ranges.

d.   Liquid Chromatography

Liquid chromatography describes a category of analytical techniques for the separation of mixtures involving the passing of a mixture dissolved in a "moving" phase through a fixed material phase. Chemical compounds differ in their retention on the fixed material phase. Weakly retained compounds move quickly through the system, while those more strongly held move more slowly and complete their passage through the system later. Because of differences in this retention time, effective separation of a mixture into components can be made. Types of chromatography used in the analytical laboratory include high performance liquid chromatography and thin layer chromatography.

High performance liquid chromatography (HPLC) is a separation and comparison technique that, like GC, provides preliminary identification of analytes and sample components and can be used as a quantitation method. Unlike GC, nonvolatile and thermally labile compounds can be analyzed. Because HPLC is non-destructive, samples can be recovered for additional testing. Limitations include the necessity for appropriate standards with each set of samples, high purity solvents, and pre-test equilibration time. The possibility of sample carry-over also requires constant monitoring and implementation of rigorous quality control measures.

e.   Thin Layer Chromatography

Thin Layer Chromatography (TLC) is another step in an analytical scheme which enables a rapid separation and comparison of sample components on a silica gel plate exposed to a solvent. The movement of the sample relative to the solvent front is referred to as the "retention factor" (Rf)[40] and varies among components. The technique provides preliminary data on the identity of an analyte and the presence of additional sample components. TLC was one of the most widely used separation techniques due in part to its simplicity and low cost, but the analytical method has been replaced by more specific instrumental methods. TLC may be used as a preparative method and, if non-destructive detection methods are used, TLC may be combined with other methods for greater selectivity. Detection of the compounds can be made by fluorescence or spray reagents. Examples of these reagents include but are not limited to FPN reagent (ferric chloride/perchloric acid/nitric acid), Marquis Reagent (formaldehyde and concentrated sulfuric acid), and Mandelin's reagent (ammonium vanadate in sulfuric

---

[40] Heesun Chung *et al.*, "Drug Analysis," in WILEY ENCYCLOPEDIA OF FORENSIC SCIENCE, (Jamieson A. & Moenssens A.A., eds) 2009 & online updates.

acid). Both short wave and long wave ultra violet light can also be used to visualize the components.

The benefits of TLC include the option to run multiple samples simultaneously, easy visualization of results, and increased selectivity from the use of specific eluents. Limitations are the moderate level of discrimination, the need to match standard and sample concentrations, and different pattern development from salt forms of certain compounds.

f. Microcrystalline Tests

Microcrystalline tests involve reacting a suspect material with a specific chemical reagent to produce crystals of characteristic color or shape. The crystals are examined under a microscope using either ordinary or polarized light. Microcrystalline tests can be used to screen for the presence of certain chemicals in controlled substances. The test benefits include ease of use, minimal equipment costs (glass slides and just drops of the appropriate reagent), and readily observable crystal structures that can be distinguished by the trained analyst. Limitations include the narrow time window in which the probative crystal structures can be observed, the use of a relatively large sample (several milligrams), and the need for careful imaging or a second procedure to obtain confirmation of the results from a second analyst. There is also the challenge of producing data, usually in the form of photographs, which can be used to validate or to justify a conclusion.

g. Pharmaceutical Identifiers

With intact, untampered, marked capsules or tablets, information relevant to the identity of the substance may be found in the manufacturing marks of the pharmaceutical company. "Pharmaceutical preparations possess unique identifying information both in the general appearance of the preparation and the inscriptions or markings."[41] The size, color, shape, and markings of the tablet or capsule are compared with published physical characteristics available from the manufacturer, governmental agencies, or other commercially available references such as the Physician's Desk Reference[42] or Ident-a-Drug Reference.[43]

---

[41] Virginia Department of Forensic Sciences, *Controlled Substances Procedures Manual*, DFS Document 221-D100, Revision 19, September 19, 2016 at p. 30 (available at: http://www. dfs.virginia.gov/wp-content/uploads/2016/09/221-D100-Controlled-Substances-Procedures-Manual.pdf)(last accessed December 6, 2016).

[42] *See* http://www.pdr.net (last accessed December 6, 2016).

[43] *See* http://identadrug.therapeuticresearch.com/ (last accessed December 15, 2016).

CONTROLLED SUBSTANCES ANALYSIS

3. EXAMPLES OF CATEGORY "C" TESTS

a. *Color Tests*[44]

Similar to microcrystalline tests, color tests (also referred to as chemical screening tests) use a reagent or series of reagents added to a small amount of the suspect material. Color tests use specific color test reagents that react chemically with a specific portion of a drug molecule, producing a characteristic color. The reactions observed may be the development of a particular color with a single reagent or observation of a series of colors or other changes occurring as different reagents are added. The tests are used only as preliminary tests as a part of an analytical scheme to indicate the possible presence of a drug in a sample. The formation of a color when a reagent is combined with a sample only indicates that a certain class of drugs may be present in the sample. Also, the actual color produced may vary depending on a number of factors including the concentration of the drug, whether the drug is present in a salt form, additional substances in the compound, and the conditions under which the test is performed (temperature, humidity levels, etc.).

Color tests rely on simple chemical reactions and produce visible changes without the need for any visualization equipment or instrumentation. The tests are inexpensive, rapid, do not require extensive training to use, and may be conducted on multiple samples simultaneously. In addition to low specificity, the limitations of color tests include the relative instability of some of the color test reagents, the need to determine color reactions only within a specified exposure time range, and the lack of utility of the tests for some people with relatively common visual impairments in color recognition.[45]

b. *Immunoassays*

Immunoassays (discussed more fully in Chapter 13) are based on the binding of antibodies and antigens. Immunoassays can be used to screen seized samples for the presence of controlled substances. A specific controlled substance may be detected by its ability to displace or block the binding of a fixed amount of the labeled drug molecule present in the reagent. Immunoassays are useful in screening large numbers of

---

[44] On color tests generally, *see* National Institute of Justice, Law Enforcement and Corrections Standards and Testing Program, *Color Test Reagents/Kits for Preliminary Identification of Drugs of Abuse,* NIJ Standard-0604.01, 2000 (available at: https://www.nij. gov/topics/technology/standards-testing/pages/active.aspx)(last accessed December 15, 2016).

[45] In 2016, a media investigation uncovered the use of color tests to support criminal convictions in several jurisdictions. When later laboratory results determined that no controlled substances were actually present, the practice was widely criticized and some jurisdictions changed practices. See Ryan Gabrielson & Topher Sanders, "Busted," ProPublica, July 7, 2016; Ryan Gabrielson, " 'No Field Test is Fail Safe': Meet the Chemist Behind Houston's Police Drug Kits," ProPublica, July 11, 2016; Ryan Gabrielson, "Prosecutors in Portland Change Policy on Drug Convictions," ProPublica, November 28, 2016 (all articles available at: https://www.propublica.org/site/author/ryan_gabrielson)(last accessed December 6, 2016).

samples, but will only give an indication of the drug or drug group present and the results must be confirmed with more specific techniques.

The benefits of immunoassays include suitability for automated analysis, the availability of commercial kits, and ease of use.

c. Melting Point

The melting point technique determines the temperature at which liquid and solid forms of a material are in equilibrium, generally the temperature at which a solid begins to change into a liquid. Identification is made through comparison to literature values or a standard.

The melting point of an unknown compound is determined, and then compared against the literature to find other, known compounds with similar melting points (usually within a 5–8 degree range). Systematically, the unknown compound is then mixed with a sample of a standard compound, and the melting point of the mixture is determined. If the mixture melts sharply at the known melting point, then the unknown can be identified.

The technique is straight-forward, easy to use, and has the benefit of extensive published referenced data. Little sample is required. If the sample is pure, the technique is not destructive and the sample may be recovered and reanalyzed.

d. Other Spectroscopy Techniques

There are additional spectroscopy techniques for identification of chemical compounds. Most types involve the measurement of light or other radiation absorbed by or emitted from a sample. The specific wavelengths of radiation absorbed/emitted are related to the chemical structure of the molecule. Measurement of the radiation's frequency or wavelength and/or the amount absorbed/emitted is used to identify a particular chemical species or determine the relative quantities present.

Fluorescence spectroscopy compares the fluorescence spectrum of an unknown analyte to that of a standard analyzed using the same analytical parameters to give preliminary identification information. Benefits include sample recovery for additional testing, possible quantitation for analyte samples, and utility as a screening tool. Limitations include the fact that not all compounds show characteristic fluorescence spectra and different compounds may produce identical spectra.

Ultraviolet spectroscopy uses the ultraviolet spectrum to yield data correlated to the chemical structure of substance in the sample. The technique is frequently combined with chromatography for greater selectivity. Benefits include sample recovery and potential automation when combined with chromatography. Limitations include modest selectivity, inapplicability to compounds lacking a suitable chromophore (light-absorbing group) to produce a signal, pH effects, and potential chemical composition changes during analysis.

III. COMMON DRUGS OF ABUSE[46]

§15.07 NARCOTICS/OPIOIDS

All drugs derived from the opium poppy (including opium, morphine, and codeine) and natural and synthetic morphine derivatives that mimic morphine's actions (such as methadone, oxycodone, and hydrocodone) are known collectively as narcotics or opioids.[47] Although the majority of these drugs have appropriate medical uses (the notable exception being heroin), each is highly addictive, creating both a psychological and physical dependence on the drug in the user. Some of these opioids, such as heroin and opium, are tightly controlled while others, such as oxycodone are prescribed as pain relief medication. The increased abuse of prescription drugs, however, has drawn more attention to these synthetic opioids.

Opium is the gummy liquid derived from the oriental opium poppy, a plant which grows to approximately four feet in height with four-inch flowers. Raw opium is harvested by slitting the capsule of the flower and collecting the milky latex exudate. In the moist state this residue is dark brown; however, it hardens and lightens in color when dried and ground to powdered form. Opium poppies are grown around the world in locations including, but not limited to France, Turkey, Australia, Mexico, Spain, Afghanistan, and regions of South America. The raw product can be smoked or taken orally by dissolving in a liquid. Raw opium is not widely used now in the United States, although abuse was more common in the late 1800s. The alkaloid derivatives of opium (morphine, codeine, and heroin) are produced by pharmaceutical treatment of raw opium.

1. MORPHINE

Morphine is a natural alkaloid contained in opium with a molecular weight of 285.33 and the active ingredient of opium. Morphine was discovered about 1805, and with the development of the

---

[46] An excellent resource for drug information is United States Department of Justice, Drug Enforcement Administration, *Drugs of Abuse: A DEA Resource Guide*, 2015 Edition (available at: https://www.dea.gov/pr/publications.shtml)(last accessed December 8, 2016).

On the subject of illicit drug production generally, *see* International Narcotics Control Board, *Precursors And Chemicals Frequently Used in the Illicit Manufacture of Narcotic Drugs And Psychotropic Substances* 2015 (March 2, 2016)(available at: https://www.incb.org/documents/PRECURSORS/TECHNICAL_REPORTS/2015/2015-PreAR_E.pdf)(last accessed December 15, 2016).

[47] Other terms used are opiates and narcotic analgesics. Dimitri Gerostamoulos, "Opioids" in WILEY ENCYCLOPEDIA OF FORENSIC SCIENCE, (Jamieson A. & Moenssens A.A., eds) 2009 & online updates.

hypodermic syringe, became widely introduced in the Civil War period. Raw opium contains about 10 percent alkaloidal morphine. Morphine is legally used for prescribed medical purposes, but it is also illegally used by addicts. Physically, morphine in a salt form (usually morphine hydrochloride) is a white crystalline powder. As the drug takes effect, the subject becomes drowsy ("on the nod") and experiences a euphoric feeling.

Morphine alkaloid melts at about 230 degrees C. Morphine may be extracted from aqueous solutions by the addition of a carbonate/bicarbonate buffer and extracting with chloroform. Precipitated with Wagner reagent (aqueous solution of iodine and potassium iodide) it forms red, overlapping plate-like crystals; with Marme reagent (aqueous solution of cadmium oxide and potassium iodide) colorless, medium sized needles are quickly formed singly and in sheaves; with sodium carbonate, small, sharply defined rods in rosettes form.[48]

Concerning color tests, morphine produces the following color results with the listed reagents:[49]

Marquis reagent (100 ml of concentrated sulfuric acid with 5 ml of 40% formaldehyde): purple

HNO_3 (concentrated nitric acid): an orange-red color fading to yellow

Meckes reagent (1 g selenious acid in 100 ml of concentrated sulfuric acid): dark green

Froehdes reagent (0.5g of molybdic acid or sodium molybdate in 100 ml of concentrated sulfuric acid): purple becoming gray/purple

Mandelin reagent (1g of ammonium vanadate in 100 ml of concentrated sulfuric acid): yellow changing to violet-brown

---

[48] Several analytical methods for each controlled substance are discussed in this Section. These are not the only validated analytical methods that can be used for identification of the substances. Laboratories vary in their procedures and the particular analytical method used by the laboratory should be considered in each case to verify that the method has been validated (both as a method and for use by the laboratory) and that the procedures were properly followed in the analysis.

[49] For more information about Morphine and a sampling of a few of the other tests used, see: Gregory D. Busse & D. J. Triggle, *Morphine (Drugs: The Straight Facts)* 2006; M.E. Alburges, R.L. Foltz & D.E. Moody, "Determination of Ibogaine and 12-Hydroxyibogamine in Plasma by Gas Chromatography Positive Ion Chemical Ionization Mass Spectrometry," 19 J. Anal. Tox. 381 (1995); L.R. Goldbaum & M.A. Williams, "The Identification and Determination of Micrograms of Morphine in Biological Samples," 13 J. Forensic Sci. 253 (1968); Miller, "The Determination of Excipient Sugar Diluents in Illicit Preparations Containing Heroin by Gas Chromatography," 17 J. Forensic Sci. 150 (1972); Patricia Jenson, et al., "Identification of Drugs and Their Derivatives," 21 J. Forensic Sci. 564 (1976); C.C. Clark, "A Study of Procedures for the Identification of Heroin," 22 J. Forensic Sci. 418 (1977).

2. CODEINE

Codeine (methylmorphine), a natural alkaloid contained in opium with a molecular weight of 299.36, is prepared by methylation of morphine. It is a mild analgesic and a common ingredient of many cough medicines such as elixir of terpinhydrate, which are legally available to consumers. In large doses, codeine may be used as a substitute for morphine. Physically, it is a crystalline powder of long, slender, white crystals.

Codeine alkaloid has a melting point of 154–156 degrees C. It is soluble in ether, chloroform, alcohol, water and benzene but insoluble in petroleum ether. The crystalline precipitate (salt form) includes but is not limited to codeinces sulfate. Microcrystal identifications include Wagner reagent, which produces large, yellow, branched plate like crystals; potassium iodide, which produces long needle-like crystals. Marquis reagent produces a purple color on application to codeine; HNO_3 produces yellow; Meckes reagent produces an instant green changing to blue-green; and Froehdes reagent produces blue-green.

3. HEROIN

Heroin (diacetylmorphine), a synthetic alkaloid of opium with a molecular weight of 369.40, is prepared by treating raw opium chemically with acetic anhydride. In most cases heroin will be treated with hydrochloric acid to yield heroin hydrochloride. This latter compound is soluble in water, a necessary quality for users who inject the substance into their vascular system. Heroin is insoluble in water and cannot be hypodermically injected. Apart from medical research, no legal use of heroin exists; its manufacture, sale, distribution, and possession are strictly prohibited.

Heroin was first produced in Germany in 1898. It is at least three to four times more potent in effect than morphine, and it has the same addictive properties and action as morphine. Physically, it is an odorless, brownish-white to white powder, with a bitter taste. On the illicit market pure heroin is "cut" or diluted so that the user receives a sample containing only 3 to 5 percent heroin. Much of the heroin that enters the United States comes from either Mexico ("black tar:" found primarily in the western United States) or Columbia (white heroin: primarily sold on the East Coast).[50] Though the sources of heroin also include Southeast Asia, Southwest Asia, and Mexico. Heroin in the salt form (usually heroin hydrochloride or heroin citrate) is usually injected.

Heroin hydrochloride melts at 243–244 degrees C and is soluble in alcohol, chloroform, ether and water. It forms spherical clusters of golden-yellow, needle-like crystals on treatment with platinum chloride.

---

[50] United States Department of Justice, Drug Enforcement Administration, *Drugs of Abuse: A DEA Resource Guide*, 2015 Edition (available at: https://www.dea.gov/pr/publications.shtml)(last accessed December 8, 2016).

Concerning the qualitative color tests, heroin gives the following colors on treatment with the corresponding reagent: Marquis reagent-purple; Froehde reagent-purple becoming gray-purple; Mecke reagent-dark green; Mandelin reagent-light brown; concentrated nitric acid-yellow changing to green.[51]

GC/MS is the primary tool for the identification of heroin in a sample. If the sample is minute, liquid chromatography may be used in quantification. Fourier Transform Infrared Spectroscopy (FTIR) is another commonly used validated analytical method available to most laboratories to identify heroin and to report the salt form. Because most heroin samples are relatively weak in terms of the amount of actual heroin as a percentage of the total sample, the sample will usually need to be "cleaned up" before analysis to remove adulterating substances.

4. OTHER SYNTHETICS

Additional synthetic opioids-like substances, such as meperidine (Demerol), methadone, hydrocodone, and oxycodone, are made by chemical processes, but they have the same addictive potential as the opiates produced from botanical opium. Some color test reactions for these synthetics are noted below, and GC/MS is routinely used for identification confirmation.

	Marquis	Meckes	Froehdes
Hydrocodone:	purple	green	light yellow
Meperidine:	orange	yellow-green	grey
Methadone:	slow pink	yellow-green to green	no reaction
Oxycodone:	yellow to purple	yellow to olive green	yellow

Another recently-encountered synthetic substance with effects similar to opioids, but usually much stronger is fentanyl. Fentanyl was first introduced in the early 1960s as an intravenous analgesic-anesthetic under the trade name Sublimaze. By rearranging, adding, or taking off groups of atoms from the morphine molecule, underground chemists created a new drug that was initially legal (although now a controlled substance), that provided the same type of rush as heroin, and would not have the hazards of withdrawals. Fentanyl hydrochloride is a synthetic narcotic analgesic similar to morphine, but 50–100 more potent. It is medically used for the treatment of chronic pain in the form of patches, lozenges, or

---

[51] On the subject of narcotic identification color tests generally, *see* United Nations International Drug Control Programme, *Rapid Testing Methods of Drugs of Abuse*, 1994 (available at: https://www.unodc.org/pdf/publications/st-nar-13-rev1.pdf)(last accessed December 15, 2016).

injections.[52] In the early 2000's, fentanyl abuse was limited medical personnel taking patient patches for recreational use, and doctors and caregivers who misprescribed or failed to monitor the medication.[53] More recently, clandestine laboratory production of fentanyl has resulted in numerous overdoses and the drug has become a focus of law enforcement efforts.[54]

Seized drug analysis of fentanyl for identification and purity quantitation is generally accomplished by GC/MS and FTIR.

§15.08 STIMULANTS

1. COCAINE

Cocaine is a psychotropic drug prepared from coca leaves of the plant, *Erythroxylon coca,* which is a shrub native to northern South American Andes. The leaves are dried, the cocaine extracted along with other excipients in "poso pits" usually containing dilute acid. After crude processing, this extracted cocaine will be converted into coca paste, from which cocaine (specifically "cocaine hydrochloride") is derived.[55] Cocaine rapidly metabolizes in the body. The principal breakdown products of cocaine are benzoylecgonine (BEG) and ecgonine methyl ester (EME).

Cocaine is commonly encountered as a street drug in two forms: The first form, sometimes referred to as "cocaine powder," is cocaine hydrochloride. Because it is water soluble, cocaine hydrochloride is usually ingested by inhalation thereby dissolving in the moist nasal passages and then entering the body. Cocaine base is the second form of cocaine which exists as a water insoluble substance. Cocaine base in this form sometimes has the appearance of a rock-like substance, and is sometimes referred to as "crack." Cocaine base is not water soluble, so it is smoked, usually by heating in a glass pipe and then inhaling the cocaine vapors.

The distinction between cocaine hydrochloride and cocaine base has been significant in the law since 1986 when Congress, in reaction to media reports of the violence associated with the crack trade, instituted increased penalties for offenses involving cocaine base. The Anti-Drug

---

[52] Mindy J. Hull *et al.,* "Fatalities Associated with Fentanyl and Co-administered Cocaine or Opiates," 52 J. Forensic Sci. 1383–1388 (2007); National Institute of Health, National Institute on Drug Abuse, "Drug Facts: Fentanyl," June 2016 (available at: https://www.drugabuse.gov/publications/drugfacts/fentanyl)(last accessed December 8, 2016).

[53] *See* Rebecca Porter, "Medical Patch Users Discover Danger Beneath the Surface," 41 Trial 12 (Feb. 2005).

[54] *See* NPR, "Deaths Involving Fentanyl Rise As Curbing Illicit Supply Proves Tough," November 18, 2016 (available at: http://www.npr.org/sections/health-shots/2016/11/18/502355406/deaths-linked-to-fentanyl-rise-as-curbing-illicit-supply-proves-tough?utm_source=twitter.com&utm_campaign=health&utm_medium=social&utm_term=nprnews)(last accessed December 8, 2016).

[55] Daniel S. Isenschmid, "Cocaine" in WILEY ENCYCLOPEDIA OF FORENSIC SCIENCE, (Jamieson A. & Moenssens A.A., eds) 2009 & online updates.

Abuse Act of 1986 (ADAA), 100 Stat. 3207, established mandatory minimum sentences for controlled substance offenses based on drug type and quantity. Based on anecdotal and what some consider debatable scientific information, the penalty structure for crack quantities relative to cocaine hydrochloride quantities was established as the ratio of 100:1.[56] For example, a mandatory 10-year sentence is required for offenses involving 5 kilograms or more of "a mixture or substance containing a detectable amount of" cocaine hydrochloride, but the same sentence is required for offenses involving only 50 grams or more of cocaine base.[57] Similarly, a mandatory 5-year sentence is required for 500 grams of a mixture containing cocaine hydrochloride or 5 grams of a mixture containing cocaine base.[58] This penalty ratio of 1:100 came under tremendous criticism for its lack of scientific basis and disproportionate impact on minorities.[59] In 2010, Congress changed the ratio to roughly 18:1 amending the statutory mandatory minimum quantities of cocaine case to 280 grams (from 50 grams) and 28 grams (from 5 grams).[60]

a. Cocaine Hydrochloride

Cocaine hydrochloride is a white, crystalline powder. Tolerance does not develop; rather, the drug's effects are magnified with increased use. Ingestion is by absorption through the nasal mucous membrane as a result of sniffing the powder or by injection directly into the vascular system. The effect produced by cocaine use is fleeting. Dosage must be repeated to recapture it. Abuse may result in toxic effects such as hallucinations, delusions, and deterioration of the nasal septum.

Cocaine is soluble in ether, water, alcohol and chloroform. Treatment with platinum chloride produces feathery, pale-yellow crystals; gold chloride produces long, rod-like crystals with short arms extending at right angles. Colorwise, $Co(SCN)_2$ (cobalt thiocynate) produces a blue, flaky precipitate. There is no reaction to the Marquis reagent, Froehdes reagent or Meckes reagent. Confirmatory testing and quantitation for cocaine is usually by GC/MS or liquid chromatography/MS.[61]

---

[56] The United States Sentencing Commission subsequently promulgated Sentencing Guidelines that utilized the 100:1 ratio in setting all quantity thresholds for cocaine offenses. In 2007, the Commission reduced the cocaine base/cocaine sentencing ratio under the Guidelines. *See* United States Sentencing Commission, Guidelines Manual Supp. App. C, Amdt. 706 (effective Nov. 1, 2007).

[57] ADAA, § 1002, 100 Stat. 3207–2 (amending 21 U.S.C. §§ 841(b)(1)(A)(ii)–(iii)).

[58] ADAA, § 1002, 100 Stat. 3207–3 (amending 21 U.S.C.§§ 841(b)(1)(B)(ii)–iii)).

[59] *See* United States Sentencing Commission, Report to Congress: Report on Cocaine and Federal Sentencing Policy, Chapter 7, Sentencing of Cocaine Offenders (Feb. 1995)(available at: http://www.ussc.gov/Legislative_and_Public_Affairs/Congressional_Testimony_and_Reports/Drug_Topics/199502_RtC_Cocaine_Sentencing_Policy/CHAP7.HTM)(last accessed September 5, 2011); *see also* www.famm.org.

[60] *See* Fair Sentencing Act of 2010, § 2, 124 Stat. 2372.

[61] Id.

b.   *Cocaine Base*

Cocaine base is prepared by adding a basic substance (pH above about 7.5) to an aqueous solution of cocaine hydrochloride. The aqueous solution is then brought to a boil. One of the more commonly encountered methods of making cocaine base for smoking involves adding sodium bicarbonate (baking soda) to aqueous cocaine hydrochloride, boiling the solution and in the process converting the cocaine hydrochloride to cocaine base. Heating the precipitated cocaine base under heat lamps or in a microwave oven to remove the water results in "rocks" of cocaine base (referred to as crack cocaine) that is then smoked.[62] Cocaine base can be formed by using materials other than baking soda to convert the cocaine hydrochloride to cocaine base.[63]

Color tests can assist in distinguishing cocaine and crack. The $Co(SCN)_2$ reagent produces a blue precipitate with cocaine hydrochloride, but no reaction with cocaine base. If hydrochloric acid is added to cocaine base in solution in the presence of the $Co(SCN)_2$ reagent, a blue precipitate will form. Attenuated total reflection Fourier transform infrared (ATR-FTIR) spectrometry is the most easily performed analysis for distinguishing cocaine, although near-infrared Raman spectroscopy and infrared absorption spectroscopy can be used and reportedly are better at distinguishing the adulterants in the sample.[64] Gas chromatography/Flame Ionization Detector (GC/FID) analysis and high performance liquid chromatography (HPLC) analysis are usually used for quantitation analysis.

2.   PHENETHYLAMINES

Phenethylamines are a group of related organic compounds, each consisting of a phenyl ring, a methyl group, a two-carbon side chain, and an amino group. They are central nervous system stimulants which act to increase physical activity, euphoric spirit, and wakefulness. One of the more commonly encountered phenethylamines is methamphetamine in the form of the hydrochloride salt. In its illicit form, methamphetamine hydrochloride is relatively simple to synthesize from licit pharmacutical products and substances available from a commercial sources like a grocery store. A related stimulant is found in khat (*Catha edulis*).

---

[62]   Id.

[63]   The United States Supreme Court addressed the definition of "cocaine base" within the penalty provisions of 21 U.S.C. 841, holding that the term encompasses more than just "crack," but all forms of cocaine base. DePierre v. United States, 131 S.Ct. 2225 (2011).

[64]   Ciro A.F.O. Penido, Marcos Tadeu T. Pacheco, Renato A. Zangaro & Landulfo Silveira, Jr., "Identification of Different Forms of Cocaine and Substances Used in Adulteration Using Near-infrared Raman Spectroscopy and Infrared Absorption Spectroscopy," 60 J. Forensic Sci. 171–178 (2015).

a. *Amphetamine and Methamphetamine*

Some phenethylamines and phemethylamine-like substances have proved medically effective as stimulants in the treatment of narcolepsy and in improving the performance of children whose learning has been impaired by an inability to concentrate.[65] Ritalin (methylphenidate) is used to treat attention deficit disorder. Other well-known amphetamines are benzedrine (amphetamine sulphate), dexedrine (dextroamphetamine sulphate) and methedrine (methamphetamine hydrochloride).

The most common designer stimulant drug is methamphetamine (methylamphetamine or "speed"), which is the N-methylated form of amphetamine.[66] The ease of obtaining chemical precursors for methamphetamines has seen the emergence of clandestine speed laboratories. Most "meth labs" are found in houses and apartments, although mobile labs are becoming increasingly common. The drug is a central nervous system stimulant and produces an intense high which is mainly derived from the dangerous chemicals used in its production including Toluene (brake cleaner), sulfuric acid (drain cleaner) and lithium (camera battery).[67] Methamphetamine can be smoked, snorted, taken orally, or injected. Methamphetamine produces a feeling of euphoria, loss of appetite, paranoia, alleviating fatigue, and intensifying emotions, while creating feelings of mental alertness and wellbeing. The effects on the central nervous system and cardiovascular system are very similar to cocaine.[68]

In the mid 1980's, a form of methamphetamine hydrochloride appeared called ICE. The substance is highly purified methamphetamine hydrochloride, usually above a purity of 80%, which looks like rock candy or a chip or ice. It is a concentrated form of methamphetamine resulting when a solvent is used as a crystallizing agent. Methamphetamine hydrochloride is can be smoked, injected, or taken orally and is sometimes referred to as crystal meth or speed.[69]

Suspected amphetamines will be analyzed by crystal tests, TLC combined with color tests, and GC/MS or liquid chromatography-MS/MS for confirmation.[70] For crystal tests, a portion of the sample is

---

[65] Olaf H. Drummer, Jochen Beyer and Dimitri Gerostamoulos, "Amphetamine" in WILEY ENCYCLOPEDIA OF FORENSIC SCIENCE, (Jamieson A. & Moenssens A.A., eds) 2009 & online updates.

[66] Id.

[67] Anna S. Vogt, "The Mess Left Behind: Regulating the Cleanup of Former Methamphetamine Laboratories" 38 Idaho L. Rev. 251(2001).

[68] Id.

[69] Olaf H. Drummer, Jochen Beyer and Dimitri Gerostamoulos, "Amphetamine" in WILEY ENCYCLOPEDIA OF FORENSIC SCIENCE, (Jamieson A. & Moenssens A.A., eds) 2009 & online updates.

[70] Most amphetamines show poor mass spectral definition without derivatization. To improve the performance of GC/MS analysis, chemical derivatization of the amphetamine extract with acetyl or perfluoracyl derivatives is necessary. Liquid chromatography-MS/MS has the benefit of not requiring chemical derivatization. *See* Olaf H. Drummer, Jochen Beyer

dissolved in water and 10% tetrachloroauric solution is added, resulting in the formation of fine needlelike crystals. The presence of chloride can be detected by the addition of silver nitrate reagent to produce a white, curdy precipitate.[71] With TLC, the compound is dissolved in methanol and concentrated ammonia is used as the developing solvent. Using ninhydrin as a developing reagent, amphetamine produces a pink or violet color and methamphetamine produces a pink-orange color.[72] Raman spectroscopy is a simple, rapid, nondestructive screening test for detecting methamphetamine in clandestine laboratory liquid submissions.[73]

Quantitation of amphetamine and methamphetamine involves counting units (pills, tablets) or weighing the powder or crystal.

b.   Khat and Designer Cathinones

Cathinone, the psychoactive ingredient in the Khat plant, is the beta-keto derivative of amphetamine, and is classified by the federal government as a Schedule I drug. Khat is a flowering evergreen shrub found predominantly in Africa and the Middle East. Several designer cathinones (synthetic beta-keto derivatives of other synthetic amphetamine compounds) have appeared and are being abused as "party drugs:" methcathinone, mephedrone, methylone, diethpropin, and bupropin. The most commonly encountered synthetic cathinone, mephedrone (4-methylmethcathinone, 4-MMC), is generally in a white or off-white powder form. These drugs are stimulants with effects similar to amphetamine and to MDMA, producing euphoria, alertness, talkativeness and sociability. Users face the risks of both types of drugs including overstimulation of the cardiovascular system (leading to heart and circulatory problems) and overstimulation of the nervous system (leading to paranoia and hallucinations).

Since not all synthetic cathinones are included in the drug schedules or otherwise regulated, analysis must distinguish between the controlled substances and others which are currently legal. Analytical methods used in the identification of cathinones are TLC and GC/MS (derivatization with acetylation and silylation will improve spectral information).

and Dimitri Gerostamoulos, "Amphetamine" in WILEY ENCYCLOPEDIA OF FORENSIC SCIENCE, (Jamieson A. & Moenssens A.A., eds) 2009 & online updates.

[71] Heesun Chung et al., "Drug Analysis," in WILEY ENCYCLOPEDIA OF FORENSIC SCIENCE, (Jamieson A. & Moenssens A.A., eds) 2009 & online updates.

[72] Id.

[73] Jeremy S. Triplett et al., "Raman Spectroscopy as a Simple, Rapid, Nondestructive Screening Test for Methamphetamine in Clandestine Laboratory Liquids," 58 J. Forensic Sci. 1607–1614 (2013).

§15.09 DEPRESSANTS

1. BARBITURATES

Barbiturates are classified as hypnotic anesthetic or sedative drugs. Some of the commonly encountered capsules are nembutal (sodium pentobarbital: "yellow jackets"), seconal (sodium secobarbital: "red birds"), Tuinal (a 50/50 mixture of sodium secobarbital and sodium amobarbital-"Christmas trees") and amytal (sodium amobarbital: "blue birds"). These substances depress the higher cerebral nerve centers, removing control over learned behavior and inhibitions governing instinctive behavior. Barbiturates are often medically prescribed for sedation or as nerve tranquilizers. Taken in prescribed therapeutic doses, barbiturates do not appear to produce physical dependence or toxic results. Significant physical dependence is reported when the daily misuse of the drug is in excess of five therapeutic doses per day. In such cases abstinence may result in withdrawal symptoms such as *delirium tremens*, convulsions, and vomiting.

There are more than one hundred different barbiturates, all of which are barbituric acid derivatives. Identification of barbiturates singularly and as a class is done by one of the following types of tests:

(1) Color reaction, particularly the Dille-Koppanyi test, in which the appearance of a red-violet color on treatment of the sample with cobalt acetate and isopropylamine indicates a barbituric acid derivative, but this test is not specific for any single barbiturate;

(2) Microcrystalline examination of the precipitate of the treated sample;[74]

(3) Melting point examination [Nembutal: 126–130 EC; Seconal: 100 EC; Amytal: 156–158 EC]

(4) UV (extraction usually required and should be run in both acidic and basic media due to characteristic bathochromic shift from acid to base);

(5) FTIR (extraction usually required);

(6) Thin layer chromatography; and

(7) GC/MS (derivatization required).

2. BENZODIAZEPINES

Benzodiazepines are central nervous system depressants that are legally available only through prescription and controlled through Schedule IV of the CSA. Alprazolam (Xanax®) and diazepam (Valium®) are the two most frequently encountered benzodiazepines in street

---

[74] For a pictorial illustration of the various crystalline tests used to identify specific barbiturates, *see* John E. David, "Barbiturate Differentiation by Chemical Microscopy," 52 J. CRIM. L., CRIMINOL. P.S. 459 (1961).

trade. Analytical methods for the identification of the controlled substance include pharmaceutical identifiers, GC-MS, and direct analysis in real time (DART) mass spectrometry.[75]

Other synthetic depressants including gamma-hydroxybutyrate (GHB) and flunitrazepam (Rohypnol®), are also frequently seized in pills, powder, or liquid form. Analytical schemes for the identification of these designer drugs must take into account their form and specific composition, but TLC with color test visualizing sprays followed by GC/MS or FTIR are generally used.[76]

§15.10 MARIJUANA AND SYNTHETIC CANNABINOIDS

1. MARIJUANA

Although marijuana is considered scientifically as a hallucinogen, many states and the federal government classify marijuana as a Schedule I drug along with heroin or treat it independently of other hallucinogenic compounds. Marijuana and other psychoactive products derived from the plant *Cannabis sativa* are the most widely used illegal drugs in the world despite decades of regulation efforts.[77] Marijuana constitutes a significant portion of all plant material seized during law enforcement investigations in the United States.[78]

Cannabis sativa is a hardy weed growing to a height of five feet. It is sticky to the touch and has a distinctive odor. The seed of the marijuana plant is a single seed that whitens as it ripens contained in a pod that browns as it ripens. The main stalk varies from 1/2 inch to 2 inches in diameter. It has fluted leaf stalks and narrow, compound palmate leaves containing variable numbers of leaflets up to seven in number. The leaves are lance shaped with serrated edges and they may be up to five inches long. (See Figure 1.) The upper surface of the pointed leaves is of a darker green than the lime colored under leaf. The plant is covered with one celled, curved hair like fibers (cystolithic hairs) which permit microscopic identification, even when fragmented. These cystolithic hairs are found in the greatest abundance on the upper side of the leaves. These glandular hair-like fibers contain the resinous substance with the main psychoactive ingredient (delta-9-tetrahydrocannabinol or THC) which creates mild hallucinogenic effects

---

[75] Warren C. Samms et al., "Analysis of Alprazolam by DART_TOF Mass Spectrometry in Counterfeit and Routine Drug Identification Cases," 56 J. Forensic Sci. 993–998 (2011).

[76] Paul A. Gahlinger, "Club Drugs: MDMA, Gamma-Hydroxybutyrate (GHB), Rohypnol, and Ketamine," ANAL. BIOANAL. CHEM. (June 1, 2004).

[77] Zlatko Mahmedic *et al.,* "Potency Trends of [Delta-9]-THC and Other Cannabinoids in Confiscated Cannabis Preparations from 1993–2008," 55 J.FORENSIC SCI. SOC. 1209–1217 (2010).

[78] Lindsay Allgeier, "Field Testing of Collection Cards for *Cannabis sativa* Samples with a Single Hexanucleotide DNA Marker," 56 J.FORENSIC SCI. SOC. 1245–1249 (2011).

and acts as a depressant to the central nervous system.[79] Although THC is found throughout the plant, the highest concentrations are in the female flowering heads.[80]

Figure 1: The characteristic leaf shape of a marijuana (Cannabis sativa) plant. *Courtesy: Chicago Police Department Criminalistics Division.*

Because the appearance of individual cannabis plants varies depending on growing conditions and the environment, some researchers theorized that there were three varieties of cannabis plants: *Cannabis sativa L., Cannabis indica L.,* and *Cannabis ruderalis.*[81] In some jurisdictions where marijuana was defined as cannabis sativa L., attorneys argued that a conviction required proof of the specific marijuana species, creating the "species defense."[82] The "species defense" generally was unsuccessful as courts concluded the statutory prohibitions covered all potential species of marijuana,[83] and legislatures amended their statutes to explicitly prohibit any species of cannabis.[84] It is now widely accepted that only one species of marijuana exists: *cannabis sativa.*[85]

---

[79] Other cannabinoids also have pharmacological properties. Zlatko Mahmedic *et al.,* "Potency Trends of [Delta-9]-THC and Other Cannabinoids in Confiscated Cannabis Preparations from 1993–2008," 55 J.FORENSIC SCI. SOC. 1209–1217 (2010).

[80] Stuart Dickson and Helen Poulsen, "Cannabis," in WILEY ENCYCLOPEDIA OF FORENSIC SCIENCE, (Jamieson A. & Moenssens A.A., eds) 2009 & online updates.

[81] R. Hauber, "Summary of Distinguishing Features of the Three Proposed Species of Cannabis," 13 MIDWEST ASSOC. FOR. SCIENTISTS NEWSLETTER 33 (Oct. 1984) in which it is concluded that a lack of "reproductive isolation" proves marijuana is monotypic.

[82] *See generally,* Randal N. Graham, "A Unified Theory of Statutory Interpretation," 23 Statute L. Rev. 91, 95–06 (2002).

[83] *See* U.S. v. Sanapaw, 366 F.3d 492, 494–096 (7th Cir.2004).

[84] State v. Adler, 108 Hawaii 169, 118 P.3d 652 (2005).

[85] Stuart Dickson and Helen Poulsen, "Cannabis," in WILEY ENCYCLOPEDIA OF FORENSIC SCIENCE, (Jamieson A. & Moenssens A.A., eds) 2009 & online updates.

Although marijuana is sometimes mixed with liquids, or eaten, it usually is smoked.[86] Reported effects of mild to moderate marijuana use include euphoria, relaxation, increased sociability, and changes in perception.[87] Studies suggest that the effects of moderate doses of marijuana and alcohol are similar,[88] but marijuana combines many of the effects of tranquilizers and hallucinogens.[89] Mood and perception effects can include anxiety and paranoia. That marijuana use can impair the motor and cognitive skills necessary for safe driving has been recognized,[90] and the courts have allowed testimony relating to the impairment of cognitive functions used in motor vehicle operation.[91] The subjective effects are dependent on variable factors such as the dosage, the means of administration, the psychological condition of the user, and the circumstances in which it is used.

Marijuana has approved medical uses as a treatment for the severe nausea and vomiting that often accompany cancer chemotherapy and as an appetite stimulant to treat the wasting syndrome accompanying AIDS.[92] It also has been used to temporarily relieve the pain caused by

---

[86] Marilyn A. Huestis, "Cannabis (Marijuana)—Effects on Human Behavior and Performance," 14 For. Sci. Rev. 16 (2002).

[87] Elke Raes and Alain G. Verstraete, "Drug-Impaired Driving," in WILEY ENCYCLOPEDIA OF FORENSIC SCIENCE, (Jamieson A. & Moenssens A.A., eds) 2009 & online updates.

[88] Alex Kreit and Aaron Marcus, "Raich, Health Care, and the Commerce Clause," 31 Wm. Mitchell L. Rev. 957, (2005), stating that "marijuana is a relatively safe and 'benign' medicine in terms of side effects and potential toxicity."

See also Carole Shapiro, "Law v. Laughter: The War Against the Evil Weed and Big Screen Reefer Sanity," 29 Okla. City U. L. Rev. 795 (Fall 2004); Sara Markowitz, "Alcohol, Drugs, and Violence," 25 Intl. Rev. L. & Econ. 20 (March 2005)("[u]nlike with alcohol, there is some uncertainty surrounding the pharmacological link between drugs and violence. It is known that biological effects differ by drug type and amount of use. For example, short-term use of marijuana may inhibit aggressive behavior, while long-term use can alter the nervous system in a way that promotes tendencies towards violence (National Research Council, 1993)").

[89] Stuart Dickson and Helen Poulsen, "Cannabis," in WILEY ENCYCLOPEDIA OF FORENSIC SCIENCE, (Jamieson A. & Moenssens A.A., eds) 2009 & online updates.

[90] Olaf H. Drummer, *The Forensic Pharmacology of Drugs of Abuse.* Oxford University Press, 2001.

[91] Kelli M. Hinson, Jennifer Evans Morris, and Elaine Chen, "Annual Survey of Texas Law Article, Civil Evidence," 57 SMU L. Rev. 653 (Summer 2004), indicating that the Fifth Circuit found that the expert testimony regarding studies which have demonstrated that marijuana use impairs cognitive functions, including those related to the operation of a motor vehicle for at least twelve hours after the acute high wears off was admissible to help the jury understand the effect of recent ingestion of marijuana on an individual's cognitive functions, including perception and reaction time, which are both critical factors in any motor vehicle accident. *See also* Bocanegra v. Vicmar Services, Inc., 320 F.3d 581 (5th Cir.2003).

[92] In 2015, Virginia approved the medical use of cannabidiol or THC-A oil to treat intractable epilepsy. Va. Code § 54.1–3408.3:

A. As used in this section:

"Cannabidiol oil" means a processed Cannabis plant extract that contains at least 15 percent cannabidiol but no more than five percent tetrahydrocannabinol, or a dilution of the resin of the Cannabis plant that contains at least 50 milligrams of cannabidiol per milliliter but not more than five percent tetrahydrocannabinol.

"THC-A oil" means a processed Cannabis plant extract that contains at least 15 percent tetrahydrocannabinol acid but not more than five percent tetrahydrocannabinol, or a dilution of the resin of the Cannabis plant that

disabling spasticity associated with being a quadriplegic and the intra-ocular pressure that glaucoma sufferers experience.[93]

Marijuana is generally identified by macroscopic/microscopic examinations and color tests. If microscopic characteristics are absent or the chemical tests are inconclusive, many laboratories use GC/MS.[94] Macroscopically, analysts look for the palmate arrangement of the leaflets, the pinnate appearance and serrated edges of the leaflets, seeds, and fluted stems and stalks. Microscopically, the analysis of suspected marijuana involves looking for cystolithic hairs (single celled hair like fibers, some of which resemble bear claws) and examining the seeds for morphological characteristics (coconut shape, veined with lacy markings, and circumference ridge).

The two most common color tests/chemical spot tests used to determine whether a substance is marijuana are the Duquenois-Levine Reagent test and thin layer chromatography (TLC) with Fast Blue B Salt for visualization. The Duquenois-Levine Reagent test screens for tetrahydrocannabinol, the hallucinogenic constituent of marijuana. The test procedure involves extracting the sample into a suitable solvent (usually hexane, petroleum ether or methanol). Equal amounts of the

---

contains at least 50 milligrams of tetrahydrocannabinol acid per milliliter but not more than five percent tetrahydrocannabinol.

B. A practitioner of medicine or osteopathy licensed by the Board of Medicine in the course of his professional practice may issue a written certification for the use of cannabidiol oil or THC-A oil for treatment or to alleviate the symptoms of a patient's intractable epilepsy.

C. The written certification shall be on a form provided by the Office of the Executive Secretary of the Supreme Court developed in consultation with the Board of Medicine. Such written certification shall contain the name, address, and telephone number of the practitioner, the name and address of the patient issued the written certification, the date on which the written certification was made, and the signature of the practitioner. Such written certification issued pursuant to subsection B shall expire no later than one year after its issuance unless the practitioner provides in such written certification an earlier expiration.

D. No practitioner shall be prosecuted under § 18.2–248 or 18.2–248.1 for dispensing or distributing cannabidiol oil or THC-A oil for the treatment or to alleviate the symptoms of a patient's intractable epilepsy pursuant to a written certification issued pursuant to subsection B. Nothing in this section shall preclude the Board of Medicine from sanctioning a practitioner for failing to properly evaluate or treat a patient's medical condition or otherwise violating the applicable standard of care for evaluating or treating medical conditions.

[93] Stuart Dickson and Helen Poulsen, "Cannabis," in WILEY ENCYCLOPEDIA OF FORENSIC SCIENCE, (Jamieson A. & Moenssens A.A., eds) 2009 & online updates; see also Editorial. "Therapeutic Marijuana Use Supported While Thorough Proposed Study Done," 281 JAMA 1473 (1999).

[94] See Todd v. Rush County Schools, 983 F.Supp. 799, 123 Ed. Law Rep. 120 (S.D.Ind.1997), recognizing use of gas chromatography test has better than 99% accuracy. See, e.g.: Robert Connell Clark, Marijuana Botany (1991); J. Calvin Giddings, Ed., Advances in Chromatography, 1980; R.C. Backer, et al., "A Simple Method for the Infrared Identification of Cannabinoids of Marihuana Resolved by Gas Chromatography," 15 J. FORENSIC SCI. 287 (1970); S.W. Bellman, et al., "Spectrometric Forensic Chemistry of Hallucinogenic Drugs," 15 J. FORENSIC SCI. 261 (1970); D.P. Carew, "Microscopic, Microchemical, and ThinBLayer Chromatographic Study of Marihuana Grown or Confiscated in Iowa," 16 J. FORENSIC SCI. 87 (1971); M.J. de Faubert Maunder, "The Forensic Significance of the Age and Origin of Cannabis," 16 MED. SCI. LAW 78 (1976).

Duquenois' reagent (2.5 ml acetaldehyde and 2.0 g of vanillin in 100 ml of 95% ethanol) and concentrated hydrochloric acid are added to the extract with a positive result indicated by blue/deep purple color reaction. The next step involves adding sufficient $CHCL_3$ (chloroform) to form a discernible layer with the extract and then mixing. A positive result is indicated by a pink/purple color reaction in the bottom layer (the chloroform layer) if THC is present.[95]

Using TLC, the sample is extracted using a suitable solvent (same as with the Duquenois-Levine Reagent test) and spotted on a silica (or equivalent) gel with a standard. The mobile phase is usually 4–8% diethylamine in toluene. To visualize, Fast Blue B Salt (tetrazotized o-dianisidine zinc chloride salt) or Fast Blue BB Salt (4-benzoylamino-2,5-diethoxy-benzenediazonium chloride hemi [zinc chloride] salt) is sprayed on the gel after migration. The three major cannabinoids will appear in the following order with the noted color reaction:

Cannabidiol—Orange

Tetrahydrocaanabinol—Red

Cannabinol—Purple

Quantitation of marijuana plant material is usually by weight. THC concentration levels may be measured by GC/MS.[96]

2. SYNTHETIC CANNABINOIDS

Synthetic cannabinoids, commonly known as "spice" or "K2," refer to any artificial cannabinoid. Since the late 1980's, over one hundred different artificial cannabinoids have been synthesized in laboratories as researchers developed chemicals to mimic the effects of THC to study how cannabinoids affect biological activity. The synthetics can be broadly categorized into three structural types: THC classical, JWH-018 Napthoylindoes, and CP47, 497 (C8) Non-classical.[97]

For street sales, the synthetic cannabinoid (generally the chemical JWH-018[98]) is sprayed on other legal plant material, such as catnip, and are sold as incense or herbal supplements The material is then smoked in a manner similar to marijuana. Reported effects are similar to marijuana inhalation: increased pulse rate, alteration of mood and perception, and reddened eyes.[99] Pharmacological studies and anecdotal

---

[95] C.G. Pitt, R.W. Hendron and R.S. Hsia, "The Specificity of the Duquenois Color Test for Marijuana and Hashish," 17 J.FORENSIC SCI. 693–700 (1972).

[96] Heesun Chung *et al.,* "Drug Analysis," in WILEY ENCYCLOPEDIA OF FORENSIC SCIENCE, (Jamieson A. & Moenssens A.A., eds) 2009 & online updates.

[97] Thomas J. Gluodenis, Jr., PhD., "Identification of Synthetic Cannabinoids in Herbal Incense Blends," *Forensic Magazine,* June/July 2011 (available at: http://www.forensicmag.com/article/identification-synthetic-cannabinoids-herbal-incense-blends)(last accessed September 1, 2011).

[98] Named after the inventor of the chemical, John W. Huffman.

[99] Volker Auwarter *et al.,* Letter to Editor, J. MASS SPECTROMETRY (30 December 2008).

information from hospitals and poison controls centers suggest that the chemical is much stronger and lasts longer than THC.[100]

Prior to 2010, only one synthetic cannabinoid, HU-210, was listed on the federal Controlled Substances Act as a Schedule I drug. By 2011, eighteen states criminalized one or more of the synthetic cannabinoids and the DEA began adding more synthetic marijuana chemicals to Schedule I.[101] Regulation efforts improved and most jurisdictions have classified these substances by structure generally and also list numerous specific substances. For example, Virginia includes in Schedule I:[102]

> Any substance that contains one or more cannabimimetic agents or that contains their salts, isomers, and salts of isomers whenever the existence of such salts, isomers, and salts of isomers is possible within the specific chemical designation, and any preparation, mixture, or substance containing, or mixed or infused with, any detectable amount of one or more cannabimimetic agents.
>
> a. "Cannabimimetic agents" includes any substance that is within any of the following structural classes:
>
>> 2-(3-hydroxycyclohexyl)phenol with substitution at the 5-position of the phenolic ring by alkyl or alkenyl, whether or not substituted on the cyclohexyl ring to any extent;
>>
>> 3-(1-naphthoyl)indole or 1H-indol-3-yl-(1-naphthyl)methane with substitution at the nitrogen atom of the indole ring, whether or not further substituted on the indole ring to any extent, whether or not substituted on the naphthoyl or naphthyl ring to any extent;
>>
>> 3-(1-naphthoyl)pyrrole with substitution at the nitrogen atom of the pyrrole ring, whether or not further substituted in the pyrrole ring to any extent, whether or not substituted on the naphthoyl ring to any extent;
>>
>> 1-(1-naphthylmethyl)indene with substitution of the 3-position of the indene ring, whether or not further substituted in the indene ring to any extent, whether or not substituted on the naphthyl ring to any extent;

---

[100] *See* National Institute on Drug Abuse, *Drug Facts—Synthetic Cannabinoids*, November 2015 (available at: https://www.drugabuse.gov/publications/drugfacts/synthetic-cannabinoids)(last accessed December 15, 2016); *see also* Susan Scutti, "'Fake Pot' Causing Zombielike Effects is 85 Times More Potent Than Marijuana," CNN, December 16, 2016 (available at: http://www.cnn.com/2016/12/16/health/zombie-synthetic-marijuana/index.html?sr=twCNN121616zombie-synthetic-marijuana0211PMVODtopLink&linkId=32462631)(last accessed December 16, 2016).

[101] Federal law defines "cannabimimetric agents" as "any substance that is a cannabinoid receptor type 1 (CB1 receptor agonist as demonstrated by binding studies and functional assays within any of" five structural classes and lists 15 specific substances. 21 U.S.C. § 821(d)(2(A) and (B).

[102] Va. Code § 54.1–3446(7). The statute also lists over 40 individual substances.

3-phenylacetylindole or 3-benzoylindole with substitution at the nitrogen atom of the indole ring, whether or not further substituted in the indole ring to any extent, whether or not substituted on the phenyl ring to any extent;

3-cyclopropoylindole with substitution at the nitrogen atom of the indole ring, whether or not further substituted on the indole ring to any extent, whether or not substituted on the cyclopropyl ring to any extent;

3-adamantoylindole with substitution at the nitrogen atom of the indole ring, whether or not further substituted on the indole ring to any extent, whether or not substituted on the adamantyl ring to any extent;

N-(adamantyl)-indole-3-carboxamide with substitution at the nitrogen atom of the indole ring, whether or not further substituted on the indole ring to any extent, whether or not substituted on the adamantyl ring to any extent; and

N-(adamantyl)-indazole-3-carboxamide with substitution at a nitrogen atom of the indazole ring, whether or not further substituted on the indazole ring to any extent, whether or not substituted on the adamantyl ring to any extent.

Because of the relatively recent use of the synthetic cannabinoids as recreational drugs, the development of analytical schemes for the detection of the chemicals generally lagged behind legislative efforts to ban the substances. The macroscopic botanical identification methods used with regular marijuana are inapplicable. Rapid identification of synthetic cannabinoids is accomplished with MS and NMR and quantitation can be accomplished using HPLC with UV detection.[103]

§15.11 HALLUCINOGENS

1. MDMA

New forms of methamphetamines continue to enter the illegal drug market. One of the first derivatives was MDA (3, 4-methylene-dioxyamphetamine), but it had undesirable side effects. MDMA (3, 4-methylenedioxymethamphetamine) followed, and is classified as a hallucinogen despite its stimulant properties. Initially synthesized in

---

[103] See Michael Marino et al., "Rapid Identification of Synthetic Cannabinoids in Herbal Incenses with DART-MS and NMR," 61 J. Forensic Sci. S82–S91 (2016); Laura A. Ciolino, "Quantitation of Synthetic Cannabinoids in Plant Materials Using High Performance Liquid Chromatography with UV Detection (Validated Method)," 60 J. Forensic Sci. 1171–1181 (2015).

an attempt to develop new synthetic routes for blood clotting agents, MDMA has no legitimate medical use today and is best known as the club drug "ecstasy."[104] Although currently a controlled substance, in the late 1960's, MDMA was prescribed by psychiatrists to encourage openness in therapy sessions and despite such side effects as rapid heartbeat, fatigue, profuse sweating, and withdrawal.[105]

MDMA ingestion increases the release of serotonin, dopamine, and norepinephrine. The effects of an oral dose appear within 30 to 60 minutes and last up to eight hours.[106] Serotonin producing neurons can be affected leading to tachycardia, mydriasis, diaphoresis, tremor, hypertension, arrhythmias, Parkinsonism, esophoria (tendency for eyes to turn inward), and urinary retention. However, the most troublesome potential outcome of MDMA ingestion is hyperthermia and the associated serotonin syndrome, which is manifested by grossly elevated core body temperature, rigidity, myoclonus, and autonomic instability. These adverse effects can result in end organ damage, rhabdomyolysis and acute renal failure, hepatic failure, adult respiratory distress syndrome, coagulopathy, psychosis or brain damage.[107]

Color tests show the following reactions to the listed reagents for both MDA and MDMA: Marquis (dark violet to black); Mecke (green to dark blue/violet to black); Froehde (brown to dark blue/violet to black_. Tetrabromophenolphthalein ethyl ester (TBPEE) can assist in distinguishing MDA (which produces a purple color) and MDMA (which produces a blue color). TLC, UV, and GC (with extraction and derivatization) can be used for separation. GC-FTIR is a useful tool to differentiate MDMA compounds, although other techniques are used for in-field analysis.[108] Using GC with internal standards can provide MDMA quantitation.

2. OTHER HALLUCINOGENS

Hallucinogenic drugs include mescaline in peyote, psilocin/ psilocybin in mushrooms, LSD, and PCP. Mescaline (3,4,5-trimethoxyphenylethylamine) is a natural alkaloid that induces visual hallucinatory effects, particularly emphasizing vividness of color. It is

---

[104] Ruth J.H. Waddell-Smith, "A Review of Recent Advances in Impurity Profiling of Illicit MDMA Samples," 52 J.FORENSIC SCI. SOC. 1297–1304 (2007).

[105] Charles Grob et al., "The MDMA-Neurotoxicity Controversy Implications for Clinical Research with Novel Psychoactive Drugs," 180 J. NERV. MENT. DIS. 355 (1992).

[106] Paul A. Gahlinger, "Club Drugs: MDMA, Gamma-Hydroxybutyrate (GHB), Rohypnol, and Ketamine," AMER. FAM. PHYSICIAN (June 1, 2004).

[107] Hatzidimitriou, "Altered Serotonin Innervation Patterns in the Forebrain Of Monkeys Treated with (∀)3,4-methylenedioxymethamphetamine Seven Years Previously: Factors Influencing Abnormal Recovery," 19 J. NEUROSCI. 5096 (1999). *See also* Paul A. Gahlinger, "Club Drugs: MDMA, Gamma-Hydroxybutyrate (GHB), Rohypnol, and Ketamine," AMER. FAM. PHYSICIAN (June 1, 2004).

[108] Suely K.S.S. Porto et al., "Analysis of Ecstasy Tablets Using Capillary Electrophoresis with Capacitively Coupled Contactless Conductivity Detection," 59 J. Forensic Sci. 1622–1626 (2014).

the active ingredient of the peyote cactus. Analytical schemes to identify mescaline include color tests (Marquis reagent-orange; Mecke-green to dark brown; Froehde-green to blue; HNO_3-bright red), TLC and UV. Psilocin and psilocybin are also naturally occurring substances in hallucinogenic mushrooms of the genera *Psilocybe*. Many analytical techniques may be used for the identification of psilocin and psilocybin, including GC/MS, but HPLC is the most widely used technique.[109]

Other hallucinogens are synthetically produced. LSD (lysergic acid) and PCP (phencyclidine) are of this type. LSD (lysergic acid diethylamide), with a molecular weight of 323.42, is a powerful hallucinogenic. LSD may be negatively identified by a color test using Ehrlich reagent (p-dimethylaminobenzaldehyde and HCl in ethyl alcohol). Formation of a blue color on treatment indicates that the substance is one of the lysergic acid derivatives. Absence of a color reaction demonstrates that the substance is not LSD. Chromatography (TLC and GC) may also be used to identify LSD, although LC/MS/MS has been described as the method of choice for identification of LSD.[110]

Phencyclidine (PCP) was at first commercially manufactured under the name Sernyl as a general anesthetic but had detrimental effects on patients. It was remarketed as a tranquilizer for animals in veterinary practice, and was sold under the name Sernylan before becoming illegal as a Schedule II Controlled Substance in 1978. PCP has been customarily synthesized in clandestine drug laboratories. When tested with the Marquis reagent, PCP will undergo a color change ranging from colorless to faint pink. With $Co(SCN)_2$, the reaction will be blue. Of the microcrystalline tests, PCP is distinctive in the presence of potassium iodide which causes it to display crystals first in the form of needles, shortly changing to blades which are colorless under plain light but gray under polarized light.[111] PCP can be qualitatively identified through the normal separation processes of the various chromatographic techniques. Nuclear magnetic resonance (NMR) spectroscopy can provide an even greater degree of identification, but should be used in combination with mass spectrometry and gas chromatography due to its limitations identifying small sample sizes.[112]

§15.12 ANABOLIC STEROIDS

Anabolic steroids are synthetic analogues of testosterone, the male sex hormone (thus described as androgenic). Since one of their

---

[109] Nicole Anastos, Simon W. Lewis, Neil W. Barnett and D. Noel Sims, "The Determination of Psilocin and Psilocybin in Hallucinogenic Mushrooms by HPLC Utilizing a Dual Reagent Acidic Potassium Permanganate and Tris (2,2'-bipyridyl)ruthenium(II) Chemiluminescence Detection System," 51 J.Forensic Sci. 45–51 (2006).

[110] Heesun Chung *et al.*, "Drug Analysis," in WILEY ENCYCLOPEDIA OF FORENSIC SCIENCE, (Jamieson A. & Moenssens A.A., eds) 2009 & online updates.

[111] P. Ruybal, "Microcrystalline Tests for Narcotics and Dangerous Drugs," CRIME LAB. DIGEST 6 (Dec. 1980).

[112] Frederick P. Smith, *Handbook of Forensic Drug Analysis* 205 (2005).

characteristics is the stimulation and synthesis of cellular proteins, which help in the growth and repair of bodily tissues, athletes use anabolic steroids to increase muscle mass and strength as well as for increased workout stamina. Other types of steroids, the cortico steroids, are used for many legitimate medical purposes, generally to relieve inflammation in tissues caused by arthritis or injuries. Unlike cortico steroids, anabolic steroids are used to promote muscle growth, resulting in their proliferation among athletes. Anabolic steroids are many and varied, one estimate finding "eighty anabolic/androgenic steroids marketed worldwide."[113]

Scientific studies have indicated that anabolic steroid use can cause rages, mood swings, higher levels of aggression, and depression.[114] To meet what one U.S. Senator called "one of America's most serious drug problems," Congress enacted the Anabolic Steroids Control Act of 1990, which classifies anabolic steroids as a Schedule III controlled substance under the Controlled Substances Act.[115] The Act also criminalizes physician prescription of anabolic steroids for any use other than for the treatment of a disease or other recognized condition. The Anabolic Steroid Control Act of 2004, signed by the President on October 22, 2004, added eighteen drugs to the controlled substance list, including several steroid precursors, or derivatives of testosterone, which once ingested, metabolize into anabolic steroids. After the passage of the federal laws, states also classified anabolic steroids as controlled substances.

There are no good screening tests for anabolic steroids and counterfeit or substituted pharmaceutical markings make these markings unreliable indicators of identity. FTIR may be used following additional extractions to remove any oils in the substance. GC/MS also may require special derivatization techniques and instrument settings.

IV. STATUTORY CONTROL OF DRUGS

§15.13 FEDERAL

1. CONTROLLED SUBSTANCES ACT

In response to the increasing amount of drug abuse in the United States, Congress in 1970 approved legislation which provided for

---

[113] P. Colman, et al., "Anabolic SteroidsBAnalysis of Dosage Forms from Selected Case Studies from the L.A. County Sheriff's Scientific Services Bureau," 36 J. Forensic Sci. 1079 (1991).

[114] Helen Keane, "Diagnosing the Male Steroid User: Drug Use, Body Image and Disordered Masculinity," 9 HEALTH 189 (2005); C.J. Hannan, "Psychological and Serum Homovanillic Acid Changes in Men Administered Androgenic Steroids," 16 PSYCHONEUROENDOCRINOLOGY 35 (1991) and T.P. Su et al., "Neuropsychiatric Effects of Anabolic Steroids in Male Normal Volunteers," 269 J.A.M.A. 2760 (1993).

[115] 21 U.S.C. 812(3)(e).

enhanced efforts in prevention of drug abuse and rehabilitation of drug users. The legislative intent was to establish regulatory oversight for the distribution of controlled substances, to provide more effective law enforcement for drug abuse prevention and control, and to enact a balanced system of criminal penalties for drug offenses. Under its authority to regulate interstate commerce,[116] Congress passed the Comprehensive Drug Abuse Prevention and Control Act. The section of the law regulating the possession and use of drugs is known as the Controlled Substances Act (CSA). The CSA exempts tobacco and alcohol from the definition of controlled substances, but both street drugs and prescription drugs are included. The CSA established five schedules for controlled substances based on the substance's potential for abuse or addiction, the current medical uses for the substance, the available scientific knowledge of the effects of the substance on the human body, and the scope of current and past abuse of the substance.

The CSA makes it "unlawful for any person knowingly or intentionally . . . to manufacture, distribute, or dispense, or possess with intent to manufacture, distribute, or dispense, a controlled substance."[117] The United States Supreme Court has held that the ordinary meaning of the law requires conviction where the defendant knows "that the substance he is dealing with is some unspecified substance listed on the federal drug schedules."[118] Punishment schemes (prison terms, fines, and supervision) are established under the CSA based upon the schedule of the substances underlying the violation. The penalty structure for simple possession offenses is also affected by the accused's criminal history of prior convictions for similar offenses.[119] The penalty structure for trafficking offenses is impacted by the schedule designation of the drug, whether death or serious bodily injury resulted from the use of the drug, the weight of the drug involved, and whether the accused has prior convictions for similar offenses.[120] Penalties are also enhanced for distributions to minors.[121] The most serious penalties were enacted for a "continuing criminal enterprise."[122]

---

[116] Congressional findings make it clear that it would be contrary to the statute's enforcement objectives to differentiate between drugs that move across state lines and those that only move intrastate, since both types will ultimately affect interstate commerce. 21 U.S.C. § 801(3)-(5).

[117] 21 U.S.C. § 841(a)(1).

[118] McFadden v. United States, 135 S.Ct. 2298, 2304 (2015). See also United States v. Andino, 627 F.3d 41, 45–46 (2d Cir. 2010); United States v. Gamez-Gonzalez, 319 F.3d 695, 699 (5th Cir. 2003); United States v. Martinez, 301 F.3d 860, 865 (7th Cir. 2002).

[119] 21 U.S.C. § 844.

[120] 21 U.S.C. § 841(b).

[121] 21 U.S.C. § 859(a). Triple penalties may also be imposed for a repeated violation of this section. 21 U.S.C. § 859(b).

[122] 21 U.S.C. § 848. A person is engaged in a "continuing criminal enterprise" if (1) he violates a provision of the Act which is punishable as a felony and which is (2) part of a continuing series of violations in which he supervised 5 or more people who acted in concert with him and (3) from which he obtains substantial income or resources.

FEDERAL CONTROLLED SUBSTANCES ACT
AT A GLANCE

Scheduling Criteria	Examples of Drugs Included
Schedule I High potential for abuse, no accepted medical use, lack of accepted safety for use of the drug.	Heroin, LSD, MDMA, Marijuana, Mescaline, Psilocybin, Psilocyn, Synthetic cannabinoids
Schedule II High potential for abuse, accepted medical use, abuse may lead to severe psychological or physical dependence.	Opium, Cocaine, Fentanyl, Methadone
Schedule III Less potential for abuse than I or II, accepted medical use, abuse may lead to moderate or low physical dependence or high psychological dependence.	Amphetamines, Anabolic steroids
Schedule IV Low potential for abuse relative to drugs in Schedule III, accepted medical use, abuse may lead to limited physical or psychological dependence relative to drugs in Schedule III.	Barbital, phenobarbital
Schedule V Low potential for abuse relative to drugs in Schedule IV, accepted medical use, abuse may lead to limited physical or psychological dependence relative to drugs in Schedule IV.	Cough syrups containing codeine

Under the Controlled Substances Act, the Drug Enforcement Administration (DEA) has the authority to schedule, de-schedule, or reschedule substances.[123] Proceedings to add, delete, or change the schedule of a drug or other substance may be initiated by the DEA, the Department of Health and Human Services (HHS), or by petition from

---

[123] The authority has been provided to the Attorney General under the Comprehensive Crime Control Act of 1984 (Pub.L. 98–473), and the Attorney General has delegated this authority under 21 U.S.C. 811 to the Drug Enforcement Agency (DEA) Administrator. 28 CFR 0.100. The delegation of legislative authority was made in order to ensure current updating by a less cumbersome procedure and a more informed body.

any interested party, including drug manufacturers, medical or pharmaceutical associations, state or local government agencies, public interest groups, and individual citizens.[124] When a petition is received by the DEA, the agency conducts its own investigation of the drug and requests an evaluation and recommendation from HHS as to whether the substance should be scheduled and the appropriate schedule.[125] The CSA requires the DEA to give notice and an opportunity to be heard to all concerned persons; notifications appear in the Federal Register. The CSA provides for hearing and appellate procedures for interested parties to object to decisions on the DEA concerning scheduling actions, but the possibility of overruling the decisions is extremely limited because great deference is afforded the determinations by the DEA. In addition to the regular scheduling authority of the CSA, the DEA also has the power to establish temporary emergency scheduling of substances by the Comprehensive Crime Control Act of 1984.[126] In 1993, there was an emergency scheduling of the designer drug "Nexus" in the Federal Register[127] and five synthetic cannabinoids were added to Schedule I under the emergency scheduling provisions in 2010.[128] The up-to-date schedules are codified in the Code of Federal Regulations.[129]

On April 13, 2009, the Ryan Haight Online Pharmacy Consumer Protection Act of 2008 became effective. This Act amended the CSA by adding a series of regulatory requirements and criminal provisions intended to combat the unlawful distribution of controlled substances through online pharmacy websites. An online pharmacy is defined as:[130]

> (A) means a person, entity, or Internet site, whether in the United States or abroad, that knowingly or intentionally delivers, distributes, or dispenses, or offers or attempts to deliver, distribute, or dispense, a controlled substance by means of the Internet; and
>
> (B) does not include—
>
>> (i) manufacturers or distributors registered under subsection (a), (b), (d), or (e) of section 823 of this title who do not dispense controlled substances to an unregistered individual or entity;

---

[124] U.S. Department of Justice, Drug Enforcement Administration, *Drugs of Abuse: A DEA Resource Guide*, 2015 Edition at p. 8.

[125] Id.

[126] The Comprehensive Crime Control Act of 1984 (Pub.L. 98–473) was enacted on October 12, 1984.

[127] 58 Fed.Reg. 58819 (11/4/93), 59 Fed.Reg. 671 (1/6/94).

[128] Schedules of Controlled Substances: Temporary Placement of Five Synthetic Cannabinoids Into Schedule I, Federal Register, Vol. 76, No. 40, pp. 11075–11078)(March 1, 2011)(available at: http://www.gpo.gov/fdsys/pkg/FR-2011-03-01/pdf/2011-4428.pdf)(last accessed December 8, 2016).

[129] *See* 21 C.F.R. §§ 1308.11–1308.15.

[130] 21 U.S.C. § 802(52).

(ii) nonpharmacy practitioners who are registered under section 823(f) of this title and whose activities are authorized by that registration;

(iii) any hospital or other medical facility that is operated by an agency of the United States (including the Armed Forces), provided such hospital or other facility is registered under section 823(f) of this title;

(iv) a health care facility owned or operated by an Indian tribe or tribal organization, only to the extent such facility is carrying out a contract or compact under the Indian Self-Determination and Education Assistance Act [25 U.S.C. 450 et seq.];

(v) any agent or employee of any hospital or facility referred to in clause (iii) or (iv), provided such agent or employee is lawfully acting in the usual course of business or employment, and within the scope of the official duties of such agent or employee, with such hospital or facility, and, with respect to agents or employees of health care facilities specified in clause (iv), only to the extent such individuals are furnishing services pursuant to the contracts or compacts described in such clause;

(vi) mere advertisements that do not attempt to facilitate an actual transaction involving a controlled substance;

(vii) a person, entity, or Internet site that is not in the United States and does not facilitate the delivery, distribution, or dispensing of a controlled substance by means of the Internet to any person in the United States;

(viii) a pharmacy registered under section 823(f) of this title whose dispensing of controlled substances via the Internet consists solely of—

(I) refilling prescriptions for controlled substances in schedule III, IV, or V, as defined in paragraph (55); or

(II) filling new prescriptions for controlled substances in schedule III, IV, or V, as defined in paragraph (56); or

(ix) any other persons for whom the Attorney General and the Secretary have jointly, by regulation, found it to be consistent with effective controls against diversion and otherwise consistent with the public health and safety to exempt from the definition of an "online pharmacy".

The Act makes it illegal under federal law to deliver, distribute, or dispense a controlled substance online unless the online pharmacy holds a modification of DEA registration authorizing it to operate.[131]

2.   CONTROLLED SUBSTANCE ANALOGUES

In 1986, Congress enacted the Controlled Substances Analogue Enforcement Act (Analogue Act). The Analogue Act makes illegal all substances structurally or pharmacologically similar to Schedule I or II controlled substances that are intended for human consumption.[132] A "controlled substance analogue" is defined as a substance:[133]

(i)   the chemical structure of which is substantially similar to the chemical structure of a controlled substance in schedule I or II;

(ii) which has a stimulant, depressant, or hallucinogenic effect on the central nervous system that is substantially similar to or greater than the stimulant, depressant, or hallucinogenic effect on the central nervous system of a controlled substance in schedule I or II; or

(iii) with respect to a particular person, which such person represents or intends to have a stimulant, depressant, or hallucinogenic effect on the central nervous system that is substantially similar to or greater than the stimulant, depressant, or hallucinogenic effect on the central nervous system of a controlled substance in schedule I or II.

With the Analogue Act, Congress intended to prevent the distribution of newly created and unscheduled drugs that have not yet listed on the schedules but that have similar effects on the human body.[134] "A controlled substance analogue shall, to the extent intended for human consumption, be treated, for purposes of any Federal law as a controlled substance in schedule I."[135] The interaction between the CSA and the Analogue Act prohibits the distribution of controlled substance analogues, even if not listed on the CSA scheduled.

In *McFadden v. United States*,[136] the defendant was convicted of distributing an analogue substances in the form of "bath salts"[137] after

---

[131] U.S. Department of Justice, Drug Enforcement Administration, *Drugs of Abuse: A DEA Resource Guide*, 2015 Edition at p. 13.

[132] Id. at p. 10.

[133] 21 U.S.C. § 802(32)(A).

[134] United States v. Klecker, 348 F.3d 69, 70 (4th Cir. 2003).

[135] 21 U.S.C. § 813.

[136] 135 S.Ct. 2298 (2015).

[137] "Bath salts" is a term used for various recreational drugs used to produce effects similar to those of cocaine, methamphetamine, and other controlled substances. The products sold by McFadden were "white and off-white powders packaged in small plastic bags . . . . containing, among other substances, 3,4-Methylenedioxypyrovalerone, also known as MDPV; and 4-Methyl-N-ethylcathinone, also known as 4-MEC [that were] capable of producing effects

the jury was instructed that it need only find that McFadden intended the substance to be consumed by humans. McFadden appealed to the Fourth Circuit Court of Appeals and ultimately to the United States Supreme Court alleging that the jury should have been instructed that it must find "he knew the substances he distributed had chemical structures and effects on the central nervous system substantially similar to those of controlled substances."[138] The Supreme Court held that the jury instructions were erroneous, but that McFadden's proffered instruction went too far. Instead, where the controlled substance at issue is an analogue, the prosecution must only establish that the defendant knew he was dealing with "a controlled substance." This knowledge requirement is met "if the defendant knew that the substance was controlled under the CSA or the Analogue Act, even if he did not know its identity [or] if the defendant knew the specific features of the substance that makes it a 'controlled substance analogue.' "[139] On remand, the Fourth Circuit found that the "jury instructions omitted the required element that McFadden knew either that the bath salts were regulated as controlled substances or that the bath salts had the features of controlled substance analogues."[140] The appellate court vacated several convictions, but affirmed the convictions for distributions that occurred after the date of certain recorded phone calls involving McFadden.[141] The court held that McFadden's statements in those calls demonstrated his knowledge of the chemical structures and physiological effects of the bath salts.[142]

§15.14 STATES

The need to solve the "drug problem" has been a recurrent theme of political and social commentary in the United States since the 1960's. Drug control is one of the largest areas of overlap between the federal and state governments, with criminal prosecution possible in either or both jurisdictions for the same conduct. Because the prosecutions are by separate sovereigns, dual prosecutions do not violate constitutional double jeopardy protections.[143] The Department of Justice has adopted an internal policy known as the "Petite Policy," which allows a federal

---

on the central nervous system similar to those that controlled substances (such as cocaine, methamphetaimine, and methcathinone) produce." 135 S.Ct. at 2302–2303.

[138] 135 S.Ct. at 2300.

[139] 135 S.Ct. at 2302.

[140] United States v. McFadden, 823 F.3d 217, 224 (4th Cir. 2016).

[141] 823 F.3d at 227–228.

[142] Among other statements, McFadden explicitly compared the substances to cocaine and crystal meth. 823 F.3d at 227.

[143] The dual sovereignty doctrine allows the federal government and a state government or two state governments to bring successive prosecutions for offenses arising from the same criminal act. *See* Rinaldi v. United States, 434 U.S. 22, 28 (1977)(per curiam)(dictum); Abbate v. United States, 359 U.S. 187, 195–196 (1959); Bartkus v. Illinois, 359 U.S. 121, 128–129 (1959).

prosecution following a state trial based on the same conduct only with prior approval from the Assistant United States Attorney General.[144] However, this is merely an internal policy, and provides no substantive rights to defendants.[145] Some states, however, prohibit successive federal-state prosecutions for the same conduct by state statutes.[146]

The Federal Controlled Substances Act served as a model for the drafting of a uniform state law which has now been adopted in 48 states and the District of Columbia;[147] but with time the state statutory schemes have begun to show variety as the states made additions and modifications to the schedules.[148] The Uniform Controlled Substances Act has the same objectives and scheduling scheme as its Federal counterpart. In each state a state board or agency is delegated the authority to administer the Act and add, delete, or reschedule substances.

Unlike the Federal Act, the Uniform Act does not include the offense of "continuing criminal enterprise."[149] None of the offenses correspond to exact penalties as in the Federal Act, the specifics being left to the state legislatures, but the Uniform Act was written with the idea that the penalties would mirror those of Federal law. The Uniform Act contains different provisions for the distribution of controlled substances to minors, requiring that there be a two year age difference between the purchaser and the seller.[150] Additionally, the Uniform Act limits the penalty of possession of marijuana based on the amount in possession.[151]

---

[144] US Department of Justice, US Attorney's Manual § 9–2.031 (2007)(describing the Petite Policy procedures). *See also* United States v. Gomez, 776 F.2d 542, 550 (5th Cir. 1985)(Petite policy only applies if the defendant is actually brought to trial in state court).

[145] *See. e.g.,* United States v. Peterson, 233 F.3d 101, 104 (1sr Cir. 2000); United States v. Cote, 544 F.3d 88, 104 (2d Cir. 2008); United States v. Jackson, 327 F.3d 273, 295 (4th Cir. 2003).

[146] *See* Va. Code 19.2–294: "[I]f the same act be a violation of both a state and federal statute, a prosecution under the federal statute shall be a bar to a prosecution under the state statute. . . For purposes of this section, a prosecution under a federal statute shall be deemed to be commenced once jeopardy has attached."

[147] New Hampshire and Vermont have not adopted the Uniform Controlled Substances Act. N.H. retains its own Controlled Drug Act enacted in 1969 and Vt. its Possession and Control of Regulated Drugs Act of 1967. See, N.H.Rev.Stat.Ann. 318–B:1 (2006) and Vt.Stat.18 § 4201 et seq. (2005).

[148] For example, Virginia does not treat marijuana as a Schedule I substance (see Va. Code §§ 18.2–248, 248.01, 250.1), has six schedules of drugs (Va. Code § 54.1–3400 *et seq.*), and criminalizes the possession and distribution of more synthetic cannabinoids.

[149] States have enacted "drug kingpin" laws similar to the continuing criminal enterprise provisions of the federal law. *See* Va. Code § 18.2–248.1.

[150] Uniform Controlled Substances Act of 1994 § 409 (2006). A double penalty is imposed on anyone 18 or over who distributes to anyone who is at least two years his junior.

[151] Uniform Controlled Substances Act of 1994 § 406 (2006). The Uniform Act provides more liberal treatment of small scale marijuana offenses than the Federal Act. Section 406 provides that (1) may not knowingly or intentionally possess a controlled substance unless the substance was obtained directly from, or pursuant to, a valid prescription or order of a practitioner, (2) if possession of marijuana is less than 29 grams, then the penalty is a misdemeanor, and (3) possession of more than 29 grams of marijuana may be penalized by a felony charge. States have taken various approaches toward the punishment of small scale

The greatest variation between the state and federal statutory schemes may be in the treatment of marijuana. As of November 11, 2016, 29 states and the District of Columbia have enacted laws legalizing marijuana in some form, primarily for medical use of marijuana, and 7 states and the District of Columbia permit recreational use of small amounts of marijuana.[152] In 2005, the United States Supreme Court held that states cannot prohibit the federal government from enforcing federal controlled substances laws against citizens in states which permit medical marijuana use,[153] and the conflict between state and federal law is expected to become more of an issue.

In 2009, United States Deputy Attorney General David Ogden issued a memo to federal prosecutors (the "Ogden memo")[154] advising them that it would not be an efficient use of resources to prosecute individuals with serious medical conditions who use marijuana as part of a recommended treatment regimen consistent with applicable state law, essentially instructing federal prosecutors to "stand down" from medical marijuana cases and defer to state law. This memo concerned only personal use, not the manufacturing or distribution, of marijuana. Since then, several states, including Colorado, New Mexico, and Maine, have allowed for the operation of state-licensed medical marijuana

---

marijuana offenses and not all have adopted § 409, although most states have retained marijuana as a Schedule I substance.

[152] See http://www.governing.com/gov-data/state-marijuana-laws-map-medical-recreational. html (last accessed December 9, 2016).

The state provisions differ on the covered medical uses (restricted by type of illness) and whether the provisions protect visitors who were prescribed marijuana in their home state (reciprocity). *Compare* Haw. Rev. Stat. §§ 329–121 to 329–128 *with* Me. Rev. Stat. tit. 22, § 2383–B(5), (6)(1999) (amended 2001) and Mich. Comp. Law § 333.26424(j)(2008).

The state laws have codified the medical necessity defense that had been upheld in some court decisions. *See* Jenks v. State, 582 So.2d 676, 679 (Fla.Dist.Ct.App.1991) (holding statute listing marijuana as a Schedule I substance does not preclude the defense of medical necessity for a defendant who allegedly used marijuana to treat nausea in connection with his AIDS' treatment); State v. Bachman, 61 Haw. 71, 595 P.2d 287, 288 (1979) (holding a medical necessity defense could be asserted to a marijuana possession charge with competent medical testimony); State v. Hastings, 118 Idaho 854, 801 P.2d 563, 565 (1990) (holding defendant who was charged with possession of marijuana was entitled to present evidence relating to the common-law defense of necessity in connection with her claim that she suffered from rheumatoid arthritis and used marijuana to control pain and muscle spasms). *See also* People v. Mower, 28 Cal.4th 457, 122 Cal.Rptr.2d 326, 49 P.3d 1067, 1071 (2002); State v. Hanson, 468 N.W.2d 77, 77B78 (Minn.Ct.App.1991); State v. Williams, 93 Wash.App. 340, 968 P.2d 26, 28 (1998); (Seeley v. State, 132 Wash.2d 776, 940 P.2d 604, 606B07 (1997)); Tate, 505 A.2d at 942; State v. Bachman, 61 Haw. 71, 595 P.2d 287, 288 (1979); State v. Hastings, 118 Idaho 854, 801 P.2d 563, 564 (1990); State v. Poling, 207 W.Va. 299, 531 S.E.2d 678, 680–081 (2000).

[153] Gonzales v. Raich, 545 U.S. 1 (2005). In a 6–3 decision, the Court ruled that federal congressional authority to regulate the interstate market in illegal drugs extends to small quantities of doctor-recommended marijuana consumed under California's Compassionate Use Act. The holding did not affect the legality of the state medical marijuana laws, but did put medical marijuana users at risk of criminal prosecution by the federal government.

[154] David W. Ogden, Memorandum for Selected United States Attorneys, "Investigations and Prosecutions in States Authorizing the Medical Use of Marijuana, October 19, 2009 (available at: https://www.justice.gov/opa/blog/memorandum-selected-united-state-attorneys-investigations-and-prosecutions-states)(last accessed December 9, 2016).

producers and providers.[155] Other states, including Arizona, Delaware, New Jersey, Rhode Island, and Vermont, have similar laws, but have either suspended or not yet implemented their medical marijuana distribution programs. In response, the federal government issued a series of memos advising federal prosecutors that the Ogden memo was never intended to shield the manufacturing and distribution of marijuana,[156] and setting priorities for the enforcing the CSA as to marijuana-related conduct:[157]

- Preventing the distribution of marijuana to minors;

- Preventing revenue from the sale of marijuana from going to criminal enterprises, gangs, and cartels;

- Preventing the diversion of marijuana from states where it is legal under state law in some form to other states;

- Preventing state-authorized marijuana activity from being used as a cover or pretext for the trafficking of other illegal drugs or other legal activity;

- Preventing violence and the use of firearms in the cultivation and distribution of marijuana;

- Preventing drugged driving and the exacerbation of other adverse public health consequences associated with marijuana use;

- Preventing the growing of marijuana on public lands and the attendant public safety and environmental dangers posed by marijuana production on public lands; and

- Preventing marijuana possession or use on federal property.

§15.15 LEGAL CHALLENGES

A variety of constitutional challenges have been mounted against both the Federal Act and the Uniform Controlled Substances Act. Of these claims, the assertions of a denial of equal protection of the laws or of a due process infraction (including vagueness) have been most often used. A subsidiary, but often mooted, charge is that the scheduling

---

[155] Colo. Rev. Stat. 12–43.3–101 *et seq.;* Me. Rev. Stat. Tit. 22, §§ 2422; 2425; N.M. Stat. Ann. § 30–31C–1.

[156] James M. Cole, Deputy Attorney General, "Guidance Regarding the Ogden Memo in Jurisdictions Seeking to Authorize Marijuana for Medical Use," June 29, 2011 (available at: https://www.justice.gov/sites/default/files/oip/legacy/2014/07/23/dag-guidance-2011-for-medical -marijuana-use.pdf)(last accessed December 9, 2016).

[157] James M. Cole, Deputy Attorney General, "Guidance Regarding Marijuana Enforcement," August 29, 2013 (available at: https://www.justice.gov/iso/opa/resources/305201 3829132756857467.pdf)(last accessed December 9, 2016); and James M. Cole, Deputy Attorney General, "Guidance Regarding Marijuana Related Financial Crimes," February 14, 2014 (available at: https://www.justice.gov/sites/default/files/usao-wdwa/legacy/2014/02/14/DAG Memo %20-%20Guidance%20Regarding%20Marijuana%20Related%20Financial%20Crimes%202%2014% 2014%20(2).pdf)(last accessed December 9, 2016).

technique for controlled substances impermissibly delegates an exclusively legislative function to an administrative agency.

Objections have been lodged to the Controlled Substance Analogue Enforcement Act on constitutional grounds. In *United States v. Fisher*,[158] it was argued that the Controlled Substance Analogue Act was impermissibly vague. The court, however, stated that the Act was not unconstitutionally vague as applied to gamma-butyrolactone (GBL) as an analogue of listed controlled substance of gamma-hydroxybutyrate acid (GHB), and that "persons of ordinary intelligence would be able to determine that GBL, which metabolizes into GHB upon ingestion, would meet definition of a controlled substance analogue."[159]

State statutes have also been challenged as vague. Such challenges have generally been unsuccessful due to the determination that the federal statute is not unconstitutionally vague.[160] For example, in *People v. Frantz*, defendant acknowledged that the similar federal statute was determined not to be unconstitutionally vague. The Colorado Court of Appeals adopted the analysis of the Court in *United States v. Granberry*,[161] which held that the statute states that drugs which have been chemically designed to be similar to controlled substances, but which are not themselves listed on the controlled substance schedules, will nonetheless be considered as Schedule I substances if the requirements are met under 21 U.S.C. § 802 (32). The Court held that this language was not impermissibly vague.

The scheduling of both cocaine and marijuana has been vigorously opposed. The decisions from the federal courts are unanimous in upholding the CSA classification of cocaine as a Schedule II drug.[162] Defendants have argued that the classification violates the equal protection guarantee. The courts have responded that since there is no constitutional right to possess, use, or sell cocaine, the legislation must simply bear a rational relationship to a legitimate state interest. The decisions further conclude that the criteria for classification are rationally related to the legitimate legislative interest in mitigating drug abuse. Most state courts have rejected a similar contention of unconstitutionality.[163]

---

[158] 289 F.3d 1329 (11th Cir.2002).

[159] Id.

[160] See, e.g., People v. Frantz, 114 P.3d 34 (Colo.App.2004).

[161] 916 F.2d 1008 (5th Cir.1990).

[162] *See, e.g.,* United States v. Caseer, 399 F.3d 828 (6th Cir.2005); United States v. White, 2006 WL 1360165 (D.Kan.2006). See also, United States v. Vila, 599 F.2d 21 (2d Cir.1979); United States v. Solow, 574 F.2d 1318 (5th Cir.1978); and United States v. Stieren, 608 F.2d 1135 (8th Cir.1979).

[163] *See* Cardwell v. State, 264 Ark. 862, 575 S.W.2d 682 (1979); People v. Stout, 116 Mich.App. 726, 323 N.W.2d 532 (1982); State v. Dudley, 104 Idaho 849, 664 P.2d 277 (1983); State v. Harris, 637 S.W.2d 896 (Tenn.Cr.App.1982); State v. McMinn, 197 N.J.Super. 621, 485 A.2d 1072 (1984).

Over the last several decades, groups such as National Organization for the Reform of Marijuana Laws (NORML) and other groups have presented unsuccessful objections to scheduling of marijuana under Schedule I in the federal statute.[164] In *Louisiana Affiliate of NORML v. Guste*,[165] it was held that the federal law does not unconstitutionally infringe upon rights of privacy or equal protection or transgress the prohibition against cruel and unusual punishment by including marijuana in Schedule I. Although marijuana remains a Schedule I drug, numerous groups and individuals have continued to challenge the classification based on medicinal values.[166]

The delegation of scheduling authority to an administrative agency within the executive branch of government has also been the subject of constitutional challenge as an unconstitutional delegation of legislative power. Such an objection has been uniformly unsuccessful at the federal level,[167] but a few state courts have balked at this delegation of authority.[168] In *United States v. Pastor*,[169] the federal court held that the extensive legislative history and congressional intent evident in the statute indicated that the scheduling authority was delegated to provide flexibility and speed in scheduling of substances. This valid purpose, combined with procedural safeguards and the availability of judicial review, was held to be sufficient protection against arbitrary action. The majority of state courts have adopted a like reasoning.[170]

---

[164] *See* NORML v. Bell, 488 F.Supp. 123 (D.D.C.1980). *See also* Alliance for Cannabis Therapeutics v. D.E.A., 15 F.3d 1131 (D.C.Cir.1994). Alliance for Cannabis Therapeutics v. D.E.A., 930 F.2d 936 (D.C.Cir.1991). In both cases, a rescheduling to Schedule II was unsuccessfully litigated to enable doctors to prescribe marijuana for therapeutic purposes.

[165] 423 U.S. 867 (1975).

[166] For more information regarding marijuana and the courts, *see* David R. Ford, Marijuana: Not Guilty as Charged (2006); Dana Graham, "Decriminalization of Marijuana: An Analysis of the Laws in the United States and the Netherlands and Suggestions for Reform," 23 Loy. L.A. Int'l & Comp. L. Rev. 297 (2001). *See also*, M. Soler, "Of Cannabis and the Courts: A Critical Examination of Constitutional Challenges to Statutory Marihuana Prohibitions," 6 CONN. L. REV. 601 (1974).

[167] *See generally* Anno., "Validity of Delegation to Drug Enforcement Administration of Authority to Schedule or Reschedule Drugs Subject to Controlled Substances Act," 47 A.L.R.Fed. 869 (updated 2003).

[168] In Utah, South Dakota, and Georgia, the delegation of legislative power has been held unconstitutional. State v. Gallion, 572 P.2d 683 (Utah 1977); State v. Johnson, 84 S.D. 556, 173 N.W.2d 894 (1970); Sundberg v. State, 234 Ga. 482, 216 S.E.2d 332 (1975). In Mississippi, Louisiana and Washington the state's delegation of scheduling authority to a federal administrative agency has been voided. Howell v. State, 300 So.2d 774 (Miss.1974); State v. Rodriguez, 379 So.2d 1084 (La.1980); and State v. Dougall, 89 Wash.2d 118, 570 P.2d 135 (1977). *Contra* State v. Ciccarelli, 55 Md.App. 150, 461 A.2d 550 (1983).

[169] 557 F.2d 930 (2d Cir.1977).

[170] State v. Reed, 14 Ohio App.3d 63, 470 N.E.2d 150 (1983).

V. TRIAL AIDS

§15.16 EXPERT QUALIFICATIONS

Formal education in chemistry, pharmacology, or a related branch of science is generally required for laboratory analysis of seized drugs. However, law enforcement officers frequently testify about the results of field tests and some courts have allowed police officers to testify in narcotics cases based on technical training and field experience rather than solely based on their education.[171] In drug cases, users have testified as to the identity of a controlled substance based on their prior experience with the drug.[172]

Professional guidelines from ASTM and SWGDRUG include recommendations for the training and education of forensic drug analysts.[173] Both organizations recommend:

> [N]ew analysts shall have at least a bachelor's degree or equivalent (generally, a three to four year post-secondary degree) in a natural/physical science. The individual shall have successfully completed lecture and associated laboratory classes in general, organic and analytical chemistry.[174]

In addition to the basic education, SWGDRUG recommends extensive initial training,[175] and continuing professional development of a minimum of twenty hours per year.[176] Attorneys should review these industry standards to ensure the analyst in their case has met the recommended level of education and training, including continuing education and professional development.

---

[171] On the admission of estimates of quantities of drugs possessed by arrestees for sale, see, United States v. Pugliese, 712 F.2d 1574 (2d Cir.1983) where a DEA agent was permitted to give his expert opinion as to the quantity of a typical heroin purchase for an addict's own use. Cf.: State v. Ogg, 243 N.W.2d 620 (Iowa 1976), holding that police testimony that the amount of LSD "far exceeds what one might possess for personal use" (46 tablets) was improperly admitted as an outright opinion as to defendant's guilt on one of the essential elements of the crime.

[172] The narcotic quality of a substance may be shown by testimony of the addict-user: Howard v. State, 496 P.2d 657 (Alaska 1972). Testimony of witness, an experienced user, that white powder was high quality heroin, was sufficient to support finding that substance imported was heroin: U.S. v. Clark, 613 F.2d 391, 5 Fed. R. Evid. Serv. 463 (2d Cir.1979). See generally, Anno., "Competency of Drug Addict or User to Identify Suspect Material as Narcotic or Controlled Substance," 95 A.L.R.3d 978 (updated July 2003).

[173] ASTM E2326-14: "Standard Practice for Education and Training of Seized-Drug Analysts," ASTM Int'l, 2014; SWGDRUG Recommendations Part II, "Education and Training," Version 7.1, June 9, 2016.

[174] SWGDRUG Recommendations Part II, "Education and Training," Version 7.1, June 9, 2016 at p. 4.

[175] SWGDRUG specifically endorses the European Network of Forensic Science Institutes (ENFSI)'s "Education and Training Outline for Forensic Drug Practitioners" and recommends its use in the development of training programs. Id at pp. 5–6. The ENFSI document is available at: http://enfsi.eu/documents/other-publications/ (last accessed December 8, 2016).

[176] SWGDRUG Recommendations Part II, "Education and Training," Version 7.1, June 9, 2016 at p. 4.

§15.17 EVIDENCE ISSUES

1. GENERAL ADMISSIBILITY

The nature of controlled substances can be proved by competent expert testimony. Where a qualified expert stated he knew the tests which were used to determine whether a substance was morphine, and that he conducted the proper tests, his identification testimony was admissible even though on cross examination he could not state the names or number of the tests he used.[177] An expert's testimony will be inadmissible, however, if the court determines the methodology used is not sufficiently reliable to identify the substance at issue.[178]

The United States Supreme Court has held unconstitutional a state statute making the status of drug addiction a crime in itself.[179]

2. QUALITY CONTROL

Even under optimal conditions using well-validated analytical methods by well-trained analysts, analysis of an unknown substance involves a level of uncertainty. Analytical procedures have technical limitations and analysis always involves the potential for human error. As a matter of due diligence, attorneys must investigate the reliability and limitations of the analytical results that will be used as evidence. The first step in that investigation requires review of the underlying data and supporting documentation of the analysis, including relevant laboratory validation and quality assurance records.[180]

---

[177] State v. Baca, 81 N.M. 686, 472 P.2d 651 (1970), cert. denied 81 N.M. 721, 472 P.2d 984 (1970).

[178] State v. Ward, 364 N.C. 133, 694 S.E.2d 738 (2010). The NC Supreme Court referred to the 2009 report of the National Academy of Sciences on forensic science and stated that the field of forensic science has come under acute scrutiny on a nationwide basis. 364 N.C. at 141, 694 S.E.2d at 743. After reviewing the "visual comparison" method used by the analyst, the Court concluded that the state had not carried its burden of demonstrating the sufficient reliability of the evidence and that the trial court had abused its discretion by admitted the chemist's testimony. 364 N.C. at 148, 694 S.E.2d at 747–748.

[179] Robinson v. California, 370 U.S. 660 (1962), rehearing denied 371 U.S. 905 (1962). The United States Supreme Court has also made a distinction between criminalizing a drug addiction and behavior related to the addiction, such as using an illegal controlled substance. Mitchell v. Hood, 145 F.Supp.2d 1188 (D.Or.2001).

[180] For forensic science analyses conducted in crime laboratories, laboratory accreditation standards provide guidelines for the validation process. The American Society of Crime Laboratory Directors (ASCLD) and its accrediting body (ASCLD/LAB: ASCLD-Laboratory Accreditation Board) have adopted an international standard for the International Accreditation Program. (http://www.ascld-lab.org/acredidation-programs/) This standard, ISO/IEC 17025:2005, was developed by the International Organization for Standardization (ISO) and the International Electrotechnical Commission (IEC) as a guideline for testing laboratories.

ISO/IEC 17025:2005 specifies the general requirements for competence to do testing using standard methods, non-standard methods, and laboratory-developed methods. It is applicable to all organizations performing tests, including submitting laboratories, consulting laboratories, and laboratories where testing forms part of inspection and product certification. ISO/IEC 17025:2005 is applicable to all laboratories regardless of the number of personnel or the extent of the scope of testing activities. ISO/IEC 17025:2005 is for use by laboratories in developing their management system for quality, administrative, and technical operations. Laboratory customers, regulatory authorities, and accreditation bodies may also use the

A comprehensive discovery request should include the following:

(1) The Analysis

- Contemporaneous notes made during the analysis, including all photographs, diagrams and descriptions of the analysis conducted;

- Data, including electronic data, generated as part of the analysis;

- Chain of custody documentation regarding all samples analyzed;

- Documentation regarding the collection of all physical evidence;

- All information concerning any review conducted by a peer or supervisor, including all documentation and opinions rendered;

- Information generated by any database searches; and

- The underlying basis of the opinion including identification of any material relied on in forming that particular opinion.

(2) Manuals and Validation Studies

- Procedure manuals for any technique used in the analysis; and

- Validation studies, including data generated, for any technique used in the analysis.

(3) Quality Control

- Standard operating procedures concerning quality assurance and control;

- External audit reports;

- Internal audit reports;

- Internal quality control documents concerning any errors or "unexpected results";

- Contamination logs;

- Corrective action documentation for any error or "unexpected result;"

---

standard in confirming or recognizing the competence of laboratories. Compliance with ISO/IEC 17025:2005, however, does not itself demonstrate the competence of the laboratory to produce reliable and accurate results. It is a guideline, not the definitive checklist.

Section 5.10.1 of ISO 17025:2005 requires documentation of all information "necessary for the interpretation of the test or calibration results and all information required by the method used."

- Records of any relevant internal review or audits conducted for any reason other than accreditation purposes; and

- Calibration and maintenance records for all instrumentation used in the analysis.

(4) The Analyst

- Curriculum vita or resume of the analyst;

- Listing of cases in which the analyst has previously testified;

- Information concerning inadequate performance;

- Records concerning any error or "unexpected result;"

- Proficiency test results; and

- Certification records.

3.   QUANTITATION

The government may seek to establish through expert testimony that, even though only a fraction of a larger amount of a seized substance was analyzed for the presence of a controlled substance, the entire quantity confiscated can be inferred to be of the same quality as the sample which has been tested. Such an inference from the testing of a sample generally appears in prosecutions where a statutory minimum quantity must be established to sustain the validity of the prosecution[181] or where a certain quantity is alleged in order to prove the intent to sell the controlled substance[182] or to disprove its possession for personal use.[183] The common theme running through the cases and research articles, which discuss the propriety of crime laboratory sampling techniques, is that the sample tested must be representative of the whole lot[184] and that the selection of the sample must be random in nature.

The sample size and the randomness of its selection can, according to statistical principles, be the linchpin upon which conclusions concerning the nature of the entire lot can properly turn.[185] Sample size

---

[181] United States v. White, 2 Fed.Appx. 671 (8th Cir.2001).

[182] Gerbier v. Holmes, 280 F.3d 297 (3d Cir.2002).

[183] United States v. Banuelos, 322 F.3d 700 (9th Cir.2003). See also, United States v. Hillmann, 102 Fed.Appx. 527 (9th Cir.2004)(the government failed to introduce sufficient evidence of intent to distribute).

[184] See Jos J.A.M. Weusten, "Representative Drug Sampling: Sample Size Calculations Revisited," 56 J.FORENSIC SCI. 501–505 (2010). See also State v. Absher, 34 N.C.App. 197, 237 S.E.2d 749 (1977)(chemist's visual examination of the entire lot of marijuana and PCP tablets was sufficient to prove the commonality of the whole). Some courts have held that a failure to test the entire batch goes to the weight rather than the admissibility of the expert's testimony. People v. Kline, 41 Ill.App.3d 261, 354 N.E.2d 46 (1976), People v. McCord, 63 Ill.App.3d 542, 20 Ill.Dec. 257, 379 N.E.2d 1325 (1978).

[185] Sampling methods and plans have been recommended by SWGDRUG. See SWGDRUG Recommendations Part III A, "Methods of Analysis/Sampling Seized Drugs for Qualitative Analysis," Revision 5.1, January 27, 2011, pp. 7–13.

selection tables are available as are the rules for representative sampling[186] but the courts have not generally enforced adherence to these statistical guidelines. In *Morrison v. State*,[187] for example, the police took a pinch from each bale of green plant material totaling 467 pounds in all. The sum total of the pinches amounted to 18.1 grams, which upon testing proved to be marijuana. The court found the inference strong and persuasive that the untested material was the same as that tested, in spite of the fact that a random "pinch" does not comport with a table of random numbers, a more statistically fine-tuned approach to randomness.[188]

Some state courts and some state legislatures[189] have adopted a rule requiring the prosecution to prove that the defendant possessed a usable quantity of a controlled substance. The reasoning underlying this rule is either that the courts interpret the legislative intent in proscribing drug use to be to sanction the possession of more than a mere trace of a controlled substance, even though the amount suffices for qualitative analysis in the crime laboratory, or that the prosecution has conclusively failed to prove a knowing possession of a controlled substance when a usable quantity has not been demonstrated.[190]

No agreement exists among the cases as to the exact amount necessary to constitute a usable quantity. In *Cooper v. State*,[191] less than two ounces of a loose leafy substance which tested as marijuana was inadequate as a usable quantity, but in *People v. Stark*,[192] 0.16 grams of cocaine scraped from a crusher and a screen was considered to be more than a mere trace.

The majority of courts which have rejected the usable quantity rule have adopted a measurable quantity standard which requires only that the amount in question be large enough to be analyzed. To the chemist, the usable quantity rule mandates the quantification of a suspect sample as well as a determination of its nature. A measurable quantity criterion might have the same outcome as a usable quantity rule where the identification of a substance by testing will not be adequate to prove it to be measurable.

Under the Uniform Controlled Substances Act, offenses are punishable based on the amount of the drug possessed by the accused;

[186] Drug Sampling Guideline UNODC-ENFSI, published 08–21–2010 (available at: www.enfsi.eu)(last accessed July 24, 2012).

[187] 455 So.2d 240 (Ala.Cr.App.1984) (haphazard, "grab a handful" approach to random sampling is not adequate as a random sampling technique).

[188] *A Million Random Digits with 100,000 Normal Deviates,* The Rand Corporation (1955).

[189] The federal statutes specifically require only a "detectable" amount of controlled substance be present. *See* 21 U.S.C. §§ 802, 841.

[190] It has also been suggested that the government's consumption of the traces of a substance in testing which deprives the accused of an opportunity to retest justifies the existence of the usable quantity rule. Gerald F. Uelman and Victor G. Haddox, *Drug Abuse and the Law Sourcebook* 6B41 (1984).

[191] 648 S.W.2d 315 (Tex.Cr.App.1983).

[192] 157 Colo. 59, 400 P.2d 923 (1965).

the higher the amount, the greater the potential penalty. The Federal Controlled Substances Act as well as the Federal Sentencing Guidelines also graduate punishments based on the weight of the controlled substance in question.[193]

The pure weight argument has been given more credence in those cases where the statute specifically exempts certain substances from legislative control. Thus, the exclusion of sterile marijuana seeds from Ohio's marijuana prohibition resulted in the reversal of a marijuana possession conviction where the weight of the sterile seeds had not been subtracted from the total amount which the accused was charged with possessing.[194]

Not infrequently persons charged with drug offenses based on the aggregate quantity of the drug possessed have interposed a constitutional challenge to the charges grounded on a claimed denial of equal protection of the laws.[195] The defense theory is that it constitutes an arbitrary and unreasonable legislative classification to punish possessors of aggregate quantities equally with the possessors of pure quantities. In *People v. Campbell*, for example,[196] it was noted that, under the Michigan statutory scheme, one who possesses more than 50 grams of cocaine in the aggregate is punished more severely than one who possesses less than that amount in the pure form. As a consequence, a person convicted of possessing 51 grams of a mixture containing but 15% of pure cocaine would be more heavily punished than a person convicted of possessing pure cocaine in an amount of 49.9 grams. Like the Michigan reviewing court in *Campbell*, other courts have been unpersuaded by the defense arguments.[197] The courts have not perceived evidence of unconstitutional legislative irrationality in punishing dealers, who tend to cut their product before sale, more heavily than those who sell the drugs in purer form.

The practice of determining recommended sentence lengths based on the weight of a carrier medium added to the weight of the substance itself has also been challenged. In *Chapman v. United States*,[198] the petitioner argued that the blotter paper used as a carrier medium for LSD should not be tacked on to the total weight for sentencing purposes as such an aggregation would violate the equal protection and due process.[199] The Supreme Court held that the Sentencing Guidelines are not arbitrary in defining the weight of a mixture to include the carrier medium. In addition, the federal statute plainly refers to a "mixture or

---

[193] The government must still prove the weight of the illegal drug quantity beyond a reasonable doubt. *See* U.S. v. Gonzalez, 420 F.3d 111 (2d Cir.2005); U.S. v. Stewart, 361 F.3d 373 (7th Cir.2004).

[194] State v. Yanowitz, 67 Ohio App.2d 141, 426 N.E.2d 190 (1980).

[195] People v. Stahl, 110 Mich. App. 757, 313 N.W.2d 103 (1981).

[196] People v. Campbell, 115 Mich. App. 369, 320 N.W.2d 381 (1982).

[197] People v. Bradi, 107 Ill.App.3d. 594, 437 E.E.2d 1285 (1982).

[198] 500 U.S. 453 (1991).

[199] Id.

substance containing a detectable amount." Thus, although the petitioner's pure LSD weighed only 50 milligrams, the entire "mixture" weighed in at 5.7 grams, subjecting the petitioner to a greater sentence.

If a statute uses ounces as the measure of the prohibited quantity, whether aggregate or pure, it may become necessary to decide whether the legislature intended the avoirdupois ounce (28.349 grams) or the apothecaries (troy) ounce (31.103 grams).[200] On the general theory that statutory ambiguities are to be resolved in favor of the accused, the court in *Horton v. State*[201] reversed a conviction for possessing more than one ounce of marijuana since the weight of the substance totaled only 29.8 grams, short of the weight of the apothecary's ounce.

VI. RESOURCES

§15.18 BIBLIOGRAPHY OF ADDITIONAL RESOURCES

Victor Adint, *Drugs and Crime* (1997).

Edward Bartick, "Applications of Vibrational Spectroscopy in Criminal Forensic Analysis," *Handbook of Vibrational Spectroscopy*, 2993–3004 (John Wiley and Sons Ltd. 2002).

Marco A. Balbino *et al.*, "The Application of Voltammetric Analysis of Δ9-THC for the Reduction of False Positive Results in the Analysis of Suspected Marijuana Plant Matter," 61 J. Forensic Sci. 1067–1073 (2016).

T. Bora, M. Merdivan, and C. Hamamci, "Levels of Trace and Major Elements in Illicit Heroin," 47 J. FORENSIC SCI. 959–963 (2002).

J.F. Casale, "An Aqueous-Organic Extraction Method for the Isolation and Identification of Psilocin from Hallucinogenic Mushrooms," 30 J. Forensic Sci. 247–250 (1985).

W.C. Cheng, N.L. Poon, and M.F. Chan, "Chemical Profiling of 3,4-methylenedioxymethamphetamine (MDMA) Tablets Seized in Hong Kong," 48 J. FORENSIC SCI. 1249–1259 (2003).

D.M. Chiong, E. Consuegra-Rodriquez, and J.R. Almirall, "The Analysis and Identification of Steroids," 37 J. Forensic Sci. 488–502 (1992).

Laura A. Ciolino *et al.,* "The Chemical Interconversion of GHB and GBL: Forensic Issues and Implications," 46 J. FORENSIC SCI. 1315–1323 (2001).

Clarke's Isolation and Identification of Drugs (A.C. Moffat's 2d ed. 1986).

---

[200] State v. Ordonez-Villanueva, 138 Or.App. 236, 908 P.2d 333 (1995)(stating the metric equivalent of one ounce for an avoirdupois ounce or an apothecary's (troy) ounce).

[201] 408 So.2d 1197 (Miss.1982); People v. Gutierrez, 132 Cal.App.3d 281, 183 Cal.Rptr. 31 (1982).

Johan Dahlen and Sylvia von Eckardstein, "Development of a Capillary Zone Electrophoresis Method Including a Factorial Design and Simplex Optimisation for Analysis of Amphetamine Analogues, Cocaine, and Heroin," 157 Forensic Sci. Int'l 93 (2006).

Terry A. Dal Cason, "Review of: Mass Spectra of Designer Drugs 2005," 51 J. FORENSIC SCI. 454 (2006).

S.L. Datwyler and G.D. Weiblen, "Genetic Variation in Hemp and Marijuana (Cannabis sativa L.) According to Amplified Fragment Length Polymorphisms," 51 J. FORENSIC SCI. 371, (2006).

Stephen J. deRoux and William A. Dunn, " 'Bath Salts' the New York City medical Examiner Experience: A 3-Year Retrospective Review," J. Forensic Sci. 2016 (available online at: http://onlinelibrary.wiley.com).

Sebastian Dresen et al., "Electrospray-Ionization MS/MS Library of Drugs as Database for Method Development and Drug Identification," 161 Forensic Sci. Int'l 86 (2006).

Olaf H. Drummer and Morris Odell (eds.), The Forensic Pharmacology of Drugs of Abuse (Hodder Arnold Publications, 2001).

Elizabeth Evans, et al., "Determination of Inorganic Ion Profiles of Illicit Drugs by Capillary Electrophoresis," 61 J. Forensic Sci. 1610–1614 (2016).

S. Gross, "Psychotropic Drugs in Developmental Mushrooms: A Case Study Review," 47 J. FORENSIC SCI. 1298–1302 (2002).

Danielle Hamby et al., "Identification of 2-(ethylamino)-1-(4-methylphenyl)-1-pentanone (4-MEAP), a New "Legal High" Sold by an Internet Vendor as 4-Methyl Pentedrone," 60 J. Forensic Sci. 721–726 (2015).

Miriam Joseph, Ecstasy: Its History and Lore (2000).

Steven B. Karch, Drug Abuse Handbook, 2nd ed. (CRC Press 2006).

Erja Katainen et al., "Quantification of the Amphetamine Content in Seized Street Samples by Raman Spectroscopy," 52 J. FORENSIC SCI. 88–92 (2007).

S.C. Kim et al., "Simultaneous Analysis of D,3-methoxy-17-methylmorphinan and l-3-methoxy-17-methyl-morphinan by High Pressure Liquid Chromatography Equipped with PDA," 161 Forensic Sci. Int'l, 185 (2006).

R.E. Lee, "A Technique for the Rapid Isolation and Identification of Psilocin from Psilocin/Psilocybin Containing Mushrooms," 30 J. Forensic Sci. 931–941 (1985).

Barry Levine, Principles of Forensic Toxicology 3rd ed. (American Association for Clinical Chemistry, 2010.

Tien-lai Li et al., "Artifacts of GC-MS Profiling of Underivatized Methamphetamine Hydrochloride," 162 Forensic Sci. Int'l 113 (2006).

Jennifer R. Mallette and John F. Casale, "Headspace-Gas Chromatographic-Mass Spectrometric Analysis of South American Commercial Solvents and their Use in the Illicit Conversion of Cocaine Bass to Cocaine Hydrochloride," 60 J. Forensic Sci. 45–53 (2015).

James Robert Nielsen, *Handbook of Federal Drug Law* (1992).

Report of the U.N. Office of Drug Control and Crime Prevention (2001).

A.G. Ryder, "Classification of Narcotics in Solid Mixtures Using Principal Component Analysis and Raman Spectroscopy," 47 J. FORENSIC SCI. 275–284 (2002).

T. Sasaki and Y. Makino, "Effective Injection in Pulsed Splitless Mode for Impurity Profiling of Methamphetamine Crystal by GC or GC/MS," 160 Forensic Sci. Int'l 1 (2006).

Steven M. Sottolano and Ira S. Lurie, "The Quantitation of Psilocybin in Hallucinogenic Mushrooms Using High Performance Liquid Chromatography," 28 J. Forensic Sci. 929–935 (1983).

Synthetic Drug Control Strategy: A Focus on Methamphetamine and Prescription Drug Abuse, Office of National Drug Control Policy Publication (2006).

S.F. Teng *et al.*, "Characteristics and Trends of 3, 4-Methylenedioxy-methamphetamine (MDMA) Tablets Found in Taiwan from 2002 to February 2005," 161 Forensic Sci. Int'l 202 (2006).

B.M. Thomson, "Analysis of Psilocybin and Psilocin in Mushroom Extracts by Reversed-Phase High Performance Liquid Chromatography," 25 J. Forensic Sci. 779–785 (1980).

Kenji Tsujikawa *et al.*, "Development of a Library Search-Based Screening System for 3,4Methylenedioxymethamphetamine in Ecstasy Tablets Using a Portable Near-Infrared Spectrometer," 61 J. Forensic Sci. 1208–1214 (2016).

Gerald F Uelman, Victor G Haddox, *Drug Abuse & the Law Sourcebook*, 2 vols. (2005).

Robert G. Weston, "Quick Screening of Crystal Methamphetamine/ Methyl Sulfone Exhibits by Raman Spectroscopy," 55 J. FORENSIC SCI. 1068–1075 (2010).

Karen L. Woodall, Teri L. Martin, and Barry A. McLellan, "Oral Abuse of Fentanyl Patches (Duragesic®): Seven Case Reports," 53 J. FORENSIC SCI. 222–225 (2008).

CHAPTER 16

FORENSIC PSYCHIATRY AND PSYCHOLOGY

I. INTRODUCTION

§16.01 SCOPE OF THE CHAPTER

Psychiatry is the medical specialty concerned with the study, diagnosis, treatment, and prevention of mental disorders. It is based on the premise that biological causes are at the root of mental problems, although some psychiatrists do not strictly adhere to the biological model. Psychology is the study of the nature, functions, and phenomena of behavior and mental experience. It emerged from the disciplines of biology and philosophy in the late 1800s. Forensic psychiatry and forensic psychology are the application of psychiatric and psychological principles and techniques to situations involving the civil and criminal justice systems.[1] Although the two fields have differences in their areas of

---

[1] "Forensic psychiatry is a medical subspecialty that includes research and clinical practice in the many areas in which psychiatry is applied to legal issues." American Academy of Psychiatry and the Law at: http://www.aapl.org/org.htm (last accessed December 14, 2016). Forensic psychology "functions include assessment and treatment services, provision of advocacy and expert testimony, policy analysis, and research on such topics as eyewitness accounts, offender behavior, interrogations, and investigative practices." Gary R. VandenBos,

focus,[2] they are used similarly in the justice system and the courts often use the terms interchangeably.[3] Forensic psychiatrists and psychologists are involved in the assessment of mental states and conditions and provide expert testimony to assist the courts when an individual's mental state is relevant to the proceedings.[4]

Mental health evaluations are an essential component of the work of a forensic psychiatrist or psychologist. The forensic mental health evaluation (also called a forensic mental health assessment, forensic psychiatric evaluation, or a forensic psychological examination),[5] refers "to all techniques used to measure and evaluate an individual's past, present, or future psychological status."[6] The forensic mental health evaluation may be conducted by individuals from different fields (e.g., psychiatry, psychology), but has the common purpose of assisting in making legal determinations when an individual's mental state is relevant. Because the parameters of a specific mental evaluation will vary with the practitioner, the individual being assessed, and the relevant question at issue in the case, this chapter will discuss broadly forensic mental health evaluation techniques. Similarly, an overview of evaluation tools will be provided because of the wide variety of tools available. Expert qualifications, standards, common evidentiary issues in forensic psychiatry and psychology cases, and constitutional protections implicated in forensic mental health examinations in criminal cases will also be discussed.

---

ed., *APA College Dictionary of Psychology*, 2d ed., American Psychological Association, 2016 at p. 175.

[2]   Two distinctions between the fields have been the medical degree and prescription authority of psychiatrists, but "the lines of separation between the two professions are becoming increasing blurred." Curt R. Bartol & Anne M. Bartol, *Introduction to Forensic Psychology: Research and Application*, 3d ed., Sage Publications, Inc., 2012 at p. 11.

[3]   For a discussion of the historical context of the introduction of mental health experts in court proceedings, *see* Liza H. Gold, "Rediscovering Forensic Psychiatry," in Robert I. Simon & Liza H. Gold, eds., *Textbook of Forensic Psychiatry,* 2d ed., American Psychiatric Publishing, 2010 at pp. 3–42.

[4]   Within the criminal justice system, mental illness is prevalent. The 2005 survey by the Bureau of Justice Statistics found that more than half of all prison and jail inmates had a mental health problem, including 705,600 (75%) inmates in State prisons, 78,800 (45%) in Federal prisons, and 479,900 (64%) in local jails. Doris J. James & Lauren E. Glaze, *Bureau of Justice Statistics Special Report: Mental Health Problems of Prison and Jail Inmates,* NCJ 213600, September 2006 (available at: https://www.bjs.gov/content/pub/pdf/mhppji.pdf)(last accessed December 14, 2016). With this frequency of mental illness, "mental capacity is an issue most [attorneys] encounter on a regular basis and is often a relevant factor in preparing a defense case." Wendy R. Calaway, "Witness for the Prosecution? A Primer on Understanding the Limits on the Government's Gathering of Rebuttal Evidence When Mental Condition Is at Issue," The Champion, November 2016, at p. 38.

[5]   Kirk Heilbrun & Casey D. LaDuke, "Foundational Aspects of Forensic Mental Health Assessment," in Brian L. Cutler & Patricia A. Zapf, eds., *APA Handbook of Forensic Psychology,* American Psychological Association, 2015 at p. 3.

[6]   Curt R. Bartol & Anne M. Bartol, *Introduction to Forensic Psychology: Research and Application,* 3d ed., Sage Publications, Inc., 2012 at p. 196.

§16.02 TERMINOLOGY

The following terms are among those commonly encountered in forensic mental health evaluations or expert testimony from forensic psychiatrist and psychologists. More complete listings of terminology are found in the *APA Dictionary of Psychology*,[7] *APA College Dictionary of Psychology*,[8] *APA Dictionary of Statistics and Research Methods*,[9] *Oxford Dictionary of Psychology*,[10] and the Society for Neuroscience's *Brain Facts*.[11]

Acetylcholine: A neurotransmitter that plays an important role in memory formation and learning in the central nervous system.

Actuarial Data: Statistical information compiled from databases and gathered through objective measures. Compare *Clinical Data.*

Adrenal Cortex: An endocrine organ (defined *infra*) that secretes steroid hormones for metabolic functions, e.g., in response to stress.

Adrenal Medulla: An endocrine organ that secretes epinephrine and norepinephrine with activation of the sympathetic nervous system.

Affect: The outward manifestation of a person's feeling or emotion. Blunted or flat affect means the absence or near absence of expression; inappropriate affect means discordance of physical and verbal expression; labile affect means abrupt shifts or repetition in expression. Along with cognition and conation, affect is one of the three traditionally identified components of the mind.

Agonist: A neurotransmitter, drug, or other substance that stimulates receptors to produce a desired reaction.

Amino Acid Transmitters: The most prevalent neurotransmitters in the brain, including glutamate and aspartate (excitatory) and glycine and gammaaminobutyric acid (inhibitory).

Amygdala: Forebrain structure that plays a central role in emotional learning, particularly in response to fear.

Antagonist: A drug or other substance that blocks receptors and inhibits the effects of agonists.

Aphasia: Inability to utter, write, or understand once familiar language, words, or objects due to an injury or disease of the brain centers involved in language production and interpretation.

---

[7] American Psychological Association, *APA Dictionary of Psychology*, 2d ed., American Psychological Association, 2015.

[8] Gary R. VandenBos, ed., *APA College Dictionary of Psychology*, 2d ed., American Psychological Association, 2016.

[9] Sheldon Zedeck, *APA Dictionary of Statistics and Research Methods,* American Psychological Associations, 2014.

[10] Andrew M. Colman *Oxford Dictionary of Psychology,* 4th ed., Oxford University Press, 2015.

[11] Society for Neuroscience, *Brain Facts*, 2012 (available at: http://www.sfn.org/public-outreach/brainfacts-dot-org)(last accessed December 13, 2016).

Autism Spectrum Disorders (ASD): A condition characterized by impaired social skills; verbal and nonverbal communication difficulties; and narrow, obsessive interests and repetitive behaviors.

Autonomic Nervous System: Part of the peripheral nervous system responsible for regulating internal organ activity; it includes the sympathetic and parasympathetic nervous systems.

Axon: Fiberlike extension of a neuron that sends information to target cells. Axons are microscopically narrow, but vary in length from micrometers to several feet long (in neurons running from the base of the spinal cords to the toes). Longer axons tend to be coated with myelin (see *infra*).

Basal Ganglia: Deep brain structures that play a central role in the initiation of movement, includes the caudate nucleus, putamen, globus pallidus, and substantia nigra. Cell death in the substantia negra contributes to Parkinson's disease.

Bipolar Disorder: Severe mood or affective disorder characterized by periods of cyclical swings between mania and depression. The manic phase is characterized by over activity, euphoria with flight of ideas, excitement, decreased need for sleep, impaired judgment, and pressured speech. The depressive phase is characterized by moodiness; slowed thinking, movement, and eating processes; guilt feelings; decreased self-esteem; and general lack of interest.

Broca's Area: Brain region in the frontal lobe of the left hemisphere that is important for speech production.

Catecholamines: The neurotransmitters dopamine, epinephrine, and norepinephrine.

Cerebellum: Lower portion of the brain below back of cerebrum, which is about the size and shape of a squashed tennis ball, that is involved mainly with muscular coordination and body equilibrium, but is also involved in cognitive functions such as working memory, attention, and language.

Cerebral Arteriosclerosis: Hardening of the arteries of the brain with a decrease in the blood flow to the brain from lessening of the diameter of the arteries servicing it; results in an organic brain syndrome manifested neurologically in convulsions, aphasia, chorea, Parkinsonism, etc., or functionally in the form of intellectual dulling, memory defects, paranoid delusions, confusion, dementia, etc.; highly correlated with advancing age.

Cerebral Cortex: A sheet of tissue covering the outermost layer of the cerebrum.

Cerebrum: Largest part of the human brain, approximately 85% of its volume. It has two hemispheres (right and left) connected by axons. Each hemisphere is divided into four lobes: frontal lobe, parietal lobe, temporal lobe, and occipital lobe.

Clinical Data: Information derived from interviews, less structured and more subjective than Actuarial Data.

Cognition: All forms of knowing and awareness, such as perceiving, conceiving, remembering, and reasoning, judging, imagining, and problem solving. Along with affect and conation, one of the three traditionally identified components of the mind.

Conation: The proactive (as opposed to habitual) part of motivation that connects knowledge, emotions, and instincts to behavior. Along with affect and cognition, one of the three traditionally identified components of the mind.

Concurrent Validity: In psychological testing, validity measured by comparison with previously validated test.

Dementia: A loss of brain function that occurs with certain diseases. It affects memory, thinking, language, judgment, and behavior. The causes of dementia are numerous and complex, and diagnosis and treatment options depend upon test results and careful examination.

Dendrite: Treelike extension of the neuron cell body that is the primary site for receiving and integrating information from other neurons.

Dopamine: A catecholamine neurotransmitter present in three brain circuits: one regulating movement (deficits here are associated with Parkinson's disease), a second important in cognition and emotion (abnormalities here are associated with schizophrenia); and a third that regulates the endocrine system.

Endocannabinoids: Lipid-derived messengers that control the release of neurotransmitters (usually by inhibition) and play an important part in the control of behavior.

Endocrine Organ: An organ that produces secretions that are distributed in the body through the bloodstream.

Endorphins: Neurotransmitters that generate effects similar to morphine.

Epilepsy: A brain disorder in which a person has repeated seizures (convulsions) over time. Seizures are episodes of disturbed brain activity that cause changes in attention or behavior.

Epinephrine: A hormone, released by the adrenal medulla and specialized brain sites, that serves to put the body in a general state of arousal, also known as adrenaline.

Flight of Ideas: A continuous flow of accelerated speech wherein the subject makes abrupt changes of topic, often based on perceived associations, stimuli which distract, or plays on words. In extreme states, the speech may become incoherent. Often seen in manic episodes, though it also occurs in some cases of organic mental disorders and schizophrenia, psychotic disorders, and even as an acute reaction to stress.

Glutamate: Amino acid neurotransmitter that excite neurons.

Hallucination: An apparently real sensory perception, auditory or visual, without any real external or internal stimuli that cause it. Should be distinguished from illusions, during which external stimuli are misperceived or misinterpreted, and from normal vivid thought processes. Types of hallucinations include auditory, gustatory, olfactory; somatic; tactile, and visual. Hallucinations may be mood congruent or mood incongruent. In its serious form, hallucinations are commonly experienced by psychotics. Transient hallucinations are experienced at times by persons without mental disorders. Some drugs may also induce hallucinations.

Hippocampus: Sea-horse shaped structure in the brain that is involved in learning, memory, and emotion.

Insanity: Unsoundness of mind as frees one from legal responsibility, as for committing a crime, or as signals one's lack of legal capacity, as for entering into a contractual agreement. Insanity is a legal concept distinct from psychiatric classification.

Intelligence: Aggregate capacity of the individual to act purposefully, think rationally, and deal effectively with his environment, expressed in terms of I.Q.; a psychological determination of the relationship of a person's mental age to his chronological age.

Malingering: Fabricating or exaggerating the symptoms of mental or physical disorders for a variety of "secondary gain" motives, which may include financial compensation (often tied to fraud); avoiding school, work or military service; obtaining drugs; getting lighter criminal sentences; or simply to attract attention or sympathy.

Myelin Sheath: Compact fatty material that surrounds the axons of some neurons and accelerates the transmission of electrical signals.

Neuron: Cells in the nervous system that transmit information and are responsible for brain function. They are characterized by a cell body (soma); long, fiberlike extensions (axons); and shorter, treelike extensions (dendrites). Neurons can connect with other neurons or with other types of cells.

Neurotransmitter: A chemical that is released from a neuron for the purpose of relaying information to other neurons. Over 100 different neurotransmitters have been identified.

Norepinephrine: A catecholamine neurotransmitter produced in the brain and the peripheral nervous system that is involved in arousal, sleep regulation, mood, and blood pressure.

Parietal Lobe: One of four subdivisions of the cerebral cortex that plays a role in sensory processes, attention, and language.

Peripheral Nervous System: A division of the nervous system consisting of all nerves that are not part of the brain or spinal cord.

Pons: A part of the hindbrain that is the major route for the forebrain to send and receive information from the spinal cord and peripheral nervous system.

Psychoanalysis: A theory of mental structure and function, consisting of a loosely connected set of concepts and propositions, a theory of mental disorders, and an associated method of psychotherapy based on the writings of Sigmund Freud, its distinctive characteristic is the emphasis on the unconscious mental processes and the various mechanisms people use to repress them.

Psychosis: A severe symptom of psychiatric disorders characterized by an inability to perceive reality. Psychosis can occur in many disorders, including schizophrenia, bipolar disorder, depression, and drug-induced states.

Psychotropic: Substances that cross the blood-brain barrier to affect a person's brain function; for example, anesthetics and pain medications are different types of psychotropic drugs that doctors commonly prescribe. Some illicit recreational drugs also cross the blood-brain barrier, like cocaine and marijuana. Other psychotropic drugs effecting mood include antidepressants, antipsychotics, mood stabilizers and tranquilizers.

Sensorium: The sensory apparatus that is related to mental faculties.

Somatic Therapy: The biological treatment of mental disorders (e.g., medication).

Sympathetic Nervous System: A branch of the autonomic nervous system responsible for mobilizing the body's resources during times of stress and arousal.

Synapse: A physical gap (less than a micrometer, a millionth of a meter) between two neurons that functions as the site of information transfer from one neuron to another. At synapses, the axon releases neurotransmitters that are received by the dendrite of another neuron.

Temporal lobe: One of four major subdivisions of each hemisphere of the cerebral cortex that functions in auditory perception, speech, and complex visual perceptions.

Wernicke's Area: Brain region responsible for comprehension of language and production of speech.

§16.03 EVIDENTIARY USES

Forensic psychiatry and psychology examinations may be used in cases when an individual's mental state or condition is relevant, which includes a vast array of civil and criminal cases. Depending upon their background and training, forensic psychiatrists and psychologists serve the judicial process by addressing a wide range of issues in both civil and criminal actions. In criminal cases, these include mental state at the time of the offense;[12] competency to stand trial, waive *Miranda* rights, plead guilty, waive the right to counsel, waive appeals, and be sentenced or executed;[13] and in mitigation or aggravation of punishment. Noncriminal issues addressed by forensic psychiatrists and psychologists include civil commitment;[14] civil competencies;[15] mental injuries raised in insurance and tort cases;[16] antidiscrimination and employment adjudication;[17] child and family disputes including abuse, neglect, divorce, and custody;[18] and claims in workers' compensation cases and other entitlement cases.[19]

---

[12] *See* 18 U.S.C. § 17 (defining the standard for the insanity defense); Clark v. Arizona, 548 U.S. 735 (2006) (on the use of testimony for diminished capacity determinations).

[13] *See* Thomas Grisso, *Evaluating Competencies: Forensic Assessments and Instruments*, 2d ed., Kluwer Academic/Plenum Publishers, 2003. *See also* Dusky v. United States, 362 U.S. 402 (1960) (establishing standard for competence to stand trial); Miranda v. Arizona, 384 U.S. 436 (1966) (confession in custodial interrogation inadmissible unless defendant knowingly, intelligently, and voluntarily waives certain rights); Colorado v. Connelly, 479 U.S. 157 (1986) (mental condition a factor to be considered in determining whether confession was voluntary); Faretta v. California, 422 U.S. 806 (1975) (concerning defendant's right to waive counsel and self-representation); Indiana v. Edwards, 554 U.S. 164 (2008) (standards for competency to stand trial and to represent oneself need not be the same); Rees v. Peyton, 384 U.S. 312 (1966) (test for competency to waive further proceedings); Atkins v. Virginia, 536 U.S. 304 (2002) (executing the intellectually disabled violates the Eighth Amendment); Panetti v. Quarterman, 551 U.S. 930 (2007) (defendants sentenced to death must be competent at the time of execution).

[14] *See* O'Connor v. Donaldson, 422 U.S. 563 (1975) (holding unconstitutional the confinement of a nondangerous mentally ill person capable of surviving safely alone or with assistance); Kansas v. Crane, 534 U.S. 407 (2002) (civil commitment of dangerous sexual offender).

[15] "Mental competency for a specific activity is perhaps the most common reason for a consultation and expert opinion in forensic psychiatry." Alan A. Abrams, "Competencies in Civil Law," in Robert I. Simon & Liza H. Gold, eds., *Textbook of Forensic Psychiatry,* 2d ed., American Psychiatric Publishing, 2010 at p. 227. *See generally* Douglas Mossman & Helen M. Farrell, "Civil Competencies," in Brian L. Cutler & Patricia A. Zapf, eds., *APA Handbook of Forensic Psychology,* American Psychological Association, 2015 at pp. 533–558; John Parry & Eric Y. Drogin, *Mental Disability Law, Evidence, and Testimony: A Comprehensive Reference Manual for Lawyers, Judges and Mental Disability Professionals*, American Bar Association, 2007.

[16] *See* Dillon v. Legg, 441 P.2d 912 (Cal. 1968) (allowing recovery based on emotional distress not accompanied by physical injury); Sheely v. MRI Radiology Network, P.A., 505 F.3d 1173 (11th Cir. 2007) (damages available under § 504 of the Rehabilitation Act when emotional distress is foreseeable). *See generally* Eric Y. Drogin et al., "Personal Injury and Other Tort Matters," in Brian L. Cutler & Patricia A. Zapf, eds., *APA Handbook of Forensic Psychology,* American Psychological Association, 2015 at pp. 471–509.

[17] *See, e.g.,* Gaul v. AT&T, Inc., 955 F. Supp. 346 (D.N.J. 1997) (finding that depression and anxiety disorders many constitute a mental disability under the Americans with Disabilities Act). *See generally* Margaret S. Stockdale et al., "Employment Discrimination," in Brian L. Cutler & Patricia A. Zapf, eds., *APA Handbook of Forensic Psychology,* American Psychological Association, 2015 at pp. 511–532.

[18] *See generally* Marc J. Ackerman & Jonathan W. Gould, "Child Custody and Access," in Brian L. Cutler & Patricia A. Zapf, eds., *APA Handbook of Forensic Psychology,* American Psychological Association, 2015 at pp. 425–469; Tonia L Nicholls & John Hamel, "Intimate Partner Violence," in Brian L. Cutler & Patricia A. Zapf, eds., *APA Handbook of Forensic Psychology,* American Psychological Association, 2015 at pp. 381–422.

[19] For a comprehensive discussion of the variety of mental health court evaluations, *see* Gary B. Melton et al., *Psychological Evaluations for the Courts: A Handbook for Mental Health Professionals and Lawyers,* 3d ed., The Guilford Press, 2007. *See also* Paul S. Appelbaum, "Reference Guide on Mental Health Evidence," in Federal Judicial Research Center, *Reference Manual on Scientific Evidence*, 3d ed., National Academies Press, 2011 at pp. 815–816; Henry T. Greely & Anthony D. Wagner, "Reference Guide on Neuroscience," in Federal Judicial

Scientific evidence on mental states and conditions has also been used to support positions of policy and constitutional intent in the courts and legislative bodies. In the line of cases concerning the constitutionality of the penalty structures for juveniles, the United States Supreme Court relied in part on mental health research concerning juvenile brain structure and functioning.[20] After the Court barred the death penalty for defendants with intellectual disability,[21] some states turned to psychological tests of intelligence and functioning to define the mental condition which renders a person ineligible for the death penalty.[22]

II. EVALUATIONS

§16.04 PURPOSE AND TECHNIQUES

The forensic mental health assessment will vary from a clinical or treatment evaluation in several respects, including the sources of information consulted, the testing instruments used, and the purpose of

---

Research Center, *Reference Manual on Scientific Evidence*, 3d ed., National Academies Press, 2011 at pp. 807–811.

[20] In Roper v. Simmons, 543 U.S. 551, 569 (2005), the Court held that the death penalty was unconstitutional for crimes committed by juveniles and noted: "[A]s any parent knows and as the scientific and sociological studies respondent and his amici cite tend to confirm, '[a] lack of maturity and an underdeveloped sense of responsibility are found in youth more often than in adults. . . ." In Graham v. Florida, 560 U.S. 48, 68 (2010), holding that life without parole sentences are unconstitutional for nonhomicide juvenile offenders, the Court went further: "[D]evelopments in psychology and brain science continue to show fundamental differences between juvenile and adult minds. For example, parts of the brain involved in behavioral control continue to mature through late adolescence." In Miller v. Alabama, 132 S.Ct. 2455, 2464–2465 (2012), barring mandatory life sentences for juvenile offenders, the Court noted that its prior decisions relied "not only on common sense—on what 'any parent knows'—but on science and social science as well. . . . [and that with a juvenile], as the years go by and neurological development occurs, his 'deficiencies will be reformed.' "

[21] Atkins v. Virginia, 536 U.S. 304 (2002).

[22] *See, e.g.,* Fla. Stat. 921.137(1) ("As used in this section, the term "intellectually disabled" or "intellectual disability" means significantly subaverage general intellectual functioning existing concurrently with deficits in adaptive behavior and manifested during the period from conception to age 18. The term "significantly subaverage general intellectual functioning," for the purpose of this section, means performance that is two or more standard deviations from the mean score on a standardized intelligence test specified in the rules of the Agency for Persons with Disabilities. The term "adaptive behavior," for the purpose of this definition, means the effectiveness or degree with which an individual meets the standards of personal independence and social responsibility expected of his or her age, cultural group, and community. The Agency for Persons with Disabilities shall adopt rules to specify the standardized intelligence tests as provided in this subsection."); S.D. Codified Laws 23A-27A-26.2. ("As used in §§ 23A-27A-26.1 to 23A-27A-26.7, inclusive, mental retardation means significant subaverage general intellectual functioning existing concurrently with substantial related deficits in applicable adaptive skill areas. An intelligence quotient exceeding seventy on a reliable standardized measure of intelligence is presumptive evidence that the defendant does not have significant subaverage general intellectual functioning.").

the evaluation.[23] Unlike the clinical evaluation, where the purpose is to serve the health care needs of the individual, the forensic evaluation serves the interests of the legal system by assisting in legal determinations. The focus of the mental health evaluation conducted by a forensic psychiatrist or psychologist will vary depending on the legal determination at issue. Some determinations, such as mental state at the time of the offense or the competency of a now-deceased testator, will require a retrospective assessment of mental functioning.[24] Determinations involving an existing memory state, such as the competency to stand trial or for civil commitment, are contemporaneous assessments. Other determinations will have a future focus, such as a defendant's future dangerousness, and are prospective assessments. In some cases, particularly death penalty cases, all three types of evaluations may be involved over the course of a case.[25]

The fundamental techniques of a forensic mental health evaluation are consistent for all types of assessments of mental state and condition, although the relative importance and availability of the techniques will vary. The main techniques of an evaluation are clinical examination, structured diagnostic interviews,[26] psychological testing, collateral source information and record review, and possibly neuroimaging and laboratory tests.[27] Although not designed specifically for forensic evaluations, the American Psychiatric Association's *Practice Guideline for the Psychiatric Evaluation of Adults* provides an extensive discussion of the domains (focus areas) of a general psychiatric evaluation:[28]

---

[23] For a detailed discussion of the distinctions between forensic and clinical assessments, *see* Gary B. Melton et al., *Psychological Evaluations for the Courts: A Handbook for Mental Health Professionals and Lawyers,* The Guilford Press, 2007 at pp. 43–68.

[24] *See generally* Robert I. Simon & Daniel W. Shuman eds., *Retrospective Assessment of Mental States in Litigation: Predicting the Past,* American Psychiatric Publishing, 2002.

[25] For a discussion of the role of mental health evidence in all stages of a death penalty case, *see* American Bar Association, Death Penalty Due Process Review Project, *Severe Mental Illness and the Death Penalty,* December 2016 (available at: http://www.americanbar.org/content/dam/aba/images/crsj/DPDPRP/SevereMentalIllnessandtheDeathPenalty_WhitePaper.pdf)(last accessed December 22, 2016).

[26] The structured diagnostic interview may use standardized data forms, questionnaires, and rating scales, but does not include psychological and neuropsychological testing instruments (discussed in Section 16.07 *infra*). A list of structured interview instruments is provided in Table 3 of the American Psychiatric Association Work Group on Psychiatric Evaluation, Practice Guideline for the Psychiatric Evaluation of Adults, Second Edition, June 2006 at pp. 23–28 (available at: https://psychiatryonline.org/pb/assets/raw/sitewide/practice_guidelines/guidelines/psychevaladults.pdf)(last accessed December 15, 2016). These tools vary widely in their validity and reliability. Potential race, gender, cultural, and other biases may also limit their effectiveness. See S. Lopez & J.A. Nunez, "Cultural Factors Considered in Selected Diagnostic Criteria and Interview Schedules," 96 J. Abnorm. Psychol. 270–272 (1987); R.J. Samuda, Psychological Testing of American Minorities: Issues and Consequences, 2d ed., Sage Publishing, 1998.

[27] Laboratory tests may be helpful in ruling out general medical causes of abnormal behavior or for collecting genetic information. Paul S. Appelbaum, "Reference Guide on Mental Health Evidence," in in Federal Judicial Research Center, Reference Manual on Scientific Evidence, 3d ed., National Academies Press, 2011 at pp. 834–839.

[28] American Psychiatric Association, Practice Guideline for the Psychiatric Evaluation of Adults, Third Edition, American Psychological Association, 2016 at pp. 4–6 (available at:

- Reason for the evaluation;
- History of present illness;
- Past psychiatric history;
- History of alcohol and other substance use;
- General medical history;
- Review of systems;
- Family history;
- Personal and social history;
- Physical examination;
- Quantitative assessment of symptoms, level of functioning, and quality of life.

Across all domains, a clinical mental health evaluation is generally based on four sources of information: (1) observation and interview of the patient; (2) information from others (e.g., family, significant others, case managers, other clinicians); (3) diagnostic testing; and (4) medical records.[29] For a forensic mental health evaluation, additional sources of information will be court records, witnesses, victims, law enforcement personnel, attorneys, and corrections personnel. Forensic psychological evaluations also are increasingly using neuroimaging techniques to associate mental states with the physical states of the brain.

With all three types of assessments, reviewing historical information (collateral source information and records before or during the time in question) is usually an important part of the evaluation, but is essential to a retrospective assessment. If the individual is available for evaluation, the clinical examination and structured diagnostic interview are useful even for retrospective assessments to evaluate the consistency of reported symptoms and to explore the possibility of evolving deficits. For contemporaneous assessments, the clinical examination is fundamental and the most important component.[30] How people report current symptoms and events is important to the evaluation process. Mistakes in comprehension, recall, and expression, or intentional fabrication, may provide information supporting a diagnosis.

§16.05 PREDICTIVE ASSESSMENTS

Of the three types of assessments, the prospective assessment is the most controversial, "especially when the outcome being predicted

---

http://psychiatryonline.org/doi/pdf/10.1176/appi.books.9780890426760)(last accessed December 19, 2016).

[29] Id. at pp. 3–4.

[30] Paul S. Appelbaum, "Reference Guide on Mental Health Evidence," in in Federal Judicial Research Center, *Reference Manual on Scientific Evidence*, 3d ed., National Academies Press, 2011 at p. 834.

occurs at a relatively low frequency."[31] Prospective assessments are used throughout the criminal justice system, for bail determinations,[32] at sentencing, and for probation decisions.[33] In civil cases, prospective assessments are used for civil commitments, sexually violent predator commitments, and predictions of future impairment and response to treatment. Until the 1970s, forensic examiners making prospective assessments relied primarily on clinical judgment: subjective assessments based on the individual examiner's experience and knowledge. Studies found that the accuracy rate of such predictions was incredibly low; a frequently cited conclusion was that mental health professionals' predictions of violence were twice as likely to be wrong as right.[34]

To assist forensic examiners to improve the accuracy of predictions, researchers developed risk assessment instruments based on statistical data correlating specific factors with certain outcomes (e.g., violence, recidivism). These risk assessment instruments are also referred to as actuarial instruments and use empirically based formulas encompassing both static factors (e.g., age, gender) and dynamic factors (e.g., substance abuse, unemployment). There are a wide variety of instruments available to forensic psychiatrists and psychologists in making risk assessments, depending on the nature of the risk at issue.[35] Predictive assessments ordinarily focus on actuarial or statistical data that identifies factors that have been shown in research to have the strongest correlation to the future outcome being assessed;

---

[31] Id. at pp. 818–819.

[32] *See* Va. Code § 19.2–152.3. ". . . The Department of Criminal Justice Services shall develop risk assessment and other instruments to be used by pretrial services agencies in assisting judicial officers in discharging their duties pursuant to Article 1 (§ 19.2–119 et seq.) of Chapter 9 of this title." The pretrial risk assessment instrument used by pretrial service programs in Virginia is available at: https://www.dcjs.virginia.gov/correctional-services/programs/comprehensive-community-corrections-act-ccca-pretrial-services-act/ccca-psa-pra (last accessed December 20, 2016).

[33] The Virginia Criminal Sentencing Commission includes a "Nonviolent Risk Assessment" Section in the sentencing guidelines worksheet for nonviolent offenses. See http://www.vcsc.virginia.gov/worksheets.html (last accessed December 15, 2016). The risk assessment program became a permanent part of Virginia's sentencing guideline system following a pilot study that found it to be effective in identifying good candidates for diversion from incarceration. Brian J. Ostrom *et al., Offender Risk Assessment in Virginia,* National Center for State Courts, 2002 (available at: http://www.vcsc.virginia.gov/reports.html)(last accessed December 15, 2016).

[34] John Monahan, *The Clinical Prediction of Violent Behavior*, US Government Printing Office, DHSS Publication No. (ADM) 81-921, 1981 at p. 60.

[35] For example, the Static-99R is the most widely used sex offender risk assessment instrument in the world, and is extensively used in the United States, Canada, the United Kingdom, Australia, and many European nations. The Static-99R is a ten item actuarial assessment instrument created by R. Karl Hanson, Ph.D. and David Thornton, Ph.D. for use with adult male sexual offenders who are at least 18 year of age at time of release to the community. In 2012, the age item for the scale was updated, creating Static-99R. *See* http://www.static99.org (last accessed December 22, 2016).

Other sex offender risk assessment instruments include the Minnesota Sex Offender Screening Tool-Revised (MsSOST-R), the Rapid Risk Assessment for Sex Offense Recidivism (RRASOR), Sex Offender Risk Appraisal Guide (SORAG), and the Static-2002R.

but some assessment instruments use both statistical data and structured clinical judgment.[36]

The difficulty with predictive assessments based on previously-identified correlated factors is that correlation does not necessarily equate to causation, and the accuracy of such measures is incredibly uncertain. "The inescapable uncertainties of the course of mental disorders and their responsiveness to interventions create part of the difficulty in such assessments, but an equally important contribution is made by the unknowable contingencies of life."[37] Other complicating factors are the quality of the predictive instruments used in such assessments and whether they improperly reinforce racial, economic, and gender sterotypes.[38] Forensic psychiatrists and psychologists may "adjust the scores on risk assessment instruments upward or downward to incorporate data that might not be covered by the instrument[,]" such as a recent, highly stressful event that might impact judgment and control.[39] Research has shown that such case-based adjustments to actuarial assessments do not improve the quality of the prediction.[40]

One psychological test that is commonly used as a predictive measure in risk assessments of criminal defendants and for civil commitment of sexual offenders is an instrument for measuring criminal psychopathy: Hare's Psychopathy Checklist (PCL),[41] its revision (PCL-R),[42] and the screening version (PCL:SV).[43] The checklist is an actuarial instrument assessing the individual's emotional, interpersonal, behavioral, and social deviance factors of criminal psychopathy.[44] Information to assign a zero-to-two score on each factor is gathered from various sources, including self-reports, behavioral

---

[36] *E.g.*, the Structured Assessment of Violence Risk for Youth (SAVRY). *See* Randy Borum et al., "Structural Assessment of Violence Risk in Youth," in Thomas Grisso et al., eds, *Mental Health Screening and Assessment in Juvenile Justice*, The Guilford Press, 2005 at pp. 311–323.

[37] Paul S. Appelbaum, "Reference Guide on Mental Health Evidence," in Federal Judicial Research Center, *Reference Manual on Scientific Evidence*, 3d ed., National Academies Press, 2011 at p. 819.

[38] *See* Kirk Heilbrun *et al.*, *Forensic Mental Health Assessment: A Casebook,* Oxford University Press, 2002, at pp. 470–478.

[39] Curt R. Bartol & Anne M. Bartol, *Introduction to Forensic Psychology: Research and Application*, 3d ed., Sage Publications, Inc., 2012 at pp. 150–151.

[40] Terence W. Campbell, "Sex Offenders and Actuarial Risk Assessments: Ethical Considerations," 21 Behavioral Sci. & Law 269–279 (2003).

[41] Robert Hare, "A Research Scale for the Assessment of Psychopathy in Criminal Populations," 1 Personality & Individual Differences 111–119 (1980).

[42] Robert Hare, *The Hare Psychopathy Checklist—Revised*, Multi-Health Systems, 1991.

[43] Robert Hare, *The Psychopathy Checklist*, 2d ed. Revised, Multi-Health Systems, 2003.

[44] The twenty traits assessed by the PCL-R are: 1. Glib and superficial charm; 2. Grandiose estimation of self; 3. Need for stimulation; 4. Pathological lying; 5. Manipulativeness; 6. Lack of remorse; 7. Shallow affect; 8. Lack of empathy; 9. Parasitic lifestyle; 10. Poor behavioral control; 11. Sexual promiscuity; 12. Early behavior problems; 13. Lack of realistic long-term goals; 14. Impulsivity; 15. Irresponsibility; 16. Failure to accept responsibility; 17. Many short-term sexual relationships; 18. Juvenile delinquency; 19. Revocation of conditional release; and 20 Criminal versatility. Marc J. Ackerman, *Essentials of Forensic Psychological Assessment*, 2d ed., Wiley, 2010 at pp. 281–282.

observations, and collateral sources. Trained examiners use the information to assign points based on the frequency the individual exhibits the disposition listed (0 = consistently absent, 1 = inconsistent, 2 = consistently present). The higher the score, the higher the risk of the individual exhibiting criminal psychopathy. Generally, a score of 30 or above will result in the label "psychopath." Proper scoring requires access to considerable background material and the examiner should have extensive training in using the PCL.[45] Although the instrument is widely used, some psychologists have expressed reservations about its validity in minority and disadvantaged groups and have called for it not to be used as a measure to predict future dangerousness in death penalty cases.[46] The instrument, however, continues to be used in capital sentencings.[47]

Concerning the results of predictive assessments, the courts have generally allowed predictions of behavior, but do acknowledge they are imperfect. In *Schall v. Martin*,[48] the Supreme Court held that:

> [F]rom a legal point of view there is nothing inherently unattainable about a prediction of future criminal conduct. Such a judgment forms an important element in many decisions, and we have specifically rejected the contention. . . 'that it is impossible to predict future behavior and that the question is so vague as to be meaningless.' We have also recognized that a prediction of future criminal conduct is 'an experienced prediction based on a host of variables' which cannot be readily codified.[49]

Some courts have declined to apply the admissibility standards of *Daubert* and *Frye* to risk assessment instruments holding that the instruments are "simply actuarial tables—methods of organizing and interpreting a collection of historical data," and do not involve a scientific principle, method, or technique to which the admissibility standards

---

[45] Curt R. Bartol & Anne M. Bartol, *Introduction to Forensic Psychology: Research and Application*, 3d ed., Sage Publications, Inc., 2012 at pp. 260–261.

[46] J.F. Edens, J. Petrila & J.K. Buffington-Vollum, "Psychopathy and the Death Penalty: Can the Psychopathy Checklist-Revised Identify Offenders Who Represent 'A Continuing Threat to Society'?," 29 J. Psych. & Law 433–481 (2001).

[47] *See* People v. Johnson, 62 Cal.4th 600, 624–625, 364 P.3d 359, 375–376 (2016) ("Dr. Flores described the results of the Hare psychopathy checklist, a test that quantifies the subject's psychopathological tendencies associated with a "basic criminality makeup," which the tester then compares to the scores of inmates in the prison population generally. The checklist showed, among other traits, that defendant was cunning, manipulative, callous, and impulsive, and that he lacked guilt or remorse. Defendant's score, 34 out of 40, placed him in the 97th percentile of the prison population generally. In connection with this assessment, Dr. Flores referred to defendant as a "principle psychopath," meaning that his antisocial, criminal, and violent actions and behaviors are governed by his own internal ethical code, which derives from principles and values of his gang.").

[48] 467 U.S. 253 (1984).

[49] 467 U.S. at 278–279 (internal citations omitted).

apply.[50] Other courts have held that the evidence derived from such risk assessments meets the admissibility standards.[51]

III. EVALUATION TOOLS

§16.06 DIAGNOSTIC SYSTEM

The standard nomenclature and diagnostic criteria for mental disorders used in the United States are provided in the *Diagnostic and Statistical Manual of Mental Disorders* (DSM), published by the American Psychiatric Association. The fifth edition of the manual (DSM-5) was published in 2013. "DSM diagnoses are generally accepted and relied on in clinical and research venues."[52] The DSM was developed as a guide in the diagnosis of mental disorders, but it is also used as a reference for the courts and attorneys. The DSM-5 notes:[53]

> When used appropriately, diagnoses and diagnostic information can assist legal decision makers in their determinations. For example, when the presence of a mental disorder is the predicate for a subsequent legal determination (e.g., involuntary civil commitment), the use of an established system of diagnosis enhances the value and reliability of the determination.... However, the use of the DSM-5 should be informed by an awareness of the risks and limitations of its use in forensic settings. When DSM-5 categories, criteria, and textual descriptions are employed for forensic purposes, there is a risk that diagnostic information will be misused or misunderstood. These dangers arise because of the imperfect fit between the questions of ultimate concern to the law and the information contained in a clinical diagnosis.... It is precisely because impairments, abilities, and disabilities vary widely within each diagnostic category that assignment of a particular diagnosis does not imply a specific level of impairment or disability.

---

[50] People v. Erbe, 344 Ill.App.3d 350, 364, 800 N.E.2d 137, 149 (App. Ct. 4th Dist. 2003).

[51] In re Det. of Ritter, 192 Wn. App. 493, 372 P.3d 122 (2016) (Structured Risk Assessment-Forensic Version); In re Commitment of R.S., 339 N.J. Super. 507, 540, 773 A.2d 72, 92 (2001), *aff'd* 173 N.J. 134, 801 A.2d 219 (2002)(Minnesota Screening Tool-Revised and Rapid Risk Assessment of Sex Offender Recidivism); In re Detention of Holtz, 653 N.W.2d 613, 619 (Iowa App. 2002) (Static-99 and the Minnesota Screening Tool_revised); In re Detention of Strauss, 106 Wn. App. 1, 4, 20 P.3d 1022, 1023–1024 (2001) (Violence Risk Appraisal Guide and the Minnesota Screening Tool-Revised). See also Jackson v. States, 833 So.2d 243, 246 (Fla. App. 2002).

[52] Robert I. Simon & Liza H. Gold, "Psychiatric Diagnosis in Litigation," in in Robert I. Simon & Liza H. Gold, eds., *Textbook of Forensic Psychiatry,* 2d ed., American Psychiatric Publishing, 2010 at p. 151.

[53] American Psychiatric Association, *Diagnostic and Statistical Manual of Mental Disorders,* 5th ed., American Psychiatric Publishing, 2013 at p. 25.

The DSM-5 discusses the diagnostic criteria and provides descriptive text to assist in diagnostic decision making for the following categories of disorders:

- Neurodevelopmental Disorders;
- Schizophrenia Spectrum and Other Psychotic Disorders;
- Bipolar and Related Disorders;
- Depressive Disorders;
- Anxiety Disorders;
- Obsessive-Compulsive and Related Disorders;
- Trauma- and Stressor-Related Disorders;
- Dissociative Disorders;
- Somatic Symptom and Related Disorders;
- Feeding and Eating Disorders;
- Elimination Disorders;
- Sleep-Wake Disorders;
- Sexual Dysfunctions;
- Gender Dysphoris;
- Disruptive, Impulse-Control, and Conduct Disorders;
- Substance-Related and Addictive Disorders;
- Neurocognitive Disorders;
- Personality Disorders; and,
- Paraphilic Disorders.

Other less common mental disorders, disorders resulting from medication effects, and other conditions that may be the focus of clinical attention are also covered. Within each category, general information about the disorder is discussed, including diagnostic features, prevalence, development and course, risk and prognostic factors, gender-related and culture-related diagnostic issues, functional consequences, differential diagnosis, and other relevant factors. "The symptoms contained in the respective diagnostic criteria sets do not constitute comprehensive definitions of underlying disorders. . . . [r]ather, they are intended to summarize characteristic syndromes of signs and symptoms that point to an underlying disorder."[54]

The DSM as a diagnostic reference has been incorporated into hundreds of federal and state statutes and regulations,[55] including

---

[54] Id. at p. 19.

[55] *See, e.g.,* Va. Code § 38.2–3418.17 (defining autism spectrum disorder as "any pervasive developmental disorder, including (i) autistic disorder, (ii) Asperger's Syndrome, (iii) Rett syndrome, (iv) childhood disintegrative disorder, or (v) Pervasive Developmental Disorder—Not Otherwise Specified, as defined in the most recent edition of the Diagnostic and Statistical Manual of Mental Disorders of the American Psychiatric Association" for purposes of requiring insurance coverage); Ohio Rev. Stat. 3923.281(A)(1) (defining "Biologically based

statutes that make a DSM diagnosis an essential element of a claim (e.g., The Americans with Disabilities Act).[56]

§16.07 PSYCHOLOGICAL TESTING

The forensic mental health assessment typically starts with observations and evaluation of the individual during the course of one or more interviews. The observations noted by the examiner include the individual's appearance, grooming, behavior, posture, gait, facial expressions, eye contact, motor activity, rate of speech and pitch, emotions, verbal associations, and other factors. Forensic examiners will complement the interviews with record review and collateral source information. If the diagnosis is made at this point, the examiner relies on experience and judgment in making diagnostic conclusions. The accuracy of these subjective conclusions can be negatively affected by many factors, including hypothesis confirmation bias (information that corroborates the suspected diagnosis is overvalued; information inconsistent with the suspected diagnosis is undervalued). To provide objective diagnostic information and improve the accuracy of the conclusions, forensic examiners will frequently use psychological testing.

"Psychological testing is the administration and interpretation of standardized tests with acceptable psychometric properties," including reliability, validity, error rate, and known limits of generalizability.[57] Standardized psychological testing can improve diagnostic accuracy and reliability. Also, some diagnoses by definition require standardized testing (e.g., intellectual disability) and other forensic questions are impossible to address without standardized testing (e.g., assessing the neuropsychological decline in progressive dementia). The primary reason for including psychological testing in forensic examinations is the relevance to the legal determination since the testing results offer an objective measure of function that can be compared to averages of

---

mental illness" as "schizophrenia, schizoaffective disorder, major depressive disorder, bipolar disorder, paranoia and other psychotic disorders, obsessive-compulsive disorder, and panic disorder, as these terms are defined in the most recent edition of the diagnostic and statistical manual of mental disorders published by the American psychiatric association.").

The Department of Veteran's Affairs Disability Schedule in 38 CFR § 4.125 provides "(a) If the diagnosis of a mental disorder does not conform to DSM-5 or is not supported by the findings on the examination report, the rating agency shall return the report to the examiner to substantiate the diagnosis. Diagnostic and Statistical Manual of Mental Disorders, Fifth Edition (DSM-5), American Psychiatric Association (2013), is incorporated by reference into this section with the approval of the Director of the Federal Register under 5 U.S.C. 552(a) and 1 CFR part 51. To enforce any edition other than that specified in this section, the Department of Veterans Affairs must publish notice of change in the Federal Register and the material must be available to the public.").

[56] Robert I. Simon & Liza H. Gold, "Psychiatric Diagnosis in Litigation," in Robert I. Simon & Liza H. Gold, eds., *Textbook of Forensic Psychiatry,* 2d ed., American Psychiatric Publishing, 2010 at p. 167.

[57] Madelon V. Baranoski, "Psychological Testing in Forensic Psychiatry," in in Robert I. Simon & Liza H. Gold, eds., *Textbook of Forensic Psychiatry,* 2d ed., American Psychiatric Publishing, 2010 at pp. 617–618.

measured populations. In this way, psychological testing allows a measure of relative functional impairment relevant to many legal determinations.[58]

A psychological test is any standardized instrument used to measure behavioral, emotional functioning, cognitive abilities, aptitude, and personality characteristics.[59] Psychological tests are diagnostic aids in measuring the range and nature of intellectual ability and emotional response. The tests are not conclusive means of determining the mental status of a subject, and are used in combination with the examiner's observations, records review, and other information. The value of the psychological testing is no greater than the validity and appropriateness of the tests themselves and the skill, training, and practical experience of the examiner who employs them. One of the main concerns when selecting a test is its validity, which is whether it actually measures what it is purported to assess. Devising, standardizing, refining, and validating psychological tests continue to be major research activities of psychologists.

In assessing the appropriateness of the testing instrument used in an evaluation, the issues and questions to consider include:[60]

1. Reliability and Validity

    •   Have adequate levels of reliability been demonstrated?

    •   Have adequate levels of validity been demonstrated?

    •   Is the test commercially available?

    •   Is the comprehensive user's manual available?

    •   Has the instrument been peer reviewed?

2. Qualifications of the Evaluator

    •   What are the qualifications necessary to use this instrument?

    •   Does the evaluator have these qualifications?

---

[58] Some courts have relied on the results of testing over the conclusions of the expert mental health professional. *See, e.g.,* Clayton v. Roper, 515 F.3d 784, 791 (8th Cir. 2008) (trial court did not err in relying on the objective findings from the tests the [expert] doctor performed than on [the expert's] ultimate conclusion."); United States v. Battle, 272 F. Supp.2d 1354, 1362 (N.D. Ga. 2003) (court noted that objectively graded personality tests suggested the defendant did not suffer from a thought disorder of psychotic proportions). Experts have cautioned, however, against overreliance by judges and juries on quantitative test data because of inadequate awareness of the significant limitations of some tests. *See* Stuart B. Kleinman & Daniel Martell, "Failings of Trauma-Specific and Related Psychological Tests in Detecting Post-Traumatic Stress Disorder in Forensic Settings," 60 J. Forensic Sci. 76–83 (2015).

[59] Gary R. VandenBos, ed., *APA College Dictionary of Psychology*, 2d ed., American Psychological Association, 2016 at p. 367.

[60] These issues and questions are based on the following resources: Paul S. Appelbaum, "Reference Guide on Mental Health Evidence," in Federal Judicial Research Center, *Reference Manual on Scientific Evidence*, 3d ed., National Academies Press, 2011 at pp. 885–888; Gary B. Melton et al., *Psychological Evaluations for the Courts: A Handbook for Mental Health Professionals and Lawyers*, 3d ed., The Guilford Press, 2007 at p. 48.

3. Fitness for Purpose

- Is the person being evaluated part of the population for which the instrument was validated or designed?

- Is the test valid for the purpose for which it will be used?

- How directly does the instrument assess the construct of interest?

- Are there alternative methods of assessment that assess the construct in more direct ways?

One resource for assessing and selecting testing instruments is the Mental Measurements Yearbook (MMY) series. The MMY provides evaluative information to promote and encourage informed test selection. Typical MMY test entries include descriptive information, two professional reviews, and reviewer references. To be reviewed in the MMY a test must be commercially available; be published in the English language; be new, revised, or widely used since it last appeared in the MMY series; and must include sufficient documentation supporting their technical quality to meet criteria for review. Volumes in the MMY series are produced every three years, with the next volume due to be published in 2017.[61]

Since there are literally hundreds of psychological tests, the following discussion will be limited to some of the most frequently and widely used personality, intelligence, and neuropsychological tests. The forensic examiner will generally use an assortment of tests to assess cognitive abilities and to assist in the diagnosis of mental disorders. The specific tests used will depend on the focus of the evaluation, any areas of concern (e.g., impulsivity, cognitive function), and the training of the examiner. The proper administration of psychological tests requires training on the specific instrument used, which may be extensive for some of the testing instruments. Aside from the types of tests discussed *infra* the examiner may use other instruments designed to address specific issues such as competence to stand trial,[62] malingering,[63] risk assessments for violence and sexual offenses,[64] the level of suggestibility in children,[65] and assessments for sexual harassment.[66] These tests are

---

[61] *See* http://buros.org/mental-measurements-yearbook (last accessed December 20, 2016).

[62] *See generally* Patricia A. Zapf & Jodi L. Viljoen, "Issues and Considerations Regarding the Use of Assessment Instruments in the Evaluation of Competency to Stand Trial," 21 Behavioral Sci & Law 351–367 (2003).

[63] Examples of malingering assessment instruments include the Structured Interview of Reported Systems, the Test of Memory Malingering, the Rogers Criminal Responsibility Assessment Scales. *See* Curt R. Bartol & Anne M. Bartol, *Introduction to Forensic Psychology: Research and Application*, 3d ed., Sage Publications, Inc., 2012 at pp. 164–165.

[64] *See* notes 35, 41–47 and accompanying text *supra*.

[65] *See* Laura Volpini *et al.,* "Measuring Children's Suggestibility in Forensic Interviews," 61 J. Forensic Sci. 104–108 (2016)(using the Bonn Test of Statement Suggestibility).

[66] The dominant instrument for assessing the impact of sexual harassment on the alleged victim is the Sexual Experiences Questionnaire (SEQ), which has been described as "the most theoretically and psychometrically sophisticated instrument available for assessing incidence and

beyond the scope of this general discussion, but should always be considered in cases involving specific legal determinations of mental condition.[67]

1. PERSONALITY TESTS

Personality tests, designed to help identify abnormal tendencies in an individual's personality, are of two types:

(a) Self-report inventories (also referred to as psychometric tests) in which the individual is given a prepared list of questions and is asked to agree or disagree or pick the correct answer. The response is scored on a previously established scale.

(b) Projective tests in which the individual is given ambiguous stimulus material to observe how the individual experiences and deals with life situations. The test responses are used as substitutes for observed behavior in daily activities of the individual. The aim of these tests is to reveal subtleties of the individual's personality.

These two distinguishable approaches are complementary to each other; neither need be used to the exclusion of the other.

a. Self-Report Inventories

The best known of the self-report inventories is the Minnesota Multiphasic Personality Inventory (MMPI/MMPI-2), originally developed in 1939 at the Department of Neuropsychiatry at the Medical School of the University of Minnesota. The MMPI is currently administered in one of two forms: the MMPI-2, which has 567 true/false questions, and the newer MMPI-2-RF, published in 2008 and containing 338 true/false items. While the MMPI-2-RF is a newer instrument and takes about half the time to complete (usually 30 to 50 minutes), the MMPI-2 is still the more widely used instrument because of its existing large research base and familiarity with psychologists. A third version of the test, the MMPI-A, is designed exclusively for teenagers and is not widely used.

---

prevalence of sexual harassment," Lilia M. Cortina, "Assessing Sexual Harassment Among Latinas: Development of an Instrument," 9 Cultural Diversity & Ethnic Minority Psychology, 164–181 (2001) at p. 165 (available at: https://lsa.umich.edu/psych/lilia-cortina-lab/Cortina%202001%20CDEMP.pdf)(last accessed December 20, 2016), but has also been criticized as lacking validity and reliability. Barbara A. Gutek, Ryan O. Murphy & Bambi Douma, "A Review and Critique of the Sexual Experience Questionnaire (SEQ)," 28(4) Law and Human Behavior 457–482 (2004) (available at: https://www.researchgate.net/publication/8216916_A_Review_and_Critique_of_the_Sexual_Experiences_Questionnaire_SEQ)(last accessed December 20, 2016).

[67] These forensic assessment instruments developed in the 1970s in a drive to "develop reliable and valid methods to measure what the law wanted to know that was of a psychological or psychiatric nature." Thomas Grisso, "Saleem Shah's Contributions to Forensic Clinical Assessment," 19 Law & Human Behavior 25–30 (1995) at p. 25. *See generally* Richard Rogers & Chelsea E. Fiduccia, "Forensic Assessment Instruments," in Brian L. Cutler & Patricia A. Zapf, eds., *APA Handbook of Forensic Psychology*, American Psychological Association, 2015 at pp. 19–34.

The MMPI is considered a protected psychological instrument, meaning it can only be given and interpreted by a trained psychologist. While it is commonly administered by computer and requires no direct professional involvement during its administration, psychological testing is nearly always preceded by an interview by the psychologist who will interpret the testing results. After the computer scores the test results, the psychologist completes a report interpreting the test results in the context of the individual's history and current psychological concerns. The aim of the test is to identify psychopathological characteristics demonstrated by the individual's choices on the test. The questions are structured to disclose attempts at fabrication.[68] In determining the personality characteristics of the individual, the answers obtained are compared with the established group responses. These established scale patterns were determined by giving the test to a large number of clinical patients who represented the major psychiatric diagnostic categories and a similar number of normally adjusted people. The individual's personality is diagnosed by the degree to which the answers resemble one of the criteria groups.

The MMPI was developed on the basis of empirical findings and has been widely validated by controlled studies. The major criticism which has been made is the potential cultural and age bias involved in using a test developed from the responses of American adults. Despite these potential problems, the MMPI has been carefully researched and has a high degree of reliability.[69] Research has also shown that MMPI is useful in the assessment of malingered psychopathology.[70]

There are various other self-report inventory personality tests. Among those that are widely used are: the Personality Assessment Inventory (PAI), a 344-item inventory written at a fourth-grade legal, covering 22 clinical and treatment scales, and designed to measure adult psychopathology;[71] the California Psychological Inventory™ (CPI™), a test with 434-questions designed to assess social communication and interpersonal behavior that is frequently used in employment screening;[72] the Myers-Briggs Type Indicator® (MBTI®), an objective

---

[68] The MMPI-2 has scales that correlate with persons who are both fabricating symptoms and hiding symptoms. Roger L. Green, "Malingering and Defensiveness on the MMPI-II," in Richard Rogers ed., *Clinical Assessment of Malingering and Deception*, 3d ed., Guilford Press, 2008 at p. 159.

[69] *See* Ryan v. Clarke, 281 F. Supp.2d 1008, 1032 (D. Neb. 2008) (noting that the MMPI is the "gold standard" for objective psychological testing).

[70] Gary B. Melton et al., *Psychological Evaluation for the Courts: A Handbook for Mental Health Professionals and Lawyers*, 3d ed., The Guilford Press, 2007 at pp. 59–60.

[71] *See* http://www.wpspublish.com/store/p/2893/personality-assessment-inventory-pai (last accessed December 29, 2016). The PAI was found to be the second most used self-report inventory, behind the MMPI, in forensic evaluations of adults. Robert P. Archer et al., "A Survey of Psychological Test Use Patterns Among Forensic Psychologists," 87 J. Personality Assessment 84–94 (2006) at p. 87 (available at: https://www.researchgate.net/publication/6928742_A_Survey_of_Psychological_Test_Use_Patterns_Among_Forensic_Psychologists)(last accessed December 29, 2016).

[72] *See* https://www.cpp.com/products/cpi/index.aspx (last accessed December 29, 2016).

personality test based on Carl Jung's theory of personality type;[73] and the revised NEO Personality Inventory (NEO PI-R), an objective personality test consisting of 240 questions designed to measure five personality dimensions (emotional, interpersonal, experiential, attitudinal, and motivational styles).[74]

b. Projective Tests

The Rorschach Inkblot test, developed in 1921 by Swiss psychiatrist Hermann Rorschach, is perhaps the best known projective test. His *Psychodiagnostics,* published in 1921 and translated into English in 1942, marked the birth of projective testing, and the technique became a favorite clinical tool following World War II. The individual is shown singularly ten distinctive inkblots of bilateral symmetry. The blots are contained on square cards. Some are colored; all have slightly different intensities of shading. The subjects are asked to relate what they see in the inkblot pictures. Rorschach scores are determined with reference to reception of (1) form, shape, color and shading; (2) content, i.e., plant, animal, movement; and (3) location, i.e., whole card or only a segment. The interpretation of the responses is dependent on the subjective observation of the examiner and the scoring of the individual's responses may vary from examiner to examiner. Apart from being the most widely used, the Rorschach test is probably also the most widely criticized of all psychometric techniques. A body of research findings has raised questions about even the most basic elements of scoring.[75]

The Thematic Apperception Test (TAT) is a projective test which had its origins in studies at Harvard University. It was first published and marketed as a test in 1943, The test attempts to determine the interpersonal reactions of the subject through the individual's narration of consecutive stories when shown a set of ambiguous pictures which contain people of both sexes and different ages in situations designed to trigger stories of psychological significance. The full set contains 30 pictures, including some alternative versions for males and females or adolescent and adults. In construing the story of each picture, the individual is instructed to narrate what is happening at the moment, what led up to it, how the people feel, and the outcome of the situation. The diagnostician then analyzes the story responses for pervasive personality patterns. Supporters of the testing believe that the individual is less likely to conceal true motivation and feelings when protected by the anonymity of explaining the actions of third persons (the people in the images). This test has been described as useful in diagnosing

---

[73] Information supporting the validity of this assessment is available at: https://www.cpp.com/campaigns/mbti_manual_supp.aspx (last accessed December 29, 2016).

[74] *See* http://www.statisticssolutions.com/neo-personality-inventory-revised-neo-pi-r/ (last accessed December 29, 2016).

[75] William M. Grove et al., "Failure of Rorschach-Comprehensive-System-Based Testimony to be Admissible Under the Daubert-Joiner-Kumho Standard," 8 Psychology, Public Policy, and Law 216–234 (2002).

fantasies, motives, drives, ambitions, preoccupations, attitudes, and interpersonal relationships.[76]

There are many other types of projective tests, such as those involving word association or sentence completion. The Rorschach test, TAT, and all projective unstructured tests are based on the theory that the individual's perceptions among the multitudinous stimuli, how the perceptions are organized, and the manner in which the responses are made, reveal important signs of personality.[77] The purpose is to discover the individual's inner attitudes. The projective tests by their nature cannot be standardized. Variables which may affect the responses include the presence or absence of the examiner, the manner of test administration, the instructions given, the attitude of the examiner, the physical conditions of the test surroundings, and the differences in color, brightness, and background of the pictures. Primary reliance is placed on the examiner's expertise in assessing the responses and organizing the observations that are made. Projective tests were once used more widely than they are today; questions about the validity and reliability of the testing measures have limited their value for forensic assessments.[78]

2.   INTELLIGENCE TESTS

Intelligence tests are used to determine the degree of an individual's intelligence or intelligence quotient (IQ). They are reliable enough to play a primary role in the assessment of minimal intelligence on the various issues of capacity, responsibility, competence, and credibility. While most experts will readily concede that IQ is not a mathematical absolute, it is a useful tool in diagnosing the mental state of a subject. Some IQ tests such as the Otis Quick Score Test could be given to groups of people with only the necessity of a monitor, pencils, and paper. If the circumstances suggest a mental deficiency, an individually administered test could then be given by an expert.

The Stanford-Binet Test is an individually administered test used to determine children's IQ and might be employed to test a prospective child witness. In most instances, however, the forensic examiner will use the Wechsler Adult Intelligence Scale-IV (WAIS-IV). The WAIS-IV is an individually administered standardized adult intelligence test with

---

[76] *See* Leopold Bellak, *The T.A.T., C.A.T., and S.A.T. in Clinical Use,* 5th ed., Allyn & Bacon, 1992; Jerome Kagan & Gerald S. Lessner, *Contemporary Issues in Thematic Apperception Methods,* Thomas, 1961.

[77] For a critical assessment of the legal standing of projective testing *see* David L. Faigman et al., *Modern Scientific Evidence: The Law and Science of Expert Testimony,* 2011–2012 ed., West, 2011 at Vol. 2, pp. 255–294.

[78] *See, e.g.,* James M. Wood, *What's Wrong with the Rorschach? Science Confronts the Controversial Inkblot Test,* John Wiley & Sons, Inc. 2003; Howard Garb et al., "Roots of the Rorschach Controversy," 25 Clinical Psychol. Rev. 97 (2003); Howard Garb et al., "Effective Use of Projective Techniques in Clinical Practice: Let the Data Help with Selection and Interpretation," 33 Prof. Psychol: Res. & Prac. 454 (2003); Carl Gacono et al., "The Rorschach in Forensic Science," 2 J. Psychol. Prac. 33 (2002); Scott O. Lilienfeld et al., "The Scientific Status of Projective Techniques," 1 Psychol. Sci. Publ. Int. 27 (2000).

separate norms for various age levels from adolescence to old age. The IQ under WAIS-IV is determined from a combination of verbal and performance tests. The verbal tests consist of oral subjects covering common sense, judgment, general information, mathematics, digit span, word similarity, and vocabulary. The performance tests consist of visual or visual-manipulative tests of digit-symbol pairing, picture completion, block design, picture arrangement, and object assembly. As with all psychological tests, variables such as anxiety, ill health, distraction, uncooperativeness, mental illness, inattentiveness, lack of education, influence of the examiner, and divergent cultural background can affect the accuracy of an adult IQ test. However, the test attempts to minimize cultural differences and educational gaps, and WAIS-IV is a reliable, validated test.[79]

3. NEUROPSYCHOLOGICAL TESTS

Neuropsychological tests are cognitive/functional tests of retention, memory, and conceptual thinking. Although particularly prevalent as a tool for diagnosing brain damage, the tests are not confined to the sphere of neurology and are also used to diagnose functional mental illness. Neuropsychological tests may be requested when cognitive deficits are suspected or when needed to assess the severity or progression of deficits over time. In addition, neuropsychological tests can be helpful in distinguishing between cognitive disorders and malingering. Research has identified typical patterns of cognitive deficits for a variety of mental disorders, including schizophrenia and bipolar disorder.

A neuropsychological test frequently used for screening for cognitive impairment is the Mini-Mental Status Examination (MMSE®) available through Psychological Assessment Resources (PAR).[80] The test is a thirty-point screening tool that provides measures of orientation, registration (immediate memory), short-term memory (but not long-term memory) as well as language functioning. The MMSE® has demonstrated validity and reliability in psychiatric, neurologic, geriatric, and other medical populations. The convenient new "all-in-one" test form offered by PAR includes a detachable sheet with stimuli for the Comprehension, Reading, Writing, and Drawing tasks.

Psychologists will also use test batteries to assess neuropsychological performance. Neuropsychological test batteries vary considerably based

---

[79] *See* Atkins v. Virginia, 536 U.S. 304, 309 n. 5 (2002) (noting that the Weschler Adult Intelligence Scale test is the standard instrument in the United States for assessing intellectual functioning). *See also* Brumfield v. Cain, 808 F.3d 1041, 1050 (5th Cir. 2016) (the expert "administered the WAIS-IV, which is one of the 'gold standard' IQ tests"); Ex parte Moore, 470 S.W.3d 481, 516 (Ct. Crim App. Tex. 2015) (same); Pruitt v. Neal, 788 F.3d 248, 266 (7th Cir. 2015) (same).

[80] *See* http://www4.parinc.com/products/Product.aspx?ProductID=MMSE (last accessed December 15, 2016).

on the specific tasks and abilities being assessed, but the majority of tests can be categorized as measuring the following brain processes:[81]

- Sensory input;

- Attention and concentration;

- Memory and learning;

- Language and sequential processing occurring contemporaneously with spatial processing and manipulatory ability;

- Executive functioning; and,

- Motor output.

Common neuropsychological tests include NEPSY-II, Neuropsychological Assessment Battery (NAB), Wechsler Memory Scale 4th ed. (WMS-IV), Conners' Continuous Performance Tests (K-CPT and CPT-II), the Halstead-Reitan Neuropsychological Test Battery, and the Luria-Nebraska Neuropsychological Battery.[82]

Older tests include the Bender Visual-Motor Gestalt Test, a neuropsychological test designed to help in the diagnosis of loss of function and organic brain damage.[83] This test presents nine geometrical figures that are copied by the individual. The evaluation of the individual's linear design perception and visual motor functions are used to diagnose possible organic brain impairment. Other older tests are: the Porteus Maze Test, the first widely used non-verbal test of ability, which involves finding paths through a series of mazes;[84] and the Goldstein-Scheerer tests, which require the individual to copy colored designs, sort them into categories, and reproduce designs from memory.[85]

§16.08 NEUROIMAGING[86]

Psychological tests are one form of neuroscience evidence important in assessing brain dysfunction; another form is "neuroimaging" tests.

---

[81] John M. Spores, *Clinician's Guide to Psychological Assessment and Testing*, Springer Publishing Co., 2013 at p. 101.

[82] For a detailed description of the tests and their applications, *see* Kenneth M. Heilman & Edward Valenstein, eds., *Clinical Neuropsychology*, 5th ed., Oxford University Press, 2011; John M. Spores, *Clinician's Guide to Psychological Assessment and Testing*, Springer Publishing Co., 2013.

[83] http://www.hmhco.com/hmh-assessments/other-clinical-assessments/bender#overview (last accessed December 29, 2016).

[84] Andrew M. Colman, *Oxford Dictionary of Psychology,* 4th ed., Oxford University Press, 2015 at p. 586.

[85] Id. at p. 318.

[86] Detailed discussions of neuroimaging techniques are available in Henry T. Greely & Anthony D. Wagner, "Reference Guide on Neuroscience," in Federal Judicial Research Center, *Reference Manual on Scientific Evidence*, 3d ed., National Academies Press, 2011 at pp. 761–784; Lyn M. Gaudet & Gary E. Marchant, "Under the Radar: Neuroimaging Evidence in the Criminal Courtroom," 64 Drake L. Rev. 577–661 (2016); and Jason P. Kerkmans & Lyn M. Gaudet, "Daubert on the Brain: How New Mexico's Daubert Standard Should Inform its Handling of Neuroimaging Evidence," 46 N.M. L. Rev. 383–409 (2016).

Neuroimaging is a type of mental health evidence that involves scanning the brain using various techniques to evaluate the structural or functional characteristics. Advances in neuroimaging have had profound effects on scientific research on brain function. Imaging methods that allow high resolution measurements of brain structure and function in living people have increased the role of neuroscience evidence in litigation. The number of courts addressing the admissibility and weight of neuroimaging evidence has increased exponentially from 2000–2015 and there has been a shift to a focus on the substantive results and the appropriate use of neuroimaging results.[87] This technology is "becoming a highly significant part of the criminal justice process."[88] Criminal defendants regularly use neuroscience evidence at every stage of the criminal process in all manner of cases,[89] and neuroimaging has been recognized as an important component of that evidence.[90] Civil parties have also used neuroimaging techniques to demonstrate injury or impairment, but without as much controversy.

1.   STRUCTURAL TECHNIQUES

a.   CAT

The first neuroimaging techniques assessed the structures of the brain. Computer axial tomography or computer-assisted tomography (CAT or CT) scans, developed in the 1970s, are multidimensional, computer-assisted x-ray machines. The multiple angles and computer analysis enable the technology to detect relatively small density differences within the brain to produce images of the soft tissue of the brain. The technique provides structural information, but not direct

---

[87] *See Id.*; Deborah W. Denno, "How Prosecutors and Defense Attorneys Differ in Their Use of Neuroscience Evidence," 85 Fordham L. Rev. 453–479 (2016); Nita A. Farahany, "Neuroscience and Behavioral Genetics in US Criminal Law: An Empirical Analysis," Journal of Law and the Biosciences 1–25 (2016).

[88] Lyn M. Gaudet & Gary E. Marchant, "Under the Radar: Neuroimaging Evidence in the Criminal Courtroom," 64 Drake L. Rev. 577–661 (2016) at p. 578.

[89] *See* Nita A. Farahany, "Neuroscience and Behavioral Genetics in US Criminal Law: An Empirical Analysis," Journal of Law and the Biosciences 1–25 (2016).

[90] *See, e.g.,* Johnson v. United States, 860 F. Supp.2d 663, 894 (N.D. Iowa 2012) (reversing death sentence for the failure to present mental health mitigation from "an adequate battery of neuropsychological and neuroimaging testing"); United States v. Sandoval-Mendoza, 472 F.3d 645, 652–653, 656 (9th Cir. 2006) (reversing conviction for improper exclusion of expert testimony regarding defendant's brain tumor that supported defendant's entrapment defense).; People v. Jones, 620 N.Y.S.2d 656, 657 (N.Y. App. Div. 1994) (trial court erred in denying defense request for brain scan that may have been useful in his justification defense).

See also ABA, Guidelines for the Appointment and Performance of Defense Counsel in Death Penalty Cases 31 (rev. ed. 2003)("Diagnostic studies, neuropsychological testing, appropriate brain scans, blood tests or genetic studies, and consultation with additional mental health specialists may also be necessary.")(available at: http://www.americanbar.org/groups/com mittees/death_penalty_representation/resources/aba_guidelines.html)(last accessed December 21, 2016).

information about brain function. It is useful in detecting physical variations like lesions, atrophy, and hemorrhages.[91]

CAT scans are quick, noninvasive, and because the equipment is widely-available in hospitals and clinics, the images are relatively inexpensive and easy to obtain.[92]

b.　MRI and DTI

Also developed in the 1970s, magnetic resonance imaging (MRI) is a diagnostic tool used in studying brain structure and some activity by using magnetic fields to create high-quality, three-dimensional images. The images are created by detecting the density of hydrogen atoms and "flipping" them with radio pulses in and out of alignment with the magnetic field. The oscillating magnetic field created by the flipping atoms can be measured and the strength of the signal is partially dependent on the hydrogen concentration, which varies according to the density of the water in the brain. The structural images are very detailed and can be used to detect abnormalities, such as brain injuries and tumors.[93] The technology is noninvasive, offers higher resolution than CAT scans, and does not expose the body to x-rays or other radiation.

Diffusion tensor imaging (DTI) uses the MRI technology to measure the direction water diffuses in brain tissue. This technique is useful in tracing axon connections since water tends to travel along the direction of the myelin coating of axons, not across the myelin. Abnormal connection patterns are associated with a variety of conditions from Alzheimer's disease to traumatic brain injury (TBI).[94] The technique has been challenged as unreliable in diagnosing TBI, but the majority of courts addressing the issue have admitted the evidence.[95]

---

[91] Jane Campbell Moriarty, "Flickering Admissibility: Neuroimaging Evidence in the U.S. Courts," 26 Behav. Sci. & L. 29 (2008) at p. 31. See Reid v. Metro. Life Ins. Co., 944 F. Supp.2d 1279, 1311 (N.D. Ga. 2013) ("[C]omputed tomography (CT) and magnetic resonance imaging (MRI) may reveal cerebral atrophy as an indicator or Dementia.").

[92] CAT scans were introduced in the trial of John Hinckley for the attempted assassination of President Ronald Reagan as evidence of perceive abnormalities in the structural surface of his brain. See Lincoln Caplan, The Insanity Defense and the Trial of John W. Hinckley, Jr., Laurel Publishing, 1984.

[93] Jane Campbell Moriarty, "Flickering Admissibility: Neuroimaging Evidence in the U.S. Courts," 26 Behav. Sci. & L. 29 (2008) at p. 31. See People v. Urdiales, 871 N.E.2d 669, 698 (Ill. 2007) (using MRI evidence, in addition to other expert testimony, in support of claim of diminished capacity).

[94] See Voccia v. United States, 2016 U.S. Dist. LEXIS 60780, *2 (E.D.N.Y. 2016)(plaintiff obtained DTI examination "which resulted in a diagnosis of traumatic brain injury"); Smith v. Ryan, 823 F.3d 1270, 1295(9th Cir. 2016) (defendant claimed PET and DTI scans revealed unspecified brain damage).

[95] See, e.g., White v. Deere & Co., 2-16 U.S. Dist. LEXIS 15644, *12 (D.C. Colo. 2016)("DTI is reliable technology and [the expert] applied a reliable methodology in arriving at his challenged opinion."); Andrew v. Patterson Motor Freight, Inc., 2014 U.S. Dist. LEXIS 151234, *8 (W.D. La. 2014)("In sum, the evidence submitted shows DTI has been tested and has a low error rate; DTI has been subject to peer review and publication; and DTI is a generally accepted method for detecting TBI."); Ruppel v. Kucanin, 2011 U.S. Dist. LEXIS 67503, *6 (N.D. Ind. 2011)(finding DTI to be a reliable method); Booth v. KIT, Inc. 2009 U.S.

2.   FUNCTIONAL TECHNIQUES

a.   *fMRI and MRS*

MRI technology is also used as a functional imaging technique. Functional techniques provide evidence of brain injuries or diseases that do not affect the structure of the brain, but may impair ability to function.[96] Functional magnetic resonance imaging (fMRI), introduced in the 1990s, is a technology that uses magnetic fields to detect activity in the brain by monitoring blood flow changes in the brain during the performance of particular tasks or with exposure to specific stimuli.[97] The fMRI detects changes in the density of the ratio of oxygenated hemoglobin and deoxygenated hemoglobin (which produces a stronger fMRI signal). The blood flow changes allow the interpretation of brain activity through the blood-oxygen-level dependent response (the BOLD response). The BOLD response reflects the fact that increased neural activity requires increased oxygenated blood flow, changing the ratio of oxygenated to deoxygenated hemoglobin.[98]

Magnetic resonance spectroscopy (MRS) uses the same equipment as fMRI, but measures concentrations of certain chemicals in the brain, such as neurotransmitters, instead of blood flow.[99]

b.   *EEG and MEG*

Electroencephalography (EEG), the oldest neuroimaging technique, records the electrical activity on the surface of the brain in response to a variety of stimuli and activities by attaching electrodes to the scalp.[100] Magnetoencephalography (MEG) is the measurement of small magnetic fields generated by brain activity. MEG uses superconducting quantum

---

Dist. LEXIS 117486, *3 (D.N.M. 2009)(denying motion to exclude expert testimony based on DTI results).

[96] *See* Rogers v. State, 783 So.2d 980, 997–998 (Fla. 2001) ("Many forms of injury to the brain tissue, both traumatic and otherwise, do not affect structural integrity of the brain tissue. Rather, the shape of the brain tissue remains unchanged, but the ability to function properly is altered by the injury.").

[97] Kenneth K. Kwong et al., "Dynamic Magnetic Resonance Imaging of Human Brain Activity During Primary Sensory Stimulation," 89 Proc. Nat'l Acad. Sci. U.S. 5675 (1992).

[98] Although fMRI has not been used as frequently as other techniques in criminal cases, it has received a great deal of attention from legal commentators. Lyn M. Gaudet & Gary E. Marchant, "Under the Radar: Neuroimaging Evidence in the Criminal Courtroom," 64 Drake L. Rev. 577–661 (2016) at p. 586.

[99] "MRS is a noninvasive diagnostic test for measuring biochemical changes in the brain, especially the presence of tumor. Spectroscopy is a series of tests that are added to the MRI scan of your brain or spine to measure the chemical metabolism of a suspected tumor." R.V. v. Sec'y of HHS, 2016 U.S. Claims LEXIS 935, n.24 (Ct. Fed. Claims 2016).

[100] A brain electrical activity mapping (BEAM) is a method of presenting the results of an EEG in a colored, graphic display. State v. Zimmerman, 802 P.2d 1024, 1026–1028 (Ariz. Ct. App. 1990). Quantitative methods that compare the individual's EEG results to the results of other measured populations are referred to as "QEEG." Robert W. Thatcher & Joel F. Lubar, "History of Scientific Standards of QEEG Normative Databases," in Thomas H. Budzynski et al., eds., *Introduction to Quantitative EEG and Neurofeedback: Advanced Theory and Applications,* 2d ed., 2009 at p. 30.

interference devices ("squids") positioned over the scalp and can quantitatively measure the strength of activity in various areas of the brain at millisecond resolution. As with other techniques, MEG is used to demonstrate neuroanatomical changes.[101] EEG and MEG are more accurate than fMRI in temporal resolution (the timing of the brain activity), but less accurate in the spatial resolution (the location of the brain activity). The results of these techniques are particularly useful in diagnosing epilepsy and other seizure disorders.[102]

EEG is noninvasive, relatively inexpensive, and can be portable. MEG is more expensive and less portable.

c. PET and SPECT

Positron emission tomography (PET) is a nuclear medicine imaging technique that produces a three-dimensional image of functional processes in the body. The system detects pairs of gamma rays emitted indirectly by a positron-emitting radionuclide (tracer), which is introduced into the body on a biologically-active molecule. One common tracer is fluorodeoxyglucose (FDG), a molecule that is very similar to glucose (sugar) and is treated by the body as glucose. Areas of the brain that use more energy (consuming more glucose) will have higher concentrations of the FDG tracer. The radiation from the FDG tracer is detected and measured by the PET scanner. Other common tracers are oxygen-15, which can be used to determine what parts of the brain are using more or less oxygen; and carbon-11, which can be introduced into molecules that bind with specific receptors in the brain, such as receptors for dopamine or serotonin.

Three-dimensional images of the radiation emissions of the tracer material within the brain are then constructed by computer analysis in a PET scan. The result is a record of the concentrations of the tracer material, and depending on the target of the tracer, either the specific receptors of interest or the level of a specific activity (e.g., glucose consumption or oxygen absorption). The differences in magnitude in radiation emissions, and therefore, tracer concentration levels are typically depicted through the use of different colors. The images are generally not used for structural analysis, but to document its functioning, and are useful in detecting abnormal inactivity such as

---

[101] *See* Grange Ins. Co. v. Sawmiller, 11 N.E.3d 1199, 1201 (Ohio Ct. App. 3d Dist. 2014) (expert's opinion that plaintiff suffered physical injury from her PTSD was not supported by any objective medical tests, such as X-rays, computed tomography scans, magnetic resonance imaging, or magnetoencephalography).

[102] Jane Campbell Moriarty, "Flickering Admissibility: Neuroimaging Evidence in the U.S. Courts," 26 Behav. Sci. & L. 29 (2008) at p. 31.

In People v. Musselwhite, 954 P.2d 475, 482–483 (Cal. 1998), the defendant introduced a BEAM analysis to support the argument that he "suffered from organic brain damage" that "prevented him from forming the mental state required for the commission of murder in the first degree." *See also* People v. Steele, 47 P.3d 225, 231–232 (Cal. 2002) (introducing BEAM analysis to argue against premeditation in murder case).

might be present with Alzheimer's disease or stroke damage.[103] PET scans may also be used to determine which specific areas of the brain are used during certain activities (e.g., reading) or in response to certain stimuli. The technique is relatively expensive and does expose the subject to radiation.

Single photon emission computed tomography (SPECT) scans are similar to PET scans in that they require introduction of a radioactive tracer and produce three-dimensional images of the brain.[104] SPECT does not use positron-emitting tracers, but instead uses gamma-emitting tracers which are more stable and less expensive. The resolution of SPECT scans is not as high as PET scans, but the amount of data recovered is greater.[105]

3. INTERPRETATION ISSUES

The various imaging techniques previously discussed are accepted scientific technology that has been used for decades for research, diagnostic, and clinical purposes. The issue for the use of the techniques in criminal and civil cases, however, is whether the technique has been validated for the purpose it is being offered in the litigation. For example, CAT scans and MRI scans are capable of providing reliable structural images of the brain, but whether such scans are relevant and probative of an individual's particular mental state at issue in the litigation is a separate question. "[D]espite evidence for the localization of some brain functions (e.g., speech, vision), the general tendency of the brain to function as an integrated network limits the conclusions that can be drawn about a person's functional abilities on the basis of structural studies alone."[106] Similarly, the use of functional imaging technology is limited by the lack of a direct link from demonstrated aberrant patterns of brain activity to actual functional impairment that affected the behavior relevant in the case.[107]

---

[103] In Jackson v. Calderon, 211 F.3d 1148, 1165 (9th Cir. 2000), the defendant argued that the PET scan revealed brain damage caused by PCP abuse that rendered him unable to form the intent to kill.

[104] *See* Bryan v. Mullin, 335 F.3d 1207, 1230–1231 (10th Cir. 2003) (using SPECT scan evidence to support insanity claim).

[105] Jane Campbell Moriarty, "Flickering Admissibility: Neuroimaging Evidence in the U.S. Courts," 26 Behav. Sci. & L. 29 (2008) at p. 32.

[106] Paul S. Appelbaum, "Reference Guide on Mental Health Evidence," in Federal Judicial Research Center, *Reference Manual on Scientific Evidence*, 3d ed., National Academies Press, 2011 at p. 838.

[107] Id.; *see also* Cone v. Carpenter, 2016 U.S. Dist. LEXIS 54052, *202–203 (W.D. Tenn. 2016)("[T]the Court finds that the science used by [the neuropsychologist] is somewhat unreliable and has limited probative value regarding whether Cone suffered brain damage and mental illness when he committed these offenses in 1980 and how that brain damage or mental illness affected his behavior as it related to the Todds' murder. The Court further notes that [the expert] did not review evidence of Cone's behavior from the Florida case, had no personal contact with Cone, did not conduct a clinical evaluation, has no knowledge of the etiology of his purported abnormalities, and admittedly cannot predict the effect of these abnormalities on Cone's behavior. . . .The Court finds persuasive Meltzer's critique of [the expert's]s work and opinion that [the expert's] method is imprecise. Although neuroimaging has some relevance, the translation of neuroimages to a single subject is particularly

Neuroimaging results will present several scientific issues that must be considered in determining the admissibility and weight of such evidence. Although each of the techniques discussed has been studied extensively, the studies using the technique for the stated purpose (for example, to demonstrate impairment of a specific cognitive ability), may be limited. In assessing the value of the studies, replication, experimental design, and the representative nature of the studies must be carefully examined.[108] Any assessment of the value of neuroimaging results must also consider the fact that the individual results in the case are generally being compared to averages and the statistical value of such averages.[109] Apart from the rare case that involves the comparison of images from the same individual, such as a medical malpractice case, most cases involve comparing an individual's neuroimaging results to the group averages obtained from prior research studies to demonstrate "abnormality." The technical accuracy and robustness of the individual result must also be considered.[110] Neuroimaging technology must be carefully calibrated and maintained for consistent results and there may be variability among different types or brands of equipment.[111] This inconsistency and variability is minimized in large studies, but may have pronounced effects in interpreting an individual scan.[112]

IV. TRIAL AIDS

§16.09 EXPERT QUALIFICATIONS

1. PSYCHIATRISTS

A psychiatrist is a medical doctor (physician) who, after completing the requirements of the medical degree, has received advanced training

---

challenging. Notably, '[c]urrent brain imaging methods cannot readily determine whether a defendant knew right from wrong or maintained criminal intent or mens rea at the time of the criminal act.' ")(internal citations omitted).

[108] *See* Henry T. Greely & Anthony D. Wagner, "Reference Guide on Neuroscience," in Federal Judicial Research Center, *Reference Manual on Scientific Evidence*, 3d ed., National Academies Press, 2011 at pp. 777–779.

[109] *See* United States v. Gigante, 982 F. Supp. 140, 147 (E.D.N.Y. 1997, aff'd, 166 F.3d 75 (2d Cir. 1999)(court refused to admit PET scan evidence because the PET scans used for comparison "grossly differed from defendant in age and background. . . [and none] were under the influence of drugs.").

[110] Neuroimaging scans, particularly from the computer-assisted imaging techniques, are graphical representations of the results established with designated parameters that may be altered by the expert. Some commentators have expressed concern that this allows the expert to manipulate the parameters to make the results more or less dramatic. Bridget Pratt, " 'Soft' Science in the Courtroom" The Effects of Admitted Neuroimaging Evidence into Legal Proceedings," Penn. Bioethics J., April 2, 2005 at pp. 1–3.

[111] Henry T. Greely & Anthony D. Wagner, "Reference Guide on Neuroscience," in Federal Judicial Research Center, *Reference Manual on Scientific Evidence*, 3d ed., National Academies Press, 2011 at p. 781.

[112] Id. at p. 787.

in the diagnosis, treatment, prevention, and study of mental disorders.[113] The educational requirements for a psychiatrist in the United States are 4 years of pre-medical training in college; 4 years of medical school, the final two years of which are spent in clerkships studying in at least five specialty areas; and a minimum four-year residency in a hospital or agency accredited by the Accreditation Council on Graduate Medical Education (ACGME).[114] Training for psychiatry includes the study of psychopathology, biochemistry, genetics, psychopharmacology, neurology, neuropathology, psychology, psychoanalysis, social science, and many other theories and approaches advanced in the field.

Licensing requirements for psychiatrists vary by state. The Federation of State Medical Boards (FSMB), which represents the state medical boards, maintains an index of state licensing boards online that provides links to the specific requirements for each state medical board.[115]

In addition to completing the United States Medical Licensing Examination through the National Board of Medical Examiners, most psychiatrists take a voluntary certification examination through the American Board of Psychiatry and Neurology (ABPN).[116] This test consists of two parts: written and oral. The written test must be passed before the candidate can take the oral examination. Being board-eligible entitles the doctor to practice psychiatry while seeking board certification. Being board-certified is generally a requirement for long-term practice in a private or academic setting. Psychiatrists who desire to further specialize may complete a one or two year fellowship in the subspecialty and obtain additional board certification in the subspecialty.[117] For certification in forensic psychiatry, applicants must be certified by the Board in general psychiatry by December 31 of the year prior to the examination administration and are required to submit documentation of successful completion of one year of ACGME-accredited fellowship training in forensic psychiatry that did not begin before the time in the general residency training in psychiatry, including time spent in combined training programs, was completed. The exposure to forensic psychiatry given to psychiatry residents as part of their basic psychiatry curriculum does not count toward the one year of training. All licensing and training requirements must be met by July 31 of the year of the

---

[113] See Narriman C. Shahrokh & Robert E. Hales, *American Psychiatric Glossary*, 8th ed., American Psychiatric Publishing, 2003 at p. 157.

[114] Program requirements are available at: http://www.acgme.org/Specialties/Overview/pfcatid/21/Psychiatry (last accessed December 14, 2016).

[115] http://www.fsmb.org/licensure/fcvs/state-requirements (last accessed December 15, 2016).

[116] Information on the qualifications for board certification and the examination process is available at: https://www.abpn.com/become-certified/ (last accessed December 14, 2016).

[117] The available subspecialty certifications are listed at: https://www.abpn.com/become-certified/taking-a-subspecialty-exam/ (last accessed December 14, 2016).

examination. The ABPN maintains an online database for public verification of board certification.[118]

The American Psychiatric Association is a national professional association whose physician members specialize in the diagnosis, treatment, and prevention of mental disorders. It was founded in 1884 as the Association of Medical Superintendents of the American Institutes for the Insane, renamed the American Medico-Psychological Association in 1892, and adopted the current name in 1922. Its objectives include the promotion of research and professional education in psychiatry. The organization has extensive publications, including the *Diagnostic and Statistical Manual of Mental Disorders*. The American Psychiatric Association also maintains a directory of publications and a searchable database of psychiatrists by location and other specifications.[119]

The American Academy of Psychiatry and the Law (AAPL) is an organization of psychiatrists dedicated to excellence in practice, teaching, and research in forensic psychiatry. Founded in 1969 with only 10 members,[120] AAPL currently has more than 1,500 members in North America and around the world.[121] The organization's website maintains a listing of forensic psychiatry fellowships available in the United States and Canada, as well as links to practice guidelines developed by the organization.[122] AAPL promotes scientific and educational activities in forensic psychiatry by facilitating the exchange of ideas and practical clinical experience through publications and regularly scheduled national and regional meetings.

2.   PSYCHOLOGISTS

A psychologist is an individual who is professionally trained in one or more of the branches or subfields of psychology.[123] Individuals may pursue masters or doctoral level training in psychology. The Ph.D. and Psy.D. degrees are terminal doctorate degrees and typically require, at a minimum, four years of advanced coursework in psychology, training in research methods and statistical analysis, and (at least in the case of Ph.D. candidates) a dissertation, which is a written presentation of an original piece of psychological research. Most states require that an independent practice or licensed psychologist hold a Ph.D. or Psy.D.

---

[118] See https://application.abpn.com/verifycert/verifycert.asp (last accessed December 14, 2016).

[119] https://www.psychiatry.org/psychiatrists/search-directories-databases (last accessed December 15, 2016).

[120] Robert I. Simon & Liza H. Gold, *Textbook of Forensic Psychiatry*, 2d ed., American Psychiatric Publishing, 2010 at p. 4.

[121] *See* http://www.aapl.org/index.htm (last accessed December 21, 2016).

[122] Id.

[123] Psychology is a "diverse scientific discipline comprising several major branches of research (e.g., experimental, biological, cognitive, lifespan developmental, personality, social), as well as several subareas of research and applied psychology (e.g., clinical, industrial/organizational, school and educational, human factors, health, neuropsychology, cross-cultural)." Gary R. VandenBos, ed., *APA College Dictionary of Psychology*, 2d ed., American Psychological Association, 2016 at p. 367.

("professional psychology") degree from an American Psychological Association[124] approved clinical psychology program,[125] plus additional required post-doctoral training and supervision. Although the use of the term "psychologist" is restricted in some jurisdictions to licensed psychologists, the title may be used by master's-level trained scientists in a number of non-medical specialties including social, school, and cognitive psychology (particularly those working in an academic setting).

In 2001, the Council of Representatives of the American Psychological Association voted to recognize forensic psychology as a specialty and by 2006 the organization broadened the definition of the specialty to include both clinical practice and research.[126] Forensic psychology fellowship programs are available[127] and certification in forensic psychology through an examination process is offered by the American Board of Forensic Psychology. The American Academy of Forensic Psychology (AAFP) is the education and training arm of the American Board of Forensic Psychology (ABFP), which is responsible for the certifying process in forensic psychology. Both AAFP and ABFP are part of the American Board of Professional Psychology, which has provided certification in designated psychology specialties since 1947.[128] Details on the certification process and a directory of ABFP Forensic Specialists are available on the organization's website.[129]

In addition to the American Psychological Association, the Association for Psychological Science (APS) is another large psychological association in the United States. The APS is dedicated to the advancement of scientific psychology and publishes five journals: *Psychological Science, Current Directions in Psychological Science, Perspectives on Psychological Science, Clinical Psychological Science, Psychological Science in the Public Interest.*[130] The International Association for Correctional and Forensic Psychology (IACFP) focuses on psychology practice in the criminal justice system and law enforcement settings.[131]

---

[124] The American Psychological Association is a scientific and professional organization founded in 1892 and it is the largest association of psychologists in the world. Among its objectives are the promoting of research in psychology and the improvement of research methods and qualifications of psychologists. Its extensive publications include more than 85 scholarly journals, books, videos, and seven electronic databases.

[125] Accreditation standards are available at: http://www.apa.org/ed/accreditation/about/index.aspx (last accessed December 15, 2016). A searchable database of accredited programs is available at the same link.

[126] Curt R. Bartol & Anne M. Bartol, *Introduction to Forensic Psychology: Research and Application*, 3d ed., Sage Publications, Inc., 2012 at p. 16.

[127] For example, Emory University School of Medicine offers a Forensic Psychology Postdoctoral Fellowship. Program details are available at: http://www.psychiatry.emory.edu/education/fellowships/professional_psychology/grady_forensics.html (last accessed December 15, 2016).

[128] http://abfp.com/about/ (last accessed December 15, 2016).

[129] *See* http://abfp.com (last accessed December 15, 2016).

[130] Curt R. Bartol & Anne M. Bartol, *Introduction to Forensic Psychology: Research and Application*, 3d ed., Sage Publications, Inc., 2012 at p. 17.

[131] http://www.aa4cfp.org (last accessed December 19, 2016).

With the expanded focus on neuroimaging and neuroscience in the law, forensic neuropsychology is developing rapidly. Certification in neuropsychology is available through the American Board of Clinical Neuropsychology (ABCN). The ABCN is a specialty board of the American Board of Professional Psychology (ABPP) and is responsible for administration of the examination for competence in the specialty of Clinical Neuropsychology.[132] Once a candidate passes the ABCN examination and becomes board certified in the specialty of Clinical Neuropsychology, he/she is invited to join the American Academy of Clinical Neuropsychology (AACN), which is the membership organization of ABCN Specialists.[133]

3. QUALIFICATIONS GENERALLY

Until the 1960s, courts generally only recognized medically-licensed psychiatrists as the appropriate expert to testify as to mental health conditions, particularly in the criminal justice system. Psychologists were limited to testimony concerning test results and did not provide testimony as to mental condition when the defendant's sanity or mental ability were in question.[134] In *Jenkins v. United States*,[135] the trial court instructed the jury that the testimony of three psychologists could not be considered on the issue of whether the defendant suffered a mental disease or defect for purposes of an insanity defense.[136] The trial court found that the psychologists were not competent to give an opinion as to a mental disease of defect because they lacked medical training.[137] The appellate court reversed, holding that a psychologist with proper credentials was competent to provide such testimony.[138]

Although fellowship training, specialty board certification, and professional organizational membership indicate expertise in forensic psychiatry and psychology, forensic concentration may be offered in programs in clinical psychology, counseling psychology, and criminal justice, among others.[139] Evaluation of the expert's qualifications should

---

[132] Information on certification requirements and procedures is available at: https://theabcn.org/becoming-certified/ (last accessed December 19, 2016).

[133] A directory of board certified members of the AACN is available at: https://theaacn.org/ (last accessed December 19, 2016).

[134] Curt R. Bartol & Anne M. Bartol, *Introduction to Forensic Psychology: Research and Application*, 3d ed., Sage Publications, Inc., 2012 at pp. 118–119.

[135] 307 F.2d 637 (D.C. App. 1962).

[136] 307 F.2d at 642–643.

[137] 307 F.2d at 643.

[138] "We hold only that the lack of a medical degree, and the lesser degree of responsibility for patient care which mental hospitals usually assign to psychologists, are not automatic disqualifications. Where relevant, these matters may be shown to affect the weight of their testimony, even though it be admitted in evidence. The critical factor in respect to admissibility is the actual experience of the witness and the probable probative value of his opinion. The trial judge should make a finding in respect to the individual qualifications of each challenged expert." 307 F.2d at 646.

[139] *See* United States v. Odeh, 2016 U.S. Dist. LEXIS 168146, *14 (E.D. Mich. 2016)(government objection to clinical psychologist as unqualified because not a forensic psychologist overruled).

extend beyond the expert's professional title and the educational program titles, although case law in some states does limit certain mental health evidence to specifically titled experts. For example, in Maryland, case law says that opinions on competency in criminal cases must be provided by a psychiatrist or licensed psychologist.[140] Other courts will admit mental health testimony from experts other than forensic psychiatrists and psychologists.[141] Courts have also recognized experts based on experience and self-directed instruction.[142] In assessing the qualifications of an expert providing mental health testimony, attorneys and the court should consider training, experience, licensure, board certification, and any prior relationship with the individual under evaluation.[143] As with any expert, the credentials and background experience of a forensic psychiatrist or psychologist should be carefully vetted.[144]

A few states have imposed qualification requirements on forensic mental health evaluators, primarily through regulatory systems,[145] and other states have established state certification procedures. For example, Massachusetts has used a "designated forensic professional" scheme for forensic psychiatrists and psychologists since the 1980s. The certification process is managed through the Commonwealth of Massachusetts Department of Mental Health and involves taking a written examination on standards of practice, state forensic statutes, and mental health case law; completing two training reports and two final reports; and receiving a written assessment from a forensic mental health supervisor.[146] Other

---

[140] Colbert v. State, 18 Md. App. 632, 642, 308 A.2d 726, 732, cert. denied, 269 Md. 756 (1973). In Maryland, there is some legal foundation for allowing licensed clinical social workers to provide an opinion on competency; however, the Department of Health and Mental Hygiene, which oversees all competency evaluations for the criminal courts, does not currently utilize clinical social workers for this purpose. Md. Health Occupations Code Ann. § 19–101 (m)(4) (2014). See also Hon. Charlotte M. Cooksey, Mental Health Procedures, 2014 (available at: http://mdcourts.gov/reference/pdfs/mentalhealthprocedures.pdf)(last accessed December 20, 2016).

[141] See United States v. Azure, 801 F.2d 336, 342 (8th Cir. 1986) (social worker).

[142] See LeBlanc v. Coastal Mech. Servs., LLC, 2005 WL 5955027 (S.D. Fla. 2005) (counselor with extensive clinical experience); see also Jenkins v. United States, 307 F.2d 637 (D.C. Cir. 1962) (determination of a psychologist's competence to render an expert opinion is a case-by-case matter based on knowledge, not a professional title).

[143] Although a prior treatment provider will have experience with the individual, the prior therapeutic relationship may introduce conflicts of interest and bias that should be avoided. Paul S. Appelbaum, "Reference Guide on Mental Health Evidence," in Federal Judicial Research Center, Reference Manual on Scientific Evidence, 3d ed., National Academies Press, 2011 at pp. 869–875.

[144] See Drake v. Portuondo, 321 F.3d 338, 340 (2d Cir. 2003) ("It is now clear that the expert's qualifications were largely perjured, and that the syndrome, dubbed 'picquerism,' is referenced nowhere but in a true-crime paperback.").

[145] See, e.g., Ohio Revised Code § 2945.37 and § 5122.01 (setting the educational and training requirements for psychiatrists and licensed clinical psychologists who conduct competency to stand trial evaluations).

[146] Commonwealth of Massachusetts Department of Mental Health, Forensic Service, Designated Forensic Professional Procedures Manual, July 22, 2011 (available at: http://www.mass.gov/eohhs/docs/dmh/publications/dfp-manual.pdf)(last accessed December 20, 2016).

states, such as Virginia, Florida, and Texas, provided specialized continuing education, but do not have a formal certification process.[147]

§16.10 STANDARDS

Most jurisdictions do not place requirements or restrictions on the techniques or methods of forensic mental health evaluations and the specific approach is left to the discretion of the evaluator. A few jurisdictions have adopted specific guidelines through regulatory standards, primary limited to specific types of evaluations.[148] For example, Florida has guidelines specifically for competency evaluations in criminal cases.[149] Unlike many areas of forensic science that have promoted standards development through governmental agencies like NIST-OSAC,[150] the fields of forensic psychiatry and psychology have relied on professional organizations for the development and promotion of industry standards.

The American Psychological Association has issued *Specialty Guidelines for Forensic Psychology*[151] for the "professional practice by any psychologist working within any subdiscipline of psychology (e.g., clinical, developmental, social, cognitive) when applying the scientific, technical, or specialized knowledge of psychology to the law to assist in addressing legal, contractual, and administrative matters."[152] The application of the guidelines is triggered not by the title of the examiner, but by the service being provided. The guidelines are voluntary, but do provide industry standards for the practice of forensic psychology on responsibilities; competence; diligence; relationships; fees; informed consent, notification, and assent; conflicts in practice; privacy, confidentiality, and privilege;

---

[147] Kirk Heilbrun & Stephanie Brooks, "Forensic Psychology and Forensic Sciences: A Proposed Agenda for the Next Decade," 16 Psychology, Public Policy & Law, 219–253 (2010) at pp. 228–229.

[148] For example, Pennsylvania's Board of Psychology adopted a Code of Ethics that is set forth as a regulation in section 41.61 of Title 49 of the Pennsylvania Code. Principle 3(e) of 49 Pa.Code § 41.61 states: "As practitioners and researchers, psychologists act in accord with American Psychological Association standards and guidelines related to practice and to the conduct of research with human beings and animals." Relying in part on Principle 3(e) of the Code of Ethics, in Grossman v. State Board of Psychology, 825 A.2d 748 (Pa.Cmwlth. 2003), Pennsylvania's Commonwealth Court upheld a State Board of Psychology disciplinary action against a psychologist for violation of the APA Guidelines.

See also Curt R. Bartol & Anne M. Bartol, *Introduction to Forensic Psychology: Research and Application*, 3d ed., Sage Publications, Inc., 2012 at p. 196; Kirk Heilbrun & Stephanie Brooks, "Forensic Psychology and Forensic Sciences: A Proposed Agenda for the Next Decade," 16 Psychology, Public Policy & Law, 219–253 (2010) at p. 225.

[149] *See* State of Florida Department of Children and Families, CF Operating Procedure No. 155-19, *Evaluation and Reporting of Competency to Proceed*, July 24, 2015 (available at: https://www.dcf.state.fl.us/admin/publications/cfops/CFOP%20155-xx%20Mental%20Health%20-%20Substance%20Abuse/CFOP%20155-19,%20Evaluation%20and%20Reporting%20of%20Competency%20To%20Proceed.pdf)(last accessed December 20, 2016).

[150] *See* https://www.nist.gov/topics/forensic-science/osac-subcommittees (last accessed December 20, 2016).

[151] American Psychological Association, "Specialty Guidelines for Forensic Psychology," 68 American Psychologist 7–19 (2013)(available at: http://www.apa.org/practice/guidelines/index.aspx)(last accessed December 16, 2016).

[152] Id. at p. 7.

methods and procedures; assessment; professional and other public communications. In collaboration with the American Academy of Forensic Psychology, Oxford University Press also published a series on "Best Practice in Forensic Mental Health Assessment."[153] The series describes the relevant law, science, ethics, and other influences on best practices.

The American Academy of Psychiatry and the Law has promulgated guidelines on several subjects, including forensic evaluations of psychiatric disability, psychiatric evaluations of competency to stand trial, ethics guidelines, evaluations of defendants raising an insanity defense, and the video recording of forensic psychiatric evaluations.[154] The evaluation guidelines provide background on the legal issues involved, discussion of the necessary components of the evaluations to be conducted, listings of relevant available assessment instruments and testing tools, and information on the structure and substance of the forensic report. For the guidelines on competency to stand trial, the limitations of the most widely-used instruments are discussed in detail. These guidelines, while voluntary, are well-regarded and experts practicing in the field should at least be familiar with the standards.

The American Psychiatric Association has developed and published 23 practice guidelines on the diagnosis and treatment of various mental disorders.[155] Importantly, the Association has adopted the *Practice Guidelines for the Psychiatric Evaluation of Adults*.[156] The Association cautions that the Practice Guidelines are not intended to serve or be

---

[153] *See, e.g.,* Alan Goldstein & Naomi E. Sevin Goldstein, *Evaluating Capacity to Waive Miranda Rights,* Oxford University Press, 2010; Mark Cunningham, *Evaluation for Capital Sentencing,* Oxford University Press, 2010; Geri S.W. Fuhrmann & Robert A. Zibbell, *Evaluation for Child Custody,* 2011; Debra A. Pinals & Douglas Mossman, *Evaluation for Civil Commitment,* Oxford University Press, 2011; Andrew W. Kane & Joel A. Dvoskin, *Evaluation for Personal Injury Claims,* Oxford University Press, 2011; Lisa Drago Piechowski, *Evaluation of Workplace Disability,* Oxford University Press, 2011; Jane Goodman-Delahunty & William E. Foote, *Evaluation for Workplace Discrimination and Harassment,* Oxford University Press, 2010; Kirk Heilbrun, Thomas Grisso & Alan Goldstein, *Foundations of Forensic Mental Health Assessment,* Oxford University Press, 2008; Philip Will & Mary Alice Conroy, *Evaluation of Sexually Violent Predators,* Oxford University Press, 2008.

[154] Liza H. Gold et al., "AAPL Practice Guideline for the Forensic Evaluation of Psychiatric Disability," 36(4) J. Amer. Acad. Psych. & Law S3–S50 (2008); Douglas Mossman et al., "AAPL Practice Guideline for the Forensic Psychiatric Evaluation of Competence to Stand Trial," 35(4) J. Amer. Acad. Psych. & Law S3–S72 (2007); American Academy of Psychiatry and the Law, *Ethics Guidelines for the Practice of Forensic Psychiatry,* Adopted May 2005; AAPL Task Force, "AAPL Practice Guideline for the Forensic Psychiatric Evaluation of Defendants Raising the Insanity Defense," 42(4) J. Amer. Acad. Pysch. & Law S3–S76 (2014); AAPL Task Force, *Video Recording of Forensic Psychiatric Evaluations,* Revised May 2013.

All AAPL guidelines are available on the organization's website (available at: http://www.aapl.org/practice.htm)(last accessed December 16, 2016).

[155] The practice guidelines are available at: http://psychiatryonline.org/guidelines (last accessed December 16, 2016).

[156] American Psychiatric Association Work Group on Psychiatric Evaluation, *Practice Guideline for the Psychiatric Evaluation of Adults,* 3d ed., American Psychiatric Association Publishing, 2016 (available at: http://psychiatryonline.org/doi/book/10.1176/appi.books.97808904 26760)(last accessed December 16, 2016).

construed as a "standard of medical care."[157] The guidelines, however, do provide industry recommendations on how evaluations should be conducted and documented.

The American Bar Association has adopted standards for attorneys, judges, and others working in the criminal justice system for dealing with mental health issues. Originally adopted in 1984,[158] the standards were recently the subject of a four-year review and revision effort. The updated *Criminal Justice Mental Health Standards* were adopted by the ABA in August 2016.[159] The Standards "represent a comprehensive approach to the adjudication and treatment of people with mental disability who come into contact with the criminal justice system . . . [in] a balanced attempt to promote fair and humane treatment without compromising public safety, accurate evaluations and adjudications consistent with constitutional and other legal prerogatives, and decision-making autonomy for people with mental disabilities that does not offend competing reliability goals."[160] Part III of the standards addresses evaluations and expert testimony and Standards 7-3.9 and 7-3.10 contain provisions regarding the necessary qualifications for mental health professionals.[161]

---

[157] "[A]dherence to these guidelines will not ensure a successful outcome for every individual, nor should these guidelines be interpreted as including all proper methods of evaluation and care or excluding other acceptable methods of evaluation and care aimed at the same results." Statement of the American Psychiatric Association (available at: http://psychiatry online.org/doi/full/10.1176/appi.books.9780890426760.pe01#x79596.8322619 (last accessed December 16, 2016).

[158] The original publication was more than ninety black letter Criminal Justice Mental Health Standards. Among other issues, the Mental Health Standards dealt with: (1) the role of mental health professionals in the criminal justice system; (2) the interaction between the police and people with mental disorders; (3) general issues concerning evaluations and testimony by mental health professionals; (4) competence to participate in the legal process; (5) the insanity defense and related defenses; (6) commitment of insanity acquittees; and (7) special commitment, sentencing, and prison issues that affect offenders with mental disorders. http://www. americanbar.org/publications/criminal_justice_section_archive/crimjust_standards_mentalhealth _toc.html (last accessed December 22, 2016).

[159] *Criminal Justice Mental Health Standards*, American Bar Association, August 8, 2016 (available at: http://www.americanbar.org/content/dam/aba/publications/criminal_justice_standards/ mental_health_standards_2016.authcheckdam.pdf)(last accessed December 22, 2016).

[160] Christopher Slobogin, "The American Bar Association's Criminal Justice Mental Health Standards: Revisions for the Twenty-First Century," 44 Hastings Const. L. Qtrly. 1–36 (2016).

[161] These standards divide forensic experts into three categories: court-appointed evaluators, testifying evaluators, and scientific experts. Under standard 7-3.10, court-appointed evaluators who address competence issues should generally be psychiatrists, psychologists, social workers, or psychiatric nurses who have met the relevant licensing requirements, whereas court-appointed evaluators of mental state at the time of the offense or of future risk generally should be psychiatrists or psychologists. Standard 7-3.10(c)(ii). All such evaluators must possess the necessary clinical knowledge and have received training on and possess sufficient forensic knowledge about the legal issue addressed in the evaluation. Standard 7-3.9(a)(ii). Testifying experts must either meet the same requirements or, if they have provided therapy to the person, be limited to testifying about "matters concerning the defendant's general mental condition as presented during the therapeutic relationship." Standard 7-3.9(b)(ii). All testifying experts must have "performed an adequate evaluation, including a personal interview with the individual whose mental condition is in question, relevant to the legal and clinical matter(s) upon which the witness is called to testify." Standard 7-3.9(b)(iii). In contrast, scientific experts do not need to evaluate the person if they

§16.11 EVIDENCE ISSUES

1.   GENERAL ADMISSIBILITY

Expert testimony from forensic psychiatrists and psychologists faces the same admissibility challenges as expert testimony from other forensic disciplines.[162] These challenges have largely been unsuccessful with some exceptions for experts testifying outside their area of expertise,[163] insufficient testimony about the methodology,[164] and controversial theories. For example, in *Matter of State of New York v. David D.*[165] the respondent in a civil sex offender commitment proceeding challenged the admissibility of testimony from the state's expert witness concerning a diagnosis of Other Specified Paraphilic Disorder (OSPD) Hebephilia.[166] Following a *Frye* hearing, the court concluded that OSPD Hebephilia is not generally accepted as a reliable diagnosis in the relevant psychiatric community.[167] The court considered the fact that the diagnosis was discussed but not included in the DSM-5 as a diagnosis.[168] That fact was not deemed determinative, however, because "the reasons for the APA Board's rejection are cloaked in secrecy, and the basis for the rejection cannot be discerned."[169] Ultimately, the court determined that the large number of opponents of the diagnosis reflected in the scientific articles demonstrated that the diagnosis is not accepted by a substantial majority of the scientific community.[170]

---

have the education and experience necessary to "present scientific or clinical knowledge" relevant to the particular issue in question. Standard 7-3.9(c).

[162] *See, e.g.,* United States v. Odeh, 2016 U.S. Dist. LEXIS 168146 (E.D. Mich. 2016)(challenges to psychologist's testimony included relevance, reliability, lack of peer review on theory, and probative value outweighed by prejudicial value).

[163] *See, e.g.,* City Homes, Inc. v. Hazelwood, 210 Md.App. 615, 63 A.3d 713, cert. denied, 432 Md. 468, 69 A.3d 476 (20130)(in lead paint case, a pediatrician was not qualified to offer an opinion on resulting mental impairment because he had no experience evaluating brain impairment in children who have been exposed to lead).

[164] *See, e.g.,* State v. Braesch, 292 Neb. 930, 949–950, 874 WN.W.2d 874, 889–890 (2016) (expert failed to explain what information lead to the diagnosis of bipolar I disorder and how that disorder would have limited the defendant's ability to regulate his behavior); Blasdell v. State, 470 S.W.3d 59, 65–66 (Ct. Crim. App. Tex. 2015) (expert failed to testify to any peer-reviewed article discussing the "weapon-focus-effect theory" so court was unable to discern the potential error rate or whether the theory is generally accepted and expert "did not describe any principles of the theory or the methodology by which he would apply those principles.").

[165] 37 N.Y.S.3d 685, 53 Misc.3d 1041 (Sup. Ct. Albany Cty. 2016).

[166] The expert defined OSPD Hebephilia as the sexual attraction to pubescent girls (ages 11–14).

[167] 37 N.Y.S.3d at 686.

[168] "These are the mental health professionals who would have direct familiarity with the diagnosis, its scientific underpinnings, and its reliability." 37 N.Y.S.3d at 694.

[169] Id.

[170] 37 N.Y.S.3d at 695–696. *See also* Matter of State of New York v. Jason C., 51 Misc.3d 553, 26 N.Y.S.3d 423 (Sup. Ct. Kings Cty. 2016) (diagnosis of Other Specified Paraphilic Disorder-Non-Consent (OSPD-NC) not generally accepted in the relevant scientific community).

The ABA *Criminal Justice Mental Health Standards* provide slightly different standards for the admissibility of expert testimony depending on whether the assessment is retrospective, contemporaneous, or prospective.[171] For retrospective and contemporaneous assessments of mental condition, the standards provide that "expert testimony, in the form or an opinion or otherwise . . . should be admissible whenever the testimony is based on and is within the specialized knowledge of the witness and will assist the trier of fact on an issue relevant to the adjudication."[172] If the expert is testifying about the person's future mental condition, including risk of violence, the standards add the requirement that the testimony be "based on reliable techniques and practices and outline the factors that the expert may consider:[173]

- The clinical significance of the individual's history and current behavior;

- Scientific studies involving the relationship between specific behaviors and variables that are objectively measurable and verifiable;

- The possible psychological or behavioral effects of proposed therapeutic or other interventions;

- The factors that tend to enhance or diminish the likelihood that specific types of behavior could occur in the future; and,

- The defendant's performance on validated instruments for assessing risk and need only when administered, scored, interpreted and presented in accordance with scientific and professional standards.[174]

Some limitations exist, however, for mental health evidence, including neuroimaging results, that are not generally present with other expert testimony. These limitations raise issues concerning the relevance of mental health testimony, ultimate issue testimony, and certain constitutional protections in criminal cases.

---

[171] *Criminal Justice Mental Health Standards*, American Bar Association, August 8, 2016 (available at: http://www.americanbar.org/content/dam/aba/publications/criminal_justice_standards /mental_health_standards_2016.authcheckdam.pdf)(last accessed December 22, 2016).

[172] Id. at Standard 7-3.8(a).

[173] Id. at Standard 7-3.8(b).

[174] The Standards also provide that "[t]he expert should identify and explain the theoretical and factual basis for the opinion and the reasoning process through which the opinion was formulated. In doing so, the expert should be permitted to describe facts upon which the opinion is based, regardless of their independent admissibility under the rules of evidence, if the court finds that the Sixth Amendment to the U.S. Constitution and similar relevant state provisions permit admission of these facts and that: (i) they are of a type that is customarily relied upon by mental health professionals in formulating their opinions; and (ii) they are relevant to serve as the factual basis for the expert's opinion; and (iii) their probative value outweighs their tendency to prejudice or confuse the trier of fact. Standard 7.3-11(c).

2. RELEVANCE

Although a few cases have raised the issue of the scientific reliability of DSM diagnoses,[175] most courts and litigants treat the issue as settled.[176] The more significant question is whether the DSM diagnoses, which do not rate impairment, are relevant to legal determinations. "Diagnosis and impairment are not equivalent. No diagnosis carries specific information regarding level of impairment or information about whether an impairment associated with that diagnosis is relevant to the legal issue under examination by the court."[177] When a criminal defendant offers psychiatric evidence, the courts must ensure the evidence "is relevant to negate specific intent as opposed to 'presenting a dangerously confusing theory of defense more akin to justification and excuse.' "[178] Even if the proffered mental health testimony is relevant to specific intent, the Court must still "determine whether the testimony is grounded in sufficient scientific support to warrant use in the courtroom, and whether it would aid the jury in reaching a decision on the ultimate issues."[179] With respect to the helpfulness inquiry, "[t]he proper focus [is] on the proffered link or relationship between the specific psychiatric evidence offered and the [mental state] at issue in the case.' "[180] In *United States v. Davis*,[181] the district court held that the expert testimony of the forensic psychologist concerning the diagnosis of Attention Deficit Hyperactivity Disorder (ADHD) was inadmissible because the expert failed to establish the link between the symptoms of ADHD and the defendant's mental state in preparing the false tax returns.[182]

---

[175] Ryder v. State, 83 P.3d 856, 869 n. 3 (Crim. App. Okla. 2004) ("This is especially true in a case involving psychological and psychiatric testimony. So much of the opinion given by these expert witnesses is based on subjective opinion. These types of experts often cite to a diagnosis in the Diagnostic and Statistical Manual of Mental Disorders (1994)(DSM-IV) published by the American Psychiatric Association. Based upon the procedure utilized to enter a proposed malady into the DSM-IV, there is some question as to whether some of the possible diagnoses listed in the DSM-IV could meet the admissibility requirements of Daubert.").

[176] There have even been challenges to mental health evidence because it did not rely on the DSM criteria. *See, e.g.,* S.M. v. J.K., 262 F.3d 914, 922 (9th Cir. 2001) (court held that it was proper to admit the expert testimony and allow the variance with the DSM criteria to be explored on cross-examination).

[177] Robert I. Simon & Liza H. Gold, "Psychiatric Diagnosis in Litigation," in Robert I. Simon & Liza H. Gold, eds., *Textbook of Forensic Psychiatry,* 2d ed., American Psychiatric Publishing, 2010 at p. 153.

[178] United States v. Childress, 58 F.3d 693, 727–28 (D.C. Cir. 1995) (*quoting* United States v. Cameron, 907 F.2d 1051, 1067 (11th Cir. 1990)).

[179] 58 F.3d at 728 (quoting United States v. Brawner, 471 F.2d 969, 1002, 153 U.S. App. D.C. 1 (D.C. Cir. 1972)).

[180] Id. at 730 (*quoting* Cameron, 907 F.2d at 1067 n. 3 (11th Cir. 1990)).

[181] 78 F. Supp.3d 17 (D.D.C. 2015).

[182] 78 F. Supp.3d at 20–21. *See also* United States v. Boykoff, 186 F. Supp.2d 347 (S.D.N.Y. 2002) (expert failed to establish link between diagnoses (bipolar and attention deficit disorder) and the mental state for the criminal conduct); United States v. Wall, 593 Fed. Appx. 128 (3d Cir. 2014) (expert testimony properly excluded where expert offered no link between the psychiatric evidence and the defendant's intent to defraud).

Since the 2000s, courts have become more familiar with neuropsychological testing and neuroimaging techniques.[183] That familiarity, however, has not equated to universal admissibility. Neuroimaging results have been excluded by courts over concerns about reliability and relevance.[184] The concerns about the relevance of neuroimaging evidence are based on the variability of the brain. Analyzing an individual's brain provides little probative information since individual variability is so great. "[I]t is difficult to draw any reliable conclusion from the observation that a particular individual's brain shows some type of distinctive or unusual pattern or characteristic."[185] To account for this variability, experts use quantitative methods to compare individual data with large data sets of representative populations to determine the statistical significance of any particular findings in an individual's results. Because quantitative methods are necessary, the error rate of the neuroimaging technique is important information that must be considered whenever neuroimaging evidence is presented.

> [E]rror rate is also crucial to most neuroscience evidence, in two different senses. One is the degree to which the machines used to produce the evidence make errors. Although these kinds of errors may balance out in a large sample used in published literature, any scan of any one individual may well be affected by errors in the scanning process. Second, and more important, neuroscience will almost never give an absolute answer, but will give a probabilistic one. For example, a certain brain structure or activation pattern will be found in some percentage of people with a particular mental condition or state. These group averages will have error rates when they are applied to individuals. Those error rates need to be known and presented.[186]

Adding to the concerns about the relevance of neuroimaging evidence is the "gap" between the asserted brain abnormalities and the relevant mental state at issue.[187] Research has not conclusively established what

---

[183] *See, e.g.,* Cone v. Carpenter, 2016 U.S. Dist. LEXIS 54052 (W.D. Tenn. 2016)(detailing the numerous reports from psychiatrists, psychologists, and neurologists concerning the psychological testing and neuroimaging results from examinations of the defendant in the 1980s and 2010s).

[184] *See, e.g.,* United States v. Mezvinsky, 206 F. Supp.2d 661, 662, 674–675 (E.D. Pa. 2002) (excluding PET scan evidence as lacking both reliability and relevance where "frontal lobe organic brain damage" could not be correlated to lack of relevant mental state necessary for fraud).

[185] Lyn M. Gaudet & Gary E. Marchant, "Under the Radar: Neuroimaging Evidence in the Criminal Courtroom," 64 Drake L. Rev. 577–661 (2016) at p. 590.

[186] Henry T. Greely & Anthony D. Wagner, "Reference Guide on Neuroscience," in Federal Judicial Research Center, *Reference Manual on Scientific Evidence*, 3d ed., National Academies Press, 2011 at p. 787.

[187] Lyn M. Gaudet & Gary E. Marchant, "Under the Radar: Neuroimaging Evidence in the Criminal Courtroom," 64 Drake L. Rev. 577–661 (2016) at p. 592. *See,* e.g., United States v. Purkey, 428 F.3d 738, 752 (8th Cir. 2005) (neuroscience evidence properly excluded because the expert could not establish a connection between the PET and MRI results and the

inferences about behavior properly can be drawn from neuroimaging evidence.[188] For this reason, it is important that additional forensic mental health assessment tools are used to clinically correlate the neuroimaging findings to demonstrated impairment in cognitive or behavioral function.[189]

3. ULTIMATE ISSUE

With respect to mental health testimony in criminal cases, it has long been a matter of controversy whether expert witnesses should express an opinion as to the ultimate issue in a case.[190] For example, in a case in which a criminal defendant has asserted an insanity defense, if the expert tells the finders of fact that the defendant is "insane," that is testimony on the "ultimate issue." Many scholars have objected that this testimony is improper because it is "not based on 'specialized' knowledge, but [on] legal and moral judgments outside the expertise of mental health professionals."[191] Legal commentators argue that such testimony invades the province of the jury.[192]

Although a matter of scholarly controversy, ultimate issue testimony is generally permitted in most states.[193] The Federal Rules of Evidence permit ultimate issue testimony except as to mental states that constitute an element of the charge or constitute a defense to the charge:

> Rule 704. Opinion on an Ultimate Issue
>
> (a) In General—Not Automatically Objectionable. An opinion is not objectionable just because it embraces an ultimate issue.

---

defendant's state of mind at the time of the offense); People v. Goldstein, 786 N.Y.S.2d 428, 432 (App. Div. 2004) (excluding PET scans because they were not probative of insanity issue).

[188] Jane Campbell Moriarty, "Flickering Admissibility: Neuroimaging Evidence in the U.S. Courts," 26 Behav. Sci. & L. 29 (2008) at pp. 42–44.

[189] *See* United States v. Day, 524 F.3d 1361, 1369–1370 (D.C. Cir. 2008) (affirming the exclusion of expert's testimony based on PET scan results because the conclusions were inconsistent with the defendant's medial records and other psychiatric evidence).

[190] Paul S. Appelbaum, "Reference Guide on Mental Health Evidence," in Federal Judicial Research Center, *Reference Manual on Scientific Evidence*, 3d ed., National Academies Press, 2011 at p. 867.

[191] Gary B. Melton et al., *Psychological Evaluations for the Courts: A Handbook for Mental Health Professionals and Lawyers*, The Guilford Press, 2007 at p. 17.

[192] Ric Simmons, "Conquering the Province of the Jury: Expert Testimony & the Professionalization of Fact-Finding," 74 U. Cin. L. Rev. 1013 (2006).

[193] *See, e.g.*, Maryland Code 9–120("Notwithstanding any other provision of law, a psychologist licensed under the "Maryland Psychologists Act" and qualified as an expert witness may testify on ultimate issues, including insanity, competency to stand trial, and matters within the scope of that psychologist's special knowledge, in any case in any court or in any administrative hearing."); Ind. R. Evid. 704 ("Testimony in the form of an opinion or inference otherwise admissible is not objectionable just because it embraces an ultimate issue [except] [w]itnesses may not testify as to opinions concerning intent, guilt, or innocence in a criminal case; the truth or falsity of allegations; whether a witness has testified truthfully; or legal conclusions."); Fla. Stat. 90–703 ("Testimony in the form of an opinion or inference otherwise admissible is not objectionable because it includes an ultimate issue to be decided by the trier of fact."). Virginia permits ultimate issue testimony in civil cases, but prohibits it in criminal cases. *See* Va. Rule 2:704 .

(b)   Exception. In a criminal case, an expert witness must not state an opinion about whether the defendant did or did not have a mental state or condition that constitutes an element of the crime charged or of a defense. Those matters are for the trier of fact alone.

The practical effect of the federal rule, however, may have little impact on how the expert's testimony is perceived by the factfinder. Experts may not opine on the ultimate issue (insanity), but are not barred from addressing whether the defendant meets a specific legal standard under the statute at issue (whether the defendant could "appreciate the wrongfulness of his acts"[194]).

The ABA Criminal Justice Mental Health Standards include this guidance on ultimate issue testimony:[195]

If the jurisdiction requires the evaluator to present his or her opinion on a question requiring a conclusion of law or a moral or social value judgment, the evaluator should use cautionary language to explain the boundaries of the expert's clinical expertise and the limitations of the opinion.

§16.12 Constitutional Protections

1.   Fifth Amendment

The Fifth Amendment to the United States Constitution provides in part that no person "shall be compelled in any criminal case to be a witness against himself."[196] The constitutional protection requires at its core that the government produce evidence against the defendant by the labor of its officers, not by the "simple, cruel expedient of forcing from his own lips."[197] Under a narrow set of circumstances, generally involving competency assessments or the government's right to refute a mental capacity defense, the Fifth Amendment privilege against self-incrimination may be involved in forensic mental health evaluations.

The prosecution of a mentally incompetent person violates the constitutional protection of due process.[198] The protection is so fundamental that the issue of competency may be raised by the government or the court in addition to the defense. If a reasonable basis

---

[194]   18 U.S.C. § 17—federal statute defining insanity.

[195]   *Criminal Justice Mental Health Standards*, American Bar Association, August 8, 2016 at Standard 7-3.8(c).

[196]   "No person shall be held to answer for a capital, or otherwise infamous crime, unless on a presentment or indictment of a grand jury, except in cases arising in the land or naval forces, or in the militia, when in actual service in time of war, or public danger; nor shall any person be subject for the same offense to be twice in jeopardy of life or limb, nor shall be compelled in any criminal case to be a witness against himself, nor be deprived of life, liberty, or property without due process of law; nor shall private property be taken for public use without just compensation." U.S. Const. Amend. V.

[197]   Culombe v. Connecticut, 367 U.S. 568, 581–582 (1961).

[198]   Drope v. Missouri, 420 U.S. 162 (1975).

exists to believe competency is an issue, the court has an absolute duty to order an evaluation.[199] Similarly, if the defense raises a mental capacity defense to the charges (e.g., insanity), federal criminal procedure rules[200] and state statutory provisions require or permit the court to order an evaluation for use by the government.[201] When the defendant is compelled to undergo these court-ordered evaluations, constitutional protections against self-incrimination are implicated. If the defense has not requested an evaluation and has not asserted a mental capacity defense, the Supreme Court has held that statements made by the defendant during the court-ordered evaluation may not be used by the government at trial.[202] The federal criminal procedure rules and some state statutory provisions broaden this protection to cover evaluations requested by the defense and to evidence derived from the defendant's statements during the evaluation.[203]

---

[199] Id.; Pate v. Robinson, 383 U.S. 375 (1966).

[200] Fed. R. Crim P. 12.2(c)(1)(B): "If the defendant provides notice under Rule 12.2(a) [to raise an insanity defense], the court must, upon the government's motion, order the defendant to be examined under 18 U.S.C. § 4242. If the defendant provides notice under Rule 12.2(b) [to introduce expert evidence of mental condition bearing on guilt or on punishment in a death penalty case] the court may, upon the government's motion, order the defendant to be examined under procedures ordered by the court."

[201] *See, e.g.,* Va. Code § 19.2–168.1:

A.   If the attorney for the defendant gives notice pursuant to § 19.2–168, and the Commonwealth thereafter seeks an evaluation of the defendant's sanity at the time of the offense, the court shall appoint one or more qualified mental health experts to perform such an evaluation. The court shall order the defendant to submit to such an evaluation and advise the defendant on the record in court that a refusal to cooperate with the Commonwealth's expert could result in exclusion of the defendant's expert evidence. The qualification of the experts shall be governed by subsection A of § 19.2–169.5. The location of the evaluation shall be governed by subsection B of § 19.2–169.5. The attorney for the Commonwealth shall be responsible for providing the experts the information specified in subsection C of § 19.2–169.5. After performing their evaluation, the experts shall report their findings and opinions, and provide copies of psychiatric, psychological, medical or other records obtained during the course of the evaluation to the attorneys for the Commonwealth and the defense. The evaluator shall also send a redacted copy of the report removing references to the defendant's name, date of birth, case number, and court of jurisdiction to the Commissioner of Behavioral Health and Developmental Services for the purpose of peer review to establish and maintain the list of approved evaluators described in subsection A of § 19.2–169.5.

B.   If the court finds, after hearing evidence presented by the parties, that the defendant has refused to cooperate with an evaluation requested by the Commonwealth, it may admit evidence of such refusal or, in the discretion of the court, bar the defendant from presenting expert psychiatric or psychological evidence at trial on the issue of his sanity at the time of the offense.

[202] Estelle v. Smith, 451 U.S. 454 (1981). In *Estelle*, the defendant had been evaluated for competency prior to trial. The prosecution introduced psychiatric testimony based on the competency evaluation during the sentencing phase to establish future dangerousness. 451 U.S. at 456. The Supreme Court held that since the defendant had not requested the competency evaluation and had not introduced psychiatric evidence, the government's use of the competency evaluation information at sentencing was unconstitutional. The Court reasoned that the "psychiatric evaluation [was ordered] for the limited, neutral purpose of determining his competency to stand trial, but the results of that inquiry were used by the State for a much broader objective that was plainly adverse to [the defendant]." 451 U.S. at 465.

[203] Fed. R. Crim. P. 12.2(c)(4): "No statement made by a defendant in the course of any examination conducted under this rule (whether conducted with or without the defendant's

If the defendant asserts a mental capacity defense, the scope of the defendant's waiver against self-incrimination has been the subject of much debate. In *Buchanan v. Kentucky*, the Supreme Court held that the government's use at trial of a court-appointed psychiatrist's opinion to rebut the defendant's asserted defense of extreme emotional disturbance did not violate the Fifth Amendment.[204] Whether the psychiatric evidence derives from an evaluation on an issue asserted by the defense is an important distinction in the law. The psychiatric opinion in *Buchanan* was derived from an evaluation conducted on the issue of the affirmative defense asserted by the defense (extreme emotional disturbance) and the Court held that the defendant waived his Fifth Amendment privilege against self-incrimination only as to matters on that issue.[205] The importance of the scope of the defendant's waiver was noted in *Powell v. Texas*, where the Supreme Court held that assertion of an insanity defense at trial did not waive the Fifth Amendment protection as to the admission of psychiatric evidence on the issue of future dangerousness at sentencing.[206]

Some courts have further defined the scope of the waiver by limiting the government's access to the defendant to obtaining evidence necessary to rebut the defense raised.[207] In *United States v. Johnson*, the district court held that evaluation questions that exceed the scope of what is necessary to rebut the defendant's asserted defense violate the privilege against self-incrimination.[208] "When a defendant raises a defense that relies on an expert examination of his mental condition, the Fifth Amendment does not protect him from being compelled to submit to a *similar examination* conducted on behalf of the prosecution or from the

---

consent), no testimony by the expert based on the statement, and no other fruits of the statement may be admitted into evidence against the defendant in any criminal proceeding except on an issue regarding mental condition on which the defendant: (A) has introduced evidence of incompetency or evidence requiring notice under Rule 12.2(a) or (b)(1), or (B) has introduced expert evidence in a capital sentencing proceeding requiring notice under Rule 12.2(b)(2)." *See also* Va. Code § 19.2–169.7: "No statement or disclosure by the defendant concerning the alleged offense made during a competency evaluation ordered pursuant to § 19.2–169.1, a mental state at the time of the offense evaluation ordered pursuant to § 19.2–169.5, or treatment ordered pursuant to § 19.2–169.2 or § 19.2–169.6 may be used against the defendant at trial as evidence or as a basis for such evidence, except on the issue of his mental condition at the time of the offense after he raises the issue pursuant to § 19.2–168."

[204] 484 U.S. 402, 424 (1987).

[205] Brown v. United States, 356 U.S. 148, 154–155 (1958) ("[T]he breadth of his waiver is determined by the scope of the relevant cross-examination.").

[206] 492 U.S. 680, 685 (1989).

[207] *See* Gibbs v. Frank, 387 F.3d 268, 274 (3d Cir. 2004) ("waiver is not limitless; it only allows the prosecution to use the interview to provide rebuttal to the psychiatric defense). *See also* State v. Harris, 28 N.E.3d 1256 (Ohio 2015); State v. Martin, 950 S.W.2d 20 (Tenn. 1997); State v. Schackart, 858 P.2d 639, 645 (Ariz. 1993); State v. Steiger, 590 A.2d 408, 416 (Conn. 1991); Braswell v. State, 371 So.2d 992, 997 (Ala. 1979).

[208] 383 F. Supp.2d 1145, 1162 (N.D. Iowa 2005).

introduction of evidence from that examination for the purpose of *rebutting* the defense."[209]

The principle of the limited scope of the Fifth Amendment waiver has also been used to restrict the types of psychological testing conducted by the government's experts. In *United States v. Taylor*, the defense provided notice of an intent to introduce psychiatric testimony based on alcohol and drug screening tests.[210] The government's expert wanted to conduct personality psychological testing, including the MMPI.[211] The court held that the defendant's notice of intent to introduce psychiatric testimony was not "an open door for any type of mental testing" and barred the government from introducing any materials that extended beyond substance abuse.[212]

To promote the defendant's full cooperation with the evaluation, the ABA *Criminal Justice Mental Health Standards* adopt a strong position on the privilege against self-incrimination:[213]

> (a) Admissibility of disclosure or opinions in criminal proceedings. No statement made by or information obtained from a person, or evidence derived from such statement or information during the course of any pretrial evaluation or treatment described in 7-3.1, and no opinion of a mental health professional based on such statement, information, or evidence is admissible in any criminal proceeding in which that person is a defendant unless it is otherwise admissible and:
>
> (i) it relates solely to the defendant's present competency to proceed and the use of such disclosure or opinion conforms to the requirements of Standard 7-4.7; or,
>
> (ii) it is relevant to an issue raised by the defendant concerning the defendant's mental condition and the defendant introduces or intends to introduce the testimony of a mental health professional to support the defense claim on this issue.
>
> (b) Duty of evaluator to disclose information concerning defendant's present mental condition that was not the subject of the evaluation.
>
> (i) If, in the course of any evaluation, the evaluator concludes that the defendant may be incompetent to proceed, the evaluator should notify the defendant's

---

[209] United States v. Williams, 731 F. Supp.2d 1012, 1017 (D.C. Haw. 2010) (emphasis in original).

[210] 320 F. Supp.2d 790, 791 (N.D. Ind. 2004).

[211] 320 F. Supp.2d at 792–794.

[212] 320 F. Supp.2d at 794.

[213] *Criminal Justice Mental Health Standards*, American Bar Association, August 8, 2016 at Standard 7-3.2.

attorney and, if the evaluation was initiated by the court or prosecution, should also notify the court and prosecution.

(ii) If in the course of any evaluation, the evaluator concludes that the defendant presents an imminent risk of serious danger to him or herself or to another person or otherwise needs emergency intervention, the evaluator should take appropriate precautionary measures in accordance with applicable professional standards and statutory reporting requirements.

2.   SIXTH AMENDMENT

The Sixth Amendment to the United States Constitution provides: "In all criminal prosecutions, the accused shall enjoy the right . . . to have the assistance of counsel for his defense."[214] This right extends to any stage of the proceeding, including pretrial and out-of-court proceedings, when the absence of counsel might derogate the defendant's right to a fair trial.[215] This constitutional provision requires notice to counsel of an examination to protect the defendant's right to consult with counsel concerning the scope and nature of the examination.[216] The right to counsel encompasses "counsel's being informed about the scope and nature of the proceeding" and how the evaluation will be used.[217]

The majority of courts that have addressed the issue have held that the right to counsel does not extend to the right to have counsel present during the government's examination.[218] Some courts have ordered the video recording of the government's examination to ensure the examination remains within the limited scope of the Fifth Amendment waiver.[219]

These holdings are consistent with the ABA *Criminal Justice Mental Health Standards* which require that, whenever feasible, all evaluations initiated by the prosecution or the court be recorded, preferably through video as well as audio.[220] To avoid the possibility of obstruction of the evaluation, the Standards state that neither the prosecutor nor defense

---

[214] U.S. Const. Amend. VI.

[215] United States v. Wade, 388 U.S. 218, 226–227 (1967).

[216] Estelle v. Smith, 451 U.S. 545, 467 (1981).

[217] Buchanan v. Kentucky, 484 U.S. 402, 424 (1987).

[218] *See, e.g.,* United States v. Byers, 740 F.2d 1104, 1121 (D.C. 1982); United States v. Wilson, 920 F. Supp.2d 287, 305 (E.D.N.Y. 2012).

[219] *See, e.g.,* United States v. Hardy, 644 F. Supp.2d 749, 750 (E.D. La. 2008).

The American Academy of Psychiatry and the Law does not support "a blanket rule requiring video recording in all forensic interviews [but does find] the option of video recording to be an ethically acceptable medical practice." AAPL Task Force, *Video Recording of Forensic Psychiatric Evaluations,* Revised May 2013 (available at: http://www.aapl.org/practice.htm) (last accessed December 16, 2016).

[220] *Criminal Justice Mental Health Standards,* American Bar Association, August 8, 2016 at Standard 7-3.5(d)(ii).

attorney is entitled to be present during the evaluation unless the evaluator requests their presence.[221]

V. RESOURCES

§16.13 BIBLIOGRAPHY OF ADDITIONAL RESOURCES

1. BOOKS AND ARTICLES

Paul S. Appelbaum and Thomas G. Gutheil, *Clinical Handbook of Psychiatry and the Law,* 4th ed., Lippincott Williams and Wilkins, 2007.

Curt R. Bartol and Anne M. Bartol, eds., *Current Perspectives in Forensic Psychology and Criminal Behavior*, 32d ed., Sage Publications, Inc., 2012.

Brian L. Cutler and Patricia A. Zapf, eds., *APA Handbook of Forensic Psychology*, American Psychological Association, 2015.

Brent Garland ed., *Neuroscience and the Law: Brain, Mind, and the Scales of Justice*, Dana Press, 2004.

Michael S. Gazzaniga, ed., *A Judge's Guide to Neuroscience: A Concise Introduction*, SAGE Center for the Study of the Mind, 2010.

Thomas Grisso, *Evaluating Competencies: Forensic Assessments and Instruments*, 2d ed., Springer, 2007.

Kirk Heilbrun, *Principles of Forensic Mental Health Assessment*, Kluwer Academic/Plenum Publishers, 2001.

Kirk Heilbrun *et al.*, "Standards of Practice and Care in Forensic Mental Health Assessment: Legal, Professional, and Principles-Based Considerations," 14 Psychology, Public Policy & Law 1–26 (2008).

Matthew T. Huss, *Forensic Psychology: Research, Clinical Practice, and Applications*, 2d ed., Wiley, 2014.

The Kavli Foundation, Gatsby & the Society for Neuroscience, *Brain Facts*, 2012 (available at: http://www.brainfacts.org/about-neuro science/brain-facts-book/)(last accessed December 13, 2016).

Glenn J. Larrabee, ed. *Forensic Neuropsychology: A Scientific Approach*, 2d ed., Oxford University Press, 2012.

Gary B. Melton *et al.*, *Psychological Evaluations for the Courts: A Handbook for Mental Health Professionals and Lawyers*, 3rd ed., Guilford Press, 2007.

---

[221] Id. at Standard 7-3.5(c).

John Monahan and Laurens Walker, *Social Science in Law: Cases and Materials*, Foundation Press, 2014.

Stephen Morse and Adina Roskies eds., *A Primer on Criminal Law and Neuroscience*, Oxford University Press, 2013.

Richard Rogers, *Clinical Assessment of Malingering and Deception*, 3d ed., The Guilford Press, 2008.

Robert I. Simon and Liza H. Gold, *Textbook of Forensic Psychiatry* 2d ed., American Psychiatric Publishing, 2010.

Robert I. Simon and Daniel W. Shuman, *Retrospective Assessment of Mental States in Litigation: Predicting the Past*, American Psychiatric Association Publishing, 2002.

Jennifer L. Skeem, Kevin S. Douglas and Scott O Lilienfeld eds., *Psychological Science in the Courtroom: Consensus and Controversy*, The Guilford Press, 2009.

John M. Spores, *Clinician's Guide to Psychological Assessment and Testing*, Springer Publishing Co., 2013.

Larry R. Squire *et al.*, eds., *Fundamental Neuroscience*, 4th ed., Elsevier Inc., 2013.

Gary R. VandenBos, ed., *APA College Dictionary of Psychology*, American Psychological Association, 2016.

2. ONLINE RESOURCES

The American Psychological Association: http://www.apa.org/.

The American Psychiatric Association: www.psych.org/.

The American Neurological Association: www.aneuroa.org/.

The American Academy of Psychiatry and the Law *(AAPL)*: http://www.aapl.org.

Federation of European Neuroscience Societies: www.fens.org.

National Association of Psychometrists *(NAP):* www.napnet.org/.

National Institute of Biomedical Imaging and Bioengineering: www.nibib.nih.gov.

National Institute of Mental Health: www.nimh.nih.gov.

The Society for Neuroscience: http://www.sfn.org.

INDEX

References are to Pages